Shakespeares after Shakespeare

Shakespeares after Shakespeare

An Encyclopedia of the
Bard in Mass Media and Popular Culture

VOLUME 1

Edited by Richard Burt

Greenwood Press
Westport, Connecticut • London

Library of Congress Cataloging-in-Publication Data

Shakespeares after Shakespeare : an encyclopedia of the Bard in mass media
and popular culture / edited by Richard Burt.
     p. cm.
    Includes bibliographical references and index.
    ISBN 0–313–33116–2 (set : alk. paper)—ISBN 0–313–33117–0 (v. 1 : alk. paper)—
ISBN 0–313–33118–9 (v. 2 : alk. paper)
    1. Shakespeare, William, 1564–1616—Adaptations—Encyclopedias. 2. Shakespeare, William,
1564–1616—Film and video adaptations—Encyclopedias. 3. Shakespeare, William, 1564–1616—
Stage history—Encyclopedias. 4. Shakespeare, William, 1564–1616—Influence—Encyclopedias.
5. Popular culture—United States—History—20th century. 6. Popular culture—Great Britain—
History—20th century. I. Burt, Richard, 1954–
    PR2880.A1S48 2007
    822.3'3—dc22   2006010852

British Library Cataloguing in Publication Data is available.

Copyright © 2007 by Richard Burt

Library of Congress Catalog Card Number: 2006010852
ISBN-10: 0–313–33116–2 (set)   ISBN-13: 978–0–313–33116–9 (set)
         0–313–33117–0 (vol. 1)   978–0–313–33117–0 (vol. 1)
         0–313–33118–9 (vol. 2)   978–0–313–33118–9 (vol. 2)

First published in 2007

Greenwood Press, 88 Post Road West, Westport, CT 06881
An imprint of Greenwood Publishing Group, Inc.
www.greenwood.com

Printed in the United States of America

The paper used in this book complies with the
Permanent Paper Standard issued by the National
Information Standards Organization (Z39.48–1984).

10 9 8 7 6 5 4 3 2 1

Contents

An Anti-Preface: About Facing Shakespeare

RICHARD BURT

Shakespeare's pluralization into "Shakespeares" may be seen not only in the proliferation of citations across media but in recent debates about Shakespeare the icon focusing on several portraits and a death mask that may or may not be Shakespeare.[1] The more Shakespeare is present in our culture, the less certain what counts as Shakespeare— especially the iconic representation—becomes. As we turn to face Shakespeare, his true face appears to recede into clouds of scholarly debate and uncertainty. A number of academic biographies of Shakespeare have appeared at roughly the same time as a number of books newly disputing Shakespeare's authorship. The most celebrated of the new biographies, Stephen Greenblatt's *Will in the World* (2003), is a novelization of Shakespeare's lost years where what Natalie Zemon Davis calls "fiction in the archives" bleeds into fiction and film outside the archives.[2] And if a reading in New York of Gary Taylor's version of Shakespeare's lost play *Cardenio* is any indication, we are entering a new age of reconstructing Shakespeare's plays no longer based on authenticity but on sounding, to use Taylor's Stephen Colbert–like term, "authentish."[3] Taylor's play is based on Lewis Theobald's play *Double Falsehood, or the Distressed Lovers* (1728), which Theobald claimed was adapted from several manuscripts he owned of *Cardenio*. In writing his own version of *Cardenio*, Taylor has deleted some of Theobald's scenes (to leave only what Shakespeare wrote) as well as added scenes of his own based on what Shakespeare and John Fletcher sounded like, so that Taylor, going back to the future, effectively replaces Theobald as adapter. Though Taylor's "authentish" *Cardenio* may strike some readers as ludicrous, scholars, a TV producer, and major actors have taken it seriously. Fifteen actors, including Sam Waterston, Whoopi Goldberg, Richard Dreyfuss, Blair Brown, and James Naughton read through the play in March 2006, and David Black, the producer of the TV series *Law and Order* who brought Taylor and the actors together, hopes to lure Taylor into writing for TV.

While a number of Shakespeare critics working on film and media have productively theorized the effects of digital media on what was pluralized in the 1980s as "Shakespeares," institutional Shakespeare has lagged far behind. The Folger Shakespeare Library does not collect comic books, radio tapes, or films and television shows on DVD, and research sponsored by the Folger on Shakespeare and the visual arts focuses exclusively, as far as I am aware, on the fine arts.[4] Though the journal of record, *Shakespeare Quarterly*, occasionally publishes an article on a Shakespeare film, it restricts reviews of performances to theatrical performances.[5] This comes as no surprise, of course. One may fantasize about a Shakespeare archive that would include Shakespeare-related mass media materials, but one tends to fantasize, of course, precisely about that which will never come to pass.

And even if such a fantasy were ever realized, archiving the materials in a book such as *Shakespeares after Shakespeare* would reproduce the present cultural proliferation and fragmentation of Shakespeare, not some unified Shakespeare, which we may now see is little more than a cultural imaginary.[6] As a textual fragment that involves further textual fragmenting in the form of endnotes, this preface performs this insight. Paratextual fragmentation is inevitable in any encyclopedia.[7] As Jacques Derrida comments on Hegel's prefaces, especially in relation to Hegel's *Encyclopedia*, the preface is for Hegel a model and a norm based on a narrative of complete knowledge:

The end of the preface, if such an end is possible, is the moment at which the exposition (*Darstellung*) and the sequential unfolding off the concept, in its self-movement, begin to overlap according to an a priori synthesis: there would then be no more discrepancy between production and exposition, only a presentation of the concept by itself, in its own words, its own voice, in its logos. No more anteriority or belatedness of form, no more exteriority of content; tautology and heterology would be coupled together in the speculative proposition.[8]

For Hegel, "the philosophical encyclopedia, which conveys the organic and rational unity of knowledge, is not, in contrast to what is sold today under that title, an empirical aggregate of contents.[9] Derrida shows that in Hegel's works, the preface proliferates rather than ends.

Shakespeares after Shakespeare is not, then, a philosophical encyclopedia, but an aggregate of contents. The recognition that no encyclopedia of Shakespeare could provide a totality of knowledge and a linear narrative of Shakespeare's transmission is an asset rather than a liability, however, in providing occasions for new lines of research. Scholars are beginning to take stock of the implications of digitalization for early modern literature, as are performance critics triangulating the stage-to-stage model of performance with a third term, media, which traverses both terms, extends from page through stage.[10] Shakespeare and early modern literature have a central role to play in new media studies, which has excluded attention to the paratext when engaging literary/philosophical theories of (hyper)textuality. As new media studies has begun to engage old media, it has extended "old" media only back to the nineteenth century.[11] Clearly the history of literature's mediatization extends as far back as medieval manuscripts.[12] We hope that *Shakespeares after Shakespeare* furthers a more dialectical engagement with old and new media and alerts a wide range of Shakespeare and non-Shakespeareans to the existence of an even wider range of Shakespeare-related materials, some of them fascinating, some of them not, that may contribute to a better understanding of Shakespeare's mediatization and his place in new media.

Entries on Shakespeare-related materials in this book are organized the following ways: Each chapter groups them according to the medium in which they appear—film, television, radio, and so on. In each chapter, the entries are arranged alphabetically play (or poem) by play, from *All's Well That Ends Well* to *The Two Gentlemen of Verona*. Under each play or poem, the entries are listed chronologically, earliest to most recent. While we have tried to provide complete bibliographical information for all entries, in some cases complete information proved impossible to find. Entries by contributors other than those written by the contributor in charge of a given section are noted by their initials in parentheses following these entries.

NOTES

1. Alan Riding, "Will the Real William Shakespeare Please Stand Up?" *New York Times*, March 4, 2006, www.nytimes.com/2006/03/04/arts/design/04shak.html.

2. See Natalie Zemon Davis, *Fiction in the Archives: Pardon Tales and Their Tellers in Sixteenth-century France* (Stanford, CA: Stanford University Press, 1987). Greenblatt quite interestingly cites fictional treatments of Shakespeare's life as valuable resources as well as the 1998 John Madden film *Shakespeare in Love*. See Stephen Greenblatt, *Will in the World: How Shakespeare became Shakespeare* (New York: W. W. Norton, 2004), 392.

3. Campbel Robertson, "New Life for an Old Play, But Is It Shakespeare's?" *New York Times*, March 1, 2006, www.nytimes.com/2006/03/01/theater/newsandfeatures/01blac.html. The details on Taylor's *Cardenio* in this paragraph are taken from Robertson's article.

4. The Folger Library does have the Shakespeare Film Study Collection, but it is confined to silent films, BBC productions, and canonical adaptations of Shakespeare.

5. *Shakespeare Quarterly* did devote an issue to "Screen Shakespeare" (53, no. 2 [Summer 2002]), and occasionally published an article on Shakespeare and film.

6. Rather than have all contributors cite the same Shakespeare edition, I decided as editor to allow each contributor to cite her or his preferred edition since there is no point in pretending that there is a consensus about the best scholarly edition or that there is a stable print edition of Shakespeare's works. All citations in my entries are to Stephen Greenblatt et al., eds., *The Norton Shakespeare* (New York: W. W. Norton, 1997).

7. On paratexts, see Gerard Genette, *Paratexts: Thresholds of Interpretation* (Cambridge: Cambridge University Press, 1997).

8. Jacques Derrida, "Outwork, Prefacing," in *Dissemination*, trans. Barbara Johnson (Chicago: Chicago University Press, 1981), 3–59 to 30–31.

9. Ibid., 47.

10. Some symptoms of this development as of this writing: For the March 2007 Renaissance of America meeting, there were two calls for papers, one on "Early Modern Search Engines: The Organization of Vernacular Texts in 17th-century England" and the other on "EEBO and Early Modern Studies." JSTOR announced plans to introduce links into their footnotes: www.jstor.org/about/reference_linking/reflinking.html. My thanks to Scott Newstok for drawing my attention to these symptoms. Barbara Hodgon and W. W. Worthen are at the forefront of reconceiving Shakespeare performance in terms of stage, page and media.

11. See, for example, Thomas W. Keenan and Wendy Hui Kyong Chun, eds., *New Media, Old Media: Interrogating the Digital Revolution* (New York: Routledge, 2005); and James Lyons, John Plunkett, Richard Maltby, and Steve Neal, eds., *Multimedia Histories: From the Magic Lantern to the Internet* (Exeter: University of Exeter Press, 2006).

12. For an analysis of homologies between medieval-related films and medieval manuscripts, see Richard Burt, "The Schlock of Medievalism: Of Manuscript and Film Prologues, Paratexts, and Parodies," *Exemplaria* 18, no. 2 (Fall 2006): 1–22. Available online as a pdf file at www.english.ufl.edu/exemplaria.

Volume
1

1

Introduction

"SHAKESPEARE, MORE OR LESS? FROM SHAKESPEARECCENTRICITY TO SHAKESPEARECENTRICITY AND BACK," RICHARD BURT

When Kenneth Rothwell and Annabelle Henkin Melzer compiled their magisterial reference work, *Shakespeare on Screen*, in the 1980s, they reluctantly excluded television programming they thought noteworthy, what they called a "thriving subspecies of the Shakespeare on screen genre" and defined as "the appropriation of bits, pieces, and segments of Shakespeare by the scenarists for popular television shows." Rothwell and Melzer found the programs difficult to track down because they were "not listed separately in the television guides."[1] Because previous researchers like Rothwell and Melzer depended exclusively on archival holdings and TV guides, existing bibliographies of Shakespeare in mass media have been confined largely to film and television, and bibliographies that include Shakespeare television programming have been largely confined to adaptations of the plays along the lines of the BBC adaptations of the 1970s and 1980s and earlier Hallmark, Philco, and Westinghouse television adaptations.

What Rothwell and others couldn't find in the 1980s and early 1990s can now often be dug up, along with a huge number of previously unknown references to Shakespeare not only in film but in a much wider variety of mass media that includes those covered in this book: comic books, novels and genre fiction, popular music, radio, and theater performances.[2] The increasing integration of media, particularly though the computer (downloadable movies and television programming, websites with high-quality scans of paintings, new search engines), has meant that a much wider range of hitherto unarchived and often previously ephemeral Shakespeare-related materials, including television advertisements, may now be found online, accessed,

and, in the case of television, digitally recorded on one's computer. Although an increase in the number of references to Shakespeare may be seen in some modern mass media (witness Shakespeare films initiated by Kenneth Branagh's *Henry V*), Shakespeare's presence is so widespread across various media as to make narratives about greater or lesser frequency of Shakespeare's appearance difficult, perhaps impossible to tell. Quite clearly, however, digitalization and media integration, along with numerous search engines such as Google (text, images, and video) and searchable website databases TitanTv and Windows Media Center, have made it possible to find and often access far more Shakespeare materials in mass media than ever before. The question now is less "How does one find all this stuff?" than "What do we do with it now that it is so easy to find?"

Still, there remains no systematic way of finding Shakespeare citations in mass media. There is a multitude of internet search engines a researcher may use, but finding Shakespeare references is largely hit and miss for a number of reasons. There is no master search engine listing all the search engines one could use, and finding them is part of the task of research. One reason Shakespeare is difficult to track on television is that Shakespeare's name does not always appear consistently in entries on Shakespeare-related materials. If one enters "Shakespeare" on the Internet Movie Database (www.imdb.com), for example, only a fraction of the films related to Shakespeare on that database will turn up. Searches for individual plays by their titles will also not exhaust the data on that website. Similarly, episode summaries of television programs on a site like TV.com are not searchable, so entering "Shakespeare" into the website search engine turns up only one Shakespeare program. Because Shakespeare references are not systematically catalogued or searchable, no one researcher and no team of researchers will probably ever turn up everything there is to find. Doug Lanier, Courtney Lehmann, Ellen Joy Letostak, and I all found a few films, for example, that the others didn't. The same is true when Ellen Joy Letostak, Susanne Greenhalgh, and I searched for television programs. Nearly every contributor found examples in a field other than their own. Assembling a team of scholarly researchers is crucial because, in many cases, Shakespeare references will only be found by accident while the researcher is watching television or film, reading a comic or novel, or listening to music or radio programs that do not appear to have anything to do with Shakespeare. Ideally, the materials compiled in this book and others like it would someday be online in a single database, with an international team of researchers that would include, in addition to the scholars contributing to this book, Kenneth Rothwell, Michael Bristol, Luke McKernan, Olwen Terris, José Ramón Fernández-Díaz, Laurie Osborne, Tanya Gough, Mariangela Tempura, Yang Lingui, Scott Newstock, Nancy Charlton, Abigail Quart, Eddie Sammons, Robert Shaugnessy, Mark Thornton-Burnett, Ramona Wray, Hugh Davis, and Daniel Rosenthal, all of whom would update it more or less frequently.

However, even with the best possible team of researchers, no reference book in print or online will probably ever present itself as complete. Certainly, *Shakespeares after Shakespeare* does not aim for complete coverage. Any database of "Shakespeares" in mass media will likely be incomplete because there are simply too many passing references that go unnoticed and because, as Wes Folkerth notes in his introduction to the popular music section, there are too many that have nothing to do with Shakespeare except a line reference to be worth tracking down. "Shakespeare's" mediatization means that what counts as Shakespeare is getting increasingly fragmented.[3] Some media and genres seem to engage infrequently in wholesale adaptations of Shakespeare's plays, as Annalisa Castaldo notes in her introduction to the literature section, and instead refer to the works through quotation, character, or individual scene. DVD editions of John Madden's *Shakespeare in Love* (1998) and Kenneth Branagh's *Love's Labour's Lost* (2001) include deleted scenes, and if Shakespeare films follow in the wake of recent developments, we can expect DVD editions of Shakespeare films to be issued in different cuts, either longer or shorter than the theatrical release.[4] An additional problem is that the fine arts and "low" mass media have overlapped as well, at least since the pop art of the 1960s. Sometimes Shakespeare also comes up in the mix as in Keith Mayerson's painting cycle *Hamlet 1999* (2001–4). One critic notes the mix of political figures, movie stars, and icons of so-called popular culture in the series:

The plotless "narrative" of more than one hundred canvases, rendered in a palette of marigold and pea soup, has only a general order, accumulating meaning frame by frame like an exploded comic book. Its tragic drift is bookended by a pair of G.W.s: Bush, recognizably smug even in a few blotches of oil paint, and Washington, a la Gilbert Stuart but mortally disappointed. The latter's a Ghost, and the former's an arch-Claudius; but the figures that recur—among them Keanu Reeves, River Phoenix, Harry Potter, John Lennon, and the Virgin Mary—are less characters than mobile principles of martyrdom, sorrow, venality, and legacy extracted by the artist from Shakespeare's play and clad in contemporary skins.[5]

However, these kinds of connections are beyond the scope of this book. Similarly, we have not included Shakespeare's presence in a variety of products such as dolls, action figures, board games, greeting cards, playing cards, wrapping paper, shopping bags, beer bottles, and so on. As a number of contributors remark in their introductions, our shared aim is to provide a range of samples to give as full a representation as possible of Shakespearean adaptation and citation. Some areas of research such as television are so relatively new that, as Susanne Greenhalgh says in her unusually comprehensive introduction to British television, the researcher feels that she has only scratched the surface of what is out there.

The idea of a complete Shakespeare in mass media database thus remains largely a fantasy, even if we substitute for some authentic Shakespeare items created in "Shakespeare's" name. "Shakespeares" are readable in a wider, less homogenous number of single and collected editions (some as literature, others as performance) and films and television programs are viewable on a remarkable multiplicity of screens in a wider variety of conditions and places. DVDs may be played in cars as well as on planes and in airports, where the traveler may rent films and a portable DVD player. UMD editions of films are playable on video game players. In November 2005, Apple introduced a video iPod with an 2.5-inch color screen; one could either watch films on the iPod's screen or connect to a PC and then play. And so on.

Digitalization has meant improvements in the image quality of Shakespeare films. Whereas some Shakespeare films were available in video in widescreen or "letterbox" formats, the vast majority were pan-and-scans, in which 20–25 percent of the image was cut. Almost all DVD films have been released in widescreen. The greater density of digital reproduction, as opposed to the analogue recording used for video (the American NTSC system being, it should be noted, far worse than the European PAL system), has typically meant a higher image quality that's visible to the naked eye. (Some low-density DVD transfers are atrocious, whereas "superbit" DVDs have an even higher density than standard versions.) DVDs also make available the original theatrical trailers, whereas videos did not. The digitalization of film has also begun to fragment films by introducing deleted scenes, recuts, extended versions— even, in the case of the DVD of Francis Ford Coppola's *The Outsiders*, a "novelization." However, Shakespeare films thus far have not been in the forefront of these developments. If "Shakespeares" remain, as Courtney Lehmann puts it in her introduction to the film adaptations section, Shakespeares always remain in transit, not a stable, locatable whole that can be subsumed under the heading of a single "Shakespeare." To put the point another way, Shakespeare cannot be rightly presumed to be complete, an ideal that adaptations would be said to approximate more or less fully.

Although the title of this book opposes Shakespeare to "Shakespeares" in order to make clear that this book documents and explores Shakespeare in modern and new media and the difference these media make to Shakespeare studies, it is important not to conceptualize Shakespeare and mass media in mythic terms, as a succession of before and after, original and derivative, master and slave (or servant/handmaiden), but to force the question, What do we mean by Shakespeare? Once we take into account the fact that Shakespeare's plays were never to be literary monuments but were instead always theatrical experiments subject to revision, it becomes clear that the plays are not "master-texts" (or "mistress-texts," or even "master-mistress texts") that were followed by adaptations and citations at a much later time. Famous lines ("Let slip the dogs of war"), titles (*All's Well That Ends Well*, *Much Ado about Nothing*), and character names, are now so much a part of the language that, at least in the United States, they have become "post-hermeneutic"; that is, they no longer have any meaningful relation to Shakespeare.[6] Marjorie Garber carefully notes an historical shift in the way Shakespeare has been cited, and argues that Shakespeare's citation has become increasingly "disembodied" and "dislocated from [the citation's] context."[7]

The practice of citing Shakespeare as a cultural enforcer can sometimes obscure both the irony and the wit of the original. What might once have been called "Bartlett's Familiar Shakespeare," and is now to be found at Shakepeare.com, has changed the way Shakespeare intersects with contemporary culture. It is no longer the case that a knowledge of the playwright necessarily precedes quotation from them.... Today Shakespeare is more likely to be a citation, a tagline, an adage, or a slogan.[8]

Garber rightly refuses to lament this shift to what she regards as the sampling or branding of Shakespeare as a sign of the declining importance of the humanities.

Yet Garber's distinction between contextualized and decontextualized citation, while understandable, does not hold up in key respects. Quotations in modern performances are no longer context-bound, not because they are

unrecognized but because of their hyper-familiarity. As Orson Welles noted long ago, "Now we sit through Shakespeare in order to recognize the quotations." More strongly, I would argue that Shakespeare has always been "Shakespeares," mediatized and subject to dislocation, decontextualization, and fragmentation as the texts were revised, performed, printed and otherwise circulated in Elizabethan and Jacobean England and Europe. Shakespeare's mediatization and consequent fragmentation also extends much more broadly than the quotation of famous lines from the plays Garber notes. By the nineteenth century, Adrian Poole writes in his fine book *Shakespeare and the Victorians*, the term "Shakespeare"

meant a body of texts, edited, published, and marketed with a developing sense of scholarly protocol but also of an expanding readership's diverse needs. It meant an array of stories, characters, speeches and sayings so widely and intimately familiar that readers and auditors could be relied on to recognize them when they were quoted, echoed, mimicked, travestied and transformed. It also meant a whole set of particular images and models through which these Shakespearean "originals" were mediated. That is to say, through the works of other writers—poets, novelists, dramatists—who had themselves appropriated Shakespeare's words, figures, and plots.... Nor must we forget the work of visual artists, the painters, illustrators and cartoonists responsible for imprinting, on the mind of individuals and the culture at large, images of Hamlet and Falstaff, Romeo and Juliet, Lear and Cordelia, Ariel and Caliban—and of their creator. We must allow a special force to the legendary stars associated with particular roles, often perpetuated by the production of well-known paintings, in illustrated editions of the plays and elsewhere.[9]

The introduction of modern mass media developed in the nineteenth century and sold widely in the twentieth extends the heterogeneity that make up "Shakespeare." More so than in Victorian culture, however, Shakespeare's citation and circulation in modern popular culture and mass media shifts attention away from Shakespeare's language. Shakespeare also has a variety of quasi-hermeneutic functions in paratextual material such as film trailers, DVD menus, theater posters, movie marquees that show up in films (*Bram Stoker's Dracula*, *It's Love I'm After*, *Valley Girl*, *L'Appartement*, and *Wicker Park*, to name just a few examples), comics, and cartoons.[10]

The subtitle of this book, "An Encyclopedia of the Bard in Mass Media and Popular Culture," implicitly raises fundamental questions about the materials in the book by linking two terms, "mass media" and "popular culture," that are usually opposed by academics. Popular culture is regarded as something produced from below, by the people. It is "good" because it supposedly involves active listening, reading, and interaction. By contrast mass media are imposed from above by what Theodor Adorno called the culture industry on the people.[11] Mass media is "bad" because it supposedly dilutes literature, dumbs it down, and makes readers and listeners into passive consumers of products. Shakespeareans analyzing popular culture and mass media have largely followed suit.[12] Attempts to salvage mass media do so by shifting attention from production to reception turning into a version of popular culture (the people become fans).[13] In Shakespeare criticism, popular Shakespeare is often regarded as burlesques and parodies that makes irreverent fun of elite, institutional Shakespeare.[14] Even a figure as important as Orson Welles, who performed Shakespeare in the theater and on radio, film, and television, is typically regarded as using Shakespeare against these media.[15] In replaying scenes from plays that often parody Shakespeare, many of the materials included in this book challenge the academic tendency to value popular culture and denigrate mass media because much of the mass media show the people embracing Shakespeare rather than parodying him. Indeed, there is something like a genre of modernization and remediation whereby Shakespeare gets reduced and modernized into a musical, jazz, or rap. Although I think that no such thing as popular culture, unrelated to elite culture, has ever existed, I have used both terms because of their currency.

In addition to putting into question the meanings of Shakespeare, popular culture, and mass media and questioning their critical usefulness, *Shakespeares after Shakespeare* hopes to understand more fully the complexity of what Shakespeare does in mass media and what mass media does to Shakespeare by furthering, among others, five broad aims in future research:

1. To show how literature and literary quotation are media effects.
2. To enlarge the field of media being analyzed and adopt a transmedia approach toward Shakespeare's reproduction and citation in literature and visual and electronic media.
3. To understand how Shakespeare's presence across all media and media technologies enables and undermines various kinds of criticisms, some nostalgic, some forward-looking, of modern communications technologies, modernization, and globalization.
4. To explore what has become problem: namely, categorizing the variety of Shakespeare materials now that, as Douglas Lanier points out in his introduction to film spin-offs, the fidelity model of film criticism, along with discussions between legitimate and illegitimate Shakespeare and between Shakespeare and Schlockspeare, are no longer sustainable.
5. To consider as a question how to assign value to the materials catalogued in this book now that the criterion of fidelity has been abandoned.[16]

Alan Liu comments that "literature as traditionally understood no longer survives as an autonomous force.... Since the eighteenth through the nineteenth centuries, literature has merged with mass-market, media, educational, political, and other institutions that reallocate, repackage, and otherwise 'repurpose' its assets." He adds that literature has "lost its distinction on the gradient that blurs together textuality and information, imagination and entertainment,

authors and celebrities, and publishers and conglomerates."[17] Whereas I think Liu is right to locate literature in the culture and infotainment industry, I am not convinced that literature ever existed as "an autonomous force" or that the distinctions Liu draws were never blurred in practice as literature came to be institutionalized. Shakespeare was always a part of a nascent culture industry.[18] Thus, the status of Shakespeare's works as literature, and more broadly, the academic institution of Shakespeare studies, need to be understood in relation to the ways Shakespeare and academia involve fantasies about crossing over into non-literary media.[19]

The present book is divided into separate media, mostly for convenience of use but also to give a more specific sense of the ways in which various media evince an ambivalence about Shakespeare's value (Shakespeare comics may be regarded as childish, for example, but are far and away the most expensive to collect). *Shakespeares after Shakespeare* is also meant to further the second aim I identified above, namely, taking a transmedia approach to Shakespeare's citations in mass media. Hence, entries have been cross-referenced both within and across sections (comics, film, TV, and so on) to highlight the extent to which Shakespeare's citation not only crosses from one medium to another but is often "remediated," or framed in one medium through another.[20] For obvious reasons, Shakespeare is most frequently represented in comics, novels, television programs, and films as a theatrical performance, forming a kind of Shakespeare subgenre, but it may sometimes take the form of a film in novels. What Frederic Jameson says of film's "rivalry" with other media may be generalized to the way all media frame competing media: "Whenever other media appear in film, their deeper function is to set off and demonstrate the latter's ontological primacy."[21] Often one medium uses Shakespeare to mount a critique of another medium or modern mass media as a whole, and thereby knowingly or unknowingly represses Shakespeare's presence in another medium or other media. For example, films about theater, and about Shakespeare theatrical productions specifically, often figure television as a threat to film. In *The Playboys* (dir. Gillies MacKinnon, 1991), derived from *Bye Bye Brazil* (dir. Carlos Diegues, 1979), a traveling theater troupe that does scenes from *Othello* and other plays is reduced in number due largely to the pressures of television, which appears midway through the film in the local bar, and the arrival of *Gone with the Wind* at the local movie theater. More broadly, *Food of Love* (dir. Stephen Poliakoff, 1997) enlists a theatrical Shakespeare to take on all modern communications technologies. The critique is offered somewhat ironically, as the contrast between what English villages were once and what they are now (overtaken by satellite dishes in backyards and porn in the window display of the local video store) is made as the traditionalist hero watches scenes from a film, namely Michael Powell and Emeric Pressburger's wonderful *A Canterbury Tale* (unidentified as such). This quasi-Lawrentian criticism of the negative impact of visual media on modern life in the name of Shakespeare of course conveniently forgets that Shakespeare appears pervasively in the very media being denigrated and defined as threats to Shakespeare, high culture, and the good life.

As Shakespeare and, more broadly, literature and literary culture, are transposed, constructed, and framed in rival media, the rivalry tends to take a heightened narrative form in which Shakespeare, in one medium or another, is lost or the actors performing his play are losers.[22] Attending more widely to possible losses in Shakespeare's transmission (including translation) and in tracking him (always a hit-and-miss position when using search engines) takes us to the third aim of this book by helping to frame the ways in which Shakespeare is called up to defend or resist various social and political agendas and values in mass media.[23]

Consider Shakespeare and the telephone. One might think they are by definition antagonistic to one another. In *Food of Love*, for example, the theater director (Richard E. Grant) takes away the cell phones owned by nearly all of the cast members. Cell phones are supposed to be turned off in theaters; movie theater chains now end the commercial for the snack bar with a request to turn off cell phones. Yet Shakespeare has been on the line ever since the telephone was invented. When Alexander Graham Bell and Thomas Watson first performed public demonstrations of how the telephone worked, they cited Hamlet's "To be or not to be speech," truncating it to, "To be or not to be ... there's the rub."[24] More recently, a 2003 Nextel thirty-second cell phone commercial involved a fast-paced parody of *Romeo and Juliet* with the dialogue modernized and spoken into cell phones held by each of the characters. The ad contrasts what looks like an iconic scene from Shakespeare done in traditional period dress with (initially hidden) modern technology. Beginning with increasingly short shot-reverse-shots of Juliet smiling as she looks down at Romeo and Romeo smiling, looking up at her, the ad set ups the joke as Juliet pops open her cell phone and says,

JULIET: Romeo!
ROMEO: Juliet!
JULIET: I love you.
ROMEO: Ditto.

The rest of the commercial reduces *Romeo and Juliet* to one-word lines as Tybalt, Paris, Romeo, and Juliet all die in quick succession, and the curtain drops to thunderous applause.

No doubt due to a variety of factors in addition to communications technologies, including globalization, decolonization, flows of global capital, and transitions between old and new media, previous ways of categorizing Shakespeare no longer seem workable. As testimony to this problem—the fourth aim this book seeks to address—the contributors have chosen different options in their introductions, in some cases using only a few categories, in others inventing new categories, and in still others proliferating categories. Moreover, some media have required two sections (film and television; Chapters 3–4, 8–9), and some are represented in appendices (comics and Italian television). Rather than try to impose a foolish consistency on the entire book, I have chosen to let it perform this problem because the problem won't go away and is in fact what really demands, and even rewards, critical attention. One consequence of research in the area of Shakespeare in mass media and popular culture is a destabilization of the ways academic boundaries between traditional and innovative criticism are usually drawn: though researching hermeneutic and post-hermeneutic Shakespeares[25] may often make one feel one is at the cutting edge of Shakespeare scholarship, it's sometimes hard not to feel as well that one is at its lunatic fringe. If categories for Shakespeare's heterogeneous presence across mass media prove difficult to construct, they will also inevitably be used. To grasp this problem, without proposing to solve it, I propose an overarching and self-deconstructing set of terms, "Shakespeareccentricity" and "Shakespearecentricity" and make a case for the study of the more eccentric Shakespeare materials archived in this book, which might still strike some Shakespeareans as mere drek or schlock, generic and formulaic materials that contribute nothing to our understanding of the plays themselves (presumed to be the primary goal of Shakespeare scholarship).

As is clear to most Shakespeareans, every performance or citation reproduction of what counts as Shakespeare has a centrifugal pull on the text, is eccentric in that it more or less decenters Shakespeare's language and plot by cutting, rearranging lines and scenes, and adding new signifiers through gesture, costume, lighting, narrative, and so on. On the other hand, citations and adaptations of Shakespeare return us to Shakespeare as a center, even if the Shakespeare imagined as central proves to be a fantasy. Something always counts as Shakespeare, and its gravity exerts a centripetal pull on other materials toward it. The terms "Shakespeareccentricity" and "Shakespearecentricity" inevitably devolve into their opposites, "Shakespeareccentricism" and "Shakespearecentrism," which will in turn dialectically revolve back into their opposites. This oscillation between the eccentric and the centered means that the generic, "bad" Shakespeare as well as the unusual, "good" Shakespeare cannot be found on either side of a divide between the eccentric and the centered because the eccentric can become standardized, generic, and clichéd as it becomes eccentrism, just as the centric can become decentered by virtue of its centricity (the drive to the center can start to look obsessive, compulsive, authoritarian, and so on).

Just as the variety of materials catalogued in *Shakespeares after Shakespeare* demands we abandon the criterion of fidelity and thereby creates a problem of categorization, so that variety generates as a question what counts as good or bad. In other words, how we are to assign value to Shakespeare in film and mass media becomes a problem, the articulation of which is the fifth of aim of this book, once we no longer have the criterion of fidelity and we are thus required to make arguments about what is or is not of value.

Speaking as the editor, I believe a case can be made that many eccentric Shakespeare materials are worth attending to not because they are aesthetically complex but because they add a greater range of materials than are present in more centered materials and thus have an almost necessarily greater degree of interest. For example, accounts of plays in performance often suffer, in my view, from their narrow focus on canonical theater productions and films as well as from inadequate attention to ways in which theater Shakespeare performances have long colonized modern mass media (Marc Antony dialing the funeral oration speech in a phone booth to a newspaper reporter, for example).[26] Attention to citations and scenes from *Othello* in television programming would require, in my view, a whole revision of present narratives that take the casting of Othello as a black actor as their end point.

To be clear, I am not proposing a new hierarchy of some materials over others but the injection into "normative" Shakespeare criticism of a broad set of data such that the entire database may be seen and understood in new ways as a result, to introduce a final neologism, of their "Bardridization." The oscillation I am describing extends to academic Shakespeare criticism as well, especially criticism not focused on mass media but on "the plays themselves." If Shakespeare is often produced in iconic and generic ways in mass media (the balcony and tomb scenes from *Romeo and Juliet* are a staple, for example) and seem to be read the same way (*Romeo and Juliet* is about forbidden love at first sight), Shakespeare criticism is often no less generic. How different, we may ask, is historicist, feminist, or queer criticism of the plays in which we learn that the plays are subversive, containments of subversion, or some version of both? Or that the plays display and seek to manage widespread cultural anxieties about _____ (fill in the blank)?

Moreover, it's not as if criticism of the plays operates independently of mass media. For example, Stephen Greenblatt acknowledges John Madden's *Shakespeare in Love* (1998) as the motivation for his novelization of Shakespeare's life, *Will in the World: How Shakespeare Became Shakespeare*, did television interviews on the *Charlie Rose Show* and C-Span's *Book-notes* with host Brian Lamb

in 2004, and has published op-ed pieces in the *New York Times* on *Shakespeare in Love* and on the first presidential debate between President George W. Bush and Senator John Kerry and *Julius Caesar*.[27]

More traditional criticism than Greenblatt's goes even further in remediating the plays, interpreting them not by juxtaposing them with anecdotes but by turning them into the equivalent of nineteenth-century realist novels. More innovative criticism has begun self-consciously recasting early modern media in terms of new media, focusing on the early modern computer and publishing "circuits."[28] The new Sourcebooks Shakespeares editions of individual plays are reasonably priced and valuable hybrids, giving footnotes on the meanings of obsolete words (like literary editions) and on performances (like the Cambridge University Press performance editions). In addition, there are introductory essays focused on performance and popular culture as well as CDs with recordings of a large number of actors doing performances of passages and scenes.[29] The CD that comes with the *Othello* edition, for example, has twenty-seven tracks, including one by Edwin Booth.

As more critics begin working on Shakespeare in film and mass media, no doubt some criticism will become similarly generic. A given film will be regarded as more or less in conflict with the commercial forces it wants to resist; film criticism will be reduced once again to analyzing the moment of a film's production; a film's location will be said to resist globalization; TV shows of comic books using Shakespeare will be discussed in terms of canned cultural studies work on fandom; and so on.

This editor and the contributors to this book hope, however, that the availability of an astonishingly large database and the pull between Shakespeare's eccentricity and centricity, or "Bardridity," can lead to far more original and exciting kinds of research and pedagogy in Shakespeare studies, especially by enabling a less parochial sense of Shakespeare as English and American. Wherever possible, we have included examples of Shakespeare in Europe, and Asia, and Africa. To be sure, some of the works catalogued in this book will not receive much, if any, critical attention. I think most, and perhaps all, of us felt at points bored out of our minds by some of the materials we nevertheless felt we had to include out of professional obligation. Yet in addition to making more materials available for Shakespereans to write about, *Shakespeares after Shakespeare* offers what are often quite fascinating materials that challenge as well as develop the ways in which Shakespeare criticism has thus far proceeded, especially when it comes to historicizing Shakespeare or defining what political Shakespeare means. As Amy Scott-Douglass points out in her introduction to the theater section, even those playwrights who pay homage to Shakespeare when adapting him also take issue with him. Given the questioning of Shakespeare, Scott-Douglass concludes that "resistance is the very spirit of adaptation."

The pedagogical opportunities offered by the materials catalogued in *Shakespeares after Shakespeare* are even greater. While more and more Shakespeareans make use of film clips in their classrooms, the study of Shakespeare on film remains mostly ancillary, a way of getting students to appreciate the complexity and indeterminacy of Shakespeare's plays. Relatively few Shakespeareans teach classes specifically on Shakespeare in film. No doubt Shakespeare and film will remain the dominant area of research and teaching because comics are often far more expensive to obtain. (The *Famous Authors* Shakespeare comic books, for example, may sell, as of this writing, for as much as U.S.$150 each.) Similarly, many television programs remain relatively difficult to find; recording them will require for many Shakespeareans the purchase of a new computer to record them.

We hope that *Shakespeares after Shakespeare* offers possibilities beyond film clips in traditional Shakespeare as literature courses. For example, students might be asked to do research along the lines of this book and others, like finding examples not catalogued and writing up entries on them. Research in these areas may also be Shakespeareccentric: One often finds materials one is not looking for in the process of looking for something else.

Courses on Shakespeare in film might also begin to explore new media, especially video games, something we have not included in this volume because the subject has yet to be researched. Video games sales surpassed those of film some years ago, and it is likely that Shakespeare is already showing up in a number of games. He appears in at least one PlayStation 2 game, *Silent Hill 3*: a riddle asks the player to the give the titles of six Shakespeare tragedies. Thus far, only Kenneth Branagh's *Hamlet* and Oliver Parker's *Othello* have spun off a game (on CD-Rom), both of which are now out of print. A CD-Rom based on the film *Star Trek VI: The Undiscovered Country*, entitled *Klingon Academy*, is playable on a PC and, like the film, includes many Shakespeare citations.

More adventurous Shakespeareans might do a course on Shakespeare's afterlives in television or on literature. Multimedia Shakespeare courses might also be organized along other lines. Courses on Shakespeare as a character or on Shakespeare and children could include films, television programs, novels, theater productions, children's books, and comic books. Additionally, this book may offer inspiration for possible uses of Shakespeare in courses not taught by Shakespeareans. Scholars and educators in other fields teaching courses on film adaptation, African American film, post-colonial film, Bollywood film, transnational cinema, or on film genres such as the Western, the horror film, film noir, and so on, might devote a class or even several classes on some Shakespeare examples, including

some off-beat ones. There are, if I may be permitted one Shakespeare citation, an infinite variety of possibilities.

NOTES

1. Kenneth S. Rothwell and Annabelle Henkin Melzer, *Shakespeare on Screen: An International Filmography and Videography* (New York: Neal-Schuman, 1990), 16.

2. Similarly, Luke McKernan depended on the BFI archive for his reference book *Walking Shadows: Shakespeare in the National Film and Television Archive* (London: BFI, 1994). Kenneth Rothwell is currently updating his book *Shakespeare on Screen* (1990) with the assistance of Tanya Gough and José Ramón Díaz; McKernan is now updating his book as well and also including radio. Important resources include Mariangela Tempura and Vanni Borghi's (commercially unavailable) archive of her extensive holdings at the Centro Shakespeareano, University of Ferrara, and the catalogue for the 2001 Venice Biennale, *Shakespeare & Shakespeare: trascrizoni, adattamenti, traddimenti 1965/2000*, eds. Luca Scarlini and Elisa Vaccarino (Venice: Edizioni La Biennale di Vienezia, 2001). The former covers film and television, including those making only small citations to Shakespeare, and the latter, theater, music, dance, and literature as well as a number of short critical essays. See also the essays in Agostino Lombardo, ed., *Memoria di Shakespeare* (Rome: Bulzoni Editore, 2001).

3. On the term "mediatization," see Frederic Jameson, *Postmodernism, or, the Cultural Logic of Late Capitalism* (London: Verso, 1991). For recent uses of it by Shakespeareans, see Laurie E. Osborne, "Clip Art: Theorizing the Shakespearean Film Clip," *Shakespeare Quarterly* 53, no. 2 (Summer 2002): 227–40; and Richard Burt, "Slammin' Shakespeare in Acc(id)ents Yet Unknown: Liveness, Cinem(edi)a, and Racial Dis-integration," *Shakespeare Quarterly* 53, no. 2 (Summer 2002): 201–25.

4. Thus far, Shakespeare films on DVD do not include many of the extras that are common in DVD editions of many films. There are no extended DVD editions of Shakespeare films, such as those of Ridley Scott's *Gladiator* (2005) or *Kingdom of Heaven* (2005). Also, no Shakespeare film on DVD has an audio commentary by the director, although the Criterion editions of Laurence Olivier's *Richard III* and the Masterworks edition of Akira Kurosawa's *Ran* do include audio commentaries by film scholars. The two-disc edition of Baz Luhrmann's *William Shakespeare's Romeo + Juliet* is presently the more advanced Shakespeare DVD.

5. See Domenick Ammirati, "Mayerson: Derek Eller Gallery," *ArtForum* (February 2005).

6. Adrian Poole, *Shakespeare and the Victorians* (New York: Thomson, 2004), 118.

7. See Marjorie Garber, *Shakespeare after All* (New York: Pantheon Books, 2004), 39. On quotation, see Douglas Bruster's somewhat pedestrian, *Quoting Shakespeare: Form and Culture in Early Modern Drama* (Lincoln: University of Nebraska Press, 2000); Martin Harries's far more exciting *Scare Quotes from Shakespeare: Marx, Keynes, and the Language of Reenchantment* (Stanford, CA: Stanford University Press, 2000); and Marjorie B. Garber, *Quotation Marks* (New York: Routledge, 2003).

8. Garber, *Quotation Marks*, 40–41.

9. Poole, 5–6.

10. I draw on Gerard Genette's notion of the paratext. See *Paratexts: Thresholds of Interpretation* (Cambridge: Cambridge University Press, 1997). Work in film theory on the cinematic paratext has largely been confined to opening title sequences. The critical literature on opening title sequences is extensive, and most of it is in French and German. Nothing, as far as I know, has been written on closing credit sequences. Nicole de Mourgues' *Le générique de film* (Paris: Merediens Klincksieck, 1993) and an unpublished dissertation by Leopold Joseph Charney, "Just Beginnings: Film Studies, Close Analysis, and the Viewer's Experience" (New York University, 1992), make use of Genette, although neither addresses digital film. See also Deborah Allison, "Promises in the Dark: Opening Title Sequences in American Feature Films of the Sound Period" (University of East Anglia, 2001); Soren Kolstrup, "The Film Title and Its Historical Ancestors, or How Did We Get Where We Are?" *P.O.V.* 2 (November 1996), http://imv.au.dk/publikationer/pov/Issue_02/section_1/artc1B.html; Sarah Boxer, "Making a Fuss over Opening Credits: Film Titles Offer a Peek at the Future in More Ways Than One," *New York Times*, April 22, 2000; John C. Welchman, *Invisible Colors: A Visual History of Titles* (New Haven, CT: Yale University Press, 1997); André: Gardies, "Au commencement était le générique," in *Le conteur de l'ombre: Essai sur la narration filmique* (Lyon: Aléas, 1999), 13–23; Joachim Paech, "Vor-Schriften—In-Schriften—Nach-Schriften," in *Sprache im Film* (Wien: Wespennest-Film, 1994), 23–40; Mathias Poledna, "Light Extra Bold—Titelsequenzen und populärkulturelle Peripherie," *Internationale Kurzfilmtage Oberhausen 46* (festival catalog), May 4–9, 2000, 176–82; Jean-Pierre Berthome, "Les inconnus du générique," *Cinema 70*, no. 142 (January 1970): 32–67; Michel Saignes, "La lettre et la cinématographe. Graphisme et générique [Intervention de Michel Saignes transcite par Rodolphe Paillez]," *Image et son* 131 (January 1977): S. 81–86; Christopher Kelty and Hannah Landecker, "A Theory of Animation: Cells, L-Systems, and Film," *Grey Room* 17 (Fall 2004): 30–63; Jeff Bellantoni and Matt Woolman, *Type in Motion: Innovations in Graphic Design* (London: Thames & Hudson, 1999); David Geffner, "First Things First," *Filmmaker Magazine* 6, no. 1 (Fall 1997); Richard Hollis, "Credit Where Credit's Due," *The Guardian*, April 27, 1996, 28; John Naughton, "Credit Where Credit's Due," *Empire* (March 1994): 54–55; John C. Welchman, *Invisible Colors: A Visual History of Titles* (New Haven, CT: Yale University Press, 1997); David Geffner "The Art of Kyle Cooper," *Filmmaker Magazine* 6, no. 1 (Fall 1997); Ken Coupland, "Imaginary Forces: Taking All the Credits," *Graphis* 317 (September–October 1998), 62–71; and Andrea Codrington, *Kyle Cooper* (New Haven, CT: Yale University Press, Monographics, 2003). On the related but quite different film trailer, see Lia Kernan, *Coming Attractions: Reading American Movie Trailers* (Austin: University of Texas Press, 2004) and Hediger Vinzenz, "Das vorläufige Gedächtnis des Films: Anmerkungen zur Morphologie und Wirkungsästhetik des amerikanischen Kinotrailers," *Montage/av: Zeitschrift feur Theorie & Geschichte audiovisueller Komunikation* 8, no. 2 (1999): 111–32. Genette's spatial model of (para)textuality need to be brought into dialogue with recent work on media change and transition. See Peter Lunenfeld, *The Digital Dialectic New Essays on New Media* (Cambridge, MA: MIT Press, 1999); Don Harries, ed., *The New Media Book* (Berkeley: University of California Press, 2002); Thomas W. Keenan and Wendy Hui Kyong Chun, eds., *New Media, Old Media: Interrogating the Digital Revolution* (New York: Routledge, 2005); and David Thorburn and Henry Jenkins, eds., *Rethinking Media Change: The Aesthetics of Transition* (Cambridge, MA: MIT Press, 2004).

11. See Theodor Adorno and Max Horkheimer, "The Culture Industry: Enlightenment as Mass Deception," in Theodor Adorno and Max Horkheimer, ed., *The Dialectic of Enlightenment*, trans. John Cumming (New York: Herder and Herder, 1972). See also the essays collected in Theodor W. Adorno, *The Culture Industry*, ed. J. M. Bernstein, 2nd ed. (New York: Routledge, 2001).

12. For a full survey of these views of popular culture and mass media and the way they have played out in Shakespeare studies, see Richard Burt, ed., *Shakespeare after Mass Media* (New York: Palgrave, 2002).

13. On fandom, see Richard Burt, *Unspeakable ShaXXXspeares* (New York: St. Martin's Press, 1998).

14. In *Highbrow/lowbrow* (Cambridge, MA: Harvard University Press, 1988), Lawrence Levine offers an influential, if mythic, account of the way Shakespeare, who was widely popular in the nineteenth century, became part of elite culture in the twentieth and twenty-first centuries (Shakespeare is taken out of the popular). For a more recent example, see Adrian Poole's discussion of "Popular Shakespeare" in *Shakespeare and the Victorians* (New York: Thomson, 2004), 13–15.

15. See Michael Anderegg's excellent *Orson Welles, Shakespeare, and Popular Culture* (New York: Columbia University Press, 1999), especially pp. 164–67.

16. An enlightening email from Douglas Lanier drew my attention to the question of value.

17. Alan Liu, "The Future Literary: Literature and the Culture of Information," in *Time and the Literary*, ed. Karen Neumen, Jay Clayton, and Marianne Hirsch (New York: Routledge, 2002), 61–62.

18. See Michael Bristol, *Big-Time Shakespeare* (New York: Routledge, 1996); and Richard Burt, *Licensed by Authority: Ben Jonson and the Discourses of Censorship* (Ithaca: Cornell University Press, 1993). See also William Warner on eighteenth-century literature, marketing, and mass media.

19. This would include writing the history of Shakespeare in print in relation to the history of Shakespeare as literature. For work along these lines, see David Scott Kastan's *Shakespeare and the Book* (Cambridge: Cambridge University Press, 2001).

20. Richard Grusin and Jay David Bolter, *Remediation: Understanding New Media* (Cambridge, MA: MIT Press, 2000). See also Lev Manovich, *Language of New Media* (Cambridge, MA: MIT Press, 2002).

21. Jameson, 1991, 62, N. 19, p. 84.

22. On adaptation from novels and comics into film and vice versa, see Deborah Cartmell and Imelda Whelehan, *Adaptations: From Text to Screen, Screen to Text* (New York: Routledge, 1999), 3–4 and 28.

23. The first words etched by Thomas A. Edison's electric pen were, "Now is the winter of our discontent," from *Richard III*, Edison's favorite play. For a brief discussion, see Lisa Gitelman, *Scripts, Grooves, and Writing Machines: Representing Technology in the Edison Era* (Stanford, CA: Stanford University Press, 2001).

The earliest recording of Shakespeare was Henry Irving's 1888 version of the opening monologue of *Richard III*. To hear it, go to www.theirvingsociety.org.uk/richard_iii.htm. For a brief discussion of it, see Wes Folkerth, *The Sound of Shakespeare* (New York: Routledge, 2002). Michael Heumann comments on a similar link between Shakespeare and an early sound recording medium, the gramophone: "The phonograph's successor, the gramophone, a device developed by Charles Tainter in 1881 . . . used wax cylinders rather than the phonograph's tinfoil cylinders. Tainter's first words into the gramophone are telling: 'G-r-r-G-r-r- There are more things in heaven and earth Horatio, than are dreamed of in our philosophy-G-r-r-I am a gramophone and my mother was a phonograph.'" See "Metal Machine Music: The Phonograph's Voice and the Transformation of Writing" (1998), www.hauntedink.com/ghost/ch1.html. Susanne Greenhalgh is researching Shakespeare recordings downloadable on Apple iPods. IPods are being used for educational purposes at Duke University. See www.dukemagazine.duke.edu/dukemag/issues/091005/ipod1.html.

24. See Avital Ronell, *The Telephone Book: Technology, Schizophrenia, and Electronic Speech* (Lincoln: University of Nebraska Press, 1989), 283–85, for a full discussion, including the relation between theater and the telephone and Bell's father's interest in Shakespeare. References to *Hamlet* run through Ronell's excellent book.

25. See Burt 1998.

26. For an extremely valuable essay that makes theorizing connections between theater and media in Shakespeare performance, see Barbara Freedman, "Critical Junctures in Shakespeare Screen History: The Case of *Richard III*," in *The Cambridge Companion to Shakespeare on Film*, ed. Russell Jackson (Cambridge: Cambridge University Press, 2001), 47–71.

27. Stephen Greenblatt, *Will in the World: How Shakespeare Became Shakespeare* (New York: Norton, 2004); Stephen Greenblatt, "About That Romantic Sonnet," *New York Times*, February 6, 1999, A15–16; and Stephen Greenblatt, "Friends, Americans, Countrymen," *New York Times*, October 3, 2004, 4-11. See also an article about news interviews Greenblatt and Garber did after *Shakespeare in Love* swept the 1999 Academy Awards, www.news.harvard.edu/gazette/1999/03.18/shakespeare.html.

28. See, for examples, Neil Rhodes and Jonathan Sawday, eds., *The Renaissance Computer: Knowledge Technology in the First Age of Print* (New York: Routledge, 2003); and Elizabeth Sauer, *"Paper Contestations" and Textual Communities in England: 1640–1675* (Toronto: University of Toronto Press, 2005).

29. The series editors are Marie Macasia and Dominique Racah.

2

Cartoons and Comic Books

INTRODUCTION, "SHAKESPEARE STRIPPED: THE BARD (UN)BOUND IN COMICS," RICHARD BURT

As is the case with his appearance in nearly every other mass medium covered in this book, Shakespeare's appearances in cartoons, comic strips, and comic books registers an ambivalence. On the one hand, these materials are regarded as degraded, infantile. The Folger Shakespeare does not collect them, for example.[1] On the other hand, some comic books, nearly all of which are out of print, are the most commercially valuable of all the materials covered in this volume, some rising, as of this writing, to several hundred dollars. Shakespeare has received full-length comic book and graphic novel adaptations, and scenes and lines, some famous and some not, appear as well in cartoons, comic strips, and comic books for children and adults. Though the large majority of these comics are not as well known to Shakespeareans and are not easily accessible, they have begun to attract scholarly interest and have led to the publication of a number of excellent articles and book chapters.[2] Interestingly, comic book adaptations tend to be among the most conservative in any medium; characters from Shakespeare, for example, are almost always in period dress. The conservatism is only partly explicable in terms of comic books' censorship and the low regard in which comics were held in the 1950s, when Dr. Fredric Wertham's *Seduction of the Innocents* had wide currency and led to the introduction of the Comics Code Authority. Even in comics for adult readers produced in the 1980s and after, the costumes tend to be traditional, though the violence, in *Macbeth* comics, for example, becomes far more graphic in the 1980s.

This conservatism may have to do with the drive to adapt Shakespeare plays and literature generally as a narrative that connects the panels in a symbolizable whole. In his Lacanian account of sequentiality in comic books,

Donald Ault points out that the events between the panels are not symbolizable and thus analogous to the Lacanian real, a traumatic kernel that can never be made symbolic. As image sequences, comics "form networks of interrelations from panel to panel, panel to page, and page to page and thus participate in a symbolic order governed by laws of substitution and association (metaphor and metonymy)."[3] To be sure, there has been a move from the straightforward page layouts of the early adaptations, in which each panel is to be read in a left-to-right, top-down manner, to more recent Shakespeare comic adaptations, especially a Japanese manga–style *Macbeth* graphic novel, that give the reader much freer reign in navigating the page and that call attention to the page layout by bleeding part of an image in one panel into another or letting a word balloon extend from one panel to another. Nevertheless, even in these more recent comic books, a conventional narrative structure overrides more radical possibilities for destabilizing and deconstructing Shakespeare's plays.

While Shakespeare appears in comic books in a wide variety of ways, what follows in this introduction is confined to a brief history of comic book adaptations of Shakespeare. These comic books are likely to be of greatest interest to most Shakespeareans, since they can be taught and researched much along the lines of film adaptations.

The *Fast Fiction/Stories by Famous Authors Illustrated* series included three Shakespeare titles: *Hamlet, Romeo and Juliet,* and *Macbeth.*[4] All three were published in 1950, priced at ten cents, and adapted by Dana E. Dutch. Some of Shakespeare's language is kept, but much of it is modernized. Editorial comments are also interpolated to advance the narrative. These comic books also invoke the theater.

The opening and closing pages of *Hamlet* are framed by a curtain, and the final page ends with word "Curtain" at the bottom and the masks of comedy and tragedy. A curtain across the top and running down the left and right sides frames the opening and closing pages of *Romeo and Juliet*. *Macbeth*, the crudest of the three, is divided into three "parts"; *Hamlet* and *Romeo and Juliet* are divided into four. The composition of panels is fairly static in *Macbeth* and *Hamlet* (usually five to six panels, mostly square, and one or two circular panels). *Romeo and Juliet* is far more varied and inventive, and the arrangement more clearly guides the viewer's eye from one panel to the next. The tomb scene is particularly good, highlighting Juliet's suicide rather than Romeo's. Romeo and Juliet look to be in their twenties. All three comics were done in period dress, for the period in which the play is set (medieval Scotland for *Macbeth*, Renaissance Verona for *Romeo and Juliet*, and so on).

Probably the most familiar to readers born before 1960 are the *Classics Comics/Classics Illustrated* (Gilberton Publications) Shakespeare comic books. Gilberton published 169 titles from 1941 to 1962 (two new issues were released in 1969 along with new covers for several earlier versions in one of three failed attempts to revive and extend the series).[5] These comic books kept Shakespeare's language, but thereby faced a new problem, namely, how to cram the text in without letting it override the visuals. As with the Famous Authors comic books, all five *Classics Illustrated* comics were done in period dress for the period in which the play is set. Five Shakespeare issues in the series were all published in the 1950s: *Julius Caesar* (two versions, one with a line-drawn cover, the other with a painted cover), *A Midsummer Night's Dream*, *Hamlet* (a second edition in 1969 with a new painted cover), *Macbeth*, and *Romeo and Juliet* (a second edition in 1969 with a new painted cover). These were priced at ten and fifteen cents. The five Shakespeare plays adapted in this series were also the ones most frequently taught in American middle schools and high schools and the most frequently adapted on film. Two main illustrators did the five original *Classics Illustrated* Shakespeare comics: Albert Blum (*Macbeth*, *Hamlet*, and *A Midsummer Night's Dream*) and Henry C. Kiefer (*Julius Caesar*). Kiefer's style was theatrical; his *Julius Caesar* was influenced by the actor Henry Irving's production. Cinema influenced Kiefer's contemporaries at *Classics Illustrated*. Blum experimented with panel shapes in *A Midsummer Night's Dream*, and his *Hamlet*, particularly Claudius and Gertrude, was influenced by Olivier's 1948 film *Hamlet*. Kiefer did many of the period-style classics comics. His *Hamlet* looks more like Edwin Booth. Kiefer also did the covers and interior art work for all three Shakespeare comics in the *Fast Fiction/Stories by Famous Authors Illustrated* series. This competitive series was absorbed by Gilbertson, publisher of *Classics Illustrated*. The *Classics*

New Yorker cartoon by Tom Kleh, published January 2000. © Cartoonbank.

"Mr. Tilson will suffer you gladly now."

New Yorker cartoon by John Caldwell, published January 2000. © Cartoonbank.

Illustrated comics did not carry advertisements except for its own back issues and for binders, and all issues had one- and/or two-page supplements at the back, such as biographies of Shakespeare or an essay on the Elizabethan playhouse. During World War II, between five and ten million copies were sent to GIs through the American Red Cross.[6]

First Publishing/Berkeley Publishing Group briefly revived the *Classics Illustrated* series from February 1990 through June 1991 and issued new versions (all forty-eight pages in length and priced at $3.75). Twenty-seven titles were published, all looking like graphic novels. *Hamlet*, the only Shakespeare comic book in the series, was issued in March 1990. The panel composition is highly varied, and the small text is often broken up into small word balloons, making it far easier to follow than the *Classics Illustrated* adaptations. This *Hamlet* is relatively full version using Shakespeare's language. It is done in period dress.

In 1997 and 1998, Acclaim Books reissued the *Classics Illustrated* Shakespeare comics and others in smaller-sized, paperback-like editions with new painted covers and a scholarly apparatus at the back. The publishers targeted educators as their audience. In the later Acclaim series, the comics were reissued as "study guides" with "and notes" written on the covers. A Cliffs Notes–like essay supplement appeared at the back. A new *Henry IV* comic was issued in 1998. Issues of *Henry IV, Part 2* and *Henry V* were scheduled in April and June 1998, respectively, but never

issued (as were eight other titles). When the *Classics Illustrated* was revived in 1990, Shakespeare came earlier in the series (issue 5 out of 27 as opposed to issue 68 out of 169), and when Acclaim Books reissued the series in 1997 and 1998, Shakespeare came even earlier and more prominently (issues 2, 5, 9, 13, and 31 out of 62 issues). Additionally, Shakespeare's *Henry IV, Part 1* was the first newly issued comic in the series (# 59), and two more original Shakespeare comics were scheduled but never released (out of ten never-released issues). Taking a much smaller form, these reissues meant to compete with Cliffs Notes; hence, the scholarly apparatus added at the end of each comic book. The smaller size degrades the original *Classics Illustrated* comics, however, making them much harder to read.

In 1984, Pendulum Press/Academic Industries, Inc., published a new comic-book series of literary adaptations, Pocket Classics. It included twelve Shakespeare titles: *As You Like It, Hamlet, Julius Caesar, King Lear, Macbeth, The Merchant of Venice, A Midsummer Night's Dream, Othello, Romeo and Juliet, The Taming of the Shrew, The Tempest,* and *Twelfth Night*. The comic books are smaller than is usual— only 5 1/3″ × 8″, hence "pocket" classics. All are black and white, with sixty-one pages, and Shakespeare's language is modernized. The main interest of this series is the variety and number of the plays adapted. Douglas Lanier comments, "The illustrations look somewhat generic, though the compositions are occasionally unusual and illuminating."[7]

Workman Publishing published four comic graphic novelizations between 1982 and 1984: *Macbeth, King Lear, Othello,* and *Romeo and Juliet,* with three of them presented as "complete and unabridged" on the covers. A similar version of *Twelfth Night* was published in 1985 by Oval. Von illustrated both *Romeo and Juliet* and *Macbeth.* Ian Pollock's illustrations for *King Lear* are the only ones to make use of modern dress. These "novels" are far and away the most inventive of the comic books adaptations.

In 2002, an online version of the first act of *Hamlet,* by Aaron Thacker and Ben Templesmith, was published by Unbound Comics as *Hamlet: Issue #1.* The comic is made up of full-color paintings and can presently be downloaded in Adobe Acrobat for $1.75. The language is Shakespeare's.

Puffin Graphics, a branch of Penguin Books, began publishing a new series of graphic novel literary adaptations in 2005, with *Dracula* scheduled for publication in 2006. One title is a Shakespeare adaptation: *William Shakespeare's Macbeth, the Graphic Novel.* The black-and-white graphic novel, 148 pages long, keeps Shakespeare's language and is unusual in giving the play a science-fiction setting and illustrating it in Japanese manga style; the artist is Japanese and lives in Nagoya, Japan.

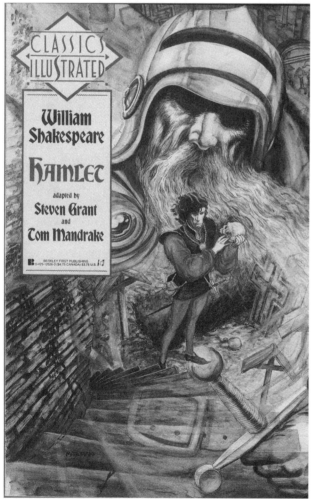

Hamlet, 1990.

There is also a twenty-four-page "Making of *William Shakespeare's Macbeth, the Graphic Novel*" at the back of the book.

In addition to these English-language adaptations, several Japanese comic book adaptations were published in Japan. I refer the reader to Appendix A.

Many scholars locate the history of comics thousands of years ago.[8] The history of Shakespeare in comics is longer than has been charted here. Caricatures, political cartoons, and editorial newspaper cartoons have yet to be researched, primarily because scholars working on Shakespeare and what has come to be known as visual culture focus their attention on Shakespeare in the fine arts.

Of the comics citing Shakespeare or using scenes form the plays, two Sandman comics, one about *A Midsummer Night's Dream* and the death of Shakespeare's son and another about Shakespeare writing *The Tempest*, are among the most interesting and have drawn the most critical attention from Shakespeareans.[9] Shakespeare comics can be assimilated to work on film and television adaptations (all are interpretations); however, I think they offer new, less text-centered ways of thinking about Shakespeare's remediation, since they cross over into "novels" and since comics have become increasingly cinematic. (Comics critics prefer the term "panel" to "frame," for example, so as not to confuse comics with film.) The nature of the comic page is also changing as comic books are coming "unbound" when they are published on the web.[10] They might be more fully linked up to the history of the comics book medium.[11]

NOTES

1. Two universities have large comic book collections and resources: Michigan State University (which has a searchable database online and whose librarians will send black-and-white photocopies of some comic books on request) and the University of Florida. The online comics journal *ImageText* is published by Donald Ault and other members of the English Department at University of Florida.

2. See Michael D. Bristol, "Shakespeare: The Myth," in *A Companion to Shakespeare*, ed. David Scott Kastan (Oxford: Blackwell, 1999), 489–502; Annalisa Castaldo, "'No More Yielding than a Dream': The Construction of Shakespeare in *The Sandman*," *College Literature* 31, no. 4 (2004): 94–110; Fabio Ciaramaglia, *Shakespeare e il linguaggio del fumetto*, Piccola Biblioteca Shakespeariana 31 (Rome: Bulzoni, 2003); Annalisa Castaldo, "A Text of Shreds and Patches: Shakespeare and Popular Culture," *Shakespeare and Renaissance Association of West Virginia: Selected Papers* 20 (1997): 59–71; Josh Heuman and Richard Burt, "Suggested for Mature Readers? Deconstructing Shakespearean Value in Comic Books," in *Shakespeare after Mass*

Media, ed. Richard Burt (New York: Palgrave, 2002), 150–71; A. J. Hoenselaars, "Shakespeare alom," *Armada: Tijdschrift voor wereldliteratuur* 6 (January 2001): 62–71; James P. Lusardi, "Iconic Shakespeare: Oscar Zarate's *Othello*," *Shakespeare Yearbook* 11 (2000): 136–53; Pietra Motta, "Shakespeare a fumetti," in *Shakespeare graffiti: il cigno di Avon nella cultura di massa*, ed. Mariacristina Cavecchi and Sara Soncini (Milano: CUEM, 2002), 137–79; Marion D. Perret, "Not Just Condensation: How Comic Books Interpret Shakespeare," *College Literature* 31, no. 4 (2004): 72–93; Marion D. Perret, "'And Suit the Action to the Word': How a Comics Panel Can Speak Shakespeare," in *The Language of Comics: Word and Image*, ed. Robin Varnum and Christina T. Gibbons (Jackson: University Press of Mississippi, 2001), 123–44; Marion D. Perret, "More than Child's Play: Approaching *Hamlet* through Comic Books," in *Approaches to Teaching Shakespeare's Hamlet*, ed. Bernice Kliman (New York: Modern Language Association, 2001), 161–64; Susan Viguers, "*King Lear* as a Book: A Visual/Verbal Production," *Shakespearean International Yearbook* 4 (2004): 215–31; and Naomi J. Miller, ed. *Reimagining Shakespeare for Children and Young Adults* (New York: Routledge, 2003).

3. See Donald Ault, "'Cutting Up' Again, Part II: Lacan on Barks on Lacan," in *Comics and Culture: Theoretical and Analytical Approaches to Comics* (Copenhagen: University of Copenhagen Press, 2000), 109–21; and Donald Ault, "Imagetextuality: 'Cutting Up' Again Part III," *ImageText* 1, no. 1 (Spring 2004), www.english.ufl.edu/imagetext/archives/volume1/issue1/ault/.

4. Classicscentral.com has scans of the covers of all of these comic books and the *Classics Illustrated* comics as well.

5. My history of *Classics Illustrated* comics is derived from William B. Jones Jr., *Classics Illustrated: A Cultural History, with Illustrations* (Jefferson, NC: McFarland, 2002).

6. For more complete coverage of these comics, see Heuman and Burt, 2002; and Perret, 2004.

7. Post on Shaksper.net.

8. See, for example, Scott McCloud, *Understanding Comics* (New York: HarperCollins, 1994); and David Kunzle, *The Early Comic Strip: Narrative Strips and Picture Stories in the European Broadsheet from c.1450 to 1825* (Berkeley: University of California Press, 1973).

9. See Castaldo, 2004; and Hueman and Burt, 2002.

10. Sarah Boxer, "Comics Escape a Paper Box, and Electronic Questions Pop Out," *New York Times* August 17, 2005, www.nytimes.com/2005/08/17/books/17comi.html?8hpib.

11. On the medium of comics, see Hans-Christian Christiansen, "Comics and Film: A Narrative Perspective," in *Comics & Culture*, ed. Anne Magnussen et al. (Copenhagen: Museum Tusculanum Press, 2000), 107–21; Dunger Hella et al., "Comic—Vorschule des Fernsehens," in *Comics im Aesthetischen Unterricht*, ed. Dietger Pforte (Frankfurt am Main: Athenaeum, 1974), 172–247; Will Eisner, *Comics and Sequential Art* (Tamarac, FL: Poorhouse Press, 1985); Pascal Lefèvre, "The Importance of Being 'Published': A Comparative Study of Different Comics Formats," in Magnussen et al., 2000, 93–105; McCloud, 1994; Scott McCloud, *Reinventing Comics* (New York: HarperCollins, 2000); and Varnum Gibbons.

ENTRIES PLAY BY PLAY, MICHAEL P. JENSEN

Additional entries by Richard Burt are followed by (RB).

ALL'S WELL THAT ENDS WELL

1 *Captain Marvel Adventures*
"Captain Marvel Gets the Golden Fleece" # 56, March 15, 1946. Greenwich, CT: Fawcett Publications, Inc. Otto Binder (writer), C. C. Beck (artist). Page 11.

Captain Marvel was a lighthearted derivative of Superman. In a typically goofy adventure, Marvel is sent to search for some golden fleas, but he mishears and goes in pursuit of the Golden Fleece. In bringing the story to its resolution, he defeats the cult that worships the golden dog who has the golden fleas, and he also secures the Golden Fleece. Billy Batson, who is Captain Marvel when not super-powered, tells the story on his daily radio broadcast, concluding, "All's well that ends well!" There are very few comic references of any sort to this play, and all of them use the title as a closing phrase as Shakespeare did with the paraphrases "All yet seems well" (5.3.370) and "All is well ended" (Epilogue.2). Helena uses the line a couple of times, but more as a hope than as a conclusion (4.4.39 and 5.1.29).

ANTONY AND CLEOPATRA

2 *Foxtrot*
August 29–September 2, 1989. Universal Press Syndicate. Bill Amend (writer/artist).

A five-day sequence portrays the difficulty Paige has studying *Antony and Cleopatra* for school. She cannot get started because she does not understand the first sentence of the play (August 29). She asks her brother to define the words "prithee," "dottage" [sic], and "forsooth." He deliberately gives her misinformation, telling her, for example, that forsooth means "Kiss me, hot Momma, I'm burnin' with love." She believes him (August 30). On the third day she concludes that the play is written in Martian, not English (August 31). She then resorts to Cliffs Notes (September 1), and in the final strip she laments the sad ending. Another brother worries that the asp has cooties from biting a girl (September 2). The strip is ineptly drawn, but the writing captures the anxiety students feel when reading texts foreign to them, mixed well with exaggeration about unhelpful siblings and the antagonism in family dynamics.

AS YOU LIKE IT

3 *Whiz Comics*
"Captain Marvel and the Grand Steeplechase." Vol. 7, # 38, December 25, 1942. Greenwich, CT: Fawcett Publications. Otto Binder (writer), Marc Swayze (artist). Page 7.

This Captain Marvel story uses the expression "forever and a day," which appears in *As You Like It* (4.1.64) although it was a cliché when the story appeared. Billy Batson is the boy who becomes Captain Marvel when he says a magic word. He has a valet named Steamboat (an African American stereotype), and Steamboat has a girlfriend named Delilah. Steamboat will be the jockey for a horse named Black Booty in a race. Delilah tells him that if he loses the race, "Yo' is disgraced in mah eyes fo'evah an' a day!" Steamboat wonders how long that is, and Billy assures him, "Pretty long." As glimpsed in the spelling of Delilah's quote, the story is more notable for its racial stereotypes than for its thin connection with Shakespeare.

4 *Our Boarding House*
December 2–11, 1952. NEA, Inc. Bill Freyse (writer/artist).

This is a Shakespeare-related sequence within a longer story. A temperance club called the Owls plans to raid Major Hoople's drinking club. The Major and his boys plan a diversion so the Owls will leave them alone in the future. They will pretend they are interested in the intellectual things approved of by the Owls. The idea is explained by a member named Twiggs in the December 2 panel, and the Major thinks it is a fine idea, adding that the boys could read Shakespeare and drink tea. On December 3, Twiggs tells the Major he has books on science and philosophy and by Shaw and Shakespeare. He wonders if the boys will think *Pygmalion* "is a treatise on hogs." Twiggs gives a copy of *As You Like It* to a member named Brannigan with instructions to read it to another member named Watson when the time comes. Watson wonders if the book is a bartender's guide (December 14). Brannigan reads, "A fool, a fool! I met a fool i' the forest, / A motley fool; a miserable world!" (2.7.15–16) Watson says that Shakespeare "sounds like his tank sprung a seam!" The other members work on geography (December 5). The raid occurs between the December 6 and 10, with the next and final Shakespeare reference on December 11. While some members talk geography, Brannigan reads *As You Like It*: "And this, our life, exempt from public haunt, finds tongues in trees, books in the running brooks, sermons in stones, and good in everything" (2.1.18–19). The Major mutters, "Egad! I hope the lads don't overplay it."

5 *Frank and Ernest*
August 16, 1974. NEA, Inc. Bob Thaves.

Frank and Ernest look homeless, standing among garbage. Using lines from *As You Like It* (2.7.139–40), perennial punster Frank says, "If it's true that 'All the world's a stage and all the men and women merely players'...I want to speak with someone in central casting." See the introduction for the background on this strip.

6 *Garfield*
December 9, 1981. United Features Syndicate, Inc. Jim Davis (writer/artist).

Jon has a cat named Garfield, who understands what Jon says and replies in thought balloons, which Jon is somehow able to hear. This comic strip defies logic and is lazily drawn and repetitive, but that has not stopped it from being one of the world's most popular strips for nearly three decades. This time, Jon asks Garfield's philosophy of life. The cat paraphrases *As You Like It* (2.7.139–40), saying, "All the world's a cookie jar, and all the men and women merely crumbs." Garfield then looks smug, and adds, "I happen to be one of the chocolate chips."

7 *Good Days and Mad*
1980s, Reprint 1994. Dick DeBartolo (writer). Page 101.

In a two-page parody of magazine advertising is a call for actresses. "We are looking for...girls to appear in an all-nude version of Shakespeare's 'As You Like It.' Here is your chance to be seen and handled by top agents and producers! Send nude photo...to: Shakespeare-in-the-Buff Festival Auditions, c/o The Wild Pussycat Strip Joint and Pizza Palace...." This mock ad was not illustrated, and was reprinted in Dick DeBartolo's book *Good Days and Mad: A Historical Tour Behind the Scenes at Mad Magazine* (New York: Thunder Mouth Press, 1994) without crediting the original publication date or issue number.

8 *As You Like It*
1984, Reprint 1994. Circle Pines, MN: American Guidance Service, Inc. Naunerle Farr (adapter), Nestor Leonidez (artist).

Naunerle Farr adapted most of the Pendulum series of Shakespeare comic books. One reason they are so bland is Farr's tendency to skip anything strongly visual such as flashbacks, Shylock's knife, and the wrestling match in this play. It is over in two panels, one before it begins, the next after Orlando has won. This goes against the strength of the comic medium, but does protect kids from a violent scene (p. 13). In keeping with this tendency to play it safe, Adam is not near death with hunger, just tired, hungry, and in need of a rest (p. 21). Though Orlando draws his sword to steal food, he does not threaten to kill anyone (p. 23). Rosalind is hardly a convincing boy. From the slight bulge of her bust, the thick hair spilling from her hat, and even the apparent mascara she wears in close-ups (e.g., p. 29), she could not fool anyone as Ganymede. Perhaps this helps children identify her. Pendulum is unusual for the number of comedies adapted to comic books, but they typically eliminate the humor to concentrate on the plot.

This book is unusual for trying to keep some comic scenes, though without laughs. The conversation between Touchstone and Corin survives in two brief panels, but the updated language does not seem to try to make it funny, or possibly does not succeed (p. 27). Farr also retains Rosalind's joke about telling her father, as Ganymede, that "his" father's parentage is "as good as he" (3.5.37). It does not come off (p. 34). Eliminated are two subplots. The antagonism between Orlando and Jaques is gone as part of the near-excising of Jaques. He gives a paraphrase of the "seven ages of man" speech that is so brief as to be meaningless (p. 24) and is otherwise on hand only to be told he is silly on a couple of occasions. Also cut is Audrey and her relationship with Touchstone, who makes only a couple of brief and late appearances. There are four couples in the play representing four aspects of love; this cut deletes the most physical of the four. One of the nice things about the play is the way the characters become tired of playing at love and grow ready for the real thing. Orlando does this (p. 48), but Farr robs Rosalind of her moment. The AGS reprint was examined for this entry.

9 *Andy Capp*
November 2, 1990. Syndication International North America Syndicate, Inc. Reggie Smythe (writer/artist).

A comic strip with a peculiarly English view of life, Andy Capp has nevertheless been popular in other parts of the world. Andy lives for the pub, so much so that he cannot keep a job, sponges off his wife Flo, and will pick up any other woman. The strip began as a panel in 1958 and, unlike *Blondie*, has not kept up with the times. Andy is as much a misogynist as ever, but Smythe created a successful formula. At its height, the strip appeared in more than fifteen hundred papers around the world and is still popular. Shakespeare quotes are rare, but this one is well judged. Andy is in a pub making time with a woman who wants Andy to tell her about himself. Flo enters, orders Andy to go play darts while she does "the telling." As Andy walks away, he complains that "all the world's a stage—and one of these days I might get the chance to play the lead in my own life." The quote from *As You Like It* (2.7.147) is not credited. It is assumed that readers will recognize it. The date above is the publication date in American newspapers.

10 *Frank and Ernest*
October 8, 2000. NEA, Inc. Bob Thaves (writer/artist).

This is a typical, pun-filled *Frank and Ernest* Sunday page. Frank wants to demonstrate to readers that Ernest has a "colorful personality," so he asks him a series of questions. The answers are titles of songs, plays, and films that allow Ernest to substitute a color for a similar sounding word, such as his favorite Broadway show, *Yellow Dolly*. What is his "favorite Shakespeare play?" The answer is "Azure Like It."

11 *Ziggy*
May 4, 2004. Universal Press Syndicate. Tom Wilson
and Tom II (writers/artists).

Ziggy, the often sentimental thoughts of an everyman
figure, began as a cartoon panel in 1968 with a strip format
on Sundays. It had enormous popularity into the 1980s, but
came to be considered passé, though it is still published
today. It became a father/son project in 1987, with the son
now doing the bulk of the work. In this panel, Ziggy walks
under a caption that says " 'All's the world's a stage'!—Wm.
Shakespeare." He says, "And it seems I just ended up as an—
USHER." The quote is from *As You Like It* (2.7.139).

12 *Pearls before Swine*
March 18, 2005. United Features Syndicate, Inc.
Stephan Pastis (writer/artist).

The regular characters in this stiffly drawn comic strip
are a pig, a rat, and a zebra, with occasional appearances by
a couple of alligators. In this daily, one of the alligators says
the zebra is not afraid of them because they are stupid, so he
brings along an intelligent alligator, who proves his smarts
by quoting, "Here comes a pair of very strange beasts,
which in all tongues are called fools," from *As You Like It*
(5.4.37). This alligator ends up apologizing to the zebra for
the other's uncouth behavior.

HAMLET

13 *Buster Brown: His Snow Man*
Early March 1906, Reprint 1977. King Features Syndicate.
Richard F. Outcault (writer/artist). Pages 16–17.

The immensely popular *Buster Brown* is usually credited
with being the first comic strip (more than one panel). It
was created by Richard F. Outcault, who is usually credited with also creating the first comic panel. Whether or
not it was truly first, there no denying Buster's popularity,
which translated into toys, films, a stage show, and a line
of children's shoes and comic books that lasted well into
the baby-boom generation. Outcault began the Sunday-
only strip in 1902 and it lingered until 1921, although he
abandoned it to others many years before. The formula
was simple and open to endless variation. Buster was
naughty but learned his lesson, with the last panel a
homily on what he had learned. This is perhaps disin-
genuous. It is difficult to believe most readers would have
read to the homily if they had not been entertained by
the mischief that preceded it. This is the first of two strips
from 1906 that mention Shakespeare in the lesson. Buster
and his friends build a snowman and -woman that are
unusually realistic. They dress them in his parent's clothes
and show them off to Buster's mother, but by the time she
arrives, the snow-couple have melted and the clothing is
drenched. Mother gives Buster a spanking, and he learns
that "some folks don't attach enough importance to
clothes. Shakespeare says 'costly thy raiment as thy purse

New Yorker cartoon by Stuart Leeds, published January 1997. ©
Cartoonbank.

can buy.' How are you to gain our first idea of a man
except by his clothes?" and concluded clothes are too
important to treat as he has done, for "they are the
key to" a person's "nature, breeding and taste." The
Shakespeare quote is form *Hamlet* (1.3.74), and Outcault
substituted *raiment* for *habit*. This Sunday strip ran two
weeks after a George Washington's Birthday strip, which
was on a Thursday that year, indicating it is probably
from the first or second Sunday or March. This strip was
found in Richard F. Outcault, ed., *Buster Brown: A
Complete Compilation: 1906* (Westport, CT: Hyperion
Press, 1977).

14 *Baron Mooch*
December 11, 1909. King Features Syndicate, Inc.
George Herriman (writer/artist).

In 1.5.15–16, the Ghost tells Hamlet, "I could a tale
unfold whose lightest word / Would harrow up thy soul."
In this strip, Herriman, who often sprinkled in Shakespearean phrases and paraphrases over his career, has a
goose tell a cat, "Were you not such a lowbrow, I would a
tale unfold to you." This one of the strips Herriman tried
before creating *Krazy Kat*. Both the cat and the goose are
precursors of characters in the later strip.

15 *Krazy Kat*
June 16, 1921. King Features Syndicate, Inc.
George Herriman (writer/artist).

The action of this daily strip has Ignatz Mouse bean
Krazy Kat with a brick, then try to revive him as a dog
comes along. The dog is impressed because he mistakenly

thinks that Ignatz is trying to help Krazy. Once Krazy is conscious again, Ignatz heaves another brick at him, much to the dog's surprise. The Shakespearean connection is a well-worn line of Herriman's, where he uses Laertes's "Have at you" (5.2.289), here spoken by Ignatz, to indicate a sneak attack. This is the earliest reference found so far of Herriman using this line.

16 *Krazy Kat*
February 14, 1926. King Features Syndicate, Inc.
George Herriman (writer/artist).

Krazy and a dog have a long, banal conversation about apples. When this Sunday page finally draws to a close, Ignatz makes a sneak attack on Krazy, using the same phrase Laertes uses when making his sneak attack on Hamlet (5.2.289). Ignatz says, "Have at you!!! 'Nogood' Have at you!!!" Krazy is knocked to the ground by Ignatz's brick.

17 *Krazy Kat*
December 19, 1926. King Features Syndicate, Inc.
George Herriman (writer/artist).

Again using Shakespeare's words "have at you" to indicate a sneak attack, Officer Pupp hurls a rubber brick at Ignatz Mouse. Ignatz bends over to look at a worm in the bottom of a tree, so the brick misses him, bounces off the tree, and beans Pupp. The bounce off Pupp's head sends the brick bonking into Krazy.

18 *Krazy Kat*
September 11, 1927. King Features Syndicate, Inc. George Herriman (writer/artist).

George Herriman loved to sneak Shakespeare's lines into the mouths of his characters when he put them in similar situations. In what is perhaps the strangest quote of all, Hamlet's words of disgust and disapproval about his Mother's wedding and life in general, "oh fie" (1.2.137), became the words of disgust and disapproval spoken by an old duck as she tells off Ignatz Mouse for heaving a brick. "Oh—fie—fie—fie." In the next panel she bad-mouths Officer Pupp for having a billy club, and in the panel following says, "Fie, oh fie, oh fie." Ignatz and Pupp discard their weapons—temporarily.

19 *Krazy Kat*
December 16, 1928. King Features Syndicate, Inc.
George Herriman (writer/artist).

Herriman repeats his gag from June 16, 1921 (see separate entry), by having Ignatz Mouse use Laertes's phrase "Have at you" (5.2.289) while making a sneak attack. Again, Krazy is hit in the head by Ignatz's brick. This time Krazy is not knocked to the ground.

20 *Krazy Kat*
December 20, 1931. King Features Syndicate, Inc.
George Herriman.

In *Hamlet* (2.2.575), Rosencrantz and Guildenstern leave the title character, and Hamlet begins the "rogue and peasant slave" speech with the words, "Now I am alone." Herriman, who often put Shakespeare's words, misspelled, into the mouths of his characters, develops the theme of *alone*. In the first panel, Ignatz Mouse "engages in 'solitaire'—solus." Krazy enters in the second panel, saying, "Now I am illone—" [*sic*]. Krazy finds Ignatz in panel three and proceeds to kibitz until Ignatz goes to fetch a brick to silence that krazy kat. Police Officer Pup puts Ignatz in jail, then begins to kibitz Krazy.

21 *Secret Agent X-9*
October 12, 1935. King Features Syndicate, Inc.
Leslie Charteris (writer), Alex Raymond (artist).

The strip was created in 1934 by mystery writer Dashiell Hammett, who soon turned the writing over to others. At this point in his career, X-9 most often fought crime and sabotage in the United States, as he does here. X-9 prowls the grounds of an apparent film studio. His partner Carp waits in the car. Carp is seen and asked why he is there. "I came to see if I could get a job. . . . My best part is Hamlet," he replies. Carp and X-9 make a hasty retreat in the next strip.

22 *Mickey Mouse*
August 2, 1936. King Features Syndicate, Inc.
Floyd Gottfredson (plotter/penciller), Ted Osborne (dialog), Ted Thwaites (inker).

Like George Herriman, long-time Disney writer and artist Floyd Gottfredson uses a variation on Laertes's "Have at you now" (5.2.289) to begin a duel, this time between Mickey Mouse and Richard the Lion-Hearted. Mickey hides between the pages of a Robin Hood book to escape a malevolent fly and surrealistically finds himself caught in the adventure story. To prove his worthiness to be one of Robin's Merrie Men, he agrees to highway robbery of a passing merchant. They fight with quarterstaves, and Mickey bests him. As he attacks, Mickey says, "Okay! Have at ya!" His opponent, it is learned in the August 9 Sunday page, is the king.

23 *Terry and the Pirates*
January 25, 1941. Chicago Tribune–New York News Syndicate. Milton Caniff (writer/artist).

Dr. Ping has befriended the regular characters, but a traitor named Tang works against their interests. Tang has been found out and confined to the brig. Ping has caught him attempting to escape, and holds him at gunpoint. Tang says, "Out of the way, ancient turtle! Tang does as he pleases." In panel two Ping replies, "But not as Dr. Ping pleases—there's the rub! Back to your bunk!" Tang knocks him unconscious and runs away in panel four to make more trouble for our heroes. He only succeeds for a little while. "The rub," of course, is taken from the language of the "To be or not to be" speech (3.1.67): "Ay, there's the rub." The rub was an obstacle in a game called bowls that stopped a ball from reaching its goal. Dr. Ping seems to mean "that's the problem," which is slightly different.

24 *Terry and the Pirates*
April 23, 1943. Chicago Tribune–New York News Syndicate. Milton Caniff (writer/artist).

On the traditional date of Shakespeare's birth, flier Lieutenant Joss Goode sees the unconscious nurse Taffy Tucker and quotes *Hamlet* in his southern accent as phoentically rendered by Milton Caniff: "Deah maid, kind sistuh, sweet Ophelia! . . . O Heavens! Is't possible a young maid's wits should be as mortal as an old man's life . . ." (4.5.157–59). Happily, Taffy is not dead.

25 *Archie Comics*
"Archie in the Play's the Thing." # 26, May 1947. Unknown (writer), Bill Vigoda (artist).

Archie Andrews and his friends are the creation of Vic Bloom and Bob Montana. The feature began in a back-up spot in a superhero comic in 1941, but it was popular and Archie soon had his own title and even precipitated the company to change its name. It has been around ever since, with dozens of writers and artists contributing to the character. The basic premise is that Archie is attracted to both Betty and Veronica but has a rival in another teenager named Reggie. Also in the cast is Archie's best friend Jughead, his parents, and various authority figures at his high school. In this comic, Veronica will not go to the school dance with Archie unless he appears in the school play as Hamlet. Archie has two problems. The first is that he is the understudy and Reggie has the lead; the story does not address this. The other is that he needs a skull to rehearse but cannot find one. Jughead volunteers his head (still attached), but Archie's father is so annoyed at the noise they make that he makes them stop. They try to steal a skull from their school science lab, but only get away with it because Archie puts it on his head and disguises his body under a lab coat. This makes him look like a ghost and allows his to get past the school principal, who faints. This starts a rumor that there is a ghost on the prowl, so *Hamlet* is cancelled and replaced with *A Midsummer Night's Dream*. The logic behind that is not clear, but it does allow the writer to get to the concluding joke. Archie is determined to get into that show, so he puts on a donkey costume. The sight of a talking donkey makes the principal faint again, and he is taken to hospital. The issue reviewed is missing its cover, so the indicia information is not there. According to the University of Michigan Library's website, there is a story entitled "Midsummer's Nightmare" in *Archie Comics* # 28 (September/October 1947), and a *Romeo and Juliet* story in *Archie and Friends* # 21, February 1997.

26 *Saddle Justice*
"Horse Opera Hamlet." # 3, Spring 1948. New York: Educational Comics. Unknown (writer), H. C. Kiefer (artist). Page 8.

Despite the number, this is the first issue of *Saddle Justice*, which took over the numbering of the *Happy Houlihan* comic book to save money at the post office. The first story in this issue is about an actor who disguises himself and plays the part of a robber to get cash without anyone knowing who he is. He ends up murdering as well. Beyond the title, the only mention of Shakespeare is when the actor changes disguises while robbing a train. He says, "This is better'n Shakespeare." *Hamlet* is not mentioned in the story. Credit: Dick Swan.

27 *Pogo*
December 16, 1948. Post-Hall Syndicate. Walt Kelly (writer/artist).

A recurring piece of dialogue in George Herriman's *Krazy Kat* was "have at you" whenever there was an attack. Herriman found this in *Hamlet* (5.2.289), where Laertes says it when attacking Hamlet. Walt Kelly also knew his Shakespeare, and used the words in exactly the same way in this strip. Albert Alligator and Beauregard the Bloodhound are rival detectives. Albert wears a Sherlock Holmes deerstalker, and Beau has a London bobby hat. As they prepare to duke it out, Beau says, "Have at you Sirrah! You overgrown toadie-frog!" A duck, the mail carrier, interrupts them.

28 *Pogo*
September 21, 1949. Post–Hall Syndicate. Walt Kelly (writer/artist).

These attending Owl's school have been given an assignment to learn about "nature's creatures," which they misunderstood as "nature's screechers." When Pogo Possum tries to screech, it comes out as "HAWCK." This prompts Porkypine to muse, "Oh—I just don't know a hawk from a handsaw, anymore," a paraphrase of *Hamlet* (2.2.361).

29 *Dick Tracy*
May 11–13, 17, 23, June 4–5, 7, 9–11, 14, 18, July 11, 1950. Chicago Tribune–New York News Syndicate. Chester Gould (writer/artist).

The drunk Vitamin Flintheart enters a bar, laments his bad fortune, and quotes *Macbeth* (May 11). He goes to his hotel and quotes *Henry V*, *Hamlet*, and *Othello* (May 12). *Titus Andronicus* follows (May 13), and then Vitamin sleeps it off, but in the wrong room. It is the room of the wounded criminal Blowtop, who calls Vitamin "Shakespeare" on May 17 and forces Vitamin to dress his wounds. Vitamin tries "to quote the bard" on May 23, but Blowtop blows his temper, which stops him. Vitamin also befriends a man from Borneo and trades one of Blowtop's shirts for a shrunken head to be used in a production of *Hamlet* that Vitamin and Blowtop plan to produce together (June 4–5). Vitamin develops the habit of speaking to the head (June 7 and 9–11) and even uses it as a dummy, throwing his voice while giving lines from *Hamlet*, which annoys Blowtop (June 14). As the story reaches its conclusion, Blowtop tosses the head into the river and tries to kill Vitamin. Blowtop is eventually stopped by detective Dick Tracy, and Vitamin recovers the shrunken head, saying, "Good old Yorick" (July 11).

30 *Pogo*
September 2, 1950. Post-Hall Syndicate. Walt Kelly (writer/artist).

The Deacon wants to start a school and gives Albert the alligator a math lesson. Albert, who has probably been doing too much gambling, insists the number eleven follows the number seven in sequence, "Like the night the day," an unacknowledged quote of *Hamlet* (1.3.79). Albert next recites the alphabet, which is rendered as playing cards: "Ace, King, Queen, Jack" on down to the deuce. The Deacon is not impressed, but pretends he is, appointing Albert truant officer with the responsibility to "fetch in a new student body."

31 *Stories by Famous Artists Illustrated*
8. *Hamlet*. October 1950. Bridgeport: Seaboard Publishers, Inc. Dana E. Dutch (adapter), Henry C. Kiefer (artist).

Dutch approaches adapting *Hamlet* differently here than he did with *Macbeth*. He still rewrites Shakespeare's dialogue, but drops in more of the original words and phrases than before. Much of the cutting is summarized in narration. He opens with Hamlet (1.2) after a caption describes the first part of the scene (p. 3). Restructuring the story as a comic book makes this more satisfying than *CI*'s version, which compromises the medium in deference to the play. Even so, the soliloquies are too text-heavy to work. Polonius's advice to Laertes is given in full, which is a mistake in a medium this visual. Dutch elides this scene with Ophelia telling her father about Hamlet's strange behavior, again saving space and allowing Dutch to keep the story moving (pp. 9–10). Hamlet's telling Horatio about the deaths of Rosencrantz and Guildenstern is moved to the graveyard scene, where it makes better sense, and the exposition about the pirates is given there in dialog (p. 22). All the humor is cut, along with every reference to Norway. The only mention of politics is in the caption already mentioned describing Claudius's adeptness at it and his dispatching "couriers on a mission of state" (p. 3). Everything else is a domestic matter. As does Malcolm in Dutch's *Macbeth*, Hamlet sometimes looks like a woman (see the second and last panels of p. 6). The length of Hamlet's hair is always changing: Compare pp. 14 and 15.

32 *The Best Cartoons from PUNCH*
Reprint 1952/original publication date unknown. New York: Simon & Schuster. George Morrow (writer/artist). Page 83.

Shakespeare spelled his name six different ways in his six extant signatures. In an apparent parody of this, longtime *Punch* cartoonist George Morrow has Shakespeare look at a sign painter doing his work. The sign reads, "GLOBE THEATRE / HAMLET, / PRINCE OF DENMARK / A TRAGEDIE / By / SHAXPERE." The artist tells Shakespeare, "I'd better come back when you've made up your mind." The pages of *The Best Cartoons from PUNCH* are not numbered, so the reference above was derived by counting from the first cartoon in the book.

33 *The Best Cartoons from Punch*
Reprint 1952. New York: Simon & Schuster.
J. W. Taylor (writer/artist). Page 119.

A family is eating a meal. The mother tells the son not to quote Hamlet's "'Oh, what a noble mind is here o'erthrown' every time your father opens his mouth, or I'll stop you going to the pictures altogether" (3.1.150). The original date of this cartoon is unknown, but, given the subject matter, it is probably after Olivier's 1948 film version of *Hamlet*. The original date was not found. The pages of *The Best Cartoons from PUNCH* are not numbered, so the reference above was derived by counting from the first cartoon in the book.

34 *Classics Illustrated 99*
Hamlet. September 1952. New York: Gilberton Company, Inc. Sam Willinsky (writer), Alex A. Blum (artist).

Willinsky had a clear strategy for abridging this story: Begin most scenes in the middle and sometimes cut the end. Let three examples stand for many. 1.2 begins with "O, that this too too solid flesh" speech (1.2.133–63). The scene finishes in a second panel when Hamlet is informed about the ghost (p. 7). Also gone is the dialogue between Laertes and Ophelia in the next scene (1.3.1–63). It begins with a few of their father's precepts, but very few (p. 7). This is immediately followed by Hamlet vowing to follow the ghost (p. 8); the forty-four lines preceding their meeting are missing (1.4), and so is most of what follows the ghost's departure (p. 10). This adaptive strategy strips away nearly everything political in this highly political drama, including all references to Norway. Rosencrantz and Guildenstern are in the story (pp. 11 and 18 have the two panels in which they say something), but so furtively that the comic may have benefited by their absence. The cuts tell the story quickly and focus on the family relationship. The confrontation between Hamlet and Gertrude is surprisingly full, taking nearly seven pages (pp. 20–26), one a striking two-page single panel with the ghost (pp. 24–25). While that panel is effective, most of the art is Blum's usual hackwork. The conclusion is simply inept. For some reason, he

Hamlet by Alex A. Blum (artist) and Sam Willinsky (writer), 1950.

draws two cups of wine, one poisoned and one not. He then mixes them up, with Gertrude drinking from the cup that was not offered to Hamlet; she is poisoned anyway. Perhaps the intent was to parallel the two swords, but it does not work (p. 42). "The King's *to blame*" (5.32.320) is changed to "*to be blamed*"—a mistake probably, since CI is usually scrupulous about not rewriting Shakespeare's dialogue (p. 44, emphasis mine). This issue had eight printings, the last with a new cover by Edward Moritz in March 1969, plus the Acclaim study guide in 1997. The first printing was examined for this entry.

35 *Captain Marvel Adventures*
"Captain Marvel and the Royal Riddle." # 137, October 1952. Greenwich, CT: Fawcett Publications, Inc. Otto Binder (writer), C. C. Beck (artist). Pages not numbered, page 5.

In a twist on Alexander Hope, Mark Twain, and countless others, Billy Batson (the alter ego of Captain Marvel) has a double named Tommy Archer. Tommy does not know that he is a missing king. Captain Marvel frees

the boy when two men attempt to kidnap him. After becoming Billy Batson again, he is mistaken for Tommy, captured, and taken to Tommy's kingdom where he is given the royal treatment—literally. There is also an attempt on his life, as a balcony collapses while Billy stands on it. He says the magic word that turns him into Captain Marvel, saving himself and the cheering throng who came to see their king. While holding up the balcony, Captain Marvel says, "There is something rotten going on, and this isn't Denmark!" adapting *Hamlet* (1.4.90). Of course, the evil prime minister is behind the plot. He figures out that Tommy is the real heir, but Captain Marvel saves him in the nick of time.

36 *Pogo*
August 4, 1955. Post-Hall Syndicate. Walt Kelly (writer/artist).

A mouse and a snake discuss their chances of getting a job as linguists on a television program. The snake makes mention of his having no feet and tells the mouse a story. "I was booked as the Ghost in Hamlet one time by an agent in Saskatoon an' when it came time for me to walk, well, sir, you can imanin...."

37 *Mary Worth*
October 18, 1958. King Features Syndicate, Inc. Ken Allen (writer/artist).

Mary Worth is a classic comic strip soap opera that began in 1938, the creation of writer Alan Sanders and artist Ken Ernst. Mary does not appear in this daily strip; she is often absent since the strip is about an ever-changing series of characters whose lives Mary touches. In this story a young woman is engaged to be married to an actor named Paxton. In a previous strip he indicated his dislike for children, but she has a daughter. When they are introduced, he says, "Fine! Splendid! Excellent!" Referring to his previous complaint, the mother says she knows Shakespeare too, and then severely paraphrases Gertrude's line from Hamlet (3.2.230), "Methinks he doth protest too much!" Paxton explains that he actually likes children, just not on the stage where they steal scenes.

38 *Rocky and His Fiendish Friends*
"Tee-Vee Jeebies." # 1, October 1962. Poughkeepsie, NY: K. K. Publications. Unknown (author/illustrators). Page N/A.

The dog Mr. Peabody has adopted a human boy named Sherman. They use their Way-Back Machine to travel in time. On this journey, they visit the Renaissance inventor of television, who explains it works like a magnifying glass over a piece of paper. Just then, William Shakespeare enters excited by the possibility of reaching people who do not attend the theater. The inventor puts him in behind a pane of magnifying glass, but the sun comes in, setting

Shakespeare's britches on fire. He flees. Always ending in a villainous pun, Mr. Peabody explains that this experience is responsible for Shakespeare's most famous line, "TV or not TV." This is a comic book tie-in to the *Bullwinkle* television program.

39 *Our Boarding House*
December 11 and 13, 1965. United Features Syndicate. Bill Freyse (writer/artist).

Mrs. Hoople has ordered the Major to take a job at a department store and not to quit. In the December 11 strip, he faces a manager who says that with his red nose the Major will make a perfect department store Santa Claus and to suit up. Hoople protests that "the actor's guild would never permit an old Shakespearean performer, a man who thrilled European royalty," like himself, to be a department-store Santa. Apparently they would. In the December 13 panel he is in costume and walking toward the children. He thinks, "the play's the thing, as the Bard noted!" evoking *Hamlet* (2.2.633). The Major eventually loses the job for abusing the customers.

40 *Pogo*
September 14, 1969. Post-Hall Syndicate. Walt Kelly (writer/artist).

A seventeen-week sequence of Sunday pages were inspired by George Herrman's *Krazy Kat*, with a brick-throwing cat assaulting a dog named Beauregard. The sixteenth week has a fox named Seminole Sam trying to sell them "dog wigs." They suspect these are the hides of actual dogs. Beauregard looks one of the wigs in the eye and says, "Alas, poor Yorick, I hardly knew him," a paraphrase of *Hamlet* (5.1.178).

41 *Justice League of America*
"The Dream Factories of Doctor Destiny!" # 176, March 1980. New York: DC Comics, Inc. Gerry Conway (writer), Dick Dillin (penciller), Frank McLaughlin (inker). Pages 7 and 9.

The Justice League is a team where some of DC's most popular superheroes work together against villainy too great for a single hero. For more than a decade the story structure of most issues was to have the heroes assemble to learn that their foe has three plots going on in different parts of the world. The heroes form groups and go to each, overcome the obstacles they find, and reunite to defeat the villain in a final battle. So it is here, with the variation that they capture Doctor Destiny before breaking into three teams. He is forced to tell the truth by Wonder Woman's magic lasso and explains that his Omega Program will drive everyone on Earth insane. The only way to stop it is to find the three remaining Omega machines hidden in three places around the world. He gives clues to their locations. One is "where a prince debated the long sleep, perchance to dream" (p. 7). Superman and Hawkgirl realize this must be Kronborg Castle, the place Shakespeare called Elsinore in *Hamlet*. Superman quotes a bit of 3.1, beginning with "to die; to sleep no more..." (p. 9). They are attacked by demons but defeat them, enter the castle, and destroy the Omega machine (p. 16). The others do the same in Bihar, India, and in Philadelphia. Someone scratching this comic hard to find significance might note that madness is an issue in *Hamlet*, and world madness was the goal of Doctor Destiny. There is nothing in the story that indicates this is anything more than a coincidence, and certainly there is nothing corresponding for Bihar and Philadelphia.

42 *Heavy Metal*
"Shakespeare for Americans: Hamlet." November 1981. New York: Heavy Metal Magazine. Howard V. Chaykin (writer/artist). Page 6.

Set in the nineteenth-century American West, this one page of *Hamlet* highlights changes scenes with each panel. Horatio meets Hamilton at the train station in panel one. The ghost reveals that Hamilton's uncle and mother are "in cahoots" in panel two. Without context, Hamilton says, "Yes...No..." in the third. He confronts his mother in the fourth, someone unidentified (Laertes) calls Hamilton to a gun battle in the fifth over the death of "my sister," and someone unidentified (Fortinbras) surveys the scattered bodies in the last panel. Those who know *Hamlet* will get it; it can make no sense to anyone new to the play. Peter Kuper is credited as Chaykin's assistant.

43 *Hamlet*
1984, reprint 1994. Circle Pines, MN: American Guidance Service, Inc. Naunerle Farr (writer), E. R. Cruz (artist). Pages N/A.

This is so ineptly handled it could almost be an early CI comic. Characters have a tendency to dress for battle, no matter where they are. Horatio does this on pp. 8–13, corresponding to 1.1, and Polonius wears chain mail in the domestic scene with his children (pp. 17–18) and in his conversation about Hamlet's letter (pp. 24–26). Rosencrantz and Guildenstern wear it throughout (e.g., pp. 26–28). Cruz draws the actors playing the king and queen exactly as he does Claudius and Gertrude. What may be intended as parallelism is confusing when Claudius and Gertrude seem to be in the play. Someone knowing the story can sort it out, but the intended young readers do not know the story (pp. 35–36). Then Claudius tells Laertes, "You shall have revenge" against Hamlet, apparently in his mother's presence (pp. 48–49). The way Cruz draws one panel, Claudius seems to tell Gertrude she is drinking poison (p. 58). Who is that man behind the curtain in the queen's room? No caption identifies him, and he is seen in a shadowy long shot. It is no clearer when Hamlet kills him (pp. 40, 42). It is two pages later that readers learn it is Polonius (p. 44).

Hamlet is a story haunted by the past actions of the previous kings of Denmark and Norway. The first two pages deftly summarize the plot before the play begins (pp. 7–8), but then some of this information is repeated on page 11. All this makes for very strange reading. Cuts are necessary to fit the long story into fifty-five pages of story. Gone are Polonius's advice to Laertes, reduced to "Remember everything I told you" (p. 17), the spy he sends after his son (2.1), all references to his statesmanship (e.g., 1.2.47–49), and Hamlet's scenes teasing him (2.2). This reduces Polonius to a feckless father. The gravediggers are virtually eliminated, and Osric is reduced to a messenger. The changes to Polonius, the gravediggers, and Osric eliminate all the play's humor. A series of meditations on death distinguish this play, and most of those are gone. The most famous speech, "To be or not to be" (3.1.55–89) is reduced to an out of context "Life's sad. If death is like sleep, it might be better to die" (p. 39).

44 Pluperfect Pogo

Date unknown, reprint 1987. New York: A Fireside Book. Walt Kelly (writer/artist). Page 157.

This book reprints a story from one of Kelly's earlier books (not published in newspapers), entitled "Bark Us All Bow Wows-of Folly." In part one, Albert the alligator and a snake look at an alligator-skin satchel. Albert recognizes his Uncle Yorick, and says, "Alas! Poor Uncle Yorick, I knowed him well!" He then gives the satchel a decent burial. Pluperfect Pogo does not credit the original publication.

45 The Cowboy Wally Show

1988, reprint 1996. New York: Marlowe & Company. Kyle Baker (writer/artist). Pages N/A, Chapter 3.

This is the story of a beer-guzzling, obese, debauched media star named Cowboy Wally and is a lighthearted satire on Hollywood and the cult of celebrity in America. Using the framing device of a documentary about Wally's life, the story visits the high points, which are the same as the low points, of Wally's career, including his several failed television shows, a French Foreign Legion film, and his adaptation of Hamlet. Wally and his partner Len hold a meeting with the financiers of their next film to decide on a suitable story. The moneymen want a failure for tax purposes, so they decide to make Hamlet and to cast game show queen Vanna White as Ophelia (pp. 11–17). Something goes wrong that night; what is not clear, but it involves prostitutes and drugs in a laundromat. Wally and Len are put in jail without bail (pp. 18–24). Undaunted, they plan to make the film in their cell, cast with guards and their cellmates. Wally does not feel "Shakespeare's dialogue has the right rhythm" and rewrites it to make it appealing to modern audiences. Len finds this repugnant,

so Wally calls him a snob. Wally turns the story into a comedy (pp. 25–29). Baker shows Wally's version of the play (pp. 30–42). Since they have no costumes, they draw them on pieces of paper, which they hold up when reciting Wally's goofball lines.

46 Sandman

"Passengers." # 5, May 1989. New York: DC Comics. Neil Gaiman (writer), Sam Keith, Malcolm Jones III (artists). Page 12.

Dr. Destiny may nor may not be human. He has escaped from an asylum; he is naked and has a head like a skull. He seeks a ruby with supernatural powers and forces a woman to drive him to where the ruby is hidden. On the drive he asks her name, and she tells him. He repeats it. "Rosemary...that's for remembering." This is a slight misquotation of Hamlet (4.5.173). He murders Rosemary after he reaches his destination. The author is well aquainted with Shakespeare and often drops unacknowledged references and quotations into his work. He later made Shakespeare part of the ongoing Sandman saga. (See separate entries on related Sandman issues, especially under A Midsummer Night's Dream and The Tempest.)

47 Walt Disney's Comics and Stories

"Walt Disney's Donald Duck." # 539, June 1989. Prescott: Gladstone Publishing, Ltd. Translator (Geoffrey Blum), The Gutenberghus (writers/artists).

Daisy Duck asks Donald and his cousin Gladstone Gander, rivals for her affection, to help her drama guild with Gimlet, Prince of Denmark. The play is performed at the Tyrone Gusty Theater, obviously named for Irish director Tyrone Guthrie, for whom a theater in Minneapolis really is named (p. 2). Lines from Gimlet are cribbed directly from Hamlet, and so are quips, as when Donald appraises Gladstone's audition and says "Something's sure rotten in the state of Denmark" (p. 4, paraphrasing 1.4.90). The director dismisses Gladstone, saying he is "not Olivier material," and Gladstone agrees that he is "more an antique Roman than a Dane" (p. 5, 2.2.283). There are more quotes and quips when Gladstone sabotages Donald's audition and ends up with the part (pp. 5–8). He is a hit and tries to make time with Daisy, but he is sent on tour instead. He is hauled unwillingly away. And thus the whirligig of time brings in his revenge as Donald shouts, "Goodnight, sweet prince" (5.2.358–59), dances with Daisy, and thinks, "Three cheers for Shakespeare! 'Cause his play's the thing that sent Gladstone off and left me king" (p. 10, paraphrasing 2.2.604–5). This is a translation and reprint of a Danish comic, date unknown, by a Copenhagen-based comic packager called the Gutenberghus. The actual writers and artists are not known, so the credits above are those found in the American edition. It is difficult to guess why the translator kept the title Gimlet, Danish name for Hamlet.

48 *Classics Illustrated*
"Hamlet." # 5, March 1990. New York: Berkeley Publishing Group and First Publishing, Inc. Steven Grant (writer), Tom Mandrake (artist).

In the same number of pages as the original *CI* "Hamlet," forty-four, Grant and Mandrake expand the story through more and littler panels and smaller lettering. This allows Grant to fill out characterization and keep the humor of Polonius's dithering dialogue (i.e., p. 16). Blum just illustrated one panel at a time, but Mandrake designs an entire sequence so the story flows from one panel to another and one page to the next. The design is strong enough that it hardly matters that Mandrake is weak on anatomy and lumpy in his shading. A more serious lapse is when Polonius reads Hamlet's letter to Claudius and Gertrude but holds no letter (p. 16). Grant follows the custom in cutting all the politics in the play. The march on Poland is included, but abridged to reflect Hamlet's personal struggle (pp. 32–33), and while Fortinbras shows up in the end, there is little political content in the scene (pp. 43–44). Unfortunately, Grant sometimes cuts information needed later, as when Polonius asks Ophelia what Laertes "hath said to you," but the dialogue where he learns Laertes said something is gone (p. 10). Polonius's cry for help from behind the arras is cut, so Hamlet has no way of knowing someone is back there; he stabs anyway (p. 29). Missing is the scene where Claudius and Laertes plot to use poison. Poison is on the sword and in the cup, but how it got there is not explained (p. 41). This is the only Shakespeare title produced during the *Classics Illustrated* revival of 1990.

49 *Apache Dick*
"The Dick and the Doll Part IV." # 4, May 1990. Newbury Park CA: Malibu Graphics. Will Jacobs (writer), Darick Robinson (artist). Page 7.

As a fan of novels by James M. Cain and certain paperbacks of the 1950s, Will Jacobs was inspired to tell the story of a guy and the doll that does him wrong. It is Cain-lite, but that is fitting since this is basically an action story based on characters from the humor comic *The Trouble with Girls*. Apache Dick is asked by his cousin to investigate Baby Doll, who is marrying and murdering to collect the insurance policies of her deceased husbands. To expose her plot, Apache marries her and plans with his friend Lester Girls to fake his death. Apache goes to Lester's house after his apparent death. Lester is not home, but his terrible nephews are tying up the dogs and creating their usual pandemonium. They mistake Apache for a ghost, and tell him that Lester has married Baby Doll. Apache quotes *Hamlet* (1.2.179–81), "Thrift, thrift, Horatio! the funeral bak'd meats / Did coldly furnish forth the marriage tables." Nephew Willie wisecracks that Apache must be alive, since "no ghost would talk that weird!" Gerry agrees, and says Apache is speaking "like some half-

assed imitation of Shakespeare, or something!" At the time he wrote this issue, Jacobs had read very little Shakespeare, though he knew and admired *Hamlet.*

50 *Milk and Cheese Volume 1: Fun with Milk and Cheese*
"Milk and Cheese Are Dead." 1991, Reprint 1998. San Jose: Slave Labor Graphics. Evan Dorkin (writer/artist). Page 2.

Milk and Cheese are quite a pair. They are a mayhem-loving, nihilistic, and anthropomorphic carton of milk and block (sometimes wedge) of cheese who live to get drunk and destroy. A story may show them beat street mimes to death ("Milk and Cheese in Street Performers Must Die!"), destroy a bowling alley ("Milk and Cheese in Bowl-O-Rama!"), or spend two pages vomiting ("Milk and Cheese Vomit!"). Of course Dorkin's work has some faithful admirers, and on occasion there is something clever in the stories. A marginal note in the vomit story warns readers not to "emulate Milk and Cheese! They are trained alcoholics!" It is fun when Dorkin uses his characters to express contempt for his admirers, at least the first few times he does it, and his catch phrase is clever: "Dairy products gone bad." The story "Milk and Cheese Are Dead!" has an unattributed quotation from *Hamlet*. They notice that after the actor Michael Landon died, his photo was twice on the cover of *TV Guide* magazine. They want attention, too, and decide that death is the way to get it, so they buy a plot and headstone and pretend to be dead. They are so disappointed by the turnout that they go on a rampage and kill two bystanders and the gravedigger. While they are buying their plot, the undertaker tells them they look too healthy to be buried. Milk assures him, "We are beyond this mortal coil." Cheese then threatens to kill him if he does not cooperate. The words "this mortal coil" were coined by Shakespeare in *Hamlet* (3.1.66). "Milk and Cheese Are Dead!" is anthologized in the first Milk and Cheese collection and is a reprint of a 1991 story.

51 *Frank and Ernest*
June 15, 1991. NEA, Inc. Bob Thaves (writer/artist).

Frank looks at the directory for a school of performing arts to see the room numbers of three classes. The music classes are in rooms "A-One anna Two" (Bandleader Lawrence Welk's famous line). The drama class is in room "2B (or not 2B)" (*Hamlet* 3.1.55). The dance classes are in rooms 1, 2, 3–1, 2, 3. Perhaps Thaves should have called it the school of vaudeville routines.

52 *Sally Forth*
January 6, 1993. King Features Syndicate, Inc. Greg Howard (writer), Craig MacIntosh (artist).

This is another strip from the popular domestic comedy genre, featuring Sally, her husband Ken, and their daughter Heather. In the continuity for this period, Sally is unhappily on a diet. Heather tells her father that Mom is

pacing in "the kitchen saying, 'To eat or not to eat: that is
the question.' Then she tried to tell me she was quoting
some guy named Omelet." Her father corrects her,
"Hamlet." Heather complains that it is all this talk about
"guys with food names" that is making her mother "so
hungry." The quote is from *Hamlet* (3.1.55).

53 *Mary Worth*
January 11–19, 1993. North America Syndicate, Inc.
John Saunders (writer), Joe Giella (artist).

This story began well before and ended well after the
dates above; these are the dates of the Shakespearean
content. An older couple, Ian (male) and Toby (female)
have quarreled over the accusation that Toby had an affair
with a man named Guy Cahors. They have finally made up
and are thinking of how to get revenge against Toni Dulac,
the woman who spread the rumor. Ian has an idea inspired
by *Hamlet*. He wants to invite Toni, Guy, and Guy's wife
over for dinner (January 11–12). Mary Worth intervenes,
since Toni will probably not go to Ian and Toby's house.
Mary will host a party, but she is not sure what Ian means
by his reference to *Hamlet* (January 13–16). Ian was
thinking of the play within the play. He and Toby will
make sure to say some things they want their guests to
hear (January 17–19). This is the last reference to Shakespeare.

54 *Frank and Ernest*
February 24, 1993. NEA, Inc. Bob Thaves (writer/artist).

In a purely visual pun, Thaves has the words, "If Shakespeare had been Egyptian:" on the wall of an ancient tomb.
Frank and Ernest look at hieroglyphics of two bees, an ore, a
rope tied into a knot, and two bees. This adds up to a visual
Hamlet (3.1.55): "To be, or not to be."

55 *Calvin and Hobbes*
March 6, 1994. Universal Press Syndicate. Bill Watterson
(writer/artist).

This was an extraordinarily popular and influential strip
about a boy and his imaginary friend, a tiger, that only
lasted for several years. Here, the boy Calvin is about to eat
dinner when the meal stands up and recites much of
Hamlet's "To be or not to be" speech (3.1.56–88) over
eight of this Sunday page's fifteen panels. Calvin reacts for
a few panels, and then his meal begins to sing the notoriously bad pop song *Feelings*. When his mother asks if he
liked the dish, Calvin tells her, "Let's not have this ever
again."

56 *Peanuts*
May 19, 1994. United Features Syndicate, Inc. Charles
M. Schulz (writer/artist).

Peppermint Patty is known for her ability as a neighborhood baseball player, not for her school work. She reads
to her class. "This is my report on Hamlet. . . . A hamlet is a
small village with a population of maybe a few hundred,

and . . . Ma'am?" Back in her seat, Patty's friend Marcie
tells her this was "one of the great tries of all time!"

57 *Mad Magazine*
"The Lion's Kin." # 332. December 1994. New York:
E. C. Publications. Stan Hart (writer), Sam Vivano
(artist). Page 26.

This is a parody of *The Lion King*, a cartoon the Walt
Disney Studio claims is based on *Hamlet*. The television
cartoon characters the Simpsons go to see *The Lion's Kin*
and comment on the action. In one panel, Marge Simpson
says, "A prince who feels guilty about his father's murder!
This movie is a jungle version of Shakespeare's Hamlet!"
The connection between *The Lion King* and *Hamlet* is dubious. Some believe the claim is a piece of Disney disin-
formation so people would not notice their plot is much
closer to a Japanese manga and anime entitled *Jungle
Emperor (Kimba the White Lion)* by Osamu Tezuka. According to Doug Lanier, this was "quite a heated matter in
Japan."

58 *Frank and Ernest*
February 4, 1999. NEA, Inc. Bob Thaves (writer/artist).

Frank and Ernest do not appear in this strip. Instead we
see William Shakespeare by the sign "Shakespeare 1999,"
to indicate this is what he might say in modern times: "To
be or not to be . . . or maybe virtual reality?"

59 *Hagar the Horrible*
February 20, 1999. King Features Syndicate.
Chris Browne (writer/artist).

Dik Browne created *Hagar the Horrible* as the Viking
version of *Bringing Up Father*. Hagar is uncouth and unkempt and only wants to drink with the boys and sack
England, much to the chagrin of his wife, who would like
him at home, clean, and companionable. The strips are
very similar at their core, but the Viking twist makes it
seem new. Browne's son Chris assisted his father on the
strip and took over completely when Dik passed away with
nary a discernable difference. This daily has Hagar echo
Hamlet as he sits up in bed and muses, "To sleep in . . . or
not to sleep in . . . that is the question." Helga thinks, "I'm
not dealing with the run-of-the-mill loafer here!" Though
he does not appear in this strip, we note that Hagar and
Helga have a son named Hamlet, a name he would probably not have if Shakespeare had not written his play.

60 *The Adventures of Superman*
"Pranked!" # 579, June 2000. New York: DC Comics.
J. M. DeMatteis (writer), Mike Mckone (penciller),
Marlo Alquiza (inker). Pages 20–21.

The Prankster is one of Superman's oldest foes, dating
back to 1942. He uses practical jokes and gimmicks to
commit crimes, an approach that seemed dated as the
twentieth century ended, so this issue attempts to update
the character by making him tech savvy. Superman is

having a very bad day. His wife is missing and he wants to search for her, but he is distracted by a couple of second-tier villains who will not leave him alone. One is the new and improved Prankster. He creates human-looking nanobots for his audience and broadcasts a television program from a pirate station where he plans to enact *Hamlet* 5.1. He is dressed appropriately and manages to get out portions of the text, occasionally adapted to the situation ("Alas, poor Superman"), while Superman tries to stop him, battling the robotic members of the audience to get to the Prankster. Superman thinks that the robots are annoying and the Prankster is a "poor man's Kenneth Branagh up there comes in a close second!" in the annoyance sweepstakes. The Prankster also quoted Shakespeare in his first appearance in *Action Comics* # 51.

61 *Evening Standard*
March 16, 2001, Reprint 2003. London: Evening Standard. Patrick Blowere (writer/artist).

Prime Minister Tony Blair is Hamlet in this political cartoon. He holds a sheep's skull, instead of Yorick's, for an epidemic of foot-and-mouth disease was decimating Britain's sheep and cattle population at that time. There were rumors Blair would call a general election on May third, so the caption is, "To run on May 3rd or not to run on May 3rd," paraphrasing 3.1.56. This became the dust-cover image on *Shakespeare Survey* 53, Peter Holland, ed. (Cambridge: Cambridge University Press, 2003).

62 *Doonesbury*
June 8, 2003. Universal Press Syndicate. G. B. Trudeau.

Though *Doonesbury* is known for its left-of-center political commentary, it has always provided an equal measure of social satire, as it does in this Sunday page. The "bimbo" actress Boopsie is pitched for the role of Ophelia by her agent, Sid, but is told she is too old for the part. Sid is not ready to give up. "We'll send her in for Botox! Clear up those lines in no time!" He is told, "Botox actresses can't do drama. They lose the ability to frown!" Sid suggests she can "act around" that problem, but is told the character is suicidal. Sid suggests they "turn it into a comedy!" Phoning Boopsie at the end of the strip, Sid says, "Sorry, babe, the scripts has problems." She asks, "'Hamlet' has problems?"

63 *Non Sequitur*
June 7, 2004. Universal Press Syndicate. Wiley Miller (writer/artist).

Two children are taking a test. Question seventeen is "What was the name of Hamlet's mother?" A girl whispers to the boy, and he writes the answer "Mommy." Later she tells her father what she learned in school. "Boys are an endless source of amusement."

64 *Frank and Ernest*
August 27, 2004. NEA, Inc. Bob Thaves (writer/artist).

In a strip subtitled "Hamlet on the Golf Course," the melancholy Dane holds a gold tee and contemplates, "To tee or not to tee?" Hamlet is drawn exactly the way Thaves drew William Shakespeare on July 17, 2002.

65 *The Incredible Hulk*
"Shattered." # 76, October 2004. New York: Marvel Comics. Bruce Jones (writer), Dougie Braithwaite (penciller), Bill Reinhold (inker). Pages not numbered, page 22.

Noting that Hamlet has a kind of logic underlying his ravings, Polonius observes, "Though this be madness, yet there is method in't" (2.2.208–9). This has evolved into our proverbial, "There's method in his madness." Writer Bruce Jones drew on one of these when he had one of the Hulk's oldest foes, the Leader, take over the Hulk's mind so he could transfer his own brain into the Hulk's body. The leader's brain has been separated from his body, and stored in a tank full of fluid to preserve it, and from here the Leader sends out brain waves to control the Hulk. Just as the Hulk arrives to the underground cavern where the Leader's brain is located, Nadia, a mysterious Russian, arrives to rescue him. The Leader explains his plan to Nadia as the Hulk is forced to twist the dials that will begin the transformation process. She tells him his is mad, and he agrees, but adds that after existing for so long in a fishbowl and enduring the loneliness that came with it, "I believe I've earned a little madness!—But there was always method in it!" In the end the Leader does not get away with it and apparently dies.

66 *Catwoman*
"Betrayal." # 35, November 2004. New York: DC Comics. Ed Brubaker (writer), Paul Gulacy (penciller), Jimmy Palmiotti (inker). Pages not numbered, page 22.

"War Games" is a multipart story that covers several issues of several titles and is not complete as this entry is written. What is called "Act Two, part 7" tells the story of a gang war in Gotham City. Batman, his aides, and the police department are trying to contain it and find the person who manipulated the gangs into fighting. In the main plot of this issue, Catwoman is working the East Side, battling two women who appear to be influenced by the Uma Thurman character in the film *Kill Bill*. In the subplot, Batman has his assistants and the police heard the gangs to Robinson Park, presumably for a showdown in a future issue. Working with Batman is Orpheus, who is barely seen in this issue. Batman sends a message to Orpheus saying he will join him in ten minutes. The closing page shows someone, presumably the mastermind, standing over Orpheus's body in typical Hamlet pose, contemplating the helmet of Orpheus. He paraphrases Hamlet (5.1.202–3), "Alas, poor Orpheus . . . I knew him, Horatio . . . Knew him to be a two-faced spy secretly working for the Batman."

67 *The Dark Horse Book of the Dead*
"The Ghoul." 2005. Scott Allie, ed. Milwaukie, OR: Dark
Horse Books. Mike Mignola (writer/artist). Pages N/A.

This story is about an immortal named Edward who feeds
on the bodies of the dead. Hellboy, a demonic creature
raised to protect mankind from malevolant supernatural
forces, tracks Edward down at midnight in a London
graveyard. As Hellboy stalks him through the cemetery,
Edward quotes liberally from eighteenth-century death
poetry: "The Grave" by Robert Blair, "The Pleasures of
Melancholy" by seventeen-year-old Thomas Wharton the
younger, and "Elegy Written in a Country Churchyard" by
Thomas Gray. The story opens with the television in Edward's home, where his wife watches a puppet production of
Hamlet. Some of the dialogue between Hamlet and his father is given, including the appropriate, "I can a tale unfold"
(1.5.15). At the end of the tale, Edward mutters "Hamlet" as
he falls into a grave and dies. The story returns to the television, and a slightly edited version of the dialogue about
Polonius being eaten by worms (4.3.16–35). There is a
closing caption crediting Shakespeare, Blair, and Wharton,
but curiously not Gray. A line in Blair's poem, not used in
this story, quotes *Hamlet* on the "witching time of night"
(3.2.406). Wharton's poem mentions Juliet kissing Romeo
in the tomb, and those lines are spoken by Edward (p. 18).

68 *Captain America*
"Out of Time, Part One." # 1, January 2005. New York:
Marvel Comics. Ed Brubaker (writer), Steve Epting
(artist). Page 12.

This *Hamlet* allusion has little to do with the story,
which is about the Red Skull buying arms from a former
Soviet agent, who has his own plans for conquest, and the
Skull trying to re-create the powerful cosmic cube, which
allows the user's wishes to come true. The twelfth page is a
series of flashbacks from Captain America's life. Without
being explicit, the second panel appears to be a street shot
of Brooklyn during the Great Depression. Men are gathered on a street corner, and on display is a portion of a
poster advertising someone with the last name of Howard
(whose first name is off the panel) playing Hamlet. Aside
from the theme of seeking power, a feature of all Red Skull
stories and which may be a coincidence, there is no apparent link between the choice of play and the story. This
is the most recent incarnation of the *Captain America* title.
The way Marvel currently operates, there will probably be
another within a few years or sooner.

69 *Rhymes with Orange*
May 18, 2005. King Features Syndicate, Inc.
Hilary B. Price.

In a strip reminiscent of *Frank and Ernest*, Price goes a
long way to make a pun. A dog leans over a fence to kiss a
cat. The cat hisses the dog away, so the love-sick canine

quotes *Hamlet* (3.2.230): " 'The Lady doth protest too
much.' I think you really like me." The cat puns, "Sometimes a hiss is just a hiss," evoking the kiss line from the
song *As Time Goes By*.

70 *Zits*
May 27, 2005. King Features Syndicate. Jerry Scott and
Jim Borgman (writers/artists).

To read *Zits* for several months is to realize that Scott and
Borgman do not like teenagers. They consistently show their
protagonist, Jeremy, to be selfish, shallow, and arrogant. His
parents are long suffering and hapless in dealing with Jeremy's personality problems. The intent appears to be a humorous "teenagers are like that" attitude, but the result is
unsavory. In this end-of-term strip, Jeremy deliberately
squeezes all the knowledge accumulated over the previous
months out through his ears, then breaths a sigh of relief. His
father looks at the mess of words and ideas littering the floor,
and comments that finals must be over. His mother re-
commends saving some of it for next year. Among the ideas
Jeremy expels are bits of mathematical formula, history,
biology, and line 64 from *Hamlet* 3.1, "To be or not to be."

HENRY IV, PART 1

71 *Dick Tracy*
March 22, 1962. Chicago Tribune–New York News
Syndicate. Chester Gould (writer/artist).

Brush is a criminal working a fake charity scam. He uses
two chimpanzees to open envelopes with donations and
put the money down a chute, where it drops into baskets.
The chimps become enraged for no reason and attack those
working for Brush. Brush escapes through the chute. A
policeman finds the apes wrecking the office and decides to
leave the room, quoting Falstaff without attribution, "They
say the better part of valor is discretion" (*Henry IV, Part 1*,
5.4.117). Gould does not appear to grasp the irony that
Falstaff's statement is basically cowardly, so the officer
takes the line at face value.

72 *Adventure Comics*
"Supergirl." # 422, August 1972. New York: DC Comics.
Steve Skeates (writer), Mike Sekowsky (penciller),
Bob Oksner (inker). Page 10.

Supergirl is the cousin of Superman. He trained her to
become a hero, though until later years her stories were
domestic as she helped people in her neighborhood and
later college. This story is an exception, presented as her
stories were evolving into standard superhero fare. It is
basically the *King Kong* story, with a giant robot substituting
for Kong. As it captures Supergirl, the caption reads, "Some
say that discretion of the better pert of valor . . . in this
instant [*sic*] Supergirl doesn't even get a chance to be
prudent." This is a paraphrase of *Henry IV, Part 1* (5.4.117).

73 *Classics Illustrated*
1998. New York: Acclaim Books. Gregory Feeley
(adapter), Patrick Broderick (artist).

Despite the error on the back cover implying this is a
reprint of an old *CI* comic, this is a new adaptation of a
play not previously given the *CI* treatment. The original
comics made storytelling errors, and this follows that tradition. Falstaff gives some of Hal's lines in the second
balloon on page six because Broderick drew the wrong
character. King Henry and Hotspur argue on pages nine
and ten. Henry exits in the play (1.3.122), and Hotspur
says insulting things about him. Feeley and Broderick forgot to include the exit, so a reader might wonder why
Henry tolerated Hotspur's insubordination. Characters are
colored alike for easy identification.

HENRY IV, PART 2

74 *Buster Brown: And the Bold Burglar Laughed*
Mid-May 1906, Reprint 1977. King Features Syndicate.
Richard F. Outcault (writer/artist).

This is another *Buster Brown* formula strip, with Buster
getting into trouble so there can be a moral lesson in the
last panel. Hearing that there have been burglaries in the
neighborhood, Buster takes a sword down from the wall
and goes to sleep holding it. A burglar enters. His dog
Tiger (usually called Tige) attacks the burglar, sending
him back through the window. Buster's father appears
with revolvers while the felon heaves a brick through the
window. For a change it is Tige who gives the homily,
writing about the blessedness of sleep: "Shakespeare says,
it is 'nature's soft nurse' . . . how forgiving sleep will let us
rest, the wile she mends our shattered frames," and similar mawkish comments. The Shakespeare quote is
from *Henry IV, Part 2* (3.1.8). This strip ran twelve
weeks after a George Washington's Birthday strip, which
puts the date around mid-May. It was found in Outcault,
ed., *Buster Brown, A Complete Compilation: 1906* on
pages 37–38.

75 *Mandrake, the Magician*
February 18, 1939. King Features Syndicate, Inc.
Lee Falk (writer), Phil Davis (artist).

Molly Brunswick, clearly inspired by Amelia Earhart,
disappeared on a solo flight over the South Pole. Mandrake
the Magician and his servant Lothar find her in a hidden
prehistoric land, full of dinosaurs and cavemen. One caveman hurls a spear at Mandrake just as a tiger attacks
Molly. Mandrake uses his magic to direct the spear into the
tiger. As it strikes the beast, Mandrake paraphrases Pistol
from *Henry IV, Part 2* (5.3.51): "It's an ill wind that blows
to no good!" Pistol's actual line, "Not the ill wind which
blows no man to good" was originally from John Hey-
wood's *Proverbs and Epigrams*, "An ill winde that bloweth

no man to good." Part of Pistol's characterization is to
constantly quote lines from others. Falk has adapted
Shakespeare's version of the line.

76 *Terry and the Pirates*
July 16, 1944. Chicago Tribune–New York News
Syndicate. Milton Caniff (writer/artist).

On the run as usual, Burma, the bad girl with a heart of
gold, has taken refuge with a mysterious young woman.
Burma is exhausted and falls asleep. As she watches Burma
sleep, the young woman quotes *Henry IV, Part 2* (3.1.9–12):

Why rather, sleep, liest thou in smoky cribs,
Upon uneasy pallets stretching thee
And hush'd with buzzing night-flies to thy slumber,
Than in the perfumed chambers of the great?

77 *Pogo*
July 15, 1952. Post-Hall Syndicate. Walt Kelly
(writer/artist).

In a parody of the 1592 presidential election, Pogo
Possum is running for president. On his way to Chicago for
the party convention, he and his pal Porkypine use a train
rail as a pillow as the lie down for the night. Porkypine
paraphrases *Henry IV, Part 2* (3.1.31) when he muses,
"Uneasy lies the head that sleeps on a railroad track."

78 *Frank and Ernest*
January 25, 2005. NEA, Inc. Bob Thaves (writer/artist).

This one-panel cartoon features the lovable losers Frank
and Ernest and very occasionally others. Most days the
strip is an outrageous pun. This one is an exception. A king
leaves the Royal Gym. Frank, dressed as a court jester,
paraphrases *Henry IV, Part 2* when he tells Ernest, "Heavy
is the head that wears the crown . . . and the body isn't in
great shape either" (3.1.31). Shakespeare's line is "Uneasy
lies the head," which has an entirely different meaning.
When asked if the paraphrase was deliberate or just a
memory lapse, Thaves replied in an e-mail (January 31,
2005), "I incorrectly remembered the quote. However if I
had known the quote, I think I would have gone ahead
with the strip as is. I don't think there is any harm in a little
artistic license being taken in a cartoon."

HENRY V

79 *Doom 2099*
"The Action of the Tiger" and "Unto the Breach." Issues
2 and 3, February and March 1993. New York: Marvel
Comics. John Francis Moore (writer), Pat Broderick
(penciller), John Beatty (inker). Page 30 of both issues.

Traditional Marvel Comics villain Dr. Doom, the King
of the Eastern European empire of Latveria, has disappeared. In the year 2099, a man claims to be Doom
without fully understanding how he came to this future era,

"Once more unto the breach, and that's it for me."

New Yorker cartoon by James Stevenson, published January 1999. © Cartoonbank.

and he has gaps in his memory. A dictator with ties to a corporate empire now runs his kingdom, but Doom wants it back. This is the background for a modestly successful, forty-four-issue series that ended each issue with a quote from which the issue's title was taken. In issue # 2, "The Action of the Tiger," Doom declares war on the current regime in the last panel, and a caption quotes *Henry V* (3.1.3–6): "In peace, there's nothing so becomes a man as modest stillness and humility. But when the blast of war blows in our ears, then imitate the action of the tiger." In the third issue, "Unto the Breach," we learn Doom is waging his war by sabotage, undercutting the quote in the previous issue, or perhaps misapplying it. Issue # 3 ends with Doom and his cronies trapped by the new ruler and his legions. The title of this issue is taken from the first two lines of the same speech in *Henry V*, which serve as this issue's ending quotation: "Once more unto the breach, dear friends, once more; / Or close the wall up with our English dead." Both quotations seem more gratuitous than apt.

80 *Comic Book Shakespeare: Henry V*
2004. St. Julians, Sevenoaks, Kent: Timber Frame Publications Ltd. Simon Greaves (adapter/artist). Pages N/A.

The fourth in Greaves's series designed to teach Shakespeare to British students shows marked improvement over his previous comics. His use of wash (gray tones) has improved, giving the illusion of greater dimensionality. The battle scenes, though greatly simplified, appear to consciously draw on medieval stylists like Paolo di Dono

Unnello and the illuminator of the Luttvell Psalter (p. 45). They picture the battles effectively. There are fewer disembodied talking heads than in the past, and more variety to the drawings. These things make for a livelier comic, although Greaves is still necessarily wordy. The prologue is crammed into a page and a half, followed by another short page and a half for the Bishops to plot in 1.1. The talky Salique justification consumes another three pages (pp. 4–6). There are just twelve drawings in these six pages; the rest is text. Greaves still edits for space, and must with a sixty-page limit. 2.2 is reduced to a caption and a single panel (p. 12). In Shakespeare, the English lesson (3.4) works because there are just enough lines in English to be understood and funny. Because of his pedagogical approach, Greaves must add a Modern English translation of the French lines. The scene loses all its charm in English and because it is cut after the first joke (p. 25). While there is the usual bad drawing, the chorus looks like Shakespeare, and it is a role that tradition, on insufficient evidence, has assigned to him. As usual, Greaves comic is informed and thoughtful. It is much improved, but dully rendered.

81 *X-Men Unlimited*
"Follow the Leader." # 5, December 2004. New York: Marvel Comics. Scott Killinger (writer), Real Lyra (penciller), Jay Leisten (inker).

The X-Men are a team of mutants with different superpowers. Wolverine has metal claws that make him lethal. He does not want to be a leader. Cyclops has a holographic program of Shakespeare's *Henry V* and gets Wolverine to play Henry. Only the scenes at Agincourt seem to be in the program. Wolverine arrives with a crown on his head surrounded by his men. He ignores them and butchers the enemy. Because he did not explain his battle plan, or have one, his men were unable to cut off the French retreat. They live to fight another day. Like Henry (4.1), Wolverine walks through the camp at night and hears more complaints about the French retreat. Wolverine is asked to give a motivational speech before the next battle, such as the one Henry gives (4.3). Wolverine refuses, but ends up briefly saying he knows they will win because "I have all of you on my side." He becomes a real leader and wins using the strategy Henry used in the actual battle. This story sheds no light on the play, nor does it use any of Shakespeare's language. It puts Wolverine, a reluctant leader, into a position where his refusal to lead hurts his men, and he is forced to assume real leadership to save lives and become victorious as he first fails to do what Henry did, then acts to ensure victory.

HENRY VI, PART 2

82 *Batman Adventures*
"Poker Face." # 11, April 2004. New York: DC Comics.
Ty Templeton (writer), Rick Burchett (penciller), Terry
Beatty (inker). Pages 7–8, 11.

A villain named the Riddler appears to be going straight.
He then sends this clue to Batman about a crime he plans
to commit: "You've made me into Shakespeare's 'Dick the
Butcher'... and every action has an equal and opposite
reaction. Midnight. Lives at stake." Alfred the butler in-
correctly identifies Dick the Butcher as a character from
Henry VI (it is *Henry VI, Part 2*), and misquotes the line
"The first thing we do, let's kill all the lawyers" (4.2.70) as
"First, we kill all the lawyers." The riddle indicates the law
offices of Wright and West "at the corner of Newton
Avenue and Third" because " 'Right' and 'west' are equal
but opposite directions on a map." It turns out the Riddler
was not planning a crime. He was just lonely and wanted
Batman's company.

HENRY VI, PART 3

83 *Krazy Kat*
October 19, 1930. King Features Syndicate, Inc.
George Herriman.

Shakespeare's line, "The smallest worm will turn, being
trodden on" (*Henry VI, Part 3*, 2.2.17), evolved as the
proverb "the worm turns." People today seldom realize the
expression started with Shakespeare or that he meant a
snake. George Herriman's Sunday page has a very cute
premise: Krazy Kat and Ignatz Mouse are on a teeter-totter
when Krazy stops to talk to a worm, sending Ignatz to the
down position with a jolt. He climbs up the board, tipping
it down on Krazy's head just as Officer Pupp comes along.
Ignatz sends the board into Pupp's head to avoid arrest. The
worm observes all this, and in the last panel asks, "How can
I help turning? Am I not a 'worm'?"

JULIUS CAESAR

84 *Classics Illustrated*
"Julius Caesar." # 68, February 1950. New York:
Gilberton Company, Inc. Henry C. Kiefer (artist).

This is the first edition of the *Classics Illustrated* "Julius
Caesar" that ran in the newspaper strip *Illustrated Classics*
from October 12–November 2, 1947. The art was then
adapted for the comic book format. Cassius's story about
saving Caesar from drowning is very well done in four
vertical panels with a tall caption that keeps the lination of
the verse (p. 4). There is some rewriting of dialogue during
the Act 5 battle scenes (pp. 25, 34). Panels are drawn out
of sequence on page 8; they need to be read down, then
right, but Kiefer does nothing to indicate this to the reader.
Then the same layout is read in the usual way on page 20.

Cassius has sky-blue hair throughout. Shakespeare's "gray
lines" of the sky (2.1.116) are colored yellow (p. 9). Caesar
sends a servant to talk to the priests. The page after the story
is a biography of Shakespeare, different than the biographies
used in other *CI* Shakespeare titles. There were three
printings before the story was redone in 1960 (see entry 86).
A new cover, painted by Leonard B. Cole, was added to one
of these reprints; it does not clearly depict any characters
from the story, just two Roman soldiers fighting.

85 *Out Our Way*
September 15, 1953. NEA, Inc. J. R. Williams
(writer/artist).

The title refers to small-town America and the sometimes simple but good-hearted people who live there. The
panel ran from the end of 1922 until 1977. In this Tuesday
panel, two men looking like ranch hands sit in a bunk-
house. The one reading quotes *Julius Caesar* 1.2.202–5:

Let me have men about me that are fat;
Sleek-headed men, and such as sleep o' nights.
Yon Cassius has a lean and hungry look;
He thinks too much: such men are dangerous.

His partner comments, "Shakespeare had something
there—I've thought th' same thing lookin' at them skinny
longhorns!"

86 *Classics Illustrated*
"Julius Caesar." # 68, May 1960. New York: Gilberton
Company, Inc. Alfred Sundel (writer), Reed Crandall and
George Evans (artists).

Reed Crandall is acknowledged as one of the finest
comic-book artists of all time. He collaborated with
George Evans, an above-average comic artist, on this
second edition, with Evans laying out the pages of the
first half and Crandall adding the details, then completing
the story. Evans then went over everything to keep the
look consistent. The result is far superior to the previous
edition because vast blocks of text do not overwhelm the
drawings, and the artists have the skill to make the story
flow. Yet it has some peculiarities of its own. The captions
and word balloons are typeset, rather than hand lettered,
which makes the text lifeless, although sometimes this
allows the lineation of the verse. The most damning
problem is rushing through the last eight scenes, beginning with the confrontation between Cassius and Brutus
in 4.2. The blundering that brings about their downfall
and later pathos are merely touched on, not told, so these
events lack impact, the sole exception being Octavius's
tribute to Brutus at the end (p. 45), so eight of the last
nine pages are unsatisfying. An interesting cut is the last
of 2.1, from line 310. Cutting this joins the scene between Brutus and Portia to the scene with Caesar and
Calpurnia, the concerns of the wives now clearly juxtaposed. Leonard B. Cole's painted cover from the Kiefer

Julius Caesar by Henry C. Kiefer (artist), 1950.

comic was reused. This version retained the same number as the first and the indicia gives the first edition publication date, February 1950. This second edition received five printings. The Acclaim study guide uses the first edition of the story.

87 *Heavy Metal*

"Shakespeare for Americans: Julius Caesar." September 1982. New York: Heavy Metal Magazine. Walter Simonson (writer/artist), assisted by Frank Miller. Page 75.

Reimagining the assassination scene as an American gangster story, a man in a fedora and trench coat enters the door of "Caesar and Co." in the first panel. It is the only panel with a drawing. Most of the rest are black, sometimes with sound effects. Caesar slams the door in the second panel and whistles. There is silence until the fifth panel, which is red with gunfire, then silence, followed by one last shot. Caesar asks, "You too, Brutus?" After a panel of silence, Caesar is heard falling to the ground. Frank Miller is not credited in the table of contents, but Simonson thanks him for the "flourish of the quill" in a marginal note.

88 *Julius Caesar*

1984. West Haven, CT: Academic Industries, Inc. Naunerle Farr (adapter), Vicatan (artist). Pages N/A.

This is an above-average adaptation in the Pendulum/ Pocket Classics series. Most of the story is here with the dialogue modernized and captions added to move the action forward. Among the cuts are the most famous line of the play, "*Et tu Brute*" (3.1.76), along with all references to the close relationship between Caesar and Brutus, the story of Cassius saving Caesar's life, the scene where Antony and Octavius decide who will live and die (4.1), and the argument between Cassius and Brutus (4.2). Brutus's servant Lucius is drawn as a middle-aged man, although he is a boy in the play. Antony's forum speech gets right to the point. It is over in eight panels on two pages, but the revision makes its argument with surprising force (pp. 45–46). The downside is the speed at which Brutus and Cassius get out of town (p. 47); the burning of buildings is also cut, so there is nothing to tip them off.

89 *Frank and Ernest*

February 18, 2000. NEA, Inc. Bob Thaves (writer/artist).

Frank and Ernest are the new anchormen for The Shakespeare Network. Frank says that retailers blame "poor results on inventory problems while defending their sales strategy." Ernest adds, "The fault, Frank, is not in their stores, but in their shelves," punning on Cassius's line, "The fault, dear Brutus, is not in our stars, But in ourselves," from *Julius Caesar* (1.2.140–41).

90 *Frank and Ernest*

April 7, 2002. NEA, Inc. Bob Thaves (writer/artist).

Frank and Ernest are punning again, this time on their television cooking program, *The Classy Cuisine Show*. There are four descriptions of dishes by Frank that are given punning names by Ernie. One is about a Shakespeare scholar who "makes the world's most magnificent Caesar salad," which Ernie calls "The Noblest Romaine of Them All," paraphrasing *Julius Caesar* (5.5.68).

91 *Julius: Let Slip the Dogs of War*

"Friends, Londoners, Guv'nors . . . lend me your ears." 2004. Portland, OR: Oni Press, Inc. Antony Johnston (writer), Brett Weldele (artist). Page 90.

Several films have updated *Macbeth* to a modern gangster setting. Johnston had the idea of doing this with *Julius Caesar* in a comic book. The title quotes from Antony's funeral oration, "Friends, Romans, countrymen, lend me your ears." He imitates the *Macbeth* films by keeping the basic story, but updates dialogue and makes small changes to accommodate the new milieu of gangster life in London's East End. Since the gangster world operates with a strong leader at the top, and *Julius Caesar* is all about avoiding one, space is given to rationalizing this change (pp. 24–29). There are some savvy correspondences, such as the scene in Brutus's tent (4.2) taking place in Brett's restaurant headquarters (pp. 108–20), and Julius's ghost appears to Brett on late night television (pp. 121–23). The story becomes silly when the gang war begins. There are more than 200 criminals dead over the course of several days, but the police apparently do nothing. They do not even have Brett's house under surveillance when Mark and his gang bring the war to his home. Credulity is not just strained, but spastic (pp. 131–50). It is very difficult to follow the sides in this battle since everyone wears a black suit. Basically the story stays too close to *Julius Caesar* to work in the gangster setting. The basic idea was first used in the "Shakespeare for Americans" strip in 1982.

92 *Bizarro*
February 20, 2004. Chronicle Features Syndicate.
Dan Piraro (writer/artist).

This one-panel cartoon began in 1985. It is seldom funny or even clever. Creator Piraro usually settles for strange, as he does here, which is consistent with the title. There is a séance. The gypsy leading it says, "Et tu, Brute?...Remember the Alamo!...Storm the Bastille!... Give me liberty or give me death!...Elvis has left the building." The point is in the caption: "Channeling Surfing."

93 *Get Fuzzy*
March 26, 2004. United Features Syndicate, Inc.
Darby Conley (writer/artist).

Julius Caesar was warned a few times to beware of the ides of March, the fifteenth day of the month; the first warning is in 1.2.18. Because he did not take heed, he was assassinated. Cassius Dio records his last words as the Greek "kai su teknon," though it seems odd that Caesar would speak Greek at such a time. Shakespeare renders this phrase as the Latin "*Et tu, Brute?*" (3.1.76). Conley uses both of Shakespeare's expressions in this comic strip. Bucky, the evil Siamese cat, runs up behind Satchel, the gentle bulldog, shouts, "Beware the ides of March," and scribbles "Kick Me" on his back. Satchel tells him to knock it off, that "the ides was the 15th," and then muses that the day of this strip, the twenty-sixth, must be "the idiots of March." This prompts their owner to say, "Et tu, Bucky."

94 *They'll Do It Every Time*
March 7, 2005. King Features Syndicate. F. Friedheimer (writer), Al Scaduto (artist).

Actor Horace Hambone is a bore. In the first panel, he drones endlessly at a party about playing Antony in *Julius Caesar*, and the first part of "Friends, Romans, Countrymen" is quoted (3.2.73). The second panel shows him too nervous to give a coherent speech after winning an academy award. *They'll Do It Every Time* is a two-panel gag strip based on certain stereotypes, some of which, like the one

above, seem to have no basis in cultural belief. It is often written by readers, who submit an idea to the syndicate, and they are credited in the cartoon. Jimmy Hatlo began it in 1929. The title is the source for what has become a common American idiom.

KING LEAR

95 *Peanuts*
December 22, 1974. United Features Syndicate, Inc.
Charles M. Schulz (writer/artist).

A recurring story line in the *Peanuts* comic strip are the attempts by Snoopy, a beagle, to become a published writer, although he is a terrible writer. This Sunday page shows Snoopy writing in every panel. His text appears at the top of the panel. This story is about a couple attending a performance of *King Lear* near the holidays. One of the performers becomes ill. The theater manager steps forwards and asks, "Is there a doctor in the house?" The husband declares that he has an honorary doctorate. Upon hearing this, his wife decides not to give him anything for Christmas.

96 *Heavy Metal*
"The King and I." February 1983. New York: Heavy Metal Magazine. Angus McKie (writer/artist). Pages 41–44.

A man observes soldiers traveling to war (p. 42). He later watches their battle (p. 43). In every panel he recites lines from *King Lear*. For example, when cannon balls explode, he gives the "Blow winds and crack your cheeks" speech (3.2.1–9), and when he looks at the battle field afterward (a close-up of his wide-eyed face, not of what he sees), he says, "As flies to wanton boys, are we to the gods; they kill us for their sport" (4.1.36–37). The speaker ages as the story progresses, beginning at a smooth faced thirty-something, and ending in grizzled and wrinkled old age, all in what seems to be the passing of a few hours. Judging by the sky, the action appears to take place over a single night and into the dawn. It ends with "The wheel had come full circle" (5.3.175). The credit above is given in the table of contents. On the last page McKie gives the credit as "A William Shakespeare—Angus McKie Co-Production." The play that supplied the lines in not named.

97 *King Lear*
1984, Reprint 1994. Circle Pines, MN: American Guidance Service, Inc. Naunerle Farr (adapter), Gerry Taloac (artist).

This is one of the more successful in the Pendulum/Lake Classics/Pocket Classics/AGS Shakespeare titles. For the most part it is a terse and enjoyable retelling of *King Lear* for young readers, with only a few eccentric touches. One of these is a matter of censorship to protect kids from the graphic images of Gloucester's blinding. Since he is blind later in the story, his blinding cannot be cut, yet no one will give youngsters a book with explicit images. Farr gets around this problem by cutting to the next panel as Cornwall is about to remove the first eye. That next panel shows the deed accomplished and the servant attempting to stop Cornwall before the second eye is removed. After their brief fight, the other eye is gouged, again between panels. It is a sensitive solution that robs the scene of it melodramatic power, just as it is intended to do (pp. 43–44). The concluding fight between Edgar and Edmund is handled the same way, about to begin in one panel and concluded in the next (p. 56). Three cuts may have been poorly judged. The transition into Lear's madness is abrupt. He is merely angry in one page (p. 39) and certifiable the next time we see him (pp. 41–43). Gone are the lines that indicate the transition (2.4.264–84) and his rage against the storm (3.2). In 1.4, Lear has a conflict with the servant Oswald. Kent, in disguise, trips Oswald, delighting Lear and assuring a place at his side. This development sets up the antipathy between Oswald and Kent that pays off when Kent bates Oswald and is punished for it (2.2). Farr cuts Oswald's rudeness, yet Kent later says, "You're the same rascal who was so rude to the king" (p. 33). Perhaps the unkindest cut of all is the elimination of the Fool, who does not appear in the *Dramatis Personae* (p. 6) or even in the background of the court scenes. With the Fool goes the whole aspect of the play that Lear brought his problems upon himself. This is hinted at by a couple of others, most notably Kent (1.1.144–54), but the Fool is an anvil chorus, clanging the message home again and again. Farr tries to make up for this in the introduction, writing, "Lear had always been a man who acted without thinking things through. Because of this, he was about to make one of the biggest mistakes of his life" (p. 7). This is brilliantly simple, but the Fool is badly missed.

98 *King Lear*
1984. New York: Workman Publishing. Ian Pollock (artist).

This is the fourth, and in some ways the most compelling, of the Cartoon Shakespeare Series. Ian Pollock eschews realism to interpret the story, using surrealist techniques to convey the searing emotional impact of *King Lear*. His figures are set against a surreal landscape where slabs of stone are propped up with sticks, and one has elevator doors at the bottom. This is not a confined, claustrophobic *King Lear*, but one where the open spaces are barren of relief. Exaggeration makes Pollock's point when Gloucester says there was good sport at the making of Edmund (1.1.23) and Gloucester salivates (p. 1). Lear's throne is atop a tower, far above the heads of his subjects. Scissors hang from a string, ready to cut the map of his kingdom in three (p. 2). The world sometimes changes from panel to panel, led by the dialogue and Pollock's imagination, as when the Fool says, "All that follow their

noses are led by their eyes but blind men" (2.4.63–64) and he removes his nose. In the next panel he adds, "Let go thy hold when the great wheel runs down a hill" (2.4.65–66). The Fool does not let go of the wheel he holds, and is pulled down the hill (p. 54). When Lear tells Regan she is a "boil/a plague-sore" (2.4.215–16), he throws a gooey red boil away (p. 61). Thus Pollock makes Shakespeare's words concrete. There are a few unsubtle bits of symbolism. Gloucester pulls down one of the pillars supporting his house, literally as well as figuratively, when he rejects his son Edgar (p. 17). Edmund soon leans against it juggling as he plots his next move (p. 19). As Lear dies, a low-hanging cloud lowers above him and rains (p. 138). The final shot is not of the remaining Act 5 characters, but an unnumbered page (p. 139 reverse) of the Fool hanging. The pages are numbered to 139, but the second page is called page 1 and the last page is not numbered, making a total count of 141 pages.

99 *Foxtrot*
November 7, 1988. Universal Press Syndicate. Bill Amend (writer/artist).

Running in the strip's first year, this is probably its first mention of Shakespeare. All the Shakespeare references found in *Foxtrot* are about a student's anxiety over studying him in school. The others (see *Antony and Cleopatra* and *Macbeth*) run in a sequence of about a week, but this is a single daily. A student named Steve reminds a student named Peter about the *King Lear* exam in fifteen minutes. Steve complains of staying up "half the night studying," but still feels nervous. He mistakes Peter's just now realizing there is a test—and he should have read the play—for command of the material. Peter asks Steve to excuse him. "I'm a little pressed for time."

100 *New York Times*
December 21, 2003. New York: The New York Times Company. Ron Barrett (writer/artist).

On December 12, 2003, Joe Horn of the New Orleans Saints scored a touchdown, then immediately used a cell phone to call his family to celebrate. The game was still on. No one had ever done this. Many were shocked by his egoism. Because this is against the rules, his team was charged with a fifteen-yard penalty and Horn was fined $30,000. In response the *New York Times* ran an editorial cartoon titled "Examples of Unsportsmanlike Behavior." In the first panel, a player delays the game for a dramatic reading. He is pictured holding a copy of *King Lear* as he speaks into a microphone.

LOVE'S LABOR'S LOST

101 *Love's Labor Lost*
1930s. Place of publication and company unknown. Unknown (writer/artist). Pages N/A.

Tijuana Bibles were anonymous, usually eight-page pornographic comic books, nearly always based on American comic characters, radio personalities, or movie stars. Because the creators, printers, and distributors would have been arrested if identified, those behind them took no credit and did not copyright these comics, so publication place, year, and sometimes the decade are uncertain. This parody of the comic strip *Moon Mullins* has nothing in common with Shakespeare's play beyond the paraphrase of the title, which in this case refers to Uncle Willie not enjoying a sexual escapade. Willie has an erection in his sleep, and Auntie Mamie decides to take advantage of it. Nephew Kayo watches and comments, but Uncle Willie does not awake until it is over. There were several *Moon Mullins* Tijuana Bibles, but this is the only one to touch, even if barely, on Shakespeare. Though the name of Uncle Willie may seem suggestive to British readers, it is less so in America, and this is the correct name of a character in the comic strip. There was another Tijuana Bible that was not seen entitled *Boots in Love's Labor Lost*.

102 *Terry and the Pirates*
May 6, 1939. Chicago Tribune–New York News Syndicate. Milton Caniff (writer/artist).

Teenager Terry Lee is unhappy in love, as usual. He reads a book, then throws it down in disgust before he leaves the room. His guardian Pat Ryan picks it up to see what Terry was reading. The cover reveals "*Love's Labor's Lost* William Shakespeare." Caniff has *Labor*, not *Labour's*, which is the word in the British version of the title.

MACBETH

103 *Terry and the Pirates*
April 20, 1938. Chicago Tribune–New York News Syndicate. Milton Caniff (writer/artist).

Burma is the perennial bad girl with a heart of gold. She has had a tough life on the wrong side of the tracks, but she has the pluck and determination to rise above it. Yes, many clichés apply to Burma, except one—she has this background yet knows her Shakespeare. Burma is in a car with the Chinese servant Connie who is driving, title character Terry Lee and a nasty little girl they are protecting. Burma is in the back seat with the girl. After she acts up again, Burma says: "Let's go on, Connie! If you hear a scream back here, it'll be this half-pint Lady Macbeth changing her attitude!"

104 *Stories by Famous Authors Illustrated*
"Macbeth." # 6, August 1950. Bridgeport: Seaboard Publishers, Inc. Dana E. Dutch (adapter), Henry C. Kiefer (artist). Pages N/A.

This comes from the company set up to compete with *Classics Illustrated*, and produced Shakespeare titles before *CI* got around to him. The adaptation is not nearly as

reverent as *CI*'s, so it makes for a better comic book. Dutch keeps a little of Shakespeare's language, but largely writes revised and modern dialogue that sounds of another era, yet is understood instantly. If Macbeth's "All right, you've shamed me to agreement" lacks poetry, it is comic-book clear (p. 6). The proportion of text and picture is typical of comics in that era, unlike *CI*'s text heavy panels. There are only thirty pages compared to forty-four in the *CI* "Macbeth," but the rewriting allows Dutch to get more story in than *CI*'s slavish use of Shakespeare's dialogue permits. Yet Dutch does not take full advantage of the medium's possibilities. The murder of Duncan could have been visually exciting, but Dutch only shows what Shakespeare shows (and less with abridgement), instead of rethinking the story from scratch. If Shakespeare left it off the stage, Dutch leaves it off the page. Cuts include all the humor and the supposed luxury of Malcolm (4.3). It is a bit more violent than the *CI* version, with a knife raised above Macduff's son (p. 20) and Macbeth's head shown twice (p. 30). Kiefer adds a bizarre touch to Malcom's battle gear: breast plates as one might expect on an Amazon warrior. He looks like a woman in the bottom panel of p. 24.

105 *Alley Oop*
April 2–June 2, 1953. NFA Services, Inc. V. T. Hamlin (writer/artist).

This sequence retells *Macbeth* from the point of view of a minor character played by Alley Oop (see introduction for a longer discussion). Oop has his own meeting with the weird sisters, who send him to Macbeth's castle (April 7–9). He is on hand to see Duncan's sons flee (April 10), and is assigned to the palace guard where he witnesses a number of the events from the play, including the parting of Macbeth and Banquo from the castle (April 15) and the visitation of the ghost at the banquet (April 18), and is outside Macduff's castle when his family is murdered (May 6). He joins the army of Malcolm and Macduff, and even holds the door for the latter when he enters with the king's head (May 28). About a week and a half concentrates on Macbeth's story when Oop is not there to observe, including his preparation for war (May 15–25). Naturally, several lines from the play are used, especially in these Macbeth scenes. Hamlin then twists the story by having Shakespeare step out from behind a flat (May 29), which angers Oop. The story seemed real while Oop experienced it, and he is angry his had to live through it, even tossing a copy of Shakespeare's works through a window as soon as he gets his hands on one (June 1). Unfortunately, this sequence has not been reprinted.

106 *Classics Illustrated*
"Macbeth." # 128, September 1955. New York: Gilberton Company, Inc. Lorenz Graham (writer), Alex A. Blum (artist).

Macbeth by Alex A. Blum (artist) and Lorenz Graham (writer), 1955.

Blum's art has vastly improved, though he may had un-
accredited assistance. The look is obviously inspired by Hal
Foster's comic strip *Prince Valiant*. Clothes, castles, hair, the
design of some faces, and even the color (for which Blum
was probably not responsible) imitate *Valiant* down to the
capes worn by the male characters. It is attractive, sunny,
and arguably wrong for the dank, corrupt world of *Macbeth*.
Blum tends to use stock poses for actions such as contem-
plation. This is most notable on p. 16, where Banquo sits in
a chair to think, facing slightly to the right, his helmet on
the table beside him. Macbeth does the same in the last
panel in a virtually identical pose, his crown on the table.
Blum fails to draw the fog mentioned on p. 3, although the
colorist helps out by putting streaks of violet in the sky (not
added when Acclaim recolored the book). Blum takes advantage of the medium to do things impossible on stage. He
makes the witches disappear by drawing outlines, not detailed renderings (p. 4) and uses similar tricks for Banquo's
ghost (pp. 20–22) and the prophecies (pp. 24–25). He shows
Macbeth's investiture (p. 15) and has Banquo and Fleance
make their journey by horseback (p. 19). He seems to imitate Kiefer's 1950 *Famous Authors* adaptation at points such

as the similar approach to the prophecies (FA pp. 17–18,
here pp. 23–26) and some design elements, especially the
decision put wings on Macbeth's helmet. Captions are hand
lettered, but dialogue is typeset, which sometimes allows the
letterer to keep the lination of the verse. For some reason,
Lady Macbeth's line "We fail!" (1.7.60) becomes "We fail?"
(p. 8). Major cuts are the Porter, who silently opens a door
in one panel (p. 12) and references to Malcom's supposed
corruption (4.3). The slaughter of Macduff's family is
mentioned instead of shown, perhaps to protect young
readers. This version underwent eight printings, plus an
Acclaim edition in May 1997 with a new cover by Richard
Chase. The story was recolored in dark, moody hues that
better match the play, but ill suit Blum's open style.

107 *Macbeth*
1982. New York: Workman Publishing Company, Inc.
Von (artist).

An unabridged text adaptation. Von's chief weakness
is a sloppy and stiff rendering with occasional anatomy
problems, but his strengths are strong indeed. He knows
how to tell a story visually, choosing angles that are
sometimes surprising but effective. Long expository passages such as 1.2 become dynamic flashbacks of the battles
(pp. 2–5), and dialogue such as the falcon/owl allusion
(2.4.12–13) is visualized (p. 35). The vivid use of color
adds to the effect. Something is colored blood-red on
nearly every page, yet the palette changes with the scene:
Moody browns and grays dominate for the witches in 4.1
(pp. 56–62), rich greens mark forest scenes like 4.3 (pp.
66–69) and 5.4 (p. 81), with a sickly gray ascendant for the
sleepwalking scene (5.1; pp. 74–76).

108 *Macbeth*
1984, Reprint 1994. Circle Pines, MN: American
Guidance Service, Inc. Rich Margopoulos (adapter),
Vicatan (artist).

As the wounded Sergeant tells his tale of Macbeth's
valiant deeds, Vicatan (the professional name of the late
Philippine artist Vic Catan, Jr.) illustrates them with
heroic verve. Macbeth hacks his way through dozens of the
enemy, looking strong and noble, like a leader of men. The
heavily muscled hero looks right at home in a comic book.
Comic book semiotics signal to readers that this hero is
invulnerable (pp. 9–12, 14). He is so heroic that he cannot
possibly be headed for a fall. Setting up the expectations of
readers and then thwarting them was probably not intentional—the story is drawn in Vicatan's natural style—but
works anyway. When Macbeth falls, he will fall far. Margopoulos and the artist do a fine job of turning the story
into a comic book by picturing the scenes between
Shakespeare's scenes, such as Duncan's arrival at Macbeth's castle (p. 25), the banquet he is served (p. 26), and
his murder (p. 30). The climactic battle is long, energetic,

and well choreographed (pp. 56–59). The comic is more violent than most Pendulum titles and includes the twin beheadings of Macdonalwald (p. 12) and Macbeth (pp. 60–61). Despite opening up the story for adaptation, the essence of the tale is still there, more faithfully captured than in a comic like the Pendulum *Hamlet*. There are losses, of course, but most major characters and their stories are translated into the new medium. The Porter is reduced to one panel (p. 32). More of a surprise is the cutting of Macbeth's reaction to his wife's death. The *tomorrow* speech is not paraphrased (5.5.19–28); instead a caption tells readers, "But Macbeth had little time to mourn" (p. 54). Not surprisingly, Malcom's testing of Macduff is also excised (4.3). This is part of the Pendulum/Lake Classics/Pocket Classics series of educational Shakespeare comics.

109 *Alien Encounters*
"Ray Bradbury's The Exiles." # 10, December 1986. Guerneville, CA: Eclipse Comics. Ray Bradbury (original story), Tom Sutton (adapter/artist). Pages 1 and 4.

Alien Encounters was a short-lived science fiction anthology comic, sometimes adapting short stories by well known sci-fi writers as Tom Sutton does here. The premise of the story is that fantasy authors and their creations live in a sort of afterlife, but for only as long as copies of their books exist. The year is 2020 and Earth is now a totalitarian state, prone to the burning of all books that are not about science. Fantastic literature is especially purged. Astronauts are headed for Mars with the last copies of books by J.R.R. Tolkien, H. P. Lovecraft, Arthur Machen, and a few others. Edgar Allan Poe and Ambrose Bierce are especially determined to stop them. They try to enlist the aid of Charles Dickens, and unsuccessfully, of William Shakespeare, successfully. Shakespeare does not appear in the story, but the weird sisters and Hecate from *Macbeth* act on behalf of the authors. A bit of 1.1 and 4.1 are amalgamated by the weird sisters with new ingredients feeding the cauldron to create a spell to stop the astronauts, but all is in vain. The astronauts land and burn the last copies of the books by these authors, who disappear during their attack. Bradbury also wrote about censorship in his novel *Fahrenheit 451*.

110 *Saviour*
"Shakespeare's Sister." # 2, February 1990. Leicester: TRIDENT COMICS. Mark Millar (writer), Nigel Kitching (artist). Pages 10 and 12.

Saviour is a rare British comic with circulation in the United States, though the circulation was limited to comic book stores willing to experiment with material and publishers far out of the mainstream. It was not a success, and the multipart story was not finished. Writer Millar admits the story in the first issue is difficult to follow. Making sense of the second issue, if this is the second issue (see below), is

almost impossible. This description is partly guesswork. It appears that Tony is a thirty-third-generation descendent of Shakespeare and a reincarnated Jesus (p. 12). At least he believes so. He is here to save the world from a plot to get the keys to Hecate's throne (p. 10, and see *Macbeth* 3.5 for Hecate). Shakespeare's line died out a couple of generations after him. Possibly Millar does not know this, but it would be interesting if he does, and this is intended as a clue about Tony's self-deception. Tony is at least naïve, trying to recruit prostitutes for his crusade and paying them for their time (pp. 17–19), and altering things said to him into something he wants to hear. It is not clear if Tony is the title character or if that is the villain. Saviour is the name of a superhero who, later in the series, emerges as the probable anti-Christ. The title of the story seems to be taken from Virginia Woolf's essay, but there is no clear reference to her or to her writing.

111 *Suburban Cowgirls*
July 23, 1991. Tribune Media Services, Inc. Janet Alfieri (writer), Ed Colley (artist).

This was a short-lived strip (1990–95) about a frizzy-haired woman coping with life. The key to the day's gag is sometimes printed on her T-shirt. It was a well-done strip that deserved to last longer. This daily evokes *Macbeth* (4.1.10) as the woman pushes a plunger into a toilet. She says, "Bubble...bubble...toilet trouble." Her T-shirt says, "MacBath."

112 *Green Lantern Crops Quarterly*
"Whatever Happened to Charley Vicker?" # 3, Winter 1992. New York: DC Comics. Gerard Jones (writer), Tim Hamilton (penciller), Romeo Tanghal (inker). Pages 48–54.

Green Lantern of Earth is a hero made super by a power ring that allows him to do pretty much anything, and he is part of a team of ring-wielding adventures who keep the universe safe from evil. In a two-part story (*Green Lantern* 55–56, September and October 1967), there is a television show based on his exploits. He is portrayed by an actor named Charley Vicker, whose brother serves as his stand-in. The brother wears the Green Lantern costume one day, is mistaken for the real Green Lantern, and killed. Charley dedicates himself to real, not acting heroism, becoming a member of the Green Lantern Corps. In the current story, a sequel written decades later, Jones imagines that Vicker wanted to be a classical actor, but compromised his art for money. Charley finds an oppressed alien race on the planet Hwagaaga. The Hwagaagians have no tradition of heroism, so they do not know how to fight their oppressors. Charlie battles their enemies for them and inspires the Hwagaagians with heroic tales. *Henry V*, Aeschylus's *Prometheus Bound*, and Ibsen's *Brand* are among the dramas mentioned (p. 52). With these tales as models, the Hwagaagians join the fight. After they are free, Charlie becomes a roving player, enacting adaptations of Shakespeare that are tailored to Hwagaagian culture for their education and inspiration. The story, mostly told in flashback, begins with a longish scene showing Vicker's adaptation of *Macbeth*, and a portion of 4.1 is shown, including the adapted line, "Fillet of a Flying Jiss, in the Thoga boil and hiss!" (pp. 46–47). There is also a shot of Vicker playing Hamlet (p. 47). The original Charley Vicker stories do not mention Shakespeare.

113 *Wonder Man*
19, March 1993. New York: Marvel Comics. Gerard Jones (writer), Jeff Johnson (penciller), Dan Pandsian (inker).

Eisner Award–winning writer Gerry Jones was in a Shakespeare phase during 1991–93, with the above entry, *The Trouble with Girls Christmas Special,* and *Justice League Europe* (see both under Shakespeare). Wonder Man wants to make his living as an actor. One of the investors behind a film version of *Macbeth* makes the director audition him. He expects a disastrous reading, but is shocked at how wonderfully Wonder Man reads Macbeth's "tomorrow, and tomorrow, and tomorrow" speech and the lines leading up to it (5.5.9–28). A member of the superhero team called The Crazy 8 says they are like Henry V, and paraphrases 4.3.57–60, "And this day shall ne'er go by to the ending of the world but we in it shall be remembered. We few, we happy few, we band of brothers. And...uh...sisters. We Crazy 8!"

114 *Foxtrot*
January 18–22, 1994. Universal Press Syndicate.
Bill Amend.

The strips this week are devoted to a student grappling with *Macbeth*. In the first strip, Paige tells her mother she has to write an essay on the play. Her mother, Andy, acts a portion of the dagger speech (2.1) with a crazed look on her face. Paige shows her distaste. She says she had forgotten Andy was an English major as Andy recites the opening stage direction. The next day, Paige wonders why her mother is "all excited" since "it's just a play." Andy shouts her response, calling it "one of Shakespeare's greatest and darkest and relevant tragedies." The daughter holds up her copy of the text as "a spit shield" to stay dry during her mother's diatribe. Paige asks for Andy's help writing an essay about the play. Andy wants to know if she is having trouble "coming up with a good thesis," or "key examples supporting that thesis," or ending "with a strong and clear conclusion." Paige just wants to know what the play is about (January 20). The next strip shows her dancing in delight at having finished the play; then she becomes depressed when she remembers the essay, and her brother reminds her she has just fourteen hours. In the last strip, Paige asks Andy for help with the essay and endures a

tirade about doing the work herself. When it is over, Paige says, "Just double-check my spelling." The essay is written. Andy asks, "Why didn't you just say so?" and is told, "I like to watch your chew-outs fall flat." Then Andy looks at the essay and asks, "How do you spell 'Macbeth'?" There is a similar sequence in this strip under *Antony and Cleopatra* in 1989.

115 *Introducing Media Studies*
2000. Cambridge: Icon Books Ltd. Ziauddin Sardar (writer), Borin Van Loon (artist). Page 115.

Icon publishes a series of introductory guides intended to help undergraduates understand complex subjects via lighthearted, heavily illustrated books. They cover a range of subjects, some as traditional as Shakespeare (see entry), Freud, and Plato, and others as new and trendy as Postmodernism, Semiotics, and Linguistics. They are generally made effective by integrating a paragraph of text with an illustration often accompanied by a word balloon that comments on the text or serves as an example of what the text has to say. To show how much programs in television can change on the journey from original concept to air, Sardar introduces a program that began as a "pitch about making Shakespeare for the masses" that ends up as "a soap opera." A photo of elderly people in a pub has a number of word balloons. One man speaks in pseudo-Shakespearean language. Another has a sentence that incorporates a partial line from *Macbeth* (3.4.118): "Prithee, sirrah, stand not on the order of thy going, but sling your 'ook."

116 *Macbeth*
2002. New York: Scholastic Inc. Trina Robbins (writer), Michael Lilly (penciller), Nimbus Studios (inker).
Pages N/A.

Scholastic Inc. produced a number of comic book versions of literary works as part of their *Read 180* program for children with reading difficulties. *Macbeth* is the only work by Shakespeare, but the script by Trina Robbins stands out for its well-judged cutting of the unessential to tell the story clearly.

117 *Superman and Batman*
"Part Five: State of Siege." # 5, February 2004. New York: DC Comics. Jeph Loeb (writer), Ed McGuinness (penciller), Dexter Vines (inker). Page 16.

U.S. President Lex Luthor has a plan to finally destroy Superman and much of the rest of the superpowered population. He has declared Superman a traitor and ordered his arrest by the other heroes. They have taken sides, some supporting Superman, and the conflict could be devastating. Batman is on Superman's side, and his assistants Nightwing, Robin, Batgirl, and the Huntress have cornered Luthor in the Oval Office, but he has used nerve gas to incapacitate them. As he prepares for the next assault, he identifies with Macbeth, saying, "Blow wind! come wrack!" (5.5.51) when Superman arrives to confront him. The story is continued in the next issue.

118 *Sherman's Lagoon*
October 12–17 and 18–20, 2004. King Features Syndicate, Inc. J. P. Toomey (writer/artist).

Sherman's Lagoon is about a group of undersea creatures who are very stupid. This sequence is about their production of *Macbeth*. A turtle named Filmore explains to a shark named Sherman that they need more culture, so he holds auditions for the play. Attention is diverted by a hermit crab named Hawthorne, who stages an "armpit noise-athon" (October 12). The next day Sherman tells his wife he wants to be in the play (October 13), then tells Filmore he wants to play Macbeth in a rainbow wig and with a kazoo (October 14). He wears a kilt and a Scottish hat in the next strip. Filmore gives him a description of Macbeth's character, which he is not smart enough to understand, so Filmore says, "He's the head dude." Sherman gets it, "So, more of an Archie than a Jughead?" (October 15). Hawthorne is cast as Banquo. He is proud to play a general, but is afraid his actual service record will become an issue (October 16). Sherman and the Hawthorne rehearse their lines the night before the opening. Unfortunately, they are lines from *Taxi Driver*. They agree they are "cool lines" (October 18). On opening night, Sherman tells Filmore he has only learned half his lines, so wants to know if they can move his death up to page 37 (October 19). The sequence ends with the reviewers praising the director for turning Shakespeare's tragedy "into a comical spoof." After thinking it over, Filmore shouts, "I'll take it!" The sequence really could be about any performance of "high culture," for the jokes could have been adapted to opera or independent cinema. Toomey chose Shakespeare to make fun of his dense and unintellectual characters. The October 17 Sunday page was independent of this story.

119 *Mutts*
October 31, 2004. King Features Syndicate, Inc. Patrick McDonnell (writer/artist).

Mutts is the sweet adventures of two friends, a dog and a cat, and the nice people in their lives. This Halloween Sunday page is one of the edgier cartoons McDonnell has done, not that anyone will mistake it for edgy. The weird sisters from *Macbeth* put the eye of newt, toe of frog, and wool of bat into the cauldron. They let the fire burn to double bubble the toil and trouble (4.1.15–16, 21–22). They then put the slop into tins of cat food. This is later offered to Mooch the cat, who refuses it and later tells Earl the dog, "Who knows what they put in that stuff!?!" The reference to the "tongue of dog" is kindly abridged.

120 *William Shakespeare's Macbeth, the Graphic Novel*
New York: Puffin Graphics, 2005. Adapted by Arthur Byron Cover. Illustrated by Tony Leonard Tamai.
     See introduction. (RB)

121 *Hagar the Horrible*
January 9, 2005. King Features Syndicate, Inc. Chris Browne (writer/artist).

Hagar the uncouth Viking is sick, so his wife, the semi-couth Helga, prepares his medicine. An old woman wants to know the ingredients. Helga tells her, "Castor oil, eye of newt, wing of bat, 3 caterpillar eggs, ⅓ cup of vinegar, one finely chopped snake skin . . . and a dash of oregano!" The woman wants to know how Helga gets Hagar to drink that and is told, "I serve it in a beer mug, and he chug-a-lugs it before it realizes it isn't beer!" Shakespeare's "Wool of bat" is transformed into "wing of bat," of course, but the concoction clearly is inspired by Macbeth (4.1.12–17):

Fillet of a fenny snake,
In the cauldron boil and bake;
Eye of newt and toe of frog,
Wool of bat, and tongue of dog,
Adder's fork and blind-worm's sting,
Lizard's leg and howlet's wing.

122 *The Wizard of Id*
January 23, 2005. Creators Syndicate, Inc. Johnny Hart (writer), Brant Parker (artist).

Though supposedly set in a small despotic kingdom in medieval times, this strip uses many modern trappings for its humor, including the Internal Revenue Service. The tax man visits the Wizard to complain about some of the very odd business expenses on his tax return. The Wizard says they are vital to his work. The IRS man demands he prove it, so the Wizard turns him into a rat. "Eye of newt" is one of the ingredients the weird sisters throw in the cauldron in *Macbeth* (4.1), and "newt's eye" is one of the business expenses declared by the Wizard of Id.

123 *The Incredible Hulk*
#82, August 2005. New York: Marvel Comics. Peter David (writer), Jae Lee (artist). Page 16.

A witch named Tricia has been murdered, she presumes by a rival witch. Her astral form asks the Hulk to help her identify her murderer. Under her guidance, the Hulk visits her rivals and questions them. Should any of them lie, the rival's aura will tip off Tricia. One of those the Hulk questions is an actress at "a dress rehearsal of" *Macbeth*. One of the actresses playing a witch "unbeknownst to the others . . . was a genuine practicing sorceress on the side." She is innocent, and so are the others. The murderer turns out to be the son of Tricia's fiancé. There is a one-panel shot of the cauldron scene (4.1), with one of the actors, for some reason, holding a knife.

THE MERCHANT OF VENICE

124 *Krazy Kat*
February 22, 1925. King Features Syndicate, Inc.
George Herriman.

Year in and year out, Krazy Kat mistakes the bricks Ignatz Mouse throws at him for tokens of love. When Krazy gets into a fight with another cat, Ignatz heaves a brick even though he does not have a clear shot, saying he "can't wait all day to sock" Krazy. The brick hits the other cat. A caption illustrated with eyes reveals Krazy's response, "The green, green eyes of jealousy." This line cribs *The Merchant of Venice* (3.2.110), where Shakespeare uses the expression "green-eyed jealousy." Krazy and the other cat end up throwing the brick at each other.

125 *Pogo*
July 22, 1952. Post-Hall Syndicate. Walt Kelly (writer/artist).

Using Shakespeare to parody attitudes in the 1952 presidential election that first put Dwight D. Eisenhower in the White House, Kelly has Beauregard, a dog, stumping for presidential candidate Pogo Possum. He reads what he thinks is an old speech that refers to *The Merchant of Venice*: "A pox on the usury of any party who asks the pound of flesh." A mouse with a derby and a cigar tells Beauregard that he was "readin' a letter I was writin' to a 1930 creditor in Keokuk." Beauregard replies, "It seemed like a excellent summary of party sentiments." The emphasis and spellings are Kelly's.

126 *Heavy Metal*
"Shakespeare for Americans." February 1982. New York: Heavy Metal Magazine. Howard V. Chaykin (writer), Walt Simonson (artist). Page 6.

Then-President Ronald Reagan answers questions at a press conference. Nobel Prize–winning economist John Kenneth Galbraith asks about supply-side economics, and Reagan answers by telling the story of *The Merchant of Venice*. He compares the strength of Antonio's wealth to a slob like Bassanio, who drains capital with his wasteful social programs. Reagan says Antonio borrows from Shylock at "ridiculous interest rates," thus running "up a deficit," and finds he has "mortgaged his future! Just the way America has!" Portia saves the day because she knows that tax breaks for the rich are the solution to the problem. Reagan interprets the verdict against Shylock as persuasion that "high interest is wrong," and he should "use his wealth to aid his own daughter and son-in-law." Thus Shylock becomes a convert to supply-side economics. This cartoon is fair to this portion Reagan's economic theory and his stand against social programs even as it turns Shakespeare's play on its head. It was published before Reagan created huge deficits that were not resolved until the Clinton administration.

127 *The Merchant of Venice*
1984. West Haven, CT: Academic Industries, Inc. Naunerle Farr (adapter), Jun Lofamia (artist). Pages N/A.

The Merchant of Venice is an odd play in which big and angry emotions combine with greed and bigotry to smother the lighthearted plot. Farr's adaptation so dilutes what is disturbing in the play that the remainder is hardly worth telling. The play effectively repeats certain words like a drumbeat, beating characters and the audience with their impact. *Jew* is used twenty-four times in 4.1, but only twice in the corresponding scene of this adaptation, and never as an insult. Similarly, the word *bond* is used seventeen times in the same scene, and just twice here (pp. 47–52). Reduced in this way, the words have little effect. The juxtaposition of Christian to Jew is also gone when an expression like *Christian blood* (4.1.310) is reduced to *blood* (p. 50). This makes the story anemic in every sense of the word. A few expressions of bigotry survive, but so many fewer that they lack power. Among the cuts are Shylock's excesses as he prepares to go out to dinner, and most of the terrible, but well-deserved things Jessica says about him. Only enough is preserved to advance the plot (pp. 30–31). The most successful comic book versions of Shakespeare usually adapt his language, sometimes heavily. This one fails by making the new language awkward and stiff, as when Bassanio says, "Good day to you! When are we going to get together and have some fun" (p. 10). It is common to abridge by cutting the humor in a play. Here, Launcelot Gobbo's pranks with his father are included (pp. 24–26), but the humor at Morocco's expense is gone, though he is still vain (pp. 23, 32–33). Lofamia's art is lovely, but serves little purpose. This is one of the books first published by Pendulum. The Pocket Classics edition was reviewed for this entry.

128 *Shylock Fox and Comics for Kids*
Begun in 1987 and still in syndication. King Features Syndicate, Inc. Ben Weber, Jr. (writer/artist).

This comic strip is really an activity strip for children, with trivia questions, brain teasers, and other activities. It features Shylock Fox and Max Mouse, and is syndicated to more than 400 newspapers worldwide. The name of the fox is obviously based on Shakespeare's character in *The Merchant of Venice*, but he is really a Sherlock Holmes figure, sporting a deerstalker hat and Inverness cape as he takes Max on their educational adventures. Weber is not really referencing Shakespeare, but raided *The Merchant of Venice* for a name that is evokes the sound of Sherlock.

129 *The Toledo Blade*
"The Merchant of Venice 2005." April 19, 2005. Toledo: The Toledo Blade. Kirk Walters (writer/artist).

In April 2005 the Republican-dominated U.S. Senate and House of Representatives passed a bankruptcy reform bill. The legislation greatly disadvantages those who declare bankruptcy after October 17, 2005, while advantaging the credit card companies whose lobbyists helped write the legislation. This is typical of the reforms under the administration of George W. Bush, which consistently favors the privileged at the expense of the poor. The President lost no time signing it into law. In response, Ohio's *Toledo Blade* ran a political cartoon that used *The Merchant of Venice* to comment on the new bankruptcy standards. Antonio stands before a member of Congress and a smiling man who is the embodiment of credit card companies. The Congressman indicates the credit-card man and says, "I don't want to hear some sob story . . . give him his pound of flesh."

A MIDSUMMER NIGHT'S DREAM

130 *Midsummer Day Dreams*
August 1–September 1, 1911. National News Association.
Windsor McKay (writer/artist).

Comic strips were more fluid at the turn of the twentieth century than they are today. Newspapers employed artists to create strips. If a strip did not work, or if the artist or editor had a better idea, the strip was changed. Windsor McKay created several strips in the first two decades of the century, some of them running concurrently. Some ran for a few weeks, only to be abandoned for something else. McKay continually experimented with drawing dreams, most often nightmares, but sometimes daydreams. In the autumn of 1911 he created a strip with a title paraphrased from Shakespeare, *Midsummer Day Dreams*. One book says it was a daily strip; the only sample found is a Sunday page. The dates above come from the same source and should not be considered certain. In typical McKay style, it pictured the impossible. An actor talks to his wife in a restaurant about possibly changing his career. As he drones on, his wife daydreams about a small dog that enters and changes breed from panel to panel, getting bigger with each change. The wife tries to shoo away the dog. When it becomes a St. Bernard, it climbs on the table. Since the dog is not really there, the actor does not understand what his wife is going on about. She blames her fantasy on being sleepy.

131 *Classics Illustrated*
"A Midsummer Night's Dream." # 87,
September 1951. New York: Gilberton Company, Inc.
Sam Willinsky (adapter), Alex A. Blum (artist).
Pages N/A.

Another stolid rendering by Blum makes this a chore to read, and certain other features give readers a strange experience. Philostrate, who acts as entertainment producer

for Duke Theseus, is identified as the court jester (p. 2). He does not wear traditional jester's gear, but he does dress strangely. Blum draws Oberon pointing to the Indian Boy when he says, "Give me that boy," but the boy is not depicted here or anywhere in the comic (p. 12). Apparently Blum did not know what a dolphin looks like, but he nevertheless depicts the mermaid riding one. Its slightly squared and wrinkled head, the heavy scales on its body, and the almost feathery tail are all wrong, and so is the colorist's choice of yellow (p. 12). The flower is nicely done. Only the flower struck by Cupid's arrow changes color (p. 13); others remain white, though this becomes a problem when Puck brings two flowers to Oberon, both purple (p. 16). The size of the fairies changes from panel to panel. Titania and Oberon are the size of human adults early in the story (pp. 10, 11), with other fairies much smaller, yet Oberon is half the size of Lysander and Hermia when they share a panel (p. 26). Hermia and Helena are drawn at about the same height in some panels, though the dialogue about Hermia's small stature is retained (p. 31).

A Midsummer Night's Dream by Alex A. Blum (artist) and Sam Willinsky (writer), 1951.

Hermia is described as tawny, but colored with blonde hair (p. 31). At the end of the play, there is reference to the fairies coming to bless Theseus's palace, but the image is of Puck in the woods as he gives the unofficial epilogue (5.1.430–45). Surely these things will confuse some readers. The first printing was consulted for this entry. This title endured five printings, plus the Acclaim edition released in April 1997 with a new cover by Richard Chase.

132 *Pogo*

December 24, 1953. Post-Hall Syndicate. Walt Kelly (writer/artist).

This Christmas Eve comic strip features Porky dressed as Santa Claus and knocking on Pogo's door. Pogo complains that it is 4 A.M., which makes Porky realize, "You don't need a watch!" He rummages through his bag of presents, produces a flower, and adds, "That's good, 'cause here's somethin' I been savin' for you since August.... Now, please, don't fawn on me.... A sprig of Love-in-idleness." This is the name Oberon gives the pansy in *A Midsummer Night's Dream* (2.1.168). Kelly repeats the gag the following year when Porky gives Pogo another flower, but there is no reference to Shakespeare. He had saved this one since "early June."

133 *Doctor Strange*

"A Midsummer's Nightmare!" # 34, April 1979. New York: Marvel Comics Group. Ralph Macchio (writer), Tom Sutton and Craig Russell (artists). Page 1.

In most ways this is a typically bad Marvel comic of the 1970s. Stories were protracted fights with the hero and villain slugging it out, instead of a plot. Here the good magician Doctor Strange and his enemy magician Cyrus Black batter each other with spells for most of the story's seventeen pages. It opens with Doctor Strange contemplating a copy of *A Midsummer Night's Dream*, musing that Shakespeare's works are filled with "dark imaginings," as Strange probes "the wispy borders between illusion and reality" (p. 1). It is into his dreams that a creature called Nightmare comes to abduct Strange to a world where Black can attack him. If Nightmare seems vaguely like Neil Gaiman's Sandman, note the physical similarity between them on pp. 6, 7, and 10, and remember that both come to people in their dreams. This is not a claim that Gaiman was inspired by Macchio's story, but it seems possible. The first page has the only reference to Shakespeare, but it introduces the imaginative realm where Macchio stages the battle.

134 *Heavy Metal*

"Shakespeare for Americans." December 1981. New York: Heavy Metal Magazine. Howard V. Chaykin (writer), Walt Simonson (artist). Page 6.

This *A Midsummer Night's Dream* entry in the "Shakespeare for Americans" series is even more bizarre than others. Five of the eight panels give the cast: former President Dwight Eisenhower as Theseus, his wife Mamie as Hippolyta, the cast of the sitcom *I Love Lucy* as the four lovers with the baby, Little Ricky, as Puck. Singers Steve Lawrence and Edie Gormé are Oberon and Titania, with another former president, Richard Nixon, as Bottom. The rest shows the cast over three panels wearing strange costumes from various *I Love Lucy* episodes, with sixteen lines taken out of context from throughout the play. The lines are scattered around these panels. It is insightful in noting the affinity of Shakespeare's story to modern sitcoms, but has little to offer beyond that observation.

135 *A Midsummer Night's Dream*

1984, Reprint 1991. West Haven, CT: Pendulum Press. John Norwood Fago (adapter), Fred Carillo (artist). Pages N/A.

First published in 1980 in black and white, this is a later color reprint, and the change has an advantage. Carillo draws Demetrius and Lysander alike and sometimes does the same with Hermia and Helena. Giving Helena and Demetrius brown hair and making Hermia and Lysander blondes is beneficial, but at other times color is problematic, as when a word balloon is partly colored by the mantle of a door on p. 9. The most important test of any comic artist is how well the story is told visually, and Carillo gets high marks. Using just three or four panels on most pages, and carefully varying perspective to keep visual interest, there is a real flow from one panel to another, from page to page, and from scene to scene. It does not feel like a series of illustrations with text, the fault that makes *CI* stories dull. This is ably abetted by the anonymous adapter who rewrites all but a couple of Shakespeare's lines, but creates a lively script that keeps the story moving with the plot points virtually intact. Naturally, much of the complexity is gone; there is little sense of the tumult in nature or of the enmity between Titania and Oberon. The plot complications seem as harmless as April Fool pranks, and Bottom does not come across as larger than life. The language is designed to avoid childhood tittering, so *donkey* is substituted for *ass*. The purple flowers are not really purple, though they do have purple on them, but the scene depicting a mermaid riding on a dolphin's back is very prettily rendered (p. 18). Carillo also illustrated Pendulum's *The Taming of the Shrew*.

136 *A Midsummer Night's Dream*

1985. London: Michael Joseph Ltd. Von (adapter/artist). Pages N/A.

This is the first comedy in the series begun by Oval and continued by Michael Joseph. Von distinguishes the fairy and human scenes in the way he designs a page: The panel design for the humans is a traditional grid, but the fairy pages often have just one or two panels, and when more, the lines between the panels swirl and curve, sometimes sprouting leaves or flowers (e.g., p. 29). When a scene has both humans and fairies, the page usually receives the fairy design (p. 82), although 4.1 is an exception (pp. 58–61). Panel borders are used creatively throughout. When the Mechanicals enter the woods to rehearse, the borders resemble trees, the trunks and branches separating the panels (pp. 32–33). They are based on columns for the scenes in Athens (e.g., p. 6), and there are a number of Pre-Raphaelite flourishes on both covers, the borders of each page, and design elements on some pages (e.g., pp. 56–57). Von does not open up the story much via flashbacks as Kiefer did for *CI*. No mermaids or dolphins are shown, although Cupid's dart pierces the flower on p. 21. The difficulty of doing comedy without actors is obvious in the Mechanical's scenes. Von does not attempt humorous illustration, and there is nary a laugh. The typesetter helpfully sets the lines from *Pyramus and Thisbe* in italics, so those lines can be instantly distinguished from other dialogue. Von makes some odd mistakes, such as putting characters on the wrong side of a panel on p. 6, which means he has to make their word balloons criss-cross on p. 7. Francis Flute has a beard, not one "coming" as he says on p. 10. Peter Quince has a pointed "Mr. Spock" ear on the same page, but it is normal elsewhere. The word *For* in "For lying so, Hermia, I do not lie" (2.2.52) is mis-set as *Foy* (p. 28). There are numerous other mistakes throughout. These nagging errors aside, the book has much charm and a clever design, but it is clear that Von has not solved the problem of making Shakespeare's humor work in a comic book.

137 *Sandman*
"Sleep of the Just." # 1, January 1989. New York: DC Comics. Neil Gaiman (writer), Sam Kieth (artist), Mike Dringenberg (artist). Page 36.

Sandman is an immortal creature who lives in and controls the world of sleep and dreams. Occultists in the early twentieth century imprison him in a glass globe, promising release if he will give them his powers. He refuses because his "gifts are neither mankind's to receive nor mine to give." Since his captors do not understand this, he concludes, "Lord, what fools these mortals be," an unacknowledged quote of Puck's (3.2.115) in *A Midsummer Night's Dream*. Gaiman was just warming up with this quote. He will revisit Shakespeare and obviously acknowledge him for an extended story about this play (see next entry), and again for the conclusion of the series where it integrated it with the end of Shakespeare's career and *The Tempest* (see entry).

138 *Sandman*
"A Midsummer Night's Dream." # 19, September 1990. New York: DC Comics. Neil Gaiman (writer), Charles Vess (artist). Pages N/A.

Shakespeare and his son go with the actors of the Lord Strange's Men to a Sussex countryside meeting in 1593, where they are to give the first performance of *A Midsummer Night's Dream*. As arranged, Shakespeare is met by the Sandman, the Lord of Dreams, who wears Elizabethan garb and directs them to a natural amphitheater where the performance is attended by dozens of supernatural creatures, including Oberon (here called Auberon), Titania, and Puck (pp. 1–6). That is the extraordinary conceit of this issue, where the first payment is made for the Faustian bargain Shakespeare made with Sandman in # 13 (see entry 218). He is to write two great plays about dreams in exchange for the ability to write great plays (see also *Sandman* # 75 under *The Tempest*). The rest of the story is the (truly) magical performance of the play, handled like Act 5 with constant comments from the gallery. Some of the comments move the narrative forward, allowing Gaiman to skip huge chunks of the story. Other comments come from the actors backstage as they express their alarm about this strange audience. During the interval—performances then did not usually have intervals, but never mind—Oberon gives the company a bag of gold and Puck learns his character's lines and takes over the role (p. 15). He does not really make mischief, though he stays on Earth after the other fairies retreat to their new fairy realm. The performance includes many quotations from the play. The longest is Theseus's "The Lunatic, the Lover, and the Poet" speech (5.8–18), here voiced by Shakespeare as Theseus. The lines

The poet's eye, in fine frenzy rolling,
Doth glance from heaven to earth, from earth to heaven;
And as imagination bodies forth
The forms of things unknown, the poet's pen
Turns them to shapes and gives to airy nothing
A local habitation and a name

especially resonate with this story of a play about a dream in which Shakespeare's imagination has become incarnate (p. 20). When the performance is over, the actors fall into a slumber. Did they but dream? The bag of gold is opened, but now contains only yellowed leaves (p. 24). The story names a number of people Shakespeare knew and worked with, including his son Hamnet, Richard Burbage, Will Kemp, Robert Armin, Henry Condell, and Christopher Marlowe (who Shakespeare probably knew, and whose death is announced).

139 *Superboy*
"Going Mental." # 34, December 1996. New York: DC Comics. Ron Marz (writer), Ramon Bernado (penciller), Doug Hazelwood (inker). Page 11.

The teenaged, hyper, hormone-driven Superboy has finally figured out he is in love with a television news reporter named Tana, but he also knows that Roxie has unrequited love for him. Tana has just kissed him in front of Roxie, which leads to Roxie literally flying off in a huff. Superboy sits down with his guardian/mentor/tutor Dubbilex for his literature lesson. Dubbilex reads *A Midsummer Night's Dream* (3.2.323–25): "O, when she is angry she is keen and shrewd. She was a vixen when she went to school: And though she be but little, she is fierce." Superboy responds, "Yeah, that Shakespeare guy sure knew women. Nothing but grief."

140 *The Incredible Hulk*
"Big Things" Part Three. # 73, August 2004. New York: Marvel Comics. Bruce Jones (writer), Dougie Braithwaite (penciller), Bill Reinhold (inker). Page 11.

The Hulk, in his normal identity of Bruce Banner, is visiting Tony Stark, who is really Iron Man. They are working on a gamma-ray project. Nicole, who is one of Stark's girlfriends, invites Banner on a picnic, saying, "It's a beautiful spring day... and 'I know a place where the wild thyme grows.'" This paraphrases *A Midsummer Night's Dream* (2.1.249). They have quite a nice time. This is the numbering of the current Hulk series, and may change again at any time. Look for the date when researching this issue.

141 *Comic Book Shakespeare: A Midsummer Night's Dream*
2005. St. Julians, Sevenoaks, Kent: Timber Frame Publications, Ltd. Simon Greaves (adapter/artist). Pages N/A.

It is immediately obvious that Simon Greaves has improved greatly since his last book. The first few pages do not rely on close-ups, but integrate them with long and medium shots. Panels with two or more characters far outnumber talking heads, and even those are more varied and interesting. While pages are still text heavy, the text no longer overwhelms the pictures (pp. 1–7). The first scene with the Mechanicals is even more impressive. Rather than trying to draw them realistically, Greaves makes them obviously comic, which suits them. He still has room to improve, but he has taken a giant step. The color choice is green, which seems natural for a play with so many scenes set in the woods, but Greaves does not do the expected. To color the trees would be to color the background, drawing the eye away from the focal characters. Instead, he colors the fairies green—all of them, and seldom anything else (e.g., p. 20). This seems a strange choice, and is, but most pages are effectively colored, with the fairies popping out from the background. Greaves opens up the story by illustrating the imbalance in nature described by Titania, showing a hamlet flooding in the incessant rain. Some of the animals outside the town have died (p. 15). 3.2, the long scene with battling lovers, does not get the laughs it receives on stage. It probably needs actors to play the lines as funny and add movement to seal the comedy. Finding laughs on a comic page is difficult for anybody adapting Shakespeare; Greaves does not seem to have tried (pp. 32–40). He pulls this off with *Pyramus and*

Thisbe in the last act, partly because the lines are more obviously humorous, partly because of the characters he already established for the Mechanicals, and because Greaves simply draws the action humorously (pp. 51–57). Greaves is getting good, and this book creates anticipation for the *Tempest*.

MUCH ADO ABOUT NOTHING

142 *The Born Loser*
February 1, 1988. NEA, Inc. Art Sansom and Chip Sansom (writers/artists).

Brutus Thornapple says something stupid again. He sees Gladys reading *Much Ado about Nothing* and complains that Shakespeare puts him "to sleep." Gladys informs him that after the Bible, no one "has been so widely quoted!" Her husband is unimpressed, saying that if Shakespeare had not "written all those plays" nobody would have "ever heard of him." Gladys looks exhausted.

143 *Frank and Ernest*
March 13, 1993. NEA, Inc. Bob Thaves (writer/artist).

After seeing a poster advertising the play *A Big Hassle About Zilch*, Frank tells Ernest, "I hate it when they update Shakespeare."

OTHELLO

144 *Krazy Kat*
July 26, 1921. King Features Syndicate, Inc. George Herriman (writer/artist).

Ignatz Mouse goes to the beach and tans himself. He becomes very dark. Krazy Kat goes to the beach, where the tanned Ignatz beans him with a brick. Because of Ignatz's dark skin, Krazy thinks the mouse who beaned him is not Ignatz. Krazy returns the brick to the back of Ignatz's head, and says, "Dunt think I'm no' 'Desdamonia' you Othello."

145 *Terry and the Pirates*
June 18 and July 5, 1946. Chicago Tribune–New York News Syndicate. Milton Caniff (writer/artist).

The Dragon Lady's assistant, named Slits for his odd glasses, is in love with the Dragon Lady, but she has spurned him. Though there is no rival for her affection, and so no actual jealousy, Terry's co-pilot Hotshot Charley refers to Slits as a "green-eyed monster," referring without acknowledgment to *Othello* (3.3.170). Charles calls him this again in on July 5, 1946, but without the reference to jealousy.

146 *Heavy Metal*
"Shakespeare for Americans." January 1982. New York: Heavy Metal Magazine. Howard V. Chaykin (writer), Walt Simonson (artist). Page 6.

Othello receives the "Shakespeare for Americans" treatment, here a storyboard for an advertisement of a film version set in the underworld of Las Vegas. Chaykin is smart in choosing lurid moments, just as a real ad might feature. Included are a sexy torch singer singing *Willow Weep for Me*, a shutout, a woman in a nightgown being threatened on her bed, with voice-over lines such as "where death is swift and scarlet" and "even the innocent are caught in webs of duplicity." This is not so much a satire on *Othello* as an appropriation to satirize (if that is the right word—it is not very satrical) television advertisements for films. Chaykin chooses scenes from throughout the play without tying them together, so only those who know the story can make sense of the *Othello* part of it. The credits above are as found. Judging by the style, Chaykin contributed to the art.

147 *Othello*
1983. New York: Workman Publishing. Oscar Zarate (artist). Pages N/A.

This is the second in Oval's Cartoon Shakespeare Series, and it is very different than those drawn by Von. Zarate is big on symbolism and fills the back with it. In the strongly interpretative first scene, Roderigo meets Iago at the house of a prostitute and gives Iago money to pay the woman. She has a pet monkey, an animal evoked several times in the play because early moderns associated them with a lascivious nature. It is after this transaction that Iago and Roderigo make their way to Brabantio's house (pp. 1–2). The book is filled with animals. Zarate gives Brabantio a dog that tries to attack Roderigo on sight (p. 7). Othello's explanation to the senators is not full of bird imagery, but Zarate fills the panels of Othello's memory with birds in flight (pp. 16–18). When Iago calls nature a fig (1.3.313), an early modern euphemism for female genitalia, we see a monkey eating a fig (p. 23). The same monkey throws a rotten tomato at a painting of three nymphs (pp. 24–26). This menagerie is soon joined by seagulls (p. 27), a parrot, hawk, and a tiger cub (p. 30), the cub soon adopting Iago and appearing several times with him (the last time is on p. 54). What some of these animals are intended to convey is not clear. Symbols are seen in the locations where Zarate chooses to tell the story. Iago leads Roderigo down a labyrinth-like spiral staircase as he insists that Desdemona will soon want new lovers (2.1.36–38). Iago gives advice to Cassio in 3.1 as they walk through a maze (pp. 56–57). The 3.3 meetings of Cassio and Desdemona, and soon after of Desdemona and Othello, take place in that same maze (pp. 58–60). Iago tells Othello about the handkerchief (later in 3.3) on a balcony, perhaps a conscious reversal of *Romeo and Juliet* (2.2). The inconstant moon wanes in the background (pp. 71–75). The scene in which Iago persuades Othello to murder Desdemona (4.1) takes place behind a series of pillars. As the panels progress and Othello's mind becomes more tortured, the pillars seem to grow closer, entrapping him, then shift to surreal angles, bulging and

twisting like roots, perhaps reflecting the twisting of Othello's mind (pp. 83–85). Zarate returns to the maze for the death of Roderigo (5.1; pp. 108–13). Throughout, Zarate uses images and symbols to give a deeply psychological rendering of the play.

148 *Othello*
1984, Reprint 1994. Circle Pines, MN: American Guidance Service, Inc. Dorothy Calhoun Fago (adapter), Vicatan (artist). Pages N/A.

Imagine an *Othello* where race is not an issue. He is not called "thicklips" (1.1.66), and Brabantio is not told "an old black ram/Is topping your white ewe" (1.1.88–89), or that his daughter is covered with "a Barbary horse" (1.1.111–12). Imagine if Othello does not say, "Haply for I am black" (3.3.263) and looks far more like Cassio (they look like brothers) then he does like Paul Robson. You would have an *Othello* without a hint of race, and that is what Fago and Vicatan present in their Pendulum comic book. The most exotic thing about him are two Muslim-looking headdresses not worn after page 25. The play is about more than race, but it is an important aspect. To lose it is to make the story pointless, whether you believe the Moor is a light-skinned Moroccian or very dark skinned. By eliminating most of Iago's soliloquies, Fago eliminates the ambiguity about his motives. He tells Roderigo that he acts because Cassio was given the promotion, and it is left at that (p. 8). Because the scene of Cassio kissing Desdemona's hand is cut (2.1), there is nothing to present to Roderigo as evidence that Cassio is in love with her, yet he is still convinced. Othello accepts Desdemona's guilt far more quickly than in the play—too quickly at just three pages and a panel (pp. 24–25, 27–28). He is so overwrought that he faints (in this version), after just two panels. There is no time for the building of his psychodrama (p. 32). Children may find this more persuasive than an adult can. One expects a certain amount of adaptation for comics and accepts some censorship in a children's adaptation, but there are too many references to race for the story to satisfy without it. One can argue that children are being introduced to the story, so this will not bother them. That is doubtless correct, but then without it they are not really getting *The Tragedie of Othello, the Moor of Venice*, as First Folio has it. By censoring race from the story, the entire exercise seems pointless.

149 *Superman*
"The Man Who Murdered Evil." # 419, May 1986. New York: DC Comics. Elliot S. Maggin (writer), Curt Swan (penciller), Dave Hunt (inker). Page N/A.

He looks like Satan, dresses like Dracula, and sometimes calls himself Iago. The villain in this story is a demon-possessed human who represents the malignancy of motiveless evil, and thus he is named for the Shakespeare character who is often described that way. He claims to be "the one responsible—for youth's pain and age's despair . . . for tyrants' ascendancy and pilgrims' descent . . . for the crashing of hopes and the untimeliness of death." Superman thwarts him in the end.

150 *Brenda Starr*
June 21, 1995. Tribune Media Services, Inc. Mary Schmich (writer), Ramona Fradon (artist).

Brenda Starr has become a controversial strip, not so much for its content, which is standard adventure fare, but for the politics of being created by a woman, Dale Messick, and featuring a female star character. Many commentators consider it second-rate, which places it above most strips which are third-rate, but a big rung below the creations of Hal Foster, Milton Caniff, Roy Crane, and a few others. The other side considers the critics blind to the sensibility Messick brought to her work. However one feels about *Brenda Starr*, no one can deny the success of a strip that began in 1940 and is still running, with alternate versions in comic books, a Big Little Book, a novel, a movie, a television movie, and a movie serial. Messick retired in 1980, replaced on the art by Ramona Fradon and on the writing by a succession of people. Only the June 21, 1995, strip was seen from this sequence, so these comments lack context. A young woman is jogging with a hunky man who appears to be her attorney. She lets slip something about spying on someone named Babs and is embarrassed to have revealed that. He says that "shared sweat makes people honest," then adds, "to abuse a line from Shakespeare, 'I am nothing if not discreet.'" She is impressed that he quoted Shakespeare. Since Shakespeare did not write the line, if it difficult to know what he is misquoting. That line that comes closest is Iago's "For I am nothing if not critical" (2.1.117), although the sentiment is completely different.

151 *Mother Goose and Grimm*
December 6, 1996. Tribune Media Services, Inc. Mike Peters (writer/artist).

Grimm is a rather disgusting and incorrigible dog who is happiest when digging through the garbage because it smells so much like food. In a quiet moment, the reading Mother Goose tells Grimm, "Shakespeare said 'He who steals my purse steals trash'" (3.3.157). Grimm becomes excited and digs through Mother's purse, thinking, "Where? Where's trash? Where?" We note that if Shakespeare's line is taken this way, the purse is the trash, not the contents, but this comment demonstrates the problem of giving close readings to most comic strips. Shakespeare's line lacks the pronoun, but is nearly always misquoted with it.

152 *Frank and Ernest*
July 17, 2002. NEA, Inc. Bob Thaves (writer/artist).

Frank is without Ernest, but his is still punning. This time he is in Elizabethan garb, sitting behind a desk emblazoned with the sign, *Ye Editor*. He tells William Shakespeare, "How about making it a comedy and changing the name from 'Othello' to 'The Moor, the Marryer'!" This strip assumes readers will know that Othello is a Moor and will get the joke, which is assuming a lot. It is the sort of joke often found on English radio, but is rare in any medium in the United States.

153 *Rhymes with Orange*
March 22, 2005. King Features Syndicate. Hilary B. Price.

Two women attend a performance of *Othello*. From onstage (not pictured) comes a word balloon with a bit of the "I kissed thee ere I killed thee" speech (5.2.420–21). After the show, one woman tells the other that the English are better at performing Shakespeare because they still have British accents in the second act. The theater has a sign advertising *Othello*. According to an e-mail, price was not aware that this is point of contention between theatergoers and theater professionals in America. One contingent takes pride in our native Shakespeare style, noting that American accents, especially in the South, may be closer to the Elizabethan accent than the Standard English of modern Britain, though this is often a hindsight rationalization for simply preferring American Shakespeare. The other camp points to the long tradition of Shakespeare performance, with one generation passing down the style to another, though this is often a hindsight rationalization for simply preferring the English style of Shakespeare. There are snobs on both sides. Richard Nelson satirized this second sort of snobbery in his play *Some Americans Abroad*, which was commissioned and first performed by the Royal Shakespeare Company.

PERICLES, PRINCE OF TYRE

154 *Krazy Kat*
November 18, 1928. George Herriman (writer/artist).

In addition to the earlier and better-known "Lend me your ears" (*Julius Caesar* 3.2.78), Shakespeare twice used the expression "lend ear" in both *Coriolanus* (5.3.23) and in Shakespeare's portion of *Pericles, Prince of Tyre* (5.1.97). Herriman follows the specific use in *Pericles*. A dog who is running for Mayor asks those hearing his speech to "lend ear." Much of his language is pseudo-King James English, such as "Thrice will I repay." For Herriman, swiping the short phrase from Shakespeare nicely sets up the antique tone to come. The candidate's speech bores the audience, who leave one by one.

RICHARD II

155 *Richard II*
April 28, 1952. Post-Hall Syndicate. Walt Kelly (writer/artist).

In a tenuous connection to Shakespeare, Walt Kelly named a character Bolingbroke. This story is a satire on the

1952 presidential election that put Dwight D. Eisenhower in the White House. Pogo Possum has been put forward as a presidential candidate, but has not agreed to run. His self-appointed campaign manager is a bear named P. T. Bridgewater, who is sometimes accompanied by a rabbit banging on a drum to drum up support for the candidate. Bridgewater first calls the rabbit Bolingbroke and in the same panel calls him Hewlitt. On May 20, he is called both Hebrides and Julius, and Bertram (also a Shakespearean name, but not as distinctively so) and Winthrock on June 18. Kelly, who certainly knew Shakespeare, seems to have glanced at *Richard II* for the name Bolingbroke.

RICHARD III

156 *Krazy Kat*
August 19, 1917. King Features Syndicate, Inc. George Herriman.

Ignatz Mouse is in hospital, where his doctor forbids him cheese. Krazy overhears this, and wonders what he can do to make his love happy. He laments "A Cheese, a cheese, my king's-dim for a cheese!"

157 *Krazy Kat*
January 25, 1942. King Features Syndicate, Inc. George Herriman (writer/artist).

George Herriman created a variation on the August 19, 1917, Sunday page twenty-five years later. In the afterpiece (a wide panel unrelated to the story located at the end of that day's cartoon), Ignatz, who so adept at hitting Krazy in the head with bricks, longs for a new brick to attack the kat. He strikes a regal pose and says, "A brick—my kingdom for a brick!" A brick is zipping its way towards his noggin from off the panel. He is about to get his wish, but not the way he wished it.

158 *Nuts!*
5, November 1954. New York: Premiere Comics Group. Yvonne Rae (writer), Ross Andru (penciller), Mike Esposito (inker). Page 2.

Nuts! was a short-lived imitation of *Mad* magazine, dispensing parody comic book stories. Their last issue poked fun at Captain Marvel in a story drawn by the veteran team of Ross Andru and Mike Esposito. Billy Battyson learns that his enemy Master Mynd is looting the city. Billy wants to change to Captain Marble where no one will see so he may preserve his secret identity. He borrows from both Superman and Richard III, saying, "My kingdom for a phone booth ... how can I change without it" (paraphrase of 5.4.7). After a series of mishaps that lead to the Captain being attacked by a bee, traversing an obstacle course, and arrested, he overcomes another old foe who turns out to have reformed. He ends up playing marbles with Batman and Superman in an insane asylum. He should have stayed out of the phone booth. *Nuts!* # 5 is

scarce, even by the standard of old comic books. Researchers may want to consult a black-and-white reprint in *Alter Ego* # 33, ed. Roy Thomas (Raleigh, NC: Two-Morrows, February 2004), pp. 47–52.

159 *The Born Loser*
August 7, 1984. NEA, Inc. Art Sansom (writer/artist).

Brutus Thornapple betrays his ignorance every time he opens his mouth, and does it again in this strip. His boss, Mr. Veeblefester, quotes *Richard III* (1.1.1–2), "Now is the winter of our discontent, made glorious summer by this sun of York ..." and attributes it to Shakespeare. Brutus is offended by the attribution. He does not need it since he has "read everything the 'Bard' ever penned ... unless, of course, he's written something new recently." The credit above is probably correct. Chip Sansom was assisting his father when this strip was done, but it is unusually signed by Art Sansom alone. The credit is based on this bit of internal evidence.

160 *The Wizard of Id*
May 16, 2004. Creators Syndicate. Johnny Hart (writer), Brant Parker (artist).

The despotic king of the land of Id is under attack from the Huns. He leaps from his horse to avoid some arrows and cries "A horse! A horse! My kingdom for a horse!" (5.4.7). A servant brings an old plow horse. The king complains that such a horse would be offered to a monarch, but the peasant impresses the king by saying the horse comes with a magnesium plow, presumably a reference to the attraction some automobile drivers have to magnesium wheels.

ROMEO AND JULIET

161 *Krazy Kat*
May 28, 1916. King Features Syndicate, Inc. George Herriman (writer/artist).

Krazy confides to Ignatz Mouse that he would like to be a hero. Ignatz says, "to be a 'hero,' you've got to be like 'Napoleon' and 'Romeo and Juliet,' and 'John L. Sullivan,' and 'Villa,' and ole 'Capt. Kidd'—full of fight and ginger!" Ignatz then hurls a rock at police Officer Pup, who thinks it was thrown by a bear who came along at the moment of impact. A rock fight ensues between Pup and the bear. Krazy is finally being threatened by Pup and the bear who decide he threw the first stone. When they leave, Krazy tells Ignatz, "I—I—I did'nt act exackly like them Napoleons, and them other fellas would'a acted, did I, 'Ignatz'?"

162 *Krazy Kat*
December 13, 1921. King Features Syndicate, Inc. George Herriman.

Herriman returned frequently to a gag using a variation of Juliet's "Wherefore art thou Romeo?" (2.2.33). He apparently thought *wherefore* means *where*, not *why*, and structured his joke on that assumption. Krazy Kat installs a balcony below his window, saying he can "now be Juliet and 'Ignatz' can be Romeo." He wonders "wherefore don't you come unda my belcony and make love to me," so of course, Ignatz Mouse beans him with a brick from the roof. Krazy considers this an "original way of Romeoing."

163 *Krazy Kat*
September 27, 1925. King Features Syndicate, Inc. George Herriman.

Krazy Kat is lonely because Ignatz Mouse in not with him. He recites *Romeo and Juliet* (2.2.33) in Katspeak, "Oy 'Ignatz'.!!! Where four is thou, Ignatz?—I have waited hours for thee—and yet thou comest not—oi, woi is me, woi is me—" Herriman exploited the general misunderstanding of the word *wherefore* to get this gag across.

164 *Krazy Kat*
January 10, 1926. King Features Syndicate, Inc. George Herriman (writer/artist).

Following the popular misconception that *Romeo and Juliet* 2.2 takes place on Juliet's balcony, Krazy stands on a balcony yearning for Ignatz Mouse to come along "Like 'Joliet' awaiting her 'Rummio.'" Ignatz shimmies up a drainpipe and loosens a terra-cotta roof tile to toss at him. Krazy, unaware of this, says, "Oy, why comes he not . . . Wear four is thou, 'Ignatz,' and why?" (2.2.33, sort of). Krazy decides to put up the balcony's awning for a little shade, just as Ignatz drops the tile. It bounces off the awning, and hits Officer Pupp, who happens to pass by. Ignatz dangles from the tiles above the awning while Pup searches for him on the roof, and expresses the hope that he can land "on something reasonably soft." It is at that moment Krazy decides to close the awning, hoping "heaven may yet showa a giff of love upon me."

165 *Krazy Kat*
December 5, 1926. King Features Syndicate, Inc. George Herriman (writer/artist).

In a variation on an old gag, Officer Pupp has trapped Ignatz Mouse under an orange crate. He tunnels out, popping through the ground just as Krazy says, "Ware four is thou at, 'Ignatz'??" He, of course, clobbers Krazy with a brick, goes back into the hole, and emerges from the box with Officer Pupp blissfully unaware.

166 *Krazy Kat*
June 29, 1930. King Features Syndicate, Inc. George Herriman (writer/artist).

Yet again a would-be lover is called Romeo. This time it is a French donkey named Kiskidee KuKu, who has a crush on Krazy Kat. He receives a note signed K suggesting a "tryst" that night. He turns up at the appointed hour expecting to meet Krazy, only to learn that the note was sent by a duck named Mrs. Katalpa. Krazy wanders by, sees them together, calls KuKu a "Romeo," and says he'll have Officer Pupp arrest KuKu.

167 *Krazy Kat*
February 15, 1931. King Features Syndicate, Inc. George Herriman (writer/artist).

In this Sunday page, Krazy, the eternal innocent, goes to a fortuneteller and is advised to sow his wild oats. Krazy laments, "Oh, 'Oat,' Oh, Wile 'Oat'—Where four is thou—wile oat?" Krazy searches through bramble and brier and finally finds a single wild oat, rejoices, and shows it to Ignatz Mouse, wishing he had a needle and thread "to sew this 'wile oat' with." As shown above, Herriman found *wherefore* in *Romeo and Juliet* (2.2.23).

168 *Terry and the Pirates*
November 10, 1934. Chicago Tribune–New York News Syndicate. Milton Caniff.

Terry Lee, his Chinese servant Connie, and Dale Scott are captured and held aboard a ship. The Captain tries to force himself on Dale. Terry literally swings to the rescue on a curtain, kicking the Captain in the face. Terry says, "There's a kiss for your exalted pan!—Th' love scene is off—'cause Romeo lost his uppers!—Beat it Dale!!" and they run out of the room.

169 *Terry and the Pirates*
October 24, 1936. Chicago Tribune–New York News Syndicate. Milton Caniff (writer/artist).

The evil but conflicted Dragon Lady has captured noble Pat Ryan. Like all women, she is a little in love with him, despite her baser nature. She gazes at him as he sleeps and recites a bit of *Romeo and Juliet*: "Sleep dwell upon thine eyes, peace in thy breast!—Would I were sleep and peace, so sweet to read!" (2.2.186–87). How a Chinese pirate came to know the play so well is not addressed, nor is there a need to, since virtually everyone in *Terry and the Pirates* knows Shakespeare.

170 *Li'l Abner*
April 1–May 2, 1938. United Features Syndicate, Inc. Al Capp (writer/artist).

Daisy Mae is in love with Li'l Abner, but since their relationship is not working out, she becomes engaged to a Boston socialite named Dr. Paradise, who bears a strong resemblance to the actor William Powell. Her roughhouse cousins Luke and Lem Scragg, and her Uncle Romeo Scragg crash the engagement party. Romeo tries to romance a widow until he learns her husband is alive, so the boys plan to kill the husband to make their Pappy happy. This and their eating habits ruin the party. Paradise breaks off the engagement, and the Scraggs take Daisy Mae home in a stolen car. They meet a gangster who looks just like Li'l Abner (recurring villain Gat Garson), and the Scraggs leave the story at this point, though they become regular characters in the strip. Subsequent appearances are not listed.

171 *Terry and the Pirates*
June 12, 1939. Chicago Tribune–New York News
Syndicate. Milton Caniff (writer/artist).

Terry Lee is still unhappy in love, and due to a strange
turn of events confides in the Dragon Lady (sometimes a
villain, sometimes not). She has even taught Terry how to
dance. He explains why he cannot invite April Kane to the
Governor's Ball. The Dragon Lady sums up the situation:
"Now the young one has knowledge of dancing—the invitation to the grand ball—the desire to be the great
lover . . . but, alas, no Juliet!"

172 *Terry and the Pirates*
October 31, 1940. Chicago Tribune–New York News
Syndicate. Milton Caniff.

Relief worker Raven Sherman and pilot Dude Hennick
are captives of a villain named Chopstick Joe. Raven
leaves through the window of the room where she is held
and makes her way along the ledge to Dude's room. When
she enters his window, Hennick says, "And you crawled
around the ledge! . . . . My, my! What the Romeo and Juliet
act has come to!" Raven replies, "No time for balcony
scenes," then tells Dude of Joe's scheme to ransom her. The
reference to the balcony scene in *Romeo and Juliet* is well
chosen by Caniff. Raven and Dude are smitten with each
other, though they have not admitted it yet. Caniff uses
one of literatures best known flirting scenes to show Raven
and Dude flirt with each other even as he advances the
story. Alas, their love will prove as star-crossed as the love
of Shakespeare's characters.

173 *Terry and the Pirates*
November 24, 1941. Chicago Tribune–New York News
Syndicate. Milton Caniff (writer/artist).

After months of facing dangers on his own, young Terry
Lee is finally reunited with Pat Ryan and April Kane. April
is very cold to Terry, which makes him wonder if she is in
love with Pat. Most women who meet him are, though
April is much closer to Terry's age. In panel 4 Pat says:
"Wake up, Romeo! Who do you suppose I sent for you?"
The answer, of course, is April Kane, so Terry learns Pat
has no designs on her.

174 *Action Comics*
"The Case of the Crimeless Crimes." # 51,
August 1942. New York: DC Comics. Jerry Siegel (writer),
Ed Dobrotka (penciller), John Sikela (inker).
Pages 2, 3, and 11.

This story is the first appearance of the Prankster, a
villain who seems to commit a series of crimes, but ends up
enriching his apparent victims. It is all a plot to earn trust
so he may make an even bigger score before Superman
stops him. These pranks earn him a lot of publicity. He tells
his gang that even Hollywood has noticed, but "of course
I'll turn it down unless they let me chose my own director,

cast, and play the role of Romeo in my favorite Shakespearean drama!" As a short, pencil-necked, pear-shaped
man, he is an unlikely Romeo (p. 11). The story also has
two unacknowledged and possibly unconscious Shakespeare quotations, since both expressions have become
English idioms. On page two Superman complains that
members of the Prankster's gang "disappeared into thin
air." "Thin air" was coined in *The Tempest* (4.1.150). On
page 3 the Prankster murders another criminal, saying he is
freeing the man "from this mortal coil." "This mortal coil"
comes from *Hamlet* (3.1.75). This story was reprinted in
Superman the Action Comics Archives, vol. 3 (New York: DC
Comics, 2001), pp. 206–18.

175 *Terry and the Pirates*
April 8, 1944. Chicago Tribune–New York News
Syndicate. Milton Caniff (writer/artist).

With yet another reference to the balcony scene (2.2),
Burma is held prisoner (again) in a tower where she has
been speaking to one of her captors, the very fat Katrinka.
Young Terry Lee lowers himself from the roof to enter her
window, then waits until Burma can get Katrinka out of
the room. While there is no balcony, the moment is not
lost on Burma. As she pulls Terry into the room she says,
"For Pete's sake, come in, Terry. . . . If I hadn't talked fast,
that king size Katrinka would have heard your number
twelves bumping on the wall. . . . If you're going to play
Romeo, make it a sock-o performance!"

176 *Terry and the Pirates*
November 11, 1946. Chicago Tribune–New York News
Syndicate. Milton Caniff (writer/artist).

Terry Lee, now a young man in the military, and fellow
pilot Deeth Crispin are both courting Jane Allen. Since
they are friends, they are being nice to each other about it.
Hotshot Charley tells her, "Jane, those two boy-Romeos
are going to under-play each other so far that ol' Hotshot
will have to start courting you to keep your morale from
being choked by soft soap. . . ." This is the last Shakespeare
reference found in *Terry and the Pirates*. Caniff gave up the
strip six weeks later to create *Steve Canyon*. The first year of
Terry by Caniff's successor George Wunder was read, but
no references to Shakespeare were found.

177 *Li'l Abner*
December 31, 1947–January 20, 1948. United Features
Syndicate, Inc. Al Capp (writer/artist).

The community of Dogpatch is under an atomic cloud
that is so dense nobody can see. Romeo McHaystack, who
bore a strong resemblance to Bertrand Russell before he
was punched in the nose, is caught kissing a young woman.
Her father pulls off Romeo's straw hat revealing the tattooed words, "Girls!! Beware of this man!! He is Romeo
McHaystack!" The number of exclamation marks changes
from cartoon to cartoon. Romeo describes his profession as

"romance of th' more athletic type!!" so this tattoo is a problem. He goes to Dogpatch so the cloud will keep anyone from seeing him, and pretends to be hunky Li'l Abner. The men of Dogpatch hang Abner for kissing their sweethearts. While he dangles, a moonshine still blows up, annihilating the cloud. Everyone can see again, and they figure out it was Romeo McHaystack who really did all the kissing. Abner is apparently saved, since he is free in the January 20 strip.

178 Barnyard Comics
"Francois Feline." # 17, April 1948. New York: Animated Cartoons, Inc. Unknown (writer/artists). Pages N/A.

Francois Feline was one of several characters in *Barnyard Comics*, part of a genre called "funny animal" comics. These were popular in the 1940s and 1950s, running out of steam in the 1960s. The exploits of Francois also appeared *Happy Comics*, but the character had a short career. He is a house cat who used to be in a second-rate vaudeville act. He decides to read Shakespeare aloud—very loud. This makes the family canary angry. They agree that if the canary proves Francois knows nothing about Shakespeare,

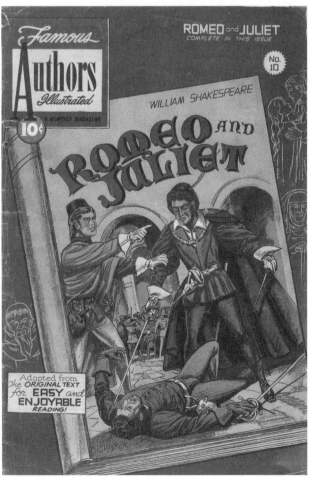

Romeo and Juliet by Henry C. Kiefer (artist) and Dana E. Dutch (adapter), 1950.

Francois will give up his recitals. The canary points out Francois just gave one of Juliet's lines thinking it was Romeo's (2.2.33). Francois claims he knew this, so the canary imitates the ghost of Shakespeare to scare Francois away from his plays. In this guise he tells Francois he will give him a chance to prove he can perform Shakespeare, invites him to play Yorick, and offers to cut off Francois's head to help him prepare. Francois refuses, but agrees to never perform Shakespeare again. When alone, the canary doffs his disguise, then Francois comes and tells him about Shakespeare's ghost, urging him to go see it. The canary enters that room, and really does see Shakespeare's ghost, holding a quill. The ghost thanks him for tricking Francois into laying off his plays.

179 Master Comics
"Ozzie and Babs: Women, Women, Women." # 109, November. Greenwich, CT: Fawcett Publications, Inc. Unknown (writer/artists). Page 4.

Master Comics was an anthology title that presented the adventures of Captain Marvel, Jr., Nyoka, the Jungle Girl, and cowboy Tom Mix, among others. One of the humor features was the *Archie*-inspired teenage strip, *Ozzie and Babs*. In this story, Ozzie is tossed out of the balcony as a joke by his friends, and he lands on stage in front of the great actress Krizta Maritza. She thinks Ozzie leaped from the balcony to throw himself at her feet, and gives him a big kiss while a photographer clicks away. This gets him in trouble with Babs, who smacks him outside the theater, and in trouble with his father, who sees the photo in the paper. His father asks, "What am I raising in this house—a Romeo?" When the neighborhood girls see the photo, they all want a piece of Ozzie's glamour, so he flees while they invade his house. He tries to hide with his friend Dip, who has no sympathy and throws him out where the teenaged girls pursue him again. Ozzie tries to escape by climbing a flagpole, but they follow him up. Their combined weight breaks the pole, and Ozzie lands on Kirzta Maritza, who slugs him. The girls see this and reject him, too. Ozzie is not destined to be a Romeo.

180 Famous Authors Illustrated
"Romeo and Juliet." # 10, December 1950. Bridgeport: Seaboard Publishers, Inc. Dana E. Dutch (adapter), Henry C. Kiefer (artist). Pages N/A.

Dutch keeps, but completely rewrites, the prologue. Where Shakespeare very generally summarizes the action, Dutch gives specific details about the characters and their enmity, permitting him to later cut some of Shakespeare's expository dialog. This permits the action to start with the Prince halting the fight (p. 1), yet swords are drawn in battle, which is what young readers want to see on a splash page. Dutch experiments with a lighter adaptation, cutting but keeping Shakespeare's sentence structure, then substituting a word or phrase more easily grasped by young readers. He rearranges scenes for brevity, so the Rosaline conversation between Romeo and Belvolio (1.1) includes Peter with the guest list (1.2; p. 3). The Queen Mab speech and Mercutio's showiness are cut, which keeps readers from knowing the depth of feeling between Romeo and Mercutio; the latter's death under Romeo's arm lacks impact (p. 15). Though the language is usually updated, Dutch barely touches on some of Romeo and Juliet's love poetry, including the sonnet they speak when they first meet (p. 6). As usual when cutting this play for film, radio, television, and comics, the balcony scene (2.2) is given fuller treatment than any other (pp. 8–10). As will become customary in comic book adaptations, all the humor is cut. While hardly sexually explicit, a caption mentions that "Romeo steals through the night to be with his bride for the first and last time." He is shown buttoning has cape as he dresses to leave (p. 17). This is unusual for an American comic book in the 1950s or 1960s. Kiefer renders the story with his usual lack of vigor. His Romeo looks exactly like his Hamlet, including the strange feminine touches in some panels (e.g., p. 3). This comic is most interesting when read after the other two *Famous Authors* Shakespeare titles to see how Dutch's approach to adaptation evolved quickly over just a few months.

181 *Love Diary*
"Back Alley Girl." # 17, c. 1951. Sparta, IL: Our Publishing Company. Unknown writer, Mort Leav (artist). Page 1.

On the first page of a story, a teenage girl passes a couple of wolf-whistling boys loitering by a billiard hall, a sign of their low characters. One of them asks, "Doin' anythin' tonight, Babe?" She replies, "G'wan! Go chase yourselves, you poolroom Romeos." There is conflicting information about this comic. The title is given as found, but one source indicates the title was changed to *Diary Loves* with the second issue.

182 *Buz Sawyer*
September 22, 1951. King Features Syndicate, Inc. Roy Crane (writer/artist).

In an episode where adventurer Buz Sawyer is mostly on the sidelines, the guests at a resort get to know each other. A milquetoast named Dudley leaves his wife for a would-be actress he thinks fancies him, but she merely hopes he can help her career. Her ham-actor boyfriend is jealous, grabs his gun when he sees Dudley, and says, "So there's the Romeo who's trying to steal my girl!" and shoots at Dudley. He misses, and Buz disarms him. All is set right in the end.

183 *Our Boarding House*
November 10 and 13, 1953. NEA, Inc. Bill Freyse (writer/artist).

In a story running for a few weeks, Major Hoople is laid up with an injury and starved for company. He acts insane to get attention, and everyone humors him. Two of the strips connect to *Romeo and Juliet*. On November 10, he waves at his friends from his window. One advises the others, "Wave back at him! The Major must think he's Juliet!" Three days later his wife comes to clear his room, and he tells her, "Egad, my dear! Must you bustle into my bedroom with those housekeeping implements?—I have just finished writing 'Romeo and Juliet', and am about to start on a play about Denmark which I intend to title 'Hamlet'!" His wife says, "Excuse me, William!" but wonders if he is faking, and if she should humor him or "wrap this mop around his jowls."

184 *Classics Illustrated*
"Romeo and Juliet." # 134, September 1956. New York: Gilberton. George Evans (artist). Pages N/A.

The adaptive strategy for this story is to dash from the beginning until the "balcony scene" (2.2), then take a more leisurely pace. It does not work, mostly because the first fourteen pages are so rushed and lacking in pace that it is difficult to maintain interest. After the initial battle— something so visual is wisely milked—the next nine scenes (of the comic, not the play) are told in one-page units:

Romeo and Juliet by George Evans (artist), 1956.

Romeo and Belvolio on p. 5, Capulet and Paris on p. 6, the invitation to the Capulet ball on p. 7, and so on. These scenes are bite-sized, predictable, and forced into units that do not fit the flow of the story. Even the meeting of Romeo with Juliet is abrupt. Their first words are of kissing (p. 12). After so much abridgement, 2.2 is given fuller treatment, really allowing the poetry and the emotions the space to work (pp. 15–20), so the reader is swept along with them. The rest is not as satisfying, but the one-page units are mostly gone, so scenes are better paced. The humor is also mostly gone, with only the scene of Juliet trying to get the Nurse's news surviving (pp. 23–24). The story may be violent, but the treatment is not. The fights are brief, with usually single panels showing clashing swords. Stabbings are off-panel (p. 27) or after the contact was made (pp. 28, 40). Similarly, Juliet is shown before she stabs herself (p. 43). There were only two printings, the second with a new cover by Edward Moritz during the 1968–76 reprint period. It was also released as an Acclaim study guide. The first printing was consulted for this entry.

185 *Blondie Comics Monthly*
"Blondie in Guess Who?" # 101, April 1957. Sparta, IL: Harvey Publications, Inc. Uncredited (writer/artists). Page 3.

This is the comic-book version of the *Blondie* comic strip, a domestic comedy about the silly things done by the Bumstead family. While comic strips were reprinted in early issues and some Sunday pages continue to be, most stories in the comic book were produced by writers and artists in Chic Young's studio. This original story is about the bad advice father Dagwood gives to teenage son Alexander about getting a date for the prom. Dagwood proudly says that when he was in school, he kept the girls guessing as to whom he would ask out, guaranteeing him a great date. He does not explain how this works. Alexander says he will call several girls to "let them guess who" he will take to the dance. Blondie does not like the advice Dagwood gives to Alexander. She pulls him out of his easy chair and says, "Guess what you're going to do, Romeo?" He is seen washing dishes in the kitchen sink in the next panel. Naturally, the plan backfires because Alexander does not make sure he has a date before making the condescending phone calls.

186 *Dick Tracy*
February 29, 1959. Chicago Tribune–New York News Syndicate. Chester Gould (writer/artist).

In this daily strip, a camera did not film the evidence Detective Dick Tracy wants because it was pointed at too steep an angle. Tracy cries out "Oh, science, wherefore art thou?" adapting *Romeo and Juliet* for his use. Here Gould reveals that he, like most people, does not know that *wherefore* means *why*.

187 *Classics Illustrated*
"Master of the World." # 163, July 1961. New York: Gilberton. Unknown (writer), N/A (artist).

"Who am I?" was a filler feature inside the front cover of *CI* comics from 1951. It was as unillustrated quiz with five clues, always promoting another *CI* title. The July 1961 adaptation of Jules Verne's "Master of the World" promoted "Romeo and Juliet" with clues such as, "I was the only daughter of an Italian nobleman who was engaged in a terrible feud with another noble." This is followed by clues about duels, banishment, a secret marriage, and love at first sight. The last clue is, "Desperate, I went to the friar, who gave me strange advice. The exciting climax of my story can be found in the play by William Shakespeare which bears my husband's name and mine." The title "Romeo and Juliet" is not stated clearly, but Juliet's name is printed upside down under the last clue. The writer is not credited.

188 *Superman's Girl Friend Lois Lane*
"Dear Dr. Cupid." # 45, November 1963. New York: DC Comics. Unknown (writer), Kurt Schaffenburger (artist). Page 5.

Lois Lane is temporarily assigned to write the lonely hearts column for the *Daily Planet* newspaper. Through some coincidences, she is convinced Clark Kent is asking Dr. Cupid's advice on how to win her. Clark takes Lois to an amusement park where they view "tableaux of great romances of history and fiction." The first of these is the balcony scene from *Romeo and Juliet*. It is actually the mail carrier who as smitten with Lois, not Clark, who does not change to Superman in this story.

189 *The Man from U.N.C.L.E.*
"The Spider and the Spy." # 8, September 1966. Poughkeepsie, NY: Gold Key. Dick Wood (writer), Mike Sekowsky (artist). Page 1.

"Jet Dream and her Stunt-Girl Counter-Spies" is a four-page filler series in *The Man from U.N.C.L.E.* comic book. This story uses the idea that anyone who fancies himself attractive to women is a "Romeo" rather nonsensically. Jet is lured into a spy cell, and simply because one of the spies says that she had "walked right into our arms," she calls him "Romeo," and says that she was not caught by them, but had "hooked you boys." It makes little sense.

190 *Adventure Comics*
"The Rejected Supergirl." # 395, July 1970. New York: DC Comics. Robert Kanigher (writer), Win Mortimer (penciller), Jack Abel (inker). Pages 1 and 7.

Poor Supergirl feels rejected. A poll of other young women at her college indicates she is last in popularity of the nine women whose names were submitted. As seen on the splash page, and later in the story, Juliet is number two.

Supergirl's wounded ego is restored when it is discovered that she is really first, but a computer glitch gave the order as an acrostic. Because the *S* in Scarlet O'Hara is the first letter in Supergirl's name, she was ranked first so the acrostic would work. *Ju*liet was number two, the *U* of Juliet sharing the second position with Supergirl's name. The *L* being the last letter in Supergir*l* put her in last place. Only Scarlet O'Hara, Juliet, and Supergirl are fictional characters; Coretta King, Marie Curie, and others on the list are actual people.

191 *Teen Titans*
"Intruders of the Forbidden Crypt" and "The Tomb be Their Destiny!" # 35, October 1971 and # 36, December 1971. New York: DC Comics. Bob Haney (writer), Nick Cardy (artist). Pages N/A.

The Teen Titans are a group of young superheroes mostly drawn from the sidekicks of more established heroes. The only member in this story who is not someone's sidekick is the star character Lilith, who has advanced ESP powers. The story is a sequel to *Romeo and Juliet*, set in 1971 Verona where the Titans go for the opening of an ecological laboratory. Like Shakespeare's play, there are two warring factions, those supporting the lab and a local businessman who opposes it. Though he is the Capulet character, his son is named Romeo. When the Titans attend a ball at his house, Romeo and Lilith fall instantly in love. As the story progresses we learn that she and her Romeo are the reincarnation of the first Romeo and Juliet, fated to meet and love again with each new generation. Still echoing the play, the story has an authority figure who tells both sides to stop fighting and a balcony scene which is just long enough for Lilith to run downstairs and hop on Romeo's motor scooter. Kid Flash, like Mercutio, is stabbed in the street, though not fatally. He even quotes " 'tis not so deep as a well . . . nor wide as a church door . . . but 'tis enough" as Batman's friend Robin gives him a blood transfusion (awkwardly drawn on page 14—Robin is not in the panel; we learn it was he who gave Kid Flash the transfusion on p. 2 of the next issue). Another character is Romeo's cousin Calibano, a Caliban type. Lilith uses her ESP powers to probe his mind. She learns he was in love with Juliet all those years ago. When Romeo and Juliet met at the Capulet tomb for a tryst, Calibano discovered them, murdered Romeo, and Juliet took her own life. He remained by her body for centuries. Calibano attempts to repeat this by murdering the current Romeo so he may have Lilith for himself. He is shot by the archer Speedy, sidekick of Green Arrow and a member of the Titans, and he hobbles off to the Capulet tomb to die. Romeo and Lilith are together at the end of the story. Presumably he is in some subsequent issues, but this has not been verified. Nick Cardy is credited as the sole artist, but the distinctive

style of George Tuska can be seen in some figures; it is presumed that he assisted Cardy with both issues.

192 *The Smith Family*
January 25, year unknown, probably mid-1970s. Washington Star Syndicate, Inc. Mr. and Mrs. George Smith (writers/artists).

This strip was not a big success when judged by the number of papers that carried it, merchandising, or public consciousness, but it ran from the fifties into the nineties, which is a considerable achievement. It was produced by George and Vi Smith, and told the story of a little boy named George Smith and his long suffering parents. In this strip, George asks if he can go to the movies to see the classic western *Rodeo and Juliet* by Jake Spear. They tell him he can. Once he is gone, his father says, "I can't wait till he gets back." The sample seen is not dated, so the date above is a guess based on a used care advertisement on the back. It cannot be before 1974.

193 *Romeo and Juliet*
1980, Reprint 1984. West Haven, CT: Academic Industries, Inc. Rich Margopoulos (adapter), Nestor Redondo (artist). Pages N/A.

The narrative is very clear in this educational comic book, and the updated language is mostly effective, but results in occasionally stilted and banal dialogue such as this exchange as Romeo and Juliet are about to marry. Romeo says, "I hope you are as happy as I am, Juliet," and she replies, "Oh, Romeo! I can not tell you how much I love you" (p. 35). The story is also sanitized to not offend: "Like a rich jewel in an Ethiop's ear" (1.5.43) is changed to the less racially charged, "She is like a snowy dove among dark crows" (p. 20). Romeo and Juliet do not make love during their night together. The first panel shows him sitting on the outside rail of Juliet's balcony. She stands on the inside (p. 49). This is a love unsullied by physicality, love as children often understand it. Typical of comic book adaptations, the humor is sacrificed to move the story along, so the Nurse does not delay giving Juliet news about Romeo, and their exchange takes just one panel (p. 34). Mercutio's taunting of Tybalt with the word *cat* is cut, yet the conceit survives in this line of narrative, "Tybalt, fast as a cat, ducked under Romeo's arm and stabbed Mercutio" (p. 39). To make the apothecary understandable to young readers, his house is called "a nearby drug store" (p. 54). This is a safe *Romeo and Juliet*, completely gutted of passion, humor, or anything unfamiliar to modern readers, but the squeamish may find it a pleasant introduction to the play. The Pocket Comics version was studied for this entry.

194 *Romeo and Juliet*
1983. New York: Alfred A. Knopf. Von (adapter/artist). Pages N/A.

This is the third in the unabridged Cartoon Shakespeare Series. Von's style does not lend itself to humor, but he paces the panels to good effect, as seen with Peter and the letter (1.2; p. 12), and the almost obscene but fully clothed shot of the Nurse as she swears "by my maidenhead" (1.3.2; p. 14). The brawling scenes are well executed, with combatants spread across the panels, arms and weapons raised to defy orderly composition. The effect is chaotic, deadly, just right (e.g., pp. 5, 59). Von does not seem able to draw anyone attractively. Faith is required to accept that Romeo and Juliet make a strong impression on each other, yet Von hedges this effectively by drawing their first meeting inside of hearts that fill two pages. In the border around the hearts are pastoral and mythological scenes of Cupid and men and woman frolicking together (pp. 24–25). This is so effective Von uses the trick twice more. Romeo's death is on two pages bordered by skulls (pp. 112–13), and Juliet's death is drawn inside the Ace of Spades, the traditional card of misfortune and sometimes death (pp. 116–17). There are some interesting visual conceptions. 2.2 is usually called "the balcony scene," though Shakespeare does not mention a balcony. After five pages of Romeo looking up and Juliet looking down (pp. 31–35), Von changes to diagonal panels, which give the dialogue a natural flow (pp. 36–37). When Juliet contemplates what may go wrong if she takes the potion given her by Friar Lawrence (4.3), Von draws her reflection distorted in the green curve of the bottle. She is hideous, as if she were "stifled in the vault / To whose foul mouth no healthsome air breathes in" (4.3.32–33; p. 95). When Sampson and Gregory make their jokes about forcing themselves on the Montague women, an evil-looking pussycat walks by as he stalks his prey (p. 2). Among Juliet's first words in 3.5.2–3 are, "It was the nightingale, and not the lark,/that pierced the fearful hollow of thine ear." Outside her bedroom window are four larks, the heralds of the morn (p. 78). These are just a few examples of how Von's interpretation is well imagined and effective. The American edition published by Knopf was reviewed for this entry.

195 *The Daring New Adventures of Supergirl*
"Hail, Hail, the Gang's All Here!" Vol. 2, # 4, February 1983. New York: DC Comics. Paul Kupperberg (writer), Carmine Infantino (penciller), Bob Oksner (inker). Page 3.

A gang of supervillains invades an aerospace technology show to steal a two-ton satellite. As they depart, the leader turns to onlookers and says, "Till we meet again. . . . Parting is such sweet sorrow," the last part of which is a quote from *Romeo and Juliet* (2.2.184).

196 *Superman*
"Luthor Lashes Back." # 386, August 1983. New York: DC Comics. Cary Bates (writer), Curt Sawn (penciller), Dave Hunt (inker). Page 13.

Lois Lane has recently broken up with Superman, a relationship archenemy Lex Luthor planned to exploit. Luthor mulls over the break-up while a woman polishes his bald head; he refers to Superman and Lane as "star-crossed lovers," the expression applied to Romeo and Juliet in line six of the prologue of that play.

197 *Ranma ½*
"Wherefore art thou, Romeo?" "Romeo? Romeo? Romeo!?" "Not Your Typical Juliet." "A Kiss to the Victor." 1987, Reprint 1996, Vol. 7. San Francisco: Viz, LLC. Toshifumi Yoshida (translator), Gerard Jones (translator), Rumiko Takahashi (writer/artist). Pages 7–70.

Ranma is a teenaged boy who turns into a teenaged girl when he is splashed with cold water. He only becomes a boy again when splashed with hot water. He has a crush on Akane, but he is shy, and that antagonizes her. Ryoga also has a crush on Akane, which makes Ranma jealous. In this four-part story, their school mounts a production of *Romeo and Juliet*, with Akane as Juliet and Ranma as a reluctant Romeo. Ryoga wants the part as an excuse to kiss Akane. Ranma's reluctance to play the balcony scene and kiss her gives the Ryoga the opportunity to act, and Martial Arts mayhem ensues on stage. This retelling is greatly simplified. Ranma's story was originally published as a serial in Japan from 1987 to 1996, translated and republished by Vic Comics in comic book form in the United States, and then published as graphic novels. Ranma could be seen as a gender-bending interrogation of sexual politics, but Takahashi's work defies this interpretation. She has a light, even silly approach. The gender switches in this volume are usually an embarrassment to Ranma and used as motivation or to create sitcom plot elements. The title is pronounced "Ranma half," the half indicating "half boy/half girl." Translator Gerry Jones had a copy of Shakespeare's play open when doing his translation of the Japanese.

198 *Peanuts*
May 4, 1988. United Features Syndicate, Inc. Charles M. Schulz (writer/artist).

In an odd sequence, the girl who sits behind Linus in school changes her name each day, and in the first panel of this day's strip announces she is now named Polly. Linus, exasperated with her, says he does not care if her "name is 'Louis the fourteenth.'" She insists "Names are interesting. . . Shakespeare said. . . ." Linus interrupts, "I know what Shakespeare said." Polly wonders why she would call herself Louis the Fourteenth. Linus wonders why it takes so long for the recess bell to ring. Though Schulz does not say so, he is almost certainly referring to Juliet's lines: "What's in a name? That which we call a rose / By any other word would smell as sweet" (2.2.43–44).

199 *Frank and Ernest*
October 25, 1992. NEA, Inc. Bob Thaves (writer/artist).

This Sunday page has four rephrasings of faux-gossip column headlines, with Frank reading the headline, and Ernie giving the gag version. The first is, "A certain foreign movie starlet dumps Romeo for being too cheap." Ernie's version is, "Wow! Greek goddess drops Latin lover for going Dutch treat." It is the only Shakespeare reference of the four.

200 *Mister Boffo*
July 18, 1993. Tribune Media Services, Inc. Joe Martin (writer/artist).

This cartoon began in 1986. At first, it was often a strip, but the daily is now almost exclusively a panel. While most panels feature the title character, Martin sometimes permits himself to do an unrelated gag panel as he does here. Shakespeare is writing at his desk, when his wife interrupts to tell him he "can come up with something more memorable...than...'Romeo, issat you?'" This presumably refers to "Wherefore art thou, Romeo" (2.2.37), which has another meaning entirely, but this lapse puts Martin in the excellent company of George Herriman, who makes the same mistake regularly in *Krazy Kat*.

201 *For Better or for Worse*
January 8, 1996. Universal Press Syndicate. Lynn Johnston (writer/artist).

This popular, wordy, family soap opera often has a sardonic touch as it does in this daily strip. A teacher tells his students to break into groups and discuss how the characters in *Romeo and Juliet* communicate, or fail to, using excerpts from the play translated "into modern-day language." He then asks if there are any questions. One boy wants to know "Why?" The first part of the assignment shows a savvy understanding of the story and how the tragedy at several points results from failed communication.

202 *Luann*
July 7–24, 1997. United Features Syndicate, Inc. Greg Evans (writer/artist).

Luann is a strip about a high-school girl, her friends, and her family. A recurring theme is the way that teenaged girls make fools of themselves over teenaged boys. Luann's major crush is on an emotionally unavailable boy named Aaron. She attempted to get his attention for several years, before the character moved to another state. This three-week sequence was often more about the date than about Shakespeare, so we shall examine the Shakespearean highlights. At dinner one evening, Luann's father tells the family he has two tickets to a new theater company's production of *Romeo and Juliet*. Mom reminds him that they have a wedding that day, so Luann claims the tickets for a date with Aaron (July 7). One problem is getting up the courage to ask him, but she finally does, though he accepts without much enthusiasm; Luann has enough for

them both (July 10 and 12). She works up the courage to take his hand during the performance, but he barely notices because his is so absorbed in the story. Luann thinks that she is fighting a losing battle "with a 400-year-old dead guy" (July 21–22). It is during the latter strip that some lines of the play are seen near the edges of the panels as if coming from the stage. As they leave the theater, Aaron says it was a "great play" with an "important message." Luann quips that the message is "wait 2 seconds before you kill yourself." Not bad advice, but not what Aaron had in mind. "I mean about intolerance. How we judge and hate each other for being different. That's what led to Romeo's sad end." It is a novel interpretation, at any rate (July 24). The date does nothing to solve the dilemma of their relationship.

203 *W Juliet*
1999, Reprint 2004. San Francisco: VIZ, LLC. William Flanagan (translator), Emura (writer/artist). Pages 6–92.

This Japanese series takes its title from the collection's first story about a high-school production of *Romeo and Juliet*. Emura (pseudonym for a woman cartoonist) kept the title when later stories moved to other things. Jto is a teenaged tomboy who joins the drama club. She is cast as Romeo because of her height, husky voice, and leading-man good looks (p. 13). Jto's new friend Amano is cast as Juliet (p. 23). Amano is a boy posing as a girl. Tsugumi, who wanted to play Juliet, suspects this. She plots to kidnap Amano, prove he is a boy, and play Juliet herself (p. 31). Jto and Amano avoid this, and the show goes on (pp. 44–46). Jto and Amano admit their attraction to each other, speak some of Romeo and Juliet's poetry, and kiss. The translator does not copy Shakespeare's lines accurately. One example: "the gentle sin" becomes "the gentle fine" (1.5.94), which makes no sense. Flanagan mangles this line twice (pp. 25, 44). Amano is disguised because of an agreement with his father. He wants to be an actor, but his father insists Amano eventually take over the family business. He will be free of this obligation if he successfully passes as a girl throughout high school. Most stories have no Shakespeare content, but concern how Amano's gender is nearly discovered, sitcom-like. *Romeo and Juliet* is mentioned a few times in the second story, partly about the Romeo and Juliet game where girls "tread the thorny path...to rescue their Romeo!" (p. 55). Jto is tied up against her will as the prize (p. 83), but Amano arrives first and wins (p. 88). Obviously there is much here for gender and queer critics. Jto tends to play the aggressive, traditionally male role, while Amano is demure. When asked if she would chose a different gender if she were reborn, Emura replied, "I think being a boy would be fun!" (p. 157). Against this is the content of the stories. Their attraction began when Amano's maleness was established. Emura says the series was inspired by Baz Luhrmann's film *William*

Shakespeare's Romeo + Juliet (see entry 496), but readers will find few correspondences beyond the emphasis on youth. This American version collects the first four *W Juliet* stories published in Japan in 1999, although the copyright page dates some material as early as 1997.

204 *Tromeo and Juliet*
1, January 1999. New York: Troma Comics. Brian McNulty (adapter), Mike Turney (penciller), Angel Ramirez and Ron Nelson (inkers).

In the first four pages of the story (after a one-page introduction), we see a dead squirrel, a woman get her nipple pierced, a reference to incest, a fight in a nightclub, a young couple having sex against the wall at the club, a finger hacked off and landing on the bosom of the women, much to her delight. There are nine uses of the F-word, plus the F-gesture. Though the story begins with some recognizable traces from *Romeo and Juliet* such as an opening chorus that follows some of Shakespeare verbal structure (p. 2) and an early scene where the Romeo character names his latest crush (p. 3), this is boldly not *Romeo and Juliet*, but an adaptation of the proudly transgressive film *Tromeo and Juliet* that was written by Lloyd Kaufman and James Gunn (see entry 1239). These four pages are just a precursor to all the piercings, incest, lesbian sex, and masturbation to follow. The story also continues to touch Shakespeare from time to time, especially when Tromeo and Juliet meet. Shakespeare's lines are adapted to this post-punk world, as when Tromeo says Juliet "hangs upon the cheek of night like a rich barbell in a trasher's ear" (p. 18). The comic ends with Juliet's father shackling and confining her as punishment, and the promise of part 2 in the next issue, which was never published. Those who must know what comes next should watch the film. The comic, like the movie, can be described as sleaze over substance, or perhaps it is more accurate to say that sleaze is the substance. The cult following that venerates this material likes it that way. See also entry 1239.

205 *Comic Book Shakespeare: Romeo and Juliet*
2000, Reprint 2003. St. Julians, Sevenoaks, Kent: Timber Frame Publications, Ltd. Simon Greaves (adapter/artist). Pages N/A.

This is another *TF* educational comic, with amateurish drawings and an abundance of text because both Shakespeare's lines and a modern translation are included. Though it is easy to fault the new language, some of Greaves renderings are quite nice. "O, she doth teach the torches to burn bright" becomes, "She outshines all the torches lighting up the night"; this is well suited for the modern ear (p. 12). The problem is the minority but large number of nagging things that could be rendered better. Questionable translations are (first Shakespeare/then Greaves): "villain/monster" (p. 2), "Ay me/Mmmm" (p. 18), and "doting/day dreaming" (p. 25). One transla-

tion is just wrong: "Not Romeo, Prince; he was Mercutio's friend; His fault concludes but what the law should end, The life of Tybalt" (3.1.184–6) is rendered, "Not Romeo, Prince. He was Mercutio's friend. What he did was wrong, but Tybalt deserved to die anyway" (p. 32). As usual, the humor is cut. Romeo and Belvolio do not tease Peter (p. 8), and the nurse immediately gives her news to Juliet (p. 27). American comics censor the rampant sexuality. Greaves had a similar problem when making his translation. "It would have been impossible to render lines such as 'the bawdy hand of the dial is now upon the prick of noon' (Mercutio, 2.4.119) without having the book banned from every school in the United Kingdom." Yet he believes the "heightened sexual atmosphere is vital…since it both reflects R & J's physical passion, and also to some extent accounts for it." He restored it visually by putting nude frescos and statues in every corner of the Capulet house and garden, including Juliet's bedroom, and shows the couple partially clothed and in bed in 3.5. A similar compensation: Friar Lawrence's monologue in 2.3 about his herbs is gone, and the scene begins with Romeo's entrance. To make up for the loss, Greaves puts a pot on the table with herbs growing in it (p. 24). Although there is much to pick at in Greaves's work, including the frescos and statues, he is thoughtful about visualizing the things he cuts. This is a reprint of a 2000 publication published by SLP Educational Publishers, Ltd.

206 *The Spectator*
Vol. 287, # 9025, July 28, 2001. London: The Spectator. A. J. Singleton (writer/artist). Page 7.

Juliet sits on her balcony doing a search on her laptop computer. The search is for "Romeo! Romeo!" This is a visual echo of 2.2.33.

207 *Frank and Ernest*
June 9, 2003. NEA, Inc. Bob Thaves (writer/artist).

Thaves gets away from puns to bring us the love story of "The Invisible Man and Juliet." Juliet in on her balcony and asks, "Wherefore art thou?" The answer comes from behind her when the Invisible Man says, "Right here." Thaves does not need to draw him, of course. Like George Herriman, Thaves understands *wherefore* to mean *where*.

208 *Foxtrot*
September 26, 2003. Universal Press Syndicate. Bill Arnold (writer/artist).

A lizard wearing a jacket tells a student, "I am Don Iguan, the reptilian Romeo." He offers to teach the student to attract women and flies. When asked, "Shouldn't that be 'attract women like flies'?" he says, "What's a date without some food?" The comic is so egregiously drawn that it is impossible to tell what the lizard wears around his neck.

209 *Zits*
April 4, 2004. King Features Syndicate, Inc. Jerry Scott (writer), Jim Borgman (artist).

Jeremy quarrels with his girlfriend and tells her that he is very close to "no longer worshiping the ground you walk on." His buddy Pierce says, "Way to strengthen your bargaining position, Romeo."

210 *Rose Is Rose*
April 19, 2005. United Features Syndicate, Inc. Pat Brady (writer), Don Wimmer (artist).

This awkwardly drawn domestic comedy uses the Romeo cliché in the standard way. Rose tells her husband she will plant sunflower seeds and asks a kiss for luck. He kisses the packet of seeds. She says, "Hey, Romeo! Seeds don't need kisses.... People do!" She looks at then kisses the packet herself thinking, "If I were a seed.... I'd take all the affection I could get!"

THE TAMING OF THE SHREW

211 *Heavy Metal*
"Shakespeare for Americans: After Dark." April 1982. New York: Heavy Metal Magazine. Walt Simonson and Howard V. Chaykin (writers/artists). Page 6.

The Taming of the Shrew receives a kinky treatment with the leather-clad host of a bondage club offering fun with blonde, bosomy Bianca only after a session with the whip-wielding Mistress Katherina, who invites visitors to bend over. This is followed by a personal advertisement, "Italian stallions wanted," followed by a number of abbreviations that are a shorthand for various types of kinky sex. Leather-wearing, hooded Pete shows up to answer and has a session with Mistress Katherina which results in her being bound, and they fall in love. The last panel is another newspaper ad placed by the new couple looking for another couple who also wants kinky sex. Gender and transgressive critics will have a field day with this, but they should note it says more about Howard Chaykin than it does about the play. He shows an affinity for this imagery in his other comic work, and the art is clearly in his style. Simonson's contribution is not obvious. The credits are given as found.

212 *The Taming of the Shrew*
1984. West Haven, CT: Academic Industries, Inc. Naunerle Farr (adapter), Fred Carrillo (artist). Pages N/A.

This is the Pocket Classics edition of the Pendulum *Shrew*. Perhaps surprisingly, the introduction is used. There is a slight logical problem when the Lord and his attendants find Sly unconscious, and in Farr's rewrite, use his name which they could not know. There is a dialogue mistake on page 26 when Baptista welcomes guests to his home. One replies, "And you, good sir," as if he is welcoming Baptista to his own home. The caption "Then on Saturday" is misplaced (p. 39), occurring in the middle of a scene begun on the previous page. Mostly the updating is handled well, although every scatological remark is expunged, including much of the dialogue between Petruchio and Katherine on their first meeting (2.1), which makes their scene very short (eight panels on pp. 31–33). Farr and Carrillo open up the story a few times. There are several scenes with horses, and one tosses Katherine into the mud (p. 43). The wedding is pictured in three panels (p. 41). It is difficult to imagine that Sly could have really seen any of this. One disturbing fact from the production history of the play is Petruchio's whip. No one carries a whip in the play, the word is not used, and its variant *whipped* appears only once (1.1.132) in a non-threatening context. Despite this, there have been countless productions where Petruchio snapped a whip, sometimes using it near Katherine, and sometimes using it on Grumio. Here Petruchio has it on the cover and splash page (p. 7, which was used for the cover), and threatens Grumio with it on p. 20. There are two major cuts. Petrucho's explanation as to why he mistreats Katherine is so truncated that it has no impact (pp. 45–46), and the ending is much changed. The wagers are made and the wives still called, but Katherine does not force the other women to come to the men, they simply are invited to join them, and Katherine's speech on obedience is not just cut, it is not even alluded to (pp. 60–61). The comic book is mildly entertaining, but Farr abridged not just these two scenes but the whole point as well.

213 *Frank and Ernest*
August 28, 2001. NEA, Inc. Bob Thaves (writer/artist).

Frank and Ernest look at a newspaper devoted to stock market news. Frank tells Ernest about an article that says "smart people pulled out of the market just in time." Ernest makes a typical pun, "As Shakespeare would say, it was 'the timing of the shrewd!'"

THE TEMPEST

214 *Krazy Kat*
October 4, 1925. King Features Syndicate, Inc. George Herriman.

In *The Tempest*, Trinculo and Stephano call Caliban a *moon-calf* four times to indicate that he is a monster (2.2.111, 2.2.115, 2.2.139, and 3.2.25). In *Krazy Kat*, Ignatz Mouse calls Kolin Kelly a *moon calf* to indicate he is a monster for refusing to give Ignatz credit to buy more bricks. Ignatz beans Krazy with a pot instead.

215 *The Tempest*
1984. West Haven, CT: Academic Industries, Inc. Rich Margopoulos (adapter), Gary Taloac (artist). Pages N/A.

This reprint of the 1970s Pendulum edition (republished by Pocket Comics in 1984) succeeds because Margopoulos and Taloac made comic book sense of the story, yet capture much of the original in their own way. This is only slightly undermined by some mistakes and censorship. Pendulum typically suppressed anything sexual, so Caliban's attempted rape of Miranda is generalized to "Had you not tried to attack my child..." (p. 25). Prospero has a kinder heart, forgiving his brother without being shamed into it by Ariel. Some will miss the two best-known passages in the play, Prospero's "Our revels now are ended" (4.1.148–63) and the epilogue, which are cut. There are also some odd lapses, such as Taloac mistakenly drawing a dock on the isle (pp. 19, 61), and Margopoulos not making it clear that Prospero compels Miranda to sleep; he just suggests that it is bedtime (p. 18). The translation of the story into new words and pictures offset these disappointments, however. The revision is always smooth and readable, with brief captions that tell readers what is cut. Flashbacks expand the story of Prospero's life in Milan, a six-page short story within the story, complete with illustrations and invented dialogue of the plotting, deposing, and finally the exile of Prospero and Miranda (pp. 12–17). The Ariel/Sycorax story receives brief but similar treatment (p. 21). Many things are shown that cannot be seen on stage, such as the ship at the end of the story (p. 61) and Ariel off the ground (usually) to underline his airy quality (e. g., pp. 20, 29, 53). The play is full of music, yet comics are a silent medium. The music is created visually by mentioning it in a caption and showing notes floating across the panel. This is surprisingly effective (for example, on pp. 26, 31, 47). Ariel always plays the music. Post-colonial critics will be pleased that Caliban is more a man than a monster, albeit quite ugly and a hunchback. *The Tempest* shows Pendulum at its best.

216 *Forbidden Planet*
1993. Wheeling, WV: Innovative Corporation. David Campiti (script), Daerick Gross (adapter/artist). Pages N/A.

The film *Forbidden Planet* (see entry 1341) is famously based on Shakespeare's *The Tempest*, but the closeness of the adaptation has been overstated. The movie is a favorite amongst sci-fi film buffs and comic book geeks, so Innovative adapted it for comics in 1992, using glossy paper and painted art. It was successful enough that the four issues were soon reprinted as the graphic novel reviewed here. Script writer Campiti's introduction to the first issue explains, "We have been given access to set designs, the original screenplay, background details, and more...fans will be treated to scenes and snippets of dialogue they never got to see in the finished film. Even when scenes are identical...actual dialogue sometimes changed; we've tended to select what seemed to be the more interesting version." Gross even paces the comic on the screenplay, not the film. He "wanted to 'open up' the story and show more of the planet." These materials make sense of something that makes no sense in the movie. Altria, who

grew up on the planet, has a pet tiger who is very gentle with her. (Never mind what a tiger is doing on another planet.) It attacks after she kisses Commander Adams, leader of the expedition to rescue Altria and her father. Adams kills the tiger. Altria wonders why the tiger attacked them and Adams says, "You really don't know, do you?" Neither does the audience, because the scene that explains it was cut from the film, but it is restored in the comic where there is a longish exposition of the myth of the maiden and the unicorn that identifies Altria with the maiden and the tiger with the unicorn (p. 30). This scene expands the love story between Adams and Altria, and it makes *Forbidden Planet* is even less like *The Tempest*. On the last page someone—it is not clear who—asks a very sensible question also not in the film: "Why would the Krell have built in a self-destruct mechanism to obliterate their entire planet?" Maybe to end the film with a cliché? *Forbidden Planet* certainly has connections with Shakespeare's play, so by default does the comic, but the formative influence was not Shakespeare, but the sci-fi films of the 1950s.

217 *The Tempest*
1994. East Grinstead, West Sussex: King Rat Comics. Garen Ewing (adapter/artist). Page N/A.

Garen Ewing has a vision for *The Tempest*. His adaptation is highly interpretive and could be called Ewing's commentary on the play. To give one example out of literally dozens, Prospero reminds Caliban who taught him to speak, and Caliban replies, "So now you can understand my curses on you" (p. 8). This is more specific than Shakespeare, whose emphasis is on the making, not the understanding of curses. Ewing's interpretation may or may not follow the text, but his work is boldly interpretive and visionary, something not true of most adaptations. Critics from an earlier era would have complained that this is not Shakespeare. It is not, but it is an integrated and compelling view of the play, or to put it another way, Ewing recasts his source, though less fully than Shakespeare usually recast his sources. Ewing arranges the story for graphic sense and filters the dialog for readability. He introduces several flashbacks, such at the visualization of Prospero's backstory (p. 4) and the conception of Caliban (p. 6). A dream sequence shows Prospero's concern for Miranda and establishes his motivation to get her off the island (p. 17). The discovery of Caliban by Stephano and Trinculo would be difficult to make effective on a comic page, so Ewing has them discover him behind a bush (p. 15). There are some very small changes to the story, such as the sailors seeing Ariel above their ship (p. 2) and Ariel kissing Prospero (p. 26), a display of emotion that many will consider wrong. Since it is in vogue to note that Antonio does not accept Prospero's offer of forgiveness, Antonio's repentance on page 31 will seem wrong to many.

Ewing sets up some scenes that pay off later, as when Stephano is seen with his barrel of wine as the storm is about to wash him overboard (p. 2). The loveliest moment is when Prospero drowns his book (singular) by tossing it overboard as the ship sails from the island. Ewing gives it an entire page, and the effect is stunning. Ewing's art is cluttered and over detailed, something he has overcome with maturity as seen in his current work. Even so, he tells his story (not Shakespeare's) very well.

218 *Sandman*
"The Tempest." # 75, March 1996. New York: DC Comics.
Neil Gaiman (writer), Charles Vess (illustrator).
Page N/A.

With the credit "additional material by William Shakespeare," Neil Gaiman tells the story of how Shakespeare became a genius (see entry for *Sandman # 3* under Shakespeare). Essentially, he made a Faustian pact with a supernatural creature, the Sandman, the lord of dreams. In exchange for this gift, he writes two plays for the Sandman, *A Midsummer Night's Dream* (see entry 138) and *The Tempest*. This story unfolds in Stratford, where Will Shakespeare has gone to escape the plague and write what readers are told will be his final play. Included in the story are members of Shakespeare's family and friends, such as Anne and Judith Shakespeare, their neighbors the Quineys, and Ben Jonson with black, not red, hair. Excerpts from throughout *The Tempest* are given as Shakespeare writes the play, which parallels Gaiman's version of the close of his life. Gaiman uses the mythos that regards *The Tempest* as Shakespeare's farewell to the theater to shape this story. It is also Gaiman's last issue of *Sandman*, and he uses the farewell to the theater to parallel his own farewell to his comic book. It is sad to let go, Gaiman seems to say, and Shakespeare is letting go of not just the theater but everything. If the prevailing mood is melancholy, it stems from completeness as he prepares to give Sandman the final payment. He readies himself by touching all the things and people who mean the most to him. When that is done, he is all but ready to go, with just a lingering trace of reluctance. This aspect of the story is told with great beauty. In a postscript, Gaiman acknowledges that Shakespeare wrote plays in collaboration after *The Tempest*, but to make much of that would nullify his main conceit, so it is downplayed even in this confession. Gaiman's knowledge of Shakespeare is broad though superficial; it includes such broadly held misinformation as Shakespeare translating some Psalms for the *King James Bible*.

219 *The Incredible Hulk*
"Tempest Fugit" Parts 3 and 5. # 79 and 81, May and July 2005. New York: Marvel Comics. Peter David (writer), Lee Weeks (penciller), Tom Palmer (inker). Page 20 in # 79, page 16 in # 81.

General Thunderbolt Ross, Bruce Banner (the Hulk), and a brother and sister are all stranded on a tropical island. The isle is somewhat like Prospero's island in *The Tempest*, as Ross tries to explain to the siblings, saying, "We pluck images from people's heads and give them form and substance." This is after first answering poetically, and without attribution, with this paraphrase from the play (4.1.156–67): "We are such things as dreams are made of" (# 79, p. 20). The question of this five-part story is: Will they live, or will the illusions turn real and round their little lives with a sleep? The same quote is given again two issues later, again without attribution (# 81, p. 16). Page 18 refers to the "monsters of this island," a phrase very like Shakespeare's "monster of the isle" in *The Tempest* (2.2.69).

TWELFTH NIGHT

220 *Pogo*
July 23, 1949. Post-Hall Syndicate. Walt Kelly (writer/artist).

A boll weevil fancies himself a singer, but he is terrible. He gives a banjo to Porkypine, and comes upon Pogo playing a violin. He stops and mangles the best-known song from *Twelfth Night*: "When that I was and a little tiny boy— / with hey, ho! The / wind and the rain—a the rain it / raineth everyday—a / BABE" (5.1.366–69). Porky and Pogo chase him, trying to smash the instruments over his head.

221 *Heavy Metal*
"Shakespeare for Americans." May 1982. New York: Heavy Metal Magazine. Howard V. Chaykin (writer), Walter Simonson (artist). Page 64.

Playing with the gender confusion of *Twelfth Night*, Simonson and Chaykin create a paper doll set. The dolls are naked renderings (except for a fig leaf) of Viola, Sebastian, Orsino, and Olivia. While the clothes have names attached, given their identical poses the male garb of Viola and Sebastian are interchangeable, and she has a dress that would fit Sebastian. Only the outfits of Orsino and Olivia would not fit another character. There are twelve lines of dialogue that are not from the play but summarize the goals of these characters. A note in the margin thanks Simonson's then-wife Louise for helping; Louise Simonson is also a comic book writer.

222 *Twelfth Night*
1984. New Haven, CT: Academic Industries, Inc. Naunerle Farr (adapter), E. R. Cruz (artist). Pages N/A.

In keeping with the Pendulum penchant for safe Shakespeare, this *Twelfth Night* cuts much of the cruelty to Malvolio. He is gulled, of course (pp. 36–38), but the consequences of his embarrassment do not cut deeply. He is not held captive, although Toby is "to take good care of him" (p. 42), and Feste does not verbally abuse him as Sir

Topaz (4.2). Cutting this and his agony in captivity spares young readers the cruelest behavior in the play, simplifies the morality of the story, and makes it possible to skip Malvolio's threat of revenge. He raises his fist deep in the background of a group shot (p. 61), but this is not explained and is easy to miss. One ill-judged cut makes Feste a bad singer, raising the question as to why so many want him to vocalize. Right after he sings "O Mistress Mine," Mariah enters and complains, "What awful noise" (p. 29). Missing is the caterwauling that comes after the song (2.3.59–64). Two things will only bother those who know the play. Sir Andrew does not have the flaxen hair described in 1.3.85, but that description is cut along with the racy joke that follows it. An odd matter of stagecraft in this play (possibly explained by a revision that was not followed through) is why Feste is to be part of the gulling scene (2.4.153), but is replaced by Fabian in the actual scene (2.5). This comic book eliminates them both from the gulling—problem solved. Fabian makes a late entrance in the quarrel scene (p. 44). In a screw-up worthy of *CI*, the Captain and Viola are dry and their clothes look spry as they come out of the water and onto the shore (pp. 9–12). Conversely, the artist did himself proud in the transformation of Viola to Cesario. Viola has very long hair. In disguise, her hair is very short and boyish, making for a striking transformation (e.g., p. 21). The Pocket Comics version was studied for this entry.

223 *Twelfth Night*

1985. London: Oval Projects Limited. John H. Howard (artist). Pages N/A.

This is the last published book in the Cartoon Shakespeare Series, and the second comedy. Perhaps Howard is not as adept a storyteller as the others, or possibly this play resists the unabridged cartoon treatment. Scenes long in dialogue are talky and slow. Funny lines work, but lines that rely on an actor to make them funny are a problem. Too many of the panels on pp. 7–12 (1.3) just lie there. There are also some curious mistakes. Malvolio drops the ring before Viola refuses to take it, so the word balloons seem to be in the wrong panels (p. 31). The letter scene (2.5) is badly blocked. It is not possible that Malvolio would not see Sir Toby and Fabian spying on him (p. 53). Despite the basically modern setting, a few characters have touches of Elizabethan garb, especially Malvolio. This is necessary for the scene with his yellow stockings (3.4; pp. 74–79). They would be invisible under trousers. Howard fills Illyria with dogs and cats. When Sir Andrew says, "I am dog at a catch" (2.3.60–61), he grabs a dog by the tail. The dog bites him in the next panel (p. 35). Yet Howard is careless about details. When Malvolio swears "by this hand" (2.3.124), he does not hold up his hand, nor is there any indication that Malvolio exits right after, though he is gone (p. 39). Howard adds some interpretative visuals.

Olivia puts on lipstick before Viola's entrance in 1.4 (p. 22). She is heavily made up when she removes her veil, explaining why Viola wonders if Olivia's beauty is real or painted (p. 24). Later, Orsino walks past Viola as Cesario dressing and nearly sees her topless (p. 42). The typesetter of the balloons gets around the silence of the comic medium when Feste affects a phony voice. As Sir Topas, his font becomes ornate (pp. 97–98, 100). Italics are used to indicate that Feste speaks softly as he pretends to leave (p. 101). When he reads madness—Malvolio's letter—fonts are replaced by bold but inconsistent hand lettering (p. 118). The story ends with a cloudburst chasing everyone inside except for Feste, who sings of the wind and the rain (pp. 123–24). The book includes a glossary for the first time in one of the Cartoon Shakespeare Series.

224 *Frank and Ernest*

August 8, 1999. NEA, Inc. Bob Thaves (writer/artist).

Frank and Ernest appear to be bums hanging out on a park bench amid litter. They look at a series of quotations on the theme of fate. Ernest asks Frank if he believes in fate. Frank replies "I'd hate to think I turned out like this because of something I have control over!" The quotations are from Webster's *New World Dictionary*, Byron, Aeschylus, Zeno, and two early modern writers. One quotation from Marlowe's *Hero and Leander* is "It lies not in our power to love or/hate. For will in us is overruled/by fate" ("First Sestiad," 167–68), and another, from *Twelfth Night*, is "Fate, show thy force; ourselves we do/not woe; what is decreed must be;/and be this so" (1.5.186–87).

225 *Comic Book Shakespeare: Twelfth Night*

2003. Simon Greaves (adapter/artist). St. Julians, Sevenoaks, Kent: Timber Frame Publications, Ltd. Pages N/A.

Another *TF* educational comic, this one is derailed by a technical problem. Since these books are basically black and white with a single color, the obvious choice for this play is yellow for Malvolio's stockings (3.4); a printer's error put too much green in the mix, which should be corrected in subsequent printings. The modern translation is not printed in color as the other books are, since with this color would be too faint to read. Instead, the lettering is black with a yellow/greenish screen laid over it. This puts so many blocks of color on a page that it is seldom appropriate to shade the drawings. This is done sparingly, though Malvolio's stockings are in color (pp. 34–35, 56–58). While yellow *seems* the right choice for this play, the necessity of these blocks makes it the wrong, an insolvable dilemma with this color process. Drawings sometimes communicate the wrong thing, as when Orsino's hair, earrings, and full lips make him look like a woman (as on p. 2), probably unconsciously adding to the gender confusion of the story. It is rare that Greaves takes advantage of working in a visual medium, but one nice scene is when

Viola disguises herself as a boy, which is shown in three panels: putting her hair into cornrows, binding her bosom, and wearing a doublet (p. 5). She is identical to her brother when we see him on p. 14. Malvolio's body language is appropriately haughty in his first appearance (p. 8), but the body language of Olivia does not express infatuation through her long, mostly talking-head scene with Viola disguised as Cesario (pp. 10–12). Greaves creates a logistical problem by making Feste the only musician. This puts him in both 2.3 and 2.4, apparently moving at the speed of light between households. Most of the clowning is cut from the letter scene (3.5), which basically becomes a monologue by Malvolio (pp. 24–27). To please school authorities, most of the sexuality is censored. Maria leaves before Sir Andrew's first panel, so Toby's attempt to pander is cut (1.3.45–79; p. 6). His invitation for Maria to "Come by and by to my chamber" (4.2.7) is also cut.

THE TWO GENTLEMEN OF VERONA

226 *Heavy Metal*
"Shakespeare for Americans: Two Gentlemen of Verona." July 1982. New York: Heavy Metal Magazine. Peter Kuper (writer/artist). Page 64.

After assisting Howard Chaykin on a previous installment, Peter Kuper gets solo credit for the first time in this funny animal version of *Two Gentlemen of Verona*. Proteus and Julia are cats, Valentine is probably a mouse (the ears are not quite right), and some of the outlaws in the forest are dogs and bears, but Sylvia and her father appear to be human. As with previous episodes, each panel dips into a different point of the story, so the plot makes no sense. It ends with a scene not in Shakespeare, the wedding of Silvia to Valentine and Julia to Proteus. The minister is a drunken rabbit.

THE WINTER'S TALE

227 *Arcade: The Comics Review*
"Classics Crucified/The Winter's Tale." # 1, Spring 1975. Justin Green (adapter/artist). Pages N/A.

Underground comics (or comix, as their creators preferred) tended to portray subject matter aboveground comics were forbidden to discuss. Writer/artists (they were usually the same) were drawn to stories of drug use, explicit sex, graphic violence, and didactic political commentary, or any combination of these. DC writer/editor Dennis O'Neil once described them as an attempt to shock, but claimed that once the shock wore off, they had little to offer. There is justification for this in the many forgettable, poorly written and poorly drawn stories that were churned out, often under a purple haze in the late 1960s and 1970s. When seminal underground figure Art Spiegelman won a Pulitzer Prize for *Maus* (1986) and Robert Crumb somehow became respectable, many took a second look. *Arcade: The*

Comics Review was the elite of underground anthologies, edited by Spiegelman and Bill Griffith and featuring the top talent. The first issue includes a retelling of *The Winter's Tale* in which Justin Green casts Leontes as a Mafia kingpin, Paulina and Polixenes as actors Simone Signoret and Karl Malden, Mamillius as the old comic strip character Henry, and so on. He gives the role of Camillo to himself. Not all this casting goes to type—Henry speaks, which he did not do in the funny papers—but it enlivens Leontes as a sort of proto-Tony Soprano. Dialogue is changed to match, so the report of the oracle is, "Camillo is mellow, Polixenes is ace, Hermione ain't phony, but Leontes is one bad mofo; if he don't find the little girl he ditched, ain't nobody gonna be his heir!" The story is fairly faithful to the plot and characters for two pages, then Green lets loose on the last page. Leontes sexually assaults Perdita until he learns she is his daughter, and still seems interested afterward. He expresses no remorse about Hermione until he sees her as a statue. When he grabs what he thinks is the statue's leg, she whacks him on the head with a rolling pin. Perdita's adopted family and Autolycus are excised, though the bear and an intermission are included. If this sounds strange, it should be understood in the context of a 1975 underground comic book, where irreverence was revered.

MISCELLANEOUS

228 *Bringing up Father*
Date unknown, 1913, Reprint 1977. King Features Syndicate, Inc. George McManus (writer/artist).

Bringing up Father is based on the premise that lowbrow culture brings happiness and anything highbrow brings misery, or at least snobbery and boredom. Newly rich Maggie decides her uncouth husband Jiggs needs a tutor to read Shakespeare's works to him. Jiggs wants to know what the tutor thinks of the New York Giants baseball club. We do not find out, but the next panel shows the tutor reading part of the balcony scene from *Romeo and Juliet* (2.2), while Jiggs wonders if Romeo is the name of a dog. The tutor then reads a bit of *Richard III* (5.4), as Jiggs looks angrily at a bust of Shakespeare, saying, "So this is the gink that wrote them books—eh!" The next shot shows the bust crashing to the sidewalk outside, with the books coming through the window after it. This strip was found on p. 82 of George McManus, the book *Bringing up Father: A Complete Compilation: 1913–1914* (Westport, CT: Hyperion Press, 1977).

229 *Bringing up Father*
Date unknown, 1914, Reprint 1977. King Features Syndicate, Inc. George McManus (writer/artist).

This domestic comedy, often called *Maggie and Jiggs*, is about a poor couple who suddenly come into money, and how they adjust, or do not, to living among the upper crust. Maggie thinks the ways of the rich are fabulous, but her husband just wants to be one of the boys. They take a world tour in a months-long sequence, and visit Stratford-upon-Avon in this daily strip. Maggie tells Jiggs to dress well for their visit to Shakespeare's home, and adds, "His plays are wonderful." Jiggs, despite having a brief education in Shakespeare the year before (see 1913 entry above), has never heard of Shakespeare, and assumes the word *plays* refers to sports. Jiggs wonders "what team he plays on." They arrive at the birthplace, which looks nothing like the actual building. Jiggs asks the porter if Shakespeare is in, and if he is, to announce them. This is another of the endless variations on Jiggs ignorance of culture, with a resulting embarrassment to his wife. It was McManus's genius that he always kept Jiggs the sympathetic character. This strip was found on p. 150 of McManus, the book *Bringing up Father: A Complete Compilation.*

230 *Bringing up Father*

Date unknown, 1914, Reprint 1977. King Features Syndicate, Inc. George McManus (writer/artist).

Maggie takes to living amongst the upper crust, but her husband sneaks away to shoot pool with the boys. Their world tour takes them to London where Maggie announces they will see *Othello* that night. Jiggs asks where he lives. They enter their box while the orchestra tunes. Jiggs comments on the trombone player, then asks him how he swallowed "that horn so easy," mistaking the movement of the slide toward the musician as the slide entering his mouth. The presence of an orchestra raises the possibility they attend an opera, not a play, but if so one would expect the title to be *Otello,* and either way, Shakespeare is the ultimate inspiration. This strip was found on p. 155 in *Bringing up Father: A Complete Compilation.*

231 *Krazy Kat*

November 21, 1917. King Features Syndicate, Inc. George Herriman (writer/artist).

Ignatz bemoans the high price of bricks at ten cents. He sails one towards Krazy Kat's noggin, who ducks, and the brick falls harmlessly into the lake. Ignatz plays with *Othello* (3.3.157–61) as he bemoans the loss of his money. "A dime for 'that' brick robs me of my purse. That miss robs me of my good name." A little later Krazy is sitting on a rock, bemoaning not seeing Ignatz. "Oh, 'Ignatz' Wherefore is you, Ignatz"—Long has I waited for you, and yet you comest not—A-Less." This paraphrases *Romeo and Juliet* (2.2.33). There follows a *Macbeth* paraphrase (5.5.19), when Krazy and his cousin Krazy Katfish exchange the hope that Ignatz will come soon. Krazy says, "To-Morrow." Katfish says, "Ah-h-h-Tomorrow." Krazy replies, "Un-hun-Tomorrow."

232 *Krazy Kat*

August 9, 1921. King Features Syndicate, Inc. George Herriman (writer/artist).

In a comic strip that is not so much a spoof of the authorship controversy as a spoof on Krazy Kat's stupidity, Ignatz Mouse comes upon Krazy reading *Romeo and Juliet* and muttering "wunderfil." Ignatz inquires who is wonderful. Krazy replies that Shakespeare is, and "That's why those 'eggs' get me so engry." Krazy means "them eggs with that 'Bacon' theory—" and mutters that some day someone will attribute Shakespeare's works to "Ham." Ignatz wants to pop Krazy with a brick, but does not have one. He cries, "A brick—a brick—my kingdom for a brick!!!"

233 *The Complete Cartoons of the* New Yorker

October 3, 1925, Reprint 2004. New York: Black Dog and Leventhal Publishers, Inc. Rea Irvin (writer/artist).

Shakespeare reads a poem titled "The Beulah Boosters" at a banquet of the Celestial Rotary Club.

ROTARIANS we pledge ourselves to Beulahland so fair.
It's like you will I am sure not find anywhere,
With its wealth of entertainment and climate so rare
About it we are enthusiastic is what I declare.

Beulahland appears to be a New York jazz club, but that has not been confirmed. The cartoon is cartoon 191 for 1925, found on the first CD-ROM in Robert Mankoff, ed., *The Complete Cartoons of the* New Yorker (New York: Black Dog and Leventhal Publishers, 2004).

234 *Terry and the Pirates*

January 4–6, 18–22, and February 1–2, 5, 8, 1940. Chicago Tribune–New York News Syndicate. Milton Caniff.

This is the sequence described more fully in the introduction, where the usually heroic Pat Ryan tries to save teenaged April Kane from being added to the harem of an arms dealer named Singh-Singh. He is only interested in women who speak English, so Pat manipulates a woman named Cheery into becoming Singh-Singh's ideal by getting her to perform the "quality of mercy" speech (*Merchant of Venice* 4.1.179–200) in her father's house. It works. Cherry vows revenge when she realizes that Pat set her up. She makes an apt contrast of characters when she prepares a sleeping potion and declares, "The ingredients are at hand! All I need do is administer my devil's broth—and watch its effect! I should never play Portia. . . . Lady Macbeth is my type!" Prior to this, the quotations in the sequence had all been from *Merchant of Venice.* Caniff now switches to *Macbeth.* Cherry recites "Double, double toil and trouble; fire burn and cauldron bubble" (4.1.10–11) while cooking her potion, which she soon gives to Pat. This is the end of the Shakespeare references, but not the end of the story. It does not end in triumph for Pat and April—*Terry* stories seldom do—but it does end in their escape and in punishment for those who deserve it. The story runs longer than the dates above, which are the dates of the Shakespeare references.

235 *Terry and the Pirates*
July 22, 1941. Chicago Tribune–New York News
Syndicate. Milton Caniff (writer/artist).

Burma is laid up with an injured leg. Raven Sherman sends Burma some books and periodicals for entertainment. Unfortunately for lowbrow Burma, they are strictly what she calls egghead stuff: "Weekly Review of Literature," *History of China*, Gibbon's *Rise and Fall of the Roman Empire* (vol. 5), an unspecified volume of Keats, and a one-volume *Complete Shakespeare*. The Gibbon book is usually found abridged in one volume or unabridged in three. Five or more volumes are a bit unusual.

236 *Dick Tracy*
November 26, 1944. Chicago Tribune–New York News
Syndicate. Chester Gould (writer/artist).

In this Sunday page, actor Vitamin Flintheart introduces Dick Tracy to Showflake Falls, the marvelous ingenue he has discovered. Flintheart and Tracy do not know that criminals are looking for her, and the news report that Snowflake has been cast in Flintheart's new play tells them where to find her. In response to Tracy saying that Snowflake is "doing alright," Flintheart replies, "As the great Bard once said, 'He who—??'—How *do* those lines go??" We never find out, probably because Gould did not know.

237 *Superman*
"Shakespeare's Ghost Writer." # 44, January 1947. New York: DC Comics. Don Cameron (writer), Ira Yarbrough (artist). Pages N/A.

"Marvelous, Superman! I couldn't write better myself!" says William Shakespeare as he looks over the shoulder of the Man of Steel, who is moving a quill so fast one wonders how Shakespeare could read the words (p. 1). Early Modern England was certainly fortunate that Clark Kent and Lois Lane were sent back in time where they made significant contributions to British culture. Superman saves Shakespeare from Sir Harry Stafford and his gang of bullies, who attack him for mocking Sir Harry with character of Falstaff (pp. 3–5). Superman takes Lois to the Boar's Head Tavern to await Clark Kent (Superman in his secret identity), then quickly assumes his alter ego as Kent (p. 5). They begin England's first newspaper, opening their office in Fleet Street. Superman discovers a plot by King James and his Privy Counsel to curb dissent and a free press. The first issue of *Ye Daily Planet* has this story and an advertisement for "Shakespeare's Globe Theater" (p. 8). Though Superman does not drink, for some reason he visits the Mermaid Tavern where Shakespeare is drinking with Ben Jonson. Shakespeare takes Superman aside to tell him the plot of his next play, the "dual personality of Clark Kent, who is really Superman!" Superman suggests another plot, the story of Macbeth, and even writes the play, which Shakespeare promises to go over to put in his own style, but that is not necessary; Superman transcribes the play from his perfect

memory (pp. 8–10). Perhaps incorporating the supposed curse of *Macbeth* without acknowledgment, rain begins to fall during "the fourth act." Superman moves the cloud, saving the play. After the show Shakespeare comments, "I have reached the highest pinnacle of fame," and thanks Superman (pp. 10–11). The king has the newspaper office wrecked by cannon fire, and then the cannon is turned on Clark and Lois. Dare he change to Superman to whisk her to safety, but reveal his identity? He thinks, "To stay or not to stay, that's the question" (p. 12). Meanwhile, the time ray that sent them into the past is fixed, returning them to the present before Clark is forced to act super (p. 13). While the story can be accused of condescending to the English press and Shakespeare, and it does, it is best viewed as yet another story about Superman going to a new place and impressing everyone. Variations on this formula were written by the hundreds, and it was Jacobean England's turn. The strategy was more about impressing young readers with the specialness of Superman than it was to insult other cultures; that was a mere by-product. See also *Time-Flies* (entry 1135).

238 *Pogo*
New York Star. November 17 and 19, 1948. Walt Kelly (writer/artist).

In the November 12 strip, Albert the Alligator accidentally swallowed a pollywog. Over the next few days, Albert and Pogo tried to figure out how to rescue the poor thing. A crow comes along in the 17 November strip and accuses Albert, saying "Et tu Albert? Is they no haven of safety?" Albert does not understand this bit of Latin Shakespearean slang (from *Julius Caesar* 3.1.77), and says, "Et two? Naw, jes one." The pollywog is rescued the next day. On November 19, Porkypine hears of this and quotes *King Lear* (1.4.311), "How sharper than a serpent's tooth it is to have a thankless child" to no obvious purpose. The sequence appeared in the *New York Star*, where Kelly was art director. The paper went out of business four months after *Pogo* began, but Kelly was able to market the strip though the Post–Hall Syndicate. Kelly rewrote and redrew some of the *Star* continuities, dropping the Shakespeare references, though dozens more followed over the decades.

239 *Kid Eternity*
14, March 1949. Buffalo, NY: Comic Magazines.
Unknown (writer), Sheldon Moldoff (artist). Pages 8–9.

"It's no use boss! We can't move this tub of lard!" says the crook as he and some colleagues try to move Sir John Falstaff. Kid Eternity is able to summon anyone from the past to help stop crime now, though the comic book often mixed real and fictitious people. When a gang of thieves rob a bank, Kid Eternity summons the fat knight to block the exit on page 8, trapping them inside. Falstaff holds them until the police arrive and then is sent back into eternity on page 9. This story also has cameos by Kit Carson, Hephaestus, John Dillinger, and Oliver Wendell

Holmes. Falstaff is based on an Elizabethan knight named Sir John Oldcastle, who was fictionalized, some say scandalously, in *Henry IV, Parts 1 and 2*, in *The Merry Wives of Windsor*. Falstaff's death is mentioned in *Henry V*. This story was not given a title.

240 *Our Boarding House*
October 3, 1950. NEA, Inc. Bill Freyse (writer/artist).

Our Boarding House (1921–81) was run by Major and Mrs. Hoople, who seem to only rent to eccentric characters. The daily gag panel is unusual for telling long stories at a rate of one panel a day. These were often about the Major, usually wearing a fez, trying to separate someone even more foolish than he from their money. In this panel, the major is a door-to-door salesman. His pitch is that "with this charming set of five books . . . you can dream with Shakespeare, stroll with Poe, peer over the shoulders of famed atomic scientists with their magic test tubes, revel with Mozart—" and that is as far as he gets for his potential victim invites him in to talk it over.

241 *Our Boarding House*
December 12, 1951. NEA, Inc. Bill Freyse (writer/artist).

This panel of *Our Boarding House* (1921–81) was created by Bill Freyse, one of several who worked on the strip over the years, but his tenure was the longest and his drawing style the one most associated with it. It was a one-panel-a-day cartoon, but with continuing storylines that unfolded very slowly. In this panel, a theatrical producer named Mr. Pike laments that one of his actors is in hospital. The Major looks at his cigar and tells Pike that he will take the wounded man's place. "Most of my stage experience has been in heavy Shakespearean roles, but a versatile man of my talents could easily adapt himself . . . though I've never played comedy parts." The only acting the Major has done is in moments like this, where he tries to make a quick buck by lying to people.

242 *Pogo*
June 21, 1952. Post-Hall Syndicate. Walt Kelly (writer/artist).

In a satire on the 1952 presidential election that put Dwight D. Eisenhower in the White House, Pogo Possum is running for President. He prepares to go to Chicago where he will give a campaign speech, and Howlan' Owl gives this advice: "They has been 48 presidents an' that's how come they's 48 stripes in the Union Jack. The 13 stars is a symbol of luck and comes from Shakespeare's 'Lucus a non Lucendo,' in which I sand the part of ol' Non Lucendo, (hisself) an' guv out the aria 'Thank your lucky stars.' Keep this all in mind, it may come to the aid of your repartee." (The spelling is Kelly's.)

243 *Pogo*
September 11, 1952. Post-Hall Syndicate. Walt Kelly (writer/artist).

To get out of running, Pogo schemes with Beauregard, an actor dog who claims to be descended from Thespis. He says he is known for his quick study all the way from the swamp to Stratford-on-Avon (September 9, 1952). When the strip goes into a concurrent parody of the election and the comic strip *Little Orphan Annie*. Beauregard suggests Pogo play a character named "Hey, Nonny, Nonny" or maybe "Li'l Arf an' Nonny."

244 *Captain Marvel Adventures*
"Capt. Marvel and Mr. Tawny's Culture Craze." # 137, October 1952. Greenwich, CT: Fawcett Publications, Inc. Otto Binder (writer), C. C. Beck (artist). Page 5.

Tawky Tawny is an anthropomorphic tiger. He speaks English, wears a suit, and is a friend of Captain Marvel. He is an innocent, discovering some aspect of the world in most of his stories, usually by making mistakes that Captain Marvel helps him correct. Mr. Tawny decides to become cultured in this story and joins the All Arts Institute. This turns out to be a group of very bad, and therefore failed musicians, poets, and painters who teach Mr. Tawny to condemn everything in the arts, especially junk like Beethoven, the *Mona Lisa*, and, in one panel, Shakespeare. A copy of his works are to torn apart by Marmaduke Snootwich, the leader of the Institute, who calls Shakespeare's writings "drivel." In the end, Captain Marvel teaches Mr. Tawny the difference between being cultured and being a snob. Mr. Tawny breaks with the All Arts Institute, and at the end of the story goes with Billy Batson (Captain Marvel in his secret identity) to a museum to enjoy "Music. Arts. Literature. . . . All works of genius!" which Mr. Tawny soaks "up like a sponge" (p. 6).

245 *Our Boarding House*
October 23–December 6, 1954. NEA, Inc. Bill Freyse (writer/artist).

Mrs. Hoople does most of the work at *Our Boarding House* while her husband handles most of the drinking and socializing, so she arranges for the Major to have a job at the toggle-bolt factory. He must avoid this at any cost. He decides to become a painter (October 23). He goes to the library where he has little trouble convincing the librarian a portrait of Shakespeare is needed on the library wall (October 25). Since the Major is lazy, work progresses very slowly, so slowly that residents make fun of him. When the head is half painted, it looks so little like Shakespeare that Professor Grimpz mistakes it for Walt Whitman (November 2). As the portrait nears completion, it earns the sarcasm of several other characters, but the Major is bursting with confidence, knowing his work equals Rembrandt, Velázquez, and Leonardo da Vinci (November 6). When he unveils the picture to the head of the library, Major Hoople finds that someone added a handlebar moustache (November 12). In the hope that the culprit will reveal himself, the Major and his friend Twiggs pretend the library paid $100 for the portrait, and Hoople's nephew is revealed as the moustache painter (November 19). The Major presents the picture to the boys at the club; they hope it will cover a hole in the wall (November 23). One of the boys says the portrait resembles a local saloon owner, Bascom O'Hare (November 25). The Major and Twiggs sell the portrait to him for $250 (December 2). When two of the boarders become sarcastic about the painting after the fact, Major Hoople asks why they "toss mud at the genius?" (December 6).

246 *The Neighbors*
June 6, 1960. New York News, Inc. George Clark (writer/artist).

That Neighbors was a comic panel that ran from 1939 to 1976. It dealt with domestic issues, sometimes in ways that are considered politically incorrect now. The nagging wife, the selfish husband, the obnoxious in-laws, women preoccupied with fashion, and men playing games were recurring themes; this strip has three of the above. The selfish husband is leaving for a round of gold. His nagging wife says, "Did Shakespeare waste HIS time on the golf course? I'll bet he was at HIS typewriter all day long!"

247 *Dick Tracy*
Various dates: June–November 1960. Chicago Tribune–New York News Syndicate. Chester Gould (writer/artist).

This is the bizarre story of poet Providence J. Ogden, discussed in the introduction. Much of Ogden's dialogue is doggerel. Gould made up the lines, but Ogden attributes them to dozens of different poets, a few real, but most made up, the fictitious names being atrocious puns on the names of real poets. It is difficult to know if Gould was expressing his contempt for poetry or actually thought this was funny. Shakespeare is not named, but couplets are attributed to Shakeswhiskey (June 7) and Shakesbeer (July 6 and 19, 1960). There are two other writers from Shakespeare's era, but Gould does not pun on their names, and the first is not really known for his poetry. Doggerel is attributed to Bacon on July 30, August 1, and September 13 and 25, and to Milton on September 4. Ogden and the others in his gang are captured on November 27, to the relief of readers everywhere.

248 *Mad*
"The Mad Shakespeare Primer." # 60, January 1961. New York: E. C. Publications. Phil Hahn (writer), Wallace Wood (artist). Pages 22–24.

Hahn creates an amusing hybrid by rewriting some of Shakespeare's plays in blank verse. Hahn captures the rhythm of first-grade readers in his verse rendering of four Shakespeare plays, as when he writes, "He is climbing Juliet's trellis. / Climb, climb, climb" (p. 23). This three-part repetition is in every stanza and sets the tone of the entire piece. It would be churlish to complain that Hahn gets the plots wrong, as when he writes that Hamlet has two suicides (he presumably includes Gertrude's death) and three fatal duels (there is just one, but it comes at the end of three bouts of dueling). It would be even more churlish to fault him for making the plots incoherent. These observations are beside the point, which is to fill three pages of a humor magazine with silly lines about Shakespeare, such as, " 'Out damned spot!' says Mrs. Macbeth/Mrs. Macbeth has dirty hands, all right. / She also has a dirty mouth!" and "Tomorrow, Caesar will be as dead as a mackerel. / Some of the Senators will stab him in the Forum. / Also in the Duodenum, Esophagus, and Belly. / Stab, stab, stab" (p. 24). The plays are *Macbeth, Romeo and Juliet, Hamlet,* and *Julius Caesar.* The *Macbeth* lesson was reprinted in Maria Reidelbah's *Completely Mad: A History of the Comic Book and Magazine* (Boston, Toronto, London: Little, Brown and Company, 1991), p. 66.

249 *Our Boarding House*
August 4 and September 27, 1961. NEA, Inc. Bill Freyse (writer/artist).

Our Boarding House (1921–81) is almost forgotten today, but entertained readers for sixty years, although it is ill-suited for the narrative speed that is popular today, with Freyse expecting readers to remember what happened in a story six weeks before. Major Hoople is outraged because a record album is being sold that embarrasses him. He has recorded some speeches that are being marketed as a cure for insomnia. He complains that "generations of Hooples have been noted Shakespearean actors." His friend Twiggs comments that there is money in the records and notes Shakespeare "wrote for money, and $100 is the best kind of applause." That is an argument the Major understands. In the September 27 panel he actively tries to sell something by invoking the name of Shakespeare again. He indicates a tape recorder to a room full of sleepy men and notes the thoughtfulness that went into the selections on the tape and how students will benefit from hearing "the poetry of Shakespeare, the simplicity of Lincoln and the eloquence of Hoople!" One of the men says, "After listening to that I could doze off during a parachute jump!"

250 *The Amazing Spider-Man*
"The Grotesque Adventure of the Green Goblin." # 14, July 1964. New York: Marvel Comics. Stan Lee (writer), Steve Ditko (artist). Page 1.

The Shakespeare reference is in the credits. Marvel Comics editor Stan Lee was the first to introduce credits for artist, writer, and letterer in the modern era of comics. In what he called the Mighty Marvel Manner, he often wrote the credits in a playful style. He typically wrote something grandiose for the himself and the artist, then added a deflating line about the letterer. He handled it a bit differently in the fourteenth issue of *Spider-Man,* using Shakespeare's reputation as a writer for the ages to begin the credits: "Written by Stan Lee (the poor man's Shakespeare)/Drawn by Steve Ditko (the poor man's da Vinci/Lettered by Art Simek (the poor man's rich man)." A novelization of the Spider-Man character has three Shakespeare references. *Murdermoon* by Paul Kupperberg (New York: Pocket Books, 1979) is a story about our hero teaming up with the Hulk for an adventure. Spider-Man paraphrases *Romeo and Juliet* (p. 22) and *Hamlet* (p. 67) and quotes *Macbeth* (p. 160) in the course of the story. The Hulk does not quote anyone, in keeping with his then-brutish nature. See also *Spider-Man 2* (entry 1287).

251 *Mad*
"Shakespeare Up-to-Date." # 92, January 1965. William Garvin (writer), Jack Rickard (artist). New York: E. C. Publications, Inc. Pages 15–17.

"Had Shakespeare known that his 400th Birthday Year would be commemorated by his work appearing in MAD, he probably would have quit writing and become a plumber. Instead, he turned out all those wonderful works filled with quotes that are as apropos today as when they were written. And we can prove it" (p. 15). This is the introduction to the "Avon Calling Dept." feature that drops lines from Shakespeare into new contexts, such as some older folks watching the Beatles on television. One quotes *Henry VI, Part 1* (3.1.106): "O! how this discord doth afflict my soul!" The Edsel was the Ford Motor Company's biggest failure; an engineer looks at the car and quotes *Henry IV, Part 2* (1.3.46): "What do we do then but draw anew the model . . . ?" Other gags show a woman looking at a movie poster of Burt Lancaster and Kirk Douglas. She has quotes about Shakespeare's characters with the same last names, and so it goes with advertising, Frank Sinatra's Rat Pack, politicians, then-President Lyndon Johnson and Vice President Humphrey, baseball, horse racing, telephones, budgets, and even *Mad* magazine, which gets a quote from *Othello* (2.3.203): "Give me to know/How this foul rout began, who set it on,/and he that is approved in this offence." The quotations are from a wide variety of plays and Sonnet 132. The plays quoted include some that are not very popular such as *Timon of Athens* and *Cymbeline*.

252 *Batman and Robin the Cheetah Caper*
1969. Racine: A Whitman Book. George S. Elrick (writer), unknown (artist).

Big Little Books were children's books often based on comic strips, though movies were also adapted for the BLB format along with a few original titles and even a very few nonfiction books. They were published from the early 1930s, and the format survives today. That format was to put illustrations on most odd-numbered pages, with the text on even-numbered pages. This BLB was not directly based on the Batman comic book, but on the recently cancelled *Batman* television series. In that show, Batman

and Robin gained access to the Batcave by tipping up the head of a Shakespeare bust and flipping a switch hidden inside. This was used in the book; the bust may been seen, or partly seen, on pp. 21, 23, 87, and 126. Even less related to comics were two novelizations of the series by William Woolfolk writing under the name Winston Lyon. The bust is mentioned twice in *Batman vs. Three Villains of Doom* (New York: Signet Books, 1966), on pages 20 and 49. There are also characters named Hecate (a black cat) and Ross. These are the names of characters Shakespeare used in *Macbeth*, though these characters predate Shakespeare, and it is not certain that Woolfolk had *Macbeth* in mind. The other book, *Batman vs. the Fearsome Foursome*, is a novelization of the 1966 TV spin-off movie *Batman* and was not reviewed, but the bust appears in the film, and may be in the novel as well.

253 *Grimm's Ghost Stories*
"By the Bones of Shakespeare!" # 25, August 1975. Poughkeepsie, NY: Western Publishing Company, Inc. Arnold Drake (writer), Garcia Lopez (artist). Pages N/A.

Shakespeare was all the rage in the eighteenth century, and mementos were especially prized. Wood from a mulberry tree, supposedly from Shakespeare's last garden, was used to make thousands of boxes and other objects, far more than could possibly have come from a single tree or even a field of them. They fetched premium prices, as did other objects Shakespeare probably never owned. Writer Drake seems to have this in mind for his story about three actors who are booed off the stage but come up with another plan to make money. They will ignore the curse on Shakespeare's grave, "Blest be the man that spares these stones, but cursed be he that moves my bones," and sell his bones as mementos. They break into the grave, but are discovered before then can steal the bones. They realize that once word is out that the grave was opened, they can sell any old bones as Shakespeare's, and the gullible public will buy. They hear someone pursuing them and dash into their room in a Stratford inn. A skeleton comes through the door, and the scene ends. "Hours later," as the caption reads, their bodies are discovered (p. 6). The story begins with their "Scenes from Shakespeare" performance, the stabbing of Caesar, the smothering of Desdemona (p. 1), and the asp biting Cleopatra (p. 2). When their bodies are discovered, it is noted that one was stabbed like Caesar, one smothered like Desdemona, and the last bitten by a snake as was Cleopatra (p. 6). In addition to these references, there is a brief quotation from *Macbeth* on p. 3. This is the cover story. The cover shows Shakespeare half hidden by a quill, with the three thieves being attacked by some of his characters, including the asp.

254 *Mad*
"A MAD TREASURY OF Shakespeare's Lesser Known Quotations." # 191, June 1977. New York: Educational

Comics. Dennis Snee (writer), Harry North, Esq. (artist). Page 30.

This is essentially a text page within a humor comic book. There are four illustrations, one with Yorick's skull atop a body. He contemplates the head of Hamlet. Another has Richard III being offered a stick horse. Julius Caesar is contemplated by his future assassins as a side of beef. Juliet needs to diet; she and the balcony crash on Romeo, who for some reason was playing a lute. Most of the faux-quotations are on a Shakespearean subject, but do not sound much like Shakespeare. One example is "Could Richard stop death? Could Henry? If they were here, you could ask them." A few are clearly derived from plays: "Of valor, discretion is the better part; of dinner, dessert" was clearly written with *Henry IV, Part 1* (5.4.118–19) in mind. There are twenty-one of these "Lesser Known Quotations." At least two earlier issues have Shakespeare-inspired text pages with even less illustration, though there are a few drawings in the margins of number 37 that are not clearly related to the text. It is Antony's funeral oration from *Julius Caesar* (3.2) in both Elizabethan and modern English. *Mad # 39* gives the same treatment to *Romeo and Juliet* (2.2) with no illustrations whatever.

255 *Peanuts*
September 30, 1978. United Features Syndicate, Inc. Charles M. Schulz (writer/artist).

In a pun that could almost belong to Bob Thaves, Snoopy sits atop his doghouse writing, and Lucy asks if he ever considered writing a play. She says, "Maybe you could be another William Shakespaw!" Snoopy hits her in the head with his typewriter.

256 *The New Yorker*
November 12, 1979. New York. Joseph Mirack.

In this one-panel cartoon, two men talk in a bar. One says, "Shakespeare said that? Gosh, if Shakespeare said that, I'll go along with it."

257 *Fantastic Four*
"The Battle of the Titans!" # 212, November 1979. New York: Marvel Comics Group. Marv Wolfman (writer), John Byrne (penciller), Joe Sinnott (inker). Page 16.

The Sphinx is another of Marvel's immortal villains, this one the magician who was put down by Moses in *Exodus* 7:8–13. (This is a slight change from *Exodus*, which mentions multiple magicians.) The Sphinx is banished for his failure and finds a magical jewel during his exile. This gives him immortality and great power. A montage panel shows his progress through the centuries, including a shot of William Shakespeare, although Shakespeare is not named (p. 16). The Sphinx's goal is to restore Egypt to its previous glory, even as he destroys the rest of the world. He is confronted by a habitual planet destroyer named Ga-

lactus, who wants the Earth for his own purposes. The story is continued in the next issue, not reviewed. Marv Wolfman is one of the writers Gil Kane is quoted in the introduction as criticizing. He must be credited for referencing *Exodus*, but not for Shakespeare. Marvel stories were virtually all written as plot synopsis, which the artist then drew, adding his own pacing and details. The writer then suited dialogue to the drawings. Shakespeare was almost certainly added by Canadian artist John Byrne, not by Wolfman.

258 *Mad*
"William Shakespeare . . . Movie Critic." # 224, July 1981. New York: E. C. Publications. Henry Clark (writer). Pages 36–37.

Under the heading "To see or not to see dept.," this film parody pretends to advertise ten movies with comments by film critic William Shakespeare. His lines become apt when quoted out of context. Most are not very clever, such as "'Dost thou fall upon thy face?' Romeo and Juliet/Act 1 Scene 2" for the movie *1941*. A couple are strangely appropriate, such as this comment from *A Midsummer Night's Dream* (3.2.281–82) about the James Bond film *Moonraker*: "I perceive a weak Bond." The most elaborate is for *Star Trek: The Motion Picture*, which not only insults the movie ("'The Enterprise is sick!' Troilus and Cressida/Act 1 Scene 3") but the actors as well. The best is probably the quote given to the horror flick *The Amityville Horror*, supposedly based on a true story: "'I could condemn it as an improbable fiction.' Twelfth Night/Act III Scene 4." Other quotes come from *Henry V*, *Two Gentlemen of Verona*, *The Tempest*, *The Comedy of Errors*, *The Merchant of Venice*, *Macbeth*, *Othello*, and *Henry IV, Part 2*.

259 *Mad*
"William Shakespeare . . . Social Critic." # 225, September 1981. New York: E. C. Publications. Henry Clark (writer), photos supplied by United Press International. Pages 12–13 from reverse cover.

In a follow-up to "William Shakespeare . . . Movie Critic," and under the auspices of their "Something is Rotten Dept.," *Mad Magazine* uses lines from Shakespeare's plays to comment of ten social issues and pop culture icons. A photo (usually) was captioned with a seemingly apt, but out of context quote. A photo of hazy smog over a urban center is captioned, "'Devouring pestilence hangs in our air.' Richard III/Act I Scene 3." The leather-clad rock group Kiss, with the gargoyle make-up, had the caption, "'So wild in their attire, that look not like the inhabitants o' the earth.' Macbeth/Act I Scene 3." A drawing of *Mad*'s mascot Alfred E. Newman even rates a quote: "'This thou seest is but a clod.' King John/Act V Scene 7." Other quotes are from *Henry V*, *Julius Caesar*, *Hamlet*, *Timon of Athens*, *Titus Andronicus*, *Othello*, and *Coriolanus*.

260 *Heavy Metal Magazine*
"Shakespeare for Americans." Vol. V, # 7, October 1981.
New York: HM Communications, Inc. Howard V. Chaykin (writer), Walter Simonson (artist). Page 6.

In the first of the "Shakespeare for Americans" pages, Chaykin and Simonson introduce their series of one-page riffs on Shakespeare by having "Bill" himself explain the purpose of the series. He says that since the old language makes his plays hard to understand, this will be a series of updates that tell the stories in modern ways for modern American readers. He says all this against a series of different backgrounds, literally stepping out of the panel from early modern England into one on the American frontier, where he is dressed like Kit Carson. This is followed in sequence by the 1920s, World War II, a space walk near the moon, and finally as a modern superhero with a big *WS* on his chest. *Heave Metal*, as it is usually called, began reprinting stories from a French comic book, but eventually added American material.

261 *The Born Loser*
October 11, 1983. NEA, Inc. Art Sansom and Chip Sansom (writers/artists).

Brutus Thornapple was born to lose. He is not just ignorant, he has terrible luck. Any attempt to impress someone will have the opposite result. Worst of all, he never learns from his mistakes. Brutus, the creation/victim of Art Sansom, has been losing at life in the funny pages since 1965. Sansom was assisted by his son Chip from 1974. In this strip Brutus speaks to a minister:

As Shakespeare said, "Quoth the Raven, 'Nevermore.'"

The minister corrects him, saying the quote is from Edgar Allan Poe. Brutus digs his hole deeper by replying, "That just goes to show you what I know about the Bible."

262 *Frank and Ernest*
July 6, 1984. NEA, Inc. Bob Thaves.

Frank reads a newspaper article, then tells his friend Ernest about an article claiming that Shakespeare was always the first to the ale house so he could sit near the fire. He closes with a typical pun: "The early Bard gets the warmth."

263 *Shoe*
January 22, 1986. Tribune Media Services, Inc. Jeff MacNelly.

Skyler, a bird who is also a student, reads a quote supposedly by Shakespeare. "Any man who sayeth doth not stand upon need,/Needeth not lest he stand in want of need." After reading this, Skyler thinks that "Shakespeare may have been a great writer, but he probably would have made a better lawyer." The quote is problematic; it is certainly not by Shakespeare. A Google search only turned up the nineteenth-century code of behavior for the Oven Fork Baptist Church in Kentucky. That is only a partial match and has an entirely different meaning. It is difficult to know what the late Jeff MacNelly had in mind when creating this Wednesday strip.

264 *Sandman*
"Sound and Fury." # 7 June 1989. New York: DC Comics/Vertigo. Neil Gaiman (writer), Mike Dringenberg and Malcolm Jones III (artists). Pages 9, 10, and 22.

A character named John Dee (presumably named for the Elizabethan Magnus) possesses the ruby necklace made from Sandman's powers and plans to use it to kill Sandman and wreck havoc on mankind. Taking the persona of Julius Caesar, Dee encounters a chorus of Asian women who wish all his dreams of world conquest come true (p. 9). They then get Freudian and tell Dee he had a dream about raping his mother, quoting *Macbeth* without acknowledgement: "a tale told by an idiot, full of sound and fury, signifying nothing" (5.5.26–28). After the voice of his mother wishes she had strangled him at birth, two men in gas masks emerge to tell him "beware the ides of March" (*Julius Caesar* 1.2.18, again without acknowledgement, p. 10). Dee's nightmares continue until he is defeated by the Sandman. Sandmen takes Dee to Arkham Asylum, an institute for the criminally insane. They are confronted by a Batman villain named the Scarecrow, who welcomes Dee with a quote from Marlowe's Dr. Faustus, "It is a comfort in wretchedness to have companions in woe," this time naming the author (2.2). Sandman is co-published with DC's Vertigo imprint.

265 *Sandman*
"Doll's House, Part Four: Men of Good Fortune." # 13, January 1990. New York: Vertigo/DC Comics. Neil Gaiman (writer), Michael Zulli (penciller), Steve Parkhouse (inker). Pages 11–13, 17–18.

An interruption to a longer story entitled "Doll's House" begins with men in a late medieval tavern complaining about taxes. Sandman and his sister Death join them. The argument shifts to literature, *Piers Plowman* is mentioned (p. 2), as well as death and a possible escape from death. One of the characters turns out to be immortal, like Anasuerus, the Wandering Jew. Sandman makes an appointment to meet him at the tavern once every hundred years. This issue chronicles their meetings through the centuries. Shakespeare and Christopher Marlowe are in the tavern during their third meeting. Marlowe critiques the beginning of Will's "first play" *Henry VI, Part 1* (1.1.1–4). Marlowe suggests that with lines that bad, Shakespeare should quit writing. Shakespeare recites a line from *Doctor Faustus* with admiration. Shakespeare says he would make a Faustian bargain if he could write like that. Sandman overhears and makes an offer (pp. 11–13). The offer will be fleshed out in *Sandman* # 19 and # 75. There is another reference: At a later meeting, the Anasuerus character tells Sandman he saw *King Lear*, with Mrs. Siddons as Goneril. He disapproves of the happy ending. He asks Sandman about his deal with Shakespeare, but they are interrupted (pp. 17–18).

266 *Mad*
"Mad Raps Up Shakespeare." # 300, January 1991. New York: E. C. Publications, Inc. Frank Jacobs (writer), George Woodbride (artist). Pages 11–13.

"Is this...a rap-per...that...you...see? / Gadzooks! Sure is, because the rap's...on...me!" This is said by a tennis shoe–wearing William Shakespeare in the introduction to a *Mad* blend of Shakespeare and rap music. Four plays receive the rap treatment in single-panel parodies of the best-known scenes or lines: *Hamlet, Richard III, Julius Caesar,* and *Romeo and Juliet.* The artist shows some knowledge of the plays and characters, so Richard III stands on a battlefield with a banner showing his totem, a boar, and the Nurse can be seen through the window as Juliet speaks to Romeo. It is presented by the "Frank on a Roll Dept."

267 *Blondie*
September 3, 1991. King Features Syndicate, Inc. Dean Young (writer), Stan Drake (artist).

In a strip betraying its domestic American comedy origins, Dagwood Bumstead sits in a car with the other members of his carpool. The woman next to him asks if his wife has a job. Dagwood says he would never allow that. The woman says that Dagwood reminds her of Shakespeare. Dagwood wants to know if that is because he is so dramatic, and she says, "No, because neither you left the 17th century." The reason *Blondie* has been around since 1931 is the ability of creator Chic Young and his successors to reflect their times. This strip was produced in a world that was somewhat reluctantly forced to accept women in the workplace and shows that change in both the woman in the carpool and Dagwood's resistance to Blondie having a job. Shakespeare is basically incidental, framing the insult to Dagwood. A few years later, Blondie started her own catering business and forced her still-reluctant husband to accept the change.

268 *The Trouble with Girls Christmas Special*
Story title N/A. # 1, December 1991. Westlake Village: Malibu Graphics. Will Jacobs (writer), Gerard Jones (writer), Tim Hamilton (penciller), Marvin Perry Mann (inker). Pages 4 and 14.

Poor Lester Girls wants a quiet life in a suburban bungalow with a wife and 2.3 delightful children, a life where he can relax and read dog stories; pretty much the life his brother Cal actually has. Instead, constant attacks by Ninjas and supervillains force Lester into thrills and

adventures he would do anything to avoid. There is also the problem of being irresistible to woman, which gets in the way of serious relationships. Jacobs and Jones began their creation as an unsold novel and a parody on all the bad best-selling fiction flooding the American marketplace, but it became a modest success in the comics. Every issue of *The Trouble with Girls* is rich with allusion to world, and especially American, literature. One panel of this comic (p. 13, panel 4) refers to Wharton, Melville, Dreiser, Dostoyevsky, Conrad, Twain, Jim Thompson, and others. There are two nods to Shakespeare. On p. 4, an old woman gives a clue to a treasure hunt, "By any other name, I still smell as sweet!" which paraphrases *Romeo and Juliet* (2.2.43–44). On p. 14, Lester is in conversation with his brother and his best buddy, Apache Dick. They ask Cal about life in Dullsville. After a reference to two plays by Sophocles, Apache asks if Mrs. Macbeth is still in the asylum. Cal replies that she was released, and "invented a detergent that made her a million bucks. She calls it 'Out,'" a reference to the imaginary spot of blood Lady Macbeth cannot wash off in *Macbeth* (5.1.39).

269 *Justice League Europe*
"Doomed by Deconstructo!" "Alas—*Poor Kara!*" # 37 and 39, April and June 1992. New York: DC Comics. Gerard Jones (writer), Ron Randall (penciller), Randy Elliott (inker). # 38, pages 6 and 8, # 39 cover.

Gerard Jones is given to allusion and is of a more intellectual bent than most comic-book writers, so using the idea of deconstruction to create a comic-book villain seems a natural for him. More anarchist then deconstructionist, Deconstructo finds a magic wand left by aliens that allows him to change the world in any way he wishes. In this three-issue sequence, he goes on a rampage of physical deconstruction of London and anybody who gets in his way, especially the European branch of the Justice League, a group of mostly American expatriate superheroes. Part of the fun lies in seeing the concepts of deconstruction physically manifest themselves in such incidents as rearranging the city and giving life to the Assyrian reliefs in the British Museum. There are also allusions to John Milton, *The Wizard of Oz* (Jones grew up reading the Oz books), Edward Elgar, and philosophers and theorymongers like Friedrich Nietzsche, Michael Foucault, and Paul de Man and to historical images as Deconstructo rampages through Ron Randall's uninformed versions of Trafalgar Square and the British Museum. There are three Shakespeare allusions. In # 38 (p. 6), Deconstructo stands atop a sphinx with the head of Queen Victoria and not only sings "Rule Brittania" and comments on "empire," but he riffs on Gaunt's "sceptred isle" line in *Richard II* (2.1.40), calling it a "shoppered aisle" and a "kippered eel." This is an intelligent bringing together of sources. Two pages later, Sue Dibny, who is looking for a leader to give the JLE some order, cries in frustration "A *leader*! My *kingdom* for a *leader*!" paraphrasing *Richard III* (5.4.7). The last Shakespearean allusion is on the cover of # 39. At the end of # 38, Deconstructo cuts off the head of Power Girl, a female Superman, whose other name is Kara. Instead of Yorick's skull, the cover of # 39 shows Deconstructo contemplating the severed head of Kara, and by her head is the story title, "Alas—Poor Kara!" See Richard Burt, *Shakespeare after Mass Media* (New York: Palgrave, 2002), 150–54.

270 *The Cheque, Mate*
"Shakespeare." # 1, July 1992. Seattle: Fantagraphics Books, Inc. Wes Kublick (writer), Eddie Campbell (artist). Pages 36, 37, 40, front cover reverse, and back cover obverse.

Campbell is an English comic artist who has contributed short comic stories and strips to a number of publications. *The Cheque, Mate* collects some of this material and presents a few new features as well. One of these is a ten-strip sequence titled "Shakespeare," written by Kublick. Campbell dedicates these strips "to anyone who ever tried to make a living from a creative endeavor and spent 50% of their creative energies in finding ways to make past due cheques arrive in the mail" (p. 29), inviting readers to identify Shakespeare's frustrations with his and Kublick's own. Nine of the strips show Shakespeare writing letters for money owed him. The strips come in two varieties. Most show Shakespeare seemingly writing off the point, then making the point in the last panel, as when he writes that "words are immortal" and notes they are worth more than a king's gold, and then asks, "Why is it yours are worthless?" (back cover obverse). In a few cartoons, Kublick uses lines from the plays to make the point. For example, he uses *Hamlet* (1.1.165), first reminding his correspondent of the money promised, then adding, "So I have heard and do in part believe" (front cover reverse). The last strip shows Shakespeare meeting his friend Ben, no last name, who observes that Shakespeare looks proud of himself. Shakespeare replies, "Smartest thing I ever did . . . got Francis Bacon to write my collection notices" (back cover obverse). Two unrelated strips quote Shakespeare under the overall title "Mindless Violence." These strips really have mindful violence. In one Hamlet says, "To be, or not to be . . ." (3.1.55). A man shoots him between the eyes and says, "Stupid question" (p. 37). The last strip begins with the killer onstage, giving lines 59–60: "To die, to sleep no more—" He shoots a member of the audience and adds, "That's somebody else's problem" (p. 37).

271 *Sylvia*
14 August 1993. Tribune Media Services, Inc. Nicole Hollander (writer/artist).

This strip has three virtually identical shots of a refrigerator. The main difference is the changing sign on it.

The first panel asks readers what they would prefer to find inside the refrigerator. The second panel suggests "a previously undiscovered play by Shakespeare," and the third gives the alternative, "or a sliver of lemon meringue pie?"

272 *Blondie*
October 8, 1993. King Features Syndicate, Inc. Dean Young (writer) and Stan Drake (artist).

America's most successful family strip is *Blondie*, the story of Blondie and Dagwood Bumstead and their family. Dagwood watches television when the neighbor boy Elmo tells of a school assignment to keep a journal and wonders if Dagwood keeps one. Dagwood answers that he keeps notes in his pocket, such as grocery lists and reminders to get a haircut. Elmo points out that those "aren't very great thoughts." Dagwood trades on Shakespeare's high reputation by saying he would bet money that "Shakespeare had the very same note in his pocket."

273 *The Born Loser*
October 15, 1994. NEA, Inc. Chip Sansom (writer/artist).

Young Wilberforce Thornapple asks his father if he knows anything about Shakespeare. Brutus boasts that he "learned something in" his "four years" at university. Gladys retorts that was when he graduated to sophomore. This strip is merciless in embarrassing Brutus at every opportunity, in this case taking Shakespeare's name in vain to jab at the born loser. The writer/artist credit above is correct, though many newspapers identify the creator as Chip's father Art Sansom. The strip is signed Art/Chip, but Art Sansom died in 1991.

274 *Flaming Carrot Comics*
"Herbie in Alas Poor Carrot!" # 31, October 1994. Milwaukie, OR: Dark Horse Comics. Bob Burden (writer/artist).

Professor Dogwood, an English teacher, is fired for suggesting that Shakespeare did not write his plays. His student Herbie enlists the aid of the ineffectual super-hero Flaming Carrot to go back in time, prove Dogwood is right, and save his job. Shakespeare is a nearly toothless dullard and a handyman by profession, who will do anything to make a quid, including write plays. Since he can not do this on his own, he enlists the aid of time travelling twentieth-century comedian Buddy Hackett, who supplies the poetry. Dogwood gets his job back at the end of the story.

275 *Scud: The Disposable Assassin*
10, December 1995. Milwaukie, WI: Fireman Press Ltd. Mondy Carter (writer), Rob Schrab (writer/artist). Pages 3, 23–25.

Scud was a short-run humor comic that received sparse distribution. Only # 10 was seen, and it does little to explain the premise of the series, which involves mechanical assassins that may be purchased in a vending machine. This issue is about the British space program's successful use of an anti-graviton generator that is beamed to Earth from a space station. Manning the station are former actors with the Royal Shakespeare Company, the focal figure being Basil Canis, who is inclined to tell old theater stories to his cronies on the station. His former affiliation with the RSC is mentioned on p. 3, and then he tells an anecdote about an actor using a line from *Hamlet* during a performance of *Timon of Athens* (pp. 23–24). When a crew member is found dead on p. 25, another crew member quotes *Julius Caesar* (3.1.148–50), "O mighty Caesar, dost thou lie so low? Are all thy conquests, glories, triumphs, spoils, shrunk to this little measure?" This is a multi-part story, so there are probably other Shakespeare references in the issues following. Artist Rob Schab is credited with conceiving the story. This issue does not have a separate title.

276 *Mad Magazine*
"Shakespearean Sonnets for Modern Lovers." # 360, August 1997. New York: DC Comics. Andrew J. Schwatzberg (writer), Timothy Shamey (artist). Pages 29–31.

Thine eyes shine like CDs in the morning sun,
I long to have thy software in my hands.
And when you send a GIF for me to run,
I feel a sudden twitch in my glands.

Thus writes a modern urban Romeo, who e-mails a sonnet to his Juliet. So readers will not miss the point, she is poised on the balcony of her house. This is the first of four sonnets published under the auspices of Mad's "Bard Silly Dept." The subjects are sending love letters via e-mail, kinky sadism, love betrayed on daytime television talk shows, and a woman who makes her husband use a condom. None can be compared to a summer's day.

277 *Introducing Derrida*
1996, Reprint 2000. Duxford, Cambridge: Icon Books. Jeff Collins (writer), Bill Mayblin (artist). Page 43.

This series of books attempts to make difficult and sometimes theoretical subjects understandable to undergraduates via nonfiction comics. The comics use original drawings, but more often collages of photos and engravings create images that illustrate the subject. This book on the deliberately obscure French philosopher Jacques Derrida attempts to deconstruct the deconstructionist. A two-page section that questions the usefulness of writing is illustrated by a couple of dozen books. Amongst those whose titles can be read are the Bible, *Das Kapital*, and the works of William Shakespeare. This is a bit double-edged, although this two-page section does not acknowledge it: It is in part the theories of Derrida that have led some to question the concept that long-venerated writings like Shakespeare's are meaningful and should be the cornerstone of our civilization, yet that status is why Shakespeare's works are in the illustration.

278 *The Born Loser*
July 26, 1997. NEA, Inc. Chip Sansom (writer/artist).

Gladys reads a letter to Brutus. Some friends wrote about their trip to Shakespeare's house in "Stratford-on-Avon." Brutus, as usual betraying his ignorance, asks if they got his autograph. The writer/artist credit above is correct, though many newspapers, like *The Washington Post* where this strip was found, identify the creator as Chip's father Art Sansom, who died in 1991.

279 *Liberty Meadows*
October 27–November 1, 1997. Creators Syndicate, Inc. Frank Cho (writer/artist).

This short-lived strip is a poor man's *Pogo*, about the interactions of the creatures, some of them human, who live in Liberty Meadows. While Frank Cho falls short of Walt Kelly's excellence, it is still a good strip that deserved to run longer than its three years and has in the form of the *Liberty Meadows* comic book, which began by reprinting the comic strip, then presented new material. This sequence takes place at a Halloween party and is full of allusions to *Star Wars*, *Xena: Warrior Princess*, FBI founder J. Edgar Hoover, pin-up queen Bettie Page, Francis Bacon, and William Shakespeare. A character named Al hosts the party and is in a costume intended to represent Elizabethan garb, though it can be mistaken for a harlequin outfit. His costume is not explained in this strip, and he does not appear again until the November 1 strip when he is tending the bar. A guest says, "Hey Shakespeare! Need a refill here." Al explains that he is not dressed as Shakespeare, but as "Francis Bacon—the real author all Shakespeare's plays." He adds that Shakespeare was "just an illiterate actor." The guest is not impressed. "I'm still thirsty, Shakespeare. Gimme a refill." Al appears again in costume in the next day's Sunday page, but there are no references to either Shakespeare or Bacon. This strip is also reprinted in the undated *Liberty Meadows* comic book # 4 (Baltimore: Insight Studio Group).

280 *Tales from Shakespeare: Seven Plays Presented by Marcia Williams*
1998. Cambridge, MA: Candlewich Press. Marcia Williams (writer/artist). Pages N/A.

This is a comic book packaged as a children's book. It has four- or six-page stories of *Romeo and Juliet*, *Hamlet*, *A Midsummer Night's Dream*, *Macbeth*, *The Winter's Tale*, *Julius Caesar*, and *The Tempest*. The stories and storytelling have a number of peculiar features. Williams uses the same cluttered style in all her stories. The clutter comes from trying to squeeze too many panels on a page, the amount of detail she puts in a tiny panel, and her conceit that the plays are being performed at the Globe Theatre. This conceit results in cluttered margins, as groundlings look on, and often inanely comment on the action. Each page looks pretty much the same except for a very few large panels and an occasional change in palate. The colors for *A Midsummer Night's Dream* are especially vibrant and suit that play well. She tends to go with gray tones for *Hamlet* and *Macbeth*. This is an effective change, but makes the plays too alike visually. The colors for *The Winter's Tale* are autumnal, neither wintry nor springlike. Williams fails to explain the cuts in some stories, so these narratives do not always make sense.

281 *The Clone Conspiracy*
"The Clones of Malcolm Syberg!" 1998, Reprint 1998. Baltimore: Insight Studios Group. Allan Gross (writer), Mark Wheatley, Marc Hempel, and Damon Willis (artists). Pages: Preface 8–16, Chapter 5 32–49.

This graphic novel pretends to be the report of an actual conspiracy, complete with a preface giving an overview of it. The back cover copy claims this story "proves...the secret of cloning arose from an ancient civilization, passing through the hands of Moses, Jesus, the mysterious man known as Shakespeare, and even John F. Kennedy before falling into the possession of a splinter group of the Freemasons. Hidden ciphers lead to a trail of treachery, murder and deceit that infected the superpower governments of the Cold War." We will concentrate on the early modern connection. The preface reveals that Francis Bacon was a clone and the son of Queen Elizabeth. Clones do not grow old and die, so he eventually fled to Canada where he still lives. He wrote the plays of Christopher Marlowe, Robert Greene, and William Shakespeare, plus novels such as *Don Quixote* and *Robinson Crusoe*. Before leaving England, he cloned Marlowe to make William Shakespeare. Shakespeare was the front man for Bacon and a spy who used the name William Hall. The bulk of the other Shakespeare material is in chapter 5, where readers meet Bacon and his family, all named for characters in Shakespeare's plays. Quite a bit of the chapter is a debate of Bacon's authorship, presenting some of the evidence supposedly favoring him. The final proof is a cop-out. The protagonist, Dr. Cyborg, is shown Shakespeare's plays in Bacon's hand, including first drafts in Latin. *Taming of the Shrew* is mentioned as one of Bacon's lesser efforts. Literary scholars are portrayed as afraid of the truth. There is a concluding sword fight between Bacon's son Hamlet and Dr. Cyborg that parallels the end of *Hamlet*, though both live. This graphic novel was originally published as a five-issue series titled *Doctor Cyborg*.

282 *Luann*
November 6, 1998. United Features Syndicate, Inc. Greg Evans (writer/artist).

Luann is a cross between humor strip and soap opera, with short continuing story lines but a light touch. Most of the stories involve Luann and her circle of friends, but sometimes Evans spotlights supporting characters as he does here. High-school teachers Mr. Fogarty and Ms. Phelps are approaching middle age alone. They have crushes on each other, but are too shy to do anything about it.

In the days that precede this strip, Fogarty finally decides to make his move, but it is the wrong move. He promises a student five dollars if he will scare Ms. Phelps so he can rescue her. As he struts in her praise, the student reenters asking for his money, and Ms. Phelps sees through the scheme. Fogarty confesses. She says the trick was not necessary because she is attracted to him. He realizes this but thinks the attraction is "more intellectual than physical." She refers to her slinky dress and says "So this outfit says, 'Let's discuss Shakespeare'?" Nothing comes of this. As of this writing (August 2005), they are still not together.

283 *Non-Sequitur*
April 19, 1999. Universal Press Syndicate, Inc. Wiley Miller (writer/artist).

In a parody of the film *Shakespeare in Love*, a couple pass a cinema and note the posters for films that are "coming soon." The titles are *Dickens in Love*, *Hemingway in Love*, and *Twain in Love*. The woman says to her husband, "Well, it looks like the post-Oscar creative bandwagon has kicked into high gear...." The image of Dickens on his poster looks far more like Shakespeare than Dickens.

284 *Frank and Ernest*
August 13, 2000. NEA, Inc. Bob Thaves (writer/artist).

This is a typical, pun-filled *Frank and Ernest* Sunday page. Frank has a new invention that will "probe the finer points of history," the Historiscope. He discovers three unknown historical events, and Ernest writes them in a huge book entitled *Little-Known Historical Facts*. In the one that involves Shakespeare, Frank looks at his Historicsope and discovers "Shakespeare got rowdy one too many times. His local tavern kicked him out for life." Ernest writes this as, "The bar barred the Bard!"

285 *Introducing Shakespeare*
2001. Duxford, Cambridge: Icon Books. Nick Groom (writer), Piero (artist). Pages N/A.

This is another Icon Books title that uses cartoons to introduce undergraduates to modern scholarship. It is roughly divided into three parts. The first is Shakespeare's biography, the second studies his reputation through the nineteenth century, and the last views Shakespeare as a twentieth-century cultural icon, looking at film, opera, cultural appropriations, and authorship questions, with the most pages given to scholarly disputes, all expansively illustrated. There are some factual errors and opinions stated as facts. The biography states that the traditional date of Shakespeare's birth, April 23, was chosen for political motives since it is St. George's Day, a day of nationalism (p. 4). That date may have been chosen for sentimental reasons or even sincerely believed is not considered. It boldly claims Shakespeare "was very interested in developing a national myth" (p. 25) and presents the theory that Shakespeare played Adam in *As You Like It* as a fact (p. 16). Donald Foster's claim, that we can discover the parts Shakespeare played with computer analysis of the language of his characters, is stated without credit (p. 18). The book implies that playwrights were paid by the performance; the unusually high number of performance of *Titus Andronicus* is noted, with an illustration showing Shakespeare counting his money, but writers were paid a flat fee for all rights to their work (p. 32). It treats some disputed matters as settled, giving only one side, such as the providence of Shakespeare's quartos (pp. 36–39), autobiographical aspect of *Hamlet* (p. 40), and claims that *Love's Labor's Lost* and *A Midsummer Night's Dream* are Shakespeare's "two most personal plays" (p. 60). The discussion of Shakespeare's universality is fun. It is accepted by most of his fans, while those who deny it are an elite group of scholars. Groom balances those fixated on Shakespeare being used by Tory and imperialist politicians by noting the use made of him by leaders in the Eastern Block and by Karl Marx using Shakespeare to prove his points (pp. 134–38). Next comes a consideration of New Historicism, Cultural Materialism, and Post-Colonial Criticism, among several others, and then a consideration of problems with their methods. It is dazzlingly succinct (pp. 138–57). The illustrations are clever. When an author is quoted, a drawing of the author gives the quote in a word balloon, as with Coleridge, Hazlitt, and Keats (p. 91). One particularly imaginative use of this is a quote by Marxist critic Terry Eagleton, saying "Shakespeare is the quintessential commodity." The smoke from his cigar forms the face of Karl Marx, who says, "One could say the same thing about Eagleton's Marxism" (p. 142). When discussing how many biographers have read their own interests and professions into Shakespeare's life, Piero presents a Shakespeare paper doll with hats that may be put on him as the biographer desires (p. 12).

286 *Simpsons Comics*

"Bard Boiled." # 76, (month not given) 2002. Santa Monica, CA: Bongo Entertainment. Ian Boothby (writer), John Costanza (penciller), Phyllis Novin and Howard Shum (inkers). Page N/A.

The cover blurb is "The Simpsons Shake-Up Shakespeare!" and that says it well. This comic book version of the animated television series uses the framing device of putting on a school play. The ten stories in the comic either parody Shakespeare's stories or use a Shakespearean idea to launch a Simpsons-style riff. An example of the former is "Itchy & Scratchy in 'Titus Andronicus'" where, after numerous amputations, beheadings, and a baking, a cat's lopped-off heard tells a dead mouse, "I like violence as much as the next guy, but whoever wrote this is really messed up." "Henry V" riffs on the king rallying his troops. This king gives a long, boring speech, complete with mathematical diagrams. When he finally finishes, he finds

that everyone has gone home. The last page is merely an egregious pun, as the characters assemble at the As You Lick It Ice Cream Parlor, eat ice cream, and say, "All's Well That Ends Well." The other plays parodied, or at least mentioned, are *Troilus and Cressida*, *Antony and Cleopatra*, *Julius Caesar*, *Romeo and Juliet*, *Two Gentlemen of Verona*, *Richard III*, *Othello*, *King Lear*, and *A Midsummer Night's Dream*.

287 *Frank and Ernest*

February 8, 2002. NEA, Inc. Bob Thaves (writer/artist).

At the Old Globe Theater, Frank, in jerkin and pumpkin pants, goes to William Shakespeare and tells him the queen wants to see *Macbeth* and wonders if they should charge her for the performance. Shakespeare muses, "To fee or not to fee...." Shakespeare is working at his desk, with many crumpled papers around him. It may be noted that the name of the theater is wrong: There was no "Old" before "Globe," and the spelling of theater is the American, not the English version which ends-*re*.

288 *Frank and Ernest*

March 20, 2003. NEA, Inc. Bob Thaves (writer/artist).

Frank and Ernest are schoolchildren. They appear to be alone in their classroom. On the blackboard is

| Hamlet | *SHAKESPEARE* | Romeo and Juliet |

This is followed by three quotes from Shakespeare: "To be or not to be, that is the question" (*Hamlet* 3.1.64), "We are such stuff as dreams are made on" (*Tempest* 4.1.156–67), and "What's in a name? That which we call a rose by any other word would smell as sweet" (*Romeo and Juliet* 2.2.33–34). Frank tells Ernest, "That Shakespeare guy had some really neat sound bites." Note that the second quote is from *The Tempest*, which in not mentioned on the blackboard. The cartoon is reminiscent of a story John Gielgud used to tell about two elderly women talking during an intermission of *Hamlet*. One said to the other, "I don't see what the big deal is. It is just a bunch of famous sayings strung together."

289 *The Adventures of Superman*

"Rather, Rinse, Repeat" [*sic*]. # 617, August 2003. New York: DC Comics. Joe Casey (writer), Charlie Adlard (artist). Page 9.

Superman is mentally assaulted by a villain who shows him a number of faked events about people in his life. In one vision, an unidentified character spouts some flowery dialogue: "Verily, your Ignorance. How doth you fancy your planetary kingdom of Crud?" A woman answers him, "HA! What's with the Shakespeare?" He answers, "I dunno.... I'm wingin' this mind-bender!"

290 *Get Fuzzy*

August 17, 2003. United Feature Syndicate, Inc. darby conley (writer/artist).

The premise of the comic strip *Get Fuzzy* is that a young man has conversations with his dog and cat. While the animals are certainly anthropromorphized, they remain true to the basic characters of a dog (loyal, kind, dull-witted) and a cat (scheming, vengeful, selfish). In this Sunday page, the young man banters with them about his intelligence, or lack of it. The cat says, "As I've said before," then quotes the "Be not afraid of greatness" speech from *Twelfth Night* (2.5.117–18). When he is told, "You didn't say that. Shakespeare said that," he replies, "Nuts to thou." He is then answered with a quote from *The Merchant of Venice* (2.2.198), "Thou art too wild, too rude and bold of voice," and finally *Hamlet* (5.1.315), " 'The cat will mew and the dog will have is day!'"

291 *Y, The Last Man*
"Comedy and Tragedy." # 16 and 17, January and February 2004. New York: DC Comics. Brian K. Vaughan (writer), Paul Chadwick (penciller), Jose Marzan, Jr. (inker). Page N/A.

Though set in a world very like ours, the science-fiction premise of this series is that all males of every species have apparently died, possibly from a plague that did not harm women. Number 16 introduces a male monkey who somehow survived. The cover shows the monkey on a stage in Elizabethan clothing, holding Yorick's skull. Inside, some female actors speculate that the reason the plague closed the theaters in "Shakespeare's lifetime" is that there were only male actors. This plague ended "in 1670 . . . right after women were allowed back on stage." They seem to take this premise seriously. The series has a character named Yorick, also male, whose father was a Shakespeare professor before the plague. Yorick was charged with supervising the monkey, who escaped under his watch. Yorick has a sister named Hero, the name of a character in *Much Ado about Nothing*.

292 *Batman: Harley and Ivy*
"Hooray for Hollywood." # 3, August 2004. New York: DC Comics. Paul Dini (writer/artist), Bruce Timm (writer/artist). Page 6.

Harley Quinn and Poison Ivy are true homicidal maniacs: They are crazy and they kill—a lot. They team up in this light-hearted, comical mini-series to wreck havoc on those destroying the Brazilian Rain Forest. Back in the United States, Harley watches a parody of the "entertainment news-show" *Access Hollywood*, here called *Excess Hollywood*. A late-breaking story reveals that a film will be based on their exploits, cast with a video music star who looks nothing like Harley. In an interview, the star defends the casting saying she had "done Shakespeare, you know . . . back in high school." This comic uses the cultural myth that actors are good if they have done Shakespeare. Harley and Ivy take over the studio by killing those in charge, and make the movie themselves, killing each successive actor cast as Batman.

293 *Sally Forth*
November 29, 2004. King Features Syndicate, Inc. Greg Howard (writer), Francesco Marciuliano (artist).

Not to be confused with the R-rated military comic strip by Wally Wood, this *Sally Forth* is about a self-righteous wife/mother/career woman with the same name. The Thanksgiving-week sequence shows Sally and her group being manipulated by the new boss into taking work home during the holiday. In this post-holiday strip, Sally and a co-worker are back at work. They run into their boss, who asks if they had a nice holiday. They give a socially acceptable "Good." After he leaves, the co-worker tells the truth, cracking that it was good if you like "working the whole weekend." Sally tells her that "asides are only spoken out loud in Shakespearean plays."

294 *Mallard Fillmore*
February 28, 2005. King Features Syndicate, Inc. Bruce Tinsley.

This is an extremely right-wing, highly political comic strip. A typical example is the use of Shakespeare to comment on the discussion about the Western Canon in universities today. Mallard, a duck, looks at his "Liberal Lexicon" to define "Dead White Males" (exampled by a drawing of Shakespeare) as "Irrelevant Western Men . . . who once cluttered up ancient U. S. textbooks," then adds that dead is the "preferred liberal condition for white males." Tinsley apparently believes that all liberals are women or deceased.

295 *Rhymes with Orange*
April 29, 2005. King Features Syndicate, Inc. Hilary B. Price.

One way that probability theorists make the point that everything will eventually happen by chance is to state that a million monkeys typing on typewriters will eventually, by chance, produce the works of Shakespeare. Price relates this idea via a conversation between a woman and her friend as they lean against a tree. She tells the monkey/Shakespeare story, then her friend mentions that the chance might be even slighter because of the monkeys working on George W. Bush's environmental policy.

296 *Mother Goose and Grimm*
May 6, 2005. King Features Syndicate, Inc. Mike Peters (writer/artist).

Pulitzer Prize–winning political cartoonist Mike Peters added a daily humor strip in 1984, now syndicated to over five hundred newspapers around the world. Peters does gag panels without his regular characters when an idea goes in another direction, and Mother Goose and her disgusting dog Grimm are not in this daily strip. Instead, Mary Shakespeare sits with her son in the consulting room of the family physician. Young Will is writing with a quill. His mother complains, "All he does is write." The doctor prescribes Ritalin so that he will "be like every other normal, average kid."

297 *Plastic Man*
"The Edwina Crisis: Prologue Part Two." # 16, July 2005. New York: DC Comics. Kyle Baker (writer/artist). Pages 4 and 21.

Edwina is Plastic Man's adopted daughter, and the crisis is that she has been abducted by a super powered teenager she does not want to date but goes out with anyway to defy Plastic Man. Her date is the stereotypical troubled boy but with comically exaggerated trouble. He recites poetry as they drive down the street. The poems include an excerpt from Alexander Pope's *Eloisa to Abelard* (p. 4). On the same page is the strange choice of

Othello (3.3.502–9), strange because it is hardly a love poem:

Like to the Pontic sea,
Whose icy current and compulsive course
Ne'er feels retiring ebb, but keeps due on
To the Propontic and the Hellespont,
Even so my bloody thoughts, with violent pace,
Shall ne'er look back, ne'er ebb to humble love,
Till that a capable and wide revenge
Swallow them up.

Plastic Man is in hot pursuit, and stops the car. The beau steals a motorcycle, using his lightning power to start it, saying:

Brief as the lightning in the collied night,
That, in a spleen, unfolds both heaven and earth,
And ere a man hath power to say "Behold!"
The jaws of darkness do devour it up:
So quick bright things come to confusion.

(A *Midsummer Night's Dream* 1.1.148–52)

3
Film Adaptations

INTRODUCTION, "WHAT IS A FILM ADAPTATION? OR, SHAKESPEARE DU JOUR," COURTNEY LEHMANN

Defending the project of film adaptation, André Bazin touted film as a medium uniquely capable of making literature and drama more "digestible" for audiences. In the cinema, he observed, it is "as if the aesthetic fat, differently emulsified, were better tolerated by the consumer's mind."[1] The same could certainly be said of Shakespeare, whose plays have found a second home in the cinema and, in the age of home theater, in the individual "consumer's mind." But what exactly *is* a film adaptation, and what does it mean to adapt *Shakespeare*, a figure whose work—much like a film—is cobbled together from so many hands, fragments, and motives? To extend Bazin's gastronomic metaphor, there can be no doubt that what constitutes an adaptation of Shakespeare, let alone a successful one, is very much a matter of personal taste. Some like their Shakespeare on screen "over easy," as a welcomed respite from the rigors of reading the plays, while others prefer the poetic license of directors who rearrange scenes and reassign speeches to create a "scrambled" Shakespeare. Still others enjoy the surprising range of Shakespeare films that experiment with genres drawn from other media, such as detective novels, which make for a "hard-boiled" Bard, or musical adaptations that, with the exception of *West Side Story*, tend to generate "sunny side up" renderings of the plays. There is even a Shakespeare du jour fit for textual purists, who will surely applaud Kenneth Branagh's decision to fold the First and Second Quartos, as well as the First Folio, into his 1996 "omelet" of *Hamlet*. In short, when it comes to Shakespeare, there are as many adaptation styles as there are audiences.

If we add up all the known adaptations, spin-offs, and citations of the thirty-six plays ascribed to Shakespeare, we arrive at more than a thousand films. Whereas the cinematic adaptation of other canonical figures—Jane Austen, Charles Dickens, Mark Twain, and Tennessee Williams—generally increases their oeuvre by a factor of two and, therefore, effectively doubles their lifetime literary output—the Shakespeare canon increases by a *power* of two, reproducing itself on screen exponentially. Hence, it is not an exaggeration to claim that Shakespeare films invoke an entire species of adaptation. It's as though in the hands of filmmakers, "Shakespeare" possesses something akin to what Charles Darwin himself characterized in *The Origin of Species* as the unique ability to identify, select, and reproduce traits that are favorable to non-random, long-term proliferation, which, in a word, is the process known as "adaptation."

Nevertheless, the answer to the question with which we began—"What is an adaptation?"—remains, like Shakespeare himself, elusive. Does filmed theater constitute an adaptation or a recording? Does celluloid define a film, or do cinematic techniques? Can non–English language films still be called adaptations when, for many, what is quintessentially "Shakespearean" is the language itself? Is there, in other words, room for a definition of adaptation that accounts for the spirit rather than just the letter of the text? On the one hand, as Annalisa Castaldo observes in her introduction, the compilers of the First Folio established a text-centered precedent for adaptation when they chose to address Shakespeare's works to "the great Variety of *Readers*." On the other hand, what is often overlooked in this dedication is not *who* is poised to inherit Shakespeare's legacy but *what* is bequeathed to them, for John Heminges and Henry Condell offer neither Shakespeare's body nor his text but his "remaines." A rather different prospect than inheriting a stable body of work delimited by letters and line breaks, a legacy comprised of remains is nothing less than an invitation to participate in an adaptation process that, by its very definition, is always unfinished. Like the ghost of Ophelia that Hamlet attempts to embrace in vain in George Méliés's 1907 film, this remainder—indeed, the spirit that eludes our grasp—is precisely what makes Shakespeare such an apt candidate for ongoing adaptation.

It is particularly imperative, then, that in assessing Shakespeare adaptations we avoid the pitfall of paternity—literary or filmic—in favor of following Heminges and Condell's cue to shift our critical gaze from "who" to "what." For to seek, like Hamlet, for the noble intentions of an author or auteur in the dust that settles around a "finished" film is to betray the fact that, like Shakespeare's plays, films, too, are merely the privileged remnants among so many others—fragments left on the cutting room floor, unrealized frames in the shooting script, promotional trailers, product tie-ins, and, of course, all the fantasy footage that the individual spectator brings to and takes away from the viewing experience. It is for this reason that Bazin, similar to Darwin, argues for a critical approach to adaptation that accounts for the random forces of nature and technology—both felicitous and disastrous—that inflect the entire chain of (film) production, as well as the distinctly subjective historical climate from which a given film springs. Although this concept of an entire "culture of adaptation" may seem obvious to postmodern audiences, in the 1950s, such observations cut against the grain of the then-dominant auteur theory, the romantic excesses of which continue to haunt the reception of Shakespeare adaptations with remarkable tenacity. Nevertheless, recent work in the field is more attentive to the Bazinian "big picture." Kenneth Rothwell's *History of Shakespeare on Screen*, for example, employs phrases such as "Hollywood's Four Seasons of Shakespeare" to describe the period from 1929 to 1953, for which Sam Taylor's *Taming of the Shrew* and Joseph Mankiewicz's *Julius Caesar* provide the bookends, while referring to the shift toward more disturbing visions of Shakespeare in the volatile, uprising-rich 1960s and 1970s as "Shakespeare Movies in the Age of Angst." Others, such as Colin MacCabe, explore more recent films through coordinates that include both chronology and geography, such as "Post-National European Cinema," whereas Samuel Crowl announces his patented combination of traditional and contemporary approaches to periodization in phrases like "The Kenneth Branagh Era."[2]

Nevertheless, the big picture perspective offered by such interpretive categories is not to be confused with the whole picture, which must take into account the remarkable variations that occur *within* a certain generation of Shakespeare films. For such mutations, depending on their retention or elimination in subsequent adaptations, may impact the entire species. But to whom—or what—do we attribute the emergence of adaptive advantages in a medium wherein the distinction between random and non-random influences is often difficult to ascertain? The work of Orson Welles is a case in point: do we ascribe his privileged place at the vanguard of Shakespearean filmmaking to singular strokes of genius or cumulative blows of fortune? Consider, for example, the day on the set of *Othello* (1952) that the costumes didn't arrive in time to maintain the shooting schedule for a film already plagued by financial problems. Iago's attempted murder of Cassio is relocated to a Turkish bath wherein the absence of clothing adds a sensual aura to Iago's conspiracy that not even the sultry Mediterranean location of the film could accomplish. Is this brilliant innovation attributable to a flash of the auteurist imagination, to pure coincidence, or to the plague of insufficient financing and repute of "box office poison" that has historically hounded Shakespeare films and Welles's career in particular? The categories I offer for the films contained in this section reflect an attempt to accommodate the range of possible responses to such questions and, therefore, may be applied diagnostically, in order to describe broad trends, or idiosyncratically, as a means of excavating a single film. Bearing in mind the unique challenges that a performative medium like film poses for any attempts at schematization, I propose the following categories of adaptation: "conventional," "transpositional," "oppositional," and "experimental." In the process of exploring specific applications of these categories as well as the premises on which they are based, I will also seek to dispel some of the more dogged assumptions that continue to beleaguer the interpretation of Shakespeare on screen.

Whereas conventional adaptations closely rely on the text and period proper to a given Shakespeare play, transpositional films alter the historical or cultural setting of the play but may or may not update the language, as the difference between *West Side Story* (Robert Wise and Jerome Robbins, 1961) and Baz Luhrmann's *William Shakespeare's Romeo + Juliet* (1996) illustrates. By contrast, experimental adaptations that approach Shakespeare through the stylistic conventions of other media—animation and musical theater being the most popular choices—almost always modify and often completely dispense with the playtext, while oppositional films, which are concerned a priori with subversive political readings of the plays, may cloak their agendas in faithful treatments of the text, as Derek Jarman's adaptation of *The Tempest* (1979) certifies. Generally speaking, however, the terms "conventional," "transpositional," "oppositional," and "experimental" tend to correlate with ascending degrees of departure from a given Shakespeare play; but they do not necessarily imply a chronological progression. Although the latter two categories are indeed more relevant to contemporary filmmaking than to adaptations made during the silent era, the majority of Shakespeare films released both before *and* after the advent of sound are conventional. Hence, it is important not to approach such adaptations as though they are inherently passé or have nothing new to teach us. Lacking the sexiness of the other categories, conventional films are beset by the assumption that they are insufficiently cinematic or, better put, overly "theatrical" in some derogatory sense of the term. To disabuse ourselves of this notion, we need only look to Roman Polanski's *Macbeth* (1971), an adaptation that is utterly conventional in terms of its period setting, costume, and screenplay but one that employs some of the most extraordinary montage effects—impossible to even approximate in the theater—of any Shakespeare film ever made. Even the earliest silent Shakespeare films, which tend to record theater productions or reproduce them in a studio, offer glimpses of this potential while also serving as artifacts of cinema's own adaptation process—its efforts, that is, to distinguish itself from or pay homage to its theatrical ancestry.

In fact, the common perception of early cinema as a medium struggling to distinguish itself as something other than a poor imitation of theater is routinely overstated. Particularly during the silent era, the disruptive use of title cards alone made the audience's experience of silent film very different from theatrical spectatorship. If anything, the challenge to be "non-theatrical" came much later, when the introduction of synchronized sound, coupled with the rise of feature-length film, forced the cinema—and especially Shakespearean cinema—to prove itself a "spirit of another sort." For who would go to see a Shakespeare play captured by a fixed camera in a single take, with the faint outline of bobbing heads slightly obstructing the view of the downstage area? Such an experience is not film, nor theater, but something more akin to *Mystery Science Theater* (of which there is a Shakespeare episode), in which we watch—on TV—other people watching a film in the theater, as in the Electronovision *Hamlet* (Sir John Gielgud, 1964).[3] The point is that film has always been too expensive and too labor-intensive to be oriented toward merely reproducing, rather than creating, "reality." Had most emergent cinemas—from Hollywood to Bollywood—*not* sought early on to develop (1) a non-declamatory acting style suitable to the conditions that govern film performance, (2) a unique vocabulary of shots that range beyond theatrical frontality and medium distances, and (3) a mode of editing that enables film reception to take place in real time without subjecting the production process to its constraints, then cinema would never have survived the transition to sound film. This does not mean, of course, that there are no Shakespeare films that are not based on or inspired by pre-existing theater productions, for this is a practice that remains popular today. Max Reinhardt's 1935 film of *A Midsummer Night's Dream*, for example, which

was derived from his experimentation with Shakespeare in the German theater, is far more cinematically adventurous than much later adaptations of *Dream* by Celestino Coronado (1984) and Adrian Noble (1996), likewise based on theatrical antecedents. Kenneth Branagh's films of *Henry V* (1989) and *Much Ado about Nothing* (1993) are based on Royal Shakespeare and Renaissance Theatre Company productions, respectively, yet their origins as such are undetectable on screen. Indeed, lest we assume that any film with a stage heritage must necessarily be compromised by it, we need look no further than Julie Taymor's 1999 adaptation of *Titus*—the theatrical predecessor of which is nothing if not "cinematic."

If the notion of a founding rivalry between cinema and theater is subject to frequent exaggeration, then so too is the bildungsroman of the brave new medium battling—against throngs of naysayers—to prove itself worthy of the term that enthusiasts used to herald film's fin de siècle appearance as "the seventh art." While it is true that, at first, the cinema encountered the challenge of appealing to a "respectable" audience that would enable it to rise above the ranks of peep shows and the ephemeral entertainment associated with nickelodeons, the fact is that film was the *only* medium poised to inherit the audience that theater had lost long ago to all but an educated elite. Nevertheless, the emergence of Shakespeare on screen was something of a double-edged sword: if, on the one hand, the Bard's plays invested cinema with the promise of some degree of mass acculturation, then they also made it particularly susceptible to the criticism that film was merely degraded theater. Significantly, different national cinemas approached the ontological question of what cinema was to be—or not to be—in different ways.

The first example of Shakespeare on film is a studio recording of King John's death scene (in *King John*, 1899), performed by Sir Herbert Beerbohm Tree in consultation with William Kennedy-Laurie Dickson, an associate of Thomas Edison. Captured by a fixed camera and exclusively medium shots, the scene is a replica of Beerbohm's performance in the title role at Her Majesty's Theatre in London. In the next three decades, many more British Shakespeare films would follow in the footsteps of this example, rarely venturing beyond the parameters of pre-existing theatrical productions. But, then again, what reason had British cinema to stray too far from the stage, when film could be used to showcase the artistic—and national—heritage of the world's greatest dramatist? Significantly, on the Continent, too, the earliest Shakespeare adaptations were infused with a similar patriotic impulse. Italy, for example, experimented with out-of-doors spectacle and enormous ensemble casts, at once exploring the camera's range and celebrating the locations that form the backdrop of so many of the Bard's Italianate plays, whereas Northern European cinema displayed its uniquely "Nordic" temperament by opening the trap door to the chiaroscuro effects of the human psyche, culminating in Sven Gade's German Expressionist film *Hamlet: The Drama of Vengeance* (1920). The French, perhaps flouting their cultural reputation for deviance, revealed an inclination for challenging the prevailing moral sentiments associated with Shakespeare's plays. As early as 1911, Louis Feuillade created a version of *King Lear*, titled *Le Roi Lear au Village*, which not only modernized the setting of the play—a mode of adaptation that falls into the category of transpositional—but also resists demonizing the daughters while making Lear himself morally suspect, thus anticipating much later and more explicitly oppositional adaptations like Jocelyn Moorhouse's *A Thousand Acres* (1997).

Predictably, it is not the moral economy but the market economy that defines the first wave of American adaptations of Shakespeare mass-produced by studios like Vitagraph, which relied heavily on the new medium's ability to create the overnight sensations that would soon crystallize into the Hollywood star system. For example, the "Vitagraph girl," Florence Turner, paved the way for "the girl with the curl," Mary Pickford, who attempted to use Shakespeare to establish a new, less innocent, flapper-inspired persona in Sam Taylor's 1929 *Taming of the Shrew*, the first feature-length Shakespearean sound film. The fact that neither her brazen, whip-wielding interpretation of Shakespeare's Kate nor the relentless rumors of her tempestuous off-screen relationship with co-star Douglas Fairbanks could make Pickford, much to her chagrin, anything other than America's sweetheart testifies to the power that the system—and not Shakespeare—ultimately wielded over the stars themselves.

In the wake of synchronized sound—not to mention coming attractions like Technicolor, famously featured in Laurence Olivier's painterly *Henry V* (1942), and cinemascope, a staple of Welles's adaptations—many other nations have emerged as formidable forces in Shakespearean filmmaking, particularly Russia, Japan, and India. While Russia and Japan are overwhelmingly associated with the well-known films of Grigori Kozintsev and Akira Kurosawa, respectively, India, which is distinguished by *multiple* national cinemas, is the source of a veritable cottage industry in Shakespeare and a "great Variety" of directors. Recent films such as the Malayalam adaptation of *Kaliyattam* (*Othello*; Rajasekharan Jayaraaj Nair, 1997) and Bollywood's *Maqbool* (*Macbeth*; Vishal Bharadwaj, 2004) have awakened interest in much earlier, Parsi adaptations such as the Sohrab Modi (1935) and Kishore Sahu (1954) *Hamlets*. Like post-colonial India itself, all of these films are syncretistic in that they appropriate elements of British theater and Hollywood cinema without completely reconciling Western codes with indigenous linguistic and cultural traditions. In considering how to categorize such films, we can start from the straightforward assumption that all non–English language Shakespeare films are transpositional in that they literally transpose the setting of a given Shakespeare play to a different place and, not infrequently, time. But so does a film like *10 Things I Hate about You* (Gil Junger, 1999), one of the many innocuous "teensploi" treatments of Shakespeare—to cite Richard Burt's apt coinage—patented by Hollywood in the 1990s. Are we then to classify *Ten Things* in the same category as Sohrab Modi's *Khoon Ka Khoon* (*Hamlet*; 1935), the first feature-length Shakespeare film to emerge from India, created in the thick of the independence movement?

This is the point at which the gap in cultural understanding that separates Hollywood and even European adaptations of Shakespeare from Asian, South Asian, or African Shakespeare films makes classification particularly challenging. Hence, in seeking to categorize Modi's *Hamlet*, we must look to the Bazinian big picture of broad stylistic brushstrokes and technological breakthroughs, as well as the singular, culture-specific dialogue in which such a film participates. For example, were it not for its translation into Urdu, Modi's *Hamlet* could be considered conventional in that it is primarily a synthesis of existing British theatrical productions. However, when viewed in light of its release amidst rising tensions between agitators for Indian independence and British colonial rule following the Ghandi-led Salt March of 1930, this act of appropriation—even poaching—could easily be interpreted as oppositional. Of course, decisions as to which category best fits any of the films contained in this section may be made on a case-by-case basis, but I would argue that the categories I have yet to explore—oppositional and experimental—should be reserved for films that are *widely* readable in these terms. Hence, while Modi's *Hamlet* certainly can be read as oppositional, its content does not suggest an interpretation of Shakespeare's play that is visibly politicized in the way that, for example, Tunde Kelani's *Thunderbolt* (2000) is. More than a transpositional spin-off of *Othello* that features a cross-tribal romance in contemporary Nigeria, *Thunderbolt* adds a twist to Iago's duplicitous story of Desdemona's infidelity when Othello (Yinka) is prompted to place the curse of "Magun" (a sexually transmitted curse that, like AIDS, is popularly associated with certain death) upon Desdemona (Ngozi)—despite not having any proof of her betrayal. Shakespeare's story of a husband who neglects the truth before his very eyes thus becomes a parable of neglect that defines the policy of the West toward the AIDS crisis in Africa. Crucially, this "oppositional" spin on the content of Shakespeare's play would be recognizable to filmgoers not only in Europe and America but also in India and Southeast Asia, where the lack of availability of inexpensive, generic drugs for combating AIDS is a crisis of significant proportions. In other words, although interpretations of and attitudes toward such politicized readings of Shakespeare will vary from person to person and place to

place, films that are classified as oppositional must be legible as such to audiences beyond their immediate culture
of reception.

What, then, do we make of Shakespeare films that are
intentionally illegible, such as Peter Greenaway's adaptation of *The Tempest, Prospero's Books* (1992)? While this
obscurantist film could be classified as oppositional, I am
inclined to reserve this category for adaptations that
tamper with our expectations in ways that make us distinctly uncomfortable, not just perplexed, pensive, or put
off. In other words, oppositional films are distinguished by
affective "tampering," whereas experimental adaptations
like Greenaway's are born of *aesthetic* tampering; they are
adaptations in which the form drives the content rather
than, as with oppositional films, the other way around
(although, as the work of filmmakers like Derek Jarman
demonstrates, there is room for significant overlap between
these categories). Overwhelmingly represented in this category are musical and animated adaptations of Shakespeare. Whereas experimentation with genre, such as
adaptations in the style of the Western or film noir, belong
in the "transpositional" category, musicals and animated
films require more than changes of costume, scenery, and
landscape to make their experiments work: they require
additional *media*—ranging from human bodies engineered
for song and dance routines to the acetate used for cel
animation. However, while musical, animated, and even
pornographic adaptations are the most obvious candidates
for inclusion in the "experimental" category, so, too, are
technically avant-garde adaptations such as Greenaway's
version of *The Tempest* and Jean-Luc Godard's *King Lear*
(1987)—the latter offering an example of a spin-off contained in Chapter 4. Although neither film introduces new
media in the way that other adaptations in the experimental category do, both approach their *own* medium in
radically different terms—so much so that the spectator's
experience of the cinema is often defamiliarized. In short,
whereas "experimental" adaptations such as Kenneth
Branagh's *Love's Labours Lost* (2000) and films from
Shakespeare: The Animated Tales series (1992, 1996) interject interpretive codes drawn from other media alongside our existing cinematic vocabulary, films such as
Prospero's Books and *King Lear* demand the invention of
new terms altogether.

It is not a stretch to claim that in the age of home
theater, *everyone's* experience of cinema is defamiliarized
or, more accurately, hyperfamiliarized by technologies that
make reception both highly personal and portable—a
phenomenon that would seem to have reached its limit
with the UMD DVD, playable only on the four-inch movie
screens of individual Sony Playstations. "Filmgoing" is no
longer defined so much by the collective experience of
going to the cinema as it is about the convenience of films

coming to us in the privacy of our homes, cars, and internet
cafés. Does this mean that the BBC Shakespeare "video
drama" series (1978–85), which continues to introduce
students to the Bard on screen in secondary schools and
universities all over the world, qualifies for inclusion in this
section? And, on the other end of the spectrum, what do
we make of the interactive CD-ROM games of *Hamlet* and
Othello, for example, that have reinvented the concept of
what it means to perform or—better put—*play* Shakespeare for our contemporary gaming culture? The answer
rests not so much with determining the relevance of this
series to the categories of adaptation explored above but
with clarifying what is meant by "Shakespeare on screen."
Hence, if we began with the question "What is an adaptation?" then we must conclude, somewhat preposterously,
by asking, "What is a *film*?" What, in other words, is the
difference between the ever-expanding phenomenon of
Shakespeare on *screen*—from the silver screen to television
and computer screens—and a Shakespeare *film*?

Prior to the invention of videorecording technology
associated with the rise of television and, later, digital
video and home theater, the answer to this question is
straightforward: Shakespeare films exist exclusively on
celluloid, the medium onto which silver halide crystals
combine with photons to imprint images. Beginning in the
1950s, however, Shakespeare enjoys a prolific new life on
video in productions that, on the Internet Movie Database
(IMDB) and elsewhere, are commonly referred to as
"films." This is a misattribution not only because video-
recordings of Shakespeare's plays made during the pre-
digital era tend simply to recreate theatrical productions
in a sound studio for airing on TV, but also, more importantly, because analog recording technology makes it
virtually impossible to conceive of, let alone create,
Shakespeare in distinctly cinematic terms. Beyond the
obvious differences in quality of resolution and depth of
field that distinguish film's superior technical capabilities
from those of video, adaptations created for the old standard video monitor or television screen aspect ratio of four
units wide by three units high—as opposed to the standard
widescreen film ratio of sixteen by nine—become subject
to a kind of Hamletian claustrophobia, "bounded in a
nutshell" by a frame that makes even the most bravura
attempts at approximating filmic qualities fall, quite literally, flat. Nevertheless, the argument could reasonably be
made that the distinction between film and video is no
longer relevant, since films are now shown on TV and
videos can be digitized and marketed as "films." To address
this objection we would do best to return to the (personal)
taste test with which we began, for cinephiles know that
whereas films can be remastered and reformatted for television, the reverse is not true: no amount of technological
manipulation can change the look of analog video to make
it appear more like a film. In other words, in seeking to

answer the question as to what constitutes a film, the particular screen that a given Shakespeare adaptation is *originally* created for—though not necessarily subsequently shown on—makes all the difference. All of these elements account for the fact that the vast number of Shakespeare videos and made-for-TV "films" created between 1954 and the early 1990s are not included here.

Digitization changes these hard-and-fast distinctions between film and video adaptations, for in the fully digital era, we find ourselves in the thick of a filmmaking culture in which the stigmatization of video no longer applies. Particularly in the post-millennial age of high definition (HD), there is little separating celluloid Shakespeare from digital Shakespeare—other than that fetishized, grainy "film look" and, to be sure, a whole lot of money. For, lest we forget, a mere two minutes of film shooting costs (on average) fifty dollars, and any rejected footage cannot simply be recorded over the way it can be on a digital camera. Digitization has the advantage of being both efficient and affordable, and where there is little time and less money, Shakespeare has proven particularly popular—not only because his works are classified as "public domain" and, therefore, there is no estate to negotiate legalities or royalties with, but also because Shakespeare continues to be the storyteller of choice for the cinema's own ongoing adaptation process in the wake of technological and cultural "regime change." Whether or not digitization is equivalent to democratization is another matter, but there can be no doubt that the late 1990s witnessed the emergence of a new, more autonomous genre of Shakespearean filmmaking: "indie" adaptations. Admittedly, adaptations created on miniDV like Richard Griffin's *Titus Andronicus* (2000), Allison LiCalsi's spin-off *Macbeth: The Comedy* (2001), and The Derry Film Initiative's *Hamlet* (Stephen Cavanagh, 2004) do not have the same sharpness of resolution or perspectival depth associated with celluloid or, for that matter, with digital films captured on cameras like the Sony 24p HD Stohland. But the gap between film and video is narrowing because, from the standpoint of production, digital technology marks a quantum improvement upon the now-outmoded analog recording technology and, from the standpoint of reception, because filmmakers are creating adaptations with an eye to their availability for viewing in VHS and DVD formats or, as is the case with the *Star Wars: Macbeth* (Ben Concepcion, 1997), as MPEGs on the internet. For all its advantages, however, something must be said of digitization's emergent casualties—among them, the most recent film in the *Star Wars* prequel trilogy, *The Revenge of the Sith* (George Lucas, 2005), which, only hours after its much-anticipated opening night, had been leaked to an internet file-sharing network. Whether or not this distinctly post-modern form of piracy will lead to "bad quarto"–style versions of Shakespeare films remains quite literally to be seen.

Nevertheless, in the spirit of inclusion—the good, the bad, and the ugly—I have created an entry for *every* digital Shakespeare adaptation that I can verify the existence of (through tracking down stills, internet reviews, records of festival screenings, home page production data, or personal correspondence with the director) in an effort to honor this precedent-setting technology that promises to turn up more films every day.

In seeking to determine what stuff "films" are made of in the era of digital adaptation, a certain intractability continues to surround Shakespeare films that are intended for simultaneous distribution on TV and DVD, such as Uli Edel's "TNT Original Movie," *King of Texas* (2002), a western adaptation of *King Lear* with stunning, sweeping production values that has been released on DVD with widescreen formatting. For those who object to such adaptations being classified as films on the grounds that they were originally aired on TV, we need only recall that the earliest, along with some of the most recent, Shakespeare films originally "aired" in the theater. But for those who require further convincing that we, too, must adapt our understanding to an expanding horizon of film adaptation, I would point once again—this time by way of conclusion—to the mercurial work of Orson Welles, whose final Shakespeare film, *The Merchant of Venice* (1969), was originally recorded on celluloid *and* made for TV *and*, thanks to Welles's widow Oja Kodár, is currently available (in fragments only) as an "extra" on the Criterion Collection DVD of *"F" for Fake* (Orson Welles, 1976). I have included this film in hopes that one day the remaining negatives will surface. Perhaps they will be found in a basement, like the 1912 *Richard III*, which was discovered by accident in 1996 and turned out to be the first feature-length Shakespeare film ever made. Or perhaps the missing *Merchant* will turn up decades from now in an estate sale on eBay. Until then, as is the case with so many of Welles's Shakespeare films, we will have to settle for "piecing out its imperfections with our thoughts." But this is the beauty of the adaptation process in which we all participate, for Shakespeare's "remaines" on film—whether dreamt of in doublet and hose or digitized for downloading—remain quite literally in the eye of the beholder, and, as such, they conjure the aspiring filmmaker in us all.

NOTES

1. André Bazin, "Adaptation, or the Cinema as Digest," in *Bazin at Work*, ed. Bert Cardullo, trans. Alain Piette and Bert Cardullo (New York: Routledge, 1997), 49.

2. Kenneth S. Rothwell, *A History of Shakespeare on Screen: A Century of Film and Television* (Cambridge: Cambridge University Press, 1999); Colin MacCabe, "A Post-National European Cinema: A Consideration of Derek Jarman's *The Tempest* and *Edward II*," in *Shakespeare on Film*, ed. Robert Shaughnessy (New York: St. Martin's, 1998), 145–55; and Samuel Crowl,

Shakespeare at the Cineplex: The Kenneth Branagh Era (Athens: Ohio University Press, 2003).

3. *The Mystery Science Theater Hamlet* is based on Franz Peter Wirth's 1960 television adaptation starring Maximilian Schell, available on DVD in the *MST 3000* Collection, vol. 4.

BIBLIOGRAPHY

Bazin, André. "Adaptation, or the Cinema as Digest." In *Bazin at Work*, ed. Bert Cardullo, trans. Alain Piette and Bert Cardullo, 41–51. New York: Routledge, 1997.

Burt, Richard. "Te(e)n Things I Hate about Girlene Shakes-ploitation Flicks in the Late 1990s, or Not-So-Fast-Times at Shakespeare High." In *Spectacular Shakespeare: Critical Theory and Popular Cinema*, ed. Courtney Lehmann and Lisa S. Starks, 205–32. Madison, NJ: Fairleigh Dickinson University Press, 2002.

Crowl, Samuel. *Shakespeare at the Cineplex: The Kenneth Branagh Era*. Athens: Ohio University Press, 2003.

MacCabe, Colin. "A Post-National European Cinema: A Consideration of Derek Jarman's *The Tempest* and Edward II." In *Shakespeare on Film: Contemporary Critical Essays*, ed. Robert Shaughnessy, 145–55. New York: St. Martin's, 1998.

Rothwell, Kenneth S. *A History of Shakespeare on Screen: A Century of Film and Television*. Cambridge: Cambridge University Press, 1999.

ENTRIES PLAY BY PLAY, COURTNEY LEHMANN

For references to "Spin-offs," please see Chapter 4, "Film Spin-offs and Citations."

ANTONY AND CLEOPATRA

298 *Antony and Cleopatra*
1908. U.S. Vitagraph. Silent, b&w, c. 7 mins. Charles Kent.

Vitagraph promoted this dramatically condensed film of *Antony and Cleopatra* by focusing on the burgeoning medium's capacity to be literally in two places at once, pitching this one-reeler as "a fine picture of Roman pride and Eastern magnificence." The adaptation encompasses most of the major action of Shakespeare's play, though it begins with Antony falling in love "at first sight" with Cleopatra, played by the director's wife, Betty Kent. Typical of the Vitagraph Shakespeare films, Kent's adaptation was created entirely in a studio, but nevertheless proved a success with audiences who, unlike the reviewer quoted below, resisted fretting over discarded details in order to enjoy the condensed classic: "If Shakespeare could only realize the fate of the works he left behind, the modern use of them would cause his prophetic soul to weep. Just think of it! *Antony and Cleopatra* given in its entirety . . . in less than twenty minutes! What a vast difference between the older presentation and that represented by the modernized form of amusement" (*Moving Picture World*, November 7, 1908). Such mixed responses, which couple exclamatory wonder with horror, typified the reception of the earliest Shakespeare films.

299 *Cleopatra*
1910. France. Pathé. Silent, b&w, 9 mins. Ferdinand Zecca.

This film is a condensed version of Shakespeare's play focusing on the relations between Antony, Cleopatra, and Octavius. Given the extremely short running time, this Cleopatra (Madeline Roch) is represented as even more impetuous than her Shakespearean counterpart, poisoning (rather than merely beating) the messenger who delivers news of Antony's defeat. The film has German titles and was never released in the United States.

300 *Cleopatra*
1913. France. Pathé. Silent, b&w, c. 10 mins. Director unknown.

Robert Hamilton Ball indicates that this film is likely a reissued version of its 1910 predecessor, adding an impressive return across the desert on camels. With the standard bravado, Pathé pitched the short film as "a massive and glittering production showing the barbaric splendor of the Great Queen's court."

301 *Antony and Cleopatra* (Swiss title: *Antoine et Cléopatre*; Spanish title: *Marco Antonio y Cleopatra*)
1972. Spain/Switzerland/U.K. Transac/Izaro/Folie Films. Sound, col., 160 mins. Charlton Heston.

With its many "jumpcuts" between Egypt and Rome, as well as its montage of short, successive scenes, *Antony and Cleopatra* is, in many ways, Shakespeare's most "cinematic" play. By contrast, Heston's film is glacial in its pacing and leaden in its appearance, falling considerably short of the naturalistic impressions of Rome and Egypt that Shakespeare offers without the help of cinematic realism. More interesting than this unimaginative adaptation is the fact that it completes the trilogy of films in which Heston has played Mark Antony, delivering memorable portrayals of the young orator in two earlier films of *Julius Caesar* (David Bradley, 1950; Stuart Burge, 1969 [below]). Like Antony himself, Heston would have been better served by quitting while he was ahead.

302 *Kannaki*

2002. Malaysia. Mahesh Raj. Sound, col., feature length (exact length unknown). Jayaraaj Rajasekharan Nair.

Winner of several awards for music, cinematography, and direction, the most recent Shakespeare adaptation from the director of *Kaliyattam* (see *Othello* entries, this chapter) may also be his best. Set in contemporary Malaysia, *Kannaki* is the story of Manickan and Kannagi—the former, an expert cockfighter (undoubtedly with pun intended), the latter, a local beauty with whom the vast majority of the village is infatuated. Village tensions are at once precipitated and relieved through the practice of cockfighting; typically, Manickan fights on behalf of Choman and against the Gounder, but when rumors of Manickan's desire to marry Kannagi abound, Choman is outraged and goes public with an announcement proclaiming the betrothal of Manickan to his sister Kumudam. The film takes a variety of treacherous turns from this point forward, mirroring—in the relations between men—the serpentine plot of Shakespeare's play. Meanwhile, like Shakespeare's Cleopatra, who fears the prurient humiliations of her Roman captors, Kannagi, too, is the subject of rumor and trauma as the village belle-turned-pariah.

AS YOU LIKE IT

303 *As You Like It*

1908. U.S. The Kalem Company. Silent, b&w, 10 mins. Kenean Buel.

This film is noteworthy for its pastoral sequences, which employ out-of-doors shooting on the Ernest Seton Thompson estate in Connecticut. The gambit of using a conspicuous local attraction to incite audience curiosity, and even tourism, is repeated in August Blom's 1910 film of *Hamlet* (below), shot on location in Elsinore, Denmark. Despite the Kalem Company's good intentions, however, the film invited comparison with precisely the kind of mass entertainment it sought to transcend, as one critic indignantly implied: "The love scene in the forest between Rosalind and Orlando is acted in a lame manner. I have seen people hold hands in that fashion on the last Coney Island boat of a Saturday night, but in a Shakespeare play—never" (*Moving Picture World*, November 7, 1908).

304 *As You Like It*

1912. U.S. Vitagraph. Silent, b&w, 30 mins. Charles Kent.

Although this film uses sophisticated techniques such as cross-cutting and chiaroscuro effects, it is probably better known for casting the sixty-year-old Rose Coghlan as Rosalind. A common practice in early Shakespeare films that continues today, this three-reeler includes several interpolated scenes that are merely hinted at in the text, such as the depiction of each of the "seven ages" of man.

305 *Love in a Wood*

1915. U.K. London Film Company. Silent, b&w, c. 40+ mins. Maurice Elvey.

As its title suggests, this film is significant as one of the earliest modern-dress versions of screened Shakespeare. The characters and events are all drawn from Shakespeare's play, with modest variations. For example, the "court" plot is transferred to an estate, wherein the well-intentioned and authentically noble "Duke Squire" is ousted by "Fredericks," a character identified as nouveau riche and, therefore, potentially villainous to the strictly stratified class structure of early twentieth-century England. Of particular interest is the "updating" of Rosalind and Celia as gypsies—a decision that conspicuously dates the film, since the Romany people, long considered a menace to "civilized" society, are now virtually extinct in Great Britain.

306 *As You Like It*

1936. U.K. Inter-Allied Film Producers. Sound, b&w, 95 mins. Paul Czinner.

This million-dollar film features Laurence Olivier as a charming but ultimately unpersuasive comic hero. As Michael Anderegg astutely notes, Olivier is in many ways too talented to play Orlando, one of Shakespeare's less rewarding roles. Elisabeth Bergner, Paul Czinner's wife, is an uncharacteristically coy Rosalind. Like Emma Croft's Rosalind in the only adaptation of *As You Like It* made since Czinner's film (Christine Edzard, 1991 [below]), Bergner plays Rosalind/Ganymede with a nervous energy that renders her an even more elusive "catch" than she/he is in Shakespeare's play. The result is a surprising lack of chemistry among two future mainstays of the British star system.

DVD: features liner notes essay by Roy Hemming.

307 *As You Like It*

1991. U.K. Sands Films. Sound, col., 112 mins. Christine Edzard.

Edzard's film replaces Shakespeare's court with a firm in contemporary London while substituting the dilapidated dockyards of suburban Rotherhithe for the forest of Arden. Critics have almost unanimously panned this bleak adaptation, perhaps expecting something more lavish from a director who worked as an apprentice to Franco Zeffirelli, a veritable master of visual indulgence. Nevertheless, if *As You Like It* is sparse in terms of its production values, it does not mince the text, for this adaptation remains one of the few Shakespeare films that retains almost the entire play. Created at the end of the Reagan/Thatcher era, Edzard's adaptation has sparked controversy not only for its pallor but also for its polemic that, for some critics, is overstated. An example is the tableau of urban sprawl and agrarian decline evinced by the absurd figure of Corin, who wanders the dockyard with his lone sheep on a leash. Alternating between images of corporate cutthroats and the oil drum fires of "Arden's" homeless population, *As You Like It* is, at its best, a trenchant critique of gentrification schemes that masquerade as "urban renewal." Nor does the film's ending concede a glimmer of hope or the prospect of a brighter future, for the dual wedding of Rosalind with Orlando and Celia with Oliver takes place back at the firm in a room bizarrely decked in polyurethane, suggesting the artificial, forced nature of the concluding unions. Relentless in its effort to resist the romanticism of one of Shakespeare's most beloved romantic comedies, *As You Like It* offers a parable of Thatcherite neglect and, in the process, assays a new genre: the post-industrial pastoral.

308 *As You Like It*
1996. Russia/Wales. Soyuzmultifilm and Christmas Films. Sound, col., 27 mins. Alexei Karakov.

This film from *Shakespeare: The Animated Tales* series employs a variety of techniques, including explicit allusions to the comic strip genre and the Elizabethan woodcut, as Laurie Osborne perceptively notes, and even the painterly style of Olivier's metatheatrical film of *Henry V* (below), in order to render Shakespeare's comedy in pictoral terms. Significantly, despite being a short film intended for children, the characterization of Rosalind is relatively sophisticated, for her trademark physical and affective mobility achieves a fluidity in this film—born of the animated medium's painstakingly detailed modulations of action—impossible to approximate with real actors.

309 *As You Like It*
U.K./U.S. Shakespeare Film Company/HBO Films. In Production. Kenneth Branagh.

Having once described the Tuscan mise-en-scène of *Much Ado about Nothing* as a sultry combination of "heat, haze, and horseflesh," Kenneth Branagh characterizes his return to romantic comedy in *As You Like It* as a vision of "sumo, martial arts, and cherry blossoms" (*Screen Daily*, April 22, 2005). Inspired by nineteenth-century Japan, Branagh's film stars Kevin Kline, who played Bottom in Michael Hoffman's lush Hollywood adaptation of *A Midsummer Night's Dream* and, as with all of Branagh's Shakespeare adaptations, will invite comparison with Laurence Olivier's 1936 version, directed by Paul Czinner (above).

THE COMEDY OF ERRORS

310 *The Boys from Syracuse*
1940. U.S. Universal Pictures. Sound, b&w, 74 mins. A. Edward Sutherland.

A musical adaptation of *The Comedy of Errors*, this film is based on the highly successful Broadway musical by George Abbot, Richard Rogers, and Lorenz Hart. Created

during the era in which it was customary for musicals to segregate black "specialty" performers from the rest of the cast, the film updates much of Shakespeare's language to New York–style slang but maintains the anachronistic title of "slave" for the two Dromios. Yet this title proves oddly fitting given the film's emphasis on work and labor, which is evinced by the retention of only four of the songs from the original Broadway musical: "This Can't Be Love," "Falling in Love with Love," "Sing for Your Supper," and "Oh Diogenes." For example, in the second verse of "This Can't Be Love," Shakespeare himself emerges as a sadistic playwright who tortures his characters for a buck—a suggestion that is borne out not only by *Romeo and Juliet* but also by *The Comedy of Errors*: "Though your cousin loved my cousin Juliet / Loved her with a passion much more truly yet / Some poor playwright / Wrote their drama just for fun, / It won't run!" Similarly, as its title implies, "Sing for Your Supper" continues this theme of making a living by any means necessary, cleverly linking the Renaissance system of patronage to the American entrepreneurial spirit in its concluding lines: "Songbirds are not dumb, / They don't buy a crumb / Of bread, / It's said. / So sing and you'll be fed." Ironically, the film failed to achieve its projected gross at the box office, despite its efforts to capitalize on the success of its Broadway run. See also entry 587.

311 *Do Dooni Char*
1968. India. Bimal Roy. Sound, b&w, length unknown. Debu Sen.

Known in its posterity as the "original" Hindi adaptation of *The Comedy of Errors*, this musical version stars Bollywood legend Kishore Kumar in the role of Shakespeare's troubled twins.

312 *Los Gemelos Alborotados (The Alborotados Twins)*
1981. Mexico. Producciones Aguila. Sound, col., 85 mins. Mário Hernández.

Like its immediate predecessor, *The Boys from Syracuse* (above), this film is also a musical adaptation. Set in rural Mexico, *Los Gemelos Alborotados* features two Gúmaros and two Chons, separated since boyhood by bandits. Although later spin-offs customarily represent one set of twins as "good" and the other as some shade of "evil," Hernández's adaptation uses black and white hats to distinguish the two Gúmaros for the benefit of the audience and, more cleverly, to parody the quintessentially American film genre of the Western, in which there are no "good" Mexicans. Quite a departure for Hernández, whose lengthy career is associated more with the *El Topo* (Alejandro Juderowsy, 1970) tradition of shoot-'em-up Latino exploitation films than it is with frothy musical comedy, *Los Gemelos Alborotados* marked the beginning of the crossover trend in the Mexican films of the 1990s, many of which strove to surmount the gunslinger stereotype by appealing to Tejano culture through films focusing on family drama (*Mi Familia*; Gregory Nava, 1995), magical realism (*Like Water for Chocolate*; Alfonso Arau, 1993), and pop icons (*Selena*; Gregory Nava, 1997). Hernández has since worked to further the careers of young Latino filmmakers as head of the Cinema Project based in UCLA's Chicano Studies Research Center.

DVD: no extras listed.

313 *Angoor*
1982. India. A. R. Movies. Sound, col., 170 mins.
Sampooran Singh Gulzar.

Mirroring Shakespeare's plot involving two pairs of twins, each composed of a master and servant, this story of misrecognition is set in Mumbai, where the unmarried Ashok and Bahadur arrive to purchase a grape field (Angoor) and are repeatedly mistaken for their married counterparts, also named Ashok and Bahadur. Gulzar served as the lyricist for the musical adaptation on which *Angoor* is based (Debu Sen's 1968 *Do Dooni Char*), which received only a lukewarm reception at the box office but has since become something of a cult film among Bollyphiles. Perhaps based on his earlier experience with Sen's adaptation of *The Comedy of Errors*, Gulzar seems particularly determined to make this Shakespearean comedy outrageously entertaining, despite being known for his more sensitive, serious films. In *Angoor*, this mission is accomplished due, in part, to the outstanding performances of Sanjeev Kumar (the two Ashoks) and Devan Varma (the two Bahadurs) but mainly due to Gulzar's transpositional brilliance. An Urdu language adaptation of *The Comedy of Errors*, *Angoor* is a particularly rich example of Bollywood's syncretistic approach to Shakespeare. This theme is announced even before we enter the film proper, when Gulzar engages in a post-colonial gamble by doctoring the bust of Shakespeare to make the Bard's features more "Indian" looking. This opening gesture sets the tone for the film's subsequent acts of appropriation, modernization, and even iconoclasm. For example, the play's multiple references to the confusion associated with dreaming, typified in lines like "What, was I married to her in my dream?" (2.2.182) are altered—to great comic effect—to phrases such as "Did I have a dream of radish parothas?" Similarly, antiquated accusations of witchcraft in Shakespeare's play are updated to charges of "smoking"—specifically, ganga and bhang. Gulzar's entertaining potpourri also includes the song "Preetam Aaa Milo," suggestive of Rodgers and Hart's influential musical adaptation of Shakespeare's play (above). But Gulzar reserves one final gesture of cultural cross-pollination for the conclusion of his film, wherein the Indianized figure of Shakespeare resurfaces—this time with a twist. No longer the literary monument that presides over the beginning of *Angoor*, this Bard has become the matinee idol of the silver screen, sending us off with a wink that invokes one of filmed Shakespeare's "primal scenes": Mary Pickford's wink in Sam Taylor's 1929 *Taming of the Shrew* (below). See also entry 589.

DVD: full screen, English subtitles.

314 *The Comedy of Errors*
2000. U.S. Bob Schulenberg. Sound, col., length unknown. Wendell Sweda.

Possibly still in search of a distributor, this film is significant as the only attempt to adapt Shakespeare's play to the screen using its historical setting.

315 *Do Dooni Char*
India. In production. Anant Mahadevan.

Mahadevan promises that his latest film will hearken back to the success of Gulzar's *Angoor*, despite its titular affinity with its predecessor, *Do Dooni Char* (both above). Sammir Dattani will play the Antipholus characters in Samir Kohli's screenplay adaptation of *Comedy of Errors*, which, Mahadevan promises, has never before "been interpreted in this way." See also entry 593.

CORIOLANUS

316 *Coriolano, Eroe Senza Patria (Thunder of Battle)*
1963. Italy/France. Dorica Film/Explorer Film 58/ Comptoir Français du Film. Sound, col., 101 mins. Georgio Ferroni.

Based on a combination of Plutarch's *Lives* and Shakespeare's play, this film stars Gordon Scott, better known as one of the many screen Tarzans, as Coriolanus. Because of its significant changes to Shakespeare's plot—most notably, the interjection of a love story and its happy ending—this adaptation is best classified as a spin-off, and is included here because it is the only screen version of *Coriolanus* ever attempted.

CYMBELINE

317 *Cymbeline*
1913. U.S. Edwin Thanhouser. Silent, b&w, 41 mins. Frederick Sullivan.

This *Cymbeline* is a signature film in the series of Shakespeare silents produced by Edwin Thanhouser. Replete with impressive external ensemble scenes and action shots, this adaptation distinguishes Thanhouser, working with Sullivan, as one of the great early *metteurs-en-scène*. The adaptation is significant as one of the first, if not the very first, Shakespeare film to be created in Hollywood. *Moving Picture World* generously described it as deserving of "great credit for seeking to aim high. Such pictures, though there may be blemishes in the execution, strengthen our hope in the future of kinematography" (April 5, 1913).

Remarkably, a print of *Cymbeline* survived the fire that claimed so many other Thanhouser classics.

318 *Cymbeline*
1925. Germany. Sender Freies Berlin. Silent, b&w, length unknown. Ludwig Berger.

Though this film is now lost, it is only natural that Ludwig Berger, well-known in Germany for his adaptation of operettas, ballet, and theater, should try his hand at Shakespeare shortly before joining his colleague Max Reinhardt in Hollywood in 1928. His choice of *Cymbeline*, one of the least frequently adapted films, is perfectly in keeping with his interest in the fantastical and exotic, culminating in his 1940 film, *The Thief of Bagdad*.

HAMLET

319 *Le Duel d'Hamlet*
1900. France. Phono-Cinéma-Théâtre. Silent, b&w, 3 mins. (174 ft.). Clément-Maurice Gratioulet (prod.).

Presented during the Paris Exposition of 1900, this film features the duel scene in which Sarah Bernhardt plays Hamlet, included here as a precedent for future cross-dressed Hamlets (see *Hamlet: The Drama of Vengeance* [1920] and *Intikam Melegi: Kadin Hamlet* [1978, both below]) and for its use of sounds effects, courtesy of Lioretographe sound cylinders. See also entry 595.

320 *Hamlet*
1907. France. Star Film. Silent, b&w, 10 mins. (574 ft.). George Méliés.

George Méliés cast himself as *Hamlet* in this dramatically condensed film that opens with the graveyard scene and ends with the duel scene. Of particular interest is what lies between these Shakespearean bookends: Hamlet sees not only his father's ghost, which prompts him to pursue revenge, but also Ophelia's ghost. A truly precocious example of cinema's ability to render poetry pictorially, this Hamlet attempts to embrace Ophelia as she throws flowers to him from her garland. The decision to feature two ghosts where Shakespeare's play calls for one demonstrates the extent to which cinema's "deficiency"—its capacity for representing only the remnants of live action rather than the thing itself—proved to be the source of its most potent special effects. See also entry 597.

321 *Amleto*
1910. Italy. Cines. Silent, b&w, 9 mins. Mario Caserini.

This film contains the major plot elements of Shakespeare's play (the ghost's appearance, the players' re-enactment of the murder, Polonius's accidental murder, Ophelia's implied drowning, the gravedigger scene, and the confrontation with Laertes). Cines, a major player in the European market, also produced an even shorter version of *Hamlet* in 1908, but this film is more a series of fragments than a continuous segment.

322 *Hamlet*
1910. U.K. Barker. Silent, b&w, c. 20 mins. William George Barker.

This studio-based film is the first British *Hamlet*, created in a mere six hours. In keeping with such thrift, the cast, as Robert Hamilton Ball observes, was chosen not for their distinguished acting careers (they had no such thing) but, rather, based on first impressions and other superficial criteria: the Ghost, for example, was picked for being tall, while Ophelia was selected because she could swim.

323 *Hamlet*
1910. France. Éclipse. Silent, b&w, 10 mins. Henri Desfontaines.

Unlike the vast majority of early *Hamlet* films, this—a jewel in the French *série d'art*—survives, appropriately, in fragments in the New York Museum of Modern Art.

324 *Hamlet*
1910. Denmark. Nordisk. Silent, b&w, 12 mins. August Blom.

Shot on location at Kronborg Castle in Helsingør (Elsinore), Denmark, this adaptation is an early example of the Scandinavian talent for open-air filming. Olef Jensen came up with the idea of shooting *Hamlet* in its historical location as an incentive to tourism. Actual soldiers stationed at the fortress were used as extras, adding an almost documentary feel to the already-inspiring realism of the castle environs. A bit too inspired, Blom got carried away with his camera and created an adaptation that was initially some 12,000 feet. Sadly for film historians, he was persuaded by Nordisk President Ole Olesen to cut the final product down to a single reel.

325 *Hamlet*
1913. U.K. Cecil Hepworth. Silent, b&w, 59 mins. E. Hay Plumb.

As with much of early filmed Shakespeare, this *Hamlet* is more a recording of a play than a film. Nevertheless, its impressive length and use of location shooting distinguish it as a transitional film, situated between theatrical modes and cinematic mise-en-scènes. Hamlet is played by the preeminent Sir Johnston Forbes-Robertson, whose performance as an effete, highly guarded prince offers an ideal illustration of the Victorian tradition that Kenneth Rothwell has dubbed "Hamletism." Significantly, Forbes-Robertson was sixty years old at the time of filming.

326 *Amleto*
1914. Italy. Società Ambrosio. Silent, b&w, length unknown. Arrigo Frusta.

The mystery surrounding this elusive film is greater than Hamlet's own. Robert Hamilton Ball suggests that the difficulty in pinning down accounts of this adaptation may stem from the fact that it may have been created under a different title, *The Mad Prince*, an impressive seven-reeler that is also lost.

327 *Amleto*
1917. Italy. Rodolfi-Film. Silent, b&w, 40 mins.
Eleuterio Rodolfi.

Though not a remarkable film, this *Hamlet* is a milestone in the history of adaptation as one of the earliest concerted efforts to render Shakespeare's language in cinematographic terms, making particularly deft use of close-ups to track Hamlet's "antic disposition." More interesting than Hamlet's behavior, however, is Ophelia, who is invested with a dogged independence rarely emphasized in even contemporary, "enlightened" films of the play. For example, she teasingly rejects a necklace that Hamlet offers her before embracing it; later, after she has assured Laertes that she will ignore Hamlet's advances, she kisses the necklace right under his nose—clearly indicating contrary intentions. Finally, her death is definitively represented as an accident, the product of her falling into the stream rather than wading—Virginia Woolf style—deliberately toward her demise.

328 *Hamlet: The Drama of Vengeance*
1920. Germany. Art Film. Silent, b&w, 73 mins.
Svend Gade.

This adaptation, based on a combination of the sources used in Shakespeare's *Hamlet* and the anonymous German play *Fratricide Punished* (1781), as well as Edward P. Vining's theory (contained in his Yale master's thesis of 1881) that Hamlet was a woman, stands alone as one of the first films to truly experiment with the notion that the marriage of Shakespeare and celluloid was not about merely recording reality but creating it. Hence, this film, heavily influenced by German Expressionism and the emergence of the New Woman, tells the story of a princess Hamlet, whose impenetrable mystery stems from the fact that she is a woman—secretly in love with Horatio (who, in turn, is in love with Ophelia), and trapped in a man's clothing and occupation. Ironically, despite this Hamlet's feminization, he/she proves to be far more capable of revenge than his/her Shakespearean counterpart, killing Claudius by setting his room on fire in the midst of the king's drunken revels. In fact, in this film, Hamlet's mother proves more treacherous than her new husband, for it is she who poisons the cup offered to slake Hamlet's thirst. Played by the incomparable Asta Nielsen, Hamlet survives the sinister plots of his/her treacherous family only to die at the hands of Laertes's rapier, and only then is his/her mystery literally plucked out by Horatio, who, in a scene more amusing than heart-wrenching, discovers the dying Hamlet's distinctly female breasts, as well as her unrequited love for him, too late. As a side note, an easily missed example of Nielsen's consummate grace as a performer occurs in the scene wherein Hamlet revises the warrant for his death; in the

Asta Nielsen plays Hamlet in Sven Gade's *Hamlet* (1920). Courtesy of Douglas Lanier.

midst of penning the document by candlelight, Hamlet's quill momentarily catches fire, at which point Nielsen calmly blows it out and continues writing.

Though considered by many to be more at home in the spin-off genre, *Hamlet: The Drama of Vengeance* contains most of the major events of Shakespeare's play, including Hamlet's schooling at Wittenberg, his return home to witness how his father's funeral banquet furnishes his mother's wedding feast, the murmuring of Old Hamlet's ghost beyond the grave, the play within a play, the murder of Polonius behind the arras, Hamlet's exile in the company of Rosencrantz and Guildenstern, his alteration of the death warrant, his return to find Ophelia dead, the gravedigging scene, Hamlet's leap into the grave after Laertes, the final duel, and Fortinbras's entry to claim the throne—not to mention several direct quotations of Shakespeare's play translated into German, such as Hamlet's indictment "Mother, you have my father much offended." The key differences involve the aforementioned love triangle, the conversion of enmity between young Fortinbras and Hamlet to friendship, the materialization of the snake pit from which Claudius plucks his murder "weapon," the manner of Hamlet's revenge, and Gertrude's revenge plot against Hamlet. The film also includes a particularly amusing scene in which Hamlet is examined by a doctor to determine whether or not he is feigning madness. Interestingly, in what amounts to a distinctly feminist parody of the assumption that the smaller female brain equates with lesser intelligence, the doctor leaves the scene entirely puzzled, concluding that "his brain is too small for someone of such intelligence." Indeed, the joke is on him.

329 *Hamlet* alias *Khoon Ka Khoon (Blood for Blood)*
1935. India. Movietone and Stage Film Company. Sound, b&w, 122 mins. Sohrab Modi.

Based on a stage production and spoken in Urdu, this Victorian adaptation of *Hamlet* is significant not only as one of the earliest Shakespearean "talkies" but also as the film that marked Naseem Bano's acting debut. Several stills of the film survive to suggest the extent to which Modi's film, as with Sahu's later adaptations (below), sought to juxtapose indigenous cultural traditions with Western codes. The most provocative example of this syncretistic approach is the elimination of Ophelia as an audience member at Hamlet's production of *The Murder of Gonzago*, since the public display of affection between aristocratic women and their suitors was unacceptable within the prevailing modes of cultural decorum. See also entry 628.

330 *Hamlet*
1948. U.K. Two Cities. Sound, b&w, 153 mins. Laurence Olivier.

The only adaptation of a Shakespeare film (discounting the *Romeo and Juliet* spin-off, *Shakespeare in Love*) to win an Oscar for best picture, this is perhaps Olivier's most memorable role, one for which he received the Academy award for best actor. The stark, engraving-style quality of Olivier's mise-en-scène poses striking contrast to his actorly vision of Hamlet as indecisive to a fault, an interpretation that is announced in the interpolated statement that precedes the film proper: "This is the tragedy of a man who could not make up his mind." Tight framing, deep focus, chiaroscuro lighting, and serpentine interiors make this film particularly apt for psychoanalytic interpretation, as does the heavy-handed establishing shot, repeated at the end of the film, of Gertrude's bedchamber. The film's hyper-Oedipalization is underscored by an extraordinarily young Gertrude (Eileen Herlie), who lavishes several lingering kisses on her son's lips—an interpretive decision that is taken to an extreme in Zeffirelli's adaptation (below), wherein Mel Gibson's Hamlet and Glenn Close's Gertrude engage in an extended open-mouthed kiss following Hamlet's violent pinning of and (fully clothed) thrusting into his mother on her bed. More consistent than Zeffirelli's reading, however, Olivier's film culminates in Gertrude's suicidal display of maternal instinct, as she consumes the poisoned drink—aware that it is intended for

Hamlet—in an effort to spare her beloved son. A surprising success in America, the film tied with *Key Largo* for box office returns, perhaps owing to the concerted efforts of its marketing team, which launched a number of books—including an early example of the now-popular "Making Of" genre—as well as a record containing speeches and excerpts from the film's musical score. See also entries 639, 650, 705, 735, 1526, and 2199.

DVD: full-screen format.

331 *Khoon-E-Nahag (Hamlet)*
1954. India. Hindustan Ehitra. Sound, b&w, 127 mins. Kishore Sahu.

What is most fascinating about this important film is the fact that despite being a shot-by-shot reconstruction of Laurence Olivier's *Hamlet* (above), its origins in Bombay's unique cinematic culture, as well as India's post-revolutionary period, are inscribed in a variety of directorial gambits—not the least of which is, of course, the play's translation into Urdu. The upshot is a film that is as much about cultural collision as it is about assimilation, as indigenous codes clash with the Western literary canon.

332 *Der Rest ist Schweigen (The Rest Is Silence)*
1959. West Germany. Freie Film Produktion GmbH & Co. and Real-Film GmbH. Sound, b&w, 103 mins. Helmut Kautner.

A critical figure in German post-war cinema (and wrongly described as a Third Reich filmmaker), Helmut Kautner was one of the few directors working in the Nazi era who resisted the propaganda imperative mandated by Joseph Goebbels. His films, predominantly comedies, domestic intrigues, and romances, subscribed to a looser, more spontaneous narrative style than that legislated by the Nazi demand for National Socialist transparency, while often encoding subtle critiques of the Reich by juxtaposing comic revelations with, for example, the sound of air raid sirens. Kautner turned to more explicit cultural critiques in the post-war period. Shakespeare's *Hamlet* thus becomes the perfect vehicle for Kautner's obsession with the specter of historical guilt, as Hamlet represents an entire culture haunted by the sins of its fathers. Prefiguring the themes of much later adaptations such as Michael Almereyda's millennial *Hamlet* (below), this adaptation recreates the gloomy Dane as the son of a deceased corporate executive, featuring playful touches such as a scene in which the Hamlet character, named John H. Claudius, contacts the ghost via telephone. Significantly, the actor who played Hamlet (Hardy Krüger) was a former member of Hitler Youth who later voiced his resistance to the regime; meanwhile, Polonius's family, the von Pohls, evokes the ghost of Hitler through their Austrian identity. Kautner himself played a minor role in the film. See also entry 644.

333 *Hono-o no shiro (Throne of Flame)*
1960. Japan. Daiei Studios and Toei Co. Ltd. Sound, col., 98 mins. Tai Kato.

Kato's adaptation offers a bold transposition of Shakespeare's play to the yazuka genre, which emerged, in part, as the Japanese response to catastrophic defeat in World War II. The yazuka tradition strives to emulate the noble samurai culture of the past while satisfying the need for contemporary sources of Japanese honor—hence, yazuka films feature gangs of modern-day warriors who are uncompromising, fiercely nationalistic, and profoundly anti-Western. In this context, Tai Kato's famous adaptation of *Hamlet* becomes a form of invasion in its own right, for Kato converts a preeminent icon of Western culture into a spokesperson for "pure" Japanese values of loyalty, courage, and self-sacrifice. Despite the seemingly poor fit between Hamlet's pensive, sedentary disposition and this extremely violent, action film genre, other aspects of yazuka films, such as their focus on outsiders intent on reforming a corrupt system, are perfectly attuned to Hamlet's desire to overthrow the decadent Danish court. Uncannily, American director John Foster observes that his own yazuka knockoff, *Kyoto Nocturnes, Part One: Elegant Slaughter* (2005), was inspired by *Hamlet's* deft modulation of the divide between action and introspection, violence and spirituality: "Believe it or not, the reason I decided to mix the yazuka and horror genres in 'Elegant Slaughter' was because of Shakespeare! To me, Shakespeare uses the supernatural elements to reveal his character's [*sic*] desires and fears. And, of course, supernatural elements just make a story more interesting" (www.dragonsdenuk.com/ kyoto_interview.htm).

334 *Gamlet (Hamlet)*
1964. USSR. Lenfilm. Sound, b&w, 140 mins. Grigori Kozintsev.

This film presents a highly political and imaginative interpretation of Hamlet, making Hamlet a man of action who is nevertheless alienated at court. The opening sequence performs a stunning interpretation of Hamlet's view that "the time is out of joint." Hamlet rushes back to court on horseback even as black flags of mourning are being unfurled at Elsinore castle. Claudius's speech is delivered by a herald and then translated by ambassadors (see the similar use of French and a translator for France in Kosintsev's *King Lear* [1969]). When we get to Claudius giving the rest of his speech to his court, it's not clear how much time, if any, has passed. Is his speech continuous? Or is he giving it at a later date? Nor is it clear who is in command of Elsinore. Who is giving the orders that the flags be unfurled? Cannons fired? The proclamation read? When Claudius finally addresses Hamlet, who we are led to think will be first seen at court after Claudius's speech as the camera tracks him moving right, down the table of courtiers, Hamlet's chair is empty. He's already off. The opening sequence also moves from open external spaces (a shot of the sea, a long shot of the land) to increasingly shut-in interior spaces (the castle gates drop as the music gets ominous) to suggest that Denmark is indeed a prison. Shots of the ocean recur (see somewhat similar shots of a river with whitewater in Kosintsev's *King Lear* [below]). Dmitry Shostakovich's soundtrack score produces lots of fascinating effects. For example, a mechanical theme played on a harpsichord that sounds like a music box is heard when Ophelia first appears, instructed in a dance. Later, when she is mad, the same music and dance appear, as if she were on automatic pilot. The "Making Of" documentary on the Russico DVD is very informative.

Two-disc DVD with extras from Russico. English or Russian with English subtitles.

335 *Hamile (The Tongo Hamlet)*
1964. Ghana. Ghana Film Industry Corporation. Sound, b&w, 120 mins. Terry Bishop.

Set among the Frafra people north of Ghana and based on a stage production by the University of Ghana School of Music and Drama, this modern-dress version of Shakespeare's *Hamlet* is significant as Ghana's first feature film. See also entry 651.

336 *Hamlet*
1969. U.K. Woodfall. Sound, col., 117 mins. Tony Richardson.

This intense, tightly framed film dominated by close and medium shots takes Hamlet at his word when he claims that he could be "bounded in a nutshell." The Tony Richardson–Anthony Hopkins pairing is one of the most combustible Hamlet and Claudius combinations of all time, and is based on the Roundhouse Theatre production of 1969.

337 *A Hercança*
1970. Brazil. Longfilm Produrora Cinematografica. Sound, col., 90 mins. Ozualda Ribiera Candeias.

Portuguese for "inheritance," *Hercança* retells Shakespeare's *Hamlet* in the context of Brazilian culture. The adaptation follows the plot of *Hamlet* closely and, in keeping with Latin American tradition, emphasizes the theme of family honor and the problem of patriarchal succession. Hence, whereas Shakespeare's play identifies the characters by name, Candeias's film situates them in terms of their familial relationship to Hamlet (here "Omelete"): for example, Gertrude becomes "Mãe de Omelete" and Claudius becomes "Tio." This approach to *Hamlet* through the lens of "inheritance" may have influenced the recent Danish spin-off of the same title (Per Fly, 2003). See also entry 662.

338 *Dans la Poussière du Soleil (Lust in the Sun; Lust in the Dust)*
1971. France and Spain. IMF Pictures and Kerfrance Production. Sound, col., 84 mins. Richard Balducci.

One of the four-hundred and fifty spaghetti Westerns to surface between 1962 and 1976, this adaptation closely parallels the plot of *Hamlet*, adding Mediterranean-inspired "spice" to the Nordic temperaments of Shakespeare's gloomy Danes. Interestingly, the extraordinary number of spaghetti Westerns made during this period (a few of them Shakespearean) emerged in response to the distinctly Southern Italian demand that shaped their conventions, for at this time, spectators from "the boot" of Italy attended films in greater numbers than any other Europeans. Perhaps the most explicit connection between Shakespeare and this unlikely genre of adaptation is the fact that Ennio Morricone wrote the score to accompany the recently rediscovered, first feature-length Shakespeare film (the 1912 *Richard III* [below]) as well as scores for many Sergio Leone films. The film's three titles—*Lust in the Dust, Lust in the Sun, and Dans la Poussière du Soleil*—uncannily suggest the three texts of *Hamlet*: Q1, Q2, and the First Folio. See also entry 664.

339 *O Jogo da Vida e da Morte*
1971. Brazil. Futura Films. Sound, col., 98 mins. Mario Kuperman.

Set in suburban São Paolo, this adaptation closely parallels the plot of Shakespeare's play, transferring the overt theme of political corruption to the less avowedly political but equally inimical "underworld" of South American drug trafficking. Significantly, Shakespeare functions as something of a bridge in the director's career, for the realism with which the camera tells this story seems to have inspired Kuperman's more recent turn to documentary shorts, such as *O Rio Ribeira de Iguape* (1998). See also entry 665.

340 *Hamlet*
1976. U.K. Essential Productions and Royal College of Art. Sound, col., 65 mins. Celestino Coronada.

Originally shot on video, this free adaptation presents Hamlet as someone whose manic disposition is born of his literally split personality, which Coronada simulates by casting twins to play him. Announcing the film's privileging of the visual rather than verbal dimensions of Shakespeare's play, Coronada includes only the opening lines of Hamlet's most famous soliloquy, "To be or not to be," as an establishing "shot" with which to begin his film. Appropriately, the opening frame represents two eyes peering out at the spectator, an image that effectively positions the audience as honorary Rosencrantz and Guildenstern figures, the hired hands—and eyes—assigned to pluck out Hamlet's mystery by any means necessary. A scream, the first of many disconcerting off-screen sound

effects, follows to create a disturbing disjunction between what our eyes can see and what our ears can hear. Subsequently, our sense of a play with which virtually every theatergoer, to some degree or another, is familiar is further fractured and alienated by Coronada's decision to divide the role of Hamlet into two parts, adapting the perceptual schemes of psychomachian allegory to the philosophical tradition of the mind-body split: Hamlet's bodily persona is manifested by a black costume occupied by one of the twins, while his psychological being is portrayed by his white-costumed brother. Equally provocative is Coronada's decision to double the parts of Ophelia and Gertrude in order to accentuate Hamlet's unresolved Oedipal complex, a casting choice that makes explicit Hamlet's implicit equation of mother and lover in Shakespeare's play. Less Shakespeare, perhaps, than Coronada, this film is a cinematographic tour de force that nevertheless offers a compelling reading—and an ingenious rendering—of Hamlet's madness. See also entry 675.

341 *Intikam Melegi: Kadin Hamlet (Angel of Vengeance: The Female Hamlet)*
1977. Turkey. Ugur Film. Sound, col., 86 mins. Metin Erksan.

Rather strange bedfellows, to be sure, this adaptation features a sexy, Turkish female Hamlet and a mise-en-scène that is more evocative of the era of its making than of its country of origin, as high fashion and the wa-wa sound of guitars establish the priority of time—the 1970s—over place. Combining the melodramatic sentiments of afternoon soaps with panoramic vistas and gunslinging pursuit scenes reminiscent of the Russian "Westerns" of Nikita Mikhailkov, this adaptation suffers from a missing throughline. Unlike Svend Gade's 1920 *Hamlet: The Drama of Vengeance* (above), which similarly features a female protagonist, the premise of Hamlet's sex change in this film is never explained, functioning more as a source of extra-diegetic intrigue than thematic resonance or plot advancement. Nevertheless, a certain degree of consistency is supplied by changes made to the complementary roles of Rosencrantz and Guildenstern, who are also converted to women, as well as Ophelia, played by a man in this film who, like his Shakespearean counterpart, is prone to hysteria and drowns himself in the wake of Hamlet's perceived rejection. The feigned, even contrived nature of Hamlet's insanity in this adaptation is emphasized by a series of interpolated scenes intended to convince Hamlet's enemies of her mental deficiency. Perhaps the most intriguing example of this approach—one that underscores the fact that Hamlet is merely *performing* the role of madwoman—is the scene in which she dons a tuxedo and proceeds to conduct an open-air "orchestra" comprised of instruments and chairs, but no musicians. See also entry 677.

342 *Hamlet*
1990. U.S./U.K./Spain. Warner Bros. Sound, col.,
135 mins. Franco Zeffirelli.

Compared with Zeffirelli's earlier period films, the stark medieval setting and monochromatic hues featured in this adaptation signal a marked departure from his typical flair for costume drama. Mel Gibson stars in this thought-provoking, supremely Oedipalized *Hamlet*, which begins with an interpolated scene in the royal mausoleum in which the camera triangulates between Hamlet, Claudius, and Gertrude to accentuate the Freudian "family romance" theme. Distractions from this intense family focus are excised from the film—the elimination of the Fortinbras plot is a case in point. Another distinctive feature is the film's emphasis on surveillance, which makes this *Hamlet* even more claustrophobic than Olivier's tightly framed, almost imploding adaptation (above). The most memorable moment by far is the long, sensual kiss between Hamlet and Gertrude, which she initiates in an effort to ameliorate his rage as he mock rapes her on the bed. As several critics have noted, such a conspicuous use of Shakespeare as a star vehicle means that cinematic intertextuality provides almost as many cues for reading this film as does Shakespeare's play, to the extent that this *Hamlet* is perhaps best described as *Mad Max* meets *Fatal Attraction* (George Miller, 1979; Adrian Lyne, 1987).

DVD: features widescreen anamorphic format and introduction from Mel Gibson, as well as several "Making Of" pieces such as "Hamlet: An Actor's Journey" and "Mel Gibson: To Be or Not to Be."

343 *Hamlet*
1992. Russia/Wales. Soyuzmultifilm and Christmas Films. Sound, col., 25 mins. Natalya Orlova.

A remarkable example of the stained-glass animation technique for which only Orlova is known, this *Hamlet* was the only film in the original series *Shakespeare: The Animated Tales* to win an Emmy award. Like the use of puppetry in the animated *Tempest* (Stanislav Sokolov, 1992 [below]), this adaptation of *Hamlet* cannot help but embed messages in its medium. Because of the nature of Orlova's animation technique, in which a single pane of glass supplies the "stage" for the entire film and therefore contains memories, indeed physical traces, of the preceding scenes, this adaptation offers a particularly convincing embodiment of Hamlet's affliction with memory.

344 *Hamlet*
1996. U.K. Castle Rock/Columbia. Sound, col., 242 mins. Kenneth Branagh.

In many ways the polar opposite of Olivier's *Hamlet* (above), Branagh's adaptation is characterized by wide open spaces and bright lighting, and is the first film to offer the full text of Shakespeare's play (and then some—Branagh adds scenes, such as Hamlet and Ophelia in

flagrante). Yet the most distinctive feature of this epic 70mm film is the look-alike effect it generates between Hamlet (Branagh) and Claudius (Derek Jacobi), whose "face time" far exceeds the role allotted to him in Shakespeare's play. This casting arrangement is the stuff of a "play within" in its own right, as a subtle means for Branagh to at once admire and, in the Freudian spirit of *Hamlet* itself, kill off the theatrical father—indeed, the former Hamlet who inspired Branagh's pursuit of the Shakespearean mantle in the first place. In contrast to the other members of the court, Hamlet and Claudius are the only two figures who have bleach-blonde hair cut in a military flat-top style. Likewise, their costumes distinguish them from the crowd: both wear black, plain, and form-fitting outfits that they occupy with the stiff posture of bowling pins, quite unlike the relaxed poses and lavish costumes worn by the other members of the vaguely Edwardian court. That Hamlet is the natural son of Old Hamlet—whose peppery hair, incandescent eyes, gargantuan physique, and sulfurous breath make him resemble nothing in Horatio's philosophy or Hamlet's family tree—strains credulity in and of itself. But when coupled with the unmistakable likeness between stepfather and son, we are led to wonder just how long Gertrude has been parking her bustle under Claudius's bed.

With Blenheim Palace used for the exteriors, an edifice that commemorates the English victory over the French, and all the choice roles reserved for English actors (Oscar-winning American and Continental cast members are allotted bit parts—Gerard Depardieu's Reynaldo and Charleton Heston's Player King, for example), it is tempting to read this *Hamlet* as Branagh's final bid for assimilation into the ranks of natural-born Englishmen. Appropriately, as Russell Jackson observes in his film diary, on the final day of rehearsal, Jacobi gave Belfast's prodigal son the entrée he had been waiting for:

He holds up red-bound copy of the play, that successive actors have passed on to each other with the condition that the recipient should give it in turn to the finest Hamlet of the next generation. It has come from Forbes Robertson, a great Hamlet at the turn of the century, to Derek, via Henry Ainley, Michael Redgrave, Peter O'Toole and others—now he gives it to Ken.

Filled with allusions to other epics such as *Dr. Zhivago* (David Lean, 1965), *Ben Hur* (William Wyler, 1959), and *Gone with the Wind* (Sam Wood and George Cukor, 1939), Branagh's self-described "big, big Hamlet film" most lacks a sense of its own identity. Ultimately, then, the film testifies to Branagh's brilliance as a master adapter—a talent that did not go unrecognized by the Academy of Motion Picture Arts and Sciences, which nominated him for "Best Screenplay Adapted from Another Medium"—even as it inscribes his insecurities as a director. Fittingly, audiences can go in search of slaying their own demons in the CD-ROM murder mystery game of "Hamlet" that was released when the film appeared in theaters. See also entries 3124 and 3139.

345 *Hamlet*
2000. U.S. Miramax/Double A Films. Sound, col.,
112 mins. Michael Almereyda.

A dramatically condensed version of Shakespeare's play set in contemporary Manhattan, Almereyda's *Hamlet* offers a compelling critique of corporate America in the era of global capitalism. Hence, the figure of the Ghost is upstaged by the far more haunting specter of commodification that threatens at every turn to replace relations between people—to cite Marx's famous dictum—with relations between things. One of the film's more playful invocations of this theme is its representation of the "merger" of the Ghost's incorporeal body with that of the Pepsi Corporation when the Ghost bids Hamlet adieu while disappearing into a soda machine—a tableau that is trumped only by Hamlet's delivery of the "To be or not to be" soliloquy while walking down the "Action Film" aisle of Blockbuster Video. (Such conspicuous product placement is often a means through which independent filmmakers like Almereyda seek to defray production costs, a strategy that considerably problematizes their critique of the corporate superstructure.) Hamlet, played by Gen-X star Ethan Hawke, is a disaffected amateur filmmaker whose search for an authentic existence is aligned with his rejection of contemporary technology—most obviously, digital film—in favor of his archaic pixelvision camera. Nevertheless, the fact that Hamlet's relationship to "reality" remains hopelessly mediated, indeed, conspicuously constructed according to the nostalgic impulses of the "home movie" genre, is a stunning example of the extent to which the simulacrum is mistaken for the thing itself within the hypermediated culture of postmodernity. Within the perceptual schemes of cinematic intertextuality, Hawke's Hamlet, who prefers the purgatory of an easily manipulated (reel) existence—one that can be paused, rewound, or fast-forwarded at will—to the "real world" outside these safe confines, becomes the perfect sequel to his alienated figure of Troy in *Reality Bites* (Ben Stiller, 1994). Ironically, Almereyda's approach to Hamlet as a budding filmmaker, considered highly original by the film's many admirers, unwittingly repeats the central gambit of Claude Chabrol's 1963 spin-off *Ophélia*, the story of the malcontent Yvan who, having seen Olivier's *Hamlet*, creates a short film that baits his father's murderer in the same manner as *The Mousetrap*.

DVD: no special features.

346 *Hamlet*
2001. Northern Ireland. The Derry Film Initiative. Sound, col., 93 mins. Steven Cavanagh.

As with much earlier Indian adaptations, this film of *Hamlet* is inseparable from the history of British imperialism that continues to make Northern Ireland at once a colonial outpost—indeed, a poor imitation of the thriving South (currently the second most expensive country in Europe, next to Finland)—and a locus of utopian potential, imagined in earlier *Hamlets* like Almereyda's (above), which features visual references to Ireland as a place magically removed from the corporate endgames of Manhattan. The Derry location, as Mark Thorton Burnett observes, is central to this dual inflection as a city that, during the Troubles, fostered a Catholic haven and, simultaneously, has long been associated with Protestant radicalism. These seemingly mutually exclusive sentiments of reconciliation and rebellion merge in Hamlet's (played by Cavanagh) delivery of the "To be or not to be" soliloquy in Gaelic. Read alongside the elimination of the Ghost's speeches, this important gesture suggests a broader wish for Northern Ireland to move past its history of haunting by an overbearing English fatherland toward the celebration of the heritage it shares with the South.

HENRY IV

347 *Campanadas a Medianoche* (U.K. title: *Chimes at Midnight*; U.S. title: *Falstaff*)
1966. Spain/Switzerland. Internacional Films/Alpine. Sound, b&w, 113 mins. Orson Welles.

A remarkable, tragic, challenging adaptation of *Richard II*, the *Henry IV* plays, *Henry V*, and *The Merry Wives of Windsor*, this adaptation, starring Welles as Falstaff, revolves around the life of "Fat Jack" and his epic friendship with Prince Hal, and is considered by many to be Welles's best Shakespeare film. Although the sound quality is poor, due to budget constraints and the bizarre mishaps that have plagued the transmission of so many of Welles's finished and unfinished projects, no other film—save *Citizen Kane* (1941)—approximates the visual magnificence of *Chimes at Midnight*. This observation, however, must be qualified, for in contrast to the bravura camera work, smooth edits, glossy mise-en-scène, brilliant chiaroscuro effects, and searing deep focus of Welles's debut film, *Chimes at Midnight* is quietly magnificent. Though the film itself is dramatically lit, the prevailing tones—if not spectral, then certainly emotional—are a pronounced gray, as if the shades of black and white had conspired to portend the twilight of Welles's career. Scholars have repeatedly contrasted the film with Olivier's *Henry V* (below), particularly in terms of Welles's refusal to glorify war—attributable, perhaps, to the difference between the patriotism-infused world wars and the ambivalent "police action" of Vietnam, a conflict that was already underway during the making of *Chimes*. A more subtle and rewarding point of comparison, however, is the shot composition that characterizes the two films. Olivier's exquisite Technicolor construction of *Henry V*, wherein nearly every scene is modeled after Renaissance paintings, tapestries, and landscapes, is precisely that—constructed. The eye is repeatedly drawn away from the "downstage" action in order to cultivate the distance, if not divinity, necessary to hedge Olivier's future king. In other words, in more ways than one, every image in this film is framed. Welles's film inverts the focus of Olivier's painterly and meticulously crafted mise-en-scène; equally beautiful and painstakingly composed, Welles's film is nothing if not immediate, on the brink of tipping over into our space and bursting through its frame, just as Welles's Falstaff—by virtue of his sheer immensity—seems almost to burst through his skin. The best scenes in this film, then, are the ones in which the "center cannot hold"—when, that is, Welles's composition gives in to gravity, and he must tip his camera and shackle us to its distortions and fetishes. This approach is most evident in the Boar's Head Tavern scenes, in which Welles often employs a low-angle camera that renders Falstaff truly larger than life and yet utterly unintimidating, softened by the rounded shapes of the film's privileged "containers"—pots and casks of ale, the curved architecture of the tavern, and, of course, Fat Jack himself. By contrast, the court scenes, which are more staid in their camera work but composed with equal care, ensnare the eye with sharp, vertical features—halberds and flags that embody Hal's rise to glory and warn against (indeed, cordon off) the excesses of the past—culminating in his brutal rejection of Falstaff: "I know thee not old man, fall to thy prayers" (5.5.47). Complementing his direction, Welles's acting in this film serves as a constant and, in the end, painful reminder that Falstaff quite literally does not fit within this architecture—not so much because of his extraordinary girth but rather because, unlike Hal, he is not made of stone. See also entry 752.

DVD: includes filmographies and interviews with significant members of Welles's staff; however, there are no English subtitles for these Spanish-language features of the DVD.

HENRY V

348 *Henry V*
1913. U.K. Stratford School. Silent, b&w, length unknown. Director unknown.

According to Robert Hamilton Ball, this version of *Henry V* is the first Shakespearean amateur film ever made, performed by the children of Stratford school.

349 *Henry V*
1944. U.K. Two Cities. Sound, col., 137 mins. Laurence Olivier.

Considered a masterpiece of Technicolor—still a relatively new phenomenon at the time—and, for many, the first truly cinematic adaptation of a Shakespeare play, this film is even more remarkable for the fact that it was Olivier's directorial debut. With England at war not with France but with Germany, *Henry V* also served as a powerful propaganda piece that, in hindsight, has perhaps been unfairly accused of glorifying war. What makes this film so extraordinary as a director's vehicle is its ingenious mod-

Laurence Olivier as Henry V in his production of *Henry V* (1944). Courtesy of Douglas Lanier.

ulation between theatrical and cinematic modes. The film is framed as though it were a performance of an Elizabethan play at the Globe Theatre, taking place in "real time": a flag is raised, a curtain is drawn, and the Elizabethan-clad Chorus takes the stage to escort us into the drama. With the exception of the battle scenes, there is no effort, perspectival or otherwise, to conceal the status of the setting as constructed for the stage. Nevertheless, the sets themselves are exquisitely rendered, made to appear as though they were torn out of a medieval illuminated manuscript. By contrast, lengthy tracking shots are employed for the impressive battle sequences between the English and the French, as Olivier takes full advantage of the camera's sweeping view to recreate the battle of Agincourt with exceptional realism. Predictably, given the historical context of the film, the major cuts are to those segments that highlight Henry's often brutal behavior, and may be usefully compared with Branagh's post-Falklands' decision to showcase—through flashbacks—the young king's ruthless rejection of his tavern days in the hanging of Bardolf (see entry 351).

DVD: features commentary by film historian Bruce Eder, theatrical trailers, a historical chronology of England's monarchs, and production photos.

350 *Campanadas a Medianoche* (U.K. title: *Chimes at Midnight*; U.S. title: *Falstaff*)
1966. Spain/Switzerland. Internacional Films/Alpine. Sound, b&w, 115 mins. Orson Welles.
   See entries 347 and 752.

351 *Henry V*
1989. U.K. Renaissance Films. Sound, col., 138 mins. Kenneth Branagh.

   Kenneth Branagh's film-directing debut is as prodigious as Olivier's, at once charting a young king's ascent to national glory and a young director's rise to international prominence. In his autobiography, *Beginning*, which deals in part with the challenges of making *Henry V*, Branagh asserts that his objective in creating this adaptation is nothing less than to "save the British film industry." Despite this audacity, Branagh often represents Henry as a figure dwarfed by his royal robes, throne, or darkly lit medieval dwellings, encoding, perhaps, anxieties about his own inaugural transition from theater to film. Nevertheless, there are many instances in which Branagh seems perfectly at home in his new medium, as in the lengthy "Non Nobis" dead march that concludes the battle of Agincourt. This scene, in which Henry wades through the carnage while carrying a dead boy over five hundred feet of tracking platforms, is envisioned by Branagh as "the greatest tracking shot in history." (If so, it has certainly been trumped by Alexander Sokurov's remarkable single-take film, *Russian Arc* [2002].) A significant omission from the film's conclusion is the Chorus's allusion to Essex returning from Ireland "[b]ringing rebellion broached upon his sword" (5.1.32), a line that may hit too close to home for Branagh, whose war-torn childhood in Belfast continues to inflect his films in stunning, though clearly unconscious, ways. As many critics have noted, Branagh's *Henry V* departs from Olivier's (entry 349) in its utter refusal to glorify war, and its gritty, often grotesque battle scenes were undoubtedly influenced by the post-Falklands context of the film's creation. See alos entries 3171 and 3172.
   DVD: contains theatrical trailers.

HENRY VI

352 *Henry VI*
1928. U.S. Warner Brothers. Sound, b&w, 10 mins. John Adolfi.

   This film is significant as one of the first Shakespearean "talkies," featuring John Barrymore's delectably villainous reading of Richard of Gloucester's soliloquy.

HENRY VIII

353 *Henry VIII*
1911. U.K. Barker Motion Photography. Silent, b&w, length unknown. Will Barker.

   This lost film is distinctive for being of feature length, presenting the great Sir Herbert Beerbohm Tree as the notorious king in what was, for its time, a blockbuster success in England. Honoring the actor's request not to be remembered on celluloid, the film was burned when its distribution phase ended; all that remains of this landmark picture is the film that Barker made of its destruction.

354 *Cardinal Wolsey*
1912. U.S. Vitagraph. Silent, b&w, 10 mins. Laurence Trimble.

   This is the last Vitagraph picture and is worthy of the classification "adaptation" in the more adventurous spirit of the term, using Shakespearean scenes and speeches to frame a film that focuses less on the intrigues of Henry and Anne Boleyn and more on Wolsey's heroic resistance to the king's sundry whims. Despite these variations on the theme of *Henry VIII*, the film is largely wedded to Shakespeare's plot.

JULIUS CAESAR

355 *Julius Caesar*
1908. U.S. Vitagraph. Silent, b&w, 10 mins. William V. Ranous.

   This short film with German titles follows the major plot elements of Shakespeare's play, which is distilled into a mere fifteen scenes and framed by impressive establishing shots that emphasize cinema's mobility over theater. One amusing detail to note is that when the request for a hundred pairs of brown tights could not be met in time for the shooting schedule, the actors' legs were painted brown instead. Also of interest are the censorship issues that plagued the film, suggesting the long shadow cast by the Victorian era: the murder scene was characterized as too violent, and the tunics worn by the Romans were considered to be too short.

356 *Giulio Cesare (Julius Caesar; Brutus)*
1909. Italy. Itala Film. Silent, b&w, 10 mins. Giovanni Pastrone.

   This film is distinctive for its use of double exposure to depict Calpurnia's dream, although, rather curiously, this same technique is not employed to represent the ghost of Caesar later in the film. Like Charleton Heston's *Antony and Cleopatra* (above), this early Italian *Julius Caesar* suffers from an emphasis on crowd scenes and long shots that dwarf the major characters; both films, in other words, fall prey to the temptation to privilege the representation of Rome over Romans.

357 *Bruto (Brutus)*
1910. Italy. Cines. Silent, b&w, 11 mins. Enrico Guazzoni.

   With the exception of eliminating Act 1, this short film follows the major events of Shakespeare's *Julius Caesar* quite closely, beginning and ending with the deaths of Caesar and Brutus, respectively. Lauded for its lucid approach to a complex story of intrigue and political subterfuge, Guazzoni's film also offers previews of the kind of historical spectacle for which Italian cinema was to become known, as well as providing the director with a blueprint for his 1914 feature-length spin-off, *Caius Julius Caesar*.

358 *Julius Caesar*
1911. U.K./France. Co-Operative. Silent, b&w, 10 mins. Will Barker and F. R. Benson.

Banking on the success of recent Shakespeare films, this film was a recording of a stage performance by F. R. Benson's players that opened to favorable reviews abroad but failed to prove a transatlantic success; whether this is attributable to compromised quality or limited distribution is unclear.

359 *Caius Julius Caesar (Julius Caesar)*
1914. Italy. Cines. Silent, b&w, 78 mins. (originally 104 mins.). Enrico Guazzoni.

This adaptation is significant as the first feature-length version of *Julius Caesar* and is derived, in part, from Shakespeare's play. Though the film is more about the life of Caesar, his death is clearly indebted to Shakespeare. Typical of Italian filmmaking, the adaptation features impressive ensemble scenes involving as many as a thousand extras, the scope of which is clearly intended to flex cinema's strengths relative to theater. As was common, the English language prints of the film quote directly from Shakespeare to emphasize the connection to the play that the German titles and dramatic visuals occlude.

360 *Julius Caesar*
1950. U.S. Avon/Brandon. Sound, b&w, 90 mins. David Bradley.

Remarkably, this amateur film made on a shoestring budget and shot around Northwestern University in Chicago features the young Charlton Heston as Antony, just before Heston emerged as a star. Based in the university football stadium during the off-season, the film is remarkably resourceful in its efforts to recreate the feel if not exactly the look—of the Roman forum. Bradley's adaptation won the award for Best Film at the Locarno Film Festival, an established venue for international and independent film in the Italian-speaking region of Switzerland, three years after its release.

361 *Julius Caesar*
1953. U.S. John Houseman/MGM. Sound, b&w, 120 mins. Joseph L. Mankiewicz.

Required reading in virtually every American secondary school in the 1950s, *Julius Caesar* was one of the first Shakespeare films to feature an educational marketing campaign. Marlon Brando stars as Mark Antony, the young, impressionable, and, ultimately, Machiavellian friend of Caesar in the first major American adaptation of Shakespeare's play, while Deborah Kerr plays Caesar's

prophetic but ignored wife Portia only four years before her most memorable role opposite Carey Grant in *An Affair to Remember* (Leo McCarey, 1957). But for those who expect Brando to provide the main attraction, they will likely come away from their viewing experience convinced that they have seen a film called *Cassius*, based on John Gielgud's extraordinary performance as Shakespeare's most subtle conspirator. Indeed, more interesting than the film's frequently cited antifascist subtext, which is carried over from Houseman's more overtly political Broadway theater adaptation of *Caesar*, subtitled *Death of a Dictator* (1937), is the relationship between Gielgud's Cassius and James Mason's Brutus, which is fraught as much with homoerotic desire as it is with political ambition. The strength of this film, particularly when compared with Burge's adaptation (below), is its subtle acting, muted tones, spare sets, and carefully embedded leftist sentiments, which have led scholars to classify it as *film gris*. Unlike its generic cousin, film noir, which thrives in an overdetermined universe devoid of moral accountability, *film gris* invokes a world in which choices and change are still possible.

362 *Julius Caesar*
1969. U.K. Commonwealth United. Sound, col., 114 mins. Stuart Burge.

This adaptation may be usefully compared with its immediate predecessor, which, though created nearly two decades earlier, is a far superior film. Attempting to substitute spectacle for talent, Burge's *Caesar* is visually impressive but suffers from an overzealous desire to cast Hollywood stars in roles for which they are poorly suited. Heston's Mark Antony—returning to form from his role in David Bradley's adaptation of *Caesar*—privileges a flesh-revealing toga over emotionally revealing oratory, while Jason Robards's Brutus approaches his lines as though he were reading yesterday's news from a teleprompter. In this case, Burge would have done better to stick with Brits in the leading roles, as commanding performances by Diana Rigg (Portia) and Sir John Gielgud (Caesar) suggest.

363 *Julius Caesar*
1996. Russia/Wales. Soyuzmultifilm and Christmas Films. Sound, col., 27 mins. Yuri Yulakov.

Another film from the *Shakespeare: The Animated Tales* series, this adaptation is rendered through the traditional technique of cel animation. The benefit of this particular form of animation, which relies on meticulous, incremental drawings and stop-action cinematography to produce the illusion of continuous, transformative motion, is—as Sergei Eisenstein once observed of the work of Walt Disney—its capacity for activating "prelogical" or child-like modes of thought. Liberated from "prescribed norms of nomenclature, form and behavior" associated with the adult world and, for Eisenstein, the strictures of repressive socioeconomic orders, pre-logical thought processes engage in what Eisenstein describes as a "lyrical" revolt from the "partitioning and legislating" that are the basis of capitalistic society. In the animated *Julius Caesar*, the shape-shifting that characters and objects undergo—for example, the transformation of scroll to snake to Brutus's reflections on Caesar as an "unhatched serpent" (2.1.3)—forces us to acknowledge not their distinctiveness but their ontological continuity, indeed, the broader "conspiracy" of associative thinking in which the audience itself participates.

KING JOHN

364 *King John*
1899. U.K. British Mutoscope and Biograph Company. Silent, b&w, 1.5 mins. William Kennedy-Laurie Dickson.

A single shot capturing Sir Herbert Beerbohm Tree as King John in his death throes is the first-ever known recording of Shakespeare on screen. Included here because of its obvious importance, this fragment, filmed in a studio rather than on stage, reproduces the theatrical production at Her Majesty's Theatre in 1899. Featuring a dramatic shot of King John prone and aloof in his chair, clutching at his chest and rejecting the sympathy of the woman at his feet, the king eventually rises and lurches forward as the retainers move from the frame toward him.

DVD: *Silent Shakespeare*: digitally remastered with a newly recorded score.

365 *Saed e Havas* (*King John*)
1936. India. Stage Film Company. Sound, b&w, length unknown. Sohrab Modi.

Acclaimed Shakespearean actor as well as the director of the first Indian Technicolor film (*Jhanski ki Rani*, 1953), Sohrab Modi was one of the founders of what would become known as Bollywood. The second of Modi's three Shakespeare films, *King John* reflects Hindi cinema's roots in Parsi theater, which, prior to the rise of film, was one of the leading sources of cultural transmission and reformation in India. Parsi theater, derived from the name for Persian immigrants to India, invokes the kind of cultural syncretism that inflects Indian filmmaking to this day, combining multiple language traditions and a confluence of Indian, Western, and Arabic music, contexts, and, eventually, performers. *King John*, with its English, French, and Austrian characters—not to mention its compelling portrait of the mongrel figure of John the Bastard—is a Shakespeare play uniquely suited to the Hindi, Urdu, Gujarati, and implicitly hybrid English languages that form the basis of Parsi culture. Intriguingly, similar to Shakespeare's own theater, the Parsi theater maintained a taboo against female actresses that, for a time, carried over into cinema, forcing men to play women's parts. Conveniently for Modi's film of *King John* and Shakespeare's histories in general, this obstacle is mitigated by the sparsity of important female roles (with the obvious exception of the women featured in the *Henry VI* plays). Like his earlier adaptation of *Hamlet*, *Khoon Ka Khoon* (above), Modi's *King John* was derived from a stage production.

KING LEAR

366 *King Lear*
1909. U.S. Vitagraph. Silent, b&w, 10 mins. William V. Ranous.

This film is admirable for its ambitious effort to condense all the twists and turns of Shakespeare's plot into a single reel. However, unlike the majority of the other Vitagraph Shakespeare adaptations, this film was unsuccessful in its effort to explain the complex political power struggles at stake in Shakespeare's play—despite opening with an interpolated introduction of the major characters, each with a name "tag."

367 *Re Lear* (*King Lear*)
1910. Italy. Film d'Arte Italiana. Silent, b&w, 11 mins. Gerolamo Lo Savio.

Shot largely in outdoor locations, this film is precocious in its emphasis on naturalistic settings, coupled with exquisite costumes. The surviving prints have been beautifully color-tinted with yellow, blue, crimson, and lavender hues, lending the characters an individuality that is particularly challenging to express in silent film. Ermete Novelli plays Lear with a distinctly Italian flair for exaggerated hand gestures, often waving his hand, fingertips touching, close to the face of his disrespectful daughters. An interesting casting choice accentuates the already tense family dynamics within the film, as Goneril is played by Olga Giannini Novelli—very likely, Lear's real-life daughter-in-law. The most entertaining scene in Lo Savio's otherwise high-tragic adaptation occurs when Lear strikes Oswald in the codpiece, bringing him swiftly to his knees.

DVD: *Silent Shakespeare*: digitally remastered and beautifully colorized with a newly recorded score.

368 *Re Lear* (*King Lear*)
1910. Italy. Milano. Silent, b&w, c. 10 mins. Giuseppe de Liguoro.

Though little is known about this version of *King Lear*, the film has been definitively identified with director-actor-adapter Giuseppe de Liguoro, who had an undeniable passion for the classics, both directing and starring in films of Homer's *Odyssey* (1911), Dante's *Inferno* (1909, 1912), and Sophocles' *Oedipus Rex* (1909).

369 *Le Roi Lear au Village* (*The Village King Lear*)
1911. France. Gaumont. Silent, b&w, 12 mins. Louis Feuillade.

This adaptation served as one of the first pictures in Feuillade's new "slice of life" series, titled *La Vie telle qu'elle est*. The importance of this film is that it is not only a

modernization but also an interpretation that resists demonizing the daughters while representing Lear in far more
ambivalent terms than Shakespeare's play. In this respect,
this version of *Lear* anticipates contemporary retellings
such as Jane Smiley's Pulitzer Prize–winning novel, *A
Thousand Acres* (1991).

370 *King Lear*
1916. U.S. Thanhouser Film Corp. Silent, b&w, 43 mins.
Ernest Warde.

Like its Italian predecessor, this feature-length film takes
advantage of location shooting and makes masterful use of
dissolves as well as intercutting for reaction shots that
further distinguish cinema's ability to structure audience
response.

371 *Korol Lir (King Lear)*
1969. USSR. Lenfilm. Sound, b&w, 140 mins. Grigori
Kozintsev.

Created after the "Thaw" in the thick of renewed repression under Brezhnev, Kozintsev's adaptation of *King
Lear* takes sparsity for theme, featuring desolate panoramas
and oppressive stone façades that cast the pall of pending
apocalypse over the entire film, at once invoking the
medieval uncertainties of Shakespeare's setting and the
film's imbrication in contemporary crises such as Vietnam
and the Soviet-led invasion of Czechoslovakia. Acted
predominantly by thespians from Baltic countries and
dubbed into Russian—and accompanied by Shostakovich's
final film score—*Korol Lir*, despite Kozintsev's published
disinterest in Brechtian productions like Peter Brook's
Stratford *Lear* (1962), offers a vision of the failure of Soviet
socialism as the ultimate alienation effect. There is no
more poignant representation of this failure than the scene
in which the decrepid, aristocratic king, accompanied by his makeshift entourage composed of the blind Gloucester, the "mad" Edgar,
and the emaciated Fool, crosses paths with a
mass of refugees fleeing the newly war-torn
kingdom—a tableau that suggests both the
dream of a classless society and the violence
that, throughout the twentieth century, has
been enlisted to defend and, ultimately, to defeat this utopian project. Yet like the film's own
fascination with open spaces, Kozintsev, perhaps in a nod to his pioneering predecessor,
Sergei Eisenstein, bequeaths the residue of such
montage collisions to the unsurveilled imagination, wherein meaningful social action may
yet prevail over madness. (CL)

Kozintsev's film is a masterpiece of cinema
that recalls Ingmar Bergman's *Seventh Seal* and
perhaps exceeds it in giving the viewer a sense
of a medieval past. The film is most striking in

its sparing use of close-ups and music, composed by Dmitry
Shostakovich (as in Kozintsev's *Hamlet* [above]). Wide
angle lenses and deep focus shots of exteriors predominate,
with a large cast of extras looking on and, during the final
battle, displaced as Lear's castle is burned by Edmund and
his troops. Medium shots predominate in interiors. Kozintsev gives both a sense of the broad social world Lear
inhabits, beginning with a shot of peasants making their
way to the castle to hear him divide his kingdom, and deep
psychological inwardness. Medium-long shots of characters also distance them. France's lines are cut, and Lear's
lines are translated into French, giving the film an international feel and highlighting the film itself as a translation (see the similar translation of Claudius's opening
speech into different languages in Kozintsev's *Gamlet*
[above]). Inwardness is achieved less through the use of
voice-overs (used by Edmund and Edgar occasionally)
than by recontextualizing Lear's line. He ends his speech
after his rejection by Cordelia by going to the castle
parapets. As he leaves the interior, he orders, "Saddle my
horses; call my train together," and then walks through a
room with his hounds and hawks. In a stunning sequence
of camera tilts, we see the peasants outside of the castle
kneel and then bow their heads in amazement as Lear
walks up the castle steps, and delivers his lines from afar
and with Cordelia absent, freely translated: "he that makes
his generation messes / To gorge his appetite, shall to my
bosom / Be as well-received, / As thou my sometime
daughter." Lear delivers his speech cursing his daughters
Regan and Goneril alone, after they have left. Lear is
played in a very understated way. He is first heard laughing
from behind a door and emerges laughing; he speaks softly
most of the time, the major exceptions being when he

Yuri Yarvet (King Lear) and Valentina Shendrikova (Cordelia) in Grigori
Kozintsev's *Korol Lir* (1969). Lenfilm/The Kobol Collection.

tears about the map after Cordelia refuses to speak and when he delivers the "Blow wind, crack you hurricanoes" speech. Kozintsev's film, which fuses the play's Christian themes with Marxist analysis, is weakest in siding clearly with Lear, more sinned against than sinning; Cordelia, played by a beautiful, younger woman; and the fool, Edgar, Gloucester, Kent, and Albany. The actresses playing Goneril and Regan are overweight, unattractive, and well into late middle age, and they are hard to distinguish. The Dover cliff scene is cut, as are Edgar's lines to Albany when he gives him a letter before fighting Edmund (5.1), making Edgar more simple, less of an agent, and clearly on the side of good. Edgar buries Gloucester's corpse as choral music comes in to reinforce our sense that he is a good, forgiving son. Cordelia gets a long close-up when Lear plays his love game, and she and Lear each get close-ups when he awakens and recognizes her. Nevertheless, the film is effective cinematically both in its efforts to darken the bad characters and in its efforts to redeem the good ones. For example, lines from Edmund's speech to the captain—"men / Are as the time is: to be tenderminded / Does not become a sword" (5.3)—are recontextualized as a speech Edmund gives to rally his troops, as if he were a budding Henry V, and their positive response ("Edmund! Edmund! Edmund!") provides one of the most disturbing moments in the film. The "Let's away to prison" sequence is particularly brilliant as the knights in charge of Cordelia and Lear become absorbed by Lear's speech, and Edmund is seen becoming increasingly angry.

Sound is used imaginatively. We hear Gloucester calling for Edmund in Edmund's room; Cordelia hears Regan speak from another room. Music at points begins diegetically and then gradually becomes extradiegetic, and vice versa. A blast of a horn from a peasant near the beginning of the film, for example, recurs at later points in the film when Gloucester kisses Lear's hand after finding him on the heath and again when Lear recognizes Gloucester. The trumpet calling for a champion to fight Edmund also develops into a theme independent of the trumpet we see on screen. Choral music is first heard as a number of travelers meet up with Lear and Gloucester on the heath, and this music recurs as Lear is carried in a litter asleep after Cordelia's knights find him, in Lear's "Let's away to prison" speech, and then in various parts of the battle scene. The extradiegetic theme, played on a clarinet and heard in the opening credits, returns as music played by the Fool on a flute. In all cases of diegetic music, the effect is undercut by a realistic sense that the interment is the source of the sound. The music offers emotional support for Lear, but its very abstractness suggests its inability to offer much. Hence, music is silenced through most of the film. The film provides a relatively happy ending. The fool survives and plays his flute in the final shot, as he is almost walked on by

one of the four knights carrying a litter with Lear's and Cordelia's corpses on it. We see peasants putting out fires and beginning to rebuild their destroyed homes. Shots of Edgar show him still in shock as he looks on as Lear and Cordelia are carried off but stays back to take command of what is left. (RB)

372 *King Lear*
1971. U.K./Denmark. Filmways/Athene. Sound, b&w, 137 mins. Peter Brook.

The subject of a polarized reception, this film is distinctly Nordic in sentiment, even Bergmanesque—a kind of Shakespeare–meets–*Wild Strawberries* (1957) interpretation of *King Lear*. Some critics interpret Brook's minimalist, nihilist production as a mark of artistic integrity, while others cite the unbearable sparseness of the film as evidence that the director is far more at home in the theater. Cutting the opening back story contained in the conversation between Kent, Gloucester, and Edmund, Brook's adaptation begins with Lear's pronouncement: "Know that we have divided / In three our kingdom" (1.1.36–37). Even audiences familiar with Lear's speech will hear "No" rather than "Know" in this first utterance, an elision that rather cleverly announces the director's own "darker purpose" (1.1.35).

373 *King Real and the Hoodlums*
1983. U.S. Welfare State International. Sound, col., 54 mins. John Fox and Paul Haywood.

Credit for this avant-garde film most belongs to Adrian Mitchell, who adapted the screenplay from the theatrical interlude he wrote in 1982, titled *The Tragedy of King Real*, a play that brings together the classical and experimental performance traditions that inform his work (Mitchell wrote for Peter Hall, Peter Brook, and Laurence Olivier). Like Penny Woolcock's 1997 film of *Macbeth* (below), which is shot on location on a housing estate and features actual residents of the low-income housing projects, Mitchell conceived of *King Real and the Hoodlums* as a community project based in Barrow-in-Furness, a small town distinguished by its role as a manufacturer of nuclear submarines. The cast, assembled in the thick of the second Cold War, is comprised mainly of unemployed youth in the depressed region; hence, the plot, in which one representative of the younger generation, Cloudella, remains intent on resisting the sins of the fathers while her sisters use their inheritance (of nuclear technology) to start World War III, suggests in no uncertain terms the very real ontological uncertainty lived by 1980s' youth, who grew up all too aware of the leaders—from the United States to the USSR—poised with their fingers "on the button." A rock opera that condenses Lear and Gloucester into a single figure, *King Real and the Hoodlums* ends with a glimpse of the aftermath of a nuclear holocaust in which Real and Cloudella are briefly reunited before they die. Though none of Shakespeare's play is cited directly, one of the film's most stunning revisions of *Lear* is the song that Cloudella sings to her father, which takes its cues from Lear's entreaty to his daughter: "Come, let's away to prison / and we two will sing like birds i' th' cage" (5.3.8–9). Invoking the present horrors of a once-hopeful world, Cloudella's lament heralds the victory of an apocalyptic capitalism, in which people make commodity fetishes of one another:

You were Father Christmas
And I longed for you
You were the hangman
And I hid from you
You were the ice-cream man
I worshipped you
You were the scissorman
I dreamed of you
How could I love you
When I always knew
I was the unicorn in your private zoo.

See also entry 802.

374 *Ran (Chaos)*

1985. Japan. Greenway Film/Nippon. Sound, col., 160 mins. Akira Kurosawa.

In Kurosawa's classic style, this version of *Lear* is set in medieval Japan during the Sengoku Jidai (Age of the Country at War, or Warring States Period, 1467–1568) and, in keeping with precedent-setting adaptations like *The Yiddish King Lear*, the story line is transformed according to the cultural dictates of its setting. Hence, the daughters are changed to sons, but the essential theme of family honor—*giri* in Japanese—is, as in Shakespeare's play, the fulcrum of the film. Most insightfully, the film's conclusion transforms Shakespeare's vision of a culture uneasily straddling the divide between astrological determinism and the Protestant work ethic into a commentary on the constitutive uncertainties of Eastern spirituality, as the blind Tsurumaru (the Gloucester character) stumbles at the edge of a cliff, dropping his scroll over the edge, which unfurls to reveal the image of a giant Buddha. Whether the Buddha is meant to menace, mock, or mollify the desperate man is open to interpretation. See also entry 803.

DVD: Masterworks edition includes commentary by film historian Stephen Prince and filmmaker Peter Grilli, as well as a documentary about "The Making of *Ran*."

375 *King of Texas*

2002. U.S. Flying Freehold Productions, Hallmark Entertainment, and Turner Network Television. Sound, col., 120 mins. Uli Edel.

One of the more provocative aspects of Uli Edel's Western adaptation of *King Lear* is the paradox of its title, which juxtaposes the mutually exclusive political systems of American democracy and British monarchy. Were *King of Texas* set prior to the Revolutionary War, this combination would make more sense; however, the film's opening frames establish the period of 1842, sixty-six years after the United States declared that it would never again swear allegiance to a king. At this time, the historically accurate term for the leader of Texas was not king but *president*, for Texas was then a nation unto itself—with its own congress, laws, leader, and, as the beginning of the film makes clear, "Independence Day," which is the cause of the Lear family's celebration. In a film that otherwise strives to create a believable sense of place and period, one can only speculate that the title "president of Texas" might have hit too close to home for its largely American audience (*King of Texas* initially aired on TNT). Indeed, such a title, when considered in relation to the film's setting in 1842, which commemorates the birth of Texas as a rogue state, too easily invokes the leftist critique of a period much closer to 2002, when the United States—under the isolationist policies of its Texas-born president—has acquired the reputation of a rogue *nation*. Hence, the creative anachronism "*King* of Texas."

Edell's adaptation parallels Shakespeare's play very closely, although the influence of spin-offs such as *A Thousand Acres* (Jocelyn Moorhouse, 1997) is evident in the modicum of sympathy evinced for Lear's daughters, Suzannah, Rebecca, and Claudia, all of whom have long suffered their father's favoritism toward his son, who was "martyred at Goliad." Such references to Texas history prior to its annexation by the United States are sprinkled throughout *King of Texas* and, like the film's title, create a pastiche of fact and fiction, past and present. For example, whereas the warring factions in Shakespeare's play correspond to distinct generations, Udell's film strains plausibility by representing the older generation as Alamo veterans and the younger generation as untried upstarts who take their freedom for granted (when, in fact, the only survivors of the Alamo were women, children, and slaves). This latter point, however, rather cleverly explains the presence of the one black character in the film, Rip, a combination of the Fool and Kent, sage and slave, whose presence simultaneously invokes the "buddy film" genre. All in all, Udell's relocation of Shakespeare's play to the Texas-Mexico border in the post-Alamo years—a period of constant uprisings and decentralized power—approximates the incremental chaos of *King Lear*'s feudal setting.

Hence, if in Shakespeare's play, Lear's conspicuous displays of power are tied to his retinue of one hundred knights, then in Udell's adaptation, retainers become roundups, as John Lear flexes his authority by revealing the hundreds of cows he commands. The implicit irony of both scenarios is that Lear's own family members will prove far less tractable, despite lavishing him with praises—proportionate to the land he promises each daughter—such as "If you hadn't been here we'd all been carried away by Comanches years ago." Such praise is forgotten once Rebecca and Suzannah experience their first taste of ownership and seek to expand their empire, at Emmet's prompting, into the oil-rich land across the Mexican border, which belongs to Lear's lifelong but respected enemy, Menchaka (a vague stand-in for the Mexican leader Santa Anna). What makes this scenario so apropos of the film's release in 2002 is the fact that in order to engage in this expansionist endeavor, Emmet's faction must pre-empt the "international" accord established by John Lear's revolutionary army in the wake of the post-Alamo, post-Goliad victory at San Jacinto, the very battle that earned Texas its independence. Far more poignant than King Lear's passive role in the fictitious French-English war of Shakespeare's play, then, John Lear's decision to join forces with Menchaka and take up arms against his own family members suggests a much greater transformation. See also entry 816.

DVD: Dolby surround sound, Anamorphic widescreen formatting, plus filmographies, subtitle options, and scene access.

LOVE'S LABORS LOST

376 *Love's Labours Lost*
2000. U.K./France/U.S. Miramax Films/Shakespeare Film Co./Intermedia/Pathé. Sound, col., 93 mins. Kenneth Branagh.

Set conspicuously *after* the repeal of Prohibition and before the outbreak of World War II, Branagh's film is situated in the thick of the wildly expressive culture of 1930s-style musicals like *Top Hat*—the Astaire-Rogers classic that, on the very first day of rehearsal, he screened for the entire cast and crew. Not unlike the "vaulting ambition" associated with his debut film of *Henry V* (through which Branagh hoped to "save the British film industry"), his adaptation of *Love's Labors Lost* is marked by the similar ambition to single-handedly "revitalise British musical film" (qtd. in Lister, www.branaghcompendium.com). That the film fails to do so is not surprising, given the mixed generic imperatives of the Hollywood musical and Shakespearean comedy, the upshot of which is an adaptation that deploys the Bard as a decoy for Branagh's homage to Irving Berlin and Busby Berkeley. In the style for which he has become known, Branagh combines a recognizable ensemble of classically trained British actors with a sprinkling of Hollywood stars—in this case, Alicia Silverstone, fresh from her leading role in *Clueless*, itself an adaptation of Jane Austen's *Emma*. The reason why this approach to casting is not nearly as effective in this film as it is, for example, in *Much Ado about Nothing* (1993 [below]) is because of the heightened demands of the musical genre, which require directors to cast actors who can sing and dance or, conversely, to hire singers and dancers who can act. In *Love's Labour's Lost*, the cast—despite their proven talents—does not succeed in persuading the audience that they can do any of the above in this already unpopular Shakespeare play. Although Branagh rather brilliantly attempts to make the play's downer ending meet the upbeat conclusion of musical comedy by converting the men's yearlong penance to war service—after which, in the wake of V-E Day, all the couples are happily reunited—no amount of clever innovation could save this film from its virtually direct-to-video fate. Opening, after much publicity, to a highly curtailed run in the wake of poor audience response, *Love's Labours Lost* also spelled the end of the three-picture deal that Branagh signed with Miramax, who had agreed to back his subsequent Shakespeare adaptations of *Macbeth* and *As You Like It*, the latter currently in progress. As is the case with many films in the age of home theater, however, *Love's Labours Lost* has enjoyed much more favorable attention on DVD.

DVD: includes Dolby Digital Sound, deleted footage, outtakes, and a "Making Of" featurette.

From left to right, Alessandro Nivola, Alicia Silverstone, Matthew Lillard, Carmen Ejogo (partially visible), Adrian Lester, Emily Mortimer, Kenneth Branagh and Natascha McElhone in Kenneth Branagh's *Love's Labour's Lost* (2000). Courtesy of Douglas Lanier.

MACBETH

377 *Macbeth*
1908. U.S. Vitagraph. Silent, b&w, c. 9 mins. William V. Ranous.

Another of J. Stuart Blackton's one-reel efforts to raise the cultural status of cinema through Shakespeare, this film failed to achieve the desired effect. According to one particularly blunt reviewer, whereas Shakespeare's play is "art," the Vitagraph film is "5 cent art" (*Moving Picture World*, June 13, 1908).

378 *Macbeth*
1909. Italy. Cines. Silent, b&w, 16 mins. Mario Caserini.

An early example of Italianate indulgence that anticipates the work of Franco Zeffirelli, this expensive film for its time (it cost $10,000) furnishes us with a lavishly constructed mise-en-scène that, nevertheless, is altogether out of keeping with the bleak medieval landscape of Shakespeare's Scottish play. Known for his elaborate historical spectacles and epic crowd scenes, Caserini—and his film of *Macbeth* in particular—demonstrate the extent to which cinematic forms, particularly in the context of emergent national cinemas, often prevail over their Shakespearean content.

379 *Macbeth*
1910. France. Film D'Art. Silent, b&w, 10 mins. André Calmettes.

In contrast to the emergent Italian cinema, French cinema was noticeably tied to theater, particularly when Shakespeare was at stake. But this *Macbeth* film, which remarkably reproduces all of the major plot elements of Shakespeare's play in a mere ten minutes, is not without distinctly filmic moments, such as the use of double exposure to simulate the disappearing act of Banquo's ghost. Also worthy of mention is the decision to predicate Macbeth's distrust of Banquo on the thane's refusal to kneel in acknowledgment of his coronation. Hence, though its staginess is offputting, this early film moves squarely in the direction of adaptation-as-interpretation.

380 *Macbeth*
1911. U.K. Co-Operative. Silent, b&w, 14 mins. F. R. Benson.

Films by Co-Operative, created in conjunction with Benson's theater company, tended to be even less adventurous than their Continental counterparts, leaning more toward the goal of recording rather than reinterpreting Shakespeare's plays. Significantly, this *Macbeth* was released by the production company with a great deal of commercial fanfare and, unlike the Vitagraph pictures, with no pretensions to "art," hailing the film as a "sure money-maker."

381 *Macbeth*
1913. Germany. Heidelberger Film Industrie. Silent, b&w, 47 mins. Arthur Bourchier.

In addition to its exceptional length, what is distinctive about this film is its original plan to feature British stars with a German supporting cast. However, this unique international casting arrangement was abandoned when it proved to be too expensive. The film opened in the United States three years after its European prémiere to universally poor reviews, and, not coincidentally, the Shakespearean sequels promised by Film-Industrie never materialized.

382 *Macbeth*
1916. U.S. Triangle-Reliance. Silent, b&w, 9 reels proposed, exact length unknown. John Emerson.

Well ahead of his time in recognizing the uncanny spectral effects of the filmic medium, Emerson planned to highlight the natural affinity between cinematic representation and the supernatural. Though the resulting film was critically acclaimed, it failed to achieve commercial success, and the ensuing humiliation of its star—none other than Sir Herbert Beerbohm Tree—provides us with an unattractive glimpse of the bottom-line orientation of the emergent studio system.

383 *Macbeth*
1916. France. Éclair. Silent, b&w, c. 10 mins. Director unknown.

Little is known about the only French Shakespeare film released in 1916 other than the fact that it starred the diva of the Operá-Comique, Madame Georgette Leblanc Maeterlinck.

384 *Macbeth*
1922. Germany. Elel Film/Filmindustrie Heidelberg. Silent, b&w, c. 30 mins. Heinz Schall.

Robert Hamilton Ball refers to the existence of this film as "maddeningly inconclusive." However, it is reasonable to speculate that Schall, having collaborated with Svend Gade and Asta Nielsen on *Hamlet* (1920), was prompted to take on *Macbeth* based on the success of this earlier film.

385 *Macbeth*
1947. U.S. David Bradley. Sound, b&w, 73 mins. David Bradley.

Produced on a budget of $5,000, this *Macbeth* is another example of Bradley's well-received amateur Shakespeare films. Bradley went on to play Brutus while directing Charleton Heston in *Julius Caesar* and is better known today for his performances of Argus Filch in the hugely popular *Harry Potter* films (Chris Columbus, 2001, 2002; Alfonso Cuarón, 2004; Mike Newell, 2005).

386 *Macbeth*
1948. U.S. Mercury Productions for Republic Pictures. Sound, b&w, 107 mins. Orson Welles.

Originally recorded in a Scottish burr, this B-movie-style production of *Macbeth* is nothing if not bizarre. The costumes vary wildly from character to character and make little or no functional sense, combining faux fur, silver lamé, tartan, and bare flesh, topped off with headpieces that look as though they were commissioned by outer-space gladiators—all remnants, it would seem, of theatrical productions past. This theme of cost-efficiency masquerading as creativity repeats itself in the sets, which, while far less gaudy than the costumes, are even less naturalistic. The enormous spikes that jut straight up out of the ground are a case in point: these free-standing, pointed columns do not support a roof that offers protection from the elements, nor do they serve as a barrier to deter unwanted guests. Yet this transparent lack of function is precisely what makes them so unnerving, for they embody the perverse "interior" architecture that Welles is so intent on exploring in his film of *Macbeth*. Indeed, even more than his acclaimed Harlem-based stage production, commonly referred to as the "Voodoo *Macbeth* (1936), Welles's film—despite its conspicuously flawed execution—is a psychological tour de force that has visibly influenced the best subsequent films of *Macbeth*, most notably Roman Polanski's hallucinogenic adaptation and Kurosawa's eclectic Samurai "Western" (both below).

Welles's film opens with an allusion to his theater production, as the witches wind up their spell while clutching a mass of wet, clay-like earth, clawing at the mass until it resembles a crude human form. That this "voodoo doll" represents not just an abstract human figure but also Macbeth himself is evident when, in the very next scene, the same necklace that the witches have placed around the figurine's neck is offered to Macbeth to signify his new title as "Thane of Cawdor." But without our knowledge of Welles's earlier theatrical production, the immediate association that the mud-strewn, totemic figurine conjures is the Jewish legend of the Golem. What follows from this scene, then, is more than just an examination of the psychological parameters of one man's ambition but, rather, an exploration of the undulating and often hypocritical architecture of organized religion. Subsequently, Welles's eclectic mise-en-scène moves from Judaic parable to pagan rabble, as we are introduced to the motley crew of "Scottish" thanes. Part Goth, part Viking, part Hun, and part barbarian, these warriors are recognizable for what they are not—Picts—for the only thing that is missing from their fur-strewn, fleshy, hairy, horn-topped, gold-adorned surfaces is the *Braveheart*-style face paint that distinguished these ancient, extinct predecessors of the Scots. Nevertheless, the eclectic appearance of the thanes is one of the better filmic representations of the hybrid tribes of Celts that alternately ravaged, settled, and abandoned much of the territory we now recognize as Europe. In fact, the ragtag occupants of Welles's mise-en-scène seem to belong not to eleventh-century Scotland but to a much earlier period— somewhere around the eighth century—as though the half-pagan, proto-Christian world of *Beowulf*, rather than the medieval Scotland of Shakespeare's play, was Welles's

immediate inspiration. This association is borne out by the ensuing interpolated scene over which a "Holy Father" prevails. Though intoning a prayer in Latin over the faint din of Gregorian-style chants, the gaunt figure of the priest, with his long, gray braids, sharp fingernails, and burdensome robes, also evokes ties to the pagan—if not druidic— worship of the natural world. The complexity and uneasy fit of these borrowed cultures is apparent in the classic Wellesian juxtaposition that follows; switching to English, the priest exclaims, "Dost thou renounce Satan and his works and all his pomp?" to which the thanes grunt in reply, "I do renounce him." Immediately, the camera provides the visual "punctuation" for this pronouncement—an image of the Thane of Cawdor's head on a cross-shaped pike—the savagery of which is paired with the thanes' collective utterance of "Amen." In the context of a culture that accepts murder with the same poker-faced indifference as it does God, Macbeth's conscience-stricken moments are nothing shy of heroic.

The film ends, appropriately, with a return to the Golem/voodoo figurine, from which Macbeth recoils in horror in the instant that Macduff decapitates it. Immediately after the dismembered mound of clay is flung to the ground, Macbeth's real head, dangling from the end of Macduff's sword, is flung over the cliff, down to the frenzied masses gathered below. All that is missing from this neat conclusion is a vision of the thanes consuming the body and the blood of Macbeth, a scene that would render all too plain the history of savagery that these would-be Christians—ostensibly headed for the Crusades—share with the pagan cultures they seek to subdue. Though this first of Welles's three Shakespeare films has incurred praise and criticism in almost equal measure, the film is of pivotal importance as a particularly rich source of Welles's artistic debts to radio and theater, as an adaptation that positions cinema not as a culmination but as an extension of these other media. See also entries 823 and 867.

DVD: restores the film from its cut version, which ran eighty-six minutes, to its full length.

387 *Macbeth*
1951. U.S. Unusual Films/Bob Jones University. Sound, col., 80 mins. Katherine Stenholm.

A strange choice for a Bible-belt production, this amateur *Macbeth* film stars Bob Jones Jr. Rather bizarrely, the film eliminates Lady Macbeth's "Unsex me here" speech (presumably in the interests of p[ropr]iety) but features three men in drag as the witches.

388 *Joe Macbeth*
1955. U.K. Columbia Pictures. Sound, b&w, 90 mins. Ken Hughes.

This adaptation is important as the earliest known transposition of Shakespeare to the conventions of the gangster film genre. The plot and characters follow Macbeth with minimal alterations, the most significant of which is the film's treatment of the relationship between Joe and his best friend Banky, who is not suspicious of Joe's motives and remains loyal to him when he takes over for Duca as kingpin. Rather, it is Banky's son Lennie who suspects foul play from Joe, who immediately orders him killed. A variation on the miscarried plans that plague the intended murder of Banquo and Fleance in Shakespeare's play, the hit is botched when Banky is killed instead. In many ways more logical than the conclusion of Shakespeare's play, Lennie, the Fleance character, avenges his father's murder and kills Joe in the end. Another provocative alteration is the film's perverse rendering of "justice" in its depiction of the relationship between Joe and the Lady Macbeth character, Lily. For if, as in almost all the other film versions, Macbeth's ambition may be "blamed" on his wife's persistent promptings, which, in turn, lead to the ultimately suicidal pangs of conscience that she experiences as her punishment, here Joe accidentally shoots Lily, inviting a more misogynistic interpretation of Macbeth's wife getting "what she deserves." Interestingly, the central role of the swimming pool in the film (wherein Joe stabs Duca) is repeated in a different context in *Scotland, PA* (below), wherein the Macbeths literally drown Duncan in a vat of frying fat and, after taking over his fast-food business, purchase an above-ground pool as the symbol of their success. See also entry 830.

389 *Kumonosu jô (Throne of Blood [The Castle of the Spider's Web])*
1957. Japan. Toho. Sound, b&w, 105 mins. Akira Kurosawa.

Without employing a single word from Shakespeare, Kurosawa's adaptation—preposterous as it may sound—is a more effective rendering of *Macbeth* than the vast majority of English language films of Shakespeare's play. In fact, there is something about foreign language adaptations that liberate spectators from the rigors of rhetorical exactitude and enable them to enter into what revolutionary film theorist Sergei Eisenstein termed "the filmic fourth dimension." Inspired, not coincidentally, from Eisenstein's study of Kabuki theater, the filmic fourth dimension is a space of plural provocation in which visual and aural stimuli are experienced simultaneously and unhierarchically—a place that exists, as it were, *between* the discrete borders of film frames where, contrary to the classical "'aristocracy' of individualistic dominants... [there is] a 'democratic' equality of rights for all provocations, or stimuli" (*Film Form* 1949, 66). Kurosawa's adaptation of *Macbeth* offers a unique example of how these competing stimuli produce very dif-

ferent films in the minds of individual spectators—much more so than an adaptation in which Shakespeare's language works with cinematic grammar to organize and streamline the perception of meaning. The competing codes associated with the medieval samurai culture of Kurosawa's setting—the sparsity and survivalist orientation of the vast, menacing landscape, coupled with the culture of personal ornamentation associated with both male warrior dress and female masking (itself a conflicting sign of modesty and sexual availability)—compel the spectator to adopt a posture of affective and semantic pliability throughout the film, without privileging any single source of cues. The most provocative point of entry into this filmic fourth dimension is not Macbeth (Washizu) but his wife Asaji, whose hauntingly understated voice, dress, and expression—rendered all the more ghostly by her high-set, painted-on eyebrows located just below her hairline—continually conflict with her homicidal promptings and profoundly "unladylike" ambition. Yet the representation of Asaji is not limited to visual stimuli, for the mere *memory* of the barely audible squeaking of her slippers and swishing of her dress along the wooden castle floors evinces shudders from the audience long after her suicide and the film's spectacular conclusion, in which Washizu is converted from a proud to pathetic peacock, run through with a flurry of his enemies' arrows. See also entry 831.

DVD: the Criterion collection includes the trailer, commentary by Michael Jeck, and an essay by Stephen Prince.

390 *Macbeth*
1960. U.S. Hallmark. Sound, col., 107 mins. George Schaefer.

Toshirô Mifune (Taketori Washizu) and Isuzu Yamada (Lady Asaji Washizu) in Akira Kurosawa's *Throne of Blood* (1957). Courtesy of Douglas Lanier.

"For the first time on the giant screen in blazing technicolor," reads the promotional poster for this film, which, regrettably, is not available in VHS or DVD formats. Like Olivier's *Richard III* (entry 469), this adaptation sits somewhat uneasily between film and television, and was created with both distributional media in mind. Though originally aired on TV and produced, in part, on a sound stage, this adaptation starring Maurice Evans and Judith Anderson was recorded on film and was released in U.S. theaters for a limited run in 1963. More significant than the five Emmys it gleaned from its television debut is the fact that this is the very first film adaptation of *Macbeth* to employ location shooting in Scotland, and its impressive battle sequences are believed to have inspired later Scottish-themed films such as *Rob Roy* (Michael Caton-Jones, 1995) and *Braveheart* (Mel Gibson, 1995).

391 *Macbeth*
1971. U.K. Playboy Productions/Caliban Films. Sound, col., 140 mins. Roman Polanski.

A particularly interesting choice of adaptation in light of the brutal murder of Polanski's wife and unborn child by the Charles Manson cult, this film, shot in Wales, has fared better in posterity than in its own day. In fact, Polanski's *Macbeth*, which is no more gratuitously violent than Kenneth Branagh's adaptation of *Henry V* (the latter praised for its "realistic" vision of war), seems to suffer from guilt by association—with the Playboy financing, for example, or the criminalization of Polanski himself—rather than being evaluated on its own terms. Though conceived as a conventional adaptation set in medieval Scotland, the film comments on its own creation in the "hippie" culture of the late 1960s and early 1970s not only in its allusion to the witches' potion as a form of LSD but also in its approach to sexual attraction as an addictive hallucinogen in its own right. Significantly, Francesca Annis's (Lady Macbeth's) nude sleepwalking scene was in the Polanski–Kenneth Tynan script even before Playboy stepped in to finance the project. In addition to the film's unapologetic realism, its most important contribution to the broader history of Shakespeare adaptation lies in its ending, which pictures the minor character Donalbain—Malcolm's estranged and, in this film, clubfooted younger brother—loping clumsily into the witches' lair. The implication is that the restoration of Malcolm as king will not put an end to the cycle of bloodletting that began with Macbeth's visitation with the "weird sisters" but, rather, provides the perfect excuse for a nearer and dearer display of homicidal violence: fratricide.

392 *Men of Respect*
1991. U.S. Efraim Horowitz and Gary Mehlman. Sound, col., 113 mins. William Reilly.

Created by New York University Assistant Professor William Reilly, this impressive mobster modernization, set

in the New York City underworld, stars John Turturro and Katherine Borowitz, who are married in real life. Remarkably faithful to the plot and text of *Macbeth*, Reilly's screenwriting paraphrases much of Shakespeare's shortest play with precision; for example, Donalbain's exclamation that "There's daggers in men's smiles" is reproduced in Donalbain Di'Mico's observation to his brother that "There's a gun behind every smile." The film, though violent, also successfully distills the sense of humor embedded in Shakespeare's play, chiefly through the addition of New York comedian Stephen Wright. Replacing the porter who unwittingly opens the door to murderers in *Macbeth*, Wright, in this adaptation, becomes the custodian assigned to clean up the dirty work of others. See also entry 854.

DVD: includes original trailer, widescreen format, and Dolby digital stereo.

393 *Macbeth*
1992. Russia/Wales. Soyuzmultifilm and Christmas Films. Sound, col., 25 mins. Nikolai Serebirakov.

A product of the series *Shakespeare: The Animated Tales*, this adaptation is composed through cel animation with a distinctly Russian flair for the dramatic, typified in the film's recurring images of dismemberment. Yet the violence of the imagery is often tempered by dissolves that privilege the fantastical, a prominent example of which occurs when Lady Macbeth delivers her "Unsex me here" speech to reveal a horse and a toothed beast springing from her bodice.

394 *Star Wars: Macbeth*
1997; 2001. U.S. AriZonA Pictures and NS Productions. Sound, col., 17 mins. Bien Concepcion and Donald Fitz-Roy.

Beginning with the simultaneous citation and displacement of Scotland, the opening frame of this *Macbeth* reads, "A long time ago in a galaxy far far away... SCOTLAND?" Originally an English project, this adaptation is a radically condensed version of Shakespeare's play using *Star Wars* characters, created by a group of Glen Ridge High School students known as "giggers," a derogatory combination of "geek" and "nigger." Appropriately, Scotland becomes in this short film a revisionary landscape, a "safe zone" of childhood nostalgia that presents teens with an opportunity to work through adolescent angst and, in so doing, imagine a better future. Against the history of machismo and jock cliques that gave this overwhelmingly upper-class high school a reputation for elitism, racism, and, ultimately, violence (culminating in the notorious gang rape of retarded girl Leslie Faber in 1989), the subtitle of this film could easily be called *The Giggers Strike Back*, for it ends in a vision of the geeks inheriting the earth or, better put, the galaxy—replete with interpolated footage from the original *Star Wars* movie, reproduced with permission from Steven Spielberg. In keeping with the 1990s' filmmaking trend of conspicuous product placement, Malcolm and Macduff celebrate the restoration of their dynasty in front of a Coca-Cola machine. See also entry 862.

395 Macbeth
1997. U.K. Cromwell Productions. Sound, col., 129 mins. Jeremy Freeston.

Though acclaimed as a theatrical production (1996), the film version has not been well received. Nevertheless, Freeston's adaptation, which takes pains to recreate the eleventh-century look of the play, remains only one of two films of *Macbeth* to be actually shot on location in Scotland. Also worthy of mention is the fact that Jason Connery (son of Sean) stars as Macbeth and that the film was financed, in part, by soliciting public investment: for £1,000 per share, financiers were permitted to appear in the film as extras.

DVD: includes a documentary on the making of the film.

396 Macbeth
1997. U.K. Channel Four Films. Sound, col., 87 mins. Michael Bogdanov.

Originally aired on BBC2, this adaptation participates in the emergent trend of setting *Macbeth* in unspecified, post-apocalyptic locations that eerily invoke the Third World within wealthy nations. The "castles" in Bogdanov's film, for example, are abandoned warehouses that serve as relics of rampant post-industrial fallout, born of global economic practices like outsourcing. One of the more poignant and memorable examples of the conflict between these two worlds is the tableau of Greta Scacchi's Lady Macbeth, elegantly reclining on silk pillows on the dirty floor of the empty warehouse she calls home. So, too, Macbeth is a figure who, for a time, elicits our sympathy, particularly when Duncan, who emerges as a distinctly white-collar criminal in this adaptation, passes over the bloodied day laborer in favor of promoting his undeserving and spoiled son, Malcolm. In stark contrast to Macbeth's sullied paramilitary garb, Malcolm enters the picture with a meticulously coiffed appearance, replete with a perfectly tilted beret—an indication that he has never even broached the battlefield. That Malcolm should resurface at the end of the film to claim his title, fresh from a bout of croquet on the manicured lawns of his English mansion, provides an all-too-fitting entrée for the next generation of armchair warriors. The film ends with a vision of alienated labor in the extreme, as Macbeth's body is dumped on a trash heap, where the witches—portrayed as homeless, unemployed women—proceed to pillage his body for scraps of subsistence. A film that is better in theory than execution, Bogdanov's *Macbeth* was created on the cusp of the DVD revolution and, hence, remains in the aesthetic no-man's-land between film and video.

397 Macbeth on the Estate
1997. U.K. BBC2. Sound, col., 80 mins. Penny Woolcock.

Deceptively titled for U.S. audiences who associate the word "estate" with multimillionaires, this film is shot on location on Birmingham's Ladywood Estate, with "estate" invoking the equivalent of government-subsidized housing projects in the United States. Created by documentary filmmaker Penny Woolcock and originally aired on BBC2, *Macbeth on the Estate* is a highly condensed modernization of Shakespeare's play featuring a handful of professional actors (James Frain as Macbeth, for example) and more than a hundred residents of the housing project. The film's unforgettable contribution to the remarkably rich adaptation history of *Macbeth* is its decision to make the witches not old crones but *children*—a far from subtle comment about governments on both sides of the Atlantic, whose convenient claims about "urban renewal" amidst the post-industrial squalor of northern England or Midwestern America continue to leave not one, but innumerable, children behind. Similarly, the portrait of Birnam Wood as a lone tree suggests in no uncertain terms the environmental toll of such political profiteering. But perhaps the most disturbing aspect of this *Macbeth* is its vision of the racism that perpetuates these cycles of abjection, for Woolcock's film ends with a vision of Fleance—ostensibly a future king—outfitted as a skinhead and pointing his fingers in the shape of a gun, leveled at the blue-eyed, brown-skinned, distinctly mulatto figure of young Malcolm.

398 In the Flesh
1998. U.S. and Hungary. VCA. Sound, col., 120 mins. Stuart Canterbury.

An example of the lesser known cottage industry in "adult" Shakespeare films, *In The Flesh* is a surprisingly faithful adaptation of *Macbeth* that stars porn film staples Mike Horner and Kylie Ireland. Its most memorable scene by far stems from the decision to recast the banquet as an orgy that includes the ghost of Duncan. Indeed, the most noteworthy qualities of this adaptation are its efforts to translate the shifting sentiments of Shakespeare's play into distinctly erotic scenarios; Lady Macbeth's suicide, for example, is also depicted as her final orgasm, as the "little death" and the "big sleep" become one and the same phenomenon. Although tartan accents adorn what little clothing the cast members wear in an effort to invoke "Scotland," *In the Flesh* makes more of its scenic filming location shooting in Budapest, which also serves to sell the swarthy "Magyar" look of the film's cast. Hence, this *Macbeth* offers a provocative example of the multinational dimensions of adult filmmaking. Moreover, as a film with explicitly artistic aspirations, *In the Flesh* is evidence of the emergent genre of "high" as opposed to "hard" porn. Compare *Macbeth xxx* (entry 866); See also entry 864.

DVD: includes interactive menus, photo gallery, and previews.

399 *Macbeth*
1998. U.S. Showcase Films. Sound, col., length unknown. Paul Winarski.

This indie *Macbeth* uses locations in Cape Cod and Harvard University environs. Though Winarski is established as a theater director, his film debut has been described by reviewers as aesthetically stunning if technically unsophisticated.

400 *Macbeth-Sangrador (Bleeder)*
1999. Venezuela. Post Meridien Cinema. Sound, b&w, 89 mins. Leonardo Henríquez.

Surprise winner at the Argentinian film festival, this film is a predominantly faithful version of *Macbeth* that takes place within South American bandit culture. The one significant departure from Shakespeare's play is the film's effort to establish Maximiliano (Macbeth) as a "good guy" who happens to fall in with the wrong crowd. Through this point of emphasis, Henríquez (who also wrote the screenplay) adopts a less ambiguous approach to the relationship between fate and coincidence in Shakespeare's play, by suggesting that Maximiliano is a victim of circumstance more than a cold-blooded killer by nature. Nevertheless, the film is laced with over-the-top violence, gratuitous nudity, and South American stereotypes. Reflecting *Macbeth*'s extensive history of adaptation within the protocols of indigenous gangster cultures, *Macbeth-Sangrador* is more interesting for the way in which the camera becomes a source of machismo in this film, as though its frenetic movements and bravura angles were an attempt to outperform Maximiliano himself. The style of the adaptation, coupled with its conspicuously irreverent use of Catholic imagery, suggests the pronounced influence of Baz Luhrmann's 1996 film *William Shakespeare's Romeo + Juliet* (below), a film shot in Mexico City—a place rife with images of the Virgin Mary—and visibly enamored with the caricatures of Latino culture. See also entry 868.

401 *Makibefo*
1999. Madagascar and U.K. Blue Eye Films. Sound, b&w, 73 mins. Alexander Abela.

Oceanographer Alexander Abela bases his little-known adaptation of *Macbeth* in a remote coastal village of Madagascar, in which the inhabitants are, appropriately, fishermen. Using a technical team of precisely two people, Abela's equally stripped-down version of Shakespeare's play reduces the complexities of Scottish succession to five essential characters: Makibefo, Valy Makibefo, Bakova, Malikomy, and Kidoure—a condensation of King Duncan and the Thane of Cawdor. Featuring a cast of non-professional actors utterly cut off from technology—including electricity, running water, and the mass media—

Abela's vision of "Scotland" approximates both the barrenness and brutality of Shakespeare's medieval landscape more than any other screen landscape to date. Yet *Makibefo* simultaneously suggests the influence of other screen *Macbeth*s, for it clearly enters into dialogue with Welles's 1948 adaptation (above). In fact, Abela's film issues a corrective to the casual primitivism of Welles's version, in which the beating of tribal drums, the bearing of flesh, and the sensationalist sprinklings of "black magic" serve as a synecdoche for "primitivism"—an example of what Toni Morrison refers to as the function of blackness in the white imagination. By contrast, *Makibefo* does not subscribe to a neototemic approach to its African context, unfolding instead through the rituals of everyday life. In other words, in this film, the fiction of *Macbeth* is driven by the lived realities of its Malagasy performers. Particularly at the beginning of the film, the stunning resolution of the stark, black and white cinematography seems almost at odds with Makibefo's considerable hesitation; he strikes us, at least initially, as having more in common with Hamlet than with his warrior namesake. But this approach both to performance and to production is in keeping with Abela's cinema verité aspirations, for unlike the abrupt edits and accelerated narrativization of other screen versions of Shakespeare's shortest play, *Makibefo* unfolds at a relatively leisurely pace, attentive to the rhythms of its setting and the fluid action of Abela's earlier work with underwater cinematography. Importantly, despite Abela's scientific eye, the camera does not study its subjects; rather, it modestly observes the inhabitants of the frame without judgment, much like the Namibian bystander-narrator of the Dogme 95 adaptation of Lear, *The King Is Alive* (2000).

Perhaps the most fruitful avenue of inquiry raised by this film, particularly when explored in conjunction with Michael Roes's *Someone Is Sleeping in My Pain: An East-West Macbeth* (below), is attempting to identify what makes this exceptionally violent and insular play about Scottish politics such a rich source of dialogue—if not diplomacy—between East and West in the age of global antagonisms. See also entry 869.

402 *Mad Dawg: Running Wild in the Streets*
2001. U.S. Leo Films and Fusion Films. Sound, col., 95 mins. Greg Salman.

Never commercially released, *Mad Dawg* is a gangsta—as opposed to gangster—adaptation of *Macbeth* that reflects a combination of the Shaksploitation and blaxsploitation genres. Searching for a plot to justify its creation, Salman pilfers from the play to structure what is otherwise a cheaply made, poorly shot film whose every third word is an expletive. For example, in place of Lady Macbeth's demonic suggestion that Duncan's murder be blamed on the guards, *Mad Dawg*'s Lady M. instructs Mac to give Duncan's prostitutes some bad coke and then "blame the shit on the hos." The film's one thought-provoking flourish is its replacement of the witches with a lone televangelist, whose self-aggrandizing designs cleverly transpose the more dubious motivation of Shakespeare's witches into the profit-or-perish milieu of contemporary consumer culture. Nevertheless, Salmon's tasteless vision of *Macbeth* as a "Dawg Eat Dawg World" is better left unconsumed. See also entry 874.

DVD: no special features.

403 *Scotland, PA*
2001. U.S. Lot 49 Films. Sound, col., 102 mins. Billy Morrisette.

A brilliant transpositional treatment of the "Scottish play" set in the cultural backwater of western Pennsylvania in the 1970s, Billy Morrisette's film retains none of Shakespeare's language but captures the enterprising spirit of the Macbeths in this tale of a small-town corporate takeover. (Significantly, the filmmakers began shooting in rural Pennsylvania but found it too built up to produce the more depressed look of middle America in the 1970s, hence, the production moved to—of all places—Nova Scotia, literally "New Scotland.") Repeatedly passed over for promotion at Duncan's burger joint, Joe "Mac" McBeth (James LeGros) is persuaded by his wife, Pat, played by *ER* star Maura Tierney, to murder his boss. When the high-camp act of Duncan's elimination at the hands of a deep-fat fryolater is achieved, Duncan's burger joint is converted to "McBeth's"—evocative, of course, of McDonald's—and Mac's modest dream of a middle-class existence materializes overnight. But the more his fast-food kingdom expands (with the help of innovations such as the drive-through window and a traveling French fry truck), so does his appetite for brutality and penchant for paranoia, which drive him to murder his best friend, Anthony Banconi, on the slightest hint of suspicion. Once the local detective, McDuff (Christopher Walken), is called onto the scene to investigate the string of "accidental" deaths, Pat, too, falls prey to paranoia and, unlike her husband, pangs of guilt, which culminate in her suicidal decision to remove the invisible fryolater burn on her hand with a meat cleaver. A stunning example of what post-modern theorist Fredric Jameson refers to as "libidinal historicism," *Scotland, PA* employs persuasive markers of the 1970s—such as Bad Company songs, Camaros, bell bottoms, and allusions to popular television series like *McCloud*—that nevertheless fail to offer us sufficient escape into a retroculture insulated from the corporate endgames that, in the age of Enron, make the McBeth's franchise look like "small potatoes" indeed. Appropriately, in a nod to Polanski's concluding vision of Donalbain starting the vicious cycle of ambition anew (above), Morrisette's film ends with a vision of MacDuff, having vanquished the

carnivorous McBeth, opening a vegetarian fast-food franchise.

DVD: includes director's commentary, snapshots from Sundance, and an Insider's Guide to *Scotland, PA*. See also entry 876.

404 *Someone Is Sleeping in My Pain: An East-West Macbeth*
2002. Yemen/U.S./Germany. Michael Roes. Sound, col., 96 mins. Michael Roes.

This digital *Macbeth* is the story of an American film director (played by African American actor-dancer Andreá Smith) who travels to Yemen in order to film a South Arabian version of *Macbeth* among Yemeni tribal warriors. "For them," as Michael Roes comments, "honor, hospitality, and blood feuds—those medieval concepts which occupied the Scottish king Macbeth—are not obsolete ones, but are values that are still valid and lived out" (www.hagbeck.com/e_f_jemen.html). Nor is the American director immune to the throes of ambition, for in his relentless desire to create the film, he underestimates the magnitude of the cross-cultural challenge he has initiated. A brilliant independent "adaptation" in the most nuanced sense of the term, Roes's film is as much about its process of production—replete with the problems of communication and intercultural conflicts that Shakespeare's medieval play raises for present East-West relations—as it is about the founding of the Stuart dynasty.

405 *Macbeth*
2006. Australia. Film Victoria and Mushroom Pictures. In production. Geoffrey Wright.

Set in Melbourne's gang culture, this adaptation (currently in production) suggests not only an obvious debt to the many gangster film adaptations of *Macbeth* that precede it but also at least a titular nod to Tim Blake Nelson's *O* (1999 entry 461), in which the Othello character is a former gang member. See also entry 882.

406 *Macbeth*
Renaissance Films. In production. Todd Louiso.

No previous attempt to set *Macbeth* in eleventh-century Scotland has proven a commercial success; however, the backers of this film, set to star Jennifer Connelly and Philip Seymour Hoffman, are certain that this adaptation will—through name recognition and Hollywood-style production values—transcend the curse of Shakespeare's "Scottish play."

407 *Macbeth aka: William Shakespeare's Macbeth*
In production. U.S. South Main Street Productions. Richard Griffin.

This film purports to maintain Shakespeare's text in a modernized, B-grade horror film setting, similar to the style of indie filmmaker Christopher Dunne (*Titus Andronicus*, below).

MEASURE FOR MEASURE

408 *Dente per Dente (Measure for Measure)*
1942. Italy. F. E. R. T. Studios. Sound, b&w, 90 mins.
Marco Elter.

This adaptation, the title of which translates literally as
"Tooth for Tooth," retains little of the play's language but
the majority of its plot. The film is significant for being the
only adaptation of *Measure for Measure* that has a close
relation to the play beyond the appropriation of its title.
The decision to adapt a play about an imposter-dictator in
Austria is particularly interesting in light of the film's
creation during the Mussolini era, at which time Italy
aligned itself with the Axis forces, though the country was
eventually bombed by both Allied and German troops.

THE MERCHANT OF VENICE

409 *The Merchant of Venice*
1908. U.S. Vitagraph. Silent, b&w, c. 9 mins. William
Ranous.

One of the least successful films in the Vitagraph series,
this version of *Merchant* is hampered by its use of painted
drops, which create an unsatisfactory illusion of "Venice."

410 *Il Mercante Di Venezia (The Merchant of Venice)*
1910. Italy. Film d'Arte Italiana. Silent, col. (tinting),
8 mins. Gerolamo Lo Savio.

Shot on location among the watery "streets" of Venice,
this film offers yet another example of the Italian proclivity
for taking full advantage of the new medium's possibilities
for liberating representation from static frontality and
suffocating interiors. The prints are color-tinted with a
range of rich hues, adding drama through association;
Shylock, for example, wears crimson robes, evocative of his
thirst for blood. As was a common practice in silent cinema, the bond is represented as a handwritten document
to which the audience is privy. Whereas in Shakespeare's
play, Shylock states the terms of his agreement with Antonio, in Lo Savio's film, Antonio is shown writing the
letter that entitles Shylock "to any part of my body he
pleases," a variation that evinces the perversity of the bond
and, especially, Antonio's affinity for masochism. Shylock
is distinguished from the others by his wildly unkempt hair
and exaggerated gestures that, at times, border on clown-
ish. The "abduction" of Shylock's daughter Jessica (as it is
referred to in the film) is prefaced by a letter from Lorenzo,
which reads, "Pretty Jessica, My friends Antonio and
Bassanio have business with your father and he will leave
with them soon. Be prepared as soon as they are gone and I
will come for you." This addition allows Lo Savio to pass
over the cumbersome debate over whether or not Jessica
should disguise herself as a boy, for when the coast is clear,
she simply emerges from her house and steals away with
Lorenzo. Two somewhat inexplicable aspects of this

adaptation are the casting of Olga Giannini Novelli, a
large and distinctly matronly woman, in the role of Portia
(her appearance strains belief that she is worth all the
trouble) and the film's ambiguous ending, wherein the law
leaving Shylock's fate up to the "Duke's discretion" is
shown to the audience, but no verdict follows. By choice or
by accident, Lo Savio leaves the ending up to us.

DVD: *Silent Shakespeare*: digitally remastered with a
newly recorded score.

411 *The Merchant of Venice*
1912. U.S. Edwin Thanhouser. Silent, b&w, 30 mins.
Barry O'Neil.

A precedent-setting film in the history of American-
screened Shakespeare, this *Merchant* is a two-reel study in
pictorographic splendor, with great care taken to recreate
lavish Venetian interiors and exteriors that include establishing shots of an Italian garden, courtesy of one of
Thanhouser's associates. The film may be usefully compared with the Vitagraph *Merchant* (above), which, unlike
Thanhouser's production that pursued a more elite audience, actively courted a mass audience comprised of not
only working-class Americans but also newly arrived immigrants.

412 *Shylock, ou le Marchand de Venise (The Merchant of
Venice)*
1913. France. Éclipse. Silent, b&w, 22 mins. Henri
Desfontaines.

The French Film d'Art productions were known for
being more theatrical than cinematic, and, as such, they
are valuable as artifacts of transition. The most noteworthy
and disturbing irony of this film is that the actor who
played Shylock (Harry Baur) would later be tortured by the
Gestapo in a French prison; he died shortly after his release.

413 *The Merchant of Venice*
1914. U.S. Universal. Silent, b&w, four reels. Lois Weber.

This lost film is significant as the first feature-length
Shakespearean comedy on screen, and was directed by Lois
Weber, the highest paid director—male or female—at
Universal Studios and a pioneer of silent cinema.

414 *The Merchant of Venice*
1916. U.K. Broadwest Film Company. Silent, b&w, five
reels. Walter West.

Essentially a film recording of a theatrical production at
the St. James Theatre, this abbreviated production is distinguished by its transposition of Shylock's entire speech
"Hath not a Jew eyes?" onto title cards. Nevertheless, *Cinema News and Property Gazette* favorably reported, "The
Broadwest *Merchant of Venice* is not a photo-play, but a
moving photograph of Shakespeare's stage play" (January
11, 1917).

415 *Der Kaufmann Von Venedig (The Jew of Mestri)*
1923. Germany. Peter Paul Felner Produktion. Silent, b&w, 64 mins. Peter Paul Felner.

Despite its title and the altered names of several protagonists (Shylock is Mordecai, and Portia is Beatrice), this film is clearly an adaptation of Shakespeare's *The Merchant of Venice* with a few provocative additions, such as the death of Mordecai's wife, Rachela, from a heart attack. Werner Krauss stars as Mordecai.

416 *The Merchant of Venice*
1927. U.K. De Forest Phonofilms. Sound, b&w, 10 mins. Widgey R. Newman.

This film is the first known Shakespearean talkie, using Lee De Forest's precedent-setting recording system, to which all sound films are indebted.

417 *Le Marchand de Venise (The Merchant of Venice)*
1953. France/Italy. Elysée Film/Venturini Produzione Films. Sound, b&w, 102 mins. Pierre Billon.

This otherwise unremarkable coproduction stars the exceptional French actor Michel Simon, long associated with the work of Jean Renoir, as Shylock. Whether or not the makeup accident that left part of Simon's face paralyzed occurred in this film or, more likely, in his role as the Banquo character in a 1952 spin-off of Shakespeare's cursed "Scottish play" (see *Le Rideau Rouge*, or *The Crimson Curtain*), is the subject of much speculation.

DVD: no special features noted.

418 *The Merchant of Venice*
1969. Sound, b&w, 60 + mins. Orson Welles.

As was customary with Welles, *The Merchant of Venice* was a film that he undertook simultaneously while working on *The Deep*, a thriller that, Welles hoped, would prove popular enough to pay for all of his unfinished pet projects. Ironically, both films shared the same fate: with only a scene or two left, *The Deep* was nearing completion when Lawrence Harvey, its star, died; later, the negatives—like those for the newly completed *The Merchant of Venice*—mysteriously vanished. The Munich Film Museum is working on a restoration of *The Deep*, two working prints of which survived, whereas what remains of Welles's *Merchant*, though providing us with far less to look at—less than a reel, in fact—offers much to think about as the final adaptation in Welles's eclectic Shakespearean "tetralogy." The film opens with a glorious flotilla of maskers on Venice's Grand Canal during the height of *carnevale*; even in black and white, the kaleidoscopic range of hues remains detectable through the grainy film stock. When the costs of filming in Venice proved too high and Welles's backers pulled out, Welles moved both *The Deep* and *Merchant* to a tiny island off the coast of Dalmatia (now Croatia), since both films required location shooting on or near water. In perhaps the most extraordinary example of Welles's

resourcefulness, wooden puppets filled in for masked carnival goers where actors could not be found or paid—the result is not grade-B Shakespeare but a remarkably haunting experience, from Shylock's point of view, of the "wooden" Venetians' consistent refusal to recognize his humanity as a Jew. Played by Welles, Shylock delivers his "Hath not a Jew eyes?" speech as understatement—less angrily than world-weary. Years later, long after the allegedly stolen negatives failed to surface and the fate of *Merchant* had been confirmed, Welles drove out into a field and delivered Shylock's monologue in a trenchcoat at dusk. As with so many of Welles's films, we cannot help but hear in this strange speech his outrage at those in whom he had placed his trust and whom he believed—with or without cause—had betrayed him. That fragments of this remarkable film have survived against all odds is, perhaps, the best revenge.

Excerpts of the film are available in Vassili Silovic's documentary *One Man Band* (1996), which has been bundled in the recently released DVD version of *"F" for Fake*.

419 *Te Tangata Whai Rawa O Weniti (The Maori Merchant of Venice)*
2002. New Zealand. He Taonga Films/Te Mangai Paho. Sound, col., 158 mins. Don C. Selwyn.

The first Maori adaptation of a Shakespeare play, this *Merchant of Venice* also participates in the broader "Kiwi film revolution" associated with Peter Jackson's *Lord of the Rings* trilogy (2001, 2002, 2003) and independent gems like *Whale Rider* (Niki Caro, 2002). Based on an earlier theatrical version, Selwyn's film, set in seventeenth-century Venice but performed in distinctly non-European period costumes, is dominated by medium and close shots. Hence, a more useful point of analysis than the film's restrained cinematography is its textual status as an exercise in "double translation." In the Renaissance, a common pedagogical exercise was translating a text from Latin into English and, from the English, back into Latin—hence the expression "double translation." *The Maori Merchant of Venice* operates according to a similar principle: the text of the film is derived from Dr. Pei Te Hurinui Jones's translation of Shakespeare's play (1) into Maori (2); subsequently, the English subtitles (3) are derived from the Maori translation, the result of which (4) is not a return to Shakespeare's text but an English language version that takes it cues as much from a Maori inflection as it does from Shakespeare. Like the Shakespeare films of Bollywood, this adaptation may be usefully explored as a register of the Maori peoples' complex attitude toward the European colonizers of New Zealand, particularly in its dramatization of the relationship between cultural "insiders" and "outsiders." See also entry 901.

420 *William Shakespeare's The Merchant of Venice*
2004. U.S./Italy/Luxembourg/U.K. Avenue Pictures,
Navidi-Wilde, Movision Entertainment, Spice Factory.
Sound, col., 138 mins. Michael Radford.

Pacino's long-anticipated performance as Shylock ultimately falls short of the hype associated with this film from
the director of *Il Postino* (1994). Pacino overplays Shylock
in his standard New York accent, which, in and of itself,
makes the much-maligned Jew even more of an outcast
than he really is in Venice's flourishing merchant community. Whereas the production values, typical of Radford, are stunning, the performances delivered by Pacino,
Joseph Fiennes (Bassanio), and Jeremy Irons (Antonio)—
although excellent in isolation—clash in ways that are
superfluous to the plot. The subject of more fruitful discussion and debate has been the film's emphasis on the
Jessica subplot and, especially, the ending that pictures her
staring down at Leah's ring—an indication that she did
not, in fact, sell it for a monkey as Tubal reports. The
implication that Jessica is perhaps not as happy in her
marriage or, for that matter, in her conversion to Chris-
tianity as the Venetians would like us to believe makes the
film as a whole far more interesting in retrospect. The final
image of Jessica gazing at her father's cherished heirloom is
complemented by the background against which it is shot:
an exquisite tableau of two fisherman hunting with arrows
that arc into the water and then disappear. A vision of
beauty and futility and, above all, the brutality of Christian
proselytism, the film's closing scene subtly comments on
those "fishers of men" who, in turn, make *other* men—like
Shylock—prey to their sacrilegious whims.

421 *The Merchant of Venice*
In production in 2005. Patrick Stewart and Ian McKellen.

Sir Ian McKellen and Patrick Stewart, two of Britain's
greatest Shakespearean actors, are to star in a film adaptation of *The Merchant of Venice* set in modern-day Las
Vegas. McKellen will apparently play Bassanio, and
Stewart will play Shylock. The £20 million movie will shift
the action of the Bard's 1596 play from medieval Italy to
the flamboyant Venetian Resort, Hotel and Casino in the
heart of the Nevada desert. Stewart will keep Shakespeare's dialogue but set the action on the resort's versions
of the Rialto Bridge, St. Mark's Square, and the Grand
Canal. No attempt will be made to pass off the replica
settings as the real Venice. Stewart believes that America's
gambling capital is the perfect backdrop for Shakespeare's
classic tale of reckless wagers, greed, and moneylending.
The film is also expected to make use of the city's thriving
gay scene as it tries to explore the nature of the relationship
between Antonio, the eponymous hero of the play, and
Bassanio, his young protégé. Industry sources believe the
film will be more like Baz Lurhman's *Romeo + Juliet* (1996
[below]).

THE MERRY WIVES OF WINDSOR

422 *Merry Wives of Windsor*
1910. U.S. Selig Polyscape Company. Silent, b&w, c.
10 mins. William Selig.

This early version of *Wives* evidently had *A Midsummer
Night's Dream* "on the brain," as its most noteworthy scene
contains an image of Falstaff wearing an ass's head rather
than buck horns.

423 *Merry Wives of Windsor* (U.K. title); *Sir John Falstaff*
(U.S. title)
1911. France. Éclipse. Silent, b&w, 10 mins. Henri
Defontaines.

A review in the April 20 *Bioscope* reports this film as
"entitled to rank among the greatest successes" of Éclipse
films. The evidence that the film is modeled more after the
Verdi opera than the Shakespeare play (as Eddie Sammons
argues in *Shakespeare: A Hundred Years on Film*) is not
compelling, since one of the scenes includes Mistress
Quickly's marriage to Pistol, which does not occur in the
opera.

424 *Falstaff the Tavern Knight*
1923. U.K. British and Colonial Kinematograph
Company. Silent, b&w, c. 20 mins. Edwin Greenwood.

The only thing that distinguishes this short film version
of *Merry Wives* is the fact that the cast includes Margarte
Yarde, who would become famous as a horror film actress.
See also entry 904.

425 *Die Lustigen Weiber (Merry Wives of Windsor)*
1935. Germany. Carl Hoffmann and Leslie Urdung,
producers. Sound, b&w, 90 mins. Carl Hoffmann.

Though the evidence concerning this film is tenuous, if
it is true that Carl Hoffman (a major German Expressionist
filmmaker distinguished for his work with Fritz Lang) cast
Leo Slezak, one of the most famous tenors at the Vienna
Court Opera, as Falstaff, then this would have been a film
well worth seeing. Given this information, however, it is
likely that Hoffman's film was a recording of an opera,
rather than an adaptation.

426 *Campanadas a Medianoche* (U.K. title: *Chimes
at Midnight*; U.S. title: *Falstaff*)
1966. Spain/Switzerland. Internacional Films Española/
Alpine. Sound, b&w, 115 mins. Orson Welles.

See entries 347 and 752.

427 *As Alegres Comadres*
2003. Brazil. Ananã Produções, Conexão Cinema, and
Zohar Cinema. Sound, col., 109 mins. Leila Hipólito.

The only Brazilian film shown in the historic First Women's International Film Festival in Israel, Hipólito's
adaptation reveals the increasing inclination to set Shakespeare films in the nineteenth century (see, especially,
Hoffman's *Dream* [below] and Branagh's *Hamlet* [above]).

Set in the scenic valley town of Tiradentes (which, not coincidentally, hosts an annual film festival of its own), the film features an ex-soldier named João Fausto who devises a plan to seduce and bribe two affluent homemakers, who, in turn, plot their own revenge. *Merry Wives'* theme of women working together is particularly central to Hipólito's philosophy of filmmaking, which is not only deeply collaborative but also concerned with acquiring female financing. This ethos permits her broader latitude for representing, in the context of a deeply patriarchal culture, male foibles, as she suggests in her description of the film as a "lusty comedy of many errors (largely male) and non-errors (mainly female)." The question is whether or not this theme jars with Hipólito's nationalistic desire to "make a film which [i]s completely Brazilian in every way, from design and characterization to setting." The success of the film abroad is an indication that *As Alegres Comrades* met both objectives. See also entry 911.

A MIDSUMMER NIGHT'S DREAM

428 *A Midsummer Night's Dream*
1909. U.S. Vitagraph. Silent, b&w, 8 mins. J. Stuart Blackton and Charles Kent.

Though this short film reproduces the major plot elements of Shakespeare's play—including Egeus's rejection of Hermia's preferred suitor, Puck's mischievous anointing exploits, the rude mechanicals (here referred to as "tradesmen"), Bottom's conversion to an ass and Titania's infatuation with him, Hermia's fight with Helena, Lysander and Demetrius's pursuit of one another, the final reconciliation, and, lastly, Bottom's recounting of his dream—this *eight-minute* film also *adds* the character of Penelope in a twist that marks its emergence as one of the earliest free adaptations in the more contemporary spirit of the term. Even without the benefit of post-modern approaches to gender and sexuality that audiences may bring to bear on this newly available film, the Penelope character gives this adaptation a strikingly "queer" spin—certainly a first for screened Shakespeare—as she replaces the character of Oberon, devising her revenge after a falling-out with Titania. That this quarrel, like the Oberon-Titania conflict in the play, is a lovers' quarrel is suggested not only by the film's wholesale substitution of Penelope for Oberon but also by the penultimate scene in which Penelope removes the love spell: in this instant, Titania awakes and veers toward Penelope as though she were angling for a kiss, but then abruptly points the way forward to some off-screen place, grazing Penelope's breast with her arm in the process. Penelope responds by putting her arm around Titania with an almost paterna-

listic confidence, and the two stroll happily away in an interpolated scene that restores the bonds between women that Hippolyta, Hermia, and Helena have all sacrificed to marriage. In addition to offering a semantically provocative interpretation of Shakespeare's play, this sepia-toned adaptation is also technologically advanced, distinguished not only by its open-air shooting but also by a scene that employs dissolves and superimpositions to represent Puck's circumnavigation of the globe.

DVD: *Silent Shakespeare*: this Milestone collection offers a restored print and a newly recorded score.

429 *A Midsummer Night's Dream*
1913. Italy. Gloria Film. Silent, b&w, c. 22 mins. Paulo Azzuri.

Yet another testament to the precocity of Italian filmmaking, the fragments that remain of this *Dream* contain evidence of dissolves, chiaroscuro effects, and location shooting, all of which combine to propel early Shakespearean film into a category beyond theater.

430 *A Midsummer Night's Dream*
1935. U.S. Warner Bros. Sound, b&w, 117 mins/140 mins. Max Reinhardt/William Dieterle.

Derived, in part, from Reinhardt's German stage production, this film, created on a huge budget for its time ($1.5 million), takes full advantage of cinema's capacity for spectacle. Like the Svend Gade *Hamlet* (above), Reinhardt's adaptation is indebted to German Expressionism, which accounts for the film's brilliant chiaroscuro effects and corresponding inquiries into the more sinister resonances of Shakespeare's play—its nightmarish threads of sadism, misogyny, beastiality, and political tyranny. Parti-

Jean Muir (Helena) and a young Mickey Rooney (Puck) in Max Reinhardt's *Midsummer Night's Dream* (1935). Courtesy of Douglas Lanier.

cularly interesting is the treatment of Hippolyta, whose distinctly phallic accessories, typified in the live snake she wields at the beginning of the film, suggest the tenacity of the anxieties elicited by the Roaring Twenties' equivalent of Hippolyta's Amazonion past: the transvetite figure of the flapper. In this context, Theseus's opening allusions to impotence,

but O, methinks, how slow
This old moon [wanes]! She lingers my desires,
Like to a step dame, or a dowager,
Long withering out a young man's revenue (1.1.3–6)

suggest the precarious masculinity of U.S. culture in the interwar years. Combining stylistic flourishes from the European art cinema, courtesy of not only Reinhardt's international reputation but also the artists he imports, such as choreographer Bronislava Nijinksa, composer Philip Mendelssohn, and dancer Nini Theilade, with the Hollywood studio system and other, less glamorous remnants of America's industrial landscape—typified in the film's use of a special cobweb-making machine known as the Akron Spider—this adaptation is the first Shakespeare film to succeed as a thoroughly cross-cultural enterprise. In addition to the wedding march that *still* accompanies newlyweds as they process out of their marriage ceremony, the most memorable performances are delivered by James Cagney as Bottom and the young Mickey Rooney as Puck. The film exists in varying lengths, with the shortest and longest noted above.

431 *Sen Noci Svatojanske (Midsummer Night's Dream)*
1959. Czechoslovakia. Ceskoslovensý Statní Film.
Sound, col., 80 mins.; English language version,
74 mins. (1971). Jírí Trnka.

A triumph of the Eastern European school of stop-action puppetry, Trnka's adaptation of *Dream* is the first puppet kinescope film. Featuring a literally plastic cast whose faces, hands, and feet are made of a compound that can be continuously sculpted to produce naturalistic effects, this film is rendered in exquisite detail and is performed by characters who seem to radiate wonder at their own creation. Individualized by memorable features, costume, and affect, Trnka's endearing figurines are at once lively and ephemeral, leaving us with the impression that they have performed for us courtesy of a weekend pass from Santa's workshop. The English language version, released in 1971, is narrated by the venerable Richard Burton, whose voice is supported by an entire cast of British theatrical luminaries. See also entries 924, 2404.

432 *Nichts als Sünde*
1965. East Germany. DEFA. Sound, col., 106 mins.
Hanus Burger.

The name of the Czech documentarist Hanus Burger is given here with hesitation, for this musical film, though credited by several sources to Burger, would have marked a rather extraordinary departure from the director's earlier work. The switch from documentarist to *metteur-en-scène* is significant in its own right, but the subject of Burger's work is even further removed from the lighthearted milieu of musical comedy. In fact, one of Burger's better known documentaries, *Mills of Death* (1945), focuses on the liberation of the Nazi death camps. Then again, the precedent for such strange bedfellows—Shakespearean film and the Holocaust—had been famously set only three years before *Mills* by Ernst Lubisch's *To Be or Not To Be* (1942; see Chapter 4, "Spin-offs"). Perhaps harder to believe than the notion that Burger eventually tried his hand at musical comedy after the gravity of his earlier work is that the U.S. War Department hired Billy Wilder—fresh from *Double Indemnity* (1945)—to edit and remaster *Mills of Death* for distribution among Allied troops.

433 *A Midsummer Night's Dream*
1968. U.K. Michael Birkett. Sound, col., 124 mins.
Peter Hall.

Though this film (originally broadcast on television) opened to abysmal reviews, it has garnered an enormous amount of critical attention ever since its inauspicious beginnings. Relying heavily on jumpcuts, handheld camera work, and Brechtian alienation effects, Brooks's adaptation is the first example of a *nouvelle vague* Shakespeare, and stars Helen Mirren as Hermia, Diana Rigg as Helena, and a scantily clad Dame Judi Dench as Titania. A particularly fruitful point of entry into this challenging adaptation, as Peter S. Donaldson has shown, is to explore the many "dissonances" between the film's form and its content, both of which vie for the spectator's attention and complicate the gender and class struggles that the play itself seeks to resolve.

434 *Sueño de una noche de verano* (U.K. title: *A Midsummer Night's Dream: After William Shakespeare*)
1984. Spain/U.K. Lindsay Kemp. Sound, col., 85 mins.
Celestino Coronada.

An example of an adaptation in the more flexible sense of the term, this film is best described as an extended interpretive dance version of Shakespeare's play. Heavy makeup, fabricated sets, and a reliance on close and medium shots make Coronada's *Dream* more theatrical than cinematic, yet this film—with its use of operatic interludes, vocal distortion for Oberon and Titania's voices, and a mise-en-scène that combines Elizabethan-style frocks with sci-fi metallics—never quite settles into a single medium. Appropriately, Coronada's unorthodox approach culminates in a queer spin on Shakespeare's familiar plot, when the lovers awake to find themselves enamored with their same-sex counterparts. Unlike Gabriele Salvatores's 1983 *Sogno Di Una Notte d'estate* (entry 936), however, Coronada's film returns to compulsory heterosexuality for its conclusion—but not without a reminder of what may (or may not) have transpired in the woods in the mechanicals' persuasive, all-male performance of *Romeo and Juliet*.

435 A *Midsummer Night's Dream*
1992. Russia/Wales. Soyuzmultifilm and Christmas Films. Sound, col., 25 mins. Robert Saakianz.

Using cel animation, this film is the least reliant on the text of any in the *Shakespeare: The Animated Tales* series, frontloading extensive voice-over narration that enables the pictures to tell the story. Of special interest is the handling of Bottom's transformation to an ass, which strongly suggests James Cagney's memorable impersonation in Max Reinhardt's 1935 film (above).

436 *Ill Met by Moonlight*
1994. U.S. Titania Pictures. Sound, col., 122 mins. S. P. Somtow.

Born in Thailand, Somtow Papinian Sucharitkul is a filmmaker, as well as an author of sci-fi and horror novels. His adaptation of A *Midsummer Night's Dream*, which takes its point of departure from Oberon's affront, "Ill met by moonlight, proud Titania" (2.1.60), is a modernized, pseudo-punk film of Shakespeare's play that features a largely amateur cast—with the exception of serial horror film actor Tim Sullivan as Oberon. Somtow may have decided on this particular title because it evokes a very successful and highly suspenseful war film also titled *Ill Met by Moonlight* (Michael Powell and Emeric Press Burger, 1957). The menacing, "after hours" mise-en-scène of the latter film may have had something to do with Somtow's decision to shoot the film almost entirely after sunset—although it is more likely that Somtow was more intent on maintaining a low profile in the Los Angeles street locations he chose for filming, as well as keeping costs down. Whatever the case, the result is that Somtow's version of *Dream* has an unintended film noir look that is out of keeping with its farcical content. Interesting in light of the film's allusion to the natural disasters born of Oberon and Titania's quarrels, *Ill Met by Moonlight* rather miraculously survived the devastasting Northridge earthquake.

437 A *Midsummer Night's Dream*
1996. U.K. Paul Arnott/Channel Four Films/Edenwood. Sound, col., 105 mins. Adrian Noble.

A better stage production than film adaptation, Noble's minimalist *Dream* is dominated by medium shots and a static reliance on theatrical frontality. As with his 1994 stage version, Noble structures his adaptation as though the ensuing dream is the brainchild of a young boy—a framing device that was employed in an earlier film by John Canemaker, titled *Bottom's Dream* (1983; see Chapter 4). Of greater interest is the influence that Nunn's casting of Osheen Jones appears to have had on Julie

Taymor's decision to use a boy, also played by Jones, as a similarly interpolated framing device in *Titus* (below). However, Noble seems oblivious to the disturbing implications that the ensuing nightmare is the product of the boy's imagination—particularly given that Titania's "ravishment" of Bottom is presented in this film as an encounter more akin to rape. A conspicuous allusion to Stanley Kubrick's A *Clockwork Orange* (1971), this scene occurs in a fantasy space that is filled with dangling, carrot-shaped objects, which evoke the strap-on nose that doubles as a dildo in the rape scene of Kubrick's film. Noble further suggests an association with rape by representing Bottom's thrusts as particularly violent, despite being accompanied by carnivalesque "Hee Haws." For an adaptation filled with allusions to children's films, such as *Mary Poppins* (Robert Stevenson, 1964) *ET* (Steven Spielberg, 1982) and *Home Alone* (Chris Columbus, 1990), this scene is glaringly incommensurate. The most successfully transferred element from Noble's earlier stage version of the play is the surrealist inflection of the mise-en-scène, which, especially in its use of umbrellas, employs frequent allusions to the paintings of Rene Magritte.

DVD: Dolby digital surround sound and widescreen formatting.

438 A *Midsummer Night's Dream*
1998. U.S. Singularity Motion Pictures. Sound, col., 92 mins. Timothy Hines.

Although the ideal subject for Hines's penchant for the fantastical, this film does not live up to its distribution by Troma Entertainment. Set in medieval Athens but performed with a campy inflection, this low-budget *Dream* is at its best in scenes that feature Skunk T'weed's female Puck and E. Maurice Stevens and Aimee Riegel Pomeroy's Ike-and-Tina-style interpretation of Oberon and Titania's tempestuous relationship.

439 *William Shakespeare's A Midsummer Night's Dream*
1999. U.K./Italy. Fox Searchlight/Regency Enterprises/Panoramica. Sound, col., 121 mins. Michael Hoffman.

Kevin Kline had hoped to play Oberon in this film, so when the part went to Rupert Everett, Hoffman—who wanted Kline to play Bottom all along—decided to expand this role. Despite Calista Flockhart's (of *Ally McBeal* fame) memorable performance as Helena, Kline's Bottom steals the show as a man trapped in a loveless marriage but who never gives up hope that his luck will change. In order to establish Bottom as the film's central character, Hoffman supplies Kline with several added scenes, which render him a more sympathetic—as opposed to simply pathetic—character. In one scene, for example, Bottom wears his Sunday best into town, where he pauses to "people watch" at a café; his spirits are soon quite literally doused by pranksters who cover him in chianti. We can't help but feel for Bottom as he attempts, with all due dignity, to wipe the excess from his badly stained white suit. By far the most significant addition to Hoffman's film, however, is the character of Bottom's wife, for while it is customary to cut characters in film adaptations, they are rarely added. But in order to convince us that what takes place in the forest is *Bottom's* dream, Hoffman bucks tradition and creates a "back story" for him, by inventing the browbeating wife whose constant abuse of Bottom serves to justify his fantasy fling in the forest with Titania (Michelle Pfeiffer). And what takes place in the forest does not necessarily stay in the forest, for in the film's final interpolated scene, Titania appears, now Tinkerbell-sized, in a blaze of fairy dust outside Bottom's window—apparently endorsing not only her very real love for Bottom but also the eye shadow and other makeup tie-ins that accompanied the film's release.

DVD: theatrical trailers and widescreen letterbox format.

MUCH ADO ABOUT NOTHING

440 *Saty delaji cloveka (Much Ado about Nothing)*
1912. Czechoslovakia. ASUM. Silent, b&w, length unknown. Max Urban.

This film is not only the first known Czech adaptation of Shakespeare but also the first screen version of *Much Ado about Nothing*.

441 *Mnógo šúma iz ničegó (Much Ado about Nothing)*
1955. USSR. Moscow Film Studios. Sound, b&w, 96 mins. Lev Samkovoi.

The Soviets seem to have had a particular fondness for this Shakespearean comedy, and, until Kozintsev, their approach to screened Shakespeare tended to be more theatrical than cinematic. This film, based on a production by the Evengi Vachtangor Theatre Company, is no exception.

442 *Viel Lärm um nichts (Much Ado about Nothing)*
1964. East Germany. DEFA-Studio für Spielfilme. Sound, b&w, 102 mins. Martin Hellburg.

This film is significant as one of the few Shakespeare films produced from behind the East German iron curtain. As with the abundant Mosfilm and Lenfilm Shakespeare adaptations, the adaptation of classics was generally much easier to pass through Soviet censors than proposals for new work, which raised suspicions about bourgeois "decadence." This particular film, similar to Berezantseva's (1983 [below]), features several balletic interludes. Arno Wyzniewski, who played Claudio in this production, performed in the East German musical adaptation of *Twelfth Night, Nichts als Sünde* (above), in the very next year.

443 *Mnógo šúma iz ničegó (French title: Beaucoup de Bruit pour Rien; English title: Much Ado about Nothing)*
1973. USSR. Mosfilm. Sound, col., 101 mins. Samson Samsonov.

Known for his adaptations of literature into film, Samsonov teamed up with acclaimed costume designer Ludmila Kusakova to create this Mosfilm classic.

444 *Lyubovyu za Lyubov (Love for Love)*
1983. USSR. Mosfilm. Sound, col., 79 mins. Tatyana Berezantseva.

A music-filled adaptation of *Much Ado about Nothing* with a special appearance from Alla Pugacheva, the Russian pop icon, this film is a curious hybrid that includes classical ballet interludes, a narrator figure who is a famous Russian opera singer, and low, vaguely "Romany" cultural performances sprinkled into the Don John sub-plot. The film's title is evoked by the musical centerpiece of the film, Pugacheva's song "Love for Love," which is a version of Shakespeare's Sonnet 40 ("Take all my loves, my love, yea take them all; / What hast thou then more than thou hadst before?") and is used to chide Don Pedro and Claudio for their abuse of Hero after her innocence and "death" are revealed. As is the case with Kozintsev's films, Shakespeare was a particularly popular subject for adaptation in the former Soviet Union as a figure whose work was easily approved by the Kremlin.

445 *Much Ado about Nothing*
1993. U.S. Renaissance Films. Sound, col., 111 mins. Kenneth Branagh.

Filmed at Villa Vignamaggio in Greve-in-Chianti, Branagh's second Shakespeare film marks a departure from the high seriousness of *Henry V* (1989 [above]), for Branagh describes *Much Ado about Nothing* as a giddy celebration of "heat, haze, and horseflesh." The film's Italianate splendor, which is considerably enhanced by Branagh's decision to relocate the setting from the impoverished island of Sicily to the painterly province of Tuscany, is reminiscent of Merchant/Ivory productions such as *A Room with A View* (1985) and *Enchanted April* (1992). Despite its Mediterranean leanings, however, *Much Ado* was intended to be—at least according to Branagh's enthusiastic screenplay—a Shakespeare film "for the world," featuring a cast that is "as international as possible," energized by "[d]ifferent accents, different looks." But the scope of Branagh's world proves to be a small one after all, for in the film itself, we are presented with a cast comprised exclusively of Anglo-American actors, only one of whom—Denzel Washington—is black. In discussing his casting decisions with *Film Review*'s Tony Crawley, Branagh implies that his rationale for choosing Washington was color-blind: "he's a brilliant actor, very masculine but also very tender. I didn't think beyond that. His being black doesn't work for or against the story." Yet Branagh's aloofness with regard to race belies the attentive cuts he makes to Shakespeare's play, which seek to erase the social antagonisms that threaten his utopian vision. For example, Benedick's line "if I do not love [Beatrice], I am a Jew" (2.3.263) is deftly eliminated, as is Claudio's response to Leonato's question "Are you yet determined / To-day to marry my brother's daughter?" (5.4.37), to which Claudio replies, "I'll hold my mind were she an Ethiope" (38). With Denzel Washington's Don Pedro standing by as his best man, Robert Sean Leonard's Claudio would surely choke on these words. In his analysis of the role of ideological fantasy in the sequel genre, titled "Papering the Cracks," Robin Wood explains that the fate of sociopolitical fantasy on screen hinges on the successful "covering over" of a certain "disturbance," similar to the New Historicist theory of power as a delicate balancing act between "subversion and containment." This formula seems equally apropos of Branagh's Shakespearean "sequel" to Henry V, for in Much Ado about Nothing, blackness functions as a synecdoche for the social antagonisms that characterize the world of realpolitik, even as it enables Branagh to create a reel world where such antagonisms don't exist. Significantly, Much Ado—which many consider to be the best Shakespeare comedy on film—was the last of Branagh's dynamic screen pairings with his then-wife Emma Thompson, who played Beatrice.

DVD: theatrical trailers, full-screen and widescreen anamorphic formats, and "Making Of" featurette.

OTHELLO

446 *Otello*
1907. Italy. Cines. Silent, col. (tinting), 5 mins. Mario Caserini.

Caserini's adaptation features scenic open-air location shooting and focuses its use of color-tinting on the Venetian canals. More than any other national cinema, Italian filmmakers approached Shakespeare as a means of exploring the technological potential of the new medium, experimenting with color processing long before the film stock became available in the 1930s.

447 *Othello*
1908. Austria. Pathé. Sound, b&w, 29 mins. Director unknown.

This film is highly mysterious due to its unusual length and apparent use of sound technology. It is clear from the Weisbaden brochure that this *Othello* was, at least originally, "sung and acted by Erik Schmedes." Although a print of the film has survived, its sound apparatus has not, so this *Othello*, while a film historian's dream, remains nonetheless a puzzle.

448 *Othello* (alternative title: *Jealousy*)
1908. U.S. Vitagraph. Silent, b&w, 10 mins. William V. Ranous.

Lacking the sophistication of its European counterparts, this *Othello* is noteworthy as an example of the American penchant for commercialism in its clever placement of the Vitagraph "V," which stands for "Venice" in this film, for "Verona" in the *Romeo and Juliet* of that same year, and, always, in the minds of cinemagoers, "Vitagraph."

449 *Otello*
1909. Italy. Film d'Arte Italiana. Silent, b&w, 11 mins. Gerolamo Lo Savio.

A distinctive advance in this history of adaptation, this *Othello* abbreviates Shakespeare while adding a scene to highlight the new medium's capacity for action scenes, staging a sea attack on the Turkish fleet near Cyprus. Rather curiously, when the film was released in France in 1918, local censors banned it from exhibition because the film depicts Desdemona's death at the hands of the Moor. As with Lo Savio's other Shakespeare adaptations, more than half of the film was hand-colored.

450 *Otello (Othello)*
1914. Italy. Societá Ambrosio. Silent, b&w, 32 mins. Arrigo Frusta.

Upon *Otello*'s release in America, *Motion Picture World* had high praise for the film, which was distinguished by its length, visual sophistication, and spectacular Venetian locations: "That a play of this character can be so satisfactorily placed on the screen is strong evidence of the progress of the motion picture. It enables thousands to become acquainted with great dramatic masterpieces who would never otherwise know about them" (April 30, 1914).

451 *Othello* (U.K./U.S. title: *The Moor*)
1922. Germany. Wörner-Film. Silent, b&w, 93 mins. Dmitri Buchowetski.

This film, starring Emil Jannings and Werner Krauss, arguably owes less to cinema and more to the theatrical tradition of German Expressionism. Alternately described as artistic and grotesque, superbly acted and unbearably overplayed, masterfully directed and ill conceived, the reception of *The Moor* has been divided at best. However, given the film's miraculous restoration and availability on video, audiences have the luxury of deciding for themselves.

DVD: In addition to being independently released, the Yutkevich film is available for viewing as part of the extras menu on the DVD version of Tim Blake Nelson's O (entry 461).

452 *Othello*
1952. U.S./Italy/France/Morocco. Films Marceau/Mercury Productions/Mogador Films. Sound, b&w, 91 mins. Orson Welles.

Opening with Welles's signature skewed camera angles, *Othello* begins at the end, as Iago (Micheál MacLiammóir) is introduced to us being hauled away in a cage reserved for beasts. As with all of Welles's Shakespeare films, often the most original moments stem from exigency—as in the Turkish bath sequence, which emerged from a clothing shipment delay that threatened the shooting schedule, hence the improvisation with towels. This fortuitous accident established an undercurrent of homoeroticism that all subsequent films of *Othello* have had to contend with in one way or another. Also of interest is the fact that Welles's *Othello*, like the color-enhanced image of O. J. Simpson on the cover of *Time* magazine, "darkens" as the film proceeds; as is the case with so much of Welles's work, whether this effect is intentional or coincidental is open to speculation.

The career trajectories of the two stars, Welles and MacLiammóir, who met while acting at Dublin's Gate Theatre, are particularly interesting in light of the film's competing stories of assimilation, mirroring—in their acts of cultural crossing between England and its former colonies—the "journies" undertaken by Othello and Desdemona, respectively. Indeed, the American-born Welles, in seeking an identity aligned with the quintessentially English figure of Shakespeare, suggests the assimilationist agenda of Othello, whereas the English-born MacLiammóir, who moved to "barbaric" Ireland to become the face of Irish theater (he kept his real birthplace secret), imitates Desdemona's unusual act of *reverse* assimilation, indeed, of self-"othering," in marrying Othello. See also entries 989, 995, 999, and 1088.

DVD: includes a twenty-two-minute "Restoring *Othello*" featurette.

453 *Otello (Othello)*
1955. USSR. Mosfilm. Sound, col., 106 min. Sergei Yutkevich.

This lavish and heavily stylized Russian adaptation is most interesting for the impact it had on later film versions of *Othello*, especially Liz White's little-known adaptation (below). The fountain scene in which Iago's image appears fractured after he stirs his reflection in the water is paradigmatic of foreign cinema's substitution of symbolism and spectacle for Shakespearean dialogue as a means of efficiently advancing the narrative; Iago's Janus-faced disposition and future treachery, for example, are conveyed here in a fraction of the time it takes to utter the line "I am not what I am" (1.1.65). A more controversial point of analysis, as with the Burge adaptation below, is the use of blackface in this film. Unlike Welles's Othello, who becomes progressively darker, Sergei Bondarchuck's Othello suffers from inconsistent coloration. Yet here, too, such "accidents" of makeup application are telling—suggesting, in this case, Othello's alternating points of identification with African and Italian culture.

454 *Othello*
1965. U.K. British Home Entertainment. Sound, col., 166 mins. Stuart Burge.

Essentially a recording of a play with a few cinematic flourishes, this film stars Sir Laurence Olivier in blackface and contains the famous "dirty still": a moment when Olivier's makeup smudges onto the blushing cheek of Maggie Smith's Desdemona. What is fascinating about this production is its astonishing lack of self-consciousness toward "race" as a category of performance, despite being released in the thick of the Civil Rights movement. There seems to be little acknowledgment of the fact that race change may be performed in one direction *without* consequence (as in the minstrelsy tradition on which Olivier's performance is based) but with *fatal* consequences in the "other" direction (as in Othello's assimilationist marriage to Desdemona). That Olivier received an Academy Award nomination for best actor in his impersonation of Othello is an extension of this double standard. See also entries 1028 and 1458.

455 *Catch My Soul* (aka *Santa Fe Satan*)
1973. U.S. Metromedia Producers Corporation. Sound, col., 100 mins. Patrick McGoohan and Kurt Neumann.

Set in New Mexico in the midst of an evangelical-style religious cult, this rock-opera is based on Jack Good's musical adaptation of *Othello*. Good's version—in many ways better suited to today's resurgent evangelical Protestantism than to the period of its composition—plays on suggestions in Shakespeare's text that "souls" are up for grabs (in lines such as Othello's exclamation to Desdemona "Perdition catch my soul / But I do love thee" (3.3.90–91) and, in reference to Iago's treachery, "He hath thus ensnared my soul" [5.2.302]) to emphasize the psychomachian struggle embedded in the play itself. That Othello, the leader of the desert parish, fails to recognize the extent to which his own soul hangs in the balance between Desdemona's "good" and Iago's "evil" becomes, of course, the stuff of tragedy in this story of a man who, like so many other religious leaders, claims to be above temptation—professing a "perfect soul" (1.2.31). Despite its conceptual brilliance, McGoohan's film fails to do justice to either its musical or Shakespearean predecessor, producing the stock "types" of a medieval morality play rather than the subtle inquiries into the human psyche long associated with *Othello* and its stage and screen afterlives. As a side note, the reason this adaptation has not been released on VHS or DVD is due to ongoing legal battles regarding the film's musical content. A glimpse or, better put, a sound of what the film offers is provided by the album *Catch My Soul*, which is derived from the adaptation's theatrical run in London's West End in the early 1970s. The major difference between the stage musical and McGoohan's film is the former's setting in the Louisiana bayou—hence the bizarre "swamp funk" feel of several of the musical numbers retained by the film, which include direct citations of Shakespeare ("Put out the Light,"

"Othello," and "Catch My Soul") as well as allusions to specific scenes, such as Cassio's drinking revels ("Chug-a-Lug"). See also entry 1003.

456 *Othello*
1980. U.S. Liz White. Sound, col., 115 mins. Liz White.

Filmed over four summers from 1962–64 in and around the former all-black resort (owned by her grandparents) on Martha's Vineyard, Liz Shearer White's breakthrough adaptation of *Othello* never received commercial distribution and was at last screened in 1980 at Howard University. Influenced by Yutkevitch's version (above), White's film—the first to employ an all-black cast—likewise features a fountain scene; however, in her adaptation, Iago's reflected image is not revealed to be fractured but, rather, completely withheld from the spectator—a signature example of the immense subtlety with which White accentuates the gap between image and perception that characterizes racism, even as she transforms Shakespeare's treatment of this problem into a story of *intra*racial antagonisms. With Kikuyu/Panamanian actor Yapphet Kotto playing Othello as a native African among black Americans, White's film chronicles a crisis of Duboisian double consciousness on both sides, with tragedy residing in the gap that separates "African" from "American." Significantly, the South African–born musician Hugh Masekela, a founder of the "world music" genre, worked on the film's soundtrack at the very same time he was in the process of recording his own story of assimilation, preserved on the album *The Americanization of Ooga Booga* (1966). In effect, the haunting Zulu melodies, chants, and instrumentation that comprise the film's soundtrack herald the end of segregationist America only to warn of an apartheid forming within the African American community.

The setting of the film on Martha's Vineyard, which is referred to obliquely as "the island" rather than Cyprus, removes White's folk musical from the specific geopolitical crisis staged in Shakespeare's play, namely, the crusade against the Ottoman Empire, and situates it somewhere between a brutal past and a hopeful future. Simultaneously reminiscent of Ibo Landing along the Middle Passage and evocative of the Edenic vision of black autonomy sought by the burgeoning Civil Rights movement, this liminal island setting is complemented by the structural duality of Shearer Cottage, with its twin kitchens, baths, bedrooms, and balconies. In this context, the eighty-foot porch connecting the identical structures increasingly resembles the hyphen that at once separates and unites "African" and "American." That White's film gravitates toward conflict rather than conciliation between cultures is announced in the very first scene by Iago (played by White's son, Richard "Sookie" Dixon), who lumbers down the road carrying what is soon identified as Othello's luggage. Later, we will see Iago toting Othello's dirty laundry as well as his freshly

shined shoes, a change that effectively demotes him from his position as officer or "Ancient" in Shakespeare's play to mere lackey in White's film. The ongoing implication of such interpolated stage business seems to be that, as a former slave himself, Othello should know better than to subject his fellow blacks to such demeaning tasks, even if he does enjoy a coveted position of authority in his new surroundings. But in White's adaptation, unlike Shakespeare's play, there is no indication that Othello is in fact a former slave, for White removes this reference from Othello's back story and, in so doing, stresses the equal footing that he shares with the rest of his non-slave-born community. The seeds of tragedy are sown, then, when Kotto's Othello misses this crucial matter of social etiquette and cultural sensitivity, which becomes the basis of Iago's efforts to return the insult in kind.

457 *Otelo (El Commando Negro)* (Spanish title; French title: *Othello [Le Commando Noir]*; English title: *Othello [The Black Commando]*)
1982. Spain/France. MB Difusion/Eurociné. Sound, col., 106 mins. Max H. Boulois.

This film is an action-based adaptation of *Othello* set amidst civil uprisings in Africa, with Boulois casting himself as Othello and—a particularly bizarre choice—Tony Curtis as Iago. A prolific author, political figure, and agent provocateur, Boulois expands the premise of *Othello* into a story of "Third World" and "First World" relations, representing Othello as a mercenary in Africa who falls in love with a Boston senator's daughter. Like the contemporary France that Boulois calls home, Boston, too, is a place that hides a disturbing culture of racism beneath a veneer of old New England–style civility, thus presenting Boulois with an opportunity to displace his critique of contemporary France much in the same way that Shakespeare appropriated Italy vis-à-vis England. Yet the central problem posed by this adaptation is its reliance on the action film genre, which, by accentuating Othello's violent, shoot-'em-up streak (albeit circumstantial), makes Othello a less sympathetic character than he is in Shakespeare's play. Indeed, in his dual role as actor and director, Boulois seems torn between the glamour of his performance and the grit of his polemic. Poised somewhere between blaxploitation film—replete with a funk soundtrack composed by Boulois himself—and European art cinema, this ambitious adaptation is as telling in its shortcomings as it is in its successes. See also entry 1007.

458 *Othello*
1995. U.S. Castle Rock/Dakota Films/Imminent Films. Sound, col., 125 mins. Oliver Parker.

Following on the heels of the O. J. Simpson trials, Parker's *Othello* emerged as an allegory of its moment. Billed (inaccurately) as the first film of *Othello* to star a black actor (Laurence Fishburne), the most memorable performance is delivered by Kenneth Branagh, who as Iago uses a form of interaction uncharacteristic of the cinema—direct address—to convince audiences, much as he does Othello, to privilege his story. A more subtle means through which Branagh and Parker accomplish this objective is by eliminating any suggestion of Iago's latent homosexuality; as in Branagh's *Hamlet* (1996 [above]), the film interpolates a scene in which Iago and Emilia are shown having sex. We are left with the inescapable impression that Shakespeare's title was a mere decoy for the film that Parker's adaptation discovers: *Iago*. Interestingly, like the bundling of Branagh's *Hamlet* with an interactive murder mystery challenge, Parker's film was also accompanied by a CD-ROM game.

DVD: includes theatrical trailers and widescreen anamorphic format.

459 *Othello*
1996. Russia/Wales. Soyuzmultifilm and Christmas Films. Sound, col., 27 mins. Nikolai Serebryakov.

Using the traditional cel animation technique, this film in the *Shakespeare: The Animated Tales* series, like its short silent film predecessors, uses the medium as an opportunity to render in pictorial terms aspects of Shakespeare's play that are merely described. A poignant example of this approach occurs when Desdemona's death is foreshadowed by a white moth, which transforms via close-up into a death's head. The moth also functions as an allusion to Othello's detailed description (eliminated from the film) of how his prized handkerchief—the product of silkworms—was created in the first place.

460 *Kaliyattam* (*Play of the God*)
1997. India. New Generation Cinema. Sound, col., 130 mins. Jayaraaj Rajaskharan Nair.

This adaptation is a contemporary remake of *Othello* set amidst the Theyyam festivals of northern Kerala, South India, wherein residents don costumes representing various gods in order to reconcile issues astir in their villages. This transpositional treatment of Shakespeare's play, which relies heavily on the use of masks, elicits a post-modern reading of "identity" as nothing if not performed, suggesting the extent to which all of us share Iago's capacity to be something other than what we profess. Indeed, in the spirit of Salmon Rushdie's *The Moor's Last Sigh* (1995), the emphasis on ritual that haunts this adaptation lends a chilling sense of ubiquity to Shakespeare's story of "the Moor of Venice" as a doomed exception to cultural rules— from Italy to India. Significantly, the film's use of a silk robe rather than a handkerchief as "proof" of Desdemona's (Thamara's) betrayal of Othello (Kannan Perumayalan) is repeated in Geoffrey Sax's adaptation (below). Also of interest is the way in which the notoriety achieved by this film provided its National Award–winning star, Suresh Gopi, with a platform for sociopolitical intervention in his home of Kerala, where he has taken advantage of his vis-

ibility to raise money and support for orphans and children afflicted with AIDS. For an *Othello* film that integrates the AIDS pandemic into the film itself, see *Thunderbolt* (entry 462). See also entry 1016.

461 *O*
1999 (released 2001). Lions Gate/Dimension. U.S. Sound, col., 91 mins. Tim Blake Nelson.

This teen-genre modernization of *Othello* features a main character named "Odin James" (Mekhi Phifer), a star athlete whose initials are, not coincidentally, O. J. Shot entirely on location in the very heart of the Old South— Charleston, South Carolina—*O* transforms Othello's role as one who does the state "some service" (5.2.339) to that of a swingman who leads his team to the state basketball championships. A clever literalization of Iago's role as Othello's Ancient, or "right-hand man" in Shakespeare's play, the Iago character Hugo (Josh Harnett) plays the right-handed point guard who feeds Odin the ball but never gets credit for his assists. Jealous of Odin's popularity and his relationship to the coach (Hugo's father), Hugo retaliates by feeding Odin lies about Desi (Julia Stiles), daughter of the dean of the prep school. A particularly apposite spin in light of the crackdown on drug abuse in sports, the film represents Hugo's barely suppressed penchant for violence as being aggravated by his use of steroids. Perhaps more disturbing than the predictable homicides that conclude the film is the representation of Odin as a former drug abuser/dealer himself, a detail that clarifies Othello's oblique observation that "Chaos has come again" (3.3.92) and, consequently, incriminates Odin. Withheld from U.S. release for two years, *O* was bailed out by Lions Gate when the original distributor, Miramax, balked at releasing a film that ends in a flurry of teen gun violence in the aftermath of the Columbine High tragedy. See also entry 1021.

DVD: an amazing package, this two-disc DVD features director's commentary, interviews with the cast, deleted scenes, basketball analysis, and, finally, Dmitri Buchowetski's 1922 version of *Othello*.

462 *Thunderbolt*
2000. Nigeria. Production Company unknown. Sound, col., 105 mins. Tunde Kelani.

One of "Nollywood's" standout directors, Tunde Kelani recreates *Othello* as a tale of inter-tribal conflict, as well as a call to pan-Nigerian peace, in *Thunderbolt* (2000). More than merely a transpositional treatment of Shakespeare's play, *Thunderbolt* adds a twist to Iago's duplicitous story of Desdemona's infidelity when Othello (Yinka, a representative of the Yoruba tribe) is prompted to place the curse of "Magun" (a sexually transmitted curse which, like AIDS, is popularly associated with certain death) upon Desdemona (Ngozi, a member of the Ibo tribe)—despite any proof of her betrayal. Making an overtly political statement, Kelani's film converts Shakespeare's story of a husband who neglects the truth before his very eyes into the parable of neglect that defines the policy of the West toward the AIDS crisis in Africa.

463 *Othello*
2001. U.K./Canada/U.S. London Weekend Television/CBC/PBS. Sound, col., 104 mins. Geoffrey Sax.

Originally aired on television, this adaptation is set in a fictional, contemporary London in which the Turkish-Venetian conflict of Shakespeare's play is transposed as racial tensions between black and white urbanites, with conspicuous allusions to the Brixton race riots of 1982 and the 1993 murder of a black teenager (Stephen Lawrence) by white hooligans at a bus stop in southeast London. The Iago character, Ben Jago (Christopher Eccleston), sets his revenge plot into motion when he is passed over for a promotion following the prime minister's decision to make John Othello (Eamonn Walker) the new police commissioner—a decision that, the film suggests, is based on election-year politics rather than individual merit. Like Othello, John Othello naïvely steps into the position convinced of his worthiness, and, also like his Shakespearean namesake, his discourse is strikingly "color-blind." For example, just as Othello rebukes his fellow (white) Venetians by appropriating the very racist terms with which he has been described—"What, are we turn'd Turks...? (2.3.170)—Commissioner Othello proactively describes those (white) officers who even *think* of committing police brutality as "violent animals" who "belong in prison," unselfconciously evoking the historical classification of the black male as an animal. A significant difference between play and film is that Desi (Keeley Hawes) and Michael Cass (Richard Coyle) cultivate a strong friendship when Cass is hired to protect Desi from skinheads who object to her marriage to Othello. When the two discover during their many hours alone that they share a love of the arts—something evidently missing from Desi's relationship with her workaholic husband—the alleged affair becomes more plausible, and at one point, Cass even angles (unsuccessfully) for a kiss. When Ben Jago couples his lies about Desi's promiscuous past with the claim that Cass's semen has been confirmed—through DNA tests—on Othello's African robe, Desi's fate is sealed. Hence, John Othello becomes a far more sympathetic character than Shakespeare's Moor of Venice, for whereas the latter acts upon circumstantial evidence, the former acts upon incontrovertible "proof" of Desdemona's infidelity. But if this adaptation seeks to absolve Othello, then it condemns Iago, whose homicidal behavior is motivated more by his repressed desire for Othello than for the job title he covets and, at the end of the film, acquires. "I loved him too, you know," he exclaims of Othello in the film's very first line (a variation of which he repeats at the conclusion of the film),

thus repeating the Wellesian gambit of beginning at the end, as well as suggesting the disturbing extent to which overt racism is more socially acceptable than latent homosexuality. Although Andrew Davies's screenplay retains virtually none of the play's language, its stunning story of the "skinhead within" is one of the most persuasive contemporary retellings of Shakespeare's play on screen.

DVD: no special features indicated.

464 *Omkara (Othello)*
In production. Vishal Bharadwaj. India.

RICHARD II

465 *Richard the Second*
U.S. 2001. Sub Rosa Studios. Sound, col., 97 mins. John Farrell.

An indie Shakespeare film created by the author of *Digital Movies with Quicktime Pro* (Charles River Media, 2002), John Farrell's digital modernization is the first-ever film of *Richard II.* Shot on location at Fort Strong, Long Island, to recreate the look of a medieval fortress, *Richard the Second* is a modern-dress, action film adaptation about one of Shakespeare's least action-oriented monarchs. Though a visibly low-budget production that has been alternately panned and praised, Farrell's adaptation is interesting as a case study in colliding visions—as an example, that is, of how "the Shakespeare film" does not constitute a genre in its own right but, rather, wrangles with existing film genres and conventions to varying degrees of success. In *Richard the Second,* the uneasy fit between the action film genre and Shakespeare's history play leads not to an intriguing hybrid but to a hopelessly compromised half-breed that is convincing as neither "Shakespeare" nor "film." The addition of uzis and the elimination of John of Gaunt's elegiac "This blessed plot, this earth, this realm, this England" (2.1.50) speech is a case in point.

Released in 2004, the DVD features include interviews, a still gallery, deleted footage, trailers, and outtakes.

RICHARD III

466 *Richard III*
1908. U.S. Vitagraph. Silent, b&w, c. 10 mins. William V. Ranous.

Like Olivier's *Richard III* (below), Ranous's film is based on Colley Cibber's adaptation, and likewise features the director in the leading role. In the style typical of Vitagraph, this *Richard* ambitiously packs the major events of Shakespeare's play into a single reel. Unlike other screen versions of the film, however, this adaptation is distinguished by its sequencing in which Richard is shown *first* accepting the crown and *then* sending the princes to the tower, rather than merely "inferring" their bastardy

(3.5.75), which, in other versions, contextualizes his right to the throne.

467 *Richard III*
1911. U.K. Co-operative Cinematograph Co. Silent, b&w, 27 mins. F. R. Benson.

Benson's film (starring the director as Richard) makes little effort to establish itself as anything other than recorded theater, employing the same scenic backdrops and staging used in the theatrical production that precedes it. An exception is the dream sequence that precedes Richard's fatal encounter with Richmond, which employs dissolves to represent each of Richard's victims morphing into the next. Worthy of mention is Benson's decision to represent Richard killing Henry VI "twice," which is repeated in Keane's adaptation of the very next year: first Richard watches the king expire and, then, when it is clear that Henry is dead, he leaps up onto the desk whereon the body lies prone and adds a gratuitous thrust—as if Richard were performing a ritual slaughter of the "King's two bodies." A scene often deleted from silent versions, Clarence is shown nearly persuading one of his assassins to relent; another uncommon choice is the representation of Lady Anne dying in the instant that Richard is crowned. Though little more than a series of discontinuous tableaux, this film does an admirable job of selecting excerpts from Shakespeare's play—particularly Richard's sinister speeches—to establish Richard's evil nature, rather than relying on exaggerated postures, gestures, or prosthetic makeup to convey his internal and external disfigurement.

DVD: *Silent Shakespeare*: digitally remastered footage with a newly recorded score.

468 *The Life and Death of King Richard III*
1912. U.S. M. B. Dudley Amusement Co. Silent, b&w, 59 mins. James Keane.

Recently rediscovered, this film, donated to the American Film Institute by collector William Buffum in 1996, is the first feature-length film—Shakespearean or otherwise—made in America. This sepia-toned *Richard* shows remarkable sophistication in terms of its length, spectacular crowd and battle scenes involving a thousand people and hundreds of horses, and special effects, such as the impressive rendering of Richard's nightmare before the battle of Bosworth, which features superimposed footage of the ghosts of his victims. The text of the film Americanizes Richard's early title, amending it from "Gloucester" to the phonetic "Gloster," an example of the trend toward simplification and accessibility typical of the very first Shakespeare films. Similarly, Frederick Warde's performance as Richard is a caricature of evil rather than Shakespeare's study in subtlety, but the film nevertheless offers an array of original touches. For example, when Richard goes to kill Henry VI, he murders him with his dagger and blithely steps out onto the balcony to wave at the crowd gathered below the king's bedchamber; he then returns to gaze at Henry's dead body and repeatedly stabs it with his sword, wallowing in his own evil as he all but licks the weapon clean of blood. This imagery is repeated in the subsequent scene in which Richard woos Lady Anne, whose repeated dagger thrusts at the presumptuous duke stop shy of piercing his flesh. Typical of silent film's thrift, Clarence's eloquent entreaty to his assassins moments before his murder is eliminated in favor of a swift execution, whereas more attention is awarded to scenes that lend themselves to visualization, such as the decision to depict the entry of the ill-fated princes on Shetland ponies—an image that emphasizes their childlike innocence, diminutive size, and, of course, Richard's unthinkable malice in ordering their imprisonment and eventual execution. A modicum of sympathy for Richard's disfigurement is evinced, however, by the scene in which Virginia Rankin's spritely York embarrasses Richard in front of the crowd gathered to pay homage to the young Prince Edward by aping Richard's crookback posture with a childish lack of tact. Hence, the film intriguingly poses the question as to whether or not Richard would, in fact, have gone through with the princes' murder had he not been a victim of their taunts. Medieval weaponry, such as morning stars and maces, abounds in Richard's fatal encounter with Richmond, which is unrivaled in its scale among early Shakespeare films. Enno Morricone's morose but fitting original score is restored to its full, piercing resonance, rising and falling with Richard's political career.

469 *Richard III*
1955. U.K. London Films/Lawrence Olivier Productions/ Big Ben Films. Col., sound, 138 mins. Laurence Olivier.

An adaptation of an adaptation (based on a combination of David Garrick's and Colley Cibber's versions of Shakespeare's *Richard III*), this film stars Olivier as the crookback king with John Gielgud and Ralph Richardson in the supporting roles of Clarence and Buckingham, respectively. As a side note, Richardson's Buckingham bears such an uncanny resemblance to Kevin Spacey that one wonders if Olivier's casting choices influenced Al Pacino's decision to award Spacey—an exceedingly unlikely choice—the role of Buckingham in his spin-off *Looking for Richard* (entry 1051). Unlike Pacino's vision of an ostensibly democratic approach to filming Shakespeare's play, Olivier's approach is nothing if not aristocratic, for in eliminating Margaret, he effectively removes all potential competitors for and obstacles to his own virtuoso performance. Not surprisingly, then, Olivier's film is considered by many to be his best Shakespearean screen performance, offering him the rare opportunity to demonstrate his extraordinary range within a single role—for Richard is by turns villainous, seductive, and witty in his uniquely macabre way. Although Olivier plays Richard with a deformed shoulder, visible limp, and sharp prosthetic nose, his character seems to grow more attractive as the film proceeds, mirroring the process through which Richard seduces his internal audience in addition to his captive film spectators. Hence, one of the film's more chilling moments occurs when the young duke of York teasingly suggests that his uncle "bear [him] on [his] shoulders" (3.1.131), a remark that elicits a screeching orchestral accompaniment—reminiscent of the horror film genre—and a long, malicious stare from Richard, who, we know too well, will soon reap his revenge on the boy and his brother.

Described by some critics as the least "cinematic" film in Olivier's oeuvre, this high period-style adaptation of *Richard III* documents the influence of presentational modes associated with the then-nascent medium of television, which are evident in the film's reliance on tight framing and confining sets that, typical of sitcoms, are comprised of multiple units in a continuous space. Others, however, cite Olivier's cinematographic use of deep focus—courtesy of VistaVision—as the film's most compelling feature. The point that critics unanimously agree on is Olivier's exhilarating acting in a part that he clearly enjoyed playing. Indeed, the otherwise humble and guarded thespian seems to have gravitated to Richard in the last of his three Shakespeare films precisely because it gave him a chance to "ham it up," fully conscious of the fact that, as he explains in his book *On Acting*, "Richard . . . would lay his head on the camera's bosom if he could." See also entry 1041.

DVD: original trailer, chapter access, and collector's booklet.

470 *Richard III*
1986. France/Switzerland. CDNA et al. Sound, col., 135 mins. Raúl Ruiz.

Raúl Ruiz, one of the premiere auteurs working in contemporary film, offers the most avant-garde version of *Richard* to date, replete with his signature skewed camera angles and emphasis on the fantastical features of his source. Shakespeare's story of the self-installed dictator is a particularly resonant subject for the Chilean-born director, who fled to France in the wake of Agusto Pinochet's dictatorship, and has been living in exile ever since. Indeed, Ruiz's preoccupation with the theme of political subterfuge and murder is evident in his recent "sequel" to *Richard III*, titled *A Taste for Murder* (2003), a neo-noir tale of a serial killer who, not unlike Richard, is an egomaniac perversely seeking to have his memoirs written. In the *nouvelle vague* tradition to which Ruiz's work is indebted, *Richard III* debuted at Cannes in the series *Perspective Du Cinéma Français*.

471 *Richard III*
1996. Russia/Wales. Soyuzmultifilm and Christmas Films. Sound, col., 27 mins. Natalya Orlova.

Another marvel of the *Shakespeare: The Animated Tales* series, this film employs the painstaking stained-glass technique for which Orlova is known. This unorthodox animation strategy, in which images are painted on and scraped off a *single* pane of glass, is an ideal medium for illustrating the ever-mutating evil machinations of Richard's mind, as the audience is literally able to trace—in the opaque remainders of individual scenes—where one pernicious plot ends and another begins. The uniquely Russian animation technique featured in this adaptation also offers a particularly lucid point of departure for exploring the palimpsestic status of the Shakespearean text.

472 *Richard III*
1995. U.S./U.K. Stephen Bayly/Paré Production, et. al. Sound, col., 105 mins. Richard Loncraine.

Set in a fictional 1930s, this film, starring Ian McKellan (who cowrote the screenplay with Loncraine), updates Shakespeare's play about the ruthless early modern dictator in light of two twentieth-century political crises: the rise of the Nazi Party in Germany and the British abdication controversy. It is this historical context that informs the film's utter entrenchment in and homage to the mass media, representing Richard's rise to power as a wedding of the German propaganda film to British tabloid journalism. Significantly, Richmond is singled out as Richard's nemesis even before we are aware of his role as such, chiefly because he is the only character who enjoys a certain degree of autonomy in relation to the media, impervious to the lure of photo-ops and the Machiavellian theater of politics that Richard's reign has inaugurated. That the first citation in the film is not of Shakespeare's play but of Marlowe's poem ("Come live with me and be my love") cleverly refigures these rival modes of performance in terms of early modern "mass media."

Like so many other Richards before him, McKellan relies heavily on direct address to the camera, confiding the revelation of his prodigious iniquity in the audience itself. Yet this same intimacy and rapport with the spectator that render him powerful also make him vulnerable. Signaling a departure from the traditional depiction of Richard's vulnerability as inextricable from his mother's rejection of him, McKellan's Richard is weakened only by his attraction to Tyrell (Adrian Dunbar), whose face time in the film far exceeds his presence in Shakespeare's play. Hence, unlike any other adaptation of *Richard III*, this film leaves us wondering if Richard's string of murders is motivated by revenge or by his desire to conspire repeatedly with his favorite hired hand. The most striking example of this ambiguity occurs when Richard has announced his wish to have the princes in the tower killed, after which even the loyal Buckingham abandons him. When Richard poses this double homicide request to Tyrell, however, he does so while offering him his pick of sweets from a heart-shaped box of chocolates. "It is done," replies Tyrell, his fingers lighting on a different chocolate with each word until he teasingly pops his chocolate of choice into his mouth, savoring its taste as a prelude to satisfying his taste for murder. When Tyrell exits, Richard thrusts himself back against his chair, breathing heavily, visibly attempting to master any sign of his susceptibility to desire. But Richard's confidantes, the audience, have seen more than he meant to disclose: offering an example of what Freud described as "displacing upward," Tyrell is the prosthetic hand that empowers Richard's withered arm, without whom Richard is unmistakably castrated.

It is interesting to note that Richard's vulnerability in this production extends beyond the diegesis to McKellan himself. For despite his extraordinary credentials as a classically trained Shakespearean actor, McKellan's trepidation at the thought of adapting Shakespeare to the screen—and, therefore, making considerable cuts to the largely intact theatrical text he had performed throughout his 1990 National Theatre run—is evident in his screenplay confession that "change by change, cut by cut," he found himself consulting the Bard as to whether or not "he would approve" of his decisions. Whatever McKellan's concerns, however, director Richard Loncraine does not suffer the same pangs of conscience, as the opening of the film proceeds for nearly ten minutes without so much as a peep from the playtext. In this successful transpositional treatment of *Richard III*, the film's self-indulgent production values—characterized by glossy, highly stylized camera work; elaborate sets and costumes; a stellar cast; a sultry "swing" soundtrack; and rich texture of cinematic allusion—force us to wait for Shakespeare as merely one of many coming attractions.

DVD: theatrical trailers and widescreen letterbox format.

473 *The Street King* (aka *King Rikki*)
2001. U.S. Mistral Pictures LLC. Sound, col., 91 mins.
James Gavin Bedford.

An ambitious transposition of *Richard III* to the barrio gang milieu of East Los Angeles. Rikki Ortega, abandoned by his mother as a child and recently returned to Los Angeles, seeks to carve out his place in the Ortega family business, crime, and to take revenge for his childhood. As the Ortegas try to eradicate the Rojas, a rival family running local drug labs for the Gavilans, a Mexican cartel, Rikki engineers a complicated double-cross that will eliminate both the Rojas and his own brothers, leaving him in sole control of a barrio criminal empire. He seduces Anita, the wife of Alejandro Rojas, a rival he has just killed in a raid on his meth lab, and then discards her for Lupe; he arranges for his brother Jorge to be arrested and killed in prison; he runs over his brother Rios with his car as Rios prepares to move stolen merchandise; and he murders his brother Eduardo by poisoning his recreational cocaine and finishing him off with an injection of air in the hospital.

Throughout, Rikki is pursued by Juan Valleja, a childhood friend who is now a cop. At film's end, Rikki orchestrates an elaborate drug buy that sets members of his family from the North against the Rojas and the remainder of his own gang, using the young Rafael Ortega as a hostage in hopes that he too will be killed. Rikki's plan goes sour when he finds himself trapped, and he is killed by Valleja.

The film's hip ambitions are made clear in an opening sequence in which a mural of Shakespeare's face is spray-painted over with a backwards cap and sunshades. Though it uses none of Shakespeare's dialogue, *The Street King* finds analogues for nearly all major characters and many major scenes and motifs from *Richard III*. Rikki is Richard Gloucester, Jorge is Clarence, Eduardo is Edward, Anita is Anne, Palacio is Buckingham, Valleja is Richmond, and so on. Like Richard, Rikki orchestrates mutual suspicion among family members, seduces women, and harbors a deep resentment of his family that he hides under a veneer of bonhomie. The women perceive and helplessly lament Rikki's evil nature, but his brothers all go to their deaths without recognizing Rikki's hand in their demise, with the sole exception of Rios, who tells Rikki, "You'll be next." Like Richard, Rikki addresses the audience directly and with a beguiling if utterly heartless black humor, and occasionally the film plays with that metacinematic element, as when Rikki addresses us directly in his bedroom about his plans, then asks us for privacy so he can make love to Anita. Strikingly absent is any analogue for Richard's confrontation with the ghosts of those he's murdered or his self-doubt and self-loathing. Indeed, when Rikki is confronted by Valleja at film's end, he remains unrepentant and offers to make a deal for his life by sharing his ill-gotten gains. The film also refuses to paint Valleja as a moral alternative to Rikki (as Richmond is to Richard), for after killing Rikki, Valleja walks away with his satchel of cash. Of the many "Shakespeare in the hood" film adaptations (*Blazin'*, *Brooklyn Babylon*, *Mad Dawg*, *Barrio Wars*, *Gedebe*, and the like), this is the most ambitious and has the highest production values.

DVD includes an interview with Jon Seda (who plays Rikki) in which he speaks about the film's relationship to *Richard III*. (DL)

ROMEO AND JULIET

474 *Romeo and Juliet*
1908. Italy. Cines. Silent, b&w, 7 mins. Mario Caserini.

In the race to release the first-ever screen version of *Romeo and Juliet*, the Italians—the source of the original legend on which Shakespeare's play is based—fittingly prevailed.

475 *Romeo and Juliet*
1908. U.K. Gaumont. Silent, b&w, 12 mins. Director unknown.

Though distinguished as being the longest British film to date, this *Romeo and Juliet* aspired to little more than recording a pre-existing theatrical production from the Lyceum.

476 *Romeo and Juliet*
1908. U.S. Vitagraph. Silent, b&w, 11 mins. William V. Ranous.

One of the many Shakespearean one-reelers released by Vitagraph, this film stars Florence Turner, whose notoriety paved the way for what would become known in the 1920s as the star system. Pre-figuring Baz Luhrmann's extensive vocabulary of cinematic shots in his 1996 film, *William Shakespeare's Romeo + Juliet* (below), this adaptation is also noteworthy for its use of relatively advanced techniques— including seventeen different camera angles, cross-cutting, indoor/outdoor scenery, and off-camera editing—all in a mere fifteen minutes.

477 *Romeo and Juliet*
1911. U.S. Edwin Thanhouser. Silent, b&w, 27 mins. Barry O'Neil.

Although O'Neil's adaptation maintains a static camera, this film shows technical sophistication in terms of its length and active camerawork, as well as in its sets, which do not rely on ephemeral backdrops but instead make use of solid interior and exterior mise-en-scènes.

478 *Romeo e Giuletta*
1911. Italy. Film d'Arte Italiana. Silent, b&w, 25 mins. Gerolamo Lo Savio.

Filmed on location in the streets of Verona, this *Romeo and Juliet* reveals the Italian flair for spectacle as well as a specific form of tragic sentimentality that will not reappear until Baz Luhrmann's 1996 adaptation (entry 496). In this version, Juliet awakes to find Romeo alive but in the throes of death—suggesting a nod to Italian compatriot Luigi Da Porto, who was the first to popularize this ending in the tale, written in 1524, that inspired Shakespeare's *Romeo and Juliet*.

479 *Indian Romeo and Juliet*
1912. U.S. Vitagraph. Silent, b&w, c. 10 mins. Larry Trimble.

One of the earliest transpositional adaptations of a Shakespeare play, this film, starring the Vitagraph girl Florence Lawrence, retells Shakespeare's story of feuding families as a clash of feuding Native American tribes.

480 *Romeo and Juliet*
1916. U.S. Metro. Silent, b&w, 80 mins. John W. Noble.

The first blow in the rivalry between Metro and Fox, this extravagant production (now lost) starred Francis X. Bushman. The film cost $250,000, employed a cast of six hundred, and featured a live musical score derived from Charles Gounod and Tchaikovsky.

481 *Romeo and Juliet*
1916. U.S. Fox. Silent, b&w, 50 mins. J. Gordon Edwards.

Fox released an ambitious *Romeo and Juliet* of its own, starring Theda Bara, in an effort to enter into direct competition with the announced Metro production. This was the first time that this kind of competition had occurred, marking a significant turning point in the emergent industry's sense of itself as a contender with other forms of entertainment. Made of the same self-deteriorating stock as the Fox *Romeo and Juliet*, this film, too, has been lost to the ravages of time.

482 *Romeo and Juliet*
1931. Hungary. Sound (unknown), b&w, length and production company unknown. István Kató.

This animated short film was created entirely in silhouette and, even more remarkable, relied exclusively on natural lighting. Through his unusual approach to the medium of film, Kató not only presents us with the first known Hungarian Shakespeare film but also creates the visual equivalent of Romeo and Juliet's frequent invocations of "day" and "night."

483 *Romeo and Juliet*
1936. U.S. MGM. Sound, b&w, 123 mins. George Cukor.

Hell-bent on sparing no expense to showcase the talents of his wife, producer Irving Thalberg financed *Romeo and Juliet*, as Robert Willson observes, as a "lover's monument" to Norma Shearer. Despite Thalberg's intent to subvert the iron law of "profit or perish" with a $2 million, high-art adaptation of Shakespeare's most popular play, this painstakingly ornamental film fared well neither at the box office nor at the hands of critics, and lost nearly a million dollars. The main complaint was not the over-the-top opulence of the mise-en-scène but the age of the leads: Norma Shearer played Juliet at thirty-seven and Leslie Howard enacted Romeo at forty-two, with John Barrymore's Mercutio rounding out the then-geriatric trio at the ripe age of fifty-four. (Basil Rathbone played Tybalt at forty-four.) Despite meticulous attention to detail in the score—Tchaikovsky's crescendos are synchronized with the couple's budding passions—as well as in setting and costume (Shearer's exquisite dresses, for example, were adapted from Renaissance paintings), nothing could sufficiently distract audiences from the fact that these "young lovers" were long past their prime. Of more interest is that the MGM *Romeo and Juliet* was accompanied by one of the earliest "tie-in" books, replete with scholarly commentary from Professor William Strunk Jr., who, quite out of keeping with the studio's penchant for profligate productions, was best known as the author of the succinct composition manual, *The Elements of Style*. See also entry 2495.

484 *Anjuman*
1948. India. Nargis Art. Sound, b&w, 140 mins. Akhtar Hussein.

This Hindi adaptation of *Romeo and Juliet* is mentioned here by dint of the fact that in the preceding year, Hussein directed a film that was actually titled *Romeo and Juliet*, but never completed. Both films star "Nargis" (born Fattima A. Rashid), who would become one of the most popular faces in Indian cinema in the 1950s.

485 *Romeo and Juliet*
1954. Italy/U.K. Verona Productions. Sound, col.,
138 mins. Renato Castellani.

Appropriately, this film reflects the Italian post-war neorealist movement, adapting Shakespeare to the style that surfaced in the wake of post-war desolation, characterized by open-air cinematography and a pseudodocumentary camera. Fitting for a film that combines warring factions with a famous love story, Castellani's directorial style is often described as *realismo rosa*, or "soft neorealism," which succeeds in toning down the chiaroscuro effects of its starker predecessor with faint colors and a more studied, steady camera. Unfortunately, the raw beauty of the film's open-air scenes, featuring Renaissance architecture as well as civic and pastoral visions of daily life, is frequently interrupted by the poor synchronization of sound and image, which makes for several absurdist moments, such as Tybalt's "what, drawn..." *before* Benvolio draws his weapon. Perhaps due to the challenges of postdubbing, Mercutio's role, performed by Ubaldo Zollo, is radically diminished. Notwithstanding such affronts to the suspension of disbelief, two interpolated scenes form the highly memorable bookends of the film: (1) the opening, wherein William Shakespeare himself (played by John Gielgud) escorts us into the Veronese *mercato*; and (2) approaching the film's conclusion, the glimpse of Friar John and his mule at the mercy of misfortune, in a scene that has more in common with commedia dell'arte than high tragedy.

486 *Hassan and Naima*
1959. Egypt. Sound, b&w, length unknown. Director unknown.

This Egyptian version of *Romeo and Juliet* stars the "Cinderella" of the Arab world, Soad Hosni, in her first film appearance. Significantly, the transposition of this Renaissance play into Islamic culture is particularly believable in terms of its emphasis on an overbearing patriarchy and the perils of arranged marriage; hence, in this production, the role of Naima's father (Old Capulet in Shakespeare's play) is augmented.

487 *West Side Story*
1961. U.S. Mirisch/Seven Arts/Beta. Sound, col.,
155 mins. Robert Wise and Jerome Robbins.

Surpassed only by *Titanic* (1997) and the epic *Ben Hur* (1959), *West Side Story* won ten of the eleven Oscars for which it was nominated and is universally considered to be one of the greatest films of all time. Not surprisingly, then, this musical film has acquired an autonomy in popular culture that is all its own, as the source of innumerable spinoffs and citations in its own right. Baz Lurhmann, for example, in discussing the decisions made during the filming of *William Shakespeare's Romeo + Juliet* (entry 496), invokes *West Side Story* when he explains his abundant use of water imagery as evocative of Romeo and Juliet's " 'there's a place for us' moments"—alluding, of course, to the famous love song from *West Side Story* by that title. Abel Ferrara's *China Girl* (entry 492) goes one step further, adapting *West Side Story's*—rather than Shakespeare's—version of the Romeo and Juliet legend. Created in the midst of rising class tensions in New York City in the wake of a massive wave of Puerto Rican immigration, Robert Wise and Jerome Robbins's film, based on the stage musical, reenvisions the Montague-Capulet feud as a war between the "Sharks" and the "Jets," rival street gangs comprised of first-generation, working-class Americans and Puerto Rican newcomers, respectively. The decision to adapt *Romeo and Juliet* as a musical is in many respects the ideal choice for a play in which the protagonists suffer from both severe parental circumscription and an uncanny sense of their own "star cross'd" fate (Pro.6). Indeed, the often strained naturalism and predictability of the musical genre are perfectly in keeping with the overwhelming sense of foreboding and repetition that plagues the lovers—to the extent that both Romeo and Juliet, on several, separate occasions, "spontaneously" convey the feeling that they are playing parts against their will. In this respect, Tony (Richard Beymer) and Maria's (Natalie Wood) duets are not at all unlike Romeo and Juliet's sonnets, for both poetic forms articulate the desire to escape social conventions even as they remain circumscribed by them. Whereas the play depicts Romeo and Juliet's revolt from the strictures of feudalism as a symptom of an aristocratic culture in decline, *West Side Story* presents the failure of Tony and Maria's cross-cultural romance as a vision of the broken promises of the American dream, which Maria survives to mourn. See also entries 780, 1021, 1161, 1163, 1207, 1228, 1239, 1244, 1260, 1263, 1274, 1276, 1279, and 1692.

DVD: theatrical trailers, production notes, and widescreen anamorphic format.

488 *Los Tarantos*
1963. Spain. Tecisa Productions. Sound, col., 83 mins. Francisco Rovira Beleta.

Building on the extraordinary success of *West Side Story*, Spain created its own flamenco-style musical adaptation of *Romeo and Juliet* only three years later, winning an Oscar and the hearts of everyone who watched Carmen Amaya dance her way through trials of love and violence. Though *Los Tarantos* is based on *La historia de los Tarantos* by Alfredo Mañas, this story of young lovers from rival gypsy factions is itself an adaptation of Shakespeare's play. The plot follows the play until the end, when Rafael and Juana are killed by Curro, the Paris figure. In keeping with Shakespeare's conclusion, the feuding families reconcile in the wake of the young lovers' deaths.

489 *Giuletta e Romeo: Los Amantes de Verona*
1964. Italy/Spain. Imprecine/Hispaner. Sound, col., 99 mins. Riccardo Freda.

Best known for his unique brand of horror/fantasy films, Freda's *Romeo and Juliet* is significant in part because it reflects an older trend in Shakespearean adaptation—specifically, the early Italian penchant for historical spectacle—which could not be further removed from the vogue for neorealism that characterized Italian cinema of the 1950s and 1960s. In this case, Shakespeare seems to have been adapted as a means of justifying the film's reversion to classicism, with musical accompaniment courtesy of Tchaikovsky and Rachmaninoff.

490 *Romeo and Juliet*
1968. Italy/U.K. BHE/Dino De Laurentis Cinematografica/Verona Productions. Sound, col., 152 mins. Franco Zeffirelli.

Popularly known as the flower child *Romeo and Juliet*, Zeffirelli's 1968 version was the first Shakespeare film to explicitly target teens. The most memorable, quintessentially "Zeffirellian" scene is the Capulet ball where the lovers meet for the first time. Here, they perform a pas de deux to the song "What Is Youth," a ballad that would become legendary in its own right as the theme of the soap opera *The Young and the Restless*. Zeffirelli's tendency to luxuriate in the details and linger over visual splendor is never more pronounced than it is in this scene, which consumes sixteen minutes of camera time and, beyond its opening and closing frames, is superfluous to the plot. Yet the film is surprisingly sparing in other

Olivia Hussey (Juliet) and Leonard Whiting (Romeo) in Franco Zeffirelli's production of *Romeo and Juliet* (1968). Courtesy of Douglas Lanier.

respects, for Zeffirelli insisted on casting relative unknowns in the leading roles, as well as actors whose ages were much closer to Shakespeare's protagonists than those of performers in previous films (Leonard Whiting's Romeo was seventeen, and Olivia Hussey—a rather fitting surname for this aggressive, cleavage-bearing Juliet—was fifteen). Even by contemporary standards, the upshot of these casting decisions is a refreshingly convincing pair of lovers whose eager sexuality places them provocatively between their doublet-and-hose dress and the free-love fervor of the late 1960s. An often overlooked detail is that the voice of the Chorus is supplied by Sir Laurence Olivier.

DVD: widescreen anamorphic format.

491 *Montoyas Y Tarantos*
1989. Spain. Comunicacion Visual Creativa. Sound, col., 103 mins. Vincente Escrivá.

Shot in the vicinity of Jerez de la Frontera, this film adaptation of *Romeo and Juliet*, like its predecessor *Los Tarantos*, is based on *La historia de los Tarantos*, but is an inferior remake of Francisco Rovira Beleta's 1963 masterpiece.

492 *China Girl*
1987. U.S. Vestron Pictures. Sound, col., 89 mins. Abel Ferrara.

An adaptation of *Romeo and Juliet* that privileges *West Side Story*'s version of Romeo and Juliet over Shakespeare's, this film tells the story of Tony and Tye, teenage members of New York's Italian American and Chinese immigrant populations, respectively. The impetus for both the romance and the tragedy in this film is the opening of a Chinese restaurant in Little Italy. The major difference between *West Side Story* and *China Girl* is the latter's darker ending in which both Tony and Tye (not just Tony, as in *West Side Story*) die, refusing the consolation of brighter days to come. As this ending suggests, the film parallels the plot of *Romeo and Juliet* quite closely, albeit at one degree of Shakespearean separation. See also entry 1207.

493 *Romeo-Juliet*
1990. Belgium. Paul
Hespel. Sound, col., 120 mins. Armando Acosta.

Though hard to believe, this film was shot using only one live actor, John Hurt, with the rest of the cast comprised of *cats*, whose voices were provided by the likes of Francesca Annis (Juliette), Vanessa Redgrave (Lady Capulet), Ben Kingsley (Capulet), and Maggie Smith (Rosalyne). Italian director Armando Acosta was reported to have spent nearly five thousand hours in the editing room to deliver the final product, which is a mixture of Sergei Prokofiev's ballet, Shakespeare's play, and Acosta's poetic imagination.

494 *Romeo and Juliet*
1992. Russia/Wales. Soyuzmultifilm/Christmas films. Sound., col., 25 mins. Efim Gambourg.

This film in the series *Shakespeare: The Animated Tales* uses the traditional technique of cel animation. More interesting than the film's form is the puritanical debate spawned by its sexual content, which initially involved a consummation scene. The compromise struck between Russian animators and the more circumspect British producers was the retention of Romeo and Juliet's post-consummation lark/nightingale speech.

495 *Romeo and Juliet*
1994. U.K. Alan Horrox. Sound, col., 81 mins. Alan Horrox.

Originally aired on television and released for commercial sale on video in the wake of the *Romeo + Juliet* mania incited by Luhrmann's 1996 film (below), this conventional, period dress adaptation stars Jonathan Firth (Colin's brother) as Romeo.

496 *William Shakespeare's Romeo + Juliet*
1996. U.S. Bazmark Productions. Sound, col., 120 mins. Baz Luhrmann.

Shot in Mexico and featuring memorable, larger-than-life captures of the statue of the Madonna that presides over Mexico City, this film offers an iconoclastic treatment of religion as just another commodity in post-modern consumer culture. In this respect alone, Luhrmann's film not only alludes to popular adaptations such as *West Side Story* and Zeffirelli's *Romeo and Juliet* but also to lesser known films like *China Girl*, which features a scene wherein Chinese gangsters deface a statue of the Virgin Mary. Indeed, despite the title's declaration of fidelity to Shakespeare alone, *William Shakespeare's Romeo + Juliet* invites discussion about the Bard's own status as a masterful adapter of source materials, invoking—in its use of water imagery—Shakespeare's principal source (Arthur Brooke's *The Tragicall Historye of Romeus and Juliet*) and, in its hypertragic ending in which Juliet awakes just before Romeo

dies, the play's Italian antecedents (Masuccio, Da Porto, etc.).

Music figures heavily in Luhrmann's adaptation. Unlike *West Side Story* (entry 487), however, *William Shakespeare's Romeo + Juliet* would be considered a "non-integrated" musical, because the songs are performed by figures who are not characters in the play and remain, essentially, sequestered from the main cast. What is especially interesting about these musical interludes is the fact that they are sung by black performers—the effect of which, howsoever unintentional, is a formally "segregated" film that duplicates the overtly racist treatment of minority performers in the classic MGM musicals of the 1930s and 1940s. The appearance of R&B "Diva" Des'ree, for example, uncannily recalls the solitary elegance of Lena Horne in particular, suggesting the ways in which the racial tensions that shape the content of *West Side Story* resurface formally in Luhrmann's adaptation.

Following the film's $11.6 million opening weekend, Leonardo DiCaprio became a household name and Claire Danes's career was revived from the doldrums of syndication on the teen television series *My So-Called Life*. Innumerable fanzines, fansites, and other ephemera devoted to the film and its stars, director, and triple-platinum soundtrack continue to surface. Especially useful for students, the most recent DVD version has an interactive component for the express purpose of screenplay-to-screen comparisons. Situated in Luhrmann's own career between the *Romeo and Juliet* spin-offs *Strictly Ballroom* (1992) and *Moulin Rouge* (2001), *Romeo + Juliet* remains the highest-grossing Shakespeare film of all time—although, like *West Side Story*, this adaptation is anything but "Strictly Shakespeare."

DVD: theatrical trailers, widescreen letterbox format, behind the scenes with the director, music videos, commentary by the crew, and screenplay-to-screen comparisons.

497 *Barrio Wars*
2002. U.S. Paul Wynne. Sound, col., 90 mins. Paul Wynne.

A poorly executed version of *Romeo and Juliet* set among Latino gangs, this direct-to-DVD film stars underground rapper Chino XL. *The Street King* (above), released in the very same year, offers a much more persuasive transpositional treatment of Shakespeare's *Romeo and Juliet* "in the barrio."

DVD: Dolby digital sound and trailers.

498 *Lil' Romeo and Lil' Juliet*
In Production. U.S. Master P and Mark Canton. Katia Lund.

Co-director (with Fernando Meirelles) of the extraordinarily graphic and critically acclaimed 2002 film about Brazillian gangs, *City of God*, Lund's latest film is set to feature hip-hop phenom Lil' Romeo. Based on her earlier work, this adaptation of *Romeo and Juliet* is expected to be particularly violent; however, Lund may attempt to distance herself from this assumption by conveying the on-screen violence through music and dance.

THE TAMING OF THE SHREW

499 *La Bisbetica Domata*
1908. Italy. Società Italiana Fratelli Pineschi. Silent, b&w, 5 mins. Azeglio and Lamberto Pineschi.

This early Italian version of *Shrew*, directed and produced by the Pineschi brothers, suggests a new spin on the sibling rivalry that characterizes the relationship between Kate and Bianca in Shakespeare's play. Significantly, neither brother is credited with having directed or produced a subsequent film.

500 *The Taming of the Shrew*
1908. U.S. Biograph. Silent, b&w, 10 mins. D. W. Griffith.

Starring the "Biograph girl" Florence Lawrence, this film privileges the slapstick interpretation of *Shrew* that Sam Taylor's 1929 version would make famous. As is common with many screen versions of *Shrew* (not just the silent ones), Griffith's adaptation eliminates the Christopher Sly frame and considerably reduces the Bianca subplot. Perhaps the most important contribution of this *Shrew*, which fails to demonstrate the sophisticated camera work for which Griffith was becoming known, is its inclusion of a whip as one of Petruchio's props—an accessory that, in Sam Taylor's 1929 version (below), will be entrusted to Kate. The film survives in the Library of Congress.

501 *La Mégerè Approvoisée*
1911. France. Éclipse. Silent, b&w, 10 mins. Henri Defontaines.

Admirable for its one-reel length, this film begins with Petruchio's entreaty to Bapista for Katherine's hand and ends with the bet. Between these scenes, the film not only closely follows Shakespeare's plot but also depicts scenes that remain part of the "off-stage" action—for example, the wedding fiasco—importantly showcasing cinema's ability to materialize events that the theater must leave to the imagination.

502 *The Taming of the Shrew*
1911. U.K. Co-Operative Cinematograph Co. Silent, b&w, 13 mins. Will Barker.

As with other Co-Operative ventures, this film was based on a stage production starring F. R. Benson's players and employs the camera as a means of recording, rather than reinventing, theatrical performance.

503 *La Bisbetica Domata*
1913. Italy. Film Ambrosio. Silent, b&w, 22 mins. Arrigo Frusta.

Similar to the Éclipse production before it, this *Shrew* makes shrewd use of cinema's capacity for mobility in order to create realistic renderings of scenes that cannot be performed in Shakespeare's play. The most memorable example of this "screen business" is the film's dramatic depiction of the grueling moonlight pilgrimage to Petruchio's house, which becomes the comic centerpiece of Frusta's adaptation.

504 *The Iron Strain* (U.K. title: *A Modern Taming of the Shrew*)
1916. U.S. Triangle. Silent, b&w, four reels (exact length unknown). Reginald Barker.

One of the earliest examples of a transpositional Shakespeare adaptation, this film depicts a high society shrew from New York being sent to Alaska to meet the "barbarian" (a man free from social conformity) to whom she is betrothed. Eventually, she comes to like him, and, conveniently, he turns out to hail from the same social class as she does. Although progressive in terms of its approach to adaptation, Barker's *Shrew* is socially conservative in its execution, suggesting the growing insecurity of the American "aristocracy" in the wake of rampant immigration and a rising middle class.

505 *The Taming of the Shrew*
1923. U.K. British and Colonial Kinematograph Company. Silent, b&w, 20 mins. Edwin J. Collins.

Although the majority of the intertitles for this film are excerpted from Shakespeare, the conclusion emerges from the burgeoning cinematic imagination when the ensemble "bet" scene is replaced with a tableau of Kate sitting on Petruchio's lap and kissing him—the perfect cue for later successes such as *Kiss Me Kate* (see Chapter 4, "Spin-offs").

506 *The Taming of the Shrew*
1929. U.S. Pickford Corporation/Elton Corporation for United Artists. Sound, b&w, 73 mins. Sam Taylor.

Known as the first feature-length Shakespearean "talkie," this film starring Mary Pickford and Douglas Fairbanks set the precedent for later attempts to showcase on- and off-screen duos, such as Zeffirelli's 1966 adaptation (below), starring Elizabeth Taylor and Richard Burton. This film is important not only for its pioneering use of synchronized sound but also for its implicit inquiry into the ways in which life imitates art when casting arrangements blur the boundary between them. In her autobiography, *Sunshine and Shadow*, Pickford reveals her struggles with Fairbanks, who, like Petruchio himself, frequently arrived late for filming, refused to study his lines, and was constantly pulling pranks on the set; he became, in effect, a vision of method acting gone awry. Hence, although critics have explained away Pickford's tendency to shout Kate's lines as evidence of her uneasy transition from silent to sound film, it is equally likely that the tangible desperation in her voice encodes her frustration with Fairbanks—particularly in light of the fact that despite *Shrew*'s ranking among the *New York Times*' ten best films of the year, she withdrew it from circulation, claiming that she was never again "at home" in front of the camera. For all Pickford's doubts and subsequent self-effacement (she became a recluse not long after the film was completed), this version of *Shrew* has inspired a great number of feminist readings, which focus not only on Pickford's appropriation of phallic props—among them, a whip that she frequently cracks in Petruchio's midst—but also on one of the most famous moments in all of filmed Shakespeare: Pickford's notorious wink following Kate's "concession" speech, a bit of stage business that has called into question her sincerity ever since.

DVD: excerpts of the film are available on the DVD *Mary Pickford: A Life on Film.* A DVD version of the 1966 rerelease has been made available since June 2005 that deletes seven minutes of the 1929 version to achieve tighter synchronization effects; this version includes scene access and a digitally remastered audio track.

507 *Hathili Dulhan*

1932. India. Madan Theatre. Sound, b&w, feature (exact length unknown). Jeejeebhoy F. Madan.

The most distinctive quality of this film from the early Hindi "talking picture" scene is the fact that Khurshid, one of the greatest stars of Indian musical cinema of the 1940s, played a minor role to Indian silent star Patience Cooper. Yet the star behind the scenes was, of course, J. F. Madan, who owned as many as three hundred cinemas all across India. Significantly, though, despite his prolific entrepreneurial presence, Madan was not interested in cinema as a truly mass medium, for his films were intended for predominantly British audiences as well as members of the Indian elite.

508 *La Bisbetica Domata*

1942. Italy. Excelsa Film. Sound, b&w, 85 mins. Ferdinando Maria Poggioli.

It is somewhat ironic that this Italian adaptation features a Petruchio who earns his riches in America and returns to Italy to tame the hell-cat Catina, when, in the world outside the film, American troops would soon be arriving to forcefully occupy the country.

509 *Makacs Kata*

1943. Hungary. Mester Film. Sound, b&w, 75 mins. Viktor Bánky.

This modern dress adaptation, also filmed in Budapest, emerged at the same time as *Makrancos Hölgy* (below), the major difference being that the latter translates Shakespeare's title quite faithfully, whereas the former interprets it as "Stubborn Kate."

510 *Makrancos Hölgy*

1943. Hungary. Hunnia Studio. Sound, b&w, 83 mins. Emil Martonffry.

Filmed and set in Budapest, this contemporary adaptation was released at the same time as its Hungarian competitor (above) *Makacs Kata*.

511 *Cartas marcadas*

1948. Mexico. Diana/Almeda. Sound, b&w, 92 mins. René Cardona.

This adaptation is one of the earliest known Shakespeare films from Mexico; it stars national idol Pedro Infante.

DVD: Full-frame version.

512 *Ukroshcheniye stroptivoj (Taming of the Shrew)*

1961. USSR. Mosfilm. Sound, b&w, 92 mins. Sergei Kolosov.

Shot in the former Soviet Union's premiere studio, Mosfilm, this version of *Shrew* starred Lyudmila Kasatkina and marked the onset of a lasting professional relationship with Sergei Kolosov—one of the few film partnerships to survive the fall of the iron curtain. Kasatkina worked under Kolosov's direction all the way through the 1993 television series *Raskol*.

513 *The Taming of the Shrew*

1966. U.S./Italy. Royal Films/F.A.I. Sound, col., 122 mins. Franco Zeffirelli.

Capitalizing on the tempestuous off-screen relationship between the two principals, Elizabeth Taylor and Richard Burton, this film might be considered the comic sequel to the duo's critically acclaimed, highly serious *Who's Afraid of Virginia Woolf*, which depicts a disturbing relationship similarly based on excessive drinking and bickering. Yet despite the infectious combination of the two leads, a bizarre sense of dissociation between the actors and the diegesis plagues the film. For example, the Italianate splendor typical of Zeffirelli's lush mise-en-scènes often sits awkwardly with the frequently crude comic interactions between Burton and Taylor, who cannot seem to decide if the film is to be a classical vehicle or a Hollywood blockbuster—ultimately, it was neither. Also worthy of mention is the film's status as a symptom of increasing directorial dis-ease with adapting Shakespeare to the screen; as in so many contemporary Shakespeare films, this *Shrew* is beleaguered by interpolated scenes that are superfluous to the plot, appearing to have no purpose other than to assert a certain degree of independence from Shakespeare's words. The upshot of such directorial antics (memorable examples of which are the drawn-out chase scenes) is an "adolesecent" film, caught between childish imitation and adult autonomy. Nevertheless, it could be argued that *Shrew*, as the first of Zeffirelli's Shakespeare films, lends itself to analyses of the director's opus as a bildungsroman that evinces increasing degrees of maturity, evidenced in his later adaptations of *Romeo and Juliet* and *Hamlet* (1968, 1990, above).

DVD: includes production notes, theatrical trailers, bonus trailers, and widescreen amamorphic format.

514 *Taming of the Shrew*
1996. Russia/Wales. Soyuzmultifilm and Christmas Films. Sound, col., 27 mins. Aida Ziablikova.

Another film in the series *Shakespeare: The Animated Tales*, this stop-action puppetry version of *Shrew* invokes a return to the opening scene of Sam Taylor's 1929 film (above), which opens with a "Punch and Judy" show. In Ziablikova's adaptation, the literal woodenness of the puppets suggests a subtle form of commentary on the process of social conformity to which Kate is subjected, as do the interpolated moments that draw attention to the status of the taming plot as a *performance*, embodied in the use of theatrical curtains that "reveal the apparatus" and, therefore, arouse suspicion as to the sincerity of Kate's actions. Nevertheless, quite unlike Taylor's adaptation, in which Mary Pickford's Kate famously winks at the camera after delivering her "concession" speech, this Kate—for better and for worse—appears unmistakably tamed.

515 *10 Things I Hate about You*
1999. U.S. Mad Chance/Jaret. Sound, col., 97 mins. Gil Junger.

A clever, if ultimately conservative modernization of *Shrew* set in an American high school, this film stars the "Florence Turner" of the 1990s, Julia Stiles, and tells the story of a teenage "riot girl" who resists conformity at all costs—that is, until the right guy, Patrick Verona (Heath Ledger), comes along. Feminists will nevertheless be relieved that despite meeting Mr. Right, "Kat" still appears intent at the end of the film on fulfilling her dream of attending Sarah Lawrence College. See also entry 1326.

THE TEMPEST

516 *The Tempest*
1905. U.K. Charles Urban. Silent, col. (tinting), 2 mins. Charles Urban.

Hailed as a great experiment in cinematic realism, this short film captures the opening shipwreck scene of Shakespeare's *The Tempest*, created with permission from Sir Herbert Beerbohm Tree, who was starring in the production at Her Majesty's Theatre in London.

517 *The Tempest*
1908. U.K. Clarendon Film Company. Silent, b&w, 11 mins. Percy Stow.

Though not known for producing any other Shakespeare films, the quality-oriented Clarendon company released a remarkable version of *The Tempest*, hailed as a model silent film for its lucid condensation of Shakespeare's plot, suc-

cinct titles, and out-of-doors locations. The film opens with a particularly poignant tracking shot of the newly exiled Prospero, clutching his baby girl to his chest as he wanders the island he must call home. Immediately, Caliban is introduced as the land's only denizen; he is represented as a "Grizzly Adams" figure or, in less anachronistic terms, as a stereotypical wild man with long unkempt hair, tattered clothing, and an apelike posture. Prospero is shown swiftly subduing him with his staff, and, subsequently, the scene cuts away to his discovery of Ariel, represented as a young girl whom Prospero frees from entrapment within a tree. The subsequent title card reads, "Ten years later," and is followed by a scene in which Ariel taunts Caliban by changing shape before his eyes; truly prodigious for such an early film, jumpcuts are employed to transform Ariel to and from a monkey as an example of her prankster personality. Another primitive special effect is created when Prospero conjures the storm, the onset of which is signaled by a poof of smoke that suddenly transforms (again, with the help of dextrous editing) into a flock of doves—a tableau that suggests the pending conversion of Prospero's mission on the island from revenge to reconciliation. A rather absurd scene ensues in which Ferdinand is shown sauntering out of the chest-high water fully clothed and drenched from head to toe (save for the feather in his cap), as though he was starring in some Victorian spoof of *Baywatch*. The Ferdinand-Miranda plot follows and leads to the accord among all the island's inhabitants, as announced by the title card "Friends once more." Oddly, the film concludes without so much as hinting at Caliban's fate—a particularly conspicuous omission given the concluding image of the island's only other indigenous denizen, Ariel, being granted her freedom and waving farewell as the rest embark on their journey home to Milan.

DVD: The Milestone DVD restores the film from its original nitrate prints, highlighting its blue-tinted scenes in particular; a newly recorded score is loosely synchronized with the adaptation.

518 *The Tempest*
1911. U.S. Edwin Thanhouser. Silent, b&w, 10 mins. Barry O'Neil.

Robert Hamilton Ball speculates that Barry O'Neil directed this film for which not even a cast is identified. Another film in the *Thanhouser Classics* series, *The Tempest* was poorly received in its time and, along with the rest of the Thanhouser productions, was lost in a 1917 warehouse disaster—an event that adds a bizarre twist to a film that ends with a magician drowning his books.

519 *La Tempête*
1912. France. Éclair. Silent, b&w, 18 mins. Émile Chautard.

This may be the first Shakespeare film to include a flashback sequence, which is employed to demonstrate

Prospero's recognition that he has been betrayed by his brother and the king of Naples.

520 *The Tempest: By William Shakespeare, as Seen through the Eyes of Derek Jarman*
1979. U.K. Boyd's Company/Berwick Street/No. 8 Films. Sound, col., 95 mins. Derek Jarman.

In the avant-garde style for which Jarman's pioneering work is known, this version of *The Tempest* is one of the more successful attempts at adapting Shakespeare for the purposes of social commentary, with conspicuous allusions to the casualties of Thatcher's Britain. The subject of his third feature film, *The Tempest* is filled with all the eccentricities of Jarman's imagination, as Gothic, Baroque, camp, and horror elements combine to create a truly hybrid category of adaptation. Neither exclusively conventional nor transpositional, the film is set in an unidentifiable period, featuring costumes that alternately invoke Velasquez paintings and sci-fi. Experimental in its approach to casting (Prospero, for example, is played by the real-life magician/dramatist Heathcote Williams) and genre (the Busby Berkeley–style musical finale with Elisabeth Welch singing "Stormy Weather" amidst dancing sailors is a case in point), *The Tempest* is, above all, oppositional. The decision to shoot interiors in the fire-damaged, abandoned Stoneleigh Abbey inflects all the denizens of his mise-en-scène with the stigma of homelessness; and Caliban (Jack Birkett) is depicted not as a racial outsider but as an ostracized insider: a fragile, pallid AIDS victim for whom Thatcher famously had no sympathy. These visions of homelessness and homosexuality signal Jarman's confrontation with Thatcher's much-touted monetarist "revolution" in the act of paying tribute to its unacknowledged victims. That Jarman himself died of AIDS in 1994 is unwanted proof of the precipitous spread of this *socially* transmitted disease of neglect with which *The Tempest* takes issue.

DVD: includes three rare short films by Jarman: *A Journey to Avebury* (1971), *Garden of Luxor* (1972), and *Art of Mirrors* (1973); also contains the text of the original press kit.

521 *Prospero's Books*
1991. Netherlands/France/Italy. Allarts/Cinea/Camera One, et al. Sound, col., 125 mins. Peter Greenaway.

When he envisioned bringing Shakespeare's *The Tempest* to the screen, Greenaway was already imagining some form of Shakespearean subterfuge, hoping that in being faithful to the text (indeed, he follows the play more closely than any other film version) and to the theatrical tradition of casting a classically trained actor on the verge of his retirement as Prospero (a place supplied by Sir John Gielgud), he would be free to explore the play in a vein unlike any before imagined. Greenaway does precisely this in *Prospero's Books*, fashioning the film as a kind of prequel

to *The Pillow Book* (1996) by superimposing images of and excerpts from all of the books in Prospero's library—which, we know, he "prize[s] above [his] dukedom" (1.2.168). That neither Shakespeare nor Prospero reveals to us the contents of the library provides Greenaway with his entrée into the Renaissance imagination, out of which he fashions twenty-four books. Typical of Prospero's magic in *The Tempest* and Greenaway's own auteurist flourishes, *Prospero's Books* continually calls into question the lines and layers that separate illusion from reality, often superimposing fact on fiction and vice versa. For example, visually superimposed "over" Gielgud's often distorted, simultaneous recitations of other characters' lines are images and evocations of art history—a classic example of which is Greenaway's invention of *A Book of Water*, which he envisions as a series of lost drawings by Leonardo da Vinci (lost, of course, because Prospero presumably drowns these books at the end of Shakespeare's play). For just a moment, then, we are led to read *The Tempest* itself as though it were historical truth, as a proleptic explanation, that is, of why some works have survived the ravages of time and others have not. Lest the viewer get too carried away with speculation, however, Greenaway continually overlays these ghostly inventions with matter culled from the human body: blood, urine, and vomit abound, as do evocations of the natural world (rain) and its industrial offspring (ink). In this context, perhaps the most provocative book in Greenaway's catalogue is also the most anachronistic: *A Book of Motion*. Ostensibly based on the Renaissance preoccupation with the natural beauty and nobility of man, this book becomes an opportunity for Greenaway to celebrate the *manmade*—specifically, the invention of cinema itself—by incorporating images from Eadweard Muybridge's studies of motion, which culminated in the immediate predecessor of the cinematic apparatus, the zoöpraxiscope. Remarkably, all the while that Greenaway is indulging in the construction of Prospero's library, Gielgud and the rest of the cast are performing *The Tempest*. The film ends with only a nominal departure from the play, in that Prospero drowns his books, as expected, but two of them are salvaged by Caliban: one, the 1623 Folio, whose first nineteen pages have been left blank (for *The Tempest*), the other, the playtext of *The Tempest* that Prospero has just completed. A brilliant and audacious anachronism, Greenaway's film of *Prospero's Books* hereby becomes the progenitor of Shakespeare's plays, even as the source of this birth—Caliban—reminds us that the birth of cinema itself was once deemed monstrous by its many detractors, indeed, a thing of darkness—and light—that neither theater nor literature would acknowledge their own. See also entry 1349.

522 *The Tempest*
1992. Russia/Wales. Soyuzmultifilm and Christmas Films. Sound, col., 25 mins. Stanislav Sokolov.

Part of the highly successful *Shakespeare: The Animated Tales* series, this film employs stop-action puppetry as a pun on Prospero's internal role in *The Tempest* as a master puppeteer. Another prominent example of "bearing the apparatus" occurs in the figure of Ariel, who, evocative of Sandy Duncan's Tinkerbell in *Peter Pan*, is a girlish, free-spirited sprite who nevertheless can fly only with the help of visible cables and, of course, Prospero's permission.

TITUS ANDRONICUS

523 *Titus*

1999. U.S./Italy. Blue Sky Productions. Sound, col., 162 mins. Julie Taymor.

This stunning, highly stylized adaptation marks a departure from films like Dunne's (entry 524) by adapting Shakespeare's slasher play as an art film. Featuring a remarkable cast willing to work for far less pay than their names would typically command—including Anthony Hopkins (Titus), Jessica Lange (Tamora), and Alan Cummings (Saturninus)—Taymor's film is, surprisingly, a director's vehicle. Featuring bravura camera work and montage sequences typified by the Penny Arcade Nightmare (PAN) flashbacks, the film's startling visual juxtapositions of human, animal, and machine suggest a mode of visual experimentation not unlike the paintings of Frida Kahlo—the subject of Taymor's next film. These interpolated sequences disrupt the diegesis on several occasions, seeping into the narrative as though they were eruptions of the filmic unconscious, indeed, the irrepressible "insistences"—as Pier Paolo Pasolini describes them—that encode the director's "temptation to make another film."

Nowhere is this temptation more visible than in Taymor's post-mutilation vision of Lavinia, who struggles to keep her tattered white dress from blowing up above her thighs in a scene explicitly intended to recall the iconic image of Marilyn Monroe coyly poised over a subway grating. This superimposition of vapid popular entertainment on Ovidian tragedy is disturbing for the way in which it tempers our sense of Lavinia as a victim of a heinous crime, revealing Taymor's barely concealed disdain for her

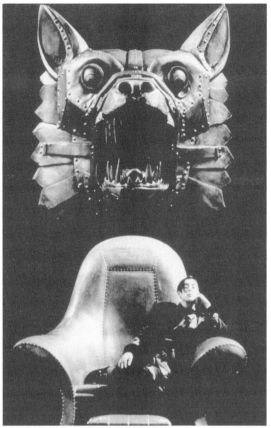

Saturninus under a massive wolf-head from *Titus* (2001). This shot shows the kind of postmodern design Julie Taymor used in the film. Courtesy of Douglas Lanier.

character as "Daddy's girl, all dressed up for defilement," as Taymor describes Lavinia in her screenplay. Yet Taymor's implication that Lavinia is not as innocent as she seems is offset by her augmentation of Young Lucius's role, the child observer who ushers us into the film when he swept away from his own kitchen, where his make-believe game of search-and-destroy has precipitated an eruption of real violence just beneath his kitchen window. When his anonymous captor/savior takes him into the Roman coliseum and thrusts him over his head in a gesture of triumph—a move that evinces an unsettling roar from an invisible crowd—we are led to wonder if we have just been party to a rescue or a pedophilic abduction.

If the audience enters the Roman coliseum—itself a structure that blurs the boundaries between violence and entertainment—through the eyes of a presumably innocent child, then by the end of the film, the spectator is no longer accorded the benefit of the doubt. Rather, following the apocalyptic spectacle of the banquet in which the horrors of Senecan tragedy and the absurd splendor of Dionysian revels are condensed into Titus's homicidal feast, the camera tracks back to reveal that we are not in the privacy of Titus's home but within the circumference of the coliseum, where spectators now fill the once-empty seats, watching in perfect silence and—in so doing—voicing their complicity in the carnage. Indeed, as Taymor observes, "They are silent. They are we." The film ends with our former ally, Young Lucius (carrying Aaron and Tamora's baby in his arms), turning his back on an audience that has failed to earn his trust, as he heads toward a rising sun and, perhaps, another film.

DVD: includes commentary by Taymor, theatrical trailers, scene-by-scene commentary from Anthony Hopkins, a "Making Of" documentary, a costume gallery, and widescreen anamorphic format.

524 *Titus Andronicus*

1999. U.S. Joe Redner Film and Productions. Sound, col., 140 mins. Christopher Dunne.

Billed as the definitive adaptation of Shakespeare's "splatter epic," Dunne's *Titus Andronicus* is a self-consciously a B-grade horror film. Visibly fake blood, gore, and grotesquely bulging eyes (caused by pain before death) dominate the mise-en-scène of this low-budget slashploitation production in which Titus's famous pie becomes meatloaf.

525 *William Shakespeare's Titus Andronicus*
2000. U.S. South Main Street Productions. Sound, col., 170 mins. Richard Griffin.

An example of the "indie" Shakespeare movement, Richard Griffin's DVD version of *Titus Andronicus*, created on a budget of $12,000, enjoyed a weeklong run at the Cable Car Cinema in Providence, Rhode Island, and features locations from all over the tiny state. According to the director, the film emerged, in part, as an effort to provide a less violent, sensationalist spin on Shakespeare's play than Taymor's film (above), opting instead for a searing psychological approach more in keeping with an adaptation of *Hamlet* than the horror genre. The setting is contemporary, featuring the disaffected youth culture of "Goths" (replacing the warring Germanic peoples of the same namesake) and fervent lobbyists for the Saturninus and Bassianus "parties," all of which suggest the alienating, polarized political climate of America in the wake of the Bush Jr. administration.

TWELFTH NIGHT

526 *Twelfth Night: Or, What You Will*
1910. U.S. Vitagraph. Silent, b&w, 10 mins. J. Stuart Blackton.

Noteworthy for its use of outdoor locations, this film opens with Viola emerging from the sea—in Long Island as opposed to Illyria. The scene immediately shifts to Orsino's residence, where we encounter the melodramatic Duke and his many servants sporting Elizabethan frocks, tunics, tights, and the like. Subsequently, the audience is permitted a glimpse of the letter that Cesario is about to carry to Olivia on the Duke's behalf—a clever substitution for a title card that reads, "Though ofttimes scorned by you I sent my best beloved page once more to plead my cause. I follow him anon to learn thine answer." When Cesario arrives at Olivia's home, all the ladies veil themselves, and Olivia is represented as swiftly taken by the young page's charm. But Malvolio (Charles Kent) is truly the star of this adaptation as a delectably disdainful aspirant to Olivia's attention. For example, in the scene in which he is asked to give Olivia's ring to Cesario, Malvolio refuses to touch the boy, dropping the ring into Cesario's hands with the help of his guidon, the long, ornamental staff that enables him to keep the world quite literally at arm's length. Hence, Sir Andrew, Sir Tony, and Maria's prank seems all the more justified in this film. Given the difficulty of explaining the riddle "M.O.A.I." that their forged letter from Olivia contains, the film explicitly identifies Malvolio as the man

who "doth sway [Olivia's] life." Malvolio's gaudy smiles and gartered stockings follow hard upon this false revelation of Olivia's love for him, and, in the end, Malvolio is forced to watch Olivia deny both her letter and her love for him, as she drapes herself in the arms of Sebastian. Feste appears only for a moment in this film, somersaulting swiftly into the scene just prior to the disclosure of Cesario's real identity; he disappears just as quickly when Olivia refuses to cater to his tricks.

DVD: digitally remastered with newly recorded score.

527 *Dvenadtsataia Noch (Twelfth Night, Or What You Will)*
1956. USSR. Lenfilm. Sound, col., 90 mins. Yan Frid.

A lavish, almost balletic version of *Twelfth Night* in the traditional Russian style, this version of *Twelfth Night* was directed by the musical comedy mastermind, Yan Frid, whose first teacher in the art of filmmaking was none other than Sergei Eisenstein.

528 *Was Ihr Wollt*
1962. West Germany. Bavaria Atelier. Sound, b&w, 166 mins. Franz Peter Wirth.

The director of more than sixty made-for-TV films, Franz Wirth added a celluloid version of *Twelfth Night* to his list that spawned a response from East Germany, releasing a television version of *Was Ihr Wollt* (directed by Lothar Bellag) one year later.

529 *Viola und Sebastian*
1972. West Germany. Guertler/Runze. Sound, col., 93 mins. Ottokar Runze.

A pop musical version of *Twelfth Night*, Runze's debut film suffered from poor critical reception, despite the success of earlier German musical adaptations of Shakespeare.

530 *Twelfth Night*
1986. Australia. Twelfth Night. Sound, col., 120 mins. Neil Armfield.

This little-known version of *Twelfth Night*, based on a highly successful theater run in the early 1980s, features a largely indigenous cast, including Australian native Geoffrey Rush as Sir Andrew Aguecheek in his first film appearance. The critics' chief complaint about Armfield's attempt to move from theater to film is not the quality of acting, which has been consistently rated as excellent, but rather the fact that Gillian Jones's Viola is too feminine—something more visible on screen than stage—to pull off the role of either Cesario or Sebastian.

531 *Twelfth Night*
1992. Russia/Wales. Soyuzmultifilm and Christmas Films. Sound, col., 25 mins. Mariya Muat.

Part of the series *Shakespeare: The Animated Tales*, this film uses hand-manipulated puppets, each of them six inches tall, to render Shakespeare's story in child-friendly terms. Unlike Shakespeare's play, this adaptation satisfies our curiosity as to what Viola looks like in her "women's weeds" (5.1.273) by transforming her upon Orsino's request. This socially conservative tendency to explain some of the more risqué ambiguities of Shakespeare's plays occurs throughout the films in this series, ostensibly because they target a young audience.

532 *Twelfth Night*
1996. U.K./Ireland/U.S. Renaissance Films. Sound, col., 134 mins. Trevor Nunn.

Kenneth Branagh's producing presence is all over Trevor Nunn's directorial film debut, which contains echoes of Branagh's highly successful 1993 film of *Much Ado about Nothing* (above). For example, the love prank played on Benedick, which requires much farcical sneaking about behind statues, topiaries, and shrubs in Leonato's garden, clearly provides the template for the framing of Malvolio (Nigel Hawthorne) in Olivia's (Helena Bonham Carter) statue-strewn grounds. Similar to the slow-motion scene in which Benedick splashes around in a fountain to celebrate his newly proclaimed love for Beatrice, in Nunn's adaptation, an uptight Malvolio—suddenly giddy with the thought of Olivia requiting his desire—christens the moment by thrashing about the water feature in Olivia's garden. More original is the film's approach to Feste (Ben Kingsley), whose mood is melancholy at best; nevertheless, his subdued, if not downright depressed sagacity suggests the personnel shift in Shakespeare's own company away from Richard Burbage's gag-oriented roles to the more mature and often biting wit associated with the characters played by Edward Alleyn—which included, of course, Feste. The most striking aspect of Nunn's brooding adaptation, however, is his decision to depict Illyria not as a topsy-turvy state of nature but, rather, as a militaristic state that is as prone to paranoia and as it is pranks.

533 *She's the Man*
U.S. DreamWorks Pictures. In production. Andy Fickman.

Starring teen-phenom Amanda Bynes of Nickelodeon and, more recently, *What A Girl Wants* (Dennie Gordon, 2003), this adaptation of *Twelfth Night* is distinguished by its multiple screenplays; the first, written by Jack Leslie, is in the process of being rewritten by Karen McCullah Lutz and Kirsten Smith, best known for their work on *Legally Blonde* (Robert Luketic, 2001).

THE TWO GENTLEMEN OF VERONA

534 *Yi Jian Mei*
1931. China. Lian Hua Film Company. Silent, b&w, 113 mins. Bu Wancang.

This feature-length adaptation set in twentieth-century China is the first known Shakespeare film from this country.

THE WINTER'S TALE

535 *Racconto d'Inverno (A Winter's Tale)*
1910. Italy. Cines. Silent, b&w, length unknown. Director unknown.

Though advertised by Cines with the company's typical fanfare, promising scenes of splendor that "bewilder" and "charm" the eye, this film is really more a lively series of individual tableaux.

536 *A Winter's Tale/The Winter's Tale*
1910. U.S. Edwin Thanhouser. Silent, b&w, 10 mins. Barry O'Neil.

One of the more expensive pictures in the *Thanhouser Classics* series, this film was applauded as a triumph that distinguished Thanhouser as the most important American producer of early Shakespeare films. This film, like 90 percent of the Thanhouser productions, was destroyed in the 1917 fire.

537 *Una Tragedia Alla Corte Di Sicilia* (alternative title: *Novella D'Inverno: Una Novella Di Shakespeare*; English title: *The Winter's Tale*; reissue title: *The Lost Princess*)
1914. Italy. Milano Films. Silent, b&w, 32 mins. Baldassare Negroni.

In this short film, Shakespeare reads the play to his friends, and his audience applauds him; when the external audience responds in kind, they applaud the cinematic framing device rather than the performance of the play itself—an early vision of cinema performing a *coup de théâtre*.

538 *The Winter's Tale*
1996. Russia/Wales. Soyuzmultifilm and Christmas Films. Sound, col., 27 mins. Stanislav Sokolov.

Winner of the 1996 Emmy for Best Animated Feature, this film employs stop-action puppetry to bring Shakespeare's statue of Hermione to life—reminiscent, appropriately, of the children's tale of Pinocchio. Also in light of the young audience targeted by the *Animated Tales* series, the role of the child Mamilius is augmented. Disturbingly, though, the film's representation of Hermione is more incriminating than Shakespeare's play suggests, as Solokov repeats a gambit used in Kenneth Branagh's 1993 adaptation of *Much Ado about Nothing* wherein a Hero look-alike is shown in a sexually compromising position to make Claudio's accusation of her infidelity more believable. In a similarly wordless scene, Hermione is shown in what appears to be a furtive conversation with Polixenes, hence planting a seed not only in Leontes's mind but also in the audience's imagination that she is, potentially, guilty of cuckolding her husband. Although the effect of such interpolations stop shy of "blaming the victim," they succeed in downplaying the plight of the women while eliciting more sympathy for, and lending credence to, the violent behavior of their male accusers.

4

Film Spin-offs and Citations

INTRODUCTION, "ON THE VIRTUES OF ILLEGITIMACY: FREE SHAKESPEARE ON FILM," DOUGLAS LANIER

Until fairly recently, most of the film adaptations of Shakespeare listed in this section have dwelt in the critical netherworld of "Shakespeareana," that dark space reserved for the illegitimate, fake, scandalous, or unfaithful versions of the Shakespearean script, the realm of bastard, deformed, or wayward children of the Bard. Even a cursory glance over the labels often used for such films—"unfaithful adaptations," "spin-offs," "derivatives," "travesties," "revisions," and "Schlockspeare"—reveals how routinely and sometimes unconsciously they are clouded with pejorative connotations from the very start of discussion. Once upon a time, one job of the professional Shakespearean was to determine the proper lineage and moral character of members of Shakespeare's ever-extending adaptational family, to determine which film performances were entitled to be called "proper" Shakespeare, and which were to be excluded from the rights and privileges accorded to their father's name. Ben Jonson, in the first full-scale criticism of Shakespeare's work, his poem "On the Memory of my beloved, The Author Master William Shakespeare, and what he hath left us," published among the prefatory pieces to the 1623 Folio, established this genealogical function of criticism when he observed, "Look how the father's face / Lives in his issue, even so the race / Of Shakespeare's mind and manners brightly shines / In his well-torned and true-filéd lines" (ll. 65–68). However, as is so often the case with genealogies of the privileged (and "Shakespeare" is a family name that accords considerable cultural privilege), the line between legitimate and illegitimate offspring is never entirely clear. Indeed, how one distinguishes proper child from bastard shifts from age to age and culture to culture, shaped not by stable objective principles but by the changing needs and interests of the moment. And, as any viewer or reader of *King Lear* knows, by his very exclusion from legitimacy the bastard can highlight, invert, protest, and even take revenge upon the often problematic assumptions that led to his abjection in the first place.

Recently, many (though certainly not all) Shakespeareans have reconsidered the value of films previously excluded from the inner circle of Shakespeare's family. For one matter, the line between "proper" and "improper" Shakespeare films is hard to determine and defend, particularly considering that any adaptation of Shakespeare to the screen entails radically recasting his theatrical scripts for a medium Shakespeare could never have imagined. Evaluations of cinematic Shakespeare are often in danger of falling into matters of prevailing tastes or idiosyncratic preference rather than principled assessment. The postmodern insistence upon recognizing differences and resisting hierarchizing them has offered theoretical justification for growing unease about easily designating different adaptations as, to use a much invoked distinction, "faithful" or "unfaithful." Second, in an age when Shakespeare's reach is global and Shakespeare's cultural authority remains powerful (even as the terms of that authority are changing), scholars interested in studying the nature of Shakespeare's afterlife have turned their attention to performances of Shakespeare in all their variety to assess how and why Shakespeare's significance—a genuinely singular cultural phenomenon, after all—has been reproduced and how it might be produced differently. Such studies spring from the insight that even passing references or wildly transformed adaptations, when they are (mis)recognized as "Shakespearean" by some fraction of their audience, nevertheless contribute to the wider, evolving sense of

Shakespeare's reach, relevance, importance, or sheer recognition value. Indeed, freed from the burden of fidelity in its various forms, "unfaithful" screen Shakespeares may provide a clearer view of processes of negotiation, transposition, cooperation, revision, and contestation between Shakespeare and a prevailing culture or marginal subcultures than do their "proper" counterparts.

This bibliography has retained what has become a commonplace distinction between "faithful" Shakespeare films and "free" adaptations, in part simply as a practical division of labor necessitated by the sheer volume of films referencing Shakespeare. Since the distinction has become conventional and has consequences for how we see the relationship between Shakespeare and film, it merits discussion. One seemingly objective criterion for making this distinction is Shakespeare's language. Faithful adaptations hew closely to Shakespeare's language, while free adaptations do not. This distinction is particularly powerful, considering that Shakespeare's language is all that survives of his "original" productions[1] and, more important, Shakespeare's accrued cultural authority is closely tied to his undeniably extraordinary wordcraft. But the distinction is more complex and less objective than it may first seem. For one thing, not a few Shakespeare films use his words while radically reshaping their order and context. Orson Welles's *Othello*, widely regarded as a canonical Shakespeare film, fractures Shakespeare's script and reassembles it to fit Welles's view of Othello's fall as an existential tragedy. For another, there are several canonical Shakespeare films that, for various reasons, use little or none of Shakespeare's language—silent Shakespeare films such as *Richard III* (André Calmettes and James Keane, 1912) or the non–English language adaptations of Akira Kurosawa or Grigori Kozintsev. Indeed, Kurosawa's *Throne of Blood* (1957) and *Ran* (1985) pose the most problematic examples, faithful to neither Shakespeare's language nor the plots of Shakespeare's originals, yet regularly regarded as faithful to the "spirit" of the plays they adapt to the screen, *Macbeth* and *King Lear*, respectively. One body of "free" adaptations—*Men of Respect* (William Reilly, 1991) and *O* (Tim Blake Nelson, 2001) provide apt examples—remains remarkably faithful to the plotlines of their respective originals (*Macbeth* and *Othello*) while using contemporary dialogue and settings. To the extent that their audiences find the films in some sense "Shakespearean," such films challenge the notion that being Shakespearean depends upon using Shakespeare's dialogue. After all, Shakespeare himself wrote his tales of Roman and British history in what was for him and his audiences a contemporary idiom; arguably, then, a recasting of his plotlines in modern language may be more faithful to the spirit of Shakespeare's enterprise than some quaint, fetishistic, or antiquarian attachment to his particular mode of expression. Passing citations of Shakespearean lines also complicate the question of textual fidelity. Though a filmmaker may faithfully transcribe Shakespeare's words when they are included in his or her film, the meaning is altered, sometimes radically, by who says them and in what particular context. And, it should be remembered, nearly all performances of Shakespeare—and certainly those on film— make changes in the Shakespearean script, out of necessity and interpretive license. My point is that fidelity to Shakespeare's language is not a reliable guide to which films might count as "proper" Shakespeare and which do not.

As with fidelity to language, so too with fidelity to Shakespeare's plot, characters, themes, or, most slippery of all, "spirit." In each case, one can point to examples of Shakespeare films regarded as canonical that violate such principles of fidelity more radically than some of their noncanonical counterparts. The problem of determining what we mean by properly "Shakespearean" films can be even more challenging in the case of distinguishing between Shakespearean and non-Shakespearean films. Take the case of *The Lion King* (Roger Allers and Rob Minkoff, 1994), the popular Disney animation that chronicles the coming of age of Simba the lion. In Simba's youth, his father Mufasa, beloved King of Beasts, is killed by Scar, Simba's uncle, who takes over the kingdom. Simba grows up away from the court in the company of Pumbaa (a fat warthog) and Timon (a meerkat), who teach him the ways of the world and encourage him to adopt their hedonistic philosophy of "hakuna matata" ("no worries"); when Simba comes of age, he learns the truth of his father's fate and, encouraged by Mufasa's ghostly admonition to him to remember, he vows vengeance upon Scar, ultimately regaining his father's kingdom. As several commentators have noted, although there are no direct borrowings from Shakespeare's dialogue, at first glance the film bears several resemblances to details from Shakespeare's *Hamlet*: the usurping uncle, the revered father, the son given the task of avenging his father's death, the uncle's treacherous minions (a pack of hyenas in *The Lion King*), the dead father's appearance as a ghost, and even the son's courtship (of Nala, a lioness). There are also elements from *Henry IV, Part 1*: a disgraced prince who grows up in the company of ne'er-do-wells but who eventually demonstrates his heroic nature in a battle against a formidable enemy. And yet there are substantial differences: Scar does not marry Simba's mother, as Claudius does Gertrude; there are no characters comparable to Polonius, Laertes, or Fortinbras, and no moments corresponding to *The Mousetrap* or Ophelia's madness; *The Lion King* includes no sequence like the Gad's Hill robbery or Hal and Falstaff's repartee at the Boar's Head Tavern; and Scar little resembles the hasty if courageous Hotspur. How, then, to understand the relationship between this film and Shakespeare's plays, if there is one at all? Should Shakespeare be counted as an uncredited source? Are *Hamlet*, *Henry IV, Part 1*, and *The Lion King* analogues, that is, coincidentally similar versions of widespread cultural narratives but without Shakespeare serving as a specific source? Or is *The Lion King*'s resemblance to Shakespeare's plays a chimera, borne of our desire to see elements of Shakespeare in nearly every narrative (which, with sufficient ingenuity and abstraction, we may readily do)?

These difficult interpretive questions also raise issues of cultural authority that are attendant upon designating any film in some sense Shakespearean. How we construe a film's relationship to Shakespeare can matter for its reception and cultural status. If we construe Shakespeare as a source for *The Lion King*, then it becomes possible to read the film as a revision of or negotiation with two of Shakespeare's most popular plays. We might, for example, see it as an example of the Disneyfication of Shakespeare's more troubling Oedipal narratives or an attempt by a multimedia conglomerate to use tried-and-true popular stories, ones safely out of copyright, to ensure its success in the lucrative but unpredictable children's film and video market (or, indeed, both of these alternatives). Using Shakespeare as a source also potentially offers Disney a measure of cultural prestige for its products, buffing its image as a provider of wholesome, edifying animated "classics" rather than just pop ephemera. If we think of *The Lion King* as a Shakespearean analogue, whatever "universality" it might lay claim to is less a matter of its specific echoes of *Hamlet* and *Henry IV, Part 1* and more a matter of the film's use of a more general plot type it just happens to share with Shakespeare, a plot type that addresses perennially compelling issues, tailoring them to the particulars of a given culture. (The director's commentary track on *The Lion King*'s DVD release makes just such a claim, mentioning *Hamlet* alongside folktales and the Old Testament as sources for the story line.) If we conclude that the resemblances between *The Lion King* and Shakespeare are, despite first appearances, finally an illusion, that conclusion raises the larger question of whether or not seeing such Shakespearean parallels is a matter of highly motivated perception, borne of an overfamiliarity with Shakespearean narratives and characters (to the exclusion of other "classics") and of the desire for a variety of reasons to make Shakespeare a central source of popular culture. That is, it draws our attention to the possibility that the seeming proliferation of free Shakespearean film adaptations, a perception to which this very bibliography contributes, is little more than a critical mirage, testifying to the critic's desire to demonstrate Shakespeare's cultural prominence, universality, or perennial popularity.

Though the sheer variety of free Shakespearean film adaptations listed here makes generalizations challenging, several patterns nevertheless emerge. First, free treatments of Shakespeare often occupy extremes of attitude toward Shakespeare. Sometimes they offer forms of bardolatry in which Shakespearean parallels are treated as articulations of emotional universals or Shakespearean references serve to highlight, intensify or verify some theme, elevating it to the level of profundity. And sometimes they offer forms of iconoclasm in which Shakespeare in his "proper" or high cultural guise is treated as an object of burlesque, often with the intention of making popular culture by contrast seem all the more modern, entertaining, accessible, or inclusive. And, paradoxically enough, these extremes may appear alongside each other in the same film, as they do, for example, in Ernst Lubitsch's 1942 antiwar comedy *To Be or Not to Be*.

Secondly, these films also reveal the enormous pressure of established film genres on adapting Shakespeare for the screen. Many free adaptations take the form of reshaping Shakespearean texts to the formal conventions, ideological contours, and demographic targets of dominant film genres, a process particularly clear in the raft of teen Shakespeare adaptations that flooded the megaplexes in the decade following Baz Luhrmann's enormously successful *Romeo + Juliet* (1996). The drive to recode Shakespearean narratives within the conventions of established film genres seeks to render Shakespeare in some sense "popular," commercially viable, or more easily legible as a means for extending or "classicizing" a film genre, as a form of burlesque, or simply as a way of quickly supplying copyright-free material for an industry hungry for ready-to-use content. It testifies to the extraordinary power of popular film genres as interpretive filters through which Shakespeare (and, of course, much else) is experienced by mass audiences. That power is typically more visible in free than in canonical adaptations (though it operates in both), and it fuels the persistence of certain hybrids such as the Shakespearean musical, the Shakespearean Western, or urban Shakespeare, some of which have become sub-genres in their own right. Indeed, several films even include elements of self-consciousness about their own hybridizing, such as the inset musical version of *A Midsummer Night's Dream* in the recent teen film *Get Over It* (Tommy O'Haver, 2001). Certainly, several plays have seemed to fall inescapably into the gravitational pull of specific genres—in ways revealing about the interpretive predispositions that modern audiences bring to these works: *Macbeth* and the gangster saga, *Hamlet* and film noir, *A Midsummer Night's Dream* and sex comedy, *Othello* and the backstage thriller, and *King Lear* and family melodrama. *Romeo and Juliet*, by far the most frequently adapted of Shakespeare's plays to the screen, has become the template for what is now a well-worn romantic scenario—a youthful romance blocked by some ethnic, religious, racial, class, or ideological feud between the lovers' families or peers, with the lovers' difficulties often serving as a means for commenting on the effects of social fissures and for reasserting the transcendent power of love. But in such films, one also often sees the pressure of romantic comedy in the drive to reconcile warring clans without the lovers having to die, paving the way for a happy ending. For instance, *Shakespeare in Love* (John Madden, 1999), a film that maps the plot outline of *Romeo and Juliet* back onto Shakespeare's own romantic biography, ends with Will Shakespeare and his love Viola de Lessups being tragically parted by her forced marriage to Lord Wessex. However, the film's coda supplies a compensatory transcendence of the forces that divide them: Shakespeare imagines Viola's release from her marriage in the form of a shipwreck from which she alone walks away into the pristine New World, a scene he records as the opening sequence of his new play, *Twelfth Night*. Charting differences between Shakespeare's plays and their transpositions into familiar film genres helps us identify ideological pressure points in both Shakespeare and popular film.

Thirdly, these films reveal the repeated attraction of a metadramatic approach to film adaptation, that is, films that chronicle theatrical (or, less often, cinematic) productions of Shakespeare in which the performers' lives come to mirror those of their characters. Such films reverse the commonplace that Shakespeare's works reflect the essence of real life by showing how in certain circumstances life comes perversely to mirror Shakespeare. Adaptations of this sort bear a certain affiliation to parodies of theatrical Shakespeare, a recurrent motif in Shakespearean film from as early as the silent era. Both types of adaptations remind us of the screen's deeply ambivalent relationship to the stage, for which Shakespeare, still so associated with the theater, remains a focal point. The cinema certainly pays homage to its roots in theatrical performance with these representations of the Shakespearean stage. But it also distinguishes itself from its forebear and competitor by representing stage performance of Shakespeare as inherently comic or prone to calamity (as in the case of parody) or as excessively powerful, seductive, or dangerous (as is often the case for metadramatic films). That is, metadramatic films register the extraordinary cultural authority of Shakespearean language and performance, Shakespeare's capacity to captivate us, while at the same time they demonize specifically theatrical performances of his work, suggesting that on the stage Shakespeare's power can enter real life in ways that are uncontrollable, poignant, (self-)destructive, and even prone to violence. These films also reflect shifts in dominant acting styles over the course of the twentieth century, from the grandiloquence of late nineteenth-century acting to method acting, in which the performer is encouraged to intertwine his or her own personal emotional life with that of the character. One variant of this adaptational approach, in which a scholar's life becomes intertwined with the Shakespeare materials he or she is teaching or studying, highlights yet another motif in this sub-genre. Often in metadramatic films, those who fall under Shakespeare's spell are Shakespearean professionals (or those who aspire to be). Stage actors or professors, who might otherwise be the standard bearers for "proper" Shakespeare, become in some manner disabled or compromised by the power of Shakespeare over which they might claim special authority. In effect, these metadramatic scenarios often imagine the revenge of Shakespeare upon those who lay claim to exclusive authority over his work. They speak to popular resentments about what Pierre Bourdieu has called "symbolic violence," the ways in which cultural elites use certain symbolic markers, Shakespeare among them, to assert the subordinate cultural status of non-professionals. In that sense, then, these films often have an antielitist edge, a quality that tacitly asserts a difference between the stage or classroom, the realm of high cultural, "proper" Shakespeare, and the cinema, where the power of the Bard can be seen to elude professional control and interact freely with workaday life, becoming by implication once again the property of "the people."

Lastly, a number of free adaptations interject Shakespeare himself in contemporary contexts or, less often, historical contexts clearly reimagined in contemporary terms, as in the theater world of *Shakespeare in Love*, recast as a Hollywood manqué. Certainly these appearances of Shakespeare continue the theatrical tradition of Shakespeare as a dramatic character. But instead of celebrating Shakespeare by recognizing his universality or contemporaneity (the burden of most Victorian representations), these screen appearances—typically little more than cameos—most often turn on the *mismatch* between Shakespeare and some aspect of the contemporary pop scene. Usually that mismatch is played for comedy, with the butt of the joke being either Shakespeare, who is presented as if flummoxed or upstaged by modernity, or more often pop culture itself, on whose inadequacies Shakespeare is made to stand in judgment. In the latter case, Shakespeare serves as an artistic or ethical standard from which pop culture can offer self-critique.

Shakespeare's cameos in *Time Flies* (Walter Forde, 1944) and *Looking for Richard* (Al Pacino, 1996) provide cogent examples. In *Time Flies*, a time-travel comedy in which a dotty inventor and group of entertainers are accidentally projected back to Elizabethan England, Shakespeare is encountered at the Globe Theatre, where he is struggling to write *Romeo and Juliet*. In a parody of Shakespeare's status as author, Susie Barton, a nightclub singer, provides him with familiar passages from the balcony scene, which she already knows from the future, underlining the point that Shakespeare's lines have become through time public property, not the creation of a solitary literary genius. Later, after hearing a band of Elizabethan musicians perform, Susie sings and dances her way through "Ring along

Bells" on the Globe stage, a swing tune that gets an enthusiastic response from the Renaissance audience and delights an at first bewildered Shakespeare, who sways with the beat as he listens. This sequence accords with several attempts during the 1930s and 1940s to hybridize Shakespeare and jazz in an attempt to popularize the former. This particular scene, however, tends to stress the *replacement* of traditional high culture with modern pop, for Shakespeare is quite content to be pushed to the margins of his own stage by a contemporary musical number. In *Looking for Richard*, Al Pacino addresses the relationship between contemporary sensibilities and Shakespeare's once-popular *Richard III* while providing a behind-the-scenes look at the process of staging the play and educational film–style commentary on its contexts. Besides Pacino's visit to Shakespeare's birthplace and several passing shots of his image, Shakespeare makes two short but pointed cameos that frame the documentary. When Pacino makes his first entrance as Richard on a mock-Elizabethan stage, he finds Shakespeare himself as the only member of the audience. Pacino's reaction, an anxious "Fuck!" highlights his awareness that his performance (and his popularizing documentary) will be measured against an ever-present standard of Shakespearean authenticity, here embodied by the Bard himself. After Richard is killed, a scene Pacino doubles by showing its rehearsal on a New York street, we very briefly glimpse Shakespeare seated in the theater, shaking his head in dismay at both Pacino's performance and his behind-the-scenes antics. This instance of Pacino's self-mockery has a double implication. On the one hand, Shakespeare passes final judgment on Pacino's film project, finding it inauthentic, perhaps insufficiently faithful in its rendering of the material or too revealing of the actors' exploratory, playful rehearsal processes. On the other hand, Pacino seems quite willing to embrace, even trumpet Shakespeare's dismay, as if it is a mark of his own desire to replace misguided reverence toward Shakespearean "authenticity" with popular relevance and immediacy. Pacino underlines his unconcern about rigorous fidelity in the very next scene by badly paraphrasing Hamlet's famous final line, "The rest is silence," and then following it up with "Whatever I'm saying, I know Shakespeare said it." This pair of Shakespeare cameos neatly encapsulates one of the central animating tensions of the film, between a desire for historical and artistic fidelity to a Shakespeare whom Pacino clearly reveres, and a desire to recast Shakespeare in terms more amenable to a popular film audience. More generally, these films suggest how Shakespeare's appearances in film are often linked to questions of cultural hierarchy and legitimation.

In addition to full-scale free adaptations, this bibliography also includes "cameo appearances," passing references to recognizably Shakespearean lines, characters, scenes, or motifs separated from their source narratives. For

convenience, I've divided "cameo appearances" into two groups: one included with the plays from which they spring, and the second (labeled "miscellaneous") combining films that include references from several plays, films that feature appearances of Shakespeare as a character or discussions of Shakespeare, and films in which Shakespearean actors or teachers are prominent characters. At work in these cameos are not only the meaning of the specific references but also our recognition that they come from Shakespeare, invoking more general associations, among them artsiness, aristocratic bearing, old-fashionedness, grandiloquence, theatricality, and Britishness. These passing references, so marginal to the narrative of their films, often serve to articulate or reinforce central themes. But they also offer the audience a number of pleasures. Sometimes the pleasure is of sheer recognition, that is, membership in the select group capable of identifying a given reference as Shakespearean and, sometimes, recognizing the specific source. At other times, pleasure springs from sensing how a Shakespearean passage or character's meaning has been altered by its being placed in a new context; irony, a favorite effect, typically depends upon our prior familiarity with the Shakespearean original. Pleasure can also be had from parsing the thematic relationship (or, occasionally, the pointed lack thereof) of a Shakespearean reference to the rest of its host film. This group of cameos reveals that a handful of certain scenes recur with special regularity—Hamlet holding Yorick's skull (sometimes conflated with his "To be or not to be" speech); Romeo and Juliet's balcony scene; and, in older films, the assassination of Julius Caesar. To be sure, these moments are favorite parodic targets, but they are also powerful memorial centers in popular culture, rehearsed and rerehearsed in many examples, with each repetition encapsulating for their audiences the "essence" of Shakespeare and his main concerns—the poet of love, the purveyor of philosophical reflection, the proto-democrat antipathetic to tyranny. That is, these kinds of allusions, perhaps each negligible in itself, concatenate in mass culture to shape how popular audiences understand Shakespeare and hold in place certain conceptions of his work.

One of the difficulties of researching this area of Shakespeare's afterlife is that there are almost no reference works devoted to free film adaptations, since most Shakespeare film bibliographies concentrate on what they identify as faithful versions. Short of trying to view hordes of films in search of references, one must typically rely on careful searches of film bibliographies and databases for leads. Several reference works do address these kinds of adaptations. The standard bibliography for film Shakespeare, Kenneth S. Rothwell and Annabelle Henkin Melzer's *Shakespeare on Screen*, provides comprehensive entries on a few examples; Robert Hamilton Ball's still unsurpassed *Shakespeare on Silent Film* documents examples of Shakespeare freely adapted to silent film; Luke McKernan and Olwen Terris's *Walking Shadows* catalogues Shakespeare films, both faithful and free, in the United Kingdom's National Film and Television Archive, emphasizing British examples; though it is marred by errors, Eddie Sammons's ambitious *Shakespeare: A Hundred Years on Film*, international in its scope, includes listings of many free adaptations and passing references; and José Ramón Díaz Fernández's bibliographies for *Post Script* (Winter–Spring 1998) and for James R. Keller and Leslie Stratyner's *Almost Shakespeare* document many examples, along with references to relevant scholarly studies.

Research in this area has been enormously aided by online databases that allow one to search vast archives. However, it is worth remembering that online lists and discussions of free Shakespeare film adaptations often uncritically borrow from one another, and thus errors quickly proliferate. Researchers using these tools are thus advised to proceed skeptically and to double-check references before relying on them. The Internet Movie Database (www.imdb.com), a comprehensive and quite reliable online film database, allows one to search its titles, plot summaries, and character lists by keyword, though it is important for a researcher to know that not all of the films it includes have been publically released or even completed. Allmovie.com, another online film database, also includes plot synopses; its search engine is very basic (title, actor, and director only), and the summaries are not always reliable. The American Film Institute provides a searchable catalogue of American films, available by subscription (www.afi.com/members/catalog/); and though the British Film Institute has no publically accessible online database, one of its websites (www.screenonline.org.uk) is a valuable source of information about Shakespearean films produced in the United Kingdom. Surprisingly, two commercial sites with very powerful search engines are useful for researchers who are deft at crafting sufficiently delimited search terms: Amazon.com and eBay.com. Yahoo.com includes "Shakespearean" among the film genres it lists (http://dir.yahoo.com/Arts/Humanities/Literature/Authors/Playwrights/Shakespeare_William_1564_1616_/Films); however, its coverage is hit or miss, and the websites it features are of widely

varying quality. SHAKSPER, an online scholarly discussion group on all matters Shakespearean, offers occasional postings identifying free film adaptations; postings on this topic are in no way methodical and can contain errors, but they provide potential leads for the researcher. An archive of postings on SHAKSPER is publically available (www.shaksper.net), and it is searchable by single words.

NOTE

1. For the sake of space, I will leave aside discussion of whether the textual records that survive from the period give us reliable access to what Shakespeare wrote or what was spoken on the stage. For provocative discussions of this very complex, much debated issue, see Stephen Orgel, "Acting Scripts, Performing Texts" and "The Authentic Shakespeare," in his *The Authentic Shakespeare, and Other Problems of the Early Modern Stage* (New York: Routledge, 2002), 21–48 and 231–56.

BIBLIOGRAPHY

Ball, Robert Hamilton. *Shakespeare on Silent Film: A Strange Eventful History*. New York: Theatre Arts, 1968.

Bourdieu, Pierre, and Jean-Claude Passeron. "Foundations for a Theory of Symbolic Violence." In *Reproduction in Education, Society and Culture*, trans. Richard Nice, 1–68. London: Sage Publications, 1990.

Díaz Fernández, José Ramón. "Shakespeare and Film—Derivatives: A Bibliography." *Post Script* 17, no. 2 (Winter–Spring 1998): 110–20.

———. "Shakespeare Film and Television Derivatives." In *Almost Shakespeare: Reinventing His Works for Cinema and Television*, ed. James R. Keller and Leslie Stratyner, 169–89. Jefferson, NC: McFarland & Co., 2004.

McKernan, Luke, and Owen Terris. *Walking Shadows: Shakespeare in the National Film and Television Archive*. London: BFI, 1994.

Orgel, Stephen. *The Authentic Shakespeare, and Other Problems of the Early Modern Stage*. New York: Routledge, 2002.

Rothwell, Kenneth S., and Annabelle Henkin Melzer. *Shakespeare on Screen: An International Filmography and Videography*. New York: Neal-Schuman, 1990.

Sammons, Eddie. *Shakespeare: A Hundred Years on Film*. Lanham, MD: Scarecrow Press, 2004.

ENTRIES PLAY BY PLAY, DOUGLAS LANIER

Supplemental materials on DVD are noted only where they are relevant to the Shakespearean content of the film. Additional entries by Richard Burt (RB), Ellen Joy Letostak (EL), Michael P. Jensen (MJ), Minami Ryuta (MR), and Scott Newstock (SN) are noted by their initials in parentheses following their entries.

ALL'S WELL THAT ENDS WELL

539 *All's Well That Ends Well*
1940. U.S. Terrytoons. Sound, b&w, 7 mins.
Mannie Davis.

Animated short, part of the series produced by Terrytoons for the educational market. See also the *Much Ado about Nothing* by Terrytoons.

ANTONY AND CLEOPATRA

540 *The Passions of an Egyptian Princess*
1911. U.K. Production company unknown. Silent, b&w, 14 mins. Theo Frenkel.

Lost film. Presumably about Cleopatra, but content is unknown.

541 *Cleopatra* (aka *Helen Gardner in Cleopatra*)
1912. U.S. Helen Gardner Picture Players. Silent, b&w, 88 mins. (in cut for TV). Charles L. Gaskill.

A silent version from the Émile Moreau and Victorien Sardou play *Cléopâtre*, supervised by J. Stuart Blackton. Rereleased in 1918, apparently in the wake of the notorious version by Theda Bara. Recently restored and shown on Turner Classic Movie Network. No direct citations of Shakespeare, but many plot parallels.

542 *Queenie of the Nile*
1915. U.S. Lubin Manufacturing. Silent, b&w, length unknown. Director unknown.

Lost film. Sammons summarizes the film: a man (dressed as Antony) is enlisted to help a woman who thinks she is Cleopatra. Instead, he is attracted to her maid, Charmian. When a blow on the woman's head restores her senses, the film ends happily.

543 *Cleopatra*
1917. U.S. Fox Film Corporation. Silent, b&w, 125 mins. J. Gordon Edwards.

Lost film (though stills and summaries survive). An extravaganza featuring vamp Theda Bara as Cleopatra. Her co-star Fritz Leiber (Caesar) would go on to become a sci-fi and fantasy writer who would occasionally use Shakespearean motifs in his writing.

544 *Peg O' My Heart*
1919. U.S. Famous Players Lasky Corporation. Silent, b&w, length unknown. Never commercially released. William C. DeMille.

Adapted from the play by J. Hartley Manners. A poor Irish farmer's daughter, Peg, moves to England to live with an aristocratic family and falls in love with a nobleman.

In his complaints about changes to his play, Manners noted that the filmmakers included elements of *Antony and Cleopatra*.

545 *Cleopatra*
1920. U.S. Pathé Freres. Silent, b&w, 5 mins.
Bud Fisher.

An animated version of the classic story starring Mutt and Jeff, popular comic strip characters of the period. From a story from Bud Fisher's original cartoon strip.

546 *Cleopatra and Her Easy Mark*
1923. U.S. Lee-Bradford Corporation. Silent, b&w, length unknown. Frank A. Nankivell, Richard M. Friel, and W. E. Stark.

Part of an animated series devoted to spoofing famous historical figures.

547 *Cleopatra*
1928. U.K. Production company unknown. Silent, b&w, length unknown. Roy William Neill.

Lost film. Neill went on to become a horror actor and suspense film director.

548 *Oh! Oh! Cleopatra*
1931. U.K. Masquers Club of Hollywood and RKO Pathé Pictures Inc. Sound, b&w, 16 mins. Joseph Santley.

Parody; part of the Masquers Club series.

549 *Cleopatra*
1934. U.S. Paramount. Sound, b&w, 100 mins. Cecil B. DeMille.

Adapting plot elements from Sardou's and Shakespeare's plays, DeMille's period production recasts the story for a jazz age sensibility, truncating the plot, adorning the heroine in art deco sets and fashions, and reimagining Cleopatra as, in William Everson's phrase, a "gold-digger made good" who uses her sexuality and wit to manipulate the powerful men in her life. Especially noteworthy is the visually extravagant scene on Cleopatra's barge. See also *Julius Caesar*.

Only passing allusions to phrases from Shakespeare's play (such as Cleopatra's "easy way to die") appear in the dialogue.

Henry Wilcoxon and Claudette Colbert from *Cleopatra* (1934). Courtesy of Douglas Lanier.

550 *The Rake's Progress* (aka *Notorious Gentleman*)
1945. U.K. Individual Pictures. Sound, b&w, 109 mins. Sidney Gilliat.

Adapted from a story by Val Valentine. After having been expelled from Oxford, Vivian Kenway, a selfish upper-class cad whose virtues are his blunt honesty and adventurous spirit, drifts from career to career and lover to lover. He briefly works for a coffee plantation; he seduces Jill Duncan, the wife of his best friend, Sandy; he marries Rikki Krausner, an Austrian Jewish refugee, for her money, after which she attempts suicide; and his drunken driving leads to his father's death. Throughout, he is loved by Jenny Calthrop, his father's secretary, who sees him for what he is. In the end, Vivian ends up in the army in World War II, and he dies making a redemptive sacrifice to clear a crucial bridge.

When at Oxford, Sandy gives Jill tickets for a performance of *Antony and Cleopatra*; she tosses them aside to meet secretly with Vivian in a punting boat. Their tryst in the boat is juxtaposed with Enobarbus's description of Cleopatra's barge from *Antony and Cleopatra* (2.2). In this case, Vivian is, like Cleopatra, the vain, irresistibly charming seducer; the scene foreshadows Vivian's later cuckoldry of Sandy.

551 *A Fig Leaf for Eve*
1946. U.S. Carry Westen Corporation. Sound, b&w, 69 mins. Donald Brodie.

Stripper Eve Lorraine learns that she may be the heir to a hair tonic fortune, but when the children of the Sardam estate learn of her indecent past, her claim to the money is threatened.

As part of Eve's campaign to become cultured, she learns Shakespeare and eventually performs a scene from *Antony and Cleopatra* for a high-society benefit. The performance is awkward, and she laughed from the stage. When she becomes angered by one of the Sardam sisters' offer to buy her off, she returns to the stage to perform an exotic dance, to the audience's delight.

552 *La Vida íntima de Marco Antonio y Cleopatra*
1947. Mexico. Filmex. Sound, b&w, 97 mins. Roberto Gavaldón.

A parodic musical comedy adaptation of the Antony and Cleopatra story. No direct verbal references.

553 *She's Working Her Way through College*
1952. U.S. Warner Bros. Sound, col., 104 mins. H. Bruce Humberstone.

Adapted as a musical from the play *The Male Animal* by James Thurber and Elliot Nugent. Angela Gardner, aka "Hot Garters" Gertie, a burlesque queen and aspiring playwright, decides to leave performing to pursue a college education. On her closing night, she meets former teacher John Palmer, now a theater professor at Midwest State, and immediately decides to attend college there. Amidst a long-standing rivalry over funding and administrative favor from the trustees between Palmer and football coach Shep Slade, a rivalry complicated by romantic rivalry over Palmer's wife, Helen, Palmer decides to produce Angela's play as a musical in a bid for big audiences. When Ivy Williams, aka "Poison Ivy," discovers Angela's former identity and exposes her, Palmer is pressured to close the show, but he speaks to the student body in defense of Angela's show business background, refusing to capitulate to Dean Copeland, head of the trustees, and becoming a college hero. When Angela discovers that Copeland is a hypocrite who earlier tried to seduce her, Copeland allows the play to go forward and promotes Palmer.

We learn that Ivy, a prissy society girl used to being top dog in Midwest's dramatic productions until Angela arrives, starred as Juliet in the college's previous season. When Palmer laments the lack of interest in college stage productions, Angela suggests that they "get away from Shakespeare and give 'em what they want," and she engineers a vote against Shakespeare in favor of her musical. The boorish coach Slade jokes about sleeping in Shakespeare class and confesses that he never finished *Macbeth*. One of the songs has the refrain, "That's the stuff that dreams are made of," a misquotation (perhaps via *The Maltese Falcon*) from *The Tempest* (4.1). When we see the first production number of the finished musical, it stresses how education is useless next to female charms. The first illustration of that principle is Cleopatra, recast as a golddigger who drugs Antony for his treasure; as her song suggests, "the only easy mark she made was Antony." The film has a deeply divided, nearly schizophrenic attitude toward the value of education (and thus of Shakespeare). On the one hand, Palmer, consistently presented as a decent man of principle, insists that education is an inalienable right of all students; on the other hand, many of the film's songs proudly proclaim the uselessness of academic knowledge. Shakespeare is portrayed as utterly unpopular, the property of eggheads and snobs. (The title of Angela's musical, the alternative to Shakespeare, is *Give 'Em What They Want*.) The earlier version of *She's Working*, *The Male Animal*, exuded a far more progressive attitude: the climactic scene protesting an ouster from college (in this case, of professors accused of communism) featured English professor Tommy Turner reading a letter by Bartolomeo Vanzetti, of Sacco and Vanzetti fame. The earlier film featured no substantial Shakespeare references.

554 *Serpent of the Nile*
1953. U.S. Columbia Pictures. Sound, b&w, 81 mins. William Castle.

Adaptation by the renowned director of sensationalistic B films of the 1950s. After very briefly recapping the events of *Julius Caesar* following his assassination, this film retells the tale of Mark Antony and Cleopatra, with the added element of a love triangle with a young soldier, Lucilius, troubled by her decadence. The spectacles on Cleopatra's barge are reminiscent of those in DeMille's *Cleopatra*; the film was photographed on sets left over from Columbia's *Salome*.

Though the film generally follows the plot outline of *Antony and Cleopatra*, by adding the Lucilius and Cleopatra sub-plot, it clearly condemns Cleopatra's pursuit of power and Antony's blindness to her stratagems and slide into drunken impotence, and praises Lucilius's bourgeois decency. The only direct Shakespearean reference is, in the film's opening moments, to Antony's lament over Caesar's corpse (*Julius Caesar* 3.1.149–51).

555 *Due Notti con Cleopatra (Two Nights with Cleopatra)*
1954. Italy. Excelsa Film and Rosa Film. Sound, col., 78 mins. Mario Mattoli.

An odd combination of sword-and-sandal epic and bedroom farce, with Sophia Loren in a double role as Cleopatra and a slave girl, Nisca. The plot revolves around Cleopatra's machinations to sleep with Marc Antony while being guarded by Cesarino (played by Italian comic Alberto Sordi), whose penalty for failing to guard the queen is death. Much of the comedy revolves around confusion between Cleopatra and Nisca: Cleopatra uses Nisca to secretly see Mark Antony, but Cesarino confuses

the two and falls in love with the wrong woman. No direct verbal allusions. Little remains of Shakespeare's play save the relationship between Cleopatra and Mark Antony.

556 *Le Legioni di Cleopatra (Legions of the Nile)*
1959. Italy, France, and Spain. Alexandra Produzioni Cinematografiche, Atenea Films, CFPC, Estela Films, and Lyre Films. Sound, col., 91 mins. Vittorio Cottafavi.

After the battle of Actium, Cleopatra and Antony await the arrival of Octavius's armies in Egypt. The film's central plot concerns the efforts of Curridius, a Roman envoy, to travel from Rome to Egypt to reconcile Antony and Octavius; along the way, he encounters many action-filled adventures. No direct verbal allusions.

557 *Totò e Cleopatra (Toto and Cleopatra)*
1963. Italy. Euro International Film and Liber Film. Sound, b&w, 100 mins. Fernando Cerchio.

A comedy starring the beloved Italian stage and screen comedian, Toto. Fulvia captures her husband Antony and substitutes Toto for him, sending him back to Egypt, where he mistreats Cleopatra and is sentenced to death. After Antony's return earns Toto a reprieve, Toto substitutes for Antony in battle, and returns to Rome with Cleopatra as his slave. No direct verbal citations.

558 *Carry on Cleo*
1964. U.K. Anglo-Amalgamated Productions. Sound, col., 92 mins. Gerald Thomas.

One of the "Carry On" comedy series, filmed on the abandoned London sets for Mankiewicz's *Cleopatra* (entry 559) and slyly mimicking its ad campaign. The film features Hengist Pod as a blundering British slave mistaken for a mighty fighter who must protect Julius Caesar from an assassination plot created by Cleopatra and Mark Antony. The plot is primary an excuse for sight gags, sexual innuendo, bad puns, and parodies of scenes from Mankiewicz's *Cleopatra*.

Includes practically none of Shakespeare's plot. The film includes running gags on "Friends, Romans, and countrymen" (spoken by Julius Caesar, no less) and "Beware the Ides of March"; in a vision, Caesar sees his own assassination and, with a knife protruding from his chest, asks, "Is this a dagger I see before me?"

559 *Cleopatra*
1964. U.K., U.S., and Switzerland. 20th Century Fox. Sound, col., 192 mins. Joseph L. Mankiewicz.

A notoriously bloated and troubled production starring Rex Harrison, Richard Burton, and Elizabeth Taylor, which traces Cleopatra's doomed relationships with Julius Caesar and then Mark Antony, both of which are threatened by Roman imperial politics. In this version, the character weaknesses of the two men; Cleopatra's love for her son, Caesarian; and a rather elegiac portrayal of the principal characters receive special attention. The film shows the influence of DeMille's 1934 film in its epic-scale visual spectacle, particularly in its huge sets, lavish processional scenes, and pre-CGI staging of the Battle of Actium; Taylor's bath scene and form-fitting, see-through fashions were considered quite provocative for a mainstream film. Notably, elements of the tempestuous relationship between Elizabeth Taylor and Richard Burton are allegorized in the romance between Cleopatra and Mark Antony, which dominates the film's last half.

Though the screen credits identify "ancient sources" as the inspiration for the script, the film strikes interesting relationships with Shakespeare's *Julius Caesar* (JC) and *Antony and Cleopatra* (AC). A number of details preceding and following Julius Caesar's assassination show the influence of Shakespeare's version. Brutus's "honorable" status, for instance, is repeatedly referenced. The scriptwriters clearly sought to avoid writing dialogue for some over-familiar Shakespearean scenes from *Julius Caesar*. For example, though it follows the details of Shakespeare's version closely, the assassination of Caesar is handled as a wordless dream vision revealed to Cleopatra by an Egyptian sibyl; the words of Mark Antony's funeral oration for Caesar are drowned out by the noise of the Roman crowd. The death scenes of Mark Antony and Cleopatra offer clever transformations of lines and motifs from Shakespeare's AC. For example, Charmian's "O quietness, lady" in AC (4.15) becomes Cleopatra's "There has never been such a silence," uttered over Mark Antony's dead body. In 5.2 the exchange between First Guard, "Charmian, is this well done?" and Charmian, "It is well done, and fitting for a princess / Descended of so many royal kings," is transformed into this exchange between a Roman guard and Cleopatra's dying servant: Guard: "Was this well done of your lady?" Servant: "Extremely well, as befitting the last of so many noble rulers." As Cleopatra dies, she speaks of having a dream, though in the film version that dream is of lost greatness, not of Mark Antony.

560 *The Notorious Cleopatra*
1970. U.S. Global Pictures. Sound, col., 88 mins. A. P. Stootsberry (aka Peter Perry).

A comic sexploitation adaptation, from the same production team that produced *The Secret Sex Lives of Romeo and Juliet*. Mark Antony is sent to Egypt to procure Cleopatra for an oafish Julius Caesar, but he becomes enamored of her himself. When Antony returns to Rome, Cleopatra follows in disguise and harbors Antony after he engineers the assassination of Caesar; Antony murders Cleopatra out of sexual jealousy for her tryst with a Roman soldier, and then kills himself. To my knowledge, this is the first film version to feature a black Cleopatra.

Uses many of the characters from AC—Cleopatra, Charmian, Mark Antony, and Enobarbus—but the plot motifs from Shakespeare's version are significantly changed or scrambled. Two verbal references among the Elizabethanisms of the dialogue: "transform'd / Into a strumpet's fool" (1.1), and Enobarbus's drinking song from 2.7.

DVD includes two shorts, "Cleopatra's Asp" and "Cleopatra's Milk Bath," both of which offer comic sexploitation versions of plot motifs. "Cleopatra's Asp" includes a verbal allusion to "come to bury Caesar, not to praise him" from JC 3.2. DVD also includes *The Secret Sex Lives of Romeo and Juliet*.

561 *Kureopatora (Cleopatra, Queen of Sex)*
1972. Japan. Mushi Productions and Xanadu Productions. Sound, col., 112 mins. Osamu Tezuka and Eiichi Yamamoto.

An animated sexploitation parody of *Antony and Cleopatra*, with Julius Caesar as an aging lecher, Cleopatra as a pneumatic nymphomaniac, Antony as a fool, and Ptolemy and Octavian as gay queens. Sexually explicit cartoon scenes are mixed with references to contemporary culture. Direct verbal references unknown.

562 *Cleopatra Jones*
1973. U.S. Warner Brothers. Sound, col., 89 mins. Jack Starrett.

In this blaxploitation film, Cleopatra Jones, a special drug agent for the U.S. government, attempts to destroy the drug trade of a major dealer, Mommy. Mommy takes revenge by engineering the shutdown of a local drug clinic and attempting to kill Cleopatra, leading to a mano a mano between the two women and Mommy's gang.

Francesca Royster argues that the film visually alludes to Shakespeare's play in several places, including the barge scene.

563 *Once upon a Time in America*
1984. Italy and U.S. Embassy International Pictures, PSO International, Rafran Cinematografica, and Warner Bros. Sound, col., 229 mins. (director's cut). Sergio Leone.

Adapted from the novel *The Hoods* by Harry Grey. This film epic, reminiscent of *The Godfather* and starring Robert De Niro as Max, chronicles of the lives of a group of Jewish gangsters—David "Noodles" Aaronson, Maximilian "Max" Bercovicz, Philip "Cockeye" Stein, and Patrick "Patsy" Goldberg—from their youth in New York's Lower East Side through Prohibition to their bittersweet reunion in the 1960s. Shakespeare's Cleopatra is briefly referenced in a scene in a dressing room near the end of the film. Max, now an old man, shows up after a performance of *Antony and Cleopatra* to tell Deborah Gelley (Elizabeth McGovern), who left him to become an actress, that she was right to do so. He sees a poster for *Antony and Cleopatra* on the wall with her the line "Age cannot wither her" and cites the line, applying it to her. Deborah is taking off her whiteface makeup derived from a Kabuki version of Cleopatra's death scene that Leone actually shot for the film. See Christopher Fryaling, *Sergio Leone: Something to Do with Death* (Faber & Faber, 2000), 447. (DL and RB)

564 *Sogni erotici di Cleopatra (Erotic Dreams of Cleopatra)*
1985. Italy. Production company unknown. Sound, col., 86 mins. Rino Di Silvestro.

Softcore pornographic adaptation. Left by Caesar in a villa near Rome, Cleopatra fantasizes about various sexual adventures. No direct verbal references.

565 *Bugsy*
1991. U.S. Baltimore Pictures, Desert Vision, Mulholland Productions, and TriStar Pictures. Sound, col., 134 mins. Barry Levinson.

In the 1940s, transplanted New York gangster "Bugsy" Siegel seeks to create a gambling empire in Las Vegas, Nevada, while romancing Hollywood actress Virginia Hill. When his mob-backed budget becomes bloated and Virginia embezzles some of the money, he is targeted for murder by his superiors.

In "Age Cannot Wither Him," in *Shakespeare the Movie*, eds. Lynda Boose and Richard Burt (Routledge, 1997), Katharine Eggert argues that this film has significant parallels with *Antony and Cleopatra*. There are no direct verbal citations.

566 *Joan chez les pharaons (Joy and the Pharoahs)*
1992. France. Benjamin Simon and ATC 3000/M6 Films. Sound, col., 90 mins. Jean-Pierre Floran.

Softcore pornographic adaptation. Using a film-within-a-film structure à la *The French Lieutenant's Woman* (1981), the film chronicles the life of a hedonistic supermodel starring in an erotic version of the life of Cleopatra, set in a very debauched and sadistic Egypt. Her personal sexual exploits and relationships frequently mirror historical events in the film. This film alludes to and outdoes the milk bath scenes in *Cleopatra* (1963) and *Carry on Cleo* (1964).

The film includes only passing references to a few events from *AC*—Cleopatra's romance with Antony, Octavius's assault on Egypt, and Antony and Cleopatra's deaths; there are no direct verbal citations. At one point, in the midst of an erotic actress's audition, the director says, "I've no intention of putting you straight into Shakespeare right away." And at film's end, the narrator comments about the fall of Cleopatra's empire, alluding to Macbeth's "Tomorrow and tomorrow and tomorrow" speech: "Civilizations, you too are mortal and will one day die away. Let us then laugh at the monumental farce we call History, in which we are all poor players."

567 *Anthony [sic] and Cleopatra*
1998. Italy. Moonlight Entertainment. Sound, col., 88 mins. Joe D'Amato.

Hardcore pornographic adaptation. Cleopatra, Caesar, and Anthony engage in a series of sexual encounters with each other and their court minions.

No direct verbal citations; the relationship to Shakespeare does not extend beyond the title, costuming, and vaguely Egyptian and Roman mise-en-scènes.

568 *Cleopatra*
1999. U.S. Babelsberg Film GmbH and Hallmark Entertainment. Sound, col., 174 mins. Franc Roddam.

Uses Margaret George's *Memoirs of Cleopatra* as its main inspiration. Emphasis falls on Cleopatra's ruthlessness, the sexual and political intrigues associated with her reign, and elaborately staged battle sequences. The first half focuses primarily on Cleopatra's romance with Julius Caesar and the threat their son poses to Octavian's political ambitions; the second half details Cleopatra's affair with Antony, his defeat at the hands of Octavian at Actium, and Cleopatra's suicide. The film is particularly notable for the youth of the main characters and the African and Middle Eastern ethnicity of the Egyptian court.

No direct verbal citations. Many of the events of *JC* and *AC* are included in the film; also stressed is the Shakespearean theme of Egyptian luxury versus Roman rectitude.

569 *Cleopatra: The Dream of Any Farao [sic]*
2000. Brazil. LGI Brazilian. Sound, col., 86 mins. Roger Lemos.

Hardcore pornography. A modern young man, in love with Cleopatra, asks an Egyptian god to take him back to live with the Egyptian queen.

Little Shakespearean content, beyond the character of Cleopatra and the general situation.

570 *Cleopatra Does Hollywood*
2002. U.S. Vivid Video. Sound, col., 80 mins. Ralph Parfait.

Hardcore pornography. Inexplicably transported to modern Hollywood after the murder of Caesar, Cleopatra and attendant Mesogenes search for Mark Antony and are pursued by Octavian, owner of a wax museum.

Little relationship to Shakespeare, aside from the main characters; upon his death, Caesar utters, "Oi vey, Brute."

571 *Kannaki*
2002. India. Wellgate Video. Sound, col., 120 mins. Jayaraaj Rajasekharan Nair.

Indian adaptation to a Malayalam cockfighting milieu. A championship cockfighter, Manickan, falls for a local beauty and black magic woman, Kannagi, much to the displeasure of Manickan's benefactor, Choman, and Choman's sister, Kumudan. The plot revolves around the tragic consequences of Manickan and Kannagi's love. Nair is a noted Indian film adaptor of Shakespeare—see also his *Kaliyattam*.

Many resemblances of plot and characters; Nair claims that his production is a Shakespearean adaptation.

572 *Cleopatra*
2003. Sweden. Private. Sound, col., 105 mins. Antonio Adamo.

Hardcore pornography, indebted in part to *The Mummy* (1999). Structured as a tale-within-a-tale: Cleopatra seduces all those she meets, and a group of modern archaeologists excavating her tomb also engage in a series of trysts. Spawned a sequel from the same director, *Cleopatra 2: The Legend of Eros* (2004).

Very little discernible relationship to Shakespeare, beyond the title character. The sequel is even farther removed from Shakespeare.

573 *Marc Anthony*
2004. Sweden. Private Man. Sound, col., 90 mins. Sebastiano Brogi.

Hardcore pornography. Though Marc Anthony is to be married to Cleopatra, he dallies with various palace servants. When she dies of an asp's bite, he becomes the ruler of Egypt.

Very little discernible relationship to Shakespeare besides the narrative setup and title character. Reputedly the largest-budget adult gay film ever shot, produced in tandem with Private's *Cleopatra* and *Cleopatra 2*.

DVD has been issued in two different editions, neither of which includes extras related to Shakespeare.

AS YOU LIKE IT

574 *Seven Ages*
1905. U.S. Edison Manufacturing Company. Silent, b&w, 5 mins. Edwin S. Porter.

Using the "seven ages" speech as its armature, the film offers a portrait of a modern couple through different stages of their lives. As children, they play together; as youths, they attend school and later become lovers. As adults, they pursue careers, have a family, and grow old together. Holding the film together is the motif of the kiss, which all the ages share.

An interesting attempt to convert the "seven ages" speech to modern visual terms. Title cards identify the "seven ages"; in a twist, the final age is "What Age?" featuring not death but an unmarried woman kissing her cat.

Available in the DVD collection *Edison: The Invention of the Movies*.

575 *Nina of the Theatre*
1914. U.S. Kalem Company. Silent, b&w, 2 reels. George Melford.

The first part of a melodramatic serial about an actress's trials and tribulations. Features at least one scene (unspecified) from *As You Like It*.

576 *Of Human Hearts*
1938. U.S. MGM. Sound, b&w, 105 mins. Clarence Brown.

Jason Wilkins (Jimmy Stewart) grows up disenchanted by the poverty-stricken life his minister father (Walter Huston) leads, and decides to leave home to become a doctor. His mother (Beulah Bondi) scrimps and sells her few meager possessions in order for him to train as a physician. He joins the Union Army as a surgeon, and is surprised to be summoned to the White House by President Abraham Lincoln (John Carradine). Lincoln berates him: Jason has been ungrateful and not corresponded with his mother in two years. She assumes he must be dead, and has written to the president in order to find out where her son's grave is. Lincoln gives Jason White House stationery and makes him write a letter to his mother while he watches. As Jason writes, Lincoln appropriately cites from *As You Like It*:

Blow, blow, thou winter wind,
Thou art not so unkind
As man's ingratitude. . . .
Freeze, freeze, thou bitter sky,
That dost no bite so nigh
As benefits forgot. (2.7)

As Jason heads back to the front, he repeats, "Freeze, freeze, thou bitter sky, / That dost no bite so nigh / As benefits forgot"—apparently, he now sees the error of his ways and will stay in touch with his mother. He gets a furlough, and goes home for a surprise visit. His mother is glad to see him alive.

Beulah Bondi was nominated for a Best Supporting Actress Oscar for her performance as Mary Wilkins. (EJL)

577 *The Roman Spring of Mrs. Stone*
1961. U.K. and U.S. Warner Bros. Sound, col., 103 mins. Jose Quintero.

Adapted from the novel by Tennessee Williams. When Karen Stone, a middle-aged actress, takes a vacation in Rome and her husband dies en route, a friend hires the gigolo Pablo, a cynical young man, to assuage her grief. Though Pablo is rude and rejects her, Mrs. Stone pursues him until she is murdered by a madman.

As the film opens, we see Mrs. Stone, an aging actress, star in *As You Like It* as Rosalind, although she's too old for the part.

578 *Yentl*
1983. U.S. Barwood Films and Ladbroke Investments. Sound, col., 132 mins. Barbra Streisand.

Musical adaptation of the story "Yentl, the Yeshiva Boy" by Isaac Bashevis Singer. Yentl, a young woman who wants to study Scripture, poses as a boy named Anshel. Once at school, he falls in love with fellow student Avigdor, who is himself in love with Hadass; Hadass eventually falls for Anshel, unaware that he is a girl.

Uses the motif of cross-dressed wooing from *As You Like It*, though there are no direct verbal references.

579 *Reckless Kelly*
1993. Australia. Serious Entertainment and Warner Bros. Sound, col., 103 mins. Yahoo Serious.

In this farce, Ned Kelly, the descendant of an Australian Robin Hood, seeks to raise money to prevent the sale of his land to a Japanese buyer. Moving to the United States, he first plans a bank robbery, but then lands the starring role in a Hollywood film, finding romance along the way.

Briefly references Jaques's "All the world's a stage."

580 *Nymph*
1995. U.S. Vivid Video. Sound, col., 84 mins. Paul Thomas.

Hardcore pornography. Nick, an architect living in a deteriorating Los Angeles apartment building, discovers Daphne, a promiscuous nymph, in a spring in its foundation; the two band together to save the building from destruction.

Daphne misquotes a short passage from *As You Like It* (5.2, Silvius's praise of Phebe).

581 *Never Been Kissed*
1999. U.S. Bushwood Pictures, Flower Films, Fox 2000 Pictures, and Never Been Kissed Productions. Sound, col., 107 mins. Raja Gosnell.

When Josie Geller, a withdrawn reporter, poses as a high school student for an undercover exposé, she confronts her own past as a nerdy, unpopular teenager who had been romantically humiliated by a boy. She learns to be popular and becomes enamored of her English teacher, Mr. Coulson, but she cannot express her feelings without revealing her disguise.

Several scenes in Mr. Coulson's English class reference *As You Like It* and in particular Rosalind, stressing how disguise offers a freedom to voice emotions one otherwise cannot express; later, like Rosalind, Josie finds that her disguise is also an impediment to romance. Josie and her high school boyfriend go as Rosalind and Orlando to the prom. Particular speeches referenced are Jaques's "all the world's a stage" speech from 2.7 and Rosalind's "no sooner met but they looked" speech from 5.2. Josie also briefly quotes Lorenzo's description of "the floor of heaven" from *The Merchant of Venice* (5.1).

582 *The Blonde Bombshell*
2000. U.S. London Weekend Television. Sound, col., 240 mins. (miniseries). Robert Bierman.

A biopic chronicling Diana Dors, the British blonde bombshell. Dors briefly references "All the world's a stage" after posing nude for photographers.

583 *Connie and Carla*
2003. U.S. Barber, Birnbaum, Brillstein-Grey Entertainment, Playtone, and Spyglass Entertainment. Sound, col., 98 mins. Michael Lembeck.

Having been witnesses to a gangland murder, failing cabaret singers Connie and Carla are forced to pretend that they are drag queens as they hide out in Los Angeles. Soon Connie falls in love with Jeff, a straight man looking for his cross-dressed brother, but she cannot reveal her true identity.

Like Rosalind, Connie finds that cross-dressing allows her freedom to speak openly but quickly becomes a romantic impediment when she falls for Jeff. Shakespeare is briefly referenced—one drag queen claims that Shakespeare wrote "d-r-a-g" in the margins of manuscripts to indicate cross-dressed parts. (*Yentl* is also referenced at the denouement.) No direct verbal allusions.

584 *Exile from the Sun*
2004. U.S. One Ganesh Productions. Sound, col., 30 mins. Michael Poitevin.

John Blake, a writer and actor who has become an accountant, wallows in disillusionment about his abandoned artistic career until his wife Maggie and friend Jim encourage him to recover his creativity and happiness.

Includes several citations from *As You Like It*.

THE COMEDY OF ERRORS

585 *Two Little Dromios*
1914. U.S. Edwin W. Thanhouser. Silent, b&w, 10 mins. Unknown.

Apparently a lost film. The summary by Sammons indicates that the twins are girls, one from the city, one from the country, who switch locales and cause confusion. Double exposure is used to create the illusion of twins in those scenes. The title may be related to a number of "Two Little" films produced by Lupin late in the first decade of 1900.

Direct citations unknown.

586 *Our Relations*
1936. U.S. Stan Laurel Productions and Hal Roach Studios. Sound, b&w, 73 mins. Harry Lachman.

Laurel and Hardy slapstick adaptation of the W. W. Jacobs story "The Money Box." Stan Laurel and Oliver Hardy, upstanding citizens and happily married, become mixed up with their ne'er-do-well sailor twin brothers, Alf Laurel and Bert Hardy, who are on shore leave. One of the most elaborately plotted and produced of the Laurel and Hardy comedies.

Uses several motifs from *The Comedy of Errors*: mistaken identities between two pairs of twins, seemingly lost money, unpaid debts, a ring, a prostitute (here, a pair of floozies), and angry wives.

587 *The Boys from Syracuse*
1940. U.S. Universal Pictures. Sound, b&w, 74 mins. A. Edward Sutherland.

Four characters from *The Boys from Syracuse* (1940). In this photo from the musical version of *The Comedy of Errors*, we see the main characters, Antipholus and Dromio, giving money to two confused merchants. The still shows the ersatz Roman set and costume design. Courtesy of Douglas Lanier.

Film adaptation of the Richard Rodgers, Lorenz Hart, and George Abbott Broadway musical. The plot closely follows that of Shakespeare's play, with the addition of several comic anachronisms such as parchment newspapers, a toga store, chariot taxis, slave labor unions, and Greek broadcasters. Angelo and Pinch become bumbling tailors, and the role of Aemilia is excised, though Egeon's final revelation of the two Antipholis' identities is retained. The prevalence of sight gags and the treatment of various scenes as somewhat detachable comic routines suggest the strong influence of vaudeville and musical review. There are no direct citations from Shakespeare's text.

Of particular interest because it is the first major transposition of Shakespeare to the American musical form (and the first film of such an adaptation), and because of the musical's interestingly cynical take on love's fragility in its most famous number, "Falling in Love." See also entry 310.

588 *Los Gemelos Alborotados*
1981. Mexico. Producciones Aguila. Sound, col., 85 mins.
Mário Hernández.

Two sets of twins, named Gúmaro and Chon, are separated when bandits steal one set of boys during a fiesta. One Gúmaro (who wears a white sombrero) marries Munita, a excitable hypochondriac, and lives with Chon as his household servant; the other Gúmaro (who wears a black sombrero) is a wandering cowboy who, with his comrade Chon, wanders into the first Gúmaro's hometown. Confusion reigns as one set of twins is repeatedly mistaken for the other.

A relatively faithful transposition of *The Comedy of Errors* to a rural Mexican town. Antonio Aguilar, the much-beloved Mexican star who plays both Gúmaros, wrote the screenplay and sings the many songs in the film; there is only one bit of trick photography in the film, used for the final song, which is a duet between the two Gúmaros. The adaptation deftly adapts many of Shakespeare's plot points, motifs, and minor characters, including Pinch (here, a doctor), the courtesan, the goldsmith and the gold chain, the money given to Chon (here, bail money given by Munita), the exorcism of one of the twins (here, by a priest), Gúmaro's attraction to Munita's sister, and the attribution of the characters' misperceptions to madness (the last is particularly emphasized). Summaries indicate that one set of twins is evil, and the other good, but the film itself makes little of this distinction. A touch of political satire is included with the added figure of Munita's father, a tin-pot general who forces Gúmaro to marry Munita. The frame-tale exposition is handled as a flashback, told by Gúmaro's parents to a priest, and the final revelation is almost entirely wordless, a silent exchange of glances, after which Munita faints.

589 *Angoor*
1982. India. A. R. Movies. Sound, col., 240 mins.
Sampooran Singh Gulzar.

Raj Tilak and his wife have two sons, both named Ashok; they adopt another pair of twins named Bahadur (left at a temple) before leaving on a sea journey in which the pairs are separated. One Ashok is married to Sudha, and his servant Bahadur is married to Prema; they live with Sudha's sister Tanu, a singer. The other Ashok and Bahadur are unmarried, and when they visit the other Ashok's town, the two sets of twins are repeatedly confused with one another.

This fairly faithful adaptation of *The Comedy of Errors* opens by identifying the play as Shakespeare's and even including an Indianized, bearded portrait of the author. Many of Shakespeare's characters, plot points, and motifs are transposed to contemporary India: the necklace (with the goldsmith and the merchant), the courtesan (here, Ashok's friend Alka), the servant's buying of rope, the husband's being rejected at night at the door to his home, and the like. Gulzar tends to multiply the situations of misrecognition he inherits from Shakespeare's narrative, and he adds a number of interesting touches: at a game of cards, Tanu comments about being sick of having pairs (she has two kings and two jacks); Sudha is shown using eye medicine, a portent of her later misrecognitions; smoking ganga and using opium are major motifs, linked to altered perception; Bahadur's wife Prema, the counterpart to the kitchen wench Nell, is pregnant rather than fat; and Ashok's request for directions to the police station becomes yet another example of comic misdirection. Throughout the film, there is a concern to rationalize some of the more fantastic elements of Shakespeare's farce: in the prologue, the Tilaks justify why they are taking a sea journey rather than flying (Mrs. Tilak enjoys the long journey and is afraid of flying); the Bahadur twins are not taken into the temple where they are left because of caste and religious issues (they are Nepalese); and the unmarried Ashok is an avid mystery reader and so often thinks that characters behaving oddly to him are members of a gang. As in *Los Gemelos Alborotados*, the final revelation scene is handled as an exchange of wordless glances, though Gulzar adds some extra twists: quick flashbacks during the scene underline how the two mistaken twins put the wives in a sexually compromising position, and when the unmarried Ashok goes to reunite with his parents, he at first recognizes the wrong woman as his mother. Though there are no direct Shakespeare citations, some of Shakespeare's speeches have counterparts in Gulzar's dialogue (note, for example, Bahadur's reference to the city being haunted by spirits). At film's end, the portrait of Shakespeare gives the viewer a wink. See also entry 313.

590 *Big Business*
1988. U.S. Silver Screen Partners III and Touchstone Pictures. Sound, col., 97 mins. Jim Abrahams.

Separated at birth by a nurse's accident, two sets of twins, both named Sadie and Rose, grow up in different environments. Sadie Shelton is a ruthless New York City businesswoman, whereas her sister Rose is sensitive and dysfunctional; Rose Ratliff is a rabble-rousing working-class labor leader from rural Jupiter Hollow, while her sister Sadie is wide-eyed about the luxurious world of city life she's seen on TV. When Sadie Shelton decides to divest her company Moramax of Jupiter Hollow's Hollowmade Furniture in order to enable a strip mine, Rose and Sadie Ratliff travel to New York City to stop her at the shareholders' meeting. When both are put up in the same hotel, they are confused with one another by hotel workers, corporate minders, and their prospective suitors. When eventually the women discover each other, Sadie Ratliff impersonates Sadie Shelton at the shareholders' meeting and saves the company. In the end, each woman ends up with an appropriate suitor.

Directed by Jim Abrahams, a noted director and writer of spoof films in the 1990s, *Big Business* grafts the basic doubled-twins premise of Shakespeare's farce onto a comic fable about the rapaciousness of corporate America. In this adaptation, the twins are given distinct personalities coded to their parental heritage: the two Sadies, born of wealthy parents, are bred for corporate business and expensive

Lily Tomlin and Bette Midler from *Big Business* (1988), a modernized version of *The Comedy of Errors*. This shot features Tomlin and Midler (doubled), twins mismatched at birth, in an elevator. Courtesy of Douglas Lanier.

urban tastes, whereas the two Roses, born of working-class parents, value family, rural life, and populist business practices. (Ironically, Sadie Ratliff impersonates her sister by imitating what she's seen on the TV show *Dynasty*.) Though the plot does not closely follow Shakespeare's, the general premise of concatenating misrecognitions is maintained. A number of specific motifs appear in modified form: Sadie's son Sly gives Sadie Ratliff a wad of cash, thinking that she is his mother; Dr. Jay, Rose Shelton's suitor, tries to give Rose Ratliff an engagement ring (like the necklace in Shakespeare's version), though she refuses it, thinking it is a corporate bribe. The revelation scene is unusually handled: in imitation of Groucho Marx's famous routine in the mirror in *Duck Soup*, Sadie mimics her image as if in a mirror until she realizes that she's not looking at a reflection but at her twin, after which all the twins' identities are revealed to themselves and corporate minders, but not publicly. One amusing metacinematic moment during this scene involves Rose's assumption that their twins are evil robots or pod people, clichés from science fiction film. *Big Business*'s glorification of a luxurious urban lifestyle rests very uneasily with its message about the joys of an idyllic American simple life in the country. Even so, it is an instructive example of how a message comedy can be wedded to Shakespearean farce.

591 *Michael Madana Kamarajan*
1991. India. Production company unknown. Sound, col., length unknown. Srinivasa Rao Singeetham.

The wife of a separated couple, pregnant by the jealous brother of her rich husband, gives birth to quadruplet sons, each of which is separated from the other and grows up separately. One son, a thug, contracts to kill another son, a millionaire, not knowing he is his lost brother; the millionaire switches identities with a third son, a fireman. Kamal Hassan plays all the brothers; he also produced the film.

The basic premise of identical sons separated at birth and mistaken for one another parallels that of *CE*, though the plot here is quite different.

592 *Class of Nuke 'Em High 3: The Good, the Bad, and the Subhumanoid*
1994. U.S. Troma Productions. Sound, col., 102 mins. Eric Louzil.

The third installment in Troma Studio's exploitation series. The two sons of heroic Roger Smith, Dick and Adlai, are separated at birth; Dick, kidnapped by thugs, is raised to be violent, while Adlai is pacifist and kind. Dick becomes evil Dr. Slag's means for framing Roger (by destroying his reputation with the townspeople of Tromaville) and ruining the city (by turning it into a toxic waste dump). Adlai comes to his rescue. Brick Bronsky plays three roles, those of Roger, Dick, and Adlai Smith.

The basic premise of mistaken twins and a father under threat of the law owes to *CE*; there are no direct verbal references to Shakespeare's dialogue.

593 *Do Dooni Char*
2006 in production. India. Sound, col., Ananth Mahadevan.

See announcement at www.hindustantimes.com/news/181'1358498,00110003.htm. See also entry 315.

CORIOLANUS

594 *Coriolano, Eroe Senza Patria* (*Thunder of Battle*)
1963. Italy and France. Dorica Film, Explorer Film 58, and Comptoir Français du Film. Sound, col., 101 mins. Giorgio Ferroni.

In this Italian *peplum* (Italian film epic) adaptation, Rome is in the midst of a grain shortage. Sicinius and Brutus use the opportunity to present reforms to the Senate, but they are blocked when Caius Marcius proposes to give away grain freely. When the Senate discovers that a shipment of grain has been hijacked, Caius is sent to retrieve it; after his heroic victory, Caius discovers that the culprits have been working for Aufidius, leader of the Volscians. Aided by Sicinius's traitorous intelligence, Aufidius plans to attack the Roman army, but Caius heroically assaults Corioli and leads the Romans to victory, in the process killing a cowardly soldier in Sicinius's command. Caius, now called Coriolanus, is tapped to be consul, but he alienates the populace by adopting an arrogant tone in asking for the people's vote. When Sicinius displays the body of the soldier Coriolanus killed, the people call for his exile and Coriolanus leaves, joining Aufidius's army. Aufidius reveals to Coriolanus the treachery of Sicinius, and Coriolanus is convinced by his mother Volumnia and wife Virginia to offer Rome a peace treaty. On the steps of the Senate, Coriolanus exposes Sicinius's traitorousness and engages him in single combat; assassins hired by Sicinius to kill Coriolanus instead kill Sicinius. Afterward Coriolanus, Virginia, and their son, Marcius, leave Rome, as the consul praises his heroic, honorable conduct.

Though the narrative loosely follows that of Shakespeare's play, there are several significant changes that mute the political shades of gray of Shakespeare's version. Sicinius is presented as a pseudopopulist willing to betray Rome to foreign enemies in his pursuit of personal power; his schemes become increasingly treacherous, culminating in an assassination plot. (His reference to "comrades" early on may signal an allegory of Italian communists or labor unionists.) Brutus offers a foil, a man who soon refuses to go along with Sicinius's nefarious schemes. Caius is presented as unambiguously heroic and honorable, particularly in his handling of the grain shortage and his battle conduct; even his arrogance in campaigning—here, simply a matter of tone rather than conduct—seems justified by the cowardly, fickle nature of the people. His return to Rome is not a defeat, but an opportunity to offer peace without bloodshed and to expose the treachery of his enemy Sicinius. (Gordon Scott, a former Tarzan, stars in the Coriolanus role.) The considerable screen time devoted to strategy and battle scenes emphasizes Coriolanus's heroic qualities. Though initially presented as a barbaric warmongerer, Aufidius demonstrates respect for a fellow warrior when he senses that the women have convinced Coriolanus to return to Rome; he does not afterward turn on Coriolanus, as he does in Shakespeare's version. Though at first the film emphasizes the division between plebeian and patrician, two sub-plots suggest their possible rapprochement. At first Livia, Coriolanus's sister and a patrician, and Marcus, a soldier and a plebeian, carry on a forbidden romance divided by class, but Marcus's honor in battle leads Coriolanus to give his blessing to their union; Marcus is at first alienated from his father Brutus, a senator for the plebeians, by his loyalty to the Roman army (and political status quo), but Brutus's growing disaffection from Sicinius works to reconcile the two. Most fascinating is the ending, where the assassins' fickle shift in allegiance is treated with contempt by Marcus (himself, a mirror image of Coriolanus) and where Coriolanus and family leave Rome to start a life anew elsewhere, away from senatorial politics. An fascinating case of converting

Shakespeare's study in political ambiguities to the con-ventional moral clarity of the *peplum*. No direct verbal allusions.

HAMLET

595 *Le Duel d'Hamlet*
1900. France. Phono-Cinéma-Théâtre. Silent (but see below), b&w, 3 mins. (174 ft.). Clément-Maurice Grationlet (prod.).

A film of the final scene of *Hamlet*, with Sarah Bernhardt as Hamlet. Originally made for presentation at the Universal Exposition in Paris, 1900. This film also included a soundtrack (primarily of sound effects) synchronized with the action. See also entry 319.

596 *Actor's Troubles*
1903. U.S. Selig Polyscope Co. Silent, b&w, length unknown. Director unknown.

Lost film. A down-and-out Shakespearean actor and his valet encounter a real ghost. Though the Selig summary doesn't specify, it is quite possible that this film references *Hamlet*.

597 *Hamlet*
1907. France. Star Film. Silent, b&w, 10 mins. (574 ft.). George Méliès.

A lost film, known only through photos and its summary. It portrays Hamlet's agitated mental state, opening with the grave-digging scene, moving to a double ghost scene (Hamlet confronts both his father's ghost and also Ophelia's ghost, who tosses him flowers), and culminating in the duel and death scene. Apparently the ghost scene allowed Méliès to showcase his signature photographic special effects. See also entry 320.

598 *La Maschera che Sanguina*
1914. Italy. Ernesto Maria Pasquali. Silent, b&w, 3 reels. Director unknown.

A successful actor seeks the hand of the daughter of a rich banker; he opposes their union. The actor's success is sealed early in the film by his performance of a soliloquy from *Hamlet*.

599 *Martin as Hamlet*
1914. Germany. Neue. Silent, b&w, 718 ft. Director unknown.

An actor rehearsing at home for *Hamlet* is mistaken for a madman by his servants and becomes imprisoned at the police station; his wife eventually straightens matters out.

600 *Ham and Hamlet*
1915. U.S. Silent, b&w, length unknown. Director unknown.

No available information; apparently a lost film. The title suggests a parody of *Hamlet*.

601 *When Hungry Hamlet Fled*
1915. Thanhouser. Silent, b&w, 2 reels. Director unknown.

A burlesque, of which only one reel survives at the British Film Institute. Sammons summarizes the film: an experienced actor attempts to direct an amateur troupe, but his efforts are sabotaged by a young man.

The title suggests a relationship to *Hamlet*.

602 *Colonel Heeza Liar Plays Hamlet*
1916. U.S. Bray Studios, Inc. Silent, b&w, length unknown. John Randolph Bray.

Lost film. Part of the animated series (1913–17; 1922–24) starring Colonel Heeza Liar, a spinner of tall tales and a look-alike for Teddy Roosevelt. This series was shown as part of Bray's Paramount Pictograph screen magazine. Summaries indicate that Charlie Chaplin's tramp also appears in the film.

603 *Freddy versus Hamlet*
1916. U.S. Vitagraph. Silent, b&w, length unknown. Director unknown.

When Mabel goes with Wiggins to the theater, she successfully flirts with the actor playing Hamlet. Freddy eventually humiliates the actor and Wiggins.

604 *Hamlet Made Over*
1916. U.S. Production company unknown. Silent, b&w, 305 meters. Earl Metcalfe.

Lost film. Written by Mack Sennett, the noted slap-stick director. No plot summary available, though the title and cast list—Tragedian, Manager, King—suggest a parody.

605 *Pimple as Hamlet*
1916. U.K. Phono-Cinéma-Théâtre. Silent, b&w, 3 mins. Fred Evans and Joe Evans.

One of the series of popular films by Fred Evans, a music hall performer, as his character Pimple, a clown-like character with tight clothes and lank strands of hair framing his whitened face. The Pimple films specialized in theatrical burlesque.

The film does not survive, but the character and title suggest a parody.

606 *To Be or Not to Be*
1916. U.S. American Beauty. Silent, b&w, length unknown. Edward Watt.

An itinerant Shakespearean and his company, chased by police for not paying their bills, discover a cache of lost jewels and pay their debts with the reward money.

It is unclear whether this film includes any direct *Hamlet* reference beyond the title.

607 *A Barnyard Hamlet*
1917. U.S. Powers Picture Plays. Silent, b&w, length unknown. W. E. Stark.

Animals perform the plot of *Hamlet* in this animated parody.

608 *'Amlet*
1919. U.K. Hepworth Pictures Plays. Silent, b&w, length unknown. Anson Dyer.

Lost film. Anson Dyer, a pioneer in British animation, produced a series of cutout animated parodies of Shakespeare between 1919 and 1920. *'Amlet* is the first of this series.

See also *Oh'Phelia* (below).

609 *Love Is Love*
1919. U.S. Fox Film Corporation. Silent, b&w, length unknown. Scott R. Dunlap.

When passive locksmith Gerry Sands is framed for safecracking by his boss Nick, he moves away from his sweetheart Polly Ann Kerry to escape the police; the two are reunited when Gerry returns and Polly recognizes that she misjudged him.

Gerry's weak will is bolstered when he reads from a dropped copy of *Hamlet* in the midst of a robbery into which he has been bullied by Nick.

610 *Oh'Phelia*
1919. U.K. Hepworth Picture Plays. Silent, b&w, 13 mins. Anson Dyer.

The sequel to Dyer's *'Amlet*, one of his many animated cutout parodies of Shakespeare produced between 1919 and 1920. This is the only complete film of Dyer's parodies to survive. Oh'Phelia is gardening when she is wooed by 'Amlet and rejects his advances. After Laertes chases him off, 'Amlet explains himself to the Queen and kicks Polonius. Distributing her garden's wares to the court, Oh'Phelia offends the King, is banished, and falls into the river, only to be saved by 'Amlet, after which they resolve to get married.

A number of the play's motifs are played for slapstick or convoluted puns. For example, when Oh'Phelia rejects him, 'Amlet tries to cut her hair; the title card reads, "To bob or not to bob." See also *'Amlet* (above).

611 *One Night Only*
1919. U.S. Bull's Eye Film Company. Silent, b&w, 6 mins. (surviving print is incomplete). Charles Parrott (aka Charley Chase).

A farce about a performance of *Hamlet* by a traveling Shakespearean company that is so disastrous it closes after only one night.

612 *A Sagebrush Hamlet*
1919. U.S. Jesse D. Hampton Productions. Silent, b&w, 5 reels. Joseph J. Franz.

The first of many adaptations of *Hamlet* to the conventions of the Western. Larry Lang, in an effort to take revenge upon Claude Dutton, the killer of his father, pretends to be "plumbed loco." When Dutton's henchman Two-Gun Dan fails to kill Lang, Dutton takes up the challenge and threatens Lang's sweetheart, his distant cousin Dora Lawrence. Eventually Lang kills Dutton and wins the heart of Dora.

Several motifs mirror the plot of *Hamlet*: revenge for the killing of the father, feigned madness, and romance with a young woman.

613 *Amleto e il suo Clown*
1920. Italy. D'Ambra Film. Silent, b&w, 6,365 ft. Carmine Gallone.

An odd drama-parody. Sammons summarizes the film in this way: horrified that her father has died and her mother has married a family friend, John, Alexandra hires clowns to reenact scenes from *Hamlet*. When she thinks she sees John's guilt, she kills him, only later to discover that someone else committed the crime. Afterwards, Alexandra joins a circus and eventually commits suicide at her mother's urging.

Notable particularly for its use of the play-within-the-play motif, here wittily undermined by Alexandra's misidentification of her father's murderer.

614 *Edgar's Hamlet*
1920. U.S. Goldwyn Pictures. Silent, b&w, length unknown. E. Mason Hopper.

Apparently a lost film. One of several "Edgar" films written by Booth Tarkington in 1920 and 1921. Apparently a parody in which Edgar and his schoolmates mount a disastrous performance of *Hamlet*. Not to be confused with *Edgar Hamlet* (1935).

615 *Daydreams*
1922. U.S. First National Pictures. Silent, b&w, 19 mins. Edward F. Cline and Buster Keaton.

A Young Man (played by Buster Keaton) seeks to prove his financial viability to his sweetheart's father by writing letters from the city about his various jobs; his sweetheart imagines he is more successful than he really is. The film ends with a comically botched suicide. All surviving prints are incomplete.

When the Young Man writes that he has a job in theater, his sweetheart imagines that he is playing Hamlet (Keaton is dressed in a black doublet and tights and carries a skull; he takes bows before an applauding audience).

616 *Han, Hun og Hamlet (He, She and Hamlet)*
1922. Denmark. Production company unknown. Silent, b&w, 5,725 ft. Lau Lauritzen.

Eva, a student at a girl's school, is stagestruck and with other women students puts on plays after hours, only to be caught and forbidden to act. Soon expelled for making contact with her boyfriend Paul, Eva travels with her girlfriends Fy and Bi to see him, after which she performs Ophelia in a parody version of *Hamlet*. This film stars the popular Danish comic duo known as Fy and Bi (Pat and Patachon in most European countries). Includes several scenes from *Hamlet*.

617 *So This Is Hamlet?*
1923. U.S. C. C. Burr. Silent, b&w, length unknown. Gregory La Cava.

Summary unavailable. La Cava was an animator who turned to live-action comedies in the 1920s. He also directed *Stage Door* (1937), which includes a Shakespearean passage. The title of this film suggests that it is a Shakespearean parody.

618 *Upstream*
1927. U.S. Fox Film Corporation. Silent, b&w, 61 mins. John Ford.

Adapted from *The Snake's Wife* by Wallace Smith. Lost film. Living amidst eccentric entertainers at a theatrical boardinghouse, egomaniacal and aristocratic actor Eric Brasingham unceremoniously leaves sweetheart Gertie King to star in a London production of *Hamlet*. He returns to discover that Gertie has married knife-thrower Jack. The portrayal of Brasingham is reputedly a parody of John Barrymore.

619 *The Last Moment*
1928. U.S. Samuel Freedman and Edward M. Spitz. Sound, b&w, 54 mins. (6 reels). Pál Fejös.

An experimental film that chronicles the thoughts of a drowning actor as his life flashes before his eyes. Renowned in its day for its innovative use of subjective time and first person perspective.

One sequence portrays the actor's performance in *Hamlet* and the approval of the crowd.

620 *The Melancholy Dame*
1928. U.S. Sound, b&w, 20 mins. Arvid E. Gillstrom.

Only the title relates to Shakespeare's melancholy Dane, Hamlet. The story relates the troubles of "Permanent Williams," darktown cabaret owner, who is forced to hire his divorced wife and her new husband as entertainers. His second wife doesn't relish the fact, so, in the words of one character, "troubles is somethin' Permanent ain't got nothing else exceptin." Spencer Williams stars as Webster Dill. See *The Framing of the Shrew* and *Paradise in Harlem*. (RB)

621 *Die Königsloge* (*The Royal Box*)
1929. U.S. Warner Bros. Sound, b&w, 76 mins. Bryan Foy.

Adapted from the plays *The Royal Box* by Arthur Rundt and *Kean* by Alexandre Dumas père. A theatrical biopic detailing the career of Edmund Kean and his secret love affair with the Countess Toerek, also the lover of the prince of Wales. Two versions exist, one in German, another in English.

At the film's conclusion, Kean goes insane during a performance of *Hamlet* and reveals his covert romance to the audience and the prince.

622 *Der Blaue Engel* (*The Blue Angel*)
1930. Germany. UFA. Sound, b&w, 107 mins. Josef von Sternberg.

Adapted from the novel *Professor Unrat* by Heinrich Mann. Professor Immanuel Rath, a stuffy, strict high school teacher of English language and literature in a provincial German town, pursues his wayward students to the Blue Angel nightclub, where he meets the spirited, beautiful Lola, a cabaret singer. He becomes enamored of her and is taunted for it by his students, leading to him losing his job. Even though Lola clearly doesn't love him and delights in making a fool of him, Rath marries her and soon becomes her servant, selling her postcards at cabarets and heating her curling iron. Eventually, Rath becomes a pathetic clown in the show, the assistant of a magician who degrades him onstage, as Lola takes up with Mazeppa, a callow and handsome Frenchman, without hiding the affair. Rath reacts by going on a rampage and, humiliated, returns to his school in the middle of the night, hanging on desperately in his sleep to his former desk.

In the English version of the film, Professor Rath uses "To be or not to be" to teach his class proper English pronunciation. In the German version, Rath does the same, but he also punishes his inattentive class by making them write on *Julius Caesar*: what would have happened if Mark Antony had not delivered his funeral oration? "To be or not to be" is clearly a relevant question for Rath, for he has shut out the joys of life, but he treats it merely as philological material, concentrating instead on the correct pronunciation of "the."

623 *Murder!*
1930. U.S. British International Pictures. Sound, b&w, 92 mins. Alfred Hitchcock.

Adapted from the play *Enter Sir John* by Clemence Dane and Helen Simpson. Serving on a jury for a murder case involving actress Diana Baring, actor Sir John Menier uses his skills at impersonation to reenact the crime and prove Baring's innocence, enlisting the help of Ted Markham, the stage manager, and Doucie, his wife, in the process. The killer turns out to be Handel Fane, a cross-dressing actor worried that his status as a half-black will be exposed. Two versions exist, one in English, another in German.

Though *Murder!* includes no citations from *Hamlet*, the plot turns on Menier's reenactment of the crime before the murderer, a reenactment that Menier explicitly connects to *The Mousetrap*. Clemence Dane, the film's scriptwriter, penned several plays and novels that are free adaptations of *Hamlet*.

624 *Murder*
1930. U.K. British International Pictures. Sound, b&w, 104 mins. Alfred Hitchcock.

Early Hitchcock plot revolves around actors and performance: two actresses meet for dinner; Edna Druce is later found bludgeoned by a poker, and Diana Baring sits stunned nearby, suffering from amnesia and covered with blood. Diana Baring claims she does not remember what happened; she is charged with murder, found guilty, and sentenced to death. There is a lengthy scene in the jury room as the jurors decide her fate. After her sentencing one of the jurors, Sir John (also an actor), decides that the verdict must be in error and sets out to find the guilty party and free Baring. He elicits the help of stage manager Markham and his wife Dulcie, who were in the same acting company as Druce and Baring. Markham, while describing Dulcie's versatile acting ability to Sir John, relates that he once told her, "If you can't pull yourself together, we will have to go into Shakespeare." The three decide that the guilty culprit must be Handel Fane, a member of the acting company and a female impersonator. Sir John asks Markham if he is familiar with *Hamlet*; when Markham replies that he is, Sir John states he wants to lay a plot using 3.2 as his guide in order to trap Fane. Like Hamlet, Sir John wants to produce a performance that will open "the inner history of the Baring case" by creating a scenario like *The Mousetrap* and having Fane reenact his crime in it. Realizing he is caught, Fane (who is now working as a trapeze artist) turns his trapeze rope into a noose and leaps off the platform during a performance, hanging himself in front of the carnival crowd. Interesting use of proscenium as a scene-changing device throughout. (CL)

625 *Han, Hun og Hamlet* (*He, She and Hamlet*)
1932. Denmark. Palladium Productions. Sound, b&w, 96 mins. Lau Lauritzen.

Talkies remake of the 1922 version, with the same director and the same featured stars Fy and Bi. For summary, see *Han, Hun og Hamlet* (1922).

626 *The Arizonian*
1935. U.S. RKO Pictures. Sound, b&w, 75 mins. Charles Vidor.

A new marshall, Clay Tallant, arrives in Silver City to confront corrupt sheriff Jake Mannen and his outlaw minions; Clay is helped in his task by ex-outlaw Tex Randolph. Along the way, Clay defends the honor of Kitty Rivers, the "English Nightingale" affianced to Clay's brother Orin.

A saloon show features the ghost scene from *Hamlet*, with the ghost played minstrel-style by a black man wearing a sheet.

627 *Edgar Hamlet*
1935. U.S. RKO Radio Pictures. Sound, b&w, 22 mins. Arthur Ripley.

Parody starring Edgar Kennedy, famous for his slow burn. Kennedy has a dispute with his bossy mother-in-law about the source of the "To be or not to be" soliloquy— Edgar says it is from *Hamlet*, and she says it is from *The Merchant of Venice* ("To be rich or not to be rich").

She also misidentifies "Life is real, life is earnest" (a non-Shakespearean citation) as being from *Hamlet*, while Edgar identifies it as from *Macbeth*. Edgar has trouble remembering the entirety of the "To be or not to be" speech. To settle the argument, Edgar books tickets for a local performance of *Hamlet*, but the preparations for the family to dress up leads to Edgar's temper flaring. At the word "rage," he remembers "outrageous fortune" and is able to give a full, blustering performance of Hamlet's soliloquy. In the end, the family reconciles.

Revealing for its assumptions about the highbrow status of Shakespeare (the family has to dress properly to attend the *Hamlet* performance), and for Edgar and his mother-in-law's battle over Shakespearean citations to establish domestic authority.

628 *Khoon ka Khoon* (*Hamlet*)
1935. India. Minerva Movietone and Stage Film Company. Sound, b&w, 122 mins. Sohrab Modi.

A recording of Modi's very successful Urdu stage production of *Hamlet*. Modi formed the Stage Film Company in 1935 to film famous stage plays when the decline of live theater became apparent. Modi followed up this film with *Saed-e-Havas* (1936), based on Shakespeare's *King John*. Both were financial failures. See also entry 329.

629 *The Great Garrick*
1937. U.S. Warner Brothers. Sound, b&w, 89 mins. James Whale.

Adapted from the play *Ladies and Gentlemen* by Ernest Vajda. When David Garrick insults the actors of the Comedie Française, they resolve to ridicule Garrick by creating a frightening show at the Adam and Eve Inn where he is playing. He discovers their plan and turns it against them, in the process wooing Countess de la Corbe.

The film opens with Garrick concluding his performance of *Hamlet*.

630 *Gallant Sons*
1940. U.S. MGM. Sound, b&w, 71 mins. George B. Seitz.

Schoolmates Johnny Davis, By Newbold, and Kate Pendleton attempt to prove the innocence of Davis's father when he is convicted for murder. As they investigate, they learn that Johnny was adopted and find a song connected to the real murderer, Al Posna. They engineer a scheme that prompts Posna to confess his crime.

The three sleuths create a play that, they say, is inspired by *Hamlet*; in its third act, they reenact the murder, provoking the murderer's confession.

631 *To Be or Not to Be*
1942. U.S. Romaine Film Corporation. Sound, b&w, 99 mins. Ernst Lubitsch.

Provocatively, this political lampoon opens by making a theatrical joke of Hitler's fearsome mystique, a strategy it pursues throughout. In wartime Warsaw, Joseph Tura, the self-proclaimed "world's greatest actor," is performing his *Hamlet*, while his wife Maria carries on an affair with a Polish American pilot, Lt. Stanislav Sobinski. Unwittingly, Sobinski implicates Maria with a German spy, Professor Siletsky, who is out to destroy the Nazi resistance. In an effort to protect Maria and to aid the resistance by eliminating Siletsky, Tura's troupe soon turns to impersonating Nazi officers and, in the film's climactic scene, even Hitler himself, concocting an elaborate series of seductions and deceptions to foil the SS. Brilliantly plotted, enlivened by Lubitsch's characteristic light comic touch despite the controversial material, and filled with marvelous performances by Jack Benny and Carole Lombard, this film suggests how irony and theatrical demystification might function as weapons of the weak against tyranny.

This film contains Shakespearean references of two sorts. First, a running gag in the film involves Tura speaking "To be or not to be," which Maria designates as the signal to Sobinski that he can visit her backstage. Tura never gets all the way through the soliloquy without being interrupted. The other set of references cites Shakespeare more seriously, as an indictment of Nazi anti-Semitism. At the film's climax, the Jewish actor Greenberg gives Shylock's "Hath not a Jew eyes?" speech to a group of SS officers and Hitler himself. A fascinating and controversial film that cites various forms of acting, good and bad, Shakespearean and comic farce, to rob Nazi leaders of their mystique and thus political power. See also entry 2173.

The Region 2 DVD includes a commentary track (in French) by Jean Douchet, as well as a superior print of the film. The Region 1 DVD contains no extras referencing Shakespeare.

632 *To Duck . . . or Not to Duck*
1943. U.S. Looney Tunes, Warner Brothers. Sound, color, 7 mins. Chuck Jones.

Elmer Fudd is hunting with his dog Laramore and shoots down Daffy Duck. When Fudd exclaims that he is a "gweat sportsman," Daffy suggests that duck hunting is not sportsmanlike, as one party has a gun. He suggests that they take their dispute to the boxing ring and have a "fair fight."

Jack Benny as Hamlet from *To Be or Not to Be* (1942). This publicity shot shows Benny as Hamlet, in black doublet and hose. Nice deadpan humor. Courtesy of Douglas Lanier.

Elmer Fudd has no chance, as the audience is made up entirely of ducks except for his dog, and the referee roughs him up while explaining what "not to do." Hilarious! (EJL)

633 *Strange Illusion*
1945. U.S. Producers Releasing Corporation. Sound, b&w, 87 mins. Edgar G. Ulmer.

A highly inventive film noir from the most skillful of the "Poverty Row" directors. Paul Cartwright, son of an esteemed judge who has died mysteriously, learns that his mother Virginia has taken up with Brett Curtis, a handsome but oily and suspicious wealthy man whom she wants to marry. Curtis reminds Paul of a threatening figure he has seen in his recurrent nightmares. When Paul objects to the impending marriage and has fainting spells, he is admitted to an asylum where he is kept under surveillance by Professor Muhlbach, a psychiatrist secretly in league with Curtis. Clues at the asylum reveal to Paul that Curtis is in fact a criminal, Claude Carrington, whom his father had convicted and later written about, and that Curtis not only murdered Paul's father but also intends to kill Paul, ruin Virginia, and molest Paul's sister. Eventually Paul escapes the asylum and enlists the help of his friends to confront Curtis. Particularly effective are the deeply Oedipal dream sequences that plague Paul throughout the film, the critical portrait of psychiatry, Warren Williams's unctuous performance as Curtis, and the off-kilter and paranoid tone of the film.

Plot and character parallels to *Hamlet* abound. Paul plays the role of Hamlet; Brett, Claudius; Paul's mother, Gertrude; Paul's girlfriend, Ophelia; Paul's kindly mentor Dr. Vincent, a combination of Horatio and Polonius; and Professor Muhlbach, a sinister version of Rosencrantz and Guildenstern. The film makes much of Paul's seeming madness, of his deep attachment to his mother and lionizing of his father, and of Curtis's suspicion and surveillance of the boy, both exploring and deftly debunking an Oedipal vision of Hamlet. Also interesting is the quiet desperation of Paul's middle-aged mother, who easily falls for Brett's romantic overtures and social sophistication. No direct verbal citations of Shakespeare, though a bust of Shakespeare is glimpsed on Paul's desk. Though very low budget, the film is a fascinating, well-made film noir adaptation of *Hamlet* that concentrates on the play's Oedipal psychology, and it deserves to be much better known.

634 *My Darling Clementine*
1946. U.S. 20th Century Fox. Sound, b&w, 97 mins. John Ford.

Adapted from the novel *Wyatt Earp, Frontier Marshal* by Stuart N. Lake. Wyatt Earp, cattleman and retired lawman, becomes sheriff of Tombstone to gather evidence against the boorish Clantons for cattle rustling, in the process falling in love with the schoolmarm Clementine, Doc Holliday's girlfriend. At film's end, Earp and Holliday confront the Clantons at the OK Corral, and Earp eventually returns to the prairie.

In the saloon, the Clantons torture Shakespearean actor Granville Thorndyke as he speaks the "To be or not to be" soliloquy at gunpoint; when he falters, Doc Holliday finishes the speech. At the end of this episode, Thorndyke says to the Clantons, "Shakespeare was not meant for taverns . . . or tavern louts." When Thorndyke leaves Tombstone the next day, he offers literary quotations to the crowd. To an old Civil War soldier, he offers a quotation about friendship from Addison and adds, "Good night, sweet prince" (from *Hamlet*). To the crowd, he offers, "Parting is such sweet sorrow" (from *Romeo and Juliet*). The Shakespeare sequence in the saloon articulates a key theme of the film: the uneasy place of marks of civilization in the West. In this scene, Earp defends Thorndyke from the Clantons, but it is Doc, self-doubting, dying, and aware of his failings, who is capable of completing the speech. Significantly, it is the phrase "makes cowards of us all" on which Thorndyke falters.

635 *Cross My Heart*
1947. U.S. Paramount. Sound, b&w, 85 mins. John Berry.

Adapted from the play *True Confessions* by Louis Verneuil and Georges Berr. Showgirl Peggy Harper, anxious to send her fiancé lawyer Oliver Clarke business so he will marry her, ends up accused of the murder of producer-boss Wallace Brent and is defended by Oliver. Upon her acquittal, he breaks their engagement, but a detective discovers that a disgruntled Shakespearean actor murdered Brent, and Oliver and Peggy are reunited.

The villain of the film is Peter, an Eastern European Shakespearean who wants to be cast in Brent's revival of *Hamlet*; we learn later that he has twice murdered other actors while playing Hamlet. At the film's denouement, Oliver has been lured into performing *Hamlet* with Peter, and Peggy and the police rush to save him from being murdered.

636 *Red, Hot and Blue*
1949. U.S. Paramount. Sound, b&w, 84 mins. John Farrow.

An aspiring chorus girl, Eleanor Collier, witnesses the murder of a potential theatrical benefactor, Bunny Harris,

a man she later learns is a gangster. Afterward, she is kidnapped by one of Harris's men. Her boyfriend, theatrical director Danny James, uses a clue supplied by Eleanor to rescue her and bring the criminals to justice. In the end, Eleanor marries Danny.

Danny is directing *Hamlet* for summer stock, a production that Bunny Harris finds boring; Eleanor produces a much more lively, jazzed-up musical version on the spot. Compare *Playmates*, *She's Working Her Way through College*, and *Casanova in Burlesque*.

637 *My Favorite Spy*
1951. U.S. Paramount. Sound, b&w, 93 mins. Norman Z. McLeod.

The spitting image of international spy Eric Augustine, vaudeville comic Peanuts White (played by Bob Hope) is enlisted by the FBI to pose as Eric to retrieve a valuable microfilm. To do so, he must rendezvous with Eric's girlfriend, Lily Dalbray; fend off an evil spymaster, Karl Brubaker; and avoid Eric, who has escaped and returned to Algiers.

When administered truth serum, Peanuts hoists a skull and says, "Alas, poor Yorick, I knew him well."

638 *Io, Amleto* (*Moi, Hamlet*)
1952. Italy. Sound, b&w, 103 mins. Giorgio Simonelli.

Directed by a well-known Italian specialist in parody. This version imagines a happy ending for the play: Hamlet kills Claudius, marries Ophelia, and becomes the elected president of Denmark. No other information available.

639 *Hamlet*
1954. India. Production company unknown. Sound, b&w, 140 mins. Kishore Sahu.

An adaptation from the Parsi stage version, with many visual homages to Olivier's film (entry 330). Sahu stars as Hamlet.

640 *Aasha*
1957. India. Raman Productions. Sound, b&w and col., 171 mins. M. V. Raman.

An old man's son is accused of a crime, but a cousin of the young man is the true culprit. The old man, disguised as an Arab, sets up a play to reveal the truth.

A play-within-a-play becomes crucial for revealing a crime.

641 *Desk Set*
1957. U.S. 20th Century Fox. Sound, col., 103 mins. Walter Lang.

Adapted from the play by William Marchant. Efficiency expert Richard Sumner installs a computer called EMEREK in a TV research department, much to the annoyance of researcher Bunny Watson and her staff. As Sumner comes to doubt the wisdom of the project, Bunny falls in love with him.

One of the test questions given EMEREK concerns *Hamlet*.

642 *A King in New York*
1957. U.K. Archway Productions and Charlie Chaplin Productions. Sound, b&w, 110 mins. Charles Chaplin.

A deposed monarch exiled to New York without money, King Shadov (played by Charlie Chaplin) struggles to adjust to life in the United States while encouraging the peaceful use of nuclear energy. Shadov becomes involved with Ann Kay, a young woman who hosts a TV show, and he becomes a celebrity, does commercials, and has plastic surgery in pursuit of making a living. When he befriends a small boy, Rupert, whose parents are to be imprisoned for Communist activity, he jeopardizes his living to shelter the boy.

As part of *Ann Kay's Real-Life Surprise Party*, a reality TV show secretly made during a society dinner party, Chaplin bombastically recites the "To be or not to be" soliloquy, unaware that his performance is being broadcast. Later, Shadov's ambassador observes that a king reciting *Hamlet* will appear mad.

643 *Danger Within* (aka *Breakout*)
1958. U.K. British Lion Films. Sound, b&w, 89 mins. Don Chaffey and Peter Graham Scott.

Adapted from the novel by Michael A. Gilbert. Prisoners make three escape attempts from an Italian POW camp under the command of the sinister, sadistic Capitano Benucci. Because of a traitor in the prisoners' midst (the traitor is Tony Long, who smuggles information to Benucci disguised as notes to his girlfriend), the first two escape attempts end in disaster, leading to tension between the two leaders of the prisoners, the cautious Colonel Baird and the daring Colonel Huxley. But when it becomes apparent that Germans may be taking over the camp, Baird and Huxley team up, finding the traitor and organizing a daring, successful daylight escape during a performance of *Hamlet*.

This very entertaining film juxtaposes scenes of wry British eccentricity with scenes of courageous, complicated derring-do, and the Shakespeare moments exemplify that approach. Rupert Callender, the twee prisoner who heads the *Hamlet* performance, is far more concerned with the play than escape. Each of the passages from his rehearsals is wittily intercut with events in the camp. The prisoners' struggle to hide the corpse of a man they think is an informer is set against Rosencrantz's demand of Hamlet, "What have you done, my lord, with the dead body?" (4.2); shots of the traitor Tony plotting against the life of Bunter, a fellow prisoner digging a tunnel, is intercut with Hamlet saying to his mother of the ghost, "Do you see nothing there?" (3.4); after Benucci sneeringly taunts Baird and Huxley about the informer, Callender's Hamlet offers, "O villain, villain, smiling, damned villain!" (1.5); and as the men dig a tunnel, we hear, "Well said, old mole! canst work i' the earth so fast? / A worthy pioneer!" (1.5). Of

the actual performance, we see several excerpts during the escape—Claudius's comment about Hamlet's "gentle, unforced accord" and Hamlet's "too, too solid flesh" soliloquy from 1.2, Hamlet's exchange with the gravedigger from 5.1 (including the line, ironic in the context of the escape, about Hamlet being sent to England), the final lines of the play after which the remaining men applaud, and the play's opening exchange between Bernardo and Marcellus (they have to start over to let the last men through the tunnel). In a final bit of poetic justice, the men bind and gag the traitor Tony, and leave him behind an arras; when Benucci comes to investigate and hears a noise, he unwittingly shoots his own informer to death, much as Hamlet kills Polonius.

644 *Der Rest ist Schweigen* (*The Rest Is Silence*)
1959. West Germany. Freie Film Produktion GmbH & Co. and Real-Film GmbH. Sound, b&w, 103 mins. Helmut Kautner.

An interesting post-war modernization of *Hamlet*, in which a young man, Hardy Krüger, seeks to prove that his uncle, Paul Claudius, killed his father. Novel ideas abound, including the ghost contacting his son using the telephone. Can be fruitfully compared to Kaurismäki's *Hamlet liikemaailmassa* and Almereyda's *Hamlet* (both below).

Many allusions to plot motifs, including the reenactment of the crime for the uncle and the presence of the father's ghost. See also entry 332.

645 *Heller in Pink Tights*
1960. U.S. Carlo Ponti Productions and Paramount. Sound, col., 100 mins. George Cukor.

Adapted from the novel by Louis L'Amour. The film chronicles the fortunes of the "Great Healy Dramatic and Concert Company" in frontier Wyoming, headed by the paternal actor-manager Tom Healy. Healy encourages the career of Angela Rossini, the "hellion in pink tights" (giving her the illusion of nudity), a beautiful but temptuous actress whose romantic and financial escapades threaten the economic survival of the troupe. Healy and Rossini are in love but cannot admit it to one another. Other members of the troupe—aging actress Lorna Hathaway, who has sacrificed her career for her untalented daughter, and classical actor Manfred Montague—resent Rossini's behavior. Financial troubles and Rossini's romance with gunfighter Clint Mabry threaten to destroy the troupe, but at the last minute the cast rallies in a triumphal performance of *Mazeppa*.

The film opens with Healy rehearsing Rossini in Hamlet's "Speak the speech" oration as they ride toward Cheyenne.

646 *Honoo no Shiro* (*Castle of Flames*)
1960. Japan. Daiei Studios and Toei Co. Ltd. Sound, col., 98 mins. Katô Tai.

Below are listed notable points about *Castle of Flames*.

1. Rokkaku Yûgo (Laertes) is consistently on Ômi Morokage's (Claudius) side. Yûgo supports Morokage by torturing and killing blind refugees from the neighboring country as well as oppressing peasants who plan rebellions.

In the first scene of his appearance, Yûgo asks Rokkaku Yukino (Ophelia) if she has heard from Ômi Masato (Hamlet) and also worries about his sister's love for Masato.

2. Ômi Tokiko (Gertrude) and Rokkaku Naonoshin (Polonius) know that Morokage killed the late king. Just before the bedchamber scene, Tokiko also confesses to Naonoshin that she was raped by Morokage when the late king was ill in bed.

3. Morokage is presented as an apparently evil character from the very beginning. At the very beginning of the film, he wishes Masato were drowned on his way back home from China. And his strangely long beard is probably taken from Kabuki, in whose convention that kind of huge, long beard is the sign of an evil character.

4. This film, which ends with the success of the peasants' rebellion with the young leader Masato, reflects the contemporary nationwide movement against the U.S.-Japan Security Treaty in June 1960. While the film was first shown in October of that year, it was surely being shot during the wild uproar in Tokyo against the ratification of the U.S.-Japan Security Treaty. The peasants' rushing to the gate of the castle probably reminded the contemporary audiences of the mass demonstrations by hundreds of thousands of ordinary people and students in Tokyo only some months before. As this movement against the treaty failed, the peasants' rebellion in the film would have offered its audiences a kind of replacement. Incidentally, the same director (Katô Tai) shot another period film, *Sanada Fûunroku* (the record of Sanada's *Unsettled Situations*), in 1963, based on a contemporary stage play of the same title. And in this 1963 film, the people's disappointment with the failure of this nationwide movement against the treaty is reflected as Sanada and his ninja fight against Tokugawa Shôgunate. *Castle of Flames* reflects its contemporary political situations by emphasizing the peasants' rebellion.

5. Yukino does not go mad. She instead has a chance to talk with Masato before he goes to fight a duel with Yûgo. Yukino asks Masato if she is in his way, and though Masato says nothing, she realizes what he means and drowns herself.

6. In the duel between Masato and Yûgo, the swordplay between them is very strange as typical Japanese-style swordfighting, because they hold their swords with one hand and fight as if they were fighting in the manner of Western swordplay.

7. The use of music is rather strange because it unnecessarily melodramatizes/romanticizes some scenes as if to blur or delete the misogyny of the protagonist.

8. Toward the beginning of the film, young samurai who have heard about Masato's return from China talk with each other about Masato as an enlightened, promising prince. They say that the prince will be able to clear the cloud over their country and enlighten the people in the castle. This kind of disappointment at Morokage is illuminated by a young man who Masato sees; Masato finds that he abandoned his status as a samurai and became a peasant because of the corruption of the country/authority. And this ex-samurai is the peasant who leads the army of peasants with the senior member of the village at the end of the film. Also, this young man is one of the pair who was almost shot by Morokage's retainers and was saved by Masato.

9. Morokage is planning to conquer neighboring Kumano castle and its territory. And there is a rumor that the lord of Kumano, the neighboring country, has been killing all the blind people in his country, claiming the blind are utterly useless. Hence, many blind people are flooding into Ômi, Morokage's country. Morokage and Yûgo suspect that not a few of those blind people are spies sent into their country, and so they arrest, torture, and even kill the blind flooding in. This shows that in this film, Yûgo is Morokage's evil right-hand man. (MR)

An inventive and recognizable, if only relatively faithful, adaptation of *Hamlet* retold so that both Masato and peasants rebel against a corrupt authority, represented by Claudius. (There actually were peasant rebellions protesting taxes. The leaders were usually killed, but taxes were then lowered). Proletarian film was not supposed to be ironic or campy, or to patronize the people who paid to see it. The film is quite good, and seriously tries to give its audience something beautiful and a good film. The duel between Masato and Laertes is first rate. Interestingly, *Castle of Flames* flirts with the idea that Hamlet is the reformer prince who saves the people. For example, pairs of farmers are tied up and being executed at a beach cliff. One pair is shot and killed with arrows. Then Masato arrives and throws a rock at a gun to prevent another pair from being shot with guns. One guy says loudly, "Masato will surely come here to save us!" At this point, the film seems a bit reactionary, as if the people's revolution is displaced by a reformist prince who saves the peasants. So the film would be against both the liberal democrat, pro-U.S. occupation party and complicit filmmakers. (See 4, above.) The film is also very Hamlet centered. Only Masato sees the ghost. Unlike the play, there is no independent verification of the ghost. Masato even takes on the role of reformer. The pirate explains to Masato that he was an ex-farmer and had to become a pirate. The storm gets stronger and Masato, who was picked up by the pirate when floating in a small boat, is given a large bowl of rice and sees again the ghost. Masato thinks he must save the farmers. His revenge plot can also serve their revenge. The ending of the film takes several turns, however, to limit Masato's role and undo Masato's fantasized fusion of his revenge with the peasants'. During the duel, the sword slips out of Yûgo's hand and sticks into a wall. Masato knowingly takes this poisoned sword and gives Yûgo his unpoisoned one instead. And the duel continues, and Masato thrust Yûgo's arm and Yûgo falls down. Then Morokage makes a signal and several retainers with guns appear from behind the nearby sliding doors and shoot at Masato, but he hits the floor while Tokiko rushes to him to stop the gunners, only to be shot (not killed, though). Then Morokage's retainers surround Masato, and one of the retainers throws his short sword at Masato and stabs him in the thigh. Suddenly a ringing bell warns of the peasants' attack at the castle. All the retainers go out to defend the castle and attack the peasants. Morokage also escapes from the room and then goes outside. Here Yûgo, struggling to stand up, falls down because of the poison, suggesting his death. When Masato follows Morokage and comes out of the building, several retainers shoot arrows at him; he gets severely injured and falls down as if he were dead (but not yet).

A rebellion starts at this moment, however, and the pair of peasants Masato saved earlier are leading it. The priest who talked with Yûgo before is seen being trampled to death (probably) by the army of peasants rushing through the gate.

Here the film shifts to a more progressive take on Japanese feudalism. The peasants become an active historical subject and revolt on their own, without Masato's help. But then, in a compromise, the film has Masato get up, alive after all, and go upstairs in a castle wall to catch up with Morokage, who has now gone up to the top of the castle, apparently to open the gates to let the peasants inside. Masato fights off a bunch of retainers, then kills Yûgo, and then has a long duel with Morokage. Just after Masato kills Morokage, there is a wonderful graphic match between a shot of Morokage's head split open by Masato's sword and a shot of the farmers pushing open the walls of the castle gate without Masato's help. There is no causal link between Masato and the farmers, but both seem equally related to each other (Masato saves the pair of farmers, and the pirate ex-farmer saves Masato).

As discussed above, one of the peasant leaders was Masato's close friend or one of his men, but got disappointed with the corrupted authority/government and gave up his samurai status to become a peasant. This is why, at the rebellion scene, he is in a suit of armor.

After Masato kills Morokage, there is also a similar match with Tokiko dying again with seppuko and then Masato dying (finally, a second time). In a related twist, Masato is stabbed during the duel with Yûgo, but we can't see who it is. The moment is similar to key deaths in two of Kurosawa's Shakespeare film adaptations, but the effect is quite different. We don't see who is shooting the arrows at Macbeth at the end of *Throne of Blood*. Similarly, Kurosawa

makes the trees really seem to move on their own, as if the agents are supernatural, not men. And in *Ran*, the lord is shot in the back, so we can't know if the death is the result of a deliberate betrayal or an accident. Whereas Kurosawa does not admit any role for the peasants and mystifies the historical process of rebellion, the director of *Castle of Flames* does not show us who stabs Masato while showing us a retainer shooting him with an arrow, so as to darken (but not darken completely) our view of Claudius's retainers. Unlike Kozintsev's excellent Russian *Hamlet*, which imaginatively visualizes the time being "out of joint" as a function of Hamlet being a man ahead of his time while downplaying the revolutionary moment led by Laertes upon his return, *Castle of Flames* expands on that moment and dialectically associates it with Masato while also making it independent of him. The agency and importance of Old Hamlet (Katsumasa) are similarly downplayed. When Masato returns home (he is shot rather dramatically from behind at first) to visit his father's grave, there is a comic deflation of Old Hamlet. Old Hamlet's grave marker is shot first from below (unlike Naonoshin's [Polonius] later) as if it were really huge. But in a subsequent shot, we see it is not even as high as Masato. In neither of his two appearances does the ghost talk to Masato. The second time the ghost appears, after Hamlet has been captured by pirates, he holds out his right arm and points to his right. He has a bloodstain on his white kimino, and Masato figures out that his father was murdered.

Unlike Western representations of *Hamlet*, which tend to cut its political elements, *Castle of Flames* plays them up. Just before Masato kills Naonoshin in the closet scene, for example, several people enter. As soon as Masato kills him, everyone in the palace wakes up and comes in. Naonoshin's murder is a very public event. *Castle of Flames* isolates Masato from the women but suppresses his misogyny. Tokiko and Yukino are on Masato's side and are portrayed positively. Tokiko knows that Morokage killed the old king, Katsumasa. Knowing her son's sake is poisoned, Tokiko runs toward her son to stop him from drinking it, but Morokage stops her. Watching Morokage's behaviors, Masato pours the poisoned sake down to the floor, staring at Morokage.

Even Ophelia's suicide is political. After he rebuffs her cruelly, she confesses her love for him. But she drowns herself in a beautiful scene after she sees she is in his way. At the end of the film, Masato cries as he addresses Yukino's corpse. It's not clear whether he then dies or not. (RB)

647 *The Pure Hell of St. Trinian's*
1960. U.K. British Lion Films. Sound, b&w, 94 mins. Frank Launder.
After the girls of St. Trinian's burn down their school, an unscrupulous headmaster, Professor Canford, offers to

rebuild, only to take the girls to Greece on an educational tour where he intends to sell them as wives to Arab sheiks.

During the St. Trinian's "Festival of Culture," Hamlet's "To be or not to be" is performed as a striptease. St. Trinian's *Hamlet*, we later learn, is to be featured at Stratford.

648 *The Nutty Professor*
1963. U.S. Paramount. Sound, col., 107 mins. Jerry Lewis.

In an effort to overcome his awkwardness and shyness with Stella, inept Professor Julius Kelp stumbles on a potion that turns him into Buddy Love, a handsome, ultracool nightclub singer (reputedly, a caricature of Frank Sinatra).

Buddy Love humiliates a pompous university dean by coaxing him into a parody performance of "To be or not to be."

649 *Warui yatsu hodo yoku nemuru* (*The Bad Sleep Well*)
1963. Japan. Kurosawa Production Co. Ltd. and Toho Company Ltd. Sound, b&w, 151 mins. Akira Kurosawa.

The most neglected of Akira Kurosawa's three Shakespeare film adaptations, and the only one to be set in contemporary Japan. The gift of a wedding cake at a corporate wedding reception for Koichi Nishi, a corporate assistant, and Keiko, the crippled daughter of Iwabuchi, corporate vice president and Nishi's boss, creates a public scandal by reminding the guests of the suicide of Nishi's father, Wada, that enabled their rise to power. All become even more unnerved when the police arrest one of the wedding guests. Soon we learn that these events were secretly orchestrated by Nishi himself, who has taken on a false identity to avenge his father's suicide forced by his corporate colleagues five years earlier. Nishi plans to expose the corporation's involvement in a kickback scheme, and he shames and kidnaps corporate underlings in an attempt to gather information and evidence. But Nishi's marriage to Keiko, also part of his plan for vengeance, proves an obstacle when Nishi has pangs of conscience for using her. In the end, Nishi is killed by Iwabuchi's henchmen, but Iwabuchi is rejected by his children and forced into retirement.

In *The Bad Sleep Well*, Kurosawa fragments his Shakespearean source into disjunct motifs, then reassembles them into a new whole (while adding other elements). Many parallels can be discerned: the avenging, morally troubled Nishi resembles Hamlet; Iwabuchi, Claudius (and Polonius); his fragile daughter Keiko, Ophelia; Tatsuo, his hot-headed son concerned with his sister's honor, Laertes; and Wada (Nishi's father, seen only in photographs), Old Hamlet. The film opens, as does *Hamlet*, with a gala wedding (though in this case the wedding is of the Hamlet and Ophelia figures, not Claudius and Gertrude). The revenger Nishi must engage in subterfuge and pretense (he pretends to be Itagawa), and is in constant danger; revenge is motivated by the wrongful death of a father covered over after the fact (in this case, the revenger is a bastard son of a corrupt corporation man, not the heir apparent of a heroic king). Nishi is compelled to return to memory of his fa-

ther's death (a memory contained in his photograph); and the cryptlike bombed factory where Nishi imprisons Moriyama is reminiscent of the graveyard, where the ambitions of the powerful are mocked and brought low. In this version, the Claudius figure manages to kill the Hamlet figure (he arranges for Nishi to die in a staged drunk-driving accident), but his victory is pyrrhic. Interestingly, at times Kurosawa plays against our knowledge of the details of *Hamlet*. For example, he twice uses the motif of the poisoned drink from *Hamlet* 5.2, first with the supposedly poisoned whisky that Nishi offers Shirai when he brings him to the room where his father committed suicide, and second with the medicine-laced wine that Iwabuchi fixes for himself when he believes that Nishi has cornered him. In both cases, the film audience is encouraged to conclude, because the *Hamlet* parallel demands it, that Nishi has ruthlessly, madly poisoned Shirai or that Iwabuchi has unwittingly poisoned his daughter Keiko with the wine. In both cases we are wrong, and Kurosawa uses our reaction to press against easy assumptions about good and evil. The film savagely attacks the corrupt nature of post-war Japanese corporate culture, with Nishi serving as a morally compromised revenger against the system. The bombed factory ruins not only visually suggest the moral wasteland that Japanese business has become but also remind us, as Nishi does with his Horatio-like friend Itakura, of the now-lost culture of personal honor and mutual solidarity that emerged immediately after the war. The prevalent use of photos and phones in the film reinforces the impression of an impersonally corrupt society.

650 *Ophélia*
1963. France. Boreal Film. Sound, b&w, 105 mins. Claude Chabrol.

A modernized adaptation of *Hamlet*. A literarily inclined young man, Yvan Lesurf, becomes grief-stricken and angry when his father dies and his mother, Claudia, marries his uncle, Adrien, and he takes over the local business. When he sees Olivier's film *Hamlet* (entry 330), he creates a film of his own to expose what he assumes is Adrien's crime of fratricide. In the end, he discovers that his father took his own life. Throughout the film, his girlfriend Lucy repeats the line, "I am not Ophelia." Compare to *Ithele na ginei vasilias* (below).

Stills and short excerpts from Olivier's *Hamlet* are included. Much of the narrative parallels the plot and characters of *Hamlet*, though the film's point is that Yvan's obsession with reliving the Hamlet narrative is finally self-destructive and fruitless. An interesting example of film adaptation in which the protagonist (and filmmaker) works through an Oedipal crisis with the play *Hamlet* itself.

651 *Hamile* (*The Tongo Hamlet*)
1964. Ghana. Ghana Film Industry Corporation. Sound, b&w, 120 min. Terry Bishop.

A film version of the University of Ghana's production of *Hamlet*, with the action and characters transposed to Tongo.

The plot closely follows that of Shakespeare. See also entry 335.

652 *Ithele na ginei vasilias* (*He Wanted to Be King*)
1964. Greece. Angelo Films. Sound, b&w, 88 mins. Angelos Theodoropoulos.

Adapts the play's action to modern Athens. After he returns to Athens upon the drowning of his industrialist father, Alecos seeks to trap his stepfather Guerolymos, a former business associate, into admitting his guilt by pretending to be mad. Only when his father's will is read does Alecos discover that Guerolymos is honest and Alecos will inherit the family's business holdings. Hamlet is played by the director and adaptor Angelos Theodoropoulos.

The film makes particularly strong use of the motif of Hamlet's madness.

653 *Jak byc kochana* (*How to Be Loved*)
1965. Poland. WFF Wroclaw and ZRF "Kamera." Sound, b&w, 97 mins. Wojciech J. Has.

Handled as an extended flashback, this film chronicles the life of Polish actress Felicja during the Nazi occupation of Warsaw and after. Felicja hides her self-absorbed co-star Wiktor in an aborted production of *Hamlet* when he is suspected of killing a Polish collaborator; because she loves Wiktor, for five years she endures humiliation and abuse and joins a German theatrical troupe to protect him. When the war is over, he abandons her and she is branded a collaborator. When they meet years later, he is an alcoholic and soon after commits suicide, as she struggles to resurrect her career by working in radio.

As the film opens, Felicja is preparing to play Ophelia.

654 *Beregis Avtomobilya* (*An Uncommon Thief*)
1967. USSR. Mosfilm. Sound, b&w, 93 mins. Eldar Ryazanov.

Acting as a modern Robin Hood, Yuri Detochkin, an insurance salesman, steals the cars of criminals who go unpunished, sells them, and gives the profits to an orphanage. He is investigated and eventually apprehended by Maksim Podberezovikov, a police detective and Detochkin's friend. As the investigation unfolds, the two men are performing in an amateur production of *Hamlet*.

Detochkin plays Hamlet, and Podberezovikov Laertes, in the amateur production of *Hamlet*, and the film features several passages from the rehearsals and the final performance. The role of Detochkin is played by Innokenti Smoktunovsky, who played Hamlet in Kozintsev's *Gamlet* (1964).

655 *Enter Hamlet*
1967. U.S. School of Visual Art, California. Sound, col., length unknown. Fred Mogubgub.

In this whimsical animated film, each word of Hamlet's "To be or not to be" soliloquy is illustrated with a different drawing (a bee illustrates "be," for example). The "To be or not to be" soliloquy is presented in its entirety.

656 *Hamlet*
1967. Hungary. Pannónia Film Studio. Sound, col., 14 mins. György Kovásznai.

Sammons summarizes the film in this way: a short, modernized version of the story, said to be witty and playful.

657 *Koroshi*
1968. U.K. MPI. Sound, col., 120 mins. Michael Truman, Peter Yates.

This originally aired and was released as TV episodes of *Danger Man* on January 5, 1968, and January 12, 1968. The British TV show *Danger Man* was known in the United States as *Secret Agent*, or *Secret Agent Man*. The show began as a thirty-minute program in b&w, later expanding to one hour-episodes. The only episodes shot in color were the last two: no. 85, "Koroshi," and no. 86, "Shinda Shima." These were combined (not necessarily artfully) with some linking footage for theatrical release as a film in 1968 that was entitled *Koroshi*. Patrick McGoohan decided not to continue filming the *Danger Man* series and instead created *The Prisoner*, arguably continuing to play his John Drake character from *Danger Man* and calling him Number Six. The production staff of *Danger Man* was retained for *The Prisoner*, and many cast members made the switch as well. These two episodes take place in Hong Kong, and secret agent Drake must stop Koroshi, an ancient cult of death that is hell-bent on world domination. Drake, incognito, is taken to meet Nigel—an expert on Japan, particularly of Kabuki theater, and a bad guy. There is a six-minute, traditional Kabuki performance of *Hamlet*, Act 5. Nigel explains that they are watching "the poetry of death, Koroshi." After they witness the Kabuki swordfight and poisoning of Gertrude, Drake remarks that it all seems rather familiar. At that point, he is told he has been watching *Hamlet*. Later, Nigel leaves Drake in a wardrobe room filled with all the Kabuki costumes, and one of them has a person inside and tries to kill him; he escapes. (RB)

658 *Ofelias Blomster*
1968. Denmark. Laterna Film A.S. and Kortfilmrådet. Sound, col., 7 mins. Jørgen Leth.

An experimental film built around Ophelia's madness monologue, "There's rosemary for remembrance." Her speech becomes fragmented into pure sound by wood block sounds, and the visuals emphasize meticulous camera movements in a room decorated with blue canvases. In the end, Ophelia throws herself into a lake.

Uses Ophelia's madness monologue, but fragments its delivery.

659 *Quella sporca storia del west* (*Johnny Hamlet* and *The Wild and the Dirty*)
1968. Italy. Daiano Film and Leone Film. Sound, col., 78 mins. Enzo G. Castellari.

Johnny Hamilton, a Confederate general in the Civil War, returns to Ranch Elsenor to discover that his father Chester has been murdered, and his mother has married his uncle Claude, thereby inheriting the ranch. Claude claims that he killed his father's murderer, Santana the Mexican outlaw, after a botched robbery. By tracing the ownership of an amulet Johnny discovers that Santana is alive and that he and Claude are in an uneasy league. In an attempt to frame Johnny, Claude kills Ophelia, the sheriff's daughter, and plants a gun beside her body in the mill-stream, but after being tortured by Ross and Gil (Claude's henchmen) and the sheriff, Johnny escapes with the help of his friend Horace to have a final showdown with Gil, Ross, and Claude. In the end, Johnny kills Claude, who reveals that he had killed Johnny's father and hidden the gold from the robbery. Compare *Un Uomo chiamato Apocalisse Joe* and *Dans la Poussière du Soleil* (above).

This spaghetti Western includes many parallels of character and plot to Shakespeare's play. In addition to the parallel motifs apparent in the summary, this version also includes Johnny's premonition of his father's death and the impetus to revenge, a comic gravedigger, Johnny's accusation of Ophelia of sexual promiscuity, Johnny's friendship with Horace, and a traveling troupe of players who appear throughout the film. The players open the film with a citation of Hamlet's "To be or not to be" soliloquy (a citation that signals the film's source in Shakespeare), and they reappear at midfilm to supply more lines from Shakespeare's dialogue. Moreover, certain moments in the film provide analogues for famous Shakespearean passages: pausing over a drink at the saloon, Johnny wonders whether or not it is better to be a coward (Horace joins in his reflection), clearly in parallel to Hamlet's "To be or not to be" speech. At its midpoint, the plot begins significantly to diverge from Shakespeare's script. Though the film is dated, it nevertheless includes several clever visual and symbolic touches (for instance, a recurring mirror motif) that elevate it well above the norm, and it skillfully transposes Hamlet's burden of revenge to the Western hero's personal code of honor. It deserves to be better known.

660 *The Magic Christian*
1969. U.K. Commonwealth United and Grand Films Limited. Sound, col., 92 mins. Joseph McGrath.

A brutally black comedy in which Sir Guy Grand (Peter Sellers), the world's richest man, adopts a homeless man (Ringo Starr) and tests people's willingness to debase themselves for money; the centerpiece of this episodic film is a luxury cruise on the ocean liner *The Magic Christian*.

As an early demonstration of the power of greed, Grand pays a Shakespearean to strip while performing "To be or not to be." We see Laurence Harvey—who had played Romeo in Castellani's *Romeo and Juliet* (1954)—perform this travesty before a scandalized crowd.

661 *End of the Road*
1970. U.S. Allied Artists. Sound, col., 110 mins. Aram Avakian.

Adapted from the novel by John Barth. Jacob Horner, an emotionally troubled career academic, undergoes therapy from an unorthodox psychologist, Doctor D, and has a destructive affair with Rennie Morgan, the wife of a colleague. The film was scripted by Terry Southern, who also contributed to *The Magic Christian* (above).

Doctor D includes several Shakespearean references in his therapy: he recites Macbeth's "Tomorrow and tomorrow and tomorrow" soliloquy over a barrage of bizarre images; he uses *Hamlet* as an example of how everyone is the hero of their own story; and in response to a suffering woman, he sardonically observes, "Methinks the lady doth protest too much." Late in the film, Joe Morgan, suicidal, masturbates while reciting, "To be or not to be," an episode that leads to Jacob and Rennie's affair. This was one of several sequences that earned the film an X rating upon its initial release.

662 *A Herança*
1970. Brazil. Longfilm Produrora Cinematografica. Sound, col., 90 mins. Ozualda Ribiera Candeias.

Transposes *Hamlet* to rural Brazil. Upon returning to his home, Omeleto learns that his mother has married his uncle Tio, much to his dismay. Of special note is the music by Fernando Lona. See also entry 337.

663 *Ninì Tirabusciò: la donna che inventò la mossa*
1970. Italy. Clesi Cinematografica. Sound, col., 94 mins. Marcello Fondato.

Ninì dreams of becoming a classical tragedian; instead, she achieves fame as a café songstress.

As her audition piece, Ninì performs the role of Juliet before a band of strolling players, who reject her staid interpretation. Instead, the manager offers his contemporized version of "To be or not to be." Later the troupe rehearses their version of *Hamlet*, reducing and sensationalizing the plot and filling the performance with adlibs.

664 *Dans la Poussière du Soleil* (*Lust in the Sun*)
1971. France and Spain. IMF Pictures and Kerfrance Production. Sound, col., 84 mins. Richard Balducci.

Spaghetti Western adaptation. Hawk Bradford seeks vengeance against his uncle for murdering his father Joe and forcing his mother Gertie to marry him to take over the ranch. Compare *Un Uomo chiamato Apocalisse Joe* and *Dans la Poussière du Soleil* (both below).

The film closely parallels the plot of *Hamlet*. See also entry 338.

665 *O Jogo da Vida e da Morte*
1971. Brazil. Futura Films. Sound, col., 98 mins.
Mario Kuperman.

The title translates as *The Game of Life and Death*. In modern suburban São Paolo, João learns through a spiritual medium that his uncle Claudio has killed his father in an effort to gain control of the city's drug trade. He recreates the circumstances of his father's death in order to get Claudio to reveal his guilt, which he does. Claudio sends João away when he accidentally kills Polonio, the father of Laerte and Ofelia, his girlfriend. In the end, João returns to seek vengeance and confronts Laerte's and Claudio's conspiracy to have him killed.

The film follows Shakespeare's narrative quite faithfully. No direct citations. See also entry 339.

666 *Un Uomo chiamato Apocalisse Joe (Apocalypse Joe)*
1971. Spain and Italy. Copercines, Cooperativa Cinematográfica, Italian International Film, and Transeuropa Film. Sound, col., 90 mins. Leopoldo Savona.

Spaghetti Western adaptation. When Joe Clifford, a touring actor, comes to claim a gold mine he has inherited from his uncle, he discovers that local thug Berg, his uncle's murderer, has seized it. Using both his acting and shooting skills, Clifford avenges his uncle's murder and frees the town and his mine. Compare *Dans la Poussière du Soleil* and *Quella sporca storia del west* (both above).

Throughout the film, Clifford is playing Hamlet.

667 *Dastaan*
1972. India. United Producers. Sound, col., 162 mins.
B. R. Chopra.

A remake of B. R. Chopra's first film, *Asfana* (1951), *Dastaan* uses a version of the mousetrap. See Rajiva Verma, "*Hamlet* on the Hindi Screen." *Hamlet Studies* (2002) 24: 81–93, to 91. See also *Agni Varshna*. (RB)

668 *Dr. Phibes Rises Again*
1972. U.S. American International Pictures. Sound, col., 89 mins. Robert Fuest.

The sequel to *The Abominable Dr. Phibes*. Dr. Phibes's search for a way to resurrect his dead wife takes him to an Egyptian archaeological site, where to procure an elixir of life he ingeniously murders all who get in his way.

Phibes misquotes "Thus conscience makes cowards of us all" as "Conscience makes bedfellows of us all"; he also sardonically quotes the "If music be the food of love" speech from *Twelfth Night*. Compare *Theatre of Blood*.

669 *Everything You Always Wanted to Know about Sex (But Were Afraid to Ask)*
1972. U.S. Rollins-Joffe Productions. Sound, col., 87 mins.
Woody Allen.

Adapted from the book by David Reuben. A series of comedy sketches about sex, linked to various questions taken from Reuben's book.

In the first sketch, "Do aphrodisiacs work?" Allen, as an unfunny court jester, parodies the "To be or not to be" speech from *Hamlet*: "TB or not TB: that is the congestion. / Consumption be done about it? / Of cough, of cough…" After a passing reference to Rosencrantz and Guildenstern, he then sees the ghost of his father, who directs him to seduce the queen.

670 *Un Amleto di meno (One Hamlet Less)*
1973. Italy. Donatello Cinematografica and Ministero del Turismo e dello Spettacolo. Sound, col., 70 mins.
Carmelo Bene.

A parody using elements from Shakespeare's play and Jules Laforgue's story. Hamlet, an aspiring playwright, undergoes Freudian psychoanalysis by Polonius and in the process finds himself tormented by erotic visions of Gertrude and Ophelia.

671 *La nuit américaine (Day for Night)*
1973. France. Les Films du Carrosse, PECF, and PIC.
Sound, col., 115 mins. François Truffaut.

Truffaut's behind-the-scenes comedy-drama about the making of the movie *Meet Pamela*, involving various emotional issues among the cast and technical problems in the filming. Throughout, the director Ferrand maintains a strong and steady hand. Awarded an Oscar for best foreign film in 1973.

Severine, an actress in the film, makes a passing reference to an actor giving the "To be or not to be" soliloquy.

672 *Golden Ophelia*
1974. Belgium. Promofilm and Ministerie van Nederlandse Kultuur. Sound, col., 78 mins. Marcel Martin.

After Stefan Pielek unsuccessfully attempts suicide, the police require him to apply for official authorization to kill himself. As he waits to receive permission for euthanasia, he falls in love with Ophelia, a young woman he accidentally meets, and reconsiders the value of his life.

An interesting reversal of motifs from *Hamlet*: the male character, not Ophelia, is suicidal.

673 *Per amare Ofelia (To Love Ophelia)*
1974. Italy. Diasa P.C., Maya Films, and Zodiac Produzioni. Sound, col., 105 mins. Flavio Mogherini.

An Italian sex comedy. Orlando Mannetti, heir to an industrial fortune, has romance problems with women brought on by his erotic obsession with his mother, Federica. The film's resolution comes when Federica remarries.

Uses an Oedipal understanding of Hamlet's fixation with his mother as the centerpiece of this romantic farce. In this version, the marriage of the Hamlet figure's mother resolves rather than complicates Hamlet's psychological dilemmas, and he ends up marrying his Ophelia. An interesting use of *Hamlet* to reflect upon the arrested relationship between Italian sons and their mothers. No direct verbal citations of Shakespeare's dialogue, though several scenes provide comic echoes of Hamlet's key speeches.

674 *Predstava Hamleta u Mrdusi Donjoj* (*Acting Hamlet in the Village of Mrdusa Donja*)
1974. Yugoslavia. Sound, col., 96 mins. Krsto Papic.

Adapted from Ivo Bresan's play. To boost a village's prestige on the eve of the presidential election, a local commissar mounts a production of *Hamlet*. The casting of the commissar as Claudius and a local man whose father he framed for theft as Hamlet leads to a confrontation in midplay between the men and eventually to the death of the commissar.

675 *Hamlet*
1976. U.K. Essential Productions and Royal College of Art. Sound, col., 65 mins. Celestino Coronada.

Also known as the "Naked Hamlet." A freely adapted psychoanalytic approach to the play using Shakespeare's dialogue, with Hamlet and Laertes handled as schizophrenics (the parts are played by identical twins). Gertrude's eroticism is particularly emphasized; she and Ophelia are played by Helen Mirren, noted Shakespearean actress.

676 *Hamlet*
1977. Brazil. Production company unknown. Sound, b&w, length unknown. Jose Rubens Sigueira.

Animated adaptation. Other information unavailable.

677 *Intikam Melegi: Kadin Hamlet* (*Angel of Vengeance: The Female Hamlet*)
1977. Turkey. Ugur Film. Sound, col., 85 mins. Metin Erksan.

A contemporary dress adaptation, with a female Hamlet (played by Turkish film star Fatma Girik, often in male dress). The narrative follows Shakespeare's relatively faithfully, though scenes are rearranged (the film opens with Claudius shooting old Ahmet with a hunting rifle) and the action is often radically compressed (there is no Fortinbras subplot, and Orhan, Hamlet's boyfriend, abruptly dies without explanation by drowning in a pond). The production emphasizes Hamlet's feigned madness, making use of it to create several visually bizarre scenarios—Hamlet appears in a bandleader's costume and douses Orhan's painting with red paint; she confronts her uncle and mother with mirrors while dressed in a Roman centurion's helmet; she lounges in a bedroom set up in the woods to confuse and taunt Polonius; and her confrontation with Orhan ending their relationship occurs after she directs a group of hanging musical instruments in a concert from a tape recorder. A much overused fisheye lens also adds to the impression of distorted perceptions, as does the

strange musical score, which ranges from excerpts from Shostakovich to vapid disco. When the women Rosencrantz and Guildenstern take Hamlet from the court, they go to sunbathe at the beach, where Hamlet discovers a letter packing him off to America. Many of Hamlet's speeches are delivered from on a lookout tower while she paces or directly to the camera; shots of Hamlet pacing behind bars occur several times, a visual evocation of his observation that "Denmark's a prison." The final duel becomes a fight with hunting rifles—Laertes shoots Hamlet; Claudius mistakenly shoots Gertrude, thinking she is Hamlet; and Hamlet shoots Laertes and Claudius after being shot herself. The final shot is of Hamlet destroying the rifle range targets on Claudius's estate. Though the production is apparently intended to be straight, it plays as high camp. See also entry 341.

678 *Julia*
1977. U.S. 20th Century Fox. Sound, col., 116 mins. Fred Zinnemann.

Adapted from the memoir *Pentimento* by Lillian Hellman. Julia, a rich idealistic woman who is part of the Resistance movement in Nazi Germany, asks her lifelong friend Lillian Hellman, an aspiring playwright, to smuggle money from Vienna to Berlin to combat the Nazis. Julia is murdered, and Lillian searches for her daughter Lili, who she promised to care for.

In Warsaw, Lillian sees a Polish performance of *Hamlet*; shown is an excerpt from Hamlet's "Alas, poor Yorick" speech. Intercut with the performance (though which Lillian is drowsing) is a film montage of Julia being murdered by Nazis. The film also references Robert Herrick's "Upon Julia's Clothes," which Julia recites, applying it to herself.

679 *The Ninth Configuration*
1979. U.S. Ninth Configuration Company. Sound, col., 109 mins. William Peter Blatty.

Adapted from William Peter Blatty's novel *Twinkle Twinkle Little Kane*. This surrealistic cult film—Blatty has called it a "metaphysical mystery"—details how Colonel Vincent Kane, a Marine psychologist who is himself psychologically unsteady, attempts to address the psychoses of his patients, all Vietnam veterans, in a military mental hospital in an old gothic castle. Late in the film, we learn that the psychologist Kane is in fact "Killer" Kane, a man who committed atrocities in Vietnam and who in his mind created for himself an alternative identity as a psychologist to deal with his guilt; when he discovers who he really is, he commits suicide. Often reminiscent in style of Sam Fuller's *Shock Corridor* (1963).

One mad patient, Lieutenant Frankie Reno, claims that he is planning a performance of *Julius Caesar* using dogs; there are several comic references to the casting of his dog production of *Hamlet*. At one point Reno and Kane discuss whether Hamlet is genuinely mad or merely pretending. Reno claims that if Hamlet hadn't pretended to be crazy, he would be mad in reality. This conversation points to Kane's true identity and the reason for his pretense. In another scene, Major Nammack wants to play Superman in Reno's *Julius Caesar*, swooping down to save Caesar from assassination.

DVD includes a director's commentary and outtakes that reference Shakespeare.

680 *Willie and Phil*
1980. U.S. 20th Century Fox. Sound, col., 115 mins. Paul Mazursky.

Phil D'Amico, an Italian American photographer who wants to be an intellectual, and Willie Kaufman, a Jewish teacher who wants to be a jazz pianist, meet at a showing of Truffaut's *Jules et Jim* and become friends. When they meet Jeanette Sutherland, a Southerner transplanted to New York City, Willie and Jeanette move in together (a decision made on the flip of a coin), and a romantic triangle is established that lasts for nine years.

This remake of *Jules et Jim* uses Truffaut's film to offer a portrait of various cultural lifestyles and indecision between them that characterized the American 1970s. Willie's difficulty with the direction of his life is established by a discussion of *Hamlet* he conducts in his class. In answer to his question "Why does Hamlet procrastinate?" Wilson, a student, answers that Hamlet is sexually unfulfilled and makes the application to Willie. He then proceeds to deliver Hamlet's "To be or not to be" soliloquy in a British accent. Laurence Fishburne plays Wilson; he went on to star fifteen years later in Parker's *Othello* (1995). One passing allusion: when Phil tries to laud Shakespeare, Willie praises Shakespeare for having "a terrific head for real estate investments."

681 *Mephisto*
1981. West Germany, Hungary, and Austria. Mafilm, Manfred Durniok Filmproduktion, and Objektiv Studio. Sound, col., 144 mins. István Szabó.

Adapted from the novel by Klaus Mann. Hendrik Hofgen, an amoral, self-absorbed actor, sells out to the propaganda machine of the Nazis in exchange for fame and creature comforts, ignoring the suffering of those around him.

One of Hofgen's pet projects is a production of *Hamlet*, excerpts of which are shown.

682 *Act V*
1982. U.K. Miller Productions. Sound, col., length unknown. John C. Miller.

Animated film based upon the gravedigger scene from *Hamlet*, set on a bleak heath. The dialogue corresponds to Shakespeare's, though the emphasis is on the comedy of the scene. Its loose animation style may be fruitfully compared to John Canemaker's *Bottom's Dream*.

683 *Fanny och Alexander* (*Fanny and Alexander*)
1982. Sweden, France, and West Germany. Cinema AB, Persona Films, Sandrew Film & Teater, SVT 1, Swedish Film Institute, Swedish Film Production, and Tobis Filmkunst. Sound, col., 188 mins. Ingmar Bergman.

A semiautobiographical portrait of Bergman's youth, shown through the fictional lives of the Ekdahl family, seen from the perspective of siblings Alexander and Fanny. After a joy-filled family Christmas celebration, their beloved father Oskar dies, and mother Emilie marries Bishop Edvard Vergerus, an austere, distant minister. When the bishop refuses to give Emilie a divorce, the children are rescued from their bleak existence by their uncle Isak and grandmother Helena, and afterward the bishop dies.

The circumstances of Oskar's death—he becomes forgetful and disoriented while rehearsing the part of Hamlet's ghost at the family theater, and is dead soon thereafter, all while being watched by Alexander, his son—announces a *Hamlet* subtext that runs throughout the film. Emilie's remarriage to the cruel and distant Edvard resembles Gertrude's marriage to Claudius, and Alexander, like Hamlet, remains bitterly alienated from the couple. Oskar's ghost returns several times to express his concern for the children and, in a departure from the *Hamlet* template, even has a long conversation with Helena when she awakes from a dream. (The speech she gives, about the roles she has played in her life, has affinities with Jaques's "All the world's a stage" soliloquy.) The ghost theme is linked to the cinema itself by a magic lantern show about a ghost Alexander gives to his siblings early in the film. At one point when Alexander is despondent about his change of life, Emilie tells him not to play Hamlet and denies that the situation resembles that of Shakespeare's play. There is an oblique Ophelia reference as well: a servant tells the story of Vergerus's first wife who, in seeking to save her children, was dragged under by the swirling water next to Vergerus's residence.

DVD (Criterion Collection) includes a commentary track by Bergman biographer Peter Cowie that references Shakespeare.

684 *Hamlet Act*
1982. U.S. University of Wisconsin–Milwaukee Film Group. Sound, col., 20 mins. Robert Nelson.

Written by Joseph Chang. For more information about this independent avant-garde film, see Jane Gallop, "Beyond the Mirror," *Wide Angle* 7, nos. 1–2 (1985).

685 *The Vals*
1982. U.S. Lion's Gate. Sound, col., 99 mins. James Polakof.

The film opens with a close-up of a skull. The camera pulls back and reveals a high school student, Samantha Simms (Jill Carroll). She is wearing a cape, and holding the skull as she recites from *Hamlet*:

Alas, poor Yorick . . . as a fellow of infinite jest, of most excellent fancy. He hath borne me on his back a thousand times. (5.1.77)

The other students in class, mostly females in private school uniform, mock her in Valleyspeak. Their teacher (Ray Stewart) reprimands them, and Trish continues,

And now how abhorred my imagination it is, like, my gorge just rises at it. Here hung those lips that I have kiss, that I, like, know not how, like . . . oh my God, like, gag me with a spoon! Like, this guy doesn't even have any lips! It's like barfing me out.

The teacher asks her to continue, but she refuses, putting the cape on him and handing him the skull. He wraps the cape around himself, saying, "No one interrupts Shakespeare!" He continues where Trish left off:

Where be your gibes now, your gambols, your songs, your flashes of merriment, that were wont to set the table on a roar? *[The students laugh at him, and begin to file out of the classroom. He is too caught up in his performance and does not notice.]*
Not one now, to mock your own grinning? Quite chopfallen? Now get you to my lady's chamber, and tell her, let her paint an inch thick, to this favour she must come. Make her laugh at that. *[He laughs and looks up, noticing for the first time all the students are gone. He drops the skull, and it breaks into many pieces.]*

The plot focuses on four Valley girls who, in the midst of their own mindless frat parties, sexual intrigues, and shopping, notice a small black boy who seems to be selling drugs. They follow him home, and find he lives in an orphanage run by the wheelchair-bound Mr. Stanton (John Carradine). Stanton informs them he needs $25,000 in the next five days to keep the orphanage open. The girls resolve to get the money so that the orphanage can stay open and the little boy can stop selling drugs. Their convoluted plan involves making a deal with a drug kingpin to supply him with cocaine, which their frat boyfriends will make synthetically. All ends happily. Chuck Conners, portraying one of the girls' wife-swapping, coke-snorting fathers and a TV producer, tells his complaining star, Sue Ann Langdon, to stop complaining because "This isn't Shakespeare, you know!" (EL)

686 *Private Teacher*
1983. U.S. Caballero Home Video. Sound, col., 85 mins. Gary Graver (aka Robert McCallum).

Hardcore pornography. Aunt Diane becomes concerned that her reclusive nephew Jimmy is spending too much time alone and hires a private psychoanalyst to discover his problem. When the psychoanalyst learns that Jimmy has secretly been ogling two women neighbors, she seduces him.

As she seduces Jimmy, the teacher recites the entirety of Hamlet's speech to the players. When she leaves, she re-

cites the Ghost's speech to Hamlet and directs it to Jimmy, ending with "Remember me."

687 *Strange Brew*
1983. U.S. MGM and United Artists. Sound, col., 90 mins. Dave Thomas and Rick Moranis.

In this comedy featuring Bob and Doug McKenzie, the beer-swilling Canadian duo from *Second City Television*, the two discover that Smith, an evil psychologist posing as a brewmaster at the Elsinore brewery, is secretly adding a drug to beer that will allow him to control drinkers. With the help of Pamela Elsinore, they foil his scheme.

The film contains many throwaway parodic allusions to *Hamlet*. In the film's exposition, we learn that Claude Elsinore has killed his brother John and married his wife Gertrude; Pamela, John's daughter, arrives Hamlet-like from university to claim her legacy—control of the brewing company—but is blocked by Claude (who is in turn controlled by Smith). The brewery itself is, preposterously, a castle in a Canadian suburb. Bob and Doug serve as a comically clueless Rosencrantz and Guildenstern; at one point in the film, they are in the employ of the brewery. John, whom Claude killed by electrocuting him, periodically appears in video form to warn Pamela, Bob, and Doug of Smith's plans. Claude (and Smith) seek to kill Pamela (and Bob and Doug), just as Claudius seeks to kill Hamlet, and in an oblique reference to Hamlet's madness, Pamela ends up at one point in a lunatic asylum. Henry, the old brewmaster at Elsinore, functions as Pamela's Horatio, her confidante. No direct verbal citations. None of the parodic elements are developed in any consistent way, nor are they necessary to the plot or thematically relevant. They provide a good example of purely decorative Shakespearean allusion, grafted onto the conventional, if comically handled, plot of a thriller involving a mad scientist.

688 *To Be or Not to Be*
1983. U.S. 20th Century Gox and Brooksfilms, Ltd. Sound, col., 107 mins. Alan Johnson.

A fairly faithful (though ill-considered) remake of the 1942 Ernst Lubitsch film of the same name. See summary for *To Be or Not to Be* (1942, above).

689 *Nightmare on Elm Street 4*
1984. U.S. New Line Cinema, Heron Communications, and Smart Egg Pictures. Sound, col., 97 mins. Wes Craven.
Classroom scene with *Hamlet*. See *Soul Survivor*.

690 *Secret Honor*
1984. U.S. Sandcastle 5 Productions. Sound, col., 90 mins. Robert Altman.

A tour-de-force film monologue of a fictionalized Richard Nixon. As he ostensibly dictates his rambling thoughts to a tape recorder for posterity, he surveys his political career and offers his reasons for resignation. At one point, as he reflects with bitterness on his marginal place in the Eisenhower administration, Nixon launches into a rendition of "To be or not to be."

691 *Ofelia kommer til byen* (*Hamlet Comes to Town*)
1985. Denmark. Danish Film Institute, Palle Fogtdal A/S, and Per Holst Filmproduktion. Jon Bang Carlsen.

A prostitute fleeing from a homicidal client, Molly seeks refuge in a small fishing village that is putting on a production of *Hamlet*. As they rehearse, John, the local gravedigger who is tapped to play Hamlet, falls in love with Molly, who is playing Ophelia. Eventually Molly's client discovers her in the village, and she must act to protect John and the villagers.

692 *Blue City*
1986. U.S. Paramount. Sound, col., 83 mins. Michelle Manning.

Adapted from the thriller by Russ Macdonald. Rough-and-tumble son Billy Turner returns to his Florida hometown, Blue City, to discover that his father J. T., the mayor, has been killed, and that his stepmother Malvina has taken up with Perry Kerch, a ne'er-do-well from Miami. When Billy gets out of jail for brawling, he enlists the help of Annie Rayford and her brother Joey, an old friend, to discover his father's murderer. He begins a campaign of harassment against Perry that leads to his being sent away from Blue City. But when he learns that Joey has been killed, he returns to wreak vengeance on Perry and Malvina, only to find out that the chief of police, Luther Reynolds, is the real murderer of his father.

This otherwise quite conventional B thriller is enlivened by a *Hamlet* subtext. Billy's initial situation resembles that of Hamlet, in that he returns to his home to discover that his father has been murdered and his stepmother has started a relationship with the man who has usurped his father's wealth and local power, the man who Billy suspects is his father's killer. Other details reinforce the *Hamlet* parallel: J. T. Turner is remembered as a virtuous mayor; Billy engages in behavior that others label as "crazy" but that is in fact crafty; Billy's long-standing friend Joey becomes, like Horatio, his confidante and co-conspirator against Perry; Billy accuses his mother Malvina of sexual promiscuity; and Billy is sent away from Blue City after his behavior leads to the death of someone involved in the conspiracy, Debbie Torres. But in many respects the film departs significantly from its Shakespearean forebear. Billy's girlfriend, Annie Rayford, a potential Ophelia figure, is far more plucky and clear-headed than her Shakespearean counterpart; indeed it is Joey, not Annie, who dies a watery death, and Annie functions much like a female Horatio, even going undercover to aid Billy's investigation. Also, we learn that Perry and Malvina Kerch were in fact married before Malvina was involved with Billy's father—Malvina's romance with J. T. was, in reality, a scam to get control of J. T.'s money.

And, most important, Billy's Hamlet-like assumption that Perry killed his father and married his mother was erroneous. In fact, it is Luther Reynolds, a local policeman J. T. had mentored, who is revealed to be the killer, having become greedy after tasting the mayor's kindness. The resemblances to *Hamlet* work, in other words, to mislead both Billy and the viewer about the identity of the mayor's killer and to magnify the surprise at film's end.

693 *Withnail & I*
1986. U.K. Cineplex Odeon Films and Handmade Films. Sound, col., 107 mins. Bruce Robinson.

In this very black comedy, two down-on-their-luck actors from Camden Town, the selfish, preening coward Withnail and his roommate, the naïve Marwood ("I"), go to Withnail's gay Uncle Monty's country cabin in Penrith for a holiday from hell and find themselves as miserable as ever. When Monty arrives, Withnail, fearful of his intentions, becomes increasingly desperate to leave; when he returns to London and gets a leading role, Marwood leaves Withnail.

When Withnail and "I" first meet Monty, Withnail lies about his agent encouraging him to join the Royal Shakespeare Company, a comment that leads Monty into a reverie about his past as an actor. Monty observes that a turning point was when he realized he'd never play "the Dane," and he launches into Marcellus's "We do it wrong" speech after the Ghost leaves in *Hamlet* 1.1. At film's end, when I's departure leaves Withnail alone, he performs Hamlet's "I have of late—but wherefore I know not—lost all my mirth" speech in the rain for wolves at the zoo. The reference adds an element of poignancy to Withnail's increasingly desperate circumstances as well as for the waning 1960s, whose spirit he represents.

694 *Hamlet liikemaailmassa* (*Hamlet Goes Business*)
1987. Finland. Villealfa Filmproduction Oy. Sound, b&w, 86 mins. Aki Kaurismäki.

A deadpan parodic modernization of *Hamlet*. Klaus and Gertrud poison Old Hamlet, a businessman who owns a timber and mining company. Soon after his funeral the two get married and Klaus takes control of the company, much to Hamlet's disapproval. Hamlet discovers that Klaus intends to sell parts of the company to Wallenberg, another businessman, and shift production to rubber ducks, and his father ghost tells him of his murder, which was covered over by a rigged inquest. Lauri, the brother of Hamlet's girlfriend Ofelia, quarrels with Hamlet over offices and leaves to study in Stockholm. When Klaus presents the deal with Wallenberg to the company board, Hamlet, who owns the majority of the company, blocks the changes. Hamlet reveals to Simo, his limousine driver, his intention to pretend to be mad, and Klaus watches Hamlet's antics with Polonius, Klaus's assistant, on a surveillance camera. Meanwhile, Hamlet repeatedly attempts to seduce Ofelia, but she refuses his advances. Hamlet invites Klaus and Gertrud to the theater, where the poisoning of Old Hamlet is re-enacted and Klaus is exposed. Hamlet uses a gun to confront Klaus (he is interrupted by Helena, Simo's girlfriend) and then to kill Polonius as he confronts his mother. Klaus arranges for Hamlet to take a business trip and sends corporate thugs Rosencranz and Guildenstern to kill him, but Hamlet kills them first. Ofelia, having been rejected by Hamlet for keeping him at bay, drowns herself in her bathtub. Klaus and Lauri attempt to use a plate of poisoned chicken to kill Hamlet, but because of Helena's mistake, Gertrud eats some of it and dies. In Hamlet's final confrontation with Klaus, he kills Lauri with a radio and shoots Klaus, placing the gun in Lauri's hand to implicate him. Afterward, Hamlet confesses to Simo that he gave the fatal dose of poison to Old Hamlet and that he truly loved Ofelia. Simo poisons Hamlet, and he and Helena lock up the Hamlet estate and leave.

Kaurismäki's black comic update of *Hamlet* takes the play into the realm of corporate film noir, in which the machinations of the corrupt court of Elsinore are transformed into cynical and sinister power politics in a family corporation. The film follows Shakespeare's narrative relatively closely throughout, making its only major change at the narrative's end. Though at first glance Wallenberg seems the adaptation's Fortinbras, in fact that function is served by Simo, the working-class limousine driver and union man, who, with his girlfriend, are the only ones left standing at film's end, inheriting and freeing the pathetic tethered puppy who is the only true spoil. Many of Shakespeare's scenes and speeches have counterparts in Kaurismäki's adaptation, though often with off-kilter comic twists: Hamlet's ghost speaks of having a vacation from hell when he confronts his son, and he never speaks of revenge; in his leave-taking advice to his son Lauri, Polonius advises him not to pay back loans too quickly, and he suggests to Ofelia that she resist Hamlet's advances until he marries her because divorce would cost Hamlet dearly; Hamlet reads comic books when playing the melancholic madman; and Hamlet's extra lines in the play-within-the-film are clumsily clipped into a conventional play. Kaurismäki's musical choices—often rock-and-roll songs are sardonically juxtaposed with the action—also deflate the narrative. His parody operates in several directions at once. The film lampoons *Hamlet*, turning Hamlet's moral and psychological dilemma of revenge into a goofy melodrama of corporate backstabbing and sexual frustration; Hamlet gradually emerges from the film not as an existential hero but as a bloated, contemptible corporate climber, hardly distinguishable from his enemies. The film also burlesques the visual and narrative conventions of film noir, filming the often preposterous action in comically portentous deep shadows (punctuated by melodramatic rising music) and providing us with a sardonic surprise ending; for example,

Kaurismäki typically photographs only the shoes of Klaus's henchmen, Rosencranz and Guildenstern, as they walk to do their dirty work, a cliché of noir. But most of all, Kaurismäki seeks to skewer modern corporate capitalism. Set against the heroic qualities of Shakespeare's *Hamlet*, the behavior of Kaurismäki's characters is at every turn sordid, petty, and blackly comic, and it is appropriate if ironic that working-class Simo and Helena triumph over them in the end.

695 *Maitasun Arina*
1987. Spain. Sound, col., 11 mins. Juan Luis Mendiaraz.

An inmate escapes from prison during a production of *Hamlet*, but the actor finds himself hiding out in a boutique named "Ofelia." A Basque film subsidized by the local Ministry of Culture.

696 *Outrageous Fortune*
1987. U.S. Buena Vista, Interscope Communications, and Touchstone Pictures. Sound, col., 100 mins. Arthur Hiller.

Two struggling actresses, Lauren Ames and Sandy Brozinsky, dislike each other when they learn they are dating the same man, Michael, who they soon discover is a foreign spy. When they unwittingly undermine his plans to stage his death and disappear, he implicates them in his schemes, and they must outrun him and the law.

Lauren dreams of starring in Shakespeare's *Hamlet*. Early in the film, she performs "To be or not to be" with vowels only; at film's end, we see excerpts of a triumphant stage production with Lauren as Hamlet and Sandy as Ophelia. See also entry 2705.

697 *Iskanderija, kaman oue kaman (Alexandria Again and Forever)*
1989. I Misr International Films/Paris Classics. Sound, col., 105 mins. Youseff Chahine.

An autobiographical yet fictional film about a failed making of a film on Alexander the Great. *Hamlet* also figures centrally, and in one scene the director, Yehia (Chahine's on-screen alter ego) talks about seeing John Gielgud's *Hamlet* as the camera focus on a photograph still of Gielgud. (RB)

698 *Highlander II: The Quickening*
1990. U.S. Davis-Panzer and Lamb Bear Entertainment. Sound, col., 109 mins. Russell Mulcahy.

The much-reviled sequel to the cult film *Highlander*. In 2024, Connor MacLeod, having saved the earth from the depletion of its ozone layer by devising a giant shield, recalls his part forty years earlier in an attempted coup against dictator Katana on his home planet Zeist. When Katana sends assassins into the future to kill MacLeod, he kills them and becomes immortal again. With the help of scientist Louise Marcus, MacLeod then confronts an evil corporate boss, David Blake, who wants to maintain the shield even though it is now useless. Eventually MacLeod battles Katana himself, who teams up with, then betrays, Blake. Juan Ramirez, MacLeod's partner in the coup against Katana, appears to help him.

When Ramirez first appears in the future to help Mac-Leod, he materializes in the midst of an arena performance of the "Alas, poor Yorick" sequence of *Hamlet* 5.1. Not realizing that he is ruining a play, Ramirez exchanges some homophobic banter with Hamlet about his over-attachment to his friend Yorick. Soon after, Ramirez picks up a sword and leaves the stage, getting a round of enthusiastic applause for his "performance." The scene has little to do with the remainder of the film other than, like the film's references to Wagner's *Götterdämmerung*, to give the gothic production design a classic quality and to establish that Ramirez and MacLeod's close relationship is, unlike Hamlet and Yorick's, strictly straight.

699 *Rosencrantz and Guildenstern Are Dead*
1990. U.K. and U.S. Brandenberg, and WNET Channel 13. New York. Sound, col., 117 mins. Tom Stoppard.

Adapted from Stoppard's 1966 play of the same title. Summoned to Elsinore, Rosencrantz and Guildenstern are unable to understand the machinations of the court or Hamlet's strange behavior, and they accordingly ponder their own pre-determined destinies as characters fated to die. Along the way, they meet a traveling band of players who reflect upon the nature of theater and the ironies of fate.

Stoppard directed this film adaptation of his much-admired absurdist rewrite of *Hamlet*. Though the production is handled with great wit by principal actors Gary Oldman, Tim Roth, and Richard Dreyfuss, the metatheatricality of the original play is lost in its transfer to film, with no cinematic equivalences to take its place.

700 *The Voice-Over Queen*
1990. U.S. Alyse & Her Big Ideas Inc. Sound, col., 12 mins. Alyse Rosenberg.

Naomi Strutsky, a voice-over actress with particular talent for imitating household appliances in commercials, is dispirited by her lack of recognition as a artist. She recites "To be or not to be" to a room of appreciative appliances as compensation for failing an audition for *Hamlet*. A showcase for the vocal virtuosity of Joan La Barbara, avant-garde classical vocalist.

In addition to "To be or not to be," the film includes a passing reference to "Out, out, damned spot" from *Macbeth*.

701 *JFK*
1991. U.S. Alcor Films, Canal Plus, Ixtlan Corporation, Regency Enterprises, and Warner Brothers. Sound, col. and b&w, 189 mins. (director's cut is 206 mins.). Oliver Stone.

Adapted from the books *Crossfire* by Jim Marrs and *On the Trail of the Assassins* by Jim Garrison. A fictional account of the conspiracy involving John F. Kennedy's assassina-tion, using the investigations of Jim Garrison, New Orleans district attorney, and the trial he subsequently conducted, as its centerpieces.

Jim Garrison cites, "One may smile and smile and be a villain" (*Hamlet* 1.5) when he first interviews conspiracy suspect Clay Shaw. Garrison returns to *Hamlet* in his summation speech at Shaw's trial when he makes this analogy: "We've all become Hamlets in our country, children of a slain father-king whose killers still possess the throne. The ghost of John F. Kennedy confronts us with the secret murder at the heart of the American dream." Referencing Hamlet's phrase "shuffled off this mortal coil" in passing, Garrison closes his speech with this appeal: "Do not forget your dying king," reminiscent of the Ghost's "remember me." Stone's characterization of Garrison as a tenacious man obsessed with the death of Kennedy and the corruption of the government accords with Shakespeare's Hamlet. Two other citations appear: to "Brutus and Cassius, they too are honourable men" (Antony's funeral speech for Caesar in *Julius Caesar* 3.2), and "What's past is prologue" (the film's closing epigraph, taken from *The Tempest* 2.1).

DVD (special edition) includes a commentary track by Oliver Stone that references *Hamlet*.

702 *LA Story*
1991. U.S. Carolco Pictures, IndieProd, LA Films, and TriStar. Sound, col., 95 mins. Mick Jackson.

In this partly whimsical, partly satirical portrait of Los Angeles, weatherman Harris Telemacher enjoys roller-skating in museums and celebrity status until he is fired and breaks up with his longtime girlfriend Trudi, who, he learns, has been having an affair with his agent. Taking advice from a roadway sign to rethink his vacant existence, he temporarily takes up with SanDeE, a silly Valley girl, but soon falls in love with Sara McDowel, an eccentric British journalist who interviews him for a feature on life in Los Angeles.

Telemacher and Sara encounter a gravedigger at the grave of William Shakespeare in Los Angeles; the dialogue of this scene is a lightly modernized version of Hamlet's encounter with the gravedigger in *Hamlet* 5.1. Telemacher quips that it was in Los Angeles that Shakespeare wrote *Hamlet, Part 8: The Revenge*. Telemacher twice quotes Shakespeare: first, he cites John of Gaunt's speech about "This other Eden" (*Richard* 2.2.1), substituting "this Los Angeles" for "this England"; and second, he recalls "something else Shakespeare said: 'Hey, life is pretty stupid. Lots of hubbub to keep you busy, but really not amounting to much.' Of course, I'm paraphrasing" (the paraphrase is of Macbeth's "Tomorrow and tomorrow and tomorrow" speech, *Macbeth* 5.5). After a magical tempest prevents Sara's plan of leaving Los Angeles, the road sign quotes Hamlet, "There are more things N heaven and earth Harris, / Than are dreamt of N your philosophy" (*Hamlet*

1.5). Appropriately, we learn early in the film that Telemacher has a college degree in arts and humanities. Some commentators have claimed that one sequence, in which Telemacher and Sara visit a resort with different partners, resembles the Athenian wood section of A Midsummer Night's Dream, in which two couples exchange lovers.

703 *The Stranger Aguntak (The Stranger)*
1991. India. CEG Worldwide. Sound, col., 120 mins. Satyajit Ray.

The Stranger is divided in two parts, one largely confined to the living room and bedrooms of the niece's house, and the second taking place outside after the uncle, Manomohan, has left so as not to be thought a fortune hunter. The film deconstructs these oppositions, so that everyone is in the end a stranger, if not foreigner. The collapse of inside and outside is marked through a collapse of media. Little happens dramatically in the film, and in both halves conversation predominates. The interior spaces are shot very much as if the film were an adapted play; one character is an actor, and there is even a play-within-the-film element. Though the second part takes place outside, it is shot in a similarly static and stagey way, and we see Indian dancers in the background.

Shakespeare is mentioned in two conversational scenes in both parts of *The Stranger*. In the first, the uncle; the niece, Anila Bose; and her husband Sudhindra Bose's (Depankar De) friend are in their living room, and the uncle sees that they have set a kind of *Hamlet*-like mousetrap for him. A character who is a professional actor, Ranjan Rakshit (Robi Ghosh), tests the uncle at the husband's request in order to find out if he is the real thing or just an impersonator. The uncle sees through the trap and embarrasses the husband and wife by simply asking Rakshit how he finds him. Manomohan outs him and declares about his status, "It's full of the stuff of drama. Suspense, suspicion [both words are in English], conflict. To be or not to be the uncle? [the last sentence is in English]" Manomohan asks, laughing.

The second scene of the film involving Shakespeare is a harsh replay of the first "mousetrap" scene. This time, a friend of the husband's named Prithwish Sen Gupta (Dhritiman Chatterjee) acts as a prosecutor who grills Manomohan in a failed attempt to determine if the uncle is an impersonator or not. The conversation turns to the theme of barbarism versus civilization, with Prithwish defending civilization against the kinds of backward savagery he sees Manomohan perversely defending. Manomohan says that he wishes he could be a savage, but his education has prevented him from ever reaching his goal: "I've Shakespeare, Marx, Freud, and Tagore [the very authors Ray himself read and acknowledged as key influences] in my bloodstream. That's why I cannot do without field notes (He smile ruefully.) I wouldn't need them, would I, if

I were a savage?" Prithwish counters by asking him if he has ever eaten human flesh, and he says he hasn't, regretfully because he hears it is very tasty, but he then concedes that cannibalism is barbaric. Feeling pressured, Manomohan continues, in Montaignian fashion, by saying in a more conventionally ironic mode, that what is really "civilized" is "the man who by using his thumb presses a button that releases a weapon that liberates a city with its entire inhabitants, without turning a hair." The scene ends with Prithwish losing his composure and telling the uncle to "come clean" with the truth or "clear out."

The Stranger is an arguably regressive film in that it appears to cave into the very simplistic and self-defeating myths of decline that Ray had thus far resisted, even as *The Stranger* takes an even more marked European, specifically French, perspective. *Days and Nights* has often been compared to Jean Renoir's films, and it was made just after Ray had worked with Renoir. *The Stranger* was an Indo-French production, and though it did not do well in India, it was a top grosser in Paris. The plot of *The Stranger*, in which a long-lost uncle returns from abroad after leaving many years earlier to visit his niece but is suspected by her husband of trying to gain half of her inheritance, resembles the plot of *Le Retour de Martin Guerre*. This film was perhaps an influence on Ray given that Gerard Depardieu had played Guerre in the French film (Daniel Vignes, 1982), and was a co-producer of *The Stranger* as well as of Ray's previous film, *Shakha Prashaka* (*Branches of a Tree*, 1990), also an Indo-French production. The film also brings to mind Claude Lévi-Strauss's *Tristes Tropique*, particularly "The Writing Lesson" chapter, as the uncle is an anthropologist who has studied forty-three different tribes in Brazil. His pen name is "Nemo," which the husband identifies as Jules Verne's Captain Nemo, and the uncle translates from the Latin as "no one." Perhaps Utpal Dutt, who plays the uncle Manomohan Mitra, functions in *The Stranger* as a kind of alter ego for Ray, who died the year after he finished the film. Dutt had a similarly deep investment in France. In Dutt's own film *Jhor* (1979), the significance of *Romeo and Juliet* pales besides that of the French Revolution, whose ideals are taught to Dakshina and his fellow college students by their teacher Derozio (Ujjwal Sengupta), who also has them read Voltaire and Rousseau, and in *The Stranger* there is a shift back to a kind of simplistic decline narrative signaled by the uncle's resistance to modern media.

The threat to India posed in *The Stranger* is not Western globalization and mass media but the more general threat of civilization per se to humanity. The film recycles a Montaigne-like "noble savage" critique of India itself, now regarded as the site not of untamed savagery but of civilization itself, with all its glaring contradictions and barbarisms. Ray contrasts humanizing and international Western high culture to Westernization as dehumanizing globalization. Globalization undoes identity and creates a sense of estrangement and homelessness in general, and is not something imposed on India by the West. Ray's film registers his inability to redeem homelessness as global cosmopolitanism. (RB)

704 *Noises Off*
1992. U.S. Amblin Entertainment, Buena Vista, Touchstone Pacific Partners I, and Touchstone Pictures. Sound, col., 101 mins. Peter Bogdonovich.

Adapted from the play by Michael Frayn, with the action transposed from London to Des Moines. Director Lloyd Fellowes guides a misfit cast through a technical rehearsal of *Nothing On*, a classic British sex farce. When the cast performs the play in Miami and Cleveland, however, their various tics, obsessions, and romantic rivalries destroy the play and lead to increasingly disastrous performances. When the play premières in New York, the cast pulls together to create a hit.

While the cast has taken the play on the road, Fellowes is directing a production of *Hamlet* in New York. When he returns to help with the Miami performance, he talks about his problems with various characters in his Shakespeare production. Fellowes's last line is "But then what did Shakespeare say?" at which the song "There's no business like show business" plays.

705 *The Last Action Hero*
1993. U.S. Columbia Pictures and Oak Productions. Sound, col. and b&w, 130 mins. John McTiernan.

Danny Madigan, a devoted fan of the action films of Jack Slater, is drawn by a magical ticket into Slater's fictional movie world, where Slater's victory over master villain Benedict is guaranteed by the rules of the genre. When Benedict uses Danny's ticket to travel into the real world, Slater and Danny follow, and Slater must battle Benedict according to very different rules, lest Slater actually be killed. Eventually Slater has a showdown with Benedict on a rainy rooftop, with Danny in peril. When Jack is wounded, Danny returns him to the fictional world so that he will not die.

This post-modern adaptation of an action film features a sequence that deftly parodies both Arnold Schwarzenegger's action hero persona and Laurence Olivier's film *Hamlet* (see entry 330). In Danny's English class, his teacher (played by Olivier's wife, Joan Plowright) shows the class a clip from Olivier's film *Hamlet* in an effort to convince them that Hamlet is "the first action hero." The clip features Hamlet's hesitation in killing Claudius (*Hamlet* 3.3). Danny, dissatisfied, then imagines the trailer for an alternative version of the same scene, in which Hamlet, now played by Jack Slater (Arnold Schwarzenegger), mercilessly kills Claudius, Polonius, and several guards before destroying Elsinore castle with a bomb. The sequence features turns on several Shakespearean commonplaces—Hamlet holding Yorick's skull in the graveyard,

"To be or not to be," and "Good night, sweet prince"—as well as increasingly over-the-top violence. The sequence is shot in Olivier's brooding film noir style in period setting and costume (though Hamlet anachronistically sports a cigar and a machine gun).

706 *Trauma*
1993. Overseas Film Group. Sound, col., 106 mins. Dario Argento.

The hero sees a copy of Edward Millais's painting of Ophelia drowning in a store window, which mirrors the drowning of a young woman in the film. (RB)

707 *The Lion King*
1994. U.S. Walt Disney Pictures. Sound, col., 89 mins. Robert Allers and Rob Minkoff.

This animated feature film concerns the adolescence and eventual adulthood of a lion cub, Simba, heir to King Mufasa, his lion father. Simba's evil uncle Scar treacherously murders Mufasa and exiles Simba to the jungle, where he is befriended by Pumbaa the warthog and Timon the meerkat. Urged on by his betrothed Nala, Rafiki the baboon, and the spirit of his dead father, Simba eventually returns to Pride Rock, confronts Scar, and reclaims his throne.

Though by no means a thoroughgoing version of *Hamlet*, *The Lion King* includes several motifs freely adapted from Shakespeare's narrative: the murder of the father-king and usurpation of his kingdom by his uncle, the exile of the murdered king's son, the duty to "remember" urged by the spirit of the murdered father-king, Rosencrantz and Guildenstern henchmen who aid the usurper (here rendered as a comic trio of hyenas), and even a romance between the prince and a young female (Nala). The panorama of the ruined kingdom of Pride Rock to which Simba returns might be said to be a visual analogue to Hamlet's "Something is rotten in the state of Denmark." Whereas Hamlet's hesitation to confront his uncle springs from self-doubt (among much else), Simba's springs from his guilt for the death of his father (for which, we know, he is not responsible). It is possible to see passing parallels to other Shakespearean plays in addition to *Hamlet*: Simba's adolescent idyll in the jungle with Timon and Pumbaa, guided by their hedonistic philosophy of "hakuna matata" ("no worries"), resembles Hal's time with Falstaff and company at the Boar's Head Tavern in *Henry IV, Part I*; Rafiki's riddling chiding of Simba and his leading him through a wilderness to self-knowledge have affinities with the Fool's relationship with Lear (Rafiki holds what seems to be a fool's baffle). Even so, *The Lion King* has analogues in African folktale, Japanese anime, and classical and Old Testament mythology in addition to Shakespeare, so whether Shakespeare can be said to be a specific source for the film is certainly a matter for debate.

DVD contains an audio commentary by the directors and producer Don Hahn in which Rob Minkoff claims that the story of *The Lion King* is original, though it borrows from *Hamlet*, among other sources.

708 *Prince of Jutland* (aka *Royal Deceit*)
1994. U.K. Netherlands, Denmark, France, and Germany. Les Films Ariane, Woodline Films Ltd., Kenneth Madsen Filmproduktion, Canal+, and Films Roses. Sound, col., 85 mins. Gabriel Axel.

In sixth-century Jutland, Fenge crafts a conspiracy to kill his brother King Hardvendel and to marry his wife Geruth. Prince Amled, informed of his uncle's treachery by his father's ghost, feigns madness to bide his time for revenge. Fenge is doubtful about Amled's behavior, and so arranges for a maiden to seduce him and reveal his true nature. When this plot fails and Amled kills Ribold, Fenge's lieutenant, in his mother's bedroom, Fenge sends him with two of his men to Aethelwine, the English king, to be killed. Amled changes the orders so that the two are killed instead, and he wins favor from Aethelwine by cleverly engineering a victory over a rival invading tribe. Having married Aethelwine's daughter Ethel, Amled returns to Jutland where he burns Fenge's men in their council hall and kills Fenge, afterward taking the throne of the kingdom.

This low-budget historical drama by the Danish director of *Babette's Feast* returns to Shakespeare's source, Saxo Grammaticus, for its narrative, and so the parallels to Shakespeare's play are many. Axel's emphasis falls on historical accuracy—the "kingdom" of Jutland is little more than a primitive tribal settlement in Scandinavia—and on Amled's great cunning and skill at pretense. Under the cover of madness, Amled offers many cryptic riddles that communicate threats and accusations against Fenge; when he is confronted in Aethelwine's kingdom by overwhelming numbers in the rival army, he creates a theatrical display of corpses on horseback to distract and fool his enemies, ultimately leading to victory on the battlefield. Fenge too is portrayed as a masterful actor, pretending to grieve at his brother's death to woo Geruth, engineering his own "free" election as king, and feigning respect for Amled. His motives for regicide are only briefly sketched in: he expresses his dissatisfaction with the system of the eldest inheriting the kingdom, and he lusts after the buxom Geruth, who is unaware of his feelings. The use of a narrator to provide plot points and the oddly underplayed characterizations leave the impression of a historical reenactment or retelling of a old fable. No Shakespearean lines are directly referenced, though portions of Amled's confrontation of his mother Geruth closely resemble Shakespeare's dialogue.

709 *Reality Bites*
1994. U.S. Universal. Sound, col., 98 mins. Ben Stiller.

Recent college graduate Lelaina Pierce finds herself underemployed and interested in two very different suitors, Troy Dyer, a cynical, sensitive slacker who bounces between philosophy and his rock band, and Michael Grates, a nerdy but sincere executive with In Your Face TV, a thinly disguised MTV network. When Michael tries to pitch Lelaina's documentary about her Gen-X friends, *Reality Bites*, the music network destroys its integrity, forcing Lelaina to choose between the two men.

Early in the film, Troy answers the phone, "Hello, you've reached the winter of our discontent," using *Richard III*'s opening soliloquy to establish his brooding, intellectual character. In their showdown over Lelaina, Michael accuses Troy of being a court jester who laughs at others from a safe distance. He goes on to reference the graveyard scene in *Hamlet*: "You know what happens to him? They find his skull in a grave and they go, 'Oh, I knew him and he was . . . funny.' And the guy, the court jester, he dies all by himself."

DVD includes the trailer, which features the *Richard III* reference.

710 *Renaissance Man*
1994. U.S. Cinergi Pictures Entertainment Inc., Parkway, and Touchstone Pictures. Sound, col., 128 mins. Penny Marshall.

Bill Rago, a middle-class divorced advertising writer who loses his job, is forced by circumstance to take a job as a civilian teacher at a local army base. There he meets a class of eight working-class recruits with various severe learning problems and hard-luck stories. Stumped by the assignment, he happens upon the idea of teaching *Hamlet* to the group to increase their language skills and comprehension. The class slowly warms to the assignment and begins to find analogies between the play and their lives, even transforming it into a rap musical. Throughout, drill instructor Sergeant Cass regards the class as a potentially dangerous distraction from the students' basic training. After Rago takes the group to see a live performance of *Henry V*, one of the class, Donnie Benitez, offers a stirring rendition of Henry's "Crispin Crispian" speech during a rainy bivouac that demonstrates the value of Shakespeare to Cass and the progress the class has made. The group passes Rago's final examination on *Hamlet*. Afterward, Rago reconciles with his daughter and watches with new respect his working-class soldiers as they graduate, expressing his intention of remaining as an instructor.

In this inspirational classroom drama, *Hamlet* functions primarily as the academic Mount Everest that Rago's educationally challenged and socially disadvantaged students must climb. As the film presents it, the choice of Shakespeare as a subject seems entirely arbitrary, the product of Rago's desperation for something to teach (but also a mark of his own educational and cultural privilege—he is reading the play for pleasure). The central obstacle for his students to overcome is Shakespeare's language, so Rago's first lesson consists of instruction in poetic imagery and metaphor in *Hamlet* 1.2; the lessons that follow consist largely of paraphrase of the play's narrative into contemporary language and analogies to the students' lives. The soldiers' spontaneous translation of the play into a rap musical, that is, into a contemporary "street" idiom, marks their first victory in overcoming barriers of social and cultural class to their education. As Sergeant Cass points out to Rago, Shakespeare seems a pointless luxury for soldiers who need to learn battlefield survival skills. It is for that reason that Benitez's recitation of Henry V's "Crispin Crispian" speech becomes symbolically crucial, for it directly connects the soldiers' growing Shakespearean knowledge with their military success. Benitez's speech, delivered in a working-class accent, articulates the image of the "band of brothers," a Shakespearean ideal of working-class triumph and solidarity that Rago has instilled in his class, an ideal that readily transfers to the battlefield. For that reason, at film's end Cass and other drill instructors have incorporated a *Hamlet* chant in their marching instruction: "Hamlet's mama, she's the Queen, buys it in the final scene, drinks a glass of funky wine, now she's Satan's valentine." Compare to other Shakespeare classroom dramas such as *Dead Poets Society* and *Slings and Arrows*.

711 *Billy Madison*
1995. U.S. Universal Pictures and Robert Simond Productions. Sound, col., 89 mins. Tamra Davis.

Billy Madison, childish son of hotel magnate Brian Madison, must return to school and complete twelve grades in twenty-four weeks to inherit his father's corporation. His plans are temporarily thwarted by Eric Gordon, an ambitious company man, but Billy bests him in an academic decathlon. Along the way, Billy romances his third-grade teacher, Veronica Vaughn.

As part of the decathlon, Eric and Billy compete at giving performances of "To be or not to be." Both performances are overwrought, but Billy delivers his in Elizabethan doublet and hose, carrying a skull. Billy's performance is judged superior.

712 *Clueless*
1995. U.S. Paramount. Sound, col., 97 mins. Amy Heckerling.

Jane Austen's *Emma* transposed to a contemporary Beverly Hills high school. Cher Horowitz, a rich but spoiled and materialistic high school student, focuses on her clothing and popularity until she decides to matchmake two of her teachers and recast a nerdy girl, Tai Fraiser, as one of her fashionable friends. She also looks for a boyfriend, whom she finds in the form of Josh Lucas.

In a discussion with Josh and a pompous girl, Cher identifies "to thine own self be true" as Polonius's line, not Hamlet's, by recalling that Mel Gibson didn't say the line in Zeffirelli's film adaptation (entry 342). See also entries 2849, 2851, and 2852.

713 *The Fifteen-Minute Hamlet*
1995. U.S. Cin-ciné 19. Sound, col., 22 mins. Todd Louiso.

Adapted from the comic play by Tom Stoppard. Two versions of *Hamlet*, radically stripped down for comic effect (the last version is one minute long). The piece reduces many speeches to single lines and relies heavily on sight gags (Ophelia drowns, for example, in a bucket of water). The entire production was filmed in one continuous shot.

714 *Green Eggs and Hamlet*
1995. U.S. Rock's Eye Visual Effects. Sound, col., 77 mins. Mike O'Neal.

A burlesque of *Hamlet* filmed by students at the California Institute of Technology on a shoestring budget. The plot is adapted very faithfully (indeed, scene by scene), but the dialogue is recast in Doctor Seuss–style doggerel—Polonius warns his daughter about Hamlet, for instance, by counseling, "He wants you only for a trophy, / Stay away from him, young Ophy." Throughout, SamIAmlet, a court servant, pursues Hamlet, trying to persuade him to eat green eggs. Comic egg references abound: Claudius kills Old Hamlet with poisoned eggs and attempts to do the same with Hamlet; the players are paid in eggs. The final duel between Hamlet and Laertes is particularly entertaining. The two duel with baguettes and then poisoned sporks, with mock heroic camerawork and a cheesy soundtrack; at the moment of his death, Hamlet finally tries green eggs and likes them. Another amusing touch: when Ophelia goes mad, she spouts long passages of turgid feminist criticism. Substituting for the Player's speech about Priam is a straight rendition of the "Crispin Crispian" speech from *Henry V*, delivered to a green egg.

715 *In the Bleak Midwinter* (aka *A Midwinter's Tale*)
1995. U.K. Castle Rock Entertainment and Midwinter Films. Sound, b&w, 99 mins. Kenneth Branagh.

Joe Harper, a depressed, unemployed actor, decides to mount a self-financed performance of *Hamlet* during the Christmas season in the abandoned village church of Hope, casting himself in the title role. For his cast he assembles various theatrical oddballs and losers, all with emotional problems, including the melancholy but romantic Nina (playing Ophelia), dyspeptic theater veteran Henry Wakefield (playing Claudius), flamboyant queen Terry duBois (playing Gertrude), the self-absorbed Tom Newman (playing Laertes and Fortinbras), and others. When rehearsals go badly and money runs low, Joe is tempted to give up, but the cast rallies, conquering their various demons and differences to offer a stunning rehearsal. On the night of performance, Joe is offered a part in a B-movie science-fiction epic and at first quits, leaving his sister suddenly in the title role, but Joe returns to join the cast for a triumphal performance. In the end, Tom gets the sci-fi role, Joe gets Nina, and other cast members are reconciled with their estranged families.

After the disappointing reception of *Mary Shelley's Frankenstein* and before producing his lavish, full-text film *Hamlet*, Branagh produced this low-budget comedy about the frustrations and joys of producing Shakespeare on stage, a Woody Allen–style valentine to the theater that pits "populist" Shakespeare against commercial American film. It is perhaps the best guide to Branagh's ambitions for his popular Shakespeare film adaptations, stressing Shakespeare's status as a playwright for the people, the emotional universality and consolatory nature of his tragedies, and the capacity for stage performances of Shakespeare to forge or heal bonds of community and family. The film also laments the impoverished status of local stage Shakespeare. The live performance that the troupe produces, paradoxically, relies heavily on cinema-style shock effects for its impact—Bernardo opens the play with machine-gun fire, atmospheric lighting abounds, and Hamlet delivers many of his lines directly to a frenetically moving camera. The film features many scenes from the play in rehearsal and in performance, and parallels between the characters and the actors who play them run throughout—Joe, often dressed in black and prone to depression, mirrors Hamlet; Nina, to whom he is attracted, exudes Ophelia's romantic naïveté and sadness for a lost loved one; and Terry, the gay man who plays Queen Gertrude in drag, longs for contact with his estranged son.

716 *Slings & Arrows*

1995. U.S. Stan Open Productions. Sound, col., 107 mins.
Geoffrey Sharp.

Greg Thornwood, an idealistic but lonely and melancholy teacher, undertakes to teach *Hamlet* to his basement room class of inner-city New York high school students. He attempts to demonstrate that the themes of *Hamlet* are relevant to their lives by asking the class to perform the play. When they resist and ridicule his efforts, he increasingly becomes unhinged, eventually accidentally wounding a student during a performance of Hamlet and Laertes's swordfight.

This adaptation is unusual in several respects. It explores the parallels between Hamlet's half-mad melancholy at his imperfect world and Thornwood's increasingly desperate and angry melancholy as he faces his own corrupt world, a class of bored, tragically ignorant and disruptive students and of fellow teachers who offer canned answers and teach to the tests. As Thornwood tries to present the play to his class, he encourages them to identify closely with the characters, often pressing uncomfortable analogies between Shakespeare's characters and his students' lives, yet his own identification with Hamlet becomes more and more dangerous and uncontrolled with each class meeting (we see three). Several of the students pick up qualities of Shakespeare's characters—for example, Manny, an obsequious showoff who turns in others, plays Rosencrantz; Alice-Ann, a quiet, sensitive girl, takes the part of Ophelia; Lisa, a girl who has been rendered homeless by her mother, plays Gertrude in the character of her mother; and Steve, a sullenly silent student who shows passive-aggressive contempt for Thornwood, takes the part of Laertes in the final scene. Though much of the film is preoccupied with Thornwood's extended modernized paraphrase of the play's plot, many passages of Shakespeare's dialogue are included. Several take on metaphorical resonance in the classroom context: Hamlet's speech "I have of late—but wherefore I know not—lost all my mirth" (2.2) provides insight into Thornwood's own growing disillusionment and mania, and Alice-Ann's performance of Ophelia's "O what a noble mind is here o'erthrown" (3.1) voices her sympathy for Thornwood's desperate frustration as a teacher. That Thornwood is an African American devotee of Shakespeare is unusual for this genre, as is the decidedly tragic tone of the ending, in which Thornwood is destroyed by his idealistic (over)-attachment to what the Bard represents for him—beauty, idealism, emotional depth, and relevance to contemporary life. It is an interesting riposte to more sentimental handlings of the Shakespeare classroom found in such films as *Dead Poets Society* and *Renaissance Man*.

717 *Canterville Ghost*

1996. U.S. Amzazi Productions. Sound, col., 92 mins.
Syd Macartney.

This is a made-for-television film (Hallmark Channel) based on Oscar Wilde's short story of the same title. A pragmatic American physicist, Hiram Otis (Edward Wiley), brings his family to England while he does research for four months. They rent a castle, Canterville Hall, which is haunted by the ghost of Sir Simon de Canterville (Patrick Stewart), who disappeared in 1580 after the mysterious murder of his wife. Older daughter Ginny (Neve Campbell), who was unhappy about leaving America and her friends, is unfairly blamed by her parents for the ghostly disturbances. Unlike their parents, Ginny and her brothers Adam (Ciarán Fitzgerald) and Washington (Raymond Pickard) can see and interact with Sir Simon because they believe in ghosts; the sensible physicist and his wife do not. Ginny studies an old manuscript and discovers the ghost's secret lair, then visits him to offer a proposition. Since her parents do not believe in him, she wants him to perform as a spectre they *can* believe in, thereby relieving her of the blame for his poltergeist activities:

GINNY: We saw a performance of *Hamlet* in London once and everyone loved the ghost of Hamlet's father, partly because he came in early while everyone was still awake, but you'd be great in that part.

SIR SIMON: Thou speakst wiser than thou knowest, I gave Will my thoughts on that role when he did visit here in 1599.

GINNY: You knew Shakespeare?

SIR SIMON: I did. And save for my familiar Gabriel, his words have been my only companions for four hundred years. I knowest how Hamlet's father must be confined by day and walk abroad at night. Where does thou think Will Shakespeare gottest that?

GINNY: From you?

SIR SIMON: In me you see, the genus, the original . . . you could almost say the part was written for me.

GINNY: I knew you'd be terrific.

SIR SIMON: And you must play Prince Hamlet. We will perform it in the banqueting hall; Gabriel will provide the stage effects. And you must wear a cloak.

GINNY: Just my size.

SIR SIMON: For myself, my armor will well suit, which last I wore before the Virgin Queen in Kenilworth.

Ginny practices her lines as Hamlet with the help of her new boyfriend, Francis, duke of Cheshire (Daniel Betts), having particular difficulty remembering the line "Oh, my prophetic soul!" (1.5.46) They rearrange the banqueting hall for the performance, with the family and household staff in attendance—only they and her brothers know the ghost will be the real thing. Says Francis to the boys, "You know, one rarely gets the chance to see Shakespeare performed by someone who actually knew him."

GINNY/HAMLET: Whither wilt thy lead me? I'll go no further.

GHOST: Mark me.

GINNY/HAMLET: I will.

GHOST: My hour is almost come,
When I to sulphorous and tormenting flames
Must render up myself.

GINNY/HAMLET: Alas, poor ghost!

GHOST: Pity me not, but lend thy serious hearing
To what I shall unfold.

GINNY/HAMLET: Speak; I am bound to hear. (1.5.1–10)

GHOST: I am thy father's spirit;
Doom'd for a certain term to walk the night,
And for the day confin'd to fast in fires,
Till the foul crimes done in my days of nature
Are burnt and purg'd away. (1.5.15–19)
List, list, O list!
If thou didst ever thy dear father love (1.5.28–29)
Revenge his foul and most unnatural murder.

GINNY/HAMLET: Murder!

GHOST: Murder most foul, as in the best it is;
But this most foul, strange, and unnatural.

GINNY/HAMLET: Haste me to know't (1.5.31–35)

GHOST: [. . .] but know, thou noble youth
The serpent that did sting thy father's life
Now wears his crown.

GINNY/HAMLET: O my prophetic soul!
My uncle!

GHOST: Ay, that incestuous, that adulterous beast (1.5.45–50)
[. . .] to his shameful lust
The will of my most seeming-virtuous queen.
O Hamlet! what a falling-off was there,
From me, whose love was of that dignity

That it went hand in hand even with the vow
I made to her in marriage. (1.5.53–58)

Sir Simon is overcome by emotion and unable to continue the performance. He apologizes to the audience and dematerializes. Hiram Otis does not believe it was a ghost, but rather an illusion concocted by his daughter. Mother Lucille (Cherie Lunghi), however, is now a believer.

Ginny seeks out Sir Simon, who tells her of the history of his captivity. In an Iago-like move, someone who he had believed to be a friend had suggested that his innocent wife was unfaithful to him. He believed the rumor, forbade her to leave the house, and kept her a virtual prisoner. Eventually, she went mad and stabbed herself to death. Her family chained him up in the secret room, and he slowly starved to death. A witch conjured a spell to make him walk the night, just like Hamlet's father, and brood over his sins during the day. He is doomed never to sleep unless a young girl fulfills an ancient prophecy, escorts him to the Valley of Darkness, and asks the angel to forgive him. Ginny goes to the Valley with him, her family helps her return from the other side, and Sir Simon's dead body is found where he had been chained. He is properly buried next to his Lady Eleanor, and their gravestone is shaped like an open book, with the words "To err is human . . . to forgive, divine" inscribed on it. Lady Eleanor can be heard in voice-over asking Sir Simon to read another sonnet, and he begins Sonnet 109:

O! never say that I was false of heart
Though absence seem'd my flame to qualify.
As easy might I from myself depart
As from my soul, which in thy breast doth lie
That is my home of love. (1–5)

There have been at least ten filmed versions of the satirical Oscar Wilde novelette (it contains absolutely no reference to Shakespeare), most notably:

1944: Charles Laughton, Margaret O'Brien, Robert Young
1974: David Niven, Flora Robson, James Whitmore
1985: Richard Kiley, Shelley Fabares
1986: John Gielgud, Andrea Marcovicci, Alyssa Milano
1997: Ian Richardson

(EJL)

718 *Fuck Hamlet*
1996. Germany. Production company unknown. Sound, b&w, 83 mins. Cheol-Mean Wang.

Six years after the fall of the Berlin wall, unemployment has taken a toll on Till, a formerly East German actor who cannot find work. Each morning, he recites Hamlet's soliloquy on the roof of his house. At the end of the film, he gives up, saying, "Fuck Hamlet," as he is run over and killed at Checkpoint Charlie by a car driven by a Korean couple. (with RB)

719 *Open Season*
1996. U.S. Frozen Rope Productions Inc. and Legacy Productions. Sound, col., 97 mins. Robert Wuhl.

Stuart Sain, an executive for Fielding, a TV ratings company, leaves his job to work as a public relations agent for PBT, a public television network, headed by Rachel Rowen, an ex-hippie. Because of a malfunction in the ratings boxes, PBT suddenly moves to first in the ratings, and other networks, formerly offering violence- and sex-oriented shows, scramble to create programming with a highbrow slant. A sub-plot involves Stuart's strained marriage to Cary, a psychologist.

One snippet of Plunkett Play House, a highbrow show created to compete with PBT, features Joe Piscopo, the former *Saturday Night Live* comic, playing Hamlet. He performs lines from the "O that this too too sullied flesh" speech, in tights with skull in hand. He is accompanied by an "impress track," which offers pre-recorded "ahs" and "ohs" (a serious substitute for a laugh track) to punctuate the lines. An interesting satire on the market-driven nature of popular culture.

720 *Space Jam*

1996. U.S. Ivan Reitman Productions. Sound, col., 87 mins. Joe Pytka.

Animated feature film. Bugs Bunny and other Looney Tunes characters are kidnapped by the Nerdlucks, an alien race who want to use the characters to boost attendance at their failing theme park. Bugs bargains with the Nerdlucks to play basketball for the characters' freedom, and when the Nerdlucks recruit NBA stars to assure their victory, Bugs coaxes basketball superstar Michael Jordan out of retirement for the big game. As Jordan debates whether or not to join the big game, Bugs offers a parody of "To be or not to be."

721 *Swingers*

1996. U.S. Independent Pictures and Miramax. Sound, col., 96 mins. Doug Liman.

After losing his girlfriend of six years, sensitive actor Mike Peters falls apart emotionally and seeks solace with his friend Trent Walker, a smooth-talking hipster who thinks he knows all about the ways of women and cool attitude. Trent takes Mike to Las Vegas and various Los Angeles nightclubs in an effort to help him forget his ex-girlfriend and find women and hip entertainment.

Though Mike played Hamlet in an off-Broadway production, after coming to Hollywood he can't find work and fails at an audition for Goofy at Disneyland. During a golf game, his friend Trent tells him, "There's not a lot of call for Shakespeare out here." When Mike finally gets a new girlfriend, he misquotes Hamlet: "The past is all prologue to what's to come." Compare *Shakespeare In and Out*.

722 X *Hamlet* (*Hamlet: For the Love of Ophelia*)

1996. Italy. Tip-Top. Sound, col., 110 mins. Luca Damiano.

Hardcore pornographic adaptation. Hamlet is a sexually frustrated prince who is envious of Claudius's robust sex with Gertrude and longs to consummate his relationship with the buxom Ophelia; with his friend Horace, he satisfies his sexual frustrations on many women. The ghost of Hamlet's father appears to encourage his sexual conquest of Ophelia, and he later reveals that he was killed by an aphrodisiac administered by Claudius. When the players arrive, they reenact Old Hamlet's death, and Claudius reveals that the aphrodisiac was in fact a poison, leading to a sword fight between Claudius and Hamlet. Before the two are killed, however, the characters reveal that they are in fact actors putting on the play for a modern audience.

The centerpiece of this adaptation is Hamlet's indecision about sex, spun out in several soliloquies spoken to a skull that Hamlet holds aloft. All are parodies of the "To be or not to be" speech, recast as "To screw or not to screw" and variations thereon. Gertrude is presented as a sexually insatiable queen who betrays Old Hamlet with Claudius in their own bed as the King sleeps; we learn later that she was an unwitting accomplice in Claudius's poisoning of the King. Ophelia keeps Hamlet at arm's length with the protestation that she is a virgin, but when she finally gives in to Hamlet's entreaties, he discovers that she too is promiscuous (with her bodyguards), seemingly confirming Shakespeare's Hamlet's jaundiced view of women's sexuality. The final metacinematic revelation of the play-within-the-film seems a gesture calculated to avoid Shakespeare's tragic conclusion; so, too, the odd disco music video featuring the cast, "To Fuck or Not to Fuck," that runs beneath the closing credits.

This film was released twice in slightly different versions, a two-part video version entitled *Hamlet: For the Love of Ophelia*, and a one-part DVD version entitled X *Hamlet*.

723 *Best Men*

1997. U.S. Orion and Rank Film Distributors. Sound, col., 89 mins. Tamra Davis.

Released from prison on the day of his wedding, Jesse Reilly is picked up by four friends, ex-lawyer Sol Jacobs, ex–Green Beret Buzz Thomas, nerdy Teddy Pollack, and actor Billy Philips. Unbeknownst to his friends, Philips is a Shakespeare-quoting bank robber nicknamed "Hamlet," and on the way to Jesse's wedding he robs a bank in Independence, Missouri, to get him a wedding present. The four friends become embroiled with a standoff with local sheriff Bud Philips (Billy's father) and the FBI, and each of the friends ends up making sacrifices for their friend Jesse and his bride Hope's freedom.

This free adaptation of *Dog Day Afternoon* as a serio-comic drama about four male friends features a number of references to *Hamlet*, all from Billy, the Shakespeare-quoting robber. Billy offers several quotations during his initial holdup: "How weary, stale, flat, and unprofitable / Seem to me all the uses of this world"; "Bid the players make haste"; and "If you have hitherto conceal'd this sight, / Let it be tenable in your silence still . . . I will re-quite your loves." When he first speaks to his father during the standoff, he performs a shortened version of Hamlet's "Angels and ministers of grace defend us," a performance that garners applause from onlookers. To his friend Buzz, who cannot publicly admit he is gay, he offers Polonius's advice "to thine own self be true, / And it must follow, as the night the day, / Thou canst not then be false to any man," advice that Buzz repeats when he comes out to a reporter. When his father asks him, "Why *Hamlet*?" Billy mutters, "The origin and commencement of his grief / Sprung from neglected love," then tells his father that he wanted a close father, not a ghost. And as Billy and Buzz are about to meet their deaths, Billy offers a rendition of the "To be or not to be" soliloquy. The film makes clear that Billy's quoting of Shakespeare has two origins—a desire for acting fame, and a bid for attention from his father. Two Shakespeare play titles are referenced by title: *A Comedy of Errors* and *Much Ado about Nothing*.

724 *Prince of Denmark Hill*
1997. U.S. Crucial Films. Sound, col., 12 mins. Adam Rowley.

Short film briefly released on www.Ifilms.com. A con-temporary reworking of *Hamlet*, set in South London gangland as a fast-moving, stylish black comedy. The plot is told in flashbacks during a game of Russian roulette between Keith and Dave during the wedding between Bernard, a mob boss who killed Keith's father, and Val, Keith's mother. Keith's mate Horace serves as the film's narrator. Keith plots to poison Bernard with poisoned whiskey, but Horace mistakenly puts poison in nearly ev-eryone's food, killing them all. Particularly notable is the ghost of Keith's murdered father, handled with comic horror as a sardonic rotting corpse in the manner of *An American Werewolf in London*.

725 *Beautiful Girls*
1998. U.S. Miramax. Sound, col., 110 mins. Ted Demme.

In this group portrait of men maturing in their percep-tions of women, Willie Conway, a New York City pianist, is struggling with a flagging musical career and a troubled relationship with his girlfriend. Returning to his home-town for a midwinter high school reunion, Willie becomes friends with Marty, a thirteen-year-old girl next door, who he sees as promising, and uses the reunion as a way of reevaluating the course of his and his friends' lives. Willie's friend, Tommy Rowland, a former sports hero, cheats on his girlfriend Sharon Cassidy with Darian Smalls, a former prom queen who is now married. Dumped by his girlfriend Jan, Paul Kirkwood, who is obsessed with supermodels, fantasizes about Andera, a beautiful new woman in town. And Gina Barrisano, a worker at the tavern where the friends gather, provides feminist commentary on men's views of women.

In their conversations, Marty and Willie reference both *Romeo and Juliet* and *Hamlet*.

726 *The Impostors*
1998. U.S. Fox Searchlight. Sound, col., 101 mins. Stanley Tucci.

In this Depression-era farce, Maurice and Arthur, two struggling actors, insult a famous Shakespearean actor, Jeremy Burtrom, playing in *Hamlet* on Broadway. Chased by Burtrom, the two hide in a crate and inadvertently end up on a luxury liner headed to France. As they evade Burtrom (who is also on the liner) and various members of the crew, the two pose as stewards, along the way meeting many ec-centric passengers and shipboard personnel. The two learn of various plans to sabotage the ship and thwart them.

An attempt to revive the slapstick comedies of the silent era, *The Impostors* features several references to *Hamlet*, including Burtrom's disastrous rendering of "To be or not to be." Burtrom is a parody of John Barrymore in the final, dissipated phase of his career.

727 *A Lesson Learned*
1998. U.S. All Worlds Video. Sound, col., 102 mins. Mike Donner.

Hardcore gay pornography. A series of sexual encounters set in a college.

Features one dream sequence in which a nude, erect young man recites, "Alas, poor Yorick, I knew him well."

728 *Sound Man*
1998. U.S. Mountainair Films. Sound, col., 105 mins. Steven Ho.

Igby Walters, a hapless, perfectionistic, and un-appreciated sound recordist for a low-budget sci-fi film, *Dead Cowboys*, falls for Juliet, a bad violinist, and promises her work scoring films. When the director Terry Leonard refuses to give him a hearing, he descends into increasingly desperate behavior.

The film on which Walters is working, *Dead Cowboys*, is putatively a version of *Hamlet*. We see short sequences from the film, but none seems clearly related to Shake-speare's play.

729 *Two Girls and a Guy*
1998. U.S. Fox Searchlight. Sound, col., 84 mins. James Toback.

As they wait to surprise their boyfriends, two women, Carla Bennett and Lou Johnson, discover that they have the same boyfriend, Blake Allen, a struggling young actor. When they jointly confront him about his infidelity, he struggles to justify his own dishonesty, vanity, and self-deception, using fast talk and a faked suicide. Eventually he takes up with Carla, who forgives him, and Lou leaves. As the film ends, Blake has discovered that his sick mother, whom Blake obsessively phones, has died.

One of the film's thematic touchstones is *Hamlet*, signaled by a picture of Blake in the role (with trademark skull), which sits on his piano. Blake's psychology resembles Hamlet's in several ways: he is plagued by indecision between the two women; he is an inveterate self-dramatizer, often, Carla points out, to avoid expressing real feelings; after a faked suicide, he confronts himself in the mirror about really committing suicide; and he is fixated on his mother (he lost his father in his youth). His anger and abnormal concern about her is, the film suggests, one key to Blake's psychology; Carla points out that Blake's mother controls his sexuality. To prove that he is not a hack actor, Blake offers a rendition of *Hamlet* 3.4.130–45, tellingly Hamlet's confrontation with Gertrude in her bedchamber. Though he adopts an affected, lightly British accent, the performance reflects his anger and desire for forgiveness. Carla briefly joins the performance by offering Gertrude's line, "O Hamlet, thou has cleft my heart in twain"; her brief taking of the mother's part (something that Blake didn't realize she knew) foreshadows both her forgiveness of Blake and her taking of the maternal role of comforter when Blake's mother dies.

DVD includes a commentary track in which Shakespeare is referenced.

730 *Hamlet*
1999. U.S. Sci-Fi Channel. Sound, col., and b&w, 91 mins. Created by Joel Hodgson.

An episode of *Mystery Science Theatre 3000*. The premise of this TV series is that Mike Nelson, an astronaut marooned in space, watches old movies to occupy the time, making snide comments with two robot companions. In this episode, they comment on *Hamlet, Prinz von Dänemark* (Franz Peter Wirth, 1961), a TV film adaptation that has been dubbed into English. In an epilogue sequence, the robots reveal a Hamlet action figure they have made (with a very long string to make it speak), and an actor playing Fortinbras complains about being cut from the production.

731 *Hamlet*
1999. Brazil. LGI Brazilian. Sound, col., 90 mins. Jose Gaspar.

Hardcore pornography. A series of sexual encounters with a quasi-*Hamlet* theme.

Little Shakespearean content beyond the title, character names, and various passing motifs (prince in black, skull held aloft).

732 *Hamlet and His Problems*
1999. U.S. Production company unknown. Sound, b&w, 8 mins. Allison L. LiCalsi.

Short film by the writer-director of *Macbeth: The Comedy*. Stephen Linton, a classically trained actor who has sold out to Hollywood, receives the chance to star in *Hamlet*, but, insecure, he retreats to his country cottage where he meets with Michael, a visiting Jesuit priest who sent him a fan letter. Michael's odd behavior leads both Stephen and his wife to confront their demons, and convinces Stephen to attempt the role.

733 *Les Enfants du siècle* (*Children of the Century*)
1999. France. Alexandre Films, Films Alain Sarde, France 2 Cinema, and Odeon Films. Sound, col., 135 mins. Diane Kurys.

This biopic depicts the love affair between George Sand and Alfred Musset. In one scene, the two women discuss a play Sand has written about Lorenzo de Medici. Musset says her Lorenzo is Hamlet, an Italian Hamlet, but still Hamlet.

734 *Let the Devil Wear Black*
1999. U.S. New Moon Productions. Sound, col., 89 mins. Stacy Title.

A neo-noir modernization, set in contemporary Los Angeles. Jack Lyne, a philosophy graduate student, slips into conspiratorial paranoia when he receives a tip in a bar bathroom that his sleazy uncle Carl might be involved with his father's death. Jack later discovers that Carl substituted adrenaline for his father's heart medicine (causing his heart attack), that he intends to marry his mother Helen, that Jack's girlfriend Julia's father Saul is involved in the conspiracy, and that Carl has employed Bradbury and Brautigan, two of Jack's high school friends, to kill him. The prize is his father's extensive real estate holdings in seedy Los Angeles. Julia, pregnant with Jack's child and depressed, kills herself by walking into traffic. Carl arranges to have Jack killed during a robbery at a strip club, and he poisons a bottle of champagne as a back-up plan. But Helen accidentally drinks the champagne and is killed by the hired robber, and Jack shoots Carl. Two corrupt Mexican cops bargain with Jack as he lies bleeding, taking his real estate holdings to maintain Jack's and his friend Satch's innocence of any crime.

Let the Devil Wear Black freely adapts *Hamlet* as a bleak contemporary film noir. Jack corresponds roughly to Hamlet, Carl to Claudius, Helen to Gertrude, Jack's friends Bradbury and Brautigan to Rosencrantz and Guildenstern, Saul to Polonius, Julia to Ophelia, and Satch to Horatio, though the characters' motivations are significantly altered. Many of the key events of *Hamlet* are included in reworked and reordered form—Claudius's murder of Old Hamlet with drugs, romance of Gertrude, and takeover of the kingdom; the betrayal of Hamlet's friends; Claudius's conspiracy to have Hamlet killed; and Ophelia's madness and suicide. Even some smaller commonplaces are indirectly referenced: Hamlet's "To be or not to be" soliloquy becomes a conversation with Bradbury and Brautigan about the death penalty, and after the two are killed by corrupt cops, Hamlet's disquisition on Yorick's skull becomes a philosophical meditation on a skull fragment plucked from his eye in the emergency room. Title's emphasis falls on Jack's slow piecing together of the corruption that surrounds him, his manic and ill-considered desire for revenge, and his idealization of his father, the latter of which we see in idyllic flashback sequences of Jack's childhood. His abysmal treatment of the pregnant bipolar Julia—he encourages her to have an abortion and twice uses her for sex in a bathroom—significantly qualifies our sympathies for him. The noir twist at the end, where the Latino police blackmail the wounded Jack out of his father's legacy, sits uneasily with Jack's final reverie about how remembering his father will ensure his entry into heaven. The film's stylized, elliptical dialogue often depends upon the viewer's knowledge of *Hamlet* to fill in the narrative gaps. Compare Michael Almereyda's *Hamlet*.

735 *Shakespeare In and Out*
1999. U.S. Troma Productions. Sound, col., 80 mins. Peter Shushtari.

Richard Longfellow, a young actor, aspires to play Hamlet, but he winds up acting in pornographic movies when he must make ends meet in Los Angeles. Soon he loses his girlfriend Betsy and his best friend Duane, a director, as his ego becomes inflated. Eventually he realizes the error of his ways and performs "Shakespeare for Seniors" in nursing homes in the San Fernando Valley.

This no-budget comedy, shot in mockumentary style, parodies the disillusionment and degradation experienced by actors in Hollywood, using Rich's passage from Shakespeare to pornography as its central example. Rich offers a short rendition of "To be or not to be" early in the film, and at the end he performs a longer version of the speech for senior citizens. At one point, he shows the filmmaker, Harold Asailian Jr., his collection of Shakespeare memorabilia and identifies Olivier as his role model.

DVD includes *Romeo: Love Master of the Wild Women's Dorm* (see entry).

736 *To Be or Not to Be*
1999. Belgium. Sophimages. Sound, col., 11 mins. Peter Woditsch.

Short film released for a brief time on www.atomfilms.com. In his home, Shakespeare struggles with writer's block as we witness the process of him writing, "To be or not to be." As the film opens, Shakespeare, awakening from nightmares, looks in a mirror and asks, "What is the question, which the question?" The film includes short appearances by an unsympathetic servant, Romeo and Juliet (who wish to change their unhappy endings), Ophelia, Falstaff (who corrects Shakespeare's manuscript for him), the three witches from *Macbeth*, and Shakespeare's child Hamnet. When Shakespeare identifies the dilemma as "to die, to sleep, to sleep perchance to dream, ay, there's the rub," the film ends. It is particularly interesting that this film appeared in the same year as *Shake-

speare in Love, another film about Shakespeare and writer's block, though the two were apparently developed independently. This film won a Canal+ award in 2000.

737 *Xplicitly Anal*
1999. U.S. VCA. Sound, col., 85 mins. Jim DiGiorgio.

Hardcore pornography. Collection of five sexual scenarios.

In the third scenario, an actress recites Hamlet's "Get thee to a nunnery" speech and expresses her desire to access Hamlet's soul as she gets aroused. In passing, she also references "a rose by any other name" as well as lines in pseudo-Shakespearean English. The man with her looks at the camera and says, "Suddenly, I love Shakespeare."

738 *The Demon Within* (aka *The Sculptress*)
2000. U.S. A Plus Entertainment. Sound, col., 97 mins. Ian Merrick.

A young British woman, Sarah (Katie Wright), comes to San Francisco to attend art school. Mysterious things begin to happen: she confides in and falls in love with her professor (Jeff Fahey), and she begins to sculpt people she doesn't know, who then die horribly. Next door lives a serial killer/incubus, a former Shakespearean actor named Matthew Dobic (Patrick Bauchau). His story is best explained through a perusal of his press clippings:

"HAMLET TO EQUAL THE GREATEST"
"BRILLIANT ACTOR GETS HOLLYWOOD OFFER"
"Rising Star Sacrifices Career for Priesthood"
"Prostitute Names Priest"
"Cardinal Admits Priest Developed Mental Disorder"
"Dobic's Mother Says He's No Longer My Son"

There is a large poster for a *Hamlet* performance on the wall; it depicts Dobic nearly life-sized, in costume, holding aloft a skull. The poster reads "HAMLET Matthew Dobic encore performance." His apartment looks like a theatrical dressing room, with makeup lights, costumes, masks, and many lit candles. Apparently, Dobic is a serial killer who has multiple personality disorder, and talks to the masks and blames them for his crimes.

He hears the student next door chipping away at a block of stone; he pours himself a shot of whisky, holds it aloft, and toasts himself, saying, "Hamlet!" for some reason.

She continues sculpting, and a loud voice emanates from behind Dobic's apartment door, loudly proclaiming,

O, that this too, too solid flesh would melt! (1.2.131)

Dobic is now in costume and strides across the floor citing *Hamlet*, but now in a much softer voice:

To be, or not to be: that is the question.
Whether 'tis nobler in the mind to suffer
The slings and arrows of outrageous fortune (3.1.63–65)

To be, or . . . *[pause, and evil chuckle]*
Long day, Horatio. Howl, howl, howl!!

Dobic begins drinking heavily and sits at his dressing table, speaking to one of the pictures of murdered women he has plastered on his mirror:

Did you like my performance? It's Shakespeare, you know, and it's very, very difficult. Was it good?

Sarah ends up running around the Golden Gate Bridge being chased by Dobic, who is wearing one of his many disguises. He is impotent, so she impales herself on him: in a rage, he throws her off the bridge. She comes back, now blue-colored, and stabs him to death in his apartment. She ends up in a Paris apartment sculpting, which is what she always yearned for, apparently now a succubus. (EL)

739 *Ophelia Learns to Swim*
2000. U.S. We Can Do It, LLC, and Wroughten Films. Sound, col., 88 mins. Jurgen Vsych.

Ophelia is a passive girl who has nightmares about the film *Titanic*, idolizes her boyfriend Hamilton, is ordered about by her father and brother, and cannot swim. When her brother steals a broom from a witch, Ophelia becomes mixed up with feminist heroines such as Mother Nature, The Chocolatier, The Muse, and The Librarian, who are raising money to battle their archenemy, cigarette-smoking Virginia Svelte, and her band of antifeminists. At first taken in by Svelte's gang, Ophelia soon becomes Estrogen Woman, recognizes Hamilton as a woman-exploiting creep, and crosses the brook she before could not swim.

A bizarre if well-meaning feminist satirical morality fable, using Ophelia as a metaphor for unassertive, self-destructive young women. The drowning of Ophelia is a central motif, first announced by a parody of *Titanic* in which Rose, the heroine, drowns, and by a reference to John Millais's painting of Ophelia in the brook. The feminist heroines laugh at Ophelia's name, while Svelte's gang thinks it is "cool." Insensitive Hamilton evokes Hamlet, but there is a cameo appearance of Hamlet *in propria persona* as a broom delivery man, holding a skull while offering his "too too solid flesh" soliloquy (*Hamlet* 1.2). Ophelia is given a short "mad" scene in which she wanders home, uttering vapid Valley girl phrases. Ophelia's doll, embodiment of her feminine intuition, mocks Ophelia's deference to Hamilton in Shakespearean terms—"I do not know what to think, m'lord." When Ophelia almost drowns crossing the brook, she sings a lamenting song that contains the line "men are deceivers ever" from *Much Ado about Nothing*; another song, from earlier in the film, is entitled "Me Cordelia, You King Lear."

740 *The Glass House*
2001. U.S. Columbia Pictures and Original Film. Sound, col., 106 mins. Daniel Sackheim.

When their parents die in an automobile accident, Ruby and Rhett Baker are taken in by Terrence and Erin Glass, their former neighbors, who live in a spectacular glass home in Malibu. At first the two children are pampered by the Glasses, but Ruby's conversation with her family estate lawyer Mr. Begleiter reveals that the children have inherited $4 million in a trust fund. Soon after several vaguely disturbing incidents, Ruby suspects that Terrence may have killed their parents in order to gain control of the trust, and fearing for her and her brother's lives, Ruby tries to escape. In the end, she takes revenge upon Terrence by running him over.

This thriller uses *Hamlet* as a significant sub-text at two crucial moments in Ruby's development, both linked to her studying the play in English class. In the first moment, Ruby connects her teacher's comment that "Hamlet senses something is wrong that he alone can set right" to her own situation, and she takes the initiative to contact Begleiter with her suspicions about the Glasses. In the second, after Ruby's teacher offers a performance of the ghost's admonition to "revenge his foul and most unnatural murder," Ruby first attempts to escape and afterward directly accuses Terrence of her parents' murder. The general circumstance of a seemingly benevolent stepparent engaging in murder of one's beloved parents and usurpation of one's rightful legacy resembles that in *Hamlet*, as does the atmosphere of cat-and-mouse surveillance. One other set of references concerns a *Hamlet* paper that Terrence writes for Ruby, a paper he plagiarizes from Harold Bloom's *Shakespeare: The Invention of the Human*.

The DVD commentary track by the director and writer references *Hamlet*. See Richard Burt and Lynda E. Boose, eds., *Shakespeare, the Movie II* (New York: Routledge, 2003).

741 *Soul Survivors*
2001. U.S. Artisan Entertainment. Sound, col., 84 mins. Stephen Carpenter.

During a midterm exam, we see a close-up with a (mis)quotation from Hamlet in it: "Essay Question 7: Explain the quote: "There are more things in heaven and earth than dreamt of in your philosophy." The correct quotation is "There are more things in heaven and earth, Horatio, / Than are dreamt of in your philosophy" (*Hamlet*, I.5.166–67).

See *Nightmare on Elm Street 4*. (RB)

742 *Agni Varsha: The Fire and the Rain*
2002. India. IDream Productions. Sound, col., 129 mins. In Hindi with English subtitles. Arjun Sajnani.

The film is adapted from the play of the same name by India's foremost playwright, Girish Karnad. Derived from "The Myth of Yavakri"—a part of the renowned epic *The Mahabharata*—this film retains the essence of the story as told in the epic though somewhat altered by the playwright.

The film was shot entirely on location at Hampi, the seat of the Vijaynagar Empire in the thirteenth century, which is now a World Heritage Site, under the stewardship of the

Archaeological Survey of India. The period has been accurately recreated in the film without losing its contemporary insights that are so intrinsic to the original script.

A *New York Times* review posted on the film's official website mentions *Hamlet*. (RB)

743 *Danger*
2002. India. Eros Entertainment. Sound, col., 127 mins. Govind Menon.

The copy on the back cover of the DVD refers to this Bollywood gangster film as "a Hamlet cocktail." (RB)

744 *Dying like Ophelia*
2002. Canada. 3 Legged Dog Films and Veni Vidi Vici Motion Pictures. Sound, col., 6 mins. Ed Gass-Donnelly.

Adapted from the play *Lion in the Streets* by Judith Thompson. A young woman dying of cancer seeks to die a poetic death, modeled after Millais's painting of Ophelia.

745 *Gangs of New York*
2002. U.S. Miramax Films and Initial Entertainment Group. Sound, col., 166 minutes. Martin Scorsese.

Adapted from a story by Jay Cocks. A young boy, Amsterdam Vallon, seeks to avenge the death of his father in Five Points, New York City, against William Cutting, a vicious gang leader. Set in the midst of the struggle between white, native-born Anglo-Saxon gangs and Irish immigrant gangs in the 1860s and 1870s.

Though the film is not a thoroughgoing adaptation, some commentators have suggested that several plot motifs distantly echo those in *Hamlet*: William Cutting brutally murdered Amsterdam's beloved father to take control of Five Points, and Amsterdam feels the burden of revenge; Amsterdam uses pretense to get close enough to Cutting to carry out his revenge; and Amsterdam comes to feel conflicted about the revenge he is to undertake, at once despising Cutting for killing his father and loving him as a substitute father. When Amsterdam saves Cutting from an assassin, Monk McGinn says sardonically, "That was bloody Shakespearean" and identifies Shakespeare as the writer of the King James Bible.

746 *Ophelia's Opera*
2002. U.S. Eve's Magic. Sound, col., 15 mins. Abiola Abrams.

In this experimental video production, Ophelia, trapped in an abusive relationship, and Moses Lisa, suffering from a fatal illness, use various forms of language and magical power to escape their tragic situations.

Ophelia uses a number of quotations from *Hamlet*, mixed with other forms of language, including rap and various forms of slang.

747 *Hamlet X*
2003. Australia. Production company unknown. Sound, col., 118 mins. James Clayden.

An anonymous ex-convict rehearses portions of *Hamlet* in a deserted office block with an unnamed woman; he comes to identify with Shakespeare's protagonist. The experimental style of the film is unconcerned with narrative coherence—clips from the man's past and present, some of which are repeated and reprocessed, are freely juxtaposed, and Shakespearean dialogue is often dislocated or distorted and mixed with industrial noise. Clayden is a painter and a video and performance artist. Reviewers have characterized the work as a collage-meditation on the fragmented nature of contemporary guilt and identity, using *Hamlet* as a touchstone. Compare Godard's *King Lear* and Pivens's *Macbeth: The Witches Scenes*.

748 *Stay*
2005. U.S. 20th Century Fox. Sound, col., 98 mins. Marc Foster.

Psychological thriller set in New York that is a kind of dark spin-off of *The Wizard of Oz* as channeled by David Lynch in *Mulholland Drive*. After a car accident on the Brooklyn Bridge, a young man named Henry Letham walks away from a burning car, apparently surviving. Henry becomes a suicidal patient of Sam Foster, a psychiatrist, who is now the central character of the film. Flashbacks show a woman riding in the front seat of a car talking about Ophelia, who she will play in a new production of *Hamlet*. When attempting to find Henry before he kills himself, Sam meets the actress, named Athena, at a rehearsal for a production of *Hamlet*. She plays Hamlet, and a black actor plays Rosencrantz. They run through the following lines, which have a vague parallel to the film's plot:

HAMLET: Denmark's a prison.
ROSENCRANTZ: Then is the world one.
HAMLET: A goodly one; in which there are many confines, wards and dungeons, Denmark being one o' the worst.
ROSENCRANTZ: We think not so, my lord.
HAMLET: Why, then, 'tis none to you; for there is nothing either good or bad, but thinking makes it so: to me it is a prison.
ROSENCRANTZ: Why then, your ambition makes it one; 'tis too narrow for your mind.
HAMLET: O God, I could be bounded in a nut shell and count myself a king of infinite space, were it not that I have bad dreams. (2.2.)

The black actor says his favorite line is Hamlet's "O, what a rogue and peasant slave am I" soliloquy, and comments, "I don't know what it means, but I love the word 'slave'!" Sam comments that he has seen women play Hamlet, and Athena says that "this is the lesbian, all woman production of *Hamlet*." When Sam points at the black actor, she says she's joking. The scene is repeated in one of many of Sam's experiences of déjà vu in the film. It turns out at the end of the film that Henry is dying at the car accident and that the entire film has been his fantasy. Characters in the film now reappear as the people who've left their cars to help Henry or to see what is happening. (RB)

HENRY IV, PARTS 1 AND 2, AND HENRY V

749 *The Two of Us* (aka *Jack of All Trades*)
1936. U.K. Gainsborough Pictures and Gaumont-British Picture Corporation. Sound, b&w, 76 mins. Jack Hulbert and Robert Stevenson.

Adapted from the play *Youth at the Helm* by Paul Vulpius. Mistaken for a business genius at a society cocktail party, Jack Warrender, a temporarily employed waiter, becomes the chairman of a bank and rescues it from financial ruin, all the while falling in love with Frances Wilson.

As an inspirational speech at a board meeting, Jack delivers Henry's "once more into the breach" oration.

750 *The Black Shield of Falworth*
1954. U.S. Universal International. Sound, col., 99 mins. Rudolph Maté.

Adapted from the novel by Howard Pyle. Myles Falworth, son of a disgraced knight, trains for knighthood, as his fellow knights, all aristocrats, heap scorn on his efforts. When he exposes a plot to usurp the throne of King Henry IV, his reputation is redeemed, and he eventually confronts the treacherous earl of Alban in a battle. Myles's love interest is Lady Anne, the daughter of his benefactor, the earl of Mackworth.

Of interest to this bibliography because it includes characters from *Henry IV, Part I*, Prince Hal, Walter Blunt, and Henry IV, all of whom have cameo roles.

751 *Too Much Too Soon*
1958. U.S. Warner Bros. Sound, b&w, 121 mins. Art Napoleon.

Adapted from the book by Gerold Frank and Diana Barrymore. A biopic about the downward spiral of actress Diana Barrymore, daughter of John Barrymore (played by Errol Flynn). The film portrays the neglect by her parents, particularly her alcoholic father; her failed marriages, disastrous acting career, and descent into alcoholism; as well as her tentative recovery.

While drunk on a yacht, John Barrymore delivers several lines from *Henry V* (from 2.2 and the Act 3 prologue), as well as the entirety of the "once more into the breach" speech, at the end of which he falls overboard. Later, at Barrymore's Hollywood mansion, there are visual reminders of his Shakespearean stage triumphs, in the form of Richard III's suit of armor and a book of *Hamlet*.

752 *Campanadas a medianoche* (*Falstaff* or *Chimes at Midnight*)
1966. Spain and Switzerland. Alpine Films and Internacional Films. Sound, b&w, 113 mins. Orson Welles.

The history of Sir John Falstaff, culled from *Henry IV, Part 1*, *Henry IV, Part 2*, and *Henry V*. The film covers Hal's life at the Boar's Head Tavern, the Gad Hill's robbery and Hal and Falstaff's subsequent conversation, Hal's interview with his father, Falstaff's recruitment of an army, the Battle of Shrewsbury and Hotspur's death, Henry IV's sickness, Falstaff's relationship with Doll Tearsheet, Hal's succession and subsequent rejection of Falstaff, and Falstaff's death. The text is Welles's reduction of Shakespeare's scripts, supplemented with a short narration adapted from Holinshed.

The autumnal quality of Welles's adaptation is announced as early as the film's short prologue, in which Falstaff and Shallow trudge across a lonely snowy landscape reminiscing about the "chimes at midnight" and the "times we have seen." This sequence gives the film the feeling of an extended flashback in which Falstaff's hopes and ultimate disappointment are foregrounded, though in reality Falstaff and Hal's stories occupy roughly the same amount of screentime. Welles deftly differentiates the court from the Boar's Head Tavern with cinematography and production design choices. The court is a stone castle of cavernous, shadowy empty space, and Welles tends to photograph it in tightly composed still shots of great formality; when Hal becomes king, the formality of the shots seems to intensify, with columns of upraised pikes marking off the space Falstaff cannot enter. The Boar's Head Tavern, by contrast, is a wooden structure on a human, even cramped scale, set up to resemble a kind of theater with Falstaff at its center; the camerawork is far more fluid, consisting often of handheld and moving shots communicating its vitality. Welles's Falstaff is a mountain of a man, nearly incapacitated by his great bulk yet exuding both melancholy and joviality with his eyes. Whereas Olivier's *Henry V* (entry 351), clearly the film with which Welles is in dialogue, emphasized Henry's idealized heroic quality and nearly edits Falstaff out of the narrative, Welles stresses and condemns Henry's betrayal of Falstaff, deftly suggesting the growing turn of Hal's affections away from him in small gestures, particularly the silent exchange of glances at the end of the Battle of Shrewsbury. In the end Hal becomes a version of his emotionally distant father, a man who rises to power by rejecting the warmth of personal human contact. By setting Hal's rejection of Falstaff against Doll Tearsheet's devotion to him and by underlining that Falstaff knows but tries to repress that Henry will ultimately push him aside, Welles makes of his biography a quiet tragedy. His lonely departure from Henry's life, a tiny figure exiting through a castle doorway at night, is deeply moving. Welles's handling of the Battle of Shrewsbury could not be more different from Olivier's handling of the Battle of Agincourt: whereas Olivier adopted primarily a god's-eye view of the clash and minimizes the bloodshed, Welles places the viewer in with the fighting men and insists upon the brutality of hand-to-hand combat. (In his armor, Falstaff looks appropriately preposterous, a walking caricature of a knight.) Welles's battle scenes, a marvel of cinematic economy and an indictment of the glorification of military battle, were clearly a key model for Kenneth Branagh's revisionary depiction of the battle of Agincourt in his *Henry V*. See also entry 347.

753 *Bedknobs and Broomsticks*

1971. U.S. Walt Disney Pictures. Sound, col., 117 mins. (restored video release is 139 mins.). Robert Stevenson.

Adapted from the children's novel by Mary Norton. An aspiring witch, Eglantine Price, adopts three orphaned children and, with the help of sham conjurer Emelius Browne, foils a Nazi invasion with an army of animated armor.

In *Shakespeare Bulletin* 16.1 (1998), Lisa Hopkins argues for a relationship between this film and *Henry V*. The only direct verbal citation is Eglantine Price's battle cry, "For England and Saint George," as she leads her army of armor into the fray.

754 *Faustão*

1971. Brazil. Saga Filmes. Sound, col., 103 mins. Eduardo Coutinho.

Transposes the story of Falstaff to the *cangaço* region of Brazil. Faustão, a bandit, cultivates the company of Henrique and ne'er-do-wells, always staying one step ahead of the law. The film adopts Falstaff's perspective (rather than Hal's, as in Shakespeare's narrative). Compare *As Alegres Comadres* (entries 427 and 911).

755 *So Fine*

1981. U.S. Warner Bros. Sound, col., 90 mins. Andrew Bergman.

A wonderful screwball comedy concerning the fortunes of Bobby, a college English professor. In his efforts to rescue his father Jack, a clothing designer, from a debt to the mob, Bobby accidentally stumbles upon a type of see-through-bottom jean that becomes fashionable. In the meantime Bobby falls in love with Lira, the wife of Eddie, the loan shark to whom his father is indebted.

Bobby twice references the "Crispin Crispian" speech as well as *The Merchant of Venice*. When Eddie discovers that Bobby has slept with his wife Lira, he nearly murders her during her performance as Desdemona in Verdi's *Otello*.

756 *My Own Private Idaho*

1991. U.S. New Line Cinema. Sound, col., 102 mins. Gus Van Sant.

Mike Waters, a working-class, narcoleptic male prostitute, wanders from Idaho to Seattle to Portland in search of his long-lost mother, who abandoned him as a child. In Portland he meets Scott Favor, another male hustler and the alienated son of Jack Favor, a rich businessman and politician. As Scott waits to inherit his father's fortune, he hangs out in an abandoned hotel in Portland with other male hustlers and social outcasts, chief among them Bob

Pigeon, the group's aging leader, in order to embarrass his bourgeois father. When Bob and others undertake a mugging, Scott and Mike mug the muggers and listen to Bob make up extravagant lies about the adventure. Mike, in love with Scott, believes that Scott will continue his life as a hustler after inheriting his fortune and declares his love for him; Bob and company share his belief. Scott and Mike undertake an extended road trip from Portland to Italy to find Mike's mother, but Scott, who insists that he is straight despite his dalliances with Mike, picks up an Italian girl, Carmella, and abandons Mike. Having returned to Portland, Scott, now rich with his father's legacy, cruelly rejects Bob and company. Mike returns to Idaho, left alone in the middle of nowhere with his narcolepsy.

Van Sant's film uses *Henry IV, Part 1* and *Henry IV, Part 2* as two of its narrative armatures and grafts them to a tragic gay teen coming-of-age film, retelling the tale of Hal from the perspective of an outsider rather like Poins, Hal's confidante among the rogues of the Boar's Head Tavern. Included are versions of Hal's initial encounter with Falstaff in *Henry IV, Part 1*, the Gad's Hill robbery (conducted by the men in robes à la Welles, albeit pink robes) and Falstaff's lies afterward, Falstaff and Hal's mock performances of Hal's meeting with his father, Hal's meeting with his father in *Henry IV, Part 1* 3.2, Hal's rejection of Falstaff during his coronation in *Henry IV, Part 2*, and Falstaff's death in *Henry V*. As is the case for Falstaff in Welles's *Chimes at Midnight*, Bob's entrance is first heralded by his "chimes at midnight" lines from *Henry IV, Part 2* 3.2, in this case in modernized form. Indeed, the film's many borrowings from Welles's reduction of the plays and allusions to certain performance details suggest that Van Sant's film derives from the first half of Welles's film, not directly from Shakespeare. He uses the Boar's Head sequences of the *Henry IV* plays as a way of drawing analogies between Shakespeare's working-class outlaws and contemporary gay subculture, recast in terms of countercultural pariahs. Van Sant sympathizes particularly with the Boar's Head counterparts and judges Scott, the Hal figure, harshly, though he is unflinching in depicting the uglier side of Bob (the Falstaff figure) and his comrades. Bob presents the endpoint of a gay drifter's life as pathetic rather than funny as he tries to maintain his dignity while surrounded by society's young discards. With Scott and Bob, Van Sant develops what many modern commentators have seen as an implicitly homoerotic relationship between Falstaff and Hal, as well as Falstaff's role as Hal's substitute father. Seen through Mike's eyes, Scott's dalliance with homoerotic love and a rootless life on the road, the consequences of which he never takes seriously, is all the more cruel given Mike's sad past and desperate desire for love. Scott's savage rejection of Bob and assumption of his father's mantle of social privilege and conventional morality underline the hypocrisy of the conservative

American ruling classes about the gays and homeless in their midst. Although Van Sant lightly updates Shakespeare's dialogue in the scenes, these passages are sufficiently different from the rest of the movie to leave the seams showing between Shakespeare's dialogue and Van Sant's original contributions. Critics are divided on whether this is an artistic flaw, deadpan parody, or a postmodern technique of estrangement. In any case, the film has come to be regarded as a milestone of the gay cinema, and it exemplifies how Shakespeare can be used in the service of a progressive perspective, in this case using the affection traditionally accorded Falstaff to recast the audience's sympathies for a maligned subculture. Compare *Valentin*.

The Criterion Collection DVD contains deleted scenes; an interview with director Gus Van Sant; two documentaries, *The Making of My Own Private Idaho* and *Kings of the Road*; an audio conversation between writer J. T. LeRoy and filmmaker Jonathan Caquette; and a booklet with essays by LeRoy, film critic Amy Taubin, and Lance Loud, and interviews with Gus Van Sant, River Phoenix, and Keanu Reeves, all of whom reference Shakespeare.

757 *Toys*
1992. U.S. 20th Century Fox and Baltimore Pictures. Sound, col., 118 mins. Barry Levinson.

In this fable of childlike whimsy pitted against the military industrial complex, the eccentric CEO of Zevo Toys, Kenneth Zevo, bequeaths his company not to his flaky son Leslie but to his brother Leland, a retired and frustrated general who tries to convert the company into a manufacturer of violent military toys. Leslie leads the fight against him, assisted by his sister Alsatia and eventually his militaristic cousin Patrick. The film is renowned for its art and production design, which combined allusions to Magritte with the visual sense of music videos.

In his free-form parody of a rally-the-troops speech, Leslie (played by Robin Williams) includes brief allusions to "We few, we happy few" and "For God, England, and Saint George." The battlefield embrace of York and Suffolk is briefly parodied visually by two toy bears.

758 *Tombstone*
1993. U.S. Buena Vista. Sound, col., 130 mins (134 mins. in director's cut). George Cosmatos.

An all-star update of the Wyatt Earp legend, with emphasis in this version on the lawlessness of the West, Earp's desire to avoid violence, and Doc Holliday's drug addiction. This adaptation devotes considerable time to the aftermath of the shootout at the OK Corral.

The actor Mr. Fabian delivers "once more into the breach" from *Henry V* in a saloon show and attracts the attention of Billy Breckenridge, a homosexually inclined young man. Compare *My Darling Clementine*.

DVD (director's cut) includes a director's commentary that references Shakespeare.

759 *Independence Day*
1996. U.S. 20th Century Fox and Centroplois Entertainment. Sound, col., 145 mins. Roland Emmerich.

The earth is invaded by vicious aliens, and a small army of pilots, led by a computer scientist and the president of the United States, mounts a daring resistance from a desert base.

Though this blockbuster has no direct verbal references to *Henry V*, the situation—an outnumbered, ragtag army, a leader beset by self-doubt, a cocky enemy, a climactic battle, and even a Falstaffian figure—bears some resemblance to Shakespeare's depiction of Agincourt. The president's inspiring speech to the troops on the eve of battle, taking a national holiday as its reference point and emphasizing their small numbers, echoes the rhetorical strategy of Henry's "we happy few" speech.

760 *Mystery Men*
1999. U.S. Dark Horse Entertainment. Sound, col., 121 mins. Kinka Usher.

Adapted from the comic book series by Bob Burden. After crime-fighting superhero Captain Amazing is abducted by his archenemy, the evil Casanova Frankenstein, a group of misfit superheroes named the Mystery Men, aided by mad gadget-maker Dr. Heller, must rescue Champion City and Captain Amazing from the clutches of Frankenstein.

In a parody of *Hamlet*, one of the Mystery Men, the Bowler, is a woman dressed in black who is obsessed with avenging the death of her father; she keeps her father's skull encased in a transparent bowling ball and converses with him. The Shoveler offers an inspirational speech before the group's final confrontation with Frankenstein that parodies Henry V's "Crispin Crispian" speech: "We're all in over our heads and we know it. But if we take on this fight, those of us who survive it will forever after show our scars with pride and say, 'That's right. I was there. I fought the good fight.'"

761 *Éloge de l'amour (In Praise of Love)*
2001. France. Avventura Films, Le Studio Canal+, Les Films Alain Sarde, and Périphéria. Sound, col. and b&w, 97 mins. Jean-Luc Godard.

In the first section of this two-part, avant-garde film (shot in b&w in Paris), philosophically inclined filmmaker Edgar searches for a star for a film he seeks to make on the nature of love (which he has divided into four stages). He meets Elle and is fascinated by her, but when he decides to cast her in the leading role, he discovers that she has died. The film's second section (shot in color in the French countryside) flashes back to two years earlier, when he first met Elle as he was speaking with two married Holocaust survivors who had sold their story to a Hollywood filmmaker. He meets her when she, the couple's granddaughter, looks over their film contract. Typical of Godard's work, the film's narrative is fractured and filled with digressions on a variety of subjects, most notably the nature of love and loss, the relationship of love to the state, and the problem of using and abusing language for communicating.

In one sequence early in the film's second section, Edgar discusses the French resistance with the Holocaust couple. Two dialogue tracks are overlapped: Edgar asks about the English participation in the French Resistance, while the (off-camera) Holocaust survivor speaks of the place of religion in the Resistance and Anglo-French solidarity. As part of the discussion of the latter, he notes that more than half of Shakespeare's plays are set in France (NB: this is incorrect), and references Princess Katherine's language lesson in *Henry V* 3.4. He notes that the English words taught to Katherine were "the most erotic." Intercut with shots of Edgar are closeups of a grainy photo of a woman in the Resistance. This sequence suggests the possibility of love across cultural barriers (both in Shakespeare and in World War II) and illustrates the challenge of linguistic difference.

762 *Enigma*
2001. U.K. Manhattan Pictures and Senator Entertainment. Sound, col., 117 mins. Michael Apted.

Adapted from the novel by Robert Harris. As codebreakers at Bletchley Park struggle to break a new Nazi code, emotionally fragile mathematician Tom Jericho tries to unravel the mysterious disappearance of his former lover, Claire Romilly. Aided by Claire's roommate Hester Wallace, Jericho discovers that she was involved with a mole in the codebreaking project.

In an inspirational speech to the codebreakers, a superior refers to Hotspur's line "Out of this / nettle, danger, we pluck this flower, safety" (*Henry IV, Part 1* 2.3). One codebreaker sardonically anticipates the jingoistic allusion with this comment: "Shakespeare coming up."

JULIUS CAESAR

763 *La Mort de Jules César (La Rêve de Shakespeare—Shakespeare écrivant Jules César)*
1907. France. Star Films. Silent, b&w, 334 ft. George Méliès.

Lost film. Suffering writer's block as he works on a script, Shakespeare falls asleep and dreams of the assassination scene from *Julius Caesar* (it appears above Shakespeare in an effects shot). Upon awakening, Shakespeare dances with delight and even stabs a loaf of bread his servant brings him, in imitation of what he has just seen. The final shot of the film is of Shakespeare's face, surrounded by flags of many nations.

A fascinating film from George Méliès, the early pioneer of cinematic special effects, now known only from detailed descriptions. Méliès was an admirer of Shakespeare, and here makes the case that Shakespeare's imagination is fundamentally cinematic in nature, as is Méliès's, and thus potentially universal, since the cinematic imagination is fundamentally driven by images, not language. Significantly, filmmaker Méliès himself plays the part of Shakespeare.

764 *Stranded* (aka *The Old Player*)
1916. U.S. Triangle Film Corporation. Silent, b&w, length unknown. Lloyd Ingraham.

U. Ulysses Watts, an aging Shakespearean actor who can find work only in a vaudeville troupe, develops a fatherly affection for a young girl who is a trapeze artist in the company. When Stoner, the troupe's manager, absconds with the troupe's funds and strands the actors, Ulysses and the girl, pretending to be father and daughter, join a Shakespearean revival in a nearby town. When the girl falls in love with a hotel proprietor, Stoner arrives and threatens to reveal the truth to ruin the impending marriage, but Ulysses first does so himself at the wedding, at which Stoner shoots him. As he dies, Ulysses recites portions of the death scene from *Julius Caesar* (3.1) to the wedding guests.

765 *A Roman Scandal*
1926. U.S. Jefferson Film Company, and Mutt and Jeff Films. Silent, b&w, length unknown. Charles R. Bowers and Bud Fisher.

Lost film. From Bud Fisher's popular comic strip of Mutt and Jeff. Some sources indicate that this film parodies *Julius Caesar*.

766 *Julius Sizzor*
1931. U.S. RKO Radio Pictures. Sound, b&w, length unknown. Benny Rubin.

In this parody of *Little Caesar*, the twin brother of the gangster boss Liddle Sizzor, Julius, becomes unwittingly involved in a double-cross of his brother engineered by Cleo, Liddle's conniving girlfriend.

Reference is only in the title and in Sizzor's passing reference, "you came to bury Sizzor."

767 *Beginner's Luck*
1935. U.S. MGM. Sound, b&w, 14 mins. (2 reels). Gus Meins.

In the *Our Gang* serial series. When Spanky's mother enters him in a talent contest for his *Julius Caesar* oration against his will, Spanky's friends, concerned he will be labeled a sissy, sabotage his performance. Alfalfa makes his first screen appearance in this short.

Includes snippets of Mark Antony's "Friends, Romans, countrymen" speech; Spanky delivers the speech onstage while defending himself from a barrage of peashooters. Compare *Pay as You Exit* and *Radio Bugs*.

768 *Bowery Blitzkrieg*
1941. U.S. Banner Productions Inc. and Monogram Pictures Corporation. Sound, b&w, 62 mins. Wallace Fox.

In the *East Side Kids* series. Sent to reform school for fighting with his friend, Muggs McGinnis, one of the East Side Kids, is mentored by a police officer, Tom Brady, who believes he can become a professional boxer. Later, when his friend becomes ill, Muggs reconciles with him.

Muggs delivers a mock oration to his friends that begins, "Friends, Romans, countrymen, lend me your ears—and five bucks." Later, one boy paraphrases Casca's "it was Greek to me" (1.2) as " 'twas Greek to me."

769 *The Phantom of 42nd Street*
1945. U.S. PC Pictures. Sound, b&w, 58 mins. Albert Herman.

Tony Woolrich, a theater critic, and his sidekick cab driver, Romeo, investigate a series of murders seemingly linked to Shakespearean Cecil Moore, his daughter Claudia, and Cecil's old repertory company. By staging a scene, Tony reveals that the real killer is the stage manager Thomas, who is in fact a romantic rival of Cecil's, long thought dead.

To solve the crimes, Tony concocts a rehearsal of the assassination scene from *Julius Caesar*, with Cecil as Caesar, who Thomas attempts to kill.

770 *Juke Joint*
1947. U.S. Sack Amusement Enterprises. Sound, b&w, 67 mins. Spencer T. Williams.

In this "race" film, two conniving drifters, "Bad News" Johnson and "Cornbread" Green, pose as actors in order to stay free at the home of Mama Lou Holiday, whose daughter "Honey Dew" is in a local beauty pageant. At film's end, Mama Lou discovers all her family members misbehaving at a juke joint.

To establish his theatrical credentials, "Bad News" Johnson offers a minstrel-style version of a brief passage from *Julius Caesar*, verbally referencing "I come not to bury Caesar."

771 *An Honourable Murder*
1959. U.K. Danziger Productions Ltd. Sound, b&w, 69 mins. Godfrey Grayson.

In this tale of corporate intrigue, Julian Caesar is the chairman of a large company who fights to retain his power and control. R. Cassius, one of the company's treacherous directors jealous of Caesar's success, convinces the honest, reluctant Brutus Smith to join in a vote to eject Caesar, after which Caesar dies of a heart attack. Soon after, Mark Anthony, Caesar's old friend, becomes the company chairman and removes the dishonest directors from their positions on the board. Distraught with guilt, Brutus commits suicide. As the summary suggests, this low-budget corporate film noir follows the plot of *Julius Caesar* quite closely. This film has never been released on video. Compare *Hamlet Goes Business* and Almereyda's *Hamlet*.

772 *Nearly a Nasty Accident*
1961. U.K. British Lion Films. Sound, b&w, 86 mins. Don Chaffey.

Adapted from the play *Touch Wood* by David Stringer and David Carr. A comically inept RAF officer, Captain Kingsley, causes a series of preposterous accidents when he attempts to tinker with mechanical equipment, drawing his superiors' wrath. He becomes the subject of a national manhunt when he turns up missing.

Kingsley cites, "Cry havoc, and let slip the dogs of war."

773 *Carry on Cleo*
See entry 558.

774 *Up Pompeii*
1971. U.K. Anglo-EMI and Associated London Films. Sound, col., 90 mins. Bob Kellett.

A tits-and-toga-themed sex farce adapted from the TV series. During an altercation in the marketplace, Lurcio, slave to senator Ludicrus Sextus, accidentally picks up a scroll that reveals the names of conspirators plotting to assassinate Emperor Nero. Lurcio is chased by both Nero's guards and the assassins.

An ongoing gag involves Ludicrus Sextus, played by Michael Hordern, revising a speech for the Senate that starts, "Friends, Pompeians, countrymen, lend me your feet." Ludicrus finally gives his speech as the volcano erupts and destroys the city.

775 *Walker*
1987. U.S., Mexico, and Spain. InCine Compañía Industrial Cinematográfica and Universal. Sound, col., 95 mins. Alex Cox.

A loose biopic about the nineteenth-century American soldier-of-fortune William Walker, making anachronistic references to Ronald Reagan's illegal contra efforts and often echoing Sam Peckinpah's anti-Western, *The Wild Bunch* (1969). Cornelius Vanderbilt sends Walker to Nicaragua along with a band of mercenaries to "liberate" Nicaragua, where Walker proclaims himself president, serving two years before being deposed. Walker and his friends watch a production of *Julius Caesar* as Caesar is being crowned offstage. The play itself has a race-blind cast, drawn from members of Walker's racially mixed army. The following scene is heard before two men interrupt the performance:

BRUTUS: Another general shout!
    I do believe that these applauses are
    For some new honours that are heap'd on Caesar.
CASSIUS: Why, man, he doth bestride the narrow world
    Like a Colossus, and we petty men
    Walk under his huge legs and peep about
    To find ourselves....

The camera gives a close-up of Walker, seated front and center in the audience, who regards Cassius's description of Caesar as serious rather than sarcastic praise, clearly identifying with this portrait of Caesar as larger than life. Walker walks onstage as he takes over the part of Caesar, delivering the lines "Yond Cassius has a lean and hungry look; / He thinks too much: such men are dangerous" (1.2). A Caesar-like despot, Walker then declares that the solution to their problems is slavery. A black officer standing at the back of the audience throws down a chair and shouts, "No." A black woman in the audience stands up and guides her children away. In Walker's last speech to his men, Walker repeats a paraphrase of Lady Macbeth's speech when she reads Macbeth's letter ("This ignorant present, and I feel now / The future in the instant": 1.5), which he first stated early in the film when supporting the "liberation" of Nicaragua. He says that a "great idea transports" a man "from the ignorant present and makes him feel the future in a moment" as he proceeds to talk about how the United States will never leave Nicaragua. The black officer is still there, still loyal to Walker. (RB)

776 *Killing Mr. Griffin*
1997. U.S. Bonnie Raskin Productions, Hyperion Entertainment Inc., and NBC Studios. Sound, col., 89 mins. Jack Bender.

When Mr. Griffin, a tough high school Latin teacher, humiliates several students in his class in an effort to get them to learn, Mark Kinney, a big man on campus who is a habitual liar, crafts a plan to kidnap Griffin as a prank to get himself elected class president. To do so, he recruits Susan McConnell, a mousy woman, using her crush on Mark's friend Dave Ruggles to his advantage. The plan goes horribly wrong when Griffin dies when the students abandon him without his heart medication, and Mark orchestrates a plan to keep the circumstances of his death a secret. Susan's recognition that Mark is a liar and the discovery of a tape that incriminates him lead to a confrontation between Mark and his clique of students.

A leitmotif throughout this made-for-TV film is *Julius Caesar*, which the students are studying in Mr. Griffin's class. There are some general parallels of situation and character. In some respects, Griffin resembles Caesar; Mark, Cassius; and Dave and Susan, Brutus. Like Caesar and Cassius, Griffin senses and suspects Mark's manipulativeness; and like Cassius, Mark convinces others such as Dave and Susan to join his conspiracy against Griffin. Susan delivers a heartfelt if somewhat ambivalent eulogy over Mr. Griffin's body (one that Mark then parrots in a public speech); both Mark and Susan have guilty dreams of the murder; Mark's girlfriend, Tori, remarks that her horoscope predicted that things would take an unexpected turn, an oblique allusion to the Ides of March. More generally, like Caesar, after the death of tyrannical Griffin, he is remembered fondly and his benevolence toward students is belatedly recognized.

In the one scene in which the text of *Julius Caesar* is specifically referenced, a scene in which students read portions of 3.1, the parallels between students and roles from the play are underlined—Susan plays Caesar (badly),

Dave Brutus, and Mark Cassius. The scene offers a portrait of Griffin's frustration with the class—their teenage preoccupations and self-consciousness prevent them from appreciating themes that "stand the test of time," and so after chastizing the class for their wooden performances and lack of interest, he ends the unit on *Julius Caesar*. Jack Bender also directed NBC's modern adaptation of *The Tempest* (entry 2909). Compare *Teaching Mrs. Tingle*.

777 *Free Enterprise*
1998. U.S. Mindfire Entertainment and Triad Studios. Sound, col., 116 mins. Robert Meyer Burnett.

Mark and Robert, two twenty-something science fiction fans, are arrested adolescents, immature in their relationships with women and obsessed with *Star Trek* and its star, William Shatner. Lonely Mark pitches a movie called *Bradykiller*, and Robert, having lost his girlfriend Trish because of his irresponsibility with money, chases various women. A chance meeting in a bookstore brings them in contact with the real William Shatner, who is a nerd preoccupied with putting on his one-man musical version of *Julius Caesar* and is terrible with women. Soon Robert takes up with Claire, a far more mature fellow science fiction fan, but the relationship falls apart over Robert's irresponsibility. At a surprise thirtieth birthday party, all three men sort out their relationships, Robert with Claire, Mark with a graduate student, and Shatner with a pretty bar owner.

The film includes several discussions of Shatner's preposterous musical *Julius Caesar*, which he works on throughout the film with Mark. When he exits after having had drinks with Mark and Robert, he fumbles with his credit card, quipping, "Friends, Romans, countrymen, lend me your money." At the birthday party, Shatner, rapper Rated R, and a rap crew perform an extended excerpt from Shatner's musical setting of Mark Antony's "Friends, Romans, countrymen" speech, a rap song entitled "No Tears for Caesar." It is an utterly jaw-dropping scene. Before this sequence, Shatner woos a woman he's earlier struck out with by quoting Titania from *A Midsummer Night's Dream*: "Mine ear is much enamored of thy note, / So is my eye enthralled to thy shape, / And thy fair virtues perforce doth move me." There is also a passing reference to *Forbidden Planet*.

DVD includes a commentary track by Robert Meyer Burnett and Mark Altman that references Shakespeare. (The two reveal that in an earlier version of the script, Shatner was to do a musical *Titus Andronicus*.) See also entries 1770, 2723, 2733, 2734, 2785, and 2907.

778 *Whatever*
1998. France and U.S. Anyway Productions, Circle Films Inc., and DuArt. Sound, col., 112 mins. Susan Skoog.

Following the lead of her friend Brenda Talbot, a promiscuous, sexually abused teen, Anna Stockard, an artistically inclined but blasé New Jersey girl, drifts into a life of partying, drugs, aimless rebellion, and casual sex. By doing so, she becomes alienated from her divorced mother, Carol, and potentially jeopardizes her opportunity to study art at Cooper Union, despite encouragement from her art teacher, Mr. Chaminski. A road trip to Florida with Brenda and two ex-cons, Zak and Joe, leads Anna to abandon her dissolute ways and return home.

Early in the film, a classroom scene involves a lecture on *Julius Caesar* 3.2 in which the teacher explains Brutus's reason for assassinating Caesar—"not that I loved Caesar less, but that I loved Rome more." The line is obliquely relevant to Anna's situation, in that eventually she must abandon her friend Brenda and her lifestyle in order to fulfill her artistic potential. The scene also establishes a key obstacle for Anna's academic success, her writing of a term paper to pass her English class, a task she completes at film's end.

779 *The Emperor's Club*

2002. U.S. Beacon Pictures, HorsePower Entertainment, LivePlanet, Longfellow Pictures, Sidney Kimmel Entertainment, and Universal Pictures. Sound, col., 109 mins. Michael Hoffman.

The Emperor's Club, a kind of updated and darker version of *Dead Poets Society* meets *Election*, is based on a short story by Ethan Canin called "The Palace Thief." In this case, Kevin Kline plays a prep school (all-boys') classics teacher, Mr. Hundert, who moderates an annual "Mr. Julius Caesar" competition where the three best students compete for the honor being Mr. Julius Caesar. In a key scene, the students discuss Shakespeare's *Julius Caesar*, and a "problem" student named Sedgwick Bell who has been assigned Brutus's part faults the conspirators' plot. They should have killed Marc Antony, in his view. Hundert is shocked, and the two have a brief debate over morality and power. The students all have copies of the play, and a bust of Shakespeare figures prominently in a number of shots (also at the end of the film in the same classroom). Shakespeare's appearance in the film is hardly surprising given that Hoffman directed *A Midsummer Night's Dream*, with Kline as Bottom, and given Kline's own experience doing Shakespeare and referring to Shakespeare in mall films like *Soap Dish* and *In and Out*.

As the narrative of *The Emperor's Club* proceeds, Hundert becomes a kind of Brutus figure (he is morally compromised in a number of ways as a teacher, including altering a test score so that Bell can compete as a finalist), while Bell grows up to be a would-be Caesar (more like Tiberius or Caligula, actually), a liar and a cheater who, near the end, announces his bid to run for the U.S. Senate seat his father had held until his death. When writing on Taymor's *Titus*, I was struck by the near absence of *Julius Caesar* film remakes or references. This film suggests that more cinematic *JC*s of one sort or another may be on the way. Though *The Emperor's Club* is not a great film, it is a lot smarter than the reviews give it credit for being. It often

feints toward a simplistic, predictable, melodramatic turn and then explodes the place we're made to expect we'll be taken to. It offered a very interesting take on the "culture wars," eviscerating the right-wing view held by the likes of Bill Bennet that great books produce virtue, that classes on Western civilization lead to character building and thus lead to great statesmanship. In having Bell be a kind of Caesar not unlike the young, handsome, on-the-make Caesar of Kubrick's *Spartacus* (which also has a line from Shakespeare's *JC*), the film quietly recalls an earlier cinematic and theatrical tradition of viewing Caesar as a proto-fascist (Mankiewicz [entry 361] and Welles). I thought the parallels with George W. Bush (a terrible student and stupid preppie frat boy) were really quite astonishing. At the same time, Hundert (who, unlike the teacher played by Matthew Broderick in *Election*, is a pedagogically conservative old fart, a cousin to Mr. Chips) cannot counter effectively the cynicism of Bell, the student he fails as a teacher, nor does he do anything at all to expose this neo-Caesar and take him down. The days of Orson Welles and his like are clearly past. Interestingly, the right-wing defense of Western civilization (articulated by Hundert as necessary so that we can understand the U.S. Constitution) is put under immense pressure. (The left-wing critique is not even on the film's map.) One could argue that Bell is a kind of scapegoat, since all the other students seem to benefit from Mr. Hundert's education, and all are described as captains of industry, and in one case, higher ed. But only Bell seems to count.

An Indian student named Deepak Mehta wins the Mr. Julius Caesar competition twice. He is one of the four main student characters, but hardly has any lines. (He is also the student who goes into higher education, apparently as an administrator. Though the actor is American born, his character speaks with a rather thick accent.) Another white student who Hundert fails (actually cheats of a chance to be one of the three competitors), whose father won the Mr. JC competition when he went to the school, drops off his son (same name) at the end of the film in a classroom now conspicuously multiracial and co-ed. So the loser white guys bond. A revision of Kipling's white man's burden happens, in which multicultural integration and imperialism meet (of course, they already had met in George W. Bush's cabinet), and (semi)virtuous loser white guys are content to smile at each other.

It's almost as if revolutionary violence against Caesar were impossible in a historical moment the film represents as the death of white patriarchy. Both Bell and Hundert had remote, cold fathers, and Bell's relation with one of his sons is harmed while Hundert has no children. Hundert is passed over as headmaster at a board meeting, at which a woman takes over as a (sympathetic to Hundert) British white male character takes a backseat. The only successful patriarchal model—the three white Martins—is nearly destroyed by Hundert himself, who, as Bell, points out, does not expose Bell as a cheat because of Bell's senator father. Though Senator Bell appears to be a father to his son when insisting to Hundert that he, the senator, not Hundert, will be the one to mold Sedgwick, he turns out never to have heard a word his son said to him. And while Bell's father comes to the contest, Deepak's father does not, only his mother. Later we see his beautiful wife (she has no lines, nor does the mother).

The film's scholarship is bad at points. One question asked at the competition, for example, involves an emperor in 345 (or something like it) B.C., but there were no emperors until A.D. 40 (RB)

780 *Gedebe*
2003. Malaysia. Pustaka Cipta Sdn Bhd. Sound, col., 65 mins. Namron.

Adapted from the stage play by Namron. This transposition of *Julius Caesar* to the underground music scene of Kuala Lumpur features Julius Caesar as a skinhead running a drug empire, and Brutus as the undercover policeman who seeks to trap him. Reviews suggest the influence of Baz Luhrmann's *Romeo + Juliet* (entry 496) and *The Chicken Rice War*, as well as a number of independent films. See also entry 361.

781 *Mean Girls*
2004. U.S. Broadway Video Motion Pictures, Lorne Michaels, and M.G. Films. Sound, col., 97 mins. Mark S. Waters.

Adapted from *Queen Bees and Wannabes* by Rosalind Wiseman. Home-schooled teenager Cady Heron goes to high school and encounters the Plastics, a clique of cruel beautiful girls who tyrannize the school. In return for a romantic betrayal, Cady undertakes revenge upon Regina, queen of the Plastics, by joining the clique and undermining her popularity, but her plan soon backfires when Regina discovers Cady's treachery and takes her own revenge.

Two classroom scenes involve passing and thematically relevant references to *Julius Caesar*, one of which includes a quotation from Cassius: "He doth bestride the narrow world / Like a Colossus" (1.2).

782 *Good Night, and Good Luck*
2005. U.S. Sound, col., 93 mins. George Clooney.

In this liberal-minded film, reporter Edward R. Murrow (David Strathairn) tells Fred Friendly (George Clooney) that Murrow's closing on his show attacking McCarthy "is Shakespeare." On the show, Murrow cites McCarthy's own citation of Cassius's line from *Julius Caesar*, "Upon what meat doth this our Caesar feed, / That he is grown so great?" And then he recontextualizes the line, saying that McCarthy should have read a few lines back in Shakespeare's *Julius Caesar* to Cassius's line, "The fault dear Brutus lies not in our stars, but in ourselves." Murrow re-

peats the line at the end of his broadcast. As in *Quiz Show* (Robert Redford, 1994), Shakespeare is the token of high-minded civic debate conducted by whites and opposed to the degrading, merely entertaining and profitable television shows, also implicitly addressed to white viewers. And, as in *Quiz Show*, the high-minded quoter of Shakespeare turns out to be a loser. After taking down McCarthy, Murrow is told his show will be canceled. (RB)

KING LEAR

783 *Le Roi Lear au Village (A Village King Lear)*
1911. France. Gaumont. Silent, b&w, 20 mins. Louis Feuillade.

After transferring his property to his two married daughters, a blind man is treated badly first by one daughter, then the other. Dejected and suicidal, he wanders until found by his servant (exiled by the daughters), who takes him to his lawyer. Seeking to avoid scandal, the elder daughter takes her father back home and slowly comes to regret her actions.

784 *Hobson's Choice*
1920. U.K. Master Films. Silent, b&w, 65 mins. Percy Nash.

A successful Victorian bootmaker, Henry Hobson, runs his shop and his three daughters' lives with an iron hand, standing in the way of their marriages in order to avoid the expense of dowries. The eldest daughter, Maggie, rebels, marrying his best bootmaker Will Mossop and setting up her own boot shop; soon she uses her clout to force her father to allow the other daughters to marry their chosen husbands. The first of several film adaptations of the popular play by Harold Brighouse.

This classic British film turns the motif of the tyrannical father and three daughters into material for a comedy. No direct citation of Shakespeare's dialogue.

785 *Hobson's Choice*
1931. U.K. British International Pictures. Sound, b&w, 65 mins. Thomas Bentley.

See summary above. The first talkies adaptation of this play.

786 *A Yiddish King Lear (Der Yiddishe Koenig Lear)*
1935. U.S. Lear Pictures Inc. Sound, b&w, 70 mins. Harry Thomashefsky.

Adapted from a play by Jacob Gordin. David Mosheles, a pious, excitable Russian Jewish father of three daughters, Gitl, Estelle, and Taybele, holds a feast at which he gives his daughters jewels. Gitl and Estelle praise their father, but Taybele and her consort Mr. Joffe reject his gift, arguing that beauty comes not from ornament but from nature. Angry, David gives his legacy to Abraham Chariff, Estelle's husband, to divide among Gitl and Estelle; he vows to leave with his wife Hanna Lear for Jerusalem.

David also directs Abraham to choose a husband for Taybele, and when Taybele pronounces Abraham untrustworthy, David disowns her. Two months later, Abraham cuts off Taybele's allowance. When David learns of this and of Abraham's intention to cut off his allowance, he and Hanna return home and are mistreated by Abraham and Estelle, with Abraham even selling his property to his brother to keep it from David. Taybele returns, but David refuses to forgive her, and Abraham orders her and her mother away. Now blind, David wanders homeless with his comic servant Shamay. At Taybele and Joffe's wedding, Abraham and Joffe spar over Abraham's gift and Taybele's plans to build an almshouse. Soon Gitl, her husband Moses, David, and Shamay arrive, and all are reconciled. After a doctor suggests that David's blindness may be curable, Abraham and Estelle reveal that Abraham's brother has evicted them, and David vows to regain the family's wealth.

The parallels between *Lear* and this film are many and obvious, though the narrative deviates from Shakespeare's ending in order to mute the inescapability of tragedy and to demonstrate the value of family solidarity and forgiveness. Though the Gloucester plot is excised, David's blindness certainly echoes Gloucester's. There are no direct verbal citations, but when David first rejects Taybele, Joffe calls him "the Jewish King Lear." Compare *Mirele Efros* (below).

787 *Mirele Efros*
1939. U.S. Credo Pictures. Sound, b&w, 80 mins. Josef Berne.

Adapted from a play by Jacob Gordin. Mirele Efros, a noble, pious, strong-handed widow and successful businesswoman in turn-of-the-twentieth-century Poland, is a mother devoted to her children. For her eldest son, Yosef, she handpicks a bride, Shaindel, a seemingly docile country girl who upon marriage proves to be ungrateful and devious, attempting to evict Mirele from her home and separate her from her son and grandson.

The film, adapted from a play known as *The Jewish Queen Lear*, uses the motifs of the dominating parent, the child who revolts against parental tyranny, and the dispossession of the parent. The work from which the film is taken was the single most widely performed play in the Yiddish theatrical canon, and this was the third (and most popular) film adaptation of it. The film contains no direct textual citations of Shakespeare's dialogue. Compare *A Yiddish King Lear* (above).

788 *The Wild Man of Borneo*
1941. U.S. MGM. Sound, b&w, 78 mins. Robert B. Sinclair.

Adapted from the play by Marc Connelly and Herman Mankiewicz. J. Daniel Thompson, a turn-of-the-twentieth-century medicine show barker and conman, decides to retire from life on the road and live with his daughter Mary, who he has not seen for many years. When he discovers that Mary is in poverty, he takes Mary to New York City and takes up residence in a theatrical boardinghouse where he pretends to be a famous actor. He is forced to sell his snake oil on the street until he is offered the part of the "wild man of Borneo" in a nickelodeon show; to explain his nightly absences, he tells all that he is starring in *King Lear*. When the proprietor of the boardinghouse, Bernice Marshall, and others get tickets to the show, Daniel feigns illness. Soon Daniel is found out, but Bernice offers to marry him anyway; Daniel, a perpetual drifter, at first refuses, but when his daughter falls in love with Ed, a movie camera inventor, he decides to stay at the boardinghouse and uses his connections with the nickelodeon to help the couple.

789 *Life Begins at Eight-Thirty*
1942. U.S. 20th Century Fox. Sound, b&w, 85 mins. Irving Pichel.

Adapted from the play *The Light of Heart* by Emlyn Williams. Madden Thomas, a former stage actor and cynical alcoholic, lives with his handicapped daughter Kathi in New York City. She meets a neighbor, composer Robert Carter, for whom she falls, and who she helps with his shyness. Carter uses his influence with the theater community and his influential aunt Alma to get Thomas parts, one of them in a major production of *King Lear*. When Carter and Kathi secretly plan to get married and move to Hollywood on the eve of Thomas's debut, Thomas finds out and nearly ruins his debut. His daughter confronts him about an accident he caused that led to her debilitation and vows to leave him, but she soon after recants and says goodbye to Carter. Overhearing their declarations of love, Thomas realizes the error of his ways, tells her to go with Carter, and proposes marriage to Alma.

We see several rehearsal scenes from *King Lear*. The play's theme of a father's tyrannical dependence upon and love for his daughter is clearly paralleled in the film's narrative.

790 *An Angel Comes to Brooklyn*
1945. U.S. Republic Pictures. Sound, b&w, 70 mins. Leslie Goodwins.

In this backstage musical comedy, young actress Karen James is aided by Phineas Higby, a bumbling angel from Actors' Heaven, as she struggles to start her career. Through a misunderstanding hinging on the word "angel," Karen and her friends at a theatrical boardinghouse begin work on a theatrical extravaganza they assume Higby will finance. Because of a series of Phineas's screw-ups, the group abandons the show, but not before Karen learns of the love of David, a fellow actor, for her. Eventually the troupe's own efforts secure them a producer's support.

One of the figures in Actor's Heaven is dressed as King Lear.

791 *Gunasundari Katha*
1949. India. Vauhini Studios. Sound, b&w, 172 mins.
Kadri Venkata Reddy.

Offended by his youngest daughter Gunsundari's vow to devote herself unconditionally to her future husband, an old king arranges a marriage for her with a crippled and deaf boy who is cursed. When the king comes down with a mysterious illness, his three sons-in-law search for the magical Mahendramani jewel that has the power to cure him. Gunsundari's outcast husband discovers the jewel, but the greedy sons-in-law steal it from him; as a result, one turns into a bear. Eventually, the old king is cured and reconciled with Gunsundari, and her husband's curse is broken. This film is in Teluga, and was remade as *Gunsundari* in 1955.

The film parallels *Lear* primarily in the estrangement between father and daughter over the question of her relative obedience to father and husband, and in the juxtaposition of the two superficially loving but selfish children with the one outcast but devoted child.

792 *House of Strangers*
1949. U.S. 20th Century Fox. Sound, b&w, 101 mins.
Joseph L. Mankiewicz.

Adapted from Jerome Weidman's novel *I'll Never Go There Any More*. On the East Side of New York City in 1932, Gino Moretti, a Italian immigrant barber turned banker, exerts strict personal control over his business and his four sons, Max (a lawyer), Joe (an ambitious clerk at his bank), Pietro (a bank guard and erstwhile boxer), and Tony (a weak-willed dandy). Gino browbeats and humiliates his sons in a variety of ways, except for Max, his favorite. Max is hired by a beautiful, rich ingenue, Irene Bennett, and they soon pursue a clandestine, tense, but passionate romance, despite the fact that Max is engaged to Maria Domenico, a timid Italian girl. Irene, soon troubled by Max's willingness to treat her as a mistress, breaks off the romance and takes up with another man, despite the fact that she loves him. Soon regulators close Moretti's bank, troubled by his lack of records and issuing loans without collateral, and they seek to put him on trial. In an attempt to protect his father's assets, Max proposes to divide the financial responsibility among the four brothers, but Joe, Pietro, and Tony, resentful at Gino's mistreatment of them, refuse to go along. When the trial begins to go badly, Max tries to bribe a sympathetic juror; apparently turned in by Joe, he is caught and goes to prison for seven years. Before he does so, Irene declares her love for him and vows to wait. While Max is in prison, the remaining sons, having gotten control of the family's wealth from their mother, oust Gino from the bank and put him on an allowance, humiliating him in the process. Gino urges Max to take vengeance, and after Gino dies and Max is released, Max confronts his brothers, eventually choosing to reject the hate his father has engendered in favor of life with Irene.

Various motifs from *Lear* are revised and recombined in this drama of Italian immigrant family life, with the parallels to Shakespeare's play strongest in the film's final reel. Abrasive and authoritarian Gino can be seen as a version of Lear, alienating his sons by demanding their complete obedience and love and by showing favor to Max. The film fleshes out the history of humiliation suffered by Joe, Pietro, and Tony (the Regan and Goneril figures) at Gino's hands, so that the rejection of their father at his moment of need becomes psychologically justifiable, though not sympathetic. As the focal point of the film, Max is featured in two plots, the first a romance with Irene that has little relationship to *King Lear*, and the second Gino's banking troubles and subsequent fall. This second plot uses several motifs from Lear in novel ways: it is Max, not Gino, who crafts the idea of dividing Gino's "kingdom" among the sons, and it is the three disloyal sons, not Max, who reject the idea and refuse to voice their love. Unlike *King Lear*, Gino's speech in response offers a spirited justification of his mistreatment of his sons, and it is Gino's wife, not Gino, who comes to understand the effect her husband's bullying has had on the Moretti family (he dies unrepentant). Indeed, when Max faces off with his brothers in the final scene, he is faced with a choice between pursuing the family legacy of vendetta or choosing a new romantic life with Susan; the choice, the film makes clear, is also one between remaining mired in his New York Italian family roots and assimilating with an Anglo bride in California. This is the first of screenwriter Philip Yordan's three adaptations of *Lear*, the other two being *Broken Lance* and *The Big Show*.

793 *Broken Lance*
1954. U.S. 20th Century Fox. Sound, col., 96 mins. Edward Dmytryk.

Broken Lance chronicles the fall of Matt Devereaux, a rancher whose fierce determination to build a ranching empire has left him estranged and aloof from three of his four sons, Ben, Mike, and Denny, all of whom he treats as hired hands. Only Joe, his son by his latest wife, Señora Devereaux, an Indian, loves his father. When his father discovers a copper smelter polluting his ranchland and illegally destroys it, Joe takes responsibility for the crime and goes to jail in order to save his aging father the strain of prison life. Years later, Joe is released from prison and, returning home, he finds that his brothers, led by Ben, have rebelled against their father, taking over the ranch and causing Matt to suffer a stroke. Señora Devereaux convinces Joe to make peace with his brothers, but Ben, nervous that Joe will make trouble, confronts him in a showdown.

The second of Philip Yordan's film adaptations of *King Lear* (Yordan is credited with the story, and Richard

Murphy with the screenplay), *Broken Lance* freely reworks motifs from Shakespeare's play, with the resemblances becoming strongest in the film's last third. Matt Devereaux is a Lear-like tyrant who has neglected to show love for his sons as he has built his ranching empire. His stubbornness and blunt treatment of his sons come back to haunt him when Ben gains control of the ranch (in this adaptation, Matt's attempt to stop Ben from selling a portion of the ranch he now controls leads to his death). Joe's special affinity and love for his father resemble Cordelia's for Lear, manifesting itself in his willingness to sacrifice himself by taking blame for destroying the copper smelter. Matt never rejects Joe, and though he does offer to divide the land among his three sons, Ben callously refuses to sign the deal his father has crafted in order to get more money, a deal that would have prevented Joe from serving in prison. A significant subplot concerns Joe's forbidden romance with Barbara Lawson, the daughter of the state governor who had been Matt's ally. He opposes his daughter's relationship with a man he regards as a half-breed, and so abandons Matt when he needs him most. The issue of anti-Indian racism also surfaces in the treatment of Matt's wife: though she is a Comanche, Matt refers to her as "Señora" in an effort to have her pass as Spanish. Equally progressive for its day is the film's environmentalist sub-theme, concerning pollution of ranchland by industrial pollution, a theme shares with *A Thousand Acres* (below). The film's title underlines one of its central concerns, Joe's impulse to take revenge upon his brothers for their mistreatment of his father and his "kingdom," a choice that threatens to continue the family legacy of hatred and tyranny; upon advice from his mother, Joe decides heroically instead to move on and make a life with Barbara, until Ben's confrontation forces the issue. The lance in question is a Comanche war spear that Joe tosses at Ben's feet at Matt's funeral, a challenge and a curse. In the film's final scene, Joe visits Matt's grave with Barbara and breaks the lance. The connections to *King Lear* are somewhat more muted than in Yordan's first treatment of this material in *House of Strangers*. The film won an Oscar for best original story in 1955.

794 *Hobson's Choice*
1954. U.K. British Lion Film Corporation and
London Film Productions. Sound, b&w, 107 mins.
David Lean.

See summary above. The third film adaptation of Brighouse's play, starring Charles Laughton as Henry Hobson.

795 *The Man from Laramie*
1955. U.S. Sound, col., 104 mins. Anthony Mann.

Yet another Western adaptation of *King Lear* by Philip Yordan (compare *Broken Lance*), this time using the Gloucester plot as its armature and adopting the perspective of an outsider, Will Lockhart, a loner obsessed with finding those who sold rifles to the Apaches and thereby caused his brother's murder. Lockhart wanders into Coronado, a dusty town in the New Mexican salt flats governed by Alec Waggoman, an aging patriarch. His son, Dave, a psychotically violent man, brutalizes Will for unknowingly trespassing on Waggoman land, and Vic Hansbro, Alec's adopted cowhand, saves Will from Dave's fury. Alec uses the promise of inheriting the ranch to control Vic and Dave, but the two are antagonistic toward each other. When Dave tries to give more rifles to the Apaches, with the idea of eliminating a rival ranch, Vic kills him and then implicates Lockhart in the murder. Slowly going blind, Alec discovers a discrepancy in his books, and when he tries to find the wagon of rifles, Vic accidentally pushes him over a cliff. Alec is injured (he becomes completely blind), but he is not killed, and from him Lockhart discovers that Vic spearheaded the sale of rifles. After a chase, Lockhart forces Vic to destroy the rifles, and the Apaches kill Vic for his betrayal. At film's end, Alec is to be married to Kate Canaday, a rival woman rancher, and Lockhart returns to Laramie.

Of Yordan's *Lear* adaptations, *The Man from Laramie* has the slimmest connections with Shakespeare. Nevertheless, Alec Waggoman does have many of the qualities of Gloucester—his superstition (he has a repeated dream of disaster that guides his actions), his misguided trust in the seemingly virtuous Vic, his Lear-like parental tyranny and the promise of inheritance, his literal and metaphorical blindness, and the fall from a cliff that heralds his recognition of the truth. The rivalry of two sons, one legitimate, the other not, over their inheritance also distantly echoes *Lear*, though unlike in Shakespeare's version, we are not privy to Vic's true nature until relatively late in the film and Dave never undergoes Edgar's experience as Poor Tom or his redemption. Of some interest is the way in which Yordan uses the issue of selling rifles to the Apaches to comment obliquely on arms proliferation during the Cold War, making Gloucester-like Alec a representation of the blindness of America. There are neither direct citations from Shakespeare's dialogue nor echoes of key speeches.

796 *Moby Dick Rehearsed*
1955. U.K. Production company unknown. Sound, b&w, 75 mins. completed. Orson Welles.

Adapted from the novel by Herman Melville and the play by Orson Welles. A rehearsal for a performance of *King Lear* is transformed into one for *Moby Dick*. Filmed during Welles's performance of the play in London, this film, intended for TV broadcast, was never completed. An interesting example of Welles drawing analogies between archetypal American and British tragedies.

797 *The Big Show*
1961. U.S. 20th Century Fox and Associated Producers
Inc. Sound, col., 113 mins. James B. Clark.

Bruno Everard is the aging patriarch of a trapeze act
dynasty, preventing his five children, Josef, Garda, Klaus,
Hans, and Fredrik, from marrying anyone outside the circus
world. When Bruno sees the opportunity to merge his
circus with the menagerie owned by Pietro Vizzini, he tries
to wed his favorite son Josef to Vizzini's daughter Teresa, a
bear trainer. However, Klaus, the Everard family's black
sheep, marries Teresa instead in a bid for his father's approval, in the process rejecting Carlotta Martinez, a greedy
high-wire artist. Meanwhile, Josef falls in love with a high-
society American, Hilary Allen, and Garda falls for Eric,
an American soldier, both matches of which Bruno disapproves. After the Martinez family is killed in an accident, Carlotta, herself injured and vengeful toward the
Everards, sues the family over the improper rigging. To
protect the family's assets, Bruno distributes shares of the
circus to his four children (he had earlier disowned Klaus
for being callous about the death of his wife, Teresa).
During the trial, Josef takes the fall for his father and goes
to prison, while Klaus uses the opportunity to take over the
family dynasty, placing his father on an allowance and
banning him from the circus. Bruno, attempting to make a
comeback after being squeezed out, dies in a trapeze accident. Three years later, Josef returns from prison and vows
to retake control of the circus. When Klaus attempts to kill
him, he is mauled by Teresa's bears. In the end, the three
remaining brothers reconstitute the family trapeze act, and
Garda leaves the circus to marry Eric.

Like *Broken Lance* and *House of Strangers*, this film is an
adaptation of Jerome Weidman's novel *I'll Never Go There
Any More*, which shares many parallels with *King Lear*.
Though the narrative does not follow Shakespeare's plot
closely at all, it uses many motifs from the play, particularly
in the film's third act. Bruno corresponds to Lear with his
tyrannical control over his children's love lives. Klaus,
Hans, and Fredrik view their father with varying mixtures
of fear, contempt, and greed for his fortune, while Josef, his
favorite, engages in an act of Cordelia-like sacrifice for
Bruno, even though his father's restriction on marriage
brings him suffering in his relationship with Hilary. Bruno's misconceived division of his "kingdom" among his
children leads, as it does with Lear, to his loss of power and
his humiliation at the hands of Klaus. His spiteful treatment of his father generally resembles that of Regan and
Goneril and, like Edmund, he is regarded as something of
a pariah within the family (he is the only child who is
not a trapeze artist). Even so, Bruno never has a moment
of Lear-like revelation about his maltreatment of his
children, and the final mano a mano between Josef and
Klaus and the reconciliation of the brothers depart sharply
from Shakespeare's far bleaker ending. The adaptation includes no textual citations from Shakespeare's dialogue.

798 *Rosie!*
1967. U.S. Universal and Ross Hunter Productions.
Sound, col., 98 mins. David Lowell Rich.

Adapted from the play *A Very Rich Woman* by Ruth
Gordon, itself an adaptation of Philippe Hériat's play *Les
Joies de la famille*. Rosie Lord is a wealthy, wacky grandmother
with a preference for purple wigs who freely gives away her
money and enters into a variety of madcap schemes, including a partnership with a cab driver and ownership of an
abandoned theater. Her greedy daughters, Mildred and
Edith, concerned that she will fritter away their inheritance,
seek to have her declared incompetent and commit her to a
mental institution, where she is nearly driven insane by a
bureaucratic psychiatrist and a nurse obsessed with tea
drinking. When her loving granddaughter Daphne learns of
their scheme and Rosie's maltreatment, she enlists the help
of Oliver Stephenson, a lawyer and Rosie's ex-lover, to
spearhead a court battle to liberate her. Eventually, Rosie is
freed and the daughters get their comeuppance.

Rosie! creates an unlikely and tonally very unstable hybrid between *Auntie Mame* (in which Rosalind Russell also
starred) and *King Lear*. In this version, Rosie, the Lear
figure, is sweet, fun-loving, and generous to a fault, if
somewhat eccentric. It is her daughters who, money-
obsessed and intolerant of their mother's free spirit, use the
law to dispossess her and drive her to the brink of insanity,
and it is her granddaughter Daphne, the Cordelia figure,
along with her lawyer Oliver, the Kent figure, who team up
to restore her to her former free-spirited state. During the
trial scene, the connection with *King Lear* is made explicit
with a citation of the "How sharper than a serpent's tooth"
speech. The film is an odd mix of madcap comedy in the
first half with satire on the psychiatric maltreatment of the
socially unconventional in the second half. The Gloucester plot is entirely jettisoned.

799 *One Is a Lonely Number*
1972. U.S. MGM. Sound, col., 97 mins. Mel
Stuart.

When Amy Brower's marriage to her college professor
husband James falls apart after he leaves with a student,
Amy struggles with shock, depression, and loneliness. She
tries several ways of addressing her new situation: her friend
Madge introduces her to a support group for divorcees, but
she finds Gert, the group's leader, too bitter; she tries to
throw herself into her career; she befriends an older man,
Joseph Provo, a recent widower; and she starts to date
Howard Carpenter, a man she meets at an art exhibition.

In an early sequence, as Amy first copes with the loss of
her marriage, she sees a performance of *King Lear* and sobs
uncontrollably, identifying with Lear's abandonment.

800 *Harry and Tonto*
1974. U.S. 20th Century Fox. Sound, col., 115 mins.
Paul Mazursky.

Harry Coombes, an older ex-professor living alone with his cat Tonto, is rendered homeless when he loses his New York City apartment to the wrecking ball. At first, he moves in with his oldest son Burt and his family, but he soon finds it uncomfortable and undertakes a trip to see his daughter Shirley in Chicago and son Eddie in Los Angeles. Abandoning plane and bus for Tonto's sake, Harry buys a car and drives cross-country, in the process picking up Ginger, a girl running away from home to a Colorado commune, who finds a kindred spirit with Norman, Burt's countercultural son. As he travels to see his children, Harry meets a variety of colorful characters, among them a religious hitchhiker, a senile former girlfriend, a vitamin salesman, a high-class hooker, and a Native American medicine man. After he arrives in Los Angeles and meets Eddie, who has run out of money, his beloved Tonto dies. At film's end, Harry, now alone in Los Angeles, befriends Celia, an eccentric cat lady who impulsively offers to share her apartment with him.

Mazursky's study of the poignancy of old age dovetails elements of Lear's dispossession with a countercultural road movie. Harry's loss of his home only completes the process of his losing the neighborhood of his youth and his wife, and so he is forced somewhat Lear-like to wander the "heath" of middle America to discover various dispossessed and wandering characters he never before knew. Tonto the cat, to whom Harry sings and talks, has the function of the Fool, Harry's traveling companion and confidante. Harry signals his kinship to Lear early on with three citations from the play, the second of which is taken from the "reason not the need" speech in 2.4 and the third from Lear's "Blow, winds, and crack your cheeks" speech in 3.2 as Harry is evicted from his apartment; he offers a fourth citation, "I loved her most, and thought to set my rest / On her kind nursery" (1.1), when he meets his unhappy daughter Shirley, with whom he has a tense but warm relationship. In passing, Harry confesses to his friend Jacob that he has been thinking about Lear (to which Jacob replies, "Lear who?"); when he meets his daughter Shirley, a bookshop owner, he refers to Shakespeare as "the world's greatest writer," an opinion she readily shares. In this version of the *Lear* story, Harry's children are not unloving or the cause of his homelessness, and on his journey Harry widens his cultural horizons rather than confronts his own self-ishness, gaining a new openness to non-main-stream American culture but also an awareness of the losses wrought by time. The closing scenes of the film, after Tonto's death, are more poignant than tragic, and the final shot, in which Harry watches a boy build sandcastles on a beach, suggests the gentle completion of a life cycle rather than the devastation of Shakespeare's ending.

801 *The Dresser*
1983. U.K. Goldcrest Films Ltd. and World Film Services. Sound, col., 118 mins. Peter Yates.

Adapted for the screen by Ronnie Harwood from his own stageplay, *The Dresser* is essentially a modified two-hander, focusing on the complex backstage relationship between Sir, an aging Shakespearean actor-manager on a tour of the provinces during World War II, and Norman, his closeted gay dresser who rules Sir with an iron hand, getting him through his performances while silently suffering his abuse and selfishness. The two resemble in many ways Lear and the Fool. The performances of Albert Finney as Sir and Tom Courtenay as Norman (Courtenay originated the role on the stage) are genuine tours de force. The piece makes much of the parallel between Sir and Lear, the Shakespearean character he plays in this his final performance, for both are authoritarian, self-centered, nearly senile, and half-mad, facing death and meaninglessness, at once powerful and pathetic, self-pitying and self-dramatizing. Indeed, in his performance of the part, Sir comes to see the resemblance between himself and Lear, though he never recognizes the further connection between long-suffering Norman and the Fool, nor does he experience Lear's discovery of compassion or acknowledgment of those he had earlier neglected. Unlike Shakespeare's faithful Fool, who endeavors to puncture Lear's illusions about himself, Norman faithfully maintains Sir's illusions

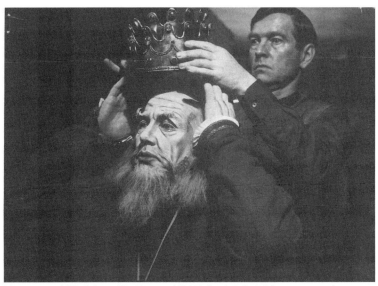

Norman and "Sir" from *The Dresser* (1983). In this shot, Norman puts the crown on "Sir" as he prepares to play King Lear. Courtesy of Douglas Lanier.

so that he can face yet another night on the stage. Madge, the stage manager of the troupe who faithfully loves Sir despite his using her, has qualities of Cordelia. The film version underplays the wry comedy of Harwood's playscript in favor of Norman's unacknowledged and thus ultimately tragic devotion to the Shakespearean he loves. The mid-war context—sketched in somewhat more fully and elegiacally in this adaptation—allows the film to be read as more than a crypto-portrait of Shakespearean Donald Wolfit (about whom Harwood wrote a biography). It is also a portrait of the ambivalent cultural legacy of Shakespearean theater at a definitive moment of its decline. Norman's anguished "What about me?" at Sir's death thus voices not only his personal betrayal by Sir but also the demands of modernity and present life against the tyranny of an outdated cultural heritage.

The film opens with the final moments of *Othello*, with Sir in the title role. It also includes portions of four scenes from Sir's decidedly old-fashioned performance of *King Lear*: the opening scene (in which Sir misses his opening cue and the cast is forced to improvise in Shakespearean language), 2.4 (in which Lear tries to resist weeping at the end of the "reason not the need" speech), the storm scene (in which we watch Norman and others create the sound effects), and the final scene (in which Lear carries on Cordelia and dies). The dialogue is peppered with passing Shakespearean allusions, not only to *Lear* (the line "reason not the need" and the Fool's song "hey, ho, the wind and the rain" are repeated motifs) but also to *Othello*, *Richard III*, *The Merchant of Venice*, *Henry V* (especially Henry's band of brothers speech), *Romeo and Juliet*, and *Macbeth* (including the curse surrounding the play). Theatrical in-jokes—about cocked-up Shakespearean lines and the weight of Cordelia—are also featured. At one point backstage, Sir engages in a funny free-associative romp through several Shakespearean commonplaces as he struggles to remember his lines.

802 *King Real and the Hoodlums*
1983. U.S. Welfare State International. Sound, col., 54 mins. John Fox and Paul Haywood.

Adapted from the play by Adrian Mitchell by the author himself. King Real is forced by the Hoodlums, a mob of punks in quasi-medieval garb, to divide his power between Raygal, Gonilla, and Cloudella, his three daughters. When Cloudella refuses her share out of love for her father, her sisters send her into a wasteland with Thomas, a musician at court. Raygal and Gonilla come to share a nuclear fallout shelter with King Real and Adderman, a fearsome soldier, but after a grotesque banquet in which the sisters eat a globe-shaped cake, the sisters surgically cut out their father's eyes, evict him from the shelter, and start a nuclear war. Wandering the devastated landscape, blind Lear comes across his daughter Cloudella, who sings a touching

song about her love and fear of him as she dies; Real dies soon after. The final musical number, a protest song, is sung by a resident of Barrow who has been forced by hard financial circumstances to build nuclear submarines.

This rock musical was staged by the performance group Welfare State International, which specialized in surreal large-scale extravaganzas. It was shot in the bleak Cornish town of Barrow-in-Furness, where the main industry is building nuclear submarines. The "blasted heath" is represented by the bleak docklands. Unemployed Barrow youth played the Hoodlums, and the film project was a community effort. As the summary suggests, the parallels with Shakespeare's narrative are many, converting *King Lear* into a savage anti–nuclear war fable and social satire. There are no direct citations of Shakespeare's dialogue. This film has never been commercially released. See also entry 373.

803 *Ran*
1985. Japan and France. Greenwich Film Productions, Herald Ace Inc., and Nippon Herald Films. Sound, col., 160 mins. Akira Kurosawa.

Hidetora Ichimonji, an aging sixteenth-century warlord in Japan, resolves to cede his authority to his eldest son, Taro, dividing his other castles and lands between sons Jiro and Saburo. Making a mockery of Hidetora's fable of the three arrows, Saburo warns him of his folly, but Hidetora banishes him along with Tango, his loyal servant who is equally truthful and loyal. Soon Taro, at the instigation of his wife Lady Kaede, exerts his power over Hidetora by humiliating him; furious, Hidetora goes to Jiro, who, by forcing his father to keep his retinue outside the castle, gets rid of him. With Saburo residing with Fujimaki, his father-in-law, Hidetora goes to his castle, only to be routed by Taro's army, who spare him because he is mad. Wandering the hills and plains in madness with Tango and Kyoami, Hidetora's jester, Hidetora comes across the hovel occupied by the brother of Lady Sué, Tsurumaru, who Hidetora rendered homeless and blinded as a child. Meanwhile, with Taro dead in the battle for Saburo's castle, Kaede takes up with Jiro and plots to kill his wife, Lady Sué. As Hidetora roams the ruins of Tsurumaru's castle and the plain with Kyoami, the armies of Jiro and Saburo and his allies gather. As the result of a treacherous truce, Saburo reunites with his father but is killed by assassins before Hidetora can ask forgiveness; grief-stricken, Hidetora dies as news arrives of Saburo's men's victory over Jiro. Horrified by Kaede's order to kill Sué, Fujimaki executes her. Tsurumaru, blind and unaware that his sister is dead, waits on a cliff for her return.

A brilliant and visually dazzling transposition of Shakespeare to Japan's violent Muromachi era, *Ran* marries many of *Lear*'s themes with the ritualized qualities of Noh drama and the martial intensity of samurai epics. As he does in *Throne of Blood*, Kurosawa treats Shakespeare's plot as an inspiration for his scenario rather than as a narrative blueprint, though he does include parallels to many of Shakespeare's characters and plot motifs: Hidetora's banishment of Sanjuro and Tango recalls Lear's banishment of Cordelia and Kent; Hidetora's curse upon Taro and Kaede recalls his curse upon Goneril; and Kyoami's tuneful mockery of Lear recalls the Fool's lampoons of Lear, though Kurosawa complicates their relationship by having Kyoami contemplate abandoning Lear. Indeed, many of Kurosawa's changes in Shakespeare's narrative are especially telling. Hidetora is undone by his pride and his sons' flattery, but also by his own ruthlessly violent campaign in the past to unite the kingdom, a campaign that has bred potent enemies and ambitious sons. Hidetora's violent past returns especially powerfully in his confrontation with Tsurumaru; picking up the motif of blinding from the Gloucester plot and making Hidetora the agent of it deepen the old warlord's culpability for unleashing a cycle of hatred and destruction—the title *Ran* means "chaos"—on his world. The recurrent image of the hunt (the film opens with a boar hunt, and hunt metaphors pepper the dialogue) gives metaphorical focus to this theme. Changing Lear's daughters to Hidetora's sons allows Kurosawa to explore not only the darker side of the samurai ethic, the ambition and greed lurking underneath codes of ritual and obedience, but also, as he earlier had with Asaji in *Throne of Blood*, the figure of the viperous royal wife in the form of Lady Kaede, who pushes Taro and Jiro into horrifying war in her quest for power and vengeance upon the Ichimonji family. *Ran* is one of the few free film adaptations that picks up *Lear*'s exploration of metaphysical questions about the grim nature of the cosmos and gods, a theme announced visually by recurring shots of the sky. Again and again, Hidetora and Kyoami muse upon the cruel ironies of fate as they confront the fruits of Hidetora's violence. Indeed, when Sanjuro's victory is announced after Hidetora and Sanjuro's senseless deaths, Kyoami, in an echo of Gloucester's line about the gods as wanton boys, accuses the gods, "You are mischievous and cruel! Are you so bored up there that you must crush us like ants? Is it such fun to see men weep?" The film ends on an unforgettable image of the human condition: Tsurumaru, blind, edging toward a precipice, waits for his sister to return, unaware that she is dead; when he comes too close to the ledge and stumbles, he drops the scroll of Buddha meant to comfort and protect him, and so is left alone, motionless lest he fall. See also entries 371 and 374.

The DVD Masterworks edition includes two commentary tracks, one by film historian Stephen Prince, the other by filmmaker and Japanese specialist Peter Grilli, both of which reference Shakespeare, as well as a documentary by Chris Marker, "The Making of *Ran*."

804 *Hollywood Shuffle*
1987. U.S. Conquering Unicorn and Samuel Goldwyn Company. Sound, col., 78 mins. Robert Townshend.

This study of black discontent in Hollywood uses the story of Bobby Taylor, a black actor struggling to make a living in the film industry, as the armature for a series of often biting lampoons of racial prejudice against black actors, producers, and directors. While Bobby works at a hotdog stand and imagines himself in various classic heroic Hollywood roles as he works on his own film project, he endures humiliating auditions for stereotypical "black" roles. When he is offered a part as a black thug, he must decide between accepting a demeaning role and maintaining his principles.

In one satirical sequence, in a mock advertisement for a Hollywood school for black actors, one black Shakespearean who has played in *King Lear* speaks of his need to master black street lingo and behavior.

805 *King Lear*
1987. Bahamas and U.S. Cannon Films. Sound, col., 90 mins. Jean-Luc Godard.

Godard's post-modern deconstruction of *King Lear* defies any easy plot summary, since one point of the film is to undermine conventional cinematic narrative. Underneath the credits, we hear an apparently real taped phone conversation between producers at Cannon Films (who produced the work) and Godard about his failure to deliver the film. The narrative proper opens with a short prologue in which Norman Mailer, one of the film's writers, shows the script in progress to his daughter Kate. The film's governing fiction concerns an apocalyptic, post-Chernobyl world in which all elements of life have been restored except for art and film. William Shakespeare Jr. the Fifth, played by the director Peter Sellars, has been contracted by the Cannon Cultural Division and Her Royal Majesty to reconstruct the works of his ancestor. Staying in Nyon, he encounters Don Learo, an aging Jewish American gangster, and his daughter Cordelia who are speaking Shakespearean lines, and he strives to record what they are saying. Shakespeare Jr. also encounters Edgar, a half-mad character with a butterfly net, and has long theoretical conversations with Professor Pluggy, a zany professor—played by Godard himself—about the nature of mimesis and the visual image. Toward film's end, we see the editing of the film footage supervised by Mr. Alien, an official of the Cannon Cultural Division (played by Woody Allen). The final image of the film is of Cordelia in white, laid upon a rock as if in sacrifice, while behind her Lear looks at a lake.

Godard's exceptionally challenging adaptation—in the film he calls it "a study," "an approach," and "a clearing"—uses *King Lear* as a starting point for contemplating the question of cultural transmission, a problem he examines from several angles at once. The gangster Don Learo is a manifestation of the "Las Vegasizing" (Godard's term) of American culture, a figure of enormous cultural power who now seeks to pass on culture to his daughter, Cordelia.

Cordelia, whom Godard explicitly identifies with virtue, says "nothing" to Lear's demand for devotion, a nothing that, Godard demonstrates at some length, might be analogized to the wordless image itself and to the avant-garde penchant for virtuously refusing to say what the wider culture wants to hear. For that reason, the opening map scene becomes a leitmotif throughout the film, repeated in different permutations and with different images juxtaposed to Shakespeare's words. It is also why Godard foregrounds the tension between himself and Cannon Films, a commercial studio run by Menahem Golan and Yoram Globus, two powerful Jewish producers. Shakespeare Jr's role also thematizes the problem of cultural transmission in the post-modern age, since instead of Shakespeare being the source of the script, this Shakespeare records the script by listening to Don Learo and Cordelia, who are themselves remembering passages of *King Lear* and mixing them up with Learo's memoir of American gangster culture. That Peter Sellars, a noted avant-garde director, plays the part of this latter-day Shakespeare only underlines how the conventional relationship between author as source and director as interpreter has become unsettled and reversed in post-modernity. Godard's own character, Professor Pluggy, a professorial version of Lear's wise Fool, introduces yet a third element problematizing the transmission of literary icons such as Shakespeare: the superiority of the visual image over the spoken word. The image, Godard stresses, bears some analogy to Cordelia's spoken "nothing," in that the image communicates without words, even though it nevertheless communicates intellectual content. Godard's own method in the film is to refuse the most "literary" element of filmmaking, conventional narrative and dialogue. He reinforces the point by crafting a soundtrack that is disjunct from the screen images and often intentionally muddled, noisy, or incoherent, using passages from *Lear* as commentary on what we see, including non-linguistic elements (such as non-diegetic screams of seabirds or storm sounds), or featuring forms of wordplay. Setting himself the task of filming *King Lear*, one of the acknowledged masterpieces of Western high culture, Godard instead films his meditation on the challenges to that task, challenges that spring from the conflict between the literary and the cinematic, the conflict between the commercial nature of American pop culture and the filmmaker's commitment to cinema as art, and the tension between faithfulness to the cultural past and directorial creativity in the post-modern present. Godard uses snippets from many passages of *King Lear*, turning several into textual leitmotifs (among them "Nothing" and "Come not between the dragon and his wrath. / I loved her most, and thought to set my rest / On her kind nursery," both from 1.1). Also referenced are "To be or not to be," Hamlet's "In my heart there was a kind of fighting, / That would not let me sleep" (from *Hamlet* 5.2), and play titles such as *Love's Labor's Lost*, and *As You Like It*. A difficult film that repays close study.

806 *Where the Heart Is*
1990. U.S. Silver Screen Partners IV and Touchstone Pictures. Sound, col., 107 mins. John Boorman.

Stewart McBain, a real estate developer who specializes in demolition, finds his plans for Brooklyn's tallest skyscraper stymied when a small building, Dutch House, is declared a protected property. In a fit of pique, he forces his three college-educated, artistically inclined children, Daphne, Chloe, and Jimmy, out of his home and into Dutch House, where he leaves them with $750 each on which to live. Desperate for cash, the three children work on creative money-making schemes: Daphne on a magic act with a homeless ex-magician called Shitty, Chloe on a trompe l'oeil calendar for an insurance agency, and Jimmy on a computer game called Demolition. They also take in various eccentric boarders—Shitty, Tom (a stock trader), Lionel (a gay fashion designer), and Sheryl (a mystic)— and temporarily try nine-to-five jobs. When a corporate raider targets Stewart's company, he mortgages all his property in an effort to fend off the raid, but he ends up losing everything when the market falls. Homeless, he wanders the streets until he is taken in by his children at Dutch House, and he reconciles with them. The city issues an eviction notice on Dutch House, but when a storm blows up, Stewart uses it as a cover to demolish the house, freeing up the property for development and allowing him to regain his company and riches. At film's end, Lionel gives a triumphal fashion show, and all the main characters reconcile with each other in a celebratory dance.

Where the Heart Is recombines various motifs from *Lear* and recasts them in comic mode. Stewart McBain, the Lear-like, acerbic patriarch, stubbornly forces his children to share Dutch House less out of anger or power than for their own good, since all are spoiled rich kids. Though the children resent their plight (and Daphne, Stewart's favorite, even attempts to change his mind), all continue to love their father; and when he is destitute, they search for him and willingly take him in, quickly forgiving him. Once rendered penniless, both the children and Stewart become acquainted with the poor and outcast of Brooklyn, though Stewart has the more chastening experience, sleeping in a cardboard hovel, roaming a waste dump, and, he observes, nearly "losing my mind." (Interestingly, none of the characters are protected from financial disaster when the stock market crashes, including Tom, the financial whiz.) Shitty, the magician bum, has some of the qualities of Lear's Fool, though he is Daphne's, not Stewart's, companion. At one point, he appears in one of Chloe's painting-photos as Lear in the storm, and he often complains of the destructiveness of the modern age in poetic terms, for example "I have seen with the magic of the eye" and "I have grown weary of these chains." As Stewart's life falls apart, his wife observes that he never really knew his children, and when he quits his bankrupt company, he says, in a line reminiscent of Lear, "I go naked into the world." Ironically, in this adaptation the storm is not a metaphor for Lear's madness but a contrived device for Stewart to regain his former status. The dance that ends the film underlines the magical reconciliation of all the characters; somewhat disappointingly, Lionel declares that he is in fact not gay (he was pretending to make it as a fashion designer) so that he can pair off with Chloe. To Daphne, Stewart declares the lesson of his experiences: enjoy the aesthetic pleasures of the moment.

807 *American Friends*
1991. U.S. BBC, British Screen Productions, Mayday, Millenium, and Prominent Features. Sound, col., 95 mins. Tristram Powell.

Francis Ashby, a bookish Oxford College fellow on holiday in the Swiss Alps, meets two American women, Caroline Hartley and her adopted daughter, Elinor. Elinor and Ashby quickly become awkwardly drawn to each other though they cannot express it directly, while Caroline develops an unreciprocated attraction to Ashby. After Ashby returns to Oxford anticipating the death of his college's president and his succession, the two women arrive at his college, and both attempt to coax out his feelings, attempts he resists because of the college's rules about the fellows having relationships with women. Soon Symes, one of Ashby's rakish colleagues, seduces Elinor. When Ashby discovers that Elinor is pregnant with Symes's child, he finally confesses his love and gives up his chance at the college presidency to marry her. Michael Palin claims that the quiet, affecting study of emotional repression was inspired by the travel diaries of his great-grandfather.

A leitmotif throughout the film is a college production of *King Lear*, referenced in three scenes. The first of these scenes sets up the parallel between the tyrannical and aged college president, obsessed with propriety and control of his "kingdom," and King Lear. The president himself says, "You want a Lear? Then you should search among that sort of men well steeped in ambition, betrayal and greed. I'm your Lear." In the last of the *Lear* scenes, a storm disrupts the performance of the play (during the storm scene) just as Ashby's problems with Elinor and Caroline begin to escalate. Like Lear, Ashby must learn to shed his attachment to the trappings of academic power and prestige and risk openly embracing the woman he truly loves, the "daughter" Elinor.

808 *The Madness of King George*
1994. U.K. Channel Four Films, Close Call Films, Mad George Films, and Sam Goldwyn Company. Sound, col., 107 mins. Nicholas Hytner.

Adapted from the play by Alan Bennett. King George III's descent into madness leads to court and parliamentary intrigue and to a horrifying depiction of eighteenth-century psychiatric practices. *King Lear* figures in George's recovery. When he regains his wits, he is acting 4.7 with his equerry and Mr. Thurlow, with George taking the part of Lear. Earlier, there is an exchange between the doctor Willis and two of George's ministers. Mr. Pitt observes that "I used to sit with my father when he was ill. I used to read him Shakespeare." Willis's reply, "I never read Shakespeare. I'm a clergyman," receives worried looks from the ministers. Prince George's efforts to usurp the throne by feeding his father's madness bear some parallels to the plot of *KL*.

809 *Family*
1996. India. Vijaya Bapineedu. Sound, col., 189 mins. Vijaya Bapineedu.

Shankarum is the authoritarian middle-class father of three daughters, Kalyani, Kavitha, and Kasthuri, and a son. He quickly arranges marriages for his three daughters with boorish working-class husbands—an exterminator, a cook, and an auto driver—without asking his daughters' approvals. The marriages soon go sour as the women suffer at the hands of their chauvinistic husbands, and the women attempt to assert their power by getting jobs. Matters are made worse by Shankarum's refusal to give his sons-in-law a promised share of his property. Shankarum's son marries into an upwardly mobile family, and his father signs over the family's property to him to finance a factory, at which the mother dies of anguish; when Shankarum orders him to finance a sister-in-law's marriage, he evicts Shankarum, and his daughters and heretofore ne'er-do-well sons-in-law team up to resist his brother's ill treatment of their father. In the end, all are reconciled.

Though this socially progressive comedy about respect for women's equal place in the family has been advertised as an adaptation of *King Lear*, in fact parallels with Shakespeare's play come into focus only briefly late in the film when Shankarum's arrogant mistreatment of his daughters and wife is revisited on him in the form of his dispossession by his son. Even so, the father's experience of homelessness becomes a mechanism for him to confront and reform his own jaundiced gender attitudes (as do his sons-in-law). There are no allusions to Shakespeare's dialogue.

DVD contains no extras referencing Shakespeare, though the package identifies the film as an adaptation of *King Lear*.

810 *The Substance of Fire*
1996. U.S. Miramax. Sound, col., 97 mins. Daniel G. Sullivan.

Adapted from the play by Jon Robin Baitz. Lonely after his wife's death and haunted by memories of his family's demise in the Holocaust, Isaac Geldhart, head of a small publishing firm, has become a perfectionist, ignoring financial realities and publishing expensive books on the Holocaust. Anxious to improve the company's bottom line, his son Aaron, who works for the firm, seeks to publish a contemporary novel by Val Chenard, and he enlists his siblings Martin and Sarah to convince his father. When his father refuses and attempts to fire Aaron, Sarah and Martin shift their shares to Aaron, effectively dispossessing Isaac. Isaac sets up a new company and sells everything to finance an expensive multivolume set on Nazi genocide by author Louis Foukold, a decision that leads to financial disaster and abandonment by his longtime secretary Miss Barzakian. When Isaac rejects his children and begins to have problems with his memory, Martin, himself suffering from cancer, moves in to take care of him. Meanwhile, Aaron takes up with Val, and Sarah abandons husband Max, a director, for her co-star Peter. When a social worker seeks to quiz Isaac about his competency, Martin becomes gravely ill and soon dies. At the funeral, the remaining children, Louis, Miss Barzakian and Isaac reconcile in Martin's favorite park.

A fascinating free adaptation that transposes many elements of Shakespeare's play to contemporary New York. Isaac corresponds to Lear, Martin to Cordelia, Sarah and Aaron to Regan and Goneril, Miss Barzakian to Kent, and Foukold to the Fool. Isaac's collection of literary memorabilia serves as his "train," and he suffers his first bout of mania during a storm, spurred on, appropriately enough, by an obsession with clothing. Like the Fool, Foukold revels in dirty jokes and mirrors Isaac's personality, and Miss Barzakian, like Kent, suffers silently until she is compelled to leave. The film generates some sympathy for Isaac's demanding nature by adding the back story of his wife and Holocaust experience, but he is also presented as irresponsible and self-destructive. It also generates sympathy regarding the children's romances: unlike Regan's and Goneril's, Edmund, Sarah and Aaron's lovers are presented favorably; Martin is poignantly alone, devoted to his father to the point of self-immolation. Of some interest is that this adaptation imagines a happy ending for the *Lear* narrative: after Martin dies, all of those Isaac has alienated reconcile with him at Martin's funeral. Isaac's burning a postcard by a Jewish artist exemplifies his final letting go of his obsession with past wrongs, in a gesture that eerily, obliquely echoes the crematoria. This adaptation contains no equivalent to the Gloucester plot, and no direct reference to Shakespeare's dialogue.

811 A Thousand Acres
1997. U.S. Beacon Communications LLC, PolyGram Filmed Entertainment, Prairie Films, Propaganda Films, Touchstone Pictures, and Via Rosa Productions. Sound, col., 105 mins. Jocelyn Moorhouse.

Adapted from the novel by Jane Smiley (entry 1860). Shifting the plot and characters of *King Lear* to agricultural middle America, *A Thousand Acres* portrays the breakup of the family and farming empire of Larry Cook, a crusty aging farmer who suddenly decides to divide his land between his three daughters, Ginny (i.e., Goneril), Rose (Regan), and Caroline (Cordelia). When Caroline, a lawyer, hesitates, Larry savagely rejects her and slowly slips into bitterness, senility, and rage, while the remaining daughters struggle to take care of an increasingly difficult father who, we eventually learn, sexually abused them as children. After Larry wanders off drunk in a storm and moves in with his neighbor Harold (a combination of Gloucester and Kent), Caroline spearheads a suit on behalf of her father against the sisters, a suit they lose. Meanwhile, Ginny and Rose's marriages suffer crises, both women having affairs with Jess, Harold's son. Eventually Rose dies of cancer, leaving Ginny with her children after the farm is sold.

Smiley's novel and Moorhouse's film reorient the story to Ginny's point of view (Ginny's voice-over offers commentary on events throughout), and they also rearticulate the sympathies of Shakespeare's play, presenting Larry and Harold as vindictive, Caroline as naïve, and Rose as justifiably angry. Ginny's character travels the longest path, moving from devotion to her father and the farm to a feminist recognition of her oppression as wife and daughter and to action to gain her independence. The film's focus on personal melodrama tends to mute the novel's interest in the farming empire and the theme of poison—psychological and environmental—just beneath the surface of these women's lives. A number of critics have complained that the revelation of Larry's incest with his daughters undermines the complexity of the father-daughter relationships in Shakespeare's original by providing an easy and unassailable justification for Ginny and Rose's treatment of their father; others have found it a moving adaptation of Shakespeare to contemporary feminist liberation narratives.

In addition to the many plot and character parallels with *King Lear*, the film also includes a reference to *The Merchant of Venice*: in a pique of bitterness Rose, referring to her mastectomy, sardonically calls her lost breast her "pound of flesh."

812 Jakob the Liar
1999. France, U.S., and Hungary. Blue Wolf Productions, Global Entertainment Productions, Kasso Inc., and TriStar Pictures. Sound, col., 120 mins. Peter Kassovitz.

Adapted from the novel by Jurek Becker. In the Warsaw ghetto in 1944, Jakob Heym, a Jewish shopkeeper, accidentally hears favorable news about Allied victories against the Nazis on a radio and relays them to his friends. When as a result rumors of a secret radio within the ghetto begin to circulate, Jakob spins fake war reports that boost the morale of his fellow Polish Jews. When the Nazis learn of these stories, they become convinced that there is in fact a radio in the ghetto, and they hunt down its operator.

In this remake of the DDR film *Jakob der Lügner* (Frank Beyer, 1974), *King Lear* comes up in the context of a marriage negotiation. Misha, a boxer, asks for the hand of Rosa from her father and mother, Mr. and Mrs. Frankfurter. When Mr. Frankfurter opposes the marriage on the grounds that all of the Jews in the ghetto have no future, Misha replies that the war will end very soon because the Russians are at Bezonica. To Misha's question, "Do you know where Bezonica is?" Frankfurter replies, "Do I know where Bezonica is? I played King Lear there three times. 'As flies to . . .'" When he pauses to try to remember the rest of the line, Mrs. Frankfurter helps by adding, "As flies to wanton boys," at which Frankfurter completes the line incorrectly: "As flies to wanton boys, they kill us for their sport." (The correct line is "As flies to wanton boys are we to the gods, they kill us for their sport.") Misha supports his claim that he heard from Jakob Heym, who has a radio. Frankfurter consents to the marriage, but destroys his own radio, which he fears will be found and will lead to his death and the discovery of Heym's radio.

DVD includes a director's commentary track that references Shakepeare.

813 *The King Is Alive (aka Dogme 4)*
1999. Denmark. Ballistic Pictures, Danmarks Radio, Det Danske Filminstitut, Good Machine, Newmarket Capital Group LLC, Nordisk Film- & TV-Fond, SVT Drama, and Zentropa Entertainments. Sound, col., 110 mins. Kristian Levring.

Eleven tourists on a bus in the Namib Desert in Africa become stranded when their bus becomes lost at night and then breaks down in the wilderness. Isolated in a deserted Nazi supply depot deep in the desert and far from civilization, the group slowly begins to realize that the situation is life-threatening. To fight off panic and their consciousness of hunger and dehydration, Henry, a former London stage actor, suggests that the group perform *King Lear*, and he writes out the roles from memory. Soon, however, the performance becomes yet another source of tension within the group, and members of the group begin to take out long-running and newly emerging antagonisms amongst themselves on each other, both within and outside the rehearsals. Eventually the group is rescued, but not before three of the group, Jack, Gina, and Charlie, die, Charlie by suicide. The story is narrated by Kanana, a mysterious old African who inhabits the supply station.

This Dogme 95 film does not attempt to replicate the plot of *King Lear* or pursue consistent parallels between Shakespeare's characters and the tourists. Indeed, within the film's narrative the choice of *Lear* as the play the group performs seems rather bizarre. Rather, it is the situation of Lear on the heath, where he becomes aware of different responses to the condition of "unaccommodated man," that resonates with the dire, primal situation of the stranded tourists and their responses to it. Henry first recognizes the appropriateness when he sees their dire predicament as "some fantastic striptease act of basic human needs." As is typical of Dogme films, the interest is in stripping away polite social veneers to raw, base emotions beneath. Levring's technique is to fragment the Shakespearean text and refract the stranded, desperate tourists' hidden desires, aggressions, fears, illusions, and attachments through the Shakespearean passages they speak as they rehearse to fend off despair. The line "I cannot heave my heart into my mouth," uttered early on, takes on particular resonance in that regard. For example, Liz, the sexually frustrated and childless wife of Ray, tries to generate her husband's jealousy by flirting with the bus driver Moses, a strategy that becomes apparent to Ray when Liz and Moses play Goneril's kiss with Edmund at 4.2.17–24; Henry and Gina develop an attachment, one that leads to Catherine's eventually murderous jealousy toward her (the parallel to Lear and Cordelia becoming apparent when Henry plays Lear's anguished "howl, howl, howl" speech over Gina's dead body). Citations from *Lear* abound: Regan and Cordelia's responses to Lear's request for declarations of love are played several times; Amanda speaks the Fool's lines about "court[ing] holy-water in a dry house" (3.2) as she sorts tin cans of food; Ray repeats Kent's final line, "My master calls me, I must not say no," as he trudges through the desert; and the final scene is an elaborate pastiche of lines from the play, primarily from Lear's lament over Cordelia's corpse. The handheld digital video lends the film the immediacy of a documentary, an effect heightened by the location shooting in Namibia.

814 *Shiner*
2000. U.K. Geoff Reeve Films, Vision View Entertainment, and Wisecroft Ltd. Sound, col., 99 mins. John Irvin.

In this gritty British crime drama, Billy "Shiner" Simpson, a petty boxing promoter working at the edges of the law, invests everything he has—his possessions, his authority, his reputation, and his hopes for redemption—in a single boxing match involving his son Eddie, the "Golden Boy." When Eddie quickly loses to an American champion, Billy suspects that his son threw the fight, but before he can discover the truth, his son is murdered. As Billy, distraught and increasingly brutal, follows out what he sees as a plot, he discovers that his daughter Georgie has betrayed him and that his associates and children, Eddie included, were justifiably terrified of him.

The plot of the film follows the outlines of a conventional if stylish film noir and so does not parallel the plot of *King Lear* except in isolated motifs. But as a character study of a frighteningly authoritarian but finally weak father who discovers the fear and mistrust he's bred among his children and followers, *Shiner* offers a number of interesting parallels to Shakespeare's character. Compare *My Kingdom* (below), another British-produced transposition of *Lear* to the world of the contemporary British underworld. *Shiner* includes no direct citations from *Lear* or any other Shakespearean play.

DVD includes a trailer and a "Making Of" featurette; in the latter, producer Geoff Reeve claims that the genesis of the story was his and Michael Caine's desire to do a modernized version of *King Lear*.

815 *My Kingdom*
2001. Italy and U.K. Close Grip Films Ltd., Primary Pictures, and Sky Pictures. Sound, col., 117 mins. Don Boyd.

Sandeman, the crusty aging patriarch of a Liverpool crime syndicate, is devoted to his wife Mandy. After Mandy is murdered during a mugging, in part because of Sandeman's cockiness, he resolves to give control of the syndicate (and of his estate upon his death) to Jo, his favorite. However, Jo, a reformed junkie disgusted by her father's criminal activities, is unwilling to become involved in crime, and so he transfers his wealth to her sisters, Traci, owner of a football team, and Kath, madame for a brothel. They battle for control of their father's empire, aided by their respective husbands, Jug, a sadistic Sikh drug dealer, and Dean, head of Sandeman's "security." As the daughters fight, they quickly cut their father off from his money and power, leaving him penniless and paranoid in the company of Kath's son. Meanwhile, Buddy Puttnam, a corrupt vice cop assigned to the case of Mandy's murder, is courted by Kath and Traci in their double-cross schemes, and Quick, a customs officer dying of cancer, pursues Sandeman until he is blinded by Jug in an interrogation. When Kath's son is killed by Jug's men, Sandeman teams with Jo and her thuggish ex-lover The Chair to give both couples their comeuppance. Kath and Traci kill each other with knives, Dean and Jug are shot, and The Chair is arrested, leaving Jo and Sandeman alive.

While by no means slavish, Boyd's stylish gangster adaptation deftly transposes much of Shakespeare's narrative and many of his characters to the contemporary Merseyside underworld. The Lear-like Sandeman, portentously first pictured playing solitaire, adores his wife as a symbol of his own misrecognized family values and sees daughter Jo as a version of his wife. Mandy's death, for which Sandeman was largely responsible, plunges him into a crisis of self-recognition, one he fruitlessly seeks to avoid by seeing Mandy's murder as part of a dark conspiracy to kill him and by drawing Jo into the crime family. When Jo refuses, disgusted by the murder of Delroy, the mugger who shot Mandy, and Sandeman disowns her, he falls to the mercy of Goneril-like Kath and Regan-like Traci, who immediately vent their resentment for Sandeman's lack of love for and tyranny over them by dispossessing him. Jug, Traci's psychopathic husband, corresponds to Cornwall, and Dean, Kath's somewhat conciliatory husband, to Albany (later, The Chair fills something of Albany's role).

The Fool's role is taken up by Kath's son, called simply "The Boy," who accompanies Sandeman on his homeless travails, comforting and listening to him. Interestingly, The Boy first comes to prominence when Jo is disowned, and when he dies, Jo reenters Sandeman's life. Puttnam corresponds to Edmund, though his role in the narrative diminishes in the film's third act. Quick combines elements of Gloucester and Kent—he treats Puttnam with contempt, he remains "faithful" to Sandeman at a distance (through his surveillance cameras), he confronts the homeless Sandeman about the moral chaos he has caused, and he is blinded by Jug and commits suicide. Many key scenes are cleverly adapted: the sisters' declarations of love occur at Mandy's funeral (Traci even sings the vapid song "Mandy" in her honor); Lear's heath scenes occur on a stormy night at a roadside café and hotel, a symbol of contemporary dislocation; Sandeman's love for The Boy is exemplified by his fishing with him in the cold and buying chips; and Sandeman's carrying of The Boy's dead body echoes Lear's bearing of Cordelia. In the film's third act, the narrative shifts to the double-double-cross plot typical of contemporary British gangster films, with Sandeman elaborately setting up the family factions to destroy each other and Delroy's father taking vengeance upon Jug. Even so, the final shot, in which Sandeman walks the desolate, lonely Merseyside quay as Jo leaves, underlines that his victory over familial and moral chaos is pyrrhic.

The film features three citations of Shakespeare. An opening title card quotes Gloucester's bleak observation in 4.1, "As flies to wanton boys are we to the gods; / They kill us for their sport," establishing this demimonde's bleak brutality. Quick, confronting Sandeman about the chaos he has unleashed in the roadside café, cites Albany in 4.2: "Humanity must perforce prey on itself, / Like monsters of the deep." And Jug, when assaulted by Delroy's vengeful father, begs for his life by citing, rather bizarrely, Portia in *The Merchant of Venice*, "The quality of mercy is not strained." Director Don Boyd was executive producer of Derek Jarman's 1979 *The Tempest*; Sandeman was Richard Harris's last leading role on film. Compare *Shiner* (above).

DVD includes a director's commentary track, behind-the-scenes featurette, and production notes that reference Shakespeare.

816 *King of Texas*
2002. U.S. Flying Freehold Productions, Hallmark Entertainment, and Turner Network Television. Sound, col., 95 mins. Eli Udel.

John Lear, aging owner of the largest ranch in Texas territory, decides to divide his ranch between his three daughters, Suzannah, Rebecca, and Claudia, in exchange for their professions of love for their father. When Claudia refuses, insisting that "love can't be commanded," Lear disowns her, and she seeks harbor with Mendaca, a Mexican rancher who is John's rival and the son of a former friend. When Lear divides his land between his two remaining daughters, Tom Highsmith, Suzannah's husband, uses the opportunity to plan a range war with Mendaca. Meanwhile, horses of Henry Westover, Lear's friend, are stolen and sold, and his son Thomas is implicated, leading to Henry disowning him; we soon learn that Henry's other son, the bastard Emmett, staged the horse theft to eliminate his brother. John Lear is evicted first by Suzannah, then by Rebecca, and is alone in a storm with his slave Rip. Highsmith, suspicious that Henry Westover has revealed his plans to Mendaca, puts out his eyes, but he is shot by one of his men while doing so. John Lear, brought to Mendaca's hacienda, is reconciled with Claudia, as Mendaca's men prepare for an attack by Highsmith and Emmett's men. Mendaca successfully defends his hacienda, but Claudia is shot in the battle, and John Lear, racked with grief, dies cradling her. Henry Westover is prevented by Thomas from committing suicide, and the two reconcile. When Suzannah and Rebecca are shown the dead bodies of John, Claudia, Highsmith, and Emmett, Suzannah shoots herself and Rebecca is arrested. The film ends with Thomas protecting his blind father at their ranch.

King of Texas originally aired on the TNT cable network on June 2, 2002. As the summary suggests, this made-for-television epic is a close transposition of *Lear* to the generic conventions of the Western. Most of the character parallels are obvious. Rip, Lear's slave, perhaps the drama's most original character, combines qualities of Kent and the Fool; though he has none of the Fool's sarcastic humor, he does sing, offers Lear direct homespun wisdom, and remains faithful to Lear throughout his travails, and his whipping by one of Suzannah's men is motivated by racism. In his backstory, John Lear is given a wife whom he worked to death and a son who died, and his emotional hardness, demonstrated in the opening sequence by his needless hanging of two of Mendaca's men, springs from his struggles to tame and maintain his ranching empire. Though Suzannah and Rebecca reject their father (as do Goneril and Regan), both are given tearful moments that register their initial ambivalence about doing so, a gesture that complicates their characterization. Interestingly, Thomas Westover is initially presented as an irresponsible drunk, and his brother Emmett an upright, loyal son, so the after-the-fact revelation that Emmett has engineered Thomas's fall comes as a shock. The first half of the film follows Shakespeare's narrative quite faithfully, including equivalents of many key plot points—Lear's division of his kingdom, the daughter's declarations of love, Lear's striking of Oswald for chiding his Fool, the dismissal of Lear's

train, Lear's curse upon his daughters, Goneril and Regan's attraction to Edmund, the blinding of Gloucester, and Lear's cursing of the heavens during the storm. The film's second half offers a more truncated and revised version of the narrative. John Lear's madness on the prairie is abbreviated and does not lead him to revelations about "unaccommodated man" (he is attended only by Henry Westover and Rip); the grand battle at Mendaca's does not include the disconcerting seesawing of power that marks the final act of Shakespeare's play, and though Lear's oration over Claudia's corpse echoes his final speech, the cause of her death—she is shot while trying to rescue her father who madly tries to stop the battle—makes her into an emblem of the senselessness of war rather than the heart-rending cruelty of fate. Most important, the Henry Westover plot is given a happy (if bittersweet) ending, muting the tragic desolation that closes Shakespeare's play. Though there are no direct citations other than "Nothing will come of nothing," the film features many indirect echoes of Shakespeare's dialogue—particularly so in the daughters' declarations of love, John's railing at the storm, and his final speech. Of interest is the recurring image of the eagle, which John comes to see as a metaphor for his own condition. See also entries 375, 1452, and 2739.

817 *The Producers*
2005. U.S. Universal Pictures. Sound, col., 134 mins.
Susan Stroman.

Several shots show a poster for *King Leer*. The first scene of the 2001 Broadway stage adaptation of Mel Brooks's 1968 film takes place on the opening, and closing, nights of Max Bialystok's (Nathan Lane) latest production, *Funny Boy*, a musical version of *Hamlet*. (RB)

LOVE'S LABOR'S LOST

There are animated shorts with the titles *Love's Labor's Lost* (1920) and *Love's Labor Won* (1933, 1948), but none have any relationship to Shakespeare's plays. The same is true of several silent films with the title *Love's Labor's Lost* (1899, 1911, 1916, and 1926) and *Love's Labor Found* (1929).

818 *Days and Nights in the Forest (Aranyer Din Ratri)*
1970. India. Sound, b&w, 120 mins.

Based on the novel by Sunil Ganguli, *Days and Nights in the Forest* is an (anti) pastoral comedy about four Bengali elite men on a vacation from the city who meet several *Suntal*, or local women, some of whom are from the elite. *Days and Nights* is an antipastoral pastoral, and it parallels, consciously or not, Shakespearean comedies and forests such as Arden or the woods of *A Midsummer Night's Dream*, and a critic for the *Observer* compared the film to *Love's*

Labor's Lost. The film is typically read as a critique of the penetration of globalization, understood to be a later phase of Western imperialism, into the now corrupted and "Englished" Indian forest itself, with the men criticized for being its racist, decadent, and fragmenting agents who are incapable of remembering India's founding fathers or fulfilling the dream of a multicultural, unified nation.

The film makes it clear, however, that the (feminine) Indian forest is already mediatized, artificial, and up to speed. Shakespeare is cited in *Days and Nights* at two key turning points to underscore this point. The first citation is a line from the balcony scene from *Romeo and Juliet*: "It is the east, and Juliet is the sun." The line is cited by the central male character, Ashim (Subhendu Chatterjee), who is romantically interested in the central female character, Aparna (Sharmila Tagore). Her father says he earlier looked out from the "balcony" (the English word is used) to observe wild animals, but Aparna has taken it over for her own uses. Aparna is set up as a mysterious person who neither her father nor Ashim can understand, and initially the film seems to oppose her to Shakespeare and Indian playboy "colonizers" of women. When Ashim asks her if the house has any secrets, she responds, "See for yourself," and takes him to see it. Once there, he goes through her books, which are all in English, including a Penguin collection of American plays and an Agatha Christie mystery novel, and he then flips through her record albums, again in English. On top is an album called *Sitar Duets*, and underneath, partly visible, is the Beatles' *Rubber Soul*. Ashim then successively flips through a Mozart album, an Andrés Segovia album, and an Indo jazz album.

The cosmopolitan eclecticism of Aparna's literary and musical interests makes her incomprehensible to Ashim, who says, "I can't quite make you out," as she is looking out the window. "Do you have to?" she replies. They step out onto the balcony, and Ashim then draws on Shakespeare. He asks her, "Why shouldn't this be called Juliet's balcony now? Suppose someone should stand there and say (he then quotes from the play, in English) 'It is the East and Juliet is the sun.'" Ashim's romantic interest in Aparna is transparent to her, and she puts him off.

APARNA: Who? you?

ASHIM: Too incongruous?

APARNA: Jackals still prowl around at night.

ASHIM: (smiling) You're very discouraging.

APARNA: Finished your inspection? (turning her head back to him as he stands behind her)

ASHIM: I feel like touching you to see if you're real.

APARNA: Try these instead. (She offers him some candy and takes one herself too.)

The scene implies, according to Cooper (130–31), a critique of Ashim's "male gaze," with a now Indo-colonial Shakespeare opposed to a more liberatory and post-colonial international and contemporary mass media. The film's Bengali context gives Ashim's quoted line an obvious Orientalist charge with Juliet as the sun to the Indian east. Ashim's rewriting of an English, colonial Shakespeare and renaming of the balcony serves as a pretext for his seduction of Aparna, while her more global cultural and media literacy offer her a defense and provide her leverage to put him off. Aparna's interests in Western and international media have made her culturally literate and able to fend off a Shakespeare pick-up one-liner. One could argue that Aparna's aesthetic tastes are parallel to Ray's. The film is quite international in style, particularly in its use of jump-cuts in the car at the start (indebted to the getaway scene near the beginning of Jean-Luc Godard's *Breathless* [1957]).

Nevertheless, *Days and Nights* does not undo colonial Shakespeare so much as reinscribe Shakespeare in a female imperial context. The key element of Aparna's character is her memory, and Shakespeare comes up for the second time in a central scene of the film in which the characters play the memory game. (RB)

MACBETH

819 *The Real Thing at Last*
1916. U.K. British Actors. Silent, b&w, 2,000 ft. L. C. MacBean.

Lost film, authored by James M. Barrie, the author of *Peter Pan*, and created as part of a live benefit show sponsored by the British royal family for the YMCA. Of historical interest because it offered a version of *Macbeth* as American film might imagine it, suggesting the developing tensions between film and Shakespearean theater, as well as British and American concepts of culture. Descriptions of the film suggest that in this contemporized adaptation, the witches were portrayed as chorus dancers, and a Chaplinesque character makes a gratuitous cameo.

820 *When Macbeth Came to Snakeville*
1917. U.S. Essanay. Silent, b&w, length unknown. Roy Clements.

When an acting troupe arrives in Snakeville for a performance, they stay at Slippery Slim's boarding house, where Sophie Clutts, Slim's wife, becomes enamored of the lead tragedian. The night after his performance of *Macbeth*, she sleepwalks, dreaming that she is Lady Macbeth. She enters his room with a knife, but she awakes before doing him harm. The tragedian flees, making Slim, Sophie's jealous husband, happy.

821 *The Village Squire*
1935. U.K. British and Dominions Film Corporation and Paramount British. Sound, b&w, 66 mins. Reginald Denham.

Adapted from the play by Arthur Jarvis Black. A village squire insists upon producing a performance of *Macbeth*, despite the objections of the locals. A visiting film star halts the production and falls in love with the squire's daughter. Notable primarily as a lampoon of amateur Shakespeare, as well as the screen debut of Vivien Leigh.

822 *The Case of the Velvet Claws*
1936. U.S. Warner Brothers. Sound, b&w, 63 min. William Clemens.

There are several references to *Macbeth*. Warren William stars as Perry Mason. See Perry Mason, "Ancient Romeo" (entry 2824), as well as entries 2748 and 2825. (RB)

823 *We Work Again*
1937. U.S. WPA. Sound, b&w, 15 mins. Director(s) uncredited.

Film of the end of Orson Welles's 1936 *Voodoo Macbeth* (from when Macbeth fears Birnam Wood to the end of the play) is seen at the end of this WPA documentary about the achievements of African Americans since the New Deal began. The Weird Sisters appear just before Macduff kills and then decapitates Macbeth. Malcolm then pops out to deliver the closing lines. A live audience is seen at the beginning and end of the film segment. The very light-skinned black actor Jack Carter, who played Macbeth in the Harlem theater production, does not star as Macbeth in the film. He was replaced by a much darker-skinned actor. The music sounds a lot like that heard on *Flash Gordon* serials. Whether Orson Welles was involved in the film is unclear. Available on disc 3 of the four-DVD set, *Treasures from American Film Archive* (www.filmpreservation.org). See also entries 386, 867, and 1028. (RB)

824 *Jwala*
1938. India. Huns Pictures. Sound, b&w, 161 mins. Master Vinayak.

In this early Indian free adaptation of *Macbeth* set in ancient India, Kuntala, a witch, tells Angar, an otherwise loyal general, that his king will die and he will become crowned in his place. Angar becomes ambitious and murders the king, after which Angar's wife Mangala and his best friend Tarang join forces with the people to overthrow the now tyrannical Angar. The film was a major box office failure.

825 *The Bookworm Turns*
1940. Sound, col., 9 mins. Hugh Harman.

In this animated cartoon, a copy of *Macbeth* comes to life as the three weird sisters are making their brew. (RB)

826 *Presenting Lily Mars*
1943. U.S. MGM. Sound, b&w, 102 mins. Norman Taurog.

Adapted from the novel by Booth Tarkington (entry 1869). Aspiring actress Lily Mars, daughter of a small-town hatmaker and piano teacher, asks her neighbor Mrs. Thornway to use her influence with her son John, a theatrical producer, to get her a part in his new show *Let Me Dream*. Though he discourages her from pursuing an acting career, her acting is later seen by Russian actress Isobel Rekaya and the author of *Let Me Dream*, Owen Vail, who conclude mistakenly that John has had an illegitimate child with Lily. After Lily straightens out the misunderstanding, she tells John that he is afraid to think of her as a woman. Despite her disappointment with John, Lily goes to Broadway and lands a job in the chorus of *Let Me Dream*. As John slowly falls in love with Lily, she becomes the object of Isobel's jealous wrath, a wrath that grows when Owen and John rewrite the ending of the play according to Lily's suggestions and cast her as Isobel's maid. Lily's public imitation of Isobel leads Isobel to quit the play, and though John casts Lily in the lead, she is not up to the role and he must reinstate Isobel at the last minute. Though Lily ends up playing a maid in the play, her family and John show their pride.

Early in the film Lily engineers an impromptu performance for John Thornway, using Lady Macbeth's sleep-walking scene as her audition piece. She performs it melodramatically, with her sister providing silent film–style piano accompaniment. Afterward, Thornway critiques her acting, claiming that she presents Lady Macbeth as if she were a high school girl playing to her boyfriend in the gallery, and he offers a restrained rendition of the final lines of Lady Macbeth's speech that better convey her guilt. Lily reveals that she's been taught acting by Professor Eggleston, whose acting manual we briefly see. The scene demonstrates both Lily's ambition and the limits of her immature talent.

827 *The Bad and the Beautiful*
1952. U.S. MGM. Sound, b&w, 118 mins. Vincente Minnelli.

From a story by George Bradshaw. A portrait of the rise of ruthlessly ambitious studio head Jonathan Shields, told in flashback through the eyes of three people who worked closely with him: director Fred Amiel, actress Gloria Lorrison, and screenwriter James Lee Barlow. In each case, Shields double-crossed them—he replaced Amiel as director on a major film, broke Lorrison's heart, and led to the death of Barlow's wife—yet all reluctantly come to acknowledge his skill at making films when they hear him pitch a new project over the phone.

In a key scene, Lorrison's dead father, in whose shadow she languishes, speaks the "Tomorrow and tomorrow and tomorrow" speech on an LP recording as Shields convinces her to give up her self-destructive alcoholism. The studio logo, shown at film's end, resembles the Shakespeare family arms.

828 *Laxdale Hall* (aka *Scotch on the Rocks*)
1952. U.K. Group 3 and Kingsley International Pictures. Sound, b&w, 77 mins. John Eldridge.

Adapted from the novel by Eric Linklater. When it is discovered that residents of Laxdale, a small Scottish village, have not paid their road tax, a parliamentary committee headed by Samuel Pettigrew, a former resident of the village, and General Matheson investigates. They learn that the five owners of cars refuse to pay taxes until a good road is constructed. The issue soon becomes one of urban versus village life; Pettigrew finds Laxdale provincial and prides himself on being a modern city dweller.

When the parliamentary committee first arrives, it sees an outdoor production of *Macbeth* performed in a storm.

829 *Le Rideau Rouge (Ce soir, on joue Macbeth or The Crimson Curtain)*
1952. France. Gaumont. Sound, b&w, 84 mins. André Barsacq.

Written by playwright Jean Anouilh. This backstage murder mystery centers around a provincial stage production of *Macbeth* in which several tragedies occur, key among them the death of authoritarian and condescending director Bertal (who also plays Banquo). Though the actors blame the calamities on the theatrical curse that plagues the play, the chief police inspector is unconvinced and eventually solves the crime. Bertal was killed by Ludovic Arn, a weak-willed actor who offers a pretense of bravado to cover over his failings. His motive was revenge for Bertal's humiliation of him and his desire for Aurélia Nobli, Bertal's drug-addicted mistress with whom Ludovic was also having an affair. Several scenes explore the parallels between relationships between characters in Shakespeare's play and relationships between the actors in Bertal's production. A number of scenes from *Macbeth* are included. Compare *Macbeth in Manhattan* and *Naked Frailties*.

830 *Joe Macbeth*
1955. U.K. Columbia Pictures. Sound, b&w, 90 mins. Ken Hughes.

Written by Philip Yordan, who also penned several film adaptations of *King Lear*. After a tarot reading predicts that he will be "king of darkness," Joe Macbeth, a middle-aged mob hitman, is coaxed by his young, beautiful, but viperous new bride, Lily, to kill the kingpin Duca and elevate himself to his boss's position. After murdering Duca during a midnight swim and installing himself as kingpin, Joe becomes increasingly savage and paranoid, arranging the murder of his friend Banky and Banky's son Lenny. Though Banky is killed, Lenny escapes and gathers discontented rival mobsters around him; as he does, Joe arranges to kidnap Ruth, Lenny's wife, and his son, but they are instead murdered, fueling Lenny's revenge. At film's end, Joe is

Paul Douglas and others in *Joe Macbeth* (1955). This photo shows Douglas (as Macbeth, at center) seeing an apparition at the banquet, with onlookers looking confused or concerned. A nice shot from this otherwise unavailable film. Courtesy of Douglas Lanier.

abandoned by others, and he accidentally kills Lily before being killed himself by Lenny.

The first of several transpositions of *Macbeth* to a gangster milieu, *Joe Macbeth* follows Shakespeare's plot relatively closely. Though the supernatural elements are thrice referenced in the predictions of Rosie, the street vendor and fortune teller, the film focuses primarily on the tense relationship between Joe and Lily (Macbeth and Lady Macbeth), Joe's crisis of conscience and manhood, and the escalating violence of his rule as "king of the city." Shakespeare's language is directly referenced three times in the film, in quotations that open the film ("Not in [the] legions / Of horrid hell can come a Devil more damn'd / In evils to top Macbeth," 4.3) and close it ("It will have blood, they say / Blood will have blood," 3.4), and in a quotation from Rosie, identifying her as the substitute for the three witches ("When shall we three meet again / In thunder, lightnin' [sic], or in rain?" 1.1). But there are various oblique references to the text as well. Echoing Duncan's exchange with Banquo at Macbeth's castle in 1.6.1–10, when Duca and Lenny arrive at Joe's mansion, they comment,

DUCA: I like this house. The fresh air of the lake gives it a sweet smell.
BANKY: You ever see so many birds flyin' around here? I guess they must like it here.

(Indeed, birds become a key symbol in the film, circling and shrieking, for instance, as Joe kills Duca at the lake.) As Joe awaits Lenny's revenge near the end, he lights his last cigarette by a burnt-down candle, a visual analogue for "out, out, brief candle" in the "tomorrow and tomorrow" soliloquy. Grim humor too is included. The porter becomes Angus, the butler of Joe's opulent mansion that, Angus sardonically observes, has passed from mobster to mobster as they've risen and fallen from power. Indeed, Angus and the mansion become important forces in the film, underlining the fruitless cyclical pattern of fleeting glory and quick death that befalls the ambitious; Joe's final scenes in the darkened house, shooting randomly at sounds he imagines, compellingly present his paranoia and isolation. Unfortunately, *Joe Macbeth* has garnered a reputation among many critics as a crude, verbally inept version of *Macbeth*; it is often trotted out as the nadir of "free" adaptation of Shakespeare. In reality, the film repays repeated viewings, and within the limitations of B-film production in Britain in the 1950s, it makes a good case for analogues between barbaric Scotland and the mean streets of film noir. See also entry 388.

831 *Kumonosu jô (Throne of Blood* or *The Castle of the Spider's Web)*
1957. Japan. Toho Company Ltd. Sound, b&w, 105 mins. Akira Kurosawa.

Throne of Blood skillfully transposes *Macbeth* to feudal Japan. Having courageously defended the Great Lord's territory against the traitors Inui and Fujimaku, Taketori Washizu wanders with his warrior friend Yoshitaru Miki through the Spider's Web Forest until they happen upon an ancient female spirit. She makes two predictions: Washizu will become the commander of the North Garrison and later Great Lord, and Miki will become commander of the First Fortress and his son will eventually rule. Soon the Great Lord fulfills the first of both prophecies. Soon after Washizu arrives at the North Garrison, the Great Lord visits, with the intention of secretly garrisoning his troops there to surprise nearby traitors. After his wife Asaji plays on his suspicions and ambition, Washizu murders the Great Lord and uses his coffin to gain admission to the Spider's Web Castle (which is guarded by Miki). Washizu becomes Great Lord, making a deal with Miki that his son will be heir, but when Asaji plays on his ambitions and reveals that she is pregnant, Washizu arranges Miki's murder. Miki's son escapes, and his ghost appears at Washizu's coronation banquet. Unconvinced that Inui's men murdered Miki, Washizu's army begins to desert, Asaji gives birth to a stillborn child, and Washizu receives word that the Great Lord's son has joined forces with Inui and Noriyasu to attack his empire. Washizu returns to the forest and learns from the ancient spirit that he cannot be defeated until the trees of the forest rise up against the Spider's Web Castle. Washizu rallies his troops with the tale of the prophecy, but omens suggest otherwise, as does Asaji's descent into mad hand-washing. In the morning, the trees advance toward the castle, and Washizu's own men shoot him dead.

Kurosawa's exquisitely photographed samurai *Macbeth* recalls and outdoes the otherworldly bleakness of Orson Welles's *Macbeth*. That quality emerges as early as the film's prologue, in which a lonely memorial to the destroyed Spider's Web Castle emerges from the otherwise featureless foggy plain. With the certainty of ruin established, Kurosawa plunges into the tale of Washizu's rise and fall, everywhere emphasizing with dialogue, music, and imagery the fated fruitlessness of his ambitions and the illusory nature of human power achieved by violence. The forest is a tangled web of underbrush that traps Washizu and Miki, and the ancient spirit a weaver of lives and spirit of death; buildings and warriors repeatedly emerge from and are engulfed by banks of fog; supernatural bird shrieks presage disaster throughout, but even more horrifying is the deceptively gentle brush of Asaji's kimono as she pursues the Great Lord's murder. The symbolic imagery, austere stage, and ritualistic characterizations of Noh drama suffuse the scenes between the honorable Washizu and the devilishly cold Asaji, who cleverly plays upon his fears of losing power while feeding her own political ambitions. By focusing primarily on the inescapable effects of the fatal prophecies and leaving out much of Macduff and Malcolm's rise, Kurosawa recasts Shakespeare's play as a existential parable of human futility, one set, paradoxically, against the exciting heroics and historical sweep of the samurai epic. Few images of that futility are more memorable than that of Washizu, shot through with arrows from his own archers, trying to draw his sword before dying, collapsing before his army, and slowly being covered by the gathering fog. The ritualistic quality of Kurosawa dovetails the excitement and historical sweep of the samurai epic in the battle scenes with the ritualistic quality of Noh drama in the confrontations between Washizu and Asaji and the banquet scenes. See also entries 389 and 649.

The Criterion Collection DVD includes a trailer, a commentary track by Michael Jeck that references *Macbeth*, and an essay by Stephen Prince.

832 *No, My Darling Daughter*
1961. U.K. Rank Organization Film Productions. Sound, b&w, 85 mins. Ralph Thomas.

Adapted from the play *Handful of Tansy* by Kay Bannerman and Harold Brooke. Tansy Carr, the socially awkward daughter of Sir Matthew Carr, a business tycoon, goes to a finishing school in Paris where she falls for American Cornelius Allingham and learns that General Henry Barclay is a business associate of her father. When Cornelius neglects to deliver a letter to Sir Matthew, he is forced to go to New York on business and sends Tansy with Barclay on a trip to Scotland. Cornelius follows the two and tries to get Tansy to marry him, but she begins a romance with Thomas Barclay, Henry Barclay's son, and the two soon elope, at which both fathers are delighted.

In an unthematic use of *Macbeth* 5.1, Tansy recites "Out, out damned spot" at the Whispering Gallery of the dome of St. Paul's Cathedral in London.

833 *Sibirska Ledi Magbet* (*The Siberian Lady Macbeth* or *Fury Is a Woman*)
1961. Poland and Yugoslavia. Avala Films. Sound, b&w, 93 mins. Andrzej Wajda.

Adapted from the story by Nikolai Leskov, "Lady Macbeth of Mzensk District." Katarina is a restless wife in a Russian village, awaiting the return of her husband who is away on business. She endures the abuse of her father-in-law, Boris Ismailov. Sergei, a travelling swineherd, arrives looking for work, and while Boris is away, Katarina quickly begins an affair with him. Returning and discovering the two together, Boris cruelly beats Sergei and threatens to expose their affair to the village, at which Katarina kills him by poisoning his pottage. The two lovers have a brief romantic idyll until Katarina's husband Zinovi returns, angry that his father is dead and suspicious of his wife. Having confessed her love for Sergei, she poisons Zinovi's tea and joins Sergei in beating him to death with a candlestick. With Sergei having hidden Zinovi's body in the pigsty, the two host a feast, but Sergei reacts with guilt when he sees the head of a roast pig, declaring, "We are eating him," but with Katarina's encouragement, he soon buries his qualms, laughing at the head. After another short period of happiness and freedom, Zinovi's sister Marfa and his insufferable nephew Fedja arrive, and Marfa declares that Fedja has been designated the proper heir and master of the family business. Katarina and Sergei plan to kill Fedja during the Easter service, but they are discovered and exiled to Siberia. On the long march to exile, Sergei begins to flirt with Sonja, a much younger female prisoner; Katarina offers her socks when Sergei falls behind due to pain, but she discovers that Sergei has given them to Sonja. As the prisoners cross a lake on a ferry, Sergei mocks Katarina and dishonors their romantic past; in retaliation, Katarina pulls Sonja into the water and the two drown.

Following the general outline of Leskov's story, Wajda's film reshapes and recombines a number of motifs from Shakespeare's *Macbeth*: the ambition and manipulativeness of Lady Macbeth, the use of murder to gain power and then the necessity to continue to murder to keep it, the appearance of a guilty apparition during a banquet, and the removal of blood from the murderer's hands (in a symbolic touch, Katarina twice licks the blood from her hands). The film entirely jettisons the supernatural elements of Shakespeare's version, using instead repeated references to the Russian Orthodox Church to suggest the standards of Christian morality against which Katarina's and Sergei's murderous behavior should be judged. To underline the relationship between Shakespeare's play and this tale,

Wajda opens with a Shakespearean quotation from Lady Macbeth:

Come, you spirits
That tend on mortal thoughts, unsex me here,
And fill me from the crown to the toe top-full
Of direst cruelty! . . . Come to my woman's breasts,
And take my milk for gall. (1.5)

Though Wajda does generate some small sympathy for Katarina's plight as a woman in an authoritarian household, his emphasis falls on her passion for Sergei and her remorselessness in murdering those who get in her way; Sergei, by contrast, becomes involved with murder only with the arrival of Zinovi and then guiltily. Wajda uses the symbol of the foggy storm, repeated throughout the film, to suggest the destructive engulfing passions that lead Katarina to murder and eventually destroy the couple; interestingly the film emphasizes that this Lady Macbeth very much wants children to give her life meaning, yet ironically she is led to kill Fedja by circumstance and, once exiled, she leaves behind the child she has had with Sergei to be cared for by Aksina, Boris's servant. The slow pace, folk setting, and broadly drawn characters lend the film the quality of a moral fable.

834 *The Comedy of Terrors*
1964. U.S. Alta Vista Productions and American International Pictures. Sound, col., 84 mins. Jacques Tourneur.

In this comedy-horror film, Waldo Trumbull, a bibbling undertaker who lives with his songstress wife Amaryllis, senile father-in-law Amos Hinchley, and meek assistant Felix Gillie, has run his father-in-law's funeral parlor into the ground. Facing bankruptcy and eviction, he begins, with the help of Gillie, to sneak into the homes of wealthy men at night and kill them, afterwards providing funeral services for the victim. At home, Trumbull's neglect of his wife pushes her into the arms of Gillie, and Trumbull fails to poison Amos, despite several attempts. Trumbull runs into problems when he decides to kill John F. Black, the man who intends to evict Trumbull and family. Black, a cataleptic, keeps coming back from the dead and, after Trumbull places him in a crypt, Black returns to take revenge upon him. Ironically, after Trumbull is victorious over Black, Amos mistakenly administers Trumbull a dose of his own poison.

As Gillie comes to kill him, Black reads the entirety of Macbeth's confrontation with Macduff in 5.8 in bed, taking all the parts and performing them with gusto. As he mimes the swordfight, he nearly stabs Gillie, who is hiding behind a screen (recalling Hamlet's stabbing of Polonius). When Black is released from the coffin, he recites an excerpt of "Is this a dagger I see before me?" from 2.1, adding lines from the "Macbeth shall sleep no more" speech in 2.2. When Black confronts Trumbull and Gillie, he gives lines from 5.3 ("The devil damn thee black"), and when Trumbull shoots him, he offers the complete "Tomorrow and tomorrow and tomorrow" speech, coming back from the dead three times to finish his performance. Basil Rathbone, who plays Black, skillfully blends stentoriousness with manic zeal in his Shakespeare renditions. Two other minor allusions: when Gillie climbs out of Black's window, he mutters, "Up and down, up and down, all night long, up and down," perhaps riffing on Puck's "up and down, up and down, I will lead them, up and down" from A *Midsummer Night's Dream* 3.2. And the family cat is named Cleopatra.

835 *The Deadly Affair*
1966. U.K. Columbia Pictures. Sound, col., 115 mins. Sidney Lumet.

Adapted from the novel *Call for the Dead* by John Le Carré. Charles Dobbs, a spy, is troubled by the suicide of his superior Samuel Fennan, since he approved Fennan's security clearance, so he privately hires Inspector Mendel to investigate. Though his suspicion falls on Elsa, Fennan's wife, Dobbs learns that his own wife Ann had an affair with fellow spy Dieter Freey. Eventually, Dobbs uncovers the identity of the mysterious Sontag, the spy in their midst.

The film features moments from an RSC production of the witches' cauldron scene from *Macbeth*, as well as Marlowe's *Edward II*.

836 *Mistrz*
1966. Poland. Studio Folmove Iluzjon. Sound, b&w, 80 mins. Jerzy Antczak.

Several refugees in war-torn Poland, among them an aspiring actor from a small town, seek shelter from the war. The actor at first disguises himself as a bookkeeper, but when he demonstrates his acting skills, he is discovered as an artist and is killed. Another of the refugees, a boy who grows up to be an actor, recalls the "mistrz" (i.e., "master") when preparing to play Macbeth.

The actor particularly wants to play Shakespearean roles and recites "Tomorrow and tomorrow and tomorrow" to demonstrate his acting talent.

837 *Teenage Gang Debs*
1966. U.S. Jude Productions. Sound, b&w, 72 mins. Sande N. Johnsen.

In this teen exploitation film, Terry, a delinquent girl and former member of the Manhattan girl gang the Golden Falcons, moves to Brooklyn and immediately begins to engineer her rise as a "deb" in the Rebels, a local boys' gang. At first she fastens on to Johnny, the current president of the gang, but when he insists that she carve his initials in her flesh, she shifts her affections to Nino, whom she quickly manipulates to challenge Johnny for leadership of the gang. After Nino kills Johnny in a knifefight and takes revenge on Annie, a girl who protests Terry's behavior, Terry again urges Nino to fight for more power, this time with the help of an allied gang, the Rat Pack, against the Warriors. Nino is clearly troubled by the ensuing

rumble and the Rebels who get killed or hurt, but when one Rebel, Piggy, announces that he intends to leave the gang to marry, Terry yet again manipulates Nino into fighting and killing him. Fed up with Terry's manipulations of Nino and her rise to power, and upset at the decimation of their gang boyfriends, the "debs" unite to beat and disfigure Terry.

The film is only tangentially related to *Macbeth*, primarily in its portrait of the vicious and manipulative Terry, who manipulates men to gain power for herself by insulting their manhood and rewarding them with sex. Though Nino's killing of Johnny occurs at a gang party (just as Duncan's murder occurs in conjunction with a banquet) and Terry puts the knife in Nino's hand, the killing of Johnny occurs in the open, for all the gang members to see, unlike Duncan's death. There are no references to the Shakespearean text, and though Terry gets her moral comeuppance in the end, the film is far more interested in long depictions of sex, violence, and motorcycle riding.

838 *The Charge of the Light Brigade*
1968. U.K. United Artists. Sound, col., 139 mins. Tony Richardson.

A savagely satirical demythologizing of the Crimean campaign, with the then-brewing war in Vietnam as its shadow target. The film focuses on Captain Louis Nolan, an independent-minded military officer seasoned by his service in India, and his friend Captain William Morris, an overly idealistic and newly married young officer. The film divides into two halves, the first being a portrait of working-class soldiers in training and their aristocratic officers, many of whom are snobbishly concerned with their own military glory, class position, or meaningless niceties of conduct. The second half recounts the disastrous battle of Balaclava, where inept, bickering, and snobbishly aloof officers led men to their deaths, despite Nolan's attempt to demonstrate leadership. These sequences are juxtaposed with animated jingoistic cartoons and sentimental songs about England.

We see and hear portions of Macbeth's second meeting with the witches (4.1), with emphasis on when the witches reveal the apparition of Banquo and warn of Macduff. (Donald Wolfit plays Macbeth.) The tyrannical aristocratic commander of the 11th Hussars, Lord Cardigan, arrives in midscene and is heckled by the crowd for his unjust arrest of a young officer, Captain Nolan. The conjunction is thematically relevant, since, like Macbeth, Cardigan is a petty tyrant who seeks to prevent Nolan's rise to power. In context, the witches's line "Come, high or low; / Thyself and office deftly show!" is particularly ironic.

839 *La Caduta degli dei (The Damned)*
1969. Italy, Switzerland, and West Germany. Eichberg-Film GmbH and Praesidens-Pegaso Italnoleggio. Sound, b&w, 155 mins. Luchino Visconti.

As the Third Reich rises in Germany, patriarch Baron Joachim von Essenbeck, head of a powerful steelmaking family dynasty, celebrates his birthday with his extended family, widow Sophie von Essenbeck and her son Martin, Sophie's lover Frederick Bruckmann, army man Konstantin von Essenbeck, Communist Herbert Thallman, his wife Elizabeth and their two girls, and Gunther von Essenbeck. Encouraged by Aschenbach, a sinister SS officer, Frederick, a manager at the family's company, plots to murder Joachim and take over the company; he kills Joachim with Herbert's gun, and Sophie convinces Martin, the company's rightful heir, to go along with the fiction that Herbert was the murderer. As Frederick pursues his ascent in the company, he sends Thallman's children to a concentration camp and conspires with Aschenbach to kill Konstantin when Konstantin attempts to wrest control of the company. When Frederick marries Sophie, his last act to legitimize his rule, Martin, at Aschenbach's direction, defiles his mother and gives Frederick and Sophie poison to kill themselves, leaving him, now an SS officer, in control.

Visconti's tale of Frederick's moral degradation in pursuit of power during the Third Reich features a number of resemblances to *Macbeth*, though it is not a thoroughgoing reworking of Shakespeare's play. In several respects Frederick corresponds to Macbeth, Sophie to Lady Macbeth, Joachim to Duncan, Martin to Macduff, arguably Aschenbach to the three witches, and Konstantin and Herbert to Banquo. Key plot motifs also suggest affinities to *Macbeth*: the killing of a benevolent patriarch during a celebration, the temptation of an ambitious man by a prediction of his rise to power, the encouragement of the murderer by his wife, the couple's subsequent guilt and further need to murder to maintain their power, the return of those the murderer has betrayed during a banquet (Herbert returns to tell of Elizabeth and the fate of his children), the mental breakdown of the murderer's wife (wracked with guilt after her encounter with Martin, Sophie is emotionally destroyed), and the return of the rightful heir (in this case, Martin) to kill the murderer and take control. Unlike Shakespeare's play, Visconti's focus is not primarily on Frederick, for he addresses the moral degradation of several members of the Essenbeck family, in particular Martin, whose pedophilia leads to the death of a girl and whose incestuous seduction of Sophie unhinges her. Indeed, Martin's tortured confrontation of his mother in the final scenes, in which he reveals a hatred for her complicity in the murder of his uncle; her refusal to love him; his incestuous desire for her; and the death of the usurping Frederick and his mother by poison, distantly recall Hamlet's confrontation with Gertrude and the fates of Gertrude and Claudius. Though there is no suggestion of the supernatural, the enigmatic figure of Aschenbach takes up the function of the witches, manipulating characters behind the scenes by playing on their unspoken ambitions and mutual antagonisms. Though there are no direct verbal citations, small touches remind us of Shakespearean commonplaces. When Frederick contemplates killing Konstantin, he says, "I've accepted a ruthless logic and I can never get away from it"; when he senses that the SS is closing in on him, he observes, "I've learned to kill. The game is not over yet. I'll go to the very end." When Martin leaves Frederick and Sophie to commit suicide, he blows out a candle, as if visually to recall Macbeth's line about the emptiness of earthly power: "Out, out, brief candle."

840 *Cabezas cortadas*
1970. Spain and Brazil. Filmscontacto, Mapa Filmes, and Profilmes S.A. Sound, col., 94 mins. Glauber Rocha.

An experimental film in the Brazil Cinema Novo tradition that protests Third World tyrannies and Latin America's history of oppression. Its plot, such as it is, concerns the thoughts of Diaz, a former dictator who, mad in his castle in exile, dreams of his glorious past in El Dorado where he oppressed the working classes and indigenous peoples. He tries to avoid deadly retribution at the hands of his victims by sacrificing a pure countrywoman, but he is stopped by a magical shepherd who frees the woman and kills Diaz. Rocha has characterized the film as a free adaptation of *Macbeth*, taking its inspiration primarily from Macbeth's guilty near-madness in Dunsinane Castle. The title translates as "severed heads," referring to Macbeth's ultimate fate. It includes no direct citations of Shakespeare.

841 *Makbet*
1970. Poland. Cartoon Film Studios. Sound, col., length unknown. Alfred Ledwig.

Animated short by the noted Polish illustrator and animator that, Sammons suggests, concerns "a man obsessed with the desire and search for power."

842 *El Mariscal del infierno (Devil's Possessed)*
1974. Spain and Argentine. Producciones Orbe and Profilmes S.A. Sound, col., 95 mins. León Klimovsky.

Unhonored for his heroic service, French warrior Gilles de Loncrane seeks to be crowned the king of France. With his wife's and an alchemist's encouragement, he becomes a sadistic tyrant, only eventually to be overthrown by his former friend, Gaston de Malebranche.

Uses several motifs from *Macbeth*: a commander tempted by ambition, a seductive Lady Macbeth figure, a protective charm provided by witchcraft, a string of murders of guests and friends, and the tyrant's guilty hallucinations and increasing despair. No direct verbal references.

843 *The Great McGonagall*
1974. U.K. Darlton. Sound, col., 89 mins. Joseph McGrath.

Co-written by Spike Milligan. In what is in effect a film version of the Goon Show, unemployed Scottish weaver

William McGonagall falls in love with Queen Victoria at a music hall show, and after giving a performance of Shakespeare for the queen, he aspires to become a poet laureate of England. He travels to Balmoral to be honored by the queen, but he is turned away at the door and has several adventures there and back again. In the end, his account of his journey gives him literary fame, and he is honored by Tennyson and the king of Timor before dying.

McGonagall becomes a lover of Shakespeare when in debtors' prison he learns to read. His favorite plays are, he tells us, *Macbeth*, *Othello*, and *The Two Gentlemen of Verona*, and he gives one-man impressions of Richard III ("Now is the winter of our discontent") and Othello ("The pity of it, Iago"). His performance before Queen Victoria is of the final scene of *Macbeth*; in McGonagall's version, Macbeth wins over Macduff, but the fight is kept going so long as the audience doesn't throw things. Later, McGonagall cites his poem in praise of Shakespeare to an unappreciative audience.

844 *Up!*
1976. U.S. RM Films. Sound, col., 80 mins. Russ Meyer.

In this sexploitation film, the mysterious death of Adolf Schwartz, a reclusive Nazi with deviant desires, becomes intertwined with events in a small Northwestern town. After Margo Winchester is raped during a morning jog and kills her attacker, she contracts with Homer Johnson, the local state trooper, to cover the crime in exchange for sexual favors. Soon the two become lovers, and Margo gets a job at Alice's Café, the local diner, leading to a boom in business and an attempt to open a nightclub. The club's first night ends with Homer being assaulted with an axe when a drunken lumberjack is aroused by Margo's dancing; the film ends with a nighttime chainsaw assault through the woods, after which the killer of Schwartz is revealed. Throughout, a nude Greek Chorus provides narration and commentary.

In a state of perpetual sexual excitement, the Greek Chorus offers her narration in a quasi-Elizabethan idiom that includes several phrases and lines from *Macbeth*, none of which are thematically significant.

845 *In the Forest*
1978. U.K. BFI. Sound, b&w, 80 mins. Phil Mulloy.

In this surrealistic comedy, while walking through a forest three medieval peasants travel through four centuries of British history, from the Middle Ages to the nineteenth century. One of the fragments of culture included is a scene from *Macbeth*. Mulloy has gone on to become a noted film animator.

846 *Shakespeare's Mounted Foot*
1979. U.K. A Breck/Campbell Production. Sound, col., 44 mins. Bert Eeles.

A comedy short concerning a turn-of-the-twentieth century theatrical troupe touring the Borders. Includes a section of the troupe's performance of *Macbeth*.

847 *Josepha*
1982. France. Albina Productions S.a.r.l., Mondex Films, and TF1 Films Productions. Sound, col., 114 mins. Christopher Frank.

Josepha Manet, an actress married to actor Michel Laurent, is troubled after she learns of Michel's long-term affair with Sarah, his press agent. When she travels to make a film, she meets and has an affair with Régis Duchemin, a wealthy horse breeder; she soon leaves Michel to live with Régis. Michel continues to struggle with his acting career until he is offered the role of *Macbeth* in a production at the National Theatre. Learning of his good fortune, Josepha drives to see Michel in dress rehearsal and, afterward, helps him reach his potential as an actor.

Michel has acted in several unsuccessful plays, so *Macbeth* is his final chance to prove his acting mettle. Of the dress rehearsal we see four sequences—Macbeth's first meeting with the witches, Macbeth and Lady Macbeth immediately after the murder of Duncan, Macbeth's "tomorrow and tomorrow and tomorrow" speech (somewhat woodenly performed), and Macbeth's confrontation with Macduff. Of his rehearsal with Josepha, we see the banquet scene (Josepha pushes him to jump on the table to confront the vision of Banquo) and the "tomorrow and tomorrow and tomorrow" speech (delivered in a world-weary manner that brings tears to Josepha's eyes). It is possible to see Josepha's pushing of Michel as obliquely parallel to Lady Macbeth's urging of Macbeth, though it has none of Shakespeare's sinister consequences. An epilogue informs us that the play was a success but that after the performance, Josepha returned to Régis. One last Shakespearean detail: Michel and Josepha's dog is named Iago.

848 *Educating Rita*
1983. U.K. Columbia Pictures. Sound, col., 110 mins. Lewis Gilbert.

Adapted from the play by Willy Russell. Rita, a working-class hairdresser, pursues a degree at the Open University, despite the fact that her choice not to become a mother causes friction with her husband Denny and her father. In need of a tutor, she chooses alcoholic professor of literature Frank Bryant, who has become disillusioned over his teaching and his failing relationship with girlfriend Julia, who is having an affair with his best friend. As Rita becomes intellectually more mature and confident, she and Frank start a romance, but in the end Rita grows past Frank and leaves both him and Denny.

In this variation on Shaw's *Pygmalion*, a key touchstone is *Macbeth*. Rita is so moved by seeing *Macbeth* in the theater that she spontaneously visits Frank to talk about the experience. The discussion of the nature of tragedy that follows underlines Rita's popular understanding of the play and Frank's literary-critical understanding, a difference that the film returns to when Frank and Rita discuss her essay on the play. It is also over *Macbeth* that Rita's alienation from her working-class husband first becomes apparent. When Rita asks Denny if he's ever seen *Macbeth*, he replies, "We're not good enough for you now." Interestingly, the filmscript cuts Rita's citation of Macbeth's "Life's but a walking shadow" soliloquy, which the playscript included.

849 *Macbeth*
1987. France and Belgium. Delalus, Henry Lange Production, S.F.P.C., TF1 Films Productions, and UNITEL Film. Sound, col., 133 mins. Claude D'Anna.

Film of the Verdi opera. Included in this bibliography because the production attempts not to merely record a theatrical performance but also to make a full-fledged film adaptation. The opera was filmed inside a castle in the Ardennes, and parts are lip-synched to music pre-recorded under Riccardo Chailly's direction.

850 *Macbeth*
1987. Finland. Villealfa Film Productions. Sound, col., 70 mins. Pauli Pentti.

Produced by Aki Kaurismaki, director of *Hamlet Goes Business* (Pentti was assistant director on that film), and part of a planned trilogy of films based on Shakespeare's tragedies (the third, on *King Lear*, was never made). This deadpan black-comedy version of *Macbeth* for arthouse audiences focuses on a war between gangsters started by Macbeth, a clueless thug, at the urging of his girlfriend (who eventually kills herself). Much of the comedy of the film springs from the escalating misquotation of Shakespearean lines and speeches as the dimwitted gangsters become increasingly paranoid and violent. The film parodies *Macbeth*, the conventions of film noir, and gangster retrofits of Shakespeare. Compare *Joe Macbeth*.

851 *Opera*
1987. Italy. ADC Films and Cecchi Gori Group Tiger Cinematografica. Sound, col., 107 mins. Dario Argento.

In this *giallo*, Betty, an understudy in a contemporary production of Verdi's *Macbeth*, is given the chance to play Lady Macbeth when the star is mysteriously killed in a car accident. Betty, terrified of the curse on the play, is pursued by a psychopath who forces her to watch as he kills victims with particular grisliness. When the police investigation fails to stop the serial killer, Marco, the opera's director, uses ravens from the production to identify (and attack) the murderer; though the murderer attempts to kill Betty after revealing his motive, he dies in a fire.

Several sequences from Verdi's *Macbeth* are included, as well as references to the curse upon productions of the play. DVD contains a featurette that references *Macbeth*.

852 *Macbeth: The Witches Scenes*
1988. U.S. The Piven Theatre & Optimus, Inc. Sound, col., 18 mins. Byrne Piven.

With a compelling vocal performance of the four witches' scenes from *Macbeth* as its soundtrack, artist Miroslaw Rogala's video reimagines the witches as post-apocalyptic social castoffs—they inhabit a bleak junkyard—who use a computer and a robot to cast their spells and foresee disasters that range from a small girl falling from a jungle gym to repeated images of nuclear holocaust. Macbeth is presented as a modern five-star general who is horrified by images of modern warfare in the procession of apparitions. The film is shot on video and uses a range of video effects that, though now dated, were advanced in its day.

Shifting the witches' scenes from a barbaric past to a dystopian present day, Rogala's video recasts the witches as grotesque, marginalized prophets of technological destruction, using the then-new personal computer both as the mechanism of that destruction and the means for predicting it. In an interesting way, that ambivalence is reflected in the piece's medium: Rogala uses computer-enabled video effects to critique what new computer technology has enabled on the battlefield, impersonal destruction on a mass scale. Some of the images Rogala keys to Shakespeare's texts are compelling, such as the blood encroaching on the frame as the witches predict Macbeth's rise to power; others are less imaginative, such as the thumb on the witches' computer screen as one says, "By the pricking of my thumbs" (4.1.61).

853 *The Haunting of Sarah Hardy*
1989. U.S. Paramount. Sound, col., 92 mins. Jerry London.

Adapted from the novel *The Crossing* by Jim Flanagan. In this made-for-TV film, Sarah Hardy is troubled by the memory of her mother's mysterious drowning on the day of her father's funeral. When fifteen years later she marries Austin Hardy, she returns to her family home, The Pines, only to be stalked by mysterious figures in the fog reminiscent of her mother. After she loses her unborn child and asks Austin for a divorce, she (and we) learn that Austin has been conspiring with Lucy, Sarah's best friend, to drive her mad and take her estate. After Sarah disappears in much the same way as her mother, Austin begins to be haunted by the same mysterious figures in the fog. When Sarah turns up alive and searches The Pines for evidence, she is chased by Austin, who accidentally kills Lucy and seems to die in a car crash. At film's end, he returns to attack Sarah once more.

Lucy, an actress, is rehearsing *Macbeth* throughout the film, and in two conversations with Sarah, excerpts of *Macbeth* are barely audible in the background. For her last conversation during the rehearsal (with Austin), the group is rehearsing Macbeth's second encounter with the witches, and we see a small portion of the performance. In this conversation, Lucy is dressed as Lady Macbeth. The play is thematically relevant: like Macbeth and his wife, Austin and Lucy plot to eliminate the trusting Sarah so they can "inherit" the estate; Lucy uses her sexual appeal to spur Austin on (at one point, they prepare to kill Sarah using knives); and Austin finds himself needing to plot further murders to cover his crimes.

854 *Men of Respect*
1991. U.S. Arthur Goldblatt Productions, Central City Films, and Grandview Avenue Pictures. Sound, col., 113 mins. William Reilly.

Another transposition of Shakespeare's tragedy to the gangster genre (see also *Joe Macbeth* [above]), set in contemporary New York. Fleeing from the murder of The Greek and his men, Mike Battaglia, a brutal hitman for padrino Charlie D'Amico, and his friend Bankie Como stumble across a threesome of squatters, one of whom prophesies that Mike will become padrino and fate will be kind to Bankie's son. As a reward for killing The Greek, Charlie makes Mike a "man of respect," a revered member of his mob. At a dinner at Mike's house, Charlie forcibly retires Carmelo Rossi and indicates that his two sons, Mal and Don, will inherit leadership of the organization. Urged on by his wife and aided by her drugging of Charlie's guards, Mike murders Charlie. When the murder is discovered, Mike brutally guns down the guards, but a glance at his wife reveals Mike's guilt to Bankie. Increasingly worried about the rise of Phil, Bankie's son and a financial whiz, he arranges the murder of Bankie and Phil at a butcher shop, but only Bankie is killed; afterward, at a party, Mike sees visions of the bloody Bankie and becomes unhinged. Returning to the squatters in a rainstorm, Mike learns that he will hold power till stars fall from the sky and that he leads a charmed life: "No man of woman born can harm you." Soon after, Duffy's wife and child are killed by a car bomb intended for him, and Duffy joins other disgruntled mobsters who have gathered around Rossi, who is anxious to have his status as a "man of respect" restored. Meanwhile, Ruth has become obsessed with cleanliness and commits suicide; after his men desert him, Mike, seeing fireworks in the sky ("until stars fall from the heavens"), shoots it out with mobsters until Duffy (who, he reveals, was born by C-section) kills him.

Reilly melds Shakespeare's *Macbeth* with the atmosphere and motifs of contemporary New York gangster films such as *The Godfather*, *Mean Streets*, and *Goodfellas*. (The cast is stuffed with well-known "tough-guy" character actors, and the milieu and graphic violence strongly recall Scorsese.) He follows the Shakespearean plot line quite closely throughout, though small changes are telling: Rossi's resentment becomes a prominent feature, indicating Charlie's (that is, Duncan's) flawed desire to create a legacy for himself at the expense of others; we learn that Mike had earlier forced the aptly named Ruth to have an abortion, a change that explains their childlessness but also motivates the tensions between them and her merciless ambition ("I know what it is to kill for you, Michael"); the cameo appearance of deadpan comic Steven Wright as Sterling the janitor (substituting for the Porter) mostly underlines the culture of intimidation in the mob rather than offering topical satire; Bankie's recognition of guilty glances between Mike and Ruth when Charlie's body is discovered remakes the Banquo character into a willing co-conspirator with Mike; and Mal's ceremonial induction of Phil into the "men of respect" at film's end implies that the cycle of ambition and murder is about to begin again. Very little of Shakespeare's dialogue remains, except for passing echoes—"be bold and resolute," and "no man of woman born"—in the witches' second confrontation with Mike, and Ruth's citation of "who would have thought the old man to have had so much blood in him" in her sleepwalking scene. Oddly, Reilly does provide an extended counterpart for the Captain's report of Macbeth's battle with Macdonald and the Norwegians with Sal's heroic account to Charlie of Mike's hit on The Greek and his men. The film particularly emphasizes the mob code of "respect" as a source of emotional conflict for Mike, the equivalent of feudal fealty for Macbeth. A repeated motif of mirrors, both flat and distorted, provides opportunities for Mike and Ruth's guilty self-confrontation; Mike's nudity with Ruth after his crimes hints at his vulnerability to her. Compared to *Joe Macbeth*, *Men of Respect* has a relentless earnestness of tone that robs the adaptation of some of its potential power as a study in grim irony, though of the two it is indisputably the more professionally made film. See also entry 392.

855 *Scenes from Macbeth*
1992. Canada. Production company unknown. Sound, col., 45 mins. Chris Philpott.

A deadpan parody of *Macbeth*, set in the contemporary business world of Toronto where businessmen murder each other between meetings and power lunches, mixing Shakespearean lines with modern dialogue. Several transpositions of Shakespeare's play are especially witty: the witches are barmy homeless women, and street urchins chant their spells as a rap number; the "tomorrow and tomorrow" soliloquy is repeated three different times, each time in a different style (the last is stand-up comedy); and a pickup truck filled with Christmas trees serves for Birnam Wood coming to Dunsinane (Macbeth is gunned down from the truck in a drive-by shooting). Of the same general tone as Kaurismaki's *Hamlet Goes Business* and Pentti's *Macbeth*.

856 *Witch Hunt*
1994. U.S. Home Box Office (HBO) and Pacific Western. Sound, col., 100 mins. Paul Schrader.

H. Phillip Lovecraft, a detective in an alternate 1950s Los Angeles where magic is commonplace, searches for the murderer of studio executive Nicky Gotlieb. Several of Lovecraft's acquaintances become suspects, Gotlieb's widow Kim Hudson among them, but the crime is pinned on Lovecraft's associate Hypolita Kropotkin, a witch for the film studio, by a powerful antiwitchcraft crusading senator Larson Crockett. Eventually Lovecraft exposes Senator Crockett as a hypocrite and finds the true murderer, a magician turned security man called Finn Macha.

This surrealistic hybrid of film noir and supernatural fantasy includes a scene early on in which Kropotkin conjures Shakespeare (with a spell that includes "fair is foul and foul is fair, / Hover through the fog and filthy air" from *Macbeth* 1.1) so that he can work as a script fixer for Gotlieb. The scene is something of a comic throwaway.

857 *Heat*
1995. U.S. Warner Bros. Sound, col., 171 mins. Michael Mann.

In this epic crime drama, Neil McCauley, a meticulous but ruthless master thief, seeks with his gang to complete one last bank heist before retiring, while he is pursued by Vincent Hanna, an equally determined Los Angeles detective whose married life is a shambles. The film pursues many sub-plots involving the personal lives of the opposing criminal and police groups. After McCauley kills an informant, Hanna pursues him to an airport where the two have their showdown gunfight.

In their one face-to-face conversation, Hanna talks about a dream in which McCauley confronts his dead victims at a banquet, a clear allusion to the banquet scene in *Macbeth* 3.4.

858 *Screamers*
1995. Canada, U.S. and Japan. Allegro Films, Fries Film Group, Fuji Eight Company Ltd., and Triumph Films. Sound, col., 108 mins. Christian Duguay.

Adapted from the story "Second Variety" by Philip K. Dick. On Sirius 6B, a planet destroyed by nuclear war, "screamers," small robots that slice their victims to death, besiege the few surviving humans who are divided into two warring groups, the Alliance and the New Economic Bloc. To seek peace, Colonel Joseph Hendricksson, leader of the Alliance, crosses a dangerous wasteland accompanied by Ace Jefferson, a jet pilot and sharpshooter; along the way, they pick up David Dearing, a small boy who turns out to be a new-design screamer. When they arrive at NEB headquarters, they discover only three survivors; the group returns to Alliance headquarters only to be assaulted by an army of small-boy screamers and afterward by Becker, one of the group, who is another model of new-design screamer. When only two are left, one of the survivors, the smuggler Jessica Hansen, turns out to be yet another human screamer who has fallen in love with Hendricksson, and she

fights her own robot kind to allow him to escape, but he unwittingly carries a screamer in the form of a teddy bear.

The human screamers quote Shakespeare at his most cynical. Becker, one of the NEB survivors, recites Portia's lines about the duke of Saxony's nephew, "when he is best, he is a little worse than a man, and when he is worst, he is little better than a beast" (*The Merchant of Venice* 1.2); like Shylock, he threateningly sharpens his knife. Later, he turns to Richard, Duke of Gloucester in his murderous vein. As Becker talks cynically to Jefferson about their status as cannon fodder, he quotes Richard, "which plainly signified / That I should snarl and bite and play the dog, [like me]" (*Henry VI, Part 3* 5.6). When Jefferson tries to help him in the aftermath of a battle, Becker attacks him, reciting other lines from the same speech: "Down, down to hell, and say that I sent you [there]! . . . For I have often heard my mother say / I came into the world with my legs forward: . . . and the woman cried . . . he [was] born with teeth!" When he turns on Hendricksson, he quotes still more of the same speech: "I have no brother, I am like no brother; / And this word 'love,' which [old farts] call divine, / Be resident in men like [you, asshole] / [But] not in me: I am [my motherfucking self] alone." Another screamer with the face of a friend attacks Hendricksson with the "Down, down to hell" speech. The choice of Richard is apropos given his extraordinary duplicity and unrepentant murderousness.

859 *High School High*
1996. U.S. TriStar Pictures and Zucker Brothers Productions. Sound, col., 86 mins. Hart Bochner.

A parody of films about an inspirational teacher at an urban high school. Richard Clark, anxious to prove to his headmaster father that he can make a difference, takes a job at Marion Barry High and proceeds to reform the school and its students while wooing a fellow teacher, opposed all the while by the cynical principal, Evelyn Doyle.

In a brief sequence, we see the fruits of Clark's reforms at a local stripclub, The Swamp: a stripper performs (badly) a passage from Lady Macbeth's "out, out damned spot" in the club's production of *Macbeth*.

860 *Macbeth Horror Suite*
1996. Italy. Production company unknown. Sound, col., 60 mins. Carmelo Bene.

A film version, made for television, of Bene's Artaudian reenvisioning of Shakespeare's play, with emphasis on spectacles of horror and blood à la Italian *giallo*. The stage version was first presented at the Festival d'Automne at the Théâtre de Paris in 1983. This film was never commercially released.

861 *The Scottish Tale*
1997. U.S. The Asylum. Sound, col., 81 mins. Mackenlay Polhemus.

On a visit to his native Scotland, Mack, a melancholy and unsuccessful Scottish poet, hears three prophecies from his three batty aunts that Mack will ruin his brother Ian's marriage to Beth Huntley, daughter of Syd Huntley, a prominent California lawyer who is also Ian's boss. Returning to his home in Inverness, California, Mack, despite his best efforts to avoid fulfilling the prophecies and to deny his attraction to Beth, ends up accidentally fulfilling all three. Meanwhile, Syd's son Sterling, angry that Beth's marriage will undermine his share of the family inheritance, plots revenge against Mack and Ian, and Beth discovers that her true father is not Syd but Arthur Golding, an eccentric Jewish tailor. The film ends with Mack and Beth getting happily married and Ian getting a puppy.

The Scottish Tale grafts many of the supernatural motifs of *Macbeth* onto a romantic comedy. Mack's three aunts serve as the three witches, offering their prophecies as they brew afternoon tea; their prophecies have the same equivocal quality that those of *Macbeth*'s witches have, and Mack ironically fulfills them. Like Macbeth, Mack also has a guilty hallucination, in the form of a half-dead skunk who appears to tell him that he should follow his heart. At film's end, the aunts reappear at Mack and Beth's wedding and reveal that they may or may not have cast a love spell. The film also comically adapts some of the revenge motifs in its sub-plots with Sterling and the skunk, and Mack pauses periodically to offer stilted poetic soliloquies in rhymed couplets. Though none of Shakespeare's language is cited, the curse of the "Scottish Play" is twice referenced, and Mack expresses his admiration for Shakespeare's sonnets, which he presents as the height of poetic achievement.

862 *Star Wars: Macbeth*
1997; 2001. U.S. AriZonA Pictures and NS Productions. Sound, col., 17 mins. Bien Concepcion and Donald Fitz-Roy.

Subtitled *Macduff Strikes Back*. A *Star Wars* fan video, shot by students of Glenridge High School in New Jersey for a school project and published on the Internet. The film cleverly splices together student performances of the final act of *Macbeth* with frame-captured footage from various *Star Wars* films and surprisingly well-done special effects. Macbeth is recast as Darth Vader, Macduff as Luke Skywalker, Malcolm as Lando Calrissian, and Siward as Hans Solo; the high school building serves as Macbeth's Dunsinane Castle/Death Star, and young Siward's death mimicks the sacrificial death of Obi-Wan Kenobi in *Star Wars: A New Beginning*. Much of Shakespeare's dialogue from *Macbeth*'s fifth act is retained, interwoven with various catchphrases and lines from the *Star Wars* series. The battle scenes with light sabres, the centerpiece of the film, are well-staged; the mano a mano between Macbeth and Macduff occurs, appropriately enough, on the high school's

stage. Several humorous touches are noteworthy: after defeating Macbeth, Macduff and his men exit the high school in the *Millennium Falcon* before it is spectacularly blown up, and at the triumphal processional (borrowed from *Star Wars: A New Beginning*) where Malcolm is crowned king, Macduff holds Macbeth's severed head, which smiles for the audience. See also entry 394.

863 *Naked Frailties*
1998. Canada. Absolute Films. Sound, col., 91 mins. Larry Reese.

A metatheatrical adaptation akin to *Macbeth in Manhattan* (entry 867). This independent film, made by the students and staff of Red Deer College in Alberta, Canada, chronicles a fictional college production of *Macbeth*. After receiving a head injury in a stage fighting class, Ross, well-regarded student actor at the college, begins to have troubling visions. The director of the production, Mr. Stuart, gives the part of Macbeth to Benj, his friend, rather than him, and the part of Lady Macbeth to Helen rather than to Ross's girlfriend, Liz. Furious at being passed over for a role she regarded as hers, Liz formulates a plan to drive Mr. Stuart from his job, as Ross experiences hallucinations in which the three witches tell him that he will have the role of Macbeth. Liz cajoles the hesitant Ross into following her plan, and the two destroy Mr. Stuart's career and get the lead roles in the play. Soon afterward, however, they descend into guilt and madness.

864 *In the Flesh*
1999. U.S. and Hungary. VCA. Sound, col., 120 mins. Stuart Canterbury.

One of the more faithful hardcore pornographic adaptations of Shakespeare's *Macbeth* (see also *A Midsummer Night's Cream*, also directed by Stuart Canterbury), *In the Flesh* adopts a post-modern production design, mixing an ancient castle and crowns with contemporary anachronisms such as machine guns, Jeeps, and modern dress, and combining lines from Shakespeare (Lady Macbeth, for example, offers a portion of her sleepwalking dialogue) with modernized and simplified versions of his dialogue. Most of the main characters and the basic narrative of ambition, murder, and guilt remain relatively intact, though in conventional adult movie fashion, the plotline periodically pauses for sex scenes, only some of which are integrated to the central narrative. For example, Lady Macbeth seduces Macbeth into killing Duncan, and Banquo appears to Macbeth at a court orgy, not a banquet; but elsewhere Lady Macbeth's sleepwalking speech becomes little more than background noise for a tryst between a guard and a nameless prisoner in the castle dungeon. In this version, the three witches cast their spell with a lesbian tryst, and Lady Macbeth uses sex to manipulate her husband. See also entry 398.

865 *Jawbreaker*
1999. U.S. Crossroads Films, Jawbreaker Productions, Inc., Kramer-Tornell Productions, and TriStar Pictures. Sound, col., 87 mins. Darren Stein.

A quartet of girls, Courtney Shane, Julie Freeman, Marcie Fox, and Liz Parr, form the social elite of Ronald Reagan High School, intimidating other students. When Courtney learns that popular Liz is likely to beat her in the election for prom queen, she convinces the other girls to kidnap Liz, but they accidentally choke her to death with a jawbreaker. To cover the crime, Courtney invents a scenario in which Liz was strangled during kinky sex, but Fern Mayo, a nerd, learns of the lie and the girls are forced to admit her to their clique. Fern is transformed into Vylette, a popular girl, and she challenges Courtney for the prom queen title; meanwhile, Julie, plagued by pangs of conscience, leaves the clique and seeks to reveal the truth, with the help of Zach, another social outcast.

Macbeth is briefly referenced in a discussion in an English class. Appropriately, the topic is Lady Macbeth.

866 *Macbeth* (*Macbeth XXX*)
1999. France. Colmax. Sound, col., 83 mins. Silvio Bandinelli.

Hardcore pornography. A modernized version of elements of the story, set in the world of an Eastern European crime syndicate. Macbeth is a hitman for a crime boss; a gypsy fortune teller substitutes for the witches. The story opens with the christening of Macbeth, and closes with that of his and Lady Macbeth's son. Compare *In the Flesh* (entry 398).

Very little of Shakespeare's story remains, save the name of Shakespeare's protagonist, the ambitiousness of Lady Macbeth, and a (very) few plot elements. There are no direct verbal references.

867 *Macbeth in Manhattan*
1999. U.S. Amber Waves, Cinebard, and Plus Films. Sound, col., 97 mins. Greg Lombardo.

This heavily metatheatrical adaptation charts the struggles of a troupe of young actors as they rehearse a production of *Macbeth* in New York City. At first, Claudia and Max, a couple to be married, are cast as the leads, but almost immediately Richard, the director, replaces Max with William, a rising star, in the role of Macbeth. As Claudia and William rehearse their roles, they discover an attraction between themselves; when Max learns of this, he moves out on Claudia and harbors a resentment at William, who in the meantime increasingly becomes an insufferable prima donna. Eventually, Claudia uncovers that William is a rake, and she and Max get back together. On the night before opening, Max kills William by engineering an accident with a piece of falling scenery as the two men rehearse Macbeth and Macduff's final battle. Max thereby ends up with the part of Macbeth he so coveted, but as he begins his performance on opening night, the spectre of the murdered William rises from the audience to accuse him.

Macbeth in Manhattan closely follows Shakespeare's plot, offering versions or snippets of nearly every major scene and speech in performance or rehearsal (or both); to make sure we can follow the story, a stagehand acts as a Chorus, summarizing events from the play in modern English. The film underlines the parallels between Shakespeare's plot and the emotional lives of the characters by intercutting performances of lines and scenes from *Macbeth* with scenes between the actors, in each case suggesting how the turmoil of the romances, career ambitions, and betrayals lies behind the successful performances of the lead plots. For example, Max's rage at William's theft of his fiancée fuels his intense performance of Macduff's desire for revenge; Claudia's sexual attraction for William underpins her seductive performance of Lady Macbeth's persuasion of Macbeth to kill Duncan, and her guilt at betraying Max parallels Lady Macbeth's guilt in the sleepwalking scene. The film's unexpected ending, where the dead William (now as Banquo) accuses Max (now as Macbeth), provides a satisfying twist and suggests a cycle of ambition, revenge, and guilt. The film also references the curse upon performances of *Macbeth*, and twice refers in passing to *Hamlet*. At the heart of the film's conception is its devotion to method acting, the notion that successful performance of Shakespeare depends upon actors actually experiencing versions of the emotions experienced by the characters. (As such, the film has a particularly strong New York pedigree.) The image of the mirror and double performances of some scenes work to underline the point, as do somewhat heavy-handed speeches by the director Richard. One uncharacteristically witty detail: when Claudia arrives with the red dress in which she will betray Max, she pricks her thumb on a needle.

NB: Compare *The Goodbye Girl*. Though perhaps indebted to Orson Welles's 1936 all-black Harlem production *Voodoo Macbeth* (entry 823), the *Macbeth* production takes race-blind casting for granted (Lady Macbeth is black and involved with the two white men; and one of the three witches is black. Also, Harold Perrineau plays a character who is part chorus/narrator, part gay dresser. Only Perrineau's blackness seems to be of significance. Perrineau also plays Mercutio in Baz Luhrman's *William Shakespeare's Romeo + Juliet* (1996) and Caliban in *The Tempest* [1998]). (RB)

868 *Macbeth-Sangrador* (*Bleeder*)
1999. Venezuela. Centro Nacional Autónomo de Cinematografía, Cinema Sur, and Post Meridian Cinema. Sound, b&w, 89 mins. Leonardo Henríquez.

The action of *Macbeth* is transposed to the Venezuelan Andes at the turn of the twentieth century. After joining a gang of bandits, Max (short for Maximiliano), a man with a reputation for justice, encounters a group of naked witches who prophesy that he will murder the leader of the gang, Duran, to whom he has sworn obedience and loyalty. With his wife's encouragement, he kills Duran and takes over the gang of thieves, after which he is plagued by guilt, fear, and increasing ruthlessness.

Though it uses none of Shakespeare's language, the plot is a rather faithful transposition of *Macbeth* to rural Latin America. The style—with extremes of violence, machismo, and gratuitous nudity; overblown and even surrealistic Catholic symbolism; and a spaghetti Western visual style—bespeaks the influence of *El Topo* and Latin American exploitation films of its ilk. See also entry 400.

869 *Makibefo*
1999. Madagascar and U.K. Blue Eye Films. Sound, b&w, 73 mins. Alexander Abela.

A very unusual and compelling cinema verité adaptation, filmed in Madagascar. Using as his actors a tribe of fishermen called the Antroyds, director Alexander Abela reconceives *Macbeth* through the lens of African mythology and local ritual, situating the narrative in a coastal village of Madagascar. Prompted by a sorcerer's prophecy of King Kidoure's assassination and Makibefo's rise to power, urged on by his wife Valy, Makibefo after much hesitation murders Kidoure and is immediately haunted by guilt. Abela's scenario focuses particularly on the primal nature of Makibefo's crime, the central role of the sorcerers in Makibefo's fate, and the ritual and mythological elements in Shakespeare's narrative. But he is equally interested in the largely improvisatory performance of the villagers, who were heretofore isolated from Western culture (including film); their performances tend to be naïve and unpolished, and a number of scenes play with the fuzzy line between reality and fiction. The film's grainy b&w and rough-and-ready camerawork are reminiscent of the "primitive" style of Piero Pasolini's "peasant" films. See also entry 401.

870 *The Talented Mr. Ripley*
1999. U.S. Mirage Enterprises, Miramax Films, Paramount Pictures, and Timnick Films. Sound, col., 139 mins. Anthony Minghella.

Adapted from the novel by Patricia Highsmith. Tom Ripley, a sociopath with a talent for impersonating others, pretends to be a Princeton student and is sent by shipping tycoon Herbert Greenleaf to Italy to convince his son Dickie to return to the States. When he meets Dickie and his girlfriend Marge Sherwood, he becomes envious of his wealth, romance, sophistication, and life of leisure, and after Dickie and friend Freddie Miles become suspicious of Tom's behavior, he murders Dickie in order to assume his identity. To maintain his ruse, he engages in an elaborate series of forgeries and murders, evading the police, Marge, and Freddie.

Macbeth is briefly referenced when Tom asks Dickie to sign his name on a postcard; the postcard reads, "Stars hide your fires," citing, appropriately enough, Macbeth's desire for kingship after Malcolm is named heir to Duncan's throne (*Macbeth* 1.4). This moment is prefaced by Dickie's condescending comment to Tom, "I can't believe you brought Shakespeare, but no clothes"; Dickie's observation highlights Tom's pretensions to cultural sophistication. Later on, as Tom's deception becomes more elaborate after Dickie's murder, there are several references to the Otello Restaurant.

871 *Borough of Kings* (aka *Brooklyn Sonnet*)
2000. U.S. Avenue R Films. Sound, col., 95 mins. Elyse Lewin.

In this semiautobiographical independent film set in Brooklyn, Jimmy O'Conner, an aspiring actor, gets the part of Banquo in a New York Shakespeare Festival production of *Macbeth* and begins a romance with Anna Callahan, the assistant stage manager. At the same time, his friend Tommy DeVito, owner of a gym and a neighborhood thug, along with fellow thug Nunzio, murder Moosehead, a member of their gang, who, they learn, is a police informant. When Jimmy sees the two cutting up Moosehead's corpse to dispose of it, Nunzio threatens to kill Jimmy while Tommy vouches for his silence. Eventually Nunzio is killed and mob boss Uncle Chicky dies, and Jimmy, after a triumphal performance in *Macbeth*, leaves the neighborhood.

This is a variation on such mob *Macbeth*s as *Joe Macbeth* and *Men of Respect*. Several sequences intercut Jimmy's performance in *Macbeth* (a contemporary urban adaptation set on the New York streets) with scenes of gang violence. As Jimmy auditions for Banquo with his speech "Thou hast it now, king, Cawdor, Glamis, all" (3.2), it is juxtaposed with a theft and vicious beating by Tommy and his gang (with emphasis on the phrase "most foully"). After a rehearsal of the banquet scene, Jimmy invites Anna to a Thanksgiving dinner with his firemen friends. And in performance, when Jimmy as Banquo is killed onstage, it is intercut with Tommy tossing a body in the river and burying another in the basement; as he does, Tommy sardonically recites Macbeth's soliloquy, "Life is a walking shadow," which he picked up from reading Jimmy's script. One last detail: Jimmy's pet ferret is named Falstaff.

DVD contains a commentary track that references the Shakespearean elements in the film.

872 *House Party 4: Down to the Last Minute*
2001. U.S. New Line. Sound, col., 79 mins.

The fourth in the *House Party* film series. John-John plays sick so he can housesit for his uncle and have a party at his mansion. The film assumes a blacktopia world where blacks are the majority and are generally well-off financially. One scene involves a class on Shakespeare, and, significantly, the teacher is white. "Shakespeare!" is written in large letters across a green blackboard, and *Henry V* and *The Taming of the Shrew* are written beneath it in smaller letters. The teacher, Miss Topay, says, "Class, today we are going to be learning Shakespeare. Not just Shakespeare, but *Macbeth*." She launches into a reading of "Double, double, toil and trouble. Fire burn, and cauldron," and is interrupted at one point by John-John's sister, Tina. At one point, her face appears just to the right of the words "the shrew." (RB)

873 *Macbeth: The Comedy*
2001. U.S. Tristan Films. Sound, col., 61 mins. Allison L. LiCalsi.

In this contemporary burlesque, after hearing the predictions of the three witches (three mincing male queens), Macbeth, a lesbian warrior, rises to power when she murders the dimwitted King Duncan with the help of her wife, Lady Macbeth. Macbeth's paranoia leads her to kill Banquo and Macduff's wife and children, but Malcolm and Macduff join forces to overthrow Macbeth at Dunsinane. After Macbeth's defeat, the three witches reappear to offer further predictions to the newly crowned Malcolm.

This parody follows Shakespeare's plot very closely, deviating primarily in the goofy identities of the characters (Macbeth and wife are lesbian vegetarians, the three witches and two murderers are gay men, Banquo is a Jamaican, and Macduff's wife is a jealous shrew) and the motivations of the characters (for example, the murderers kill Banquo because Macbeth tells them he voted against them entering an apartment co-op, and Macduff kills Macbeth despite her attempts to seduce him, because he is expected to do so by the other men). LiCalsi's main comic technique is to set the play's epic seriousness and historical remoteness against mundane details of contemporary American life— the air is sweet at Macbeth's castle because of aromatherapy, and Lady Macbeth finds Macbeth's sword in their underwear drawer. Much of the film's humor springs from its juxtaposition of Shakespearean language (which it liberally quotes in nearly every scene) and casual American vernacular—Macbeth's opening line, "So foul and fair a day I have not seen; we really kicked some ass," presages the entire film's treatment of Shakespeare's idiom. Many of the sight gags and throwaway jokes lampoon Scotland, which is treated as a comic butt throughout: Duncan is disappointed, for example, that no haggis is being served at the banquet at Macbeth's castle, many of the characters wear plaid outfits or accessories, and Malcolm merrily munches on Walker's shortbreads. LiCalsi has particular fun with deheroicizing the role of Macbeth and demystifying the witches by toying with their genders, but her primary intent is clever Shakespearean burlesque rather than social satire.

874 *Mad Dawg: Running Wild in the Streets*
2001. U.S. Leo Films and Fusion Films. Sound, col., 95 mins. Greg Salman.

A direct-to-video "gangsta" adaptation. After hearing a prophecy of his rise and fall from a televangelist, Mac, one of drug lord Dunkin's "clique," rises to head Cawdor House, a dope den, after he takes vengeance on Dunkin's rivals. Dunkin designates Malcom, the brainy underling of Dunkin, as the designated heir to his drug empire as Mac begins to covet Dunkin's wealthy lifestyle. After Mac tells Lady M, his wife, of the prophecy, she hints that he should kill Dunkin. To force Mac to follow through, Lady M drugs Dunkin after a party. Mac, surprised when Dunkin suddenly awakes, stabs him to death, afterward blaming the crime on Malcom. When Banc asks Mac for reassurance that he did not kill Dunkin, Mac hires a murderer to kill him and his family; Banc is killed, but his wife and child escape. At a party celebrating his rise to power, Mac becomes abusive to his guests and hallucinates Banc's footsteps. He returns to the televangelist, who gives him three prophecies: "No lead or steel shall pierce your skin"; "Beware the one marked with a double cross"; and Mac will live "until the blind are cured." As Lady M is plagued by sleeplessness, Mac rehires the murderer, this time to kill Duffy and his family. The murderer kills the wife and child, but Duffy kills the murderer and recognizes him as Mac's man. After having given Mrs. Duffy a sack of cash in recompense, Lady M takes an overdose of sleeping pills and dies. Mac confronts a gang headed by Duffy who have come to kill him; a news report that Stevie Wonder will have surgery on his eyes presages Mac's coming end. At first successful against his attackers, Mac is eventually shot through the eye by Duffy who, we see, has a double-cross tattoo on his neck.

Mad Dawg follows the plot of *Macbeth* fairly closely, turning it into a moralistic parable about the temptations of gangsta glamour, money, and violence, and the precipitous fall of the ambitious. The televangelist, the substitute for the witches, becomes the ethical chorus of the film, laying out Mac's rise to power but also assuring him that all is for naught. Equally telling are a pair of funeral orations, Dunkin's for a fallen lieutenant in his organization and Mac's for Dunkin, both underlining the fate that awaits Mac in the end. Mac delivers several shortened versions of Macbeth's soliloquies to the mirror in his bathroom or as he drives in his car; most of these "speeches" concern his self-doubt or self-rationalization. When he discovers that Lady M is dead and his cash is gone, he pulls a bloody twenty-dollar bill from his pocket and remarks despairingly, "All of this for a lousy Jackson," the film's substitute for Macbeth's "tomorrow and tomorrow" speech. The final sequence, in which Mac at first contemplates suicide and then becomes grotesquely cocky when he recalls the preacher's prophecies, nicely captures the oscillation be tween despair and machismo in Shakespeare's final scenes. None of Shakespeare's dialogue is referenced. See also entry 402, *Blazin'*, *The Street King*, and *Barrio Wars*.

875 *Rave Macbeth* (*Nacht der Entscheidung*)
2001. Germany. 2K Filmproduktion, Falcon Films, and Frame Werk Produktion GmbH & Co. KG. Sound, col., 87 mins. Klaus Knoesel.

Conjured by Hecate, a witch and drug dealer, three witches (in the film, "the Petry girls") appear to Troy and Marcus, best friends and veterans of rave clubs, and suggest that Marcus will be king of the rave as they enter a trendy rave club. Marcus and Troy are promoted by Dean, head drug dealer at the club, to be his "seconds," that is, seconds in command. He sends them to distribute a new, more potent drug to the crowd, and to collect money from dealers, and he shows the two a massive shipment of drugs. Soon Marcus and his girlfriend Lidia, under the influence of drug-induced hallucinations of the witches, set about maneuvering for power in the club. Lidia manipulates Marcus into believing that Troy attempted to seduce her, and Marcus kills him; Troy's girlfriend Helena, on a bad drug trip, discovers Troy's dead body before Marcus can hide it, and Lidia forces her to take an overdose to cover the crime. Dean becomes suspicious of Marcus and Lidia, particularly with the absence of Troy and Helena, and he sends his bodyguard Macduff to find the missing pair. Dean takes a call from Hecate outside, and Marcus, spurred on by a hallucination of the witches in which he's told, "The day is lost only when blood rains from heaven," stabs Dean, leaving him for dead. As Marcus and Lidia walk through the club in triumph, Macduff hunts them down and is shot by Marcus, but another security man shoots Marcus and Lidia as they try to run out of the club. A short epilogue stresses how Marcus violated the rules of the rave, which stress peace and love.

This very free adaptation takes the analogy between Macbeth's magical visions and drug-induced highs as its starting point, treating Marcus's and Lidia's hallucinations of the witches as moments in which their ambitions, greed, and violence run free of inhibitions. Interestingly, Hecate orchestrates the plot from behind the scenes, watching the characters on giant supernatural video screens, conjuring and directing the witches, and functioning as both a chorus and a demonic video DJ. It is Hecate who in the prologue calls drugs such as Ecstasy the tools of modern witches, and it is he who identifies the story as that of Shakespeare's *Macbeth*, emphasizing that such stories of "death and atonement" repeat themselves. The film creatively conflates a number of Shakespeare's characters—Troy, for example, corresponds to Banquo, but his girlfriend Helena corresponds to Lady Macduff, both

victims of the Macbeths—and various motifs from Shakespeare's script appear in altered form (Marcus hallucinates seeing Troy and Helena on the dance floor after they have been killed, and phantom drops of blood fall in Marcus's drink as he begins to feel remorse for Troy's death). Citations from the Shakespearean text are set primarily in the mouths of Hecate and the witches. As Marcus and Lidia walk in triumph through the club after the murders, the witches intone the "tomorrow and tomorrow" soliloquy as a voice-over to suggest the emptiness of their achievement; Hecate underlines the point by reciting the final lines of his first long speech in 3.5: "He shall spurn fate, scorn death, and bear / His hopes 'bove wisdom, grace and fear: / And you all know, security / Is mortals' chiefest enemy." Hecate's role as a supernatural manipulator in the film plays up the fatedness of Marcus and Lidia and gives the film the quality of a theatrical fable, a quality also suggested by over-the-top rave scenes (as Marcus and Lidia are about to fall, a fat lady sings) and by the epilogue in which the main characters stand before us, as if ready to take a bow. Compare *Midsummer*, which also transfers Shakespeare to a rave milieu.

DVD includes a trailer in English that identifies the film's source tale as Shakespeare, as well as a "Making Of" documentary, a commentary track, and two interviews with director Knoesel (all in German) that reference *Macbeth*.

876 *Scotland, PA*
2001. U.S. Abandon Pictures, Paddy Wagon Productions, and Veto Chip Productions. Sound, col., 104 mins. Billy Morrissette.

Morrissette's slacker parody resituates the action and characters of *Macbeth* to small-town America and re-

Christopher Walken in Billy Morrissette's 2001 film *Scotland, PA*. An updated version of *Macbeth*, which here becomes a black comedy of tragic proportions. Abandon Pics/Paddy Wagon/Veto Chip Prod/The Kobol Collection.

imagines Macbeth as "Mac," an aimless twenty-something in a dead-end job at the dreary local burger bar run by Norm Duncan. Frustrated by Norm's lack of recognition for his service and urged on by his ambitious wife Pat, Mac clumsily kills Norm in the fryolator and afterward transforms the restaurant into McBeth's, a modern burger joint akin to Macdonald's. When McDuff, a Columbo-like police lieutenant, arrives to investigate Norm's death, Mac and Pat, financially successful but increasingly paranoid, soon turn on Banko, Mac's friend, and eventually on each other. In an amusing parody of 1970s TV detective show conventions, McDuff and Mac have their final confrontation on the roof of McBeth's. Though Mac attempts to choke McDuff with a hamburger, he ends up dead on the hood of his Camaro. McDuff inherits the restaurant, shifting it from burgers to vegetarian cuisine.

Many of the transpositions of Shakespeare's play are quite clever: Norm's sons, Malcolm and Donald, are disaffected from their father (Malcolm is a rocker, and Donald is gay), and neither has any interest in his tiny restaurant "empire"; the witches become hippies who only Mac can see, at first appearing on a comic version of the wheel of fortune, a carnival merry-go-round; and like Lady Macbeth, Pat becomes obsessed with a stain on her hand, in this case an invisible grease burn from Norm's murder. In addition, there are several comic riffs on famous lines from the play. For example, after Norm dies in the fryolator, Pat comments, "It's done, it can't be undone," an allusion to Macbeth's far more anguished and reflective soliloquy beginning "If it were done when 'tis done, then 'twere well / It were done quickly" (*Macbeth* 3.1.1–2). Though the film certainly is a deft burlesque of the heroic dimensions of Shakespeare's *Macbeth* and of vapid 1970s-era American mass culture, it also plays as an oblique commentary from an independent film perspective on the McDonaldization of Shakespeare in the 1990s, when Shakespearean film moved definitively from the arthouse to the multiplex. See also entry 403.

The DVD includes several extras, including a director's commentary track in which director and writer Billy Morrissette discusses at length the challenges of adapting *Macbeth*.

877 *Yellamma*
2001. India. Magic Lantern. Sound, col. Mohan Koda.

Indian version of Macbeth translated into Telengana dialect of Telugu and shot entirely on location in Warangal and Karimnagar districts. Set in the turbulent times of 1850s India, in the era of the Sepoy Mutiny. Raja Narendra Bhoopala Reddy, the king of Rudraram, was known as a great warrior and a benevolent king. He and his subjects lived in peace after paying a tribute to the Nizam. The king's forces were led by Veera Pratap Reddy (Nasser),

who was married to the queen's sister and so, by relation, was a brother to the king. Into their lives entered Yellamma (Revathy), the priestess and medium, known all over the countryside as an incarnation of Mother Kali. She was the one whose prophecies were always believed to come true. Yellamma is the story of Veera Pratap and his wife Mahadevi's (Sonali Kulkarni) tryst with ambition, achievement, and unfulfilled dreams. As their drama unfolds, we witness a greater drama on the cosmic stage, one that holds, draws, and engulfs the characters into a whirlpool of ambition, deceit, and bloody revenge. Ends with Macduff killing Macbeth. According to the director, the film attempts to "indigenize" Macbeth in order to export the film for U.S. and U.K. consumption. While sometimes visually beautiful, the use of actors sporting mullets makes the film unintentionally comic for its intended, Western audiences. Contact: magiclantern@indiaa.com. See also *Maqbool*. (RB)

878 *Below*
2002. U.S. Dimension Films and Protozoa Pictures. Sound, col., 105 mins. David Twohy.

In 1943, Lieutenant Brice takes over command of the U.S.S. *Tiger Shark* when its commander, Captain Winters, mysteriously dies. The sub recovers three survivors from a British hospital ship recently sunk by the Nazis—Kingsley, a medical officer; Claire Paige, a female nurse; and Schillings, a disfigured patient. When the ship is given away as it tries to run silent while being pursued by a German destroyer, Brice suspects a traitor and eventually kills Schillings when he learns he is a German POW. But after Schillings's death, supernatural events and mysterious disturbances continue to threaten the ship, and Brice's behavior becomes increasingly unstable.

Several reviewers noted connections with *Macbeth*. The link is highlighted when a book (*The Collected Works of Shakespeare*) falls for no reason; when Claire picks it up, it opens at *Macbeth* and she notices Brice's signature on the corner of the first page. When she reads the captain's log and questions Brice, she discovers that Brice killed Captain Winters and took over the ship (just as Macbeth killed Duncan and usurped his kingdom). The revenge of supernatural forces against Brice and the crew recalls the downfall of Macbeth and his court; Brice's guilty rubbing of his hands recalls Lady Macbeth in her sleepwalking scene. Though Claire does not parallel Lady Macbeth, she is instrumental in his destruction. See also *The Chronicles of Riddick*.

879 *Maqbool*
2003. India. Kaleidoscope Entertainment Pvt. Ltd. Sound, col., 132 mins. Vishal Bharadwaj.

This often brilliant adaptation transposes the action of *Macbeth* to the criminal underworld of contemporary

Bombay. Abbaji, head of a crime family, treats Maqbool, one of his loyal lieutenants, as if he is his son, even though Maqbool seems to have little taste for violence. Two corrupt policemen predict Maqbool's rise to power with horoscopes, and Maqbool soon rises within the organization in the wake of a gangland war; at the same time, Nimmi, Abbaji's mistress, expresses her romantic interest in Maqbool, which he at first rejects. When Abbaji forces a marriage between his daughter Sameera and Boji, the son of another of his lieutenants, Kaka (i.e., Banquo), Maqbool and Nimmi murder Abbaji during the betrothal celebration. Soon Maqbool arranges the death of his friend Boji to maintain power, and he consults the policemen, who predict that he is safe until the sea comes to his house. Meanwhile Nimmi has become pregnant, but it is not clear whether the child is Maqbool's or Abbaji's. Desperate to maintain his empire, Maqbool makes a deal with smugglers, but his deal is foiled by customs agents—the "sea"—who soon come to his house. After having given birth to their child, Nimmi dies of grief and guilt, and Maqbool returns to the hospital to find his child and take revenge upon Boji, but when he sees Boji and Sameera with his child, he refuses to kill them, ending up himself killed moments later in revenge for his earlier part in the gangland war. The second half of the film very closely parallels *Macbeth* in plot, motifs, and characters.

This adaptation is remarkable in many ways—for its elliptical, highly atmospheric cinematic style; its expansion of the relationship between the Duncan and Macbeth characters, one that makes Maqbool's murder of Abbaji all the more morally fraught; its treatment of the relationship between the Macbeth and Lady Macbeth characters as a forbidden romance; its recasting of the witches as comic, horoscope-casting policemen who manipulate events to maintain a karmic balance of power; and its revision of Shakespeare's tragic ending, which underlines the redemptive potential of Maqbool and the dark ironies of destiny.

The DVD includes several extras, including an interview in which Bharadwaj discusses his use of *Macbeth*.

880 *The Chronicles of Riddick*
2004. U.S. Primal Foe Productions, One Race Productions, Radar Pictures Inc., and Universal Pictures. Sound, col., 119 mins. David Twohy.

Riddick, an escaped convict on the run, is reluctantly drawn into battle with a seemingly unstoppable army of fascistic Necromongers led by the semisupernatural Lord Marshal, who is intent on annihilating most of the universe. Subplots feature Dame Vaako, an intergalactic Lady Macbeth, and Aereon, the ambassador for a ghost-like species, the Elementals.

In an interview, Twohy pointed up the connection to *Macbeth*: "There's no secret that we are inspired by *Macbeth* for that relationship, you know, a woman who has enough ambition for them both, and a man who has real uncertainties about that. I mean, that is classic Macbeth. But yeah, we dress up in new clothes with new dialogue and put it in a new setting and it plays well. I'm not the first to borrow from Shakespeare, by the way." Compare *Forbidden Planet* and *Below*.

The DVD includes a commentary track with the director and actors, and deleted scenes.

881 *Straight to You*
2004. Australia. Sound, col., 90 mins. Michael Egan.

A romantic comedy about a male temp office worker who wants to act and a "bitchy" woman lawyer he ends up taming. The film involves the office worker getting the part of Malcolm in a production of *Macbeth*. He wrecks the production when his reconciliation with his girlfriend is accidentally broadcast to the crowd. He loses his acting career but gets the girl. (RB)

882 *Macbeth*
2006. Australia. Film Victoria and Mushroom Pictures. In production. Geoffrey Wright.

A transposition of *Macbeth* to Melbourne's gangland world. Currently in post-production. See also entry 405.

883 *Dunsinane*
2006. France. In production. Vincent Regan.

MEASURE FOR MEASURE

The pornographic films entitled *Measure for Measure* (T. J. Paris, 1999; and David Perry, 2004) have no discernible Shakespearean content.

THE MERCHANT OF VENICE

884 *The Merchant of Venice*
1919. U.K. Hepworth Picture Plays. Silent, b&w, length unknown. Anson Dyer.

Lost film; one of the series of Dyer's animated parodies of Shakespeare, produced between 1919 and 1920.

885 *None So Blind* (aka *Shylock of Wall Street*)
1923. U.S. State Pictures. Silent, b&w, length unknown. Burton L. King.

When Rachel, the daughter of a poor pawnbroker Aaron Abrams, elopes with Russell Mortimer, a rich socialite, Russell's father offers Aaron $10,000 to end the marriage. Though Rachel pleads, Aaron accepts and plans to use the money to take revenge upon the Mortimers. Rachel dies giving birth to a daughter, Ruth, who, growing up, falls in love with Sheldon Abrams, protégé of Russell Mortimer. Aaron's friend Saul Cohen falls in love with Hazel

Mortimer, Russell's daughter. Learning of these romances, Aaron, now a powerful moneybroker on Wall Street, pressures Russell to make Ruth marry Saul. Though Abrams sends Ruth away for falling in love with a gentile, eventually he becomes reconciled to the matches.

"Shylock" here is used in the film's alternate title in its generic sense, as a rapacious money dealer. But the plot of the daughter of the Jewish moneylender eloping with a rich gentile suitor has affinities to the Lorenzo and Jessica sub-plot in *Merchant*; so too does Aaron's desire for revenge upon those who have wronged him through taking his child. The film stresses the foolishness of bigotry between gentiles and Jews. Rachel and Ruth were played by the same actress.

886 *Calling the Tune*
1936. U.K. Phoenix Independent Films Association. Sound, b&w, 71 mins. Reginald Denham.

Julia, daughter of Stephen Harbord, a British record executive, loves Peter, son of John Mallory, the man who Stephen Harbord hoodwinked in order to found his entertainment empire. The plot serves as a device for showcasing prominent British stars of stage and song.

In one sequence, Cecil Hardwick recites Lorenzo's "How sweet the moonlight sleeps upon this bank" speech (*The Merchant of Venice* 5.1) to the accompaniment of a string quartet. The speech's focus on the "sounds of music" is appropriate for the film's spotlighting of recording artists.

887 *Teddy Bergman's International Broadcast*
1936. U.K. Mentone. Sound, b&w, 21 mins. Milton Schwarzwald.

A musical variety short starring Teddy Bergman, comedian and future voice of Fred Flintstone. One sequence involves Bergman's Shylock's answer to Billy Reyes's Antonio's request for a loan. After Bergman first plays the sequence straight, Reyes challenges him to repeat the speech in several accents: Dutch, blackface, Irish, Scottish, Cockney, Russian, a farmer, and Italian. An interesting case of Shakespearean parody focused entirely on accent (and showcasing the then still new sound technology).

888 *A Star Is Born*
1937. U.S. United Artists and Selznick International. Sound, col., 111 mins. William Wellman and Jack Conway.

After seeing a film by her film idol Norman Maine and getting encouragement from her grandmother Lettie, Esther Blodgett, a small-town girl dreaming of stardom, goes to Hollywood, where she quickly finds it difficult to land a role. At a party where she waitresses, she makes an impression on Maine, an obnoxious drunk, and he arranges a

screen test that leads to her being put under contract. She quickly becomes a big star and marries Maine, who, with his contract canceled, is reduced to the humiliating role of a house husband. After Norman overhears that Esther might quit pictures to save him from himself, he drowns himself. Though Esther is tempted to quit, she instead attends a film première where she identifies herself as "Mrs. Norman Maine."

Includes a passing reference to Portia's "quality of mercy" soliloquy from *The Merchant of Venice*.

889 *Hotel Berlin*
1945. U.S. Sound, b&w, 98 mins. Peter Godfrey.

Adapted from Vicki Baum's novel, *Hotel Berlin '43*, *Hotel Berlin* bears similarities to *Grand Hotel*. The plot involves various story lines about different characters staying and working in the hotel, the chief one being about an escaped prisoner from Dachau who hides in the hotel room of blonde Nazi actress Lisa Dorn (Andrea King). In the hotel lobby early in the film, Dorn says she is rehearsing a new production of *The Merchant of Venice*. She mentions that play when we first see her and she runs into General Dahnwitz (Raymond Dahnwitz). Later Dahnwitz meets her after we learn he has participated in Claus von Stauffenberg's plot to kill Hitler, and asks her who is playing Bassanio. After she answers, he says he is always jealous of her leading men. They sit down for lunch in the restaurant, and when von Stetten (Henry Daniell) comes by, they disguise their conversation by taking up the play. He asks to join them, and sits down and asks, "What are you two conspiring about?" Dahnwitz replies, "We were talking about Fraulein Dorn's new production of *The Merchant of Venice*. Shakespeare." Von Stetten replies, "A writer of true Germanic sensibility." The play is not mentioned in the rest of the film. Lisa rehearses Richter (Helmut Dantine) in his uniform to behave like a Nazi officer. But he never gets a chance to go through with the disguise. The film's citation of Shakespeare relates to a general interest in disguise, but Richter not going through with it keeps the good Germans clearly separate from the bad ones. Whereas Lisa is the heroine of the novel, she becomes a clearly anti-Semitic femme fatale in the film adaptation, set against Tillie, the good girl. Tillie too is a blonde and at one point tries on Lisa's shoes. But they don't fit, a pretty clear metaphor for the difference between the two young and pretty blondes. In the film, Richter falls in love with Dorn, who inexplicably helps him even after she sees a wanted poster of him in the hotel lobby, and he kills her after she betrays the underground. Koenig says, "There are no good Germans," and the leader of the underground, Martin Baum, says about Lisa that Nazis never change. Yet he then lets Tillie, who had a Jewish boyfriend sent to the camps, stay, and says she is trustworthy and gives her a pair of shoes. At the end of the film, a FDR quotation and letter signed by Churchill, Roosevelt, and Stalin (their signatures are seen) displace Shakespeare as a cultural authority for post-war Germans. See *Hotel Berlin '43* (entry 1891). (RB)

890 *Gentleman's Agreement*
1946. U.S. 20th Century Fox and Darryl F. Zanuck Productions. Sound, b&w, 118 mins. Elia Kazan.

Adapted from the novel by Laura Z. Hobson. When Philip Green, a widower and new writer for a New York City magazine, is assigned to write articles on anti-Semitism, he decides to pose as a Jew to experience prejudice firsthand. Once he announces that he's a Jew, he becomes privy to many forms of bigotry, particularly a subtle, silent one that merely accepts prejudice as a matter of course. Dave Goldman, Philip's long-standing Jewish friend from the military, provides Philip with a perspective on the bigotry he has faced and how he has addressed it. Soon Philip's engagement to his publisher's niece Kathy Lacey is compromised when Philip realizes that despite her protests to the contrary, Kathy harbors anti-Semitic feelings. When their engagement falls apart, Kathy consults Dave, who exposes to her her failure to confront bigotry; when she resolves to change her ways, she and Philip reconcile.

At one point, Philip references Shylock's "Hath not a Jew eyes?" speech.

891 *Green for Danger*
1946. U.K. Individual Pictures. Sound, b&w, 91 mins. Sidney Gilliat.

Adapted from the novel by Christianna Brand. In a rural emergency hospital in wartime Britain, the mysterious death of an injured postman on the operating table leads a nurse to suspect murder. When she turns up dead, Inspector Cockrill is sent to investigate several witnesses to the operation. To catch the murderer before he strikes again, Cockrill stages a mock surgery that leads to the discovery of the criminal.

This superb variation on the drawing room mystery features the "in such a night as this" speech from *The Merchant of Venice* (5.1). Mr. Eden recites the speech, and Inspector Cockrill completes it. Ironically, the night leads to a murder.

892 *I Remember Mama*
1948. U.S. RKO Radio Pictures. Sound, b&w, 134 mins. George Stevens.

Adapted from the play by John Van Druten, itself adapted from Kathryn Forbes's novel *Mama's Bank Account*. A charming portrait of the Hanson family, poor Norwegian immigrants in San Francisco who undergo several family trials and joys, all under the guidance of benevolent matriarch Marta and the irascible, eccentric

Uncle Kris. The stories are told as an extended flashback by the eldest daughter Katrin, an aspiring writer.

Katrin, who has the part of Portia in her school's graduation play, rehearses the "quality of mercy" speech. Also, Mr. Hyde, a boarder who reads stories to the Hanson family, quotes "this above all, to thine own self be true" (*Hamlet* 1.3) to the eldest son Nels in a montage sequence.

893 *The Kentuckian*
1955. U.S. United Artists. Sound, col., 104 mins. Burt Lancaster.

Burt Lancaster and young son leave 1820 backwoods Kentucky to travel to a new life in Texas. John Carradine plays a snake oil salesman, selling a "secret herbal elixir" that purportedly is concocted from Cleopatra's asp. He is described as a highly educated, number one scholar who has "pretty talk"; then he quotes Shakespeare: "As the Bard of Avon said so well 'The quality of mercy is not strained'" (*Merchant of Venice*, 4.1).

Notable as the directorial debut of Burt Lancaster; also, the first screen role for Walter Matthau. (EJL)

894 *Short Circuit 2*
1988. U.S. TriStar and Turman-Foster Company. Sound, col., 110 mins. Kenneth Johnson.

Robotics inventor Ben Jahrvi has been reduced to seeing toy versions of his great robot invention, the Number Five, on the street. When toy buyer Sandy Banatoni offers Ben $50,000 if he can provide 1,000 toys, Ben partners with Fred Ritter, a street conman who finances their business through a loan from a loan shark. Unbeknownst to them, their warehouse factory hides a tunnel to be used by thieves for a bank robbery. Events are turned around when a mysterious crate arrives containing a new model of Number Five, who speaks in phrases from TV shows and aids Ben in his efforts to fend off criminals and manufacture his toy prototypes.

Contains a passing reference to *The Merchant of Venice*.

895 *The Man without a Face*
1993. U.S. Warner Bros. Sound, col., 114 mins. Mel Gibson.

Adapted from the novel by Isabel Holland. Charles Norstadt, a troubled young boy anxious to attend a military school, needs a tutor, so he enlists the help of Justin McLeod, a former teacher who was disfigured in a car accident and now lives as a reclusive artist on the Maine coast. At first suspicious of Norstadt, McLeod soon becomes his mentor, much to the consternation of his family and the local police, who believe rumors that McLeod was a child molester. The rumors soon force McLeod and Norstadt to stay apart, though they continue their friendship from a distance and Norstadt is successful in his application to the school.

The Merchant of Venice, a set text for Charles's exam, is a repeated point of reference. McLeod offers several readings of the play—Shylock's "Hath not a Jew eyes?" speech has special significance for McLeod as a fellow sufferer of prejudice. At one point, Charles examines a Golden Classics *Merchant of Venice* comic book in a store. (NB: Classics Comics never produced a *Merchant of Venice* issue.) Interestingly, Shakespeare becomes one of Chuck's weapons to declare his independence from and superiority over his mother and older sister. When he asks his sister about *The Merchant of Venice* and she reveals that she doesn't know the play, Chuck suddenly discovers the shallowness of her pseudointellectualism.

896 *Schindler's List*
1993. U.S. Universal. Sound, b&w, 197 mins. Steven Spielberg.

Adapted from the book by Thomas Keneally. Oskar Schindler, a German businessman in Nazi-occupied Poland, uses his position as an industrialist to employ Polish Jews and thus keep them from the gas chamber; he is helped by his Jewish accountant, Itzhak Stern. Schindler's nemesis is the commandant of the nearby Plaszow forced labor camp, Amon Goeth, an alcoholic tyrant who treats his prisoners with sadism and contempt.

Features a citation of Shylock's "Hath not a Jew eyes?" speech.

897 *Se7en*
1995. U.S. New Line Cinema. Sound, col. (with b&w sequences), 127 mins. David Fincher.

Though homicide detective William Somerset is a week away from retirement, he takes on one last case, that of a serial murderer who kills each victim with reference to one of the seven deadly sins. Somerset is partnered with cocky rookie David Mills, recently married to Tracy, who is reluctant for him to take the job. When after a chase the killer John Doe turns himself in to the pair, he leads them to a grisly discovery: Doe has brutally killed Mills's wife (who he learns was pregnant) and Doe tempts Mills to murder him in retribution, a temptation to which he accedes, completing Doe's horrifying project.

Doe's murder for "Greed" involves forcing a wealthy defense lawyer to cut off a pound of his own flesh. The link to *The Merchant of Venice* is made clear in the script.

DVD includes a commentary track that briefly references Shakespeare.

898 *The Hunchback of Notre Dame*
1996. U.S. Buena Vista and Walt Disney Productions. Sound, col., 91 mins. Gary Trousdale and Kirk Wise.

Animated feature, adapted from the novel by Victor Hugo. Quasimodo, a deformed orphan rescued from death by priests, lives at Notre Dame Cathedral in Paris, working as a bell ringer. His nemesis is Judge Frollo, a racist minister of justice who almost killed Quasimodo as a child; Frollo seeks to evict gypsies from the cathedral and from Paris, but he is resisted by the commander of his own troops, Phoebus. When Quasimodo is crowned king of the fools during an annual religious holiday, he meets and is helped by Phoebus and Esmerelda, a beautiful gypsy girl, and the three team up to defend the gypsies against Frollo's scheme to destroy the gypsies' home, the Court of Miracles, a scheme inflamed by Frollo's desire for Esmerelda.

Features a brief reference by Quasimodo to Shylock's "Hath not a Jew eyes?" speech.

899 *The Pianist*
2002. France, Germany, U.K., and Poland. Bac Distribution, Canal +, and Robert Benmussa. Sound, col., 150 mins. Roman Polanski.

Adapted by Ronnie Harwood from the novel by Wladyslaw Szpilman. Wladyslaw Szpilman, a privileged pianist in pre-war Poland, endures the invasion and occupation of his country by Nazis, at first believing he is immune to political upheaval, then being imprisoned in the Warsaw ghetto, then hiding and fending for himself when he sees his family taken away to a concentration camp.

Features a brief citation of Shylock's "Hath not a Jew eyes?" speech.

900 *The Quality of Mercy*
2002. U.S. Sound, col., 15 mins. Stephen Marro.

An actress takes revenge on a theater critic who gave a bad review by arranging a supposedly chance encounter with him at a restaurant and then poisoning his food. As he dies grotesquely, spewing up his food, she launches into Portia's "quality of mercy" speech, and the film then ends. (RB)

901 *Te Tangata Whai Rawa O Weneti (aka The Maori Merchant of Venice)*
2002. New Zealand. He Taonga Films. Sound, col., 158 mins. Don C. Selwyn.

Adapted by Pei Te Hurinui Jones. A relatively faithful transposition of Shakespeare's narrative to Maori culture; Shakespeare's text was translated into Maori, presented with English subtitles. See also entry 419.

THE MERRY WIVES OF WINDSOR

Die Lustigen Weiber von Tirol (directed by Hans Billian, 1964) and *The Merry Wives of Tobias Rourke* (directed by John Board, 1972) have nothing to do with Shakespeare's play.

902 *Les Amours de la Reine Élisabeth (The Queen's Favorite)*
1912. France. Famous Players. Silent, b&w
(also tinted), 3,140 ft. Henri Desfontaines and Louis Mercanton.

Starring Sarah Bernhardt as Queen Elizabeth, this film chronicles Elizabeth's tragic relationship with the Earl of Essex, who is himself involved with the Countess of Nottingham. Having given Essex a ring that will save his life if returned to her, Elizabeth locks Essex in the Tower of London and sends the Countess to retrieve the ring. Essex tosses it away, which seals his deadly fate, leaving Elizabeth heartbroken. The film was a major box office hit for the early cinema.

The film includes a performance of *The Merry Wives of Windsor* in celebration of the defeat of the Armada, and an appearance by Shakespeare (who is congratulated by the queen).

903 *The Merry Wives of Pimple* (aka *Pimple's Merry Wives*)
1916. U.K. Production company unknown. Silent, b&w, length unknown. Fred Evans.

Lost film. Starred the British comic character Pimple, who created several Shakespearean parodies starring himself.

904 *Falstaff the Tavern Knight*
1923. U.K. British & Colonial Kinematograph Company. Silent, b&w, 2,943 feet. Edwin Greenwood.

Listed as no. 11 in the *Gems of Literature* series. The cast list indicates that this may be a shortened version of *The Merry Wives of Windsor*. See also entry 424.

905 *Die Lustigen Weiber von Wien*
1931. Germany. Production company unknown. Sound, b&w, length unknown. Géza von Bolváry.

Film production of the opera by Otto Nicolai.

906 *The Merry Wives of Reno*
1934. U.S. Warner Brothers. Sound, b&w, 64 mins. H. Bruce Humberstone.

Three wives, Madge, Bunny, and Lois, travel to Reno, Nevada, in order to get divorces. Madge, young and recently married, has had a verbal spat with her husband Frank; Bunny, somewhat older, is far more belligerent and physical in her fights with Al, her husband; and Lois, married to Tom, has been caught cheating, and later tries to have affairs with both Frank and Al. The three women meet each other at a Reno hotel, and their various romantic difficulties intertwine, leading to screwball farce. The parallels with *The Merry Wives of Windsor* do not extend very far beyond the title, though the themes of adultery and humiliating comeuppance engineered by Madge and Bunny (Lois plays the Falstaff role) have general affinities to Shakespeare's play.

907 *Die Lustigen Weiber*
1935. Germany. Cine-Allianz Tonfilmproduktions GmbH. Sound, b&w, length unknown. Carl Hoffmann.

Film production of the opera by Otto Nicolai.

908 *Falstaff in Wien (Falstaff in Vienna)*
1940. Germany. Tobis. Sound, b&w, 92 mins. Leopold Hainisch.

Film production of the opera by Otto Nicolai.

909 *Die Lustigen Weiber von Windsor*
1952. East Germany. DEFA-Studio für Spielfilme. Sound, b&w, 95 minutes. Georg Wildhagen.

Film production of the opera by Otto Nicolai.

910 *Die Lustigen Weiber von Windsor*
1965. Austria and U.K. Sigma III Corporation. Sound, col., 97 mins. Georg Tressler.

Film production of the opera by Otto Nicolai.

911 *As Alegres Comadres*
2003. Brazil. Ananã Produções, Conexão Cinema, and Zohar Cinema. Sound, col., 109 mins. Leila Hipólito.

In the nineteenth century Fausto João, an ex-soldier and inveterate debtor, travels to Tiradentes with his companions Luis and Pistola. A former Imperial Court member, he uses his former position to deceive the local bourgeoisie into believing he is an important man, and to pay his debts, he tries to seduce two women, Señoras Lima and Rocha, who have married rich husbands. When the women learn of his intentions, they decide to take revenge upon him, using Maria as a go-between. Mr. Rocha too learns of Fausto's intentions and, jealous of his wife, sets a plan of his own. A sub-plot involves the three suitors of Ana Lima: Dr. Caius, the French doctor her mother prefers; Silva, a young farmer encouraged by his uncle; and the dashing young Franco, Ana's own favorite. Their attempts to court Ana lead to various stratagems and conspiracies.

Transposing the action to rural nineteenth-century Brazil, the film follows the plot of Shakespeare's play relatively closely, though the Anne Page plot is handled rather more freely. Shakespeare is cited as a source in the credits, and a consultant from the Royal Shakespeare Company worked on the film. Compare *Faustão*, another Brazilian narrative about Falstaff (entry 754). See also entry 427.

A MIDSUMMER NIGHT'S DREAM

The pornographic films *A Midslumber Night's Dream* (Bruce Seven, 1985) and *A Midsummer Love Story* (Jourdan Alexander, 1993), and the softcore erotic film *Justine: A Midsummer Night's Dream* (Bruce Cove, 1998), have no discernible Shakespearean content other than their titles.

912 *Mischievous Puck*
1911. U.K. Natural Colour Kinematograph Co. Silent, b&w, 13 mins. Walter R. Booth and Theo Frenkel.
No information available.

913 *Ein Sommernachtstraum in Unserer Zeit*
1914. Germany. Deutsche Bioscope. Silent, b&w, length unknown. Stellan Rye.
The fiancés of an old man's daughter and niece arrive, and all share a celebratory picnic on the lawn of his home. Falling asleep, the old man dreams of the fairies from *Midsummer* and, waking, seeks to chase them off, discovering that in reality he was only dreaming and that the couples remain asleep on the lawn. Notable for its risqué content.

914 *A Midsummer Love Triangle*
1914. U.S. American Film Company. Silent, b&w, one reel. Isobel M. Reynolds.
No information available.

915 *Pimple's Midsummer Night's Dream*
1916. U.K. Piccadilly. Silent, b&w, length unknown. Fred Evans and Joe Evans.
Now lost. Part of the Pimple Shakespeare parody series.

916 *I due Sogni ad Occhi Aperti*
1920. Italy. D'Ambra Film. Silent, b&w, 1,908 feet. Lucio D'Ambra.
A parody; no other information available.

917 *Mister Cinders*
1934. U.K. British International Pictures. Sound, b&w, 72 mins. Frederick Zelnick.
Adapted from the play by Clifford Grey. In this musical, an inversion of the Cinderella story, Jim Lancaster, the poor nephew of wealthy Sir George and Lady Agatha, is mistreated by his family as they attempt to make a match between their sons Guy and Lumley and a rich heiress from America, Jill Kemp. Jill disguises herself as a servant to learn more about the two sons and soon falls in love with Jim; when he is framed for a theft, Jill rushes to his aid and eventually marries him.
Featured are several short passages from the rehearsal and chaotic performance of *A Midsummer Night's Dream* in a small village.

918 *Three Missing Links*
1938. U.S. Columbia Pictures. Sound, b&w, 18 mins. Jules White.
This farce features the Three Stooges as film actors, cast as Neanderthal cavemen in a film shot on location in Africa; when a real gorilla attacks the film crew, Curly, under the influence of a witch doctor's "love candy" and dressed in a gorilla suit, frightens off the gorilla with his romantic advances.

The love candy motif and Curly's falling in love with a beast resemble the "love in idleness" flower motif in *A Midsummer Night's Dream*.

919 *A Matter of Life and Death* (aka *Stairway to Heaven*)
1946. U.K. The Archers and Independent Producers. Sound, col. and b&w, 104 mins. Michael Powell and Emeric Pressburger.
An extraordinary wartime fantasy-melodrama that shuttles literally between heaven and earth. Peter Carter, an RAF pilot forced to jump without a parachute when his plane is damaged and crew is killed, miraculously survives and falls in love with June, the American WAC who heard his cry for help on the radio. We learn that Carter was destined to die, but that Conductor 71, a foppish French angel in charge of deaths, failed to claim him because of the English fog. Carter is allowed to appeal his case before a heavenly jury of Americans, but despite the best efforts of anti-British prosecutor Abraham Farlan, the love between himself and June earns him a reprieve.
When Carter arrives at the RAF base after his miraculous fall, he finds the soldiers involved in a production of *A Midsummer Night's Dream*, the rehearsals for which become the background of Peter's interview with a psychologist. As they rehearse, Felix Mendelssohn's incidental music for the play plays from a record. The film's interest in the relationship between American and British cultural superiority also surfaces in the *Midsummer Night's Dream* rehearsals, for the Americans are cast as the mechanicals, roles they cannot perform correctly without British direction. Conductor 71 is presented as a comic Gallic Puck, one whose mistake sets the romantic plot in motion and who sports a flower that preserves June's tears of love (a detail evoking the "love-in-idleness" flower).

920 *Sommarnattens leende* (*Smiles of a Summer Night*)
1955. Sweden. Svensk Filmindustri. Sound, b&w, 108 mins. Ingmar Bergman.
Fredrik Egerman, a middle-aged lawyer, is married to the much younger Anne, but remains secretly infatuated with actress Desiree Armfeldt, his former lover. Desiree is currently mistress to Count Malcolm, who is married to but callous toward his wife Charlotte. When Fredrik visits Desiree one evening after a play, he learns that she has a child named Fredrik; Malcolm, discovering the two together, threatens a duel. Charlotte, returning home to discern the situation, expresses her jealousy to her husband and reveals Fredrik's secret visit to Desiree to Anne. Meanwhile, Henrik, Fredrik's son by a previous marriage and about to enter the clergy, struggles with lustful thoughts about Petra, the Egerman's maid, and Anne. Desiree formulates a plan to realign the mismatched couples: she has her mother invite everyone to her manor for the weekend, where under the influence of magical

wine, they learn of each other's desires and form new couples—young Henrik and young Anne, Fredrik and Desiree, Malcolm and Charlotte, and Petra and Frid the groom.

Bergman adapts several motifs from *MND* in this farcical comedy of manners—the dreamy, erotic midsummer setting on the pastoral Ryarp estate, a group of mismatched lovers (in this case, the lovers are blocked by prior marriages rather than a father's arrangements), a love potion (in this case, a wine seasoned with a woman's breast milk and the seed of a stallion), and, in the case of Fredrik, the removal of romantic illusion (corresponding to Demetrius's change of affection from Hermia to Helena). The film stresses the male rather than female perspective on romance, for it is the men who all suffer from various forms of romantic or erotic misperceptions of women that bring the women unhappiness of various sorts; the older women, that is, Desiree, Charlotte, and Desiree's mother, control the realignment of the couples. There are no direct references to Shakespeare's dialogue in Bergman's screenplay, but there are a couple of passing oblique references: Desiree confesses to her mother that she loves an "ass" (referring to Fredrik), and in a passage where Charlotte expresses both her hatred and love for Malcolm, she notes that he pats her on the head like a dog (an oblique reference to Helena's comment to Demetrius in 2.1, "I am your spaniel; and, Demetrius, / The more you beat me, I will fawn on you"). Compare *A Midsummer Night's Sex Comedy*.

921 *Invasion of the Body Snatchers*
1956. U.S. Allied Artists. Sound, b&w, 80 mins. Don Siegel.

Adapted from the novel *The Body Snatchers* by Jack Finney. In this allegory of the McCarthy era, Miles Bennel, a doctor in rural Santa Mira, California, discovers that his neighbors are being replaced by alien replicants without any human emotions. As he tries to escape the invasion of the "pod people," he discovers that the family of his girlfriend Becky Driscoll, and then his girlfriend herself, have been replaced. When he escapes to San Francisco to tell his story, he watches in horror as a load of pods arrives.

A classic of science fiction noir, *Invasion* includes a passing reference to *A Midsummer Night's Dream* in an early conversation between Miles and Becky.

922 *Sen Noci Svatojanske* (*A Midsummer Night's Dream*)
1958. Czechoslovakia. Krátký Film Praha and Jírí Trnka Studio. Sound, col., 76 mins. Jírí Trnka.

A charming animated adaptation using stop-motion, articulated puppets. The first puppet cartoon ever filmed in Cinemascope, it was designed to be released without dialogue, relying instead on dance, pantomime, and music. The plot follows Shakespeare's narrative relatively faithfully, making only a few changes: Demetrius is a soldier,

and Lysander a flute player; an opening prologue places the action in the world of the stars and zodiac, and clarifies the situation between the Athenian lovers before they meet Theseus (Egeus is alerted to Lysander's wooing of his daughter by Demetrius); the mechanicals first rehearse in Quince's home, but are interrupted by professional players and adjourn to the wood; Oberon's motive for toying with Titania's affection is revenge for her rejection of him (there is no Indian child), and Oberon orders Puck to apply the love-in-idleness flower (here, the fragrance is magical) to the Athenians to get rid of them; when Egeus sees the lovers asleep, he at first seeks to kill Demetrius, but his heart soon softens; and Puck charms Bottom in the midst of his performance as Pyramus, making his desire for Titania fuel his acting (he kills himself with Cupid's arrow). Titania is treated as a nature goddess, her dancing and train of writhing fairies imparting fertility to the wood; Oberon, symbolized by images of the stag and his horns, is presented as a somewhat frightening deity, akin to treatment of his character in the Dieterle and Reinhardt film (note also the motif of Bottom seeing his reflection in a pool, also taken from this film). It is Puck who stumbles accidentally upon the idea of having Titania fall in love with Bottom. Interestingly, Quince closely resembles Shakespeare himself, and several comic moments involve Quince literally cutting the text with a butcher's cleaver or directing the performance. Throughout the production, Trnka is enormously resourceful in finding purely visual or musical equivalents for descriptive details in Shakespeare's text; we see, for example, Peaseblossom scratch Bottom's head and Cobweb gather honey for Bottom to eat; the narrative of the chaste goddess missed by Cupid's arrow is visualized; and corresponding to Puck's comments about "we shadows" in his epilogue is a curtain call by shadows of the mechanicals, walking in front of a stage curtain. Trnka's primary visual sources are nineteenth-century fairy paintings and stage productions of the play, and his production emphasizes the dreamlike and childlike fable qualities of the play, though Oberon's darker qualities and Bottom's affecting performance as Pyramus, underlain with lost desire for Titania, add a tragic note. In the Czech narration (added later), Trnka emphasizes the universality of the Shakespearean story (a quality he seeks to emphasize in the original languageless production), and in the epilogue he directly connects the timelessness of Shakespeare and of dreams: "Dreams guide our lives, and as Shakespeare's name will never die, neither will our dreams." An English language translation, voiced by Richard Burton, was added in 1971. A beautiful film that deserves a wider audience.

923 *Mondo Sexy di Notte* (*Mondo Sexuality*)
1962. Italy. Documento. Sound, b&w, 100 mins. Mino Loy.

Parody; also references *Romeo and Juliet*.

924 *Scorpio Rising*
1965. U.S. Puck Film Productions. Sound, col., 31 mins.
Kenneth Anger.

This experimental film documents the wandering life of
Scorpio, a leather-clad, drug-addicted homosexual biker, as
he races his motorcycle, engages in vandalism of a church,
and indulges in sadistic violence against another biker at a
party. These scenes are intercut with various elements of
pop iconography ranging from comic books to Nazi swas-
tikas, set to pop tunes. A celebration and sly deconstruction of the image of the motorcyclist as iconoclast.

One sequence intercuts images of Mickey Rooney's *Puck*
from the 1935 *MND*. (Note from RB: Anger claims he is
the uncredited child actor who plays the changeling boy in
the 1935 Reinhardt/Dieterle *Midsummer Night's Dream*
[entry 430].)

925 *A Midsummer Night's Dream*
1967. U.S. Oberon. Sound, col., 93 mins. George Balanchine and Dan Eriksen.

Film of Balanchine's ballet adaptation to music of Felix
Mendelssohn.

926 *The Projectionist*
1970. U.S. Maglan. Sound, col., 88 mins. Harry Hurwitz.

A fat, lonely projectionist finds solace in heroic, romantic, and satiric fantasies he constructs from pastiches of
old films. In the dominant fantasy of the film, he imagines
he is Captain Flash, saving a beautiful woman from a
perfectionistic theater manager he nicknames "The Bat."

The film twice references Dieterle and Reinhardt's 1935
Midsummer Night's Dream, first in an inset film *Man and His
Universe, Part I*, where Puck says, "Lord, what fools these
mortals be"; and second in a celebratory dance sequence at
film's end that references the ballet of Titania's and
Oberon's fairies.

927 *Midsommardansen* (*Midsummer Sex*)
1971. Sweden. Sisu Film. Sound, col., 89 mins. Arne Sti-
vell.

From the novel *Juhannustanssit* by Hannu Salama. A
meandering plot of Scandinavian midsummer festivity
features drinking, fights, and explicit lovemaking in a
pastoral setting. Very little relationship to Shakespeare's
play, other than the title and the pastoral midsummer
setting for various couplings.

928 *Oberon* (*Des Elfenkonigs Schwur*)
1971. Germany. ZDF. Sound, col., 91 mins. Herbert Jun-
kers.
Film of the Carl Maria von Weber opera.

929 *Wanpaku Pakku—Manatsu no yoru no yume* (*The
Impish Puck—A Midsummer Night's Dream*)
1977. Japan. Sound, color, length unknown. Kato Mei.

Based on a story by Inoue Hisashi, the central plot features children putting on a musical version of *A Midsummer
Night's Dream*.

930 *La Settima donna* (*Terror*)
1978. Italy. Magirus Film. Sound, color, 86 mins. Franco
Prosperi.

Borrowing heavily from *Last House on the Left*, this example of Italian *giallo* tells the tale of three bank robbers
who, when their car develops trouble, take refuge in a
college's isolated villa. There they discover Sister Cristina,
a nun, and several of her women students studying for
exams. As the men fix the car and hide out, they terrorize
the women with degradation, violence, and sexual assault
until, when they rape and kill one of the students, Sister
Cristina renounces her vows and takes revenge upon the
robbers, with the remaining women eventually joining in.

When the robbers first arrive, they encounter the
women rehearsing *A Midsummer Night's Dream*, specifically
Bottom's first encounter with Peaseblossom. This very
brief, at first surrealistic reference seems primarily intended
to establish a pastoral atmosphere that the remainder of
the film violently disrupts.

931 *Gregory's Girl*
1980. Scotland. Lake, NFFC, and Scottish Television.
Sound, col., 91 mins. Bill Forsyth.

Gregory, a gangly Scottish teenager, falls in love from
afar with Dorothy, a talented soccer player new at his
school. Gregory goes to extraordinary lengths to attract her
attention and affection, working out, learning Italian,
buying new clothes, and seeking advice from younger sister
Madeleine. Gregory asks out Dorothy for a date, but Dorothy, not really interested in him, sets Gregory up with
several other girls, Carol, Margo, and finally Susan. The
date with Susan leads Gregory to reconsider his love for
Dorothy.

Gregory's English class is studying *A Midsummer Night's
Dream*. When Gregory first enters the class, his best friend
Andy is reading Oberon's conversation with Puck in 3.2;
the line "My mistress with a monster is in love" applies
obliquely to Gregory's attempts to romance Dorothy.
(During this scene, comic window washers—equivalents of
the "mechanicals"—appear at the window to distract the
class's attention.)

932 *Magic on Love Island* (aka *Valentine Magic on
Love Island*)
1980. U.S. Dick Clark Productions. Sound, color,
100 mins. Earl Bellamy.

The pilot for an unsold TV series akin to *Love Boat* and
Fantasy Island, this adaptation is set on Love Island, a
tropical resort presided over by Madge, an enchantress, and
her bumbling nephew Jimmy and niece Cheryl. Using a
bouquet of magical roses, she makes love matches between

various single resort guests unhappy in love, resulting after some false romances in four couples. Several motifs from *MND* are adapted: the tropical island corresponds to the Athenian wood, Madge the enchantress to Oberon, Jimmy and Cheryl to Puck, the eight guests on Love Island to the four Athenian lovers whose couplings are scrambled and then properly aligned, and the magical roses to the "love-in-idleness" flower. No direct verbal citations of Shakespeare's dialogue. The film first aired on February 15, 1980, as a Valentine's Day special, and later was released on video.

933 *Murder Psalm*
1980. U.S. Canyon Cinema. Sound, col., 18 mins. Stan Brakhage.

Experimental hand-colored film by the noted avant-garde filmmaker, which includes excerpts from Dieterle and Reinhardt's 1935 A *Midsummer Night's Dream*. Sammons plausibly suggests that this sequence may be a homage to Kenneth Anger's *Scorpio Rising*, another experimental film that uses the same excerpts. Compare *Scorpio Rising* (entry 924).

934 *A Midsummer Night's Sex Comedy*
1982. U.S. Orion Pictures. Sound, col., 88 mins. Woody Allen.

In this drama set in nineteenth-century America, Leopold Sturgis, a rationalist academic, attends a wedding party for himself and his bride Ariel at the country home of his cousin Andrew Hobbs, an inventor, and his wife, Adrian. Also attending are Andrew's friend Maxwell Jordan, a promiscuous doctor, and his date, the scatter-brained sensuous nurse Dulcy Ward. Andrew and Adrian are having sexual problems. Unbeknownst to Adrian, Andrew holds a torch for Ariel, whom he knew as a young man but with whom he never slept; unbeknownst to Andrew, Adrian slept with Maxwell the previous summer. Maxwell falls in love with Ariel at first sight and tries to arrange a tryst with her; Ariel makes love to Andrew but soon discovers that the two cannot recapture the lost opportunities of their past; Adrian, after confessing her tryst with Maxwell to Andrew, conquers the couple's sexual problems; Leopold, after jealously pursuing and shooting Maxwell, makes violent love to Dulcy and dies, only to be reborn as a spirit of the enchanted wood.

Allen's homage to Bergman's *Smiles of a Summer Night* makes somewhat clearer the former film's debts to A *Midsummer Night's Dream*, though, as in Bergman's film, the relationship between Allen's film and Shakespeare is oblique rather than direct. Leopold opens the film with a lecture about rationalism, debunking ghosts and metaphysics, a recasting of Theseus's "lovers, madmen and poets" speech in 5.1, and the narrative proceeds to prove his position wrong. Leopold's impending marriage to Ariel corresponds roughly to the marriage of Theseus and Hippolyta, but that marriage is here intertwined with the various couplings between Maxwell, Dulcy, Andrew, and Adrian, who correspond to the Athenian lovers. Here the catalyst for the romantic and erotic exchanges is not a magic potion but the natural fecundity of the wood surrounding the Hobbs home (though there are some passing references to the intoxicating effects of wine at dinner). The element of supernatural magic is supplied by one of Andrew's inventions, a spirit ball that offers a projection of romantic possibilities both past and present. It is noteworthy that Leopold's debunking of the ball includes a reference to Shakespeare: "There are no ghosts except in Shakespeare, and many of those are more real than many people that I know." Offered as a toast during a picnic, Leopold also supplies the one direct textual reference to Shakespeare, from Titania's speech about natural chaos resulting from her and Oberon's quarrel: "The spring, the summer, / The childing autumn, angry winter, change / Their wonted liveries." Andrew and Maxwell fight in the wood over Ariel, perhaps glancing at Lysander and Demetrius's quarrel over Helena, and Andrew combines elements of Puck and Bottom's character as well as some of Demetrius. Leopold's death and reincarnation at the end of the film transform him from a Theseus into an Oberon figure. Allen's adaptation stresses, far more than does Shakespeare, the close association between lust and love, though the reconciliation of Andrew and Adrian, the only happy couple at film's end, seems to endorse marriage. The film is framed by passages from Felix Mendelssohn's *Midsummer Night's Dream* incidental music (entry 1668), and the period design of Michael Hoffman's film adaptation bears some similarities to Allen's.

935 *Bottom's Dream*
1983. U.S. John Canemaker Productions. Sound, col., 6 mins. John Canemaker.

This animated film by the acclaimed independent animator focuses primarily on Bottom's transformation into an ass by Puck, his meeting with Titania, and his awakening from the dream. Using Felix Mendelssohn's scherzo from the *Midsummer Night's Dream* suite (entry 1668) as the principal soundtrack (adding only Titania's commandment to the fairies in 3.1, "Feed him with apricocks and dewberries, /With purple grapes, green figs, and mulberries. / pluck the wings from painted butterflies / To fan the moonbeams from his sleeping eyes: / Nod to him, elves, and do him courtesies"), Canemaker imagines Bottom as a small boy whose dream is both erotic and frightening, primarily the latter. Puck is presented as a constantly changing, malicious sprite from whom Bottom tries to hide; Titania is a maternal but mischievous figure who appears briefly after Bottom chases a bright light into the forest, but who disappears, leaving Bottom in a fearsome dark wood. That is, the film offers a psychoanalytic reading of Bottom's experience in the forest, visualizing it as a form of regression to childhood desires and anxieties. The dream sequence allows Canemaker to brilliantly survey a dizzying variety of animated styles, from lifelike to abstract, pastels to pencil drawings, and along the way he visually references Fuseli's famous painting of Bottom and Titania as well as the dance sequences in Dieterle and Reinhardt's 1935 film. In addition to Titania's commandment, the film is prefaced by this textual quotation: "I have had a most rare vision. . . . Man is but an ass if he go about to expound this dream" (from Bottom's speech in 4.1). A remarkable short film that rewards repeated viewing.

Included on the DVD *John Canemaker: Marching to a Different Toon*.

936 *Sogno Di Una Notte d'estate*
1983. Italy. Giangi Film, Politecne Cinematografica, and Rai Due Radiotelevisione Italiana. Sound, col., 95 mins. Gabriele Salvatores.

A rock musical version of the play, starring Italian rock star Gianni Nannini as Titania. In this adaptation, the players and fairies interrupt the marriage of Theseus and Hippolyta, and Puck's love potion causes the mismatched lovers to fall in love with each other (in this case, Demetrius and Lysander fall in love with each other). Of particular note are the rather over-the-top production numbers: Oberon dances in a women's shower room, and huge fireworks flash by in Titania's big song. Compare *Catch My Soul*.

937 *Zelig*
1983. U.S. Orion and Warner Bros. Sound, b&w, 79 mins. Woody Allen.

This mockumentary offers the biography of Leonard Zelig, the "human chameleon," a man whose hold on identity is so slight that he takes on the characteristics of those around him; he turns out to have been instrumental in nearly every major moment of culture in the last half century. The film blends authentic newsreel footage with clever faked period vignettes and profiles of fictional and real authorities.

Zelig's father Morris, a Jewish actor, is briefly glimpsed as Puck in an Orthodox production of *A Midsummer Night's Dream*. No dialogue is heard.

938 *Dead Poets Society*
1989. U.S. Silver Screen Partners IV and Touchstone Pictures. Sound, col., 128 mins. Peter Weir.

John Keating, an unconventional literature instructor at Welton Academy, seeks to inspire his class of boys to think for themselves, "seize the day," and form a love of poetry as part of the Dead Poets Society. Under Keating's influence, Todd Anderson, the extraordinarily shy brother of a valedictorian, begins to develop more confidence and write poetry, and Neil Perry, the son of an overbearing father who intends him for medical school, secretly takes on the

part of Puck in a school production of *A Midsummer Night's Dream*. When his father discovers this and disapproves, Neil commits suicide. Keating is blamed for his behavior and fired. As Keating leaves, Todd leads a protest joined by several other boys.

Dead Poets Society consistently groups Shakespeare (and Herrick) with Romantic poets, treating them as voices of freedom, ambition, and unfettered desire. In one classroom scene, Keating claims that the purpose of poetry is to woo women and mentions Shakespeare as an example. When the boys groan, he stresses that his Shakespeare will not be conventional and boring: as if holding a skull, he intones with a lisp, "O Titus, bring thy friend hither" (not a Shakespearean line). He then imitates Marlon Brando doing "Friends, Romans, countrymen, lend me your ears," and John Wayne doing "Is this a dagger I see before me?" Later at a party with some girls, Dalton, another student in the class, takes Keating's notions about poetry seriously by trying to pass off Sonnet 18 as his own as he woos a girl. Central to the plot's climax is Neil's performance as Puck in *A Midsummer Night's Dream*; we see three passages from his performance, Puck's opening conversation with a fairy in 2.1, Puck's distillation of the love-in-idleness flower (in slow motion, cross-cut with Knox and his new girlfriend), and Puck's epilogue (cross-cut with his father's disapproving looks, as if Neil were apologizing to his father); Neil is pushed out by the cast for the audience's special applause. In *Unspeakable ShaXXXspeares* Richard Burt (New York: St. Martin's Press, 1998) reads Neil's unwillingness to reveal his acting ambitions to his father as a coded reluctance to come out as a homosexual. Compare *Lost and Delirious*, *The Emperor's Club*, and *Porky's II*.

DVD contains an audio commentary and behind-the-scenes featurette that reference Shakespeare. NB: a television release of the film shown on USA Network and released on laserdisc includes several scenes deleted from the theatrical release, including one involving *Hamlet*. The deleted scenes are not included on the DVD.

939 *A Midsummer's Night's Bondage*
1993. U.S. Arlo Productions. Sound, col., 93 mins. Art Crow.

Hardcore pornographic adaptation. Bored of the fairy realm, Titania transforms herself into Lady Simone to escape from Oberon. Many years later, Oberon finds her and, with Puck, ties her up in many positions until she promises to fulfill her royal duties.

Little discernible relationship to Shakespeare other than the title, names of characters, and pseudo-Elizabethan language.

940 *Ill Met by Moonlight*
1994. U.S. Titania Pictures. Sound, col., 122 mins. S. P. Somtow.

This adaptation was filmed at night in the back alleys of Los Angeles, using a largely amateur cast in modern hip costuming. The plot focuses primarily on the four lovers, Demetrius, Lysander, Hermia, and Helena, whose proper matching is blocked by Egeus's preference of Demetrius over Lysander for Hermia's husband. When all escape to the forest where Titania and Oberon are quarreling, Puck administers the love-in-idleness potion that makes them fall in love with the first person they see. There are no Theseus and Hippolyta. IMDB.com reports that Tim Sullivan performed the role of Oberon imitating the voice of Nick Nolte, at the director's request. This film has never been commercially released.

941 *A Little Crazy (Un Poco Loco)*
1994. U.S. Signs of Life Films. Sound, col., 104 mins. Deborah Koons.

Kate, a farmer in California, and her daughter Eva welcome Kate's sister Lisa and her fiancé Raoul, a Hispanic tennis pro, to Kate's farm, inherited from her parents. When Lisa and Raoul announce plans to turn part of the ranch into a tennis resort, Kate resents their intrusion upon her life, even though the plants are not growing well this season. Meanwhile Eva begins to fancy Ted, one of the environmental impact team Lisa has hired. Kate uses a potion from Gabrielle, a local conjure woman, to make Lisa lose interest in Raoul, but Eva also uses the potion and loses interest in Ted. Wanderly, a longtime hand at the ranch, indicates his long-standing affection for Lisa, and Kate begins to see Raoul's virtues. Lisa is accidentally given a dust of passion at Gabrielle's home, intending to use it as an antidote for the original potion. But children use it to fill eggs for the Fandango festival, where Lisa, Kate, Raoul, and Eva are all given a dose. At Lisa's wedding to Raoul, she marries Wanderly instead, Kate marries Raoul, and Eva marries Ted. On the wedding night, Kate notices that her watermelon crop has grown to be huge.

This free adaptation with a Hispanic flavor (but primarily Anglo cast) uses many motifs from *Midsummer*. The plot is structured around the days before a marriage; Kate observes that the fertility of her crops depends upon Lisa and her romantic happiness; Kate and Lisa are romantically mismatched, and the love potions allow them to be properly attached; the couples make frequent sojourns to the wood, where there is a circle of mushrooms (i.e., a fairy ring); there are two potions, one that removes affection and one that prompts it, and the wrong person is administered the first potion; the proper alignment of romantic affections is associated with a dance in the fields by the three sisters; all the couples are properly aligned in the final scenes, and their alignment leads to nature's fertility; and the primary focus is women's love, not men's. Arguably, the two giant puppets of the Fandango festival loosely correspond to Oberon and Titania, as fertility deities.

What is fairy magic in Shakespeare is treated as a form of pharmacological conjuring in the film, associated with hallucinogenic mushrooms.

942 *L'Appartement*
1996. France. IMA Films. Sound, col. Gilles Mimouni.

A Hitchcockian thriller about the impossibility of love finding its object. The heroine (Monica Belluci) plays Helena in *A Midsummer Night's Dream*. Her rival takes over the role. The ending of the film is indeterminate. The hero leaves Belluci for Boringer but finds his fiancée at the airport just as he is about to run off with Boringer. Boringer leaves. It's not clear whether the hero will leave his fiancé, whether he will murder her and then leave, or whether Boringer and he will ever hook up should he leave his fiancé. Or is he going to stay with her? The film is a kind of undoing of *MND*. Remade as *Wicker Park*. (RB)

943 *Leaving Drew*
1999. U.S. Sound, col., 21 mins. Kristen Lara Getchell.

Available on Atomfilms.com. Campbell, a struggling, lonely actor in a production of *A Midsummer Night's Dream* for the New Jersey Shakespeare Festival at Drew University, cannot sleep as he waits for his flight back to his home in Los Angeles after the production closes. As he is repeatedly interrupted by cast members, he dreams of a beautiful fairy at the shore. In hopes of getting sleep, he leaves his bed for Titania's bower onstage, where he is again visited by the fairy. On the plane home, he meets a woman who resembles the fairy woman of his dreams.

The film opens with Puck delivering the epilogue from *A Midsummer Night's Dream*, and the gap between dream and reality is its central motif, a gap that closes in the final scene. The film combines the familiar motif of the Shakespearean actor as loser with Bottom's dream of Titania as an ideal woman (perhaps glancing at the treatment of Bottom in Hoffman's film version). What initiates the dream is Ashley, the woman playing Titania, putting champagne on Campbell's eyes, with Oberon's words from 2.1, "And with the juice of this I'll streak his eyes / And make him full of hateful fantasies." Yet though Campbell's dreams do contain hateful fantasies (of his eviction and of a pompous rival getting a multipicture contract), primarily they focus on romantic fantasies. One other direct textual allusion: when Campbell climbs into Titania's bower, he quotes Helena's lines from 3.2 ("And sleep, that sometimes shuts up sorrow's eye, / Steal me awhile from mine own company").

944 *Midsummer*
1999. U.S. Kerwin Productions, MainPix, Realistic Productions, and the Midsummer Partnership LLC. Sound, col., 17 mins available. James Kerwin.

A hip teen adaptation of *MND*, akin to *A Midsummer Night's Rave* (below). Angst-filled and fiery Lysander is disturbed by the arrogant, preppy Demetrius's attentions to Hermia at a disco. Puck, a mysterious drug dealer, offers him the "love-in-idleness" drug, and after Lysander wanders into the wood, he magically receives a copy of Shakespeare's play, after which he falls asleep and the narrative of Shakespeare's play begins. The film opens with a dialogue-less visual prologue, a long unbroken virtuoso shot (à la Branagh) in a country garden in which all the main characters are introduced and their relationships established; the shot, the neutral costume design (not linked to a period), the Felix Mendelssohn soundtrack (entry 1668), and the narration that follows emphasize the "universality" of the narrative before the contemporary adaptation begins. The script emphasizes the darker elements of Shakespeare's narrative and elements of the mystical and magical (via tarot and drugs); indeed, zodiac symbols in the prologue recall those used in Trnka's animated film of the play. A seventeen-minute version of the film's opening sequence was shown at several film festivals. Because of financing issues, production on this film has been suspended.

945 *A Midsummer Night's Cream*
2000. U.S. Adam and Eve. Sound, col., 91 mins. Stuart Canterbury.

Hardcore pornographic adaptation. One of the glossier and more faithful of the X-rated adaptations.

The film uses the plotlines of Titania and Oberon's quarrel, Puck's mixing of the lovers' affections, and Bottom's tryst with Titania as the rationale for six sex scenes. Theseus and Hippolyta's marriage and the mechanicals' play are eliminated. The dialogue consists largely of highly simplified and lightly modernized versions of Shakespeare's lines, primarily in prose rather than verse. Though Athens is never mentioned, the settings and costuming are vaguely classical. Of some interest is the handling of Puck, who is played as an androgynous creature (a woman with a moustache), and Titania's fairy band, who are lesbians and voyeurs of the lovers. Compare *Puck: A Midsummer Night's Debauchery*.

DVD includes a behind-the-scenes featurette in which the actors discuss the challenge of performing a Shakespearean adaptation and various elements of the production, plus other extras unrelated to the film.

946 *Midsummer's Night* [sic] *Dream*
2000. Hungary. Cadro Films. Sound, col., 87 mins. Steve Cadro (aka Korda Istvan).

Hardcore gay pornographic adaptation. When four city boys take a rural vacation on Midsummer's Day, they quarrel amongst themselves, despite the efforts of Theseus to intervene. The boys leave town for the countryside where Puck mixes up the couples (marked by colored scarves) of Lysander and Hermes, and Demetrios and Alain. After sexual trysts, Puck restores the proper couples at Oberon's behest, and that evening Theseus and his lover Hyppolite are married.

The plot, very loosely based on Shakespeare's tale of mismatched Athenian lovers, provides the rationale for various al fresco sexual encounters between nearly every combination of cast members. The soundtrack features Felix Mendelssohn's *Midsummer Night's Dream* incidental music, including the wedding march for the final sequence (entry 1668). None of Shakespeare's dialogue appears. A male Greek Chorus, nude except for masks of comedy, provides the narration. Interestingly, the film ends with a fantasy of gay marriage. Though Theseus and Hyppolite assure their mutual fidelity by traditionally jumping over fire, the chorus incongruously counsels the viewer to beware the lusty fires of Midsummer night.

947 *A Dream of Hanoi*
2001. U.S. Bullfrog Films. Sound, col., 91 mins. Tom Weidlinger.

A Dream of Hanoi documents a bi-national and bi-lingual American and Vietnamese co-production of *A Midsummer Night's Dream* in Hanoi, the idea for which came from a dramaturg, Lorelle Browning, who works at an Oregon college not named in the film. Focusing less on the performance of the play than the efforts and tensions arising behind the scenes in the three months before the production premiered, this feel-good film takes as its ostensible subject the kinds of intercultural problems that arise from trying to integrate the two theaters. Though the subtitles at the film's beginning announce that the production "built a bridge" between the Americans and Vietnamese and the premise sounds liberal minded and well-intentioned, the film is basically a disturbing, sad, and unacknowledged exercise in latter day U.S. cultural imperialism.

What makes this film particularly appalling is the way it does not acknowledge a disparity between the production and the film. Unlike the bi-national theater production, the film is mono-national. It has only one director, an American, and it uses, utterly conventionally, a male voice-over narrative in English supplied by F. Murray Abraham. Although Vietnamese used in the film is translated into English via subtitles, the English is not translated into Vietnamese via subtitles. The film is clearly directed, then, to an American audience. And it quickly becomes clear that the production *of A Midsummer Night's Dream* is tilted toward the American audience who will watch the film. Using the evasive passive tense, we hear that "it is agreed" that the American director, Allen Nause, who has a Vietnamese woman translator present, will lay out the basic ideas, with the Vietnamese director, Doan Hoang Giang, taking a secondary role as the person who implements the American's views. Somehow, this division of labor will produce a "uniquely Vietnamese interpretation."

In addition to the American and Vietnamese director having unequal billing, Browning's presence is explained in bizarrely custodial terms. She is there, the narrator says, "to defend Shakespeare's text against misinterpretation and mistranslation." No criteria are supplied to tell us how Browning or anyone else in the film decides what is interpretation and what is misinterpretation. Even more mystifying, the Vietnamese parts of the play are translated into contemporary American English subtitles, not back into Shakespeare's text. In stunningly reactionary fashion, Shakespeare is held up as a magic wand that the Americans can turn into a baton to browbeat the poor Vietnamese director, staff, and actors into doing the play the American way. When insisting on her view of the play, Browning tells the Vietnamese director that Shakespeare is a better director than he is or than she is or than the American director is. And Doug Miller, the actor who plays Lysander and claims to bring a revolution to Vietnamese theater by openly kissing a Vietnamese actress on stage, says "We're going from zero to Shakespeare in three months." Destination Shakespeare is a given here, and one would never know from Miller's comment or from the film that the Vietnamese director had already done *King Lear* or that Shakespeare had been performed in Vietnam before Browning arrived. Despite the pretence of a co-production, then, the traffic should move in one direction as far as the Americans are concerned. They are not there to Vietnamese their American Shakespeare; they are there to Americanize the Vietnamese. (RB)

948 *Get Over It*
2001. U.S. Ignite Entertainment, Keshan, Miramax Films, and Morpheus. Sound, col., 87 mins. Tommy O'Haver.

High schooler Berke Landers is devastated when he is suddenly dumped by his longtime girlfriend Allison McAllister, who quickly takes up with insufferable pretty boy "Striker" Scrumfield. When he learns that Allison is joining Striker in auditions for the school play, a vapid musical version of *A Midsummer Night's Dream* written by drama teacher Dr. Desmond Oates, Berke decides to win Allison back by auditioning too. For help with his acting he turns to Kelly Woods, sister of his best friend Felix and an aspiring songwriter. Though Kelly makes clear that she likes Berke, he remains fixated on Allison throughout the rehearsals. Through a freak stage accident Berke is cast at the last minute as Lysander, playing opposite Allison as Hermia, Kelly as Helena, and Striker as Demetrius. Allison learns that Striker is a rake and belatedly tries to make up with Berke, but when Berke hears Kelly's song "Dream on Me," which she inserts in the musical, he uses the play to declare his love for Kelly. Despite Berke's improvised revision of Shakespeare's ending and a number of stage mishaps, the play is a success and Berke and Kelly are united.

A variation on such teen Shakespeare films as *10 Things I Hate about You* and *Never Been Kissed*, *Get Over It* uses the shifting affections between the Athenian lovers as its central Shakespearean motif, an unusual choice for free cinematic adaptations of *Midsummer*. Several magical realist sequences, all Berke's romantic fantasies, are set in an idealized Athenian wood, with Berke as Lysander blocked by Striker/Demetrius's love for his girl, Hermia/Allison; in the final scene, it is Kelly and Berke who walk together into the romantic Shakespearean forest of Berke's imagination. The film offers many glimpses of the rehearsal process of Oates's musical *Midsummer*, including silly auditions (including a performance of the song "where the bee sucks" from *The Tempest*), conflicts between Berke as Lysander and Striker as Demetrius, farcical sequences with the fairies, and the arrival of Theseus to the sleeping lovers in 4.1. The final twenty minutes of the film are devoted to the performance of the play, and it includes the play's opening scene, Lysander and Demetrius's initial faceoff, a dance sequence involving the fairies, Puck's application of the love potion to Helena's eyes (the sequence that includes Kelly's song "Dream on Me"), and Theseus's encounter with the awakening lovers in 4.1. Crucial (and repeated during the film) is Lysander's speech "My lord, I shall reply amazedly" (4.1.143–47), a speech that Berke revises on the fly in couplets to declare his preference for Kelly. Interestingly, the film repeatedly stresses how difficult Shakespeare is to understand. When first reading *Midsummer*, Berke observes that he understands "about every other word," and the first song in Oates's musical version insists that Shakespeare's work is so difficult and uncool it demands musical revision. Two other passing Shakespearean references in the film are of note. When Oates recalls his prior Shakespearean stage triumph, we see that it is his one-man *Hamlet*; he is reciting "To be or not to be" in a doublet (incongruously) to an upheld skull. And Kelly's song "Dream on Me" references in passing the same soliloquy with the line "to sleep, perchance to dream."

DVD includes a director's commentary, deleted scenes, and a behind-the-scenes featurette, all of which reference the film's Shakespearean content.

949 *A Midsummer Night's Rave*
2002. U.S. Filmtrax Entertainment Inc. Sound, col., 85 mins. Gil Cates Jr.

Xander has a crush on Mia, who is currently involved with ultra-cool Damon, while Xander's friend Elena likes Xander. All are headed to a rave, along with Xander's goofy friend Nick, who plays Danny Donkey at children's parties, and a van of stoners. Throughout, Xander is pursued by Doc, a scary drug dealer and friend of Xander's roommate Stosh, because Stosh's jacket contains money from a drug payoff. While at the rave, drug dealer Puck gives a love drug to Xander and Damon, with the result that both confess their love to Elena, who gently lets both down; Xander then confesses his love for Mia, and she confesses her love for him. Nick accidentally imbibes the love drug, becomes concerned that he is an ass, and falls for Britt, a beautiful DJ pursued by OB John, the mystical king of the rave. When the cops end the rave prematurely, Xander is with Mia, Nick with Britt, and Damon with best friend Gregg. Puck appears to save Xander and Mia from Doc's assault, then mysteriously vanishes when the cops bust him for drug possession.

A free transposition of *MND* to rave culture. Much of the focus falls on the Athenian lovers' plot and Puck's administering of glowing love pills to rectify the mismatched couples. There are major changes in plotting— Xander and Mia (the Lysander and Hermia counterparts) freely confess their loves to each other, Elena (the Helena counterpart) decides not to become partners with either man (she falls under the power of a trio of fairies), and Damon (the Demetrius character) ends up in a quasi-homosexual relationship with his friend Gregg. The Bottom and Titania narrative is similarly replotted: Nick (the Bottom counterpart) accidentally drinks the love drug that OB John (the Oberon counterpart) intends for Britt, and under the influence of the drug he publically declares himself an ass (à la Dogberry from *Much Ado about Nothing*), even hallucinating seeing himself in his Danny Donkey costume in a mirror. In this version, OB John does not remove the love charm from the Bottom character's eyes, and he and Britt leave the rave arm in arm. (There is no suggestion of tension between OB John and Britt, as there is between Titania and Oberon.) The "mechanicals" find their counterparts in a van of stoners, one of whom is named Snout, though this group does not perform a play or comparable action; the fairies Elena meets at the toilets correspond to Titania's retinue and have a distinctly feminist edge. No counterparts for Theseus and Hippolyta are included. The major interpolation to the source narrative is the subplot involving Doc's search for the jacket, which enables Puck to have a heroic role at film's end. Doc's unlikely conversion to love through Puck's drug is consistent with the film's overall ideal of free love under the influence of drugs, in this case a love much freer and less heteronormative than in Shakespeare's play. The rave itself becomes the equivalent of the "green world" of the Athenian wood. Several verbal citations are included, most placed in the mouth of OB John and ironized by Puck's snide comments. For example, OB John asks Puck, "Seest thou still this sweet sight?" (referring not to Titania, but to the rave), to which he replies, "I'd say on a scale of 1 to 10, I'd say that's a fabulous." Puck refers to himself as "the merry wanderer of the night," and when he appears to assault Doc, he cites the couplet from his epilogue, "If we shadows have offended, think but this and all is mended." Compare *Rave Macbeth*.

DVD contains a commentary track and featurette with Shakespearean content.

950 *Puck: A Midsummer Night's Debauchery*
2002. Brazil and U.S. FALLMS International. Sound, col., 134 mins. John T. Bone.

Hardcore pornographic adaptation. When Theseus, characterized as a right-wing, sexually repressive hypocrite, forces Lysander and Hermia to marry, the lovers venture into the woods, where various sexual trysts ensue. The settings and language are modern, but the costuming is period, and the fairy dance sequences are vaguely reminiscent of carnival. Compare *A Midsummer Night's Cream* (entry 945).

The film is essentially a series of extended sex scenes, sutured together by Puck's narration of the plot of Shakespeare's play in bridging sequences; though Puck speaks in modern English, he punctuates his speech with Shakespearean play titles, referencing *The Tempest*, *Much Ado about Nothing*, *All's Well That Ends Well*, *As You Like It*, and *Love's Labor's Lost*, among others.

951 *The Seasons Alter*
2002. U.K. Futerra. Sound, col., 4 mins. Roger Lunn.

Short rendering of Titania's speech from *A Midsummer Night's Dream* 2.1, starring Keira Knightley.

952 *Fairies*
2003. U.S. SPEAKproductions. Sound, col., 20 mins. Thomas Gustafson.

Timothy, a gay adolescent at an all-boys' school, is tormented by his homophobic classmates and coach. In his drama class, he gets the part of Puck and is encouraged by his teacher Ms. Tebbit. While performing the play, he imagines an alternate musical version of *A Midsummer Night's Dream* in which the cast joins him in dance numbers and he openly woos Jonathon, a fellow student. Compare *Get Over It*.

953 *Midsummer Dream*
2005. Spain. Dygra Films S.L. and Appia Filmes. Sound, col., 85 mins. Ángel de la Cruz, Manuel Gómez Pereira, and Manolo Gómez.

Animated free adaptation. Scheduled for theatrical release in Europe in the summer of 2005. The promotional website is www.midsummerdream.com.

MUCH ADO ABOUT NOTHING

The Chuck Jones cartoons *Much Ado about Mousing* (1964) and *Much Ado about Nutting* (1953), and Izzy Sparber's *Much Ado about Mutton* (1947), contain no references to Shakespeare.

954 *Much Ado about Nothing*
1940. U.S. Terrytoons. Sound, b&w, 7 mins. Connie Rasinski.

Short version of the play. Part of a series by Terrytoons (cf. *All's Well That Ends Well*). Features the character Dinky Duck.

955 *Gone to Earth*
1950. U.K. London Films and Vanguard. Sound, col., 110 mins. Michael Powell and Emeric Pressburger.

Adapted from the novel *Gone to Earth* by Mary Webb. Welsh gypsy beauty and songstress Hazel Woodus, a woman devoted to her pet fox Foxy, is profoundly attracted to the roguish squire Jack Reddin, a fox hunter, but in an attempt to suppress her natural desires she instead marries the prim minister Edward Marston. Soon she falls into an affair with Reddin, and when she tries to mend her ways by returning to Marston, Foxy escapes and is hunted by Reddin, leading Hazel to die in her attempt to rescue her pet. An alternative eighty-two-minute cut of this film, with added material directed by Reuben Mamoulian and supervised by David O. Selznick, was released in the United States under the title *The Wild Heart*.

Twice Hazel sings, "Sigh no more, ladies," from *Much Ado* 2.3, both times suggesting that she understands Reddin's untrustworthy nature more than she actually does.

956 *Ljubovju Zaljubov*
1983. USSR. Production company unknown. Sound, col., 84 mins. Tatiana Berezantzera.

Ballet version of the play.

957 *Class Act*
1992. U.S. Warner Bros. and Wizan Black. Sound, col., 98 mins. Randall Miller.

In this comedy of role reversal, Duncan Pinderhughes, a nerdy genius who needs to pass his gym class, and Blade Brown, a troublemaker who must, as a condition of parole, pass his academic classes to avoid jail, switch identities, with Brown in a gifted students' class and Pinderhughes among the school's gang of hoods. When Pinderhughes gets a bad reputation his estimation with sexy women significantly improves, while Brown's new academic prowess allows him to romance sweet, innocent Ellen.

One exchange between Duncan and a fellow student involves a line from *Much Ado about Nothing*, "I will live in thy ear, die in thy lap, and be buried in thy eyes" (5.2). The conversation addresses the word "die," the Elizabethan euphemism for "have an orgasm"; another student is amazed that Shakespeare would be writing about sex.

958 *Much Adobo about Nothing*
1999. Nakazono. Magwili.

A Filipino American farcical comedy. (EL)

959 *William Sexpeare's "Much Ado about Puberty"*
1999. U.S. Production company unknown. Sound, col., 6 mins. Ken Boynton.

Parody, available on iFilms.com. William Sexspeare, as a boy, worries about the onset of puberty and consults his mother and father about the birds and the bees. The film is entirely in pseudo-Shakespearean iambic pentameter, and William is dressed in Elizabethan doublet and hose even though his home is in a modern American suburb. The film has no relationship to *Much Ado about Nothing* beyond the title, but it parodies in a general way Shakespearean verbal style.

960 *Dil Chahta Hai* (*The Heart Desires*)
2001. India. Excel Entertainment. Sound, col., 183 mins. Farhan Akhtar.

A trio of close friends—smart-aleck Akash, meek, naïve Sameer, and mature, sensitive Siddarth—vow to maintain their friendships while pursuing a number of women in their lives. Their relationships between each other and with women are told in flashback as Siddarth attends his love, Tara Jaiswal, an older woman, as she dies from cirrhosis in a hospital. Siddarth, we learn, long ago fell out with his friend Akash over Tara, with Akash believing that she is too old for him. Akash, a lothario, denies the power of love and hides his feelings behind wit and bravado. Sameer is too meek to declare his affection for the women he falls for. The men go their separate ways for a while, Akash moving to Sydney, but they all return to India and eventually reunite. Akash declares his love for Shalini, who is engaged to the fiery Rohit, and Sameer is married to Pooja. Sameer watches Tara die without her being able to declare that she loved him, but he finds new love in the film's epilogue.

Akash's plotline obliquely references two Shakespeare plays. In many ways, Akash resembles Benedick from *Much Ado about Nothing*—he declares that he doesn't believe in love and is fiercely devoted to his male friends, even though he is attracted to Shalini; he finally declares his love publicly and sincerely at the last minute at a wedding (though the circumstances are different from those in *Much Ado*, since the wedding is for Shalini and Rohit). At one point, Shalini and Akash attend a performance of Berlioz's operatic *Troilus and Cressida* (based on Shakespeare's play); Shalini presents the narrative as one of true love, and notes particularly that Troilus hesitates at the gate of heaven in order to get a chance to declare his love one last time to Cressida. Shalini asks Akash who he loves in this way, and Akash has a dream sequence in which Shalini appears in the character of Cressida. When she gives him his chance to declare his love after the opera, however, he makes a bad joke of it (declaring he preferred the fat opera lady), a choice that he and she immediately regret.

961 *Much Ado*
2003. U.S. Downstage West. Sound, col., 86 mins. Kipley Wentz.

Valerie, an independent film producer, gathers with several young filmmakers struggling to complete an independent film adaptation of Shakespeare's *Much Ado about Nothing*. When her director quits, he is replaced by the self-consciously "artistic" Digby Wells, who immediately recasts Hero's and Claudio's parts and gives the role of Benedick to Seth, taking it away from Brandon, a neurotic actor who has learned all the lines and hopes to star alongside his beloved Hannah (who plays Beatrice). When Seth woos Hannah and gets a major movie role, Brandon decides to break up the two, taking his idea from Don John's interference with Hero and Claudio's romance. Meanwhile, the actors playing Hero and Claudio, the bickering Valerie and Tristan, have through Digby's bizarre acting exercises come to confess their love for one another. As filmmaking nears completion, Brandon launches his plan, which nearly destroys the production, but his subterfuge is revealed and all ends well.

The film uses many quotations from *Much Ado*, and the actors take on characteristics of Shakespeare's couples (though not the couples they actually play): Valerie and Tristan have the qualities of Beatrice and Benedick, and Hannah and Seth the qualities of Hero and Claudio. Jealous Brandon has qualities of Don John, but also of Iago. An entertaining example of the life-imitates-art backstage Shakespearean drama, as well as a parody of independent filmmaking.

962 *Much Ado about Nothing*
2005. Kitty Video.

   Kizuna manga; yaoi anime. (EL)

OTHELLO

963 *The Duped Othello* (aka *The Theatrical Chimney Sweep*)
1910. U.K. R. W. Paul. Silent, b&w, 320 ft. Jack Smith.

Apparently a comedy based upon blackface: a chimney sweep, out for revenge upon an actor, secretly loads his makeup with soot.

964 *For Åbent Tæppe* (*Desdemona*)
1911. Denmark. Ole Olson Productions and Nordisk Films Kompagni. Silent, b&w, 2 reels (1,768 ft.). August Blom.

An actor prepares for the part of Othello as his wife enters her dressing room. There she is visited by an unwelcome admirer from among the acting troupe and receives flowers from another suitor. As the cast rehearses onstage, the unwelcome admirer steals into the actress's room, reads the note with the flowers, and afterward plots. In a private dining room, the actress receives a locket from a rich man as the unwelcome admirer watches. After the actress returns to her room to rest, the unwelcome admirer tells the husband what he has seen and gives him the note that came with the flowers; later, in his wife's room, the

actor discovers the locket. He makes himself up to resemble the rich man; when she reacts favorably, he reveals his true identity and orders her out. Backstage, as the play is about to begin, the actor, now made up as Othello, sees his wife, dressed as Desdemona, with flowers, and the unwelcome admirer sees her receive a gift from the rich man and reports this to the actor. Backstage, the actor confronts his wife, but their fight is interrupted when they are called onstage. Onstage, the actor as Othello chokes his wife to death, then turns to the rich man in the audience and accuses him. As the rich man slinks away, harangued by the audience, the actor falls in grief at the sight of his dead wife.

A fascinating early example of the life-imitates-art theme seen in many popular adaptations of *Othello*. Interestingly, the Iago figure's motive is here not jealousy but revenge for the actress's rejection of his advances; also interesting is how the actor uses his theatrical skills at makeup to test his wife's fidelity and how the audience blames the rich suitor, not the actor playing Othello. The motif of the revealing gift is twice repeated, with the note with the flowers and the rich man's locket. The film is visually sophisticated for its day, particularly in its use of mirrors, both as a thematic device and as a way of extending the viewer's visual field.

Included as an extra on the Buchowetski *Othello* DVD issued by Kino.

965 *Bianco contro Negro*
1913. Italy. Pasuali Film. Silent, b&w, 4,920 ft. Ernesto Maria Pasquali.

Silent film of Verdi opera. Of historical importance because of its accompanying synchronized sound (on a disk system).

966 *Bumke als Othello*
1913. Germany. Continental Kunstfilm. Silent, b&w, 591 ft. Director unknown.

When Bumke, an inept actor, indulges his ambitions by playing Othello, he makes a fool of himself and is chased by his angry audience. One of a series of "Bumke" pictures by the silent German comedian Gerhard Dammann.

967 *L'Erede di Jago*
1913. Italy. Savoia Film. Silent, b&w, 2,789 ft. Director unknown.

An employer's wife comes to suspect that the employer's confidential secretary has stolen from him. To discredit the wife with her husband, the secretary arranges to have the employer see his wife drugged in an embrace with another man. However, the employer discovers the trick and fires him. When the secretary sets lions free on the employer's property in an effort to take revenge, he is burned to death in a fire they have caused.

968 *Othello in Jonesville*
1913. U.S. Edison Company. Silent, b&w, length unknown. Charles Seay.

Apparently a lost film. In this comedy, an unemployed actor offers a stagestruck girl and her family acting lessons in exchange for room and board. They attempt to perform *Othello* (and do so badly) at the local town hall.

969 *The Mad Lover* (aka *A Modern Othello*)
1917. U.S. Robert Warwick Film Corporation and Harry Rapf Productions. Silent, b&w, 5 reels. Léonce Perret.

Through an automobile accident Robert Hyde, a confirmed bachelor, is brought into contact with Clarice, who afterward recovers at his home. Despite his vow never to marry, Hyde falls in love with and marries her, but his obsession with fishing and hunting undermines their relationship. Clarice is advised by her priest to have children to save the marriage. Soon after, Mrs. Grosvenor, her aunt, organizes a large gathering on the Hyde estate. One activity during the group's visit is a charity production of *Othello* in which Clarice plays Desdemona and Count Vinzaglio plays Othello; their love scenes cause Hyde to dream of himself as Othello, killing his wife out of jealousy. When Hyde discovers that Vinzaglio is really attempting to seduce his wife, he throws him out and is more attentive to his wife, leading eventually to her becoming pregnant. One of the first presentations of the life-imitates-art adaptations of *Othello* (see also *For Åbent Tæppe* in 1911), this time with a happy rather than tragic ending. (This film is not to be confused with the short *The Mad Lover* produced in 1912.)

970 *Der Fliegentüten-Othello*
1918. Germany. Berliner Film-Manufaktur GmbH. Silent, b&w, length unknown. Carl Boese.

Not clear whether this is an *Othello* adaptation, though the title suggests so.

971 *De Blanke Othello* (*The White Othello*)
1919. Netherlands. Production company unknown. Silent, b&w, length unknown. Director unknown.

Content unknown, though the title merits inclusion in this list.

972 *Othello*
1919. U.K. Hepworth Picture Plays. Silent, b&w, length unknown. Anson Dyer.

One of Anson Dyer's animated Shakespeare parodies from 1919 to 1920; Othello is a seaside minstrel, while Desdemona is the daughter of the local bathing machine proprietor. This film exists now only in a fragment at the British Film Institute.

973 *Otello*
1920. Italy. Production company unknown. Silent, b&w, length unknown. Camillo de Riso.

Apparently a parody.

974 *Carnival*
1921. U.K. Alliance Films Corporation and United Artists. Silent, b&w, 54 mins. Harley Knoles.

Adapted from the play by H.C.M. Hardinge and Matheson Lang. During the Venetian carnival, Silvio Steno, an actor performing the part of Othello, becomes jealous at what he imagines is the infidelity of his actress wife Simonetta with Count Andreas. Driven temporarily insane, he almost kills her onstage during their performance of the final scene of the play. Once the curtain falls, she protests her innocence, he regains his senses, and the two reconcile. Author Matheson Lang plays the role of Steno. A version of this scenario was used in Blom's *For Åbent Tæppe* (above), and would resurface in various forms in the remakes of this film and in *Men Are Not Gods* and *A Double Life* (below).

975 *Schatten Eine Nächtliche Halluzination* (*Warning Shadows*)
1922. Germany. Pan Film. Silent, b&w, 93 mins. Arthur Robison.

Adapted from a story by Albin Grau. In this historically significant Expressionist film, a wealthy count and his wife host a banquet at his nineteenth-century manor house, attended by four of the wife's suitors. A shadow player creates a shadow play involving a silhouette of the countess as an entertainment for the guests, but when the suitors pretend to kiss the shadow, the count becomes outraged at their indiscretion and takes violent revenge. At film's end, it is not entirely clear how much of the shadow play is reality and how much fantasy. An analogue to *Othello* in its evocation of fantasized jealousy met with murderous revenge.

976 *Weißer Othello*
1922. Germany. Production company unknown. Silent, b&w, length unknown. William Karfiol.

"A Whiter Othello." A parody of *The White Othello* (produced in 1919 in the Netherlands)?

977 *Carnival* (aka *Venetian Nights*)
1931. U.K. British & Dominions Film Corporation. Sound, b&w and col., 88 mins. Herbert Wilcox.

Adapted from the play by Matheson Lang and H.C.M. Hardinge. Sound remake of Harley Knoles's *Carnival*, 1921 (see summary for that film). Matheson Lang reprises his role as the actor Silvio Steno from the silent version. Notable for its use of elaborate hand-tinted color during a carnival fireworks sequence.

978 *The Deceiver*
1931. U.S. Columbia Pictures. Sound, b&w, 66 mins. Louis King.

Adapted from a story by Abem Finkel and Bella Muni. Reginald Thorpe, a superficially charming Shakespearean matinee idol who is a womanizer, is starring in *Othello* on Broadway and planning to leave for Hollywood to become a film star. As he prepares to leave, Thorpe deceives several women, Celia Adams (his current conquest), Ina Fontaine (his leading lady), and Helen Lawton (a former lover who Thorpe's agent is blackmailing); he is disliked by many of his fellow performers, including Barney Adams, a knife-thrower. After having received a threatening letter, he requests police protection as he completes *Othello*'s run, but he is nevertheless killed. Though suspicion first falls on Helen's husband John and on Tony Hill, an understudy, Police Inspector Dunn soon deduces that Celia is Barney's daughter and that he killed Thorpe because the actor intended to leave and humiliate his child. Dunn tricks Barney into confessing.

Unlike many other backstage dramas featuring *Othello*, this narrative does not use the usual life-imitates-art formula for including Shakespeare's play. Instead, Thorpe's role as Othello seems obliquely to indicate his essential moral "blackness" and destructiveness toward women.

979 *Men Are Not Gods*
1936. U.K. London Film Productions. Sound, b&w, 90 mins. Walter Reisch.

Adapted from a story by Walter Reisch. Ann Williams, secretary to quirky theater critic Frederick Skeates, changes a bad notice of Shakespearean actor Edmond Davey's debut performance as Othello at his actress wife Barbara Halson's entreaty. When she is fired for doing so, Williams attends Davey's performance, is enthralled, and afterwards has dinner with Davey and Halson. Soon Williams is seeing Davey's performance on a daily basis, and he suggests an affair, to which after initially resisting Williams consents. Skeates, recognizing her attraction to Davey, warns her about hero worship and rehires her. Learning of the affair, Halson obliquely asks her to sever the relationship, and Williams does so via a note that ends with the phrase "as long as she lives." Fastening on the phrase, Davey formulates the idea of murdering his wife, and accordingly he tries to choke her during their performance of *Othello*'s final scene; Williams's screams interrupt the murder. Davey and Halson reconcile backstage when Davey learns she is pregnant, and eventually Williams speaks with Davey, telling him she'd prefer to be a representative of the unreserved seats. The stage manager tells the audience that the principals cannot complete the play, and this one time he hopes that they will consent to let Desdemona live.

Men Are Not Gods does not attempt to adapt Shakespeare's narrative, but instead uses copious allusions to *Othello* to explore the darker side of romantic infatuation across class lines. No small part of Ann Williams's attraction to the cad Edmund Davey is his upper-class bearing, reinforced by his status as a Shakespearean actor

and the romantic exoticism of the heroic character he plays; in this, the nature of her love for Davey, a form of hero worship, is somewhat akin to that of Desdemona's love for Othello. As Skeates observes in his initial review of Davey as a passionless Othello, he is "not the ideal Shakespearean hero we have been waiting for," just as Desdemona, after Othello strikes her in 3.4, concludes that "men are not gods." Williams's changing of Skeates's notice is thus prescient of her later misperception of Davey. Williams first experiences Davey's Othello from unreserved balcony seating, an indication of her class status, and the scenes we watch her witness take on additional resonance as she falls for the actor: in 1.3, she first hears Brabantio's accusation of witchcraft, and then watches as Othello (played as a tawny Moor) begins his reply, ending with the line, "I won his daughter." This is followed by Othello's "Farewell the tranquil mind" speech in 3.3, Desdemona's "Men are not gods" speech in 3.4 (the first of two citations of that line); and Othello's final words ending with "to die upon a kiss" in 5.2. When later Williams hears Davey's performance on the radio, it is of Othello's account of his wooing of Desdemona, a performance (and passage) that finally convinces her to consummate the relationship. When after breaking off the affair she sees Davey's performance for the final time, we are shown two scenes: first, Desdemona's willow song from 4.3 (set to Samuel Taylor Coleridge's music), a scene that brings him to tears; and second, a relatively full and passionate performance of Othello's murder of Desdemona. An ominous indication of Davey's intention is his crushing of a lit cigarette—"putting out the light"—backstage as his wife performs the willow song. Interestingly, Tommy Stapleton, the eccentric middle-class boy for whom Ann is clearly meant, tries to add a Shakespearean gloss to his own status by performing bits and pieces of Iago's grotesque accusation of Desdemona's "gross revolt" with Othello in 1.1 and Brabantio's accusation that his daughter "is abused, stol'n from me, and corrupted / By spells and medicines bought of mountebanks" in 1.3. The lines not only express Tommy's frustration that Davey has stolen Anne from him but also clarify Shakespeare's class status. The working-class neighborhood, hearing Tommy's Shakespearean tirade, erupts in revolt. May be fruitfully compared with *A Double Life* (entry 988).

980 *We Went to College*
1936. U.S. MGM. Sound, b&w, 64 mins. Joseph Santley.

Adapted from a story by Finley Peter Dunne and George Oppenheimer. In this satire of college homecomings, Ellery Standish, a workaholic economics professor, invites Phil Talbot, a former football hero, to attend Sutter College's homecoming, much to the delight of his nostalgic wife Susan. Both Ellery and Phil neglect their family lives in favor of work. When Phil arrives, Susan renews her college crush on him and through several mixups becomes convinced that Phil intends to marry her. After Phil's wife Nina becomes incensed, Phil realizes Susan's misunderstanding and irons matters out at a party, while Susan covers with Ellery for her foolishness by suggesting she had a nightmare. The film ends with Phil's friend Glenn Harvey stumbling drunk onto the football field during the big game.

Susan has been playing Desdemona in productions of *Othello* since her college days (Phil had once played her Othello). When Phil first arrives, Susan takes him to the college production of *Othello*, where she convinces him to take a small role in the production. Her role of Desdemona is thematically parallel to her persistent idealization of Phil, whom she continues to see as a hero.

981 *Paradise in Harlem*

1939. U.S. Jubilee Pictures Corporation. Sound, b&w, 85 mins. Joseph Seiden.

Lem Anderson, a blackface Negro comedian who aspires to play Othello on the legitimate stage, is forced to leave town when he accidentally witnesses a mob killing by Rough Jackson, a black mobster, and his men. Lem travels south, where he experiences racism and degradation on the chitlin' circuit, and eventually he becomes an alcoholic and loses his job when he strikes his boss. A friend helps him off liquor, and Lem returns to Harlem to play Othello in a church production, only to be recognized by the mobster's men. In an effort to frame Lem, Jackson uses his girlfriend to entrap him, but she cannot go through with the ruse and is accidentally shot by Ganoway, one of Jackson's men. Despondent, Lem briefly returns to alcohol, but he soon recovers and vows not to be run out of town again. Framed for the shooting of Jackson's girlfriend, Lem is arrested, but his landlady Madame Mamie discovers that Lem was innocent. At the last moment, Lem is released long enough to play Othello in the church production, as Jackson and Ganoway shoot each other in jealousy over a woman. The production, a black musical version of the play, is a rousing success, and Lem learns that the production will be moving to Broadway.

This remarkable film, one of many "race films" produced by black filmmakers for a predominantly black audience, treats Shakespeare's *Othello* as a pinnacle of cultural aspiration and legitimacy for black artists, pointedly in contrast to the humiliating racism of minstrelsy that Lem experiences as an artist, a racism that becomes all the more direct when he travels south. Interestingly, the film insists that blacks as well as whites participate in racism. It also includes in its critique the moral hypocrisy of status-climbing blacks such as the Preacher, who quickly abandons Lem when he is accused of shooting Jackson's girlfriend. Frank L. Wilson, who played Lem as well as wrote the film, movingly communicates both Lem's

struggle with racial degradation and his fight for moral and artistic integrity. As something of a backstage chronicle, the film features many black musical acts, and the performance of the final act of *Othello* that ends the film seeks to create a hybrid between African American music and Shakespearean drama, "illegitimate" popular art and legitimate theater. Lem's Othello, entering to strangle Desdemona, offers a stentorious Shakespearean performance that the black audience ridicules, but Desdemona's plaint not to kill her almost imperceptibly shifts into a bluesy call-and-response that the audience joins, and at the death of Desdemona the music shifts to a major key, rousing swing number, to which viewers dance in the theater aisles. Pointedly, the scene does not include Othello's loss of command or suicide.

982 *East of Piccadilly* (aka *The Strangler*)

1940. U.K. Associated British and British National Films, Ltd. Sound, b&w, 75 mins. Harold Huth.

Adapted from the novel by Gordon Beckles. Called to a Soho address while at a book launch event, Tamsie Green, a mystery novelist, and Penny Sutton, a reporter, discover a woman strangled by her own nylons. When they return with the police, the body is gone, only to reappear later on the doorstep of a theater. Eager to solve the crime, Green and Sutton investigate the eccentric inhabitants of the victim's run-down building: a hooker, George Pughe, an American millionaire living in secret in the building, and a hammy, mad actor. Pughe is convicted of the crime (wrongly, it turns out) and sentenced to hang. The killer, influenced by the final scene of *Othello*, is caught when Green convinces him to reenact the crime, lest the wrong man garner all the publicity. An analogue to the actor's life-imitates-*Othello* motif.

983 *Rossini*

1942. Italy. Lux Productions. Sound, b&w, 112 mins. Mario Bonnard.

A film biography of Giacchino Rossini, the nineteenth-century opera composer, focusing on 1815 to 1827, the period of his early success. *Otello* is referenced.

984 *The Man in Grey*

1943. U.K. Gainsborough Pictures. Sound, b&w, 90 mins. Leslie Arliss.

Adapted from the novel by Eleanor Smith. Handled as a series of flashbacks prompted by a case of memorabilia, this film details the troubled friendship between two women schoolmates, poor, treacherous Hesther Snow and rich, loving Clarissa Richmond. Clarissa is tricked into a loveless marriage with the marquis of Rohan, and Hesther becomes an actress. When Hesther becomes Clarissa's household companion, she has an affair with Rohan, and Clarissa develops an interest in Rokeby, a charismatic actor. Clarissa asks Rohan to release her so she can marry

Rokeby, but he refuses. Desperate to marry Rohan, Hesther kills Clarissa, but when he learns of her treachery he beats her to death. In the frame tale, the descendants of Clarissa and Rokeby begin a romance.

Soon after meeting Rokeby, Clarissa sees Hesther and Rokeby playing in a local production of *Othello*. The scenes referenced are 4.3 (particularly Desdemona's "willow song") and 5.2 (Rokeby plays Othello in blackface). Though Hesther's married name is Barbary, there seems little relationship between the willow song she sings and her own situation. After this scene, Clarissa's black servant Toby refers to Rokeby as "the black-white gentleman"; Toby is played by a white boy in blackface.

985 *The Volunteer*
1943. U.K. Ministry of Information and The Archers. Sound, b&w, 24 mins. Michael Powell and Emeric Pressburger.

This propaganda short by the formidable team of Powell and Pressburger features Ralph Richardson in the role of Othello in a wartime London theater. His dresser, Fred Davey, asks Richardson for an autograph before he volunteers to become a Royal Navy pilot. During the war, Davey rescues a pilot from a burning plane. When he is invited to Buckingham Palace to celebrate his heroism, Richardson asks him for an autograph. The short is notable for a cameo appearance by Laurence Olivier (see entry 351), in which he sends himself up. (DL)

This short film is really meant to help recruitment to the Fleet Air Arm, the airborne branch of the Royal Navy. The main character in the film is Ralph Richardson's dresser, Fred (Pat McGrath). He's shown to be quite clumsy and incompetent at most things, and he's trying to decide which branch of the armed forces he should join at the outbreak of war. He joins the Fleet Air Arm, and they train him to be an air mechanic; and when he's at sea and the aircraft carrier is attacked, he is quite heroic. Ralph Richardson is playing Othello at the start of the film. He's getting ready for a performance with (or despite) Fred's help. But we only see him in the dressing room in the theater, never on stage. He is wearing blackface and a full Moorish costume. He also has a dagger that Fred neglects to give him, so he has to come back into the dressing room to get it. (RB)

986 *Les Enfants du paradis* (*Children of Paradise*)
1945. France. Pathé Cinéma. Sound, b&w, 190 mins. Marcel Carné.

Baptiste, a theater mime, falls in love with his ideal woman, Garance, a prostitute and actress. Their unrequited love affair is complicated by Garance's three suitors—Frédérick LeMaître, an exuberant actor; Lacenaire, a debonaire thief; and Count Edouard de Montray, a cold but rich admirer—as well as by Natalie, the daughter of the theater manager, who loves Baptiste. When Garance becomes unwittingly implicated in one of Lacenaire's crimes, she seeks the protection of Montray and moves to India. In the film's second half, Garance returns to Paris to see Baptiste, who is now married to Natalie. The two become newly involved, and when their affair is exposed by Lacenaire, Garance's loveless marriage to Natalie is destroyed.

Othello is one of several theatrical points of reference in the film, all thematically linked to its plot. After Baptiste and Garance do not consummate their relationship, we see LeMaître reading *Othello*'s opening speech to the play's final scene. In the film's second half, we see LeMaître act in two scenes from *Othello*: Othello and Iago's exchange about killing Desdemona in 4.1, and Othello's murder of Desdemona in 5.2. LeMaître also consistently refers to himself as Othello and Garance as Desdemona when they meet again in the second half, in large part because he feels jealousy about Garance's feelings for Baptiste. During the interval in LeMaître's performance of *Othello*, he has a conversation with several pompous Frenchmen about Shakespeare. Early in the film, LeMaître also briefly references Julius Caesar, as one of the characters he intends to play.

987 *Bodas Trágicas* (*Tragic Wedding*)
1946. Mexico. Clasa Films Mundiales. Sound, b&w, 77 mins. Gilberto Martinez Solares.

Wealthy rancher Diego secretly marries young Amparo because her father, Juan Manuel, thinks of Diego as his former servant and not sufficiently highborn; unaware of the secret marriage, Juan Manuel arranges a marriage between Jose Luis and Amparo, and he attempts to shoot Diego when he comes to claim his bride. Octavio, Diego's attendant, disapproves of the marriage, as does his wife Laura, who loves Diego. Octavio engineers suspicion with Diego that Amparo is unfaithful with Carlos, one of Diego's attendants. Though the fit of jealousy soon passes, Octavio conspires to make Diego believe that Jose Luis is about to take his bride; he uses a brooch stolen by Laura as evidence of Amparo's infidelity. Carlos, drunk, arrives with a bouquet of flowers and is struck by Diego. Later, convinced of his wife's infidelity with Jose Luis, Diego attempts to shoot her, but Laura is shot instead; as she dies, she confesses her love, Amparo's innocence, and Octavio's treachery. Diego hunts down Octavio and drowns him in a swamp, and afterward he and Amparo are reconciled.

Though the credit sequence coyly identifies the film as a "Mexican adaptation of a classic drama," avoiding the name of Shakespeare, the influence of *Othello* is thoroughgoing. Diego corresponds to Othello (rendered a problematic consort for Amparo because of his class status, not his race), Amparo to Desdemona, Octavio to Iago,

Carlos to Cassio, Juan Manuel to Brabantio, and Jose Luis to Roderigo; Laura combines elements of Emilia and Roderigo, and Solares adds a comic downstairs relationship between Amparo's nurse Agustina and hired hand Juan de Dios. Diego demonstrates his heroic nature with a bullfight during his wedding celebration, although the film does open up passing critiques of Latin machismo. Almost half of the film is devoted to depicting the various wedding celebrations; only in its second half does the *Othello* parallel come into full focus. At film's end Diego strangles not Amparo, but Octavio, as if redirecting the wounded male rage of Shakespeare's protagonist at the proper victim. Diego's jealousy of Carlos is rather inexpertly woven into the plotline (it is Diego's anxiety about Jose Luis that is more dire), as is the incriminating token of the brooch and the poorly motivated happy ending. The motif of the secret marriage and alternate arranged suitor for the bride may be traced to *Romeo and Juliet*, as may be the comic figure of Agustina the nurse.

Ronald Colman and Signe Hasso from *A Double Life* (1947). Colman (Othello) is strangling Hasso (Desdemona), with onlookers from backstage about to intervene. Courtesy of Douglas Lanier.

988 *A Double Life*
1947. U.S. Kanin/Universal International.
Sound, b&w, 105 mins. George Cukor.

An atmospheric and deftly directed film noir that centers on the mental breakdown of suave matinee idol Anthony John in the midst of a production of *Othello*. The screenplay pursues several parallels between John's private demons and the pathological elements of Shakespeare's tragic hero. He is in love with his former wife Brita, though he cannot bring her to remarry him (he plays Othello to her Desdemona in the play-within-the-film); when Bill Friend, a reporter, Cassio-like attracts the attentions of Brita, John becomes insanely jealous, his feelings only deepened by the Shakespearean role he plays. At the same time, John finds himself attracted to Pat Kroll, a down-on-her-luck waitress at the Venice Café who dimly reminds him of Brita. In a fit of displaced rage triggered by Pat's innocent suggestion that he "put out the light," John murders Pat. From the film's midpoint on, it becomes a somewhat more conventional murder mystery, with Bill Friend slowly piecing together John's part in the crime, his suspicions triggered when John tries to strangle him and confirmed when John reacts with panic at a Kroll look-alike that Friend sets up for him. The film's final scenes take place during the production of *Othello*, focusing on the final scene as Friend and the police close in on the hapless and now remorseful John.

Substantial portions of the play's final scene appear three times in the film, the first a triumphal performance of the strangling scene, the second a more disturbing performance of the same sequence where John nearly chokes Brita to

death, and the third in which John, playing Othello, kills himself onstage in earnest. Particularly effective is Cukor's cinematic rendering of John's mental disorientation as he becomes possessed by the role of Othello. Early on, as he contemplates performing *Othello*, he performs three passages from 3.3 ("beware, my lord, of jealousy," "arise, my vengeance," and "haply, I am black"), all of which portend his psychological disintegration to come. When he first meets Pat Kroll, he quotes Othello from 3.3, "O that we can call these delicate creatures ours / And not their appetites," and at her apartment, he launches into Othello's "impudent strumpet" speech from 5.2. As Tony tries to choke Bill Friend, he mutters "had all his hairs," referencing Othello's revenge upon Cassio in 5.2. There are several other Shakespearean citations, and ubiquitous images of mirrors emphasize the perverse "doubling" theme. Noteworthy is a montage sequence in midfilm in which Cukor portrays the rehearsal process for *Othello* in dreamlike fashion, emphasizing the way in which the lines and action of the play invade the actor's consciousness. Ronald Colman won the Academy Award for best actor for his portrayal of Anthony John, a role that reputedly was first offered to Laurence Olivier.

This is the best of the sequence of films that imagine actors of Othello as somehow infected by the jealousy and murderous rage of their role: see also *Desdemona, A Modern Othello, Carnival, Men Are Not Gods,* and *Anna's Sin*. This trope persists in somewhat revised form in the recent films *In Othello* and *Stage Beauty* (entry 1029). See also entry 2438.

989 *Return to Glennascaul*
1951. Gordon Films. Sound, b&w, 26 mins. Orson Welles.

Orson Welles, taking a break from the filming of *Othello* (entry 452), is driving in the Irish countryside one night when he offers a ride to a man with car trouble. The man relates a strange event that happened to him at the same location. Two women flagged down his car one evening, asking for a ride back to their manor. They invited him in for a drink, and after leaving, he went back for his cigarette case. He found the manor deserted and decayed. In Dublin, a real estate broker told him the mother and daughter had died years ago. Welles, sufficiently spooked, drops the man off at his home, and speeds on by when two other stranded women wave for a ride. (RB)

990 *Il Peccato di Anna* (*Anna's Sin*)
1952. U.S. Giaguaro Film. Sound, b&w, 86 mins. Camillo Mastrocinque.

John Ruthford, an African American actor, goes to Rome to star in a production of *Othello* and to find Sam, the black man for whom John was wrongly imprisoned for seven years for the rape of a white girl. During rehearsals, Ruthford falls in love with Anna Curti, the actress playing Desdemona, but Alberto, Anna's untrustworthy manager, out to steal her inheritance and in love with her, tells Anna about Ruthford's prison record, after which she breaks off the romance. Anna eventually learns the truth of Ruthford's wrongful conviction from Sam, but Alberto throws Sam from a scaffolding, killing him before he can clear Ruthford's name. Ruthford attacks Alberto and, believing he has killed him, decides to commit suicide, but Anna pursues Ruthford; informs him that Alberto, very much alive, is in police custody; and persuades him that she still loves him.

Il Peccato di Anna uses *Othello* as the resonant backdrop for a melodrama of racism, jealousy, betrayal, and guilt. The play features several scenes of rehearsal between Ruthford and Anna as Othello and Desdemona, in the course of which they fall in love. Though the film does not attempt to mirror the play directly in its narrative, it does pursue several parallels of character and theme: Ruthford is a very free version of Othello, Anna of Desdemona, and Alberto of Iago; in this case, the Iago figure jealously ruins the reputation not of Desdemona but of Othello. *Il Peccato di Anna* revisits in contemporary form themes with which *Othello* has long been closely associated, white anxieties toward miscegenation and black male sexuality. Although Alberto is motivated by greed and envy, he also is motivated to destroy Ruthford and Anna's romance on racist grounds, and he uses the ugly stereotype of the sexually rapacious black man to do so. And when he contemplates suicide, Ruthford falls prey to the same sort of racial self-loathing that plagues Othello in the final acts of Shakespeare's play. As do so many free adaptations of *Othello*, *Il*

Peccato di Anna stresses the ease with which the lives of Shakespearean players can imitate their art, though in this case, the emphasis falls on the power of the play to stir up both romantic love and racist turmoil. Given the date of production, the amount of screen time allotted to the interracial relationship between Ruthford and Anna and the film's happy ending (a significant rewrite of the plot trajectory of *Othello*) are significant for the history of interracial romance on film.

991 *The Moor's Pavane*
1955. U.S. Universal International Pictures. Sound, b&w, 21 mins. Walter Strate.

Choreographed by Jose Limon. Filmed version of Limon's famous one-act dance version of *Othello*. Originally made for TV and broadcast March 6, 1955.

992 *C'est arrivé à Aden*
1956. France. S. B. Films. Sound, col., 88 mins. Michael Boisrond.

Adapted from the novel *Les environs d'Aden* by Jean Benoit. In this adventure film spoof, Albine, the leading lady of a French acting company stranded in Aden, a rural British colony in India, is wooed by the local potentate, Prince de Khamarkar. When the prince refuses to sign an international treaty until Albine accepts his proposal, this causes problems for Albine's lover, an English lieutenant named Sinclair, and for the villains who seek to push the prince from his throne. Eventually, the prince abducts Albine, they fall in love and marry, and the treaty is signed.

The theater troupe performs scenes from *Othello*.

993 *Jubal*
1956. U.S. Columbia Pictures. Sound, col., 100 mins. Delmer Daves.

Adapted from the novel by Paul Wellman. Rancher Shep Horgan finds an injured cowboy, Jubal Troop, offers him a job, and soon makes him foreman. Shep's wife Mae, trapped in a marriage with a man she sees as boorish, is attracted to Jubal, but he repeatedly resists her romantic overtures. Pinky, Shep's abrasive former top cowhand, resents Jubal's rise to foreman and Mae's romantic preference for Jubal. Meanwhile, Jubal is attracted to Naomi Hoktor, a religious girl traveling with a wagon train camped on the Horgan ranch, though the man to whom she is promised, Jake Slavin, is jealous of their relationship. When Jubal escorts Mae home one evening, Pinky suggests to Shep that the two are having an affair. Shep returns home to question Mae, who lies to him that the two are involved; in a rage, Shep confronts Jubal, who shoots him in self-defense. Pinky uses Shep's death as a pretext for settling scores with Jubal; when Naomi's father hides Jubal, Jake betrays him out of jealousy. Pinky and Jubal have a showdown at Shep's ranch, where the truth is revealed before Mae dies: Mae had no affair with Shep, and she was savagely beaten by Pinky when she refused his advances.

While not a thoroughgoing adaptation of *Othello*, *Jubal* does reshape and recombine several key motifs from the play. Shep, as the cattle king of Wyoming, corresponds in many ways to Othello, Mae to Desdemona, Pinky to Iago, and Jubal to Cassio. The narrative is told from the perspective of the Cassio character, and the motivations of main characters are significantly altered. In this version, though the Othello character is wildly in love with his wife, the Desdemona character does in fact have a roving eye, though her relationship with the Cassio figure is never consummated because he resists her advances. Jubal's Naomi is no Bianca, but a chaste religious woman. Desire for Shep's wife, envy at Jubal's elevation in rank, and a certain motiveless misanthropy are Pinky's primary motives for generating Shep's jealousy about Mae and Jubal. Interestingly, the character of Jake, Naomi's promised husband, allows the theme of jealousy and betrayal to be repeated in a subplot. There is also a handkerchief that serves as a romantic token, though in this case it is given by Naomi to Jubal and afterward has no further bearing on the plot. See also entries 2800 and 2804.

994 *Serenade*
1956. U.S. Warner Bros. Sound, col., 121 mins. Anthony Mann.

Adapted from a novel by James M. Cain. Damon Vincente, a farmworker with a stunning operatic voice, becomes a singer at Lardelli's restaurant in San Francisco, where he is discovered by Charles Winthrop, a musical promoter, and seductive heiress Kendall Hale (who he had met earlier as a farmworker). Eventually giving into Hale, Damon goes on tour with Winthrop and Hale, but he cancels a date with her to rehearse *Otello* at the Met in New York, a decision that leads Hale to look elsewhere for love and causes Damon to leave in midperformance. After a breakdown in Mexico City, he is nursed back to health by Juana Montes, who encourages him to regain his voice. The two fall in love and are married, and Damon returns to singing at Lardelli's. When Winthrop offers Damon a second chance at operatic fame, the return of Hale into his life leads to Juana's jealousy and soon what appears to be her accidental death in a bus accident. Injured, Juana makes Damon promise to give his performance, which he does, and he learns afterward that Juana will recover.

The film references *Otello*. Compare *For the First Time*.

995 *Touch of Evil*
1958. U.S. Universal Studios. Sound, b&w. Original 1958, release 93 mins.; 1975 preview version, 108 mins.; 1998 restoration, 111 mins. Orson Welles.

A few years after finishing his *Othello* (entry 452), Welles directed, rewrote, and acted in his last Hollywood

film, a baroque film noir often cited as the "epitaph" for the classical period of this genre. He heavily revised the Paul Monash screenplay for *Badge of Evil* (itself based on the novel by "Whit Masterson," a pseudonym for the pulp fiction team of Robert Wade and William Miller). The radical modifications Welles made to the plot strongly indicate *Othello*'s influence. Most overtly, he foregrounded an interracial relationship by reversing the original nationalities of the lead roles, instead making the male an official with the Mexican government (Charlton Heston's Miguel Vargas) and his wife an American (Janet Leigh's Susan Vargas), thereby echoing Othello-Desdemona. Welles also transposed the locale from a nameless California city to the fictional setting of "Los Robles," a nightmarish town that straddles both sides of the Mexican American border, much as Cyprus, as an outpost of the Venetian empire, is itself situated as a border on the edge of "civilization," as Detective Hank Quinlan (Welles) refers to the United States. (Fortuitously, "Los Robles" was actually shot in *Venice*, albeit Venice Beach, California.) The timing of the action (a few confusing days) in both play and film nearly perfectly coincides, whereas in the respective sources (Whit Masterson's novel *Badge of Evil*; Shakespeare's source is one of the stories in Cinthio Giambattista Giraldi's Hecatommithi [Islele]), the narratives take place over weeks. And, just as the theme of marriage is heavily underlined in *Othello*, Welles makes the Vargas couple newlyweds (they had been married for years in the screenplay, with a daughter). In fact, Welles's extensive description of the opening scene in *Touch of Evil* could just as easily describe the play: "A honeymoon couple, desperately in love, is abruptly separated by a violent incident...—an incident which, although it has no personal bearing on either of them, the man considers as a matter of his urgent professional concern."

Other traces of the subterranean *Othello* elements emerge throughout the film. Words such as "jealous," "reputation," and "honest," which do not appear in Welles's sources, are emphasized in *Touch of Evil*'s dialogue, just as they are in *Othello*. A character such as the Night Man (Dennis Weaver) recalls "the complete Shakespearean clown," according to Welles; the Night Man also, Emilia-like, introduces a discussion of the sheets on the bed of the Desdemona/Susan Vargas figure. The Othello/Vargas figure spends most of the film seeking evidence manipulated by the Iago/Quinlan figure; there's even a handkerchief exchanged between Vargas and Quinlan at a key moment. A Cassio-like role is fulfilled by Pancho (Valentin de Vargas), a Mexican hood; there are traces of Roderigo in Menzies (Joseph Calleia), Quinlan's naïve sidekick (Quinlan and Menzies eventually kill one another). Quinlan insinuates that Vargas has "that young wife of his hooked" on drugs; Brabantio likewise insists that Othello must have used some narcotic agent upon his daughter. Drunk, Quinlan recollects the "half-breed" who murdered his wife; this slur evokes the slanderously racialized references to horse-breeding that Iago launches up to Brabantio in the first scenes of the play. Perhaps the strongest single link between *Touch of Evil* and *Othello* arises from Quinlan's meditation on the method of his wife's murder, saying "the smart way to kill" is *strangulation*: "You don't leave fingerprints on a piece of string." Nowhere in either Masterson or Monash is any strangulation mentioned whatsoever; Welles here clearly recollects *Othello*, where Iago's infamous instructions set the stage, as it were, for all subsequent theatrical strangulations ("Do it not with poison. Strangle her in her bed, even the bed she hath contaminated").

As if Quinlan's reminiscence about his wife were not enough unto itself, *Touch of Evil* climaxes with a graphically portrayed strangulation scene, which bears the (displaced) fingerprints of Shakespeare. Local crime boss Uncle Joe Grandi (Akim Tamiroff) invites Quinlan into the hotel room where Susan Vargas has been drugged, apparently to show him that he has performed his duty, but unaware that Quinlan plans to murder him. Upon entering, Quinlan instructs Grandi, "Turn out the lights," just as Othello incants, "Put out the light." Quinlan murders Grandi in an attempt to frame Susan, but ruinously forgets his cane at the crime scene (one critic even called this "ocular proof"). In the final episode of the film, Vargas convinces Menzies to wear a microphone so he can record Quinlan's confession. Welles acknowledged that this particular scene echoed *Othello*. When the *Cahiers* interviewers in 1958 asked him whether "the greatest influence discernible in your work was Shakespeare?" (to which Welles responded, "Yes, without any doubt"), they continued by referring to the Night Man (who Welles conceded as Shakespearean, as noted above), and then they specifically cited this moment: "The way you direct the scene where Heston is listening to the conversation between Quinlan and Menzies makes it seem like the scene where Othello is listening to the conversation between Iago and Bianca [*sic*]." Welles seemed pleased but surprised by the resemblance—"I hadn't thought of it, but yes, it's true!"—without admitting any further debt to the play. (SN)

996 *For the First Time* (*Serenade einer Grossen Liebe*)
1959. U.S., Italy, and Germany. Corona Filmproduktion, MGM, Orion Films, and Titanus. Sound, col., 97 mins. Rudolph Maté.

In this musical, Tonio Costa, a conceited, rootless opera star, falls in love with Christa, a deaf woman, and reforms his professional life in an effort to raise funds so that she can have an operation to hear again.

Includes the finale from Verdi's *Otello* (entry 1680). Compare *Serenade*.

997 *Gody molodyye* (*Age of Youth*)
1960. USSR. Dovzhenko Film Studio. Sound, col., 81 mins. Alexei Mishurin.

Adapted from a story by A. Pereguda. This Ukrainian musical comedy centers around Natasha, a woman dancer, who replaces Lesik, a male dancer who has broken his leg. When still dressed as a boy, she rushes to catch a train to make an audition in Kiev; she discovers she has forgotten her ticket and is befriended by Sergei, a young singer, who serenades her (thinking she is "Lesik") as they ride on the train top. The next morning, Sergei meets Natasha (now as a girl), becoming infatuated with her; Natasha presents herself as Lesik's sister, and when Sergei's audition goes badly, she encourages him to sing instead. Natasha asks Volodya, a conductor who also loves her, to use his influence to help the two auditioners, but when Sergei discovers this, he becomes offended and leaves; chastened, Natasha vows to apply honestly the next year, and, dressed as Lesik, she again sees Sergei as the two leave Kiev. After spending the day together, Natasha reveals her true identity to Sergei.

Sergei's initial audition piece is from *Othello*. The situation of the cross-dressed lover bears a general resemblance to *As You Like It* and *Twelfth Night*, though there is no direct allusion to either play.

998 *Otelo* (*Wenezianski Mawr*)
1960. USSR. Qartuli Pilmi (or Gruzia Film). Sound, col., 95 mins. Vakhtang Chabukiani.

Ballet to music of Arthur Machavariani, originally produced in 1957; this USSR production starred the Paliashvili Opera Theater and Ballet of Tbilisi. See also entry 457.

999 *Saptapadi*
1961. India. Alochaya Productions. Sound, b&w, 163 mins. Ajay Kar.

In World War II, Krishnendu Mukerjee, a humble priest working at a field hospital, is brought a wounded woman whom he recognizes as Rina Brown, his Anglo-Indian former lover. The sight of her prompts a flashback to his college days, where he, as a promising medical student, wooed her, even though she was involved with another man. He discovers that Rina has been cast as Desdemona and learns the part of Othello to impress her. When her costar (and boyfriend) fails to show up for the performance, Krishnendu takes his place, and his passionate performance initiates her romance. Krishnendu's father opposes their marriage and makes Rina promise she will never see Krishnendu again, so she leaves him. When she sees Krishnendu again (in the present), she joins the Indian army and leaves lest she break down, but she tells him of her feelings before doing so. As a doctor at the war front, Krishnendu meets Rina yet again after she is wounded in a bomb attack. He reveals a letter to her in which his father removes the obstacle to their love, and the two are happily reunited.

In one early passage, Rina's boyfriend rehearses Othello's "It is the cause" speech (*Othello* 5.2), delivering it woodenly. From the adjacent balcony, Rina sees Krishnendu deliver the speech with more polish; he turns the final line "I'll smell it on the tree" into a joke about bad breath (an indication of Krishnendu's playful character). Later, we see two extended excerpts from the stage performance of *Othello*, both from 5.2: Othello's murder of Desdemona, and his final speech and suicide. The performance is filmed cinematically rather than as a stage performance (though there are a few reaction shots of the audience). The moody noir lighting and shadows, some choices of shots, and windy sound effects suggest the influence of Welles's *Othello* (entry 452). Reportedly, this film is currently being remade by Basu Chatterjee under the title *Pratiksha*. It will have a more contemporary setting, though the *Othello* elements will be retained.

1000 *All Night Long*
1962. U.K. Rank Organization Film Productions Ltd. Sound, b&w, 95 mins. Basil Dearden.

Transposes Shakespeare's plot to the after-hours British jazz scene of the 1960s. Rod Hamilton, a millionaire jazz fan, is throwing a surprise anniversary party for Aurelia Rex, a black bandleader, and his wife Delia Lane, a jazz songstress who retired when the two got married. Johnny Cousin, Rex's scheming drummer, desires a band of his own, but he cannot get financial backing without including Delia (whom he also secretly loves), and so he resolves to break up Rex and Delia's marriage by concocting the story of an affair between Delia and Cass, Rex's saxophone player and manager of the band. After having given Cass a joint to smoke, Johnny instigates a fight between Cass and crass Lou Berger, a jazz impresario, after which Rex strips him of his place in the band. Using a stolen cigarette case and a doctored tape recording as evidence, Johnny plays on Rex's insecurities, and when Cass and Delia play a duet in celebration of the anniversary, Rex erupts in fury, nearly choking Delia to death and knocking Cass from a balcony. Emily, Johnny's mousy wife, reveals Johnny's scheming lies, and as Rex and Delia walk together into the dawn, Johnny is left alone to play madly on his drum kit.

Though most commentators have focused on the celebrity jazz guests at Rod's party—Charles Mingus, Johnny Dankworth, Dave Brubeck, Tubby Hayes, and others contribute musical numbers—this free transposition of Shakespeare's *Othello* to a jazz milieu is skillfully and imaginatively handled. Shakespeare's dialogue is replaced by hipster jargon, which has unfortunately dated somewhat badly. Oddly for a film about jazz, tensions between white and black musicians are hardly addressed at all; the interracial nature of Rex and Delia's marriage and Cass's relationship with Bianca, a black groupie, is never remarked on, and the topic of racism never appears but as the subtlest and most fleeting of subtexts (except for one crass comment by Johnny about reverse racism for white musicians). Rather, amidst the hip camaraderie of the jazz world are revealed Johnny's frustrated ambitions as an aging sideman who senses his prospects are quickly slipping away. Patrick McGoohan's brilliant performance, the centerpiece of the film, stresses the improvisatory and nervously obsequious qualities of Iago's insinuations, revealing in his final scene with Emily the repugnant depths of Johnny's self-loathing and selfishness. The film noir visual style and often frenetic jazz score add to the sense of understated menace and doom beneath the surface glamour of Rod's opulent hipster lifestyle. An underrated film that deserves far more attention.

1001 *Capricio All'Italiana*
1968. Italy. Sound, col., 83 mins. (total film). Pier Paolo Pasolini (segment, "Che cosa sono le nuvole?").

A six-segment showcase of Italian directors. In one of the segments, "Che cosa sono le nuvole?" marionettes offer a performance of *Othello*, and the public, angered by the malignity of Iago, intervenes and destroys the puppets. The famous Italian comic Toto voices the puppet of Iago. An interesting representation of popular resistance to the trajectory of Shakespeare's tragedy.

1002 *The Flesh and Blood Show*
1972. U.K. Pete Walker Productions. Sound, col., 93 mins. Pete Walker.

A group of eight young actors, rehearsing a sexy review at the Dome, an abandoned seaside theater, are assaulted by a mysterious killer. In a long flashback sequence (initiated by Othello's exchange with Iago at 4.1.175–95, ending with "get me some poison"), we learn that the killer is Sir Arnold Gates, an actor who is cuckolded by his wife (who played Desdemona) with Harry Mulligan, the actor playing Cassio. In the flashback, we see Gates in performance as Othello in 4.1 noticing his wife's dress unlaced at her line "the love I bear to Cassio." After the scene is interrupted, Gates, still in makeup and costume, catches the two in flagrante delicto backstage after hours; he intones Othello's line "This night I'll not / expostulate with her, lest her body and beauty / unprovide my mind again" (4.1) as a little girl watches, then seals the two actors in a room to die. A repeated mirror motif underlines the doubled relationship between the play and reality. Various clues allow us to conclude that the little girl is Julia Dawson, a member of the group of young actors and Gates's daughter and accomplice. Compare *Theatre of Blood*.

1003 *Catch My Soul* (aka *Sante Fe Satan*)
1973. U.K. and U.S. Metromedia Productions. Sound, col., 97 mins. Patrick McGoohan.

In the rock opera *Catch My Soul*, Othello was reconceived as the charismatic leader of a hippie religious commune undone by a demonic Iago. Patrick McGoohan's film version featured Richie Havens, the popular black folk singer, in the role of Othello, presenting him as a clearly Christlike martyr dressed in a white robe who kills Desdemona and himself in a village church. Although the independent film is rather crudely made, its engagement with contradictions and conflicts within 1960s counterculture, particularly the free love movement, communal living, and religious revivalism, make it a fascinating historical document, comparable to *Jesus Christ Superstar*. The title is taken from Othello's dramatically ironic declaration of his love for Desdemona in 3.3: "Perdition catch my soul, / But I do love thee! and when I love thee not, / Chaos is come again." There are numerous allusions to Shakespeare's dialogue in all of the songs. See also entry 455.

1004 *Switchblade Sisters* (aka *The Jezebels*)
1975. U.S. Surrogate Films and Centaur Productions. Sound, col., 96 mins. Jack Hill.

Lace is leader of the Dagger Debs, a girl gang affiliated with the Silver Daggers, headed by her boyfriend Dominic. Lace and the Debs tangle with Maggie, a tough new girl in the neighborhood who humiliates Patch, one of the Debs, in a fight. When the girls are arrested, Lace rescues Maggie from the lesbian matron Mom, and the two become friends. Upon their release, Patch, jealous of Maggie's new friendship with Lace and position of power in the Debs, insinuates that Dominic loves Maggie and denigrates Maggie's plans to confront a rival gang headed by Crabs, who poses as a community leader. Lace, pregnant with Dominic's baby, secretly betrays the Debs in an effort to undermine Maggie's plans, and Dominic is accidentally killed. In the Debs' payback fight with Crabs' gang, Patch kills Crabs to prevent him from revealing Lace's betrayal. When Maggie takes control of the Debs and changes their name to the Jezebels, Patch tries to prove that Maggie betrayed the gang. Maggie and Lace fight, and Maggie kills Lace. As the girls are arrested, Patch is rejected by the gang and Maggie voices her defiance.

This exploitation film freely adapts elements of the jealousy plot from *Othello*. In this version, the genders are reversed—Patch takes the part of Iago, Lace of Othello, Dominic of Othello, and Maggie of Cassio. Too, the Iago figure's motivation is changed: Patch's hatred for Maggie first springs from Maggie's besting her in a fight over a table at a burger joint (after this incident, she says, as Iago does of Othello, "I hate her"), but later she is also motivated by envy of Maggie's rise to power in the gang and friendship with Lace. Unbeknownst to Patch or Lace, Dominic has raped Maggie even as he's been seeing Lace; that is, Dominic, not Maggie, has betrayed Lace, a point underlined when Dominic tries to force Lace to get an abortion. At several points in the movie, Patch and Lace view Maggie and Dominic together from afar in ways that recall Iago and Othello's observation of Cassio and Desdemona. Interestingly, the film preaches the virtues of female solidarity and the untrustworthiness of men, a solidarity that Lace foolishly, repeatedly betrays out of misplaced love for Dominic. Aside from Patch's declaration of hate for Maggie, the film contains no echoes of Shakespeare's language.

DVD includes an audio commentary by the director and Quentin Tarantino, and an outro by Tarantino, which reference *Othello*.

1005 *Zvezdi v kosite, salzi v ochite* (*Stars in Her Hair, Tears in Her Eyes*)
1977. Bulgaria. Boyana Film, Bulgarofilm, and Haemus Grupa. Sound, b&w, 102 mins. Ivan Nitchev.

At the turn of the twentieth century, a traveling company of actors travels Bulgaria giving performances of the classics to rural villages. After arriving in a small town to perform *Othello*, the group's Desdemona falls ill and a local schoolteacher substitutes for her. Afterward she joins the troupe and over time becomes the leading lady of the company. The film chronicles the trials of the company as the actors travel to small towns, suffer poverty and personal indignities, and try to remain true to their educational ideals. The film stresses that it is the poor and not the wealthy who most appreciate the company's performances. When the company eventually becomes a state-owned enterprise with a fixed repertoire filled with artistic compromise, it quickly falls apart, and several members, led by the schoolteacher, decide to return to a theatrical life on the road.

1006 *Otello* (*Othello, ou La déficience de la femme*)
1979. Italy. CPTV Torino. Sound, col., 77 mins. Carmelo Bene.

Bene's avant-garde reenvisioning of *Othello*, recorded in a made-for-television film. His innovation is to reverse Shakespeare's scenario, making Desdemona the jealous spouse and using b&w symbolically rather than realistically. This film was never commercially released.

1007 *Othello, el comando negro* (*Othello, the Black Commando*)
1982. Spain and France. Eurociné and M.B. Diffusion, S.A. Sound, col., 122 mins. Max H. Boulois.

This adaptation transfers Shakespeare's characters and plot to the murky world of contemporary Third World politics. When a Red Cross convoy in Africa is attacked, mercenary general Othello is hired by U.S. Senator Fergusson and his daughter Dede to protect the aid workers. As Dede cares for the sick and wounded in an African village, Othello and his men hold off a rogue puppet general and his white ally's army; at one point, Othello single-handedly attacks the army and eventually kills the black general. After the mercenaries and aid workers are evacuated to Othello's mercenary camp, Dede and Othello fall in love. Iago broods over Michael Cassius's elevation to second in command (he has been retired to diplomatic duty) and seethes with hatred about Othello and Dede's interrracial relationship; Emily, his promiscuous wife, reveals that he is impotent. Dede's father arrives and expresses his racist horror at Dede's marriage to Othello, accusing him of witchcraft. At a party for the newlyweds, Cassius, drunk through Iago's wiles, starts a brawl when a man calls Bianca, his girlfriend, a whore. Othello has Cassius arrested, but Iago encourages him to ask for Dede's help in restoring him to the general's favor; meanwhile Iago is photographing their meetings and showing them to Othello. When Othello asks for proof of Dede's infidelity, Iago supplies a doctored tape of Cassius trashing Bianca. As a result, Othello asks Iago to have Cassius murdered, and Othello confronts Dede with accusations of infidelity with Cassius and others, killing her in a moment of jealous rage. Soon we learn that Cassius has eluded his assassins, and Emily reveals Iago's treachery and impotence; Iago shoots her, Othello shoots Iago, and despite Cassius's loyal attempt to protect Othello from arrest by Ludovico and Montano, Othello commits suicide.

At first, *Othello, el commando negro* seems a routine if crudely made action film, but in its second half the parallels to Shakespeare's play come into focus. Shakespeare's dialogue survives only in occasional phrases lifted or lightly adapted from the original—Iago refers to General Othello's "thick lips," and upon discovering Dede's death, Emily tells Othello, "Your soul is blacker than your skin." However, most of *Othello*'s major characters and many of its motifs are transposed to the contemporary milieu—Ludovico becomes a U.S. State Department envoy, and Montano the general of a banana republic. (Some of the motifs appear in other films: the idea of Iago using a doctored tape recording surfaces in *All Night Long*, and the image of Othello loading a gun as Iago speaks of Desdemona's infidelity is used in Parker's *Othello*.) At times Othello's mercenary status poses a problem: as a gun for hire, Othello might come off as amoral rather than noble, so to demonstrate his moral scruples the film features an episode in which Othello refuses to back a rebel seeking to install himself forcibly as president. The final scenes of the film follow the final scenes of Shakespeare's play quite closely, so much so that Dede carries a handkerchief into her death scene, even though it has no function at all in the plot. Boulois's script dutifully includes the many motives Shakespeare gives

Iago—envy of Cassio's appointment, awareness of his wife's infidelity with Othello, racist disgust at Othello and Dede's romance, and perverse camaraderie with the general—but it is Emily's accusation that he is impotent and a "faggot" that most angers and motivates him. Lest we forget his nature, Iago's favorite outfit is a white suit with a black cowboy hat, and he typically wears gloves, as if keeping the world at a remove. Iago's insinuations to Othello are laced with misogynistic concerns about his lost manhood now that he is married and the men's loss of respect for his command now that he's been cuckolded. Othello easily takes up that misogyny, so easily that it is not clear the film critiques rather than endorses that view. (The presentation of Emily and Bianca as openly promiscuous tramps only reinforces that problem.) Though Boulois wants to emphasize the nasty racism that plagues Othello (the general must repeatedly endure hearing himself called a "nigger"), the film actually stresses the ugly "action film" culture of military machismo that Othello and Iago share and that the film struggles to repudiate. See also entry 457.

1008 *Otello*
1986. Italy and Netherlands. Golan-Globus, Cannon Productions, Italian International Film, and Cannon City Produktie Maatschappij B.V. Sound, col., 122 mins.
Franco Zeffirelli.

Film of Verdi's opera (entry 1680), as adapted by Franco Zeffirelli. Included in this bibliography because the production is conceived as a film, not as the record of a theatrical performance, and because Zeffirelli is a noted adapter of Shakespeare to film. The production features a huge cast in often cavernous sets and opulent period costumes (see, for example, the banquet scene in honor of

Jose van Dam (Iago) and Placido Domingo (Otello) sing a duet in Zeffirelli's film of Verdi's opera *Otello* (1986). Courtesy of Douglas Lanier.

Othello's arrival in Cyprus), but Zeffirelli balances the epic scope of the spectacle against frequent close-ups of the principals so that the love and jealousy story retains its intimacy (brooding reaction shots of Iago are a particular favorite). In the love duet between Othello and Desdemona, Zeffirelli includes flashback sequences that clarify past events, reaching as far back as Othello's youthful history in Africa; another set of shots illustrates Cassio's lustful dream as reported by Iago. A number of choices of imagery are reminiscent of Welles's *Othello* (entry 452): Iago's sinister "Credo in un Dio crudel" aria is delivered in a chapel that looks like the cistern in Welles's *Othello*; Otello first confronts Desdemona in an armory; and the precipitous stairs and battlements of the castle, weblike shadows, screens, and bars have a Wellesian quality. A repeated image of Christ on the cross underlines Iago's devilry and Otello's Christlike suffering at his hands, and an icy moonlight pervading many of the shots reminds the viewer of the doomed nature of the couple.

1009 *D.O.A.*
1988. U.S. Bigelow Productions, Silver Screen Partners, and Touchstone Pictures. Sound, col., 96 mins. Rocky Morton and Annabel Jankel.

Saddled with a deteriorating marriage and struggling to retain his job, Dexter Cornell, a creative writing professor at the University of Texas and would-be novelist, is pestered by Nick Lang, one of his students, to read his first novel. Soon after, Nick is found dead, killed in a fall, and Dexter surmises that Nick had been involved with his wife. After an alcoholic binge, Dexter discovers that he has been given a slow-acting poison and has forty-eight hours to live. He enlists a graduate student, Sydney Fuller, to help him track down his killer as he struggles to elude the police. After his wife is killed, Dexter confronts the murderer, a fellow professor, Hal Petersham, who intended to steal Nick's novel and publish it as his own.

Two passing references are included. In a classroom scene, Dexter asks for literary references to "green"; Nick offers *Antony and Cleopatra*, 1.5 ("My salad days, / When I was green in judgment") and *Othello* 3.3, on jealousy ("the green-eyed monster"). The second line offers an important clue to the motives behind the murders to come. In the second, in his eulogy for Nick a Shakespeare professor cites, "To sue to live, I find I seek to die; And, seeking death, find life: let it come on," misidentifying it as from *Romeo and Juliet* (it is from *Measure for Measure* 3.1).

1010 *Internal Affairs*
1990. U.S. Out of the Town Films and Paramount Pictures. Sound, col., 115 mins. Michael Figgis.

Raymond Avilla, a Latin American policeman, is hired for the internal affairs department of the Los Angeles Police Department. As he and his partner Amy Wallace investigate a drug-addicted officer, Van Stretch, they become aware of the shady dealings of corrupt, white policeman Dennis Peck. To protect himself, Peck has Stretch killed, but Demetrios, the driver for the assassin he hires, implicates Peck before Demetrios is himself killed. Meanwhile, in an effort to unnerve Avilla, Peck, a womanizer, makes him believe that he is having an affair with Avilla's white wife Kathleen, a museum curator. Peck's schemes unravel as he tries to kill or intimidate those who might expose him, and he has a final showdown with Avilla at Avilla's home, with Kathleen watching.

This neo-noir thriller recasts a number of motifs from *Othello*, most notably interracial marriage and Iago's generation of sexual jealousy in Othello. Here, the romantic catalyst for that jealousy is the Iago figure himself, Peck, who Avilla sees having lunch with his wife; later, Peck beats Avilla as he lies about his sexual exploits with Avilla's wife, and he leaves her panties, the equivalent of Desdemona's handkerchief, as proof of his tryst. In a scene vaguely reminiscent of Lodovico's arrival in 4.1 and Othello's confrontation of Desdemona in 4.2, Avilla confronts his wife about her lunch with Peck and slaps her in front of an important artist and various dinner guests; when Avilla later returns home, he tells Kathleen that he will kill her if she is unfaithful. In an extended fantasy sequence that has affinities to the fantasy sequences of Oliver Parker's *Othello*, Avilla imagines Peck and Kathleen in the midst of sex. Peck's skill at using jealousy to prompt others to murder can be seen in a short sequence with Peck's fellow officer Steven Arrocas and his wife Tova; Peck convinces Steven to shoot his wife (who has just been caught having sex with Peck) because she is a tramp. Of some interest are Peck's motives. Unlike Iago, Peck has no trace of envy. He not only uses his sexual charisma to get information from and silence women who might testify against him, but also plays on Avilla's insecurities (only barely sketched in) about his wife's sexual attractiveness, their career-couple drifting marriage, and his Latino heritage (at one point, Peck taunts him that Latin fighters are too macho and therefore used up young). Peck's final speech targets the Avillas as selfish, childless yuppies and seeks to portray his own criminal activities as self-sacrificing care for his eight children. Even so, the film stresses the familiar noir theme that Peck and Avilla are uncomfortably similar in their ruthless determination and willingness to bend the law.

1011 *Une histoire inventée (An Imaginary Tale)*
1990. Canada. Les Productions C.M. Luca and Les films telescene Inc. Sound, col., 100 mins. André Forcier.

A serio-comic, somewhat surrealistic farce about various characters' unrequited or misdirected love, centered around Gaston, a Montreal trumpet player in the midst of a slowly declining career. Florence, a beautiful middle-aged woman, is madly in love with Gaston, but, unlike Florence's many pining ex-lovers, he is indifferent to her charms. Instead he falls for Soledad, Florence's young daughter and an actress, though he cannot bring himself to declare his love. Soledad is alienated from her boyfriend Tibo, who has romantically betrayed Soledad with his female dresser, even though he still loves her. Soledad and Tibo are playing Desdemona and Othello in a sexy amateur production of Shakespeare's play; unbeknownst to the director Toni, the audiences are being hired by Toni's mafioso uncle Gros Pierre, who is also financing the play. For one performance of the play, Gaston is handcuffed by his friends to Soledad backstage, leading to his appearance with her onstage as Desdemona, much to the audience's delight. However, Tibo becomes jealous, leading to disaster for the two men. In the end, Florence and Soledad are reconciled.

In French. No English subtitles. (DL)

NB: Based on a novel of the same name. The opening of the film is very much like that of *All Night Long*. (RB)

1012 *True Identity*

1991. U.S. Sandollar Productions, Silver Screen Partners IV, and Touchstone Pictures. Sound, col., 93 mins. Charles Lane.

In this expansion of a *Saturday Night Live* sketch (by Andy Breckman, who also wrote the film's script), Miles Pope, a struggling black actor, dreams of playing Othello, though he is stuck in stereotypical or dead-end roles. When on an airplane he learns of the true identity of Leland Carver (actually Frank Luchino, a mobster who the authorities believe to be dead), Pope must disguise himself as a white man—complete with whiteface makeup—to elude Carver's assassins. Pope kills his white hitman, then by a quirk of fate he is forced to impersonate him; in the process, he meets Kristi, a beautiful interior decorator who works for Carver. Forced to juggle various roles to survive, Pope gets a role in a production of *Othello* financed by Carver. Uncovering Pope's ruses, Carver plans to kill Pope during his performance of *Othello*, but Pope anticipates his scheme and tricks Carver into implicating himself and revealing his true identity.

Written as a Hollywood star vehicle for Lenny Henry, the black British comedian, *True Identity* does not replicate the plot of *Othello*, though Shakespeare's play has a central role in the plot. The film contains several citations: Pope practices Othello's speech "My blood begins my safer guides to rule" (*Othello* 2.3.187–90) in the mirror (he stumbles on the word "collied"), then practices "for know, Iago, / But that I love the gentle Desdemona" (1.2.24–25) as he walks into the hitman's gunfire; for his audition speech, he uses Othello's "had it pleased heaven / To try me with affliction" speech (4.2.49–55, 59–61); and of Pope's stage performance as Othello, we see substantial portions of his conversation with Desdemona regarding

the handkerchief in 3.4 and his conversation with Iago about it in 4.1. After Pope is shot, he launches into pseudo-Shakespearean verse to accuse Carver:

O Francis, why dost thou seek to have me slain,
With a promise made upon the plane,
To have your secret here remain,
When now my life's blood doth stain?

One spectator remarks about the performance, "No matter how many times I see Shakespeare, I always get something new out of it." As it is for Lem Anderson in *Paradise in Harlem* (above), the playing of Othello for Pope serves as a validation of his artistry as a black actor, even though Othello has traditionally been a blackface part. Ironically, Pope's many disguises, particularly his whiteface disguise as Anthony the hitman, work to demonstrate his theatrical virtuosity, so that, by film's end, his performance as Othello no longer has quite the symbolic significance it once did. The film interestingly engages the stigma of blackface attached to the role of Othello.

1013 *Aladdin*

1992. U.S. Walt Disney Pictures. Sound, col., 90 mins. Ron Clements and John Musker.

The Sultan gives his overly picky daughter Jasmine three days to find a husband. She escapes his palace and meets Aladdin, a streetwise boy, who falls in love with her. As Jafar, the Sultan's evil vizier, uses magic to make Jasmine his bride and thus become Sultan himself, Aladdin finds a magic lamp that, when rubbed, produces a Genie who swears fealty to him. After at first losing the lamp to Jafar, Aladdin, regaining the lamp with the help of his monkey Abu, uses the Genie's magic to defeat Jafar and win the princess.

Iago, Jafar's angry, cynical parrot, is one of the villains of the story. The Shakespearean sub-text does not extend very far beyond the name itself, though there is a love scene between Aladdin and Jasmine on a balcony (no direct references to *Romeo and Juliet*, however). Compare *The Little Mermaid*.

1014 *The Playboys*

1992. Ireland, U.K., and U.S. Samuel Goldwyn Company. Sound, col., 109 mins. Gillies MacKinnon.

By having a child out of wedlock and not revealing the father, Tara McGuire, a strong-willed young seamstress, has caused a scandal in her Irish village. The local priest pressures her to marry the local constable, Brendan Hegarty, who loves her and stalks her, but when a traveling troupe of actors called The Playboys arrives in town, she becomes attracted to Tom Casey, a free-spirited actor in the company. As their romance develops, Tom learns that Brendan is the father of the child, and Brendan becomes increasingly jealous and threatening about their relationship. After Brendan steals Tara's child, Brendan and Tom have a violent confrontation after a show; Brendan leaves the village, and Tom, Tara, and child Jimmy leave for Dublin with the troupe.

We see several excerpts from the troupe's performances, one of which is a passage from *Othello*, in which Iago reveals the handkerchief to Othello and Othello offers his "Farewell the tranquil mind" speech. Later, in a clear parallel, Brendan finds Tara's handkerchief in an isolated barn, confirmation that the two have had a tryst; in his jealous rage, he burns the barn, presaging his violent behavior to come.

1015 *Interview with the Vampire*
1994. U.S. Warner Bros. Sound, col., 122 mins. Neil Jordan.

Handled as an extended interview of Louis, a 200-year-old vampire, this film chronicles the exploits of the decadent, handsome vampire Lestat in eighteenth-century New Orleans. Though Lestat converts Louis to vampirism, Louis remains wracked with guilt about his need to kill and Lestat's disdainful attitude toward mortals. The two meet Claudia, a child vampire. She becomes bitter when Lestat tells her she will never grow up, and she kills him. Louis and Claudia go on a European tour where in Paris they meet Armand and his Theatre des Vampires, a grisly spectacle for upper-class audiences. When the vampires learn that Claudia has killed one of her own kind (a primal crime), they take revenge upon Claudia and a dollmaker who has adopted her by exposing them to sunlight; they also bury Louis alive, but he is rescued by Armand, after which Louis kills the vampires as they emerge from their burning crypts. Later, he encounters Lestat, who is not dead, but he refuses to hunt with him. In the present, the reporter interviewing Louis expresses his envy of the vampire's state, and is chased by Louis and Lestat.

One mark of Lestat's decadent distance from murder is his tendency to quote Shakespeare. When he kills a woman while watching a play, Lestat tells Louis, "You'll get used to killing. Just forget about that mortal coil," referencing the phrase from Hamlet's "To be or not to be" speech. When the two murder a whore, Lestat does an extended riff on Othello's "put out the light" speech in *Othello* 5.2. Claudia picks up his attitude when she kills Lestat: watching Lestat bleed from a neck wound, she says, "Good night, sweet prince. May flights of devils wing you to your rest," paraphrasing Horatio's final words to Hamlet.

1016 *Kaliyattam* (*Play of the God*)
1997. India. New Generation Cinema. Sound, col., 130 mins. Jayaraaj Rajasekharan Nair.

A Keralian adaptation of *Othello*, based upon the Theyyam dance festivals of North Kerala in India, in which villagers costume themselves as gods, dance, and settle village conflicts. Perumalayan, a god who is facially disfigured, wins the hand of Thamara, the beautiful daughter of a wealthy land owner, and the two elope to the mountain region of Kerala. Paniyan covets the prized role of Theechamundi, and so he works to breed Perumalayan's jealousy by convincing him that Thamara is being unfaithful with Perumalayan's assistant Kanthan; to implicate Kanthan, Paniyan plants a silken robe that Perumalayan gave Thamara in his possession. Convinced of her betrayal, Perumalayan strangles Thamara in her sleep, as Paniyan orchestrates the murders of Kanthan and Unni Thampuran (who also loves Thamara). When Perumalayan learns the truth of Thamara's innocence and Paniyan's treachery from Paniyan's wife Cheera (who Paniyan also murders), he reduces Paniyan to a vegetable as his revenge. Compare *In Othello* (entry 1024). See also entry 460.

1017 *Othello: Dangerous Desire* (aka *Othello 2000*)
1997. U.S. Moonlight Entertainment. Sound, col., 85 mins. Joe D'Amato.

Hardcore pornography. A series of unrelated interracial trysts, opening with a scene in which drifter Othello rescues Desdemona from a harassing motorcycle gang.

Little Shakespearean content beyond the title, character names, and interracial nature of the couplings.

1018 *Black and White*
1999. U.S. Screen Gems/Palm Pictures. Sound, col., 98 mins. James Toback.

Set in New York, the film uses a number of plots to explore various interracial and intraracial betrayals and triangles. The opening scene involves a black man having sex with two white women in Central Park, who are then spotted and watched by a black man. A documentary filmmaker (Brooke Shields) and her gay husband (Robert Downey Jr.) interested in white kids who "act black" videotape various characters. The film's link to *Othello* is spelled out in a classroom scene where white kids and black kids talk about not being what their race expects them to be; sometimes you don't want to be what your race is supposed to be. The teacher (Jared Leto) ends the class by mentioning Shakespeare's Othello. "Iago, who has no identity, says I am not what I am."

DVD: On audio commentary, Toback spells out the film's derivation from *Othello* while commenting on a scene shot on the campus of Columbia University, where a black basketball star is set up by a white former criminal turned cop (Ben Stiller) to take a bribe. Toback says, "Here is where the actual narrative really pops in—with Ben Stiller and we don't know who he is because he is pretending to be someone else—seducing Allan Houston. Iago and Othello corrupting someone of fundamental innocence, a bribe on the Columbia campus. The central narrative only starting here with a bribe is beginning to register right here. The whole theme of the movie and much of my work is identity. Iago. "I am not what I am." See also Toback's *Two Girls and a Guy* (1997), also starring Robert Downey Jr.

See also *O* for another *Othello* as a basketball player and set in a high school. And see *Coming Soon* for another New York kids' film with a classroom scene involving *Othello*. (RB)

1019 *Coming Soon*
1999. U.S. Bandeira Entertainment, Coming Soon LLC, Key Entertainment, and Nordcapital. Sound, col., 96 mins. Collette Burson.

Three prep school senior girls search for romantic and sexual fulfillment as they apply to ivy league colleges.

In a passing reference to *Othello*, a teacher assigns an essay on the play's building to a climax, an oblique reference to one of the film's sexual themes.

1020 *Luna Papa*
1999. Tajikistan, Uzbekistan, Russia, Germany, Japan, Austria, Switzerland, and France. Euro Space, Films de l'Observatoire, NTV-Profit, Pandora Film, Prisma, Tadjik Filmstudio, Thomas Koerfer Film, and Viss. Sound, col., 107 mins. Bakhtyar Khudojnazarov.

In this magic realist drama, Mamlakat, a stagestruck girl from a Tajikistani village, becomes pregnant after a magical moonlit tryst with a actor. Rejected by her village, she, her father Safar, and her brother Nasreddin try to find the father of her child so she can marry him.

Includes several short excerpts from a performance of *Othello*, including the murder of Roderigo and Desdemona; Mamlakat also recites a brief passage from the balcony scene of *Romeo and Juliet*. In a witty moment, when Mamlakat arrives too late for an *Othello* production, she discovers a black ram and white ewe wandering on the stage near the bed.

1021 *O*
1999 (released 2001). U.S. Chickie the Cop, Daniel Fried Productions, FilmEngine, and Rhulen Entertainment. Sound, col., 95 mins. Tim Blake Nelson.

O transposes *Othello* to Palmetto Grove Academy, an elite private school in Charleston, South Carolina. Odin James, the only black student at the school, is the star player on the basketball team, beloved of its coach, Duke Goulding, and in love with Desi Brable, the white daughter of the school's dean. Hugo, Duke's son, is envious of Odin's popularity, both with other students and with his inattentive father, who publicly declares that Odin is like a son to him, and he is hurt by Odin choosing Michael, a teammate, as his "go-to" man. Hugo resolves to destroy his reputation by ruining his relationship with Desi, making Odin believe that she is having an affair with Michael. In this, he is aided by Roger Rodriguez, a rich but unlikeable boy who desires Desi, and by a handkerchief that Hugo's girlfriend Emily steals from Desi. On the eve of a championship game, Odin chokes Desi; Hugo engineers Roger's shooting of Michael, then shoots Roger himself. When Emily reveals Desi's innocence to Odin, Hugo shoots her, then Odin turns the gun on himself.

O is perhaps the most faithful of the teen Shakespeare adaptations that flourished in the 1990s. Though the characters use contemporary teenspeak rather than Shakespeare's dialogue, the characters and narrative resemble Shakespeare's quite closely. Indeed, the film goes out of its way to find close analogies for key scenes from Shakespeare's play: Brabantio's confrontation of Othello at the Venetian Senate in 1.3, for example, is recast as Dean Brable's confrontation of Odin about his secret sexual romance with his daughter, set in Coach Goulding's office (the scene ends with Brable's remark to Odin: "No, she deceived me. What makes you think she won't do the same to you?"); versions of Iago's first hints to Othello of Desdemona's infidelity with Cassio appear in a weight-room exchange between Odin and Hugo, where Hugo speaks about the sexual deviousness of white girls; Roger picks a fight with Michael at a drunken party that gets Michael ejected from the basketball team, after which Hugo encourages him to use Desi to regain Odin's and thus the coach's favor; and at Hugo's instigation, Odin overhears Michael make cocky slurs about a girl, Brandy, who he mistakes for Desi. Michael's slurs also include ugly racist remarks about Odin, part of the film's focus on buried racism that lies behind Odin's uneasy "heroic" position as Palmetto Grove's lone black sports star. Dean Brable's unstated but clear concern about his daughter's relationship with Odin is its interracial and sexual nature; in an early scene Desi and Odin joke about b&w sexual stereotypes, but as the film progresses, Odin succumbs to Hugo's stereotype of Desi as a sexually voracious white girl, and he begins to live out the stereotype of the angry, explosive, self-destructive black man. Odin and Desi's sex tryst at the Willows Hotel moves from tender passion to a near rape as Odin contemplates Hugo's insinuations about Desi's infidelity; his strangling of her later on moves rather suddenly and shockingly from tenderness to murder. Odin's final speech, delivered before his suicide, underlines the point by stressing that he was undone not by black ghetto life but by the machinations of a white prep school boy. Of some interest, too, is the complexity of Hugo's motivations, combining jealousy of his father's affection for Odin, envy of Odin's star status and anger at his preference for Michael, and anger at Michael's class status and easy affection with Desi and Emily; the repeated motif of a black hawk and white doves associated with Hugo (Hugo is a falconer) confirms but also complicates the film's racial themes. In addition to *Othello*, there is a brief reference in a classroom scene to Lady Macbeth's lines from *Macbeth* 1.7, "I have given suck, and know / How tender 'tis to love the babe that milks me," a line that resonates with Hugo's seemingly benign manipulativeness. In the same scene, Hugo offers a metacinematic smart-ass reply to the teacher's request that he name a Shakespeare poem: "I thought he wrote movies." Indeed, *O* contains many visual references to earlier Shakespeare films, including the televisual epilogue to Baz Luhrmann's *Romeo + Juliet* (entry 496) and the sexual dream sequences in Oliver Parker's *Othello*, to name but two. The film was originally made in 1999, but its release was delayed lest it rekindle memories of the Columbine High School shootings in the same year; it was eventually released in 2001. See also entry 461.

The DVD (deluxe edition) contains many extras referencing Shakespeare: a director's commentary track, interviews with the director and three principal cast members, four deleted scenes, and a trailer.

1022 *Alcatraz Avenue*
2000. U.S. Lather Rinse Repeat Productions. Sound, col., 90 mins. Tom Edgar.

Another film connecting Shakespeare and prison, although only indirectly in this case. Alcatraz Prison is pointedly referenced. The film begins with a man, David, in a jail cell, talking in voice-over about how he landed there for murder. We flash back to an earlier moment in David's life when he rents a room from a family living in Berkeley, California. The film slowly discloses that David proceeds to spy on them so he can write a novel based on their lives, and it gradually becomes clear that his family lived in that house and that his mother killed his father, stabbing him fifty times. His mother got off on grounds that the murder was self-defense. The film's plot is also framed by David's literary agent, who comments on his novel and thus indirectly on the film itself since the plots run parallel. *Othello* provides another interpretive frame. A young, somewhat disturbed high school–aged boy in the film auditions for *Othello* and gets the part of Iago. A girl who also tries out is interested in him. Parallels with Othello arise but are quickly put aside. The boy is told that the girl is already sleeping with the black kid playing Othello, and David tries to instill various conflicts, including a divorce from the parents (the father is having an affair). But David's identity is discovered by the boy, and the father decides to stay with his wife. The first scene of *Othello* is rehearsed, and Iago's motivation is explained by the drama teacher. A little bit of Othello's "whip me ye devils" is also heard. Notably, the girl tells the boy that he can't play Othello because Othello is black. Alcatraz Avenue divides Berkeley and Oakland, California. Official website at www.alcatrazavenue.com. (RB)

1023 *Hotel O*
2002. U.S. Video Team. Sound, col., 83 mins. Roy Karch.

Hardcore pornographic adaptation. Screenplay by Richard Burt. Loose adaptation of *Othello*, set at a modern hotel, Hotel O, in Venice, California, frequented by hookers. Othello (OT) is an undercover cop masquerading as a pimp, Desdemona (Mona) a hooker, and Iago an under-

cover cop and pimp wannabe. The film spawned sequels, *Hotel O II* (2003) and *Hotel O III* (2004).

Several Shakespearean lines are referenced, often with responses like "What are you talking about?" The plot uses a number of motifs from *Othello*: a romance between OT and Mona, Iago's discontent, a misplaced handkerchief, and Iago's fomenting OT's suspicions of Cass. This version ends happily, however, as Iago is caught and punished. Shakespeare appears as a night clerk at the Hotel O who anachronistically writes with a quill.

DVD includes a behind-the-scenes featurette and stills gallery, plus other extras unrelated to the content of the film.

1024 *In Othello*
2003. India. ANB Pictures. Sound, col., 100 mins. Roysten Abel.

In contemporary New Delhi, a multicultural theater troupe rehearses a Kathakali production of *Othello*. The Director (played by the film's director, Roysten Abel) casts Adil, an inexperienced, traditionally trained Kathakali actor from a rural town, in the title role, and soon he falls in love with Sheeba (who plays Desdemona), an actress also loved by Dilip (who plays Cassius) and the Director. Adil struggles with his alienation from the cosmopolitan, English-speaking company, and that alienation is made worse by Barry John, the British expatriate who plays Iago, who exploits the romantic rivalries and jealousies over Sheeba to his own Machiavellian ends. As rehearsals progress, the lives of the actors begin to mirror the lives of the characters they play. Another in the series of adaptations in which *Othello* begins to rule the actors' lives; compare *Desdemona, Carnival, Men Are Not Gods, A Double Life, Il Peccato de Anna, Une histoire inventee, Valentín, Alcatraz Avenue, Cheers, Sanford and Son,* and *Les Enfants du Paradis*. Of particular interest for its mixture of Shakespearean and traditional Kathakali performance. Compare *Kaliyattam* (above).

1025 *Interloper*
2003. U.K. Interloper Films, North West Vision, and UK Film Council. Sound, col., 8 mins. Robert Ford.

Written by Erinma Ochu. Fola, a troubled black man angry at the way in which he is repeatedly rejected and beyond the notice of the theater world, holds an audition team hostage and threatens suicide to gain their attention. The writer claims that the film is inspired by *Othello*, though the only clear reference to the play is in Fola's final line: "Put out the light, then put out the light."

1026 *Valentín*
2003. Spain. Cuarteto Producciones Cinematográficas. Sound, col., 110 mins. Juan Luis Iborra.

In this backstage drama, an all-male acting company rehearses a show of Shakespearean highlights at a country resort, using men to play the women's roles. Recently separated from his wife, Ricardo, the director, finds himself attracted to the troupe's new member, boyish Valentin, and he begins to cast him in the female leads in the revue. Envious of his success and jealous for Ricardo's attention, Jaime, a veteran actor with the company and its principal star, begins to play upon Ricardo's infatuation and tear apart the group, leading eventually to Ricardo's madness and onstage murder of Valentin. Meanwhile, Lola, the assistant director who carries a torch for Ricardo, is pursued (fruitlessly) by lesbian makeup artist Ana.

Ricardo's revue of Shakespearean highlights includes scenes from *Othello, Romeo and Juliet,* and *Antony and Cleopatra,* all of which we see in rehearsal and all of which become vehicles to express homoerotic passion. The metadramatic parallels between the players' relationships and *Othello* quickly come into focus with the arrival of Valentin, who combines elements of Desdemona and Cassio; Ricardo fills the role of Othello, and Jaime the role of Iago. The love triangle between Lola, Ricardo, and hapless Ana has affinities with Roderigo's unrequited relationship with Desdemona, though it is played largely for comedy. Iborra's film weds Shakespeare with the kind of Spanish sex comedy popularized by Pedro Almodóvar and others in the 1990s and 2000s; it also partakes of interest among some adaptors of the same period in exploring Shakespeare's drama as a vehicle for homoerotic rather than heteroerotic love (see, for example, Joe Calarco's drama *R&J* or Alison LiCalsi's film *Macbeth: The Comedy*). For all its moments of comedy and campy parody, in the end the film veers in the direction of gay tragedy.

1027 *Huapango*
2004. Mexico. Vlady Realizadores. Sound, col., 100 mins. Ivan Lipkies.

In the Huasteca region of Mexico, Julia, the best and most beautiful dancer of the Huapango, the regional dance, is partnered with Santiago, a coarse, passionate man. Though Santiago secretly loves Julia, she is enamored of Otilio, the wealthiest rancher of the province, and the two are soon betrothed. Santiago, desperate to destroy the marriage of Otilio and Julia, undertakes to make Otilio jealous over Julia's relationship with Felipe during preparations for the National Dance Festival of the Huapango, a dance contest.

1028 *Manchurian Candidate*
2004. U.S. Paramount Pictures. Sound, col., 129 mins. Jonathan Demme.

Demme's remake of the 1962 Frankenheimer political thriller shifts the plot's focus from a communist conspiracy to a transnational biogenetic corporation. In both films, nightmarish recollections by Major Bennet Marco (Frank Sinatra in the original/Denzel Washington in the remake) lead to a discovery that his unit had been brainwashed during a war (Korea/Desert Storm) to believe that Sergeant Raymond Shaw (John Harvey/Liev Schreiber) had heroically saved them in battle; the "fact" of Shaw's military valor is used by his mother (Angela Lansbury/Meryl Streep) for promotional purposes during a presidential campaign. Demme's version includes several slight modifications that echo *Othello,* despite the fact that we never hear the name of Shakespeare cited, and no lines derive directly from the play.

The most telling moment involves a scene in the apartment of Rosie (Kimberly Elise), a woman in whom the unnerved Shaw has been confiding his confused but emerging theory about the conspiracy. In her bathroom, he notices a surveillance camera hidden above him behind a ventilation grate. Furious, he then searches through her purse, where he finds, among other evidence, not Iago-esque money but rather audiotapes of their confessional conversations. His faith in her shattered, he flees her apartment. Immediately before noticing this camera, we catch sight of a carefully framed image, reversed from the wall behind the bathroom mirror. It is a poster from Paul Robeson's highly successful 1940s Broadway production of *Othello,* co-starring José Ferrer and Uta Hagen. (The appearance of this poster is all the more striking since it was not called for in the revised screenplay [Daniel Pyne and Dean Gregoris] Demme was using.)

While the mirrored image cannily inverts any attempt to link Washington's role with that of Robeson, other elements of Demme's film are still arguably inflected by Shakespeare's play. These include the fact that Marco has been tortured on an island by a malign character who manages to "get inside his head," like a latter-day Iago. The island, moreover, with its decayed arabesque structures, appears to be some kind of former Mediterranean outpost (an allusion to Cyprus?). Later in the film Marco attempts to strangle Rosie while demanding the truth of her (again, a modification from Demme's screenplay, where the two of them have a fistfight instead). Some extrafilmic facts are suggestive as well—for instance, Streep and Washington, the stars of this film, were once invited by Joseph Papp to be cast as Othello and Desdemona. Finally, a comment made by Washington during interviews promoting the production invite some scrutiny: whenever he was asked about his fidelity to the original Sinatra role, he consistently replied with variations on this response: "To me any good piece of material, like Shakespeare, ought to be open to reinterpretation. I played Othello but I didn't sit around thinking how Laurence Olivier did it when he played it" (see entry 454). Washington's statement obliquely acknowledges that in "color-blind" casting, he is remaking a role originated by Sinatra—although invoking Olivier's blackface Othello seems a complicated way to do so, especially in light of the computerized "white-washing" Marco's character undergoes by a subsequent surveillance camera. See also entries 823 and 2806. (SN)

1029 *Stage Beauty*
2004. U.K. Qwerty Films. Sound, col., 106 mins.
Richard Eyre.

Set in Restoration England just before women are allowed to act on stage, *Stage Beauty* focuses on Ned Kynaston (Billy Cruddup), a bisexual male actor renowned for playing the role of Desdemona and whose gender—woman or man—is the subject of speculation by his adoring public. His dresser, a young woman named Maria (Claire Danes), secretly imitates Ned's performance at a low-class theatrical venue called the Cockpit Tavern that approximates a strip club. When Maria's secret is discovered at court, Charles II (Rupert Everett), urged on by his mistress Nell Gwynn (Zoe Tapper), decides to let women act onstage. When Ned appeals to Charles II, he is humiliated and, after being beaten by the servants of a lord he earlier insulted, falls into an alcoholic stupor and reprises his role as Desdemona at the Cockpit Tavern. Maria, who has had an unrequited crush on Ned, finds him and convinces him to return to the legitimate stage, where he can play the part of Othello in blackface to her Desdemona. The two have a compelling rehearsal of the death scene in which they differ about how the role of Desdemona should be played: Ned says that Desdemona should meekly submit to her murder and Maria says that she should fight. During the actual performance of the scene, it is not clear whether Ned has actually strangled Maria. Maria appears to both the audience of the play and the film to be really dead. When she revives, the audience's thunderous applause and standing ovation stops the play. After the performance, Ned and Maria meet backstage alone and kiss. It is not clear whether they will have a romantic and fully sexual relationship, however, as Ned's sexual orientation still remains in question. In addition to being one of roughly twenty films that include a performance of *Othello*'s death scene, *Stage Beauty* has many parallels with *Shakespeare in Love* and is also echoed by *The Libertine* (see entries 1248 and 1500). Several other Shakespeare plays are referenced, including *Hamlet*, *Romeo and Juliet*, *King Lear*, and *Antony and Cleopatra*. (RB)

1030 *Melinda and Melinda*
2005. U.S. Fox Searchlight. Sound, col., 100 mins. Woody Allen.

The film grows out of a dinner conversation between two characters, Sy and Al, one of whom is played by Wallace Shawn, who played Wally in Louis Malle's *My Dinner with Andre* (1981). Sy and Al, sounding a lot like Wally and Andre, differ as to whether life is really comic or really tragic. Another tells a story, which the film skips over, and asks Sy and Al if it is tragic or comic. The film then tells this story twice, with the film alternating be-

tween Al's tragic sequences and Sy's comic sequences. In the tragic story, an alcoholic, out-of-work actor married to a shopaholic rich woman from Park Avenue talks to a student about Desdemona and Othello just before it becomes clear he is sleeping with her. The film, which is full of romantic triangles and infidelities and has a black male character in both comic and tragic versions, has some very loose parallels with the play. In the comic story, Will Farrell's character mentions having done King Lear, with a limp. (He plays all his roles with a limp.) (RB)

PERICLES

1031 *Paris nous appartient* (*Paris Belongs to Us*)
1960. France. Ajym Films and Les Films du Carrosse.
Sound, b&w, 141 mins. Jacques Rivette.

In the summer of 1957 in Paris, Anna Goupil attends a party where she overhears a compelling account of the suicide of a young Spaniard named Juan. At the same party, she meets Philip Kaufmann, an American expatriate who has been the victim of anti-McCarthyism, and Gérard Lenz, a charismatic theater director. Kaufmann tells her that Juan was the victim of an international conspiracy whose secrets he knew, and that Lenz will be the next victim. To prevent his death, Anna takes a part (Marina) in his no-budget production of *Pericles*. Eventually she discovers that all three men had the same mistress, Terry Yordan; Terry confesses that she learned the conspiracy's secret from Philip and told it to Juan and Lenz. Anne embarks on a quest to find the soundtrack tape Juan made for the production, and along the way meets other odd characters who complicate the mystery. Tensions mount at the rehearsals as actors leave, producers interfere, and Anne refuses to see Gérard. After Anna and Lenz part ways, Lenz takes his own life. Soon after, Anna learns that Philip made up the story of the conspiracy and that Lenz took his life because of debts for the play, and she re-evaluates what made the men commit suicide.

Widely regarded as a classic of the *nouvelle vague*, Rivette's study in free-floating paranoia, structured around a kind of detective story, includes several scenes of *Pericles* in rehearsal. The recurring scene we see in rehearsal is *Pericles* 4.1, particularly Marina's lines "Ay me! poor maid, / Born in a tempest, when my mother died, / This world to me is like a lasting storm" and Leonine's conversation with Marina about the direction of the wind. Lenz's casting of Anna as Marina points to her becoming swept up in Philip's paranoid fiction. The thematic significance of Shakespeare play for this film becomes somewhat clear in two conversations. In the first, Anne's friend Jean-Marc describes *Pericles* as a play with some good scenes that doesn't hold together and isn't even signed by Shakespeare; in the second, Lenz speaks of a global play that he's not sure all ties together, a play about the absurd. In both cases,

Pericles seems a metaphorical equivalent for Philip's conspiracy—a tissue of coincidences with global reach but no clear authorship. One other allusion seems in retrospect portentous: when we first see Anne, she is studying Ariel's song "Full Fathom Five" from *The Tempest*—Anne's perspective undergoes a "sea change" in the course of the film. There are two other passing Shakespearean references, both more conventional: to Lenz's plans for a rehearsal, one actor quips, "Tomorrow and tomorrow and tomorrow," and another actor reveals to Anne backstage that his audition speech is "Friends, Romans, countrymen."

RICHARD II

1032 *The Scarlet Pimpernel*
1934. U.K. London Film Productions. Sound, b&w, 90 mins. Harold Young.

Adapted from the play by Montagu Barstow and Baroness Emmuska Orczy and the novel by Baroness Orczy. Sir Percy Blakeney, a supercilious fop whose French wife Marguerite is estranged from him, is in reality the Scarlet Pimpernel, a master of disguise who with a band of compatriots rescues aristocratic victims of the guillotine in revolutionary France. Citizen Chauvelin is sent to England to discover the Pimpernel's true identity. Chauvelin uses the arrest of Marguerite's brother Armand St. Just, a famous actor, to blackmail her into helping him, but the Pimpernel engages him in an elaborate game of cat-and-mouse at a gala ball. When Marguerite thinks she's betrayed her husband, she pursues him to France in order to save him; when Chauvelin captures her, the Pimpernel crafts a plan to allow both of them to escape.

When it seems he is about to die before Chauvelin's firing squad, the Pimpernel recites John of Gaunt's "This other Eden, demi-paradise" speech from *Richard II* 2.2. The speech is in contrast to the dreadful doggerel he generates as Blakeney, and it underlines the film's presentation of the Pimpernel as a quintessentially British hero.

1033 *Private Lives of Elizabeth and Essex*
1939. Sound, col., 106 mins. Michael Curtiz.

Queen Elizabeth (Bette Davis) mentions Master Shakespeare in relation to the Essex rebellion.

See *William Shakespeare: His Life and Times*, episode 5, and *Elizabeth R*. (RB)

1034 *Darling*
1965. U.K. Anglo-Amalgamated Films and Embassy. Sound, col., 128 mins. John Schlesinger.

Diana Scott, a beautiful, easily bored model who fears being alone, drifts into a relationship with Robert Gold, a cultural arts reporter who introduces her to the London social set. Robert, a married man, soon leaves his wife to take up with Diana, but she becomes briefly enamored of a cynical corporate executive, Miles Brand. After rubbing shoulders with high society, having an abortion, and making another stab at her relationship with Robert, Diana films a commercial in Italy where she meets Cesare, a millionaire widower whose son Curzio woos her; soon Cesare proposes to her, and Diana marries him, becoming trapped in Cesare's world of empty wealth. When she flies back to London to try yet again to kindle her relationship with Robert, he uses her for a fling, then rejects her, driving her to the airport for the return trip to Italy.

The film is both an ironic study of Diana as "the ideal woman," with emphasis on her restlessness and self-centered faithlessness, and also a caustic portrait of swinging London in the 1960s. In one sequence, Diana reads John of Gaunt's "This royal throne of kings, this scepter'd isle" speech from *Richard II* 2.2 to a rich potential lover, while she secretly fondles a £10 chit for the gambling tables, a chit she later uses to wager and win. The speech's ideal is set against the more vapid, hypocritical reality of British high society. The same caustic irony hovers over another passing Shakespeare allusion: when Diana goes to a showing of modern artist Ralph Riggs, one woman observes of Riggs's paintings, "He's got a fantastically lean and hungry look."

RICHARD III

1035 *The Princes in the Tower*
1913. U.K. Hepworth Manufacturing Company. Silent, b&w, length unknown. E. Hay Plumb.

Lost film, apparently concerning the death of the princes. Of historical significance as the first free film adaptation of *Richard III*.

1036 *A Horse! A Horse!*
1913. U.K. Clarendon. Silent, b&w, 355 ft. Percy Stow.

When a cleaning woman is assigned the task of finding the actor playing Richard III a horse, she instead provides him a donkey.

1037 *Les Enfants D'Edouard*
1914. France. Cosmograph. Silent, b&w, 3–4 reels. Henri Andréani.

This film focuses primarily on the arrival of young Edward V and his brother to London for his coronation and their subsequent deaths at the hands of Richard's murderers. In this sentimentalized version, Buckingham aids the boys to escape briefly before they are recaptured and assassinated, and Richard, suffering from his wounds in battle, is overcome with pangs of conscience when the boys appear to him in a vision. This film may give a clue to the content of *The Princes in the Tower* (above).

1038 *The Princes in the Tower*
1928. U.K. British Filmcraft. Silent, b&w, 1,935 ft. George Banfield and Leslie Eveleigh.

From the *Ghosts of Yesterday* series, this apparently lost film treats the *Richard III* narrative as a historical ghost story.

1039 *Tower of London*
1939. U.S. Universal Pictures. Sound, b&w, 92 mins. Rowland V. Lee.

With the help of the executioner Mord, Richard, Duke of Gloucester, plots against those who stand in his way to the throne. He places senile Henry VI in the tower, sends him into battle in hopes he will be killed, and has Mord kill him at prayers; he influences his brother Edward to control key marriages at court; he kills the Prince of Wales and marries his wife, Anne Neville; he challenges his brother Clarence to a drinking contest, after which he drowns him in a butt of malmsey; and on Edward's death, he becomes protector of the two princes and has Mord arrange their deaths. As he eliminates his rivals, he destroys figurines of them in a dollhouse in his chambers. His nemeses in his plans are Queen Elizabeth, Edward's wife, who arranges for her royal treasure to be sent to aid Henry Tudor in France, and John Wyatt, a courtier who loves Lady Alice Barton and who heroically aids the rebels in France, for which he is imprisoned and tortured by Mord. In the final battle, Richard is killed by Henry Tudor and Mord by John Wyatt; soon after, Wyatt and Lady Alice are married.

This event-filled free adaptation of *Richard III* blends elements of the historical costume drama with elements of the horror film for which Universal Studios was well-known. The film doubles the narrative's main villain—Richard is a dashing (if icy) hunchback, and his henchman Mord (played by Boris Karloff) is a bald, clubfooted giant who enjoys killing (a horror film substitution for Buckingham). The sword-fighting skills of Basil Rathbone, who plays Richard, are prominently showcased, in one case in a bout with young Prince Edward. Throughout much of the film's first half, Edward actively colludes with Richard's plans to take the throne, and key to their plans is the orchestration of forced marriages as well as murders. Interesting, too, is that Richard orders the murder of the princes not to secure his place on the throne but to spite Queen Elizabeth, who has financed the rebels with her treasures. Though no direct citations appear, the film includes a couple of motifs from Shakespeare's play: the women's suspicion of and resistance to Richard, and Richard's appearance on a platform before the cheering people. Rathbone's characterization emphasizes Richard's ruthlessness, strategizing, and sinister intellect rather than his charm (he never addresses the viewer directly), qualities underlined by his manipulation of figurines in his secret dollhouse. Given the date of release, the film may have some relationship to the rise of Hitler and Mussolini, though that relationship is very oblique. The elements of historical romance sit rather uneasily with those of Gothic

horror, one symptom of which is the splitting of the villain. Equally telling is the film's unease with the aristocratic milieu, a problem it seeks to solve by creating a non-aristocratic protagonist, John Wyatt, and several working-class allies, including Tom Clink, a chimney sweep.

1040 *Ball of Fire*
1941. U.S. Samuel Goldwyn. Sound, b&w, 111 mins. Howard Hawks.

From a story by Billy Wilder and Thomas Monroe. In this modernization of "Snow White and the Seven Dwarfs," eight bookish professors are compiling an encyclopedia. When Professor Bertram Potts uses stripper Sugarpuss O'Shea to interpret modern American slang for him, he falls in love with her and saves her from being forced into marriage by her gangster boyfriend Joe Lilac. The engagement ring that Potts gives O'Shea has inscribed on it "*Richard III* 1.2.204," which Potts explains refers to these lines: "Look how this ring encompasseth thy finger. / Even so, thy breath encloseth my poor heart. / Wear both of them, for both of them are thine." The irony of such an allusion is not acknowledged.

1041 *Tower of London*
1962. U.S. Admiral Pictures. Sound, b&w, 79 mins. Roger Corman.

Using Shakespeare's play only as its starting point, this remake of Rowland Lee's adaptation weds elements of *Richard III* with elements from *Macbeth* and B-picture gothic. Richard III, goaded by his ambitious wife Anne and accompanied by his sidekick Ratcliffe, methodically murders all who stand in his way to the crown, killing and torturing his brother Clarence (named by Edward IV the lord protector), Mistress Shore (who refuses to question the princes' legitimacy), the princes (personally dispatched by Richard and Ratcliffe), and Buckingham (who opposes his rise to power). In his ascent to power Richard is opposed by Queen Anne, Lady Margaret, and an invented character, Sir Justin, who along with Tyrus, a doctor-conjurer, tries unsuccessfully to protect the princes. Expanding upon Richard's dream the night before Bosworth Field and Macbeth's crises of conscience and guilty visions, after each of the murders, Richard is haunted by ghosts of those he has killed. They taunt him with prophecies of his death—Clarence reveals that he will die at Bosworth by the hand of one already dead—and play tricks on his mind. The ghost of Mistress Shore, for example, tricks Richard into killing his beloved Anne, and ghosts of the princes try to coax him to walk off the battlements and fall to his death. On the battlefield Richard dies as Clarence's prophecy predicted, by falling from his horse onto the battleaxe of a fallen soldier as he tries to flee ghosts of those he has slain. Vincent Price's Richard is by turns an unrepentant smirking murderer, a man driven mad by his conscience, and an unloved child seeking acceptance; at times he seems to offer an intentional parody of Olivier's Richard (see entry 469; note, for example, the shot of Richard's shadow on the castle wall). The film takes every opportunity to showcase gothic clichés—dungeons, foggy landscapes, moonlit battlements, armored skeletons, secret passageways, and conjuration of spirits—and features stilted dialogue that is apparently meant to recall Shakespeare's formal diction. Even so, several sequences recall Shakespearean moments—Richard's speeches about his murders, for example, distantly evoke the addresses of Shakespeare's Richard to the audience, though his speeches in the film are typically guilty rather than gloating; the shot of Richard enthroned in his cavernous state room before the battle of Bosworth nicely conveys the emptiness of his achievement; and the ghosts of his victims, appearing as Richard laments being alone on the Bosworth battlefield, lead directly to his demise, in effect conflating Richard's dream and his death in Shakespeare's version. There are no direct citations from Shakespeare's dialogue.

The DVD includes a featurette, "Producing *Tower of London*," which references Shakespeare.

1042 *L'important, c'est d'aimer* (*The Important Thing Is to Love*)

1975. France, Italy, and West Germany. Albina Productions, CFDC, Rizzoli Film, and TIT. Sound, col., 109 mins. Andrzej Zulawski.

Adapted from the novel *La nuit americaine* by Christopher Frank. In an attempt to woo Nadine Chevalier, a cynical aging actress who, struggling for work, has been forced to act in low-budget pornography, Servais Mont, a tabloid newspaper photographer and pornographer, borrows money from gangsters to finance a theatrical production of *Richard III* in which Nadine will star as Lady Anne. Though the play fails and she at first rebuffs him, Nadine soon falls for Servais, leading to the erosion of her marriage to her gay husband Jacques to whom Nadine nevertheless feels obligated. When Jacques learns of their relationship, he commits suicide. Unable to repay his debt, Servais is beaten by gangsters, and Nadine realizes that she loves him. (DL)

Klaus Kinksi plays a gay actor doing Richard III. We see the cast rehearse the wooing of Lady Anne scene, reading parts aloud while seated; lines from Richard's opening speech while the Battle of Shrewsbury is enacted in a ballet form. Kinski and other actors wear samurai armor. The end of the film repeats the beginning, only this time Nadine and Servais connect after gangsters beat him up, thus transcending their roles as Anne and pornographer. The exquisite soundtrack is composed by Georges Delerue, who also did Godard's *Contempt* (1963). (RB)

DVD (region 2 in French only) and VHS (in English dubbed and with subtitles).

1043 *Get Mean* (aka *Vengeance of the Barbarians*)

1976. Italy. Cee Note and Stranger Productions Inc. Sound, col., 86 mins. Fernando Baldi.

One of the most bizarre spaghetti Westerns ever made. Caught in a war between viking-clad Barbarians and the Moors, the "Stranger" is hired to escort a Spanish princess, Elizabeth Maria de Burgos, from the United States back to Spain so that she can reclaim her country. Along the way, the Stranger undergoes a strange trial (in which he is turned black) and battles a triumvirate of villains from the Barbarians as he seeks to find the lost treasure of Rodrigo. Mysterious and unexplained silver balls are scattered throughout the action, as if watching the characters.

One of the triumvirate of Barbarian villains is the superficially charming but ruthless, lying hunchback Sambra, who reads Shakespeare and admires Richard III. Indeed, the Stranger calls him Richard at key points in the film. In fighting a gypsy woman Maria, an ally of the Stranger, Sambra challenges her to "take up the sword or take up me," referencing Richard's taunt to Lady Anne in 1.2. In the final mano a mano between the Stranger and Sambra, handled as a duel, Sambra recites Richard III's opening soliloquy, "Now is the winter of our discontent," as he frantically loads his cannon to kill the Stranger. Upon Sambra's death, he utters "a horse, my kingdom for . . ." but the Stranger kills him before he can finish the quotation.

1044 *The Goodbye Girl*

1977. U.S. Metro-Goldwyn-Mayer, Rastar Pictures, and Warner Bros. Sound, col., 110 mins. Herbert Ross.

Adapted from the play by Neil Simon. Paula McFadden and her daughter Lucy discover that Paula's actor boyfriend Tony has suddenly abandoned them and sub-let their apartment to another actor, Elliot Garfield, who arrives in the middle of a stormy night. After negotiations the three end up sharing the apartment as Elliot stars in an off-Broadway production of *Richard III* and Paula searches for a job, vowing to stay away from actors. Elliot's charm and energy eventually persuade Paula to fall in love with him, and when Elliot gets his break in a film in Seattle, his and Paula's relationship is tested yet again.

Central to Elliot's plotline is his starring role in a gay-themed *Richard III*. In the opening read-through with the cast, the director Mark explains his concept for the production—Richard is "the Queen who wanted to be King"—over Elliot's objection that Richard was deformed and wanted Lady Anne. We see Elliot's several attempts in rehearsal to perform Richard's opening speech; when the company rehearses the processional of Henry VI's corpse in 1.2, Elliot plays Richard as a prancing, lisping king, after which Mark assures him that the gay theme will be "subtext." Of the play's actual performance, we see three scenes—Richard's opening speech (played by Elliot with a lisp and limp wrist), the arrival of Hastings's severed head in 3.5, and the sword fight that ends the play. Afterward, we learn that Mark's interpretation was an attempt to seek his mother's approval, but the critics universally dislike the production and the show immediately closes. There are other passing references—to *The Merchant of Venice*, *A Midsummer Night's Dream* (Puck was the part that Elliot played before moving to New York), and *The Taming of the Shrew*. The comic caricature of a gay Richard III plays against the developing heterosexual relationship between Elliot and Paula; unlike Richard and unlike Paula's previous boyfriend, Elliot does love her and does keep her long.

1045 *Riccardo III*
1977. Italy. Production company unknown. Sound, b&w, 76 mins. Carmelo Bene.

The first of Bene's made-for-television avant-garde Shakespearean adaptations, in this case using *Richard III* as his starting point. Bene's emphasis falls on the centrality of women and the female in this shortened version of the play. This film was never commercially released.

1046 *Scarface*
1983. U.S. Universal Pictures. Sound, col., 170 mins. Brian dePalma.

Screenplay by Oliver Stone. Tony Montana, a refugee in the Cuban Mariel boat lift from Cuba in the 1980s, arrives with his friend Manny Ray in Miami. To leave the refugee camp, he kills Rebenga, a hated political activist in Cuba, at the behest of Omar Suarez, a criminal who works for Frank Lopez, a major drug dealer in Miami Beach; after thwarting a drug deal double-cross, Tony comes to work for Frank and soon begins to woo his girl, Elvira. Though Tony tries to give money to his mother and beloved sister Gina, his mother refuses it; Gina, however, begins to live the high life. Soon Tony strikes a deal with Alejandro Sosa, a Bolivian drug supplier, kills Frank, and marries Elvira, becoming himself a drug lord. Almost as soon as Tony gains power, his relationship with Elvira crumbles, he is caught in a money-laundering sting that compromises his relationship with Sosa and the cartel, he becomes abusive and paranoid to those around him, and he kills Manny when he discovers that Manny is in a relationship with Gina. In a spectacular death scene, Tony takes on Sosa's army of killers, bravely dying in the end.

A number of critics have pointed to resemblances between Tony Montana and Richard III, even though the film cannot be said to be a thoroughgoing adaptation of Shakespeare's play. Like Richard, Tony is physically deformed (in his case, a facial scar), he is a veteran of bloody battles, he woos a woman who at first violently objects to him and whose lover he kills, he is cursed by his mother for his ill deeds, he is accompanied by a trusted comrade and confidante (Manny) who he ultimately betrays, and, most important, though he is ruthless in his rise to power,

murdering all who get in his way, he hardly enjoys the fruits of his ambitions and comes to regret his murder of Manny. There are, however, very important differences: though Tony speaks at length of his plans and ambitions, he never addresses the viewer directly, and he has little of Richard III's surface charm and sardonic wit; those Tony murders are neither his brothers nor innocents; when Tony has the opportunity to assassinate the man who will expose the cartel before the UN, he doesn't do so because there are children in the car (very unlike Richard, who easily sends the princes to their deaths); and Tony does not have an extended moment of self-recognition and self-doubt, as does Richard the night before Bosworth Field. At best, the film might be designated a distant analogue to *Richard III*.

1047 *The Bride*
1985. U.K. and U.S. Columbia Pictures, Lee International Studios, and Delphi III Productions. Sound, col., 118 mins. Franc Roddam.

Adapted from the novel *Frankenstein* by Mary Shelley. Charles Frankenstein creates a bride for his original grotesque monster, but when she is unveiled she rejects the monster, leading him to leave. Charles names her "Eva." At first Eva has no thoughts of her own, but with the help of his housekeeper Mrs. Baumann, he molds her into an upper-class debutante. Meanwhile, the monster, still psychically linked to Eva, is befriended by Rinaldo, a dwarf; he names the monster "Viktor" and the two join the circus, where Rinaldo's business skills lead to resentment and eventually retribution against him, after which Viktor returns home. Eva becomes more independent intellectually and sexually by asserting her own desires with Josef Schoden, a callow army captain. Jealous, Charles tells Eva of her origins and makes known his desire for her, but Viktor intervenes, killing Viktor and claiming Eva for himself.

When Eva is first introduced to polite society, the topic of conversation turns to *Richard III*, which Count Maleva, a guest at the party, debunks as a distortion of history: "I don't think [Richard III] was as grotesque a character as they make him out to be." Eva expresses the provocative opinion that Shakespeare's fictional works are more interesting than his history plays.

1048 *Runaway Train*
1985. U.S. and Israel. Golan-Globus and Northbrook Films. Sound, col., 111 mins. Andrei Konchalovsky.

Adapted from a script by Akira Kurosawa. Two convicts, ruthless Oscar "Manny" Manheim and hero-worshiping Buck, escape from Stonehaven, a maximum-security prison in Alaska, and board a high-speed train, only to discover that the engineer has died of a heart attack and the train is out of control. While railroad dispatchers decide to derail the train to prevent a disaster, Manny and Buck begin to bicker as they and Sara, a woman crew member, realize their desperate plight. Manny remains calm and philosophical as he considers alternatives, while Buck is impulsive and immature. To add to the tension, the train is pursued by a helicopter containing Frank Barstow, the prison warden.

The film ends with a epigraph from Lady Anne and Richard's exchange in *Richard III* 1.2: "No beast so fierce but knows some touch of pity. / But I know none, and therefore am no beast." The citation bears upon Manny's ruthlessness, which the script presents as his pursuit of freedom. The film, with more philosophical resonance than the average action movie, is of interest for its origins in a script by Akira Kurosawa.

1049 *Moon over Parador*
1988. U.S. Universal. Sound, col., 96 mins. Paul Mazursky.

Adapted from a story by Charles G. Booth. Told in flashback, this film features the exploits of actor Jack Noah, who, while in Parador, a South American banana republic, to film a movie, is asked to play the part of Parador's presidente, Alphonse Simms, who has secretly died. At first he follows the direction of Roberto Straussman, Simms's chief of staff, and even attempts (though fails) to fool Simms's mistress, Madonna. Soon, however, under the influence of the socially conscious Madonna and Parador's revolutionaries, Noah begins to advocate policies of social justice, much to the anger of Straussman, who plans to have killed. However, Noah discovers the plot and engineers a plan with the help of a stunt man to save himself and the country.

The film is told in flashback. The opening sequence involves Noah auditioning for a role in *Richard III* at the New York Shakespeare Festival; declaring that he wants to play "the king," he tells the story of his impersonating a dictator to other actors up for parts. The role of Richard III is thematically ironic: Richard pretends to be benevolent in order to become dictator; as Simms, Noah eventually pretends to be a dictator in order to be benevolent.

1050 *Freaked*
1993. U.S. Tommy Productions. Sound, col., 86 mins. Tom Stern and Alex Winter.

In this campy teen version of H. G. Wells's *The Island of Dr. Moreau*, boy star Ricky Coogin accepts the offer of EES Corporation to become the spokesperson in South America for Zygrot 24, a fertilizer banned in the United States. Upon arriving in Santa Flan, he is transformed into a mutant by Elijah C. Skuggs, a carnival barker and mad scientist who uses toxic Zygrot 24 to create freaks for his theme park.

Transformed into a hideous freak, Ricky performs the opening speech from *Richard III* to a theme park audience, to great approval. Included with this sequence are "subtitles for the culturally illiterate."

1051 *Looking for Richard*
1995. U.S. 20th Century Fox, Chal Productions, and Jam Productions. Sound, col., 118 mins. Al Pacino.

Al Pacino offers in this unusual documentary an introduction to *Richard III* and its historical background, a celebration of actors' rehearsal and partial performance of the play, and a meditation on Shakespeare's diminished place in modern American culture. On-the-street interviews with New Yorkers concerning their experiences with and indifference to Shakespeare are intercut with scenes of Pacino rehearsing an ad hoc group of performers in a variety of urban New York spaces (most notably, the Cloisters Museum), and interviews with famous Shakespearean actors (Kenneth Branagh, John Gielgud, James Earl Jones, and Kevin Kline) and academics. Pacino seeks to communicate the immediacy of Shakespeare in performance by untangling the historical background for the viewer and stressing the active struggle of actors to work through Shakespeare's language and find contemporary analogies. Two comic sequences, one in which he visits Shakespeare's birthplace and another in which he asks scholar Emrys Jones about Anne's motive for marrying Richard, lampoon the value of academic historicism. As the film progresses, we see more and more of Pacino's troupe's production of the play, performed in period costume in vaguely historical spaces, and the interpolated interviews, commentary, and scenes of the making of the film drop away. Richard's visions on the night before the battle of Bosworth Field are handled as a film montage (as Pacino rehearses on a London stage, confronting the enormity of the role); his death on the battlefield, in which Richmond mercilessly shoots him with arrows, is nearly wordless and highly effective. The production is framed by montages of New York urban scenes (vaguely recalling the spaces of *West Side Story*) accompanied by a voice-over of Prospero's "We are such stuff as dreams are made on" speech. In addition to large sections of *Richard III*, there are references to Shakespeare's sonnets and *Henry VI, Part 3*; Shakespeare twice makes comic cameos as a member of Pacino's audience.

1052 *For Hire*
1997. Canada. Fries Film Group and Kingsborough Greenlight Pictures. Sound, col., 96 mins. Jean Pellerin.

His acting career stalled, his wife pregnant and laid off, and his health jeopardized by terminal cancer, Mitch Lawrence, a Chicago taxi driver, consents to murder a junkie informer for an author friend, Joe Watson. Afterward Mitch discovers that he has been set up, and he concocts a theatrical scheme to expose Watson's double-dealing.

Mitch stars in a production of *Richard III*, and lines from the play, particularly Richard's "O coward conscience" soliloquy from 5.3, figure prominently throughout the film.

As the film opens, Mitch is rehearsing (poorly) Richard's speech, starting with "Fool, of thyself speak well." When he buys flowers for his wife, he banters with the flower woman using lines from Richard's seduction of Lady Anne (the flower woman plays Lady Anne in the production). After the murder, we see Mitch in rehearsal of 4.2, and he speaks, "I am in / So far in blood that sin will pluck on sin: / Tear-falling pity dwells not in this eye," delivered so convincingly that he earns applause from the cast; later, we see him in rehearsal of 5.3, "Is there a murderer here? No. Yes, I am: / Then fly. What, from myself?" When Joe Watson dies, Mitch delivers in a whisper over the body the words of Hastings's Ghost from 5.3: "Bloody and guilty, guiltily awake, / And in a bloody battle end thy days!" See also entry 469.

1053 *Galaxy Quest*
1999. U.S. Dream Works. Sound, col., 102 mins. Dean Parisot.

Actors Jason Nesmith, Alexander Dane, and Gwen DeMarco, all veterans of a long-ago canceled sci-fi TV series *Galaxy Quest*, extend their faltering careers by making public appearances at fan conventions. They are recruited by a group of adoring aliens to help in their real-life rebellion against galactic oppressors, with the aid of nerdy fans of *Galaxy Quest*.

Alexander Dane, who plays the alien Dr. Lazarus on the series, complains repeatedly that he once played Richard III and has now been reduced to TV hack work.

1054 *The Filth and the Fury*
2000. U.K. Film Four International, Jersey Shore Films, Nitrate Film Productions, and Sex Pistols. Sound, col. and b&w, 108 mins. Julian Temple.

A documentary on the career of the Sex Pistols. Sid Vicious identifies Richard III as a role model, and we briefly see a clip from Olivier's film of *Richard III*. See also entry 1686.

The DVD includes a commentary track by the director that references Shakespeare.

1055 *The Actors*
2003. U.K., Ireland, and Germany. Bórd Scannán na hÉireann, Close Call Films, Company of Wolves, Dream-Works SKG, and FilmFour. Sound, col., 91 mins. Colin McPherson.

Adapted from a story by Neil Jordan. O'Malley, a failing Shakespearean in a terrible production of *Richard III*, encourages his younger colleague Tom to run a scam on a small-time crook. When the deception goes awry, the two are forced to improvise characters to stay ahead of an angry enforcer and his woman boss.

The film opens with Tom's audition for a commercial using Richard III's opening soliloquy. The film features passages from several scenes in the Nazi-themed produc-

tion of *Richard III*, including Richard's opening soliloquy (heard twice), the seduction of Lady Anne, Richard's receiving of news of Richmond's advance, and his death on Bosworth Field. O'Malley twice speaks of his desire to do a vowels-only production of *Hamlet* and offers his rendition of the "To be or not to be" soliloquy. O'Malley also references Richard III's line "I will converse with iron-witted fools" (4.2), as well as Philip Sidney's Sonnet 94.

1056 *Monsieur N.*
2003. France/U.K. Sound, col., 120 mins. Antoine de Caunes.

Richard III comes up in a scene where Sir Hudson Lowe (effectively Napoleon's jailer) tries to get the doctor to poison Napoleon. To give the doctor a hint, Lowe recites Richard's lines to Buckingham: "Cousin, thou wert not wont to be so dull: / Shall I be plain?" The Doctor answers, smiling at first, "I wish the bastards dead." When the doctor realizes what Lowe is asking him to do, the doctor refuses. Lowe then denies the implication and says he is only concerned with the doctor's literary education. Lowe is played by the wonderful Richard E. Grant, who has appeared in a number of Shakespeare (and Shakespeare-related) films such as Trevor Nunn's *Twelfth Night*, *Withnail and I*, *LA Story*, *Food of Love*, and *Bram Stoker's Dracula*. (RB)

ROMEO AND JULIET

NB: The 1981 adult film *Romeo and Juliet* (directed by Andrew White), the 1995 adult film *The Romeo Syndrome* (directed by Jim Enright) the 1990 *Romeo* (directed by Rita Horst), and the 1989 film *Romuald et Juliette* (aka *Mama, There a Man in Your Bed*, directed by Coline Serreau), have nothing to do with *Romeo and Juliet*.

1057 *Roméo et Juliette*
1900. France. Phono Cinema Théâtre. Silent, b&w, 1 reel. Clément Maurice.

An extract from the Gounod opera. This film experimented with a synchronized sound system.

1058 *Burlesque on Romeo and Juliet*
1902. U.S. Edison. Silent, b&w, 24.38 meters. Director unknown.

One of the first film burlesques of *Romeo and Juliet*.

1059 *Le Diable Geant, ou Le Miracle de la Madone*
1902. France. Star Films. Silent, b&w, 1 reel. George Méliès.

In Venice, Romeo sings Juliet a song of love outside her window. Afterward, the devil appears and Juliet, fearful, calls for Romeo to protect her, but the devil prevents him from doing so as he dances before Juliet and grows to enormous size. Juliet appeals to a statue of the Madonna that comes to life and shrinks the devil to nothingness. As Juliet and Romeo embrace, the Madonna offers her benediction for the couple.

A surrealistic free adaptation of the balcony scene that perhaps involves an allegory of the conflict between lust and chaste love. As is often the case with Méliès's films, the emphasis falls on innovative visual effects.

1060 *The Serenade*
1905. U.S. Selig Polyscope Co. Silent, b&w, length unknown. Director unknown.

Twelve slapstick scenes, each of which involves Freddie ("Romeo") serenading Fannie ("Juliet") at her balcony. In each, Romeo is in some way chased or assaulted.

1061 *Algy Goes on the Stage*
1910. U.K. Gaumont. Silent, b&w, 630 ft. Alf Collins.

In this parody, the Honourable Algy Slacker plays the part of Romeo in a musical hall. One of several "Algy" comedies of the period.

1062 *Romeo and Juliet in Town*
1910. U.S. Selig Polyscope. Silent, b&w, 1,000 ft. Otis Turner.

An Americanized burlesque. Juliet Brown and Romeo Smith are lovers divided by the hatred of their two families.

1063 *Romeo se fait bandit* (*Romeo Turns Bandit*)
1910. France. Pathé Frères. Silent, b&w (color tinted), 541 ft. Director unknown.

A modern Romeo climbs a wall to give Juliet a kiss and is discovered courting her by her father. When her father refuses to allow Romeo to marry her, Romeo hires several hunters to bind her father and kidnap Juliet; when her father is released, he discovers a ransom note for Juliet's return. Romeo pretends to ally himself with Juliet's father and rescues her, securing his approval. Max Linder, the noted silent film comedian, plays Romeo. An interesting early hybrid of Shakespearean romance and comic melodrama.

The film is included as an extra on the Kino DVD edition of Buchowetski's *Othello*, though the ending is truncated.

1064 *Bumptious as Romeo*
1911. U.K. Edison Manufacturing Company. Silent, b&w, 1 reel (975 ft.). Director unknown.

Bumptious plays the lead in an amateur performance of *Romeo and Juliet* that goes awry. The balcony scene is played for slapstick—it collapses in midperformance. One of several Bumptious films starring John C. Cumpson in 1910 and 1911.

1065 *Indian Romeo and Juliet*
1912. U.S. Vitagraph. Silent, b&w, 15 mins. Larry Trimble.

Modern story about rivalry between American Indian tribes. Starred Wallace Reid as Oniatore/Romeo and Florence Turner as Ethona/Juliet.

1066 *Nicholas Nickleby*
1912. U.S. Thanhouser Film Corporation. Silent, b&w, 1,872 ft. George O. Nicholls.

Adapted from the novel by Charles Dickens (entry 1805). When upon his death Nicholas Nickleby's father leaves his mother and sister penniless, his evil uncle Ralph, a usurer, sends him to work as a teacher at Wackford Squeers Academy, a grim boy's school. Fleeing Ralph's rough justice, Nicholas, with his mentally handicapped friend Smike, joins the Crummles theatrical troupe. Nicholas works to protect Smike, his sister Kate, his sweetheart Madeleine Bray, and Madeleine's father in debtors' prison from Ralph's machinations. Eventually, Nicholas is integral to engineering Ralph's comeuppance.

Includes excerpts from a performance of *Romeo and Juliet* by the Crummles company. This is the first film adaptation of this novel; see others below.

1067 *Romeo and Juliet*
1913. U.S. Biograph. Silent, b&w, 500 ft. Travers Vale.

In this modernization, the feud is between an Irish and an Italian family headed by Mike Montague and Pete Capulet, respectively. In this version, the children live happily ever after by escaping in a rag wagon.

1068 *The Great Leap: Until Death Do Us Part*
1914. U.S. Reliance Motion Picture Company. Silent, b&w, length unknown. Christy Cabanne.

This Romeo and Juliet story is loosely based upon the Hatfield–McCoy feud. While the home of the mountaineering Gibbs family is besieged by the Dawson clan, Mary Gibbs rushes to the side of her lover, Bobby Dawson. Pursued by Mary's father and brother, the lovers attempt to leap across a vast chasm astride a horse. Although the horse falters and they fall into the river below, Bobby and Mary swim to safety. Impressed with their courage, Mr. Gibbs finally accepts their marriage. Produced by D. W. Griffith. Compare *Our Hospitality* and *Roseanna McCoy* (entry 1144).

1069 *Her Romeo*
1915. U.S. Lubin Manufacturing. Silent, b&w, 1 reel. Director unknown.

When a young woman reads *Romeo and Juliet* and asks her boyfriend to climb a rope ladder to her, he is chased by her father and then by angry townspeople, who misrecognize him as a lousy actor in a local production of the play.

1070 *Liza on the Stage*
1915. U.K. Piccadilly. Silent, b&w, 812 ft. Joe Evans.

In this burlesque, a street-market vendor girl becomes an actress in *Romeo and Juliet*. The actress playing Juliet also starred as Liza in *Taming Liza*. One of a series of comedies directed by Joe Evans.

1071 *Portret Doriana Greya (Picture of Dorian Gray)*
1915. Russia. Thiemann and Reinhardt. Silent, b&w, 6,969 ft. Vsevolod Meyerhold and Mikhail Doronin.

Lost film, adapted from the novel by Oscar Wilde. Regarded as one of the landmarks of pre-Revolution Russian cinema, this film contains a brief excerpt from *Romeo and Juliet*. (DL)

Note from RB: A surviving still photo features Dorian (played in male drag by actress V. Ianova) and Lord Henry in a theater box while reflected behind them (almost like an idea balloon in a comic strip) is a cramped image of the balcony scene from *Romeo and Juliet*. See Marjorie L. Hoover, *Meyerhold: The Art of Conscious Theater* (Amherst: University of Massachusetts Press, 1974), 243.

1072 *Romeo and Juliet*
1915. U.K. Lion's Head and Cricks and Martin. Silent, b&w, 970 ft. W. P. Kellino.

A burlesque staging of *Romeo and Juliet* by the Mudford Amateur Dramatic Society, featuring the antics of not only the players but also the rambunctious audience.

1073 *The Soap Suds Star*
1915. U.S. Falstaff Pictures (Thanhouser Pictures). Silent, b&w, 15 mins. Edwin Thanhouser.

Desperately in need of a cheap replacement act, a vaudeville manager hires Mary Maloney, a combative laundress, and Jack Traveliyan, a pompous actor, as a slapstick team when he sees Mary beat Jack over a laundry bill. Soon the two insist upon doing Shakespeare instead, performing so badly that they end up ruining their comedy careers.

Includes a parody of the balcony scene from *Romeo and Juliet*, with Mary as a shrewish Juliet and Jack as a drunken Romeo. One title card directly references "Romeo, Romeo, wherefore art thou, Romeo?"

1074 *The Wild Goose Chase*
1915. U.S. Jesse L. Lasky Feature Play Co. Silent, b&w, 5 reels. Cecil B. DeMille.

Two old men plan to offer their grandchildren 2,000,000 francs if they will marry each other. The two grandchildren, Betty Wright and Bob Randall, meet serendipitously and Betty becomes romantically interested in Bob. When the grandparents try to force the two to marry, Bob and Betty substitute others for themselves, Bob substituting his college roommate, Betty her maid, and the couple then runs away to join a theatrical troupe. When the troupe is arrested and the parents discover the two, Betty and Bob, now in love, consent to marry.

The theatrical troupe is playing *Romeo and Juliet*, an obliquely appropriate choice given the young lovers' determination to avoid the older generation's planned marriage for them.

1075 *David Garrick*
1916. U.S. Pallas Pictures. Silent, b&w, 50 mins. (5 reels). Frank Lloyd.

Adapted from the play by T. W. Robertson. David Garrick, the famous eighteenth-century actor, sees Ada Ingot in the audience as he plays *Romeo and Juliet* at the Drury Lane Theatre, and they fall instantly in love, but he fails to meet her and to find her after a long search. Simon Ingot, her upwardly mobile merchant father, offers him money to leave England to cure his daughter's infatuation with him; not knowing the daughter is Ada, Garrick refuses and pledges never to marry a man's daughter unless he asks him to hat in hand. Garrick also offers to rid his daughter of her infatuation by attending a dinner party. When he realizes the daughter is Ada, he honors his pledge by pretending to be drunk, but Ada discovers the ruse. When her father learns of Garrick's honorable behavior, he consents to their marriage.

1076 *Romeo and Juliet*
1916. U.S. Fox Film Corporation. Silent, b&w, 70 minutes. J. Gordon Edwards and Maxwell Karger.

Now a lost film. Theda Bara, famous for her vamp roles, played Juliet, and Harry Hilliard, a star of musicals, played Romeo. In this version, Juliet awakes before Romeo dies from poison, allowing them to have a short scene together before she commits suicide. This version, and the version by Metro Pictures starring Beverly Bayne and Francis X. Bushman, were released to capitalize upon the 300th anniversary of Shakespeare's death.

1077 *Romeo and Juliet*
1919. U.K. Hepworth Picture Plays. Silent, b&w, length unknown. Anson Dyer.

Now a lost film. One of Dyer's Shakespeare animated parodies produced between 1919 and 1920. Featured Charlie Chaplin and Mary Pickford.

1078 *The Sentimental Bloke*
1919. Australia. Southern Cross Feature Film Company. Silent, b&w, 75 mins. Raymond Longford.

Adapted from the poem by C. J. Dennis. In this classic Australian silent film, Bill, an uncultured barrowman and street tough, falls in love with and eventually marries Doreen, an urbane woman, at the waterfront of Wooloomooloo, Sydney. The film chronicles Bill's attempts to woo Doreen by reforming himself; the two eventually leave the city to find happiness.

One sequence involves a visit to a theater to see *Romeo and Juliet* in which Bill explains the action to Doreen in Australian slang.

1079 *Neighbors*
1920. U.S. Silent, b&w, 18 mins. (2 reels). Buster Keaton and Edward F. Cline.

The Boy and The Girl, two children from feuding working-class families, woo each other through a fence between their tenements in New York City. Eventually, the two marry. The situation, reminiscent of *Romeo and Juliet* and of the Pyramus and Thisbe play in *A Midsummer Night's Dream*, treats Shakespeare's romantic tragedy as a slapstick farce.

1080 *Romeo und Juliet im schne* (*Romeo and Juliet in the Snow*)
1920. Germany. Ebner & Co. and Maxim-Film GmbH. Silent, b&w, 45 mins. Ernst Lubitsch.

This free adaptation resituates the action in a Bavarian village where two families, the Kapulethofers and the Montekugers, are feuding and thereby prevent Romeo and Julia from marrying. The ending is a happy one.

One of two free transpositions of Shakespeare to Bavaria produced by Lubitsch in 1920; see also *Kohlhiesels Töchter*. A third Lubitsch film of that year, *Ich möchte kein Mann sein*, uses the signature Shakespearean motif of a woman cross-dressed as a man and involved in a romantic triangle. See also Lubitsch's *To Be or Not to Be*.

1081 *Doubling for Romeo*
1921. U.S. Goldwyn Pictures Corporation. Silent, b&w, 6 reels. Clarence G. Badger.

Sam Cody, a cowboy from Arizona, loves beautiful Lulu Foster, but because he is an awkward lover, he loses her to Steve Woods, a pretty boy who works as a soda jerk. To please Lulu (who idolizes Douglas Fairbanks) and to learn proper courtship technique, he goes to Hollywood and works as a stunt double, first as a villain, then as a lover, in both cases failing miserably. After Sam returns home, Lulu says that she will not see him until he can woo her like Romeo. Attempting to read *Romeo and Juliet*, Sam falls asleep and dreams of himself and his friends playing parts in a Shakespearean movie, with scenes of sword fighting and courtship. (Ironically, Sam uses a stunt double for his swashbuckling scenes.) When he awakes, Sam courts Lulu with rough bravado, grabbing her away from Steve and marrying her instantly.

An interesting early parody of romantic clichés, sending up (and juxtaposing) Hollywood and Shakespearean commonplaces. Sam was played by Will Rogers, his last role under contract for Goldwyn Studios.

1082 *Under the Lash*
1921. U.S. Famous Players Lasky Corporation. Silent, b&w, 6 reels (5,675 ft.). Sam Wood.

Adapted from the novel *The Shulamite* by Alice and Claude Askew, and the play by Claude Askew and Edward Knoblock. Deborah Krillet, the wife of Simeon, a religious Boer farmer, falls in love with Robert Waring, the new overseer at the Krillet farm. When Simeon discovers that she has lied about being pregnant, he threatens to kill her, but Waring saves her by killing Simeon. When the two attempt to cover over Simeon's death, Simeon's sister Anna discovers the truth and is bought off with her husband's estate. When Waring learns that he's been granted a divorce by his wife, he and Deborah marry.

What precipitates Deborah's lie is her reading of *Romeo and Juliet*, to which Simeon violently objects. Gloria Swanson played Deborah.

1083 *A Pasteboard Crown*
1922. U.S. Nathan & Semerad Productions. Silent, b&w, 50 mins. Travers Vale.

Adapted from a story by Clara Morris. Sybil Lawton, a debutante rendered penniless by her father's stock dealings, desires theatrical stardom and finds a place in a stock company through the help of producer Stewart Thrall. Sybil soon becomes the ward of a despondent fellow actor in the company, Jim Roberts, to whom she gives emotional support. Returning to New York, she rehearses a production of *Romeo and Juliet*, with Thrall as Romeo and Roberts as stage manager. When Thrall's wife Edna divorces him, Roberts blames Edna and then Thrall for his problems. He shoots Thrall as Thrall and Sybil perform the final scene in the crypt of *Romeo and Juliet*, but he recovers and hopes that his declaration of love for Sybil will win her heart.

Romeo and Juliet functions as a vehicle for Thrall to declare his love for Sybil. Travers Vale, a British director working in Hollywood, had produced an earlier *Romeo and Juliet*–oriented adaptation: see his modernized *Romeo and Juliet* (1913).

1084 *The Trouper*
1922. U.S. Universal. Silent, b&w, 5 reels. Harry B. Harris.

Mamie Judd, a go-fer for a traveling stock company, has an unrequited crush on Herman Jenks, the troupe's leading man. The company's manager, Frank Kramer, and Irene LaRue, its star, plan to swindle Neal Selden, son of a local banker, first with LaRue attempting to seduce him, then by framing him for murder and robbery. However, Mamie overhears their plotting, prevents them from escaping, and exposes their plot. Though Mamie's heroism leads Jenks to realize that he loves her, Mamie ends up engaged to Selden.

Early in the film, Mamie sees excerpts from the balcony scene from *Romeo and Juliet*, with Jenks in the role of Romeo.

1085 *Juliet and Her Romeo*
1923. U.K. Bertram Phillips. Silent, b&w, length unknown. Frank Miller and Bertram Phillips.

A burlesque starring Queenie Thomas; in the series entitled *Syncopated Picture Plays*, parodies of famous plays and novels.

1086 *To the Last Man*
1923. U.S. Famous Players—Lasky Corporation. Silent, b&w, 70 mins. Victor Fleming.

Based on the novel by Zane Grey. The Jorths, a family of sheepherders, and the Isbels, a family of cattle ranchers, are in a perpetual feud orchestrated by the family patriarchs, Lee Jorth and Gaston Isbel. Meanwhile, their two children, Jean Isbel and Ellen Jorth, are carrying on a secret romance. When Ellen is accused of possessing a horse from the Isbel ranch, the feud is renewed with special force, leaving only Ellen and Jean alive in the end.

One of the first major hybrids between *Romeo and Juliet* and the Western; Jean was played by the very popular Western star Richard Dix, and Ellen by silent film star Lois Wilson. This film was remade as a talkie version in 1933 that included far more of the feud's back story.

1087 *Romeo and Juliet*
1924. U.S. Mack Sennett Comedies. Silent, b&w, 1,867 ft. Reggie Morris and Harry Sweet.

This parody stars cross-eyed comedian Ben Turpin in the lead.

1088 *Triumph*
1924. U.S. Famous Players-Lasky. Silent, b&w, 8 reels. Cecil B. DeMille.

Adapted from the novel by May Edginton. King Garnet, indolent son of David, a manufacturing mogul, fancies Ann Land, a foreman at his father's factory, but she rejects him in order to pursue her dream of being a singer. When David dies, his will stipulates that King will inherit the company if he marries within two years; otherwise the factory will fall to its manager William Silver (who is also King's half-brother and a rival for Ann's affection). After two years, King fails to marry, and William inherits, becoming an arrogant snob. Meanwhile, Ann has become a European opera star, but her career is cut short by smoke damage to her vocal chords, and she returns home to the factory, where she attracts Silver's romantic attention. Soon King takes a job at the plant and methodically works his way to manager; when Silver's leadership falters, King steps in and Silver hands him control of the company. Soon after, King wins Ann as his wife.

The film features an excerpt from the balcony scene from *Romeo and Juliet*, in which King plays Romeo to woo Ann.

1089 *Across the Deadline*
1925. U.S. William Steiner Productions. Silent, b&w, 5 reels. Leo Maloney.

Written by Ford Beebe. In this Western, Shirley Revelle and Clem Wainwright have ignored a feud between their families to pursue a romance. When Ben Larrago, a rival for Shirley's affections, reveals the romance to Shirley's father Martin, he forbids Shirley from seeing Clem, but Clem rides across the property line between their ranches deliberately to defy him. Rance, Shirley's brother, is incensed and ambushes Clem, though he is the one who is wounded. When the sheriff uses Rance's wound to frame Rance for a stage robbery, Clem reveals the truth, and out of gratitude Martin consents to their marriage.

Another transposition of the *Romeo and Juliet* story to the American West. Compare *To the Last Man*. This film should not be confused with *Across the Deadline* (Jack Conway, 1922), a Western with the same title.

1090 *Bluebeard's Seven Wives*
1925. U.S. First National. Silent, b&w, 94 mins. (8 reels). Alfred Santell.

John Hart, a meek bank teller fired after his till comes up short, takes a job as a movie extra for director B. C. Duval (a parody of Cecil B. Demille) and is given a big break after the star pitches a fit. The director and studio decide to reshape Hart into a Latin lover, along the lines of Valentino, renaming him Don Juan Hartez and insisting that he marry and divorce seven women to prove his romantic prowess. Hart quickly becomes disillusioned, and after six marriages, he returns to marry his hometown sweetheart, Mary Kelly, a diner cook; the two retire to a farm.

One sequence features Hart as Romeo in the balcony scene from *Romeo and Juliet*, playing opposite one of his future wives; also featured are excerpts from their death scene in the crypt and Romeo's confrontation with Paris, all somewhat comically overplayed.

1091 *Cured Hams*
1925. U.S. Bischoff Inc. Silent, b&w, 1,163 ft. George Jeske.

This comedy short about two vaudevillians in a rural theater features a slapstick version of the balcony scene from *Romeo and Juliet*.

1092 *Bromo and Juliet*
1926. U.S. Pathé. Silent, b&w, 24 mins. Leo McCarey.

Comedy produced by Hal Roach. When the Chase family tries to come up with ideas for a benefit variety show for missionaries, Charley's sweetheart Madge insists upon a scene from *Romeo and Juliet*, with herself as Juliet and Charley as Romeo. As he learns the part, he notices that his legs look thin in tights, so he pads them out with sponges. When Madge sends Charley to pick up her father for the show, Charley finds him drunk and, through a series of events, he becomes drunk himself and pursued by police. Arriving at the show, he hides out from the police onstage, ruining the balcony scene from *Romeo and Juliet*, the ghost scene from *Hamlet*, a magic act, and a musical number before discovering that the audience loves his slapstick antics. Madge too is delighted, for, as she says, "There were times when I imagined you had really been drinking!"

Despite the title, there is relatively little Shakespeare in this slapstick comedy. One of the better gags involves

Charley being chased through lawn sprinklers in his sponge-lined tights only to have them become water-clogged. In the balcony scene, he plays Romeo in a doublet and hose and a bowler hat, and most of his routine involves slapstick drunkenness (though when Juliet retires, it is the policeman, not the Nurse, who comes on the balcony). In the ghost scene from *Hamlet*, both Charley and the Ghost chase across a narrow parapet as Bernardo and Marcellus look on from below. One title card makes the joke that this Shakespearean revival has "everything from Richard III to July 4th."

Available on DVD on the *Lost Films of Laurel and Hardy*, vol. 3.

1093 *Wie Einst in Mai*
1926. Germany. Ellen-Richter Film. Silent, b&w, 8,711 ft. Willi Wolff.

An experimental film in which scenes from *Romeo and Juliet* are intercut.

1094 *Felix the Cat as Roameo* (aka *Felix the Cat as Romeoww*)
1927. U.S. Production company unknown. Silent, b&w, length unknown. Director unknown.

Animated short (Felix the Cat cartoon) written by Otto Messner. Now a lost film, though elements of the continuity strip survive. The connection to Shakespeare is only in the title: Felix shuttles between three different women, the Hula Girl, the Eskimo Girl, and the Spanish Girl, after leaving his faithful girl Kitty, and he has adventures with all three. Back home, Felix again proposes to Kitty, saying he'd never look at another girl—but the girls of his travels have followed him home, belying his words.

1095 *Broadway Fever*
1929. U.S. Tiffany-Stahl Productions. Silent, b&w, 62 mins. Eddie Cline.

Sally McAllister, an aspiring actress in New York City desperate to meet producer Eric Byron, takes a job as a maid, at the time unaware that she will be working for Byron. She soon falls in love with him and misdirects his star, Lila Leroy, so that she can impersonate Leroy as the company rehearses Byron's newest play in New Jersey. On the night of the play's dress rehearsal, the truth of Sally's identity is revealed, but Byron, having fallen in love, allows her to appear anyway.

When Sally first gets her job as Byron's maid, she performs lines from *Romeo and Juliet* as she does her housework.

1096 *Hollywood Revue of 1929*
1929. U.S. MGM. Sound, b&w (with color sequences), 116 mins. Charles Reisner.

A musical and theatrical review, showcasing then-new sound technology. One vignette features a rendition of the balcony scene by Norma Shearer and John Gilbert, followed by a parody of the same scene by the same actors, the second time using jazz age slang; the sequence is of particular interest because of its juxtaposition of traditional Shakespearean performance and parodic modernization, a tension that would haunt early talking Shakespeare films. Along with John Barrymore's performance as Richard Gloucester in *Show of Shows*, this scene is one of the very first appearances of Shakespeare using the new sound technology. Shearer went on to portray Juliet in George Cukor's 1936 film production; apparently, Gilbert's appearance contributed to the collapse of his career after audiences heard his less-then-stentorious voice. Some have claimed that this *Romeo and Juliet* sequence inspired the "talkie disaster" sequence in *Singin' in the Rain* (1952).

1097 *The Guilty Generation*
1931. U.S. Columbia Pictures. Sound, b&w, 82 mins. Rowland V. Lee.

Adapted from the play by J. Kirby Hawks and Joe Milward. After a feud between the Palmero and Ricca gangs leads to the death of children, the leaders of the gangs, Mike Palmero and Tony Ricca, flee New York. Mike, a bootlegger, goes to Miami where he social climbs, much to the discomfort of his daughter Maria. Tony, meanwhile, settles in Chicago. At a society party, Maria meets John Smith, an architect who is actually Tony's son Marco, though he has been disowned by his father and consequently changed his name. Maria and Marco fall in love and learn the truth about each other. Meanwhile, the feud between the rival gangs reignites when the fathers order hits on each other's favorite sons, Benedicto Ricca and Joe Palmero. As Joe dies, he reveals Marco's identity to Mike, who plans to kill him. Nina Palmero, Maria's grandmother, helps the couple escape and kills Mike to prevents Marco's death. While the gangs continue their cycle of revenge, the couple looks forward to marriage.

Many elements are included from *Romeo and Juliet*. In an unusual twist, the conventional happy ending to this *Romeo and Juliet* adaptation is provided by a grandmother *ex machina*. One of the first of several Shakespeare-gangster hybrids (a more typical choice for this hybrid is *Macbeth*). Eight years later, Lee directed the first *Tower of London* film, a free adaptation of *Richard III*. *The Guilty Generation* is one of two Shakespeare spin-offs in which Boris Karloff appears (here he plays Tony Ricca; the other Shakespearean adaptation is *Tower of London*, where he appears as Mord).

1098 *The Painted Desert*
1931. U.S. Pathé Exchange Inc. Sound, b&w, 79 mins. Howard Higgin.

Jeff Cameron and Cash Holbrook, two companions traveling west, find an orphaned boy in the Painted Desert in Arizona. Cash's taking of the boy, who he names Bill, leads to a feud between the two after they become neighboring ranchers. Years later, Jeff and his tomboy daughter Mary Ellen seek to prevent Cash's cattle from using a watering hole on their ranch, but they are prevented from doing so by a stampede that, we learn, was caused by the now grown-up Bill Holbrook. Bill tries to reconcile Jeff and Cash by proposing a joint mining scheme; Cash refuses, but Jeff consents. Meanwhile, after some initial tension Mary Ellen falls for Bill, leading to jealousy from Rance Brett, a new cowhand with the Cameron ranch. When Jeff and Bill embark on their mining venture, their first load of ore is stolen by ambushers, and Bill must work to deliver a second load in order to prevent foreclosure on their loan. He proposes to Mary Ellen, but before they can get married, the feud between Jeff and Cash is reignited when the Cameron mine is dynamited and financial double-dealings arise. Before it's too late, Bill forces Brett to confess that he destroyed the mine out of jealousy and stops a showdown between Jeff and Cash. With the fathers reconciled, Bill looks forward to marriage with Mary Ellen.

Another hybrid of *Romeo and Juliet* and the Western: compare *Across the Deadline* and *To the Last Man*. In this version, the Tybalt role, much rewritten, is taken up by Rance, a rival suitor for Mary Ellen's (i.e., Juliet's) hand; Rance is played by Clark Gable in one of his first major screen roles. Also of interest is how the adoption of Bill becomes the catalyst for the feud. NB: this film should not be confused with *Painted Desert* (David Howard, 1938).

1099 *Range Feud*
1931. U.S. Columbia Pictures. Sound, b&w, 64 mins. D. Ross Lederman.

A range war between John Walton and Dad Turner is ignited by Walton's accusation of cattle rustling, and comes to stand in the way of a budding romance between Judy Walton and Clint Turner. After John Walton refuses to allow his daughter to marry Clint, he is found shot dead, and Clint is accused and later convicted of the crime. As Buck Gordon, the town sheriff and Clint's stepbrother, receives evidence from Jed Biggers, he is wounded by a mysterious figure. After investigation, Buck discovers that the figure is Vandall, a cattle rustler who resorted to murder to cover his cattle rustling. Clint is saved from execution and is united with Judy.

This Western uses elements of the crime thriller as well as key motifs from Shakespeare's *Romeo and Juliet*—the inter-family feud and the romance between members of rival families. In this case, the happy ending is supplied by the sheriff's detective work. Notable as one of John Wayne's first major roles in a talkie; his role in *The Deceiver* in the same year also includes Shakespearean elements. Compare *To the Last Man*, *Across the Deadline*, and *Painted Desert*.

1100 *To the Last Man*
1933. U.S. Paramount Pictures. Sound, b&w, 70 mins. Henry Hathaway.

Adapted from the novel by Zane Grey. A talkie remake (with better production values) of the 1923 film of the same name. In this version the feud is between the Haydens and Colbys, rival sheep-raising and cattle-herding families, a feud that stretches back to their days in Kentucky. After the Civil War, Mark Hayden moves his family to Nevada to leave behind the feud, leaving behind his son Lynn to care for Granny Spelvin. Jed Colby, released from prison, also heads out west with his family. As part of his vendetta against the Hayden family, he and cowhand Jim Daggs raid the Hayden ranch relentlessly. When Mark Hayden's son-in-law Neil kills the Colby's horse thief, the Colbys retaliate by rustling cattle and wounding Neil. Meanwhile, Lynn Hayden arrives and falls in love with Ellen Colby. After Mark's son Bill is killed in a Colby raid on the Hayden ranch, the cycle of reprisals threatens to escalate when Daggs dynamites a canyon, killing all but himself and Lynn. Wounded, Lynn rides to Ellen, who hides him, and after a showdown with Daggs, he and Ellen marry.

This version deviates significantly from the 1923 adaptation (which is much closer to *Romeo and Juliet*), particularly in its cataclysmic ending. In this version, Western veterans Noah Beery and Randolph Scott played the male leads of Jed Colby and Lynn Hayden, respectively.

1101 *Here Comes Cookie*
1935. U.S. Paramount. Sound, b&w, 63 mins. Norman MacLeod.

To prevent a fortune-hunting rogue from marrying his daughter, millionaire Harrison Allen arranges to transfer his money to Cookie, his other ditzy daughter, who proceeds to board out-of-work actors and set up a show in his mansion.

Includes a farcical parody of the balcony scene, as well as a conversation between Burns and Allen regarding Shakespeare's death long ago.

1102 *Romeo and Juliet*
1935. U.S. Moser and Terry Educational Pictures. Sound, b&w, 6 mins. Paul Terry and Frank Moser.

Animated film, intended for the educational market.

1103 *Dimples*
1936. U.S. 20th Century Fox. Sound, b&w, 79 mins. William A. Seiter.

In mid-nineteenth-century New York City, Sylvia "Dimples" Appleby performs songs and dances in the streets, while her grandfather Eustace Appleby, aka "The Professor," looks for opportunities for petty thieving. When Dimples and her gang entertain blueblood matron Caroline Drew at her grand mansion, Appleby steals a cuckoo clock and Dimples takes the blame to save him. Touched and concerned, Caroline offers to adopt the girl for $5,000, an offer the Professor at first refuses. Soon Dimples has the part of Eva in a production of *Uncle Tom's*

Cabin by Caroline's nephew Allen, who hires the Professor as his assistant and gives him money for business expenses. The Professor loses the money in a scam with an "antique" watch, forcing the Professor to weasel money from Caroline to keep the show running. When Caroline recognizes the Professor's tactic, she goes to the theater with the police, but she and the police are so moved by Dimples's performance that they forgive all.

When Allen first summons the Professor and Dimples to his office, the Professor, a onetime matinee idol, mistakenly believes he's being asked to join the play's cast. To demonstrate his acting talent, he offers portions of Romeo's "But soft! what light through yonder window breaks?" speech (*Romeo and Juliet* 2.2); when he forgets a line, Dimples supplies it. Allen soon reveals that he's not interested in anything as grand as Shakespeare. One other indication of the Professor's acting past: Dimples declares to Allen that she wants to play Macbeth just like the Professor when she gets to the legitimate stage. Compare *Ginger* (entry 1105).

1104 *Frankie and Johnnie*
1936. U.S. All Star Productions and Select Productions, Inc. Sound, b&w, 66 mins. Chester Erskin and John Auer.

Johnnie Drew, a rural hustler in the American 1870s, arrives in St. Louis where he meets Frankie, a dance hall girl concerned at Johnnie's naïveté about the big city. Her saloon friends save Johnnie from riverboat gamblers that he had earlier swindled. Later, Johnnie proposes to Frankie, but soon his gambling debts catch up to him, and he tells Frankie that he intends to go to New Orleans. To accompany him, Frankie borrows $1,000, unaware that Johnnie is having an affair with Nellie Bly, another dance hall girl. While watching a performance of *Romeo and Juliet* with Frankie, Johnnie sneaks away, intending to leave with Nellie, but Nellie demands $13,000, which Johnnie promises to raise. Eventually, Frankie, armed with a pistol, confronts Johnnie, and he ends up shot by a henchman of Lou, from whom Frankie had borrowed the $1,000. Afterward, Frankie returns to her former fiancé Curley, and the two leave for New Orleans.

1105 *Ginger*
1936. U.S. Fox Film Corporation. Sound, b&w, 80 mins. Lewis Seiler.

Rex Whittington, an aging Shakespearean, is drunkenly despondent after being offered a spear carrier role in a movie. His streetwise niece Ginger rescues him from the police, only later to be discovered by a probation officer who warns Ginger that she can be taken away from her loving if dissolute uncle. When Rex is once again arrested, Ginger resorts to shoplifting and is herself arrested. At Ginger's trial, rich society matron Elizabeth Parker offers to adopt her, and Ginger's rude and direct manner causes comic havoc at the stuffy Parker household. When Eliza-

beth reveals to Ginger that Rex is not really her uncle, Elizabeth's husband Daniel is outraged and springs Rex from jail, but Rex realizes that Ginger belongs with the Parkers and sneaks away. In the process, an accident gives Rex aphasia. Several events springing from Elizabeth's condescension lead Ginger back to Rex, staying at a run-down boardinghouse, and when he sees Ginger, the two embrace, leading to a reconciliation among all. Early in the film, Ginger and Uncle Rex rehearse the balcony scene from *Romeo and Juliet* on the roof of Rex's New York City terement. Compare *Dimples* (entry 1103).

1106 *Give Us This Night*
1936. U.S. Paramount. Sound, b&w, 73 mins. Alexander Hall.

With the voice of Italian tenor Forcellini falling apart so badly that his diva co-star Maria Severelli refuses to work with him, opera maestro Marcello Bonetti turns to Antonio Belizza, a fisherman with a beautiful voice, to star in his new opera of *Romeo and Juliet* after Maria hears him sing. Though his mother forbids him to leave, Antonio does so anyway. While rehearsing the balcony scene, Antonio gives Maria a kiss, revealing his feelings for her. When Antonio discovers that Marcello and Maria are to be married, he runs away, prompting Maria to confess to Marcello her love for Antonio. As the opening hour of the opera nears, Marcello and Maria search for Antonio, enlisting the help of Antonio's mother, but with no Antonio in sight, Marcello is forced to rehire Forcellini. The opera begins with Forcellini in Romeo's role, but at its midpoint, Antonio returns and forces Forcellini to give the role to him. As Romeo, Antonio sings a duet with Maria for the balcony scene, and the two get a standing ovation.

The balcony scene, converted to operatic form, is central to the opera and to the budding romance between Antonio and Maria, for it is the vehicle through which they express their affections. The operatic setting was written by Erich Korngold. This film is not to be confused with *Give Us the Night* (John M. Stahl, 1939).

1107 *Pay as You Exit*
1936. U.S. Hal Roach Studios and MGM. Sound, b&w, 11 mins. Gordon M. Douglas.

In the *Our Gang* serial series. The Little Rascals' barnyard production of *Romeo and Juliet* is threatened when Alfalfa's eating of onions causes Darla (Juliet) to quit at intermission. She is replaced by Buckwheat in a blonde wig for their rendition of the balcony scene.

There is a passing citation of "To be or not to be," in addition to general references to the plot of *Romeo and Juliet*. In this version, Alfalfa (Romeo) kills Juliet's father in a swordfight before the balcony scene. Compare *Beginner's Luck* and *Radio Bugs*.

1108 *Reefer Madness*
1936. U.S. Sound, b&w,
67 mins. Louis Gassner.

An anti-marijuana film
that became a cult film
in the 1960s involving
a young couple who are
turned into pot addicts,
with disastrous results.
There is a scene in which
the couple recite lines from
Romeo and Juliet. (RB)

1109 *Sing, Baby, Sing*
1936. U.S. 20th Century
Fox. Sound, b&w, 90 mins.
Sidney Lanfield.

After being fired from her
singing job at the Ritz Club,
losing her agent, and failing
an audition, Joan Warren,
a young aspiring actress,
meets Bruce Farraday, an
actor notorious for his
drunkenness. Her former
agent Nicky Alexander en-
courages Joan to play Juliet
to Farraday's Romeo for the
sake of her career. When
she gets photographed with

Alfalfa and Buckwheat from *Pay as You Exit* (1936). In a version of the
balcony scene, Alfalfa woos a cross-dressed Buckwheat, who is wearing
a blond wig. Courtesy of Douglas Lanier.

One of the first major
South Indian historical
films. In 1083, Ambika-
pathy, the son of Kambar,
the great Tamil poet, is in
love with the princess
Amaravathy. Because the
two lovers are from different classes, Kulothunga
Chola, the King of Wor-
irur, imposes a test of will
for Ambikapathy in order
for the two to marry. Am-
bikapathy fails the test.
Sammons notes that the
film includes a balcony
scene that has similarities
to that in George Cukor's
1936 film adaptation of
Romeo and Juliet.

1112 *Hamlet and Eggs*
1937. U.S. Educational
Pictures, Incorporated.
Sound, b&w, 17 mins.
William Watson.

Leslie   Comstock,   a
pompous   Shakespearean
director, goes to a dude
ranch in Arizona to take a

Farraday, Mr. Brewster, a broadcasting executive who had
earlier rejected Joan, now wants to hire her and Farraday,
but the deal soon turns sour when Farraday's agent Robert
Wilson arrives and spirits Farraday to California. But Joan
catches Farraday's train en route, tricks Robert in leaving
without Farraday, and with Farraday's help secures a contract for them both.

Based upon the infamous affair between Elaine Barrie
and John Barrymore, *Sing, Baby, Sing* contains several allusions to Shakespeare: Farraday drunkenly babbles lines
from the plays.

1110 *A Woman Rebels*
1936. U.S. RKO Radio Pictures. Sound, b&w, 88 mins.
Mark Sandrich.

Based on the novel *Portrait of a Rebel* by Netta Syrett.
Katharine Hepburn apparently cites *Hamlet* as she plays
Pamela "Pam" Thistlewaite, a late nineteenth-century
independent woman with an overbearing, strict father. She
raises a daughter on her own. Unseen. (RB)

1111 *Ambikapathy*
1937. India. Salem Shankar Films. Sound, b&w, 210 mins.
Ellis R. Dungan.

vacation from the theater. Irene Wilson, daughter of the
rancher, is stagestruck and badgers Comstock into performing in her cowboy *Romeo and Juliet*. The balcony scene
involves gunplay and a cowboy trio singing "Comin' 'round
the Mountain." At film's end, the director, a cultured snob,
returns to New York to direct *Hamlet* dressed in cowboy
garb and speaking with a country drawl; Irene accompanies
him. Irene was played by Irene Ryan, the established
vaudeville star who went on to play Granny in the TV
show *The Beverley Hillbillies*.

The balcony and tomb scenes from *Romeo and Juliet* are
parodied by juxtaposing them with Western dialect and
slapstick. The only substantial reference to *Hamlet* is in the
title.

1113 *It's Love I'm After*
1937. U.S. Warner Bros. Sound, b&w, 90 mins. Archie
Mayo.

In this romantic farce, Basil Underwood and Joyce
Arden are a Shakespearean acting team who, despite their
constant bickering and Basil's self-absorption and romantic
escapades, are deeply in love. (The situation owes something to the notoriously volatile relationship between
Alfred Lunt and Lynn Fontanne, also an inspiration for the

musical *Kiss Me Kate!*) Basil, recognizing the error of his ways, resolves to reform and even asks Joyce to marry him, but he becomes waylaid by his plan to disillusion his worshipful fan, heiress Marcia West. He plans to act the cad so that she will marry her fiancée Henry Grant Jr., to whom Basil owes a favor. The plan goes awry when Marcia is enamored rather than repelled by Basil's behavior, and Joyce's discovery of the two together only complicates the misunderstandings. Eventually, the two women overhear the truth about Basil, and the two couples are reconciled. The film trades heavily on the Shakespearean reputation of Leslie Howard (who plays Basil), a reputation reinforced by his appearance as Romeo in the MGM film production of *Romeo and Juliet* the year earlier.

The film is filled with sly Shakespearean references. It opens with a montage of Basil and Joyce's Shakespearean tour, with references to *As You Like It*, *Hamlet*, and *Romeo and Juliet*. We are treated to an extended excerpt from the tomb scene in *Romeo and Juliet*, in which Basil and Joyce bicker *sotto voce* as they perform the scene; the set is certainly meant to recall the tomb scene for the MGM film. Basil and Joyce reference several Shakespearean chestnuts in the course of the film. Basil cautions Joyce against "the green-eyed monster" (*Othello*), and in an effort to demonstrate his boorishness he performs Petruchio's objection to the burnt meat from *The Taming of the Shrew*, 4.1. "Tomorrow and tomorrow and tomorrow" (*Macbeth*), "Give me light" (*Hamlet*), and "Angels and ministers of grace defend us" (*Hamlet*) all appear in comic contexts. At the film's end, Basil performs a self-absorbed version of the "all the world's a stage" speech (*As You Like It*), as Henry and Marcia roll their eyes and sneak away. The elevator man offers this verdict: "Boy, what a ham!" Considered in contrast with *Romeo and Juliet* (MGM, 1936), *It's Love I'm After* offers the other side of Hollywood's appropriation of Shakespeare in its golden age.

1114 *Mickey's Grand Opera*
1937. U.S. Walt Disney Pictures. Sound, col., 8 mins. Wilfred Jackson.

Mickey Mouse conducts an operatic version of *Romeo and Juliet* with Clara as Juliet and Donald Duck as Romeo. When backstage Pluto upsets a magician's props, they come to life and with their magical powers ruin the performance.

Included in the DVD compilation *Walt Disney Treasures—Mickey Mouse in Living Color*.

1115 *College Swing*
1938. U.S. Paramount Pictures. Sound, b&w, 86 mins. Raoul Walsh.

A musical comedy. As part of a pact between Alden College and the rich Alden family dating from 1738, if a daughter of the Alden family passes her graduating exam, she can receive her inheritance; otherwise, the money is the property of the college. When, with the unscrupulous help of a tutor, Bud, Gracie Alden passes her exam, she uses her new financial position to appoint herself "Dean of Men," hire screwball faculty, and promote swing, with terrible consequences for a developing romance between Ginna Washburn and Martin Bates. Eventually the tutor's scheme to aid Gracie is exposed, Alden College returns to normal, Ginna and Martin's romance is saved, and Gracie finds love and marriage with businessman Hubert Dash.

As part of a fraternity initiation, Martin Bates dresses up in a Cupid costume and sings, "What Did Romeo Say to Juliet?" to Ginna Ashburn while she listens from her balcony. The song contains many references to Shakespearean phrases and titles; at several points, Ginna supplies lines (for both Juliet and Romeo) from the balcony scene.

1116 *Dramatic School*
1938. U.S. MGM and Loewes. Sound, b&w, 80 mins. Robert B. Sinclair.

Based on the play *School of Drama*, by Hans Székely and Zoltan Egyed. About several women learning to be actresses in Paris. Apparently, it has a scene involving *Romeo and Juliet*. Unseen. (RB)

1117 *The Goldwyn Follies*
1938. U.S. Samuel Goldwyn Company. Sound, col., 115 mins. George Marshall and H. C. Potter.

When movie producer Oliver Merlin overhears two women criticizing *Forgotten Dance*, a film he is shooting, he hires one of them, Hazel Dawes, as a consultant to supply the popular perspective. Oliver falls in love with Hazel, who soon falls in love with Danny Beecher, a hamburger cook turned singer and film star. Romantic complications are juxtaposed with various entertainment vignettes in this film-within-a-film.

In a sequence early in the film, Oliver asks Hazel her opinion of a dance version of *Romeo and Juliet*, handled as a feud between classical ballet and jazz tap dancers, which we see. Hazel replies that she wants a happy ending in which the lovers live and the families reconcile, a version that is immediately shown. In the film's final scene, Michael Day engages in repartee with Charlie McCarthy and Edgar Bergen about Shakespeare. He recites "To be or not to be" and "Friends, Romans, countrymen," both of which Charlie ridicules; as his parting shot, Charlie makes a joke about Shakespeare being boring.

1118 *Kentucky*
1938. U.S. 20th Century Fox. Sound, b&w, 95 mins. David Butler.

Adapted from the story "The Look of Eagles" by John Taintor Foote. Sally Goodwin and Jack Dillon are both children of feuding horse-breeding families. The feud between the Goodwins and Dillons stretches back to the

Civil War, and it becomes inflamed when Peter Goodwin, Sally's uncle, asks John Dillon, Jack's grandfather, for a loan and is refused. When the Goodwins are plunged into poverty, Jack, keeping his identity secret, helps the family train horses and falls in love with Sally. When Blue Grass, the horse he trains for them, wins the Kentucky Derby, Sally and Jack are united, but Peter unexpectedly dies and is afterward eulogized by John, ending the feud.

The general outlines of the story—lovers separated by a feud sustained by the family patriarchs—accord with *Romeo and Juliet*, though instead of the lovers dying, it is the patriarch of one of the families. The film details the origins of the feud, something not included in Shakespeare's narrative. One of several variations based on the Hatfield-McCoy feud; compare *Rosanna McCoy*. David Butler also directed *Playmates*, another Shakespeare spin-off referencing *Romeo and Juliet*.

1119 *The Wizard of Oz*
1938. U.S. MGM. Sound, col. and b&w, 101 mins. Victor Fleming and Richard Thorpe.

Adapted from the novel *The Wonderful Wizard of Oz* by L. Frank Baum. Transported to the Land of Oz by a tornado and beset by an evil witch, Dorothy and her dog Toto search for the way back home, with the help of the Scarecrow, Tin Man, and Lion.

In this classic musical, one verse of the Tin Man's song, "If I Only Had a Heart" (lyrics by E. Y. Harburg and music by Harold Arlen), alludes to the balcony scene.

1120 *The Adventures of Huckleberry Finn*
1939. U.S. Sound, b&w, 90 mins. Richard Thorpe.

Starring Mickey Rooney as Huck, this film is the only film adaptation of Mark Twain's novel (entry 1809) that includes the burlesque of *Romeo and Juliet* in it (the balcony scene proves to be a disaster; Huck plays Juliet). J. Lee Thompson's 1974 film version of the novel does reference Shakespeare. See *Andy Hardy Gets Spring Fever*. (RB)

1121 *Andy Hardy Gets Spring Fever*
1939. U.S. Sound, b&w, 88 mins. W. S. Van Dyke.

In this, the sixth installment in the Andy Hardy series set in a rural, all-white, small American town, Andy (Mickey Rooney) is a high school student. Andy develops a crush on his new high school drama teacher, Rose Meredith (Helen Gilbert). Miss Meredith proposes that the students write and perform their own play rather than, as has been the case in the past, an already published play. She suggests they use an already published play as a model. "Read the plays of Shakespeare and Sheridan," she tells the students. Andy is the last student to leave class and talks to Meredith about the play. She mentions *Romeo and Juliet* and quotes a line from the prologue, "A pair of star-cross'd lovers take their life." Andy says he hasn't read the play but that he will. At home, he begins writing his play, basing it on *Romeo and Juliet*. He think his father, Judge Hardy, has never read it either, but is surprised when he quotes the line Meredith did and then his father completes it: "A pair of star-cross'd lovers take their life; / Whose misadventured piteous overthrows / Do with their death bury their parents' strife." Andy tells his father he has entered a new phase, shocked that he once thought "kissing girls was more important than Shakespeare." His father smiles to himself at Andy's newfound seriousness. Meredith announces to the class that the English Department has selected Andy's play, *Adrift in Tahiti*. After class, Andy explains that he based his play on *Romeo and Juliet*, changing the setting from Italy to the island of Tahiti, Romeo into a rear admiral, and Juliet in a native girl. Apparently borrowing from Giacommo Puccini's opera *Turandot*, he changes the plot as well, telling Mrs. Meredith he thinks it is "a lot better than Shakespeare's." The read admiral dumps the native girl, Tahoola, and she commits suicide by jumping into a volcano. At a rehearsal, Andy plays the admiral and his ex-girlfriend, Polly, plays the "olive-skinned" Tahoola. (In the performance, we learn that she is the mixed-race offspring of her Tahiti mother and white navy father, who was marooned on the island.) After a rehearsal, Miss Meredith closes the classroom door and turns off the lights, not realizing that Andy is still there. She walks over to a window, lit by moonlight. Andy walks over to comfort her and tells that from the first time he saw her, she seemed "sort of tragic, kind of like Romeo and Juliet." When she tells him good night, he asks her, "Is it true that Romeo was only eighteen years old?" "Something like that," she replies. His identification with Romeo becomes explicit when he then says he's "going to be eighteen myself very soon." At a dress rehearsal, Andy gives Miss Meredith a present on behalf of the class. He suggested it, he tells her. It is a leather-bound copy of *Romeo and Juliet*. Andy eventually confesses his love to Meredith, but she tells him she is already engaged. While he is escorting Meredith to her home by the light of a full moon, Meredith quotes three lines from *The Merchant of Venice* "How sweet the moonlight sleeps upon this bank. . . . Look how the floor of heaven / Is thick inlaid with patines of bright gold." Andy misidentifies the quotation: "That's from *Romeo and Juliet*. Gee, I used to think this Shakespeare stuff was just a bunch of junk. But when you say it, it all sounds so different." Andy proposes marriage to Meredith, but she postpones until after the performance the following night her explanation of her rejection. The program note for the second act says, "A pair of star-crossed lovers."

The plot of *Adrift in Tahiti* and the plot of the film run loosely parallel: the admiral rejects Tahoola because he falsely thinks she is in love with another; Meredith rejects Andy because she is already engaged to another. Just before the performance, Andy sees Meredith kiss her fiancé backstage, and he address his lines to her as she watches in the wings rather than to Tahoola. The plot of *Romeo and Juliet* does not run parallel to that of the film, however. Andy makes up with his girlfriend. The Shakespeare references seem partly intended to recall Rooney's performance as Puck four years earlier in William Dieterle and Max Reinhardt's *Midsummer Night's Dream*. A younger student whose last name is Higgenbotham (pronounced "Higgenbottom") wants to play the moon, and messes up the moon in the dress rehearsal so that Andy has to show how to do it correctly. The moon also is messed up during the performance. There is a similar in-joke about Rooney in Norman Taurog's *Young Tom Edison* (1940). As if functioning as a trailer for Rooney's next film, Judge Hardy says that Andy is "a regular Thomas A. Edison" after the performance. Rooney also performed as Juliet in a parody of the balcony scene in *The Adventures of Huck Finn* (Richard Thorpe, 1939). (RB)

1122 *Cheer Boys Cheer*
1939. U.K. Ealing Studios and United Artists. Sound, b&w, 84 mins. Walter Forde.

Adapted from a story by Donald Bull and Ian Dalrymple. The Greenleafs and the Ironsides are feuding brewers, the Greenleafs upholding the tradition of English pubs and ale, the Ironsides innovating with corporate organization, modern brewing techniques, and mass marketing. When the Greenleafs fend off a takeover by the ruthless Ironsides, Tom Ironside secretly infiltrates the company with an eye toward ruining it, but he falls in love with Margaret Greenleaf and the two end up reconciling the families.

The trope of lovers divided by a feud forms the armature for a key sub-plot of this comic paean to traditional British brewing. Widely regarded as a forerunner of the classic Ealing comedies of the 1940s and 1950s.

1123 *Le Fin du Jour*
1939. France. Regina Films. Sound, b&w, 99 mins. Julien Duvivier.

An ensemble character study of aging actors in a retirement home for destitute entertainers. The plot concerns the financial problems of the home, the various ways in which the actors support themselves, and the actors' rivalries, jealousies, and attempts to maintain their dignity. The four main characters are Raphael Saint Clair, a fading sex symbol whose arrival leads to jealousy and hatred; Cabrissade, a second-rate actor who was never more than an understudy and struggles to hide that from others; Marny, an actor who seeks self-respect when he discovers his wife's infidelities; and Monsieur Lucien, an overly cerebral stage star who never connected with his audience.

Includes several passing references to *Romeo and Juliet*.

1124 *Pukar*
1939. India. Minerva Movietone. Sound, b&w, 165 mins. Sohrab Modi.

The film offers two interlocking love stories set in the brutal court of Mughal Emperor Shahenshah Jehangir. In the first, Manghal Singh, son of Rajput chieftain Sangram Singh, is in love with Kanwar, daughter of a family with which the Singhs are feuding. Goaded into a fight, he kills Kanwar's brother and father. Sangram brings his own son to the emperor for judgment, and Jehangir sentences him to death (an eye for an eye). In the second story, a washerwoman accuses the empress of killing her husband during a hunt. Jehangir's own standard of judgment thus becomes applicable to his wife, and so he offers his own life in exchange, at which the peasant forgives him.

The basic situation of *Romeo and Juliet*—two lovers divided by feuding families, the Romeo figure Manghal killing members of the Juliet figure Kanwar's family in a fight—becomes the armature for a parable about the nature of justice and necessity for forgiveness.

1125 *That's Right, You're Wrong*
1939. U.S. RKO Radio Pictures. Sound, b&w, 94 mins. David Butler.

In an effort to boost revenues, J. D. Forbes, a movie studio mogul, recruits popular bandleader Kay Kyser and his swing band to Hollywood. Problems soon develop when the band members develop star attitudes and when screenwriters seek to give Kyser a sophisticated romantic image at odds with his homespun personality. To pressure Kyser into breaking his film studio contract, Stacey Delmore, the producer, replaces Ginny Simms (the band's singer) with Sandra Sands in the film, but Kyser, wise to his plan, unexpectedly accepts the part of Sandra's Latin lover and pretends at a press conference to want to play a Venetian gondolier opposite her. As a result of such lamebrained casting, Stacey is humiliated and buys out Kyser's contract, but the band is convinced that Kyser is in earnest and kidnaps him back to North Carolina, where they started.

The film contains a short parody of the *Romeo and Juliet* balcony scene. The same team of Kyser and director Butler would make *Playmates* in 1941, a film that features a much more involved *Romeo and Juliet* parody.

1126 *Torchy Blane in Chinatown*
1939. U.S. Sound, b&w, 58 mins. William Beaudine.

The police and a potential victim of a Chinese tong see what appears to be a Chinese man listening to them on the other side of a rice-paper door. Police Lieutenant McBride and his assistant, Detective Gahagen, open the door only to find it is actually Torchy Blane, "intrepid girl-reporter" and McBride's fiancée, who has climbed up a balcony. She tumbles to the floor as McBride and Gahagen subdue "him." Torchy quips, "Ever time I see a balcony, the Juliet comes out in me, but you Romeos play too rough." (MJ, with RB)

1127 *Shakespearian Spinach*
1940. U.S. Fleischer Studios. Sound, b&w, 6 mins. Dave
Fleischer.

Animated short film (Popeye). Having replaced the
hammy Bluto in the Spinach Theatre's operatic production of *Romeo and Juliet*, Popeye is assaulted by his rival's
many attempts to sabotage the production. Eventually,
Bluto takes Popeye's Romeo costume and locks him in a
box, afterward manhandling Olive Oyl's Juliet. Popeye
substitutes himself for Olive Oyl, endures Bluto's kisses,
and seemingly dies in a fight with him; when Olive supplies
him with a funeral wreath made of spinach, Popeye revives
and beats up Bluto, to the audience's wild applause.

A burlesque of high culture, targeting both opera and
Shakespeare. Fascinating is the number of gags that depend
upon cross-dressing, gags that have some gender implications: at different points in the narrative, both Popeye and
Bluto are dressed in Juliet's costume. Referenced are only
two familiar lines from the balcony scene—"Romeo,
Romeo, wherefore art thou, Romeo?" and "Parting is such
sweet sorrow"—as well as two key scenes from the play, the
balcony scene and the crypt scene, both converted to
slapstick violence.

1128 *Romeo in Rhythm*
1940. Sound, col., 7 mins. Rudolf Ising.

An animated cartoon based on the balcony scene that
opens in a theater production starring two black crows as
Swingin' Romeo and Flat-Foot Juliet. Both crows speak in
African American accents. The male crow (Romeo) cites
the "It is the east, and Juliet is the sun" (2.2.3) speech and
Juliet mentions Shakespeare. Most of the cartoon is swing
music accompanying various interruptions that prevent
Romeo from kissing Juliet. The music is presented by the
"Black Crow Light Opera Company." (RB & DL)

1129 *Espoirs* (aka *Le Champ Maudit*)
1941. France. Sport Films. Sound, b&w, 92 mins. Willy
Rozier.

Adapted from the novel *Romeo und Julia auf dem Dorfe*
by Gottfried Keller. In this transposition of *Romeo and Juliet*
to rural Dordogne, France, two feuding farm families, the
Martins and the Auberts, divide their children Pierre
Martin and Isabelle Aubert, who are lovers. The narrative
is played for comedy and ends happily.

1130 *Romeo und Julia auf dem Dorfe*
1941. Switzerland. Pro Film Genossenschaft für Filmproduktion. Sound, b&w, 102 mins. Valérian Schmidely and
Hans Trommer.

Adapted from the novel by Gottfried Keller. In this
transposition of *Romeo and Juliet* to a rural Swiss village
outside Zurich, Vreneli and Sali are young peasant children in love since childhood. As adolescents, they become
divided by their families' self-destructive legal feud over a

tract of land claimed by patriarchs of both farms. Eventually, sensing their plight is hopeless, the lovers decide to
spend one day alone together, and then to separate forever,
but when the day is over they cannot part and instead float
away in a boat. Later the boat is found, empty. An acknowledged classic of Swiss cinema, filmed in a social
realist style reminiscent of Vittorio De Sica. Compare
Espoirs and Delius's opera *A Village Romeo and Juliet*.

1131 *Teresa Venerdi* (*Doctor Beware*)
1941. Italy. Alleanza Cinematografica Italiana and Europa
Film. Sound, b&w, 92 mins. Vittorio De Sica.

Adapted from the novel by Rudolf Torök. In this comedy, Pietro Vignali, a doctor deeply in debt because of his
spendthrift girlfriend, singer Loletto Prima, is forced to
take a job as an orphanage's sanitation inspector to work
his way back into solvency. He becomes the object of two
women's affection: Lilli Passalacqua, the wealthy heiress of
a mattress mogul, to whom he becomes engaged, and
Teresa Venerdi, a poor but devoted foundling who re-
sourcefully solves his financial and romantic problems and,
in the end, marries him.

Includes a monologue by Juliet (in Italian) from *Romeo
and Juliet*.

1132 *Henry Aldrich Gets Glamour*
1943. U.S. Paramount. Sound, b&w, 72 mins. Hugh Bennett.

Part of the Henry Aldrich film series. Henry Aldrich, a
geeky teenager from Centerville, wins an essay contest and
goes to Hollywood for a date with Hilary Dane, a starlet
who has just learned that she is not to star in a film *Romeo
and Juliet* because she is too old. When a picture of Henry
and Hilary innocently kissing is published in movie magazines, Henry gets a reputation as a ladies' man in Centerville and drops his girlfriend Phyllis Michael to date
Virginia Lowry, a high society girl earlier out of his orbit.
His date with Virginia ends with their car breaking down,
and rumors of indiscretion cause Henry's father to with-
draw from a local election. When Hilary comes to town for
a publicity appearance, Henry, depressed at his reputation,
asks her to help reestablish his good name, and Hilary's
agent encourages her to do so to prove she can sustain a
romance with a young man and thus get the role of Juliet.
Her plan works—the studio is newly interested in her for
the role—but Henry is dismayed when he discovers he's
been used and proposes to her to force her to reveal the
truth. Eventually, Hilary does so.

Much of Hilary's and her agent Steve's motivation revolves around Hilary establishing that she can play a very
young woman and thus get the lead in the screen *Romeo
and Juliet*. The premise is interesting given the decreasing
ages of Juliets in major film productions of *Romeo and Juliet*
throughout the twentieth century.

1133 *Romeo y Julieta* (*Romeo and Juliet*)
1943. Mexico. Posa Film S.A. Sound, b&w, 104 mins.
Miguel Delgado.

A farce starring Cantinflas, the famous Mexican comedian, one of several of his parodies of classic literature. In the frame tale, Cantinflas, a hapless taxi driver, picks up a drunk actor, despondent that Julieta, the woman he loves, is being forced by her father to marry the famous Italian star Teobaldini. The actor and his friend convince Cantinflas to pretend to be Abelardo del Monte, a Shakespearean actor with a European pedigree who will play Romeo in a production sponsored by Julieta's father. Their plan is to create an example of tragic thwarted love that will prompt Julieta's father to reconsider. Though the production of *Romeo and Juliet* itself begins onstage, it soon becomes a film version that closely resembles Cukor's 1936 film adaptation in many details of period costuming, production design, shot types, and even casting (Teobaldo resembles Basil Rathbone). The film's narrative follows Shakespeare's closely, including sixteen of Shakespeare's twenty-four scenes. Though the other characters play their parts "straight" (and many of the characters of the frame tale reappear in the play), Cantinflas plays his Romeo for slapstick comedy. The first battle between the Montescos and Capuletas in the streets of Verona is a food fight; his dance with Juliet in the dance scene parodies the choreography of Cukor's film; the balcony scene involves Cantinflas repeatedly dodging a vase knocked from Juliet's balcony; Cantinflas interrupts his fight with Teobaldo for a game of dicing, and his swordplay is comically unconventional; and the poison he imbibes at Juliet's tomb leads to comic spasms. Central also to the comedy is Cantinflas's inimitable idiom, a combination of goofy rhymed couplets, street slang, working-class fast talk, anachronisms, and silly wordplay. Once the play is over, Cantinflas's girlfriend, who had earlier abandoned him, starts a fight with his co-star, and Cantinflas is cudgeled for his performance by three outraged critics. The film references not only *Romeo and Juliet*, but also *Hamlet* (and John Barrymore and Leslie Howard) when Julieta's father discusses Shakespeare with the actor's friend; Cantinflas himself speaks of knowing Shakespeare and sharing drinks with him, a lie others take as a witty joke. The parodic tone of the piece is generally gentle and is directed primarily against pompous polite society and figures of authority.

1134 *Stage Door Canteen*
1943. U.S. Sol Lesser Productions and United Artists. Sound, b&w, 132 mins. Frank Borzage.

Financed by the Theatre Guild with proceeds going to wartime fundraising, this extravaganza offered a fictionalized tale of the real Stage Door Canteen, a wartime club in Manhattan run by the Theatre Wing of the Armed Forces for the entertainment of military personnel and featuring top acts and stars. The plotline turns on a forbidden romance between Eileen Burke, a canteen volunteer, and Dakota Smith, a soldier about to be shipped overseas; their romance violates the strict no-dating rules of the Canteen. At film's end, Eileen and Dakota are about to be married, but he is unexpectedly shipped off before they can do so. The plot provides an armature for a stunning variety of music, comedy, and dramatic acts, including cameos of everyone from Guy Lombardo, Xavier Cugat, Ethel Waters, and Count Basie to Harpo Marx, Katharine Hepburn, Alfred Lunt, Lynn Fontaine, and Gypsy Rose Lee.

Early in the film Shakespearean actress Katharine Cornell makes a cameo appearance as herself, her only film performance. As she hands out oranges in a food line, she meets a soldier who recognizes her, and the two offer an impromptu rendition of Romeo and Juliet's exchange about swearing by the moon from the balcony scene from *Romeo and Juliet*. The short passage functions thematically within the film to announce the theme of intense but forbidden romance, but it too offers a glimpse of Cornell's quiet intensity and idiomatic line readings, even though she was by this time too old to play the part of Juliet onstage. Despite the touching scene, the film is clearly uncomfortable with high culture in such a setting, for at the end of the sequence, she labels her performance "a little unrationed ham being served." See also *Morning Glory* and *Stage Door*.

1135 *Time Flies*
1944. U.K. Gainsborough Pictures. Sound, b&w, 88 mins. Walter Forde.

Susie Barton, a nightclub singer, and her husband Bill are coaxed by Tommy Handley, a fast-talking schemer, into investing in his Time Ferry Service, a time-travel scheme using a time machine invented by the Professor, a dotty inventor. Chased by the police into the time machine, the group is accidentally transported back to the reign of Queen Elizabeth, where they encounter various figures from the age—Walter Ralegh, William Shakespeare, John Smith, Pocahontas, and the Queen herself. Through various machinations Tommy bilks the court of its wealth and is made Lord of America, while the Professor is arrested for making prophesies about the future. When Tommy pushes his schemes too far, he, Susie, and Bill join the Professor in the Tower. Eventually the Professor engineers the group's escape, at the last minute saving Tommy from being beheaded at the Queen's command.

Early in the film, Susie and Bill encounter William Shakespeare at the Globe Theatre as he struggles to write the balcony scene. Susie, appearing in a Renaissance costume she's borrowed from the company's wardrobe, supplies Shakespeare with the familiar dialogue she knows from the future, starting with her reply to Shakespeare's inquiry about her name—she answers, "What's in a name?" The sequence ends with Susie doing a swing number, "Ring along Bells," on the Globe stage, with Shakespeare directing the music and the Renaissance audience delightedly throwing pennies. This passage also briefly references *Love's Labor's Lost*, the title of which Susie sees on a poster backstage; Bill observes, "I'll bet business was lousy." And, in good Shakespearean style, Susie briefly cross-dresses as a man. The cast includes two stars of Olivier's *Henry V*, produced in the same year as this film: Felix Aylmer as the Professor (he played Canterbury in Olivier's film [entry 351]), and Roy Emerton as John Smith (he played Bardolph). See also entry 237.

1136 *Übers Jahr—Wenn Die Kornblumen Blühen*
1944. Germany. 79 mins. Eduard von Borsody
A *Romeo and Juliet*–style romance, set in a rural village.

1137 *Nicholas Nickleby*
1946. U.K. Ealing Studios. Sound, b&w, 108 mins. Alberto Cavalcanti.
Adapted from the Charles Dickens novel (entry 1805). See summary in entry 1066. Includes an overblown performance of the epilogue from the Crummles' performance of *Romeo and Juliet*.

1138 *The Perils of Pauline*
1947. U.S. Paramount. Sound, col., 96 mins. George Marshall.
A musical biopic of silent serial queen Pearl White, chronicling her rise to fame from her beginnings as a seamstress and the fall of her theatrical mentor and lover, Mike. A variation on the formula of *A Star Is Born*.
Pearl's impromptu show business debut involves her singing a swing number, "Rumble," before a performance of *Romeo and Juliet*. Mike Farrington, star of the troupe and Pearl's lover-to-be, comments sardonically, "An ideal curtain-raiser for Shakespeare."

1139 *That Hagen Girl*
1947. U.S. Warner Bros. Sound, b&w, 83 mins. Peter Godfrey.
Adapted from the novel by Edith Kneipple Roberts. Mary Hagen, a young woman adopted into a small-town family, is hounded by gossip about the identity of her father, rumored to be Tom Bates, a prominent lawyer. When he returns to the town and romances Julia Kane, Mary's favorite college professor, Mary tries to commit suicide.
Julia encourages Mary to audition for *Romeo and Juliet*, and she gets the part of Juliet. Pressure from the school board forces Julia to reassign the part to another girl, but when she gets sick, Mary performs the part at the last minute with great success.

1140 *Variety Girl*
1947. U.S. Paramount. Sound, b&w, 83 mins. George Marshall.
A tale of two aspiring actresses, both of whom take the name Amber LeVon, trying to break into movies at Paramount Studios in Hollywood. Their comic misadventures provide the rationale for a sequence of star cameos (many Paramount contract players), short vignettes, slapstick, and musical numbers, culminating in a variety show benefit for the Variety Club, a show business charity from which one of the aspiring actresses unknowingly benefitted.
In one sequence, one of the actresses records a voice-over for a musical stop-action puppet parody (by noted puppeteer George Pal) called *Romeow and Julicat*. In it, the Montagues and Capulets are fighting dogs and cats (respectively) in Elizabethan garb. At one point, Julicat sings, "Wherefore art thou, Romeow?" but otherwise the sequence does not reference Shakespeare's dialogue. Much of the action occurs on Julicat's balcony where, in the midst of Romeow's visit, the elder Capulet discovers the lovers' tryst and engages in slapstick violence to stop it. The sequence alternates between the puppet film itself and the actors providing the zany songs and sound effects, and it ends with the studio executive getting accidentally doused with water by the actress, a repeated motif in the film. We never see the outcome of the elder Capulet's fight with Romeow.

1141 *Anjuman*
1948. India. Nargis Arts Concern. Sound, b&w, 140 mins. Akhtar Hussein.
A free Hindi adaptation, with popular actress Nargis in the "Juliet" role. NB: this film is not to be confused with the remake in 1986 by Muzzafar Ali.

1142 *Les Amants de Verone*
1948. France. Compagnie Industrielle et Commerciale Cinématographique (CICC) and Les Films Corona. Sound, b&w, 105 mins. André Cayatte.
In this modern adaptation, Angelo and Georgia Maglia, two nonprofessional actors in a film production of *Romeo and Juliet*, become stand-ins for the leads, and soon fall in love. Their relationship is complicated by their backgrounds: Angelo is the son of a working-class glassblower, and Georgia is the daughter of a noble family that because of her father's fascist sympathies has fallen into disgrace. Georgia's fiancé Raffaele plots to have Angelo killed and turns Georgia's family against him, and the couple eventually dies on Juliet's tomb in the film studio. It is noteworthy that Jacques Prévert, the scriptwriter for *Les Amants de Verone*, also wrote *Les Enfants du Paradis*, another film about the relationship between Shakespearean drama and life (in this case, involving *Othello*). NB: this film is not to

be confused with the film of the same name by Riccardo Freda, also known as *Giuletta e Romeo*.

1143 *Carnaval no Fogo*
1949. Brazil. Atlântide Cinematográfica. Sound, b&w, length unknown. Watson Macedo.

A backstage musical, set in Rio de Janeiro's carnival time: several friends struggle to organize and perform a musical extravaganza. One sequence features a burlesque of the balcony scene from *Romeo and Juliet*.

1144 *Roseanna McCoy*
1949. U.S. Samuel Goldwyn Company. Sound, b&w, 100 mins. Irving Reis and Nicholas Ray.

From the novel by Alberta Hannum. Appalachian mountain farmers, the McCoys, and hunters, the Hatfields, their land separated by a river, have had a long-standing feud since Mounts Hatfield killed Roseanna's mother in a mad fury. Though dating storekeeper Thad Wilkins, Roseanna McCoy falls in love with Johnse Hatfield, the two meeting at a fair when Johnse helps Roseanna with a bee sting. Rejecting milquetoast Thad for the more passionate Johnse, Johnse takes Roseanna to meet his family, but patriarch Devil Anse Hatfield is slow to warm to her and Cap Hatfield is injured as the family prepares for a battle. Eager to fuel the feud, Mounts taunts the McCoys at Thad's store, and in the battle that follows, he shoots little Randall McCoy and his brother Phamer; he later uses Roseanna, Johnse, and little Randall as hostages to escape. As full-scale war erupts between the two families, Johnse and Roseanna meet; when Mounts tries to kill them, he is shot, first by Johnse, then by Anse. Johnse and Roseanna leave, crossing the river between the two families and ending the feud.

This is a hybrid of *Romeo and Juliet*, the American legend of the Hatfield and McCoy feud, and Hollywood romantic melodrama. The first half of the film is concerned with Roseanna's choice between two suitors, the passionate "bad boy" Johnse and the bland "good boy" Thad (a Paris figure, though there is no marriage contract between him and Roseanna's father). In the film's second half, Mounts functions as a Tybalt figure, actively encouraging the fighting and shooting the innocent little Randall when he moves to defend his relative. Interestingly, the mothers rather quickly approve of the match; it is the fathers who carry on the feud. The happy ending is secured when Roseanna and Johnse perform the symbolic act of crossing the river and Mounts is killed by his father, an act of contrition for Mounts's earlier action against the McCoys. Compare *Kentucky*.

1145 *La Posesión*
1949. Mexico. Cinematográfica Grovas. Sound, b&w, 103 mins. Julio Bracho.

Adapted from the novel by José López Portillo y Rojas. As Don Miguel Diaz and Don Pedro Ruiz, two wealthy landowners, pursue a dispute over a piece of mountain land, Don Pedro's son Roman falls in love with Don Miguel's daughter Rosaura, who is also Don Pedro's goddaughter. Don Miguel favors Camposorio, a judge in the land case, for his daughter's hand, and seeks to use the judge's love for Rosaura to his advantage. A duel with machetes between Pedro and Pánfilo, workers for Don Miguel and Don Pedro, leads to an escalation of tensions between the families; when Don Pedro wins the lawsuit, he is killed by Don Miguel, who also pursues Roman on the mountain. In disguise Rosaura comes to warn Roman, unbeknownst to her father. In the end, Don Miguel is killed by angry townspeople and buried next to Don Pedro on the mountain plot. Though the narrative uses many motifs from *Romeo and Juliet* (lovers from feuding families, a second suitor for the Juliet figure, and dueling servants), the film focuses rather more on the dynamics of the feud and legal battle than on the romance between the lovers.

1146 *Beneath the 12-Mile Reef*
1953. U.S. 20th Century Fox. Sound, col., 102 mins. Robert D. Webb.

Mike Petrakis, a Greek sponge fisherman, and his cocky son Tony struggle to keep their sponge-fishing business alive. When they work the waters called the Glades, their rivals—Arnold Dix and other men working for Thomas Rhys, a so-called conch (Anglo hook-boat fisherman from Key West)—take their sponges in retaliation for invading their fishing territory. Once ashore, Tony and Mike confront the men, Tony goading Arnold by dancing with Gwyneth Rhys, Thomas's daughter and Arnold's love interest. After initial tension, Tony and Gwyneth fall for each other, and their feelings for each other become stronger after Mike is killed in an accident and his boat is burned and cargo taken by Arnold. To pay off his father's debt, Tony and Gwyneth take a boat from the "conchs" and sponge-fish on the dreaded 12-Mile Reef. There Thomas and Arnold track them down, and after a fight with Arnold, Tony convinces Thomas to give his blessing to his and Gwyneth's marriage.

In its day famous for its technical achievements in underwater photography, *Beneath the 12-Mile Reef* uses *Romeo and Juliet* as its basic armature, though it deviates significantly from Shakespeare's narrative. Though the family feud between the Greeks and the "conchs" is muted by Thomas Rhys's goodwill and Mama Petrakis's quick acceptance of Gwyneth, hot-headed Arnold, like Tybalt, repeatedly reignites the conflict that keeps the lovers apart. Mike Petrakis combines character traits of both the elder Montague and Benvolio. In this version, the ending is pointedly not tragic: conflict between families is resolved by Tony's saving of Arnold's life during their fight and the good-natured cockiness of his appeal to Thomas for his blessing.

1147 *Garden of Eden*
1954. U.S. Excelsior Pictures Corporation. Sound, b&w, 68 mins. Max Nosseck.

In this early sexploitation film, Susan Lattimore, the daughter-in-law of workaholic attorney Jay, leaves her husband for Miami to resume her career as a model, taking her young daughter Joan with her. When her car breaks down, she and a driver helping her, Johnny Patterson, enter the Garden of Eden resort, a nudist camp where Johnny is a resident. Susan and her daughter soon accept the nudist lifestyle, even consenting to appear in a (clothed) stage production in the camp, Soon Jay arrives and demands that Susan and Joan return with him. When he discovers belatedly that the two are in a nudist camp, he tries to take legal action against her, but he soon warms to the nudist lifestyle, decides to stay, and apologizes to Susan for years of hateful treatment of her. As the film ends, Susan and Johnny are married and rehearsing a play, and Jay is planning to donate a gymnasium to the camp.

The play that Susan and Johnny appear in is *Romeo and Juliet*, of which we see brief excerpts of the balcony scene. When Jay awakes in the nudist camp and realizes what it is, he recognizes one of its residents as a famous Shakespearean theater director.

1148 *Nina (Romeo and Juliet in Wien)*
1954. West Germany. Corona. Sound, b&w, 105 mins. Rudolf Jugert.

In modern-day Vienna, Nina Iwanowa, a Russian, and Frank Wilson, an American, meet each other and fall in love. Both are involved in the diplomatic service and so find themselves divided by Cold War politics. Compare *The Young Lovers* and *Romanov and Juliet* (below).

1149 *The Young Lovers* (aka *Chance Meeting*)
1954. U.K. Group Film Productions Limited. Sound, b&w, 96 mins. Anthony Asquith.

Adapted from a story by George Tabori. Ted Hutchens, a codebreaker for the United States, and Anna Szobek, the daughter of the Soviet ambassador, meet at the *Swan Lake* ballet in Covent Garden and fall in love. As a consequence they become the objects of surveillance. When bureaucrats seek to break their romance, the two decide to escape across the English Channel during a tempest, their destination unknown. Compare *Nina* and *Romanoff and Juliet*.

1150 *Past Perfumance*
1955. U.S. Warner Bros. Sound, col., 7 mins. Chuck Jones.

Animated film. In this Pepe le Pew cartoon, Pepe pursues a cat who has been made up like a skunk through several sets of a silent movie studio. One of the sequences parodies the balcony scene from *Romeo and Juliet*.

1151 *Un Fantasma llamado amor*
1956. Spain. Arturo González Producciones Cinematográficas S.A. and Llama Film. Sound, b&w, 83 mins. Ramón Torrado.

Adapted from a story by Rafael Sánchez Campoy. In this comedy, a wise country elder guides a romance between two children, unwittingly recreating *Romeo and Juliet*.

1152 *Stage Struck*
1957. U.S. RKO Radio Pictures. Sound, col., 95 mins. Sidney Lumet.

Adapted from the play by Zoe Akins. A remake of Lowell Sherman's *Morning Glory* (see above), with much the same plotline and identical characters.

As she does in *Morning Glory*, Eva Lovelace offers a drunken version of Juliet's speech from the balcony scene during a theatrical party. Though this film does not include the excerpt from *Hamlet* included in *Morning Glory*, it does include citations from *Othello* and *The Merchant of Venice*.

1153 *Mädchen in Uniform*
1958. Germany and France. CCC Filmkunst and Les Films Modernes. Sound, col., 95 mins. Géza von Radványi.

Adapted from the play *Gestern und heute* by Christa Winsloe. Manuela, placed in an authoritarian Prussian girl's school by her aunt, develops a lesbian attachment to the mysterious and seductive Fräulein von Bernberg, a beautiful young teacher. After she declares her love publicly after a school play and the headmistress threatens to expel and isolate her, Manuela attempts suicide but is saved at the last moment, and the headmistress, her cruelty exposed, is chastised. The original play was a powerful antifascist statement.

In this version the school play is *Romeo and Juliet*, and Manuela uses the role of Romeo to declare her forbidden love for Bernberg (playing Juliet). In the better regarded 1931 adaptation (dir. Leontine Sagan), the school play is Schiller's *Don Carlos*, with Manuela as Don Carlos declaring his forbidden love for his stepmother, the Queen. The change may reflect an attempt to internationalize the tale's appeal.

1154 *Marjorie Morningstar*
1958. U.S. Beachwold and Warner Bros. Sound, col., 128 mins. Irving Rapper.

Adapted from the novel by Herman Wouk. Marjorie Morgenstern, a young Jewish New Yorker who aspires to being an actress, is pressured by her boyfriend Sandy and her parents to marry. To escape the pressure, she takes a job at Camp Tackamack in the Catskills as a dramatic counselor, where she meets Noel Airman, a dancer, songwriter, and director at the local summer stock theater, with whom Marjorie quickly falls in love, in the meantime resisting the overtures of Wally Wronken, a budding playwright. Marjorie and Noel start a romance, and Marjorie tries to reform him; instead of writing a musical and continuing his summer stock work, Noel tries advertising and bourgeois life but soon falls into despair and infidelity, spurred on by Wally's success, which he resents. Marjorie helps him finish his musical, but it is a flop on Broadway and Noel abandons her soon afterward to return to his life in the Catskills, where he feels most at home. Marjorie, recognizing that this is best for Noel, boards a bus to leave, and discovers on it Wally, the man for whom she is meant.

Early in the film, Marjorie appears in a rehearsal of the tomb scene from *Romeo and Juliet* for a college production. The brief vignette establishes her acting ambitions and romantic sensibility.

1155 *Romeo i Julija* (*Romeo and Juliet*)
1958. Yugoslavia. Zagreb Films. Sound, col., 10 mins. Ivo Vrbanic.

Animated film. *Romeo and Juliet* through the ages, from the caveman to the present.

1156 *Carry on Teacher*
1959. U.K. Anglo-Amalgamated Films and Peter Rogers Productions. Sound, b&w, 86 mins. Gerald Thomas.

Third in the *Carry On* series of comedy films. When William Wakefield, popular headmaster at Maudin Street School, applies for a headmaster post at a rural school, his adoring students work to ruin his chances by inventively disrupting the school when inspectors from the Ministry of Education come to inspect. Their project is interspersed with romantic entanglements between the teachers.

The students' culminating project is the sabotage of their school's performance of *Romeo and Juliet*. This travesty mostly involves comic sound effects (an out-of-tune performance of the score by the music teacher, the school's culture maven; and on the word "break" in "From ancient grudge break to new mutiny," we hear a sound of breaking glass) and physical farce (teacher Edwin Milton accidentally splashes the orchestra conductor with paint, and Romeo gets entangled in the balcony railing when it falls after Juliet leans on it). We see only the prologue, the balcony scene, and the epilogue. (Compare the student *Romeo and Juliet* travesty in *The Pure Hell of St. Trinian's*, produced in the next year.) An additional Shakespearean reference is made, to *Twelfth Night*: as teachers and lovers Gregory Adams and Sarah Allcock watch preparations for the performance, Adams comments to her, "If music be the food of love, belt up."

1157 *Gyalog a Mennyországba*
1959. Hungary. Hunnia Film Studio. Sound, b&w, 96 mins. Imre Fehér.

Imre and Vera, lovers from a rural town, marry and move to Budapest, but find life difficult. Vera soon leaves their crumbling marriage to pursue a career as an actress with a traveling stock company, and Imre soon leaves Budapest as well, taking a menial job in a rural town. When the company comes to Imre's town to perform *Romeo and Juliet*, Imre recognizes Vera and the two rekindle their relationship.

1158 *Romeo, Julie a Tma* (*Sweet Light in a Dark Room*)
1959. Czechoslovakia. CBK, Ceskoslovenský Státní Film, and Filmové Studio Barrandov. Sound, b&w, 93 mins. Jiri Weiss.

Adapted from the short story by Jana Otčenášek. Pavel Rumler, an amateur photographer and student in Nazi-occupied Prague, watches as the Wurms, a Jewish family, are forced to leave his apartment building. As Pavel searches their abandoned flat looking for Jirka Wurm's pet rabbit, Hanka, a Jew who has refused to get on her transport, arrives, and Pavel hides her in an upstairs storeroom. Pavel soon falls in love with Hanka, abandoning his former girlfriend Alena and snitching food and selling items to keep her alive. Mrs. Kubiasová, a selfish older woman who moves into the Wurms's flat, makes a play for Pavel and is rejected. When Pavel murders Mrs. Kubiasová's dog to keep him from revealing Hanka's presence, Mrs. Kubiasová pieces together that Pavel is hiding someone and tells Pavel's mother, who insists that Hanka leave. Before she can, however, the police search the neighborhood, and in an effort to save all in the apartment complex, Hanka goes outside and is shot.

Despite the film's title, Weiss's moving Nazi-era romance uses little more of *Romeo and Juliet* than the lovers divided by warring parties and the objection of a parent (Pavel's mother) to the match. Interestingly, unlike Pavel's mother, Pavel's grandfather is willing to protect Hanka before she makes her sacrifice for the good of the residents. Pavel and Hanka's discussion of the stars—Pavel likens them to two orbiting stars—offers a fleeting reminder of their star-crossed status.

1159 *Megoltek Egy Lányt* (aka *A Girl Was Killed*)
1961. Hungary. László Nádasy.

A *Romeo and Juliet*–style blocked romance involving a feud between factions of workmen in 1918.

1160 *Romanoff and Juliet*
1961. U.S. Pavla. Sound, col., 103 mins. Peter Ustinov.

Adapted from the play by Peter Ustinov. When the President of Concordia, a tiny European republic, refuses to cast the deciding vote in a deadlocked UN resolution, his country becomes the focus of lobbying by the U.S. and Soviet ambassadors. At a dance in Concordia, the President mischievously introduces Juliet Moulsworth, daughter of the American ambassador, and Igor Romanoff, son of the Soviet ambassador, and the two fall in love, only later learning who each other is. When the parents of each child discover the romance, they are horrified. A telegram announcing the arrival of Freddie, Juliet's former fiancé, is misread by the Soviets as a secret military operation, and the United States and Soviet Union threaten to invade Concordia unless the country declares its alliance. As all sides prepare for war, the President prevents Igor from committing suicide and encourages the lovers to marry. Under cover of a ceremony to celebrate Concordia's independence, the lovers, their identities concealed, marry, then reveal themselves. At first horrified, the parents soon accept their relationship and peace is established.

This gentle satire of Cold War politics adapts the basic narrative of *Romeo and Juliet*—lovers divided by a family (and here international) feud—as well as the comic sensibility of *The Mouse That Roared* (Jack Arnold, 1959) and spy film clichés. Other specific motifs appear: the lovers meet at a dance, Igor is tempted by suicide, and the President of Concordia functions much as Friar Laurence as the lovers' champion, though he is more successful. Compare *Nina* and *The Young Lovers*.

1161 *West Side Story*
1961. U.S. Mirisch Pictures, Seven Arts Productions, and United Artists. Sound, col., 151 mins. Robert Wise and Jerome Robbins.

In 1950s New York City, the Jets, a white gang headed by Riff, and the Sharks, a Puerto Rican gang headed by Bernardo, vie for control of a neighborhood. At a neighborhood dance, Tony, a friend of Riff and a former Jet, and Maria, the sister of Bernardo, meet and instantly fall in love, their dance together inflaming Bernardo's animosity toward the Jets. Afterward, Tony and Maria meet on the fire escape and declare their love for each other. At Doc's

Sweet Shop, the two gangs arrange a rumble to settle ownership of the neighborhood, and Maria asks Tony to stop the fighting. When Tony tries to, Riff is knifed by Bernardo and Tony, in a fit of fury, kills Bernardo. After the rumble, Chino, one of the Sharks, searches for Tony to avenge Bernardo's death. Maria and Tony make plans to run away; Maria sends Anita, Bernardo's girlfriend, to Doc's to send Tony a message, but she is harassed by the Jets and, in a fury, tells them that Chino killed Maria. When Tony learns of this news, he wanders the streets, taunting Chino to kill him. At the basketball court he sees Maria and rushes to her arms, but he is shot by Chino. Maria chastizes the two gangs for their violence as Tony's body is taken away.

West Side Story brilliantly combined *Romeo and Juliet* with elements of American musical theater and juvenile delinquent films of the 1950s to produce what is perhaps the single most influential Shakespeare "spin-off" of the twentieth century. The film follows Shakespeare's narrative relatively closely, transposing the Montague and Capulet feud into an urban gang war sharpened by ethnic tensions. (Originally, the conflict was to be between Catholics and Jews.) Tony and Maria meet, like Romeo and Juliet, at a dance, and their meeting on the fire escape resembles the balcony scene; Anita, Maria's confidante, has something of the role of Juliet's nurse, Doc of Friar Laurence, Riff of Mercutio, and Lt. Schrank of Prince Escalus. Of interest is the way in which the ending plays off our knowledge of Shakespeare's tragedy. Tony's despair at the (false) news of Maria's death seems to press in the direction of Shakespeare's tragedy, so when Tony and Maria rush to embrace, it seems as if they have cheated fate; Tony's sudden shooting is therefore all the more shocking and tragic. Jerome Robbins's startlingly athletic choreography, Leonard Bernstein's jazzy soundtrack, and Stephen Sondheim's witty, often socially critical lyrics (censored for the film version) are all justly famed, but it is perhaps the film's urban iconography and youth culture orientation that have had the greatest influence on subsequent Shakespearean adaptations, even though most of the film owes more to the stage than it does to the realities of New York City streets. It popularized and legitimized the contemporizing of Shakespeare and spawned myriad streetwise, youth-oriented Shakespearean adaptations on stage and film. *West Side Story* has become a key cultural filter through which *Romeo and Juliet* has been perceived in the second half of the twentieth century. Winner of ten Oscars, including one for best picture. See also entries 487, 496, 1692, 1710, 1716, 1717, 1723, and 1734.

Tony and Maria meet at a dance in *West Side Story* (1961). Courtesy of Douglas Lanier.

DVD (special collectors' edition) includes a documentary "West Side Memories" that references Shakespeare, as well as storyboard-to-film comparisons and a copy of Ernest Lehman's script that are illuminating.

1162 *Geliebte weiße Maus* (*The Small White Mouse*)
1964. East Germany. DEFA. Sound, col., 77 mins. Gottfried Kolditz.

In this musical, Fritz Bachmann, a traffic cop in Dresden, falls in love with Helene Braeuer, a younger woman who passes him daily on her way to work. The film contains a reference to *Romeo and Juliet.*

1163 *Los Tarantos*
1964. Spain. Teresa and Films Rovira Beleta. Sound, col., 92 mins. Francisco Rovira Beleta.

Adapted from the play *La historia de los Tarantos* by Alfredo Mañas. In the district of Somorrostro in Barcelona, two gypsy families, the wealthy Tarantos and the poor Zorongos, are feuding. Brought by his friend Mojigondo to a wedding celebration at the barrio, Rafael Tarantos sees Juana Zorongo, and the two instantly fall in love. Rafael brings Juana to secure the approval of Angustius, his mother, which Juana does by dancing. To destroy the match, Rosendo, Juana's father, promises Curro, a thug, that he can marry Juana; when Curro and his gang threaten Angustius, Rafael comes to her defense, after which he wins her devotion. Though separated, Rafael and Juana continue to exchange messages using carrier pigeons. Continuing his harassment, Curro stabs Mojigondo as Rafael tries to stop their fight. After a confrontation with Rosendo and his thugs, Juana searches for Rafael, intending to elope; Rafael finds her and the two share an embrace in the pigeon coop. There Curro finds and kills them both, after which Curro is killed by Salvador, Rafael's brother, and Rosendo and Angustius share their grief.

This skillful transposition of *Romeo and Juliet* to Spanish flamenco culture finds inventive equivalents for Shakespeare's narrative. The feud is established almost immediately when Curro and his thugs attack the Zorongos women and children, and Jero, Juana's brother, is wounded; Rafael and Juana's first meeting is almost entirely wordless, handled through intense glances and flamenco hand-clapping; Mercutio's "Queen Mab" speech becomes Mojigondo's dancing through the rainslick streets of nighttime Barcelona; Rafael speaks to Juana from over a fence, briefly echoing the balcony scene; two children, not the Nurse, serve as go-betweens for the lovers; and the cramped pigeon coop becomes their tomb. Flamenco music and dancing are used throughout the movie to signal solidarity with the Zorongo clan, express passion, and heighten the tension. Baz Luhrmann's *Romeo + Juliet* (entry 496) owes several unacknowledged debts to this film, including references to Spanish religious ritual and the shot of the lovers first kissing underwater (they do so in

this film to avoid being detected). In turn, Beleta's film owes much to *West Side Story*, including the look of the villains, the use of music and dancing, the urban barrio milieu, and several specific shots (including one of the lovers chasing through hanging linen, a shot also used in Zeffirelli's *The Taming of the Shrew* three years later; see entry 513). The final scene, in which the children take the carrier pigeon and walk hand in hand on the beach, adds a glimmer of hope to the otherwise tragic conclusion. No direct references to Shakespeare's dialogue, though Mojigondo does refer to Rafael as Romeo when Rafael reveals his love.

DVD (Spanish only) includes three short essays on "Los Tarantos," two of which reference Shakespeare.

1164 *Tini Zabutykh Predkiv* (*Shadows of Forgotten Ancestors*)
1964. USSR and Ukraine. Alexander Dovzhenko Studio. Sound, col., 97 mins. Sergei Paradjanov.

Adapted from a story by Mikhaylo Mikhaylovich Koysyubinskiy. At the funeral of Ivan Paliichuk's brother Olexa, Ivan's father is killed by Gutenuik for a nasty remark he made about the rich. At his father's funeral, the boy Ivan meets the girl Marichka, Gutenuik's daughter. As the two grow up, they fall in love, but they are prevented from marrying because of the blood feud between their families. Eventually, Ivan works up the courage to marry Marichka and even gets his mother's reluctant blessing, but he is forced to work as a hired hand to earn enough money to marry her. While he is away, Marichka is drowned while trying to save a black sheep. Ivan becomes distraught and withdrawn, but is drawn back into village life when Palagna marries him. Their relationship remains barren as Ivan remains fixated on Marichka, and Palagna, desperate for children, is soon seduced by the local sorcerer. When Ivan discovers their plan to kill him, he goes into the wood, where he sees Marichka's spirit and freezes to death.

This film, set among the Hutsuls of the Ukraine, an isolated mountain tribe, uses the *Romeo and Juliet* motif of lovers separated by a family feud in its first half; the motif of a star reminds us of their star-crossed nature. The film's second half, focused on Ivan's grief and disastrous marriage to Palagna, bears no resemblance to Shakespeare's narrative, though in a general way Ivan's suicide in the wood recalls Romeo's suicide at the tomb. The film is structured by chapters, many of which are linked to seasonal changes or traditional holiday rituals, all of which Paradjanov richly documents. These elements are balanced against beautiful poetic and fantasy passages that visually portray Ivan's and Marichka's love. The film is considered a milestone of Ukrainian cinema.

1165 *Gonks Go Beat*
1965. U.K. Titan Films Productions. Sound, col., 90 mins. Robert Hartford-Davis.

In this bizarre musical, two musical communities, Beatland (those who like rock and roll) and Balladisle (those who like folk music), feud with each other. In an effort to reconcile the two, Wilco Roger, a fumbling alien diplomat, engineers a romance between Helen and Steve, members of different communities, on the model of *Romeo and Juliet*, lest he be exiled to the planet of the Gonks. Although the two communities have a short war, eventually Helen and Steve's romance paves the way to rapprochement.

Essentially a showcase for various pop and folk bands of the period, *Gonks Go Beat* briefly references *Romeo and Juliet* when Wilco Roger suggests that it may provide the model for reconciling the warring communities. The allusion does not move far beyond the general similarity to two lovers divided by a feud. The only reference to Shakespeare's dialogue is to Henry V's "once more into the breach" speech, which is briefly parodied when Beatland and Balladisle go to war.

1166 *Shakespeare Wallah*
1965. U.K. Merchant Ivory Productions. Sound, b&w, 122 mins. James Ivory.

In a chronically broken-down car, Lizzie Buckingham, a British actress born in India, tours post-independence India in a small troupe headed by her father Tony and mother Carla, giving performances of classic British drama to dwindling audiences. Along the way, they meet Sanjhu Ray, a rich, callow Indian playboy who becomes enamored of Lizzie. The troupe arrives in Kalikhet to discover that their planned performances at a local school have been cut back, leading to hard times and portending a change in audience tastes from British theater to Indian pop. As Sanjhu's romance with Lizzie deepens, his girlfriend Manjula, a vain Bollywood actress, immediately becomes jealous; under the pretense of making friends with Lizzie, Manjula stresses her long-term relationship with Sanjhu and later disrupts the company's performance of *Othello*. Lizzie's mother, uneasy about her romance with Sanjhu, expresses her disapproval. When Lizzie's parents, sensing a change in their fortunes, seek to send Lizzie home, to Sanhju she offers to stay, but he does not respond to her offer. Lizzie leaves for England, and her parents remain in India.

Merchant and Ivory's portrait of cultural change in post-independence India was the second of their films together and the one that cemented their cinematic reputations, and from its very first scene—a Restoration comedy for Indian schoolboys—it establishes the growing irrelevance of classic British culture to the new India. The film uses Shakespeare in two ways. First, the romance between Lizzie and Sanjhu bears some distant resemblance to that of Romeo and Juliet, in that both lovers face disapproval—from Manjula and Carla—for straying from their "clans." In a revision of Shakespeare's ending, when Lizzie offers to

"sacrifice" herself, it is Sanjhu's unwillingness to do so for her that motivates her decision to leave India for England. Second, the film includes many references to the plays in performance. We see scenes from *Antony and Cleopatra* (1.2 and 4.15), *Hamlet* (3.4 and 4.5), *Othello* (5.2), *Romeo and Juliet* (2.6), and *Twelfth Night* (3.4). As well, members of the troupe make passing references to Shakespeare. Tellingly, the Maharaja whom the company meets early in the film knows Shakespeare well, and applies such lines as "uneasy lies the head that wears the crown" to his own state; though he admires the poetry and Lizzie's acting, Sanjhu doesn't recognize any of the plays. It is noteworthy that the film opposes Shakespearean drama to Indian film—whereas Buckingham and company find it increasingly difficult to make a living, self-absorbed Manjula causes a stir wherever she goes. Compare *36 Chowingree Lane*.

DVD includes a "Conversation with the Filmmakers" that references Shakespeare.

1167 *No somos ni Romeo ni Julieta*
1969. Spain. Copercines, Cooperativa Cinematográfica, and Exclusivas Floralva Producción. Sound, col., 85 mins. Alfonso Paso.

Roberto Negresco, a waiter in a bar with a strange speech impediment, falls in love with Julita Caporeto, a naïve young girl engaged to Cayetano. Their love is imperiled by the feud between the Negrescos (Antonio and Trinidad) and the Caporetos (Nemesio and Charo).

1168 *Out of It*
1969. U.S. Pressman-Williams Productions. Sound, b&w, 95 mins. Paul Williams and Edward Pressman.

After Paul, a shy nerd, secretly takes Christine, a beautiful cheerleader, on a date, he learns that she remains interested in Russ, her quarterback boyfriend and a bully, despite earlier indications to the contrary. Though Paul instead begins to date Barbara, Russ is intent upon humiliating him, and he does so by injuring Paul during football practice, an action that prompts Christine's sympathy for Paul and leads to further jealous revenge from Russ. To retaliate, Paul uses a cigarette lighter gun to humiliate Russ in the locker room. The film ends on a note of irresolution, as Paul watches Christine and Russ on the beach.

On their date, Paul and Christine see a performance of *Romeo and Juliet*. The play establishes Paul's romantic vision of Christine, and its motif of an escalating feud is developed in the film's narrative. The film's release in 1969 (it was made in 1967) capitalized on the popularity of both Zeffirelli's *Romeo and Juliet* (1968; entry 490) and Jon Voight (he played Russ), who achieved fame in *Midnight Cowboy* (1969).

1169 *Romeo and Juliet*
1969. Poland. Studio Filmóv Rysunkowych. Sound, col., 10 mins. Jerzy Zitman.

Animated film using paper cutouts, by the well-known Polish animator. In this political satire in favor of pacifism, Romeo and Juliet are members of opposing families who duel each other with various modern implements of war, including bombs and tanks. Eventually, the families are reconciled by the fathers.

1170 *Romeo si Julieta* (*Romeo and Juliet*)
1968. Romania. Studioul Animafilm. Sound, b&w, length unknown. Bob Calinescu.
Animated film of the play, done with stones.

1171 *The Secret Sex Lives of Romeo and Juliet*
1969. U.S. Global Pictures. Sound, col., 96 mins. A. P. Stootsberry (aka Peter Perry).

Sexploitation parody of *Romeo and Juliet*, handled as a performance at the Globe Theatre. The plot and character roster generally follow that of Shakespeare's play, with interpolated sex scenes; the film's parodic style emulates that of the 1960s television show *Laugh-In*.

Some character and plot changes: Tybalt's role is cut, Paris is gay, Romeo and Juliet are promiscuous, Juliet and the Nurse are sexually involved, the servants of Montague and Capulet only pretend to feud, and Romeo and Juliet survive (they copulate in the tomb). The prologue opens with "Friends, Romans, countrymen," before the crowd corrects him. The balcony scene uses Shakespeare's dialogue, but both Romeo and Juliet are secretly having sex with someone else as they deliver their lines. A sense of the film's style of humor can be had from this line: "If Juliet is the sun and the moon is sick and pale, would that affect daylight savings time?"

DVD includes a director's commentary track that references Shakespeare, and *The Notorious Cleopatra*.

1172 *Das Bildnis des Dorian Gray* (*Dorian Gray*)
1970. U.K., Germany, and Italy. Sargon Film. Sound, col., 93 mins. Massimo Dallamano.

Adapted from the novel by Oscar Wilde. A modernized version of the story, recast as a campy morality tale about 1960s sexual decadence. Self-absorbed, beautiful, and naïve Dorian Gray falls in love with actress Sybil Vane at the same time that Basil Hallward, his friend, paints Dorian's portrait. After a fight with Sybil after a performance of *Romeo and Juliet*, Dorian attends a party hosted by Lord Henry Wotton, a cynical hedonist, after which he sleeps with Wotton's sister Gwendolyn and Sybil commits suicide. Thereafter the portrait, which Dorian keeps hidden, reflects Dorian's moral degradation as he pursues a life of pleasure without ever aging. Eventually, Dorian murders Hallward for painting the portrait. After Dorian meets Gladys Monmouth, a double for Sybil, his life becomes increasingly unhinged; when he damages the portrait, he dies.

The film features two instances of the balcony scene from *Romeo and Juliet*. In the first, Dorian first meets Sybil, who is rehearsing Juliet's part; the closeup of Juliet with overhanging greenery may dimly recall Zeffirelli's handling of the scene in his film two years earlier. In the second instance, Dorian and Sybil make love in an empty theater as a recording of Sybil's rehearsal plays (this excerpt is different from the first instance). The two scenes are intended to establish the geniune depth of Sybil and Dorian's love as well as to introduce the theme of doubling. A third excerpt from *Romeo and Juliet*, Sybil's performance of Juliet's death in the crypt scene, is played before Wotton and his friends. Her performance is so wooden that she is heckled, though afterward Sybil expresses her indifference so long as Dorian loves her. The film begins with a point-of-view shot of Dorian's hands, bloody from the murder, which he washes, perhaps a reference to *Macbeth*, a sequence later repeated in the film.

1173 *Heer Raanjha*
1970. India. Punjab Pictures. Sound, col., 142 mins. Chetan Anand.

Adapted from the poem "Heer Waris Shah" by Waris Shah. While attending a village wedding, Dido Ranjha, a pipe player, falls in love with Heer Saleti, a beautiful woman who is already married. Their families, bitter enemies from a long feud, attempt to break up the romance. The death of the lovers leads to the reconciliation of the two families. One of the most famous tales of Punjabi literature—this film is regarded as the classic film adaptation of the story. A less cinematically accomplished version of the tale was filmed in the same year by Masud Pervaiz; there were other cinematic versions produced in 1928, 1929, 1931, 1932, 1948, and most recently in 1992.

1174 *Julie a Romeo*
1971. Czechoslovakia. Production company unknown. Sound, col., 5 mins. Zdenêk Smetana.
A short animated version of the story.

1175 *Ma che musica maestro*
1971. Italy. Flora Devon. Sound, col., 94 mins. Mariano Laurenti.

In this musical comedy, the villages of Saint Veronica Alta and Saint Veronica Bassa are feuding over the naming of a railway station. Lovers from the rival villages, Giulietta and Gianni, fall in love, and various villagers, engaged in rival ceremonial events, attempt to prevent their marriage. The two lovers meet in a scene from the play.

1176 *Reshma Aur Shera* (*Reshma and Shera*)
1971. India. Ajantaa Arts. Sound, col., 158 mins. Sunil Dutt.

A feud divides the Rajput families of the villages of Pochina and Karda. As the film opens, the Pochina family is celebrating the murder of one of the five sons of the

Karda family. Gopal, the only son of the Pochina clan, and Reshma, his sister, go to the local fair; Shera and his brothers Jagat, Vijay, and Chotu also attend. Shera sees Reshma and falls in love; when his brothers attack Gopal, Shera saves him from harm and soon after confesses to Reshma his love. The two meet by bonfire at night, and Shera vows to end the feud by giving welcome to Gopal at his upcoming wedding. When Shera's father discovers his son's love, he exiles him and sends Chotu to Gopal and his father, which Chotu does. When Shera learns this, he returns to his family intent upon avenging the deaths; he kills his father, who provokes him by claiming he killed Reshma's relatives, then Jagat and Vijay. He pursues Chotu, but Chotu begs the mercy of Reshma, and instructed by the gods to end the feud, Reshma marries Chotu to save his life. When the two reveal themselves to Shera, he is grief-stricken and shoots himself; the bullet also kills Reshma, and the two die in an embrace, covered by a sandstorm. Their sacrifice ends the feud, and the clans burn their guns in a bonfire.

The motif of lovers divided by a family feud certainly recalls *Romeo and Juliet*. Shera's mad pursuit of revenge against those who killed his lover's family has a very distant resemblance to Romeo's pursuit of Tybalt, though the circumstances are much changed (Shera kills members of his own family, not that of his lover's, and his pursuit of revenge is certainly more than momentary). The shared death of the lovers evokes that of Romeo and Juliet, particularly since the two have a conversation earlier about being together in death and they are pictured embracing in death. The film is noteworthy for its stress upon the civilizing influence of women upon men who would otherwise pursue fighting; its critique of maschismo and *izzat* is especially progressive for its day.

1177 *Bobby*
1973. India. R. K. Productions. Sound, col., 161 mins. Raj Kapoor.

Raj Nath, the shy, poetic son of a wealthy Bombay businessman, is neglected by his tyrannical father and sent to a boarding school. Upon his return on his eighteenth birthday party, he sees Bobby, the innocent but free-spirited teenage daughter of his former governess, Mrs. Braganza, and falls in love. The couple's relationship is threatened early on by Bobby's overhearing and misunderstanding Raj's talk of marriage to Neema, a dancer who fancies Raj, but Raj pursues Bobby to Kashmir and proves his love to her with an act of heroism. Upon their return, Raj tells his father of his intention to marry Bobby, but his father bitterly opposes the marriage, accusing Bobby's father Jack, a poor fisherman, of using his daughter for fortune hunting. Bobby is sent away with Mrs. Braganza to Goa, and Raj intends to wait until his twenty-first birthday to marry Bobby when he can legally do as he wants, but his father

secretly arranges a marriage with Alka Sharma, the fragile, immature daughter of a business associate. When Raj discovers this, he goes to Goa to marry Bobby, but Mrs. Braganza opposes the match because it is illegal. Raj and Bobby soon escape and are pursued by their two fathers as well as a gang of thugs anxious for a reward for Raj's capture. Raj and Bobby jump from a cliff into a river rather than succumb to their parents' wishes; the two fathers save the children from drowning and accept their relationship.

This *Romeo and Juliet* analogue uses the familiar narrative of a teen romance threatened by parental opposition; the second half of the film develops this motif into a screed in favor of children's independence from their parents' wills. The families are divided primarily by class (the Naths are rich, the Braganzas are poor), but also by religion (the Naths are secular, the Braganzas are Christian); the film's sympathies are clearly far more with the Braganzas than the Naths. Several specific motifs suggest the influence of Shakespeare: the lovers' romance is complicated by the fact that they are teenagers; the Naths arrange a marriage for their son (just as the Capulets arrange a marriage for their daughter); there is a version of Juliet's balcony (when Raj climbs up to Bobby's second-floor room in Goa); rather surprisingly, Mrs. Braganza, the counterpart to Juliet's Nurse, opposes the match between Bobby and Raj when she learns that Raj has done something illegal (that is, run away); and the final sequence of the film emphasizes the drive of the lovers to find unity in death rather than capitulate to their parents, though they are saved from their suicide by the fathers. Regarded as groundbreaking in its day because of its sexy Western fashions and championing of youthful independence.

1178 *Hipólito y Evita* (aka *Cuando el amor llegue*)
1973. Argentina. Azteca Films. Sound, col., 90 mins. Orestes Trucco.

In this comic variation on *Romeo and Juliet*, the two lovers are divided by class and political affiliation, one family upper-class supporters of Hipolito Yrigoyen, the other family working-class supporters of Eva Perón.

1179 *Angst essen Seele auf* (*Ali: Feat Eats the Soul*)
1974. Germany. Filmverlag der Autoren and Tango Films. Sound, col., 94 mins. Rainer Werner Fassbinder.

In modern Berlin, Emmi Kurowski, a lonely sixty-year-old Polish German cleaning woman, meets Ali, a forty-year-old Moroccan mechanic, in a bar during a rainstorm. After Ali dances with her on a dare, the two fall in love. As their relationship becomes public, they encounter prejudice subtle and blatant from neighbors, coworkers, and Emmi's children from a former marriage. After they become married and take a long vacation, the two receive limited acceptance, but their relationship begins to encounter problems, including Ali's infidelity with a blonde waitress who cooks him couscous. Emmi forgives Ali's infidelity, but he ends up in the hospital suffering from a burst ulcer, the result of the stress of living away from home.

Based more on *All That Heaven Allows* (Douglas Sirk, 1955) than *Romeo and Juliet*, Fassbinder's portrait of Emmi and Ali's troubled romance nevertheless uses the narrative of a relationship undermined by the objections of family and friends. There are no references to Shakespeare's dialogue. Widely regarded as one of Fassbinder's most compelling films.

1180 *Le Scomunicate di San Valentino (The Sinful Nuns of St. Valentine)*
1974. Italy. Claudia Cinematografica. Sound, col., 93 mins. Sergio Grieco.

When Esteban Albornos and Lucita Fuentes, the children of feuding families, fall in love, Lucita's father betrays Esteban to the Spanish Inquisition and places Lucita in a convent. Unbeknownst to him, the abbess is procuring men for her pleasure whom she then murders.

Several motifs of *Romeo and Juliet* appear in scrambled form: the separation of the lovers by feuding families, the accusation of murder against Esteban, a comical servant and religious figure who helps the couple, and the father's repentance for opposing the lovers when he thinks his daughter is dead.

1181 *Thieves Like Us*
1974. U.S. United Artists. Sound, col., 123 mins. Robert Altman.

In this revisionist version of the outlaws-in-love narrative popularized by *Bonnie and Clyde*, three convicted bank robbers and killers, T-Dub Masefield, Chicamaw Mobley, and Bowie, who have escaped from prison hide out with relatives and in-laws. The group decides to split up as news reports about their robberies become more and more overblown. Bowie falls in love with Keechie and struggles to balance his relationship with her with continuing to rob banks and maintain loyalty to his fellow thieves. When the police close in, T-Dub and Chicamaw betray Bowie, leading to his death as pregnant Keechie watches.

When Bowie and Keechie first make love while on the run, they listen to a radio broadcast of *Romeo and Juliet*. Each time they start to make love again throughout the evening, the same radio show is rebroadcast, primarily the balcony scene and the line "my only love sprung from my only hate." The juxtaposition foreshadows Bowie and Keechie's tragic demise, for like Romeo and Juliet, they are doomed young lovers.

1182 *Aaron Loves Angela*
1975. U.S. Columbia Pictures. Sound, col., 99 mins. Gordon Parks Jr.

In New York City's Harlem, Aaron James, a black student basketball player, falls in love with Angela, a Puerto Rican girl, a relationship the two must keep secret because of racial tensions. Aaron's father, Ike, a former minor sports star who owns a bar, pushes his son hard to become a basketball player, but Aaron would prefer to spend time with Angela in an apartment his friend Willie has fixed up in a condemned tenement. In Aaron's building Beau, a pimp, sets up a drug deal with white dealers with his friend Duke. Beau and Duke try to double-cross the dealers while closing the deal in the condemned tenement, but all are shot and Aaron ends up with the drug money. Chased by the white dealers, Aaron and Angela toss the money to crowds and escape.

Aaron Loves Angela dovetails a *Romeo and Juliet*–type narrative (filtered through the iconography of *West Side Story*) with elements of blaxploitation drama. (Director Gordon Parks Jr. also directed *Superfly* in 1972.) The least developed of the plotlines is the romance between Aaron and Angela, and the racial tension that prevents them from openly acknowledging their love is only once illustrated, when Aaron is chased by Latino men from Angela's neighborhood. There are no references to Shakespeare's dialogue, and the film is at best a distant Shakespearean analogue. Compare *O*.

1183 *Jambon D'Ardenne*
1977. France and Belgium. Lamy Films and Reggane Films. Sound, col., 85 mins. Benoît Lamy.

Two managers of restaurants in a village in Ardenne—a fancy bistro in the hotel Beauséjour, and a nearby chip shop—are fierce rivals for business, leading to gunplay. Tensions are raised even higher when the son of Beauséjour's manager falls for a girl who works at the chip shop, and employees at Beauséjour, tired of the overbearing manager, threaten to quit. Eventually, the two managers are persuaded to make peace.

1184 *Saturday Night Fever*
1977. U.S. Paramount Pictures. Sound, col., 118 mins.

Working-class male and disco dancer Tony Manero (John Travolta) seeks to move up socially and engages with his more educated girlfriend in a conversation about *Romeo and Juliet*. He is put down for his lack of knowledge of Shakespeare. (RB)

1185 *The Turning Point*
1977. U.S. Hera Productions and 20th Century Fox. Sound, col., 119 mins. Herbert Ross.

Deedee Rodgers, a ballerina who dropped her career to become a mother, envies her friend Emma Jacklin, who has become a successful prima ballerina; ironically, Emma, recognizing that she soon will be too old to dance, envies Deedee's family life. When Deedee's daughter Emilia, an aspiring ballerina, joins Emma's New York City company and falls in love with Yuri Kopeikine, a charismatic but womanizing co-star, the growing tensions between Deedee and Emma explode in a catfight before the two realize that they can both pursue their desires vicariously through Emilia's career and romantic success.

An extended ballet sequence from Prokofiev's *Romeo and Juliet* catalyzes the love relationship between Emilia and Yuri.

1186 *Romeo of the Spirits*
1978. U.K. Thorntip. Sound, col., 21 mins. Nikolas L. Janis.

A London tramp, a former actor, living around Charing Cross station recalls lines from *Romeo and Juliet* that underline his situation.

1187 *Romie-0 and Julie-8*
1978. Canada. Nelvana Unlimited. Sound, col., 30 mins. Clive A. Smith.

Animated film. Robots Romie-0 and Julie-8, created by rival companies Megastellar and Super Solar for the Megagalactic Robot Show, fall in love and escape to the planet Trashalot, helped by Mr. Gizmo. Once there, Julie-8 becomes the captive of the Junk Monster, and agrees to marry him if he will free Romie-0. Rather than actually follow through on the marriage, Julie-8 pulls the plug on herself, but Romie-0, having escaped, revives her. Rival corporate heads Ms. Passbinder and Mr. Thunderbottom, having pursued the robots to Trashalot, are captured by the Junk Monster, but they are saved by Romie-0 and Julie-8 as the two make their escape. The Junk Monster is destroyed by a storm, and Passbinder and Thunderbottom declare their love for one another and accept the robots' love.

The narrative borrows the general scenario of lovers divided by a feud from Shakespeare's play, as well as some specific motifs such as the balcony scene, Juliet's rival suitor and "arranged" marriage, and Juliet's suicide. The only reference to Shakespeare's dialogue is Julie-8's "Romie-0, Romie-0, where are you, Romie-0?"

1188 *Sieben Sommersprossen (Seven Freckles)*
1978. East Germany. DEFA, Group, and Johannisthal Production. Sound, col., 76 mins. Herrmann Zschoche.

The film centers on an amateur performance of *Romeo and Juliet*. Two young teens from quasi-dysfunctional families meet up at a summer camp and fall in love. A camp counselor sets up a performance of *Romeo and Juliet* and casts the camp children. The teen boy (Robert) plays Romeo, but the teen girl (Karoline) is not playing Juliet—her prettier friend Bettina is. But Karoline has a dream in which she is Juliet and meets Romeo at the Capulet Ball. Shakespeare, with the guidance of a progressive camp counselor and his girlfriend, serves a therapeutic function of helping the kids grow up and work through their romantic problems. Bettina becomes jealous when she learns that Robbie prefers Karoline, and she falsely slanders Karoline's sexual behavior when Karoline and Robbie are late back to camp after their borrowed motorcycle runs out

of gas. The authoritarian camp leader (who recalls Miss Ballbricka of *Porky's 2*) then wants to send Karoline home and close down the *Romeo and Juliet* production for having a negative influence. More interestingly, while foregrounding romantic love, the film suggests that the collective is the best means for working through personal problems involving romantic couples and triangles. The other girls insist that Bettina tell the truth or they will, and Robbie volunteers to go as well. The camp counselor, who casts himself as Friar Laurence, tells Robbie he should stay for the sake of the others and their work ("die ganze Arbeit"). Robbie himself goes to Bettina to tell her she must tell the truth, but Karoline, alone in her camp room (an open space like a barracks full of bunk beds), sees Bettina and Robbie from a distance and mistakenly concludes that he has betrayed her. When she runs off, two young children (6–7, I'd guess) who have been periodically spying on them call after her and then run to tell Robbie. She returns to a pond they had gone skinny dipping in and fantasizes her suicide by drowning (in a shot that cites Millais's *Ophelia*) and funeral, with Robbie dead as well. She decides to get out of the water and not drown herself, but a loon takes off and surprises her. She falls and hits her head on a rock. Robbie discovers her before she drowns, but then he stumbles as he carries Karoline up a hill, and he gets knocked out by the fall. The two lovers wake up but play dead as they are discovered by the entire camp. The film is more like *A Midsummer Night's Dream* than *R and J*. The theater production continues, very clearly as a collective effort. (The camp leader gives in, reluctantly.) After Bettina is stung by a bee, she is replaced by Karoline. The scenes from *Romeo and Juliet* alternate between being shot as if natural (only birds and so on are the soundtrack in the balcony scene) and as cinematic (the death scene is shot at the start and end with music, and the two actors are in period costume—the misc-en-scène vaguely recalls that of Zeffirelli's 1968 film). The death scene also includes Friar Laurence, and after Juliet's speech, he comes onstage with all the rest of the cast (very young kids) and gives part of his final speech. As the film ends, we see a medium shot focusing on Robbie and Karoline smiling at each other, and music from their skinny dipping interlude plays. Then the film ends. Again, the couple are framed, as in the play, by a wider social world. Shakespeare as live theater and printed book is also opposed in the film to mass media. We first see Robbie in a car with a handheld transistor on playing loud rock music, and he later gives the radio to Karoline when she is alone in bed, sick. The radio disappears, after that scene, and Shakespeare takes over. The film manages to seem contemporary and progressive while preserving high culture and a collective sensibility that does not sacrifice romance (or vice versa).

Gender hierarchies are played off against age/youth hierarchies in an almost contrapuntal. Youth triumphs over age. The parents are almost entirely absent, with the counselor standing in as "Father." The more progressive aspects of the GDR with respect to gender are not exactly fulfilled here. The camp leader is a woman, and she gives in when a man with a horse shows up and supports the *R and J* production. The counselor's girlfriend, also a counselor, is more deferential to the leader and does not participate in the *R and J* production. Moreover, the triangle involves two girls fighting over a boy. But the film is more Karoline's story than Robbie's, and the interactions among the girls are given equal time, perhaps more time, than the boys'. And in the production, Old Capulet is played as entirely brutish while both Lady Capulet and the Nurse are played sympathetically. There's also a antifascist unconscious in the film. Despite the critique of the radio (installed in every home soon after the Nazis came to power in 1933) and of gymnastics and calisthenics (associated with the director), the children and especially Robbie and Karoline are shot in a kind of kitschy way found often in Nazi *Liebenskult* and *Lebenskult* photos. *Sieben Sommersprossen* is available on video and DVD (region 2 in German only; no English subtitles) from Amazon.de. (RB)

1189 *The Reincarnation of Serena*
1979. U.S. Gourmet Video. Sound, col., 51 mins. Roy Karch.

Hardcore pornography. One of the first direct-to-video pornographic films, consisting of two unrelated costume sequences, one of which involves *Romeo and Juliet*, particularly the balcony scene. (The other sequence is a *Bonnie and Clyde* takeoff.)

1190 *The Young Lovers*
1979. Hong Kong. Shaw Brothers. Sound, col., 96 mins. Michihiko Obimori.

In Hong Kong, Junming Chiu, a poor but dedicated student, and Lanjin Fang, rich daughter of businessman Mr. Fang, fall in love. When Junming's brother Zhuming accidentally kills a gang terrorizing his sick father, Mr. Fang, hearing the news on the TV, forbids Lanjin to see him. Lanjin's father dies, and Junming becomes a driver for Yili, an older high-priced call girl. Lanjin uses a gangster to track Junming's whereabouts, but he tries to assault her, and Junming stabs him. The two are forced to live on Lantau Island with Junming's uncle and aunt, who think they are married; though they live together, they remain chaste. Eventually, Mr. Fang tracks them down and has Junming arrested for kidnapping. Junming, homeless, takes his former position with Yili and succumbs briefly to her charms. When Junming tries to break off the relationship with Lanjin, she attempts to commit suicide, leading Junming to take her home to Mr. Fang and ask his blessing. In response, Mr. Fang tries to buy off Junming and encourages Guo Huazhing, the son of a business associate, to

date her. When Guo attempts to assault Lanjin, she accidentally kills him; at the same time, Junming, pursued by a gangster, also accidentally kills him, getting wounded in the process. Junming and Lanjin reunite on the run at Lantau Island; Junming dies from his wound and Lanjin, distraught, commits suicide at his side.

This B-movie recasting of Shakespeare's *Romeo and Juliet* sets up two blocking forces that test the lovers. The Fang family's objection to Junming is that he is both poor and a gangster, an inappropriate match for their rich daughter; all assume that Junming and Lanjin's relationship was consummated on Lantau Island and therefore brings shame on them both. Junming struggles with maintaining his faithfulness and purity for Lanjin, and he fails to do so with Yili, though Lanjin never discovers this. Interestingly, Guo, the Paris figure, is killed not by Junming, the Romeo figure, but by Lanjin, the Juliet figure, though his death is accidental. The death of Junming and Lanjin, particularly Lanjin, is clearly reminiscent of the tragic end of Shakespeare's lovers. Shakespeare is briefly referenced in an English class, where the professor recites the opening lines of Hamlet's "To be or not to be" soliloquy; immediately afterward Junming's fortunes turn, for he is called out of class in midspeech to hear of his brother's killing of the gangster.

1191 *The Elephant Man*
1980. U.S. Brooks Films and Paramount. Sound, b&w, 124 mins. David Lynch.

John Merrick, a deformed man in Victorian Britain, is rescued from a freak show by Frederick Treves, a kindly doctor who takes him to live at the London Hospital. There Merrick's intellect and sensitivity are recognized, and he even briefly becomes the toast of London society. But through the machinations of an evil night porter, Bytes, Merrick's former carnival "owner," spirits him away. With the aid of other carnival freaks, Merrick returns to London and once again takes up residence in London Hospital. After attending a theatrical performance, he quietly commits suicide.

When Mrs. Kendal, a theater actress, visits Merrick after reading of his plight, she brings him a copy of Shakespeare. The two share an impromptu reading of the "holy palmer's kiss" sequence of *Romeo and Juliet* (1.5), at the end of which Mrs. Kendal gives him a kiss and declares, "You're Romeo." The scene establishes Merrick's emotional sensitivity, intelligence, and romantic idealization of Kendal, and it begins a sequence in which London socialites, following Kendal's lead, visit Merrick.

1192 *My Bodyguard*
1980. U.S. 20th Century Fox, Market Street Productions, and Melvin Simon Productions. Sound, col., 96 mins. Tony Bill.

Harassed by a bully named Moody, Clifford Peache, a shy high school student, employs an imposing troubled loner, Eric Linderman, as his bodyguard and they become unlikely friends. When Moody hires his own bodyguard, Clifford and Eric confront renewed harassment.

A short sequence in an English class concerns the feud in *Romeo and Juliet*, a theme significant to the action in the film.

1193 *Schulmadchen Reporten 13 (Sweet Young Trouble)*
1980. Germany. Rereleased by Private Screenings. Sound, col., 88 mins. Walter Boos.

Softcore pornography. At a school rehearsal of *Romeo and Juliet*, Mr. Birch, the director, and members of the student cast trade five stories involving love and sexuality as they work on the balcony scene.

The rehearsal is largely an excuse for five unrelated sexual vignettes, ranging from the tragic to the comic and all involving teen women. In the rehearsal scenes, we are shown only a brief excerpt involving Romeo's swearing to the moon and Juliet's response. Nevertheless, the scene precipitates a running discussion among the student actors about how Shakespeare perceived the relationship between sex and love. Mr. Birch argues that Romeo exudes a romantic, lustful perspective, revealed by the line "Wilt thou leave me unsatisfied?" whereas Juliet is the more "practical" one, as revealed in her desire to fix the time of the lovers' next meeting. Along the way, the students trade fairly vacuous talk about Shakespeare's universality and outmodedness. In the third inset story, *The Rape of Lucrece* is briefly referenced. A rakish young man, Stefan, interrupts a young woman's study for English class and quotes the description of Tarquin sneaking into Lucrece's chamber (ll.365–71). The passage is thematically relevant, since Stefan rapes and ruins the young woman later in the story.

1194 *Ek Duuje Ke Liye (Made for Each Other)*
1981. India. Prasad Productions. Sound, col., 163 mins. K. Balachander.

Vaasu Shivaram, a young Tamil man, returns home to Panaji in Goa after quitting his job. He soon falls in love with Sapna, his neighbor and the daughter of an orthodox Brahmin family. When the couple's secret romance is discovered by their dueling families, they pressure the two to break up and convince the two to remain apart without communicating for a year to prove that their love for one another is true. Vaasu moves to Hyerabad to work for Mr. Hari, and unknown to him, Vaasu's father coaxes Hari to matchmake Vaasu with another girl; Sapna's mother invites Chakravanthy, a foolish cousin, to their home in hopes that he can woo Sapna's affection away from Vaasu. By accident at a hotel Vaasu learns from Chakravanthy that he intends to marry Sapna. Fearing that he has been made a fool, Vaasu becomes betrothed to Sandhya, a widowed friend, but Sandhya, concerned about Vaasu's affections, travels to

meet Sapna and afterward calls off the wedding. On the day their agreement ends, Vaasu travels to meet Sapna in Panaji, but he is followed by Ram Singh and his men, a gang hired by Sandhya's brother to defend the family honor; Sapna is followed by a sleazy jerk who intends to rape her. At a temple by the sea, both fend off their attackers but are hurt. To be together lest they be parted again, the two commit suicide by diving from the cliff into the sea.

Ek Duuje Ke Liye, Balachander's Hindi remake of his own Teluga film, *Maro Charithra* (1978), uses the basic armature of *Romeo and Juliet*—young lovers divided by family antagonism (in this case, the differences involve region and caste). Several other motifs recall Shakespeare's play: the arrangement of alternate matches for the lovers by their parents; misunderstood news leading to tragically hasty actions on the protagonist's part; and the romantic suicide of the lovers. The film references Shakespeare specifically in two places. The sleazy jerk first comes on to Sapna in the university bookstore, where he tries to interest her in a copy of *Love's Labor's Lost* (she rejects him and the book); with her professor father, Sapna studies Juliet's lines "What's in a name? that which we call a rose / By any other name would smell as sweet" (2.2)—her father's lucid explanation of Shakespeare's meaning sits poorly with his shabby treatment of Vaasu. The use of Shakespeare is one way in which Balachander emphasizes the timelessness of the lovers' problems, a central theme of the film. Of interest too is the centrality of language difference in the film's plot and the many, often comic references to other films by the characters.

1195 *I Fichissimi*
1981. Italy. Dean Film. Sound, col., 90 mins. Carlo Vanzina.

Romeo, from Milan, is in love with Giulietta, sister of a southern Italian capo.

1196 *Vam i ne snilos (You Have Not Seen It Even in a Dream...)*
1981. USSR. Gorky Film Studios. Sound, col., 90 mins. Ilya Frez.

Adapted from the novella by Galina Shcherbakova. Two teenagers, Roman Lavochkin and Katya Shevchenko, fall in love when they meet in their high school class. Because Katya's mother Lyudmila and Roman's father Kostya have a prior romantic history and are neighbors, Roman's mother Vera becomes concerned about the possibility of Lyudmila and Roman's love being rekindled, and so she works to keep Roman and Katya apart. The couple's literature teacher, Tanechka, champions the couple's cause, in part because she has her own unsatisfying relationship, and in part because she is a literary romantic. In the end, Roman and Katya's love triumphs. The film briefly references *Romeo and Juliet*, in addition to the obvious parallel.

1197 *Finyé* (*The Wind*)
1982. Mali. Souleymane Cissé Productions. Sound, col., 105 mins. Souleymane Cissé.

Bah, the grandson of an African tribal chieftain, and Batrou, the daughter of a military commander, attend university and fall in love. The couple are political activists and find themselves increasingly at odds with their parents. Eventually, the two are harassed by the military for their activities and are imprisoned after a brutally suppressed demonstration that soon leads to more general civil unrest. Bah's father prays to a sacred tree and receives advice from the wind, after which he tries to confront the commander about the couple and his involvement with colonial politics. Enraged, the commander tries to kill the chieftain, but as if by spiritual protection the chieftain emerges unharmed.

The motif of lovers divided by a feud resembles that of *Romeo and Juliet*; here the feud is fueled by contemporary African politics. There are no direct citations of Shakespeare's script.

1198 *Irresistible*
1983. U.S. Select-Essex. Sound, col., 80 mins. Edwin Brown.

Hardcore pornography. Like Walter Mitty, Walter Browne is bored with his job, wife, and life and indulges in compensatory fantasies. He uses a time machine to travel back in time to encounter Cleopatra and Juliet, but soon discovers that he prefers his wife.

Two sequences toy with Shakespeare's characters: Cleopatra becomes angry when she discovers her fate; and when Walter brings Juliet into the present, stealing her from Romeo, she soon becomes a stripper.

1199 *Valley Girl*
1983. U.S. Valley 9000. Sound, col., 99 mins. Martha Coolidge.

After breaking up with her boyfriend Tommy, Julie Richman, a Valley girl and daughter of hippie parents, meets Randy, an unconventional, adventurous boy from Hollywood, at a party and the two fall for each other, though Tommy, jealous, picks a fight with Randy. Julie's conformist friends disapprove of the match because Randy doesn't conform to Valley stereotypes, and at Tommy's instigation, they pressure Julie to break up with Randy and make up with Tommy. When Randy's persistent attempts to get Julie back fail, he fights Tommy at the prom as Tommy and Julie are about to be crowned prom king and queen. In the end, he and Julie are reunited. Various trysts among minor characters form the sub-plots.

Though the director and many commentators note the relationship between Shakespeare's play and this film, the parallels are not particularly deep. The lovers are divided not by feuding parents—the Richmans in fact encourage Julie to follow her heart, and we never meet Randy's parents—but by Julie's conformist friends, who engage in the war of styles between the Valley and Hollywood. Tommy, Julie's jealous boyfriend, has many of the qualities of Tybalt. Much of the film is devoted to affectionate social satire of 1980s Los Angeles life.

Among many extras, the DVD includes a director's commentary and a featurette, "*Valley Girl*: Totally Tubular 20 Years Later," both of which reference *Romeo and Juliet*.

1200 *The Frog Prince* (aka *French Lessons*)
1984. U.S. Enigma Film and Goldcrest Films Ltd. Sound, col., 100 mins. Brian Gilbert.

Adapted from the book by N. Rootes. Jenny, a British girl studying at the Sorbonne and living with a strict, genteel French family, wants to lose her virginity to Jean-Philippe, a local French boy, but she longs to be wooed and so she sets criteria for their relationship. Jean-Philippe refuses to woo her with romantic verse, so Jenny's affections shift to Niels, a Norwegian student. After several twists and turns in relationships, Jean-Philippe eventually accedes to Jenny's romantic requirements.

Jean-Philippe fulfills Jenny's desires by reciting a passage from the balcony scene in *Romeo and Juliet* to her on the Metro.

1201 *Romeo i Julija* (*Romeo and Juliet*)
1984. Yugoslavia. Dunav Film. Sound, col., 11 mins. Dusan Petricic.

Animated film (parody).

1202 *Narekohme gi Monteki i Kapuleti* (*We Called Them Montagues and Capulets*)
1985. Bulgaria. Boyana Films. Sound, col., 89 mins. Donio Donev.

Animated film (parody). Bulgaria's first feature-length animated feature.

1203 *Rendez-vous*
1985. France. Union Generale Cinematographique. Sound, col., 82 mins. André Techiné.

Nina, an actress newly arrived in Paris, meets two men: Paulo, a timid if kind worker at a real estate agency, and Quentin, a passionate, self-destructive actor in a live-sex show. Though Paulo shows her kindness and attempts ineptly to seduce her, Nina is attracted to the intensity of Quentin and becomes involved with him. When Paulo arrives with items for Nina, Quentin leaves Nina's apartment and is hit by a car, apparently a suicide. At Quentin's cremation, Nina meets Schrutzler, a fatherly theater director working on a production of *Romeo and Juliet* who knows Quentin's past. From him she soon pieces together that Quentin, acting in one of Schrutzler's earlier *Romeo and Juliet* productions, was responsible for the accidental death of Schrutzler's daughter, the actress playing Juliet. Schrutzler casts Nina in the role of Juliet in his current *Romeo and Juliet* production, but Quentin continues to appear to Nina in her dreams, asking her not to play the part. Meanwhile, Paulo, with whom Nina is living, rejects her for what he mistakenly takes for sleeping around, even rejecting her sexual advances. Schrutzler leaves for London after giving Nina an ultimatum: choose to play the part of Juliet or not. The film closes on a tableau of Nina's shadow on the stage as the curtain rises.

Romeo and Juliet serves as a symbolic ideal of self-destructive yet pure romantic passion in the film. Quentin acts in a sordid sex-show version of the balcony scene, an indication of his artistic degradation. Lines from Romeo's speech immediately before Balthasar enters with news of Juliet's supposed "death"—"I dreamt my lady came and found me dead— / Strange dream, that gives a dead man leave to think— / And breathed such life with kisses in my lips / That I revived and was an emperor" (5.1.6–9)—are used as a leitmotif throughout the film, presaging both passionate love and death. We are also shown Nina's struggle with rehearsal of Juliet's lines from the end of the ballroom scene (1.5), emphasizing, "My only love sprung from my only hate."

1204 *Valentin i Valentina*
1985. USSR. Mosfilm. Sound, col., 93 mins. Georgy Natanson.

Adapted from the play by Mikhail Roshchin. In this melodrama, Valentin and Valentina are in love and want to marry, but their mothers plot to destroy the relationship.

1205 *Fire with Fire*
1986. U.S. 20th Century Fox. Sound, col., 103 mins. Duncan Gibbons.

Joe Fisk, a young inmate at a parole camp in rural Oregon, comes across Lisa Taylor, an artistically inclined girl at nearby Immaculate Heart Catholic School, engaged in a photo project while he is running in the woods. He instantly falls for her. At a dance for the men of the camp at the school, Lisa and Joe develop their romantic connection and make plans to communicate, despite the strictures for both. The two secretly meet at night in a crypt and make love, but they are discovered by "Boss" Duchard, the sadistic head guard at the parole camp, and Joe is locked up. Myron, Joe's friend and a mapmaker, helps Joe escape and gives him directions to a mountain cabin. Joe steals a car and collects Lisa, and the two go to the isolated cabin, but they are found by Boss Duchard, who wants to kill them for humiliating him. The cabin burns down, but Joe and Lisa jump into the river to escape.

This teen-market B movie recasts the narrative of young lovers separated by authority figures, in this case Boss Duchard and Sister Victoria of Immaculate Heart, and so may be regarded as an analogue to *Romeo and Juliet*. Several other motifs from Shakespeare's play appear in changed form: the two first formally meet at the dance (though they've seen each other earlier), and hands are a visual

motif throughout that sequence; Joe and Lisa consummate their relationship in a crypt; and Myron, Joe's eccentric friend, resembles Mercutio in some respects, particularly his disappointment at Joe's shifting affection. Interestingly, the film associates impending tragedy with the lovers throughout—Joe's first sight of Lisa is as she is staging Ophelia's drowning (recreating Millais's famous portrait) for a photo project, and her photograph is a recurring motif; when Lisa first meets Joe at the dance, it is with flowers in her hair, a reminder of Ophelia; and they later meet in a graveyard and make love in a crypt. The ending of the film, in which Joe and Lisa seem to choose suicide by water, at first seems to confirm this tragic trajectory, but their survival actually resists Shakespeare's ending. The pop soundtrack owes something to *West Side Story*, but far more to teen triumph films of the 1980s such as *Flashdance* (Adrian Lyne, 1983) and *Footloose* (Herbert Ross, 1984).

1206 *Lucas*
1986. U.S. 20th Century Fox and Lawrence Gordon Productions. Sound, col., 100 mins. David Seltzer and Linda Sutton.

Lucas Blye, a nerdy fourteen-year-old loner, bonds with Maggie, a slightly older athletic girl and daughter of a recent divorcée, over a number of cultural and intellectual pursuits and their contempt for "superficial" people. Though Lucas falls in love with Maggie, she only wants friendship, being more interested in Cappie Roew, new quarterback of the football team. When Lucas is harassed by other jocks, Cappie, running counter to stereotype, defends him. In her pursuit of Cappie, Maggie joins the cheerleading squad, much to Lucas's dismay, but he joins the football team in the hopes of attracting Maggie's affection. Meanwhile, Rina, a nerdy girl who has a crush on Lucas, tries to make her affections clear to him. At a football game, Lucas is injured, and Maggie learns that he is from a broken, poverty-stricken home, but he is afterward accepted by the jocks at school as a hero.

Rina notes in a lunchroom conversation that in *Romeo and Juliet*, people kill themselves when they can't have who they love. (This conversation takes place while jocks engage in mindless shows of prowess.) Later, outside a school dance, Lucas follows up with Rina about *Romeo and Juliet*, asking her how old the two lovers were and noting that they were from "different worlds." When Maggie finally reveals that she only wants to be friends, Lucas notes the similarity in ages between himself and Romeo. Compare *Gregory's Girl* (entry 931).

1207 *China Girl*
1987. U.S. Great American Films, Streetlight Films, and Vestron. Sound, col., 90 mins. Abel Ferrara.

In contemporary New York City, tensions mount between Italian and Chinese gangs, headed by the vehemently anti-Chinese Mercury and psychotically violent

Tsu Shin respectively, when a Chinese restaurant opens on the Italian side of Canal Street. The tensions are made even worse when Tony, a pizzeria delivery boy, and Tye, Shin's shy sister, meet at a disco and fall in love. Alby, Tony's Mafia-affiliated brother, warns Tony to drop Tye, just as Yung Gan, Tye's older brother, warns her away from Tony. In an effort to take protection money Shin bombs the Chinese restaurant, after which a gang war erupts. After Shin kills Alby, Yung tries to pack Tye off to Hong Kong, but Tye escapes to Tony instead. Shin kills the lovers, and in retribution he is killed by the Chinese gang.

Owing more to *West Side Story* than *Romeo and Juliet*, Ferrara's adaptation stresses the violence of gang conflict and hypocrisy of bigotry rather than the romance between the lovers. His choreographed and visually beautiful action sequences anticipate Luhrmann's handling of the same material, though Luhrmann's approach is much less graphic (see entry 496). There are no references to Shakespeare's dialogue. Ferrara dubbed this his favorite of his films. See also entry 492.

1208 *Julia's Geheim*
1987. The Netherlands. Topaz Pictures and NOS. Sound, col., 103 mins. Hans Hylkema.

Arzu Sülün is the daughter of Ibrahim, a Turkish immigrant and clothing worker in the Netherlands. Though Ibrahim, a traditionalist, has arranged a marriage for his daughter to another villager's son in his home village, Arzu, acculturated to Holland, doesn't want to comply with his wishes. When she is cast in the role of Juliet in a school production of Shakespeare's play, he forbids her to participate in theater, but she uses the ruse of an embroidery class to rehearse. When her younger brother Erdal is arrested, Ibrahim discovers his daughter's plans, and he tries to keep her home at work, though he is eventually persuaded to let her appear by Arzu's teachers. Meanwhile, the family of Arzu's future bridegroom arrives and Arzu learns that she was affianced three years ago to a boy she doesn't know. When her father sees the play, he recognizes the parallel between his daughter and Juliet, and he regrets his decision to marry her off.

1209 *Romeo and Juliet*
1987. U.S. Pleasure (Western). Sound, col., 85 mins. Paul Thomas.

Hardcore pornographic adaptation. In this backstage drama, a stage troupe must put on a successful production of *Romeo and Juliet* to prevent the theater from being sold to a pornographic chain.

1210 *Phantom of the Opera*
1988. Italy. Mahsa Film. Sound, col., 100 mins. Dario Argento.

Remake of the horror film with Gounod's opera *Romeo and Juliet* being performed. (RB)

1211 *Qayamat Se Qayamat Tak* (*From Judgment Day to Judgment Day*)
1988. India. Nasir Hussain Films. Sound, col., 162 mins. Mansoor Khan.

In the village of Dhanakpur, a blood feud erupts between two families when Ratan Singh gets his neighbor Madhumathi Singh pregnant and refuses to marry her or acknowledge the affair. When Madhumathi kills herself out of shame, her brother Dhanraj Singh kills Ratan at his wedding. Years later, after having served his prison sentence, Dhanraj reunites with his two sons, Raj and Shyam, who have been raised by Dhanraj's brother, a clothing maker in Delhi. While in Dhananpur on business, Raj sees and falls for Rashmi, daughter of Thakur Randir Singh, the brother of Ratan and moral enemy of Dhanraj. Raj crashes Dhanraj's party and even pretends to be Roop Singh, Rashmi's intended betrothed, to catch a glimpse of her. Later, the two families unknowingly take their vacations at Mount Abu, and Raj and Rashmi fall in love. When Dhanraj learns of Rashmi's identity, he warns her away from Raj, but Raj secretly continues to contact her. Thakur pushes ahead with Roop's betrothal to Rashmi, and when he discovers that she has been seeing Raj, he warns her away. After Rashmi's betrothal party, Raj and Rashmi escape into the countryside where they set up household in a ruined temple, but Thakur, discovering their whereabouts, hires thugs to kill Raj and any witnesses. Rashmi's grandmother reveals Thakur's plan to Raj's relatives, and they too travel to the temple. In the midst of trying to murder Raj, the thugs kill Rashmi (as a witness), and Raj, in order to be with Rashmi in death, kills himself with a knife.

Though there are no allusions to Shakespeare's dialogue, the parallels to *Romeo and Juliet* are unmistakable in this film. The feud between the patriarchs of the Singh families is established early in the film (involving sins of love committed by children of both clans), and that feud structures their antipathy to the children's courtship. The lovers fall for each other without knowing their identities, and Dhanraj's betrothal of Roop to Rashmi precipitates the lover's elopement. Rashmi's grandmother plays something of the role of Juliet's Nurse, counseling Rashmi to accept her betrothal while still remaining sympathetic to Rashmi's love for Raj. The tragic ending mirrors Shakespeare's with the action of Raj who, like Juliet, stabs himself with a knife in order to be with Rashmi in death. The tragic fatedness of the lovers is signaled early on when Rashmi takes photographs of Raj during a sunset, an omen of death; the final shot of the dead lovers, sunset in the background, recalls this motif.

1212 *Rami og Julie*
1988. Denmark and France. C. Cosmos C., Danish Film Institute, Filmcooperative Danmark, and K-Films. Sound, col., 113 mins. Erik Clausen.

In contemporary Copenhagen, Rami, a Palestinian political refugee, falls in love with Julie, a woman at a service station who harbors him as he flees Frank and his gang of racist thugs. When Rami temporarily leaves to smuggle his refugee cousin, a terrorist, into Denmark, Julie attends a party where Frank, who learns of her love for Rami, and his men attempt to assault her. In the midst of escorting his cousin, Rami is shot. When Julie goes to meet Rami and his cousin at the airport, only the cousin arrives. The film is punctuated by a Chorus figure who offers Shakespearean quotations, mostly from *Romeo and Juliet*, that provide commentary on the action.

1213 *Romeo and Juliet II*
1988. U.S. Pleasure (Western). Sound, col., 77 mins. Paul Thomas.

Hardcore pornographic adaptation. The plot revolves around the casting of Juliet in a small theatrical production, a choice between an annoying professional actress and a shy student; the "real" character of Juliet appears (from heaven) to save the production and to prompt a romance between the actor playing Romeo and his shy leading lady.

Directly references the balcony scene (several times), the "palmer's kiss" sonnet between Romeo and Juliet, Juliet's leave-taking of Romeo, and (very briefly) the tomb scene. Shakespeare and the "real" Romeo also make cameo appearances and speak in ersatz Elizabethan English.

1214 *Maine Pyar Kiya*
1989. India. Rajshri Productions Pvt. Ltd. Sound, col., 193 mins. Sooraj R. Barjatya.

When Karan, a humble mechanic and devoted father of his daughter Suman, gets a job in Dubai, he leaves Suman with his former best friend Kishen Kumar Choudhury, a rich, powerful, and haughty man who lives with his wife and son Prem. Prem soon falls in love with Suman, and despite her shyness, Suman eventually comes to declare her love for Prem. Prem wants to marry Suman, a match approved by Prem's mother, but Kishen prefers Seema, the daughter of his crooked business partner Ranjeet. While Prem is away on a business trip, Kishen sends Suman away, insulting her father in the process. Prem leaves his family to pursue Suman, but when he arrives at Karan's home, Karan rejects him as a suitor for his daughter. Karan requires Prem to prove himself by earning 2,000 rupees in a month, which Prem does. When Ranjeet's son is revealed as an embezzler and is fired, Ranjeet tries to rekindle the fight between Kishen and Karan and even arranges for Prem to be attacked, but the men unite to fight off Prem's gang, and Suman and Prem are united.

The motif of young lovers divided by parental marriage arrangements, a parallel to *Romeo and Juliet*, dominates the film's middle third. As is often the case in Bollywood films, it is the son's arranged marriage, not the daughter's, that

poses the problem, and the family patriarchs block the romance. Here the feud between the patriarchs springs from class differences—Kishen looks down upon his former friend as poor and unrefined, and Karan comes to regard Kishen (rightly so) as haughty and insulting, particularly when he accuses Suman of gold digging. Though the film does not reference Shakespeare's dialogue, it does include a passage in which Prem asks Karan to separate him from his father's name, reminiscent in sentiment of Juliet's "What's in a name?"

1215 *Montoyas y Tarantos* (*Passion Andalouse*)
1989. Spain. Communication Visual Creativa. Sound, col., 103 mins. Vicente Escrivá.

A remake of Francisco Rovira Beleta's *Los Tarantos* (1963). Though the film has a superb (and Goya-winning) score by Paco de Lucia and is somewhat more faithful to *Romeo and Juliet*, it is generally regarded as inferior to its source.

1216 *Romeo: Love Master of the Wild Women's Dorm*
1989. True Love Productions and Troma Studios. Sound, col., 86 mins. Denis Adams Zervos.

University student Romeo is a lover much in sexual demand among the women of the dormitory, but he finds true love when he meets bookish, quiet Julie. Their romance is temporarily derailed when Julie discovers "Project Romeo," a study on Romeo's sexual prowess by one of the women, but in the end he serenades Julie and wins back her love.

Though this no-budget, badly made comedy has little relationship to Shakespeare's narrative, the catalyst for Romeo connecting with Julie is that she first speaks to him using Juliet's lines from the balcony scene (he responds with contemporary English). She gives him a copy of the play, and from it he learns that a man can have only one girlfriend. He quotes Romeo's lines from the balcony scene, and later writes (vapid) poetry of his own for Julie.

Included as an extra on the DVD *Shakespeare In and Out*.

1217 *Romeo und Julia auf dem Dorfe*
1989. East Germany. Production company unknown. Sound, b&w, length unknown. Siegfried Kühn.

Yet another film adaptation of the novel by Gottfried Keller. (RB)

1218 *Sex Lives of the Rich and Famous*, Part I
1989. U.S. VCA. Sound, col., 86 mins. Henri Pachard.

Hardcore pornography. Julie Capp, daughter of a nouveau riche, overly cultured, but sexually repressed southern California family, is in love with Roman Cox, son of a crass, hedonistic family. When Regina and Terrance Capp catch their daughter *in flagrante delicto* with Roman, they ban her from seeing him. Ty Paris confronts Candy Cox about the slight to his honor, and Monty Capp confronts Regina about her treatment of their children's love affair. After a tryst with her nurse Ophelia, Julie elopes with

Roman, with the help of Laurence Friar, a gardener. Two young lovers try to continue a love affair, despite the opposition of their feuding nouveau riche families. This film spawned a sequel, *Sex Lives of the Rich and Famous #2*.

Besides the adapted names, several motifs from Shakespeare's play appear: romance blocked by a family feud, a relationship between Juliet's mother and another man, the lovers' plan to elope, and a gardener who tries to help the lovers. Both children rebel against their parents' lifestyles: Julie is sexually voracious, whereas Roman speaks of his desire for romance rather than just sex. No verbal references. There are touches of wit in the otherwise predictable script: Roman expresses his disgust for pornography; the gardener, Mr. Laurence, is half-mad as he prunes hedges, and the elixir he offers is absinthe to help with Roman's sexual performance. The sequel, "Part II," uses the same characters but runs far afield from Shakespeare's plot.

1219 *Torn Apart*
1989. Israel and U.S. Castle Hill Productions, A Forbidden Love Film Partnership and City Lights Pictures. Sound, col., 95 mins. Jack Fisher and Barry Markowitz.

Adapted from the novel *Forbidden Love* by Chayym Zeldis. In modern Israel, Ben Arnon, an Israeli Jew, and Laila Malek, a independently minded Palestinian, become friends as children, and secretly meet as teenagers. When Laila is sent away during the 1967 War and Ben moves with his family to New York City, the two lose touch. Ben returns in 1973 when drafted into the Israeli Army, and he meets Laila by chance at a checkpoint. The two renew their love, which leads to objections from their families, including Ben's father Arie and Laila's father Mahmoud. Ben's sympathies with Palestinians lead him to save a drowning Arab child, but his gun is stolen and used by a sniper, deepening the rift between him and his father and preventing Ben and Laila from meeting. At his sister's wedding in 1974, Ben's romantic memories of Laila are reawakened. He finds her, and they make plans to leave for New York City. But their escape is foiled when they are captured by soldiers. As they return, they become embroiled in a funeral riot. When Laila attempts to save Ben from a beating, she is shot and dies in his arms.

Though it does not reference Shakespeare's dialogue, this earnest resituating of *Romeo and Juliet* in the Israeli-Palestinian conflict uses many motifs from Shakespeare's original in addition to the lovers being separated by a feud and antagonistic fathers. The Paris role is filled by Moustapha, the cousin who seeks Laila's hand in marriage (interestingly, Laila's father refuses to force her into a match); Fawzi, Laila's relative, functions much like Tybalt with his involvement in anti-Israeli terrorism; Professor Mansour takes Friar Laurence's part, providing Ben (and us) with background about the political conflict and helping the lovers (he pays for his help with his life); and the use of Ben's gun in the killing of his fellow soldiers recasts Romeo's unwitting part in the death of Mercutio. Laila is shot by someone we never see, so that responsibility for her death is distributed among all. Repeated wide shots of the land remind the viewer what the war is over, and the soundtrack contains continual reminders of the conflict. The death toll in this version is quite high: by the end, Laila's brother, Ben's father, several of Ben's fellow soldiers, Professor Mansour, Fawzi, and Laila are dead.

1220 *Under the Boardwalk*
1989. U.S. New World Pictures. Sound, col., 102 mins. Fritz Kiersh.

In Los Angeles, Nick Rainford, a surfer from the Valley, meets Allie Yorpin, an artistic girl from the beach, at a beach party. Allie's brother Reef, a drug-dealing rival surfer, dislikes him as a "Val," a feeling exacerbated when he thinks that Nick has his bag of drugs his friend has lost. As Allie and Nick become lovers, Nick wounds Marone, one of the Vals, in a surfing competition, and the feud between the locals (Locs) and Vals escalates into a full-scale fight. Seeing this, Allie is disgusted, and on the day of Nick's competition with Reef, she offers an ultimatum to Nick about his surfing lifestyle. In the end, both Nick and Reef lose to Gitch, a tough surfer girl, and Nick and Allie leave Los Angeles together. The story is told in flashback by a surfer narrator we learn is Andy, Allie's nerdy cousin who in the course of the film becomes cool and Gitch's boyfriend.

This B movie uses the motif of lovers divided by a feud, in this case between rival surfing clans (the beach party offers an introduction to various surfing cliques). It also offers a strange moment in which a Mercutio-like surfer character, Nick's friend Marone, tells of a strange dream he had of bowling alleys and surfing, the film's substitution for the Queen Mab speech; Marone is later wounded by Reef, who is the film's Tybalt figure. Of some interest is the film's focus on surfer slang (which is prominently featured, though not by the main characters), and its concern with what constitutes authentic surfer culture, a theme highlighted by Hap Jordan, a sell-out surf-clothing manufacturer, and Andy, a surf dude wannabe. Nick commits a kind of "suicide" by purposely losing the surf competition, an action that wins him Allie's hand.

1221 *Romeo-Juliet*
1990. Belgium. PH Consulting and Blue Pearl Film Corporation. Sound, col., 120 mins. Armando Acosta.

Romeo and Juliet performed by long-haired cats, voiced by such British theater luminaries as John Hurt, Vanessa Redgrave, Ben Kingsley, Maggie Smith, Robert Powell, and Francesca Annis. Bizarre but entertaining.

1222 *1-800-TIME*
1991. U.S. Infinity Film. Sound, col., 75 mins. Ron Jeremy.

Hardcore pornography. A parody of *Bill and Ted's Excellent Adventure*.

At one point, the two time-traveling protagonists encounter Romeo and Juliet, who engage in a sexual tryst.

1223 *Beauty and the Beast*
1991. Disney. Sound, col., 90 mins. Gary Trousdale and Kirk Wise.

The extended DVD edition has a scene with *Romeo and Juliet*. (RB)

1224 *Sleeping with the Enemy*
1991. U.S. 20th Century Fox. Sound, col., 99 mins. Joseph Ruben.

Adapted from the novel by Nancy Bass. Laura Burney is the wife of Martin, an investment counselor and deeply controlling and abusive husband. When the abuse becomes physical and unbearable, Laura fakes her own death by drowning and lives under the assumed name of Sara Waters in rural Iowa. As she starts a romantic relationship with neighbor Ben Woodward, a drama teacher, Martin reappears in her life, having discovered Laura's ruse. After stalking and threatening her and killing Ben, Martin is killed by Laura in a showdown.

A leitmotif in Ben and Laura's relationship is *West Side Story* (based on *Romeo and Juliet*).

1225 *Kolejnosc uczuc (Sequence of Feelings)*
1992. Poland. Telewizja Polska (TVP) S.A. and Tor Film. Sound, col., 105 mins. Radoslaw Piwowarski.

Rafal Nawrot, a once well-known Polish actor who is now desperate for work, joins a production of *Romeo and Juliet* in Polish Silesia. He takes up with Skiba, an actress who is married, but he also develops a relationship with Julia Kasprusiak, a young music student and a member of his fan club. Though she is much younger than he, he ends up falling deeply in love with her. His relationship with her is jeopardized when Julia catches him in bed with Skiba.

Several scenes from *Romeo and Juliet* are juxtaposed with Nawrot's romantic life.

1226 *Mississippi Masala*
1992. U.K. and U.S. Cinecom Pictures, Mirabai Films, MovieWorks, Odyssey Entertainment, and Orion. Sound, col., 118 mins. Mira Nair.

In 1972, Jay, an Indian man, is exiled from his native Uganda with his wife Kinnu and daughter Mina. Eighteen years later, they live in Greenwood, Mississippi, in a small Indian enclave, working at the Monte Cristo Hotel for his brother Anil. Taken by Harry Patel to a local dance club, Mina meets Demetrius Williams, a black carpet cleaner, and the two become attracted to each other. At first some members of Mina and Demetrius's families are receptive to Indians and blacks mixing, but when Anil discovers Mina and Demetrius on holiday in a hotel in Biloxi, the families turn against each other, ruining Demetrius's business. Ir-

onically, Jay exercises the same bigotry to which he was subjected. When Jay decides to return his family to Uganda, Mina runs away and joins Demetrius, who plans on restarting his business elsewhere. Jay returns to Uganda to find that his longtime friend Okelo is dead and he cannot return to his once prosperous estate; he reconciles himself to life in Mississippi.

This fascinating, well-crafted portrait of two victimized sub-cultures borrows the basic narrative of *Romeo and Juliet*—lovers divided by warring families—though it avoids Shakespeare's tragic ending. Early in the film, the families express superficial respect for one another, but it is the sexual affair between Mina and Demetrius that leads to the feud, a feud motivated largely by Jay's anger at being exiled from his homeland for being an "Asian." Interestingly, Demetrius's initial motivation for being with Mina is to make his former girlfriend Alicia jealous, a parallel perhaps to Romeo's earlier relationship with Rosalind; as do Romeo and Juliet, the two have their first romantic encounter during a dance. There are no references to Shakespeare's dialogue.

1227 *Zebrahead*
1992. U.S. Ixtlan Corporation. Sound, col., 100 mins. Anthony Drazan.

In a working-class Detroit neighborhood, Dee, a black teenager, and Zack, a white Jewish teen devoted to black culture, become strong friends as they attend high school. Their friendship becomes strained when Zack begins dating Nikki, Dee's cousin. Dee's black friends and Nikki's mother oppose the relationship, and Zack's white friends and his father, a womanizer, assume that he is after sex. Matters become more tense when Nut, a local black gang member, wants to date Nikki himself. Eventually, Nut's taunting leads to Dee's death, and Nikki, Zack, and their high school are left to contemplate the meanings of his demise.

This much-praised low-budget independent film bears a general resemblance to *Romeo and Juliet* because of its use of a teen romance blocked by a feud, here urban black-white tensions, with Nut in the Tybalt role. There are no references to Shakespeare's dialogue.

1228 *The Punk* (aka *The Punk and the Princess*)
1993. U.K. Videodrome and M2 Films. Sound, col., 96 mins. Michael Sarne.

Adapted from the novel *The Punk* by Gideon Sams. David, a West London punk alienated from his policeman father, falls in love with Rachel, a rich American girl equally alienated from her vapid father and trophy wife stepmother. The two meet when David is on the run from Stray Cat, a punk against whom he won a pool game, and he runs into a theater where Rachel is performing *Romeo and Juliet*. Not only do both fathers disapprove of their romance, but also, unbeknownst to David, Rachel's jealous ex-boyfriend is Stray Cat, and when he sees the two lovers together, he attempts to kill David. In self-defense, David kills him, then finds himself on the run, eventually hiding out in a tomb and smoking drugs. In the end, Rachel finds him seemingly dead, but in reality David is alive and the two lovers are reconciled, with David's policeman father looking on with approval.

The plot and characters of Shakespeare's script are closely paralleled throughout, until the unexpectedly hopeful ending. The parallel is signaled early on with the delivery of Shakespeare's prologue, referring to not only the play-within-the-film but also the story of David and Rachel; the ill-fatedness of the lovers is signaled yet again by the playing of the tomb scene from *Romeo and Juliet* and by David's mother commenting on their conflicting astrological signs. Several passages from Shakespeare's dialogue are included in the film: in addition to an extended performance of the tomb scene and a bit of Juliet's encounter with the Nurse and her mother, bits of Rachel's rehearsal of Juliet's lines appear throughout the film. Though the film's portrayal of David and Rachel's plight is bleak, its adaptation of Shakespeare is often enlivened by sly wit. In David and Rachel's first meeting, for example, David offers a poetic passage that Rachel immediately identifies as a steal from *Taxi Driver*; their version of the balcony scene starts with Rachel saying, "Where are you, you little fucker?" and ends with David being arrested as a stalker and taken away in a police car. And when David is attacked by Stray Cat with a knife, he is wearing a Shakespeare T-shirt that ends up being slashed, in appropriate punk fashion. The film can be favorably compared to Luhrmann's film adaptation (entry 496).

1229 *Romeo and Julian*
1993. U.S. Blue Jay Productions. Sound, col., 86 mins. Sam Abdul.

Hardcore gay pornographic adaptation. Written by Michael Anton. A "gay romantic musical" putatively based on *Romeo and Juliet*, the film chronicles an on-again, off-again, on-again romance between Romeo and Julian. In this case, the block to the title characters' romance is not a feud, but Romeo's infidelity.

Few direct references other than the character names, though the "palmer's kiss" sequence is handled as a duet ("Take a Chance") between the lovers in a gay bar.

1230 *1942: A Love Story*
1994. India. Eros International. Sound, col., 157 mins. Vidhu Vinod Chopra.

In the Nepalese town of Kasauni during India's fight for independence from the Raj, Narendra (Nandu) Singh, the carefree son of a wealthy politician loyal to the British, falls in love with Rajeshwari (Rajjo) Pathak, the daughter and niece of secret revolutionaries. Raghuvir Pathak and

Uncle Baig plot to blow up the sadistic British General Douglas during a play performance, but as the troupe rehearses, their plot is discovered. Nandu declares his intention to marry Rajjo to Raghuvir; he at first rejects the proposal, then decides to accept it. But before Raghuvir can approve the match, he is killed in a raid, one that Rajjo thinks was instigated by Nandu but that in fact was the work of Nandu's father. After Rajjo is saved by Shubhankar, a revolutionary, Nandu searches for Rajjo, soon tossing in his lot with the revolutionaries and helping Shubhankar to escape. When Douglas arrives, he tries to assassinate him and is caught before doing so. But before Douglas can execute him, he escapes with Shubhankar's help, and the two hang Douglas and destroy the Raj headquarters.

Romeo and Juliet surfaces in two ways in this lavish political epic. First, the lovers are divided by the political alliances and class differences of their families; though the narrative does not often mirror Shakespeare's, the death of Raghuvir, seemingly caused by Nandu, bears a very distant resemblance to Romeo's killing of Tybalt. Second, the play-within-the-film bears very close resemblances to *Romeo and Juliet*, though we're told that it's authored by Uncle Baig. The two scenes featured from the rehearsal use paraphrased dialogue from the balcony scene (2.2) and Romeo and Juliet's morning parting (3.5). The balcony scene is particularly crucial, since Nandu uses his part as Romeo to first declare his love to Rajjo (who is acting as prompter); a version of the scene is later replayed in real life when Nandu visits Rajjo at her home. The use of a British play in a film that glorifies Indian political independence is a fascinating ideological contradiction. There are also several passing references to Romeo and Juliet—when Nandu first introduces himself to Rajjo at a library, he sings of why Romeo loved Juliet; when Nandu's co-star in the play realizes that he prefers Rajjo to her, she consoles herself by saying, "It's not a must that every girl be a Juliet."

1231 *Einfach nur Liebe* (*Simply Love*)
1994. Germany. Avista, Relevant Film, and Westdeutscher Rundfunk. Sound, col., 95 mins. Peter Timm.

Transferred to a new school, Mamba, a hip young teenage boy, is forced to decide which clique he will join—fans of the skinhead metal band The Smashers, headed by Thommy, or fans of the multicultural hip-hop group Fresh Familee. Mamba's decision is complicated by his developing romantic interest in Nadja, Thommy's ex-girlfriend. The students' new language teacher, Herr Pilgrim, uses a production of *Romeo and Juliet* to reconcile the cliques. The film's narrative of feuding groups complicating a romance has clear parallels to Shakespeare's play, and the teacher uses those parallels both to generate interest in Shakespeare and to bring the students together. *Einfach nur Liebe* is one of several films of the 1990s to address the effects of teaching Shakespeare—see also *Renaissance Man*, *Slings and Arrows*, and *Dead Poets Society*.

1232 *Juliet and Romeo*
1994. Italy. Xcel. Sound, col., 86 mins. Joe D'Amato.

Hardcore pornographic adaptation. A series of sexual trysts grouped around the romance between Juliet and Romeo.

Little Shakespearean content beyond the title, names of characters, and various motifs (sword fights, forbidden romance, and Romeo's exile). In this version, the lovers are reunited and do not die.

1233 *Love Is All There Is*
1994 (released 1996). U.S. Cinema 7. Sound, col., 120 mins. Joseph Bologna and Renee Taylor.

This comic version of *Romeo and Juliet* involves a romance between Rosario Cappamezza and Gina Malacici, children of rival Italian restauranteurs in the Bronx. The tacky Cappamezzas own a family-style eatery, whereas the aristocratic Malacicis own a pretentious fine-dining restaurant, and the two have become long-standing bitter competitors. When Rosario's co-star in a local school production of *Romeo and Juliet* becomes injured, Gina is cast at the last minute as Juliet, and the two actors fall instantly in love. The parents become all the more agitated when Rosario and Gina's performances in the play become lusty. Despite the parents' efforts to keep them apart, Rosario and Gina consummate their relationship, and their determination to be together leads to a full-scale feud between the families, conducted during two catered events. During the feud, Rosario and Gina accidentally become trapped in a shed that fills with gas, but Sadie Cappamezza, Rosario's mother, uses her psychic ability to save the couple from death. In the end, Rosario and Gina are married, and their wedding is jointly catered by the two families.

In addition to obvious parallels with Shakespeare's narrative, this film includes several citations of Shakespeare's dialogue, nearly all of them from the balcony scene. The play-within-the-film includes short excerpts from 1.1, 1.3 (featuring a comical cross-dressed Nurse), and 1.5, as well as an extended excerpt from the death scene (5.3) in which Rosario prolongs Romeo's final kiss with Gina and Gina mounts a visibly erect Rosario on the line, "Oh happy dagger! This is my sheath." In this case, the Romeo and Juliet types are motivated far more by teen lust than everlasting love. Of interest is how the script recasts Shakespeare's tragic ending. It retains the drive toward the lovers' deaths (Gina leaves a note that the parents misinterpret as a suicide note), but it reshapes it as a matter of accident and comedy. As Rosario and Gina realize that they may die, they at first calmly speak of their being together in the afterlife, then scream frantically for help;

later, when all seems lost, they kiss on the line "Thus with a kiss I die." The parents' rescue of the children becomes the means by which the families are reconciled. Also of interest is the character of Mona, a wacky local psychic who serves as the film's narrator and stresses with her premonitions the fatedness of the lovers' romance.

1234 *Makedonska saga* (*Macedonian Saga*)
1994. Macedonia and Yugoslavia. Pegasus Films. Sound, col., 111 mins. Branko Gapo.

Arriving at the western Macedonian village of Velekorab, Damjan, a Christian teacher, is at first accepted by his new Muslim neighbors. He falls in love with Dzemile, a Muslim woman affianced to a local Muslim man; when Dzemile returns his affections, her family and the village pressure her to give him up. Sensing that their relationship is impossible, Dzemile commits suicide at the river where she met Damjan. When Damjan returns to the village and discovers her death, he wanders the countryside, griefstricken. Compare *Ae Fond Kiss* (entry 1283), another *Romeo and Juliet* analogue featuring conflict between Christian and Muslim cultures.

1235 *Bombay*
1995. India. Amitabh Bachchan Corporation. Sound, col., 141 minutes. Mani Rathnam.

In a small southern India village, Shekhar Narayan, a Hindu journalism student, sees the veil of Shaila Bono, a shy devout Muslim woman, blow aside in a rainstorm, and he immediately falls in love with her. When the patriarchs of the Narayans, a well-to-do Hindu family, and the Bonos, a family of Muslim brickmakers, learn of the couple's intention to marry, they bitterly oppose the match, so Shekhar returns to Bombay and sends for Shaila, who follows. They marry, have twins, and enjoy domestic life, but Hindu-Muslim riots in Bombay threaten their lives. After the first riots, Shekhar's and Bono's parents arrive at their home, and the fathers, doting on their grandsons, begin to work out a reconciliation. But a second wave of riots leads to their deaths, to the separation of the twins from their parents, and eventually to the separation of the twins from one another. As the riots reach a fever pitch and Shekhar and Bono desperately search for their children, Shekhar and several others stand up to the rioters and convince them to stop the violence; soon after, Shekhar and Bono are reunited with their children.

The opening sequence of this powerful fable against Hindu and Muslim tension bears some resemblances to the basic narrative of *Romeo and Juliet*, since it involves a forbidden romance between children of feuding religious and social clans. In this version, the couple's move to cosmopolitan Bombay at first dodges the religious tensions that threaten to divide them; interesting too is that the parents, not the children or grandchildren, become the victims of feud. There are no allusions to Shakespeare's dialogue.

1236 *Monster Mash: The Movie*
1995. U.S. Greenhouse Film Group. Sound, col., 82 mins. Joel Cohen.

A spin-off of *The Rocky Horror Picture Show*. A couple dressed up as Romeo and Juliet have car trouble and seek help at a local mansion. (RB)

1237 *Broken English*
1996. New Zealand. Communicado Limited, National, New Zealand Film, NZ on Air, Sony Pictures Classics, and Village Roadshow Pictures. Sound, col., 92 mins. Gregor Nicholas.

Nina, a Croatian émigré to Auckland, New Zealand, with her family, falls in love with Eddie, a Maori cook at the restaurant where she works. Her drug-running father Ivan, embittered by the political conflicts that drove him from his native Bosnia and by the indignities suffered by his relatives, projects his hatred onto others and is angered by Nina's independence and relationship with Eddie. Adding to the tension is Nina's decision to finance her leaving home by entering into a sham marriage with Wu, boyfriend of Clara, a fellow worker at the restaurant, so that he can get legal residency. When at a family party Ivan erupts in violence against Wu and threatens Eddie, Eddie leaves for Waitongi and Nina pursues him, trying unsuccessfully to mend their relationship. When she returns to Auckland, she suffers what she thinks is a miscarriage, and Eddie and Ivan's confrontation at the hospital leads to a showdown at Ivan's home, where he and son Darko try to keep Nina prisoner. In the end, Ivan disowns Nina, and she and Eddie have a child.

The romance between Nina and Eddie, blocked by Ivan and his son Darko, bears some resemblance to the main narrative of *Romeo and Juliet*, though the focus is far more on the psychology of bigoted, bitter Ivan and his relationship with independent Nina than on the romance between Eddie and Nina, which seems rooted in lust rather than profound love. Ivan's explosive temper lends the film considerable tension. The scene in which Ivan and Darko recount atrocities to a young Croatian boy while spitting a pig is particularly chilling.

1238 *The Exotic House of Wax*
1996. U.S. Surrender Cinema. Sound, col., 85 mins. Cybil Richards.

Wax figures in a wax museum include Antony and Cleopatra. See *The Frozen Ghost*. (RB)

1239 *Tromeo and Juliet*
1996. U.S. Troma Productions. Sound, col., 104 mins. Lloyd Kaufman and James Gunn.

In New York City, a feud between the Ques and the Capulets rages because "Cappy" Capulet has stolen the sex-film production company and the wife of Monty Que. At a party at the Capulet mansion, Tromeo Que, Monty's nerdy son, falls in love with Juliet Capulet, Cappy's daughter, and they begin a torrid love affair. When Cappy discovers the romance, he tries to lock her away and force her to marry London Arbuckle, dopey son of a meat-processing magnate, and the escalating feud leads to the death of Romeo's friend Murray Martini and Juliet's violent brother Tyrone. To thwart her father's plans, Juliet takes a potion that temporarily makes her hideous, and London in horror commits suicide. After a melee between the households, Tromeo and Juliet learn that they are brother and sister, but decide to get married anyway. In the end, they settle in New Jersey and have mutant children.

This schlockploitation film recasts elements of Shakespeare's narrative—which it roughly parallels—in terms calculated to offend weaker sensibilities. Juliet's relationship with her Nurse becomes a lesbian tryst with Ness, her caretaker; Tromeo's first love, Rosie, is a slut who cuckolds him before his very eyes; Tromeo and Juliet's relationship is driven far more by teen lust than love; the violence of the Que and Capulet feud is comically extreme, with very crude but graphic special effects; at his death, Murray confesses his homosexual love for Tromeo; Friar Lawrence is presented as a pedophile; and the incestuous relationship between Tromeo and Juliet and the dialogue intermix Shakespearean and pseudo-Shakespearean lines with profanity and vapid teenspeak. Besides the carnivalesque delights of sex, violence, and gross-out vulgarity, the film offers a gleeful lampoon of the "streetwise" teen updating of Shakespeare offered by Baz Luhrmann's *Romeo + Juliet* (entry 496). Whether the lampoon is reactionary, progressive, or merely anarchic is a matter for debate. See also entry 204.

DVD includes a commentary track by director Lloyd Kaufman that references Shakespeare.

1240 *The Beautician and the Beast*
1997. U.S. Koch Company. Sound, col., 105 mins. Ken Kwapis.

A New York cosmetologist mistakenly thought to be a science teacher is offered a job to teach the children of an Eastern European dictator. In one scene, she teaches the children about *Romeo and Juliet*. (RB)

1241 *Blazin'*
1997. U.S. Global Star Productions Inc., Street Films, and Utopian Pictures. Sound, col., 103 mins. Marcos Antonio Miranda.

This independently produced straight-to-video production clumsily grafts the central romance of *Romeo and Juliet* onto the conventions of an urban action film. In the midst of violent altercations between the police and drug dealers, Bronx teenagers Samantha ("Sam") and Alex meet at a sleazy club, Domain, where Sam is a featured rap singer, and the two fall instantly in love. The problem is that Sam's mother, Mrs. Langstrom, is an ambitious, psychotically violent crime boss in the midst of a sensitive cocaine deal, and Alex's father is the sergeant of the local police department. Though Mrs. Langstrom forbids Sam to see Alex, Sam persists in the relationship and even steals a disc of secret material to finance the lovers' escape to freedom. Unfortunately, Mrs. Langstrom discovers the theft and pursues the two to a warehouse where Victor Ramos, an honest cop, is protecting them. In a long showdown scene, Ramos, Alex, and Sam try to battle their way past Mrs. Langstrom's gang; at the end of the fight, Mrs. Langstrom shoots Alex in the back, at which Sam and Mrs. Langstrom shoot each other.

Screenwriter and director Miranda adopts the motifs of the romance blocked by a feud, the meeting of the lovers at a musical event, the final death of the lovers, and the general atmosphere of explosive violence, but otherwise Shakespeare's plotline is handled very freely, and there are no direct Shakespearean allusions in the dialogue. *Blazin'* may be fruitfully compared to *Romeo Must Die*, a much more polished approach to the same hybrid. It is of some interest that though the film pointedly uses a multiethnic cast, the film makes nothing of the ethnic differences between Sam and Alex (Latino and white, respectively).

DVD includes a director's commentary, trailers, deleted scenes, and outtakes; the director references *Romeo and Juliet* in his commentary.

1242 *Dakan*

1997. French Guinea. Centre National de la Cinématographie, Films du Xxeme, and La Sept Cinema. Sound, col., 93 mins. Mohamed Camara.

A romance between two young male students in Guinea, Manga and Sori, faces considerable ridicule and is opposed by Manga's widowed mother Fanta and Sori's businessman father Bakary, both single parents and both of whom forbid the sons to see each other. Manga's mother uses exorcism to rid her son of his homosexuality, and eventually he tries to date a white woman, without success. Sori too tries to become a heterosexual. Eventually the two men accept their feelings for each other, though their future remains uncertain. *Dakan* is the first African film to depict an openly erotic homosexual relationship. Because of its gay themes, the film was hampered by financial problems and protests during its making.

1243 *Eve's Bayou*

1997. U.S. Chubbco and Trimark. Sound, col., 109 mins. Kasi Lemmons.

Eve Batiste, a young African American girl in the Louisiana bayou, accidentally learns that her father Louis, a handsome and seemingly loving doctor, is a philanderer. As his infidelity becomes clearer, their happy family life unravels. Suspicious, his beautiful wife Roz consults Elzora, a voodoo priestess, who tells her to wait for three years and look to her children. Her sister Mozelle Elzora accuses her

of being a black widow, killing her husbands (we later learn that her sexual infidelity led to disaster); soon Mozelle meets Julien Greyraven, a man obsessed with finding his lost wife and soon in love with Mozelle. Roz becomes more controlling of her children, and teenage daughter Cisely rebels, becoming increasingly sullen; later Cisely reveals that her father sexually assaulted her. As Eve comes to hate her father, she consults Elzora, a voodoo priestess and community counselor, about how to take revenge. Eventually, Louis is shot by a jealous husband in the presence of Eve. In a letter, Eve learns that Cisely's accusation of sexual assault was not true.

Cisely makes several references to *Romeo and Juliet*—to the prohibition on dueling, to the balcony scene (which she performs with Eve in her bedroom), and to Mercutio's description of his wound (which she applies to her mother's self-wounding). Though each of these allusions has relevance to the specific scene at hand, they also point to Cisely's romantic notions of adult love, notions shattered by her father's dalliances.

1244 *This Is the Sea*

1997. Ireland. First Look Pictures, Overseas Filmgroup, and Pembridge Pictures. Sound, col., 105 mins. Mary McGuckian.

In northern Ireland during the 1994 cease-fire, Hazel Stokes, daughter of a conservative rural Protestant family, is taken to the Belfast Agricultural Show by her kindly neighbor, Old Man Jacobs. There she meets Malachy McAliskey, a Belfast Catholic who dreams of being a race car driver and who works a hot dog truck with his brother, Padhar. Soon Malachy and Hazel begin to meet secretly and develop a relationship. Padhar, himself with a pregnant girlfriend Cathy, approves the relationship, as does Old Man Jacobs, but Hazel's mother sends Jef, Hazel's brother, to spy on her and uncovers the romance. Meanwhile, Rohan, an IRA operative, seeks to use Padhar to recruit Malachy to the cause. To destroy the relationship, Jef plants a car bomb in Malachy's car and arranges for Malachy and Hazel to meet. However, Padhar uses the car and is killed instead, leading to a rift between Hazel and Malachy. The police try to pin the crime on Rohan, but Old Man Jacobs sacrifices himself and Jef is caught. In the end, Hazel and Malachy are reunited.

In this transposition of the *Romeo and Juliet* narrative to Northern Ireland, it is Hazel's mother, not her father, who opposes the couple's match, on grounds that Hazel is violating her traditional destiny as a woman within the Protestant faith. Jef, the Tybalt figure, is primarily a misguided agent for his mother's desire to control Hazel. Perceiving repressed Hazel's desire for freedom and sensuality, Old Man Jacobs encourages her to come out of her shell, and like Friar Laurence he aids the couple, in this case by serving as a go-between and even sacrificing himself for their welfare. A folk soundtrack punctuates the emotions of many scenes, suggesting the influence of Baz Luhrmann's *Romeo + Juliet* (entry 496). There are no references to Shakespeare's dialogue.

1245 *Titanic*

1997. U.S. 20th Century Fox, Paramount Pictures, and Lightstorm Entertainment. Sound, col., 194 mins. James Cameron.

Rose Bukater, an American debutante, is sailing on the *Titanic* to America with her self-absorbed fiancé Cal Hockley to get married in order to save her mother from financial ruin. Onboard she meets Jack Dawson, a poor brash artistically inclined American, who saves her from committing suicide. The two fall in love, despite the attempts of Hockley and Ruth, Rose's mother, to separate them. When the *Titanic* sinks, Jack dies of hypothermia, but Rose survives. The tale is told in flashback, as treasure hunter Brock Lovett attempts to recover "The Heart of the Ocean," a jewel that Rose is pictured wearing.

This Hollywood epic uses some elements of *Romeo and Juliet* in its romance plotline, freely recombined—Rose and Jack are divided by class, and Rose's mother objects to their romance; they share a dance with Irish immigrants (though this is not where they first meet); Rose's impending marriage to Cal is arranged by her mother, and Rose contemplates suicide to escape it; and Jack and Cal are engaged in a deadly battle for Rose's love. The romance plotline is only one of several in this epic film.

1246 *Exile*

1998. U.S. Wicked Pictures. Sound, col. and b&w, 84 mins. Brad Armstrong.

Hardcore pornographic adaptation. Mixing elements from H. G. Wells's *The Time Machine* and Shakespeare's *Romeo and Juliet*, this film features a forbidden romance between Romeo and Juliette. The two are separated by a futuristic caste system—Romeo lives among the "Exiles," a servant class who live underground and tend the machines, while Juliette lives among the "Elite," an aristocratic class who live above and indulge in hedonism (though Juliette does not).

The Shakespearean content does not extend far beyond the names of the lovers and the general situation of forbidden love; the Tybalt role is taken by a sadistic plant manager. The lovers eventually get together and do not die.

1247 *The Lion King II: Simba's Pride*

1998. U.S. Walt Disney Pictures. Sound, col., 81 mins. Darrell Rooney and Rob LaDuca.

Animated film (straight to video). Kiara, the gregarious daughter of King Simba and Queen Nala of the lions, ventures into the Outlands where she meets Kovu, son of Zira and one of the pride exiled from the Pridelands. Kiara and Kovu are immediately attracted, but Zira raises Kovu to avenge the death of Scar, Simba's enemy. When older, Kovu is taken into Simba's pride, and he and Kiara fall in love. Though Kovu protects Simba from an ambush by Zira's followers, Simba doesn't trust him and exiles him; Kiara escapes to be with him, and the two resolve to end the feud between the two prides, which they do as Simba and Zira confront each other. Though Zira dies in an accident, the two prides are united.

This sequel to the *Hamlet*-flavored *Lion King* freely adapts a few motifs from *Romeo and Juliet*—the feud between two families, two lovers divided by the feud, an accidental death during a fight between families (Zira's son Nuka dies during the ambush of Simba), and the exile of the male lover. However, the parallels are rather general (the focus falls more on Kovu's crisis of loyalties than on his romance with Kiara), and there are no verbal references other than a passing reference to "a pound of flesh."

1248 *Shakespeare in Love*

1998. U.K. and U.S. Bedford Falls Productions, Miramax Films, and Universal Pictures. Sound, col., 122 mins. John Madden II.

Will Shakespeare, playwright for Philip Henslowe, owner of the Rose Theatre, is struggling with writer's block and impotency until he meets Viola de Lessups, daughter of an upwardly mobile merchant. Viola, an avid theatergoer, loves Shakespeare's work and even auditions for a role in his new play-in-progress, *Romeo and Ethel, the Pirate's Daughter*, while she is disguised as Thomas Kent; she is contracted by her father to marry Lord Wessex, a pompous, cash-needy nobleman. When Will and Viola meet by chance at the de Lessups home, they instantly fall in love, and their forbidden romance becomes the basis for Will's play, now retitled *Romeo and Juliet*, with Will now in full knowledge of Viola's cross-dressed disguise. When Viola's deception is revealed, the Rose Theatre is closed, but Henslowe's competitor Richard Burbage makes his theater, the Curtain, available for *Romeo and Juliet*. When Sam, the company's boy (and player of women's parts), finds his voice cracking, Viola substitutes at the last moment in the part of Juliet, and the play is a triumph. Though Mr. Tilney tries to arrest the players for having a woman in the cast, Queen Elizabeth vouches for Viola and awards Shakespeare a bet and a royal commission for a new play. Viola and Wessex, now married, leave for Virginia, but in mid-voyage the ship is wrecked and Viola is the sole survivor. Will imagines her story and begins to write *Twelfth Night*.

This romantic blockbuster grafts *Romeo and Juliet* onto ersatz Shakespearean biography and gentle Hollywood satire to offer the fictional tale of the play's genesis. The parallels between the play and Shakespeare's biography are wittily handled: Will first meets Viola at a dance he crashes at the de Lessups home, and he is chased away by Wessex (who combines both the Paris and Tybalt roles); the real life balcony scene is handled as a comedy of errors; the death of Mercutio becomes the death of Marlowe, which Will mistakenly thinks is by Wessex's hand; and Romeo's exile is transformed into the closing of the Rose. Several sequences move freely between the play in performance and Will and Viola together. In an especially remarkable midfilm sequence, the film shuttles between the balcony scene in performance (with Sam as Juliet) and Will and Viola running lines in bed (with Will taking Juliet's part, Viola Romeo's). The opening performance of the play features Will as Romeo and Viola as Juliet, so that our knowledge of their secret doomed love affair makes their performance all the more poignant and powerful. Equally interesting is the film's use of cross-dressing and the gender complication it leads to—Will first sees Viola as Thomas Kent, and he kisses her as she is cross-dressed while the company is in rehearsal. But, as several commentators have noted, the gender confusion, typically momentary and played for comedy, does not shade over into homosexuality. Sonnet 18, which the historical Shakespeare originally addressed to a young man, is in the film addressed to Viola; symptomatically Viola tears off her male disguise as she reads it. Indeed, the film stresses that cross-dressing is one of the elements that prevents Renaissance theater from showing the truth of love, an obstacle Will surmounts with his biographical play. Viola's plight, prevented from pursuing her own romantic and poetic aspirations by the marriage marketplace, is mirrored by Will's plight: as the film opens, Will has been rendered impotent erotically and artistically by the demands of the theater marketplace, which is interested only in conventional hits, "love and a bit with a dog." See also entries 1029, 3030, 3531, and 1421.

DVD Collectors' Series contains many extras referencing Shakespeare, including two commentary tracks (one by director John Madden, and the other by the cast and crew), deleted scenes, and a "Shakespeare Facts" section.

1249 *Tranamation: Romeo and Juliet*
1998. Japan.

A brief cartoon video apparently with Romeo and Juliet as transsexuals. (RB)

1250 *After Romeo*
1999. U.S. Romeo Productions. Sound, col., 100 mins.
Peter Alsop and Ellen Geer.

Ethan Just, a struggling young actor, and his newlywed and pregnant wife Lyn move into a trailer after their elopement; he makes ends meet as a pizza deliveryman. His friend Anthony, just cast as Mercutio in a professional production of *Romeo and Juliet*, encourages him to audition for Romeo, and Ethan gets the part. As the company rehearses, Lyn, belittled by her sleazy father and isolated with their new child Verona, begins to imagine that Ethan has fallen in love with his co-star Julie Winton, who plays Juliet, a situation made worse as Ethan becomes less attentive. In an attempt to heal their growing rift, she buys him a dagger as a present, but Ethan rejects it because of superstition about it being cursed. Soon Lyn resorts to putting ipecac in Julie's stage potion to sabotage the performance, but Julie is replaced by Inga, an understudy, and the play goes forward. On opening night, Lyn watches from the wings as Ethan and Inga perform the death scene in the crypt, and Lyn stabs herself offstage with the gift dagger as Inga/Juliet stabs herself onstage. Lyn dies. In an epilogue Ethan delivers Jaques's "All the world's a stage" speech from *As You Like It* as three year-old Verona looks on.

This independent film, released only on video, develops both parallels and contrasts between Ethan and Lyn's situation as a young struggling family and that of Romeo and Juliet. Ethan and Lyn begin the film as a loving couple who have escaped their parents' dysfunctional lives, somewhat as if Romeo and Juliet had survived. But as the film progresses, it stresses the contrasts between Romeo and Juliet's transcendent love and the intractable material and practical pressures that undermine Ethan and Lyn's relationship. The pressures are psychological as well: Lyn's descent into suicide replicates, we learn, her mother's self-destructive melancholy after her father's infidelity. The director of the play-within-the-film functions somewhat like Friar Laurence, attempting as best she can to help the couple surmount their marital difficulties. The epilogue

Shakespeare, pensive, writing in *Shakespeare in Love* (1998). A well-known publicity shot from the film, showing the romanticizing of Shakespeare. Courtesy of Douglas Lanier.

reveals the film's discomfort with its essentially tragic portrait of an actor's family life. The film includes many lines and speeches from *Romeo and Juliet*: Anthony delivers Mercutio's Queen Mab speech in a pizza parlor; Ethan uses a portion of the balcony scene as his audition piece; and we see portions of Romeo and Juliet's first meeting in 1.5, Tybalt and Mercutio's confrontation in 3.1 (Ethan is accidentally cut by swordplay in this scene), and the crypt scene in 5.3. As Lyn fills Julie's vial with ipecac, in voice-over Julie delivers Juliet's speech about the potion from 4.3, and after Lyn's death, in voice-over we hear the play's epilogue. In addition, the experienced actors in the production refer in passing to various lines from the play, and there is a single reference to Titania from *A Midsummer Night's Dream*. Compare *Nobody's Fool, Slings and Arrows*, and *In Othello*.

1251 *Amanda's Diary #5: Shocking Shakespeare—Romeo and Juliet Get Juicy*
1999. U.S. Private. Sound, col., 90 mins. John Millerman.

Hardcore pornography. The cast of a film version of *Romeo and Juliet* engage in various recreational couplings.

Very short vignettes of the *Romeo and Juliet* film appear, but no direct verbal references.

1252 *Kick*
1999. Australia. Blackwood Films and Carmelina Pictures. Sound, col., 92 mins. Lynda Heys.

Matt Grant, a working-class student who transfers to a private school, is the star of the rugby team, but his secret, true desire is to dance ballet, which he has studied from childhood. When a local ballet company holds open auditions for *Romeo and Juliet*, Matt tries out and wins the leading role, but he finds it difficult to balance dance rehearsals with sports, finals, and application to college. To add to his problems, Matt fears that being known as a dancer will damage his macho reputation, and Tamara Spencer, his girlfriend, has become jealous of Claire Andrews, the dancer playing Juliet. Nevertheless, he gives a triumphant performance at the Sydney Opera House.

Features a number of excerpts from the rehearsal and performance of the ballet *Romeo and Juliet*. The combination of Shakespeare and ballet (classical theater—and a love story at that!—and classical dance) constitutes a double threat to Matt's masculine reputation.

1253 *The Rage: Carrie II*
1999. U.S. Red Bank Films and United Artists. Sound, col. and b&w, 104 mins. Katt Shea.

Adapted from characters by Stephen King. Rachel Lang, a reclusive goth girl with telekinetic powers, lives with her dog Walter and foster parents after her mother has been committed to a mental institution. At her school, the jocks score with women to compete for points; when Rachel's best friend, Lisa Parker, is seduced and then dumped by Eric Stark, one of the jocks, she commits suicide and Ra-

chel vows to help local police press charges. In retaliation for this and for a budding romance with Jesse Ryan, the jocks and their girlfriends team up to humiliate Rachel, first by secretly taping a tryst between Jesse and Rachel, then by inviting her to a party where they play the tape and suggest that Jesse was only using her for points. Using her powers, Rachel kills nearly all of the students, but when Jesse arrives, they declare their love for each other before Rachel dies. In a short epilogue, Jesse, now at university, is haunted by Rachel.

The film's exposition features an English class in which *Romeo and Juliet* is the topic of discussion. The teacher leads the class to the conclusion that the only way Romeo and Juliet could be together is in death. In this discussion Jesse establishes himself as a romantic about love, Rachel as a cynic. At film's end Jesse demonstrates the depth of his love by showing his willingness to die with Rachel, though she prevents him from carrying that through.

1254 *Romeo Thinks Again*
1999. 18 mins. Matthew Parkhill.

A comedy short, imagining that at the end of *Romeo and Juliet* Romeo does not die because he had been sold watered-down poison. Romeo now works at a checkout store.

1255 *Solomon and Gaenor*
1999. U.K. APT Film & Television, Arts Council of England, S4C Television, and September Films. Sound, col., 103 mins. Paul Morrisson.

In Wales, 1911, Solomon Levinsky, son of a Jewish store owner, is a "packman," selling fabric door to door. He meets Gaenor Rees, meek daughter of a mining family, and the two fall in love. Knowing his parents will not accept him, Solomon pretends to be Sam Livingstone, English son of an engineer; Caradoc (nicknamed Crad), the fiery eldest son, takes a dislike to him and warns him away. When Noah Jones, a man who was romantically interested in Gaenor, surmises she has become pregnant, he exposes her. Solomon and Gaenor plan to leave, but their plans are thwarted when Crad leads an anti-Semitic riot; Solomon is sent away to Cardiff, and Gaenor is sent to her aunt's in Llafinangel. By fighting with Crad, Solomon learns Gaenor's whereabouts, and wounded he trudges through the snow to join her, marrying her once they are reunited. Solomon soon thereafter dies of his injuries, and Gaenor has their child. She brings his body back to the Levinskys (who had rejected her and him) to be buried.

This quiet film uses several elements of *Romeo and Juliet*. The lovers are divided by their parents' antipathies to outsiders; despite their ethnic, religious, and linguistic differences, the film portrays the Rees and Levinsky families as remarkably similar in their treatment of strangers. Hotheaded Crad plays the Tybalt role, his anger springing from his father's disrespectful treatment. And Solomon's journey through the snow to be with Gaenor has a quality of suicide. The tragic conclusion is tempered by the film's coda: Gaenor's return of Solomon's body, Crad's climbing onto the funeral wagon, and the soundtrack's featuring of a rabbinical chant and Welsh lament. The bleak world of rural Wales and the marginal status of both cultures in England lend the fragile love story added poignancy.

1256 *Tumbleweeds*
1999. U.S. Spanky Pictures, Solaris, and River One Films. Sound, col., 102 mins. Gavin O'Connor.

After she leaves another in a line of abusive relationships, Mary Jo Walker and her daughter Ava take to the road, moving from Missouri to Starlite Beach, California. Mary Jo takes a menial job with an eccentric boss and soon takes up with yet another boorish man, Jack Ranson, a truck driver she met on the road; at school Ava auditions for and gets a role in the school production of *Romeo and Juliet*. When Jack begins to ignore Ava and becomes more moody and violent, Mary Jo leaves him and is tempted to take to the road yet again, but Ava's desire to be in the play and put down roots prevails, especially when Dan Miller, a kind friend from Mary Jo's office, offers his help (and unrequited affection for Mary Jo). By film's end, Mary Jo has reestablished herself in a new job and a house of her own, and Ava has given her performance and gained a new boyfriend, Adam.

The film features several excerpts from *Romeo and Juliet*, both in rehearsal and in performance. When Mary Jo and Ava struggle with Shakespeare's language as they rehearse the balcony scene at Mary Jo's office, Dan not only recites a line from memory but also advises Ava to speak the poetry to the "beat of the human heart." Later, at the beach, in another conversation with Dan about the play, Ava notes that her friend Zoe is angry that she intends to audition for Juliet because the part was "written for her"; Dan replies that the part was written for a boy, not a girl. This remark inspires Ava to audition for the role of Romeo, which she gets. At a restaurant with her mother and Jack, Ava performs Romeo's death scene and accidentally spills water on Jack, an event that slowly escalates to violence and leads to Mary Jo's breakup with him. Of the performance of the play itself, we see Tybalt's exit, the "palmer's kiss" scene (a scene made all the more awkward by two girls kissing), Juliet's death, and the curtain call. Shakespeare's play, with its theme of romantic commitment till and beyond death, provides a contrast to Mary Jo's string of broken relationships and nomadic life.

The DVD includes a director's commentary that references Shakespeare.

1257 *Where the Boys Aren't #10*
1999. U.S. Vivid. Sound, col., 81 mins. F. J. Lincoln.

Hardcore pornographic adaptation. Two lesbian lovers are divided by loyalties to rival gangs of blondes and brunettes.

Heavily indebted to *West Side Story* for its Shakespearean content. No direct references.

1258 *Chunhyang*
2000. Korea. CJ Entertainment, Mirae Asset Capital, Saehan Industries, and Tae Hung Productions. Sound, col., 120 mins. Kwok-taek Im.

Adapted from the *pansori* song "Chunyang" by Cho Sang Hyun. Sent by his father to study in a small village, Mongryong Lee, the governor's son, sees Chunhyang Sung, a courtesan's daughter, on a swing and falls in love. Though they are divided by class, Mongryong and Chunhyang secretly marry. Soon after he is forced by his family to Seoul, where he must study for and pass examinations. He keeps his relationship with Chunhyang secret, lest he be disowned, and Chunhyang promises to wait for him. However, Byun Hakdo, a new governor and a chauvinistic despot, arrives, and he exploits the province and claims Chunhyang for his bride. When Chunhyang refuses, Byun sentences her to be whipped to death, just as Mongryong arrives to claim her. Chunhyang's words as she is beaten and Mongryong's court poem foment rebellion, and Chunhyang is saved from death. The tale is told by a *pansori* (a traditional Korean poetry singer), whose performance we see as the film begins and who serves as the narrator.

Wisely advertised as the Korean *Romeo and Juliet*, *Chunhyang* is a distant analogue to Shakespeare's play—the lovers are divided by insurmountable class differences and are secretly married, and the woman is threatened with a forced marriage that she resists. In reality, the film is far more indebted to traditional Korean folktale and political fable. The *pansori* narrator adds an element of self-consciousness to the film that is reminiscent of Shakespeare's Chorus, though the *pansori*'s role in the action is far more thoroughgoing.

1259 *The Intern*
2000. U.S. Given Films and Moonstone Entertainment. Sound, col., 90 mins. Michael Lange.

In this broad parody of the fashion industry, Jocelyn Bennett, a young, exploited intern at *Skirt*, a hip fashion magazine, navigates the office politics and phony, self-centered behavior of models and editors as she works her way into the magazine's in-crowd. All the while, she is involved in a romantic triangle between herself, Paul Rochester, a British art director, and vain supermodel Resin, and she must uncover the traitor in the midst of the staff.

At a *Romeo and Juliet*–themed photo shoot, Jocelyn and Paul are used as stand-ins for the lovers. The photo set is an ivy-festooned castle, and the photographer instructs the two to be passionate with each other, which they are. When Resin objects, insulting Jocelyn, she retorts with "Juliet croaks, anyway." This scene is a variation on the trope in which lovers otherwise unable to declare their passion for each other use their performances as *Romeo and Juliet* to do so.

1260 *Jiyuan qiaohe (The Chicken Rice War)*
2000. Singapore. Raintree Pictures Pte. Ltd. and Singapore Film Commission. Sound, col., 100 mins. Chee Kong Cheah.

In this comedy, the Chans (headed by Vincent) and the Wongs (headed by Wu) are forced to have their chicken rice stalls next to each other, escalating an already fierce feud between the families. Audrey Chan, Vincent's daughter, is cast as Juliet of her school's rock *Romeo and Juliet*, with her boyfriend Nick as Romeo, but Nick's performance is terrible. Fenton Wong, who has long adored Audrey from afar, is brought in as Nick's replacement, and slowly Audrey warms to him, eventually falling in love. Meanwhile their families compete at the Hungry Ghost Festival with rival musical attractions (a pop star and an opera). When their guests get sick (from bad chicken sold to them by Hugo A Go Goh), Vincent and Wu inadvertently reveal their secret recipes, leading to the end of their feud.

Jiyuan Qiaohe recasts several of the motifs from *Romeo and Juliet*—the feuding families, the lovers divided by the feud, and tension between Romeo and Juliet's brother (here, between Fenton and Audrey's boyfriend Nick). The film locates the origins of the feud in the jealousy of Harry Chan (Audrey's grandfather) against Sen Wong, who he suspects is seducing his wife. The text of the balcony scene reappears throughout the film; at first Audrey and Nick rehearse their lines separately, but eventually they meet serendipitously at their parents' stalls while running their lines, a fact that Fenton takes as a sign of the fatedness of their love. The film also references Shakespeare's prologue and the Capulet's dance scene (1.5). Equally prominent is the motif of using Shakespeare's play as a way for the actors to announce their love—Fenton sees his performance of Romeo's first meeting with Juliet before the school, a moment that includes a kiss, as his opportunity to declare his feelings. In this adaptation, Audrey is at first deeply conceited and Fenton painfully shy, but in the course of their rehearsals Audrey comes to see the value of a sincere, devoted boyfriend. The film reuses many motifs from Baz Luhrmann's *Romeo + Juliet* (entry 496)—its MTV-style editing and camerawork, its identification of characters with labels and stills, its use of a pop soundtrack, its use of a newscast frame, and its mixture of drama and comedy. Indeed, were it not for the romance between Audrey and Fenton, the film might be regarded as a parody of Luhrmann's adaptation. The film has a divided attitude about Shakespeare, at once referencing his work and mocking it—after the prologue, for example, the cameraman complains, "I didn't ask you to sound like Shakespeare. Do it again!"

1261 *Josh*
2000. India. United Seven Creations and Venus. Sound, col., 162 mins. Mansoor Khan.

In this Bollywood remake of *West Side Story* set in Goa, two rival gangs, the Eagles headed by Max, and the Bicchu headed by Prakash, vie for control of property. Rahul, the brother of Prakash, falls in love with Shirley, Max's twin, without knowing who she is. After considerable violence, the lovers are united.

1262 *Little Insects*
2000. U.S. Crystal Sky Communications and MPA. Sound, col., timing unknown. Gregory Gieras.

In this animated antiwar film, colonies of the Buggy Kingdom, the Valley Ants led by King Foptop and the Mountain Ants led by King Bigwig, go to battle over a jar of jam. Prince Dondo of the Mountain Ants and Princess Dayzie of the Valley Ants fall in love, and their romance brings peace to the feud. Director Gregory Gieras also worked as technical director on *The Princess and the Barrio Boy*, another *Romeo and Juliet* spin-off.

1263 *The Princess and the Barrio Boy*
2000. U.S. Showtime Networks. Sound, col., 92 mins. Tony Plana.

Sirena Garcia, a rich high school swimmer whose mother died while she was a child, is attracted to Sol Torres, a fellow high school swimmer from a working-class background who lives in the East Los Angeles barrio. Sirena's father Nestor is a successful real estate developer who plans to marry Minerva Rojas, much to the children's disapproval. At first Nestor disapproves of Sirena's romance with Sol, and the two pursue their love behind his back. But he soon approves of the match, and he discovers that Minerva is interested only in his money.

An example of pastiche, using the mismatched lovers situation from *Romeo and Juliet* as its basic armature. (Other elements are cobbled together from *The Little Mermaid*, *Father of the Bride*, and *Clueless*.) Other specific motifs may be lifted from Shakespeare: the Garcias' Spanish housekeeper roughly corresponds to the Nurse; Sirena and Sol first see each other at a party; Alex, another suitor for Sirena who is briefly shown at the party, corresponds to Paris (significantly, he is Anglo and is pushed onto Sirena by the upwardly mobile Minerva); and Sirena's girlfriends are named Rosa and Gilda (an odd allusion to Rosencrantz and Guildenstern). The film's interest in Latin American iconography and the final kiss of the lovers underwater bespeak the influence of Baz Luhrmann's *Romeo + Juliet* (entry 496), though in this version the lovers do not commit suicide. In this film, the lovers are divided not by a feud but by class differences, and one of its themes is the potential loss of cultural identity that upward mobility and assimilation bring. No direct verbal citations.

1264 *Romeo and Juliet*
2000. U.S. 2House Productions and Will & Company. Sound, col., 47 mins. Colin Cox.

A shortened version of *Romeo and Juliet*, with Mercutio as the narrator and told from his point of view. Never widely released, and intended for the educational market.

1265 *Romeo Must Die*
2000. U.S. Silver Pictures and Warner Bros. Sound, col., 115 mins. Andrzej Bartkowiak.

When Han Sing's brother Po is killed amidst tensions between Chinese and black gangs in Oakland, California, Han, son of Ch'u Sing, a Chinese mob overlord, escapes from prison to find Po's killer. While stealing a cab, he meets Trish O'Day, daughter of Isaak, a black mob leader, who disapproves of her father's business. Isaak, Ch'u, and Roth (a white businessman) are involved in a tense three-way deal to procure property for a sports stadium. When Trish's brother Colin is killed, Isaak warns his daughter away from Han, but she and Han team up to discover their brothers' murderers. When the deal is closed, Mac, Isaak's right-hand man, double-crosses Isaak, and reveals that he killed Colin. Han learns that his older brother Kai killed Po on orders of Ch'u, who is working his own double-cross. Han kills Kai, and Ch'u, facing prison or assassination, commits suicide.

The connection between this film and Shakespeare's play is paper-thin, extending not far beyond the title. Even though Trish and Han find themselves divided by a feud and father Isaak warns daughter Trish away from Han, the couple does not pursue a love relationship. Rather, emphasis falls on spectacular fight scenes set to a hip-hop soundtrack. There are no allusions to Shakespeare's dialogue, and even the label "Romeo" is referenced only once. See also entry 2875.

1266 *Sud Side Stori*
2000. Italy. Gam Films and Istituto Luce. Sound, col., 78 mins. Roberta Torre.

In this campy comedy musical, Giulietto, a Sicilian Elvis impersonator, falls in love with Romea, a Nigerian prostitute. Giulietto's three aunts and his fiancée are horrified, as are Romea's African relatives and friends, and all resort to black magic to cure the lovers. Compare *West Side Story*.

1267 *West Side*
2000. U.S. Video Team. Sound, col., 178 mins. Ren Savant.

Hardcore pornographic adaptation, with emphasis on interracial and interclass conflict in Los Angeles drug circles.

Heavily dependent upon *West Side Story* for its Shakespearean content. In this version, in the end the parents get their comeuppance and the lovers are united.

1268 *Brooklyn Babylon*
2001. U.S. and France. Bac Films, Le Studio Canal+, Off Line Entertainment Group, and Studio Canal. Sound, col., 89 mins. Marc Levin.

In Brooklyn's Crown Heights, Sara, a Hasidic Jew bent on college and independence, and Solomon, a West Indian Rastafarian rapper, lead parallel lives until a chance car crash brings them together. Racial and religious tensions escalate when Scratch, Solomon's friend, firebombs the car of Judah, Sara's possessive boyfriend and a Jewish vigilante, who retaliates by firebombing Club Dread, a local black nightclub. Solomon and Sara slowly get to know one another and fall in love, despite their own fears and the active disapproval of their friends and families. Only Sara's grandmother Nanna and Solomon's Rastafarian boss understand their commitment to love and freedom. After Nanna dies, Solomon goes to see Sara, but he is savagely beaten by Judah and other vigilantes, after which Solomon vows to kill him. Sara goes to Solomon at a Caribbean carnival, and the two meet at a park, but Judah follows them and assaults Sara, at which Solomon defends her; though victorious, Solomon refrains from killing him. In the end, Solomon delivers a triumphal rhyme about the value of love and the example of Solomon and Sheba, and we discover that Sara has had a multiracial child, their son.

The basic situation, a forbidden, potentially tragic romance in the midst of a feud, mirrors that of *Romeo and Juliet*. Though the film never alludes to Shakespeare's dialogue (its primary point of verbal reference is the biblical *Song of Solomon*), it does adapt several motifs from the play beyond the two protagonists. Nanna corresponds to Juliet's Nurse, the hot-headed Judah to Tybalt, Scratch to Mercutio, and Sara's disapproving parents to the Capulets; Solomon calls out to Sara from beneath her bedroom window, an oblique reference to the balcony scene; and Solomon and Judah's fight recalls Romeo and Tybalt's, though Solomon pointedly chooses not to kill his opponent. Instead of the lovers' deaths uniting the feuding communities, it is the birth of Solomon and Sara's child that offers that hope.

1269 *Crazy/Beautiful*
2001. U.S. Touchstone Pictures. Sound, col., 99 mins: director's cut, 135 mins. John Stockwell.

At Palisades High School in Los Angeles, Carlos Nuñez, a poor, athletically gifted Latino boy dedicated to his studies, falls in love with Nicole Oakley, a rich, free-spirited, but troubled white girl whose father is Tom Oakley, a prominent liberal congressman who has remarried. Their romance becomes entangled with Latino-white tensions, but the two nearly break apart when Carlos's mother disapproves of Nicole's undermining of his studies, and Tom warns Carlos about Nicole's destructive effect on others, an effect, he suggests, of Nicole's mother's suicide. After Nicole is threatened with boot camp in Utah to handle her alcoholism, Carlos decides to leave with her, but the two soon decide to return so that Nicole can confront her troubled relationship with her father and her addictions. In the end, Tom praises Carlos's treatment of Nicole and approves of their relationship, even helping Carlos get into the Naval Academy.

The film uses the familiar Shakespearean motif of a teen romance divided by communal feuds and parental disapproval, though with a number of interesting twists. In this case ethnic tensions between Latinos and whites, though certainly present, tend to be understated. Parental disapproval too springs not from an established feud between families but from both parents' concern for their children's futures, though in Tom's case that concern springs from his own guilt about his wife's suicide (to which he contributed by his neglect) and his daughter's self-destructiveness. The film's upbeat ending—in which Nicole, with Carlos's help, takes responsibility for her actions and reconciles with her father, and is rewarded with his approval for her boyfriend—suggests the drive toward a therapeutic solution to the otherwise tragically fated lovers' plight. The film very briefly references Shakespeare in a video being shown to a bored English class; the video's narrator stresses Shakespeare's contemporaneity—"only in this century has [Shakespeare] been understood"—and features a very brief clip from Dieterle and Reinhardt's *A Midsummer Night's Dream*. In the next scene, in a history class, the students are discussing the issue of Britain exerting authority on America from afar. The juxtaposition is revealing.

1270 *The Fast and the Furious*
2001. U.S. Mediastream Film GmbH & Co. Productions KG, Neal H. Moritz Productions, Original Film, and Universal Pictures. Sound, col., 106 mins. Rob Cohen.

In an effort to investigate a string of daring hijackings of trucks, Brian Spindler, a young undercover FBI agent, infiltrates a gang of underground race car drivers headed by Dom Toretto. Soon, as he participates in races, he develops a respect for Toretto and falls in love with his sister, Mia. Spindler suspects a sinister gang of Chinese racers headed by Johnny Tran, but when the FBI closes in on the gang too soon, his suspicion turns to Dom and gang member Jesse. In a spectacular chase, Johnny blows his cover in order to help Dom and Jesse avoid being killed when their hijack goes awry. A minor sub-plot involves a forbidden romance between Dom and Johnny Tran's sister Letty, which several critics have likened to that of *Romeo and Juliet*, particularly since a fistfight between Tran and Dom leads to a vendetta between the two gangs. But the sub-plot is so underdeveloped that the connection is at best tenuous.

1271 *Naughty College Girls #19*
2001. U.S. New Sensations. Sound, col., 90 mins.

The last of five episodes begins with a woman named Krystal, who lies on a bed with a copy of *Romeo and Juliet*, quizzing her boyfriend about it, and strips off items of her clothes when he gets the answers right: "Who are the main characters? What are the names of the feuding families?" He answers correctly, then they have sex. (RB)

1272 *Original Sin*
2001. U.S. DiNovi Pictures, Epsilon Motion Pictures, Hyde Park Entertainment, MGM, and Via Rosa. Sound, col., 116 mins. Michael Cristofer.

Adapted from the novel *Waltz into Darkness* by Cornell Woolrich. Luis Antonio Vargas, a successful coffee mogul in nineteenth-century Cuba, sends to America for Julia Russell, a mail order bride from America. At first Luis is delighted by her beauty and sexual passion, but when she leaves suddenly with his money, he learns from detective Walter Downs that she is not Julia Russell at all, but Bonny Castle, a con woman. In love with her, Luis tracks her down with the intention of killing her, but when he finds her she reveals that she is involved with Alan Jordan, a man who keeps her in his thrall. After Luis kills Alan, Bonny seems to return to him, but Luis later discovers that Alan is not dead and that the two are plotting to kill him. In the end, Bonny kills Alan and is condemned for his murder; she escapes to Morocco, where she joins Luis, who faked his own poisoning.

After an overheated rich suitor who Bonny intends to bilk leaves her hotel room, she sardonically says, "Parting is such sweet sorrow." Soon after, Luis confronts her with the intention of killing her; like Richard III, she takes his gun, puts it to her chest, and says, "Do it," knowing that he cannot. Her cold reaction to the "murder" of Billy (the true identity of Walter Downs) and seductive instruction of her husband in the arts of deception bear a very general resemblance to Lady Macbeth. Richard Burt has suggested that there are also general parallels to *Romeo and Juliet*.

1273 *Shakespeare Revealed*
2001. U.S. Vivid. Sound, col., 84 mins. Ren Savant.

Hardcore pornographic adaptation. As the cast rehearses *Romeo and Juliet*, Julie, a timid actress playing Juliet who suffers from dreams of sexual humiliation, struggles with the part and Dante the British director's sexual interpretation of the play. At the end of the film, Dante is revealed not to be British, but a scam artist from New Jersey.

The rehearsal scenes feature substantial excerpts from the balcony scene, the "palmer's kiss" scene (played twice with different men), Juliet's revelation that her lover is a Montague, the morning parting between Romeo and Juliet (played twice), and Juliet's banter with the Nurse at 2.4.47–53. From the nude performance itself, we see a portion of the balcony scene. When Dante accidentally speaks in a Jersey accent to a cast member, he says, "Hey, you're not sounding too Shakespeare right now." Dante replies that in Shakespearean theater, it is necessary to sound like a "limey" so that people will "assume I'm a second cousin" to the Bard. One of the more interesting pornographic adaptations. Compare Paul Thomas's *Romeo and Juliet II*.

1274 *What Matters Most*
2001. U.S. Chateau Wally Films. Sound, col., 122 mins. Jane Cusumano.

In Vega, a small town in western Texas, Lucas Warner, the son of a wealthy local cattle baron, falls in love with Heather Stone, a working-class girl reared by her single mother Anita. Lucas's father Raymond disapproves, and he tries to force his son to date the upper-class Lydia Sharp, daughter of the local banker; tensions mount when Heather becomes pregnant and Lucas declares his intention to marry her. Lucas is injured in a wrestling match and falls into a yearlong coma, during which Heather's child is born and Lucas's parents reject the baby and her. When Lucas comes to, his frustrations lead him to contemplate suicide. Instead, he plans to invite Heather and her baby to his wedding to Lydia Sharp, an action that reunites Heather and Lucas and leads to reconciliation between parents and son. See also entry 496.

1275 *Amar te duele (Love Hurts)*
2002. Mexico. Altavista Films and Videocine. Sound, col., 104 mins. Fernando Sariñana.

In modern Mexico City, Ulises Tilleros, a poor native Mexican with dreams of being an artist, and Renata, a wealthy bourgeois white girl with a social conscience, fall in love at the mall after she kisses him on a dare. Soon they find themselves confronting the social and ethnic class structure of their society—Francisco, Renata's former white boyfriend, jealous of Renata's affection for Ulises, lures him into fights; China, Ulises's former girlfriend, is equally jealous and harasses Renata; Renata's racist sister Mariana reveals her sister's romance with Ulises, leading to his beating by Francisco and thugs; Ulises's parents, clothing merchants in the local market, see Ulises's love for Renata and dreams of being an artist as foolish; and Renata's arrogant parents don't want their daughter dating a poor native Mexican, despite the fact that they employ native Mexicans as drivers and maids. When Renata's parents threaten to send her to Canada, Renata and Ulises try to elope, but Mariana brings Francisco to the train station where, threatening Ulises, he accidentally shoots Renata, killing her. Ulises is left to mourn by her graveside.

In addition to using the basic structure of *Romeo and Juliet*—lovers divided by a feud, in this case the social divisions of urban Mexico—this free adaptation recasts several specific motifs from Shakespeare's play. Francisco

plays the violent Tybalt role, his motives partly violence and partly jealousy; Ulises and Francisco have a violent confrontation at Mariana's birthday party, the equivalent of the Capulet ball; Ulises scales the wall of Renata's balcony to spend the night with her, and the two share a version of the parting speeches from 3.5. The ending, in which Renata dies and Ulises is left behind, emphasizes the tragic intractability of the social structure they fight against; it is all the more poignant, given that Ulises is the voice of social and romantic idealism throughout the film. The music-driven soundtrack and MTV-influenced visual style suggest indebtedness to Baz Luhrmann's *Romeo + Juliet*, though this film eschews the Latino-influenced religious symbolism of Luhrmann's film and has at times a documentary, raw feel.

1276 *Barrio Wars*
2002. U.S. Urban Girl Productions. Sound, col., 90 mins. Paul Wynne.

A Latino independent film adaptation of *Romeo and Juliet*, bearing traces of Baz Luhrmann's film (entry 496) but opting for a far grittier, rough-and-ready approach to filmmaking and the depiction of urban violence. The film remains relatively faithful to the plotline of Shakespeare's play, setting it in the mean streets of the Los Angeles barrio. Angelina, a young Latina who longs for poetry and romance in her life, and Plato, an aspiring Latino rap artist, fall in love, despite the fact that their two families are engaged in a bloody gang rivalry and Angelina's brother Rico is pathologically protective of her virginity. Like Romeo and Juliet, Plato and Angelina meet at a costume party. Plato offers her a rose and a citation from Shakespeare's Sonnet 54 (lines 11–13), after which they consummate their relationship; Plato soon after reveals his true identity, and they make plans to marry. However, Rico attacks the gang associated with Plato's family, and when Plato tries to intervene, Rico kills Plato's sister Vanessa; in hasty revenge, Plato kills Santino, Rico's right-hand man. Plato hides out in Venice Beach and the couple plan to leave for Miami, where a family friend of Angelina can offer the lovers shelter and employment. To throw her brother off their trail, Angelina fakes her death on video, but Plato, seeing the tape and not getting Angelina's message about it, kills himself. When Angelina sees his dead body in her bed, she takes his gun and follows him into death. Her hot-headed brother Rico ends his life in a hail of gunfire when he refuses to surrender to the police.

The film seems poised between a critique of gang violence and a hardened, worldwise cynicism about the violence of the barrio, a tension exemplified by the final voice-over, which pits what it misrepresents as a quotation from Shakespeare, "It is better to have loved and lost than never to have loved at all," against the cold observation that, as far as he is concerned, Plato and Angelina are just statistics from the barrio wars. Equally unnerving is the way in which the voice-over lays blame on Angelina for the violence of the film, at one point calling her "an angel of death."

1277 *Bollywood Queen*
2002. U.K. Arclight Films, Dream Fish Productions, Enterprise Films, Great British Films, Spice Factory Ltd., and Stretch Limo Productions. Sound, col., 85 mins. Jeremy Wooding.

An aspiring Indian Londoner, Geena, is saved from falling scaffolding by Jay, a working-class West Country English boy, and the two fall instantly in love. However, the romance is opposed by Geena's family, who want her to marry an Indian husband, and by Dean, Jay's racist brother who is involved with a shady clothing business. After Dean is hurt in an altercation with one of Geena's brothers, Jay and Geena leave to find freedom in the English countryside, but the two decide to return to reconcile with their families. Unexpectedly, Jay's father accepts Geena; though Geena's father still rejects Geena's romance with Jay, he soon regrets his decision. At film's end, the two leave for France.

In its spirit of half-homage, half-parody, *Bollywood Queen* uses the Bollywood cliché of a *Romeo and Juliet*–style blocked romance. The film does not develop the parallel very far or faithfully, except that Sanjay, Geena's oldest brother, plays a Tybalt-type role in urging Geena's father to reject Jay, and the fight scene ends up with Dean (a distant analogue for Mercutio) wounded (though not killed) by another of Geena's brothers.

1278 *Nicholas Nickleby*
2002. U.S. United Artists. Sound, col., 126 mins. Douglas McGrath.

Relatively little use is made of the *Romeo and Juliet* material in the novel (chapters 22–24; see entry 1805). Kate Nickleby is accosted by Sir Mulberry Hawk after a performance of *Romeo and Juliet*, where we have seen her looking adoringly at the actor playing Romeo during the balcony scene. Clearly, Hawk is no Romeo, while Kate is something of a Juliet in spurning his advances and refusing to go along with her uncle's plans for her marriage. The Crummles' production of *Romeo and Juliet* is seen briefly as Smyke is able to say his one line as the apothecary. The highlight of this otherwise bland film is Nathan Lane playing Mr. Crummle. For much fuller uses of Shakespeare in other adaptations of Charles Dickens's novel, see *Nicholas Nickleby* (1982) and *Nicholas Nickleby* (2001) in the chapter on British TV. (RB)

1279 *Orange County*
2002. U.S. MTV Films, Paramount Pictures, and Scott Rudin Productions. Sound, col., 82 mins. Jake Kasdan.

Shaun Brumder, a high school senior and aspiring writer from California's Orange County, desperately wants to be admitted to Stanford University. When his high school

counselor sends the wrong transcripts and he is rejected, he tries several ploys to reverse the decision. In a brief scene, a high school teacher leads a class discussion on *Romeo and Juliet* that focuses mainly on the cast of the Luhrmann film (entry 496); he then (mis)identifies several films supposedly made from Shakespeare's plays.

DVD includes a director's commentary, a short trailer featuring the Shakespeare scene mentioned above, and another short trailer (under the title "Literature") featuring the same high school teacher discussing *Macbeth* in similar fashion.

1280 *Romeo & Juliet Revisited*
2002. U.S. FlickeringImage.com and Wolfesden Actors Exchange. Sound, col., 30 mins. N. Barry Carver.

Beginning with where Shakespeare's *Romeo and Juliet* ends, this film imagines that Romeo and Juliet faked their deaths and move to Mantua. Despite their pledges to create monuments to their children, the Montagues and Capulets continue their feuding, now by cheating on materials for the monuments. When Friar Laurence accidentally learns that the couple is alive and tells them of their parents' continued enmity, Juliet and the Friar concoct a plan to end the feud. Friar Laurence tells the tale of a magic tree that, if kept undisturbed, will allow the children to return from the dead; the parents disarm, Friar Laurence plants the magic seed, and Romeo and Juliet return alive, ending the feud. The pseudo-Elizabethan verse-dialogue of this short is cleverly written, incorporating not only Shakespearean diction, wordplay, syntax, and imagery but also passing references to contemporary culture. When Juliet objects to living in rural Mantua, she and Romeo have an exchange that resembles the theme song from "Green Acres"; the dialogue references "Feet, don't fail me now" and "You can have my gun when you pry it from my cold dead hand." There are also some clever Shakespearean in-jokes. Romeo speaks of Juliet's "happy dagger" after Juliet reveals that she used a trick knife in her "suicide"; when Friar Laurence discovers the couple in Mantua, Romeo at first pretends that they are Pyramus and Thisbe (from *A Midsummer Night's Dream*); and Juliet's idea of impersonating a ghost appearing to her mother is a plot device worthy of Shakespearean romance.

1281 *Juliet and Her Romeo in the New Millennium*
2003. U.S. Village Stage and Screen Productions. Sound, col., 31 mins. André Anthony Moore.

This short imagines three different modern women, all as Juliet, rethinking the ending of Shakespeare's play, objecting to Romeo's chastity and death wish. Three versions of the same scene, each with a different Romeo and Juliet, clarify their different conceptions; the script for the scenes is the same heavily rewritten and punned-up adaptation of Romeo and Juliet's parting speeches in 3.5. In the first, Romeo is displeased by Juliet's desire for sex, and Juliet by his selfishness; in the second, Romeo stresses his impulse to fighting and suicide; and in the third, the two tease each other as a form of sex game, a game that momentarily leads to real fighting. When the scenes are completed, all the couples gather to see three new versions of the scenes: the first involves Romeo and Juliet in silent sex, the second reverses the sexes of the couple, and the third features the love declarations of Beatrice and Benedick in *Much Ado about Nothing* 5.4. The script's pseudo-Shakespearean verse is so overwritten and filled with phallic puns that it is nearly incomprehensible.

1282 *Phileine zegt sorry*
2003. Netherlands and U.S. Motel Films, Fu Works, and BNN TV. Sound, col., 95 mins. Robert Van Westdijk.

Adapted from the novel by Ronald Giphart. When the insufferable Phileine travels to New York to join her actor boyfriend Max, she discovers that he is starring in an experimental production of *Romeo and Juliet* in which he will have real sex with his female co-star, Joanne. In revenge, Phileine betrays Max with Joanne's boyfriend, and later becomes famous through an appearance on the *David Letterman* show. Eventually she comes to recognize her own difficult personality, and she resolves to win Max back, apologizing publicly to him at an AIDS benefit. The experimental production of *Romeo and Juliet*, which involves real sex between Romeo and Juliet, cites, "Wherefore art thou, Romeo?" and little more.

1283 *Ae Fond Kiss*
2004. U.K. Bianca Films, Sixteen Films, and Tornasol Films. Sound, col., 104 mins. Ken Loach.

In contemporary Glasgow, Scotland, Casim Khan, an aspiring Pakistani-descended DJ, meets Roisin Hanlon, an Irish Catholic music teacher, when he helps his feisty sister Tahara chase some taunting bigots. Despite the fact that Casim's father and mother have arranged a marriage for their son with Jasmine, Casim's Pakistani cousin, Casim and Roisin fall in love. They soon experience resistance to their romance from their communities—Casim's older sister Rukhsana attempts to convince Roisin to leave Casim when she finds her own betrothal to Amar in jeopardy, and Roisin's job at a Catholic school becomes threatened when she finds she cannot get moral approval from Father Chambers, her priest, for the relationship. When Casim's mother and father try to force Casim into marriage with Jasmine, and Rukhsana shows Roisin the family strife the relationship has caused, the two nearly break up, but eventually choose to remain together. A subplot involves Tahara's desire to attend Edinburgh University over her parents' objections.

In this *Romeo and Juliet* analogue, the tension that divides the two young lovers is religious (Catholic versus Muslim) and cultural (Western modern versus Eastern traditional). Unlike the Shakespearean narrative, we see only one set of parents (Casim's), and they are presented with a certain dignity and even-handedness, and, interestingly, in this version it is the man, not the woman, whose romantic choice is constrained by an arranged marriage. Instead of aiding the lovers, the priest, Father Chambers, destroys Roisin's career by trying to enforce Catholic strictures on marriage. The film is notable for its unresolved conclusion—despite concerted attempts to break them up, the lovers choose to stay together, but the tensions that plagued them remain in force. The film does not reference Shakespeare's dialogue; its title is taken from a Robert Burns song. The film resists the tragic trajectory of the Burns song and Shakespeare's play.

DVD includes a "Making Of" featurette that mentions the *Romeo and Juliet* connection.

1284 *Indian Cowboy*
2004. U.S. Sound, col. Nikhil Kamkolkar.

A multicultural romantic comedy involving *Romeo and Juliet*. (RB)

1285 *Ghetto*
2004. U.S. Studio 2000. Sound, col., 87 mins. John Travis (aka John Trennell).

Hardcore gay pornographic adaptation. Anglo and Latino gang rivalries divide two gay male lovers.

Loosely indebted to *West Side Story*, this film features little direct Shakespearean content other than lovers divided by a feud. Compare *Where the Boys Aren't #10*.

1286 *Romeo & Julia und die neue Weltordnung*
2004. Germany. Familienproduktion. Sound, col., 13 mins. Thorsten Wettcke.

This short imagines a romance between Julia, the daughter of the U.S. president, and Romeo, a Middle Eastern flower seller and son of Osama bin Laden, a romance that occurs during the president's diplomatic visit to Berlin. The couple's intention to get married is transformed by Tybalt Tybaltovic, a WAR News (i.e., FOX News) correspondent, into a false story of Julia's kidnapping by Al Qaeda. The film was conceived as a protest against U.S. policies on terrorism and was produced in the runup to the Iraq War.

1287 *Spider-Man 2*
2004. U.S. Sony Pictures. Sound, col., 127 mins. Sam Rami.

Romeo and Juliet is briefly referenced in a shot of books that Peter Parker is reading. The Signet edition of *R and J* is on the top of the pile. Parker is reading (aloud) from *The Song of Hiawatha*. *The Wasteland* is also mentioned by Doc Oc (before he becomes a villain), whose wife was an English major. Oc tells Parker that poetry is the way to a woman's heart. The film does not follow the narrative of *R and J*. Brief moments of a production of *The Importance of*

Earnest are seen because Mary Jane plays the lead. See also entry 250. (RB)

1288 *Warai no daigaku (University of Laughs)*
2004. Japan. Sound, b&w, 121 mins. In Japanese. Mamoru Hosi.

This comedy interestingly explores nationalist opposition to comedy in particular and theater more generally during a time of war. Nearly all the action takes place in a newly appointed, overzealous censor's office over a period of five days. Each day begins with a dramatist, Hajime Tsubaki (Goro Inagaki), making a trek from the theater district (geishas and barkers are seen) to police headquarters and the censor's office. In the opening sequence, the camera cuts between shots in slow motion of an audience laughing uproariously, and the censor, Mutsuo Sakisaka (Kôji Yakusho), who rejects everything on his desk more and more quickly, and Tsubaki on his way to the censor's office. Sakisaka soon makes it clear that he thinks there is no civic role for drama when war is impending. Sakisaka interviews a number of dramatists and either approves their plays when they agree to cuts (of kissing or politics) or rejects them if the dramatist refuses. Eventually, Tsubaki, who is adapting *Romeo and Juliet* as a comedy entitled *Julio and Romiet*, is allowed to go forward with the play as the censor lightens up and acknowledges his own love of theater and even fantasizes about being a gag writer (he's actually pretty good) and an actor (playing a cop, of course).

While the film sets up the censor and dramatist as good and bad guy, *Warai no daigaku* is of interest for opening up a dialogue about censorship as collaboration by making the film less of a play-within-a-film than a filmed play about the approval of a play (the film is in fact based on a 1996 stage play of the same title by the same writer, Koki Mitani). Nearly all the action takes place in the censor's office over a period of five days, and *Warai no daigaku* echoes *Waiting for Godot* in that it is very much like a play with two characters who go over and over the same ground without seeming to get anywhere.

Initially, Sakisaka pounces immediately and absurdly on Tsubaki's script: the play has Westerners in it; the idea isn't original, Sakisaka maintains. Furthermore, an English writer named William Shakespeare wrote a tragedy about similarly named characters.

Changing the order of the first syllables and exchanging the second syllables is part of the joke, Tsubaki explains. It's not funny, counters Sakisaka. Tsubaki begins to act out the balcony scene to show how it is funny, explaining that the play is a play within the play, about an acting troupe putting on a production of *Romeo and Juliet*. Sakisaka does not laugh, however. "Why write a romance about the western barbarians with whom your country is at war?" he asks. Tsubaki says it is set in Italy and that Japan recently

signed a treaty with Italy. But Sakisaka says that the author is English. "If Churchill made sushi, would you eat it?" he asks the dramatist. Tsubaki says no and adds that he wouldn't eat sushi made by Hitler either, because neither Churchill nor Hitler would make it properly. Rather than reject the manuscript, however, the censor advises cuts: "Place the action in Japan. Get rid of the British influences." Tsubaki is at his wit's end, claiming that his play is a parody and that the genre of parody has its own rules.

As negotiations between the dramatist and censor continue over the next few days, it turns out that Sakisaka has a salutary effect on the dramatist. Political repression and aesthetic excellence are not necessarily at odds. On the second day, the dramatist concedes that by moving the play's action to Japan, his play is actually better, even funnier. Tsubaki eventually makes clear to Sakisaka that he struggles against the state's authority over the theater, which he regards as illegitimate, not by refusing to write or by staging a play without the censor's approval and risking arrest, but by taking the censor's demands, however unreasonable, and rewriting his play to improve it. At this, Sakisaka places one final demand on Tsubaki: revise his comedy by excising all humor in it. Tsubaki is drafted by the army and proceeds to make his play even funnier. In the epilogue, we see stills of the *Romeo and Juliet* play, staged after Tsubaki received Sakisaka's approval, with the actress playing Julio wearing a blonde wig and the actor playing Romiet a brown wig. (RB)

DVD with optional English and Japanese subtitles. Two DVD editions: one comes with two discs, the second with extras and the censor's stamps for approved and not approved.

1289 *Almost Romeo*
2005. U.S. Ehcin Films. Sound, col., 17 mins. Justin Huntington Benson.

As he drives and later in a hotel room, down-and-out Harlan recalls the details of his love affair with Juliet, a hemophiliac tarot-card reader, as he drifts into a drug-induced haze. As he tries to sleep, he hears noises in the next room and sees images that remind him of Juliet's death during a miscarriage; he contemplates suicide but passes out before he can attempt it. The next morning, Harlan sees pictures of the innkeeper's daughter (who committed suicide), and is grateful for his redemption from tragedy.

An interesting reorientation of Shakespeare's tragic ending, handled as a hallucinatory flashback.

1290 *David & Layla*
2005. U.S. Newroz Pictures, David & Layla LLC, and Intrinsic Value Films. Sound, col., 109 mins. Jay Jonroy.

In contemporary New York City, David Fine, a Jewish television producer, and Layla, a Kurdish Muslim refugee, fall in love, only to have their romance opposed by both of their families. When Layla is faced with deportation and must marry, she must choose between David and Dr. Ahmad, a Muslim and the choice of her family. Her choice is complicated by the fact that David is engaged to Abby, an upper-class Jew preferred by David's family. As the two make their romantic decisions, David produces a TV show about cross-cultural romance. Eventually, the two are united and accepted by their families.

A romantic comedy modeled on the central *Romeo and Juliet* narrative and based on a real-life story.

1291 *Lewd Conduct #22*
2005. U.S. Diabolic. Sound, col., 120 mins. Chico Wang. Hardcore pornography.

Scene 3 (of six scenes) begins with Asia and Tony T reading aloud from the balcony scene of *Romeo and Juliet*, starting with "Romeo, O Romeo, wherefore art thou Romeo?" The director Chico Wang hands each of them two pages from the play so that they may educate the viewers about art, which Wang finds too often lacking in pornography. They both give atrocious line readings, and Tony T reads at about a seventh-grade level and scoffs a few times at his lines. The scene cuts abruptly into the two actors having sex with another man. Asia repeatedly addresses the camera as Romeo and directs the men to do various things to her, and also calls herself Juliet. The point of keeping Asia in character is apparently to degrade Romeo and Juliet by outing the lust that underlies their romantic love. It's as if Mercutio had directed the scene. The behind-the-scene extra has a scene with the director rehearsing the scene with Wang as Romeo as they go through the balcony scene. Wang is comparatively not that bad. (RB)

1292 *O Casamento de Romeu e Julieta*
2005. Brazil. Filmes do Equador and Geração Conteudo. Sound, col., 90 mins. Bruno Barreto.

Adapted from a story by Mário Prata. Romeo, one of the leaders of the Corinthians, a São Paulo soccer team, falls in love with Julieta, daughter of one of the members of the Palmeiras, the Corinthians' great rivals. To gain acceptance from Juliet's father, he must pass himself off as a devoted fan of the Palmeiras, while not alienating his own grandmother, a devoted Corinthian and keeper of his inheritance. Though the material is comic, reviews suggest that the filmmaker has treated it as a serious tragedy.

1293 *Qing ren jie (A Time to Love)*
2005. China. Beijing Film Studio and Starlight Intl. Media Co. Sound, col., 113 mins. Jianqi Huo.

A love story set in China's Cultural Revolution, with the romantic relationship between Qu Ran (Vicki Zhao) and Hou Jia (Yi Lu) opposed by both their families. References to Romeo and Juliet abound in *A Time to Love*, mostly presented in three various forms: the written play, Franco Zeffirelli's 1968 film, and a ballet production. The film emphasizes the similarities between the two love stories, even including a scene where Qu stands on a balcony reciting verses as Hou listens underneath. The difference between the film's plot and Shakespeare's is that Qu and Hou choose not to commit suicide. (RB)

1294 *Reefer Madness: The Movie Musical*
2005. U.S. Showtime Networks, ApolloScreen Filmproduktion GmbH & Co. Filmproduktion KG, and Middle Fork Productions. Sound, col., 109 mins. Andy Fickman.

Adapted from the stage musical by Kevin Murphy and Dan Studley. In this parody of 1930s musicals and antidrug propaganda, a government agent screens a cautionary film about the evils of marijuana, "Tell Your Children," for a gathered audience. In the film within the film, Mary Jane and Jimmy Harper are lovers who are happy in their naïveté and chastity until Jimmy is offered marijuana by Jack Stone, a Mephistophelian local pot dealer. Jimmy quickly descends into a life of debauchery from which even an appearance of Jesus cannot save him. When Mary tries to save Jimmy, she too is drawn to self-destruction.

Early in the film, Jimmy and Mary establish that they have been reading *Romeo and Juliet* and see themselves in terms of the lovers; however, they admit that they have not finished the play. Shakespeare makes a very brief cameo appearance. See also *Reefer Madness*.

1295 *Romeo and Me*
2005. Aesop Entertainment. Sound, col. Antony Bowman.

Starring Peter O'Toole, Stephen Rea, Janet McTeer, a love story set during World War II. The film details the story of a beautiful, young woman on the Channel Islands who falls in love with a soldier of the occupying German forces. (RB)

1296 *Gnomeo and Juliet*
In pre-production; estimated release date 2008. Disney; Animation: Rocket Pictures. Gary Trousdale.

Computer animated film spin-off of *Romeo and Juliet*. Romance blooms between ceramic indoor and outdoor garden gnomes.

Cast as of 2005 are Ewan McGregor as Gnomeo, Kate Winslet as Juliet, and Dame Judi Dench as the Nurse. Music by Elton John and Tim Rice.

Possible two-dimensional character animation set over three-dimensional backgrounds. (RB)

THE TAMING OF THE SHREW

1297 *Taming a Husband*
1910. U.S. Biograph Company. Silent, b&w, 16 mins. D. W. Griffith.

A recently married young woman is neglected by her husband and asks a girlfriend to help her reignite his ardor. The girlfriend dresses up as a man and pretends to be the wife's lover; enraged, her husband challenges the rival to a duel. All ends happily. This film, one of many "taming of" films produced in the early silent era, has a title that promises links to *The Taming of the Shrew*, but the central cross-dressing motif seems to hearken instead to *Twelfth Night*.

1298 *The Iron Strain*
1915. U.S. New York Motion Picture Corp. and Kay-Bee. Silent, b&w, 4 reels. Reginald Barker.

Mining magnate Ezra Whitney, concerned that his granddaughter Octavia will marry a foolish city boy, takes her to Alaska in search of a proper husband. In Alaska she meets Chuck Hemingway, a rough-and-ready prospector who is in reality a wealthy college boy. After Octavia rejects Chuck because he is beneath her station, with Ezra's blessing he kidnaps and marries her and takes her to his cabin, maintaining a chaste relationship with her. Octavia soon breaks down and becomes a proper housekeeper, though she keeps her romantic distance from Chuck. Meanwhile, Chuck is attracted to Kitty Malloy, who stars in the Arctic cabaret; when Octavia becomes jealous, she realizes that she truly loves Chuck, and the two return to the city to visit Ezra.

As the plot summary indicates, the plot follows that of *The Taming of the Shrew*, transferring the action to the Wild West and amplifying the issue of class differences between the Kate and Petruchio characters. Typical of melodrama, the class differences are only apparent, not real, allowing for a happy ending.

1299 *Impossible Catherine*
1919. U.S. Virginia Pearson Photoplays, Inc. Silent, b&w, 5 reels. John B. O'Brien.

Catherine, the feisty daughter of wealthy Wall Street broker Grant Kimberly, is a spoiled terror at home and a willful feminist convinced of female superiority, so much so that she has earned the moniker "Impossible Catherine." She meets John Henry at a Yale University banquet, and having read Shakespeare's *The Taming of the Shrew*, he resolves to tame her. He takes her up in his airplane, holding her captive until she consents to marry him. After the wedding, she runs away, but John finds her and takes her to his lumber camp in remote Canada where he imposes kitchen tasks on her. Unbowed, Catherine hires town bully Rosky to beat him, but he beats her instead. Coming to Catherine's defense, John is wounded and Catherine comes to recognize her love for him.

John Henry's knowledge with Shakespeare's play explicitly informs his strategy for taming Catherine. Her name also suggests a direct Shakespearean link; John Henry's name, linked to that of an American strongman

folk hero, suggests a contest between progressive feminism and traditional gender roles.

1300 *The Indestructible Wife*
1919. U.S. Select Pictures Corporation. Silent, b&w, length unknown. Charles Maigne.

Adapted from the play by Fanny and Frederic Hatton. Jimmy Ordway, newly married to overly energetic bride Charlotte, is exhausted after a honeymoon of strenuous sports and recreation. When the two return home, Charlotte throws a dinner party, at which Jimmy conspires with his friends to entertain Charlotte nonstop until she collapses. One of Jimmy's friends, professional athlete Brandy, is delighted to discover that Charlotte can match his energy, so he resolves to steal Charlotte from Jimmy. He reveals his plan to Julia Cleves, and Charlotte speaks harshly to Jimmy. Surmising that he needs to win Charlotte back, he kidnaps her, tying her up in a boathouse, which Charlotte secretly enjoys. Brandy arrives to rescue her, but when he tries to take unwanted liberties, Charlotte throws him in the water. Happily reconciled with Jimmy, Charlotte prepares the meal for the dinner guests.

Yet another of the "taming" films of the silent period. Jimmy's taming of Charlotte by abduction and her subsequent domestication are reminiscent of Petruchio's taming of Katherine. There are no direct citations of Shakespeare's dialogue.

1301 *Kohlhiesels Töchter (Kohlhiesel's Daughters)*
1920. U.S. Messter Film GmbH. Silent, b&w, 3,703 ft. Ernst Lubitsch.

Innkeeper Mathias Kohlheisel has two daughters, young Gretel, a sweet and pretty coquette, and older sister Liesel, a hellion who refuses to kowtow to men with her behavior or dress. Peter Xaver, a local man, wants to marry Gretel, but he cannot do so until Liesel is married, so on friend Paul Seppl's advice he resolves to marry and divorce Liesel, then marry Gretel. In the process of taming Liesel, he realizes he loves her. One twist is that both daughters are played by the same actress, a technique that is maintained in all of the subsequent remakes (in 1930 by Hans Behrendt, 1943 by Kurt Hoffmann, 1955 by Géza von Bolvary, and 1962 by Axel von Ambesser).

1302 *Enchantment*
1921. U.S. Cosmopolitan and Paramount. Silent, b&w, 6,982 ft. (7 reels). Robert G. Vignola.

Adapted from a story by Frank R. Adams. Inspired by a production of *The Taming of the Shrew*, Mr. Hoyt, a millionaire, hires Ernest Eddison, the actor playing Petruchio, to tame his bratty daughter Ethel. Eddison offers Ethel the lead in *Sleeping Beauty* and then treats her roughly during rehearsals, to which Ethel responds with stubbornness; when he kisses her flamboyantly during the production, she confesses her love for him.

1303 *Daring Youth*
1924. U.S. B. F. Zeidman Productions Ltd. Silent, b&w, 6 reels. William Beaudine.

Adapted from a story by Dorothy Farnum. On the eve of her wedding, Alita Allen is counseled by her unhappily married mother to follow a newspaper columnist's free-thinking, feminist regimen for a happy marriage. Alita marries John J. Campbell with the understanding that she will have unlimited freedom in the relationship, but her enthusiasm for the regimen soon wanes. Frustrated by her husband's desire to continue the arrangement, she takes up with another man, Arthur James, and is about to elope with him when Campbell discovers the two, beats up his rival, and becomes the assertive husband she desires. An interesting variation on the "taming of the spouse" motif, in which the husband needs to become Petruchio-like for the marriage to become happy. There are no citations of Shakespeare in the dialogue.

1304 *The Untamed Lady*
1926. U.S. Famous Players-Lasky Corporation. Silent, b&w, 7 reels. Frank Tuttle.

Adapted from the novel by Fannie Hurst. After having broken several engagements because of her temper, St. Clair Van Tassel, a spoiled society girl, is moving to the country when her car breaks down and she meets millionaire Larry Gasten, who soon resolves to tame her by refusing to allow her tantrums. After they have become friends, he leaves for Cuba on his yacht without her, but, headstrong, she stows away; when she is discovered, Larry turns the yacht back to New York, but Clair changes its course, sending the boat and crew into a storm in which Clair must substitute for a coal stoker who has become injured in the tempest. Having returned to New York, Clair runs away to her hunting lodge in the Catskills. When Larry pursues, he is injured in a riding accident, and in the hospital Clair realizes that she loves Larry and must take responsibility for the injuries she's selfishly caused. Yet another variation on the "taming of the shrew" motif; as in other examples of this motif in silent films, it is the injury of her husband that leads the wife to recognize her love and domesticate herself. Of added interest because Gloria Swanson stars as Van Tassel.

1305 *The Framing of the Shrew*
1929. U.S. Sound, b&w, 20 mins. Arvid E. Gillstrom.

The earliest all-black cast Shakespeare spin-off. Privacy Robson is a meek, not-too-bright, downtrodden husband who takes advice from his friend Florian Slappey and tames his obstreperous wife. After starting divorce proceedings, pretending to have a new girlfriend, and refusing to eat anything she cooks him, he eventually gets the upper hand. Mistaking one another for robbers, she fires a shotgun at him and misses. He knocks some sense into her, in the film's term, as he hits her over the head with a rolling pin.

He claims that the robber had hit her but also got away. He gets her to pay him three dollars a week in alimony. Spencer Williams, who played Andy in *Amos 'n' Andy*, wrote this film comedy, according to Donald Bogle, *Primetime Blues* (New York: Farrar, Straus and Giroux, 2001), 29. The Internet Movie Database (IMDB.com) credits Alfred A. Cohn, however, as does the film. Spencer Williams stars as Lawyer Evans Chew. The opening title credit reads, "Octavus Roy Cohen's *The Framing of the Shrew*." Cohen was a short story writer who published a collection of short stories entitled *Florian Slappey Goes Abroad* in 1928. See *Melancholy Dame* and *Paradise in Harlem*. (RB)

1306 *Elstree Calling*
1930. U.K. British International Pictures. Sound, b&w (with tinted color sequences), 86 mins. Adrian Brunel, André Charlot, Alfred Hitchcock, Jack Hulbert, and Paul Murray.

This film was Britain's Elstree Studio's answer to Hollywood singing and comedy revues so popular in the early days of the talkies. Purporting to be a live early television broadcast, the film offers a series of unconnected song, dance, and comedy routines held together by announcer Tommy Handley and sequences about a man attempting to tune into the broadcast with his homemade television.

A repeated gag involves Donald Calthrop in doublet and hose singing the praises of Shakespeare's entertainment value, only repeatedly to be humiliated. When knocked down by another man, he comments, "As William Shakespeare said in act 1, scene 2 of *Macbeth*, 'what bloody man is that?'" The film's penultimate scene is an extravagant parody of Sam Taylor's 1929 film of *The Taming of the Shrew*, specifically its treatment of 2.2 when Petruchio first meets Kate. The film set closely resembles Taylor's distinctive set for this scene, particularly its long staircase. Calthrop, the actor playing Petruchio, is made up to resemble Douglas Fairbanks Jr., and he arrives on a runaway motorcycle with a sidecar. After a conversation with Baptista in which he drops in and out of character (he first asks for "Mary" instead of "Katherine," and he ends by saying, "Tell her Doug has arrived!"), he encounters Kate, played by British International Pictures star Anna May Wong dressed as a chorus girl, who lobs custard pies at Petruchio, Baptista, and the servants. At the end of the sketch, Shakespeare arrives and laughs at Petruchio/Fairbanks; when he identifies himself as "Willie Shakespeare," he too is hit in the face with a pie. According to the British Film Institute's *Monthly Film Bulletin* (November 1975), this sequence was one of several in the film directed by Alfred Hitchcock. This parody sequence may be fruitfully compared to the parody of *Romeo and Juliet* in *The Hollywood Revue of 1929*.

1307 *You Made Me Love You*
1933. U.K. British International Pictures. Sound, b&w, 70 mins. Monty Banks.

Adapted from a story by Stanley Lupino. Pamela Berne is the feisty, beautiful heiress to the Berne fortune, and her father is eager to marry her off. At a traffic light, Tom Daly, a songwriter, sees her, immediately falls in love, and writes a song about her, which prompts her to fall in love with him. Her father immediately consents to the union. After the wedding, Berne and Daly fight constantly, at one point almost destroying a house. Despite Daly's best efforts to tame her (mostly practical jokes), she remains defiantly headstrong. When Daly threatens to divorce her, she comes to see that she will lose the only man who loves her, and she becomes a compliant housewife. The film is billed as a musical, since it includes several songs. The links to Shakespeare's narrative are general rather than specific: the father eager to spring off a difficult daughter, Daly's campaign to tame his wife, and Berne's domestication linked to her acknowledgment of her love for Daly.

1308 *Second Best Bed*
1938. U.K. Capital Films. Sound, b&w, 74 mins. Tom Walls.

Victor Garnett, a middle-aged man who has already well-established conservative habits, marries young Patricia Lynton. After the wedding, he attempts to make her take "the second best bed," and she adamantly refuses, becoming a rebellious wife. Soon Garnett flirts with a local villager, and Lynton leaves with her young friends for Monte Carlo. In the end, the two reconcile. The "second best bed" refers to Shakespeare's mysterious bequest to his wife Anne upon his death, and the film distantly recalls the motif of the new wife rebelling against her husband, in this case justifiably so. One of three uses of *Taming of the Shrew*–related material in British films of the 1930s, the other two being *Elstree Calling* and *You Made Me Love You* (entries 1306 and 1307).

1309 *Makacs Kata*
1943. Hungary. Mester Film. Sound, b&w, 75 mins. Viktor Bánky.

Kata, a headstrong millionaire heiress, is wooed by two suitors. She rejects Zoltan, a fortune hunter, in favor of Peter, a man she believes to be a poor tramp but who is actually a prosperous engineer of peasant stock. So that she can become free of her father and inherit his money, she plans to marry Peter, then divorce him a month later after paying him off. Peter goes along with Kata's scheme so that he will have the month to tame Kata. He takes her to his mother's isolated country cottage, where he engages in a number of tricks and strategies to make her an obedient, helpful housewife. The narrative and character parallels to Shakespeare's play are readily apparent, though the emphasis on Kata's exploitation of Peter's seeming peasant status is novel.

1310 *Makrancos hölgy*
1943. Hungary. Hunnia Studio. Sound, b&w, 70 mins. Emil Mártonffy.

Benedek Palma, a shrewish city woman, is brought by her new husband Jambor Pal to the country, where he engages in a regimen to tame her and get her to assume her proper role as a traditional wife. At first Benedek is angry at having been brought to the country and refuses to engage in any domestic duties; Jambor responds by declaring that if she won't cook for him, she won't eat. Soon Benedek becomes a docile peasant housewife, discovering pleasure in household work and love for her husband. However, she begins to worry that he doesn't love her because he has beaten her and refuses sexual contact with her during taming. An old peasant woman clarifies the nature of peasant culture to her: a man who doesn't beat his wife doesn't love her. The plot similarities between this film and Shakespeare's *The Taming of the Shrew* are many and obvious, though the opposition between city and country culture receives special emphasis. As in the other Hungarian film of the same period, *Makacs Kata* (entry 1309), the site of taming is a country cottage where the shrewish wife accepts the woman's traditional domestic gender role.

1311 *Casanova in Burlesque*
1944. U.S. Republic Pictures. Sound, b&w, 74 mins. Leslie Goodwins.

Adapted from a story by John Wales. Joseph L. Kelly Jr., a Shakespeare professor and son of a vaudevillian, secretly works during summers as a burlesque comic. When a stripper, Lil Colman, threatens to reveal his secret unless he casts her in the lead of the college *Romeo and Juliet* production, he acquiesces, only to find that her bad acting has driven away the rest of the cast. At the last minute, the burlesque company creates a swing version of *The Taming of the Shrew*, which the audience receives appreciatively.

Portions of *Romeo and Juliet* and *The Taming of the Shrew* are performed, as well as two Shakespearean musical numbers, "Willie the Shake" and "The Taming of the Shrew."

1312 *Enamorada*
1946. Mexico. Azteca Films and Lopert Films. Sound, b&w, 99 mins. Emilio Fernández.

During the Mexican Revolution, Emiliano Zapata's men capture the town of Chohula, rounding up the town's bourgeois leaders to subject them to revolutionary justice. The army's commander, ruthless General Jose Juan Reyes, sentences town patriarch Carlos Peñafiel to death, but he relents when he meets Peñafiel's daughter, the spirited, sharp-tongued Beatriz, who has been promised to Eduardo Roberts, an American-born Mexican. Reyes spares her father and tries to woo Beatriz, but she rebuffs his sometimes sweet, sometimes rough advances. Eventually, when Beatriz's wedding trousseau arrives, he gives up on her and leaves town with his army, but at the last second (and in the middle of her wedding contract) Beatriz realizes her love for Reyes and joins his revolutionary troops.

A popular classic of the Mexican cinema, *Enamorada* is a somewhat distant analogue of *The Taming of the Shrew*, though the motif of a beautiful shrew courted by a rough-mannered man may suggest Shakespeare's influence. One of *Enamorada*'s set pieces, Beatriz and Reyes wooing through the door to the Peñafiel home, is reminiscent in manner (but not in details of dialogue or plot) of Kate and Petruchio's first meeting. In other respects, *Enamorada* is quite different from Shakespeare's play: Beatriz has no sister and Carlos is not anxious to marry off his shrewish daughter, nor does Reyes subject Beatriz to a taming regimen. If anything, Beatriz's rejection of his courtship tames the general, softening his manner and teaching him the value of mercy. The love story is juxtaposed with extended political discussions between priest Rafael Sierra and the general. The priest agrees with the general's revolutionary ideals but not with his methods; those methods are modified by Reyes's love for Beatriz. In Beatriz's case, she is ultimately given a choice between an American businessman and a Mexican revolutionary, and she heroically chooses the latter, realigning her class alliances.

1313 *Cartas marcadas*
1948. Mexico. Diana S. A. Sound, col., 92 mins. René Cardona.

In her will Doña Camillo leaves the Villa de Maroma to Victoria, a sharp-tongued highborn woman, and Manuel, a ranchhand, on the condition that they marry. Victoria and Manuel hate each other and at first try to sabotage their forced courtship through humiliation. Eventually, both develop feelings for one another, though they have difficulty admitting it to each other. After Victoria's father Don Manuel engineers a confrontation between Manuel and Ernesto, a doctor and Victoria's obsequious lover, in which Manuel seems to be shot, Victoria declares her love for Manuel only to find out he is not wounded. Eventually Manuel declares his love for her. When a second will arrives to release them from their marriage contract, the couple vows to remain together, and Don Manuel supplies the ladder that allows the two to elope.

Though often included in lists of *Shrew* adaptations, the relationship between this film and Shakespeare's play does not extend far beyond the motif of a tumultuous romance between a sharp-tongued woman and a rough-and-ready man; as is often the case in Latin American versions of the story, the woman is upper class and the man is working class. In some respects Manuel's comic servant, Tepalcate, resembles Petruchio's Grumio, though he has little of Grumio's grumbling wit.

1314 *El Charro y La Dama*
1949. Mexico. Guillerma Alcayde. Sound, b&w, 90 mins. Fernando Cortés.

Adapted from a story by Max Aub. Raised in Texas by her Mexican parents, Patricia has developed an explosive temper, and she uses it on her fiancé, the wimpy Mr. Haste. To curb her tempestuous nature, her father takes her and her friend Clara to the family farm in Mexico; en route they are attacked by the gang of El Gavilan, a bandit, but the group is rescued by Pedro, a cowboy (*charro*), and Constantino, the local sheriff. At festivities to celebrate the family's arrival, Patricia demonstrates her skill with a gun; when at a dance, Pedro calls her a hussy, she explodes in anger and a chance falling of a coin reveals that Pedro is in fact El Gavilan. As Pedro is about to be hanged, in part on Patricia and Clara's testimony, Patricia rescues him by shooting the hangman's noose. That night, Pedro abducts Patricia and takes her to his cabin, where he subjects her to a regimen of taming, starting with a spanking. Eventually the two fall in love; Pedro returns Patricia to town, but they pretend to fight to preserve his reputation. When Don Guillermo tries to take the family ranch, Pedro saves the day and is redeemed. When Patricia leaves soon after, Pedro once again holds up her coach and abducts her, and Clara ends up with Constantino.

Though (contrary to Sammon's report) the credits do not include Shakespeare, *El Charro y La Dama* includes elements that recall *The Taming of the Shrew*. In addition to the familiar Latin motif of the willful highborn woman and her lowborn tamer, a motif signaled in the film's title and in this case linked to the differences between the American city and the Mexican countryside, the sequence in which Pedro takes Patricia to his cabin and tames her has several general resemblances to Petruchio's taming of Kate at his home. In Pedro's case, the taming involves Patricia taking up domestic duties; early in the sequence, when Pedro exiles Patricia to the doghouse and she sees a scorpion, his analogy between Patricia's nature and the scorpion recalls Petruchio's analogy between Kate and a wasp (both of which have stings in their tails). Sweet-natured and romantic Clara provides a Bianca-like contrast to Patricia.

1315 *Aan (Savage Princess)*
1952. India. Sound, col., 161 mins. Mehboob Khan.

A Hindi adaptation of *The Taming of The Shrew* that draws on *Duel in the Sun* (dir. King Vidor, 1946) and *Ben-Hur* (1917 and 1925) with the Petruchio figure dressed in jodpurs and the villain driving around in a cadillac. (RB)

1316 *The Quiet Man*
1952. U.S. Republic Pictures. Sound, col., 129 mins. John Ford.

Adapted from the story "Green Rushes" by Maurice Walsh. Irish American boxer Sean Thornton returns to Innisfree, his birthplace in Ireland, after accidentally killing a man in the boxing ring; there he plans to retire in anonymity. He meets and is smitten by feisty Mary Kate

Danaher, sister of the blustering bully Will Danaher, who is incensed when Thornton buys the same cottage, White O'Mornin', that he has designs on. When Thornton tries to engage in an extended, traditional Irish wooing of Mary Kate under the supervision of Michaeleen Flynn, the local matchmaker and their chaperone, he is blocked by Will, who remains angry at him and refuses his permission and the traditional dowry. Though several villagers try to trick Will, he stands firm against the relationship, and Mary Kate, true to Irish custom, stubbornly refuses to consummate the relationship until her brother relents. When Mary Kate accuses Thornton of being a coward, despite his vow never to fight again, he claims his wife, forces Will to pay, and the two men have a long brawl, much to the satisfaction of the villagers. Afterward, Will and Thornton reconcile at the pub, and Mary Kate and Thornton happily settle into their marriage at White O'Mornin'.

Ford's extended paean to rural Irish culture nods in the direction of Shakespeare's narrative in certain respects, though it is not a thoroughgoing adaptation. Mary Kate's headstrong refusal to accede to her new husband's authority (in this case, because of Irish custom) and Thornton's rough treatment of his wife to establish his dominance, a rough treatment at which she is secretly pleased, recall *The Taming of the Shrew*. Interestingly, this narrative includes a second "shrew," Mary Kate's brother Will, who Thornton must treat roughly in order to consummate his marriage.

1317 *Kiss Me Kate*
1953. U.S. MGM. Sound, col. (3-D), 109 mins. George Sidney.

Adapted from the musical by Cole Porter and Bella and Sam Spewack (entry 1737). This musical about the making of a musical based on *The Taming of the Shrew* focuses on the conflicts between Lilli Vanessi and Fred Graham, a recently divorced show business couple who are to star in the show. Lilli (playing Kate) threatens to marry ranching magnate Tex Callaway and retire from acting, while Fred (playing Petruchio) is involved with Lois Lane, the spicy dancer playing Bianca who is actually the girlfriend of Bill Calhoun, a penniless dancer who has borrowed money from a gangster using Fred's name. Despite their new paramours and their constant bickering, Fred and Lilli remain in love, though they cannot admit it to themselves. When two thugs, Slug and Lippy, arrive to collect on what they think is Fred's debt, they force Lilli at gunpoint to continue to star in the show despite her desire to quit; they end up as extras in the show in order to guard their actors. Even so, Lilli quits the show before its final act. When Fred, despondent, returns to the stage to do the final scene with the understudy, Lilli returns to the show and delivers Kate's speech about wifely devotion to Fred in order to declare her love.

Among the most successful of the Shakespeare musicals, *Kiss Me Kate* grafts Shakespeare's play to a plotline con-

ventional to the Hollywood musical, the backstage drama, where conflict between male and female co-stars supplies the narrative's tension. In this case, the structure of the musical—where the onstage narrative refracts the conflict in the backstage narrative—echoes Shakespeare's own play-within-a-play structure, where the taming of Kate and Petruchio is presented as a tale performed for the headstrong Christopher Sly. (Actually, the onstage narrative within *Kiss Me Kate* retains the frame-tale quality of *Shrew*, since the first number, "We Open in Venice," presents the actors as Shakespearean players who then go on to present the musical proper.) Shakespeare's narrative is presented fairly faithfully, though with some minor changes—the rival suitors to Lucentio, Hortensio and Gremio, are virtually indistinguishable from him; the taming scenes in Act 4 are reduced to the opening "burnt mutton" scene; and the sub-plot concerning Lucentio and Bianca is radically reduced. Significant portions of Shakespeare's dialogue are used, phrases and lines appear in songs—for example, Petruchio's opening number, "I Come to Wive It Wealthily in Padua"—and there are also witty passing references to Shakespearean commonplaces such as "get thee to a notary," "to flee or not to flee," or "goin' away is such sweet sorrow." The relationship between the actors and their roles is often ironic: meek Bianca is played by Lois Lane, a sexy, outgoing coquette who has the most energetic dance sequences, whereas shrewish Kate is played by Lilli, who is prone to romantic reveries about Fred and who sings, "Taunt me and hurt me, deceive me, desert me, I'm yours till I die." Whereas his whip-cracking Petruchio is truly indomitable, backstage Graham is mostly blustery and vain male ego, the irony of which is nowhere better illustrated than in his number "Where Is the Life That Late I Led?" in which he catalogues former lovers while seated on a pink brick wall that is unmistakably—and hilariously—phallic. The musical's most famous number, "Brush Up Your Shakespeare," in which the two thugs claim that quoting the Bard will make women "kowtow," is one of the most ironic takes on Shakespeare's cultural prestige ever written. The play-within-a-play structure of the musical allows a novel solution to the problem of Kate's final speech: in the context of the ongoing production, the speech is less about Kate's public submission to Petruchio than a private declaration of Lilli's love for Fred and for the theater. *Kiss Me Kate* was photographed using a 3-D process, a gimmick that accounts for several shots featuring objects tossed toward the viewer.

DVD contains a "Behind the Scenes" essay and a Cole Porter featurette that reference Shakespeare.

1318 *La fierecilla domada* (*La mégère apprivoisée*)
1955. France and Spain. Producciones Benito Perojo S.A. and Vascos Films. Sound, col., 88 mins. Antonio Román.

A relatively faithful, big-budget adaptation of Shakespeare's play, transposed to nineteenth-century Spain. Beautiful but indomitable Catalina de Martos is the daughter of Gandia de Martos, a rich merchant. Engaged to marry Don Mario de Acevedo, she rejects him as a fool and has run out of suitors until the arrival of Don Beltran, who vows that he can tame her. He takes her to his estate and makes her undergo a taming regimen until she becomes a loving wife. By eliminating the narrative of the other daughter, emphasis tends to fall on the more violent and sexually provocative elements of the shrew-taming narrative, especially apparent in a number of details: Catalina enters on horseback in male dress with a sword, and Don Beltran chains her briefly to a pillar in the midst of his shrew taming. Also noteworthy is the starring role of Carmen Sevilla, the famous Spanish film star and singer; Sevilla also played Octavia in Charlton Heston's film adaptation of *Antony and Cleopatra*.

1319 *McLintock!*
1963. U.S. United Artists. Sound, col., 127 mins. Andrew V. McLagen.

Two years earlier Katherine McLintock left her husband George Washington McLintock, strong-willed owner of a large cattle-ranching empire in the Western town of McLintock, Colorado, to pursue a life of high society refinement in the East. Much to George's irritation, she has returned to finalize a divorce and take custody of their daughter Rebecca, who is scheduled to arrive from being back east at school. George is also troubled by other changes in his life—his own aging, rival ranchers, the arrival of homesteaders supported by government land grants, corrupt government officials, and the pushing of local Indians who are George's friends and allies onto the reservation. When Rebecca arrives, she is accompanied by Matt Douglas Jr., the son of George's bitter enemy, and Rebecca soon is the focus of conflict between two suitors: Matt and Dev Warren, a new farmhand. When Comanches threaten to make their last stand in McLintock's town, he mediates a truce; afterward, Dev and Rebecca announce their plans to get married. Eventually, having had enough with Katherine's stubbornness, jealousy, and complaining, George tames her in a spectacular pursuit through the town that culminates in her public spanking. (The spanking motif may be related to the spanking motif used in *Kiss Me Kate* ten years earlier.) Afterward, the two are reunited.

Created as a vehicle to reunite the onscreen pairing of John Wayne and Maureen O'Hara that had been so successful in *Rio Grande* and *The Quiet Man*, *McLintock!* adapts various plot elements of *The Taming of the Shrew* to the Western. There are no citations of Shakespeare's dialogue (other than a passing reference to "the milk of human kindness" from *Macbeth*), but several key motifs of Shakespeare's play are freely recast: bickering between lovers who are, despite their evident attraction, unable to express their love because of a contest of authority; a subplot that involves a younger woman and multiple suitors; and a testy marriage that culminates in a taming scene in front of an audience. George Washington McLintock makes an interesting Petruchio analogue, for his irascibility springs not only from native machismo but also from his sense that the conservative order of the West for which he stands is under assault—from government meddling, from the values of the citified East, from women, and most of all from misguided notions of being civilized. McLintock is presented as a patriarch rather than a young lover, fatherly in his benevolence toward the needy, but authoritarian in the exercise of that benevolence and zealous in defense against challenges to his authority. His Katherine is shrewish less because of her sharp tongue than for her advocacy of notions of gentility that are elitist, pompous, and hypocritically moralistic, notions that violate her essential vitality. Shakespeare's concerns with the contest of power between male and female are thus extended to themes characteristic of the Western: the contest between Eastern civilization and Western freedom, the potentially emasculating domestic influence of women upon men, and the place of violence in maintaining authority. (It is noteworthy that this film mutes much of the violence by treating it as carnivalesque comedy, just as

In this shot from *McLintock!* (1963), John Wayne (the Petruchio character) spanks Maureen O'Hara (the Kate character) as others laugh. Courtesy of Douglas Lanier.

Shakespeare mutes the physical violence in *The Taming of the Shrew* by displacing most of it onto servants.) McLintock's conquering of Katherine becomes a displaced form of (re)exerting authority over a wild West that is changing. Though a film much reviled for its clearly reactionary politics, *McLintock* offers an idealized rearticulation of John Wayne's screen persona at a moment when Wayne himself was beginning to show his age and when the conservative values his persona represented were being forcefully questioned elsewhere in the culture. Perhaps in response, Wayne gives prominence to McLintock's rebellious qualities, particularly his flouting of government authority and polite social convention. That the filmmakers intended the Wayne image to be a template for younger generations is evident in the fact that there are not one but two spankings in the film, not only George spanking Katherine, but also Dev spanking Rebecca. And it is George who puts the paddle in Dev's hand.

NB: the transfers in several DVD editions currently available are very poor; preferable is the 2005 UA edition.

1320 *Frau Wirtin hat auch einen Grafen* (*Sexy Susan Sins Again*)
1968. Germany, Austria, Italy, and Hungary. AICO Film, Hungarofilm, Neue Delta, and Terra Filmkunst. Sound, col., 96 mins. Franz Antel.

Softcore pornography. One of several "Frau Wirtin" films in the late 1960s, a sexploitation series from Europe. Susanne, hostess of a brothel, has a performance of her company of traveling players interrupted by Napoleon's army. She is enlisted to deliver a message to Count Enrico, lover of Napoleon's sister, and in doing so, finds him a bride and does military surveillance in cross-dressed disguise, uncovering and foiling a scheme to assassinate Napoleon. The play that Napoleon's men interrupt is *The Taming of the Shrew*, which has little thematic significance to the remainder of the film (except, perhaps, its overt misogyny).

1321 *L'ours et la Poupee* (*The Bear and the Doll*)
1970. France. Marianne Productions S.A. and Parc Film. Sound, col., 85 mins. Michel Deville.

Gaspard, an oddball cellist who lives at his French country estate free from distraction with his three nieces and son, has his domestic peace disturbed when an auto accident brings him together with Felicia, a gorgeous but temperamental young woman from Paris. Though Felicia is attracted to Gaspard, he kowtows to her, a fact that angers Felicia and entices her into trying to make him fall in love with her. However, Gaspard, anxious to preserve his male independence and quiet and repelled by her city nature, resists her attempts, and soon the romantic battle between the two escalates into knockabout farce. Eventually the two get together.

An interesting reversal of the typical shrew-taming narrative—here the man is the "shrew" and the woman the "tamer"—and a romantic male fantasy of female seduction designed to accommodate Brigitte Bardot's sex appeal. As is often the case with variations on this motif, the city is coded as the woman's world, the realm of liberated female behavior, whereas the countryside is the man's realm, where traditional moral values reign. Beyond the motif of romantic tension between an assertive woman and a traditionalist man, there are only a few very general resemblances to Shakespeare's play. Even so, when Gaspard first meets Felicia, one indication of his eccentric, Petruchio-like nature is that he declares it has stopped raining even though he is standing in a downpour; Felicia, nonplussed, gives no reply. Later she imitates his zany behavior, and he offers her a cup of salted coffee. This film was remade in Italy in 1980 as *Il Bisbetico domato* (below), with the farcical and chauvinistic elements of *L'ours et la Poupee* ramped up.

1322 *Travolti da un insolito destino nell'azzurro mare d'agosto* (*Swept Away... by an Unusual Destiny in the Blue Sea of August*)
1974. Italy. Medusa Produzione. Sound, col., 116 mins. Lina Wertmüller.

While on a yachting trip on the Mediterranean, Raffaella Lanzetti, a spoiled, rich married shrew, and Gennarino Carunchio, a working-class sailor, accidentally become stranded on an isolated island. Whereas earlier Raffaella mocked Gennarino, on the island she becomes dependent upon his survival skills and slowly begins to become tamed and to fall in love with his machismo. Gennarino insists that she prove she really loves him by returning to the mainland and leaving her husband, but when the two return to civilization, Raffaella regretfully leaves Gennarino and returns to her rich husband.

More a Shakespearean analogue than a direct adaptation, *Swept Away* shares with Shakespeare's play a number of motifs—a shrewish, haughty woman paired with an eccentric shrewtamer, comic bickering, a taming sequence involving the isolation of the couple and food deprivation, and the shrew slowly becoming submissive. In Wertmüller's version, the taming succeeds only because of the couple's temporary isolation from social structures of class that give Raffaella superiority over Gennarino; the melancholy ending of the film offers a pessimistic view of the class system, suggesting that social class trumps "natural" patriarchy as a determinant of the politics of romantic relationships. *Swept Away* (Guy Ritchie, 2002), a fairly faithful remake with Madonna in the leading role, uses the same scenario but was universally reviled by critics.

1323 *Il Bisbetico domato* (*The Taming of the Scoundrel*)
1980. Italy. Capital Film. Sound, col., 104 mins. Franco Castellano and Giuseppe Moccia.

Elia Codogno, a hot-headed, chauvinistic farmer in the Italian countryside, is a confirmed bachelor, even though his elderly housekeeper Mamie has long encouraged him to marry a good woman. When during a storm a car breaks down nearby and its driver, Lisa Silvestri, a gorgeous society girl, asks for his help, Mamie decides that Elia should marry her. Elia, unmoved by her considerable beauty, treats her rudely, something she finds novel and intriguing, and his slow romantic responses enkindle her desire, so she resolves to bend him to her desires. After several failed attempts to impress or seduce him, including working in his fields, Lisa concedes defeat and returns to her former fiancé in Milan, after which Elia regrets his decision and decides to follow her. In order to win her love, he bets against her fiancé in a sports game, after which he announces his love for her over a microphone before the spectators. Though their relationship is tumultuous, they are finally reconciled, albeit uneasily.

A parody of *L'Ours et la Poupee* (above), in addition to its distant affinities to *The Taming of the Shrew*. In this case, the genders are reversed—it is the man who is the "shrew" and the woman who is the "tamer"—though the now conventional association in European film versions of the traditional man's world with the countryside and the "liberated" woman's world with the city remains intact. Interestingly, the reversal of the genders and the woman's use of sex as her main means of taming her man lead to some anxiety on the filmmakers' part, and so at midpoint the film abruptly shifts to a more conventional romantic scenario, in which the man tries to bend the unruly woman to his will. The film's poster features its most famous scene, in which Elia uses his tractor to drag Lisa in a bed through the village. Playing the role of Elia is the popular film comedian and singer Adriano Celentano, famous in his films for his mugging facial expressions and characteristic walk; Ornella Muti, who plays Lisa, was frequently Celentano's co-star in his comedies.

1324 *Night Magic*
1984. U.S. Essex Films. Sound, col., 90 mins. Bob Loving.

Night Magic opens with a phone machine message being left in voice-over by a guy imitating Cary Grant inviting a couple who are having sex to take a weekend trip. As the couple packs their sex toys, we also see a copy of Shakespeare's works thrown in as well. Much of the film takes place in an RV driven by Paul Thomas. The characters each have a fantasy about having sex with another person in the RV. Eric Edwards plays an "English lit" student who says he is reading *The Taming of the Shrew*. Paul Thomas asks, "To fondle or not to fondle is the question?" in response to Edwards bringing out his copy of Shakespeare. In his fantasy episode, Edwards plays Petruchio to Lisa De-Leeuw's Kate. They do Petruchio and Kate's first encounter (II.ii) and then begin speaking in faux Shakespeare verse as they start having sex. As they get more excited, they stop talking until after the sex ends, where they revert to faux

verse. We see Edwards continuing to read the play at later points in the film. (RB)

1325 *The Taming of the Screw*
1997. U.S. Notorious. Sound, col., 91 mins. Jim Powers.

Hardcore pornography. In exchange for money, a young lawyer, Pete, marries Kate, the shrewish daughter of his boss, and subjects her to various forms of sexual "taming" to make her an obedient wife. In the final scene, she demonstrates her newfound submissiveness by ordering other women to have sex with her husband. (DL)

This crudely made film includes general connections to Shakespeare's taming narrative and main characters, though no dialogue is quoted. Several scenes have more specific parallels to Shakespeare's play: Kate physically attacks her sister Jill; Pete pretends that Kate loves him while she pitches a fit; Pete forcibly takes Kate from her wedding celebration; Peter offers Kate food, then orders it taken away; when Pete pretends that midnight is morning, Kate goes along with him, claiming that the sun blinded her, and when Pete corrects her, she replies that the moon blinded her; and Kate offers a version of her "obedience" speech after the men make a bet about her submissiveness. See Richard Burt *Unspeakable ShaXXXspeares* (New York: St. Martin's Press, 1998), 93–96. (RB)

1326 *10 Things I Hate about You*
1999. U.S. Jaret Entertainment, Mad Chance, and Touchstone Pictures. Sound, col., 97 mins. Gil Junger.

Bianca Stratford, tenth-grade daughter of Dr. Walter Stratford, is not allowed to date until her sister Katharina ("Kat"), a boy-hating feminist who has a reputation as a "heinous bitch," also dates. Cameron James, a new boy in Padua High School and enamored of Bianca, concocts a plan to date her: he entice Joey Donner, an obnoxious, rich pretty boy, to pay Patrick Verona, the school bad boy, to date Kat. Bianca and Cameron pursue their romance, and Patrick and Kat develop a love-hate relationship as Patrick begins to have qualms about the financial setup. When Joey, angry that Bianca has preferred Cameron to him, reveals the setup at the prom, Kat is hurt and angry. She publicly reveals her feelings to Patrick and others in a poem she writes for her English class, and Patrick reconciles with her by using the money for their dates to buy Kat a guitar.

This free adaptation of *The Taming of the Shrew* to the conventions of the high school comedy reworks a number of Shakespearean motifs. The parallels between Shakespeare's main characters and Kat, Bianca, Patrick (Petruchio), and Walter (Baptista) are obvious, as are key plot points: Patrick's reputation as a bad boy; the financially motivated romance between Kat and Patrick; the fatherly stricture that the younger daughter can be courted only after the elder, shrewish daughter is courted; and the tempestuous nature of Kat and Patrick's relationship, particularly their sarcastic banter. Less obvious may be the relationship between minor characters and their counterparts—Cameron corresponds roughly to Lucentio, Michael Eckman (his friend) to Grumio, and Joey to Hortensio (as Hortensio's lute is smashed, so Joey's car is dented by Kat). Of interest is how the characters are significantly remotivated: Kat's shrewishness springs from an earlier sexually exploitative relationship with Joey; her father's concern about the daughters dating has its source in his work with teen pregnancy and his fears of his own aging (he makes the rule about Kat in hopes of stopping Bianca from dating at all); Bianca moves from being a vapid, self-centered popular girl attracted to Joey to a more mature woman attracted to Cameron; and Patrick develops a conscience about taking money to date Kat as he becomes more genuinely attracted to her. The film's great change in its source material is its treatment of shrew taming, which poses a problem for a modern teen audience. Unlike as in Shakespeare's play, in *10 Things* Kat never undergoes a taming regimen from Patrick; rather, she begins to open up emotionally to Patrick, becoming less bitter and more fun-loving as their relationship blossoms. Patrick too overcomes his own form of shrewishness in the film's course, making up for his earlier callousness by buying Kat the guitar she coveted and thereby supporting her artistic ambitions. When Kat objects that Patrick can't simply buy her off, he stops her mouth with a kiss, adopting but changing the motif of Kate and Petruchio's kiss. Only one direct citation from *The Taming of the Shrew* is included: upon first seeing Bianca, Cameron, like Lucentio, says, "I burn, I pine, I perish." However, there are other passing Shakespearean references. In English class, teacher Mr. Morgan recites the first lines of Sonnet 121 in rap style, then gives the class an assignment to write sonnets of their own. To encourage Patrick, Michael Eckman offers the first line of Sonnet 56, to which Patrick replies, "Don't say shit like that to me—people can hear you." Kat's friend Mandella is romantically obsessed with Shakespeare, and to woo her Michael quotes from *Macbeth* 2.3: "who could refrain, / That had a heart to love, and in that heart / Courage to make 's love known?" Later, Michael leaves Mandella an Elizabethan-style dress with a note from "William S." inviting her to the prom. An oblique reference to the situation comes with the song "Cruel to Be Kind" played at the prom. Gabrielle Union, who plays Bianca's friend Chastity, went on to play the lead in *Deliver Us from Eva* (below).

1327 *Charm School Brats*
2003. U.S. VCA. Sound, col., 104 mins. Jim Holliday.

Heath Ledger and Julia Stiles, the two principals from *10 Things I Hate about You* (1997), a *Taming of the Shrew* spin-off. Courtesy of Douglas Lanier.

Hardcore pornography. Spoiled bratty women are taught proper behavior at the Darwin Joston Charm School. One couple perform a pornographic version of the exchange between Kate and Petruchio in *The Taming of the Shrew*, 2.2. Shakespeare's dialogue is used, and they literalize some of the bawdy puns. (RB)

1328 *Deliver Us from Eva*
2003. U.S. Baltimore Spring Creek Productions and USA Films. Sound, col., 105 mins. Gary Hardwick.

Shrewish Eva Dandridge, eldest of the four Dandridge sisters, holds a tight rein over the lives of her sisters Bethany, Careena, and Jacqui, much to the irritation of their husbands, Mike, Tim, and Darrell respectively. In an effort to get Eva out of their lives and to get their hands on the sisters' trust fund, the three men contract with Ray Johnson, a meat delivery man who is a notorious player with women, to date Eva and then dump her. Ray, intrigued by Eva's sharp tongue and tough manner, agrees and soon falls in love with her. When the brothers discover that Eva has decided to decline an out-of-town job offer to remain with Ray and to use the trust fund for her and Ray, they abduct Ray and fake his death in hopes that Eva will accept the job. Ray escapes and reveals the plan to Eva, and follows her to beg forgiveness, giving her a white horse as a gift.

Deliver Us from Eva uses a number of motifs from Shakespeare's play (particularly the paid romance), though the narrative is quite freely developed and considerably remotivated. Eva has Katherine's exceptionally sharp tongue and brutally bitchy manner (like Katherine, she insists upon using full names), and Ray exudes Petruchio's cocky self-confidence and element of reversed expectation (like Petruchio at his wedding, Ray arrives for his first date with Eva in a meat delivery truck). Lucentio's blocked romance of Bianca is here divided up among three couples, in which all the husbands find their love lives thwarted by Eva's man-hating meddling, and the men, like Lucentio and Hortensio, offer Ray money to romance the shrew. This film adds an additional financial motive for the men in the form of the sisters' trust fund. As in *10 Things I Hate about You* (with which *Deliver Us* shares many affinities), the Kate character is not so much tamed as she recovers her potential for emotional intimacy after a traumatic earlier romance, and the Petruchio character, unable to commit to a long-term job or particular woman, falls in love with the woman he had earlier planned merely to trick. The ending of the film deviates considerably from Shakespeare's narrative, since Ray is forced by circumstance to make a sacrifice to woo Eva in earnest while she pursues her career (the man on the white horse also introduces the quality of a romantic fairy tale), but like *10 Things*, Eva states that she will not be bought off by Ray's gift even as she accepts it. Of special interest is the way in which the film engages conventional African American gender and class roles. (The commentary track reveals that the film was given an "urban" flavor in the director's rewrite.) Eva's shrewishness springs from her having taken the place of strong matriarch in the Dandridge clan after her parents died, and the advice she offers is intended to guard her sisters' upwardly mobile prospects in life—to get an education, avoid single parenthood, and avoid being loved and left before marriage. Ironically, the husbands are honorable in their intentions toward the sisters, so Eva's interventions actually undermine their relationships. That is, Eva's feminism has a distinct African American quality, but it is also presented as self-defeating, a trap that prevents Eva from pursuing her own emotional needs. Even though Ray is lionized by the men as a master playboy, that stereotypical role is revealed in the film's course as a liability, a symptom of Ray's own fears of abandonment, and he overcomes that role (or at least makes himself a sincere suitor) by film's end. Ray's role as a working-class meat delivery man and Eva's as a middle-class professional (a health inspector) are reminiscent of the class disposition of shrew and tamer in many Latin American films, though in this case Eva is not attracted to Ray because of his class status. (DL)

NB: Gabrielle Union, who plays the shrew Eva in *Deliver Us from Eva*, also played the widow character in *10 Things I Hate about You*. (RB)

1329 *Stormy Romance*
2004. U.S. Outback. Sound, col., 81 mins. Wesley Emerson.

Hardcore pornographic adaptation. Bernard, the owner of a rich California inn, has promised his late wife that he will not allow his daughter Bianca to marry until her bitchy sister Katherine (aka Kit) has a husband. Luke, the suitor of Bianca, encourages his friend Peter Rucchio to court Kit, while Bianca coaxes her father to pay Peter to marry her. Meanwhile, Kit teases and hits Peter to put him in his place; intrigued by Kit's feistiness, Peter refuses Bernard's payment, and Kit, impressed, warms to Peter. The two wed in a double marriage with Luke and Bianca. The entire story is told as a frame tale by a narrator to his sexual partner.

Many elements of Shakespeare's narrative are included: two daughters, the older of whom must be married before the younger; the financial arrangement that encourages Kit's somewhat unconventional suitor; the violent shrewishness of Kit, here motivated by her perception that men court her for her money; the eventual marriage of Kit and Peter (in this case, a willing one); even a frame tale, presented as an accoutrement to the narrator and his lover's tryst. There is an unusual amount of dialogue for a pornographic film, and it is in a faux-archaic style. Strikingly missing is the issue of taming Kit. Indeed, the story is constructed so that both Peter and Kit shed their "shrewishness" voluntarily. Sensing Kit's vitality, Peter rejects the financial motive for wooing her, and Kit, touched by Peter's interest in her personality and not her wealth, willingly sheds her bitchiness. Compare *The Taming of the Screw* (entry 1325).

1330 *Jail Babes #3*
1999. LFP Video. Sound, col., 136 mins. Elliot Heathcoat and Rick Rage.

Gloria Mann, the third actress to appear in this video, recites much of Kate's last speech in *The Taming of the Shrew*. She claims to have an MFA and to be a member of SAG. (RB)

THE TEMPEST

1331 *Shades of Shakespeare*
1919. U.S. Christie Film Corporation. Silent, b&w, length unknown. Director unknown.

No available information, though some commentators link the film to *The Tempest*. Starred Alice Lake.

1332 *The Tempest*
1920. U.S. Pathé. Silent, b&w, 2,000 ft. Director unknown.

A free melodramatic adaptation focusing on the Ferdinand and Miranda plotline. A man, thrown overboard in a stormy sea, washes ashore on an island. There he meets and falls in love with the daughter of a lighthouse keeper. He discovers that a boy he tries to protect is the girl's brother.

1333 *Full Fathom Five*
1937. U.K. Len Lye. Sound, col., 9 mins. Len Lye.

This early experimental film by a pioneer in color avant-garde film features hand-painted frames to accompany three passages from *The Tempest* read by John Gielgud.

1334 *The Four Feathers*
1939. U.K. London Film Corporation. Sound, col., 130 mins. Zoltan Korda.

Adapted from the novel by A.E.W. Mason. Doubtful about military service, Harry Faversham, son of a hero of the Crimean War, resigns his military commission just before his company is to venture to the Sudan. Three of his comrades, John Durrance, Arthur Willoughby, and Peter Burroughs, and his girlfriend Ethne present him with four white feathers as symbols of his cowardice. Disguised as an Arab tribesman, Harry secretly works for the British as a scout and heroically saves each of his comrades.

At the film's end, John Durrance, now blind, quotes Caliban's speech from *Tempest* 3.2, "Be not afeard; the isle is full of noises." The passage not only underlines the poignancy of Durrance's blindness (caused by the Sudanese campaign), but also suggests a redemption of poetry, since Harry Faversham was considered unfit for military service because he preferred poetry.

1335 *The Maltese Falcon*
1941. U.S. Warner Bros. Sound, b&w, 101 mins. John Huston.

Adapted from the novel by Dashiel Hammett. As hard-boiled detective Sam Spade investigates the murder of his partner Miles Archer and the mysterious Floyd Thursby, he is drawn into the search for the Maltese Falcon, a bejeweled statue also sought by three ruthless villains, Joel Cairo, Kaspar Gutman, and Brigid O'Shaughnessy.

One of Sam Spade's most famous lines, "the stuff that dreams are made of," is a misquotation from Prospero's speech in *The Tempest* 4.1, "We are such stuff as dreams are made on."

1336 *La Tempestad*
1943. Spain. CEPICSA. Sound, b&w, 84 mins. Javier de Rivera.

Adapted from a story by Miguel Ramos Carrión. This film, based on a *zarzuela* or operetta by Carrión (text) and Ruperto Chapi (music), is very loosely based on Shakespeare's play. On a stormy night a rich merchant stays in a harbor inn as he waits to embark on a journey. The innkeeper kills him for his money and lays suspicion on a young man, who escapes on a boat to America. Twenty years later, the accused man returns to seek revenge and justice.

1337 *Love Story* (aka *A Lady Surrenders*)
1944. U.K. Gainsborough Productions. Sound, b&w, 113 mins. Leslie Arliss.

On the eve of leaving to help the war effort with a concert tour, Felicity Crichton, a pianist, learns that she has three months to live. Under the assumed name Lissa Campbell, Felicity goes to Cornwall, and at the resort hotel meets several guests, among them Kit Firth, an amateur archaeologist with whom she falls in love. Their romance is blocked by the fact that Kit is unaccountably cold toward her, a fact later explained when she learns that he is going blind and wants no emotional entanglements. Also complicating matters is Kit's friend Judy, an actress from London who secretly loves Kit and is jealous of his feelings for Lissa. Lissa learns that Judy has talked Kit out of a dangerous operation to restore his sight, and in an effort to change his mind, she tells Judy she will forsake Kit if he undergoes the operation. Kit's operation is successful, and Lissa thereby leaves Cornwall. When attending one of Lissa's concerts, Judy sees Kit's reaction to her; she realizes that he truly loves her, and Kit and Lissa become reunited.

Throughout, we see rehearsals for an open-air production of *The Tempest* in which Judy will appear. The stage is situated on the rocky cliffs in a Roman amphitheater that Judy restores. Of the rehearsals we see very briefly two songs by Ariel, and Prospero's command to restore the ship's crew in Act 5. The performance is interrupted when Judy, waiting for a phone call from London about Kit's condition, cannot perform. The Shakespearean scenes are only tangentially related to the film, though it is possible to see some characters as distant analogues for Shakespeare's. Kit and Lissa, for example, might be seen as types of Ferdinand and Miranda, since their romance is so closely linked to the sea; Tony Tanner, an elderly mining industrialist, and Judy correspond very roughly to Prospero and Miranda, since he offers her fatherly advice and attempts to engineer Kit and Lissa's romance. (In the play, Judy plays Miranda.) The script makes very little of these tenuous parallels.

1338 *The Yellow Canary*
1944. U.S. Imperator Pictures. Sound, b&w, 98 mins. Herbert Wilcox.

Pretending to be friendly with the Third Reich as war as been declared, Sally Maitland is actually a British agent working to uncover a Nazi spy operation in Canada; as she works on the case, she falls in love with British intelligence officer Jim Garrick.

Includes a passing reference to Caliban's speech, "Be not afeard; the isle is full of noises" (*Tempest* 3.2).

1339 *Yellow Sky*
1948. U.S. 20th Century Fox and Lamar Trotti Productions. Sound, b&w, 98 mins. William A. Wellman.

Adapted from the novel by W. R. Burnett. A six-man gang headed by Stretch Dawson robs a bank and is chased by a garrison cavalry onto the salt flat. Desperate for water, the gang stumbles onto Yellow Sky, a ghost town inhabited only by an old prospector and his gun-toting, tomboy granddaughter Constance Mae (aka "Mike"). Stretch and Mike are attracted, though their relationship is tense, and Stretch defends her against the other men, particularly the lusty outlaw Lengthy. When the men put together that the prospector is hiding a fortune in gold, Dude tries to take control of the gang and steal the gold, but Stretch makes a deal to split the gold with the prospector and his grand-daughter. Soon Stretch, having fallen in love with Mike and been shown goodwill by the prospector when Apaches arrive, sides with the two, but Dude, having learned of his good intentions, takes over the gang and vows to hunt down Stretch. In the ensuing gunfight, one of the men is killed and two others ally themselves with Stretch, leaving Dude and Lengthy to fight it out with each other and Stretch. Stretch wins the gunfight, returns the gold to the bank he earlier robbed, and gives Mike a wo-man's hat.

The opening scenario of *Yellow Sky* bears several key resemblances to *The Tempest*, though its narrative deviates significantly from Shakespeare's, and more so as the film goes on. Stretch's gang, from whose perspective the tale is told, with its collection of mutually divisive, upwardly mobile men, is not unlike Alonso's party in *The Tempest*, with greedy Dude and brutish Lengthy taking the roles of the usurping conspirators Antonio and Sebastian. The prospector and his feisty, sexually naïve granddaughter mirror Prospero and Miranda, though the prospector is quite powerless in the face of the gang's threat. Stretch has Alonso's position of leadership, and his first advance to-ward Mike is a Calibanish sexual assault, but he soon becomes the sensitive Ferdinand to her Miranda, a parallel strengthened when we learn that his father died in his

youth. The decrepit town of Yellow Sky, a barely civilized oasis in the barren salt flat, is the equivalent of Prospero's isolated island; the claustrophobia of the setting adds to the narrative's tension. The film uses the political usur-pation plot centered on Alonso and the romance plot of Ferdinand and Miranda as its basic armatures, but then develops both freely according to the generic conventions of the Western. Central to its concerns is Stretch's struggle between two models for behavior: the tough outlaw who can too easily descend into Caliban-like sa-vagery and treachery, or the civilized cowboy who loves and defends his woman and is willing to live by a code of mutual trust with the prospector. Compare *The Jackals* (below).

1340 *Fear and Desire*
1953. U.S. Kubrick. Sound, b&w, 68 mins.
Stanley Kubrick.

Four soldiers, Lieutenant Corby, Sergeant MacLellan, and Privates Fletcher and Sidney, crash six miles behind enemy lines and scheme to use a nearby river to sail to safety during the night. In the midst of their escape at-tempt, they are spotted by a young woman whom they are forced to take prisoner and who Sidney eventually kills. They are further distracted by MacLellan's obsession with killing an enemy general he sees through his binoculars, a plan for which he willingly sacrifices his life. After Corby and Fletcher kill the general, they float to safety with Sidney (now insane) and the dead body of MacLellan.

Kubrick's first feature film, never commercially released, includes a re-ference to *The Tempest*. When Sidney is left to guard the unnamed woman (who is tied to a tree), he tells her the story of *The Tempest* to communicate with and entertain her; later he embraces her. When the men return, he is offering her water from his hand. After Sidney shoots her when she attempts to escape and thereafter becomes deranged, he mutters that Prospero has killed the girl. The sequence suggests oblique parallels and contrasts with the story of Prospero freeing Ariel from the tree in *The Tempest* 1.2.

1341 *Forbidden Planet*
1956. U.S. MGM. Sound, col., 98 mins.
Fred Wilcox.

In the twenty-third century, J. J. Adams commands the United Planets spaceship *C57D* on its mission to rescue the survivors of the spaceship *Bellero-phon*, which crash landed twenty years

Gregory Peck (left) and others in *Yellow Sky* (1948). This shot shows Peck and his outlaw gang with the old prospector and his daughter (all of whom have correspondences to characters from *The Tempest*). This film was one of the bigger-budget Shakespeare Wes-terns. Courtesy of Douglas Lanier.

earlier on the planet Altair 4. Upon arriving, Adams and crew discover only Dr. Morbius, the ship's philologist, and his daughter Altaira alive, assisted only by an astonishingly advanced robot, Robby, and living in a small, Edenic, yet futuristic paradise. Morbius resists being rescued, and Adams discovers that his ship's radio equipment has been damaged by a mysterious force, preventing him from contacting Earth. Soon Morbius reveals that Altair 4 was once inhabited by the Krel, an intellectually advanced race whose equipment Morbius has used to increase his intelligence and shape his environment. But Adams discovers that the equipment also amplifies Morbius's unconscious mind, creating a fearsome "monster from the Id" that attacks his ship out of Morbius's irrational jealousy over Adams's budding romance with Altaira. Realizing the truth and the danger the Krel equipment poses, Morbius vows to destroy the equipment, which he does after Adams's spaceship (with Altaira aboard) reaches a safe distance.

J. J. Adams (the Ferdinand character) and a couple of spacemen, Morbius (the Prospero character), and his daughter Alta (the Miranda character) from *Forbidden Planet* (1956). Courtesy of Douglas Lanier.

Though some scholars have doubted the attribution, writers of *Forbidden Planet* have explicitly identified *The Tempest* as one of their sources. Though the adaptation is quite free, there are many correspondences in the film's basic scenario: Morbius stands in for the irascible intellectual-magician Prospero, Altaira for his daughter Miranda, Robby the Robot for Ariel, the "monster from the Id" for Caliban, J. J. Adams for Ferdinand, the alcohol-loving Cook for Trinculo and Stephano, and the isolated planet for Prospero's island. There are no corresponding characters to Alonso, Gonzalo, Sebastian, and Antonio, and the usurpation plot has been eliminated, so that the focus falls more squarely on the relationship between Prospero and his maturing daughter Miranda, and her budding romance with Ferdinand, initially blocked by Prospero. Indeed, the film's narrative is told from the perspective of the Ferdinand character rather than from Prospero's perspective as in Shakespeare's version. Morbius's scientific coldness and technocratic superiority spring from his arrogant unwillingness to acknowledge the irrational elements of his nature (just as Prospero is unwilling to confront his impulse to revenge until Ariel reminds him of it in 5.1). Whereas Shakespeare seems to stress Prospero's magical power, borne of his intellect and books, and his growing moral self-knowledge, *Forbidden Planet* questions that power by stressing Morbius's vulnerability to the unconscious Id, unwittingly triggered by Morbius's jealous reaction to Adams's attraction to Altaira and his desire to rule over the planet. As such, *Forbidden Planet* can be read as a critique of the cult of humanist intellectual power that *The Tempest* seems principally to celebrate. This critique, it should be added, has its own

blind spots: Morbius's elitist scientific mind-set is set against J. J. Adams's "commonsense" middle-class and American sensibility, a sensibility that leads him to treat the independent Altaira rather puritanically and paternally; Adams also doesn't acknowledge his own will to power or the destructive, imperialistic potential of his own technology (he is a military man, after all). But within the context of the post-war nuclear age, the film's critique of the godlike intellectual who wields but does not control enormous power has special resonance. *Forbidden Planet* is one of the most important films in the history of science fiction, one that lifted the genre out of its B-film status, and its Shakespearean pedigree contributes to that special stature. See also entry 216.

1342 *The Jackals*
1967. South Africa. 20th Century Fox and Killarney Film Studios. Sound, col., 96 mins. Robert D. Webb.

Adapted from the novel by W. R. Burnett. A very close if wooden "voortrekker" remake of *Yellow Sky* (above), with the action transferred to the South African Transvaal. Names are altered—the prospector becomes Oopa, Mike becomes Willy (aka "Wilhemina"), and the town Yellow Sky becomes Yellow Rock—and African details are added and scenes intercut with shots of African wildlife and tribes, but the film often duplicates the dialogue, shots, and even acting business of its source film. Vincent Price brings a certain loopiness to the role of the grizzled prospector, and the oddly sweet soundtrack music eliminates the edginess in the romance between Stretch and the prospector's daughter. For the relationship between the film and *The Tempest*, see the discussion in the entry for *Yellow Sky*.

1343 *Age of Consent*
1969. Australia. Columbia Pictures. Sound, col., 98 mins. Michael Powell.

Adapted from the novel by Norman Lindsay. Bradley Morahan, a testy, middle-aged Australian painter living in New York City, yearns for inspiration and leaves for an isolated island in Queensland. There he lives alone with his dog Godfrey, until he discovers several other inhabitants of the island: Isabel Morley, a lonely middle-aged woman, with her dog Jasper, and Ma Ryan, a drunken hag, and her beautiful daughter Cora. After buying food from Cora, Bradley resolves to paint her, often in the nude; Cora consents because she is saving to leave for Brisbane and become a hairdresser. Their painting is temporarily interrupted when Bradley's boorish old friend Nat Kelly arrives unannounced, moves in, and begs Bradley for money to settle his many debts. When Isabel gets too aggressive in pursuing Nat romantically, he leaves, stealing Bradley's drawings and money. When Ma Ryan sees Cora pose nude for Bradley, she accuses him of seducing Cora (who is underage) and attempts to blackmail him, but she accidentally falls off a cliff and dies. A cop arrives to return Bradley's wallet and paintings, having arrested Nat, and his investigation clears Bradley and Cora. When Bradley seeks to paint again with Cora as model, she coaxes him to consummate their hitherto chaste relationship.

Though only tangentially related to *The Tempest*, *Age of Consent* does rework various motifs from Shakespeare's play. In some respects the artist Bradley resembles Prospero (who speaks of his magic "art"); Cora, his independent, daughter-like muse, has qualities of both Miranda and Ariel; Cora's grandmother has qualities of Caliban and Sycorax; and Nat Kelly bears some resemblance to the comical, scheming pair Trinculo and Stephano. Though Bradley's exile to the island is entirely voluntary, the island itself, with its fecundity and natural beauty, is reminiscent of Prospero's isle. Like several other free adaptations of *The Tempest*, the focus falls upon the intense relationship between Prospero and Miranda, here treated as a relationship between a fatherly artist and his daughterly muse. In his films Powell is often interested in barely repressed or displaced erotic energy, and so it is unsurprising that he here explores the erotic undercurrent of Bradley and Cora's relationship (an undercurrent also present in Shakespeare's play), though the two remain utterly chaste until the last few seconds of the film. Interestingly, Cora's one chance for a relationship with a Ferdinand figure, the hunky young boatswain who ferries her and Bradley to the island, turns out to be a comedy of sexual boorishness, and she rejects him. (Isabel's "seduction" of Nat provides the female counterpart to this motif.) Recasting *The Tempest* as a narrative of middle-aged male renewal is also the strategy of Mazursky's *Tempest* (below). Helen Mirren, who plays Cora, is identified in the credits as a member of the Royal Shakespeare Company.

1344 *The Tempest*
1979. U.K. Never produced. Color, length undetermined. George Dunning.

By the director of *Yellow Submarine*. Animated feature left incomplete at Dunning's death in 1979, though fragments survive. Source: www.screenonline.co.uk.

1345 *The Amateur*
1981. U.S. 20th Century Fox. Sound, col., 112 mins. Charles Jarrott.

Adapted from the novel by Robert Littell. Charles Heller, a computer expert for the CIA, uses the threat of exposing what he knows to force the agency to train him as an assassin, so that he can avenge the murder of his girlfriend Sarah Kaplan, who was killed in a terrorist raid on the U.S. Embassy in Munich. When he is sent behind the Iron Curtain, he discovers that her death is part of a larger, more sinister plot.

Professor Lakos, Heller's nemesis and an Eastern European spymaster, gives a lecture attempting to prove that Francis Bacon wrote Shakespeare's plays. His text is Prospero's epilogue from *The Tempest*. The notion of secret authorship gibes with the film's theme that things are not what they seem.

1346 *Tempest*
1982. U.S. Columbia Pictures. Sound, col., 140 mins. Paul Mazursky.

Philip Dimitrios, a middle-aged architect, becomes increasingly disillusioned with his work for Alonzo, a boorish, thuggish developer, and estranged from his wife Antonia, a former actress, and his pop culture–obsessed daughter Miranda. When Philip quits his job and separates from Antonia after a storm, she begins to date Alonzo, and Philip decides to move to Greece with Miranda, where he becomes romantically involved with Aretha Tomalin, a free-spirited singer who, after two failed marriages, finds herself stranded in Athens. When Alonzo and Antonia track Philip down in Athens, intending to force him to return Miranda to her mother, Philip, Miranda, and Aretha flee to a deserted Greek island inhabited only by Kalibanos, a daft goatherd who lives in a cave. On the island, Philip focuses on rebuilding an outdoor amphitheater as Aretha and Miranda become increasingly bored; Kalibanos attempts unsuccessfully to seduce Miranda, for which Philip beats him. Soon Alonzo, Antonia, and others in his retinue arrive in his yacht off the island, not knowing that Philip is there. Alonzo's son Freddy and Miranda, both alienated teens, meet while swimming and are instantly attracted to each other. When Kalibanos sees that the remainder of Alonzo's retinue are about to arrive by boat on the island, Philip conjures a storm and all are thrown overboard, though all survive. Philip reveals his presence to the group and sacrifices a goat because of the miracle of their salvation. Afterward, all the principals share an elaborate dance at Philip's villa, and Philip asks for their forgiveness. All leave the island, and Miranda gives Freddy her phone number.

Mazursky uses Shakespeare's play as a rough template for this seriocomic drama of male midlife crisis. Philip resembles Prospero (on the island, he wears a bathrobe that corresponds to Prospero's magic robe); Aretha, Ariel (his newfound erotic muse); and the names of many of the other characters identify their counterparts in *The Tempest*. In this version Kalibanos is less monstrous than comic, a modernized version of Pan (he plays a clarinet to serenade his goats). The unusually structured narrative moves between several flashbacks in New York and Athens, filling in the details of Philip's dissatisfaction with his life, and the present on the isolated island, where the parallels between Shakespeare's narrative and Philip's midlife idyll come into clearest focus. Though the dialogue is modern and often has the improvisational quality of rambling conversation, many sequences clearly have their origins in Shakespeare's script: Philip regards Antonia's romance with Alonzo as the ultimate betrayal, an act that prompts him to leave for Greece; in flashback, we see the early progress of the relationship between Kalibanos and Philip that mirrors closely the history given by Prospero in 1.2 (the dialogue even includes details from Prospero's speech about caring for and teaching Caliban); Philip conjures the tempest with the line "Show me the magic"; after the tempest, Kalibanos, hiding under a octopus, is visited in his cave by Trinc, a second-rate comedian, and his friend Sebastian, who observe that he looks like a man-fish and share his wine; Dolores, a buxom blonde who is part of Alonzo's retinue, offers a version of Gonzalo's "utopia" speech in 2.1 after the tempest; and the final dance at Philip's villa concerns his desire to let go of his anger at Antonia and seek forgiveness of those from his past, even Kalibanos. Indeed, it is Philip's choice between his desire for isolation and quasi-tyrannical power over the tiny island, and his need to reconcile with those he feels have wronged him, that most deeply connects with the themes of *The Tempest*. At the end of the film, a Greek sailor delivers an epilogue (in Greek) and the film players all take a bow, breaking the cinematic illusion of realism (as Shakespeare breaks the theatrical illusion with Prospero's epilogue). Three passing references to other Shakespeare plays are of note: early on, in a conversation a vapid producer (played by Mazursky himself) speaks of his new production as a cross between *A Chorus Line* and *Macbeth*, at which Miranda observes that she has been studying *Macbeth* in school and finds it boring; on the wall in the Dimitrios apartment hangs a poster from

a show entitled *Such Sweet Sorrow*, an allusion to Juliet's famous parting remark to Romeo in the balcony scene; and at the moment where Philip faces the disintegration of his marriage, a storm blows up and he seems impotently to conjure it, alluding obliquely to Lear on the heath. Compare *Age of Consent* (entry 1343).

1347 *The Little Mermaid*
1989. U.S. Buena Vista, Silver Screen Partners IV, and Walt Disney Productions. Sound, col., 83 mins. Ron Clements and John Musker.

Adapted from the tale by Hans Christian Andersen. In this animated film, Ariel, a young mermaid, has fallen in love with Prince Eric, a human being, despite the fact that Ariel's father, Triton, the king of the sea, has forbidden contact between her and the human world. To pursue her love, she contracts with Ursula, the evil seahag, to become human, but if the prince will not give her a kiss before the sun sets on the third day, Ariel will have to give her haunting singing voice to the octopus. When Triton sees the devotion of his daughter, he turns her into a human so that she and Eric can live happily ever after.

As is the case with *Aladdin*, several of the characters bear names from a Shakespearean play, in this case *The Tempest*. Though Ariel has the name of Prospero's servant spirit, she acts more like Miranda, defying her father in order to be with her lover; moreover, Eric is first attracted to Ariel by her song, a detail that recalls Ariel's siren songs to Ferdinand in *The Tempest* 1.2. Ursula bears a general resemblance to Sycorax, and Sebastian, the crab who is Ariel's loyal companion, incongruously has the name of Alonso's treacherous brother. That there is in fact a Shakespearean subtext to this adaptation of a Hans Christian Andersen fairy tale is unclear.

1348 *Resan till Melonia (Journey to Melonia)*
1989. Sweden. Film Teknik, Filmhuset, Läskonsten, Norsk Filmstudio A/S, Penn Film, Skrivstugan, and SVT 2. Sound, col., 101 mins. Per Åhlin.

The wizard Prospero lives in exile in a treehouse on the tropical island of Melonia with his daughter, Miranda; Ariel the albatross; Caliban, a monster made of vegetables; and a theater-loving dog named William. A storm brings several pairs separately to his island: Captain Christmas Tree and the boat's cook; Ferdinand and the boatswain; and two evil capitalists, Slagg and Slug. Prospero gives Caliban a magical growth elixir for safekeeping, but Slagg and Slug see him use it and kidnap Caliban to their island of Plutonia, a polluted industrial wasteland where robots force children to work building missiles. Slagg and Slug intend to use Caliban's elixir to take over Melonia, but Caliban escapes, drinks the elixir, and becomes a giant. Meanwhile, Prospero and his friends travel to Plutonia to rescue Caliban, but after Miranda frees the worker-children by turning them into birds, the group gets sidetracked by William's impromptu production of *The Tempest* in an abandoned theater. Caliban thwarts the plans of Slagg and Slug by turning their drilling machine on Plutonia and destroying it, and he saves Prospero and the others from a whirlpool by pushing them to Melonia in the theater. Prospero gives Ferdinand Miranda's hand, frees Caliban and Ariel, and gives over his magic.

Resan till Melonia grafts *The Tempest* onto a cautionary tale about the evils of military industrial capitalism. Beyond the obvious parallels, Slagg and Slug correspond to Antonio and Sebastian, seeking to usurp Prospero's benevolent and environmentally sound stewardship of Melonia, but their bumbling comedy also reminds the viewer of Trinculo and Stephano. The first half of the film remains relatively faithful to Shakespeare's narrative; various motifs—the shipwreck, Prospero's reassurance of Miranda about the storm, Ariel as Prospero's magical comrade, Caliban as servile and disgruntled monster, the attraction between Ferdinand and Miranda, and Trinculo and Stephano's trickery of Caliban with liquor and flattery—appear in minimally changed form. However, Caliban is handled as a lovable monster, and it is he, not Prospero, who finally saves the day, interestingly enough, by co-opting Prospero's magic (by drinking his elixir). The theme of freedom extends beyond Caliban and Ariel to the worker-children whom Miranda liberates with her own magic (Prospero's magic is largely ineffective in Plutonia). Beyond the Plutonia plot that preoccupies the second half of the film, there is the interesting meta-adaptational addition of William the dog. Stagestruck, William plots throughout to put on a show of his own—there is a picture of William Shakespeare over his bed, his room has the

quality of an elaborate set, and he fits an abandoned crate as a makeshift stage. In Plutonia, he finds a script of *The Tempest* and attempts to perform the play to an audience of the freed worker-children in an abandoned theater, with comically disastrous results, at once identifying the film's source as Shakespeare's play (the characters recognize themselves in the plot) and offering a parody of its performance. Several passages in Åhlin's script loosely correspond to those in Shakespeare, particularly the opening scene on the storm-tossed ship.

1349 *Prospero's Books*
1991. U.K. Allarts Enterprises, Caméra One, Canal+, Cinea, Elservier-Vendex, Film Four International, Miramax, NHK, Penta Film, and VPRO-TV. Sound, col., 124 mins. Peter Greenaway.

An utterly dazzling post-modern reenvisioning of *The Tempest*. Greenaway structures the film around Prospero's twenty-four magical books, each of which is a source of visual imagery and myth, and he pictures Prospero as he writes the text of Shakespeare's play from them, imagining the action of the narrative into being. Prospero speaks all of Shakespeare's dialogue (except in the final act), his voice electronically modified much of the time; Caliban is a grotesque, nearly nude dancer; and Alonso and men wear preposterously large ruffs, striking poses out of golden age Dutch paintings, Ariel is played by four different actors (reflecting different aspects of his character), and Prospero's retinue of spirits is represented by a wide range of nude actors and dancers. But the star of the film is Greenaway's encyclopedic collection of arresting visual images, many culled from art history and myth, which the camera surveys in long tracking shots as Prospero speaks the text and the characters play their parts. (See, for example, the opening credits shot.) Michael Nyman's jaunty minimalist, at time vaguely Baroque score lends the film a ritualistic, period-and-not-quite-period quality. The film follows Shakespeare's narrative very closely (inserting commentary about the twenty-four books), but the action of the play is treated as a starting point for Greenaway's fecund visual imagination; that is, Greenaway's principal interest is in the visual poetry of Shakespeare's play and its place in cultural history rather than in the story line. The images themselves are overwhelmingly dense, superimposed on each other, modified by computer enhancement, covered with calligraphy, poised between animation and still photographs, and photographed in exceptionally saturated color. In the final act,

John Gielgud as Prospero from *Prospero's Books* (1991). In this shot, Prospero is about to open one of his magic books, while dancers frolic in the background. Courtesy of Douglas Lanier.

Prospero gives his characters freedom by allowing them their own voices, and when he discards his final book (*The Tempest* itself), it is Caliban—perhaps a stand-in for the avant-gardist Greenaway himself—who retrieves it. See also entry 521.

1350 *Trois couleurs: Rouge (Red)*
1993. Poland and Switzerland. CAB Productions, Canal Plus, Eurimages, France 3 Cinema, MK2 Productions, Swiss Ministry of Culture, Tor, and TSR. Sound, col., 99 mins. Krysztof Kieslowski.

As the result of her hitting a dog with her car, Valentine Dussaut, a lonely fashion model, meets Joseph Kern, a bitter retired judge who secretly listens to other people's phone conversations in his home. One of the people on whom Kern eavesdrops is Auguste Bruner, a judge-in-training who is having a love affair with Karin and a neighbor of Valentine's. As a result of Kern's meeting with Valentine, he turns himself in, leading to the meeting of Karin with another man and her breakup with Auguste. Valentine learns that as a younger man, Kern was betrayed in love; he dreams that Valentine will find happiness with a judge. After a ferry accident on a stormy night, Valentine and Auguste meet (they are among the few survivors) and Kern weeps.

In Annette Insdorf's commentary track for the DVD release, she makes the connection between Kern and Prospero. Though the association is certainly oblique, it is interesting: Kern has a godlike quality, spying on those around him, but he has become embittered by betrayal in his past and later is even tempted to take revenge upon his (romantic) rival; he is linked with personal weather reports he hears on the phone; he comes to regard Valentine as a substitute daughter; and he turns himself in to the authorities, a form of Prospero breaking his staff and drowning his books. Most important, in the film's final sequence, he seems somehow responsible for the tempest and shipwreck that bring Valentine and Auguste (a younger version of himself) together, much like Miranda and Ferdinand. Certainly the film is not a thoroughgoing adaptation—there are no parallels to Caliban, Ariel, the Neapolitans, or Stephano and Trinculo—but the central themes of the film, the mysterious forces through which destined human connections are made, have affinities to *The Tempest*.

1351 *The Avengers*
1998. U.S. Warner Bros. Sound, col., 89 mins. Jeremiah S. Chechik.

In this film adaptation of the classic television series, John Steed, agent for the British Ministry, and Mrs. Emma Peel, a former government scientist, battle villain Sir August de Wynter, a mad scientist who intends to inflict destructive weather on London unless he's paid a ransom. Along the way, Steed and Peel uncover the complicity of Father, one of the heads of the ministry, in de Wynter's plans, and Peel and Steed encounter evil clones of Mrs. Peel. Several campy Shakespearean references spice up this ill-considered action film. De Wynter's weather program is called the Prospero project (Steed identifies the reference as Shakespearean for the audience). De Wynter's threatening speech to the British Council begins with the phrase "Now is the winter of your discontent," and when Steed and Peel find one of de Wynter's victims (in a neon-colored teddy-bear suit), they have this campy exchange:

STEED: "Alas, poor Teddy."
PEEL: "I knew him, Steed."

1352 *Illuminata*
1999. U.S. GreeneStreet Films and Overseas Filmgroup. Sound, col., 119 mins. John Turturro.

A backstage drama involving the production of *Illuminata*, a play newly written by Tuccio, an arrogant young playwright, for the troupe's lead actress Rachel. Though the troupe's owners think that the play has no ending, when one of the actors, Piero, collapses in midperformance of an Ibsen play, Tuccio is given a chance to produce his play. Unfortunately, Bevalaqua, a gay critic interested in Marco, the troupe's clown, savages the production, even though Celimeme, a preening prima donna, leads Tuccio on by promising him success and fame. The lives of the actors intertwine with Tuccio's play and enrich its performance. Several other subplots, most involving romances between cast members, complicate the play's production.

As he is being arrested, Old Flavio, an aging actor (and Rachel's father) who is losing his memory, performs lines from *The Tempest*. Of an actor who defends him, he says, "This thing of darkness I acknowledge mine." He then delivers Caliban's "The isle is full of noises" speech, as the company's manager Pallenchio also speaks the lines with him. The speech articulates Flavio's idealistic nature, though he resembles Prospero far more than Caliban. Later, discussing Tuccio's poor ending with Rachel, Pallenchio rehearses great tragic endings, including the endings of *Othello* and *Hamlet*.

1353 *Beginner's Luck*
2001. U.K. Angel Film & Television, Angle Eye, and Late Night Pictures. Sound, col., 84 mins. James Callis and Nick Cohen.

A black comic backstage chronicle of the Vagabond Theatre Company, as they tour London, Edinburgh, and Paris with a disastrous amateur production of *The Tempest*.

The film features passages of *The Tempest* in performance, as well as snippets of *Stormy Weather*, a rival company's musical version of the same play. Also, a recurring metaphor in the film, of the dream of an island, is linked to the play.

1354 *Je rentre à la maison* (*I'm Going Home*)
2001. Portugal and France. Artificial Eye, France 2
Cinema, Gemini Films, and Madragoa Filmes. Sound,
col., 90 mins. Manoel de Oliveira.

A quiet psychological study of the melancholy of age
and loss. After starring in a performance of Eugene Ionesco's *Exit the King*, Gilbert Vance, a famous and aging
actor, learns that his wife, daughter, and son-in-law have
died in a car accident, and afterward he becomes the
guardian of the sole survivor, his grandson, who provides
him with moments of joy as he uses routine to stave off
grief. When his performance as Prospero in *The Tempest* is
well reviewed, he gets many offers of work and takes the
part of Buck Mulligan in a Hollywood film adaptation of
James Joyce's *Ulysses*. Struggling with the part and finding
that grief and exhaustion have caught up with him, he
leaves the production and has a breakdown. Along the
way, he resists the possibility of an affair with Sylvie Leo-
nor, his co-star in the Ionesco play. We see Vance's performance of Prospero's "our revels now are ended" speech
(in French) from *The Tempest* 4.1. The speech's themes—
of the insecurity of the world, of age, of theater's essential
insubstantiality—and the character of Prospero are clearly
appropriate to Vance's situation (as is his role as the King
in *Exit the King*). That the part is played by Michel Piccoli,
a beloved French actor at the end of his career, and was
directed by Oliveira at the age of ninety-two, gives special
resonance to the narrative.

The DVD includes a commentary track by Professor
Richard Peña and an interview with Oliveira that reference Shakespeare.

1355 *Blade II*
2002. U.S. New Line. Sound, col., 117 mins. Guillermo del
Toro.

There is a brief allusion to *The Tempest* when we see
Blade walk into the vampire headquarters, named "Cali-
ban Industries." Deleted scenes on the DVD include
"Caliban Elevator" and "Whistler Discovers Caliban."
(RB)

TROILUS AND CRESSIDA

1356 *Troilus and Cressida*
Late 1960s. U.S. Film was never produced. Gail MacDer-
mott and Tom O'Horgan.

McDermott and O'Horgan (the writers and producers of
Hair) sought to make an operatic film version of Shakespeare's play near Lake Powell in Bryce Canyon, Arizona.
The film never moved beyond the pre-production phase,
but materials related to the production are housed at the
Folger Shakespeare Library. Of historical interest, given
the rock musicalization of Shakespeare in such shows as

Catch My Soul and *Your Own Thing*. The film was to have
an antiwar theme.

TWELFTH NIGHT

1357 *A Letter to Three Wives*
1949. U.S. 20th Century Fox and Sol C. Siegel. Sound,
b&w, 103 mins. Joseph L. Mankiewicz.

Adapted from the novel by John Klempner. As they are
about to embark on a charity picnic cruise, three wives and
close friends, Deborah Bishop, Rita Phipps, and Lora May
Hollinsway, receive a letter from their friend Addie Ross
announcing that she will be leaving town with one of their
husbands. Since each wife knows her husband is currently
away, the letter prompts a series of flashbacks, with each
anatomizing their troubled marriages as each wonders
whether she might be the one to be abandoned. Newlywed
Deborah feels out of place with her well-established husband Brad; social-climbing Rita, a businesswoman in radio
advertising, seems mismatched with her bookish husband
George, an English professor; and Lora May, of working-
class background, worries about being abandoned by her
husband Porter, a boorish executive. Despite their anxieties, the women learn that Addie has not taken off with
any of their husbands.

The Shakespearean allusions are all linked to George, who
early in the film complains about the low pay of teachers:
"How does [a schoolteacher] pay the rent with the plays and
poems of Shakespeare?" For his birthday, Addie sends
George a record with a note that quotes the opening of
Twelfth Night, "If music be the food of love, play on." (By
contrast, Rita forgets his birthday.) Later we learn that the
quotation is a remembrance of Addie and George playing in
Twelfth Night in high school. When Rita returns to her home,
George tells her that he was away directing a high school
production of *Twelfth Night*; this revelation explains Addie's
Shakespearean inscription, which George quotes yet again.

1358 *Nichts als Sünde*
1965. Germany. DEFA. Sound, col., 106 mins. Hanus
Burger.

A musical version of the play, set in modern Germany.

1359 *Shakespeare's Plan 12 from Outer Space* (aka *Shakespeare's Plan 10 from Outer Space*)
1991. U.S. Charles Montgomery "Spike" Stewart. Sound,
col., and b&w, 50 mins. Charles Montgomery "Spike"
Stewart.

This little-known cult film melds Shakespeare's *Twelfth
Night* with a no-budget science fiction film to create a zany,
if crude, Shakespearean parody. Kay Lenz doubles as Viola
and Sebastian, and Buck Henry, the well-known American
comic writer, plays a priest. Stewart's use of many software
optical effects gives the film a hallucinogenic quality, and

the use of a laugh track pushes it in the direction of bad television comedy.

1360 *Food of Love*
1997. U.K. and France. Arts Council of England, Canal Plus, Channel 4, Film Four Distributors, Intrinsica Films, and MP Productions. Sound, col., 108 mins. Stephen Poliakoff.

Alex Salmon, an assistant bank manager and part-time theater instructor who finds himself increasingly frustrated by his job, resolves to gather up the cast of a college production of *Twelfth Night* he directed years earlier and to restage the production in a small English village. Several of the cast members (chief among them Sam and Madeleine, and Alex and Michele) rekindle earlier romances, two of the teens he recruits battle attitude and accent issues, one of the cast members dies and another comes down with a debilitating ailment, and the villagers disdain and actively disrupt the production. Even so, the group rallies to bring off the performance.

The film centers around Alex's production of *Twelfth Night*, and, unsurprisingly, we see several scenes of rehearsal and portions of two different performances, one for a prison audience (who are appreciative), the other for the village (who are polite after Alex interrupts the production to chastise them). Several passages from *Twelfth Night* take on added significance in their context: Viola's speech about the lover "who never told her love" (2.4) becomes William's last words before he dies during a nostalgic reverie about youth; Viola's line "I would be loath to cast away my speech, for besides that it is excellently well penned, I have taken great pains to con it" is spoken by Jessica as she tries to remove her working-class accent; Sam confesses his desire for Madeleine to Jessica, just as Orsino confesses his desire for Olivia to Viola; Malvolio's torture by Sir Thopas in prison is especially moving for the prison audience; and in the village performance, Maria's speech regarding Malvolio's faults in 2.3 is spoken by Michele to Alex and becomes her way of expressing her feelings for him. The film avoids the cliché of having the actors mirror the characters they are playing or their story mirror the narrative of *Twelfth Night*, though at times passing resemblances appear between some members of the company and Shakespearean characters—Alex has a bit of Malvolio, Madeleine (who initially rebuffs Sam's advances) of Olivia, Jessica of Viola (she pretends to have a different accent), and Sam of Orsino. Rather, the essentially melancholy tone of Shakespeare's comedy is mirrored in Poliakoff's narrative, which emphasizes how Alex's exercise in group nostalgia is motivated ultimately by his midlife world-weariness and fear of death. The deeply ambivalent portrayal of the company's fleeting "success" and the unresolved nature of the rekindled romances are unusual for films of this ilk. Compare *In the Bleak Midwinter* and *Beginner's Luck*.

1361 *The Playboy Twelfth Night*
See Richard Burt, *Unspeakable ShaXXXspeares* (New York: St. Martin's Press, 1998), 93–106.

1362 *Play On!*
2000. U.S. USA Pictures. Sound, col., length unknown. Gary Halvorson.

Vy travels from Mississippi to jazz age Harlem to get a job writing songs. When she discovers that men dominate songwriting, she enlists the help of Uncle Jester to disguise herself as a man, Vy-Man, to get her work a hearing. Meanwhile, the Duke is suffering from writer's block since he has broken up with Lady Liv, a singer at the Cotton Club. To get back into her favors, he sends Vy-Man to deliver his song to Lady Liv, who falls in love with him. At the same time, Lady Liv's assistant, the pompous Rev, is seeking to work his way into Liv's good graces. The show features many classics from Duke Ellington's repertoire and was choreographed by Ellington's granddaughter Mercedes Ellington. The film is a video recording of a stage performance, broadcast once on American Public Television.

1363 *The Lizzie McGuire Movie*
2003. U.S. Stan Rogow and Walt Disney Pictures. Sound, col., 94 mins. Jim Fall.

To celebrate their graduation from middle school, Lizzie McGuire and friends Kate Sanders, Ethan Craft, and Gordo Gordon take a class trip to Rome. Lizzie, who resembles Isabella, an Italian pop diva, is asked to take Isabella's place by Paolo, Isabella's singing partner who has a crush on Lizzie. Matters become more complicated when Lizzie's family discovers her newfound pop fame and travels to Rome, and Ethan struggles with heretofore unacknowledged romantic feelings for Lizzie.

Lizzie's father Sam signals his approval of Lizzie's celebrity by offering a rendition of "some are born great, some achieve greatness, and some have greatness thrust upon 'em" from *Twelfth Night* 3.2. The irony of Shakespeare's original is not acknowledged.

1364 *Being Julia*
2004. Canada, U.S., and Hungary. Serendipity Point Films, First Choice Films, Hogarth Productions, and Myriad Pictures Inc. Sound, col., 105 mins. István Szabó.

Adapted from the novel *Theatre* by W. Somerset Maugham. Julia Lambert, a famous and aging actress, is bored with her stardom, her distant marriage to actor Michael Gosselyn, and her lack of life outside the theater. Her short but torrid affair with Tom Fennel, a young American who is friends with Julia's son Roger, briefly gives her life passion, but she soon discovers that he is using her and is more interested in a younger aspiring actress, Avice Crichton. When Avice auditions for a new play featuring Julia, gets the role, and has an affair with Michael, Julia takes her revenge by upstaging Avice and improvising on the night of the première, ironically leading to a hit. Throughout, Julia is periodically visited by the spirit of her acting mentor, Jimmie Langton.

In reference to his mother's aging beauty, her son Roger quotes Enobarbus on Cleopatra, "Age cannot wither her, nor custom stale / Her infinite variety" (*Antony and Cleopatra* 2.2); Julia replies with a laugh, "If I'd been Cleopatra, I'd have put whoever said that to death." For her audition, Julia's younger rival Avice Crichton delivers lines from Viola's "Make me a willow cabin at your gate" (*Twelfth Night* 1.5); at first she performs the lines straight (if rather overwrought), and then as if she has a cold, to the director and producer's delight. She gets the part. Compare *Illuminata*. (above).

1365 *Wicker Park*
2004. U.S. Lakeshore Entertainment. Sound, col., 114 mins. Paul McGuigan.

A disappointing remake of the brilliant *L'Appretement* as *Single White Female*. *A Midsummer Night's Dream* in the original is replaced by *Twelfth Night*. Unlike the original, which has two women, one of whom is the rival of the other, play Helena, only the rival woman stars in the productions Viola. And unlike Hermia, who faints on stage and then is fired in the original, Viola is a huge success. The stage production is multiracial, though the makeup is more Asian. The trip to Japan never taken by the hero is replaced by a trip to China, also untaken. Whereas there are no signs of Japan in the French original, images of China pervade the remake, especially in the best friend's shoe store. The remake ends happily for the main couple, who reunite at the airport at the end. No such union takes place in the original. See *L'Appartement* and *Rendez-vous*. (RB)

1366 *She's the Man*
2006. U.S. Dreamworks. Sound, col., 105 mins. Andy Fickman.

A reasonably funny modernized, teen spin-off of *Twelfth Night* along the lines of *10 Things I Hate about You* (Karen McCullah Lutz co-wrote the screenplays both films). *Twelfth Night* is credited in the opening title sequence ("Inspired by Shakespeare's *Twelfth Night*), and Viola Hastings (Amanda Bynes) cites Feste's crushing line to Malovolio, "Be not afraid of greatness; some are born great, some achieve greatness, and others have greatness thrust upon them." In the film, Viola cites the Coach, who uses the line in his pregame speeches. As in the *Lizzie McGuire Movie*, the citation is decontextualized and reinterpreted as inspirational. The film has more to do with *Bend It Like Beckham* (Gurinder Chadha, 2002) than with *Twelfth Night*. Some of the names of characters in *Twelfth Night* are retained: Duke Orsino (Channing Tatum), Olivia (Laura Ramsey), and Sebastian. Malvolio is a spider owned by a character named Malcolm (James Snyder), the real

analogue of Malvolio, who has a crush on Olivia. Viola disguises herself as her twin brother Sebastian (James Kirk)—who takes off without their parents' knowledge for London to play at a concert with his rock band—to attend the elite boarding school Illyria Academy. Additional female characters named Monique (Alex Breckinridge), who replaces Antonio, and Eunice are added to the film and straightening out Shakespeare's queer play. Similarly, a male character is added, Justin (Robert Hoffman), who Viola dumps. Monique and Justin in particular serve as scapegoats that help define both Viola's transgression as being on this side of the shrew (Monique) and Duke's sensitivity and this side of a crybaby (Justin). Girls may be jocks, but boys don't cry in this film. The film is not entirely successful in distinguishing the tomboy Viola from the shrew Monique, however, due to Amanda Byne's sometimes insufferably smug and hyper perky performance. Sir Andrew Aguecheeck, Maria, and Sir Toby are replaced by three supportive friends of Viola: Paul (Jonathan Sadowski), Kia (Amanda Crew), and Yvonne (Jessica Lucas). These friends do not plot against Malcolm, who does himself in. Justin becomes the equivalent of Malvolio near the end of the film, when he rushes off the field yelling after he fails to stop the final point, made by Viola. Though *She's the Man* largely brushes off questions about homoeroticism raised by the play (except for Olivia's crush on Viola), the film swings both ways in terms of gender. Pushing back on repulsive teen films like *The Princess Diaries* and *The Princess Diaries 2: Royal Engagement* (Garry Marshall, 2001 and 2002) and the similarly horrendous U.S. to U.K. teen girl romantic comedy Amanda Byne vehicle *What a Girl Wants* (Dennie Gordon, 2003), *She's the Man* openly mocks debutante balls and the conformity such upper-class institutions demand of women. (*The Prince and Me*, with Julia Stiles nodding to her role as Ophelia in Michael Almereyda's *Hamlet* [2000], is more overtly disenchanted with the genre.) However, at the end of the film, Viola, now an apparently conformist goody-two-shoes, appears along with nearly all the other characters now coupled, at a debutante coming-out party. At the moment when the end credits should roll, however, we see Viola and Duke dressed in their soccer gear with the other members of the team all playing soccer. Viola's wig is gone and her long hair is down, thus clearly marking her female gender, but she is back, to some extent, in drag. (RB)

THE WINTER'S TALE

1367 *Conte d'hiver* (*A Winter's Tale*)
1992. France. C.E.R., Le Studio Canal +, Les Films du Losange, Sofiarp, and Soficas. Sound, col., 114 mins. Eric Rohmer.

Félicie and Charles have an idyllic passionate affair during a brief seaside holiday. When it ends, Félicie accidentally give Charles the wrong address and they lose all contact with other, despite Felicie's attempts to find him. Five years later, Félicie is living in Paris with her daughter Elise, the product of their affair. Félicie finds herself unable to commit herself to the two men in her life, Maxence, a hairdresser who moves to Nevers and whom Félicie and Elise briefly join, and Loic, a sweet bookworm with whom Félicie has been living and to whom she returns in Paris. In both cases, her memory of Charles, whom she idealizes, renders her unable to love another man fully. By chance on New Year's Eve, she meets Charles on a bus and they are reunited.

When Félicie returns to Paris after leaving Maxence and rekindles her friendship with Loic, he takes her to a performance of *The Winter's Tale*, where we see most of the final scene of the play in which Paulina reveals the statue of Hermione, long thought dead, to her husband Leontes and daughter Perdita. The connection between the play is not at the level of character or narrative—the film's plot or characters do not mirror Shakespeare's—but at the level of theme, the bittersweet and magical resurrection of relationships between husband and wife, parent and child, that had been thought utterly lost. Little wonder, then, that Félicie is so moved by the scene. Her indecision about the two men in her life springs from her faith that she might once again meet Charles, a hope that both lovers dismiss as wildly improbable. The fantastic nature of this story of devastating loss and miraculous recovery, set against the very ordinariness of Félicie's life (and Rohmer's depiction of it), is key to the movie's gentle power. That it is set during the Christmas holiday season—Charles and Félicie reunite on New Year's Eve, and the film ends with a family party—only underlines its theme of midwinter rebirth. *Conte d'hiver* is the second in Rohmer's series, "Tales of Four Seasons."

SONNETS

1368 *In a Lonely Place*
1950. U.S. Columbia Pictures and Santana Productions. Sound, b&w, 94 mins. Nicholas Ray.

Adapted from the novel by Dorothy B. Hughes. Dixon Steele, a jaded, troubled, impulsive, and occasionally violent screenwriter suffering from burnout and self-loathing, asks Mildred Atkinson, a hat-check girl, to tell him the plot of a mass-market novel he has been hired to adapt to the screen. When Mildred is found murdered the next day, Steele becomes the main suspect, but he is provided an alibi by Laurel Gray, a neighbor and starlet who, after the two begin a romance, begins to suspect that he may really be the killer after all. The film brilliantly portrays both the McCarthyesque suspicion of intellectuals typical of the period and the degradation of an artist working in the Hollywood studio system.

Charlie Waterman, an alcoholic Shakespearean and friend of Dixon (and perhaps a riff on John Barrymore), recites Sonnet 29 to Dixon as he drifts off to sleep after a marathon writing session. In context, the outcast state refers to Dixon's status as a murder suspect, and the final couplet to Laurel Gray.

1369 *Pandora and the Flying Dutchman*
1951. U.K. MGM. Sound, col., 122 mins. Albert Lewin.

In this mannered melodrama set in the Spanish seaport Esperanza, Pandora Reynolds, a self-centered beauty who enjoys toying with men, meets the mysterious Hendrick van der Zee, a recluse who, alone on his ship in the harbor, has painted her portrait before he meets her. We learn that he is the Flying Dutchman, a seventeenth-century sailor who murders his wife when he thinks (wrongly, it turns out) that she has been unfaithful. His fate is to sail the earth as an immortal until he finds a woman who loves him enough to sacrifice her own life. In the end, Pandora and Hendrick die in a storm.

In the Dutchman's courtroom denunciation of women's faithlessness, he misquotes the penultimate line of Sonnet 116, "If this be folly and upon me proved," a phrase that eventually dooms him. The Dutchman's mad homicidal jealousy regarding his wife, later proved unfounded, bears some resemblance to that of Othello and Leontes.

1370 *Fortune and Men's Eyes*
1971. Canada and U.S. MGM, Canadian Film Development Corporation, and Cinemax. Sound, col., 102 mins. Harvey Hart.

This portrait of homosexual sub-culture in a men's prison revolves around the shifting relationships between Smitty, an innocent, initially straight new arrival; Rocky, Smitty's brooding cellmate who offers to act as his protector and lover; Mona, a weak, sensitive man who is the victim of gang rapes; and Queenie, a flamboyant drag queen who fancies and despises Mona. In the course of the film, Smitty moves from meek fearfulness of Rocky to brutally exerting his dominance over him, eventually goading Rocky into a fight and suicide; as the film ends, he has begun to harass Mona, formerly his friend.

The film begins and ends with a rendition of Sonnet 29, set to music. In one conversation about the degradation of prison life, Mona recites Sonnet 29 to Smitty—in midrecitation, Rocky catches him and becomes jealous. For the Christmas pageant, Mona performs Portia's "The quality of mercy is not strained" speech from *The Merchant of Venice* 4.1 in a monk's robe, but he is heckled from the stage by the gathered crowd; the audience much prefers Queenie's drag-queen song routine, a routine that begins with snide comments about Mona's Shakespearean recitation. In context, the sonnet refers not only to the men's imprisonment but also to the general society's despising of homosexuality.

1371 *The Angelic Conversation*
1985. U.K. British Film Institute. Sound, col. and b&w, 78 mins. Derek Jarman.

An experimental film. Hazy, stop-motion photography captures the journey of a man through several landscapes—the seashore, rocks, a garden, fog, industrial landscapes—to find his love. Part of the process entails purification, which the man does by bathing a tattooed figure and kissing him, and by purifying himself with water from a shell. After a sequence of wrestling, perhaps obliquely referencing the tale of Jacob and the angel, the man is united with his male lover. The opening and final shots of a man pensively peering from a window suggest that the main character is recalling an idyllic love affair now past. The visuals are accompanied by various ambient noises (breathing and water sounds are prominent), music by Coil and Benjamin Britten (*Peter Grimes* Suite), and Sonnets 57, 99, 43, 53, 126, 29, 94, 30, 55, 27, 61, 56, and 104 (in the order they appear in the film) read by Judi Dench. The purposely abstract nature of the film's photography and narrative preserves the ambiguities of Shakespeare's narrative in the sonnet sequence—the film has the quality of an interior monologue or a dream rather than a coherent story—even as Jarman insists upon the homoerotic orientation of the sonnets. Several repeated visual motifs, concerning earth, air, fire, and particularly water, impart an elemental quality to Jarman's abstract narrative, and the images of a man cast upon a rocky shore and carrying a log may obliquely recall Jarman's *The Tempest* (1979). The film's epigraph, "Love is too young to know what conscience is, / Yet who knows not conscience is born of love," is taken from Sonnet 151.

1372 *Pretty Woman*
1990. U.S. Buena Vista, Silver Screen Partners IV, and Touchstone Pictures. Sound, col., 119 mins. Garry Marshall.

A version of the Cinderella story. Edward Lewis, a lonely workaholic millionaire, hires Vivien Ward as an escort and makes her over as a beautiful woman; her past as a prostitute catches up with her as the two fall in love. Sonnet 29 is quoted by Edward.

1373 *Sense and Sensibility*
1995. U.S. Columbia Pictures and Mirage. Sound, col., 136 mins. Ang Lee.

Adapted from the novel by Jane Austen by Emma Thompson. A skillful film adaptation of Austen's classic novel. Includes citations of Sonnets 97 and 116, both thematically relevant.

1374 *I et hjørne av verden (In a Corner of the World)*
2000. Norway. Production company unknown. Sound, col., 2 mins. Pjotr Sapegin.

Animated short using claymation animation. On midsummer night, frogs express their love by reciting Shakespeare's Sonnet 18. Filmed in a nonstop sixteen-hour shoot.

1375 *Passion in Pieces*
1999–present. U.K. Passion in Pieces Ltd. Sound, col., 11 mins total (for five films). Sam Small.

A series of short films, each of which is based on a single sonnet. Each film is centered on a short narrative involving contemporary Londoners to illustrate the mood or theme of the sonnet; the soundtrack is typically a reading of the sonnet with musical accompaniment. Eventually the project will include twenty-five short films, each on a sonnet. "A Day in the Park" (Sonnet 15) concerns an older man strolling in a park as he thinks of the younger man and later meets him. "The Man Who Thought He Had Nothing" (Sonnet 29) features the older man at work and frustrated in his study, then walking outside in his garden to think of the younger man. "A Night on the Town" (Sonnet 94) involves the older man driving in London with the younger man as they bicker and drink. In "Lovers in a Restaurant" (Sonnet 138), the older man shares a dessert with a younger beautiful woman in a restaurant and wonders about what she thinks of him. "Flowers for My Baby" (Sonnet 145) features the older man bringing flowers to a middle-aged dark woman; this film consists entirely of painterly stills, except for three moments of movement in which the woman speaks. The same actors portray the older man and younger man in the different films. Small's emphasis upon the tragic romantic narrative carried through the sonnets is quite different from Jarman's much more abstract approach, and so the two film projects invite comparison.

The DVD contains a promotional film that references the historical background of Shakespeare's sonnets and outlines the project.

1376 *Ma femme est une actrice (My Wife Is an Actress)*
2001. U.S. Renn Productions and TF1 Films. Sound, col., 95 mins. Yvan Attal.

In this romantic comedy Yvan, a sportswriter, is increasingly consumed with jealousy about his wife Charlotte's fame and beauty as an actress, especially as she begins to star in a movie in London with a sophisticated co-star, John. A drunken John recites the final couplet from Sonnet 128 and the first eight lines of Sonnet 23 in an attempt to charm Charlotte.

The DVD includes the film's trailer that features the sonnet sequence.

MISCELLANEOUS

Citations of Multiple Works

1377 *The Master Hand*
1915. U.S. Premo Feature Film Corporation. Silent, b&w, 50 mins. Harley Knoles.

James Rallston, a rake, marries a rich incapacitated widow in order to steal her fortune. When she refuses to relinquish control to him, Rallston, with the aid of his wife's doctor Miss Lane (who loves Rallston), drugs her and has her committed to a mental institution run by yet another conspirator, Dr. Garside. Fifteen years later, Rallston has lost the financial legacy of his wife's daughter Jean in stock speculations, and in an effort to regain the lost fortune, he offers Jean as a wife to John Bigelow, Rallston's friend and a successful stockbroker. Jean is in love with Ed Pembroke, an architect, and soon convinces Bigelow that Mrs. Rallston is still alive. After having restored Jean's fortune by manipulating the stock market, Bigelow investigates Mrs. Rallston's whereabouts, soon locating Garside's asylum and masquerading as a butler to rescue Mrs. Rallston after his own doctor vouches for her sanity. Rallston, alerted, rushes to prevent their escape, but dies when his car plunges off a cliff. Miss Lane confesses her misdeeds, mother and daughter are reunited, and Jean marries Pembroke.

Disguised as the butler, Bigelow obsessively quotes Shakespeare.

1378 *Office Steps*
1930. U.S. Vitaphone. Sound, b&w, 1 reel. George Hale.

This Vitaphone short is a backstage drama featuring dances and musical numbers; it includes a theatrical burlesque featuring a pastiche of Shakespearean quotations.

1379 *Stepping Sisters*
1932. U.S. Fox Film Corporation. Sound, b&w, 59 mins. Seymour Felix.

Adapted from the play by Howard Warren Comstock. Onetime burlesque queen Cissie Ramsay seeks respectability for herself and Norma, her daughter. However, her boorish husband Herbert threatens to use a photograph of her in costume to force her to leave him out of her plans to host a charity benefit. At a garden party for Ambassador Leonard, two blueblood women, Lady Chetworth-Lynde and Rosie La Marr, reveal themselves to be Cissie's former chorus girl friends, and they vow to keep their association secret. As daughter Norma becomes suspicious about her mother's past, Cissie discovers that her husband has secretly been seeing Rosie and is prevented from exposing her because of her vow of secrecy. In reality, Herbert and Rosie have only been attending baseball games, and though Rosie vows to reconcile the husband and wife, misunderstandings escalate. At the charity benefit, Jack, Norma's lover, asks him to marry her, but she refuses lest she expose her mother and he leaves; instead of performing as cast in Mrs. Tremaine's allegorical play for the show, Chetworth-Lynde and Rosie appear in burlesque costumes, and Cissie's familiarity with them backstage gives away her past. Accepted by her daughter, Cissie chastises the pompous Mrs. Tremaine and Rosie, and learns that Rosie's

performance was designed to reconcile her with husband Herbert. Afterward, the group enjoys sandwiches and beers with Ambassador Leonard, who expresses his enjoyment of their play.

Lady Chetworth-Lynde (aka "Queenie") establishes her credentials as a cultured actress by quoting Shakespeare, first at the garden party, then when the group shares sandwiches at film's end. In the first instance, Cissie is impressed and intimidated; in the second, she smashes limberger cheese in her face.

1380 *Room Service*
1938. U.S. RKO Pictures. Sound, b&w, 78 mins. William A. Seiter.

Adapted from the play *Room Service* by Allen Boretz and John Murray. Stars the Marx Brothers. Gordon Miller, a fly-by-night producer, has gone into debt trying to stage a lousy play, *Hail and Farewell*. He, the cast, the director Harry Binelli, and business manager Faker Englund are holed up in the White Way Hotel as they try to come up with ways of raising money. Showing up unannounced, playwright Leo Davis learns that his play is in financial danger. The hotel's manager Gribble Dunstan, Miller's brother-in-law, is fed up with their dodging bills and wants to throw them out, but the group fakes a measles epidemic to allow them to stay. Meanwhile, Miller courts a potential angel, Jenkins Phillips Wood, but he is scared off by the antics of the cast and history of the show, though to Dunstan and hotel inspector Wagner MacBride, Miller pretends to have secured Wood's backing. When his lie is exposed, Miller pretends that Davis and Binelli have committed suicide because of Wagner's persistence about the bill.

Shakespeare is twice referenced. When Wood insists that Davis rewrite the play to accommodate an actress friend, Davis refuses, insisting that Shakespeare never changed any lines of his plays; when Davis pretends to die, Miller speaks, "Good night, sweet prince," to the corpse. In the musical remake, *Step Lively* (1943), these Shakespearean allusions are dropped.

1381 *South Riding*
1938. U.K. London Film Productions. Sound, b&w, 85 mins. Victor Saville.

Local public and private dramas preoccupy a Yorkshire county council, with the tension between Robert Carne, an impoverished conservative country squire, and Joe Astell, a leftist councillor ailing from consumption, as the film's focus. Carne is undermined by an unscrupulous housing scheme masterminded by Alfred Huggins and Carne's conniving neighbor Fred Snaith; Astell is an unwitting supporter of the scheme. With his wife Madge in an expensive nursing home, he finds himself attracted to and changed by Sarah Burton, an idealistic schoolteacher, who also initially attracts Astell. To get out of financial ruin, Carne contemplates suicide for the insurance money.

Midge Carne, Robert's daughter, makes mistakes in her Shakespeare essay, referring to "The Merchant of Venus" and "Sharelock"; this leads to a fight between her and Lydia Holly, a working-class girl with a much better essay. Later, as Lydia washes dishes, she recites a portion of the "To be or not to be" soliloquy, a passage relevant to her own working-class aspirations and to Robert's later flirtation with suicide.

1382 *Forged Passport*
1939. U.S. Republic Pictures. Sound, b&w, 64 mins. John H. Auer.

Adapted from a story by James Webb and Lee Loeb. Because he has foiled several plots for smuggling illegal workers, Dan Frazer, a tough immigration officer at the Mexican border, is targeted by a gang. Though he has been warned by gang member Jack Scott, he remains resolute against intimidation and so the gang sets him up, leading to the shooting of his partner, Kansas Nelson, by a mysterious gunman called Lefty at his friend Nick Mendoza's nightclub. Dan is dismissed and vows to avenge Kansas's murder, ignoring the pleas of his girlfriend Helene to leave town and marry her. Dan and Nick set up a fake smuggling ring at a gas station to trap Jack's gang, and Dan reveals his scheme to rancher Jack Rogers, but we soon learn that Rogers is Lefty and that he plans to plant a bomb to kill Dan and his men. Scott, who plants the bomb, accidentally reveals the double-cross to Helene, and she passes on the information to Dan's co-worker Shakespeare, who helps her escape from Scott. The bomb explodes harmlessly, and Dan tricks Rogers into revealing he is left-handed, exposing his schemes. Nick's club reopens, and Helene and Dan are reunited.

Helene surreptitiously passes on the information about the bomb to Shakespeare by discussing the story of one of Shakespeare's plays.

1383 *Pimpernel Smith* (aka *Mister V*)
1941. U.K. British National Pictures and Franco London Films. Sound, b&w, 121 mins. Leslie Howard.

Adapted from the novel *The Scarlet Pimpernel* by Baroness Emmuska Orczy. An update of the Scarlet Pimpernel narrative for the war years. Professor Smith, a dotty Cambridge don of archaeology who is in reality an antifascist operative, helps Doctor Benckendorf to escape from Nazi Germany, but his colleague Sidimir Koslowski is left behind. Smith organizes a fake archaeological dig as a cover for his escape operation; his plans are complicated by the surveillance of General von Graum, a Gestapo office obsessed with trapping Smith, and Koslowski's daughter Ludmilla who, anxious to free her father, is used by von Graum to try to find the spy in his midst. After a cat-and-mouse game between von Graum and Smith, and several

daring escape plans involving diversion and disguise, Smith enables Koslowski and his daughter's escape and, at the last minute, escapes the clutches of von Graum himself.

Part of the cat-and-mouse game between von Graum and Smith involves the authorship of Shakespeare, a motif that first appears when von Graum speaks "To be or not to be" and identifies it as the work of the German author, Shakespeare. Later on, Smith visits von Graum and claims that Shakespeare is in reality the earl of Oxford and therefore British. At the dig itself, Smith takes up a skull he's found and launches into "Alas, poor Yorick. . . . Now get you to my lady's chamber, and tell her, let her paint an inch thick, to this favour she must come" from *Hamlet* 5.1. The references fit with Smith's general penchant for using British superiority to tweak von Graum's ego. One other Shakespeare reference: Maxwell, the lone American among Smith's archaeological students, uses the title *A Midsummer Night's Dream* in an attempt to romance Ludmilla Koslowski.

1384 *This Above All*
1942. U.S. 20th Century Fox. Sound, b&w, 110 mins. Anatole Litvak.

Adapted from the novel by Eric Knight. During World War II aristocratic Prudence Cathaway enlists in the Women's Auxiliary Force and meets soldier Clive Briggs while she is at training camp. Though Clive regards aristocrats as detestable and Prudence never reveals her background, the two fall in love. While the two are on leave together in Dover, a chance meeting with Prudence's Aunt Iris leads to strange behavior from both of the lovers. Later, Prudence learns that Clive is a deserter who left his unit because of his hatred for defending aristocrats; when she delivers a stirring patriotic speech to him, he is driven away. Wounded and mistaken for a spy, and counseled by a local vicar, Clive resolves to turn himself in, but he sends a message to Prudence to meet him at Charing Cross so they can marry. He is arrested en route, and despite convincing his commander that he be allowed to meet Prudence, en route he is badly wounded when he helps save a woman and child from a fire. In hospital, Prudence arranges an improvised wedding as air raid sirens sound.

In the film's final scene in hospital, a nurse reads to Clive from Polonius's speech to Laertes in *Hamlet*, "This above all: to thine own self be true."

1385 *The Falcon in Hollywood*
1944. U.S. RKO Radio Pictures. Sound, b&w, 66 mins. Gordon Douglas.

Tom Lawrence, a debonair detective called "The Falcon" who is vacationing in Los Angeles, encounters Louie Buchanan, a corrupt casino impresario whom he had helped convict, and his girlfriend Peggy Callahan at the race track. Peggy takes the purse of Lili D'Allio, and when

Lawrence and D'Allio follow her to a movie studio, they hear a shooting and investigate. The victim is Ted Miles, a matinee idol, but when his wife Roxanna arrives, she declares that she never loved him and will marry Alec Hoffman, a director. Lawrence and Inspector McBride from the L.A. police soon discover a complex web of financial deals, thefts, debts, and mutual enmity among various people at the studio, including Miles, Hoffman, D'Allio, and producer Martin Dwyer. Soon while filming Peggy accidentally wounds Hoffman with a prop gun, and Louis promises to deliver the killer to Lawrence at the Los Angeles Coliseum. When the two meet, Louis reveals that he was an investor in Hoffman's film and then drops dead, poisoned. Lawrence deduces that Dwyer killed Miles and Buchanan because he oversold interest in the movie, and when confronted, Dwyer tries to escape but is shot by Lawrence on a sound stage.

Dwyer, the corrupt Hollywood producer, frequently cites Shakespeare.

1386 *Frozen Ghost*
1945. U.S. Universal. Sound, b&w, 61 mins. Harold Young.

Stage hypnotist Alex Gregor, taping a radio show before a live audience, hypnotizes a heckler to prove he is an authentic mentalist. When the heckler dies of a heart attack, Alex, wracked with guilt, refuses to work, so his manager arranges a position for him as a guide at the wax museum of Valerie Monet. The attention shown by Valerie and her niece Nina toward Alex provokes suspicion from Rudi Poldan, the disturbed plastic surgeon who fashions the wax figures. Egged on by Rudi, Valerie accuses Alex of romancing Nina, and they argue. When Valerie mysteriously disappears, Inspector Brant suspects Alex of murder, though in fact Rudi has hidden Valerie's drugged body among the wax figures. We learn that Rudi and Alex's manager are in league, aiming to have Alex committed to an asylum in order to control his estate; they discover that inadvertently Rudi's drugs have killed Valerie. Meanwhile Alex uses his mentalist powers with his assistant Maura to expose the conspirators' plot, and soon after the two are caught, with Rudi falling into the wax furnace. This film was one of Universal Pictures' "Inner Sanctum" series.

The "Shakespeare group" of wax figures surfaces at crucial moments in the plot. When Alex first arrives at the wax museum, he is shown the wax figure of Lady Macbeth, at which he shudders (since she, like him, is plagued by guilt over a murder). Later, Rudi hides the drugged body of Valerie among the Shakespearean figures, dressed as Lady Macbeth. When Inspector Brant looks for her body, he pauses over the Shakespeare figures as Rudi struggles to cover the body. When Brant sees Romeo and Juliet, he speaks Juliet's lines from the balcony scene: "Sweet, good night! / This bud of love, by summer's ripening breath, /

May prove a beauteous flower when next we meet. / Good night, good night!" At the sight of the Hamlet figure, he offers a section of the "To be or not to be" soliloquy, and as he parts with Rudi, Valerie's body undiscovered, he quips (incorrectly), "Lead on, Macduff."

1387 *Bedlam*
1946. U.S. RKO. Sound, b&w, 79 mins. Mark Robson.

In a discussion about a parrot and Lord Mortimer (Billy House), Master George Sims (Boris Karloff) cites Iago's "he who steals my purse steals trash, but he who..." His niece, Mistress Sims (Elizabeth Russell), says she has heard that it's in the playhouse. The lawyer inmate shows a series of drawings of Nell Bowyn (Anna Lee) helping a sick woman in a book that he holds and flips the pages like a flip book. On the left we see the printing of the book, which is pages from *Hamlet* having to do with the play within the play, *The Mousetrap*. (RB)

1388 *His Kind of Woman*
1951. U.S. RKO Radio Pictures. Sound, b&w, 120 mins. John Farrow.

Expatriate mobster Nick Ferraro, seeking to return to the United States from Naples after being deported, pays Dan Milner, a professional gambler, to live in Mexico for a year, with the secret intention of stealing his identity. En route to Morro's Lodge in Baja, Milner meets a rich, beautiful songstress, Lenore Brent. Once arrived, Milner meets several characters, including investment banker Myron Winton, writer Martin Krafft, Thompson, and hammy film star and hunter Mark Cardigan. Dan soon learns that Lenore is involved with Cardigan; she is in reality Liz Brady, a former singer posing as an heiress in order to marry Cardigan, who is in the midst of a divorce. After Milner makes a play for Lenore, Cardigan's wife Helen arrives, looking to reconcile. Meanwhile, Milner learns that pilot Bill Lusk is an undercover federal agent; Lusk reveals Ferraro's intentions to Milner, but Milner fails to heed the warning. When Lusk turns up dead, Milner tries to back out of his deal, but he is caught by Ferarro's thugs and taken to Ferraro's yacht to be killed. In a long chase sequence that involves Cardigan and the Mexican police, Milner is pursued by Ferraro and his men, but Ferraro is eventually killed and Lenore and Milner are romantically united.

At first Cardigan is presented as a self-absorbed cad, but once he gets his chance to become genuinely heroic by aiding Milner, he begins to quote Shakespeare, often ironically. Of his gun wound, he quotes Mercutio, " 'Tis not so deep as a well, nor so wide as a church-door" (*Romeo and Juliet* 3.1); locking Lenore in a closet, he tells his wife that "by yonder blessèd moon" she should not be freed (from *Romeo and Juliet* 2.2). To his band of ragtag Mexican policemen, he quotes *Henry V* 4.3, "Now, soldiers, march away: / And how thou pleasest, God, dispose the day!"

When his overloaded rescue boat sinks, he offers Gonzalo's line from *The Tempest*, "Now would I give a thousand furlongs of sea for an acre of barren ground," and plays on Richard III's famous line with "A ship! A ship! My kingdom for a ship!" (*Richard III* 5.4). As Mark tries to shoot out a spotlight on Ferraro's yacht, he recites Lady Macbeth's line from the sleepwalking scene, "Out, damned spot! Out, I say!" and he offers several Shakespearean quips in the gunfight that follows: "I must / Rid all the sea of pirates" (Pompey in *Antony and Cleopatra* 2.6); "Death hath not struck so fat a deer today" (Prince Hal in *Henry IV, Part 1* 5.4); and "this place is dangerous; / The time right deadly" (Ulysses in *Troilus and Cressida* 5.2). When after the battle Cardigan is asked what the odds were, he says, "Five to one," recalling the odds at Agincourt in *Henry V*. This group of Shakespearean quotations is unusual, first, for their relative obscurity (with the exception of the quip on *Richard III*) and, second, for their ambivalence, for they are both comically inflating and genuinely heroic at once.

1389 *The Lavender Hill Mob*
1951. U.K. Ealing Studios. Sound, b&w, 78 mins. Charles Crichton.

In this classic Ealing comedy, Henry Holland, a meek bank clerk, devises a plan to rob gold bullion from his own bank, partnering with Alfred Pendlebury, a fast-talking souvenir manufacturer. The plan, ironically concocted by the bank itself for a film script, is to hijack the bullion en route and turn it into Eiffel Tower souvenirs for easy transport, but the plan repeatedly goes awry when Pendlebury is arrested during the heist for another petty theft and again when the fake golden souvenirs gets mixed up with genuine worthless ones. The men travel to the Eiffel Tower to recover their souvenirs from schoolgirls who have bought them, and they make a daring escape in a police car. At film's end, we realize that the story, narrated by Holland in a Latin American resort, is being told to a Scotland Yard detective who has arrested him.

Pendlebury peppers his conversation with occasional references to Shakespeare.

1390 *Long Day's Journey into Night*
1962. U.S. Embassy Pictures and Republic Pictures. Sound, b&w, 174 mins. Sidney Lumet.

Adapted from the play by Eugene O'Neill. This character study of a dysfunctional family in early twentieth-century New England anatomizes the co-dependencies and antagonisms between James Tyrone, a once promising actor who instead devoted himself to touring with a "money-maker" and became a miser; his wife Mary, a morphine addict who dwells on her past to deny her lonely present; younger son Edmund, a poetically inclined boy who is dying of consumption and is the object of his mother's doting affection; and older son Jamie, an alcoholic

actor who is deeply bitter about his father's tyranny over the family and envious of Edmund. The action of the film involves the revelation of Edmund's sickness to the family, and James's refusal to sell land to pay for Edmund's treatment (instead allowing him to go to a state institution).

Shakespeare is used as a weapon between the sons and their actor father. This dynamic is announced very early in the film when Jamie says of Tyrone's snoring, "The Moor, I know his trumpet," to which Tyrone offers a withering reply. One of Tyrone's favorites is *King Lear*, which he quotes to Jamie ("Ingratitude, the vilest weed that grows," to which Jamie replies, "I could see that line coming") and to Edmund ("How sharper than a serpent's tooth it is to have a thankless child," a line that Edmund completes along with him, having heard all this before). When Edmund launches into poetic despair, Tyrone paraphrases his thought with Prospero's lines from *The Tempest*, "We are such stuff as dreams are made on, / And our little life is rounded with a sleep"; Edmund replies by paraphrasing, "We are such stuff as manure is made on, / So let's drink and forget it," and he follows up with a recitation of Baudelaire's "Be always drunken," which obliquely recalls and parodies Hamlet's "To be or not to be." When near film's end, Jamie, drunken, becomes cruel toward his parents, he uses Shakespearean references: of his father, he quotes from Clarence's nightmare in *Richard III* 1.4, "Clarence is come; false, fleeting, perjured Clarence / That stabb'd me in the field by Tewksbury; / Seize on him, Furies, take him to your torments!"; when his mother arrives, he comments, "a mad scene, enter Ophelia." In Tyrone's biggest speech, he rhapsodizes about the joy of playing Shakespeare, his opportunity to become a great Shakespearean, and his playing of Shakespearean parts opposite Edwin Booth in Chicago, a moment he characterizes as the high point of his life. His choice to pursue commercial success he presents as a great failure, and he blames himself, using Cassius's line "The fault, dear Brutus, is not in our stars, / But in ourselves, that we are underlings." This use of Shakespeare as an interfamilial weapon also surfaces in *Quiz Show*.

1391 *Historia de la frivolidad*
1967. Spain. Production company unknown. Sound, b&w, 60 mins. Chicho Ibañez-Serrador.

A TV mockumentary on censorship throughout the ages, handled with black humor. One of the examples is Shakespeare.

1392 *Che c'entriamo noi con la rivoluzione?* (*¡Que Nos Importa la Revolución!*)
1972. Spain and Italy. Fair Film and Midega Films. Sound, col., 103 mins. Sergio Corbucci.

Polar opposites Guido Guidi, an anticlerical Italian actor on tour in Mexico, and Don Albino Moncalieri, an Italian priest working as the secretary of the cardinal on a mission, become unwittingly involved in the Mexican Revolution. Guido is used by the revolutionaries unknowingly to transport arms, and he becomes beseiged by Colonel Herrero, commander of the federal troops, and Captain Carrasco of the revolutionary army. After many adventures Guido develops spiritually, while Don Albino is moved by the suffering of the poor. Guido eventually finds true love and uses his acting talents to inspire the people to revolutionary fervor.

Includes several references to *Othello* and *Richard III*. The final scene of *Richard III* is interrupted by revolutionaries.

1393 *Too Scared to Scream*
1985. U.S. 21st Century Film Corporation, Doorman, and Moviestore Entertainment. Sound, col., 100 mins. Tony Lo Bianco.

This American version of an Italian *giallo* centers on Vincent Hardwick, an eccentric British doorman at an upscale Manhattan apartment building where several murders have occurred and, after eliminating an earlier suspect, where Hardwick has become the prime suspect. Hardwick seems mentally unstable; he cares Norman Bates–like for his invalid mother, and often quotes Shakespeare. Kate Bridges, a policewoman, becomes an undercover decoy in the building to lure the killer, and she is protected by Lieutenant Dinardo, her boyfriend and the detective in charge of the case. Eventually the killer is revealed not to be Hardwick but another doorman named Edward. Hardwick's suspicious behavior is particularly underlined by his penchant for citing Shakespeare, though in the end his suspiciousness is a elaborate red herring.

1394 *Shakespeare 2000*
1988. Czechoslovakia. Krátký Film Praha and Studio Bratri v Triku. Sound, col., 9 mins. Dagmar Doubkova.

Set in the year 2000, the film's narrators use Shakespeare to convince their audience that romantic human passions such as jealousy, hate, and love have not changed in 500 years. The result of their efforts, however, is Shakespearean parody.

1395 *Antonia and Jane*
1991. U.K. BBC and Miramax. Sound, col., 71 mins. Beeban Kidron.

A character study of the friendship of two quite different women, gorgeous and seemingly self-assured Antonia and frumpy, bookish Jane. In flashbacks springing from both women's therapy sessions, Jane reveals that she resents Antonia's beauty, sophistication, and theft of her first serious lover. Antonia reveals her dissatisfaction with her work as a publisher and her deteriorating marriage, and she secretly desires what she sees as Jane's life of new experiences and adventure.

When Antonia has an affair, she and her lover play a sex game centered on the identification of Shakespearean quotations. Given the quote "Life is as tedious as a twice-told tale / Vexing the dull ear of a drowsy man," Jane guesses *King Lear*, *Macbeth*, and *Troilus and Cressida*. Her lover identifies it from *King John* (3.4).

1396 *Star Trek VI: The Undiscovered Country*
1991. U.S. Paramount Pictures. Sound, col., 113 mins. Nicholas Meyer.

When the Klingons, a combative alien race, seek rapprochement with the Federation of Planets after an ecological disaster, Captain Kirk and his crew are sent as diplomatic emissaries, much to Kirk's distaste. After the Klingon leader Chancellor Gorkon is murdered after a diplomatic banquet, Kirk and Doctor McCoy are convicted of the crime and sent to prison while Mr. Spock and Lieutenant Valeris struggle to clear their names. Soon it is revealed that Kirk and McCoy were framed by various cold warriors in order to foment hostility between the Klingons and the Federation. One of the conspirators, we learn, is Lieutenant Valeris. In the end, Kirk and McCoy escape the gulag, defeat the Klingon general Chang, expose the conspiracy, and prevent the assassination of the Federation president.

The film contains several references to Shakespeare. At the opening banquet, which establishes the mutual hostility between Klingons and Federation members, Chancellor Gorkon toasts "the undiscovered country," an allusion that Mr. Spock, the ship's resident intellectual, identifies as a phrase from Hamlet's "To be or not to be" soliloquy. This identification prompts one of the most interesting lines of the film: "You've not experienced Shakespeare until you've read him in the original Klingon." (The line plays with claims made in Germany prior to World War II.) This line sets in motion a contest for cultural supremacy between the Klingons and the Federation—who can claim Shakespeare as their own?—that parallels their contest for military supremacy. General Chang is the film's most consistent citer of Shakespeare, reciting "To be or not to be" in Klingon and treating the speech as a commentary on Klingon cultural annihilation. (The film's commentary track reveals that the Shakespearean quotations were inspired by a recording of William Walton's music for *Henry V* for which Christopher Plummer supplied the narration; Plummer—a well-known Shakespearean—was the actor tapped to play Chang.) Throughout the film, Chang hurls Shakespearean lines at Federation officers—referencing *Hamlet*, *Romeo and Juliet*, *Richard II*, *Julius Caesar*, and *Henry IV, Part 2*—as a way of provoking them; late in the film, he does so while firing upon the USS *Enterprise*, a combination that makes somewhat clearer how he is using Shakespeare as a weapon. The barrage of quotations is so annoying that Doctor McCoy says, "I'd give real money if he'd just shut up."

When Kirk finally destroys Chang's ship, the explosion kills Chang in midspeech as he recites "To be or not to be." There are other incidental references: Gorkon cites Miranda's phrase "brave new world" from *The Tempest*, and Kirk quotes Gorkon's quotation of "the undiscovered country" at the film's climax. Shakespeare was used elsewhere in the *Star Trek* television series, and the film both plays with and against those appropriations. After the film premièred, several Klingon language enthusiasts produced an edition of *Hamlet* in Klingon, which purported to "restore" the text to its "original" language and featured an entertaining pseudo-academic apparatus for the edition. See also entries 777, 1770, and 2723.

DVD includes a section "Shakespeare and General Chang" as well as a commentary by director Nicholas Meyer and writer Denny Martin Flinn that reference Shakespeare.

1397 *Quiz Show*
1994. U.S. Buena Vista. Sound, col., 133 mins. Robert Redford.

Adapted from the book by Richard N. Goodwin. A superb character study of two contestants on *Twenty-One*, a popular TV quiz show in 1958. Herbert Stempel, a working-class Jew and obnoxious, self-righteous loudmouth, is the reigning champion on the show. Stempel is forced by advertisers and network executives to miss a question so that he can be replaced by Charles Van Doren, a superficially charming, WASP Columbia University instructor, the son of Mark Van Doren, a distinguished professor and quietly dictatorial father. Pursued by ambitious Boston congressional aide Dick Goodwin, who wants to curb the power of television, Van Doren begins to face a crisis of conscience when he allows executives to feed him answers to questions in advance and he receives a morning talk show. Eventually Van Doren confesses his deception before a congressional committee, but advertisers protect network executives by taking the fall for them, with the result that only Van Doren pays a permanent price for the scandal.

At a birthday for Mark Van Doren, he and Charles trade quotations from Shakespeare in an increasingly tense contest of intellectual power. The lines come from *Measure for Measure*, *The Merchant of Venice*, *Much Ado about Nothing*, and *Macbeth*, and all are oblique but pointed comments about each other. When Charles falters, misquoting *Macbeth*, Charlie's mother ends the contest with the line from *King Lear*, "How ill white hairs become a fool and jester," directed at Mark. Later, when Goodwin seeks to protect Charles by not calling him at congressional hearings, his wife observes that "quiz show hearings without Van Doren is like doing *Hamlet* without Hamlet."

1398 *Lilian's Story*
1995. Australia. Movieco Australia. Sound, col., 93 mins. Jerzy Domaradzki.

Adapted from the novel by Kate Grenville (entry 2076), and based upon the life of Bea Miles. After forty years in a mental asylum, Lilian Singer is released into the care of her brother John and Aunt Kitty. As she struggles to adjust to life in modern Sydney, through flashbacks we learn of Lilian's past, particularly her controlling father's physical and psychological abuse that led to her incarceration. Looking for love, Lilian becomes infatuated with a bank manager and stalks him, then reconnects with a long-lost love, Frank, now an alcoholic cab driver. Soon the two are joined by Jewel, a homeless pregnant woman, who are all supported by Lilian's street recitations. But Jewel soon leaves with her newborn child and Frank dies, and Lilian returns to the house of her youth to confront the memories of her father raping her, her brother ignoring it, her attempted suicide, and his incarceration of her to avoid a scandal. In the end, she leaves Sydney in a cab, at peace.

The film opens with an extended quotation from Richard's prison soliloquy in *Richard II*, 5.5, starting with "how sour sweet music is, / When time is broke and no proportion kept! / So is it in the music of men's lives," establishing Lilian's penchant for quoting Shakespeare and her feeling of despair at being imprisoned. At nearly every major event of Lilian's life or when she is emotionally excited, she offers Shakespeare citations from an enormous range of sources. *Hamlet*, *King Lear*, *Macbeth*, *Julius Caesar*, *Richard II*, *Richard III*, *The Tempest*, *Venus and Adonis*, *Romeo and Juliet*, *All's Well That Ends Well*, *Measure for Measure*, *The Merchant of Venice*, *Henry V*, *Othello*, *Twelfth Night*, and Sonnet 116 are all referenced in the course of the film. Each citation is thematically relevant to Lilian's situation or emotional state at the time, though her behavior looks like madness to outsiders. She first renews her bond with Frank by trading quotations in his cab, just as they had done when they first consummated their relationship as teenagers. Shakespeare, she tells a street hooker, is her father, a clue to the place of the Bard in Lilian's life: Shakespeare offers a source of meaning, comfort, passion, and poetic beauty, an alternative to the hypocrisy, tyrannical cruelty, and sexual repression that characterize her father. Shakespearean recitation also becomes Lilian's means of financial support, for she performs for money in the park and tries to pay for cab rides with recitations. Compare *Nomad*.

1399 *Skyscraper*
1995. U.S. PM Entertainment Group, Inc. Sound, col., 96 mins. Raymond Martino.

Carrie Wisk, a helicopter charter pilot, unwittingly takes terrorists led by the ruthless Fairfax to a highrise where they take over in pursuit of a satellite guidance system. Carrie's husband Gordy, a policeman, discovers the plot and helps his wife defeat the assailants. A low-budget, straight-to-video version of *Die Hard*; compare *Lethal Tender* (entry 1401).

The psychopathic leader of the terrorists, Fairfax, loves to quote Shakespeare. When in the helicopter with Carrie, he comments on her being a woman pilot with "when a world of men / Could not prevail with all their oratory, / Yet hath a woman's kindness over-ruled" (*Henry VI, Part 1* 1.2), misidentified by Carrie as *Henry IV*. Fairfax also references "if you pinch me, I do bleed" from *The Merchant of Venice*; "The end of life cancels all bands" and "A plague upon it when thieves cannot be true to one another" from *Henry IV, Part 1*; "Alas poor Yorick" from *Hamlet*; and "Parting is such sweet sorrow" and "Never was a story of more woe / Than this of Juliet and her Romeo" from *Romeo and Juliet*. A female henchman executes one of the gang with the line "Good night sweet prince" from *Hamlet*. Fairfax's first grandiloquent line, "O thou noble adversary, know that vain circumstance pushes us to the very brink," is pseudo-Shakespearean. The quotations seem intended to underline that the villains are "foreign," an impression confirmed by the fact that they also speak some French and Italian.

1400 *Bella Mafia* (aka *Mafia Wives*)
1997. U.S. Konigsberg Company. Sound, col., 118 mins. David Greene.

An all-star TV miniseries hybridizing elements of *The Godfather* and soap opera chronicles, later released on video. Don Roberto Luciano and his wife Graziella, living in retirement in Palermo, learn that their son Michael has been killed because Luciano refused to get reinvolved in the drug trade for Pietro Corolla, an American crime boss. Roberto swears a blood oath to take revenge. Michael's illegitimate son Luka, the product of his affair with Sophia Paluzo, is born soon after. Sophia goes on to marry Constantino Luciano, Michael's brother, and bear him twins. Not knowing Luka's real identity, Corolla adopts the child, passing on his vendetta against the Luciano family to his adopted son, who methodically murders all the Luciano men. When Luka, now a psychopathic killer, visits Palermo in an effort to recover incriminating papers, he assassinates Corolla (who cursed him for killing children) and poses as the son of a rich American, charming the Luciano widows by pretending to protect them. Sophia soon learns that Luka is the killer, kills him, then learns that he was her son. Afterward, Sophia is made head of the crime family.

Poisoning plays a prominent role in the Mafia killings in this film. Luka learns of poison, particularly strychnine, from Giorgio Corolla, bedridden son of Pietro, who reads the apothecary scene from *Romeo and Juliet*. Later, in a second poisoning, Luka reminds a victim of the Shakespeare connection as he dies; as the film ends, Sophia picks up the motif, poisoning one of her nemeses. The motif of

two powerful feuding families is also vaguely reminiscent of *Romeo and Juliet*, though there is no courtship between children of the two families. Another minor allusion: when Michael leaves to go to Harvard, his mother Graziella gives him a copy of *Hamlet* and recites excerpts from Hamlet's speech "a special providence in the fall of a sparrow" (5.2).

1401 *Lethal Tender*
1997. Canada. Deadly Current Productions and Le Monde Entertainment. Sound, col., 89 mins. John Bradshaw.

Policeman David Chase and water-plant worker Melissa Wilkens team up to free hostages and foil a plot to poison a city's water supply when a criminal gang takes over a water treatment plant as a cover for the theft of bonds. A straight-to-video *Die Hard* clone. Compare *Skyscraper* (above).

Both of the film's villains, Montessi and Mr. Turner, reference Shakespeare sardonically. Mr. Turner tells one dim thug that explaining the crime is like "explaining *Hamlet* to a zoo monkey," and he later brutally betrays one of his gang with a poisoned drink, saying "Good night, sweet prince" in mock reverence over his body. Montessi addresses hostages with "Ladies and gentlemen, lend me your ears"; when one of the hostages explodes about his brutality, he replies with Shylock's "if you prick us, do we not bleed?" speech, ending with "and if I shoot you, does it not make a hole?" after which he brutally murders him.

1402 *Live Nude Shakespeare*
1997. U.S. Independent Edge Productions (Fox-Levy Productions). Sound, col., 61 mins. Michael D. Fox.

This softcore mockumentary purports to document an avant-garde production of Shakespeare by director Lionel Backslide called *Live Nude Shakespeare*, performed in the Theatre de la Merde. J. Emerson Biggins, a caricature of the pipe-smoking, tweedy scholar, interviews Backslide and several cast members about the artistic intentions behind the production, never fully appreciating that Backslide's production consists largely of scenes in which women strip while suggestively reciting passages from Shakespeare.

The film includes "readings" and performances from *Romeo and Juliet*, *Hamlet*, *Timon of Athens*, *Othello*, and *The Merry Wives of Windsor*, among others, as well as numerous references to high cultural pretensions in the stage performance of Shakespeare. Most of the passages are chosen to maximize their potential for sexual double-entendre. The film's greatest success is in its parody of bloodless academic analysis and high-concept theatrical "artistes."

1403 *The Postman*
1997. U.S. TIG Productions and Warner Brothers. Sound, col., 177 mins. Kevin Costner.

Adapted from the novel by David Brin. In a post-apocalyptic American West, a drifter known as Shakespeare— he performs Shakespeare plays in isolated villages—runs afoul of the Holnists, neofascist marauders led by the sadistic General Bethlehem. Escaping the Holnists' work camp, Shakespeare hides out in an abandoned postal van where he dons a postman's uniform. When he arrives at the village of Pineview, he delivers letters he has found, claiming that the national government has been restored and deputizing Ford Lincoln Mercury as another postal carrier. Abby, who has an infertile husband, asks Shakespeare to impregnate her; after Bethlehem kills her husband and takes her prisoner, she escapes with Shakespeare into the mountains for the winter. When the two emerge, Shakespeare discovers that Ford Lincoln Mercury has created a fledgling postal system, giving birth to a resistance movement against the Holnists. After Bethlehem brutally murders postal workers and Shakespeare is tempted to give up, he and Shakespeare confront each other in single combat.

The Postman's central theme is social cohesiveness and cultural continuity, and like the postal service Shakespeare's plays serve as one vehicle for those values. As the film opens, Shakespeare performs for a village the final scene of a much-reduced version of *Macbeth* (with his mule Bill as co-star), including a mangled version of Macbeth's "Tomorrow and tomorrow and tomorrow" speech (in this version, Shakespeare speaks of a tale told by a "moron") and concluding with the portentous couplet, "But blow, wind, come, wrack, / At least we'll die with the harness off our back." (Later, Shakespeare paraphrases the meaning of this line as "Live free or die"; the quotation inspires Woody, a Holnist captive, to help Shakespeare in his escape from the Holnist army.) When the Holnists arrive, Bethlehem sees the children playing with swords and recognizes the play as Shakespeare (as well as its subversive potential). When Shakespeare arrives at Bethlehem's labor camp, he and Bethlehem trade Shakespearean quotations. Bethlehem's choices—"Cry 'havoc,' and let slip the dogs of war" (*Julius Caesar* 3.1), and "we few, we happy few, we band of brothers" (*Henry V* 4.3)—suggest his fascist militarism, whereas Shakespeare's choices—"To be or not to be: that is the question" (*Hamlet* 3.1) and "Now is the winter of our discontent / Made glorious summer by this son of York" (*Richard III* 1.1)—hint at his concern with freedom and resistance. When Shakespeare resolves to confront Bethlehem directly, he recites Henry V's "Once more into the breach" speech (*Henry V* 3.1) in anticipation of their battle; when Bethlehem asks who he is, Shakespeare reminds him by citing "Cry 'havoc.'" Throughout the film Shakespeare is consistently associated with rhetoric that inspires men to courageous acts of resistance, something that Bethlehem instinctively understands and fears. These Shakespearean allusions are set against various pop-cultural references—to self-help manuals, *The Sound of Music*, *Universal Soldier*, and *Rio Grande*—associated with Bethlehem's fascist camp. *The*

Postman is a revealing film for those interested in associations between Shakespeare and America.

1404 *The Last Days of Disco*
1998. U.S. Castle Rock Entertainment and Westerly Films. Sound, col., 113 mins. Whit Stillman.

A character study of a group of female roommates and their men who congregate at an exclusive Manhattan disco for conversation, cocktails, and romantic intrigue. The roommates are beautiful, snotty, social-climbing Charlotte Pingress (a book editor); reserved, victimized Alice Kinnon (also a book editor); and quiet Holly. The men in their lives are Tom Platt (a young attorney who is interested in Alice), Jimmy Steinway (an ad executive who gets his clients into the club), Dan Powers (another book editor), Josh Neff (an assistant district attorney), and Des McGrath (Studio 54's assistant manager and a gay-pretender lothario).

With self-revealing irony, Des and Jimmy reflect upon Shakespearean lines as they leave the country. Des sees "To thine own self be true" (*Hamlet* 1.3) as premised on a false assumption, and Jimmy admires "Et tu, Brute" (*Julius Caesar* 3.1) as an expression of loyalty.

1405 *My Giant*
1998. U.S. Castle Rock Entertainment, Columbia Pictures, and Face Productions. Sound, col., 103 mins. Michael Lehmann.

Sammy Kanin, a struggling talent agent neglectful of his son Nick and wife Serena, travels to Romania to visit his one remaining client, Justin Allen, a teen heartthrob appearing in a period action film. A car accident brings Sammy in contact with Max Zamphirescu, a giant who works as the caretaker of a local monastery. Sensing that Max is a bankable commodity, Sammy gets him a part in the action film and takes him to the United States, where Max hopes to reunite with a former girlfriend, Lillianna Rotaro, who moved to New Mexico after their break-up. Sammy, anxious to get Max a role as the villain in Steven Seagal's latest action film, takes him to Las Vegas with the promise of seeing Lillianna, but Max contacts Lillianna and discovers she wants no contact with him. Sammy then learns that Max is dying of an enlarged heart and works to bring Max and Lillianna back together, all the while reconciling with his own family.

Max frequently quotes Shakespeare.

1406 *Tea With Mussolini*
1999. Italy and U.K. Cattleya, Cineritmo, Film & General Productions, Medusa Produzione, and Universal. Sound, col., 117 mins. Franco Zeffirelli.

This coming-of-age tale focuses on the childhood of Luca, a motherless boy living in Florence during the rise of Mussolini. Five women, Mary (an English woman on her European tour), Lady Hester (a diplomat's wife), Arabella (an artist), Elsa (an American art collector), and Georgie (an American), all eccentric, take him under their wing as they soak up Italian culture and teach him how to be a perfect English gentleman. Eventually Luca's otherwise distant father, concerned that the boy is becoming too British in the company of the women, sends him to an Austrian boarding school where he will become a Nazi. As war commences, Luca returns and helps the women survive several traumas, as he works through a crush on Elsa.

Shakespeare is an important touchstone in Mary's relationship with Luca. In an important scene, Mary and Luca perform the balcony scene from *Romeo and Juliet* using a toy theater. Juliet's cautioning Romeo not to swear on the moon "lest that thy love prove likewise variable" becomes a lesson for Luca about the everlasting nature of true love, something he desires given his family's rejection of him; the scene is interrupted by the rioting of brownshirts outside. (Since the film is semiautobiographical, this scene is of particular interest for Zefferelli's film adaptation of *Romeo and Juliet*.) Later, when Luca is sent to Austria, the women, led by Mary, send him off on the train with a rousing rendition of Henry V's Crispin Crispian speech. When Luca becomes jealous of Elsa's dashing Italian lover, Mary comments, "the green-eyed monster"; later Luca changes his mind and helps Elsa escape, declaring, "Love thyself last" (Wolsey's line from *Henry VIII* 3.2). In the epilogue, we learn that after the war, Mary taught children Shakespeare and right from wrong.

1407 *From Hell*

2001. U.S. 20th Century Fox and Underworld Entertainment. Sound, col., 137 mins. Albert Hughes and Allan Hughes.

Adapted from the graphic novel by Alan Moore and Eddie Campbell. In this version of the Jack the Ripper story, master detective and opium addict Fred Abberline has a talent for finding psychopathic criminals, which he does with the aid of drug-induced visions. He and partner Peter Godley track Jack the Ripper as Abberline develops a romance with beautiful prostitute Mary Kelly. Sir Charles Warren, Abberline's boss, insists that the crimes have been committed by a non-British criminal. Desperate to solve the crime before Mary, the Ripper's next target, is killed, Abberline discovers that Sir William Gull, the royal surgeon, is the serial killer, linked to a Masonic conspiracy that involves the monarchy.

Peter Godley repeatedly references Shakespeare. His comment "Once more into the breach, dear friends" goes over the heads of his fellow detectives; in bringing the reluctant Mary to Abberline, he says, "She's madly in love with me, though she hides it well," referencing Petruchio's characterization of Kate to Baptista; when Abberline objects to Mary being called a whore, he replies, "a rose by any other name"; when Abberline spins out a convoluted

theory of the crimes, he calls him Othello, a man for whom everything is suspicious; a vile piece of anti-Semitic graffiti he sardonically dubs "hardly Shakespeare"; and when he discover Abberline dead from opium, he says, "Good night, sweet prince."

1408 *Lost and Delirious*

2001. Canada. Cité-Amerique and Greg Dummett Films. Sound, col., 103 mins. Léa Pool.

Adapted from the novel *The Wives of Bath* by Susan Swan. Before Mary Bradford can recover from the death of her mother, her father and new stepmother send her to a Canadian all-girls' boarding school, where she is befriended by roommates Tory Moller and Paulie Oster, who she soon learns are engaged in a lesbian affair. When Tory's sister Allison threatens to expose the affair to Tory's parents, Tory jilts Paulie and takes up with Jake Hollander, a boy at a nearby school. Heartbroken Paulie attempts to win back Tory with poetry, cares for an injured bird that she sees as a version of herself, and is offered sympathy from Fay Vaughn, one of her teachers.

In her attempt to win Tory's affection, Paulie quotes *Romeo and Juliet* and *Twelfth Night* (the "willow cabin" speech). Fay Vaughn, an English teacher, teaches a class on *Antony and Cleopatra* in which she uncomfortably over-identifies with the characters. Also briefly referenced is "to thine own self be true" from *Hamlet* 1.3.

1409 *Bollywood Hollywood*

2002. Canada. CHUM Television and Momentum Pictures. Sound, col., 105 mins. Deepa Mehta.

A parody of Bollywood musicals. After Rahul Seth, an Indo-Canadian millionaire, defies his family to date Kimberley, a white pop star, she dies in an accident, leaving him distraught. His mother uses events to pressure him into marrying an Indian girl (he must wed before his sister Twinky can do so, and she is already pregnant), so Rahul asks Sue Singh, a high-class escort, to pretend to be his Indian fiancée, even though she is, so he thinks, Hispanic. After Sue charms Rahul's family during the wedding preparations for Rahul's family, she reveals that she is Indian and she and Rahul fall in love.

In a send-up of the stereotypical wise Indian grandmother, Grandma Ji repeatedly misquotes Shakespeare: "Et tu, Brutus," "This is the winter of our discontent," "All the world's a stage," "Here's the smell of the blood still: all the perfumes of Arabia will not sweeten this little hand," and "I'm here not to bury Caesar, but to praise him." All the references are comically relevant to the plot and puncture the melodrama. The situation of conditioning one child's marriage on the marriage of another obliquely may recall the central premise of *The Taming of the Shrew*. Rahul's father returns as a ghost (twice) to encourage him. Late in the film, as Sue stands on the balcony of her bedroom, Rahul courts her with poetry; when he turns his back, she is replaced by her mother (not unlike Juliet's Nurse in the balcony scene).

1410 *Bloody Streetz*
2003. U.S. Gee-Bee Productions and Hush Hush Studios. Sound, col., 83 mins. Gerald Barclay.

Shot on digital video in a gritty documentary style, *Bloody Streetz* chronicles the rise and fall of Black, a killer for hire on the streets of New York. Though he is himself a ruthless, violent thug, Black seeks revenge on the killer of his child during a drive-by shooting. His friend Jah identifies his child's killer as Musa, an African, and after Jah is assassinated for divulging that information, Black violently murders Musa. Having exacted his revenge for his friend and his child, Black seems ready to take up a steady relationship with Semaji, a nurse, and to leave behind his life of violence. However, when an African van driver chastises him for being a killer, Black impulsively murders him and afterward is plagued by visions of bloody hands and paranoid hallucinations. Acting on one of those hallucinations, he accidentally shoots Semaji and she dies in his arms. Distraught with guilt, Black carries her body to the funeral of the van driver and kills himself. Rather daringly, this plot is intercut with an extended interview with Adunni Oshupa Tamasi on black oppression in America, and director Gerald Barclay adds a coda in which he imagines a happy rather than tragic ending for Black and Semaji.

The film opens with the epithet "Tremble, thou wretch, / That hast within thee undivulged crimes, / Unwhipp'd of justice" (*King Lear* 3.2), which the director claims contains the film's entire story in miniature. Black's guilty hallucination of his repeatedly bloody hands after the van driver's murder is adapted from Lady Macbeth's hand-washing in *Macbeth* 5.1.

DVD includes a commentary track on which director and writer Gerald Barclay identifies the Shakespearean allusions in the film.

1411 *Will to Kill*
2003. U.S. Cinematoast Productions. Sound, col. (tinted), 17 mins. Mark Vittek.

Elizabeth, despondent over her divorce from Michael, decides to kill herself in grand Shakespearean style with soliloquies and a poisoned drink. She is interrupted by a pizza delivery boy who, he says, has been contracted to kill her for her husband. After he fails to do so, the two bond until Elizabeth learns that he's picked the wrong house. After he leaves, she discovers that he's unwittingly drunk her poisoned drink.

This black comic farce is filled with Shakespearean citations. Elizabeth gives a portion of Romeo's death speech (*Romeo and Juliet* 5.3.110–15) and Horatio's parting words to Hamlet (*Hamlet* 5.2.301–2) before the delivery man arrives. She also observes that Shakespeare "must've been a real boozehound, how else could he have written all those stupid-ass tragedies?" When she resumes her suicide, she begins the "all the world's a stage" speech from *As You Like It* until the pizza delivery man interrupts her. After the doomed delivery man leaves, she offers Puck's lines, "And the youth mistook by me, / Pleading for a lover's fee. / Shall we their fond pageant see? / Lord, what fools these lovers be?" (*A Midsummer Night's Dream* 3.2.112–15). Her Gothic mansion contains a Shakespeare bust and text of *Hamlet*, and we learn that she and Michael were former Shakespearean actors at an Alabama dinner theater. The film's primary parodic object is the melodramatic nature of Shakespeare's tragic speeches.

1412 *Jack's Playground 10*
2004. U.S. Digital Playground. Sound, col., 93 mins. Robby D.

Hardcore pornography. A very loosely structured series of comic sexual vignettes.

In the first vignette, a woman named Shy Love encounters Eric Masterson in a doublet and ruff, working for "TP" at "Livid Video" on a Shakespearean pornographic film. (The allusion is to Paul Thomas at Vivid Video, who has directed several Shakespeare-themed pornographic films.) Shy Love says that the costume makes him look "like a fag."

1413 *The Prince & Me*
2004. U.S. Paramount Pictures, Lions Gate Films, Sobini Films, and Stillking Films. Sound, col., 111 mins. Martha Coolidge.

Edvard, the callow heir apparent of Denmark, enrolls at the University of Wisconsin in order to mature and escape the tabloids. Once there he meets Paige Morgan, an academically driven farm girl with ambitions of becoming a doctor. Edvard—pretending to be Eddie—woos her, and they become close when she takes him home for the Thanksgiving holiday. After the two are photographed kissing in the library by tabloid photographers, Paige learns his true identity and the two temporarily part ways, Edvard returning to Denmark to ascend to the throne. However, Paige, following her heart, goes to Denmark where she and Edvard renew their romance, Paige consenting to marry him. As she is groomed to be queen, Paige comes to recognize what she is sacrificing and she reluctantly returns to America to complete her studies. During her graduation, Edvard arrives and offers to wait for her to complete her medical studies before they marry.

Shakespeare plays a key role in this modernized fairy tale. Paige, a medical student, repeatedly expresses her dislike of Shakespeare. Edvard, by contrast, knows his Shakespeare well. To apologize for his boorish behavior toward Paige, he slightly misquotes Juliet's apology for disobedience to her father in 4.2. (At first Paige doesn't recognize the quotation as Shakespeare, and once she does she thinks quoting Shakespeare marks him as a phony.) In a key scene in a laundry, Paige's comment about Hamlet leads Edvard to identify with the Prince's plight. They go on to discuss the meaning of Sonnet 148, with Edvard teaching Paige how to parse the line "the sun itself sees not till heaven clears." As a result, Paige aces her Shakespeare midterm. In an oral final examination for the class, Paige discusses *Macbeth* and *Othello* before she connects the issue of destiny with her own romantic problems. A goodbye note from Eddie references the line from Sonnet 148, leading to Paige to leave for Denmark. And when Eddie attends Paige's graduation, he greets her (unironically) with Titania's praise of Bottom from *A Midsummer Night's Dream*, "Thou art as wise as thou art beautiful" (3.1). In this case, Shakespeare is essential to Edvard's Euro-chic and aristocratic status. The narrative includes elements of *Romeo and Juliet*—Edvard's mother at first disapproves of Paige—but the connection is not developed at any length. Noteworthy too is that Paige is played by Julia Stiles, who starred in several teen Shakespeare spin-offs in the 1990s.

DVD includes a director's commentary track that references Shakespeare.

1414 *Wonderland*
2006. U.S. Metro/Cal Vista. Sound, col., 112 mins. DCypher.

A highly literary adult porn feature that includes references to *A Midsummer Night's Dream* and *Hamlet* spoken by actress Violet Blue. The film begins by quoting from Vladimir Nabokov's *Lolita*. (RB)

Shakespeare as Character or Icon

1415 *The Life of Shakespeare* (aka *The Loves and Adventures in the Life of Shakespeare*)
1914. U.K. British & Colonial Kinematograph Company. Silent, b&w, 5 reels. Frank R. Growcott and J. B. McDowell.

A film biography of Shakespeare that showcases its own historical accuracy. In the final scene, we see Shakespeare dreaming of scenes from his plays: *The Merchant of Venice*, *Macbeth*, *Hamlet*, and *The Merry Wives of Windsor*.

1416 *Master Shakespeare, Strolling Player*
1916. U.S. Thanhouser Film Corporation. Silent, b&w, 5 reels. Frederic Sullivan.

Produced during the flurry of Shakespeare films during the tercentennial of his death. Miss Gray and Lieutenant Stanton are engaged, but they cannot agree who wrote the works of Shakespeare; Gray is a committed Baconian and Stanton a equally adamant Stratfordian, and so vehement is their disagreement that they break off their engagement. Transferred to the Mexican border wars, Stanton is wounded, and when Gray hears of his suffering, she falls into a trance in which she is transported back to Elizabethan England. When two men fight over her at a tavern, Stanton defends her, aided by Shakespeare, who is a strolling player. Later, Francis Bacon falls in love with her and reveals his envy of Shakespeare at a performance of one of his plays, bribing a scholar to claim that the play was written by Bacon. When Stanton reveals Bacon's plot, he is challenged to a duel in which Bacon shoots him. As Gray wakes from her trance, she discovers that Stanton is with her in the present and that he is not hurt as badly as had been reported. She renounces her Baconian hypothesis, and the couple is reconciled.

An interesting hybrid of Shakespearean pseudobiography and swashbuckling costume drama. Thanhouser was a noted Shakespearean actor.

1417 *Old Bill "through the Ages"*
1924. U.K. Ideal. Silent, b&w, 8 reels. Thomas Bentley.

A live-action feature that has its origins in comic strips by Bruce Bairnsfather. An aging soldier, Old Bill, has dreams in which he participates in key moments of British and American history, such as the Battle of Hastings and the Boston Tea Party. In one of his dreams, he meets Shakespeare and Queen Elizabeth.

1418 *Shakespeare Was Right*
1927–1930. U.S. Production company unknown. Sound, b&w, length unknown. Director unknown.

A lost film.

1419 *Shakespeare with Tin Ears*
1933. U.S. Production company unknown. Sound, b&w, length unknown. Harry Sweet.

A lost film; apparently a musical short.

1420 *The Immortal Gentleman*
1935. U.S. Bernard Smith Films and Equity Pictures. Sound, b&w, 61 mins. Widgey R. Newman.

Ben Jonson and Michael Drayton join Shakespeare in a tavern in Southwark to people-watch; as they discuss various people they meet, Shakespeare is reminded of his characters, and we see performances of relevant passages from his plays. One of the first films to suggest that Shakespeare's writing sprang from his observation of contemporary Renaissance London life. Compare *Shakespeare in Love*.

1421 *Master Will Shakespeare*
1936. U.S. MGM. Sound, b&w, 11 mins. Jacques Tourneur.

Created as a promotional short for George Cukor's 1936 *Romeo and Juliet*, this film details the various jobs in the theater that Shakespeare worked at. Tourneur was to go on to become a respected director of atmospheric B-horror films. See also entries 1248, 2030, and 3531.

1422 *Shake, Mr. Shakespeare*
1936. U.S. Vitaphone Company and Warner Bros. Sound, b&w, 2 reels. Ray Mack.

Created as a tie-in for Dieterle and Reinhardt's 1935 *Midsummer Night's Dream*, this musical short imagines a hybrid between Shakespeare and swing music. An assistant director is ordered to read all of Shakespeare's works in order to mine them for potential film plots. Falling asleep on the job, he dreams of various Shakespearean characters coming to life from the pages of giant books and singing and dancing in celebration of their "goin' Hollywood." The characters appearing include Romeo, Juliet, Juliet's Nurse, Puck, Peter Quince, Hamlet, Old Hamlet's Ghost, Falstaff, Antony, Cleopatra, and Macbeth. Shakespeare appears toward the end of the film to object, but he is quickly convinced by his characters to join the big song and dance number. Includes passing references to a number of Shakespearean commonplaces—"To be or not to be," Romeo and Juliet's balcony scene, Hamlet with Yorick's skull, Cleopatra's barge, and the like.

1423 *The Ghost Ship*
1943. RKO Pictures. Sound, b&w, 69 mins. Tom Robson.

In this fascinating and acutely timely film, there's an exchange between the radioman Jacob "Sparks" Winslow, and the hero of the film, Tom Merriam, 3rd officer. Sparks calls Miriam "Tertius" and explains that is Latin for "third." Sparks says that Merriam is like Shakespeare in having small Latin and less Greek. When Sparks speaks again in Latin, Merriam says, "Remember, I don't know Shakespeare." The film has echoes of Jack London's *The Sea Wolf* and anticipates the 1954 film *The Caine Mutiny*. *The Ghost Ship* is a much darker film, however, in postulating that the ship's crew—because composed of men who are indifferent or cowardly, according to the psychotic, murderous captain—will not rebel against authority. (RB)

1424 *A Witch's Tangled Hare*
1959. U.S. Warner Brothers. Sound, col., 6 mins. Abe Levitow.

Shakespeare walks up to Macbeth's castle, and begins to write down a play. When he hears a cackle, the attention moves to a witch at her cauldron, saying "double, double, toil and trouble." When she tries to add Bugs Bunny to the brew, he runs to Macbeth's castle, where he uses various means to resist being caught by her. When Bugs encounters Shakespeare, he learns that he is in fact Sam Crubish and that the witch is Witch Hazel, his former girlfriend. Hazel asks Crubish why he never met her parents, and he claims she gave him the wrong apartment number, 2B. As the two argue, Bugs launches into "2B or not 2B, that is the question."

In addition to the Shakespearean jokes above, Bugs and the witch offer a parody of the balcony scene, with Bugs as Romeo and the witch as Juliet. To the witch's "Wherefore art thou, Romeo?" Bugs replies, "Herefore I art." Throughout the cartoon, we see Shakespeare/Sam writing down what he sees happening.

1425 *Next*
1989. U.K. Aardman Animations and Channel Four Films. Sound, col., 5 mins. Barry Purves.

Animated film, using stop-motion photography and articulated puppets. Will, a player who looks like Shakespeare, auditions before Peter, a producer who reads the paper while he acts (and who resembles Peter Hall, one of the founders of the Royal Shakespeare Company). In less than five minutes, and using various costumes and props, particularly a life-sized doll, Will performs in pantomime key scenes from the entirety of Shakespeare's works. In the end Peter looks up from his paper and says, "Next!"

The film contains fleeting references to all of Shakespeare's plays, though all of the allusions are in pantomime. Typical of Aardman Studios (better known as the creators of *Wallace and Gromit*), the animation is stunning, and the film makes a case for locating Shakespeare's artistry not so much in words as in memorable scenes of physical movement and pose, the stuff of puppet animators. Like *Theatre of Blood*, this short stages a confrontation between the virtuoso Shakespearean performer, here allied with Shakespeare himself, and a critical and directorial establishment more concerned with fame and finance than art. Ironically, one needs a very close knowledge of the Shakespearean canon to catch all the references in Will's performance, particularly at the speed they pass by.

1426 *Blackadder Back and Forth*
1999. U.K. New Millennium Experience Company and Tiger Aspect Productions. Sound, col., 33 mins. Peter Weiland.

Originally produced for exhibition at London's Millennium Dome, this short film was a Christmas special reprise of the *Blackadder* series, broadcast on the Sky network and later released on video. On New Year's Eve 1999, a modern Edmund Blackadder and Baldrick build Leonardo da Vinci's time machine and on a dare travel through time to collect souvenirs; at first their travels are a practical joke on their party guests, but they soon realize that the time machine they have built really works. They visit prehistoric time, Roman Britain, the Middle Ages (where they meet Robin Hood), the reign of Elizabeth I, and the battle of Waterloo before returning to the present to find their fortunes radically changed.

During Blackadder's visit to the court of Elizabeth, he runs into (literally) the then-unknown Shakespeare, who is carrying a copy of his newest play, *Macbeth*. Blackadder gets him to sign his autograph before kicking him for all the schoolchildren who are forced to read his works throughout time. He also makes a joke of Branagh's full-length *Hamlet* film. Referenced by title are *Macbeth*, *The Two Gentlemen of Verona*, *Othello*, *A Midsummer Night's Dream*, and *Hamlet*. Shakespeare is played by Colin Firth, the romantic star of *Pride and Prejudice* and the Bridget Jones films.

DVD includes a "Making Of" featurette that references Shakespeare.

1427 *Sofies verden (Sophie's World)*
1999. Norway. Norsk Rikskringkasting. Sound, col., 113 mins. Erik Gustavson.

Adapted from the book by Jostein Gaarder. In this fascinating metafictional film, Sofie, a young girl from Norway, receives a tape from a mysterious reporter, Alberto Knox, in which he seems to speak to her from ancient Greece. After he and Sofie meet many times to take sojourns throughout European history and cultures from the ancient Greeks to the present day, the two realize that they are only characters in a fictional work by Major Albert Knag intended to give his daughter Hilde an education in philosophy. Concerned that as just fictional characters they will disappear once the Major completes his novel, Sophie and Alberto escape into reality, only to discover that they cannot interact with real people. In the end, Sophie and Alberto recognize that as fictional characters, they inhabit the world of ideas and are thus immortal.

In Sophie's travel to the Renaissance, she meets Shakespeare, where he is rehearsing with an actor playing Hamlet (who is in black doublet and carries a skull). Shakespeare pointedly speaks to Sophie, "To be or not to be: that is the question," deepening her own questions about the nature of her existence.

1428 *William Psychspeare's Taming of the Shrink*
1999. U.S. Aimee La March. Sound, col., 10 mins. Ken Boynton.

Available on Atomfilms.com. A short film, entirely in iambic couplets, in which four office workers, Ecculus, Bulbis, Permia, and Richard, share their respective psychological problems (anger control, divorce, obsessive compulsive disorder, and wealthy disenchantment) with Psychis of Therapis, who looks very much like Shakespeare. Though the setting is contemporary, the characters are dressed in Elizabethan finery. The film rather deftly deflates psychobabble and New Age clichés by putting them in goofy pseudo-Shakespearean language. For example:

Each week at this time this chair you sit on
To speak of your childhood and carry on
Plumbing the depths of your mental distress
And how compulsively you do obsess.
With pitiful tears your eyes glisten;
I do not judge you—my job's to listen.

There are no specific citations from Shakespeare's dialogue.

1429 *Sexspeare: The Uncensored Lusty Works of William Sexspeare*
2003. U.S. Jill Kelly Productions. Sound, col., 87 mins. Shawn Ricks.

Hardcore pornography. A mock revisionary account of Shakespeare's writings offered by William Sexspeare the 24th, Shakespeare's heir. The film's premise is that Shakespeare's writings were censored because of the prevailing taste of Queen Elizabeth, the Virgin Queen.

Includes sequences involving a female Hamlet and female Horatio in the graveyard scene, Bottom and Titania's first meeting, Romeo and Juliet's balcony scene, Lady Macbeth and the Doctor in the sleepwalking scene, and Macbeth with two of the three witches. Many passing verbal citations (most of them bawdy plays on Shakespearean lines) and parodies.

1430 *Shakespeare's Dilemma*
2003. U.S. Lyons Den Productions. Sound, col., 37 mins. John C. Lyons.

In this parody of modern office politics, a PowerPoint-obsessed Shakespeare and several of his characters prepare for an impending audit by Othello and engage in petty backstabbing. There are no citations of Shakespeare's dialogue, but the script is in pseudo-Elizabethan English and the characters are dressed in Renaissance attire (though the action is set in a modern office complex). In addition to Shakespeare (the office manager) himself, characters from Shakespeare include Lady Macbeth, Othello, Iago, Katherina, Nerissa, Baptista, Petruchio, and Romeo. At the end of the film, we learn that the fiction we've seen is from a screenplay by Bill Spears, an executive whose mental breakdown has rendered him homeless and mad. Compare *William Psychspeare's Taming of the Shrink*.

The DVD includes several extras, many of which feature Shakespearean characters from the film.

1431 *Confessions of a Teenage Drama Queen*
2004. U.S. Disney. Sound, col., 89 mins. Sara Sugarman.

The main character of *Confessions of a Teenage Drama Queen*, Mary (Lindsay Lohan), aka Lola, says four times that Stu Wolf, lead singer and lyricist of rock band Sidarthur, is "the best poet since Shakespeare"—twice in his presence. She paraphrases Horatio's line after Hamlet dies—"Good night, sweet prince, And flights of angels sing thee to thy rest" (5.2.370–71)—as "good night, and choirs of angels rock him to his rest" when the band breaks up, and then later says she has sunk into a depression deeper than Hamlet's. The official film website is http://disney.go.com/disneyvideos/liveaction/confessions. See *Mean Girls*, *Jawbreakers*, *Porky's 2*, *The Prince and Me*, and *Not Another Teen Movie*. (RB)

Shakespearean Actors and Performances

1432 *The Old Actor*
1912. U.S. Biograph. Silent, b&w, 17 mins. (1 reel). D. W. Griffith.

An aging actor, no longer able to find work or support his family, contemplates suicide by drowning, only to be stopped by a last-minute vision of his family. Seeing a beggar, he decides to disguise himself as a poor man and deliver Shakespearean speeches at an upmarket restaurant. A theater manager takes notice and hires him for a successful show, and the old actor uses the cash advance to provide for his starving wife and children. The film references the "seven ages" speech from *As You Like It*, and Macbeth's "tomorrow and tomorrow" soliloquy.

1433 *Kean*
1923. France. Albatross. Silent, b&w, 94 mins. Alexandre Volkoff.

Adapted from the play *Kean* by Alexandre Dumas père. Kean, a lowborn actor in love with Elena Koeffeld, an aristocratic woman, uses Shakespeare to voice his secret desire for her, though she marries a count. In a performance of *Hamlet*, he sees his former lover in the audience and interrupts the play to declare his love, express his longing to push beyond the barriers of his art, battle class-oriented social injustice, and even accuse the prince of Wales who is in the audience. In the end, he is a broken man, dying penniless in a hospital. The film references *Othello*, *Hamlet*, and *Romeo and Juliet*. This tale was perennially popular among European filmmakers, for there are additional French and Italian adaptations.

1434 *Das Alte Gesetz* (*Baruch* or *This Ancient Law*)
1923. Germany. Comedia-Film GmbH. Silent, b&w, 128 mins. Ewald André Dupont.

From the memoirs of Heinrich Laube. Baruch Mayr, son of a poor Orthodox rabbi, leaves Galizia to seek his fortune as an actor. His father, horrified at his son's rejection of his religion and family, disowns him. While working in a small minstrel show, Baruch is befriended by an Austrian archduchess who introduces him to a director at the Burgtheater in Vienna, where Baruch soon becomes a contract player. Even though he is a Reformed Jew, the Austrian court is disapproving of his relationship with the archduchess and he is forced to end contact. When a friend of Baruch's father, the man who first introduced Baruch to the theater, visits him, Baruch becomes homesick and returns to Galizia with the intention of marrying his village sweetheart and mending fences with his parents. But Baruch's father refuses to forgive him, and Baruch returns to Vienna with his sweetheart as his bride; the friend of Baruch's father vows to intervene with Baruch's father in an effort to reconcile the two.

While an actor at the Burgtheater, Baruch appears briefly in two Shakespearean plays, *Romeo and Juliet* and *Hamlet*.

1435 *Success*
1923. U.S. MGM. Silent, b&w, 7 reels. Ralph Ince.

Barry Carleton is a famous Shakespearean who, unable to handle success, turns to alcohol, soon causing his wife Jane to leave him, taking daughter Rose with her. Many years later, Carleton, penniless and alone, secretly applies to play the role of King Lear in a production in which Rose, now grown, will star as Cordelia. Instead, he is assigned to be the dresser for Gilbert Gordon, the star who gets the role of Lear. He learns that the show's financier has cast Rose in the starring role so he can seduce her. On the show's opening night, Gordon, who also knows the financier's sordid intentions, deliberately gets drunk so that Carleton can step into the part of Lear. The show is a triumph, and so Carleton's reputation is restored. He is reunited with his wife and daughter, and Rose is engaged to Gilbert.

1436 *Der Gardeoffizier* (aka *Der Liebgardist*)
1925. Austria. Pan-Film, Wien and Phoebus Film. Silent, b&w, 8,267 ft. Robert Wiene.

When an egotistical actor begins to suspect, on the basis of no evidence, that his wife is unfaithful, he disguises himself as a handsome guardsman and woos his own wife in disguise. She refuses his advances, and so he wonders whether or not she has seen through his disguise. Includes scenes from *Othello* and *Hamlet*.

1437 *The Royal Family of Broadway*
1930. U.S. Paramount. Sound, b&w, 82 mins. George Cukor and Cyril Gardner.

Adapted from the play by Edna Ferber and George Kaufman. In this farce concerning the Cavendish family, a theatrical dynasty, Julia and Gwen struggle with their choices between romances and stage careers, while brother Anthony must hide out to avoid a breach of promise and scandal. Based upon the Barrymore family.

Several passing references: as the film opens, Julia Cavendish is starring in *Romeo and Juliet* on Broadway; Fanny, matriarch of the family, exits quoting Lady Macbeth's "To bed, to bed! there's knocking at the gate: / come, come, come, come, give me your hand. / What's done cannot be undone.—To bed, to bed, to bed!"; a bust of Shakespeare is positioned at the top of the staircase; and Fanny dies while acting in *The Merry Wives of Windsor* and Julia substitutes for her as the film closes.

1438 *In the Money*
1933. U.S. Chesterfield Motion Pictures Corporation. Sound, b&w, 66 mins. Frank Strayer.

In this screwball comedy, Professor Higginbotham, patriarch of a wealthy and eccentric family, learns that his income has been lost due to the loss of the family business, a chemical company. Though Higginbotham tries to change their extravagant ways with the help of his oldest daughter Mary (aka Lambie), the other children—Babs and her ex-fighter boyfriend Bibbs, and Genie and her ne'er-do-well husband Lionel—fail to heed their warnings. Youngest child Dick becomes paralyzed when he crashes during a motorcycle race in which he hoped to win money for the family. Spunk Hobbs, Bibbs's manager, proposes that Bibbs fight one last fight to win the money for Dick's operation, and Spunk and Mary marry so that she can control sufficient stock to restore her father's chemical company to his control. Bibbs wins, Dick is restored, and the promised marriage of Spunk and Mary restores the company to his control. The film was remade in 1936 as *Red Lights Ahead*.

At film's end, Bibbs retires from the boxing ring to pursue a career as a Shakespearean actor.

1439 *Morning Glory*
1933. U.S. RKO Radio Pictures. Sound, b&w, 74 mins. Lowell Sherman.

In this backstage melodrama, an aspiring actress from Vermont filled with naïvely romantic conceptions of the theater, Eva Lovelace, tries to break into New York theater with the help of theater impresario Louis Easton and playwright Joseph Sheridan. At one of Easton's parties she gets drunk and becomes romantically involved with Easton, but Easton uses Sheridan to give her the brush-off afterward. She soon falls on hard times and is reduced to working as a model and vaudeville assistant. Meanwhile, Sheridan and Easton prepare *The Golden Bough*, a major play, for its première. When just before curtain time the vapid star, Rita Vernon, attempts to extort a contract from Easton, he consents to Sheridan's suggestion that they replace Rita with Eva, who secretly has been understudying the main part. She is an instant success, and afterward learns of Easton's interest in her only as a theatrical property and of Sheridan's long-standing love for her; her concern is not to become an ephemeral "morning glory." The film was remade in 1958 as *Star Struck*.

Early in the film, as Eva discusses her acting ambitions, she expresses her desire to play Lady Macbeth, Juliet, and Cleopatra. Later, at Easton's party, Eva, emboldened by alcohol, gives an earnest rendition of Hamlet's "To be or not to be" soliloquy. When a drunk guest comments that he saw Charlie Chaplin do the same speech, but not as comically, she shifts to Juliet in the balcony scene from *Romeo and Juliet*. Though the partygoers applaud her performance, the other actresses do not recognize the source of the part.

1440 *I'll Love You Always*
1935. U.S. Columbia Pictures. Sound, b&w, 75 mins. Leo Bulgakov.

The melodrama details the employment difficulties of Carl Brent, an engineering student, and Nora Clegg, an actress in her father's Shakespearean company, when they move to New York City soon after getting married. At first overly confident, Carl has difficulty finding work and eventually works as a mover; frustrated, he blames Nora, who has foregone an attractive job in Chicago to stay with Carl, instead working secretly in a Chinese restaurant. When Carl learns of Nora's job, he threatens divorce and vows to accept the offer of an engineering job in Russia; Nora tells him that she has accepted the job in Chicago and hides from him the fact that she is pregnant. When Carl goes to accept the job in Russia, Mr. Sandstone, the boss, angry at Carl's earlier rejection of a job, withdraws the offer, at which Carl, in dire need of money and anxious to curry Nora's favor, steals money from Sandstone to buy her new clothes. On the night of their parting, the two are pursued by a detective who, hearing Carl's story, vows not to reveal the theft to Nora. Carl goes to prison, but upon his release is hired by the now sympathetic Sandstone, and soon after Carl is reconciled with his wife and child.

Early in the film, the Shakespearean company of Nora's father is briefly alluded to.

1441 *Peg of Old Drury*
1935. U.K. British and Dominions Film Corporation and United Artists. Sound, b&w, 74 mins. Herbert Wilcox.

Based upon the play *Masks and Faces* by Charles Reade and Tom Taylor. After rejecting the proposal of Michael O'Taaffe, an aspiring Irish actor, Peg Woffington, having reconsidered, arrives in London to surprise him; O'Taaffe is now involved with Margaret Dallaway, and he delays Woffington by telling her that he cannot marry her yet because of his strained finances. By chance, Peg meets David Garrick, currently starring as Shylock in *The Merchant of Venice*, and she forms the idea of acting to earn money. Disguised as an old woman, she wins a bit part in a Drury Lane performance of Jonson's *The Alchemist*; when she tells Garrick that his performance as Richard III is mediocre, he gains a new respect and affection for her. O'Taaffe announces to Peg that he is being courted by a rich woman. When soon after she auditions for the role of a recently jilted woman, her convincing performance, informed by her experience, wins her the part and afterward audience accolades and Garrick's kiss, inflaming the jealousy of Kitty Clive, an older actress. She becomes the toast of theatrical circles, and though she at first loses out to Kitty Clive for the role of Rosalind, she later gives a performance of the part that moves her parents and Michael, who are in the audience. Michael attempts to woo her back, but when Peg dresses as a man at a party and hears him using lines he'd used on other women, she challenges him to a duel, which is stopped only through Garrick's intervention. A doctor warns Peg not to strain her weak heart by acting, but she keeps the information from Garrick, who continues to employ her as Rosalind. Garrick proposes to her before a performance of *As You Like It*, and Peg dies onstage in Garrick's arms.

Contains passages in eighteenth-century performance from *The Merchant of Venice*, *Richard III*, and *As You Like It*, as well as the Shakespearean motif of an assertive woman pretending to be a man in the company of her lovers. In effect, the film is a backstage melodrama.

1442 *Strangers All*
1935. U.S. RKO Radio Pictures. Sound, b&w, 70 mins. Charles Vidor.

Adapted from the play by Marie M. Bercovici. *Strangers All* chronicles the fortunes of the dysfunctional Carter family. Having postponed his marriage to sweetheart Frances Farrell, shopkeeper Murray Carter conscientiously supports his indulgent mother Anna, his brothers Lewis (a devoted socialist) and Dick (an egotistical aspiring actor), and his sister Lily (currently in college). Having failed an audition, Dick convinces Anna to finance his move to Hollywood with his sister's trousseau money, money that, unawares to either of them, Murray needs to prevent foreclosure on his store. Though Anna asks Murray to give the money to Dick, he refuses. Meanwhile, Lily returns home with her new husband, Patrick Green, a lawyer. When that night Lewis's speech at a socialist's meeting foments a riot, Dick plans to leave with the money before Lewis's arrest leads to the smearing of his family name, at which Anna laments her self-indulgence of her two sons. When Patrick refuses to defend Lewis in court, Murray turns to Frank Walker, Lily's former fiancé (also a lawyer), and he and the family offer a rousing defense at Lewis's trial, a favor that Lewis returns when his mother is threatened with contempt of court. Soon after, the family, now much closer, travels to Hollywood to see Dick appear in a movie, a move that, we learn, he financed without Lily's money.

Dick wanders the Carter home spouting hammy renditions of Shakespeare and thinks of himself as the next John Barrymore.

1443 *Hitch Hike to Heaven* (aka *Footlights and Shadows*)
1936. U.S. Chesterfield Pictures. Sound, b&w, 63 mins. Frank R. Strayer.

Deborah Delaney, the manager of a Shakespearean touring company who hates the movies, crosses swords with Melville De La Ney, a successful film actor. Two members of her company, Daniel (Melville's son) and young and beautiful Jerry Daley, are in love, but when Melville and his wife Nadia file for divorce, Jerry becomes an unwilling correspondent, leading to a scandal that destroys Melville's film career. By a series of coincidences, his reputation is soon restored, and Jerry becomes a film star and the wife of Daniel. The Shakespearean nature of Delaney's troupe leads to a number of minor citations of and jokes about Shakespeare.

1444 *Stage Door*
1937. U.S. RKO Pictures. Sound, b&w, 92 mins. Gregory La Cava.

Adapted from Edna Ferber and George Kaufmann's play by Morrie Ryskind and Anthony Veiller. This combination of screwball comedy and blackstage melodrama presents a group of aspiring actresses living at the Footlights Club, a theatrical boardinghouse, as they struggle to find work. Two of the actresses, wisecracking hoofer Jean Maitland and aristocratic debutante Terry Randall, become in different ways exploited by the sleazy producer Tony Powell. When Randall is given a part because of Powell's backroom dealings and her friend Kay, distraught at its loss, commits suicide, Randall gives a moving performance in tribute and becomes a star.

Though the film includes no direct quotations of Shakespeare, it does offer a passage in which the actresses ridicule Randall's passion for Shakespeare when she first arrives at the boardinghouse. This passage closely associates Shakespeare with Randall's upper-class, overintellectualized bearing as well as with the now-faded success of the boardinghouse's oldest resident. *Twelfth Night* and *Hamlet* are referenced by title, and one actress (played by a young Lucille Ball) pointedly declares her preference for *Amos 'n' Andy* over the Bard.

1445 *Kean*
1940. Italy. Scalera Film S.p.a. Sound, b&w, 87 mins. Guido Brignone.

See the plot summary for *Kean* (1923 [above]). In this adaptation, there are passages from *Henry V* and *Hamlet*.

1446 *Playmates*
1941. U.S. RKO Radio Pictures. Sound, b&w, 96 mins. David Butler.

Playing himself as a washed-up Shakespearean ham actor, John Barrymore, in an attempt to get publicity and a radio advertisement contract, teams up with cornball swing bandleader Kay Kyser to perform a USO Shakespearean festival for radio executive Nelson Pennypacker and his social-climbing wife Penelope. Though the grandiloquent Barrymore vehemently objects, he is enlisted to teach Kyser proper Shakespearean performance, while he balances dodging creditors, carrying on with Latin songstress Carmen del Toro (who targets Kyser on Barrymore's behalf), and romancing Kyser's singer and girlfriend Ginny Simms. When Barrymore concludes that Kyser is hopeless, he undertakes to sabotage his performance, but Kyser discovers his plot and produces a *Romeo and Juliet* of his own, set to swing music, garnering Barrymore his contract.

Playmates is one of several films in the 1930s and 1940s to juxtapose high cultural Shakespeare with pop cultural jazz music, in effect entering midcentury debates about mass culture. It is filled with many throwaway Shakespeare jokes and citations of Shakespearean dialogue, many of them mangled by Kyser's goofy delivery. Mark Antony's funeral oration from *Julius Caesar*, assayed by both Kyser and his agent Pete, is punctuated by bad puns. During his rehearsals with Barrymore, Kyser offers many of Shakespeare's greatest hits, including "All the world's a stage," "Who steals my purse steals trash," and "The quality of mercy is not strained." Barrymore offers citations of his own, including Lucio's line, "Our doubts are traitors / And make us lose the good we oft might win / By fearing to attempt" from *Measure for Measure* 1.4 (intended to calm Kyser's stage fright) and a portion of Romeo's "what light through yonder window breaks" speech. (The latter is offered on a phono recording, and the film is particularly interesting for the prominence it gives to recording and broadcast technology.) Early in the film, Barrymore delivers from memory an affecting "To be or not to be" to demonstrate his acting ability. A poignant sequence, it offers a fleeting glimpse of Barrymore's faded yet still considerable power as a Shakespearean. By the time of the film's making, Barrymore was a notorious drunk and womanizer plagued by tax problems, not the celebrated Shakespearean of the 1920s and 1930s, so his self-caricature as a highbrow poseur is often uncomfortably humiliating except for this one moment. The film's final sequence, Kyser's swing *Romeo and Juliet*, updates the feud between the families (here the Smiths and the Joneses) as one between highbrow opera and lowbrow swing, and emphasizes contemporary hip slang rather than Shakespeare's "quaint" language. The first "act" (actually, scene) consists of the balcony scene, with passing allusions to Shakespearean phrases. Though Juliet's father at first snobbishly objects to Romeo Smith's music as mere noise, when he discovers in the second "act" that Smith is earning "thirty grand" a week as a bandleader, he approves of the match with his daughter and even joins Romeo's band. The finale involves Shakespearean characters dancing to Kyser's swing music, with Kyser playing the role of Shakespeare himself. The film is revealing for its conceptualization of the relationship between elite and pop culture in America at midcentury, but also for its desire, however parodic, for a rapprochement between cultural strata.

1447 *Alaska*
1944. U.S. Monogram. Sound, b&w, 76 mins. George Archainbaud.

Based on the novel *Flush of Gold* by Jack London. According to Weaver, in a case of life imitating art, John Carradine portrays John Reagan, "a drunkard-husband, a washed-up Shakespearean" (178). In a performance described as Barrymore-esque, Reagan performs *Othello* for a dog, references *Julius Caesar*, and recites *Hamlet*'s "To be, or not to be" (3.1) soliloquy at length as he lay dying from smoke inhalation. A big-budget Monogram picture with stars, songs, and scenery, *Alaska* depicts life in turn-of-the-twentieth-century frontier gold country. (EJL)

1448 *Radio Bugs*
1944. U.S. MGM. Sound, b&w, 11 mins. Cy Endfield.

In the *Our Gang* serial series. Froggy, a devoted fan of radio comedian Red Skelton, embarks on a career as a radio star. With other gang members, he develops a show using a joke book and wacky props and searches for a sponsor, starting with a dentist. His lack of success leads him to abandon comedy for Shakespearean drama, where he meets an even frostier reception.

At the film's end, the boys perform Shakespearean burlesque. Note the character of Old Shakespearean (a pompous aging thespian) in the credits. Compare *Pay as You Exit* and *Beginner's Luck*.

One of the few Our Gang comedies unavailable on DVD.

1449 *A Ham in a Role*
1949. U.S. Warner Bros. Sound, col., 7 mins. Robert McKimson.

Animated short. Part of the Goofy Gophers series. Dog, a cartoon character, resigns from Warner Brothers studio to become a Shakespearean actor and retires to his country house to study his dramatic craft. There he discovers the two Goofy Gophers Mac and Tosh on his grounds. He evicts them, but the two gophers take their revenge by using the words of Shakespeare's speeches to heckle him. Mac and Tosh are themselves high-class twits.

1450 *Actors and Sin*
1952. U.S. United Artists. Feature film, b&w, 82 mins. Lee Garmes and Ben Hecht.

Actor's Blood, the first half of this two-part film, concerns Broadway actress Marcia Tillayou, a victim of her own brief success and of unscrupulous show-business colleagues. Her father Maurice, a washed-up Shakespearean, takes delight in his daughter's fame and supports her. When she is found murdered, Maurice dramatically reveals who the murderer is at a banquet.

Early in the film, we learn that Maurice once played Othello, a point referenced several times; a cruel reviewer notes that because Maurice was a ham actor, it was natural that he became a Shakespearean. When Marcia's career hits rock bottom, her father encourages her to play Shakespearean heroines; in the next shot, her dead body is revealed sprawled across the bed, like, so says the voice-over, Desdemona. These hints point strongly to Maurice as the murderer, but the denouement adds a twist to that surmise. The film contains no direct Shakespearean citations.

1451 *Singin' in the Rain*
1952. U.S. MGM. Sound, col., 103 mins. Stanley Donen and Gene Kelly.

While escaping from his fans, silent film star Don Lockwood meets aspiring actress Kathy Selden, who dismisses his film work as inferior to that of stage actors. As a romance develops between the two, Kathy mistakenly hits Lina Lamont, Don's insufferable, jealous silent co-star, in the face with cake and is banned from the studio. The success of *The Jazz Singer* leads studio head R. F. Simpson to make Lockwood and Lamont's latest picture *The Duelling Cavalier* as a talkie, but Lamont's voice is so grating that the advance showing is a disaster; Cosmo Brown, Lockwood's friend, suggests that they remake the picture as a musical, with Kathy dubbing in Lina's voice, but when Lina finds out she works to cover over the substitution. At the film's première, Cosmo, Don, and Simpson expose Lina as a fraud and Lockwood proposes to Kathy.

In Kathy's first encounter with Don, she sneeringly suggests the superiority of classical theater to mass entertainment like silent film, a suggestion that leads Don to snipe that he will look forward to seeing her as Juliet, Lady Macbeth, and King Lear. His confidence in his acting wounded, Don leaves her with a mockingly grandiloquent speech in pseudo-Elizabethan English and a reference to Ethel Barrymore, though he's made to look the fool by his torn coat. When Don later sees Kathy at a Hollywood party where she is working as a chorus dancer, he asks for a rendition of a Hamlet soliloquy or the balcony scene from *Romeo and Juliet*. In "Make 'Em Laugh," Cosmo's big musical number, the same opposition between Shakespeare and popular entertainment surfaces in one verse: "You can study Shakespeare and be quite elite, / And you can charm the critics and have nothin' to eat, / Just slip on a banana peel, the world's at your feet, / Make 'em laugh, make 'em laugh, make 'em laugh." We later learn that Kathy is not the snob she first seemed, since she reads fan magazines and has seen Don's films. The initial opposition between historical drama and popular film seems to disappear when the group makes *The Dancing Cavalier*, the musical version of *The Duelling Cavalier*.

1452 *Prince of Players*
1955. U.S. 20th Century Fox. Sound, col., 102 mins. Philip Dunne.

Young Edwin Booth accompanies his alcoholic father Junius Brutus Booth on an American tour and watches as he deteriorates from the strain of touring and his over-identification with roles. Once Edwin reaches maturity, he takes up his father's mantle as a Shakespearean player when Junius retires and struggles with the family burden of genius and madness, particularly when his brother John Wilkes Booth denigrates his abilities and declares himself a star in the South. Unlike his brother, who becomes jealous of Edwin's success and descends into racism, Edwin soon makes the most of his talent, marrying Mary Devlin, having a daughter by her and finding acclaim in London, but when Mary becomes sick he slips into alcoholism and tours without her. After Mary dies and Edwin learns of his brother's assassination of Lincoln, he and his troupe are attacked by an audience who accuses him of murder, but

Edwin's courage in enduring the assault wins the hostile audience over.

This recasting of Edwin Booth as a Romantic genius, in danger of replicating the tortured self-destructiveness of his father, is filled with references to Shakespeare. Many involve snippets of the family's stage performances of plays: Junius's performance of Lear in the storm scene (which Edwin offstage recites with him), Richard III's exchange with Buckingham, "Am I King?" (from *Richard III* 4.2; Junius plays Richard, and Edwin Buckingham), Edwin's performance of Richard III's opening soliloquy, the dream sequence at Bosworth Field, and the final battle between Richmond and Richard, John Wilkes's performance as Petruchio, Edwin and Mary's performance of the death scene in *Romeo and Juliet*, and Edwin's London performance as Hamlet (we see "To be or not to be," his confrontation with Gertrude, and Hamlet's exit on the shields of soldiers). Many of these scenes have additional significance for the actors playing the parts: Junius's struggle with his inner demons of drink and madness is mirrored in his tempest-addled Lear; Junius's question "Am I king?" to his son speaks to his awareness of his waning powers as a Shakespearean star; Edwin's performance as Richard III marks his taking the mantle of stardom from his father; and Mary and Edwin's performance as Romeo and Juliet both becomes a public declaration of their love and presages Mary's death (passages from the scene are repeated later when Edwin visits the bedside of his dead wife and her grave).

In addition to these scenes, the film features numerous offstage citations. As the film opens, Junius, drunk, is reciting lines from Falstaff's recitation of his faults (*Henry IV, Part 1* 2.4) to uncomprehending onlookers in a bar; when Edwin arrives, he calls him "Hal." The passage establishes Junius as a Falstaffian figure of fallen, flawed greatness, the legacy against which his son Edwin struggles. When John Wilkes visits his father, they exchange lines from Ariel and Prospero's dialogue in *The Tempest* 1.2. Before their onstage performance as Romeo and Juliet, Edwin and Mary offer an impromptu rendition of the balcony scene, with Mary at the window of a brothel. Later, after the two are married, she urges Edwin to learn Henry's speech declaring his love for Princess Katharine from *Henry V* 5.2; indicative of his neglect of her to come, he rushes through the speech, performing it perfunctorily. When Edwin hears of his wife's illness, he is drunkenly singing the Fool's "Hey, ho, the wind and the rain" song from *King Lear* 3.2, a temporary return to his father's self-destructive state. The news of his brother's assassination of Lincoln arrives when Edwin is rehearsing an actor in the role of Polonius who, Edwin opines, is not a fool but a wise man, a remark that perhaps looks backward to his father. Several visual allusions are noteworthy as well: Edwin's performance as Richard III briefly references Olivier's film version in the opening scene (released in the same year), and his performance of Richard's dream mimicks the famous portrait of Garrick in the role. In addition to a romantic biography of an American Shakespearean, the film plays on other levels as well. One is as a mythologizing of Richard Burton's neo-romantic Shakespearean acting style, very different from that of Olivier, who was at the time the reigning Shakespearean; another is as a riposte to the popular play and film *Kean* from an American perspective. The final sequence of the play, in which Edwin courageously endures abuse because of his brother's traitorous crime, seems directed against the rising tide of McCarthyist hysteria directed at Hollywood.

1453 *Kean: Genio e sregolatezza (Kean)*
1956. Italy. Lux Film S.p.a. and Vides Cinematografica. Sound, col., 83 mins. Vittorio Gassman and Francesco Rosi.

Adapted from the story by Jean-Paul Sartre and play by Alexandre Dumas père. The popular tale of Edmund Kean's rise to theatrical fame and tragic romantic love, here starring popular actor Vittorio Gassman as Kean, for which he won a best actor award at the Italian Grolle d'Oro in 1957. See plot summary above for *Kean* (1923). This version contains theatrical extracts from Shakespeare that are somewhat longer than earlier adaptations, include scenes from *Richard III*, *Othello*, *Hamlet*, and *King Lear*.

1454 *Panic Button*
1964. Italy and U.S. Yankee Productions. Sound, b&w, 90 mins. George Sherman.

Adapted from a story by Morton Friedman. Frank Pagano, a mobster, is sent by his father, CEO of mob-owned Pagano Enterprises, to Italy to supervise the making of a flop television pilot, in order to lose $500,000 to avoid paying income taxes. To ensure its failure, for the leads Pagano hires Philipe Fontaine, a washed-up star, and Angela, an artistically inclined prostitute looking for an acting break, and Salvatore Pandowski, an inept acting teacher, as the film's director. They make a preposterously bad *Romeo and Juliet*, but it is a surprise comedy hit at the Venice Film Festival, and Pagano decides to make more Shakespeare films.

The central premise of *Panic Button* depends upon the assumption that Shakespeare is uncommercial and unpopular, a premise that the surprise ending both refutes and confirms. Of the inept *Romeo and Juliet* film we see only a portion of the balcony scene, but there are other Shakespeare citations and references. Fontaine's audition piece is a passage from *Macbeth* 3.1 (which he mangles). After Pagano's film is declared a comic masterpiece, we see mobsters reading Shakespeare scripts (*King Lear* and *A Midsummer Night's Dream*); another tells his secretary to cut scenes from *Macbeth*; and two mobsters exchange Shakespearean greetings—"How comest thou hither?"—at

which one of them observes, "No wonder I can't understand Shakespeare; he can't write good English"; in an interview, Pagano Sr. disingenuously speaks of his desire to educate the public about a man he's idolized since childhood. *Panic Button* predates *The Producers* (a more famous film with a similar premise) by four years.

1455 *Theatre of Blood*
1973. U.K. Cineman Productions and United Artists. Sound, col., 104 mins. Douglas Hickox.

Aging actor Edward Lionheart, stung that his season of Shakespeare productions was bypassed for the Critics Circle Award, takes revenge upon his critics by killing them one by one using death scenes from Shakespeare's plays. In this he is aided by his daughter Edwina and a group of homeless meth-drinkers who rescued Lionheart after he leapt into the Thames in despair. At film's end he dies spectacularly as the Burbage Theatre, Lionheart's venue and hideout, burns, and the leader of the Critics Circle, Devlin, offers a snap review.

A superb blending of Shakespeare with comic *grand guignol*, *Theatre of Blood* is filled with Shakespearean references. Lionheart uses scenes from the following plays for revenge, performing a portion of the text with each murder: *Julius Caesar* (the assassination of Caesar, followed by Mark Antony's "Friends, Romans, countrymen"), *Troilus and Cressida* (5.9 and lines from *Hamlet* 5.1, followed by the slaying of Hector), *Cymbeline* ("Fear no more the heat o' the sun," and the decapitation of Cloten), *The Merchant of Venice* (lines from 1.3, 3.3, and 4.1, leading to Shylock taking a pound of flesh), *Richard III* (opening soliloquy and lines from 1.3, followed by the drowning of Clarence in a butt of malmsey), *Othello* ("Down, strumpet," this time performed by a critic as he jealously murders his wife), *Henry VI, Part 1* (lines from 5.6, followed by the burning of Joan of Arc at the stake), *Titus Andronicus* (lines from 5.2 as well as lines from *Romeo and Juliet* 5.3, leading to two children baked in a pie and served to their "father"), and *King Lear* (lines from 1.1 and 5.3, leading to Gloucester being blinded—this final revenge is never completed). Lionheart's swordfight with Devlin (in an exercise gym) alludes to the sword fight between Tybalt and Mercutio in *Romeo and Juliet*. In addition to these allusions, Lionheart offers a number of other passing allusions. To his audience of drunken bums, he offers this contemptuous pastiche of *King Lear* 4.2 and *Othello* 1.3: "Sweetness and goodness seem vile to the vile. / Filths savor but themselves. Here, filths, put money in thy purse." When Lionheart attempts to commit suicide at the meeting of the Critics Circle, he performs "To be or not to be"; his first words upon being saved by the meth-drinkers are Miranda's from *The Tempest* 5.1, "O brave new world, / That hath such lovely creatures in it." When he carries his dead daughter Edwina to the top of the Burbage Theatre, he recites several lines

Vincent Price and Diana Rigg in *Theatre of Blood* (1973). In this shot, Price and Rigg torture the critic Devlin. Courtesy of Douglas Lanier.

from the final scene of *King Lear* concerning the dead Cordelia. The dark irony of those who see themselves upholding "proper" Shakespeare being murdered via updated reenactments of Shakespearean death scenes is wonderfully sustained throughout, aided by the sympathetic madman persona Vincent Price brings from his other horror films to the lead role. *Theatre of Blood* is an interesting example of Shakespearean performance being redeployed in the service of popular subversion of figures of authority. Though Lionheart is clearly presented as the film's protagonist, allying his brand of overacted Shakespeare with working-class sensibilities, the film's ambivalent treatment of Devlin is instructive, for unlike his peers who are caricatured as hypocrites or snobs, Devlin's devastating judgment of Lionheart's abilities springs from artistic principle—ironically, he believes Shakespeare should speak to the modern age. That is, the authority of critics is not entirely satirized; indeed, it is Devlin's approval that Lionheart most desires, and it is Devlin who is given the last critical word in the film. The film illustrates well the frequent connection in popular cinema between Shakespearean grandiloquence and murderous insanity, as well as offering a parodic version of the popular life-imitates-Shakespearean-theater motif, here taken to its (il)logical extreme. When it was adapted for live performance at the National Theatre in 2005, the adapters added material targeting the highbrow blandness and wholesomeness of subsidized theater in Britain. Compare *The Flesh and Blood Show*.

DVD includes a trailer that references Shakespeare.

1456 *The Trouble with Girls*
1969. U.S. MGM. Sound, col., 97 mins. Peter Tewksbury.

An Elvis Presley period film set in 1927 Iowa in which he stars as the manager of a traveling Chautauqua show. Notably, film begins in b&w, and when Elvis appears, it turns to color. Not the typical Elvis fare, having only three songs, but Elvis wrangles with a feisty female union rep, another who wants to join the traveling show, and a third female accused of murdering the lecherous pharmacist (played by Dabney Coleman).

Vincent Price portrays a Chautauqua lecturer named Mr. Morality. In a brief scene when checking into a hotel, he quotes Nietzsche, Confucius, Jonson, and Shakespeare—"Out of this nettle, danger, we pluck this flower, safety" (*Henry IV, Part 1* 2.3). In a later scene he lectures on morality to a rapt, packed house. Not so popular is Shakespearean Mr. Drewcolt (John Carradine). Performing to a sparse, unenthused audience, Drewcolt is heard in voice-over reciting twenty lines from Hamlet's soliloquy (3.1.64–98) as Elvis watches, smiling. Upon checking into the hotel, a desk clerk asks Drewcolt, "Did Romeo and Juliet have premarital relations?" Drewcolt's reply is "Only in the Des Moines company." (EJL)

1457 *The Wild, Wild West Revisited*
1979. U.S. CBS. Sound, col., 95 mins. Burt Kennedy.

Made-for-TV film. Government agents Jim West and Artemus Gordon are called out of retirement to find and arrest Miguelito Loveless Jr., the evil son of their archenemy. His plan is to abduct world leaders and replace them with clones he controls. West and Gordon attempt to prevent him from kidnapping President Cleveland, and he assaults them with various advanced weapons.

As the film begins, Gordon is working as a Shakespearean actor, and he uses his acting skills to disguise himself.

1458 *Fame*
1980. U.S. MGM and United Artists. Sound, col., 134 mins. Alan Parker.

At the New York High School for Performing Arts, talented teenagers from various troubled ethnic and social backgrounds train for careers in show business with several influential teachers—music teacher Benjamin Shorofsky, English teacher Elizabeth Sherwood, acting teacher Mr. Farrell, and dance instructor Miss Berg.

An early sequence features several auditions that include Shakespeare: one student recites (badly) part of Richard's opening soliloquy from *Richard III* (1.1), another recites in cap and bells Touchstone's lines from 5.4 in *As You Like It*, and yet another (a man) does Juliet's part from the balcony scene from *Romeo and Juliet* (2.2) in a thick Brooklyn accent. All of the Shakespearean auditions are played for comedy. The opening image of the film is a poster of Olivier as Othello (entry 454).

1459 *Babe*
1981. U.S. Arrow Films and Video. Sound, col., 82 mins. John Cristopher.

Hardcore pornography. A vain, independent supermodel, Babe, is required by a stipulation of her grandfather's will to wed within a month in order to inherit a fortune; meanwhile, the head of her modeling agency schemes to ruin Babe financially by encouraging her to marry Chad, a workaholic classical actor with grandiose ambitions.

When we are first introduced to Chad, he speaks in Shakespearean pastiche, on the order of "Be resolute, mistress mine." He later speaks of starring with Babe in a production of *Hamlet* with him as Hamlet and her as Ophelia, though this production is never shown.

1460 *Walls of Glass*
1985. U.S. Manson International and Tenth Muse Productions. Sound, col., 86 mins. Scott D. Goldstein.

Despite his great love of Shakespeare and ability to recite any sonnet on demand, New York actor James Flanagan cannot find work onstage, and so he has been forced to drive a taxi into middle age, all the while continuing acting school, attending humiliating auditions, and managing his deteriorating relationships with his bitter ex-wife, aimless children, and artistic mistress. In this bittersweet character portrait, Flanagan, haunted by memories of his dissolute but Shakespeare-quoting father, comes to confront his own lack of career success, eventually finding consolation in a line from Sonnet 119 his father had cited: "Better is by evil still made better." At the end of the film, Flanagan offers a rousing audition in a city park for an amused director and wins an acting job in Toronto.

Walls of Glass abounds in citations of Shakespeare. Flanagan gives Richard II's soliloquy, "I have been studying how I may compare this prison" (*Richard II* 5.5), as his audition piece, and he uses citations from various sonnets in his personal life, to flatter his mistress (Sonnet 18), to chastize his oversexed son (Sonnet 130), and to console himself (Sonnet 119). In a taxi ride with a director, he recites Sonnet 144, at which his fare notes that Flanagan too is "a liquid prisoner pent in walls of glass," that is, his taxi. Elsewhere the film references Marc Antony's speech, "I come to bury Caesar, not to praise him," and *Measure for Measure* (a Shakespeare in the Park production in which, we learn, Flanagan acted in his youth). Flanagan's final impromptu audition is a pastiche of Shakespearean commonplaces—Cassius's "honor is the subject of my story" (*Julius Caesar* 1.2), Hamlet's "plentiful lack of wit" (*Hamlet* 2.2), Jaques's "All the world's the stage" speech (*As You Like It* 2.7), and Malvolio's "some have greatness thrust upon them" (*Twelfth Night* 2.5). *Walls of Glass* certainly portrays the Shakespearean actor as a cultural loser,

particularly in the eyes of the younger generation; both Flanagan's son and young members of his audience explicitly declare Shakespeare as outmoded and incomprehensible, and at the film's climax Flanagan, frustrated at his professional failure, destroys his cherished book of Shakespeare on the stage of New York's Delacorte Theater. But the film also demonstrates the relevance of Shakespeare to Flanagan's midlife crises and thus the Bard's consolatory potential.

1461 *Nobody's Fool*
1986. U.S. Denny Productions and Island Pictures. Sound, col., 107 mins. Evelyn Purcell.

Cassie Stoolie is a working-class woman weighed down by her past relationship with Billy Downs: when she told him that she was pregnant with his child, he refused to marry her, leading her to stab him and give up her baby for adoption, and leading her small town to treat her as a pariah. When she visits the Red Rock Shakespeare Festival, she meets Riley, a spirited actor, and the two slowly develop a relationship. When he asks her to go to Los Angeles with him, she hesitates, fearful of being dumped and still not done with Billy. But her performance as Juliet at the Buckeye Festival and Riley's persistence convince her to take a chance on Riley.

At the Red Rock Festival, Cassie sees an outdoor performance of *The Tempest*, of which we see the opening storm scene and Prospero's chiding of Ariel in 1.2. The emphasis falls particularly on special effects—Prospero is in a silver suit and makeup, and Ariel glides through sparkling lights—and the effects articulate Cassie's need for magic and transformation in her humdrum life. Something of Cassie's natural acting ability is indicated by the fact that she remembers the opening lines of Prospero's epilogue as she searches for a lost thermos immediately after the show. Later on, Cassie helps with stage effects for the Red Rock production of *A Midsummer Night's Dream*, of which we see Puck's epilogue; there is also an earlier throwaway gag about a stuck ass's head on one of the actors. Juliet's "Gallop apace, you fiery-footed steeds" speech (*Romeo and Juliet* 3.2) becomes Cassie's signature soliloquy; she offers portions of it in her acting class, in rehearsal, as she walks through the wood and meets Riley, and for her fine performance for the Buckeye Festival, a performance contrasted with Kirk's disastrous rendering of the end of Macbeth's "Is this a dagger which I see before me?" speech (2.1) in which Kirk's cape catches afire. Juliet's speech articulates Cassie's desire for love, and her acting teacher stresses her need to imagine and believe in such love for her performance to have spirit; when Riley hears her give the speech, he is moved. One passing reference at the Buckeye Festival: as part of a barker's banter, we hear "To be or not to be ain't much of a choice," a remark that reflects upon

Cassie's earlier lame suicide attempts. NB: this film is not to be confused with *Nobody's Fool* (Robert Benton, 1994).

1462 *The Addams Family*
1991. U.S. Orion Pictures and Paramount Pictures. Sound, col., 99 mins. Barry Sonnenfeld.

Tully Alford, the family attorney for the Addams family, convinces Gordon Craven, the lonely son of a client, Dr. Greta Pinder-Schloss, to impersonate the long-dead Uncle Fester in an effort to swindle the Addamses out of their fortune. Wednesday Addams wonders whether Fester is who he claims to be, but in the end we learn that Craven is in fact Fester suffering from amnesia.

One set piece involves Wednesday and Pugsley's parodic performance of Shakespeare in a school play. The two engage in a sword fight in front of a castle backdrop. As Wednesday speaks Hamlet's line upon seeing Fortinbras, "How all occasions do inform against me / And spur my dull revenge. . . . O, from this time forth / My thoughts be bloody or be nothing worth!" (*Hamlet* 4.4.33–34, 66–67), Pugsley strikes her in the arm and she spurts blood. When Pugsley responds, "A hit, a very palpable hit" (from the duel between Hamlet and Laertes), Wednesday strikes off his left arm, with considerably more blood. Pugsley retaliates by cutting her throat; Wednesday turns to the audience and showers them with blood, uttering the lines "O proud death, / What feast is toward in thine eternal cell" (*Hamlet* 5.2.366–67) and "Sweet oblivion, open your arms." This sequence is intercut with reaction shots of the shocked audience. Upon Wednesday's overwrought death, the Addams family members in the audience give a standing ovation. This is a key moment of change in Fester's attitude toward the family. Much of the comedy springs from the contrast between the children's wooden delivery of lines and the graphically bloody special effects. Compare *Tromeo and Juliet*.

1463 *The Hard Way*
1991. U.S. Badham-Cohen Entertainment Group, Cohen Group, and Universal. Sound, col., 111 mins. John Badham.

John Moss, a trigger-happy New York detective, tracks a serial killer named The Party Crasher who kills his victims in discos. When The Party Crasher escapes after Moss corners him, Moss is reassigned as partner to Nick Lang, a pampered Hollywood action movie star who wants to hang out with Moss to add authenticity to his upcoming film. Posing as Moss's rookie partner Ray Casanov, Lang proceeds to screw up both Moss's relationship with girlfriend Susan and his pursuit of The Party Crasher. The film ends with Moss's spectacular capture of The Party Crasher in Times Square.

Nick confronts his agent Angie about the quality of the roles she has gotten him: "When are you going to get me something with a little relevance, a little social conscience, something that doesn't have a goddamn Roman numeral in the title? You ever hear of *Hamlet III, Midsummer Night's IV*?" Angie replies, "They made *Henry V*! It won awards for that little Scottish guy!" (an apparent reference to Kenneth Branagh, an Irishman).

1464 *Swan Song*
1993. U.K. Samuel Goldwyn. Sound, col., 23 mins. Kenneth Branagh.

Adapted from a short story by Anton Chekhov by Hugh Crutwell (Branagh's teacher at RADA). In this valentine to stage acting, Svetlovidov, a prompter, reflects after hours on the stage upon his life in the theater after his final benefit show. Confronting despair about what he has achieved and the romances and bourgeois life he has given up, he is comforted by a stage hand, Nikita.

Like *In the Bleak Midwinter* (produced around the same time), this film celebrates the joys of live theatrical acting, stressing the toll it takes on its practitioners and the audience's lack of recognition of its artistry; since Svetlovidov is played by John Gielgud, it is also a tribute to his career. The film opens with a citation of *Macbeth* 2.2, "Sleep that knits up the raveled sleeve of care." Svetlovidov also offers renditions of Lear's "Blow winds, and crack your cheeks" speech, Hamlet's exchange with Rosencrantz and Guildenstern starting with "Why do you go about to recover the wind of me as if you drive me into a toil?" Romeo's speech over the body of Juliet ("Death, that hath sucked the honey of thy breath"), and Othello's "Farewell the tranquil mind." Svetlovidov presents these passages as a survey of different moods, though with the exception of the *Hamlet* passage, all in different ways reflect the actor's melancholy sense of loss at his retirement.

1465 *Being John Malkovich*
1999. U.S. Gramercy Pictures, Propaganda Films, and Single Cell Pictures. Sound, col., 112 mins. Spike Jonze.

When Craig Schwartz, an unemployed puppeteer in a crumbling marriage to Lotte, takes a filing job in a bizarre low-ceilinged office, he discovers a portal that allows him to occupy John Malkovich's consciousness for fifteen minutes. Maxine, a beautiful co-worker, commercializes the portal, and in an effort to woo her, Craig becomes Malkovich while she has sex with him. The situation becomes more complex when Lotte also uses Malkovich for liaisons with Maxine. Malkovich soon discovers what is going on and tries to stop it, but not before the head of the filing company and his friends take over Malkovich's mind for their own purposes.

Malkovich is briefly shown rehearsing as Richard III—"Have ever woman in this humour wooed? / Was ever woman in this humor won?" The line is ironic given the bizarre nature of Maxine's courtship with Lotte and Craig.

1466 *Nomad*
2001. U.S. Mandarin Pictures. Sound, b&w, 95 mins.
Matthew Eggers Silas.

A homeless street performer in Denver, Jack methodically delivers Shakespearean soliloquies on street corners each afternoon, accompanied by Bones, his aging dog. He is discovered by Lucy, a theater student at Denver University, and the two soon strike up a friendship. Lucy and Jack share conversations about theater and life on his favorite park bench. When Jack rebuffs the advances of Charlie, an alcoholic homeless man, Charlie eventually takes revenge.

Numerous Shakespeare references.

1467 *To End All Wars*
2001. U.S., U.K., and Thailand. Argyll Film Partners, Gummshoe Productions, Integrity Partners, and Pray For Rain Pictures Inc. Sound, col., 125 mins. David L. Cunningham.

Adapted from the book by Ernest Gordon. In this prisoner of war drama, Allied soldiers Colonel McLean, Major Campbell, Captain Gordon, and Lieutenant Tom Ridgen are interred in a brutal Japanese prison camp in the Burmese jungle. Campbell, filled with hatred for the Japanese, attempts to organize an escape, but it fails; Gordon stresses forgiveness for his captors and organizes Bible lessons and university classes to educate the men. During the prisoner's performance of a play at the camp, Campbell's and Gordon's responses to imprisonment come to a head. When at war's end the camp is liberated, the men's ability to forgive their captors is again tested.

Quotes "To be or not to be," and three times references the "Crispin Crispianus" speech from *Henry V*, the latter thematically relevant to the circumstances of war.

DVD includes a "Making Of" documentary that references Shakespeare.

1468 *I Will Avenge You, Iago!*
2005. U.S. Iago Films, LLC. Sound, col., 95 mins. Zhenya Kiperman.

In this backstage comedy, Marvin, a naïve audience member, taken in by a performance of Verdi's *Otello* (entry 1680), goes backstage and stabs the hand of the actor playing Iago, Jack Bandrowsky. Improvising, Jack convinces Marvin that the true villain of the play is the Duke, who killed his daughter Gilda. Marvin vows to avenge Iago's death by killing the Duke. Helen, Jack's wife, confronts a woman who she thinks is Jack's mistress, but who is actually Eve Zimmerman, a conwoman and a thief. Later Helen, pregnant, wakes up next to the Director, who reveals horrifying details about her family and his sexual infidelity, driving Helen to suicide; we soon learn that Helen's travails are just the rehearsal for a contemporary play. When the rehearsal is over, Helen attends Jack's performance in *Rigoletto*, during which Marvin kills the

Duke backstage with a hand grenade. Two years later, Marvin is performing the lead in a prison production of *Hamlet*, with Jack and Helen, now pregnant, in the audience; Eve Zimmerman plays Gertrude, and Helen, recognizing her, hands her flowers à la Ophelia. In the epilogue, new parents Jack and Helen entertain their baby girl at home. This independent film makes a farce of the intersections between actors' roles and their chaotic real lives, and often plays tricks with the viewer's perceptions of what is real and what is theater. Contains passages from *Othello* and *Hamlet*.

Shakespearean Characters

1469 *El Abominable Hombre de la Costa del Sol*
1969. Spain. Filmayer S.A. and Pedro Masó Producciones Cinematográficas. Sound, col., 82 mins. Pedro Lazaga.

Cecilia considers her fiancé Federico a romantic hero, even though in reality he is the dull, unattractive son of a rich aristocrat who finds his son a disappointment. When his father sends him to be a public relations man at the Costa del Sol, a hotel, he quickly becomes irresistible to women, surprising his father and leading to Cecilia's jealousy.

Federico dreams of himself as Othello, Marc Antony, and Romeo.

1470 *Censored* (aka *The Sex Censor* or *Sex Censored*)
1996. U.S. Vivid Video. Sound, col., 77 mins. Michael Zen.

Hardcore pornography. Page, an overworked writer plagued by writer's block, is visited by various literary characters as she works on an article about sexuality and famous legends.

Features Romeo and Cleopatra in sexual scenes, and brief revisionary comments about couplings between Shakespearean characters. No direct verbal citations.

Shakespearean Texts

1471 *Fast and Loose*
1939. U.S. MGM. Sound, b&w, 80 mins. Edwin L. Marin.

Joel and Garda Sloane, rare bookstore owners and amateur sleuths, are asked by Christopher Oates to buy a rare Shakespeare manuscript for him. Insurers think that the manuscript's owner, Nicholas Torrent, an eccentric millionaire, has engaged in unscrupulous business practices, and so Torrent investigates. Soon after, the manuscript is stolen from Vincent Charlton, who was examining its authenticity and is found murdered, and all suspect Gerald, Torrent's hot-headed son. Nicholas is found dead, and Joel, a potential buyer, falls under suspicion among several others. Joel realizes that the stolen manuscript is really a forgery (the authentic one is in other hands), but he keeps that information secret in hopes of trapping the killer with it. As he follows leads, the stolen manuscript's owner is found dead and the authentic manuscript is found in Gerald's room. Suspecting that Gerald is being framed, Joel finally pieces together the mystery: Charlton killed others to cover over his selling of a fake manuscript.

The film's McGuffin is the Shakespeare manuscript, which is only briefly seen. Compare *Quiet Please, Murder* (below).

1472 *Quiet Please, Murder*

1942. U.S. 20th Century Fox. Sound, b&w, 70 mins. John Larkin.

Adapted from a story by Lawrence G. Blochman. In this thriller, Jim Fleg, a gentleman thief and forger of rare books, steals the Richard Burbage edition of *Hamlet* and makes forgeries from it. Unfortunately, his girlfriend Myra Blandy sells a forgery to a Nazi-associated dealer Martin Cleaver, and she plays cat-and-mouse with Hal McByrne, who has been called in to track the theft. Disguised as policemen, Fleg and his gang return to the library to steal more books, but their efforts are thwarted by McByrne, despite Myra's repeated double-crosses. After several plot twists and turns, Fleg is caught, Myra is strangled by one of Cleaver's henchmen, and McByrne ends up with Kay Ryan, a reference librarian. The film's central theme of the deceptiveness of appearances is exemplified by the *Hamlet* forgery, though the film makes no substantial reference to Shakespeare. Compare *Fast and Loose* (above).

1473 *Sherlock Holmes and the Secret Weapon*

1942. U.K. Universal Pictures. Sound, b&w, 68 mins. Roy William Neil.

Based on "The Dancing Men," *Sherlock Homes and the Secret Weapon* begins and ends with references with Shakespeare and offers a relatively straightforward opposition between a fake German and an authentic English Shakespeare. At the beginning of the film, in a restaurant in Switzerland, two unidentified Gestapo officers show up and sit down and then recognize an old, white-haired, mustachioed man masquerading as a bookseller to avoid appearing as a Gestapo agent from Berlin. The bookseller is easily identifiable as Sherlock Holmes (Basil Rathbone), disguised as a German spy disguised as a bookseller, as it were. Apparently focused on duping the waitress and maitre d' into thinking he is a bookseller, Holmes dupes the agent into thinking that they must kidnap Dr. Franz Tobel (William Post Jr.), a Swiss scientist with a new bomb-sight design. In the process of maintaining this double deception, Holmes opens his bag of books, picks one up, and says with a German accent, "Now here are the complete works of Wilhelm Shakespeare, an old German writer." "Heil Hitler," they respond, identifying themselves as Gestapo spies. In the last shot of the film, after footage of R.A.F. bombers in the sky, Watson says to Holmes, "Things are looking up Holmes, This little island

is still on the map." Citing lines from *Richard II*, Holmes replies, "Yes, this fortress built by nature for herself, this blessed plot, this earth, this realm, this England." See also entries 1514 and 2365. (RB)

1474 *Johnny Trouble*

1957. U.S. Clarion Enterprises. Sound, b&w, 80 mins. John H. Auer.

Wealthy invalid Katherine Chandler refuses to leave her apartment when the university purchases her building to convert it into a dormitory; she is convinced that her son John, who disappeared twenty-seven years earlier, will return. By charming the workmen and students, Katherine is allowed to stay and is appointed the dormitory "Nana." When she learns from Julie Horton of her boyfriend John Chandler, a troubled ex-Marine, she seeks him out, hoping he is her son. Katherine takes him under her wing, and with her help he avoids being expelled and becomes an academic success, eventually working at the university. After Katherine's death, Tom McKay, her friend and chauffeur, reveals that John was not Katherine's son; her son had been killed in an auto accident, but Katherine's husband, who knew the truth, had sworn Tom to secrecy.

When John begins to succeed in classes, we see him reading a volume of Shakespeare. On the same evening his girlfriend Julie visits him and they make love, with the result that Julie gets pregnant and John is tempted to quit school.

1475 *Huckleberry Finn*

1974. U.S. United Artists. Sound, col., 118 mins. J. Lee Thompson.

A musical film adaptation in which the conman the King (Harvey Korman), who claims to be of English royal blood and to have come to "the colonies" from England, advertises the Royal Shakespeare Company of Shakespeare's *The Royal Nonesuch* with himself as David Garrick the Younger and the Duke as Edmund Kean the elder. He adds that Huck is his nephew, Percy, and that runaway slave Jim (Paul Winfield) is "the premiere interpreter of the Shakespeare's immortal character, Caliban, the former King of Huggermugger, King Gunawanga." In his musical number that is a prologue to a nonperformance of a nonexistent play, the King explains that he found the lost manuscript of "*The Royal Nonesuch*, a new tragedy by William Shakespeare...in a corner of Shakespeare's attic...written in Shakespeare's own hand." He holds the manuscript up in front of the audience without letting them see the pages inside, which are all blank. Twain's novel (chapter 21) contains burlesques of the balcony scene from *Romeo and Juliet*, *Richard III* fighting, and Hamlet's "To be or not to be" soliloquy. *The King's Cameleopard* or *Royal Nonesuch* follows the disastrous Shakespeare performance, which despite being a burlesque is viewed by the Duke as high culture: "So the duke said these Arkansaw lunkheads couldn't come up to Shakespeare; what they wanted was low comedy—and maybe something ruther worse than low comedy, he reckoned" (22). See Twain's novel (entry 1809) and Richard Thorpe's 1939 film version (entry 1120). (RB)

1476 *Lashou shentan* (*Hard-Boiled*)
1992. U.S. Golden Princess Films and Milestone Pictures. Sound, col., 126 mins. John Woo.

When the partner of maverick policeman Tequila is killed in a gunfight in a teahouse, Tequila resolves to avenge his death. He discovers that Tony, an assassin for the mob, is in reality an undercover policeman, and the two become partners to pursue Johnny Wong, a ruthless crime lord. The film's final confrontation occurs in the maternity ward of a hospital, where Tony and Tequila must save newborns while battling multiple assassins who have smuggled their weapons into the hospital's basement and rigged the building with a bomb.

Tony uses a gun hidden in a hollow volume of Shakespeare in a library to kill a man who betrayed Mr. Hui, a crime boss. Tequila quickly finds the book on the shelf, an indication of his psychological kinship with Tony. This is the first of several seemingly "safe" environments invaded by violence.

1477 *Little Women*
1933. U.S. Warner. Sound, b&w, 115 mins. George Cukor.
1949. U.S. Warner. Sound, col., 122 mins. Mervyn LeRoy.
1994. U.S. Columbia Pictures. Sound, col., 118 mins. Gillian Armstrong.

All three films are based on Louisa May Alcott's novel *Little Women* (1869; entry 2064), in which Shakespeare is central to Jo March's development from an amateur playwright to a commercial short story writer and novelist. The three film adaptations strip Alcott's novel of its frequent literary references leaving Shakespeare nearly the lone literary referent. Each successive film version of *Little Women* becomes more transgendered and feminist and less focused on Shakespeare. In each film adaptation we see an interpolated scene with her first book published, and her writing and the book are given greater prominence in each successive cinematic version.

The novel's Hamlet and Laertes reference comes up in the 1933 Cukor version, without mention of *Hamlet*, but Jo (Katharine Hepburn) and Laurie trade lines from the dueling scene. In a later particularly corny moment, when Mr. Bhaer criticizes Jo's writings, Bhaer advises her to write like "my Shakespeare." Jo then asks "Will I ever be a Shakespeare?" and Bhaer responds that she will be "a Josephine March, and that is quite enough."

In the 1949 LeRoy version, which lifts much of the dialogue word for word from the 1933 Cukor screenplay,

the scenes are kept identical except for the Shakespeare omissions. In their place, the youngest sister Beth asserts to her sisters that Jo (June Allyson) is a "regular Shakespeare" when Jo is trying to direct Amy in Jo's play.

In the 1994 Armstrong version, Jo (Winona Ryder) picks up a copy of Shakespeare in Bhaer's study. "You have quite a library," Jo observes and then asks him, "Did you bring all these books from Germany?" Bhaer responds, "Most of these I could not bear to leave behind. I sold many things to pay for my passage. My books never." As Jo picks up a collected works of Shakespeare, whose name cannot be seen in the shot, she says wistfully, "Shakespeare. Some books are so familiar. Reading is them like being home again." She then gives it back to him, apparently having no use for it. The 1994 Armstrong adaptation is the furthest from Alcott's novel as well in making Jo less of a loser than she is the novel. Instead of turning away from celebrity and fame associated with literary salons and choosing marriage and teaching over writing, Armstrong/Ryder's Jo manages her brilliant career as a novelist, school founder, and a wife. The Armstrong version retains and dramatically magnifies Amy's burning of Jo's "story." Whereas in the novel, Jo learns that Amy has destroyed her manuscript the day afterward, in Armstrong's film, Jo discovers her story (now a novel rather than a collection of fairy tales) as it is burning. The film devotes two prolonged shot of the burning manuscript, *The Lost Duke of Gloucester*, which frame a scene called "the missing manuscript" on the DVD edition of the film.

In each successive film, Jo becomes more transgendered, with Hepburn twirling an imaginary moustache with her fingers in rehearsal and then wearing a fake beard and moustache for the performance, Allyson doing pretty much the same, and then Ryder wearing a drawn moustache and beard as he reads a story from *The Pickwick Papers*, with her sisters all dressed as men. In this way, the Armstrong film activates a transgender aspect of the novel itself, with Jo's bi-gender name (like Teddy/Laurie), her identification with Shakespeare and Hamlet, her preference for boys (she never cared for girls, she says), and her founding a school for boys (where she hires Bhaer as a teacher) more often gets in the way of patriarchy than it is a means to domesticate her. One could say that the elision of questions of commerce (Jo's squeal of delight over her letter with payment of five dollars for *The Lost Duke of Gloucester*, which she somehow managed to rewrite despite its being burned) has everything to do with the representation of her/Alcott's work, and by Armstrong's as being unpublished and hence in non-commodity form. Here we see as well the unlinking of authorship and cultural literacy from adulthood. The immaturity of Jo's book (unpublished, yet to be published) enables her romantic maturity, her transformation from a little woman into an adult woman writer and wife. (RB)

Shakespeare's Image

1478 *Girl Shy*
1924. U.S. Pathé Films. Silent, b&w, 82 mins. Fred C. Newmeyer and Sam Taylor.

Featuring Harold Lloyd, the silent comedian. Harold Meadows, a painfully shy and stuttering small-town tailor's assistant, secretly writes a book, *The Secrets of Making Love*, and goes to the city to seek a publisher. He helps Mary Buckingham, a rich young woman, as she smuggles her puppy on the train, and the two quickly fall for each other, though Harold worries that he must depend on the book's publication to make his fortune and win Mary's hand. His confidence is shattered when a publisher rejects his book and laughs at him, and Harold bravely abandons Mary, telling her that their romance was merely research. Soon, however, the publisher changes his mind and offers him an advance. Meanwhile, Mary has become engaged to Reginald DeVore, a sleazy bigamist, and Harold engages in an extended race against time to prevent their marriage.

Richard Burt notes that a Shakespeare bust appears at a key moment in the film.

1479 *Book Revue*
1946. U.S. Warner Bros. Sound, col., 7 mins. Robert Clampett.

Animated film. A series of book-related gags, set after hours in a bookstore. Shakespeare's silhouette is superimposed over a clockwork mechanism; when a jazz fanfare strikes up (from the book *Man with the Golden Horn*) and a stripper starts her routine (from the book *Cherokee Strip*), the gears break and Shakespeare's silhouette goes haywire.

As is so often the case in midcentury Hollywood shorts featuring the Bard, Shakespeare (like the clockwork) functions as a symbol of proper, high culture order, juxtaposed against symbols of pop cultural carnivality (here in the form of jazz and sex).

1480 *Laughter in Paradise*
1951. U.K. Transocean Films. Sound, b&w, 93 mins. Mario Zampi.

Henry Russell, a notorious practical joker, dies, leaving his four children £50,000 each if they will complete absurd tasks within a month of the reading of his will. Each task is keyed to the character flaw of the relative, and in the end they all discover that Russell died penniless. One of Russell's relatives, Deniston, writes pulp novels under various pseudonyms, and as we first meet him, he is dictating his next book, *Blood Lust*, filled with American slang. As he dictates, he stands next to a bust of Shakespeare on the mantelpiece, and he becomes self-conscious about the lowbrow nature of what he's writing, turning Shakespeare's face away from him. He comments about his readers; "They seem to like the American touch." The video re-

lease of the film does not contain the reference to *The Merchant of Venice* that Sammons reports.

1481 *The Faculty*
1999. U.S. Dimension Films. Sound, col., 104 mins. Robert Rodriguez.

A science ficture horror picture derived from *Invasion of the Body Snatchers*. An image of Shakespeare is seen hanging in front a blackboard in a classroom. (RB)

1482 *Underworld*
2003. U.S. Sound, col., 121 mins. Len Wiseman.

A vampire-meets-werewolves horror film that is close to being a spin-off of *Romeo and Juliet*. The central vampire warrior, Selene, in love with a human, Michael, uses busts of Shakespeare as target practice when given new bullets that will kill the Lycan (werewolves). (RB)

Shakespearean Teachers

1483 *Night into Morning*
1951. U.S. MGM. Sound, b&w, 86 mins. Fletcher Markle.

English professor Phillip Ainley spirals into depression when his wife and son are killed in a gas explosion at his home. Superficially stoic, Ainley is in reality alcoholic and suicidal, and department secretary Katherine Mead, a war widow, worries about his behavior and tries to help, which her fiancé and Ainley's best friend Tom Lawry misinterprets as romantic interest. As Mead and others attempt to get Ainley to change a student's grade, Ainley becomes more despondent and, drunk, gets into a car accident, leading to his disgrace at the college. He prepares to commit suicide, changing his will to benefit Lawry and Mead, but before he can do so, Mead stops him. After reassuring Lawry that Katherine loves him and making the grade change, Ainley conquers his depression.

Ainley lectures on Shakespeare the morning of his family's demise, and the day after the funeral he lectures on a passage from *Richard II* in which Richard contemplates death.

1484 *Absolution*
1979. U.K. and Panama. Bulldog. Sound, col., 95 mins. Anthony Page.

From the play by Anthony Shaffer. At a Catholic boarding school run by the tyrannical Father Goddard, two students, Benjamin Stanfield and Arthur Dyson, pursue revenge by creating horrifying sins of murder and reciting them to Goddard in their confessions, eventually driving him to the point of madness. Goddard regards Stanfield as his favorite, and Stanfield takes a particularly cruel revenge upon him because Goddard evicts Blakey, a drifter with which Stanfield has struck up a friendship. The film was not released until 1988.

The headmaster refers to Prospero's "We are such stuff as dreams are made on" speech, and students are briefly seen rehearsing the assassination scene from *Julius Caesar*. Both passages are obliquely relevant to the film's themes.

1485 *36 Chowringee Lane*
1981. India. Film Valas. Sound, col., 122 mins. Aparna Sen.

A deeply poignant portrait of aging and loneliness, *36 Chowringee Lane* focuses on Violet Stoneham, the aging Anglo-Indian granddaughter of a member of the East India Company, who teaches Shakespeare in a girls' school in Calcutta and lives a poignantly lonely existence with her cat Sir Toby Belch, enlivened only by occasional letters from her children. Adding to the sadness of her life, the arrival of a new headmistress demotes Violet to a teacher of grammar, and her half-senile brother languishes in a retirement home. When Nandita, one of her former students, and Samaresh, her boyfriend, encounter Violet by chance, they decide to befriend her and use her apartment for romantic assignations. Violet becomes more and more emotionally attached to them, showering them with hospitality and gifts, but once the two marry they no longer pursue the relationship. Eventually, Violet discovers by accident during the Christmas holiday that they are no longer interested in her company, and she wanders the street alone with the Christmas cake she baked for them.

Violet presents not only a touching portrait of the isolation of the aged, but also a symbol of the fading traces of the colonial past in contemporary urban India, exemplified by her dogged devotion to teaching Shakespeare; her memories of her heroic, now dead paramour Davy Bedford; and her refusal to join those who have immigrated. The film has two primary points of Shakespearean reference. The first is *Twelfth Night*, a play that, we learn, Violet has long taught her students. The film specifically references Orsino's "If music be the food of love" speech (1.1), Malvolio's "Some are born great, some achieve greatness" speech (2.5), and Olivia's encounter with the smiling and cross-gartered Malvolio (3.4). All of the passages have deeper resonance, particularly the last in which Malvolio, an older, sober man, is unbeknownst to him humiliated by others. More important and direct, however, is Violet's lengthy citation from *King Lear*, a combination of 4.6.52–56 and 5.3.8–13. Both of these speeches articulate Violet's touching identification with Lear's aged fragility, humiliation, and desire for companionship, and her reaching out to

Shakespeare to give her quiet suffering meaning. This final Shakespearean moment in the film is made all the more touching by the fact that her only audience is a stray dog.

1486 *Porky's II: The Next Day*
1983. U.S. 20th Century Fox, Astral Bellevue Pathé, and Simon Reeves Landsburg Productions. Sound, col., 98 mins. Bob Clark.

In this sequel to *Porky's*, a group of Florida high school teenagers battle the prejudice and hypocrisy of small-town politicians, right-wing clergy, and racists in the town of Angel Beach, while pursuing practical jokes and salacious escapades. The centerpiece of the film is a high school production of Shakespearean highlights that is opposed by Reverend Bubba Flavel, a Baptist revivalist preacher, and the girls' gym teacher Miss Baldrick, for its lewd content and by the Ku Klux Klan for casting Joseph Henry, a Seminole Indian, in the part of Romeo. When the show is shut down and a local official, Commissioner Gebhardt, betrays the students, the group orchestrates a spectacular revenge of pranks on them all.

Featured are myriad Shakespearean citations, all related to the school play. A number of references involve casting and its relationship to the men's masculinity: Billy and Pee Wee are made fun of for being cast as Oberon, King of the Fairies, and Puck; Anthony (nicknamed "Meat") is cast as Flute cross-dressed as Thisbe from *A Midsummer Night's Dream*, and he offers lines from the play-within-a-play in a falsetto voice as students laugh. We also hear Billy rehearse his Macbeth role, from his confrontation with Macduff in *Macbeth* 5.8. Of the production itself we see three scenes:

Characters from *Porky's II* (1982). This shot shows several of the cast members in their Shakespearean dress, as they prepare to do a version of a Shakespeare revue. Courtesy of Douglas Lanier.

Wendy and John Henry as Juliet and Romeo in the balcony scene (Tchaikovsky's music plays behind the dialogue); Pee Wee as Puck, delivering his "Now the hungry lion roars" speech from *Midsummer Night's Dream* 5.1; and Macbeth and Macduff's final swordfight from *Macbeth* 5.8. The last of these scenes becomes a farce when Macduff's sword breaks and as a prank he's given a female manikin's leg to slay Macbeth. When Flavel confronts Principal Carter about the Shakespeare play, they engage in a contest of bawdy quotations from Shakespeare and the Bible: referenced are Petruchio and Kate's exchange about tongues and tails from *The Taming of the Shrew* 2.2; Oberon's "'tis almost fairy time" from *A Midsummer Night's Dream* 5.1; Bottom's "I could munch a good dry oats" from *A Midsummer Night's Dream* 4.1; and Lear's "Let copulation thrive" from *King Lear* 4.6. Oddly, bits of Felix Mendelssohn's *A Midsummer Night's Dream* incidental music (entry 1668) play under some of the film's prank sequences. The divided attitude of the film toward Shakespeare—at once regarded as valuable and as ridiculous—is noteworthy. Compare *Dead Poets Society*.

1487 *Stan the Flasher*
1990. France. R Films and Studio Canal +. Sound, col., 66 mins. Serge Gainsbourg.

Stan, a frustrated aging man increasingly unable to satisfy Aurore, his young girlfriend, and in the midst of a midlife crisis, works as a tutor in English for children. When he gropes a fetching young girl, Natacha, during a tutoring session, her father beats him and has him arrested. Convicted, he spends his sentence term in the company of an eccentric murderer. Once released, he discovers that Aurore has abandoned him and that he has been branded "Stan the Flasher," so he commits suicide. In the film's final shot, we see Aurore clutch Stan's dead hand.

Stan quotes Shakespeare frequently. He uses "To be or not to be" as a standard set text in his tutorials, and recites it several times; it is also during Natacha's recitation of her French translation of the speech that Stan touches her (he also offers passages of Hamlet's speech to Ophelia, which follows). "To be or not to be" articulates Stan's increasingly desperate feelings of despair at the state of his life. He also cites other passages from *Hamlet* (in French translation), as well as "My kingdom for a horse" when Natacha visits him in jail (referenced too are *Othello, Macbeth, King Lear,* and *Hamlet*, by title). When Stan returns to his empty flat and bemoans his state with friends, one of them offers a portion of Hamlet's final speech and Horatio's "Good night, sweet prince," presaging Stan's suicide. Despite the potentially prurient subject matter of the film, *Stan the Flasher* is a serious study of male midlife crisis, with Shakespeare serving as the one source of unsullied meaning in Stan's world. Stan was the protagonist of Gainsbourg's earlier film *Charlotte Forever* (1986), also a man in midlife crisis.

1488 *Convento, O (The Convent)*
1995. Portugal and France. Gemini Films, La Sept Cinema, and Madragoa Filmes. Sound, col., 94 mins. Manoel de Oliviera.

Adapted from the novel by Agustina Bessa-Luís. In this version of the Faust story, iconoclastic Michael Padovic, an English professor from America, and his fetching French wife Hélène visit a convent in Arrabida, Portugal, where Padovic pursues research proving that Shakespeare was a Sephardic Jew. Baltar, the urbane, sinister caretaker of the convent, arranges with the convent's beautiful librarian Piedade for Padovic to use the library, while Baltar pursues Hélène, who is angry with Padovic's romantic inattention. Baltar offers Padovic immortality through his writing and research. When Baltar, who claims to be the devil, attempts to seduce Hélène, she demands that he first prove his love by eliminating Piedade, whom Padovic has developed an interest in. The film's ambiguously "happy" ending shows Padovic and Hélène walking arm and arm down a beach, Piedade apparently out of the picture, but the credits offer different stories of their final fate.

Shakespeare is established as Padovic's central research interest (he is looking for a crucial marriage contract to prove his point), but the key literary point of reference is Faust, which Piedade reads aloud. In Portuguese, Baltar offers a paraphrase of Oberon's description of the love-in-idleness flower and Puck's comment about going round the world in forty seconds.

Cameos

1489 *His Girl Friday*
1940. Howard Hawks.

Walter Burns (Cary Grant) phones his newspaper to give a rival reporter/poet named Roy V. Bensinger (Ernest Truex) a job. Into the phone Grant says, "I'll bet you haven't heard of Shakespeare either!" (RB)

1490 *Charulata*
1964. India. Sony Pictures. Sound, b&w, mins. Satyajit Ray.

An adaptation of Tagore's novel *The Broken Nest*. In Ray's film, the husband newspaper editor and publisher discounts the value of *Romeo and Juliet* to his brother, who is considering emigrating to England, "the land of Shakespeare." As *Charulata* makes clear, the domestic space, linked to protheses of binoculars used by Charulata, can also enable the realization of female literary ambitions. Though *Charulata*'s ending is relatively dark, it is happier than the novel's and it holds out the possibility of reconciling husband and wife, the literary and the political. (RB)

1491 *Sterne (Stars)*
1959. East Germany and Bulgaria. DEFA and Bulgarian Co-Production. Sound, b&w, 92 mins. Konrad Wolf.

A spin-off of *Romeo and Juliet*.

1492 *Superchick*
1973. Ed Forsyth.

Joyce Jillson plays Tara B. True, a buxom, blond, free-wheeling flight attendant who is so sexually attractive that she performs her airline duties disguised as a demure brunette in order not to cause a riot on the plane. The sexually adventurous True has a besotted lover at every airport; each man wants to marry her. Superchick has a black belt in karate, and uses her skill to thrash a Japanese master, thwart a gangbang by motorcyclists, and prevent a plane highjacking. After passionate lovemaking, one of her suitors proposes marriage, and the independent, free spirited True replies, "In the words of Shakespeare, let's not louse up a good thing."

Adventurous Tara answers a personal ad written by Igor Smith (John Carradine). (EL)

1493 *Hitler: A Film from Germany*
1978. Hans-Juergen Syberberg.

Shakespeare comes up twice in the seven-hour film, first when Hitler appears as Hamlet holding a skull and second when Hitler paraphrases Shylock's line "Hath not a Jew eyes? Hath not a Jew hands...?...If you prick us, do we not bleed?" as "I am a human being with two eyes and ears, like you...and if you prick me do I not bleed?" In a Brechtian manner, Syberberg uses a highly theatrical mise-en-scène, often interchanging puppets and actors, to make a critique of Hitler's afterlives in both Nazi and Hollywood films, documentaries, images, and spectacles. Citation is a mimetic performance. Yet by foregrounding Hitler as performance and performer, Syberberg makes it difficult to distinguish between miming the Fuehrer and the Fuehrer as mimic. In Syberberg's Hollywood-to-*Hamlet* connection, the appearance of Hitler as Hamlet comes at the end of a series of similar mimings that begins with a circus showman turning his back to the camera, changing his costume, and then turning back to the camera as Charlie Chaplin's Tramp wearing a Nazi armband. We then cut to him as a window washer, then to Hitler as mimicked by Chaplin in *The Great Dictator* (Charlie Chaplin, 1942), then as Napoleon, then as Hitler biting a piece of carpet, then as Hitler posing as a knight similar to the way he appears in some Nazi paintings, and then as Hamlet holding a skull. An Orthodox Jewish man wearing a yellow star follows. Chaplin, Napoleon, and Hamlet all move from iconic gestures (the Tramp twirling his cane, Napoleon placing his hand over his stomach, Hamlet holding the skull) to Hitler holding his arm up and hand back as he looks into the camera and gives or receives the "Heil." On the one hand, the film suggests that Hitler has seemingly inexhaustive power to parody various kinds of actors and incorporate them. We move from parody of Hitler (Chaplin) to precursor (Napoleon) or painting to Hitler himself. On the other hand, however, Syberberg deconstructs an apparent distinction between original and mime in which a series of vertiginous possibilities opens up: Hitler is miming Hamlet who is miming Hitler who is miming Hamlet miming Hitler, and so on. It is hard to know at a certain point where Chaplin leaves off and Hitler begins, for example. Syberberg's dual citation of Chaplin calls attention to the complex relation between Chaplin and Hitler. Well before Chaplin mimicked Hitler as Adenoid Hynkel in *The Great Dictator* (1940), Hitler was already being compared—as early as 1933—to Chaplin's tramp. The comparison was a means of minimizing Hitler's importance. In Syberberg's film, Chaplin's Nazi armband–sporting Tramp blurs the lines between Hitler as tramp and the tramp's Hitler. The Hitler-Hamlet connection is similarly complex. Hitler had cited Hamlet's line "To be or not to be" in *Mein Kampf* in a chapter on war propaganda. Using a line from Shakespeare to justify the end of aesthetics, Hitler writes, "When the nations on this planet fight for existence—when the question of destiny, 'to be or not to be'—cries out for a solution—then all consideration of humanitarianism or aesthetics crumble into nothingness" (1925; trans. Ralph Mannheim 1943, 177). (RB)

1494 *Nocturna*
1979. Harry Tampa.

Dracula (John Carradine) and his granddaughter Nocturna (Nai Bonet) live together in a Transylvanian castle along with their angry manservant-cum-wolfman, Theodore. Theodore lusts after Nocturna ("if only I could get into her coffin!"), and covets the power possessed by Dracula, who is the respected patriarch of the global vampire community. Times are hard, and they are "reduced to running a second rate hotel just to keep up with the taxes." Nocturna cares for her decrepit old grandfather, supplying him with blood because he is too infirm to hunt for himself (his fangs are dentures kept in a glass beside his coffin). A disco group, the Moment of Truth, comes to perform in their Transylvanian home/hotel, and Nocturna becomes enamored with Jimmy (Anthony Hamilton), a band member. Jimmy teaches her to dance, and Nocturna discovers that disco music "transforms" her; in fact, while dancing she becomes visible in a mirror, hence briefly becoming mortal. The couple fall in love, and Nocturna decides to live life as a mortal. Dracula refuses to permit this, reminding her that she can "use men for nourishment only," and must procreate only with one of her own kind. Nocturna runs away to New York City with Jimmy, leaving her grandfather a note. Dracula reads Nocturna's note and decides to follow her to Manhattan, telling Theodore,

As the Bard said:

If it were done when 'tis done, then 'twere well
It were done quickly. (*Macbeth*, 1.7.1–2)
How sharper than a serpent's tooth it is
To have a thankless child! (*King Lear*, 1.4.170–71)

Dracula wanders off, presumably to pack, and Theodore speaks to the camera,

You pompous ass! You s.a.p. from the galloping senility ward! You love your Shakespeare, don't you?

John Blyth Barrymore (half-brother of Drew Barrymore) portrays a punk vampire. Gloria Gaynor, Vicki Sue Robinson, and The Moment of Truth perform disco music. (EL)

1495 *The Vampire Hookers*
1979. Cirio H. Santiago.
Film begins with white-suited vampire Richmond Reed (John Carradine, portraying a character bearing his own real name) seated in a throne-like chair intoning a paraphrase of Baudelaire's "Les Métamorphoses du vampire" (1857). The film opens with two sailors, Tom Buckley (Bruce Fairbairn) and Terry Wayne (Trey Wilson), going on leave in the Philippines and looking for women. They run into transsexual hookers and horrible local delicacies, get thrown out of a bar, and narrowly escape a shakedown when their CPO Eddie Taylor (Lex Winter) drives up and saves them from a beating. Eddie hooks up with a beautiful local, Cherish (Karen Stride), who takes him to her place, which is a mausoleum in a cemetery. As she leads him down through a crypt he expresses distaste at having sex in a coffin, and Cherish replies, "Coffins are for being laid to rest; not for being laid." As she begins to seduce him, Richmond Reed appears with two nubile young women— Suzy (Lenka Novak) and Marcy (Katie Dolan)—and paraphrases *Hamlet* 3.1:

EDDIE: What the hell is this?
RICHMOND: That, my friend, is not the question.
  To be or not to be, that is the question.
  To die, to sleep no more.
  And by his sleep to say we end the heartache
  And the thousand natural shocks that flesh is heir to.
  It is a consummation devoutly to be wished for.
EDDIE: You're out of your mind, pal.
RICHMOND: It is time for you to shuffle off *your* mortal coil.

Cherish bites his neck as the three vampires advance on him. Later, as Richmond Reed and the three female vampires prepare to sleep in their coffins, Reed recites from Walt Whitman's poem "When Lilacs Last in the Dooryard Bloom'd":

Come, lovely and soothing Death,
Undulate round the world, serenely arriving, arriving,
In the day, in the night...to each (136–38)

Reed states, "Walt Whitman must have been a vampire. Only a vampire would have written so much about the night, about death." As he clambers into his coffin, he recites, "Walk out with me toward the unknown region" (2) from Whitman's "Darest Thou Now, O Soul."

As the vampires sleep, they are watched over by a repulsive, Igor-like manservant, Pavo (Vic Diaz), who yearns desperately to be a vampire and loves the smell of his own farts.

Terry and Tom notice that Eddie has not returned to base, and they set out to look for him. They witness Cherish getting into a taxi with another sailor and track her to the cemetery. Tom follows her inside the crypt, and discovers the sailor hung upside down, his blood draining into a decanter. As she pours drinks, vampire Suzy says, "I get sick and tired of these Bloody Marys." Invited to join them for a drink, Pavo cannot stomach the blood, and Reed counsels, "Give it time." Tom knocks over a candelabra and escapes, meeting up with Terry outside the mausoleum. The two are chased by Pavo and cornered by Reed and the three female vampires. Reed introduces himself:

REED: My name is Richmond Reed. A name that you all know by sight very well but that no one can speak and no one can spell.
SAILOR: What?
REED: Doesn't anyone understand poetry any more? That was written by Robert Southey.

Reed explains that he himself died in 1847, and outlived "that pompous bastard" Southey by four years. Tom and Terry realize they are about to be killed by vampires, but the sun begins to rise and the women flee back into the mausoleum, followed by Pavo. Reed tells the men,

I shall remember while the light lives yet
And in the night time, I shall not forget.
(Algernon Charles Swinburne)

Reed disappears in thin air, and the sailors decide to inform the authorities about the murders in the cemetery. Tom brings back the police, but they leave him in disgust after he is unable to open the crypt. Pavo knocks him on the head, and he awakens inside a room whose wall artwork illustrates various sexual positions. Reed and the three female vampires say they want him to stay; and Reed paraphrases Shakespeare: "Unbidden guests are welcomest gone (*Henry VI, Part I* 2.2.58–59), and Shakespeare was a man who knew about unwelcome guests."

When Tom wants to leave, Reed paraphrases both Plutarch and Ferriar: "A bird in the hand is worth its weight in gold." The women want to use Tom as their boy toy and Reed agrees, saying, "One night with them will kill you anyway."

Meanwhile, Terry begins looking for his missing friend, and Pavo and Reed discuss how vodka is the only item that will mix with blood. Reed quotes Shakespeare,

Though I look old, yet I am strong and lusty:
For in my youth I never did apply
Hot and rebellious liquors in me blood (*AYLI*, 2.3.49–51)

and then informs his pet owl, "Shakespeare was a vampire."

The women have tied Tom to the bed and are making love to him in slow motion, accompanied by the worst instrumental soundtrack of all time. Now clothed, the females enter the room because they think they smell pizza. Pavo has carried in a large bag of garlic, and Reed exclaims, "Don't you read Shakespeare, you imbecile! '...eat no onions nor garlic, for we are to utter sweet breath' (*MND* 4.2.41). Shakespeare was a vampire!" (EL)

1496 *Teaching Mrs. Tingle*
1999. U.S. Dimension Films, Interscope Communications, and Konrad Pictures. Sound, col., 96 mins. Kevin Williamson.

Leigh Ann Watson, a diligent Grandsboro High School student from a poor family, focuses on becoming valedictorian and getting a college scholarship. Unfortunately, she finds herself in the class of Mrs. Tingle, a notoriously hard, venomous history teacher. After Leigh Ann is harshly criticized on her final project by Mrs. Tingle and discovers that she may lose the valedictorian award to Trudie Tucker, fellow student Luke Churner stashes the answers to Tingle's final examination in her bag. Tingle discovers the exam and threatens to turn in Leigh Ann for cheating. When Leigh Ann, her friend Jo Lynn Jordan, and Luke go to speak with Tingle, Luke and Jo Lynn accidentally abduct her and the three keep her prisoner while trying to blackmail her into silence. Tingle tries to psych out the three students and divide them as they formulate plans to deal with their predicament. After Tingle escapes and threatens them, she accidentally attacks Trudie, leading to her dismissal and Leigh Ann's successful graduation.

On three occasions, Mrs. Tingle uses passing allusions to Shakespeare to toy with her student captors. She tries to convince Jo Lynn that Leigh Ann desires Luke by observing that "Cleopatra rebuked Antony because she desired him." She condescendingly refers to Leigh Ann as "Ophelia" because she believes Leigh Ann thinks of herself as a victim. And when Jo Lynn, an aspiring actress, addresses Tingle's dog as Romeo and launches into Juliet's address to Romeo in the balcony scene, Tingle opines that she will never be a convincing Juliet because she lacks the requisite commitment and soul. See also *Scary Movie, Blue Angel, So Fine,* and *Killing Mr. Griffin.*

1497 *Scary Movie 2*
2001. U.S. Sound, col., 88 mins. Keenan Ivory Wayans.

This politically incorrect and pretty dumb film has an episode in which a black couple, Ray (Shawn Wayans) and Cindy Campbell (Anna Faris), decide to go to a movie together. The movie marquee shows *Shakespeare in Love* on it and in the theater, Ray, who is gay but seems to be the last one to know it, goes off to the bathroom, enters a stall,

and, hearing some voices in the next stall, lowers his head to what is a glory hole and looks in it. An erect, white penis goes through it briefly and quickly withdraws, but Ray doesn't see it. He puts his ear to the hole, and then the erect penis literally goes through one of Ray's ears and out the other, killing him (though he appears alive later in the film). Meanwhile, Cindy talks back to the movie, reading the balcony scene as if it were a horror movie, and screaming after the Nurse comes to the window and sees Shakespeare at the window and screams and then he screams in turn. Later she says, "Brad Pitt's ex-girlfriend ain't all that," as Shakespeare unwinds the white bandage she used to flatten her breasts so she would look like a boy. The other members of the audience (all white) all "shhh" her, but she is defiant, saying, "shh back to you," to one, and filming him with her digital camcorder. The murderer, dressed in costume, sits downs next to Cindy with a knife on his lap, but she assumes he is her boyfriend. She then gets a call on her cell phone, and a white guy sitting next to the murderer picks up the knife in disgust and stabs her. She gets up and several other people in the audience stab her too. As she makes it to the aisle, other people get up and either stab her or hit her with things like a baseball bat, saying, "This is for ruining *Big Momma's House!*" Finally, she makes it to the stage, and gurgles in front of the movie screen, before collapsing, dead.

The episode occurs near the middle of *Scary Movie,* and it is a direct reply to and parody of the introduction to the already self-parodying *Scream 2* (Wes Craven, 1997). (The title of the *Scream 2* DVD chapter for this introduction is "Scary Movie.") There is a shot of the movie marquee showing *Stab!* and then we see a black couple, Maureen (Jada Pinkett) and Phil (Omar Epps), in line to buy tickets. Maureen says she doesn't like scary movies and suggests they go see Sandra Bullock. She is willing to see *Stab!* but voices her complaint to Phil: "I'm gonna tell you what I think it is, OK? It's a dumb ass white movie about dumb ass white girls getting their dumb asses cut the fuck up.... The entire genre is historical for excluding the African American element." Phil replies, "Where'd you get your Ph.D. in black cinema, Sista Souljah?" From *Entertainment Tonight,* she replies.

They go in to see the movie and she talks back to it, telling the blonde woman on screen (Heather Graham) not to "go in there." Phil goes out to the bathroom while she goes to get popcorn and a drink, and he enters a stall, hears a voice, puts his head to the stall wall to listen better, and then gets stabbed by a knife into his ear. The knife is withdrawn from Phil's head by the killer, and Phil slowly sinks down, holding his ear until he drops dead. The killer then sits next to Maureen wearing Phil's clothes and his mask. During a scary part, Maureen grabs the killer, thinking he is Phil, and telling him that if she were the character on the screen, she'd know how to escape. She also accurately predicts the woman's death. Yet just then Maureen sees blood on her hands (from the jacket). She recoils in horror and he then stabs her. Maureen gets up and tries to escape, but he follows her into the aisle and stabs her another four times. No one notices because everyone is dressed like the killer, screaming, and waving fake knives. Maureen walks up to the screen, her shirt all bloody, and the audience figures out that she actually is hurt. She gurgles, and collapses, dead.

Shakespeare in Love signifies in a number of ways. There is an implied parallel between the black couple and the couple in the film, Shakespeare and Viola de Lessups. Phil's gayness and disavowal of his homosexuality roughly parallel the homoeroticism in Viola's cross-dressing, and the error he makes in failing to recognize Viola in drag roughly parallels Cindy's misreading of the romantic comedy as a horror movie. Furthermore, the movie-within-a-movie and allusions to the *Scream* trilogy, which is highly self-reflexive and self-conscious, roughly parallel the play *Romeo and Juliet* within the movie *Shakespeare in Love*. It is worth pointing out that Kevin Williamson, the screenwriter for *Scream 2*, does have (all white) characters mention Ophelia, Romeo, and Juliet in *Teaching Mrs. Tingle*, a film he wrote and directed. In terms of the intercinematic allusion to *Scream 2*, *Scary Movie* may be using Shakespeare to reply to *Scream 2*'s critique of the racism of the horror movie, producing a shock value for liberal white people they're not expecting. After all, the black couple is the first to go in *Scream 2*, and it is the vocal black woman Maureen who is killed by a hooded white guy. Moreover, Maureen is portrayed as a sexually withholding bitch who rebuffs all of Phil's advances, whereas Cindy indulges all of Ray's whims, including his request that she dress up in his football uniform. By having the white people in the audience be offended by Cindy's talk back, which marks her as black, *Scary Movie* suggests that *Scream 2* co-opts an African American critique of the horror genre's racism. Perhaps the similarity between the black woman and Viola/Juliet elevates the woman's death to tragic status or makes Cindy into a rebellious figure the other race can't understand; or perhaps the similarity pokes fun at Shakespeare and is meant as a kind of aesthetic incorrectness (as in "Shakespeare ain't all that"). *Scary Movie* takes the license to be as nasty and as silly as it wants to be. (RB)

1498 P.S. Your Cat Is Dead
2002. Steve Guttenberg.

Jimmy Zoole (Steve Guttenberg) is having a bad week. His apartment has been robbed twice in the last three months, and his handwritten novel, a year's work, was stolen. It is New Year's Eve and his girlfriend Kate (Cynthia Watros) is leaving him, his best friend Pete just died, and his beloved cat is in the hospital with a bladder infection. The film opens with Zoole performing his *One*

Man Hamlet, in which he uses hand puppets, for a snoozing audience of four. A voice-over states, "My name is Jimmy Zoole, and I'm a writer and an actor, a serious actor." Zoole, in Renaissance garb, begins enacting Hamlet with a hand puppet representing the ghost of Hamlet's father:

I find thee apt, (1.5.36)
The serpent that did sting thy father's life
Now wears his crown.
O my prophetic soul! (1.5.44–46)

The *Hamlet* production is closed, the theater manager suggesting it is "too avant garde," which Zoole explains is French for "can't sell tickets." As Zoole makes his way home, the burglar Eddie (Lombardo Boyar) who has already robbed him twice breaks in again. The burglar hides when Kate gets home and begins to pack her belongings. Jimmy and Kate fight, she leaves, and Jimmy discovers the burglar and overpowers him. Zoole hogties the burglar on the kitchen sink, and spends the rest of the film torturing him: feeding him cat food, cutting the seat off his pants, and threatening his life and genitalia. In retaliation, Eddie tells Jimmy that the cat hospital called, and his cat is dead. He interviews Eddie, and it turns out that the burglar is gay. Eddie describes his ex-wife Marcy as "my Juliet; I kissed the ground she sat on," and clearly loves his daughter. Jimmy has invited Carmine (A. J. Benza) and his cohorts over in order to gang-rape the still-hogtied Eddie, but Eddie talks himself out of being a victim and the others gang up on Jimmy and hogtie him. Eddie evicts the men, unties Jimmy, and they become friends. The film ends with the two watching the sunrise on New Year's Day, and the suggestion that they might become more than just friends. (In the original play, they end up in bed together.) (EL)

1499 Sylvia
2004. U.S. MCA. Sound, col., 110 mins. Christine Jeffs.

Biopic starring Gwyneth Paltrow as Sylvia Plath. She and Ted Hughes recite parts of three Shakespeare plays: *King Lear* (Sylvia doing Lear on the heath having gone mad), *Henry IV, Part I* (Ted doing "I know you all"), and *Romeo and Juliet* (both characters, doing parts of the tomb scene). The scene goes on for some time. See 1249. (RB)

1500 The Libertine
2004. U.K. Odyssey Entertainment. Sound, col., 114 mins. Laurence Dunmore.

Stephen Jeffreys adapts another of his plays for film (see 1290), this one from a 1994 production. The film recounts the story of John Wilmot (Johnny Depp), aka the Earl of Rochester, a seventeenth-century poet. King Charles II (John Malkovich) suggests that Rochester write a major work of literature celebrating his reign. The king would like Rochester to be what Shakespeare was to Queen Elizabeth: "Elizabeth had her Shakespeare. You can be mine." This line is also in the film trailer. *The Libertine* mentions

Cleopatra, Ophelia, and Desdemona all in relation to Mrs. Barry (Samantha Morton). There is a scene in which she gives lines from Ophelia's major speeches in a revival of *Hamlet*. (RB)

Additional References

1501 *Dracula's Daughter*
1936. U.S. Sound, b&w, 71 mins. Lambert Hillyer.
    Dracula's daughter quotes Hamlet's line "There are more things in heaven and earth than are dreamt of in your philosophy" to Professor van Helsing. (RB)

1502 *The Music Man*
1962. U.S. Sound, col., 151 mins. Morton DaCosta.
    Shakespeare is mentioned several times, along with other literary figures, as a token of high culture of which the local River City townspeople are ignorant.

1503 *Shaft in Africa*
1973. U.S. Sound, col., 112 mins. John Guillermin.
    Shaft mentions Shakespeare and his education in New York. (RB)

1504 *Bringing down the House*
2001. U.S. Sound, col., 105 mins. Adam Shankman.
    The dog of an elderly white widow, played by Joan Plowright, is named Shakespeare. (RB)

1505 *Seabiscuit*
2003. U.S. Sound, col., 141 mins. Gary Ross.
    When the Seabiscuit jockey Red Pollard (Toby McGuire) is asked by a reporter about his "little horse," Pollard replies, "though she be but little, she is fierce. That's Shakespeare, guys. Shakespeare. Shakespeare." *A Midsummer Night's Dream* is not mentioned. Later, when Pollard has been replaced by another jockey, he says that this was "the most unkindest cut of all." *Julius Caesar* is not mentioned. (RB)

Hamlet

1506 *Amleto e il suo Clown* (aka *On with the Motley*)
1920. 6000 ft. Italy. Carmine Gallone.
    A girl stages the players' scene from *Hamlet*, then kills her stepfather whom she thinks has killer her father. When she learns that the stepfather is innocent, she commits suicide.

1507 *The Man Who Knew Too Much*
1934. U.K. Gaumont British Picture. Sound, b&w, 75 mins. Alfred Hitchcock.
    References "the undiscovered country."

1508 *Once upon a Honeymoon*
1942. U.S. RKO Radio Pictures. Sound, b&w, 115 mins. Leo McCarey.

References "to thine own self be true."

1509 *The Dark Man*
1951. U.K. Independent Artists. Sound, b&w, 91 mins. Jeffrey Dell.
    An actress playing Ophelia is terrorized by a killer.

1510 *The Iron Petticoat*
1956. U.S. Remus and Romulus Films Ltd. Sound, col., 87 mins. Ralph Thomas.
    A passing reference from *Hamlet* in this Bob Hope comedy.

1511 *Susanna tutta panna*
1957. Italy and Spain. Carlo Ponti Cinematografica, Jesús Sáiz P.C., and Maxima Film Compagnia Cinematografica. Sound, b&w, 90 mins. Steno.
    Includes a scene from *Hamlet*.

1512 *Ninì Tirabusciò: la donna che inventò la mossa*
1970. Italy. Clesi Cinematografica. Sound, col., 94 mins. Marcello Fondato.
    An aspiring actress plays Juliet and Ophelia.

1513 *Merry Christmas Mr. Lawrence*
1983. U.K. and Japan. Asahi National Broadcasting, Cineventure Productions London, National Film Trustees, Oshima Productions, and Recorded Picture Company. Sound, col., 124 mins. Nagisa Oshima.
    A Japanese officer cites the line "To be or not to be" when trying to coax testimony from Mr. Lawrence (David Lawrence), who is innocent of the charges, at a war crimes trial. He has no representation at the trial. See *To End All Wars*. (RB)

1514 *Without a Clue*
1988. U.K. ITC. Sound, col., 107 mins. Thom Eberhardt.
    Sherlock Holmes cites "To be or not to be."

1515 *Jesus of Montréal*
1989. France and Canada. Gerard Mital Productions, Max Films, and National Film Board of Canada. Sound, col., 117 mins. Denys Arcand.
    "To be or not to be" referenced. Also a reference to Alec Guinness in *Richard III*.

1516 *Le Champignon Des Carpathes* (*The Carpathian Mushrooms*)
1990. France. 100 mins. Jean-Claude Biette.
    A drama about a struggling production of *Hamlet*. The actress playing Ophelia has been the victim of a nuclear power plant accident.

1517 *J'embrasse pas* (*I Don't Kiss*)
1991. France and Italy. Andre Larrieu, Canal Plus, Centre National de la Cinématographie, Cine Cinq Roger, Gruppo Bema, and Salome SA. Sound, col., 115 mins. André Techiné.

"To be or not to be" referenced.

1518 *Soapdish*
1991. U.S. Paramount Pictures. Sound, col., 97 mins. Michael Hoffman.

Jeffrey Anderson (Kevin Kline) references his one-man *Hamlet*.

1519 *Gettysburg*
1993. U.S. Esparza/Katz Productions and Turner Pictures. Sound, col., 261 mins. Ronald F. Maxwell.

From the novel *The Killer Angels* by Michael Shaara. "What is a man" referenced.

1520 *Splitting Heirs*
1993. U.K. Prominent Features. Sound, col., 87 mins. Robert Young.

A passing reference to a porno *Hamlet*.

1521 *L'amore molesto*
1994. Italy. Lucky Red and Teatri Uniti. Sound, col., 104 mins. Mario Martone.

Adapted from the novel by Elena Ferrante. References *Hamlet* in Italian.

1522 *A Man of No Importance*
1994. Ireland and U.K. BBC, Little Bird Productions, Majestic Films, and Newcomm. Sound, col., 99 mins. Suri Krishnamma.

A closeted gay man participates in a performance of *Hamlet*.

1523 *Somebody to Love*
1994. U.S. Cabin Fever Entertainment Inc., Initial Productions, and Lumière Pictures. Sound, col., 102 mins. Alexandre Rockwell.

References "To be or not to be."

1524 *Blue in the Face*
1996. U.S. Internal Films and Miramax Films. Sound, col., 83 mins. Paul Auster and Wayne Wang.

"To be or not to be" referenced.

1525 *Festen*
1998. Denmark. Danish Radio-TV, Nimbus Film, and SVT. Sound, col., 105 mins. Thomas Vinterberg.

Some general resemblances to *Hamlet*.

1526 *La Nube*
1998. France and Argentina. Cinesur and Les Films du Sud. Sound, col., 116 mins. Fernando E. Solanas.

An actor imitates Olivier in *Hamlet*. See also entry 330.

1527 *Pola X*
1999. France, Switzerland, Germany, and Japan. ARD, Arena Films, ARTE, Canal Plus, Degeto, Euro Space, France 2 Cinema, La Sept Cinema, Pandora Film, Pola Productions, Theo Filmes, TSR, and Vega Film. Sound, col., 134 mins. Leos Carax.

Adapted from Herman Melville's novel *Pierre, or The Ambiguities*. In contemporary Normandy, Pierre, a spoiled aristocratic novelist, lives with his mother Marie in a chateau on the Seine, where the two have a happy if quasi-incestuous relationship. Pierre is in love with Lucie, his cousin and fiancée, whom he visits each night, and when his mother announces that she has picked a date for his wedding, Pierre rushes to tell Lucie. As he does, he meets Isabelle, a woman in the dark who claims to be his sister and tells her story of neglect and poverty. Shocked but intrigued, Pierre soon takes up with Isabelle, becoming her lover and writing a new novel in his newly impoverished circumstances among society's outcasts.

At one point, Pierre references "The time is out of joint."

1528 *Simon Magus*
1999. U.K., U.S., France, Germany, and Italy. ARP Sélection, Arts Council of Britain, Channel Four Films, Goldwyn Films, Hollywood Partners Munich, and Lucky Red. Sound, col., 101 mins. Ben Hopkins.

In late nineteenth-century Silesia, Simon, a Jew who serves as the scapegoat and outcast of his village, survives on degrading work in the sewers and food handouts, believing all the while that he is beleaguered by the Devil. Dovid, another Jew in the village, strikes a deal with a local eccentric poet esquire to build a railway station for the village, in part so that Dovid can impress Leah, a widow he loves but who refuses his advances. When Hase Sean McGinley, a wealthy Christian merchant, learns of the railway project, he uses Simon to try to thwart their plans.

Dovid takes lessons from Sarah, a woman widely read in poetry; at one point, she and the poet esquire have a quotation contest, in which passages from *Hamlet* and *Macbeth* are referenced.

1529 *Bamboozled*
2000. U.S. 40 Acres & a Mule Filmworks. Sound, col., 135 mins. Spike Lee.

In this satire of media racism, Pierre Delacroix, a black Ivy League graduate and self-loathing corporate sellout, works for a cable TV network as a writer of new shows for African American audiences. Frustrated by his condescending white boss Thomas Dunwitty and the racist assumptions of management, he proposes as a pilot *ManTan: The New Millennium Minstrel Show*, starring two homeless blacks in blackface makeup, in an effort to get himself fired. To his dismay, the network approves the show, and it becomes a hit. Delacroix is left to explain matters to angry African American audiences, and eventually he has a confrontation with Sloan Hopkins, his female assistant who is involved with Man Ray, one of the show's stars.

One actor delivers a monologue from *Hamlet*.

1530 *Down to You*
2000. U.S. Miramax. Sound, col., 92 mins. Robert Isaacson.

A character named Monk who stars in porn films is later said to be doing Macbeth. Starring Julia Stiles (*O*, *10 Things I Hate about You*, *The Prince and Me*). (RB)

1531 *La Répétition*
2000. France and Canada. Cinemaginaire, Films Pelléas, Giorno Films, and ZRF. Sound, col., 96 mins. Catherine Corsini.

The relationship between Nathalie and Louise, friends from childhood, changes when the two study drama in their twenties. Nathalie begins to enjoy the company of men, and Louise discovers that she is infatuated with Nathalie, so much so that she attempts suicide out of jealousy when Nathalie has an affair, an act that sunders their friendship. Years later, after Louise has married Nicolas, by accident the couple see Nathalie in a touring show, and Louise rekindles her obsession with her friend, eventually leaving Nicolas to pursue her as Nathalie prepares to star in a production of *Lulu*. Soon Nathalie senses that her friend's attention is troubling and may be repeating their past.

An avant-garde production of *Hamlet* appears in one scene.

1532 *Detention*
2003. Canada. GFT Detention Films, GFT Entertainment, and Nu Image. Sound, col., 98 mins. Sidney J. Furie.

In this remake of *Die Hard*, set in a school, Sam Decker, a former Marine and teacher, monitors a group of ne'er-do-wells in after-hours detention when terrorists attack and take over the school. Decker recruits his students to resist the terrorists and survive their assault. As part of his heroic motivation of the students, he recites "To be or not to be."

Henry V

1533 *Blackboard Jungle*
1955. U.S. MGM. Sound, b&w, 101 mins. Richard Brooks.

Adapted from the novel by Evan Hunter. Idealistic new teacher Richard Dadier, a Navy veteran, takes a job at a tough urban high school in New York City, where he battles teacher cynicism as well as delinquents led by Artie West, a gang leader. To undermine Dadier's authority, he is beaten and accused of racial bigotry, and his pregnant wife Anne is sent notes suggesting that Dadier is unfaithful; the latter causes her to have a premature child. In his final confrontation with Dadier, West is abandoned by his gang when Gregory Miller chooses to ally himself with his teacher.

In his interview for the job, Dadier rather tentatively quotes "Once more into the breach" to demonstrate his ability to project. Ominously, the principal says that the choice of quotation is appropriate and misidentifies it as a citation from *Henry IV*, not *Henry V*. The jealousy and marital tension that Artie generates between Anne and Richard Dadier are distantly reminiscent of the scenario from *Othello*. In this case the other woman, Lois Hammond, is genuinely interested in Dadier, though he rebuffs her advances. (DL)

Capitalizing on exploitation films about juvenile delinquents in the 1950s, *Blackboard Jungle* tells the story of a teacher named Richard Dadier, played by Glenn Ford, who gets his job after reciting *Henry V*'s "Once more to the breach" speech, and saves a very sexy teacher, Lois Hammond (Margaret Hayes), from being raped. He later rejects her quite open advances because he is married. He also manages to get a switchblade away from Artie West (Vic Morrow), a student high on drugs. Dadier's hold on patriarchy, however, is a bit tenuous. Due to letters from Artie West, Dadier's wife gives birth prematurely to a son. She had had a miscarriage earlier. The baby boy survives. For a feminist revision of the film, see *Up the Down Staircase*. Both *Blackboard Jungle* and *Up the Down Staircase* share the same theme of racial integration (Sidney Poitier made his debut in *Blackboard Jungle*) and the same temptation of an offer to the white teacher of a position at a white, better funded school. *Blackboard Jungle* is also remarkable for a scene in which Dadier shows his students the Max Fleischer cartoon version of *Jack and the Beanstalk*. The students respond remarkably well to the film, and two male teachers excitedly ask Dadier about his "secret" after his class has ended. Dadier's willingness to cross over from drama and Shakespeare to "visual media" is echoed in the film's theme song, "Rock around the Clock," by Bill Haley and the Comets. (RB)

Julius Caesar

1534 *Boys in Brown*
1949. U.K. Gainsborough Pictures. Sound, b&w, 85 mins. Montgomery Tully.

Adapted from the play by Reginald Beckwith. Boys in a reform school plan a breakout during the performance of *Julius Caesar*; compare *Danger Within*.

1535 *La Voglia matta*
1962. Italy. Dino de Laurentiis, Lux Film, and Umbria Film. Sound, b&w, 110 mins. Luciano Salce.

Adapted from the novel *Una ragazza di nome Francesca* by Enrico la Stella. A passing reference to *Julius Caesar*, 1.2.

1536 *Roma (Fellini's Roma)*
1972. Italy. Artistes Associes, Italnoleggio, and Ultra Film. Sound, col., 128 mins. Federico Fellini.

Passing reference to *Julius Caesar*.

1537 *Tutto suo padre*
1978. Italy. Variety Films. Sound, col., 99 mins. Maurizio Lucidi.

Adapted from the novel by Alberto Bevilacqua. The protagonist, a pizza maker, loves the theater; contains a passing reference to a scene from *Julius Caesar*.

1538 *The Naked Gun*
1988. U.S. Paramount. Sound, col., 85 mins. David Zucker.

A passing reference to an actor in a Shakespeare in the Park production of *Julius Caesar*.

King Lear

1539 *Emerald City*
1988. Australia. Limelight Productions and New South Wales Film Corp. Sound, col., 92 mins. David Jenkins.

Adapted from the play by David Williamson. Some critics report a relation to *King Lear*.

1540 *Stein*
1991. Germany. 105 mins. Egon Günther.

Ernst Stein, a German actor, protests the invasion of Czechoslovakia by leaving the stage during a performance of *King Lear* and going into seclusion.

1541 *Romani Kris—Zigeunergesetz*
1997. Hungary, Bulgaria, and Germany. 93 mins. Bence Gyöngyössy.

An adaptation of *King Lear*. A gypsy leader of his village becomes alienated from his daughter when she refuses to declare publicly her love for him. He gives away his possessions to his other two daughters, wanders the countryside with the village idiot after his village has been razed by officials.

1542 *Esther Kahn*
2000. France and U.K. Arts Council of England, British Screen, BskyB, Films Alain Sarde, France 2 Cinema, France 3 Cinema, Why Not Productions, and Zephyr Films. Sound, col., 142 mins. Arnaud Desplechin.

Biopic of an aspiring Jewish actress in nineteenth-century London. She plays Cordelia in a scene. Also references *The Merchant of Venice* and *Othello*.

Macbeth

1543 *Up the Down Staircase*
1967. U.S. Warner Brothers. Sound, col., 124 mins. Robert Mulligan.

While deriving much of its dialogue from the Bel Kaufman novel about teacher Sylvia Barret, the film adaptation is generally much darker and the often starling cinematography reminiscent of a John Cassavetes film. One teacher, Paul Barringer, is portrayed as a ladies' man and foreigner who mishandles a student crush on him and

resigns after she attempts suicide. A scene in the novel involving a discussion of Macbeth is retained, and an outburst at Barret's students by Barringer before he resigns involves a mention of *Othello*: "They say a writer should stick to what he knows. What nonsense. What did Dickens know about French Revolutions? What did Shakespeare know about Moors in Venice? If he stuck to what he knew, we'd have no Othello, we'd have no Alice in Wonderland, we'd have no Treasure Island." A brilliant but under-achieving student makes a frightening pass at Sylvia Barret after school is over. She manages to keep him from raping her.

By making Barret the center of the film and having the two central men fail at being her lover, the film reverses the more traditional gender hierarchies of the *Blackboard Jungle*. Author Bel Kaufman has a cameo appearance near the beginning of the film. She's the woman talking to Mr. McHabe (Roy Poole) and reading notes in the beginning as Sylvia Barrett approached the office on the first day. (RB)

1544 *Maxhosa*
1975. South Africa and Great Britain. 85 mins. Lynton Stephenson.

The plot of *Macbeth* is transposed to a Zulu tribe.

1545 *Podmoskovnye Vechera* (aka *Evenings Outside Moscow*)
1994. Russia and France. 94 mins. Valerii Todorovsky.

A loosely updated version of Leskov's story "The Lady Macbeth of Mtensk."

1546 *Kimberly*
1999. U.S. Cinerenta Medienbeteiligungs and Kimberly Productions Inc. Sound, col., 106 mins. Frederic Golchan.

Adapted from a story by Guy de Maupassant. A professor recites "Out damned spot." Also some distant affinities to *Love's Labor's Lost* (four students agree to a pact not to woo).

1547 *Liberty Stands Still*
2001. Germany and Canada. Cinerenta Medienbeteiligungs, Lions Gate Films, Pearl Pictures, and Still Productions. Sound, col., 92 mins. Kari Skogland.

A killer named "Joe" recites "tomorrow and tomorrow" to a victim.

The Merchant of Venice

1548 *Keep the Aspidistra Flying* (aka *A Merry War*)
1997. U.K. Arts Council of England, Bonaparte Films, Overseas FilmGroup, Sentinel Films, and UBA. Sound, col., 101 mins. Robert Bierman.

Adapted from the novel by George Orwell. Gordon Comstock, a young ad writer, invents the slogan "The quality of Bovrex is not strained."

1549 *My Son the Fanatic*
1997. U.K. and France. Arts Council of England, BBC, Union Generale Cinematographique, and Zephyr Films. Sound, col., 87 mins. Udayan Prasad.

Adapted from the novel by Hanif Kureishi. A prostitute's client does a bawdy turn on "the quality of mercy" speech.

1550 *Le Grande Rôle*
2004. France. Egérie Productions and Les Films de l'Espoir. Sound, col., 89 mins. Steve Suissa.

From the novel by Daniel Goldenberg. A Jewish actor struggles with the role of Shylock.

Much Ado about Nothing

1551 *Poirot non Sbaglia*
1996. Andrew Grieve.

The protagonist quotes *Much Ado*. (RB)

Othello

1552 *Il medico dei pazzi*
1954. Italy. Ponti. Sound, col., 91 mins. Mario Mattolli.

Features the Italian comedian Totò. A passing reference to *Othello*.

1553 *Il dolce rumore della vita*
1999. Italy. Letizia Cinematografica and Medusa Produzione. Sound, col., 92 mins. Giuseppe Bertolucci.

A scene in *Otello* is referenced.

1554 *Il gioco*
1999. Italy. Adriana Chiesa Enterprises and Film Master Film. Sound, col., timing unknown. Claudia Florio.

An actress plays Desdemona.

1555 *The Guilty*
2000. U.S., U.K., and Canada. British Columbia Film Commission, Dogwood Pictures, Guilty Productions, J&M Entertainment, and Muse Entertainment Enterprises. Sound, col., 108 mins. Anthony Waller.

Adapted from the novel by Simon Burke. A lawyer quotes Iago on reputation.

Richard III

1556 *J'ai horreur de l'amour*
1997. France. France 2 Cinéma and Gémini Films. Sound, col., 130 mins. L. Ferreira Barbosa.

The protagonist Annie, a doctor, appears in an experimental version of *Richard III*.

Romeo and Juliet

1557 *Make Way for a Lady*
1936. U.S. RKO Radio Pictures. Sound, b&w, 65 mins. David Burton.

Adapted from the novel by Elizabeth Jordan. Includes a disastrous recitation of the balcony scene.

1558 *The Falcon and the Co-Eds*
1943. U.S. RKO Radio Pictures. Sound, b&w, 67 mins. William Clemens.

References the balcony scene. Part of a series of detective films starring the Falcon; compare *The Falcon in Hollywood*.

1559 *This Land Is Mine*
1943. U.S. RKO Radio Pictures. Sound, b&w, 103 mins. Jean Renoir.

A Nazi official cites *Romeo and Juliet* to a French collaborationist.

1560 *Murder Most Foul*
1964. U.K. MGM British Studios. Sound, b&w, 90 mins. George Pollock.

Adapted from the novel by Agatha Christie. Miss Marple joins an acting troupe; the reference to *Romeo and Juliet* is linked to a murder.

1561 *Ludwig*
1972. France, Italy, and West Germany. Cinétel, Dieter Geissler Filmproduktion, Divina-Film, and Mega Film. Sound, col., 184 mins. Luchino Visconti.

Includes a minor reference to Romeo.

1562 *Mr. and Mrs. Bridge*
1990. U.K. and U.S. Cineplex-Odeon Films, Merchant Ivory Productions, and Miramax. Sound, col., 126 mins. James Ivory.

Adapted from the novel by Evan S. Connell. Mr. Bridge treats his daughter Carolyn like Capulet treats Juliet.

Note from RB: The daughter is performing Juliet in a local production of *Romeo and Juliet*.

1563 *The Fantasticks*
1995. U.S. Michael Ritchie Productions, Radmin Company, and Sullivan Street Productions. Sound, col., 86 mins. Michael Ritchie.

Adapted from the play by Tom Jones and Harvey Schmidt. References *Romeo and Juliet*.

1564 *La Scuola*
1995. Italy and France. Cecchi Gori Group Tiger Cinematografica and Les Films Alain Sarde. Sound, col., 104 mins. Daniele Luchetti.

Adapted from the novels by Domenico Starnone. References *Romeo and Juliet* in a teaching situation.

1565 *The Pillow Book*
1995. U.K., France, and the Netherlands. Channel Four Films, Studio Canal, Delux Productions, Kasander & Wigman Productions, Alpha Films, and Woodline Films. Sound, col., 126 mins. Peter Greenaway.

Adapted from the book by Sei Shonagon. Similarities to the final deaths in *Romeo and Juliet*.

Note from RB: The film does not directly refer to *Romeo and Juliet* when Jerome kills himself, but chapter 16 on the DVD menu is entitled "Like *Romeo and Juliet*."

1566 *The Object of My Affection*
1998. U.S. 20th Century Fox. Sound, col., 111 mins. Nicholas Hytner.

Film about a gay man loved by a straight woman and adapted from the novel by Stephen McCauley. Shows part of Romeo and Juliet reciting a sonnet together at the Capulet ball in an interracial and avant-garde production of *Romeo and Juliet*. (RB)

1567 *Romero Loves Juliet . . . but Their Families Hate Each Other!*
1998. Philippines. Production company unknown. Sound, col., length unknown. Tony Y. Reyes and Joey de Leon.

Comedy short from the Phillipines.

1568 *A Cooler Climate*
1999. DLP Productions, Paramount, and Showtime Networks. Sound, col. Susan Seidelman.

Adapted from the novel by Zena Collier. References the balcony scene.

The Taming of the Shrew

1569 *The Cutting Edge*
1992. U.S. Interscope. Sound, col., 97 mins. Paul Michael Glaser.

An ex–hockey skater tames a stuck-up skater, Kate, when they are paired.

The Tempest

1570 *Island of Lost Souls*
1933. U.S. Paramount. Sound, b&w, 71 mins. Erie C. Kenton.

Adapted from the novel *Island of Dr. Moreau* by H. G. Wells, a *Tempest* spin-off.

1571 *L'invenzione di Morel*
1974. Italy. Alga Cinematografica and Mount Street Film. Sound, col., length unknown. Emedio Greco.

Adapted from the novel by Adolfo Bioy Casares. A surreal science fiction film in which a man is dropped on a "haunted" island inhabited by Faustine, a woman with whom he falls in love. He later discovers that she is a hologram, and that the inventor Morel is long dead.

1572 *Die Nacht*
1985. West Germany. TMS Films. Sound, col., length unknown. Hans-Jurgen Syberberg.

An actress recites Prospero's renunciation of magic.

1573 *White Squall*
1995. U.S. Hollywood Pictures, Largo Entertainment, and Scott Free Productions. Sound, col., 129 mins. Ridley Scott.

Adapted from the book by Charles Gieg Jr. and Felix Sutton. A teacher cites *The Tempest*.

Twelfth Night

1574 *Ultimo tango a Parigi (Last Tango in Paris)*
1972. Italy and France. Les Productions Artistes Associés and PEA. Sound, col., 136 mins. Bernardo Bertolucci.

Marlon Brando cites "If this be the food of love."

Sonnets

1575 *Picnic at Hanging Rock*
1975. Australia. Australian Film Commission, BEF Film Distributors, McElroy & McElroy, Picnic Productions, and South Australian Film Corporation. Sound, col., 115 mins. Peter Weir.

Adapted from the novel by Joan Lindsay. References Sonnet 18.

1576 *Orlando*
1992. U.K., Russia, France, Italy, and the Netherlands. Adventure Pictures, British Screen, Lenfilm Studio, Mikado Film, Rio Film, Sigma Films, and Sony Pictures Classics. Sound, col., 93 mins. Sally Potter.

Adapted from the novel by Virginia Woolf. Orlando recites Sonnet 22, and part of the death scene from *Othello* is seen.

1577 *Maybe Baby*
1999. U.K. BBC and Pandora Cinema. Sound, col., 104 mins. Ben Elton.

Adapted from the novel by Ben Elton. References Sonnets 18 and 116, as well as *A Midsummer Night's Dream* and *Love's Labor's Lost*.

1578 *Sally Hemings: An American Scandal*
2000. CBS Television and Craig Anderson Productions. Sound, col., 87 mins. Charles Haid.

TV movie about Jefferson and Hemings. References Sonnet 57.

Miscellaneous

1579 *The Gay Divorcee*
1934. U.S. RKO Radio Pictures. Sound, b&w, 107 mins. Mark Sandrich.

Adapted from the musical by Dwight Taylor. In this Astaire-Rogers musical, a citation is attributed to Shakespeare.

1580 *Un drama nuevo*
1946. Spain. Juan de Orduña. Sound, b&w, 92 mins. Juan de Orduña.

Adapted from the play by Manuel Tamayo y Baus. Shakespeare personally intervenes in the marital problems of actors.

1581 *Simpatico mascalzone*
1959. Italy. Jonia Film. Sound, b&w, length unknown. Mario Amendola.

A wandering actress performs parts of *Othello*, *Romeo and Juliet*, and *Hamlet*.

1582 *Chi si ferma è perduto*
1960. Italy. Cineproduzione Emo Bistolfi and Titanus. Sound, b&w, 103 mins. Sergio Corbucci.

Features Totò, the renowned Italian comedian. References *Romeo and Juliet*, *Julius Caesar*, and *Hamlet*.

1583 *The Bit Part*
1987. Australia. Comedia Ltd. Sound, col., 87 mins. Nicholas Maher.

A social assistant abandons his work to become a Shakespearean actor.

1584 *Undiscovered*
2005. U.S. Cinejota Filmproduktionsgesellschaft, Cinerenta Feature Films, Intermedia Films, and Lakeshore Entertainment. Sound, col., 97 mins. Meiert Avis.

Ashlee Simpson, playing Clea, a wannabe actress, is shown in acting class declaiming passages from Shakespeare.

1585 *V for Vendetta*
2006. U.S. Warner Brothers. Sound, col., 131 mins. James McTeigue.

The film keeps the *Macbeth* reference (citing from the sergeant's speech in 1.2, "The multiplying villainies of nature / Do swarm upon him . . . Disdaining fortune, with his burnished steel, / Which smoked with bloody execution") from the Alan Moore and David Lloyd *V for Ven-* *detta* comic book on which the film is based. The reference in the film occurs when V/William Rookwood (Hugo Weaving) rescues Evey (Natalie Portman) from undercover government agents who are about to rape her at night after curfew in a dark alley. V acts out a version of the sergeant's description of *Macbeth* near the end of the film just before V dies. The film begins with a backstory prologue about the Gunpowder Plot (not in the comic book). The implicit link between Guy Fawkes and Macbeth recalls Henry Neill Paul's topical reading of Macbeth as a response to the Gunpowder Plot. in *The Royal Play of Macbeth* (1950). In V's home, Macbeth again comes up. V says to Evey: "I do dare that becomes a man. He who dares do more is none." Evey responds: "*Macbeth*. My parents read me all his plays. I became interested in theater and acted the part of Viola in *Twelfth Night*." Near the end of the film, *Twelfth Night* comes up again. V recites Viola's lines to Evey: "Conceal me what I am, and be my aid. / For such disguise as haply shall become / The form of my intent" (1.2). Evey responds: "*Twelfth Night*." Although V and Evey are matched to Shakespeare characters, the plots of *Macbeth* and *Twelfth Night* have little significance in the film, though the conjunction of Shakespeare citations and several pointed references to the Holocaust invite comparison with Julie Taymor's *Titus* (1999). Though linked to Macbeth, V is more closely connected in the film to Alexandre Dumas' fictional Edmund Dantes (the Count of Monte Cristo) and to the historical figure Guy Fawkes, a mask of whom he wears and whose failed attempt to blow up Parliament V successfully restages and carries out at the end of the film. In two scenes, V and Evey watch clips from the 1934 *Count of Monte Cristo* starring Robert Donat. V's Guy Fawkes mask, the Underground (tube, or subway system) setting, and the failed romance between V and Evey also activate a *Phantom of the Opera* reference. V's theme music, heard near the beginning and end of the film, is Tchaikovsky's *War of 1812 Overture*. (RB)

5

Pop Music

INTRODUCTION, "SHAKESPEARE IN POPULAR MUSIC," WES FOLKERTH

The conjunction of Shakespeare and popular music dates back to the original composition of the plays. Shakespeare often incorporated contemporary tunes in his plays, sometimes writing lyrics set to popular melodies, other times having his characters refer to songs and dances then in or out of fashion. Between his time and ours, many musical upstart crows have in turn beautified themselves with Shakespeare's feathers, perhaps nowhere more so than in the popular music of the past century. As the following entries attest, his work has been incorporated by songwriters and composers in myriad ways, often with more sophistication than the genre of popular music might reasonably lead one to expect. The question of how to precisely define the category "popular music" is a vexed one, however. Attempts to classify it typically begin with popular music's antithetical relation to high culture or polite forms such as opera and art song. Such definitions also highlight contemporary popular music's typical modes of dissemination through the technologies of mass media. In the earliest period we are concerned with here, classical composers such as Giuseppe Verdi, Pyotr Ilyich Tchaikovsky, and Jules Massenet used Shakespeare's plays, especially the tragedies with their amplified emotional registers, as the basis for numerous operas and ballets. Such composers availed themselves of Shakespeare's canny ability to identify particularly resonant narratives and recast them in compelling ways for the theater of his time. Other composers, such as Felix Mendelssohn, were also commissioned to write incidental and theme music for specific theatrical productions of the plays. Many of these classical works are still performed and recorded with some frequency as part of the repertoire. Their familiarity and continuing popularity with audiences is why they are represented here.[1]

Taken as a whole, the entries collected here are designed to give the reader a sense of the range of ways in which Shakespeare has been referenced across a broad spectrum of popular musical styles. Popular culture is a remarkably fluid domain, and my goal has been to provide a large selection of representative entries rather than to attempt a complete and comprehensive account of Shakespeare's presence in popular music over the past 150 years.[2] One problem with any such attempt at comprehensiveness is that Shakespeare has become so saturated in our culture that it can at times be difficult to determine the extent to which a given piece of music contains, or is specifically activated by, an allusion to or citation of his work. For instance, The Band wrote and performed a song called "Ophelia" on their 1975 album *Northern Lights–Southern Cross*. The song is about a man who laments the abrupt departure of his lover, whose name is Ophelia, but there is little else in the lyric to indicate that this is an overt reference to Shakespeare's character of the same name. Consider that it was not uncommon for baby girls to be named Ophelia up until the mid-1950s in the United States. Nevertheless, the name Ophelia does conjure up a number of associations, and listeners who are familiar with the play *Hamlet* might well develop their own connections between the song's hapless protagonist and Shakespeare's tragic hero.

Today, songwriters and pop groups quote famous lines from Shakespeare's plays, borrow his characters for their own narratives, express their ideas and emotions through the voices of these characters, adopt the titles of his plays for their own works, and use his plays as the basis for concept albums and rock operas. There is room for further research to be done in this area; there are undoubtedly more such works to discover, and Shakespeare's art will undoubtedly continue to inspire composers of popular music for a long time to come. Finding references to Shakespeare in popular music is not difficult if one is familiar with his works, especially with certain key plays like *Romeo and Juliet*, *Hamlet*, and *Macbeth*, which are among those most often cited. The internet has made it possible to quickly canvass large directories of music at sites such as allmusic.com, which allows one to search for references to Shakespeare's works in the titles of songs and albums. It is also possible to search through the lyrics of thousands of popular songs at any of the lyrics sites that are accessible through most search engines. When consulting such lyrics sites, it is important to corroborate the information they contain with firsthand experience listening to the material, since the information they contain is often donated by well-meaning but potentially misinformed contributors (it seems everyone has their own favorite example of such botched lyrics), and the lyrics sites often perpetuate these errors as they copy lyrics from each other in order to swell their individual collections. With that caveat in mind, such sites can nevertheless be a very helpful first step in searching for Shakespearean references within the lyrics of popular songs. Typical search terms would include the names of characters and plays, and phrases or strings of words from famous speeches. That said, some songs, such as Johnny Preston's "Running Bear," simply borrow a recognizable dramatic situation and little else from Shakespeare.

Identifying Shakespearean references in popular music is one thing; understanding how those references inform the musical work, and how they in turn speak back to the play, is another.[3] In the case of the song "Ophelia" by The Band, the very title sets up a framework of expectations that the song humorously subverts. Shakespeare's Ophelia is of course the victim of a tragic set of circumstances, while the character of the same name in this song actually seems to have the upper hand over her lover, or at least exercises a degree of control over her personal situation in her decision to leave. This inversion in turn affects our sense of the song's protagonist, positioned of course as Hamlet, who seems sincerely naive as he laments her departure and wonders why anybody would "leave so quickly?" and "Was it something that somebody said?," sung over a bouncy, whimsical musical arrangement. The way the song is so clearly driven by the interrogative mood recalls Shakespeare's play, which itself famously opens with a question and features numerous soliloquies in which the title character poses significant questions concerning the nature and value of life. Ophelia's status as a sacrificial victim in Shakespeare's play is cleverly suggested at the end of the song, when the protagonist voices his hope that she will return to him one day. He likens her to a type of Christ: although she's "scared and running," the singer is "still

waiting for the second coming of Ophelia," and pleads that she "Come back home." Presumably this Ophelia will not have to return from the dead, but the singer's strong hope for her return does suggest that she plays something like the role of a savior in his life. While it is apparent that this song by The Band is not overtly about Shakespeare's play, it nevertheless does hint at a comic revisioning of the story of Hamlet and Ophelia. At one point the singer even remarks that "the ghost is clear," which could indicate that, despite her departure, his simple love for Ophelia has afforded him a certain understanding denied Shakespeare's Hamlet, for whom the ghost is never clear.

As the following entries reveal, Ophelia is the Shakespearean character who, after Romeo and Juliet, has seemed to most attract songwriters. She's obviously a fan of popular music, so it could be her penchant for singing snippets of her favorite songs that so endears them to her, but there must be more to it than that. Shakespeare writes her as the kind of character who audiences and readers often develop an intense empathy for. Like Romeo and Juliet, she is a young lover who gets caught up in the trammels of a larger conflict. But unlike them, her story is marginal, and it is our fascination with her story, with its mixture of passion, purity, madness, suffering, and injustice, that songwriters often tap into when they write songs about her.

The song "Ophelia" from the 1998 album *Bath Water Flowers* by the Los Angeles–based group Darling Violetta is one of a number of songs about the character by artists such as Mae Moore and Natalie Merchant that invite the listener to imagine her perspective in different contexts. The opening image of the Darling Violetta song depicts her "lying in a field of flowers," about to be lifted out of her desolation by the music of angels. As the first chorus begins, she is already in the water, which is "quiet and calm" and comforting. As the music builds, a temporary sense of clarity and understanding pervades her thoughts, which turn to Hamlet: if she could hold him, she'd try to convince him "No one can own you." But she appears to be at peace as she drifts towards oblivion: she floats "in opaline illumination," and melts into "the dream machine." Mae Moore's song, from her album *Bohemia* (1992), focuses more on exploring the nature of Ophelia's desire. Her wish to experience "the edge" "Of a perfect dream and perfect love" and her yearning for "all or nothing" reads her back into the play not as a victim of Hamlet or other external events, but as the ultimate source of her own destiny.

The title song from Natalie Merchant's 1998 album *Ophelia* presents the character outside of the immediate context of the play, as an ur-female whose identity subtends a series of female archetypes. The first is a nun (which reminds one of Hamlet's injunction to her in the play itself) portrayed as a "bride of god" in a cloister outside of society. The second is a "rebel girl, a blue stocking suffragette who remedied society between her cigarettes." In subsequent instances she is a movie star sex symbol, a rich socialite, a "mafia courtesan," a human cannonball, and finally, a hurricane. The accretion of all of these different images of Ophelias returns one back to the play with a renewed sense of how a character we think we know well might contain a whole host of identities and hidden depths. The song's overarching argument seems to be that Ophelia is an archetypal female precisely because she has for so long been underestimated.

Popular music is largely an undiscovered country in Shakespeare studies, even though an impressive amount of creative energy has been, and continues to be, brought to bear on his works in this domain. As the previous discussion hopefully indicates, one benefit of the study of popular musical works is that it can inform our understanding of literary characters, both in terms of their reception and their transmission in the greater culture. The field is also wide open for studies that treat the emergence of specific plays at certain periods and in certain genres, such as the relation of *A Midsummer Night's Dream* to the psychedelic rock of the 1960s, or *Macbeth*'s persistent hold on the imaginations of heavy metal musicians. For example, the Colorado heavy metal band Jag Panzer's concept album *Thane to the Throne* was released in 2000, the year after the shootings took place at Columbine. At the time, some blamed the influence of heavy metal music itself for the tragedy. Jag Panzer's choice to record a concept album based on *Macbeth* might be read as a way of insisting that their music is only one element of the cultural landscape that treats violent subjects. It is likely that many thousands

of secondary school students study *Macbeth* across North America every year, and it too is work of art that contains much violent content. In addition to providing a compelling narrative for them to work with, the choice of Shakespeare's play thus helped them to protect and legitimize their own artistic vision. Although references to Shakespeare in popular music are often simple and gratuitous, a great many popular artists, including Natalie Merchant, Elvis Costello, The Smiths, The Tragically Hip, Dire Straits, and the Rave-Ups, have invoked his works in complex and nuanced ways that reward further critical attention.

NOTES

1. The present collection focuses on popular music, especially of the past forty years, where there is a significant gap in the critical documentation. There are a number of resources providing more comprehensive accounts of Shakespeare in the classical music tradition. See, for example, Bryan N. S. Gooch and David Thatcher's five-volume *A Shakespeare Music Catalogue* (Oxford: Oxford University Press, 1991), Phyllis Hartnoll's *Shakespeare in Music* (London: Macmillan, 1964), and Christopher Wilson's *Shakespeare and Music* (New York: Da Capo, 1977).

2. I wish to thank my two research assistants, Simone Cruickshank and Jennifer Shea, for their alacrity and dedication in helping me to prepare the entries for this section. Their respective contributions are indicated by the use of initials in parentheses at the end of each entry.

3. An excellent example of such a critical account is Stephen M. Buhler's "Reviving Juliet, Repackaging Romeo: Transformations of Character in Pop and Post-Pop Music," in *Shakespeare after Mass Media*, ed. Richard Burt (New York: Palgrave, 2002), 243–64.

ENTRIES PLAY BY PLAY, WES FOLKERTH

Entries by contributors other than Wes Folkerth are noted by their initials in parentheses following their entries: Richard Burt (RB), Jennifer Shea (JS), and Simone Cruickshank (SC).

ANTONY AND CLEOPATRA

1586 *Cléopâtre*
Opera. 1912. Jules Massenet, opera in four acts, composed 1911–1912, premiered 1914.

Prolific French composer Jules Massenet published twenty-five operas in his lifetime. *Cléopâtre* would be his last. Massenet composed the opera while in failing health and died only two weeks after its completion. *Cléopâtre* premiered in 1914 in Monte Carlo. In this opera in four acts, Cleopatra, sung as mezzo, is the sensual, exotic, and highly theatrical antiheroine of Shakespeare's *Antony and Cleopatra*; Antony is the Roman triumvir forced to choose

between passion and duty. In *Cléopâtre*, Massenet interprets Cleopatra's feelings for Antony as a sincere love rather than strategic seduction, but this love is realized by Cleopatra only near the opera's end, when the queen sees her death as inevitable. (JS)

1587 *Antony and Cleopatra*
Opera. 1966. Samuel Barber, with original libretto by Franco Zeffirelli, Op. 40.

Antony and Cleopatra, commissioned by the Metropolitan Opera of New York and first performed in 1966, is one of three operas composed by the acclaimed American composer Samuel Barber. The story follows Cleopatra's love affair with Marc Antony, who chooses her over Caesar's sister Octavia and ignites the war that ends with Antony and Cleopatra's respective suicides. Renowned as a melodist rather than a musical experimenter, Barber never aligned himself with any of the many different schools of classical composition that emerged during the twentieth century. Perhaps this is part of the reason *Antony and Cleopatra* became the object of such vituperative critical attack, in which reviewers suggested Barber's "neo-romantic" music was irrelevant to the modern compositional scene. In any case, *Antony and Cleopatra* was a flop, and Barber composed much less after its failure. (SC)

AS YOU LIKE IT

1588 "That's Entertainment"
Song. 1931. Howard Dietz and Arthur Schwartz, composed for the Broadway revue *Bandwagon*.

Howard Dietz and Arthur Schwartz composed several songs together for movies and musicals. One of their most memorable collaborations was the song "That's Entertainment," composed for the 1931 Broadway revue *Bandwagon* and later appearing in the musical's popular film adaptation, *That's Entertainment*. Sung by Oscar Levant, Nanette Fabray, Fred Astaire, and Jack Buchanan in the movie, Dietz and Schwartz's tune is about a world of performance and the world as performance. Borrowing Jaques's famous lines from *As You Like It*, the cast sings in unison, "The world is a stage," which provides "a world of entertainment!" Hamlet also makes an appearance in the song's cast of characters. The singers remark that anything can happen on stage, even "Some great Shakespearean scene" wherein "everyone ends in mincemeat." (JS)

1589 "Under the Greenwood Tree"
Song. 1967. Composed and performed by Donovan Leitch. Lyrics by William Shakespeare, from the album *A Gift from a Flower to a Garden*. Epic.

The lyrics of Scottish folk singer Donovan Leitch's song "Under the Greenwood Tree" are taken from *As You Like It*. In the play, the first two stanzas of the song are sung by followers of the banished duke in the Forest of Arden. Their words express the simple pleasures and happy existence of the forest dwellers, in contrast to the "painted pomp" of the court. According to them, in the forest the only "enemy" is "winter and rough weather." However, the third stanza, a response from the melancholy Jaques, takes a different view of forest life:

And if it do come to pass
That any man turn ass
Leaving his wealth and ease
A stubborn will to please . . .
There shall he see such gross fools as he.

From this view, forest life is not a world of joyful simplicity, but a place where the ease of court life is conspicuously absent—in other words, only fools would choose to live that way. Despite the cynicism of the song's final verse, the gentleness of its first two stanzas, and in particular their emphasis on the joys of music and singing (reveling in "a merry note / Unto the sweet bird's throat"), complement the sweetness of Donovan's voice and musical style. (SC)

1590 "Limelight"
Song. 1981. Rush, from the album *Moving Pictures*. Mercury.

Five years after releasing a live album titled *All the World's a Stage* (Mercury 1976), Canadian trio Rush recorded this song about the dissociative effects of rock stardom. The chorus, which describes "the limelight" as the "dream" of "those who wish to seem," suggests lyricist Neil Peart's disappointment with fame, with the way it affects even the most casual relationships. The song's final verse quotes from the beginning of Jaques's speech on the seven ages of man from *As You Like It*:

All the world's indeed a stage,
And we are merely players,
Performers and portrayers,
Each another's audience outside the gilded cage.

It's an insight Peart finds especially appropriate for his own situation, in which he finds himself expected to "pretend" perfect strangers are "long-awaited" friends.

1591 "ATLiens"
Song. 1996. Outkast, from the album *ATLiens*. La Face.

The most famous products of the "Dirty South" hip-hop scene, Outkast's Big Boi and Andre Benjamin proclaim their love for their Atlanta roots in the song and album title *ATLiens*. Like much of Outkast's music, and that of Southern rappers in general, the song "ATLiens" focuses on the necessity of staying true to oneself and finding one's place in the world without giving up or resorting to drugs and violence. The lyrics proclaim, "Found a way to channel my anger" without "drugs or alcohol so I can get the signal clear." The Shakespearean reference comes in the song's final verse, when the speaker observes, "The world's a stage and everybody's got to play their part." The well-known line from *As You Like It*, which in the play leads into an overview of the ages of man and the many roles he occupies in the course of his life, is modified to fit Outkast's positive moral outlook. With Shakespeare's help, "ATLiens" sends the message that everyone has a particular place in society and can live their lives in a way that celebrates personal freedom and individuality while also helping to create a healthier and more cohesive community. (SC)

THE COMEDY OF ERRORS

1592 *The Boys from Syracuse*
Musical. 1938; 1953. Richard Rodgers (music) and Lorenz Hart (lyrics), originally performed 1938, studio cast album in 1953. Sony.

The Boys from Syracuse, first performed in 1938, was created by the long-lived and influential composing partnership of Rodgers and Hart, and takes its tangled plotline of confused identities from Shakespeare's *The Comedy of Errors*. Aegeon comes to Ephesus from the rival city of Syracuse in search of his long-lost son, who, along with his slave, was separated from his father by a shipwreck. Also helping search is the lost twin's identical brother, Antipholus of Syracuse, who is accompanied by his slave, Dromio. Of course, the missing son also happens to be named Antipholus, and his companion slave is also called Dromio. With this established, the games begin, as the citizens of Ephesus mistake one set of twins for the other, and the two Dromios mix up their masters. The chain of mistaken identities widens to include Adriana, wife of the 'lost' Antipholus of Ephesus, as well as her sister Luciana, who finds herself fighting off an attraction to the man she mistakes for her brother-in-law. The musical, though not particularly successful in current revivals, nevertheless includes such memorable songs as "Falling in Love with Love" and "This Can't Be Love." (SC)

1593 "Miss Misery"
Song. 1997. Elliott Smith, from the album Good Will Hunting: *Music from the Miramax Motion Picture*. Capitol.

"Miss Misery" is a melancholy love song about separation and the need to fight the "bad thoughts in my head" and "keep a good attitude." The song was written and performed by Elliott Smith and is featured on the soundtrack of the 1997 Academy Award–winning film *Good Will Hunting*. The song's lyrics, performed by Smith in his signature gentle, expressive voice with a relatively simple guitar backing, sound like a poetic letter to a faraway lover. Towards the end, the singer observes the "flashing" blue light of a neighbor's TV, and sings, "It's a comedy of errors... It's about taking a fall." The reference is to Shakespeare's *Comedy of Errors*, a play in which filial and romantic love triumph, but only after a series of false starts, mistaken identities, and near misses. In Shakespeare's play, "taking a fall" is necessary to eventual success. The singer of "Miss Misery" seems to hold out hope that after going through pain and doubt, he will emerge with renewed happiness and his relationship intact, like one of Shakespeare's characters. (SC)

1594 *The Bomb-itty of Errors*
Musical. 1999. J.A.Q. (Jeffrey Qaiyum) (music), Jordan Allen-Dutton, Jason Catalano, GQ (Gregory Qaiyum), and Erik Weiner (writing).

The Bomb-itty of Errors is a fast-paced hip-hop makeover of *The Comedy of Errors*. In this all-rap adaptation of the play, two sets of twin brothers, the sons of Egeon and his wife Betty, become separated in youth and find one another again as adults. However, since the musical remains fairly faithful to its source, the boys are not reunited until they and their beleaguered mother have suffered through a series of hilarious misunderstandings and mistaken identities. Moreover, in true Elizabethan fashion, *Bomb-itty*'s cast of four is composed entirely of men who play both the male and female roles. Aside from its physical comedy appeal, the musical's true success comes from its clever adaptation of Shakespearean language and themes to twenty-first-century circumstances. The rhymes from which the entire play is constructed are the artistic offspring of Shakespeare's own verse, while the themes (love, loss, broken families, and discovering one's true identity) are as essential to modern hip-hop music as they were to early modern drama. *Bomb-itty*'s popularity and accessibility demonstrate once again that Shakespeare's linguistic and creative legacy are still inspiring today, and that his works can be enjoyed by people of all ages and of widely divergent tastes. (SC)

CYMBELINE

1595 "Cymbeline"
Song. 1991. Loreena McKennitt, from the album *The Visit*. Warner Bros.

Loreena McKennitt ends her album *The Visit* with her rendition of the song from the fourth act of *Cymbeline* in which Guiderius and Ariviragus pay their respects to the deceased "lad" Fidele, who is really Imogen in disguise (and who is not really dead). The music is anchored by a low synthesizer drone, with McKennitt's harp accompanied by the sound of a sitar. McKennitt lends her reverb-washed Celtic vowels to Shakespeare's words, and rearranges the lyric so that the ending couplets of the second and third stanzas are also brought forward as choruses in between each of the verses. This small change gives the song the exotic effect of a pantoum, a French poetic form in which words and lines hypnotically wash back and forth over the listener.

HAMLET

1596 "To Be or Not to Be"
Song. 1965. The Bee Gees, from the album *The Bee Gees Sing and Play 14 Barry Gibb Songs*. Leedon. Australia.

The Bee Gee's "To Be or Not to Be," released on their very first LP in 1965, is the perfect example of how certain phrases from Shakespeare's plays have become part of the common parlance. "To Be or Not to Be" is about an uncertain romance. The singer laments that his love builds him up and lets him down, and asks "How can I love you?

You give me no ground." The point of the song's title is, of course, to draw a loose parallel between the singer's indecisive lover and Shakespeare's famously conflicted Hamlet, Prince of Denmark, whose best-known soliloquy begins with the words, "To be or not to be, that is the question." However, the Bee Gees's song strips away all aspects of the "To Be or Not to Be" speech having to do with the nature of life and the consequences of our choices; instead, the song situates Hamlet's contemplations in the less complex (though perhaps no less painful) world of pop-song love. The song is evidently a dramatic simplification of the meaning of the soliloquy as a whole, but it does demonstrate how easily Shakespeare's basic human insights can be adapted by different artists to express emotion in such a way that audiences can recognize and identify with what they hear. (SC)

1597 "What a Piece of Work Is Man"
Song. 1968. From the musical *Hair*, lyrics by James Rado and Gerome Ragni, music by Galt MacDermot, original cast recording. RCA.

The musical *Hair*, subtitled *The American Love/Rock Musical*, centers on a group of hippies whose values of peace and free love run counter to the traditional "American way." In particular, members of "the Tribe" react against the horror of the Vietnam War and try to resist the drafting of one of their own. To express their combined belief in the human spirit with their

In the early 1974 live shows David Bowie played the role of the "Cracked Actor," parodying a Hollywood Pierrot Hamlet. © 2006 Bob Gruen/Star File.

modern sense of disillusionment, the "Tribe" calls upon *Hamlet* 2.2, and the famous phrase, "What a piece of work is man." As in Shakespeare's play, the Tribe's words are both hopeful and ironic. Lines about man's "noble reason" and "infinite faculties" capture the elements of humanity they prize and wish to defend. However, the description of the earth as a "sterile promontory" in which the singers have "lost all mirth" reveals their disenchantment with the world in a time of warfare and bloodshed. The best aspects of mankind are also the most ironic in the modern era, when mankind turns its extraordinary energy and power to destructive uses. Hamlet's musings on the complexities of human experience retain their force in the context of the

1960s culture clashes and confrontation between the value of peace and the government's political commitments. (SC)

1598 "Cracked Actor"
Song. 1973. David Bowie, on tour for the album *Aladdin Sane*. Virgin.

In live performances of the song "Cracked Actor," which first appeared on the album *Aladdin Sane*, David Bowie often sings while holding a skull, in imitation of one of the most iconic images in all of Shakespeare: Hamlet at the grave site in the beginning of Act 5. While the title of this glam-rock song evokes Shakespeare's "antic" prince, the lyrics instead depict a debauched, aging film star in Los Angeles. Bowie also performed the song with this prop during his *Serious Moonlight* tour of 1983–84.

1599 "Ophelia"
Song. 1975. The Band, from the album *Northern Lights–Southern Cross*. Capitol.

The Ontario-based group The Band first released the song "Ophelia" in 1975 on *Northern Lights–Southern Cross*, an album that, despite its critical acclaim, peaked only at twenty-six on the Billboard charts. In "Ophelia," the heroine of the song, the girl next door, has disappeared without a trace and "Nobody knows just what became of Ophelia." By the song's end, the speaker is still waiting patiently for "the second comin' / of Ophelia." In 2000 the song was re-released on The Band's *Greatest Hits* album, and in 2004 the tune was covered in a bluegrass version by the Gibson Brothers for their album *Long Way Back Home* (Sugar Hill 2004). (JS)

1600 *Rockabye Hamlet*
Musical. 1976. Written and composed by Cliff Jones, original cast recording. Rising. U.K.

Rockabye Hamlet, a 1976 Broadway rock musical adaptation of Shakespeare's most famous play, closed after only seven performances. The show was created by Cliff Jones, who adapted it from an earlier production commissioned by the Canadian Broadcasting Corporation for radio. The stage version was directed and choreographed by the distinguished Gower Champion. However, even the pedigree of those involved with the musical could not make it a success. Although *Rockabye Hamlet* has been revamped and revived in various versions over the years, it remains something of a joke within the theatrical community. The show was plagued with poor music, ludicrous action (for example, Ophelia strangling herself with a microphone cord), and above all an incoherence that rendered the complexities of Shakespeare's play all but unintelligible. While other attempts to translate Shakespeare's stories to modern times have been successful, *Rockabye Hamlet* failed to transition its plot and characters in such a way that they would remain accessible and engaging to viewers. (SC)

1601 "There Only Was One Choice"
Song. 1977. Harry Chapin, from the album *Dance Band on the Titanic*. Electra.

Musical history's ghosts haunt this song in which the narrator, a stand-in for Chapin, sees himself and a past generation of "folkies" in an aspiring young musician. Something is foul in the music world today, but Chapin's narrator hopes this boy, who has Guthrie and Dylan "in his bones" will play songs that will "heal the cracks that split apart / America gone plastic." The narrator instructs the boy to listen to the "rustling in the shadows" and the "whispers" of music's past. He will give the same advice to his young son who will also play the guitar one day. For his son, as for the other musical youth he addresses, "the only [real] choice" is to obey the voices of Chapin, the "minstrel Hamlet daddy," and other folk specters who have been wrongly deposed by rock 'n' roll glitter. This plea for the youth to maintain folk music's integrity crystallizes in the song's refrain: "write about your feelings—not the things you never did." (JS)

1602 "Cruel to Be Kind"
Song. 1979. Nick Lowe, on the LP album *Labour of Lust*. Columbia.

In this hit song cowritten with ex-Brinsley Schwartz bandmate Ian Gomm, Nick Lowe explores the confusion experienced by a male lover whose partner chooses to treat him badly. In the chorus, the woman says her behavior is all part of her plan: "You've gotta be cruel to be kind in the right measure." The song's chorus and title allude to Hamlet's speech to his mother in Act 3 Scene 4 in which he explains to her "I must be cruel only to be kind."

1603 "Althea"
Song. 1980. The Grateful Dead, from the album *Go to Heaven*. Arista.

"You may meet the fate of Ophelia, sleeping and perchance to dream," warns the singer of The Grateful Dead's "Althea." According to the song's lyrics, Ophelia, and those like her, are recklessly "honest" and "self-centered." "Althea" is a song about the place of truth and honesty in personal relationships, sung in the straightforward folk- and country-tinged rock that characterizes the Dead's music. In this context, the reference to Ophelia is mostly an allusion to her complicated and ultimately tragic relationship with the brooding Hamlet, Prince of Denmark. The poor communication that plagues Hamlet and Ophelia's relationship, combined with the prince's various preoccupations and both characters' respective angst, is the classic example of a love relationship gone seriously wrong. Perhaps Shakespeare's Ophelia truly is "honest to the point of recklessness" and "self-centered" in her desires—along with being by turns loving, bewildered, innocent, angry, defensive, and devastated. Her fate and the circumstances surrounding her demise make her an appropriate vehicle for the song's message about the necessity of finding "a little sympathy" and not "forgetting the love we bring." (SC)

1604 "Ophelia"
Song. 1981. Peter Hammill, from the album *Sitting Targets*. Virgin. U.K.

Peter Hammill's "Ophelia" centers on the image of the drowning Ophelia as a representation of the nature of human existence and experience. Describing someone in a contemplative position in front of the fire, the singer remarks, "All change—down the river Ophelia goes." The second-person narration of the song puts the listener in Ophelia's place: "You're treading water," "you'll cope with it all." The figure of Ophelia, who cannot overcome the reality of her circumstances or the weight of her emotions, becomes inseparably linked to the slowly sinking "you" of the song; Ophelia's tragic end is shared by the person who made "promises you can't keep," and who cannot adapt to the changes in her environment or in her own feelings. (SC)

1605 "Hamlet (Pow Pow Pow)"
Song. 1982. The Birthday Party, from the album *Junkyard*. 4AD Records. U.K.

Nick Cave and The Birthday Party were part of a post-punk generation that blended punk music, garage band rock, jazz, blues, and a host of other influences to create their own sound. The Birthday Party in particular is characterized by the all-out force and energy of its music, and "Hamlet (Pow Pow Pow)" is no exception. The song is built on a driving beat and bass line, over which Nick Cave growls the lyrics with a demonic fury. The Birthday Party's Hamlet is less a metaphysical thinker and more a gun-toting criminal, although the song's reference to "the grave" and the line "I think our man's in love" refer respectively to one of the play's most famous scenes and one of Hamlet's multitude of personal problems. The song's Cadillac-stealing subject even quotes the famous line "wherefore art thou" from *Romeo and Juliet*, albeit with a certain amount of irony as the sweetness of the lover's query is distorted by the singer's shrieks and growls and by Hamlet's apparently murderous intentions. The song's violence and gruesome imagery are not entirely disconnected from Shakespeare's play; after all, aside from its more spiritual concerns, *Hamlet* is also a story of murder, incest, and suicide. The Birthday Party's Hamlet seems to be drawn directly from this darker side of Shakespeare, his metaphysical musings, if any, inseparable from the "Pow Pow Pow" of his gun. (SC)

1606 "Ophelia"
Song. 1987. The Tear Garden, from the album *Tired Eyes, Slowly Burning*. Nettwerk/Capitol/EMI.

The Tear Garden's "Ophelia," like many other songs that refer to this tragic character, relies upon listeners' commonly held associations to give a song about the uncertainties of life and love additional power. Some of the song's lyrics have a nightmarish quality: the singer is "Crawling through the minefield," or trying "to hide" and "melt away." The attempt to disappear is impeded by "a hint of searchlight" cast on "a pair of lonely souls locked together." The madness of the singer's world and his repeated question, "Is it just a dream, Ophelia?" play on Ophelia's insanity in *Hamlet*, while the seemingly unavoidable threats the singer describes reflect the theatrical Ophelia's inability to escape the courtly world of treachery and deceit. The song also draws inspiration from the tragedy of Ophelia's relationship with Hamlet wherein love "cracks its stick across our fingers" and "makes us sick." Knowing the name "Ophelia" is already associated with the darker sides of the human mind, The Tear Garden deploys the literary reference to emphasize the terrors and uncertainty of the world (both internal and external), as the singer wonders, "Do you think we can make it ... Our dream, Ophelia." (SC)

1607 "Aftermath of Betrayal (The Tragedy of Hamlet)"
Song. 1988. Hades, from the album *If at First You Don't Succeed*. Torrid.

Heavy metal band Hades bases its song "Aftermath of Betrayal (The Tragedy of Hamlet)" on the story and structure of Shakespeare's *Hamlet*. Like the play, the song opens with Act 1 in the "bitter cold at Elsinor"; shortly thereafter, the dead king makes his appearance and orders his son to avenge his death, and remember him, "Hamlet my son, kill the king!" In the second verse of the song (Acts 2 and 3) Hamlet becomes "seized with madness," kills "the fool chamberlain," and ends up banished to England. The final verse covers Act 4, including Ophelia's death and Hamlet's return. The song, however, ends with the notice "to be continued" and never addresses Act 5. "Aftermath of

Betrayal" does not perform any complex analysis of Hamlet, but clearly recognizes the dramatic power of Shakespeare's story. The dark and macabre aspects of the play make it a good, if strangely elite, subject for thrash metal, and Hades takes advantage of its possibilities. (SC)

1608 "Hamlet Meets John Doe"
Song. 1990. The Rave-Ups, from the album *Chance*. Epic.

The Rave-Ups emerged from the Los Angeles music scene in the 1980s, playing roots or rocking country music about a decade before the sound became crassly commercialized as "the new country" and inundated the country music airwaves. This song by Jimmer Podrasky and Terry Wilson describes an "everyman" Hamlet, a regular, introspective guy with lots of big metaphysical questions, such as "how some ... have faith," and "how some ... get along." In the chorus he attributes his sense of malaise to his critical capacity, confessing that he's "been thinking, too long, too long." Later in the song he laments the emptiness of his words, much as Hamlet complains of the way he unpacks his own heart: "I've got nothing to say and twelve ways to say it." The song's title describes its protagonist as a conflation, as a "Hamlet meets John Doe" sort of guy.

1609 "The Woman Who Had an Affair with Herself"
Song. 1991. Toyah, from the album *Ophelia's Shadow*. EG. U.K.

British pop singer Toyah takes a girl-power stance in the song "The Woman Who Had an Affair with Herself," from her album *Ophelia's Shadow*. It is not surprising, given the album's title, that some of its songs explore the effects of Ophelia's story on popular and creative conceptions of femininity. What is somewhat out of the ordinary is the singer's attitude in "The Woman Who Had an Affair with Herself." With this song, Toyah casts off some of the doom and gloom that usually goes hand-in-hand with songs about Ophelia. Instead, she prefers to imagine a world where a woman was able to discover "the glory in the liking of herself" when "her man's attentions were somewhere else," rather than falling entirely to pieces. The song trumpets the possibility of independence and self-esteem for women, counteracting the idea that a woman's goal in life is to win a man's "wandering attentions." In effect, it posits a different outcome for the Ophelia story; the song quotes Hamlet's devastating "get thee to a nunnery" speech at length and then formulates a rebuttal by suggesting that a scorned woman become "her own secret admirer." The self-reliance and boundless freedom that result, says the singer, are as exhilarating as "being thrown into the Hawaiian surf." (SC)

1610 "Ophelia"
Song. 1992. Mae Moore, from the album *Bohemia*. Epic/Sony.

Ophelia is mentioned only in the title of this song by Mae Moore, but the song explores a side of her character. The music, with its synthesizer pads and fretless bass, creates a floating sensation, while the lyrics speak in erotic terms of "hunger," of being "enamoured with the taste" and the need to "live along the edge." Ophelia's desire is explored here less as an erotic attachment to Hamlet than as an attraction to death, or to the similar sense of oblivion provided by narcotics. The strength of that desire is figured in the song's chorus, wherein the singer seeks something "Beyond the pale," past "the veil," "on to something in the quiet..." The song was cowritten with the album's producer Steve Kilby, of the Australian group The Church.

1611 "Ophelia"
Song. 1993. Celestial Season, from the album *Forever Scarlet Passion*. Adipocere. France.

Hailing from the Netherlands, the now-defunct Celestial Season was a so-called doom metal band. *Forever Scarlet Passion* was the group's first album, and the uncompromisingly miserable lyrics of many of its songs, including "Ophelia," reflect the band's chosen genre. "Ophelia" is a relatively short and lyrically simple song: Ophelia's "bleak" "tragedy" is "The curse of a broken heart." The song's most obvious reference is to *Hamlet*, from which it draws both the character of Ophelia and the "cruel misery" of drowning "of a broken heart." However, the song's second line is drawn from Shakespeare's "Sonnet 18": "Shall I compare thee to a summer's day?" which refers to "the darling buds of May." The life- and memory-affirming aspects of "Sonnet 18," which seem at odds with the gloom of "Ophelia," actually make Celestial Season's song even sadder; the passing allusion to the poem suggests that not even the commemorative power of music and lyrics can save Ophelia from the "cruel misery" of fate. (SC)

1612 "Hamlet Rap"
Song. 1994. Composed by Mark Wahlberg and Marvyn Warren, from the movie *Renaissance Man*. Directed by Penny Marshall.

In the 1994 film *Renaissance Man*, an unemployed adman played by Danny DeVito gets a job teaching core academic subjects to underachieving army recruits. Shakespeare soon becomes the main focus of the class, and the students, inspired by both the Bard and their instructor, put together a rap musical based on *Hamlet*. Mark Wahlberg is among the recruits (cum the Double D MCs) who recontextualize the play's story in contemporary popular culture, translating it into rather outdated street slang: "The shit's iller than Cape Fear,... Started with this Prince kid, his moms and his father." The MCs continue with a summary of *Hamlet*'s major action, while also alluding to some of play's more nuanced issues, including the text's undercurrents of incest and questions of Hamlet's culpability in Ophelia's death. (JS)

1613 "Touch Me Fall"
Song. 1994. Indigo Girls, from the album *Swamp Ophelia*. Epic.

Known for their honeyed harmonies and distinctive vocal styles, the platinum-selling Indigo Girls were probably the best-known female folk rock duo of the 1990s. In 1994 they released their fifth studio album, *Swamp Ophelia*. "Touch Me Fall," the sixth track on the album, is a poignant, dreamlike ballad with harmonizing vocals, and slide guitars accompanied by plaintive violins. With her signature gravelly vocals, Amy Ray awakens from (or into) a dream, where she sees herself on what is presumably the edge of oblivion. In this dream she seeks, like her muse, the ghost of Ophelia, Hamlet's beloved, to drown after her descent into madness. But like a dream, the tempo and the tone of the track change abruptly. Suddenly, the song speeds up and becomes playful and eager. Ray beckons, "Jump, jump, jump so high," and the song's pace escalates until it slows again only to "Jump" once more with a rush of guitar and percussion at the track's end. (JS)

1614 "Dig Ophelia"
Song. 1996. Rasputina, from the album *Thanks for the Ether*. Sony.

The lyrics of Rasputina's "Dig Ophelia," a selection from their debut album, draw heavily from Queen Gertrude's description of Ophelia's death in *Hamlet*. Gertrude describes the mad and distraught Ophelia as being covered in flowers ("weedy trophies") as she flounders in, and eventually sinks beneath, the water. "Dig Ophelia" plays on this flower imagery, with lines such as, "Water kills the tall weed," the "weed" in question perhaps being the drowning girl herself. "Flowers" and "madness" are equally central to Ophelia's death-by-water, and the song's lyrics reflect the latter element when the singer observes, Ophelia's "eyes never close," her "mind's not at rest." The song also contemplates the terrible sadness of Ophelia's position and the mysterious circumstances of her death—after all, the deadly water is "just ankle deep high." Rasputina's Victorian-gothic style and selection of the cello as their instrument of choice lend this song the same haunting quality that characterizes most of *Thanks for the Ether*. Their brand of music is particularly appropriate for exploring the topics of flowers, madness, and the end of innocence, all of which are central to Ophelia's story. (SC)

1615 "Ophelia"
Song. 1996. Moist, from the album *Creature*. EMI Canada.

In 1996 Vancouver alternative rock band Moist released the album *Creature*. On its track "Ophelia," Moist sets the scene with the image of Ophelia's flowers. While Shakespeare's mad Ophelia distributes rosemary, pansies, daisies, and the like, and her grave will later be covered in flowers, Moist's Ophelia is herself figured as a delicate flower; she is, in the song, a "daisy dusted lightly." The speaker here identifies with Hamlet, though he assumes more personal responsibility for his hand in Ophelia's death than does the prince: though he never intended "to be so cold," he says, "I'm letting Ophelia die." (JS)

1616 "Cry Ophelia"
Song. 1998. Adam Cohen, from the album *Adam Cohen*. Columbia.

As with many songs that invoke Shakespeare's characters, Adam Cohen's "Cry Ophelia" refers to the character more as it has developed into a type, less as the specific fictional agent from *Hamlet*. Cohen sings the song to a woman named Ophelia who is going through a difficult time. The singer counsels her to simply cry rather than "learn how to live your life without tears," which people have tried to do "for thousands of years." The song is not particularly impressive, but it gained popularity when it was featured in an episode of a popular television show called *Dawson's Creek* and included on a soundtrack of popular songs from the show released by Sony in 1999.

1617 "Ophelia"
Song. 1998. Darling Violetta, from the album *Bath Water Flowers*. Opaline Records.

From the first moments of the soothing, almost too calm guitar strumming on Darling Violetta's "Ophelia," the song sounds like the quasi-hallucinatory musings of a woman beyond the edge of reason. The singer is relaxing "in a field of flowers," listening while "angels gently sing." While the image is a peaceful one, the singer soon asserts that she is "in a cloud of desperation." Again and again she sings of the "quiet and calm" water, going so far as to admit that it makes her feel "I am home." Cami Ellen's dreamy vocals enhance the tension between the singer's peaceful attitude of acceptance and her ongoing inner turmoil. At the same time, the song's hypnotic rhythm complements its repeated lyrics to emphasize the disparity between true "calm" and the menacing calm of the water that engulfs the singer. Like Shakespeare's Ophelia, the singer is both spirited and resigned, possibly ready to sink beneath the water but not unaware of the horrors that have brought her so low. Her competing impulses—to "sink or swim," as it were—also reflect the aura of mystery surrounding Ophelia's demise: is her death an accident or suicide? In any case, the references to flowers in the song's lyrics, in the album's title, and arguably even in the band's name, recall the macabre description of Ophelia as covered in "fantastic garlands" as she goes to her death. (SC)

1618 "Ophelia"
Song. 1998. Natalie Merchant, from the album *Ophelia*. Elektra.

Singer-songwriter Natalie Merchant explores the possibilities of Shakespeare's character as a tragic female archetype in this song from her solo album of the same name. The lyrics are structured so as to present various imagined avatars of Ophelia's character, many of them archetypes in their own right. Pointedly, with respect to Shakespeare's play, the first Ophelia is a "bride of god," and a "novice carmelite," which recalls Hamlet's injunction that she get herself "to a nunnery." A second Ophelia as a suffragette follows, then as a mass media sex symbol, "a demigoddess in pre-war Babylon," a mistress to a Las Vegas gambler, a mafia gun moll, a female cannonball in the circus, and finally a tropical storm. The trajectory moves from characters who are defined from within patriarchal institutions and situations, to ones who emblematize a violent energy and capacity for self-definition outside of such contexts. Merchant portrayed the song's various characters in a short film intended as a companion piece to the compact disc.

1619 "Ophelia"
Song. 1999. On Thorns I Lay, from the album *Crystal Tears*. Holy. Records. France.

"Ophelia," a song by heavy metal band On Thorns I Lay, demonstrates how Shakespearean references have become an indispensable element of modern culture. To begin with, the lyrics of "Ophelia" do not actually have much to do with Shakespeare's character or the tragedy in which she plays a part. Lyrics such as "We are hunting each other into the fragrant valley of sensations and illusions," suggest that "Ophelia" is a love song. However, they do not relate to *Hamlet* or to Ophelia's experiences in particular, although the song's dreamy imagery is resonant of what might wander through the mind of someone who, like Ophelia, is experiencing the mingled effects of love and madness. In any case, the relationship between Ophelia the character and "Ophelia" the song remains unclear; here, only the character's name and its various resonances are important, used to conjure up an aura of mystery and overlay the song's love lyrics with a sense of melancholy. The name "Ophelia" alone calls up a series of associations that provide On Thorns I Lay's music with a rich, ready-made cultural background. (SC)

1620 "Flowers for Ophelia"
Song. 2000. J. Englishman, from the album *Poor Li'l Rock Star*. Warner Music Canada.

Canadian singer-songwriter J. Englishman gained the respect of fans and critics alike with the release of his first solo album, *Poor Li'l Rock Star*. On the track "Flowers for Ophelia," the speaker doesn't need rosemary for remembrance; the Ophelia of this song is, for him, a mnemonic of past pain, a "fragrance" that brings "A memory of doubt." The speaker of the song vacillates between self-blame and loathing towards a woman he sees as the source of his pain. Just as Ophelia's flowers in *Hamlet* are associated with her madness and death, they are symbols of devastation in this song. As a bearer of flowers, the speaker will seal Ophelia's fate as scripted in Shakespeare, and he will request Ophelia's complicity in her destruction: he'll "hold the nails," if she'll "swing the hammer." (JS)

1621 "Ophelia's Fall"

Song. 2004. Fletcher Van Vliet, from the album *Silent Autumn*. Composed by Fletcher Van Vliet and Sara Scutt. Ragdoll Recordings.

Ophelia's fall is not her demise in this song, but rather a season of change and temporary loss for the speaker, who will leave his beloved for a brief period of time. He will miss the "kiss on my doorstep," and the "whispers in the trees or in your hair." It is the speaker himself, the song's Hamlet figure, who suffers most in this season of loss, becoming vulnerable in his Ophelia's absence: "I have no one to protect me, and I have nothing else keeping me here." As the song concludes, nostalgia continues to haunt the speaker, who remembers his Ophelia's "voice," her "eyes," and a "dull breeze" he associates with her. (JS)

HENRY IV

1622 *Falstaff*

Opera. 1893. Giuseppe Verdi, libretto by Arrigo Boito.

For his third operatic foray into the world of Shakespearean drama, Verdi focused his energies on Sir John Falstaff, one of Shakespeare's most infamous and intriguing characters. Verdi's Falstaff, like Shakespeare's, is anything but simple: he manages to be commanding and absurd, noble and vulgar, lewd and clever, obscene and intelligent, at different times and in varying degrees. Most of the three-act opera's plot comes from *The Merry Wives of Windsor*, with elements taken from the *Henry IV* plays. What makes *Falstaff* interesting from a Shakespearean standpoint is Verdi and Boito's decision to focus on a secondary character (albeit a brilliant scene-stealer) as the center of the action. *Otello* and *Macbeth* replicate their dramatic sources in their concentration on the plays' titular heroes; these operas translate great tragedies into suitably grand and powerful music, meant to stir audiences to the same degree as their theatrical forebears. However, with the comedic drama *Falstaff*, Verdi was able to apply a lighter touch (as he had wished to do for years, since before the composition of *Otello*). In writing *Falstaff*, Verdi and Boito's goal was to represent the combination of grandeur and utter ridiculousness that characterizes Sir John. In this, his final operatic work, Verdi was able to blend happy and bittersweet elements that reflect the realities of life, the genius of Shakespeare, and the traditions of Italian opera. (SC)

1623 *Falstaff*

Symphonic Poem. 1913. Edward Elgar, *Symphonic Study for Orchestra in C Minor, Op. 68*, first performed at the Leeds Festival on October 1, 1913.

Known today as one of the finest English composers of his age, Sir Edward William Elgar (1857–1934) received little recognition during his lifetime. He is perhaps best known for his *Pomp and Circumstance Marches* (1901–1907), the first of which became a kind of unofficial anthem in Britain and the musical cornerstone of university commencement ceremonies in North America. In 1913 he composed the musical poem *Falstaff, Symphonic study for orchestra in C minor, Op 68*. Elgar's musical tribute to the fat knight, a work considered one of his best achievements, is a musically and thematically integrated score in which the cast of Shakespeare's Henriad comes to life. Especially prominent in this work, of course, is the character of Sir John Falstaff himself, emerging more like the Henriad's witty gentleman knight than the cuckolded clown of *The Merry Wives of Windsor*. Elgar's work consists of two parts, "Interlude I: Jack Falstaff, Page to the Duke of Norfolk" and "Interlude II: Gloucestershire, Shallow's Orchard." (JS)

1624 "Fiddler's Green"

Song. 1991. The Tragically Hip, from the album *Road Apples*. MCA. Canada.

A Falstaffian current courses through this song by Ontario-based roots rockers The Tragically Hip. But those expecting a song animated by the jovial and vital life force of everyone's favorite fat knight may be disappointed. "Fiddler's Green" is a melancholy ballad about losing someone dear to us, and the Falstaff evoked in this song seems more like that old man who, after banishment and heartbreak, has passed on to the other side. In Irish and English legends and sea shanties, Fiddler's Green was a near-heaven for sailors and other well-intentioned, but often less-than-perfect, characters. It was a place of music and merriment where the liquor was always free-flowing (a place Falstaff would have loved, no doubt). In the song "Fiddler's Green," the Hip tell a tale of a girl whose "son has gone alee." The boy is not alone in Fiddler's Green, however. Falstaff is, presumably, also there, singing a "sorrowful refrain / For a boy on Fiddler's Green." (JS)

1625 "Falstaff"

Song. 2004. Clinic, from the CD *Winchester Cathedral*. Domino. U.K.

The playful yet poignant "Falstaff" is a fan favorite on the band's third album, *Winchester Cathedral*. On this album, the notoriously theatrical Liverpool quartet Clinic returns with its signature slow, art-punk lounge sound and a new Shakespearean flavor. Most of front man Ade Blackburn's lyrics are, as usual, indiscernible on this track, which sacrifices clarity of speech to overall mood. One thing remains clear, though: Falstaff's all-world character and his mischievousness is mourned on this track, which alternates between playful percussion and clarinet and loungelike, lamenting vocal harmonies. In "Falstaff," this sense of loss is heightened by the song's refrain: "Falstaff... You're still needed." (JS)

HENRY VI, PART 2

1626 "Get Over It"
Song. 1994. The Eagles, from the album *Hell Freezes Over*. Geffen.

The opening studio track from the Eagles' mostly live album from 1994, the song "Get Over It" was one of the last new songs the group recorded. One of Don Henley's social commentary songs, it pokes fun at the 1990s' culture of confession and its attendant discourses of victimization. In the second verse he quotes Shakespeare's Dick the Butcher, and the most famous line from the *Henry VI* plays: "old Billy was right, / Let's kill all the lawyers—kill 'em tonight."

HENRY VI, PART 3

1627 "Over the Rise"
Song. 1994. Big Audio Dynamite, from the album *Higher Power*. Columbia.

On the eclectic track "Over the Rise," Big Audio Dynamite mixes natural and electronic samplings, tribal chanting and Shakespeare. The tune begins with a pastoral flavor, but the initial sound of birdsong is rhythmically interrupted by the muffled sound of gunfire. Against this backdrop, a British Shakespearean actor recites lines spoken by Henry VI as he meditates on the battlefield:

This battle fares like the morning's war,
When dying clouds contend with growing light,
What time the shepherd, blowing off his nails,
can neither call it perfect day nor night. (*Henry VI, Part 3*, 2.5) (JS)

KING JOHN

1628 "You've Got Everything Now"
Song. 1984. The Smiths, from the album *The Smiths*. Sire. U.K.

The first line of this song from the Smiths' debut record is "As merry as the days were long," a phrase Shakespeare invented and apparently liked enough that he used it twice in his plays. The first reference is in *King John*, when Arthur notes that Hubert looks "sad" (serious), and remembers that when he was in France,

Young gentlemen would be sad as night,
Only for wantonness. By my christendom,
So I were out of prison and kept sheep,
I should be as merry as the day is long (4.1.15–18)

In the song, Morrissey's words are addressed to a lover from his school days, and they convey his characteristically arch sense of self-loathing. While noting that his lover has "everything now," he sings, "And what a terrible mess I've made of my life." The song's first lines refer to the state of their relationship in their school days. As in the scene from *King John*, bondage is also involved: the singer professes that he doesn't "want to be a lover," he just wants "to be tied to the back of your car." The second time Shakespeare employs the phrase is in *Much Ado about Nothing*, when Beatrice talks to Leonato about her lack of a husband and surmises that when she visits Saint Peter, "he shows me where the bachelors sit, and there live we as merry as the day is long" (2.1.48–49).

JULIUS CAESAR

1629 "Cleopatra's Cat"
Song. 1994. The Spin Doctors, from the album *Turn It Upside Down*. Epic.

"Cleopatra's Cat" was the first single from the Spin Doctors' ill-fated second album. The jazzy lyrics paint a nonsensical scenario in which Cleopatra's cat steals Caesar's shoes and turns them over to Marc Antony. The song contains snippets from Shakespeare's *Julius Caesar*, including the latin "'Jesu Christe Domine, / Et tu, Brute.'" Two further allusions occur in the final verse, when Brutus says "Friends, Romans, can't you see," Cleopatra's "cat is smarter than me" (perhaps suggesting the Marc Antony of *Antony and Cleopatra*), and noting that "they killed [Caesar's] ass in the second act."

1630 "Idiot Box"
Song. 1997. The Aquabats, from the album *The Fury of the Aquabats*. Time Bomb.

"Idiot Box," by ska band The Aquabats, is a meditation on obsessive television watching. In a mock-pensive frame of mind, the singer wonders if he's "going blind, Just like Mr. Magoo." The song's central message comes in the chorus, which compares "the idiot box," to "a disease just like the chicken pox." The lyrics then reiterate this message, with an additional appeal to Shakespearean authority by introducing it with "Friends, Romans, countrymen." The "Friends, Romans, countrymen" line comes from *Julius Caesar*, a literary masterwork that in some ways represents the antithesis of the "idiot box" culture that is the song's subject. Shakespeare, literature, and learning are the alternative to TV, and understanding these elements of modern culture, the song maintains, is more satisfying than knowing the ending "Of every *Scooby Doo*." (SC)

1631 "Silly of You"
Song. 1997. Salt-N-Pepa, from the album *Brand New*. London. U.K.

"[L]end me your ears countrymen ... From coast to coast, we rock the past to the future." In "Silly of You," female rappers Salt-N-Pepa rock the literary past to the future, quoting Marc Antony from Shakespeare's *Julius Caesar* (3.2). Since Marc Antony's speech ("Friends, Romans, countrymen, lend me your ears") sways the masses at Julius Caesar's funeral, Salt-N-Pepa tests the phrase's appeal in this song about fame, fortune, and rising to the top. (JS)

1632 "Black Ice"
Song. 1998. Goodie Mob, from the album *Still Standing*. La Face.

Goodie Mob emerged from the "Dirty South" rap scene closely allied with the phenomenally successful duo Outkast. Distinguished by a unique aesthetic and a dedication to battling the "gangsta rap" ethic that glorifies guns and violence, Goodie Mob (an acronym for "the Good Die Mostly Over Bullshit") garnered fans with their sincerity and musical innovation, until the band dissolved in the early 2000s. "Black Ice," which features Outkast's Big Boi and Andre Benjamin as guest performers, maintains the group's commitment to promoting an upbeat and constructive notion of African American community. The song reviles the drugs and violence that characterize much modern rap music (calling cocaine "a stain"), and Big Boi says he's "strictly 'bout these verses like ... you hear at church, boy." In the final verse of the song, Andre references a famous line from *Julius Caesar*, saying, "Friends, Romans, countrymen, lend me your eardrums." The powerful address, which calls on all listeners to stop and pay close attention to what is sure to be an important message, works as well in a rap song as it does in the mouth of Shakespeare's strong and charismatic Marc Antony. In both cases, the speaker calls on the members of his community to recognize the complexity of their social reality and pleads with his listeners to act with honesty and moral fortitude, for the good of all. (SC)

KING LEAR

1633 "I Am the Walrus"
Song. 1967. The Beatles, from the album *Magical Mystery Tour*. Capitol.

"I Am the Walrus" contains the only Shakespearean reference in The Beatles' entire recorded repertoire, and its appearance is simply the result of coincidence: Shakespeare was literally in the air at the time. When putting together the sound collage for the song's ending they turned on the radio to capture and incorporate some found elements for the collage and discovered that a radio version of *King Lear* was being broadcast. Beginning at about 3:56 in the song, it is possible to hear the following lines from Oswald's death (4.6.246–55):

[Oswald] Villain, take my purse:
If ever thou wilt thrive, bury my body
And give the letters which thou find'st about me
To Edmund, Earl of Gloucester; seek him out
Upon the English party. O, untimely death!
Death!
[Edgar] I know thee well: a serviceable villain,
As duteous to the vices of thy mistress
As badness would desire.
[Gloucester] What, is he dead?
[Edgar] Sit you down, father; rest you.

The Beatles never mention Shakespeare or his works in any of their lyrics. While it may be tempting to include the line from "Paperback Writer" where the speaker notes that the work he pitches is "based on a novel by a man named Lear," the allusion is to the nonsense poet Edward Lear, one of John Lennon's favorite authors.

1634 "Cordelia"
Song. 1991. The Tragically Hip, from the album *Road Apples*. MCA. Canada.

Tragically Hip singer-songwriter Gordon Downie renders Shakespeare's Cordelia as the archetypal casualty of fate. The song's protagonist, a poet who is "marrying words," decides to tempt a similar destiny in various ways, from robbing banks to jumping off of trains, being dragged behind cars, and even shouting out the name of the Scottish play onstage—which, coincidentally, occurs every time Downie sings the song in front of an audience: "Treading the boards, screaming out 'Macbeth'," to test fate and "see how much bad luck you" can create. Such acts of provocation seem designed to challenge fate, in order, he tells himself, "to see how alive" he really is. In the chorus, this idea takes the form of a specific refusal to identify with Lear's daughter, with the kind of victimization, and perhaps even the blind filial servitude, that she represents to him: "I'm not Cordelia," Downie sings.

1635 "King Leer"
Song. 1991. Written and performed by Morrissey, from the album *Kill Uncle*. EMI and Sire/Reprise. U.K.

Morrissey's "King Leer" is a song in which the Shakespearean allusion seems almost gratuitous, there more as clever, showy wordplay than for any deeper meaning. The song's title alters King Lear's name to make it somewhat grotesque, an uncomfortable change for those familiar with the image of King Lear as a sad, old man torn apart by the consequences of his own pride. This notion ties in well, however, with the edgy lyrics of Morrissey's song. The protagonist himself, though he accuses others of having "the gift of the grab," seems to be the titular "King Leer." He is the one trying to get attention, trying to win affection from the addressee of his song. As the singer laments, despite his efforts, the woman "didn't thank me ... and [she] didn't phone me"; instead, she ignores his attempts to win her away from someone else. The other man, whom the singer attacks as having "displayed...a real hint of cruelty," and the object of the singer's affection, who only speaks to the singer to announce, "'I'm bored now,'" seem in some sense akin to Lear's daughters Goneril and Reagan. Just as the two monstrous daughters attack their father's weakness and pride in response to his desperate efforts to confirm their love, the singer's attempts to win a romantic contest with insults, petulance, and coercion are met only with rebuffs. (SC)

MACBETH

1636 *Macbeth*
Opera. 1847. Giuseppe Verdi, libretto by Francesco Maria Piave, with additions by Andrea Maffei.

Verdi's *Macbeth* had its debut at the Pergola Theatre in Florence in March 1847. *Macbeth* is composed of four acts that closely follow the plotline of Shakespeare's play. The opera was such a success that a few years later, Verdi had it translated for performance in France. At the same time, he carried out a thorough revision of the work, dramatically altering various aspects of the score. *Macbeth* demonstrates Verdi's mastery of the operatic form: he adapts his style to the grand-scale tragedy of his source material, composing vocal and instrumental music designed to infuse the listener with terror as the protagonist descends further and further into sin. The score emphasizes the evil of Macbeth's deeds and their dire consequences for the opera's "hero"; above all, the music is designed to give weight to the words of the libretto, in an act of homage to the skill of the original playwright. Over time, *Macbeth* has become a part of the standard operatic repertoire and is still performed. (SC)

1637 *Lady Macbeth of the Mtsensk District*
Opera. 1932. Dimitri Shostakovich, *Lady Macbeth of the Mtsensk District, Op. 29.*

In Russian composer Dimitri Shostakovich's opera *Lady Macbeth of the Mtsensk District,* the character of Lady Macbeth derives not directly from Shakespeare's play, but from a short story by Nikolai Leskov. In Leskov's tale, the antiheroine is, as in *Macbeth,* an ambitious and callous woman with murderous designs. Shostakovich, however, loved the character of Katerina Izmaylova and couldn't stand to see her portrayed as a heartless villain. In Shostakovich's opera, then, Lady Macbeth appears as a sympathetic heroine and victim of her environment. (JS)

1638 *Macbeth*
Soundtrack. 1972. Third Ear Band, from the album *Third Ear Band's Music from* Macbeth. Harvest. U.K.

The Third Ear Band was formed in 1968, at the height of the psychedelic era. The experimental Scottish folk group contributed the soundtrack to director Roman Polanski's *Macbeth,* the first film he made after the brutal slaying of his wife and unborn child at the hands of the Manson clan. The movie is a particularly violent and disturbing rendering of the play, and it is complemented by the Third Ear Band's eerie, atmospheric music. The soundtrack is a combination of medieval-sounding instrumentals and modern rock moments, blending ethnic, electric, and electronic sounds. The fusion of styles and sounds provides Polanski's graphic style and Shakespeare's plotline about the price of power and ambition with an appropriately unsettling ambiance. (SC)

1639 "Macbeth"
Song. 1973. John Cale, from the LP album *Paris 1919.* Reprise.

Since his departure from the Velvet Underground in the late 1960s, Welsh musician John Cale has maintained a successful solo career catering to an art-rock audience. His raucous boogie "Macbeth" is an interesting example of derivative creativity and a playful take on Shakespeare's play. Most of the lyrics seem to be addressed directly to Macbeth by someone from the afterlife, some time after the events of the play have taken place, once all is forgiven: the singer welcomes Macbeth home, saying "everyone knows you're here, / It's easy to see they care." The line drawn most closely from Shakespeare's play refers to Lady Macbeth's influence on him: the all-knowing Lady "made you see things all her way."

1640 "The Milkman of Human Kindness"
Song. 1983. Billy Bragg, from the EP album *Life's a Riot with Spy vs. Spy.* Go! Discs/Utility. U.K.

Billy Bragg chose "The Milkman of Human Kindness" as the first song on his debut recording release in 1983, and while political consciousness and activism have long played a role in much of his music over his career, there is no denying that love songs like this one rank among his strongest and most popular work. Whereas Lady Macbeth worries that her husband's nature may be "too full o' th' milk of human kindness" (1.5.17), Bragg's song whimsically follows through on Shakespeare's metaphor—if there is such a thing as a "milk of human kindness," shouldn't there also be a "milkman" of human kindness? In the chorus Bragg declares his intention to put his own surplus to good use: "I am the milkman of human kindness," he says, and promises he'll "leave an extra pint." Bragg's twist on Shakespeare's metaphor also plays on the cultural figure of the milkman as romantic interloper who makes his deliveries while husbands are off at work.

1641 *Sound and Fury*
Album. 1983. The Youth Brigade. Better Youth Organization.

California punk rock trio The Youth Brigade made a name for themselves and defined their aesthetic with the release of their first album, *Sound and Fury.* On the album's title track, the band borrows Macbeth's existential musings and applies them to the swirling synergy of punk show mosh pits, with their "adrenaline," movement, and noise, "The music is a part of you, it always will be—Sound & Fury." Despite the nihilism inherent in the album title's quotation, the record, and the band's ethos, is surprisingly affirmative, channeling angry energy into a call for action through grassroots politics and a revolution of sound. (JS)

1642 *Macbeth*
Concept Album. 1986. Twice a Man, LP album. Xenophone. Sweden.

Swedish duo Twice a Man (Dan Söderqvist and Karl Gasleben) collaborated with the Teater Schahrazad on this version of *Macbeth*. The nine pieces, with titles such as "The Crown," "Banquet," "The Murder of Duncan," and "Insane," was released in LP format in a limited edition of 2000 copies.

1643 "Macbeth"
Song. 1989. Sonic Youth as Ciccone Youth, from the album *The Whitey Album*. Enigma/Blast First.

Sonic Youth's seventh album is animated by the mischievous spirit of Shakespeare's Falstaff more than it is haunted by the ghosts of *Macbeth*. Yet this record, originally released as a sort of gag album and musical experiment by Sonic Youth under the alias Ciccone Youth, contains two tracks with Shakespearean titles: "Macbeth" and a CD bonus track "Macbeth II." Reportedly, the title *The Whitey Album* was the result of a long-standing joke that the band would one day cover the entire Beatles *White Album*; the band's alias was a tongue-and-cheek tribute to Madonna, surnamed Ciccone. "Macbeth" and the song's alternate version (set to a hip-hop beat) are instrumental tracks with the Youth's signature sound of screeching experimental noise. "Macbeth" was also released as a music video directed by Dave Markey on Sonic Youth's retrospective video collection *Screaming Fields of Sonic Love* (DGC/Geffen 1995). (JS)

1644 "Macbeth's Head"
Song. 1989. And Also the Trees, from the album *Farewell to the Shade*. Troy.

Singer Simon Jones almost recites rather than sings the lyrics to the song "Macbeth's Head" over a drum and bass line that ticks along like clockwork in the spaces around a slow, searching keyboard part. The song begins with a man waking up to a snowfall that is "butterflying in through the open window, sand-dune drifting towards his feet." The encroaching snow triggers an image of Macbeth with an arm around his neck, saying remember "where you are, you're with me." The phrase "Macbeth's head" is then repeated anaphorically at the beginning of each of the remaining verses, linked with imagery that suggests the head as a kind of *memento mori*.

1645 "Miss Macbeth"
Song. 1989. Elvis Costello, from the album *Spike*. Warner Bros.

In one of Lady Macbeth's most shocking speeches, she imagines committing infanticide by ripping a child from her breast and dashing its brains out. It is probable that Elvis Costello had this moment in mind when writing "Miss Macbeth," which portrays a nasty old woman whose childlessness makes her hate other people's children, especially those who live in the flat upstairs from her. While the children treat her like a witch, tormenting her and testifying to their fairy tales about her (she is elsewhere described as having "cobweb tresses" and knocking her broom on the ceiling), the moral of the story is that they aren't necessarily wrong to do so. The final verse artfully preserves the situation's potential ambiguity as it depicts her practicing voodoo on one of the children: "Miss Macbeth has a gollywog she chucks under the chin, and she whispers to it tenderly then sticks it on a pin"; meanwhile, "a boy down the lane," turned white and "doubled over in pain." The song's chorus ends with the question that traces back to the source of Miss Macbeth's hatred: asking Miss Macbeth how she can miss what she never "possessed."

1646 "Uninvited Guest"
Song. 1989. Marillion, from the album *Season's End*. Never.

Not quite as hostile as a tormenting ghost, the uninvited guest of this Marrillion song takes the shapes of everyday annoyances, visitations of bad luck, and the skeletons people would rather keep in their closets. Like a spiritual or psychic specter of *Macbeth*, the uninvited guest won't let the unwilling host wash his hands of the past; he remarks, no matter how far the host may travel he'll find the "uninvited guest" is right behind so "We can talk about old times." (JS)

1647 "Blood of Eden"
Song. 1992. Peter Gabriel, from the album *Us*. Geffen.

In a song that begins "I saw the darkness in my heart" and "the signs of my undoing," it is fitting the second verse alludes to Macbeth's hallucination in 2.1: "Is that a dagger or a crucefix I see?"

1648 "Lady Macbeth"
Song. 1992. Barclay James Harvest, from the album *Welcome to the Show*. Alex.

In "Lady Macbeth," progressive rockers Barclay James Harvest tell of a wicked woman who blew into town "in the darkest hours of night." While Shakespeare's play lends similar attributes to the witches and Lady Macbeth, the song "Lady Macbeth" completely conflates the weird sisters and the play's leading lady. The song's refrain comes not from the lines of Lady Macbeth, but from those of the witches as they chant in Macbeth (4.1), "by the pricking of my thumbs / Something wicked this way comes." The Lady Macbeth of the song is cloaked in deception, dressed "in a silly gown," "Something evil came to town." She is, presumably, a manipulator of men and melodies, a musician "dripping blood upon the keys" rather than into a cauldron, as she concocts beguiling tunes. (JS)

1649 "Death or Glory"
Song. 1993. Motorhead, from the album *Bastards*. ZYX.

"Death or glory," "Blood and iron it's the same old story." "Death or Glory" is not a tale told by an idiot, but an intelligent song on the universal horrors of war, sung by speed metal band Motorhead. Referring to war as, like life, filled with "sound and fury," front man Lemmy Kliminster quotes Shakespeare's *Macbeth*. It was not the last time he would recite Shakespeare. In 1996, Lemmy would play the narrator from "The House of Motorhead" in Lloyd Kaufman's Shakesparody *Tromeo and Juliet* (1996). (JS)

1650 "Something Wicked This Way Comes"
Song. 1996. Barry Adamson, first released on the compilation *180 degrees* (Mute 1995); also released on Adamson's album *Oedipus Schmoedipus*. Mute. U.K.

Many fans of Barry Adamson know the musician as the former bassist for both the band Magazine and the band Nick Cave and the Bad Seeds. But in 1987 Adamson left the Bad Seeds and went solo to compose for the film industry. With his eerie melodies and noir noise, Adamson was a perfect addition to movie director David Lynch's *Lost Highway Soundtrack* (Interscope 1997). In "Something Wicked This Way Comes," the haunting presence of Macbeth's witches is just below the song's surface. Adamson mixes jazz, funk, and lounge, keyboard, percussion, and bass, for a jazzy track with ominous undertones. (JS)

1651 *Thane to the Throne*
Concept Album. 2000. Jag Panzer. Century Media.

Macbeth and metal rock turn out to be an excellent match on this concept album, or rock opera, by Jag Panzer. The songs focus on the anguish and masculine posturings of Shakespeare's Scottish king as he slays his way to the throne, his soliloquies accompanied by insistently galloping electric guitars. While Shakespeare's words are not used, most of the songs are sung as if in Macbeth's voice. Other songs feature passages sung in the voice of Lady Macbeth, and even MacDuff, whose perspective is presented in a slightly more commercial-sounding vein. The songs are interspersed throughout with short, classical instrumental interludes. The album was recorded in Denver and released one year after the murders at Columbine—an event which is a significant intertext for this version of *Macbeth*, as is especially notable in a song like "Insanity's Mind," which begins "I see the terrible deeds we've done," and later all "is red," "Cannot wash the stains."

1652 "Put Your Big Toe in the Milk of Human Kindness"
Song. 2002. Elvis Costello, from the album *Mighty Like a Rose*, expanded version. Rhino.

This song never appeared as part of an Elvis Costello album proper, but it was placed on expanded versions of both the *Mighty Like a Rose* and *Spike* albums. The song's titular refrain draws its main image from Lady Macbeth's first soliloquy on her husband's character, in which she declares he is "too full o' th' milk of human kindness" (1.5.17). Costello's song suggests that human nature in general is on Lady Macbeth's side: "always so capricious, in the face of wonder we're suspicious."

1653 *Fair is foul and Foul is fair*
Album. 2003. Babes in Toyland. Fire Records, United Kingdom.

Babes in Toyland's 2003 compilation, *Fair is foul and foul is fair*, provides yet another opportunity for the Minneapolis-based, all-women trio to express their affinity with witchy women. In 1998 the band recorded tracks for *Songs of the Witchblade: A Soundtrack to the Comic Books* (Dreamworks 1998), including "I Put a Spell on You" and "Witchy Woman." In 2000 the Babes added a little Shakespeare to the pot, releasing "Lived" (Almafame 2000), a live album including the song "Bubble, Bubble, Toil and Trouble." The same year the band recorded "Natural Babe Killers" (Recall 2000) with studio versions of "Bubble, Bubble, Toil and Trouble" and "Fair Is Foul and Foul Is Fair," songs that each riff generously on Shakespeare's *Macbeth*. In 2003 Babes in Toyland returned with yet another compilation, a two-disk U.K. import album featuring live and bonus tracks as well as studio demos. On this album, the band re-released versions of previously recorded *Macbeth*-inspired songs, this time citing the play in the tracks' titles: "Bubble, Bubble, Toil and Trouble [The Babes Do *Macbeth*, Act 1]" and "Fair Is Foul and Foul Is Fair [The Babes Do *Macbeth*, Act 2]." On these tracks of musical hurly burly, eerily altered voices are accompanied by throttling guitar and quick tempo changes. (JS)

1654 *A Tragedy in Steel, Shakespeare's* Macbeth
Concept Album. 2003. Rebellion. Drakkar. Germany.

German metal band Rebellion made their debut with the concept album *A Tragedy in Steel, Shakespeare's* Macbeth. Rebellion is not the first band of its kind to metallicize this Shakespearean tragedy. Jag Panzer worked on a similar project just a few years previously. In *A Tragedy in Steel*, Rebellion mixes heavy metal music with spoken passages from the play. The album did not fare particularly well with critics, who blame the derivative concept and the album's waning energy for its failings. (JS)

MEASURE FOR MEASURE

1655 "I'll Take Love"
Song. 1967. Elvis Presley from the EP *Easy Come, Easy Go*. RCA.

"I'll Take Love," sung by Elvis Presley on the soundtrack of his movie *Easy Come, Easy Go*, praises human emotion over other kinds of treasure. Money and material goods do not hold a candle to real romance; the singer explains, "Some people" only want money, but "Measure for measure, I'll take love." The "measure for measure" line is repeated numerous times throughout the song, as the singer reiterates his commitment to love over "wealth and fame," "caviar and . . . champagne." The phrase itself seems totally unrelated to the Shakespeare play of the same name (except for the fact that the play is a love comedy). However, the expression "measure for measure"—here used as a way of comparing love to material goods and money—is certainly indebted to Shakespeare's use of it for the title of his play about power, manipulation, and, of course, love. (SC)

1656 "Rock'n'Roll Nigger"
Song. 1978. Patti Smith, from the album *Easter*. Arista.

Perhaps the most infamous song by proto-punk poet Patti Smith, "Rock'n'Roll Nigger" redefines this odious racial epithet to mean any anti-establishment figure on the fringes of society. "Are you ready to behave?" Smith asks. If not, if you are a "black sheep," a "whore" or a rock-and-roll pariah, prepare to join the outsiders, she declares: "Jimi Hendrix was a nigger," as was "Jesus Christ," "grandma," and "Jackson Pollock." Shakespeare is never named in this assemblage of outcasts, but Smith does allude to his play *Measure for Measure* and the biblical passage (Matthew 7:2) from which the play takes its name. She sings of "a valley of pleasure," "the infinite sea," and "measure for measure," she says, she was lost, and paid by being "outside society." In this song, the measure or cost of nonconformity, is to join the ranks of the rock'n'roll niggers. For Smith, being an outsider may be difficult, but the singer seems to prefer this to the alternative, a life among the complacent and judgmental. (JS)

1657 "Just a Memory"
Song. 1980. Elvis Costello, from the album *Taking Liberties*. Columbia.

This duet with Attractions keyboardist Steve Nieve was first released on the album *Taking Liberties*, which brought together a number of tracks that had not yet been released in the American market. "Just a Memory" is a ballad that depicts a situation in which the singer's reaction to the breakdown of a relationship (an inability to remember) is directly related to the reason the relationship deteriorated in the first place. The moments the singer can't remember are those his former love most treasures. "Better take another measure for measure," he sings, because "Memories don't mean" much to him. The reference to Shakespeare's play here is obscure, but it may simply be a way of asking the lover to withold her judgment of him.

1658 "Keep Away"
Song. 1980. Lou Reed, from the album *Growing Up in Public*. Arista.

In "Keep Away," a song by former Velvet Underground member Lou Reed, the singer reacts to accusations of infidelity from his significant other. He tells her to keep her "jealousy" and "snide remarks" to herself, "You know that I'm not seeing anyone else." Promising his lover that he is entirely blameless, the singer says if he doesn't keep his word, he'll "keep away." As part of his campaign to end his lover's suspicions, the singer tries to find ways of distracting her and keeping her mind occupied and offers her a copy of *Measure for Measure*. The Shakespeare reference is fairly ironic, since *Measure for Measure* is a play in which various characters manipulate and conceal the truth from one another. *Measure for Measure* also deals with matters of sexual chastity and license, and its ending, in which all the characters end up conveniently matched and duly married, rings hollow. The play is therefore a particularly pointed allusion in the context of Reed's song about accusations, judgments, and their aftermath, in which the singer threatens to "keep away" from his lover altogether if she maintains her suspicions. (SC)

1659 "Measure for Measure"
Song. 1997. Matt Nathanson, from the album *Ernst*. Acrobat.

San Francisco–based singer-songwriter Matt Nathanson retells the story of Isabella and Angelo's second encounter (from 2.4) in this song from his second album, *Ernst*. Although the characters are not named, they are unmistakable, and he begins with Isabella: "She said she felt funny asking, and he said he felt funny saying 'no', but he said no." Nathanson's Isabella is more willing to trade on her own honor than Shakespeare's is, however.

THE MERCHANT OF VENICE

1660 "I've Got Five Dollars"
Song. 1956. Performed by Ella Fitzgerald, written and composed by Richard Rodgers and Lorenz Hart, from the album *Ella Fitzgerald Sings the Rodgers and Hart Songbook, Vol. 1*. Polygram.

It is a rare love song that refers to Shylock, the moneylender from *The Merchant of Venice*, instead of Romeo and Juliet or some other obvious romantic figure. Nevertheless, Rodgers and Hart's "I've Got Five Dollars" from the 1931 musical *America's Sweetheart* does just that, opening with the line, "Mister Shylock was stingy, I was miserly too." The song is about the transformative power of love, which turns someone selfish and more "crabby than a shellfish" into the very soul of loving generosity. Shakespeare's Shylock is a complex figure: he is hard-hearted in response to the way he has been treated by society, both powerful in his anger and pathetic in his quest for vengeance. However, Shylock is usually remembered for his cruelty and intransigence, and it is to those aspects of his character as it is popularly conceived that the song refers. In this case, the singer goes from being like Shylock, the epitome of hard-heartedness, to being open and giving. The unusual Shakespearean reference provides a witty opening to "I've Got Five Dollars" and complements the pattern of sibilance that marks the song's first few lines. (SC)

1661 "Stairway to Heaven"
Song. 1971. Led Zeppelin, from the album *IV*. Atlantic.

In terms of literary allusion, Led Zeppelin singer-lyricist Robert Plant is better known for turning to the work of J.R.R. Tolkien for inspiration than to Shakespeare. However, there is a Shakespeare reference at the beginning of the group's most famous song, "Stairway to Heaven," which starts "There's a lady who's sure all that glitters is gold." The first line is an inversion of the message written on the scroll that Portia's first unsuccessful suitor, Morocco, finds in the golden casket, which reads "All that glisters is not gold, / Often have you heard that told" (2.7.65–66).

1662 "Pound of Flesh"
Song. 1973. Buffalo, from the album *Volcanic Rock*. Phonogram. U.K.

Australian metal-and-more band Buffalo sold over 250,000 copies of their first album, *Dead Forever*. On the album, the band recorded tracks reminiscent of musical predecessors and contemporaries ranging from Black Sabbath to Jimmy Hendrix and Pink Floyd. On the heels of their debut success, Buffalo released their second album, *Volcanic Rock*, in June of 1973. With *Volcanic Rock*, the band demonstrates that the diverse inspirations for their music extend into the literary canon. Two track titles on the album are lifted from Shakespeare's play *The Merchant of Venice*: "A Pound of Flesh," named for Antonio's heart, the bodily cost of failing to deliver on a blood oath; and "Shylock," named for Shakespeare's Jewish moneylender who demands Antonio's flesh as his due. (JS)

1663 "Rain from Heaven"
Song. 1986. The Sisterhood, from the album *Gift*. Casablanca.

The Sisterhood is an alternate name for the English goth group The Sisters of Mercy. When the group splintered in the late 1980s, there was a legal battle over which members would be allowed to continue to conduct business under their name. When it became clear that the other side was about to release work under a widely recognized alternate name, singer Andrew Eldritch quickly recorded and released the album *Gift* under the same name as a way of blocking them. The title of the album's final song quotes from a moment in Portia's speech on mercy, in *The Merchant of Venice*: mercy "droppeth as the gentle rain from heaven /

Upon the place beneath" (4.1.185–6). The lyrics, which begin "Rain from heaven," speak of forgiving and forgetting—but by the end of the song, there is so much "mercy" around, one needs to be Christ to survive the flooding waters.

1664 "Common Ground"
Song. 1996. Midnight Oil, from the album *Breathe*. Columbia.

Known for their political activism and passionate guitar rock, as well as the distinctive vocals of front man Peter Garret, Australians Midnight Oil have been making music since 1975. In 1996 they recorded their tenth album *Breath*, which includes "Common Ground," another Oil tune calling attention to environmental issues and the plight of exploited workers. Here, Shakespeare's Shylock is invoked as a kind of vice character, a stereotypical figure of greed: "While Shylock is smiling we're loaded like mules." Moreover he plays the part of a merchant of men, a metonymy of the corporation profiting on "our" inhuman treatment as laborers. (JS)

1665 "Celebrity Skin"
Song. 1998. Hole, from the album *Celebrity Skin*. Geffen.

Singer Courtney Love's celebrity status as rock star, emerging film actor, and the widow of Kurt Cobain is the focus of this song, which considers the price she has paid for her fame. A trenchant critic of the entertainment business and its publicity machinery, she pointedly refers to the piece of herself she has given away for her fame by alluding to the conditions of Shylock's bond with Antonio: referring to herself as "Wilted and faded" in Tinsel town, she sings, "I'm glad I came here with your pound of flesh."

1666 "Bangkok"
Song. 2002. The Libertines, unreleased.

The Brit pop Libertines released their first album in 2002. On the unreleased track "Bangkok," the Libertines draw upon Shakespeare's *Merchant of Venice* to weave their tale of love for sale. Bangkok is a city known for its rampant prostitution, and so in the song "Bangkok," the Shylock figure is not a male Jewish moneylender but another fringe figure, a female prostitute. We learn that this woman has a past that is a "mean and unpleasant land." With a poor father and a drunken mother, she seeks "the dole" in a Chinatown that "smells like Bangkok" and where the quest is to "get your pound of flesh today." This song reeks of sexual imagery, and so in "Bangkok," a "pound of flesh" is neither a human heart nor the price of a broken contract but, presumably, the male organ or "piece of ass" that has become the prostitute's livelihood. (JS)

THE MERRY WIVES OF WINDSOR

1667 *Sir John in Love*
Opera. 1920s. Ralph Vaughan Williams, composed between 1924 and 1928, first performed March 21, 1929.

During his life, Ralph Vaughan Williams composed a variety of works including songs, symphonies, and operas. In *Sir John in Love*, Williams joins the ranks of those composers, including Giuseppe Verdi and Otto Nicolai, who have translated Falstaff's story to opera. For Williams's comic opera, based on Shakespeare's *The Merry Wives of Windsor*, the composer chooses a title emphasizing Falstaff's affection, rather than his greed, as a motivation for pursuing the mistresses Page and Ford. The title is a supposed quotation from Elizabeth I, who purportedly wanted to see a play about "Sir John in love." The opera itself is a romantic work, which, in keeping with its title, revolves around a lovestruck Falstaff. Complementing the story is a musical score comprising mostly love songs. The opera was first performed at the Royal College of Music in 1946. (JS)

A MIDSUMMER NIGHT'S DREAM

1668 *Wedding March*
Score. Felix Mendelssohn, from his score for *A Midsummer Night's Dream* (Op. 61).

Mendelssohn's *Wedding March* is arguably the most easily recognizable and most frequently performed piece of Shakespeare-related music ever written. After having composed an overture for the play when he was only seventeen, Mendelssohn returned to the play in 1843, adding incidental music when commissioned to do so by the Prussian King Friedrich Wilhelm IV for a production by Ludwig Tieck. Known as the "recessional," today the *Wedding March* is often played during weddings at the climactic moment when the couple, just announced as married, walk down the aisle together. One notable performance of Mendelssohn's score for Shakespeare's comedy took place in Los Angeles in 1934; it was directed by Max Reinhardt, who would incorporate the composer's music into his expressionistic film version of the play in the following year (entry 430). See also entries 925, 934, 935, 944, 946, and 1486.

1669 *Swingin' the Dream*
Musical 1939. Gilbert Seldes (writer), with music and lyrics by Jimmy Van Heusen and Eddie De Lange; performed at the Center Theater, Rockefeller Center.

Swingin' the Dream was a jazz version of *A Midsummer Night's Dream* set in nineteenth-century New Orleans, with Theseus as the state's governor. The production was a failure, but it wasn't for any lack of talent on the stage, since the cast was a dream in itself. Music was handled by the Benny Goodman sextet, the Bud Freeman band, and a full orchestra conducted by Don Voorhees. Louis Armstrong played the role of Bottom, and other familiar names in the production were Moms Mabley as Quince, Butterfly McQueen as Puck, Maxine Sullivan as Titania, and Dorothy McGuire as Helena. The idea behind *Swingin' the Dream* was to combine Shakespeare's classical theater with black vaudeville. It was part of a contemporary vogue for jazzing up, or "swinging," classic works. The show closed after only thirteen performances in late 1939.

1670 *A Midsummer Night's Dream*
Opera. 1960. Lord Benjamin Britten, *Op. 64*.

Britten's operatic version of *A Midsummer Night's Dream* was composed for and first performed at the Aldeburgh Festival in 1960. Almost the entire libretto is taken directly from Shakespeare's text, though it is rearranged into the traditional three-act opera structure and begins in the faerie world. Britten scored the work for a medium-sized orchestra, which includes an enhanced percussion section. The various social registers of the play are represented by specific parts of the orchestra: woodwinds and strings for the human; percussion, harps, and other stringed instruments for the faeries; and brass for the mechanicals. Another notable aspect of the work is that all of the faerie roles, except for the King and Queen, are written for children's voices. While the opera's musical style is distinctly modern, with some sections informed by the Shoenberg's abstract compositional principles, the challenging quality of some of the music is moderated by its comic nature. The work has achieved a broad popular appeal among opera lovers.

1671 *The Fantasticks*
Musical. 1960. Harvey Schmidt (music) and Tom Jones (lyrics and book), original cast recording. Decca USA.

The Fantasticks, like so many Shakespearean tales, is the story of a boy, a girl, their families, and the world that pulls them apart and then brings them back together for a happy ending. This long-running off-Broadway musical is filled with staging and plot devices adapted from Shakespeare's works and used for comic effect. The play is staged much like the Mechanicals' version of "Pyramus and Thisbe" from *A Midsummer Night's Dream*: there is a moon, there is a wall, and on either side of the wall are two young lovers. And, as in *Romeo and Juliet*, the lovers are kept apart by their feuding fathers. The twist is that the fathers are in fact the best of friends; they have simply pretended to hate one another for the purposes of reverse psychology. The fathers reason that if they pretend to force the Boy and Girl apart, the two will inevitably fall in love. While at first it seems that this plan has worked, the action takes a less light-hearted turn when the youngsters fall out of love and part. In the end, however, the two reunite and the musical achieves its somewhat delayed happy ending. The songs of *The Fantasticks* also borrow liberally from Shakespeare. For instance, "Metaphor" plays on the Bard's figurative language by employing nature imagery (the sun "burning like a pomegranate," or "the world like an iceberg") like Shakespeare's own. In the same song, the Boy also refers to his love as Juliet, Helena, and Cleopatra, reinforcing the play's Shakespearean connections by referencing the playwright's legendary heroines. (SC)

1672 "Midsummer Night's Dream"
Song. 1961. Jan and Dean with the Soul Surfers, composed by Don Altfeld and Jan Berry; 45 rpm single. Challenge.

Hitting gold with their song "Surf City," Los Angeles duo Jan and Dean were pioneers of good-time surf rock in the early 1960s. Faeries, aristocracy, and rude mechanicals may be missing from their tune "Midsummer Night's Dream," but the play's obsession with romantic love is revived in this Jan and Dean favorite. In this song, the duo express their wish for a "lovin' girlfriend" who will go with them to "parties every weekend" and "take strolls in the moonlight." This idealized portrait of love is, for Jan and Dean, "a Midsummer Night's Dream." The song was most recently re-released on the compilation *Teen Suite 1958–1962* (Varese Saraband 1995). (JS)

1673 "Midsummer Morning (Midsummer Night's Dream)"
Song. 1967. Joni Mitchell, unreleased.

In the 1960s Joni Mitchell was writing so many songs that she couldn't find space for them all on her albums. "Midsummer Morning (Midsummer Night's Dream)" is one of the songs from this period that never made it onto her records. In it, she speaks to a lover who has left, of her memories of their mornings together and the "Midsummer rain," the "Midsummer dawn, kisses in a doorway," all now gone, alive only in dreams. Indeed, the chorus has her reflecting on whether the whole interlude was a dream, and wondering if her lover was only "A midsummer's night's dream." The question remains, is this lover an Oberon or a Bottom?

1674 "Midsummer Night's Scene"
Song. 1967. John's Children, 45 rpm single, unreleased.

This single was the last to be recorded by John's Children before Marc Bolan left the group after only a few months in the spring of 1967. The song begins with the chant "petals and flowers," which continues throughout each verse. The first verse, which talks about "eating the heat" and "an eye in the sky melting your feet," further develops the psychedelic tone. The chorus, "It's all down to a Shakespearean dream," reads the current psychedelic moment in terms of Shakespeare's play, with its love-in-idleness and multiple levels of reality. Because of Bolan's departure from the group, only a few dozen test pressings of the single were printed, and it was never officially released. These test pressings have since become among the most collectible British 45s of the era and can command thousands of dollars at auction. The song was later released as part of an EP (extended-play single) called "A Midsummer Night's Scene" (Bam Caruso 1988).

1675 "Midsummer Night's Happening"
Song. 1969. The Sallyangie, from the album *Children of the Sun*. Warner Bros.

Before progressive music composer Michael Oldfield wrote the *Exorcist*'s well-known theme song, "Tubular Bells," he was teaming up with his sister Sally, making music in the duo The Sallyangie. Sally was only sixteen and Michael twenty-one when they produced their only album, *Children of the Sun*. One of the more memorable tracks on this atmospheric British folk album is the enchanted "Midsummer Night's Happening," in which Sally and Mike sweetly harmonize to the accompaniment of acoustic guitar and foresty flute music. The mood, characters, and title of the song are, of course, lifted from the faery-filled forest of Shakespeare's *A Midsummer Night's Dream*. Titania, Oberon, and even Puck make appearances in the Oldfields' sylvan song as the singers' playfully converse, "Trip in the forest Titania my love. . . . Come my pretty Oberon trip, trip, trip." (JS)

1676 "The Fairy-Feller's Master-Stroke"
Song. 1974. Queen, from the album *Queen II*. EMI/Elektra. U.K.

Queen's "The Fairy-Feller's Master-Stroke" was inspired by the Richard Dadd painting of the same name. Dadd was a talented Victorian artist who often chose faeries and other supernatural creatures as the focus of his work and rendered his subjects in painstaking detail. Dadd worked for nine years on "Fairy-Feller," which he painted while incarcerated in the infamous Bethlehem asylum following his gruesome murder of his own father. Given its creative inspiration, it is probably not surprising that Queen's "Fairy-Feller" is a strange and almost altogether nonsensical song; the ploughman, politician, pedagogue, ostler, "dragonfly trumpeter," and other characters Freddy Mercury mentions are taken directly from the painting. Among the figures catalogued are "Oberon and Titania, watched by a harridan" (the latter, a miniscule figure standing next to the faery King and Queen). Dadd's typically Victorian obsession with faery lore had clearly taken inspiration from the proud and playful faeries of Shakespeare's *A Midsummer Night's Dream*, a legacy that was passed onto Queen and which the band retained as part of its unique creative sensibility. (SC)

1677 *A Midsummer Night's Dream*
Concept Album. 1977. Steve Hackett, with the Royal Philharmonic Orchestra. EMI.

Guitarist Steve Hackett tunes into the enchantment of Shakespeare's faerie comedy on this album. Hackett plays the nylon-stringed classical guitar exclusively throughout, evoking the play's romantic and folkloric dimensions, while the orchestral settings suggest the play's more heroic, classical aspect. In the liner notes Hackett observes that "it's difficult not to be charmed by this magnificent and entirely romantic adventure which, like many of the Bard's works, will continue to be interpreted musically as much in the future as it has in the past." His gentle, and indeed astute, awareness of this work as a necessarily limited take on the play ultimately results in a surprisingly satisfying and coherent interpretation. Listening to the whole album is similar to having taken in a particularly good production of the play, though one more inclined to stimulate a sense of wonder than laughter.

1678 *A Midsummernights Dream*
Concept Album. 1990. Twice a Man, album. Radium. Sweden.

Swedish duo Twice a Man (Dan Söderqvist and Karl Gasleben) returned to composing for Shakespeare in the theater with this music for *A Midsummer Night's Dream*. The first act opens with two pieces, "The Sun and the Moon" and "Athens," while later acts include pieces with intriguing titles such as "The Night's Swift Dragons Cut the Clouds" and "Sensual Overflow." The music was released on CD in 1990. Twice a Man have also composed music for *Macbeth*.

1679 "Midsummer Nights Dreamin'"
Song. 1997. Travis, from the album *Good Feeling*. Epic/Independente. U.K.

Alcohol takes the place of Shakespeare's "love-in-idleness" in this song from the debut album by the Scottish group Travis. The play's depiction of eroticism run rampant finds an echo in the singer's complaint to his girl— "Do it to me, do it to you, do it to them." He still wants her even though she sleeps with his friends, so the course of true love will definitely not run smooth here, as the chorus, with its mention of "Midsummer nights, dreamin'," "too much to drink," and "head in the sink," suggests.

OTHELLO

1680 *Otello*
Opera. 1887. Giuseppe Verdi, libretto by Arrigo Boito.

Forty years after the success of *Macbeth*, Verdi returned to Shakespeare's dramas for musical inspiration. The composition of *Otello* was a long and painstaking process fraught with difficulties. At first, Verdi resisted working on yet another dramatic tragedy, hoping instead to find somewhat lighter fare for his next project. However, the maestro was prevailed upon to undertake the composition, and the insistence of other interested parties, combined with the undeniable appeal of Shakespeare himself, finally convinced him to begin adapting *Otello*. Despite the numerous obstacles that threatened to delay its completion (including an incident between Verdi and his librettist), the four-act opera, which keeps closely to Shakespeare's original plot and characterizations, was finally finished in 1887 and performed at the Scala Theatre in Milan. The music reflects Verdi's strong sense of responsibility for his material and his fine dramatic ear. *Otello* is a product of his desire to accurately capture the tragedy and genius of

his source material while also protecting his own popularity and reputation as a composer. Verdi's opera has been translated from stage to celluloid by several directors, including Franco Zeffirelli in his 1986 version of *Otello*. See also entries 996, 1008, and 1468. (SC, JS)

1681 "Desdemona"
Song. 1967. John's Children, 45 rpm single. Track. U.K.

"Desdemona" was the first single released by little-known British group John's Children after Marc Bolan, who would later lead T-Rex, joined the group for a brief stint in early 1967. The lyric begins with the singer pleading to Desdemona to "rock and roll" and heed "the conventions of the young." Here rock and roll itself, figured as dangerously seductive race music, fills in for Shakespeare's Moorish general. In the second verse the singer mentions that he owns a juke joint on the Seine. The suggestive lyrics, including the chorus, "Desdemona, Desdemona, Desdemona, lift up your skirt and fly," got the single banned by the BBC. The B-side is "Remember Thomas A Beckett."

1682 "Iago's Demise"
Song. 1996. Faith & the Muse, from the album *Alyria*. Neue Asthetik.

Darkwave duo Faith and the Muse have built a reputation around their modern gothic renderings of Elizabethan melodies and themes. In "Iago's Demise," the group turns to one of Shakespeare's darkest villains for its title. The soundscape is, characteristically, ominous in this track, which layers howling winds and other night sounds under Monica Richard's vocals. The song begins, not with Iago, but with an enumeration of Shakespeare's heroines who have fallen in death or suppression: "Ophelia, Cordelia, Desdemona and Kate," and "Beatrice so precious your pain." Iago himself plays a relatively small part in this song, which mainly laments the unrealized possibilities of Shakespeare's fallen heroines. A single reference to the infamous misogynist is buried in the middle of the song, "betwixt and between" the speaker's dreams of Shakespeare's lost ladies. (JS)

1683 "Othello"
Song. 1996. Dance Hall Crashers, from the album *The Old Record*. Honest Don's Hardly.

"Othello" is a song with a clever twist. The title and some of the lyrics suggest that it is written from the viewpoint of Shakespeare's Moor, who becomes convinced his innocent wife, Desdemona, has committed adultery and subsequently kills her. The song opens with the line, "How can you say you need me when you've been messing around all over the place?" Lyrics such as these sound much like Othello's musings and accusations in the play, as he becomes more and more enraged at the prospect of Desdemona's adultery. However, as the song continues, it becomes clear that the speaker is Desdemona, talking to her husband. The singer accuses the wrongdoer of "crossing blades with God knows who," and says, the wrongdoer is aiming for a "rise and fall." That the song is about Othello, rather than being told from Othello's perspective, is confirmed by the darkly witty lines, which accuse the other of talking about "yourself all night," and being "such a bore," and "behind my back you call me a whore." The lyrics take a shot at the self-preoccupation that characterize many of Shakespeare's tragic, brooding male heroes and bluntly remind listeners of the nature of Othello's betrayal. "Othello" makes powerful use of one of Shakespeare's best-known tragedies by giving its victim a voice and providing an intriguing hypothetical view into the "other side" of Shakespeare's story. (SC)

RICHARD III

1684 "A Hard Day's Night"
Song. 1965. Peter Sellers, 45 rpm single. Parlophone. U.K.

When the Beatles first met producer George Martin, they were most impressed with, not his experience recording classical music, but the fact that he had worked on a number of their favorite comedy recordings by a troupe called The Goons, which featured comedian Peter Sellers. By 1965 Beatlemania had swept not only through Britain, but also North America and much of the rest of the world. They had become a formidable artistic and economic phenomenon, and their status as an English cultural export was (and still remains) on a par with that of Shakespeare. The great thing about this connection is that it is both obviously true and completely ludicrous. It is a credit to Sellers's genius that he recognized this as early as 1965, when he released his rendition of the title song from the Beatles' new film, *A Hard Day's Night*, reciting the lyrics in the unmistakable guttural accent that Laurence Olivier had employed in his 1955 film adaptation of *Richard III*.

1685 "Lily of the Valley"
Song. 1974. Queen, from the LP album *Sheer Heart Attack*. Elektra.

In this brief art song, Freddie Mercury sings of a quest, which is a common theme in 1970s rock music. The second verse includes the line "I follow ev'ry course, my kingdom for a horse." Mercury quotes the famous line from Richard's final battle at Bosworth Field, associating the king's fundamental restlessness with his own.

1686 Johnny Rotten
Live Performance. 1975–78. Johnny Rotten (John Lydon) in performance with The Sex Pistols.

In developing the stage persona Johnny Rotten, the lead singer of British punk band The Sex Pistols reportedly borrowed heavily from the mannerisms and especially the posture of Sir Laurence Olivier in his 1955 film portrayal of Richard III. This reference is noted in Julien Temple's

Johnny Rotten during a live performance in 1977. Courtesy of Photofest.

2000 documentary *The Filth and the Fury* (entry 1054). As with most accounts concerning the mythic story of The Sex Pistols, this revelation should probably be taken with a grain of salt, though the visual juxtapositions in Temple's film are indeed striking.

1687 "Cemetry Gates"
Song. 1986. The Smiths, from the album *The Queen Is Dead*. Sire. U.K.

The dramatic situation of this Smiths song, a meeting between the singer and a literary chum in a cemetery, gives rise to a fascinating discussion that touches on the subjects of literary affinity, affiliation, appropriation, and originality. The singer takes issue with the way his friend recites texts without acknowledging sources, first "claim[ing] these words as [his] own: "Ere thrice the sun done salutation to the dawn." The singer retorts that he's heard these words "a hundred times," which is all the more ironic because it seems to hint that the line in question is already an echo, already double-voiced. In his popular adaptation of *Richard III* (1700), Colley Cibber gives a very similar line (and an additional crowing of the cock) to Catesby, while in Shakespeare's play, Ratcliffe alerts the king that, since "[t]he early village cock / Hath twice done salutation to the morn," his friends have been arming for battle (5.3.209–10). The military context of the source texts is also resonant here since, even though they are cohorts, the singer and his friend are divided along aesthetic and political lines: one claiming affinity with Keats and Yeats, the other with Wilde. The singer's admonishment to his friend not to plagiarize or "take 'on loan'" might be read as a slightly veiled critique of the project of adaptation and a commentary on the anxiety of influence.

ROMEO AND JULIET

1688 "I'm Putting All My Eggs in One Basket"
Song. 1936. Irving Berlin.

Irving Berlin's "I'm Putting All My Eggs in One Basket," from the Fred Astaire and Ginger Rogers movie *Follow the Fleet*, became a jazz standard in the hands of artists such as Louis Armstrong and Ella Fitzgerald. The song opens with the singer declaring himself "a roaming Romeo" whose "Juliets have been many," but whose "roaming days have gone." "Romeo" here is an appellation more akin to "Casanova" than to a romantic hero bound in desperate love to a single woman—instead of one Juliet, there are "many." In this sense, the song's lyrics are far removed from their origin in Shakespeare's characters, who preserve their absolute loyalty to one another unto death (Rosalind in Shakespeare's play here excepted). However, since the song is about a former "roaming Romeo" settling on a single woman (that is, "putting all [his] eggs in one basket"), the Shakespeare reference is not entirely out of line. (SC)

1689 *Romeo and Juliet Suite* (*Op. 64 1935–1936*)
Ballet. 1938. Sergei Prokofiev.

Sergei Prokofiev's gorgeous and powerful *Romeo and Juliet Suite* was originally commissioned by the Kirov Theatre and had its debut in a 1938 performance by the Ballet of the National Theatre in the Czech Republic. The ballet's brilliant and sympathetic musical rendering of the lovers' passion helps it stand out among Prokofiev's orchestral suites. Because the suite is written to accompany dancers and help tell a specific story through the actions of various characters, *Romeo and Juliet* is filled with musical character sketches that reflect the different players in the lovers' story: for instance, the friar's compassion, loyalty, and desire to help the young couple are conveyed in his slow, melodic theme. Romeo and Juliet's mutual attachment and their determination to remain together are captured in Prokofiev's score and, though he and his fellow librettists originally conceived of a happy ending ("living people can dance—the dying cannot"), he eventually adapted his music to Shakespeare's original ending, to beautiful and poignant effect. (SC)

1690 "If I Only Had a Brain"
Song. 1939. Harold Arlen (music) and E. Y. Harburg (lyrics), performed by Ray Bolger, Jack Haley, Bert Lahr, and Judy Garland, original cast recording for *The Wizard of Oz*. Decca.

"If I Only Had a Brain" has provided generations of children with their earliest exposure to the image of Juliet on her balcony. The famous song from the 1939 MGM movie *The Wizard of Oz* is sung by three characters (the Scarecrow, the Tin Man, and the Cowardly Lion) in succession, each of whom changes the lyrics to reflect their own particular desires. It is the Tin Man, with his wish for the heart that will make him "awful sentimental regarding love and art," who calls upon Shakespeare to make his longing for emotion understood. He sings, "Picture me a balcony, above a voice sings low: 'Wherefore art thou, Romeo?'" The reference comes during the bridge of the song, set apart from the rest of the melody as the ultimate example of romantic feeling. The Tin Man's Shakespeare allusion is not particularly complex, but captures his yearning for feelings (paralleled by Juliet's pining for Romeo) in one of our culture's most well-recognized images of deep, romantic love. (SC)

1691 "Personality"
Song. 1946. Johnny Burke and Jimmy Van Heusen, music by Burke, lyrics by Van Heusen, first produced for the movie *The Road to Utopia*. Paramount Pictures.

Beginning in the 1930s, American pop music composer James "Jimmy" Van Heusen produced an abundance of songs, many of them for movies and musical reviews. Teaming up with lyricist Jimmy Burke, Van Heusen wrote the song "Personality," composed for the movie and musical comedy *The Road to Utopia*, in which it is sung by Dorothy Lamour. In "Personality," sex appeal may be important, but it takes a personality to be able to really work it: "What did Romeo see in Juliet?" a "well-developed personality." Fans obviously thought Van Heusen's song itself had personality, as it topped the music charts at number one. (JS)

1692 *West Side Story*
Musical. 1957. Leonard Bernstein (music), Stephen Sondheim (lyrics), Jerome Robbins (choreography and original concept), and Arthur Laurents (libretto), original cast recording. CBS.

Arguably the most successful adaptation of Shakespearean material for the American musical theater, *West Side Story* debuted on Broadway in September of 1957. The story, which is based on *Romeo and Juliet*, depicts the rivalry between two street gangs, the Sharks and the Jets, on New York's west side. Tony, a member of the Jets, a white gang in the city, falls in love with Maria, the sister of one of the Puerto Rican Sharks. The real stars of the show, however, are Jerome Robbins's choreography and the songs by Bernstein and Sondheim such as "Tonight," "Maria," "America," and "I Feel Pretty," each of which is often performed outside of the work itself. The 1961 film version (entries 487 and 1161) won a total of ten Academy Awards, including Best Picture.

1693 "Fever"
Song. 1958. Written by Otis Blackwell, Eddie Cooley, and Peggy Lee, and performed by Peggy Lee. Capitol single #3998.

Peggy Lee's best-known single, "Fever" captures the power and intensity of all-consuming love. Lee's version of the song differed from earlier recordings in that she herself added additional lyrics about the history of love. In describing her feelings, the singer points out, "Fever isn't such a new thing, fever started long ago." To prove her point, she then calls upon famous historical incidents of "fever." The first example is Romeo and Juliet, with Romeo telling his paramour, "Julie, baby, you're my flame." As in so many songs, Romeo and Juliet are the archetypal romantic couple, more memorable for their mutual ardor than for the tragedy of their fate. However, the reference to a couple whose love famously persisted in the face of separation and death adds strength to the song's internal paradox, the idea that love-fever is "a lovely way to burn." The faux-Shakespearean wordplay of this verse of the song ("Thou giveth fever . . . fever, yeah, I burn, forsooth") adds a witty and slightly comic element that balances the burning intensity of the song's emotion and of Lee's voice over the tightly controlled bass line, drums, and finger snapping. (SC)

1694 "Running Bear"
Song. 1959. Johnny Preston, 45 rpm single. Mercury.

Johnny Preston went to the top of the charts with this song, penned by J. P. Richardson (aka The Big Bopper), which combines basic elements of *Romeo and Juliet* and the story of Hero and Leander in an American Indian context. Running Bear stands on one side of the river, while his love, Little White Dove, stands on the other: "their tribes" were enemies, "So their love could never be." The song ends with them throwing themselves into the "raging river" to meet in the middle, kiss, and drown together. A million-seller for Preston, "Running Bear" was later covered by Pat Boone, George Jones, The Youngbloods, and The Guess Who, among others.

1695 "That's Why (I Love You So)"
Song. 1959. Performed by Jackie Wilson, composed by Berry Gordy, Gwendolyn Gordy, Tyran Carlo, 45 rpm single. Brunswick.

Like so many other love songs, "That's Why (I Love You So)" calls upon Shakespeare as the creator of one of the greatest love stories ever told, and then tries to surpass him. Wilson sings that the author of *Romeo and Juliet* "would blow his top if he could see just how you've been lovin' me." The song pays homage to a woman who knows how to take care of her man—from backrubs to kisses—with the

idea that true love is in how she acts, and not just what she says. The song provides yet more evidence that Shakespeare has provided modern culture with an indelible vision of the meaning of "love," against which newer examples must compare themselves. *Romeo and Juliet* is the ultimate reference book of loving behavior, the standard to which the singer of "That's Why (I Love You So)" measures his relationship and finds, to his satisfaction, that his love compares admirably. (SC)

1696 "Desolation Row"
Song. 1964. Bob Dylan, from the album *Highway 61 Revisited*. Legacy Recordings.

Endlessly interpreted, this song sings of desolation row, a place? a time? a modern state of mind? characterized by alienation and meaning reconsidered. Included in Dylan's cast of literary and historical characters is an out-of-place Romeo who, mistakenly and with grave consequences, misrecognizes Cinderella as his star-crossed lover. *Hamlet's* Ophelia also makes an appearance in this song where conventions of romantic love and death are rewritten in a present context. "To her [Ophelia], death is quite romantic." Despite her idealization of death, however, this revised Ophelia has chosen a different ending, the religious life Hamlet has encouraged her to take up in his half-hearted advice, "Get thee to a nunnery." Yet lifelessness seems inescapable for Ophelia, and religious life is just another kind of suicide as Dylan calls this life "Her profession" and declares "her lifelessness" "her sin." (JS)

1697 "(Just Like) Romeo and Juliet"
Song. 1964. On The Reflections' *(Just Like) Romeo and Juliet* album. Golden World.

The first single released by Detroit doo-wop group The Reflections, this song sold over four million copies in 1964, the year of Shakespeare's quatercentenary. The song's hopeful protagonist wants to find a job so that he can buy a car and take his girl to the drive-in, because their love will go "down in history, / A-Just like Romeo and Juliet." His aspiration to become an even more renowned lover becomes apparent when he sings that he will surpass "Romeo's fame." By the final verse, however, he begins to contemplate doubts about his success, lamenting that his story could well be recontained within the tragic arc of Shakespeare's narrative. If he doesn't get a job, he frets, their happiness will "be destroyed like a tragedy." The song has been covered by numerous artists, including The Racket Squad, Michael and the Messengers, The Undertones, Sha Na Na, and Mental as Anything.

1698 "Romeo and Juliet"
Song. 1967. The Chambers Brothers, from the album *The Time Has Come*. Columbia/Legacy.

One of a handful of interracial groups performing in the late 1960s, The Chambers Brothers were known for their sweet harmonies, as well as their blending of musical styles from gospel to R&B to psychedelic rock. In "Romeo and Juliet" the group fashions another bluesy ballad that captures the spirit and theme of Shakespeare's most popular play on young love. "Like Romeo said to Juliet," the singer croons, "I love you." The song's love is one characterized by an eternally youthful spirit and a willingness to do anything, even die, as Romeo and Juliet did, for love. (JS)

1699 "Romeo and Juliet"
Song. 1968. Toby Twirl, 45 rpm single. Decca. U.K.

Newcastle-based psychedelic group Toby Twirl released this single, which recapitulates the story of Shakespeare's lovers in under three minutes, in July of 1968. The song begins with "love at first sight" for "our Romeo and his Juliet, / But never was a love so full of woe, as for Juliet and her Romeo." The chorus lyrics change slightly with each successive iteration, but each iteration asks the listener to consider the contemporary relevance of the story.

1700 "What Is a Youth" (Love Theme from *Romeo and Juliet*)
Song. 1968. Nino Rota, for the film *Romeo and Juliet*, directed by Franco Zeffirelli.

For 1968's *Romeo and Juliet* film, director Franco Zeffirelli engaged Italian composer Nino Rota for the score. Rota had made his reputation scoring for Federico Fellini on films such as *La Strada*, *8½*, and *La Dolce Vita*. In the film the song is sung at the Capulets' ball by a young man named Leonardo. The lyrics contributed by Eugene Walter are very reminiscent of Feste's songs during *Twelfth Night*'s musical interludes, comparing youth to "Impetuous fire" and "a maid" to "Ice and desire." The tune's familiarity is partly due to American film composer Henry Mancini, who recorded an easy-listening instrumental version for his album *A Warm Shade of Ivory* (RCA 1969), which hit number one on the pop charts in the United States. Mancini's rendition is frequently heard in retail shops and on late-night television commericals selling collections of "music for lovers."

1701 "The Cinema Show"
Song. 1973. Genesis, from the album *Selling England by the Pound*. Atlantic.

Genesis's 1973 song "The Cinema Show" examines the relationships between men and women and the way people put on appearances for one another. The song's "Juliet" is not a particularly mysterious or romantic figure. She is simply "Home from work," and, before leaving again, "She dabs her skin with pretty smells, concealing to appeal." Like many women, Juliet puts on something of a disguise, strategically covering her flaws before going out into the world. For Juliet, life, it seems, is something of a performance—or, as the song might have it, a "Cinema Show." The same can be said of the song's "Romeo," who is "A weekend mil-

lionaire" (a far cry from his real life, in which he inhabits "a basement flat"), armed with "a chocolate surprise" to guarantee his romantic success. He is not as suave or articulate as Shakespeare's hero; instead, he sports a "floral tie" and a head held proudly high as he eagerly sets out to conquer the world. His proud posture and chocolates are, like Juliet's makeup, a performance, a method of presenting the best possible face to obtain his desires. Here, love at first sight and fierce passion are not even considered. Instead, the names of Shakespeare's most famous romantic characters are somewhat ironically applied to two regular people, whose success in love is by no means guaranteed. (SC)

1702 "Here in Heaven"
Song. 1974. Sparks, from the album *Kimono My House*. Island. U.K.

The Sparks' song "Here in Heaven" suggests an alternate ending to the *Romeo and Juliet* tragedy: what if Juliet had never committed suicide? The song's lyrics come from Romeo's perspective (although the singer seems to be an "every-Romeo," rather than a faithful rendering of Shakespeare's own character). He sits "up here in heaven" pondering eternity and wondering, am I your "dearly departed, or am I that sucker in the sky?" Although it posits what seems to be a less devastating end to the *Romeo and Juliet* romance (she lives on, perhaps keeping his memory alive), "Here in Heaven" is somewhat disturbing. Alone in death, Romeo laments, knowing that Juliet's "health will keep you out of here, for years and years." The ending of *Romeo and Juliet* has become so engrained in popular consciousness— love conquers all, uniting two devoted people in death— that any change is a travesty that calls the love between the two characters into question. Romeo's dry remark, "Now I know why you let me take the lead," sums up everything that is wrong with the picture "Here in Heaven" presents. The song reestablishes the power of Shakespeare's vision of love by wryly and ironically undercutting it. (SC)

1703 "(Don't Fear) the Reaper"
Song. 1976. Blue Öyster Cult, from the LP album *Agents of Fortune*. Columbia.

This spooky song was penned by guitarist Buck Dharma and became the group's biggest hit. Speaking to his lover or someone he wishes to seduce, the singer fixates on the transitory nature of life, noting how death triumphs over all: "Seasons don't fear the reaper," he sings, as another voice softly calls to the listener, "we can be like they are." From this perspective the story of Romeo and Juliet turns away from tragedy, and the singer holds them up as lovers who have successfully found their ultimate, lasting unification in death: "together in eternity." Despite its morbid, *carpe mortem* lyrical conceit, the song's hypnotic guitar riff and gentle vocal harmonies smooth the whole thing out like a shot of novocaine.

1704 "Rock 'n' Roll Romeo"

Song. 1976. Sammy Hagar, composed by John Carter and Sammy Hagar, from the album *9 on a 10 Scale*. One Way.

On the last track of his first solo album, hard rockin' Sammy Hagar shouts "All the world's a stage," using Jaques's famous line in *As You Like It* to explain his staging of *Romeo and Juliet* in a modern, rock context. In "Rock 'n' Roll Romeo," Hagar runs rehearsal for his "blue-jeans Juliet," reserving the lines for himself and leaving the woman he casts silent: "baby you / Never had no lines to forget," he declares. But who needs lines when you're just going to skip the courtship and do it on the balcony, right?: "We'll get something straight . . . up in the balcony Juliet." If only Shakespeare's Romeo was so eloquent! (JS)

1705 "Romeo and the Lonely Girl"

Song. 1976. Thin Lizzy, from the LP album *Jailbreak*. Mercury. U.K.

Songwriter and singer Phil Lynott tells the story of a Romeo who falls in love with, and must take his leave of, a "lonely girl." Once he is gone, she then quickly falls in love with another, before the narrator can even make his own bid for her. Romeo arrives back in town on the train, finds out that his lonely girl has found another, and takes the train away again. Sad Romeo, "Sitting all on his own-ee-o."

1706 "Mystery Dance"

Song. 1977. Elvis Costello, from the LP album *My Aim Is True*. Columbia.

The first words on this song from Elvis Costello's debut album hint at this prolific songwriter's career-long interest in Shakespeare's works: "Romeo is restless" and "ready to kill," as he jumps out a window, while Juliet is "waiting with a safety net." Romeo says " 'don't bury me 'cause I'm not dead yet.' " The song summons the urgency and inexperience of adolescent love not only through its reference to Shakespeare's young lovers, but through its 1950s-style rock-and-roll arrangement and production. The emotional intensity characteristic of these two frames widens the song's perspective on the punk rock moment in which Costello's first album was released; that is, it finds precedent for punk's destructive energy in earlier rock and roll, and even in the work of Shakespeare. Costello would soon come to be renowned as one of popular music's most respected wordsmiths.

1707 "Fire"

Song. 1978. The Pointer Sisters, from the album *Energy*. Planet.

The Pointer Sisters had a hit with this song in 1978, which was written by Bruce Springsteen in the vein of Elvis Presley. Sung from the comic perspective of a lover who is perplexed by his/her beloved's apparent indifference, the singer cites Shakespeare's famed couple in the song's third

and final verse: "Romeo and Juliet," "Baby you can bet, their love they didn't deny." Rockabilly revivalist Robert Gordon also released the tune the same year on his album *Fresh Fish Special*.

1708 "Romeo Is Bleeding"

Song. 1978. Tom Waits, from the album *Blue Valentine*. Elektra.

In "Romeo Is Bleeding" the reference to *Romeo and Juliet* ignores the archtypically romantic aspect of the story in favor of contemplating its more violent and tragic elements. In Waits's song, Romeo resembles a gang leader rather than a suave romancer of women. He is with his friends, celebrating having "killed a sheriff with his knife" in revenge for the death of his brother, who was left "like a dog, beneath a car without his knife." However, despite his seemingly good spirits, Romeo is already bleeding. Throughout the rest of the song, as his companions all try to emulate his stance and strength, Romeo is already doomed to die. Despite being surrounded by men who want to be just like him, Waits's Romeo will die alone, "without a whimper, like every hero's dream." His death is inevitable and inescapable, much like that of Shakespeare's own character. "Romeo Is Bleeding" does not take much from Shakespeare's play but the image of violent young men with passionate spirits, who carry within them the seeds of their own destruction even as they pretend to be invincible. (SC)

1709 "Romeo's Tune"

Song. 1979. Steve Forbert, from the album *Jackrabbit Slim*. Columbia.

With a little help from Shakespeare's Romeo, 1970s folk rocker and one-hit-wonder Steve Forbert made it to the top of the popular music charts. With its blend of raspy vocals, background doo-wop, and rolling piano accompaniment, "Romeo's Tune" is considered by many fans the singer's most memorable song. Like Shakespeare's Romeo, the speaker of "Romeo's Tune" is characterized as a romantic daydreamer-poet, whispering to his beloved of "southern kisses" and midnight meetings, and pleading, "Let me smell the moon in your perfume." (JS)

1710 "Romeo and Juliet"

Song. 1980. Dire Straits, from the album *Making Movies*. Warner Bros.

Songwriter Mark Knopfler's penchant for creating short character sketches of lower-class figures results here in one of his best songs, written from the point of view of a young lover whose brief, one-sided relationship with a woman is figured in terms of Shakespeare's archetypal failed romance. At one point this Romeo references the song "Somewhere" from *West Side Story* (entry 1692), which suggests that his knowledge of Shakespeare's play is mediated primarily through the popular musical, and the movie version at that. While Knopfler's character fails to attain the poetic expressiveness of Shakespeare's young lover ("Says something like 'You and me babe, how about it?'"), it's a shortcoming he freely acknowledges in the third verse when he admits to her, he "can't do a love song, like the way it's meant to be." In his desperation he does become a better poet, however, telling Julie, "I'd do the stars with you, anytime." The tale ends with Romeo back out on the street, walking up to a new Juliet with the same tired pickup line that opens the song. Knopfler's song was also recorded by the Indigo Girls for their album *Rites of Passage* (Epic 1992).

1711 "Romeo"
Song. 1987. Don Dixon, from the LP *Romeo at Julliard*. Enigma.

As both a producer of jangle-pop and a solo artist, Don Dixon has attracted a loyal following since he coproduced REM's debut LP *Murmur* in 1983. In 1985, Dixon released his solo debut *Most of the Girls Like to Dance but Only Some of the Boys Do* (Dixon Archival 1985). Two years later, he released his first major label album *Romeo at Julliard* (Enigma 1987). According to Dixon in an interview with *Independent Weekly*, this album and its centerpiece song, "Romeo," were inspired by the play *Romeo and Juliet* as mediated through a painting by Ted "Blank Square of Excellence" Lyons. "I wrote a song called 'Romeo' for that one [album]," remarks Dixon, and "kind of built the record around the idea of failing at something you love—a glorious kind of failure." (JS)

1712 "Romeo's Escape"
Song. 1987. Dave Alvin, from the album *Romeo's Escape*. Razor & Tie.

Los Angeles–based roots rocker Dave Alvin wrote this fun song in which Romeo figures more as a Don Juan figure. The first verse begins with a woman in a bar down in the bayou, who vowed "to drink her whole life away," and asks the bartender "'have you seen my darlin' Romeo?'" In each succeeding verse we discover that her situation is shared by other women—one in Oklahoma City, another in New York City, and yet another in Cheyenne, Wyoming. Stupefaction and admiration pair up in the chorus: "Romeo, Romeo, well wherefore art thou?" "You got all these chicks just moanin' low." In the third verse, Alvin's own girlfriend confesses, "I hate to tell you Dave, but Romeo was here today."

1713 "Enchanted"
Song. 1988. Prefab Sprout, from the album *From Langley Park to Memphis*. Sony.

Prefab Sprout's "Enchanted" uses Shakespearean language and references to illustrate not only how the world has changed but also how it has, in some sense, remained the same. The singer observes that nowadays, "Bawdy talk is big . . .'Pray forsooth' and 'I adore' ain't the ticket anymore." Today's conversations take place in the gym, totally removed from the courtly scenes and romantic interludes described by Shakespeare. However, although "the calendar pages blew," just as for "the Montagues" and "the Capulet crew," "plain enchantment" remains "the glue that binds and bonds." The singer seems to be saying that, although the modern world is very different from the quasimythical Shakespearean past, some of the wonder and "enchantment" of Shakespeare's era are preserved today. The point seems to be that, though time may pass, the spirit of Shakespeare's world—both his historical world and the fictional worlds he constructed—lives on. (SC)

1714 "Cherish"
Song. 1989. Madonna, from the album *Like a Prayer*. Warner Bros.

In this upbeat song, Madonna proclaims the depth of her love for the "boy" in question, telling him, "Romeo and Juliet, they never felt this way I bet." The singer's relationship would seem to have sunnier prospects than that of the doomed lovers she compares it with, but the reference encourages her man not to "underestimate my point of view." Citing Shakespeare's lovers as the prime example of true romantic attachment, Madonna seeks to surpass their standard and convince the listener of the magnitude of her love. The song's irrepressible cheerfulness and optimistic tone counteract the potentially dark connotations of this allusion, and illustrate Madonna's ability to tap into popular culture by broadly appropriating elements of the cultural landscape. (SC)

1715 "No Myth"
Song. 1989. Michael Penn, from the album *March*. RCA.

In "No Myth," a hit 1989 release, singer-songwriter Michael Penn asks, "What if I were Romeo in black jeans?" The singer also refers to himself as "Heathcliff," another tragically romantic hero, contributing to the song's overall tone and the suggestion of loneliness and isolation that pervades its lyrics. The song seems to address the end of the singer's relationship with a woman. The singer describes himself and the woman as having "said goodbye before hello," and muses, "maybe she's just looking for someone to dance with." The song reflects the confusion that comes with the disappointing end of love and the struggle to figure out what to do or where to go next. The singer says he's "between the poles and the equator." The repeated references to two of literature's most famously doomed male lovers help to make "No Myth" a poignant rendering of the aftermath of a relationship and its effects on those involved. (SC)

1716 "Romeo Had Juliette"
Song. 1989. Lou Reed, from the album *New York*. Sire.

In this song Lou Reed situates the characters Romeo and Juliet in New York, though it is clearly not the same city as that of *West Side Story* (entry 1692). Here, Romeo Rodriguez is guided by "the twisted stars" and the same "faulty map" "That brought Columbus to New York." The way the very same stars cross both Romeo and Columbus suggests that Romeo's love for Juliette and the discovery of America are each ultimately tragic mistakes. In just over three minutes, Reed manages to plot the birth and death of Romeo's desire and to juxtapose that intimate tale with a series of scenes and images that suggest the rise and decline of the American empire.

1717 "Love Conquers All"
Song. 1991. Performed by ABC, from the album *Abracadabra*. MCA. U.K.

ABC's "Love Conquers All" incorporates the familiar "houses divided" facet of the Romeo and Juliet story to convey its positive message about the power of love. As the singer says, "Maybe you're a Montague, maybe you're a Capulet," on separate sides of an issue. Or perhaps the problem is simply that "you don't trust me yet." Love conquers all, however, regardless of the obstacles to happiness when one person is "a Shark" and the other "a Jet" (referring to the rival gangs from the musical *West Side Story*, based on Shakespeare's play; entry 1692). The song takes inspiration from the indomitable spirit of Shakespeare's lovers in lines such as, "When hate is strong... Love conquers all." The tragic and poetic aspects of Romeo and Juliet's ill-fated affair are elided in "Love Conquers All," but the notion of overcoming hardship is central to ABC's optimistic ode to the power of romance. (SC)

1718 "Romeo & Juliaaah"
Song. 1992. Udo Lindenburg and Nina Hagen, from the album *Panik-Panther*. Polygram. U.K.

Outrageous rocker Nina Hagen has developed audiences in both her native Germany and in North America. In "Romeo & Juliaaah," she teams up with famous German musician Udo Lindenburg. Shakespeare's story of adolescent sexual awakening translates here into German, with Hagen singing as Juliet and Lindenburg as Romeo. Hagen starts out "Bleib bei mir, du süsser, kleiner Romeo," and Lindenburg responds with a declaration of his love for her. The chorus gets more primitive, however, as they each sing "ohhh ohhh Romeo" and "ja ja Juliet." (JS)

1719 "This Romeo Ain't Got No Julie Yet"
Song. 1992. Diamond Rio, from the album *Close to the Edge*. Arista.

Country band Diamond Rio formed in Nashville at Opryland during the late 1980s and had success with their eponymously titled debut album of 1991. The following year they released their second album, which contains the song "This Romeo Ain't Got No Julie Yet." The bad pun

has been a fatal Cleopatra not only to Shakespeare, of course—country music songwriters and their audiences are notorious for their shameless indulgence in them as well. The song is about a young Romeo who is trying to arrange for his girlfriend to elope with him. In addition to the reference to Shakespeare's young lovers, it is only appropriate in a country music context to refer to the most famous lovers from the American South as well: "I'd follow you... Like Scarlett followed Rhett," the singer croons, but Romeo hasn't found his "Julie yet."

1720 *The Juliet Letters*
Album. 1993. Elvis Costello with the Brodsky Quartet. Warner Bros.

"The Juliet Letters" is a song cycle that came about when singer-songwriter Elvis Costello's wife, Cait O'Riordan, alerted him to a small newspaper story about a professor in Verona who had been answering letters addressed to Juliet Capulet. Costello collaborated with the members of the Brodsky Quartet on the songs, which take the form of imagined letters that the professor might have received, and in one case, might have written himself. The letters run the gamut of epistolary genres, including a suicide note, a love letter, an accusation, a divorce decree, a junk mail offer, and a letter from the battlefield. There is even one letter that arrives from the afterlife. Each of the songs is sung by Elvis Costello, accompanied by the Quartet. The work's public premier took place at The Amadeus Centre in London on July 1, 1992. It was subsequently performed by the five musicians at numerous venues in Europe, North America, and Japan. Costello learned to read and write music notation for the project, a skill that enabled his later composition of Shakespeare-themed orchestral music, *Il Sogno* (2004).

1721 "Juliet Where's Your Romeo?"
Song. 1993. Melissa Ethridge, unreleased.

Singer-songwriter Melissa Ethridge took the 1990s by storm with her Janet Joplinesque voice and her relentless country-folk-infused rock guitar. Since 1988, she has produced eight albums, her fourth album *Yes I Am* (Island 1993) earning her a Grammy award for best female vocalist of the year. In the unreleased track "Romeo and Juliet," Ethridge adapts the play that invented romantic love to revisit one of her favorite themes: the out of place and isolated heroine rewriting these romantic Shakespearean conventions. In "Juliet," a young girl stands outside, an enigma to the young boys who desire her. They wonder, along with the girl's parents, why the Romeo she ostensibly waits for never shows up: "Tell me Juliet, where's your Romeo?" "Tell us... for we all want to know." But the song and its heroine will never satisfy their curiosity, or ours for that matter, and by the tune's end, listeners are left to ponder if it is even Romeo she stands "Outside the door" waiting for. Maybe this Juliet stands, outside of conventions, waiting for someone else, or for no one at all, and perhaps this revision is not a tragedy after all. (JS)

1722 "Romeo"

Song. 1993. Written and performed by Dolly Parton and guest, from the album *Slow Dancing With the Moon*. Columbia/Sony.

Dolly Parton's country music take on the *Romeo and Juliet* story transforms the singer into Juliet and the object of her affection into an attractive cowboy. The song is primarily about sexual attraction rather than passionate love, with the singer exclaiming, "I ain't never seen a cowboy look that good in jeans." The depth of her emotional observations is apparent in lines such as, "I may not be in love, but ... I'm in heat." Parton's song is an extreme example of how completely Shakespeare has become absorbed into popular culture. Her dancing cowboy has none of the original Romeo's brooding intensity and eloquence. In fact, we only observe him through the eyes of his dancing partner, who pictures herself as his Juliet in an almost purely sexual sense rather than in terms of a life partnership. Parton hollows out all the truly Shakespearean aspects of her song's titular cowboy, but what remains is still interesting. She provides listeners with the popular conception of a "Romeo": a good-looking man who inspires an immediate reaction in women all around him. (SC)

1723 "Always"

Song. 1994. Jon Bon Jovi, from the album *Crossroad*. Mercury.

In "Always" singer-songwriter Jon Bon Jovi invokes Shakespeare's most famous tragic love story as mediated through the film version of *West Side Story* (entry 1161) and through two songs inspired by this filmic adaptation of Shakespeare's play. The Romeo of "Always" is wounded in love but unable to reveal his pain to the lover that left him: although he "is bleeding," "you can't see his blood," complains Romeo. Bon Jovi's references to a bleeding Romeo here recall Tom Waits's 1978, *West Side Story*–inspired song "Romeo Is Bleeding" from the album *Blue Valentine*, in which Romeo, a legend among his friends at the garage, is wounded while avenging the death of his brother. Waits's Romeo, like Bon Jovi's character, conceals his wounds as the speaker remarks, "Romeo is bleeding but not so as you'd notice." In writing his Romeo, Bon Jovi also looks to Dire Straits's "Romeo and Juliet," another song that refers to *West Side Story*. Lifting a line directly from this song, Bon Jovi's Romeo reveals his inability to articulate his feelings, admitting he "can't sing a love song ... the way it's meant to be." (JS)

1724 "Exit Music (For a Film)"

Song. 1996; 1997. Radiohead, from the album *OK Computer* (Capitol 1997), and the film *Romeo + Juliet* (dir. Baz Luhrmann, 1996).

The film referred to in the title of this song is Baz Luhrmann's *Romeo + Juliet* (entry 492). Luhrmann had contacted the British group Radiohead to write music for the final credits and sent them the last quarter of the film to give them a sense of how the material was being handled. Singer Thom Yorke characteristically decided to focus on the ultimate futility of the lovers' situation and was particularly inspired by the film's visual image of Juliet pointing a gun to her head. The song begins quietly, with the injunction to "wake," dry "your tears," for "today we escape." The lyrics alternate between addressing Juliet and addressing the parents, who in the song's crescendo are held accountable for the tragedy. The final line, "We hope that you choke, that you choke," is repeated three times.

1725 "Local God"

Song. 1996. Everclear, from the soundtrack album for *William Shakespeare's Romeo + Juliet*. Capitol.

"Local God," by grunge-punk band Everclear, is from the soundtrack of director Baz Luhrmann's modernized version of *Romeo and Juliet* (entry 492). Lead singer Art Alexakis performs most of the fast-paced, drum- and guitar-driven song in a snarling voice that drips with disdain. His style turns complimentary lyrics about song-subject Romeo ("I can't find the gorgeous words") into sarcasm and gives already sarcastic comments ("You look so stupid [and] happy") extra bite. The song sounds like it comes from the perspective of one of Romeo's Capulet gang rivals, or even as if it is sung by a friend who cannot understand Romeo's goofy, love-inspired behavior. The only time Alexakis's voice loses some of its ironic tone is during the bridge, when he sings that he feels "just like a local god" when he's with his gang, "yeah we do what we want." This part of the song reflects the gang mentality Luhrmann ascribes to the rival houses of Montague and Capulet, and Alexakis's change of style from entirely ironic to slightly more straightforward imbues the song with the earnestness of young men whose lives revolve around clan loyalty and warfare. "Local God" views the Romeo and Juliet story through the eyes of one less concerned with hearing "all about your love" than with maintaining the rush he gets when "with the boys." (SC)

1726 "Lovefool"

Song. 1996. The Cardigans, from the album *First Band on the Moon* (Mercury 1996); composed for and appears on the soundtrack for *Romeo + Juliet* (dir. Baz Luhrmann 1996).

Swedish group The Cardigans wrote "Lovefool" for Baz Luhrmann's 1996 film version of *Romeo and Juliet* (entry 492) after the initial song they had submitted was rejected by the director for not being upbeat enough. Although there is nothing in the lyrics that would associate the song specifically with Shakespeare's play, its inclusion in the film's soundtrack is a masterstroke. The tune's infectious, bubbly frivolity encourages the audience to consider, even vicariously experience, the completely carefree nature of the young couple's new love at the same time that it encourages a wilfull ignorance of the fate everyone knows is in store for them. In this sense the song plays an important tonal role in establishing the film's powerful emotional-roller-coaster effect, an effect that had audiences, especially teenaged ones, returning to see the film in the theater multiple times. Luhrmann's film was a generation's first introduction to Shakespeare, and "Lovefool" is the song that audience most readily associates with the film. It remains to date the Cardigans' biggest hit, though the group often laments that fans of the song completely missed the broad irony they intended to convey.

1727 "Miller's Angels"
Song. 1996. Counting Crows, from the album *Recovering the Satellites*. Geffen.

The meaning of Counting Crows' "Miller's Angels," let alone its reference to Romeo, is obscure. The song seems to be about the difficulty of choice and the divide between right and wrong. The titular Miller's angels are perhaps beings of mercy, since they "let everyone in." Yet they are also somewhat unpredictable, since "you never know where they're going to go." They exist in "the shadow of God's grace," suggesting His grace extends to them, but only in its reflected or indirect aspect. As the Miller of the song's title contemplates his changeable angels, the lyrics call, "Hey Romeo," and at one point instruct Romeo, "Don't come around here." In this case, Romeo seems to be an aspect of Miller, whose "fingers are traveling down the length of her thigh." The point at which Romeo and Miller intersect is the point at which Miller's angels "come out of the blue sky" to help him make a romantic choice, and banish the possibly unsavory Romeoesque aspect of his character. What seems clear is that this Romeo is not the romantic hero of Shakespeare's play; like his angels, Miller (and, by extension, Romeo) himself has many sides to his character, some dark and some full of grace. (SC)

1728 "Pretty Piece of Flesh"
Song. 1996. One Inch Punch, from the soundtrack album for *William Shakespeare's Romeo + Juliet*. Capitol.

One Inch Punch's "Pretty Piece of Flesh" is a musical expression of *Romeo and Juliet*'s violent undercurrent (particularly evident in director Baz Luhrmann's updated movie version [entry 492], which features this song). The song's lyrical starting point is the first scene of *Romeo and Juliet*, in which Sampson and Gregory, members of the Capulet household, discuss their hatred of their Montague nemeses. It is Sampson who declares, "I am a pretty piece of flesh," as part of his suggestion that he rape the Montague women after the men have been defeated. With such inspiration, it is no wonder "Pretty Piece of Flesh" is driven primarily by violent images and by Sampson and Gregory's

fighting words about the "dog[s] of the house of Montague." Backed by a threatening electronic beat, the singer—who delivers his opening vocals in a groaning voice before the fierce delivery of the song's rap segment—quotes Gregory's assertion that "the weakest [slave] goes to the wall." When "Pretty Piece of Flesh" segues into rap, the lyrics are composed of lines such as, "Shoulder holster strapped, I'm pulling from the chest"; all its words emphasize the backdrop of inescapable street violence crucial to Romeo and Juliet's tragedy. (SC)

1729 "Whatever (I Had a Dream)"
Song. 1996. Butthole Surfers, from the album *William Shakespeare's* Romeo + Juliet: *Music from the Motion Picture*. Capitol.

This selection from the *Romeo + Juliet* movie soundtrack, with its driving beat and violent imagery, reflects the darker currents that run through the play. From its eerie opening notes onwards, the song turns most of what is usually associated with *Romeo and Juliet* in contemporary songwriting—eternal love, rather than pain and death—on its head. Gone are the sweet images of young lovers; instead, the song opens with the voice of John Leguizamo as Tybalt, declaring, "Peace? I hate the word / As I hate hell, all Montagues." Rejecting Romeo and Juliet's normal depiction as the most faithful and romantic lovers in all of history, the Butthole Surfers' song has Romeo waving to "A chorus girl in Vegas." Juliet, meanwhile, is "up in Heaven, pocket full of pills." The song's lyrics do not tell a story, nor do they all combine to form a coherent whole. Instead, the song is tied together by its repeated images of fire and violent death. While some of the song's lyrics border on the obscene, its harshness ties with the violence and anger that drive many of *Romeo and Juliet*'s characters, and which, in the form of an "ancient grudge," are essential elements of the play. (SC)

1730 "Romeo"
Song. 1997. Sublime, first released on a compilation of various artists *Misfits of Ska* (DLL 1995), re-released on Sublime's compilation *Second Hand Smoke*. (MCA 1997).

In writing "Romeo," the ska-reggae-punk trio from Long Beach revisits a common theme in music today, a displaced Romeo (or Juliet), a romantic idealist not quite fitting in a current age and missing the love of his or her other half. The singer seeks someone who wants more than "sloppy drunk sex on a saturday night" because he is "a romeo with no place to go." Unfortunately, front man Brad Nowell shared with Romeo a tragic fate as well as romantic aspirations: in May 1996 the singer-songwriter died of a heroin overdose in a San Francisco hotel room. Only after his death did the band achieve stardom with their major album debut *Sublime* (MCA 1996) and its hit single "What I Got." The band's song "Romeo" first appeared on *Misfits of Ska*, a compilation of various artists. It was later re-released on the band's 1997 collection of rare and un-released tunes, *Second Hand Smoke*. (JS)

1731 "Romeo and Juliet"
Song. 1998. Sylk E. Fine, from the album *Raw Sylk*. RCA.

Sylk E. Fine's "Romeo and Juliet" presents listeners with the more obscene (or just the more hormonally charged) aspects of a love story. As in many rap songs, the sexually explicit lyrics of "Romeo and Juliet" are part of the singer's attempts to woo the object of her desire. The song's blend of graphic sexual description with protestations of real feeling is typical of many songs in this genre, performed by both men and women. The song opens: "like Romeo and Juliet," it's "Hot sex on a platter." But as the singer also protests, "my love be true." While the popular conception of Romeo and Juliet's romance excises its sexual aspects, retaining only the purity and intensity of their love, the attraction between Shakespeare's most famous couple as depicted in the play has an undeniable erotic current. The lyrics to "Romeo and Juliet," which suggest an inextricable link between sexual attraction, true love, and Romeo and Juliet's legendary romance, may be on the dirtier side, but they do (whether intentionally or not) reflect an aspect of Shakespeare's play and of "love" at first sight. (SC)

1732 "Singing in My Sleep"
Song. 1998. Semisonic, from the album *Feeling Strangely Fine*. MCA.

Minnesota group Semisonic (formerly Trip Shake-speare) cleverly links the 1990s vogue for making "mixed" cassette tapes to the much earlier romantic practice of serenading a loved one. The second verse makes the comparison explicit, at the same time referencing Shake-speare's play: the lover sings of "living in your cassette" and compares it to "Singing up to a Capulet." Romeo doesn't actually sing to Juliet in the balcony scene, but the two do share some particularly florid impromptu poetry with each other. In a related Shakespearean reference, members of Semisonic previously performed under the name Trip Shakespeare, whose second album was titled *Are You Shakespearienced?* (Twin/Tone 1989).

1733 *Romeo and Juliet—A Most Excellent Tragedy*
Musical Theater. 2000. Ed Goldfarb, music (debut per-formance June 21, 2000 in San Jose, California).

Bay Area musician and composer Ed Goldfarb set close to 80 percent of Shakespeare's words for *Romeo and Juliet* to music in this score, which was commissioned by local theater entrepreneurs Gary De Mattei and Michael Smythe for their musical theater production of the play. The retention of so much dialogue from the play is ac-complished by an effective pop implementation of re-citative (sing-speaking) in many of the work's pieces. The production, which ran for several weeks at the Theatre on San Pedro Square in the summer of 2000, was not a hit, but

perhaps this very interesting hybrid of musical theater and rock opera would work better in a recital performance format.

1734 "West Side Story"
Song. 2000. LFO (Lite Funky Ones), from the CD single "West Side Story." Arista.

Another version of *Romeo and Juliet* mediated through its modern retelling in *West Side Story* (entry 1692), LFO's song is one of feuding factions standing in the way of young love. In "West Side Story," the speaker pines over his beloved, Veronica. But her brothers, who disapprove of the match, pursue him, and Veronica's parents despise him. The speaker of the song straddles the centuries and layers of theatrical and cinematic representation as he compares his situation to *Romeo and Juliet* and the Jets and the Sharks. (JS)

1735 "Romeo"
Song. 2002. Amy Read, from the album *Romeo & Julia*. Halloweena Music.

The country-flavored song "Romeo" on Seattle-based Amy Read's second album, *Romeo & Julia*, tells the story of a love gone wrong from the woman's perspective. She describes how her clueless Romeo has physically hurt her, eaten up all of her money, and been rude to her friends: "Romeo,... he's rude to all my friends, there's this thing with rules he can't comprehend." In the chorus, however, she states that she will still love him, in spite of everything. "And I have troubled you my share," "you must know: I'm only human, Romeo." By the end of the song, she accepts the idea that their relationship will not last, saying she'll "look for a replacement" because "I'm only human, Romeo." Shakespeare's Romeo, the epitome of romantic commitment, has generated many similarly ironic avatars.

1736 "Romeo A Go-Go"
Song. 2003. Every Time I Die, from the album *Hot Damn!* Ferret.

"Romeo A Go-Go" by hard-core rock band Every Time I Die draws extended metaphorical comparisons between physical debility, creative output, and romantic love. In the opening line, the singer declares (or rather screams), "Tonight I'm coming home in a coma if it fucking kills me," and describes himself as a "hopeless romantic" who's "helplessly rheumatic." The singer's "Munchausen by proxy of a muse" affects him in such a way that he com-plains, his "vowels are getting lost in the gauze." While the lyrics border on the nonsensical, it is clear that the singer's ability to produce music and poetry is bound up in his physical state, which is related to his romantic attach-ments. The physically violent aspects of the song perhaps relate to Every Time I Die's style of music, which blends different forms of rock to create a sound that is loud, un-relenting, and probably physically punishing to write and perform. Why the band chose the name "Romeo" for the song's title is unclear, but it relates perhaps to the idea of a "hopeless romantic" willing to go through all kinds of pain to achieve the object of his desire, whether that be a beautiful woman, a rock song, or both. (SC)

THE TAMING OF THE SHREW

1737 *Kiss Me, Kate*
Musical. 1948. Cole Porter (music and lyrics), Samuel and Bella Spewack (book), original cast recording. Sony.

One of Cole Porter's most popular and enduring musicals, *Kiss Me, Kate* has been successful both onstage and on film (entry 1317). The story, cleverly adapted from Shakespeare's *The Taming of the Shrew*, centers on warring divorced actors brought together to play opposite one another in the musical version of *Shrew*. Of course, while the two enact the battles between Katherine and Petruchio in the theater, they also carry on with their own, parallel clashes offstage. The squabbles, misunderstandings, and humor that pervade *Kiss Me, Kate* are typical of Cole Porter, as are the musical's classic songs. Some of these are takeoffs of Shakespeare, part of the play-within-a-play musical production of *Shrew* (for instance, Petruchio's introductory song, "I Come to Wive It Wealthily in Padua"), while songs such as "Always True to You in My Fashion" have left a lasting impression on popular culture. In any case, as the play's resident mobsters remind us and as the musical's success and longevity demonstrate, if you "Brush up your Shakespeare, they'll all kowtow." (SC)

THE TEMPEST

1738 *Brave New World*
Album Title / Song. 1969. Steve Miller Band, LP album. Capitol.

The opening title track of the Steve Miller Band's album of the same name begins with the sound of an explosion and then shifts into a psychedelic mode as Miller sings the first words: "We're driving fast from a dream of the past to the brave new world." In this brave new world nothing from the past will last. Although the allusion is probably to Aldous Huxley's novel of the same name, Miller's use of the phrase here treads the thin line between skepticism and optimism in a way more reminiscent of its employment in *The Tempest*, where Miranda is at once comically naive and absolutely correct in her assessment. Is the opening sound of Miller's song a nuclear bomb, or a rocket ship lifting us off to a glorious new future?

1739 *The Tempest*
Ballet. 1981. Paul Chihara (after Henry Purcell), first recorded. Reference Recordings.

Paul Chihara's 1981 ballet *The Tempest* holds a place in history as the first ever full-length American ballet. Chi-

hara adapted his score from the music of the great seventeenth-century composer Henry Purcell, who had in fact written incidental music for John Dryden's production of *The Tempest* and for *The Fairy Queen* (an adaptation of *A Midsummer Night's Dream*). Chihara chose to retain the sweetness of Purcell's work, relying heavily on string instruments and horn sections (and causing some reviewers to proclaim his work "banal"). Shakespeare's plays have had a long history of successful adaptation to the ballet: *The Tempest* appeared in ballet form as early as 1774 and has been reimagined as dance numerous times since then. Balletic versions of other plays, most notably *A Midsummer Night's Dream*, *Romeo and Juliet*, and *The Merry Wives of Windsor*, have also become part of the modern choreographic repertoire. Given the importance of music and dance to the Elizabethan theater and cultural life, the success of Shakespearean themed ballets seems unsurprising and entirely natural. And yet, despite their connection with the plays' theatrical history, these adaptations furnish contemporary artists with new ways of interpreting the Bard and making his work accessible to modern audiences. Ballet's combination of movement and music captures the spirit of the plays and can convey their complex emotions in a related-but-different form of creative expression. (SC)

1740 "Blue Lagoon"
Song. 1984. Laurie Anderson, from the album *United States Live IX*. Warner Bros.

Laurie Anderson's "Blue Lagoon," from the five-disc album *United States Live*, takes many of its lines from Shakespeare's *The Tempest*. Specifically, Anderson references Ariel's song, with the lyrics:

Full fathom five thy father lies
Of his bones are coral made
Those are pearls that were his eyes
Nothing of him that doth fade
But doth suffer a sea-change
Into something rich and strange. (1.2.397–402)

The lines are haunting and evocative, helping to conjure up the world of the "Blue Pacific" the singer inhabits. Ariel's song is about transformation, and the expression "sea change" has become a part of the common idiom, to denote a powerful change or shift in circumstances. The song is in part a meditation on personal development and growth, as the singer, dreaming "about a perfect place," contemplates her own hopes, desires, and wishes for the future. (SC)

1741 "Ariel"
Song. 1993. October Project, from the album *October Project*. Epic Records.

The song "Ariel" from October Project's debut album takes its inspiration from Shakespeare's play *The Tempest*. The song's lyrics, combined with the soaring voice of lead vocalist Mary Fahl, capture some of the power, loyalty, and above all the longing for freedom expressed by Shakespeare's sprite Ariel as he seeks to end his servitude to Prospero. The yearning quality Fahl injects into her voice reflects the tension between loyalty and the quest for independence represented by lines such as "I want to be free," and "Forgive me for leaving." The song transforms the relationship between Ariel and Prospero—that of slave and master—into a loving bond: though the singer sighs, "your sorrow ... has made a slave of me," she also repeats the lines "I love you" over and over again, reaching out to the listener even as she sets her sights on the outside world. (SC)

1742 "Prospero's Speech"
Song. 1994. Loreena McKennitt, from the album *The Mask and Mirror*. Warner Bros.

Loreena McKennitt closes her album *The Mask and Mirror* by setting Prospero's epilogue to *The Tempest* to music in her new age Celtic idiom. The entire epilogue is sung, with the exception of the lines 5-8 where Prospero refers to Naples, his dukedom, pardoning the deceiver, and the "bare island" of the stage, omissions which allow McKennitt to sing the speech in her own persona. The enchanting quality of the music and singing is strangely at odds with the point of Prospero's speech, however, concerned as it is with the breaking of spells and the renunciation of magic.

1743 *Sea Change*
Album Title. 2002. Beck, album. Geffen/Interscope.

The title of this 2002 album invokes Ariel's speech in *The Tempest* as a way of describing the dramatic shift Beck

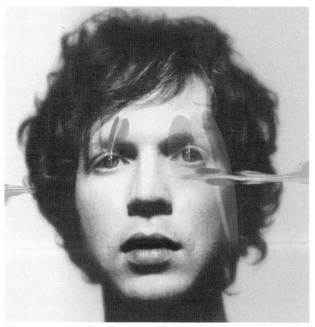

The cover of Beck's album *Sea Change*. Courtesy of Universal.

makes in his sound, from heavily ironized postmodern collages of folk, blues, and hip-hop, to his new persona as a confessional singer-songwriter right out of the early 1970s. The songs themselves recount the story of the singer coming to terms with a failed love relationship, of a sea change that has occurred in his own life, and of the artist's transformation of that pain into something rich and strange.

1744 *Make Believe*
Album Title. 2005. Weezer. Geffen Records. U.S.

Rumors of the college rock band's imminent demise began after supposed clues left in the liner notes of this album referred to Prospero's abjuration of magic from *The Tempest*, Shakespeare's last single-authored work and popularly regarded as Shakespeare's own good-bye to the stage.

This rough magic
I here abjure, and, when I have required
Some heavenly music, which even now I do
To work mine end upon their senses that
This airy charm is for, I'll break my staff
Bury it certain fathoms in the Earth
And deeper than did ever plummet sound
I'll drown my book. (5.1.57–64)

Front man Rivers Cuomo told MTV, "When we were putting the album together and finishing up the artwork, I didn't know what was going to happen in the future and I told everyone that. And that was one of the reasons why I put that quote in there, because I thought it's a really nice way to say goodbye, if it is a goodbye." Another Weezer member added, "When I saw that quote, I thought the same thing. I was studying Shakespeare at a university during the making of *Make Believe*, and it did spark some concern, and I asked Rivers about it. We never directly say, 'So, does this mean this is our last record? What does this mean?' But I knew he took Shakespeare too, and maybe it struck a chord with him." Perhaps echoing the play's epilogue, track eight is entitled "Pardon Me." (RB)

TIMON OF ATHENS

1745 *Timon of Athens Suite*
Classical Music. 1963. Duke Ellington. Varese Records.

In 1963, jazz performer and composer Duke Ellington went to Stratford, Ontario, to compose background music for a production of *Timon of Athens*. This was not the first time Ellington had merged jazz and Shakespeare; he and his creative partner, Billy Strayhorn, had already composed *Such Sweet Thunder*, a series of themes inspired by and reflective of Shakespeare's writing. Viewing the performances at Stratford in the 1957 season apparently inspired Ellington's new and more classical creative direction, and he returned to Stratford numerous times to perform and, perhaps, to soak up the artistic atmosphere. Ellington's own success at blending the Elizabethan author's work with the modern sound of jazz inspired the musical *Play On!*, which uses Ellington's jazz standards (such as "Take the 'A' Train") to tell a story inspired by Shakespeare's *Twelfth Night*. With his adamant belief that the Bard was "beyond chronology," Ellington demonstrated that as modern music and culture evolved, they could still retain their ties with the great works of the past, and keep Shakespeare's cultural legacy fresh for a new generation of readers and listeners. (SC)

TITUS ANDRONICUS

1746 *Titus X: The Musical*
Musical. 2004. Written by Shawn Northrip, directed by Peter Sanfillipo, opened November 5, 2004.

Shawn Northrip adapts Shakespeare's carnival of carnage to a punk rock score in *Titus X: The Musical*. Audiences experience the play's violent assaults as a blitzkrieg of bloody images and pounding sounds (the decibel levels are high, and earplugs are distributed at the door). The musical remains fairly true to the story from Shakespeare's source text, and the play's already inherent tragicomic elements are amplified in grotesque musical performances by Titus, who holds a mic with his bloody stubs-for-arms, and Lavinia, who sings a song after her tongue has been cut out. (JS)

TWELFTH NIGHT

1747 "Highway 61 Revisited"
Song. 1965. Bob Dylan, from the album *Highway 61 Revisited*. Columbia.

The title song from Bob Dylan's 1965 album *Highway 61 Revisited* is filled with irreverent cultural references that range from the Bible to French history to Shakespeare. In this instance, Shakespearean allusions are part of how Dylan demonstrates his cultural literacy and sense of humor. While his third-stanza reference to "Mack the finger" might be interpreted as partially inspired by Macbeth (combined with the infamous "Mack the knife"), the most overt Shakespearean moment in "Highway 61 Revisited" comes in the following stanza. In it, "the fifth daughter on the twelfth night told the first father that things weren't right." The allusion is almost a throwaway, but a clever one that complements the social and cultural references in the rest of the song. (SC)

1748 *Your Own Thing*
Musical/Rock Opera. 1968. Words and music by Danny Apolinar and Hal Hester, original cast recording. RCA Victor.

Your Own Thing premiered off Broadway at the Orpheum Theater just before *Hair* started to grow on Broadway fans, which made it the first successful rock musical. Winning the New York Drama Critics' award for Best Musical, it ran for 933 performances and even went on

tour; however, it has not been restaged often since its original run. Based somewhat loosely on *Twelfth Night*, the plot focuses on a rock band called The Apocalypse.

1749 *Then Play On*
Album Title. 1969. Fleetwood Mac, LP album. Reprise.

The title of this Fleetwood Mac album of 1969 refers to the opening words of *Twelfth Night*: "If music be the food of love, play on." In the play these words are spoken by a character who, sick for love and turning to music for solace, embodies much of what the blues would later come to be about. The tones of loss, nostalgia, and ennui that permeate and refuse to vacate Shakespeare's otherwise festive comedy are especially echoed in bandleader Peter Green's contributions to the album, in songs such as "Closing My Eyes," "Showbiz Blues," "Oh Well," and "Before the Beginning." Here, as with Shakespeare's Orsino, the connection between moroseness and self-indulgence is recognized as beautiful, not because it is desirable, but because it is true to human experience.

1750 *Play On!*
Musical. 1996. Duke Ellington (music), Cheryl West (book), conceived by Sheldon Epps. World premiere at The Old Globe, San Diego.

In *Play On!* Sheldon Epps combines a story loosely taken from Shakespeare with a score compiled from classic Duke Ellington jazz numbers to reimagine the Bard in a decidedly non-Elizabethan context. As suggested by its name, *Play On!* is adapted from *Twelfth Night*. However, the musical sets its story during the 1940s and takes place in the Harlem with which Ellington himself would have been familiar. *Play On!* follows Vy, a would-be songwriter who ventures to Harlem in search of fame and fortune. Discovering that songwriting is a man's game, she turns for help to her Uncle Jester, who aids Vy in disguising herself as one of the guys. Her goal is to enlist the professional assistance of the Duke, who is preoccupied with pining away for Lady Liv. When the Duke asks for "Vy-Man's" help in winning back his love, Lady Liv ends up falling for the cross-dressed Vy, making her blind to the affections of her assistant, Rev. Of course, with these mix-ups comes a certain amount of comedy and ample chance for renditions of popular Ellington songs such as "Take the 'A' Train," "Don't Get Around Much Anymore," "It Don't Mean a Thing if It Ain't Got that Swing," and "I Ain't Got Nothin' but the Blues." The musical retains a Shakespearean combination of comedy, romantic love story, and interest in subjectivity, and blends these with well-known music. *Play On!* once again demonstrates Shakespeare's enduring appeal and adaptability to any number of contexts. (SC)

1751 "Terror & Magnificence"
Song. 1996. John Harle, with Elvis Costello, Sarah Leonard and Andy Sheppard. Argo. U.K.

British saxophonist John Harle is the motivating force behind this record, which attempts to fuse ambient jazz, classical chamber music, and English traditional song. The first five pieces are collaborations with Elvis Costello, and three of those feature Elvis singing tunes from *Twelfth Night*, including "O Mistress Mine," "Come Away, Death," and "When That I Was and a Little Tiny Boy." The album opens with an instrumental titled "Illyria," cowritten by Harle and Costello.

1752 *Illyria*

Musical Theater. 2002. Music and lyrics by Peter Mills, book by Peter Mills and Carla Reichel.

Illyria is a comic musical based on Shakespeare's *Twelfth Night*. While there have been many variations on musical adaptations of this particular play, Peter Mills and Carla Reichel's version of the story distinguishes itself by staying true to the original time period and setting, as well as keeping fairly close to the play's original story line. The musical does alter some aspects of its source: for instance, the disguised Viola takes her brother's name rather than "Cesario," which compounds the comedy of mistaken identity. In addition, Mills and Reichel's adaptation also softens some of *Twelfth Night*'s darker overtones (for example, the specter of madness that haunts some of the characters and the unconventionality of the play's examples of "true love"). However, nothing is entirely excised, and the spirit of the Bard's play stays alive in *Illyria*'s witty banter and melodic score. (SC)

1753 "Waiting (O Mistress Mine)"

Song. 2003. Nitin Sawhney, from the album *Human*. V2 Records. U.K.

On the track "Waiting (O Mistress Mine)" from his album *Human*, Nitin Sawhney provides Shakespeare with a sweet-voiced singer and a surprisingly appropriate trip-hop-inspired beat. Many of the words to the song are taken from the play *Twelfth Night*, in which the clown Feste sings, "O mistress mine, where are you roaming? / Oh stay and hear! Your true-love's coming." Feste's song, with its carpe diem theme and assurance that "Jour-

neys end in lovers meeting," provides insight into the tangle of love affairs and mistaken identities that characterizes *Twelfth Night*. More generally, Feste's song also reflects the holiday season in which the play's events take place and helps reveal his talent at perceiving and expressing others' emotions. In Sawhney's hands, and with the addition of the word "Waiting" to its title, the song becomes both an avowal of and a plea for love. Lyrics such as "What is love? 'Tis not hereafter" take on a new weight when sung in yearning tones and backed by a gentle beat. In combination with Sawhney's own, added lyrics, Feste's song becomes even more serious and direct. Sawhney removes the song's festive aspect and adds instead an element of adult desire that alters the song's delivery without radically changing its message. (SC)

THE TWO GENTLEMEN OF VERONA

1754 *Two Gentlemen of Verona*

Musical Theater. 1971. John Guare and Mel Shapiro (libretto), Gait McDermot (music) and John Guare (lyrics); first performed at the New York Shakespeare Festival.

This musical version of *The Two Gentlemen of Verona* was introduced in 1971 as part of Shakespeare in the Park at Joe Papp's Public Theater. It was initally conceived as a multicultural production of the play that would contain a number of modern-sounding songs written especially for the production, but John Guare (later known for *Six Degrees of Separation*) and Gait McDermot (who wrote the music for *Hair*) ended up with enough songs that they had a full-fledged musical on their hands. The show's songs are fun and exude youthful energy, supported musically with lots of congos and other Latin percussion, as well as soulfully simple electric piano parts. After the show's successful run with Shakespeare in the Park, it was brought to Broadway, where it played for over 600 performances and won the Tony award for Best Musical the following year, beating stiff competition from *Grease*. The original Broadway cast recording, featuring Raul Julia and Clifton Davis, was finally released on CD by Universal in 2002.

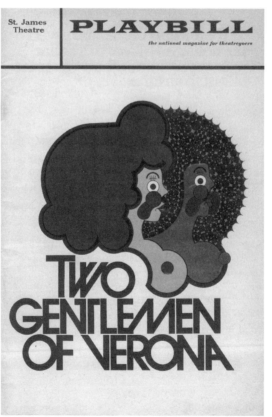

A playbill for the original production of *Two Gentlemen of Verona*. Courtesy of Photofest.

THE WINTER'S TALE

1755 "Letter to Hermione"
Song. 1969. David Bowie, from the album *Man of Words/ Man of Music*. Mercury. U.K.

An under-recognized track from David Bowie's folk-psychedelia second album, "Letter to Hermione" is a haunting invocation of the love triangle from *The Winter's Tale*, written from the imagined perspective of Polixenes. The lyrics speak of an illicit relationship fueled by inner discontent: "They say your life is going very well," "But something tells me . . . You cry a little in the dark, well so do I." When the singer asks in his letter, "He makes you laugh," "He treats you well," "he's strong for you," and his kisses are "something new," "But did you ever call my name"? it becomes clear that, in this version at least, Leontes's anxiety about the intimacy between his wife and best friend is not misplaced. It is unclear whether the song is written as an imagined version of Shakespeare's play, or if David Bowie chose to use the play's love triangle and Hermione's name as a coded reference to a more personal situation.

1756 "Loveless"
Song. 1990. Lloyd Cole, from the album *Lloyd Cole*. Capitol.

In this song cowritten with Blair Cowan, Scottish songwriter Lloyd Cole sings of a relationship that has taken an unfortunate turn with a lyric that accuses a lover of turning "the heat of a summer haze," "into a Winter's Tale." The reference to Shakespeare's play seems to be motivated by the partner's actions, which are apparently close to those of Leontes, and which place the singer in the position of the wrongly accused Hermione: "why do you say you love me when you don't?" "why should I feel blue when I do?" The word most repeated throughout the song's lyric—"why?"—is one that has perennially occupied critics of Shakespeare's play as they search for the possible motivations for Leontes's jealousy.

SONNETS

1757 "You're the Top"
Song. 1934. Cole Porter, from the musical *Anything Goes*.

Cole Porter's "You're the Top," from his 1934 musical *Anything Goes*, combines current pop cultural references of the early twentieth century with long-standing icons of cultural superiority to provide a witty catalogue of endearments. At "the top" are great historical monuments ("the Coliseum"), famous artworks and art galleries ("the Louvre museum," "the smile on the Mona Lisa," and others), movie stars (including Greta Garbo, Mae West, Fred Astaire, and even Mickey Mouse), comfort foods (Ovaltine) and, of course, "a Shakespeare sonnet." It is appropriate that a love song would refer to the sonnets, the poetic form traditionally dedicated to musings on love (among other things), and a type of poetry at which Shakespeare excelled. As the quick allusion shows, Shakespeare's poetry is a pinnacle of cultural achievement that, though part of an "elite" literature, is still an obvious and accessible reference in a song cheekily devoted to pop culture. The sonnets stand up proudly beside the world's most famous cartoon character and Mae West's lovely shoulders in a display of the best of mankind's accomplishments. (SC)

1758 *Nothing Like the Sun*
Album. 1987. Sting. A&M.

The title phrase of Sting's 1987 album *Nothing Like the Sun*, and the song "Sister Moon," borrow from Sonnet 130, commonly known by its opening line, "My mistress's eyes are nothing like the sun." "Sister Moon" is seemingly addressed both to the actual moon and to an aspect of femininity best represented by the cool mystery of the moon as opposed to the dazzling glare of the sun. The song lyrics begin with the first line of Sonnet 130, followed by "My hunger for her explains everything I've done." The latter line expresses a kind of obsessiveness not unlike that of Shakespeare's "dark lady" sonnets, of which 130 is one. However, Sting changes the resonance of the line. While Shakespeare uses it ironically, as part of a clever spoof on the Petrarchan blazon (in which the poet compares his subject's physical attributes to elements of nature), Sting employs the line as a straightforward description of Sister Moon and her calming aura. In Sting's hands, the line is emptied of its dry wit and ironic overtones and is as a result

The cover of Sting's album *Nothing Like the Sun*. Courtesy of Universal.

much more sensual and well suited to be the title of an album about relationships and personal experience. Given the nature of "Sun," it is perhaps unsurprising that other songs also seem to have Shakespearean overtones; for example, "The Secret Marriage," filled with lines such as, "No family bond has ever made us two," contains elements that evoke *Romeo and Juliet* and *The Merchant of Venice*. (SC)

1759 "Consider Me Gone"
Song. 1990. Sting, from the album *Dream of the Blue Turtles*. A&M.

Singer-songwriter Sting turns his senses to literary history for this song's inspiration. With lyrics only slightly amending Shakespeare's Sonnet 35, "Consider Me Gone" is recited by a speaker who, like that of the sonnet, has been at war with himself over the pain caused by the object of his affection. Unlike the voice of Sonnet 35, though, a speaker who remains half-forgiving, Sting's song persona leaves his internal strife behind, and with it "the rooms of forgiveness" to which the lovers have grown accustomed. Sting's speaker declares, "I have spent too many years at war with myself," and so he will no longer play the "accessory" making the excuses that fill Shakespeare's sonnet. Instead, Sting's speaker declares his intentions to leave, repeating in refrain, "consider me gone." (JS)

1760 "My Bird Performs"
Song. 1992. XTC, from the album *Nonsuch*. Geffen.

Colin Moulding makes the first of two Shakespearean references on XTC's *Nonsuch* album in this song, in which the mod British slang "bird" for "girl" is the central metaphor. The singer declares his preference for the singing of his bird to other, more high-art pleasures. Her singing moves him more than "fine art," "vintage wine," or "designer clothes." In the second verse he proclaims that "Shakespeare's sonnets" leave him unmoved, "The drama stage and the highbrow pose," but "My bird sings sweetly."

MISCELLANEOUS

1761 "Bombito and the Chorus of Girls"
Song. 1908. Leslie Stuart (music) and Adrian Ross (lyrics), from the musical *Havana*.

The second song from this turn-of-the-century musical comedy set in Cuba introduces Bombito the cigar-maker musing about what he would do if he were a "ruler despotical." Everyone would have to smoke his company's "Consuelo Coronas" cigars, and he would even build a memorial to Shakespeare, a theater, "Where Brutus, Othello, and that Jewish fellow" would blend smoke with verse. As the fantasy develops, Bombito imagines that people would see Hamlet "Smoking cigars with the Ghost in the night," and Polonius get "Ophelia to give him a light." The final verse envisions Jessica from *The Merchant of Venice* and the faeries from *A Midsummer Night's Dream* all smoking cigars as well.

1762 "Shakespearean Rag"
Song. 1912. Gene Buck and Herman Ruby (lyrics), David Stamper (music). Joseph W. Sterne & Company.

The "Shakespearean Rag" appeared during the ragtime craze that swept North America at the turn of the twentieth century. The song mixes popular and elite culture, noting that although "Bill Shakespeare never knew" ragtime, "his syncopated lines" "surely fit," the ragtime hits, which would be worthy of the Bard's consideration. The lyrics also mention various characters such as MacDuff, Desdemona, Romeo and Juliet, Hamlet, Brutus, Shylock, Othello, as well as the plays *Richard III* and *As You Like It*. The song was a hit in 1912, but its more enduring fame is a result of T. S. Eliot's allusion to it in lines 126–30 of *The Waste Land*. There, it is referred to as "That Shakespeherian Rag," Eliot drawing out the syllables as they would have been sung.

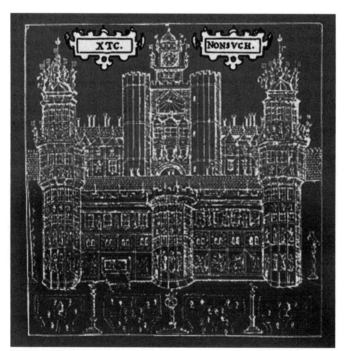

The cover of XTC's album *Nonsuch*. Courtesy of Universal.

1763 "Hillbilly Shakespeare"
Nickname of Hank Williams

By combining traditional folk styles with the blues, Hank Williams pretty much defined country and western music as we now know it back in the 1940s and 1950s. In songs like "Your Cheatin' Heart," "Cold, Cold Heart," and "I'm So Lonesome I Could Cry," Williams struck a chord with audiences across America. His popularity and reputation have only grown in the ensuing years, and his troubled life story has become legend. Williams's ability to write about situations and emotions his listeners were likely to experience themselves, with such directness, simplicity, eloquence, and truth rightfully earned him the nickname "The Hillbilly Shakespeare." Hank Williams died in 1953 at the age of 29—a tragically early death that also led him to be called "the Keats of country."

1764 "Road to Morocco"
Song. 1942. Bing Crosby and Bob Hope (performers), Johnny Burke and Jimmy Van Heusen (composers), from the film *Road to Morocco*. Directed by David Butler.

Road to Morocco was the third of Bing Crosby and Bob Hope's successful "road" movies, a series that became more and more comically self-referential with each additional film. When they sing the title song about how they're on the road to Morocco, they breathlessly manage to squeeze in a reference to Shakespeare that points up his bland cultural ubiquity: they've been so many places, they sing, they're "Like a complete set of Shakespeare that you get in the corner drugstore for a dollar ninety-eight." The two other "Morocco bound" works mentioned in the song are *Webster's Dictionary*, and "a volume of Omar Khayyam."

1765 "Cherry Pies Ought to Be You"
Song. 1950; 1951. Cole Porter (words and music), duet by Rosemary Clooney and Frank Sinatra (78 rpm, Columbia); also included on original cast recording of *Out of this World*. Sony.

Like the earlier Cole Porter song "You're the Top," "Cherry Pies Ought to Be You" largely consists of the singers' attempts to find just the right epithet for their beloved. And as in the earlier song, Shakespeare is invoked as a paragon. The new wrinkle is that Porter makes this song a duet, with the lovers singing to each other. The song was featured in Cole Porter's musical *Out of this World*, and the original cast recording was released in 1951. At about the same time, Frank Sinatra and Rosemary Clooney recorded a version that was released as a 78 rpm disk by Columbia. As the song begins, Sinatra protests his lack of poetic ability, noting that, alas a lack of flair for "tender

Undated photo of Hank Williams Sr. Courtesy of Photofest.

verses" he lacks, to which Clooney responds "try to versify and I'll versify back." He then begins tentatively with "cherry pies ought to be you," and she again replies in kind with a rhyme. They continue in this vein, comparing each other to the Pulitzer Prize, "Romeo in disguise," and so forth. Sinatra sings "Beethoven's nine ought to be you," and Clooney answers "Every Will Shakespeare line ought to be you."

1766 "Make 'Em Laugh"
Song. 1952. Donald O'Connor, from the film *Singin' in the Rain*. Directed by Stanley Donen and Gene Kelly. Composed by Arthur Freed and Nacio Herb Brown.

Donald O'Connor stole the show with this comic song-and-dance number from the film *Singin' in the Rain*. The point of the song is that audiences appreciate humor above all, and therefore aspiring entertainers would do well to observe this if they wish to succeed. The second verse invokes Shakespeare, and foregrounds his status as a serious high-culture figure (forgetting that he too had the ability to make 'em laugh): "Now you can study Shakespeare" and be the critics darling with no food on the table, or you can "slip on a banana peel," and rule the world, "Make 'em laugh, make 'em laugh, make 'em laugh!"

1767 *Such Sweet Thunder*
Album. 1957. Duke Ellington and Billy Strayhorn. Columbia.

"Such Sweet Thunder," a title taken from the words of the mischievous Puck in *A Midsummer Night's Dream*, was commissioned by the Shakespeare Festival of Stratford, Ontario, in 1956. The finished product was a twelve-part suite composed of musical portraits of some of Shakespeare's most memorable characters, as well as pieces inspired by the sonnets. Duke Ellington and his longtime composing partner, Billy Strayhorn, attempted to create music that captured the characters' natures or reflected the moods found in the poems. Their compositions, inspired by the atmosphere at the Shakespeare festival, in addition to the plays and sonnets themselves, were at once beautiful, fun, inventive, and surprising; for example, the composers incorporated a ragtime element into "Lady Mac," blending their own jazz sensibilities with their unique perceptions of Lady Macbeth's character. The parallels between Shakespeare and Ellington themselves (both highly creative and influential artists, both innovators, both closely connected with specific repertory companies), add an extra level of interest to Ellington's unusual fusion of jazz and early modern literature, a combination he would later elaborate upon with pieces such as his "Timon of Athens Suite." (SC)

1768 "Stuck Inside of Mobile with the Memphis Blues Again"
Song. 1966. Bob Dylan, from the album *Blonde on Blonde*. Columbia.

Bob Dylan's works of genius, characterized by a combination of musical mellifluousness and atonal twang, erudition and accessibility, have prompted more than a few critics to compare the artist to William Shakespeare. In fact, in his heyday the *New York Times* dubbed Dylan "the Shakespeare of his generation." No wonder Dylan continued to include Shakespeare and his plays in his songs' rich casts of characters, a cadre that included people the songwriter knew, politicians, stock characters and archetypes, and literary and historical figures. In the tune "Stuck Inside of Mobile with the Memphis Blues Again," these characters reappear, and with them the narrative gallows humor that pervades so many of Dylan's songs. In the sense that the speaker of this song is poet, prophet, and jester, Dylan's narrator finds a double in Shakespeare: "Well, Shakespeare, he's in the alley," talking to a "French girl," who claims "she knows me well." (JS)

1769 "Astronomy Domine"
Song. 1967. Pink Floyd, from the LP *The Piper at the Gates of Dawn*. Composed by Syd Barrett. Columbia. U.K.

Few groups of the last three-and-a-half decades have been as important or as influential as Pink Floyd. Pioneers of electronic and ambient astral rock, Pink Floyd has produced unforgettable albums of epic proportion and ethereal sound. Yet "Astronomy Domine" is a song that nearly suffered a fate of obscurity in America. The first track on the band's first LP, *The Piper at the Gates of Dawn*, was deleted on the album's American release by Capitol's American subsidiary Tower Records in 1967. In "Astronomy Domine," a voice sounding like a radio communication with space is accompanied by the beeping of Morse code, pulsating bass and percussion, and sliding, dissonant guitar riffs. As lyrics enter into this mélange of sound, the band moves beyond space and into Shakespeare's magical worlds from *A Midsummer Night's Dream* and *The Tempest*: "Floating down the sound resounds around the icy waters underground, Jupiter and Saturn, Oberon, Miranda, Titania." (JS)

1770 *The Transformed Man*
Album. 1968. William Shatner. Varese Sarabande.

William Shatner recorded and released his album *The Transformed Man* during the time he was starring as Captain Kirk on the *Star Trek* television series (see entries 777 and 1396). The album is curious to say the least, with Shatner reciting poetry selections over light, incidental orchestral backgrounds. The tracks on the album are arranged in pairs, each pair addressing what Shatner deems a central contradiciton of the human condition. Three of the tracks are readings of Shakespeare's works, including the "Once more unto the breach, dear friends" speech from *Henry V*, the "To be or not to be" soliloquy from *Hamlet* (which is paired with "It Was a Very Good Year"), and "But soft, what light through yonder window breaks" from *Romeo and Juliet*. Each Shakespeare piece is introduced by a prose backgrounder, in which he sets the scene for the lines he is about to recite. Shatner's famous vocal cadence, which flits like a butterfly from word to word, often making dramatic pauses with little apparent semantic motivation, is of course evident throughout.

1771 "The King Must Die"
Song. 1970. Elton John, from the album *Elton John*. Composed by Elton John and Bernie Taupin. Rocket/Island.

In "The King Must Die," the since-knighted Sir Elton John revisits some of Shakespeare's favorite themes: the treachery of friends and courtiers and a king deposed. As critics have noted, Bernie Taupin's lyrics are often hopelessly cryptic on this album, and several of the lines from "The King Must Die" are no exception. Shakespeare appears on the scene at the song's beginning, but rather than as a playwright, he is depicted here in an impossible character role that only a fool would attempt to assume: "No man's a jester playing Shakespeare," John sings, when the juggler dances upon the king's former crown. The identity of the ballad's toppled king is never revealed in this song, which, through both direct reference and allusion, compares him to fallen rulers in Shakespeare, including Julius Caesar, King Hamlet, and Macbeth. (JS)

1772 "Big Legged Sally"
Song. 1976. Champion Jack Dupree, from the album *Shakespeare Says*. Saravah. France.

New Orleans blues pianist Champion Jack Dupree was in his late sixties when he recorded this "duet," which he sings by himself, assuming the voice of a Louis Armstrong sound-alike named "Georges" in addition to his own persona. While the two characters discuss how they're going to go visit "big legged Sally," they decide they will sing a song together. "Georges" suggests they sing "one about—what Shakespeare wrote... 'Mama move your false teeth papa wanna scratch your gums' or somethin' like that." By the end of the song, Dupree lets everyone listening know that he's going to pause for a moment to take a drink, and it is evident that the drink has not been his first of the session.

1773 "Shakespeare's Sister"
Song. 1985. The Smiths. Rough Trade. Released in United Kingdom on 7 inch and 12 inch.

According to The Smiths's lead singer-songwriter Morrissey, "Shakespeare's Sister" was the story of his life. He was crushed, then, when the song only made it to number twenty-six on the U.K. charts and received very little radio play. Perhaps that is why, two years later, Morrissey re-released the track on the album appropriately titled *The World Won't Listen*. In the crooning and confessional "Shakespeare's Sister," Morrissey stands on the edge of the abyss contemplating suicide as "the rocks below say 'Throw your skinny body down, son!'" Like Shakespeare's imaginary sister Judith, as envisioned by Virginia Woolf in *A Room of One's Own*, Morrissey finds his choices in art and love restricted by traditionalist parents who stand in the way of his desires. Morrissey (who at the time alluded to his homosexuality while publicly proclaiming his celibacy) sings, that he's going to find "the one I love...Mamma, let me go!" The song ends with a negative declaration, the word "No...", signaling defiance against the mother's will. Yet, it is unclear whether this pronouncement signals that the speaker has escaped the fetters of convention by taking a plunge into the world, or onto the rocks below. (JS)

1774 *Shakespeare Alabama*
Album. 1989. Diesel Park West. EMI. U.K.

The members of Diesel Park West are not from Alabama, nor are they from any other state in the Union. Hailing from Leicester, England, they are yet another British band attempting to make their mark with a little help from the Shakespeare brand name. In 1989, Diesel Park West released their first record, *Shakespeare, Alabama*. The cover of the album featured an illustrated bust of the Bard himself, in period costume. The now out-of-print album is known for its intricate guitar solos and ambitious lyrics, in addition to its employment of celebrity Shakespeare as the album's cover model. (JS)

1775 "Shakespeare's Got a Gun"
Song. c. 1990s. Dan Bern, unreleased song.

Proclaiming that "Shakespeare's got no use" for words, letters, English classes, or those who enjoy them, Dan Bern sings, "Shakespeare watches videos, the dirtier the better." Likely, Bern's Shakespeare will see himself in the dirty movies he watches. From porn to pop music videos to explosive action flicks, Shakespeare is everywhere it seems, or at least his material is, souped-up and served raw to videophile-violence-and-sex junkies in the market for high-octane parody. In Bern's song, the Bard is a product of popular culture, both a rock star and a Rambo. Armed with both a Fender Stratocaster and an Uzi, "Shakespeare's got a gun, he's gonna use it." (JS)

1776 *Shakespeare My Butt*
Album. 1991. The Lowest of the Low, independent release.

In 1991 Toronto-based The Lowest of the Low released their debut CD, titled *Shakespeare My Butt*. Even though the album had no major label backing or distribution support, *Shakespeare My Butt* was an independent success, selling over 10,000 copies. It is likely that Shakespeare's name (despite, or perhaps because, it is undermined in the album title) boosted the band's popularity in the college music scene. It was among this demographic that The Low developed its biggest fan base, one that would embrace the group's blend of humor, left-wing politics, and occasional literary name-dropping. (JS)

1777 "Omnibus"
Song. 1992. XTC, from the album *Nonsuch*. Geffen.

Shakespeare's name is used as an epithet for the penis in this celebration of multicultural sexuality by songwriter and singer Andy Partridge. The omnibus is a bus that can "take all of us." Encouraging the listener to get cracking and "go on and taste them all," he sings, "Make your Shakespeare hard and make your oyster pearl." The allusion to Shakespeare is in keeping with the rest of the song's carnivalesque vulgarity.

1778 "Stratford-on-Guy"
Song. 1993. Liz Phair, from the album *Exile in Guyville*. Matador.

The song "Stratford-on-Guy" appears near the end of the critically acclaimed debut album that Liz Phair described as her song-by-song response to the Rolling Stones's *Exile on Main Street*. The song describes Phair flying into her hometown of Chicago (also known as "Guyville" in the Chicago scene at the time), and the view out the window during the descent. The song's chorus, "once I really listened, the noise...went away," suggests her capacity for intense focus and self-discipline. The reference to Shakespeare's birthplace in the song's title is not pursued anywhere in the lyrics, but the song may simply be one way of Phair announcing her arrival as a female artist.

1779 "William Shakespeare's in My Cat"
Song. 1994. The Arrogant Worms, from the album *Russell's Shorts*. Arrogant Worms. Canada.

Canadian folk novelty act The Arrogant Worms wrote this song, in which the lead singer, who "never much believed in reincarnation," discovers that his cat is possessed by the spirit of William Shakespeare. Shakespeare, the singer claims, "Chews on my socks while I'm asleep." Other lyrics in the song allude to the plays *Richard III*, *Macbeth*, and *Romeo and Juliet*, though the references are of similar depth and obviously meant to be silly. From the perspective of Shakespeare studies, it is perhaps most interesting to note that, to the owner's chagrin, it turns out his cat also has a soft spot for the work of Andrew Lloyd Webber.

1780 "Every Poet Wants to Murder Shakespeare"
Song. 1995. The Bad Examples, from the album *Kisses 50 Cents*. Waterdog.

In "Every Poet Wants to Murder Shakespeare," The Bad Examples make music out of "the anxiety of influence." With a certain amount of teenage-sounding sulkiness, the singer says, "Every poet wants to murder Shakespeare," because they can't measure up and are sick of kneeling before "the altar" of what came before. The lyrics play up the tension between every poet's desire to "invent the world the day that they were born," and the pressure to live up to centuries' worth of precedent and talent. As the greatest writer in the English language, Shakespeare is of course the ultimate symbol of the weighty literary past. The desire to outdo the past while retaining the greatness of English literature's "dead white men" is inescapable and eternal. Just as the singer is "as drunk as Mister Marlowe in his prime" (a reference to Christopher Marlowe, an early contemporary of Shakespeare), there is perhaps some small consolation in knowing that the next generation will have a hard time of it as well: "the poet of tomorrow will be just as drunk as I am." (SC)

1781 *The Shakespeare Revue*
Musical Theater. 1995. Created by Christopher Luscombe and Malcolm McKee, original cast recording. That's Entertainment. Jay Records. U.K.

The Shakespeare Revue assembles comic writing and songs inspired by the Bard into a single stage show that pays tribute to Shakespeare's legacy as a literary icon and, above all, as an entertainer. The show includes everything from Cole Porter to Monty Python, revealing how many different artists have turned to Shakespeare for inspiration over the course of the twentieth century. *The Shakespeare Revue* pokes fun at some of the silly or risqué works based on Shakespeare, as well as satirizing the cultural industry that has grown up around the Bard; for instance, various characters complain that they have been overperformed and exploited, while others bemoan the kinds of creative works they have, or have not, inspired. The *Revue* is an excellent example of how modern performers are continually approaching Shakespeare from new angles, keeping his work fresh and relevant to contemporary audiences with the help of comedy and a little bit of musical theater. (SC)

1782 "Fred Olivier"
Song. 1997. Toy Dolls, from the album *One More Megabyte*. Receiver. U.K.

"Fred Olivier" is a funny, quirky, and often facetious song about the joys and hazards of Shakespearean acting. Big-name commercial success is not the goal; "Don't want to go to Hollywood," says the singer. Instead, he is "crazy for King Lear," because there is nothing more delighting "Than reciting Shakespeare." Like an average-Joe version of Sir Laurence, the singer is "Fred Olivier," who depends on "to be or not to be" for the good of "my [actor's] equity." The song pokes fun at the elitism of the Shakespearean theater (only he understands what he's saying, the singer gleefully proclaims), and also mocks the big-budget world of commercial theater and film. "Fred Olivier" pays homage to the world of cultural production that has grown up around Shakespeare's works while the song simultaneously thumbs its nose at the division between high and low culture, a line that Shakespeare often straddles. (SC)

1783 *Storm*
Concept Album. 2002. Verona. Independent.
New Zealand.

New Zealand art-rock quintet Verona produced this concept album, which consists of a series of songs based on verses and songs from Shakespeare. Songwriter Dan Adams draws upon a wide range of plays, including *Twelfth Night* ("Sweet and Twenty"), *The Winter's Tale* ("Come Buy"), *Love's Labor's Lost* ("Greasy Joan"), *Othello* ("Willow Song"), *Macbeth* ("The Witches' Cauldron Scene"), and *Cymbeline* ("Come to Dust"). The group debuted this work in live performance, accompanied by the Chamberpot string quartet and narrator Peter Sledmere, at the Wellington Fringe Festival in February 2002, where it won the prize for best musical contribution to the festival. Adams continued in this vein with another album of songs derived from Shakespeare, titled *This Love Will Undo Us All* (2004).

1784 "Billy S."
Song. 2004. Skye Sweetnam, from the album *Noise from the Basement*. Capitol.

Bubblegum anthem from Canadian teen rocker Skye Sweetnam, which begins with her waking up Monday morning and refusing to go to school, a place where the teachers all get paid "Lots of money money woo!" Such irony, to the extent that it is successful, is the source of the song's appeal. The chorus, which begins "I don't need to read Billy Shakespeare, meet Juliet, or Malvolio," takes the well-traveled road of associating Shakespeare with stodgy and bookish conservatism at odds with the more energetic, urgent spirit of teen rebellion. Sweetnam's deadpan voice-over during the bridge distills the song's message with admirable economy: whether to skip or not to skip, she says, "that is the question."

1785 "Twentysomething"
Song. 2004. Jamie Cullum, from the album *Twentysomething*. Verve.

British jazz hipster Jamie Cullum's take on life in his generation begins with an "expensive education" that has made him "an expert on Shakespeare and that's a helluva lot." But he finds "the world don't need scholars as much as I thought." The rest of the song follows the speaker's deliberations over what to do with his life. Stuck at a crossroads, he finally settles on just having fun, because neither love nor work is "the answer" and "The truth eludes me so much it hurts."

1786 "Warrior"
Song. 2004. Steve Earle, from the album *The Revolution Starts . . . Now*. E-Squared.

Released during the acrimonious 2004 U.S. presidential election year, Steve Earle's *The Revolution Starts . . . Now* is a sustained political protest against America's involvement in Iraq. Although he never quotes or mentions Shakespeare directly in the song "Warrior," the adoption of a Shakespearean heroic rhetoric is evident in the way the spoken lyrics are composed in strict iambic pentameter, complete with archaic phrases such as "faithful retainer," "liege lord," and "take heed" that seem designed to lend the song an oracular tone. The Shakespearean rhetoric is also employed to suggest the timelessness of the warrior's plight. The musical background is meant to recall "The End" by The Doors, a song featured prominently in Francis Ford Coppola's Vietnam War film, *Apocalypse Now*.

1787 *This Love Will Undo Us All*
Concept Album. 2005. Dan Adams. Concordance. New Zealand.

New Zealand singer-songwriter Dan Adams developed the idea for this concept album based upon Shakespeare's works after having participated in a similar project with the band Verona a few years earlier, which was called *Storm*. The more recent album's title is pulled from *Troilus and Cressida*, and the thirteen songs draw upon a range of Shakespeare's works, including *Romeo and Juliet*, *The Winter's Tale*, *As You Like It*, *The Merchant of Venice*, *Much Ado about Nothing*, and *Twelfth Night*, as well as several of the sonnets. From a compositional standpoint one of the most interesting pieces is "I Dreamt My Lady Came and Found Me Dead," in which the three verses are a collage of lines picked carefully from *Romeo and Juliet*, *The Taming of the Shrew*, and *King Lear*. The instrumentation is acoustic and minimalist throughout, and Adams's Kiwi accent handles Shakespeare's verse with a winning ease and strength in this pop format.